W9-BYM-294

Introduction to

FINANCIAL ACCOUNTING

Second Edition

The Irwin Series in Undergraduate Accounting

Introduction to

FINANCIAL ACCOUNTING

Second Edition

PAUL DANOS
EUGENE A. IMHOFF, JR.

Both of
University of Michigan

IRWIN

Burr Ridge, Illinois
Boston, Massachusetts
Sydney, Australia

To Our Families
Mary Ellen, Amanda, and Melissa
Barbara, Catherine, and Darren

Cover illustration: *Rob Day*

© RICHARD D. IRWIN, INC., 1991 and 1994

All rights reserved. No part of this publication may be
reproduced, stored in a retrieval system, or transmitted,
in any form or by any means, electronic, mechanical,
photocopying, recording, or otherwise, without the prior
written permission of the publisher.

This publication is designed to provide accurate and
authoritative information in regard to the subject matter
covered. It is sold with the understanding that neither the
author nor the publisher is engaged in rendering legal, accounting,
or other professional service. If legal advice or other expert
assistance is required, the services of a competent professional
person should be sought.

From a Declaration of Principles jointly adopted by a Committee
of the American Bar Association and a Committee of Publishers.

Senior developmental editor: *Jeffrey J. Shelstad*
Developmental editor: *Shelley McDonald Taylor*
Project editor: *Waivah Clement*
Production manager: *Diane Palmer*
Designer: *Maureen McCutcheon*
Art coordinator: *Mark Malloy*
Art studio: *ElectraGraphics, Inc.*
Compositor: *Beacon Graphics Corp.*
Typeface: *10/12 Times Roman*
Printer: *Von Hoffmann Press*

Library of Congress Cataloging-in-Publication Data

Danos, Paul
　　Introduction to financial acccounting / Paul Danos, Eugene A.
　Imhoff, Jr.—2nd ed.
　　　p.　　cm.
　　Includes index.
　　ISBN 0-256-11416-1
　　1. Accounting.　I. Imhoff, Eugene A.　II. Title.
　HF5635.D192　1994
　657—dc20　　　　　　　　　　　　　　　　　93–10647

Printed in the United States of America
1 2 3 4 5 6 7 8 9 0 VH 0 9 8 7 6 5 4 3

· *About the Authors*

PAUL DANOS

*Associate Dean,
School of Business
Administration,
University of
Michigan*

Paul Danos was named Associate Dean for Degree Programs in July of 1991. He is responsible for the MBA, BBA, and MAcc programs, the Office of Admissions and Student Services, the Office of Career Development, Computing Services, Kresge Library and the Division of Research.

Professor Danos has been the Arthur Andersen & Co. Professor of Accounting since 1985. He was Chairman of the Accounting Department at the University of Michigan from 1984 to 1991. Professor Danos also served as the Director of the Paton Accounting Center from 1988 to 1991. He has held many positions on various university committees, including Chairman, MBA Review Team; Chairman, Comprehensive Studies Program Executive Committee; Director, Accounting Ph.D Committee; Member, Executive Committee, School of Business Administration; Member, Doctoral Studies Committee, School of Business Administration; and Accounting Faculty Recruiting Coordinator. His current and past professional associations include American Accounting Association, Board of Governors—Administrators of Accounting Programs Executive Committee and Database Committee; City of Ann Arbor, Audit Committee; Adhoc Editor, *The Accounting Review;* Editorial Board, *Advances in Accounting;* and Consulting Editor, *Review of Business and Economic Research.* Professor Danos' current research areas include the economics of auditing and how audit firms compete, new models of business school education, and philosophy of science. He has published two textbooks, several research monographs, and over twenty-five scholarly articles and has made presentations at many academic and professional meetings. He has taught financial accounting at all levels in the graduate and undergraduate programs and has taught philosophy of science to Ph.D students.

**EUGENE A.
IMHOFF, JR.**

*Ernst and Young
Professor of
Accounting,
University of
Michigan*

Gene Imhoff has taught at the University of Michigan's School of Business Administration since 1977. He holds a bachelor's degree (accounting/history) and a master's of business administration (accounting) from Western Michigan University and a Ph.D. from Michigan State University. He is a Michigan CPA and currently holds the Ernst & Young Professorship in Accounting at the University of Michigan and is chairman of the Accounting Department.

Professor Imhoff's current research interests include measuring and evaluating accounting quality, off–balance sheet financing schemes, and economic consequences of accounting disclosure rules. He has published articles in a variety of academic and professional journals, and has won three manuscript awards for his publications. Professor Imhoff is also author of the research monograph *Sales Forecasting Systems* (National Association of Accountants, 1986).

Professor Imhoff worked as an accountant for General Motors Truck & Coach Division and as an auditor for Ernst & Ernst (now Ernst & Young) prior to beginning his teaching career. He has served as an expert witness on numerous financial accounting and auditing issues and has been employed by over a dozen large and small corporations as a general management consultant and a strategic planner. He has also served as a faculty intern for Citibank, London, where he helped develop specialized financing products for use in Europe.

· *Preface*

We developed INTRODUCTION TO FINANCIAL ACCOUNTING, Second Edition, giving considerable attention to users of accounting information. We recognize that a wide variety of students take introductory financial accounting, including accounting majors, other business majors, and nonbusiness majors. Common to all these students is their interest in knowing how to read and evaluate accounting information and in being prepared for more accounting education if they desire it.

This text is based on the premise that accounting knowledge and business knowledge are inseparable. We therefore **emphasize business decisions** throughout the text. We show the students why accounting is so crucial to business and how accounting is used as a basis for making business decisions.

How can a textbook like this improve the education process? Our goal is **to impart knowledge and appreciation of accounting concepts and methods.** To help achieve this goal, we have developed the text with the following guidelines:

1. **Get and keep the student's attention.** We believe interest is heightened by appealing to the student's natural entrepreneurial instincts through a **business decision orientation.** For example, in Chapter 5 students are introduced to credit sales and merchandise inventory accounting by way of a start-up business where accounting information is created in response to the needs of two young entrepreneurs. The student is taken from the planning phase all the way to the analysis of the initial operating results.

2. **Emphasize accounting outputs.** We believe that students develop a deeper understanding of accounting concepts and methods when they visualize the outputs of the accounting system. We accomplish this by a liberal use of disclosure examples from the real world.

3. **Emphasize conceptual foundations.** We believe the hardest task for the text author is to develop a clear and usable conceptual framework for the student. After introducing students to the general nature of accounting outputs, we give them a **thorough, nontechnical introduction to the concepts involved.** In Chapter 1, we show simple financial relationships and link them to the fundamental concepts that underlie accounting. In Chapter 2, we introduce the fundamentals of matching, recognition, and measurement and link them to the elements of financial statements. Concepts are continually developed and referenced throughout the text, and Chapter 15 provides a recap of these concepts by examining in greater detail the conceptual framework of accounting.

4. **Emphasize analysis.** As early as Chapter 4, students are given an introduction to simple financial statement analysis. Because the example used in the chapter is complete and self-contained, the student is able to understand simple cash flow analysis based on the transactions illustrated in it. By comparing relative balances of cash to other assets, current to noncurrent assets, liabilities to equities, expenses to revenue, and so forth, students are given a good start in **appreciating the analytical uses of accounting outputs.** Analysis techniques are integrated throughout the text to reinforce evaluation of accounting information at the same time as students are learning to develop accounting information.

Using these basic guidelines, we have developed the Second Edition into what we believe is a useful tool for imparting knowledge about the production and use of accounting information in business.

CHANGES IN THE SECOND EDITION

It is amazing how the world of business (and the role accounting plays in it) has evolved and changed in the few short years since the First Edition was published. In our revisions of this text we have tried to reflect what we deem the most important developments in accounting education. We have benefitted greatly from the comments of students and faculty users and reviewers, and we have incorporated many of their suggestions.

- In order to reflect several major themes emerging as critical to accounting education, we have **increased our coverage of international issues** and have **integrated the coverage into each chapter** in addition to the more in-depth appendix coverage. In virtually every chapter students will find facts explaining the differences and similarities between U.S. GAAP and international accounting practices from countries around the globe. These international facts are indicated by marginal icons like the one alongside this item.
- We have **added more emphasis on ethics** issues by adding quotes from business leaders throughout the text. These are provided throughout the text in addition to Appendix A, "Ethics and Accounting Judgments."
- In order to **better communicate the meaning of accounting concepts,** we have increased the number of vignettes.

- In response to the most often stated deficiency of college graduates, we have added and revised problem materials to **require students to use writing skills.** Included within each chapter are assignments calling for written memos or reports from students, allowing them to practice their written communication skills in an accounting context. These assignments are designated with the marginal icon that appears alongside of this item.
- **Bridging problem and case materials** call on the student to bridge the gap between the examples, illustrations, and demonstration exercises provided in each chapter and related realistic accounting assignments. These bridging assignments are designated as ***Challenging*** to facilitate identification and selections.

We have also made numerous changes to fine-tune each chapter in response to specific comments. In the crucial first four chapters, where many key concepts are introduced, we have reduced the number of different business examples to better integrate the material. After thorough evaluation, we have simplified and made more communicative the exhibits and graphics. We have tried to relocate and streamline material that reviewers considered of secondary importance; for instance, the coverage of electronic data processing in Chapter 7 was put into an appendix. Of course, all problem materials were evaluated for consistency with the text and for accuracy. We have made a major effort to ensure that all topics and terms are introduced adequately before they are incorporated into problem materials.

KEY FEATURES

In addition to these new features, the Second Edition has retained the innovations from the First Edition in order better to achieve the business decision orientation of the text. These tools are designed to help students and faculty meet the challenges facing the business decision makers of tomorrow and on into the 21st century. Many of these features have been promoted by the *Accounting Education Change Commission (AECC),* which is attempting to provide a set of objectives that will enhance the learning process and the professional stature of accounting. With these goals in mind, the aim of this second edition is to become THE basic business text that meaningfully introduces the subject of accounting to students in a broad business decision-making context.

What attributes of this second edition help us to achieve these goals?

- Informal **vignettes** depicting people in realistic business situations discussing accounting issues continue to be provided throughout the text, with some new vignettes added to supplement or replace those from the first edition.

- **Immediate introduction to financial statements:** Students are introduced to the outputs of financial accounting in Chapters 1 and 2, where balance sheets, income statements, statements of cash flows, and retained earnings statements are illustrated and discussed. These two chapters demonstrate how business transactions from operating, financing, and investing activities are captured and reported in the financial statements. This is done before students are introduced to the mechanics of debits and credits to give them a good perspective on the objectives of financial accounting and how these objectives are accomplished with financial statements. This approach has proven to be most successful in teaching students the basics of the accounting information system, since they gain an appreciation for what financial statements are and how they work (the "forest") before delving into the mechanics of the accounting system (the "trees").

- Since students need to relate textbook knowledge to the real world for successful learning to occur, we include end-of-chapter material based on **actual financial statement examples.** In addition, the 1992 Annual Report of the *Ralston Purina Company* (which is provided in Appendix E) is referenced in chapter assignment material throughout the text. These problem and case materials are appropriately identified in the assignment descriptions and are particularly relevant for those seeking a stronger user orientation in the introductory financial accounting course.

- Chapter openers identify the **learning objectives** for each chapter, thereby outlining what is ahead.

- A list of **synonyms** is provided at the end of each chapter to help students become comfortable with the subtle variations in the language of business. Students are often confused when they encounter accounting terms that differ from those used in their textbook but mean the same thing. Even the most common synonyms— such as using *earnings* in place of *net income*—can be troublesome to students learning the language of business.

- A **glossary of key terms** is provided at the end of each chapter, providing definitions as developed in that chapter. (Key terms are identified in color in the body of each chapter.)

- **Labels are included after each account** used in a journal entry. For example, a contra asset account would have (*XA*) after it to clarify the type of account it is. Such labels reduce confusion in understanding journal entries and their effects on the various financial statements.

- End-of-chapter assignment materials are labeled to describe the **nature of each assignment** and the related learning objectives. We include a brief description of each exercise, problem, and case in order to explain the basic thrust of each end-of-chapter assignment. These descriptions facilitate the instructor's assignment selection process and help students identify similar assignments, should extra work be desired on a particular topic.

- **Graphics** are liberally used to depict concepts or relationships in order to enhance understanding.

- **End-of-chapter appendices** are frequently used to cover topics that not all instructors care to include in the introductory course, making inclusion or exclusion easier.

These key features are all considered to be highly compatible with the objectives of the AECC and are also of great value in achieving a basic understanding of the role of accounting in business and society. These features both facilitate learning and challenge the student to learn in a relevant context. *We believe the real interface between business and accounting encountered by students in their careers will be more understandable and more relevant because of the challenges provided by our approach to introducing accounting.*

We believe that the key features, in combination with pedagogical foundations developed in the text and end-of-chapter assignments, will provide faculty and students with a user-friendly introductory financial accounting textbook.

COMPREHENSIVE COVERAGE

This text is a comprehensive introduction to financial accounting and business decisions. We include coverage of the following subjects:

- Ethics in accounting (Appendix A and quotes throughout the book)
- International accounting (Appendix B and throughout the book)
- Accounting for price changes (Appendix C)
- Not-for-profit accounting (Appendix D)
- An introduction to methods for estimating inventories (Appendix 6B)
- Reporting LIFO inventories (Appendix 6C)
- Deferred income taxes (Appendix to Chapter 9)
- Partnership accounting (Appendix to Chapter 11)
- Earnings per share: primary and fully diluted (Appendix 12A)
- Introduction to consolidations (Chapter 12 and Appendix 12A)
- Conceptual framework of accounting (Chapter 15 and throughout the book)
- References to income taxes, such as inventories and depreciation (throughout the text)

These subjects are covered at an introductory level so students can recognize their respective roles in the overall financial reporting process. At the same time, each subject is presented independently (with related end-of-chapter material clearly labeled), so that selected topics may be easily omitted at the discretion of the instructor.

To supplement the text, the following items are included in our package.

For the Student:

- **Study Guide** (prepared by Karen Bird, University of Michigan)
  Provides review of learning objectives, chapter summaries, and self-review exercises with solutions for each chapter. New to this edition are tips for completing writing assignments.
- **Spreadsheet Applications Template Software (SPATS)** (developed by Wilbur L. Garland, Coastal Carolina University)
  Approximately 150 exercises, problems, and cases in the text can be solved using *SPATS,* which contains innovatively designed templates based on Lotus® 1-2-3® and includes a very effective tutorial for Lotus® 1-2-3®. The exercises, problems, and cases solvable with *SPATS* are identified in the margin of the text with the following symbol.

- **Practice Set** (prepared by Gene Imhoff and Karen Bird)
  Based on Hershey Foods and other annual reports. (A solutions manual is also available to the instructor.)
- **Working Papers**

For the Instructor:

- **Solutions Manual**
  Provides suggested answers to discussion questions and complete solutions for all exercises, problems, and cases in the text. The problem material and solutions were carefully reviewed for accuracy in three stages.

- **Instructor's Lecture Guide** (prepared by Kate Mooney, St. Cloud State University)
  Includes chapter overviews, lecture outlines, strategies, content analysis, transparency masters, and suggested quizzes for each chapter. This guide also offers tips for teaching and grading writing assignments, and suggested group projects.

- **Solutions Transparencies**

- **Teaching Transparencies**
  This set of teaching transparencies can be used as the basis for classroom lectures and discussions.

- **Test Bank** (prepared by Joseph Anthony, Michigan State University)
  Expanded with over 150 new questions. All questions have been carefully evaluated to ensure they correlate closely with the text.

- **Computerized Testing Software**
  This microcomputer test generator program allows the instructor to select and edit exam questions from the Test Bank database. Questions can be selected using several criteria, such as chapter, type of question (e.g., multiple choice, true-false, problem solving), and level of difficulty. The software is menu-driven, requiring little computer knowledge. It comes with a program disk; data disks containing the Test Bank data base, and clearly written documentation. It provides password protection, can be used on a network, and is available on both 5.25″ and 3.5″ diskettes for IBM® compatible microcomputers.

ACKNOWLEDGMENTS

We want to give special recognition to the following instructors:

Hobart Adams
University of Akron

Annette L. Beatty
University of Pennsylvania

Messod Daniel Beneish
Duke University

Carol E. Brown
Oregon State University

Jill Cunningham
University of Florida

Leslie C. Grow
Central Missouri State University

Randall Hayes
Central Michigan University

Ronald King
Washington University

Allie F. Miller
Rutgers University

Kate Mooney
St. Cloud State University

Kathy R. Petroni
Michigan State University

Eric G. Press
Temple University

Louis P. Ramsay
Clemson University

Stephen E. Sefcik
University of Washington

David N. Weist
University of Massachusetts

Edward W. Yonkins
Wheeling Jesuit College

**IRWIN'S
COMMITMENT
TO QUALITY**

We recognize the importance of accuracy in accounting texts. Carefully checked examples, exhibits, exercises, problems, and cases are crucial to a quality classroom experience. The authors and publisher have gone to great lengths to ensure the accuracy of all the elements in this text and its ancillaries.

Edward S. Schwan (Susquehanna University) carefully reviewed all end-of-chapter materials of the Second Edition manuscript. He evaluated each item for accuracy as well as clarity and exposition to ensure a challenging and rewarding learning experience. **Don MacGilvra** (Shoreline Community College) independently worked every exercise, problem, and case in the text and double-checked his solutions against the Solutions Manual during the galley stage. Finally, **Leslie C. Grow** (Central Missouri State University) performed a final check of the solutions in page proof.

**Paul Danos
Eugene A. Imhoff, Jr.**

· Contents in Brief

· Contents

· About the Contributors

For the Second Edition, we asked several leading accountants in businesses and accounting firms across the country to comment on ethics as they specifically apply to the accounting profession. We would like to thank the following individuals whose insights and observations appear throughout the text.

Richard R. Current
Vice President & Chief Financial Officer The Shane Group, Inc.

Merlin E. Dewing
Partner KPMG Peat Marwick

Eugene H. Flegm
General Auditor General Motors Corporation

Eugene M. Freedman
Chairman and Chief Executive Officer Coopers & Lybrand

William D. Hall
Retired Partner Arthur Andersen & Co.

Ronald L. Leach
Vice President & Chief Accounting Officer Eaton Corporation

Robert D. Neary
Co-Chairman
Ernst & Young

Shaun F. O'Malley
Chairman and Senior Partner
Price Waterhouse

Edward M. Parks
Managing Partner
Plante & Moran

Anthony J. Ridley
General Auditor
Ford Motor Company

Dominic A. Tarantino
Co-Chairman and Managing
Partner
Price Waterhouse

Lawrence A. Weinbach
Managing Partner & Chief Ex-
ecutive Officer
Arthur Andersen & Co.

Introduction to

FINANCIAL ACCOUNTING

Second Edition

> The ethics of a profession are integral to the public's perception of that profession and its worth to society. Rightfully so, the public judges a profession by the code of behavior it establishes for itself. Young people starting out in accounting should be concerned about the profession's ethics because by becoming a part of the profession, they are accepting those ethics as a reflection of themselves and their own value systems.
>
> Robert D. Neary
> Ernst & Young

P·A·R·T

I

The Accounting Process

1

The Accounting Environment and the Business Entity

Our long-term focus and rigid adherence to ethical principles have made our profession uniquely able to provide the best long-term services to the business community. There is a near-universal recognition that ethical behavior is a basic in the exercise of credibility and trust in all manner of business activity.

Lawrence A. Weinbach
Arthur Andersen & Co. SC

· Learning Objectives

After studying Chapter 1, you should understand

1. The goals of accounting, p. 4.

2. How external and internal groups use accounting information, pp. 4–8.

3. The three forms of business entities—proprietorships, partnerships, and corporations, pp. 8–13.

4. The three basic categories of a balance sheet—assets, liabilities, and stockholders' equity, pp. 13–15.

5. How accounting transactions affect the balance sheet equation and the balance sheet, pp. 16–20.

6. The difference between the balance sheet, income statement, retained earnings statement, and statement of cash flows, p. 21.

7. The organizations involved in accounting policymaking and how they serve the external, internal, and governmental user groups (Appendix), pp. 24–25.

Objective 1
The goals of accounting

Above all else, accounting is a decision-making tool. When people make important decisions concerning economic entities such as businesses, government units, and not-for-profit enterprises, they use accounting information. Almost every entity in our society is called on to develop and report on matters related to its financial status and performance, and accounting is a study of the concepts and techniques used in such reporting. In addition, because entities compete for economic resources, the successful manager must plan and control the activity of his or her entity in an effective manner, and accounting information is essential in those processes.

Accounting is a future-oriented enterprise in that the information generated by the accounting process is intended to be relevant for future decisions. As a matter of fact, decision relevance is the overriding goal of accounting. Reports on past performance and current financial status are useful only as input to decisions about courses of action that will lead to future performance and status. Accounting is also intimately involved in sorting out the financial interests of the parties engaged in all kinds of relationships. Taxing authorities are interested in past financial performance in order to assess and collect appropriate taxes. Stockholders want some indication of the potential for return on their investments. Workers and potential employees need financial information to make decisions about the viability of entities as employers. Decisions concerning rewards to managers are often based on past performance. The regulation of imports is often based on the financial information about the businesses in an industry. Decisions to open new plants, lay off workers, locate in foreign countries, and close banks and savings and loans are all based to some degree on financial information provided by the accounting system. The list goes on almost to infinity, encompassing all aspects of life from the personal finances of a student to the trillions of dollars involved in the federal budget.

The concepts and techniques covered in this text will give you a window into the basics of market-based economic systems, which are increasingly dominating the world. Information is the life's blood of such systems, and accounting information is one of the most fundamental and pervasive sources of information.

The first section in this chapter discusses the users of accounting and the forms of business entities. The chapter also introduces the balance sheet, a major financial statement that communicates an entity's financial position in terms of its resources and obligations. An appendix to this chapter discusses the organizations involved in accounting policymaking.

THE ACCOUNTING ENVIRONMENT

This section discusses (1) users of accounting information (including senders and receivers) and (2) forms of business entities. The goal of accounting is to provide information about the economic activities and the economic states of entities in ways that are useful to decision makers. The accounting communication process involves individuals, businesses, and governments who, to some extent, can be both senders and receivers of financial information and regulators (policymakers) who determine the standards for accounting reports.

Users of Accounting Information

Objective 2
How external and internal groups use accounting information.

Users of accounting information can be classified into two broad groups, (1) external users and (2) internal users, depending on the user's relationship to the reporting entity. These two groups need different kinds of accounting information because each group makes different types of decisions. Although we have previously said that all kinds of entities report accounting information, our discussion will focus on profit-seeking business entities. Future references to the reporting entity will be made simply by using the terms *business* or *company*.

External Users.   The external users of a company's accounting information include all individuals, other businesses, and other entities that are not managers or officers of the company. This user group is sometimes called outsiders because, although they are interested in the business, they are not part of the company's management. External or outside users include potential and current owners, creditors, government units, and the general public. In large entities, owners are included in the external user group because they usually are not members of the company's management even though they have a voice in determining who management is. Bankers and bondholders, as the major creditor groups, are outsiders because they usually have no management functions.

In general, external users have limitations on their access to the financial records of the business. Under normal conditions, they have general-purpose reports (financial statements) that are prepared according to a set of rules or guidelines known as generally accepted accounting principles (GAAP), which are discussed throughout the text.

The financial accounting process generates the financial statements used by outsiders, but it also is the source of much related information about the entity that is used by management. For instance, the financial statements show the total for amounts due from customers and that number is, therefore, known to outsiders. The financial accounting process also keeps records on each individual customer, but such detailed information is available only to management. The same is true for the identification of the business's creditors, the age and costs of specific assets, and a great many other details that management needs to run the business but are not usually needed by outsiders. In some cases, such as in merger negotiations or when applying for a loan, a business may provide more detail.

Governmental users.   Governmental agencies use accounting information for various types of social, political, and economic decisions. Although governmental users are included in the external user group, in this textbook we view governmental users as a special class of external users. Generally, governmental agencies have some authority to require specific accounting information from businesses.

Two prominent governmental users of accounting reports are the Internal Revenue Service (IRS) and the Securities and Exchange Commission (SEC). The IRS requires special-purpose reports—tax returns, indicating the amount of income taxes owed by individuals and businesses. The goal of the IRS is to provide for government revenues according to tax laws and regulations. The SEC requires detailed quarterly and annual financial reports of all publicly owned companies to be submitted for its files and made available to stockholders and the general public. The goal of the SEC's activities is to ensure that order is maintained in the financial markets.

The accounting environment related to governmental users is often highly specialized and relatively complicated. Banks, airlines, railroads, hospitals, utilities, shippers, and many other types of businesses make regular reports containing accounting information to various agencies of local, state, and/or federal governments who use it to regulate and tax.

Accounting environment facing external users.   From the external user's viewpoint, the accounting environment consists of four main parties: the external users themselves, managers, independent auditors, and accounting policymakers. External users seek accounting information in making business decisions; managers provide accounting information; independent auditors (certified public accountants) report on whether or not the financial reports are fairly presented in conformance to generally accepted accounting principles (GAAP); and accounting policymakers decide on the nature and content of financial reports by determining what constitutes GAAP.

Accounting policymakers weigh the costs and benefits of proposed reporting requirements for external users before issuing new requirements or revising old requirements. The ultimate goal of these policymakers is to develop GAAP that facilitate meaningful communication of relevant financial information. The appendix at the end of this chapter identifies the various organizations that directly or indirectly affect the development of accounting policy.

Although this text concentrates primarily on the accounting principles and practices in the United States, we will indicate when U.S. practices differ significantly from those of other major economic powers. As financial markets around the world have become more interactive, there has been a growing demand for the harmonization of accounting standards, which means making the accounting principles and practices of different countries more similar. The goal of harmonization is to provide more usable information to all who must compare financial results of businesses operating in different countries.

Internal Users.   Business managers are the internal users of accounting information. Managers are responsible for (1) designing an accounting information system that fits the needs of their particular business and (2) preparing all accounting information for both internal and external users.

The decisions made by managers often require more detailed and timely information than that contained in general-purpose financial statements. This accounting information is usually referred to as managerial accounting information. Unlike financial accounting information, managerial accounting information is not governed by GAAP.

Managers who also own stock in the company they manage are in a unique position of being both internal and external users. Because they could profit from the more timely and detailed managerial accounting information available to insiders, managers of corporations are subject to certain rules and restrictions in dealings in the ownership shares of their own companies. Governmental agencies and stock exchanges carefully monitor the trading activities of insiders to guard against the misuse of information that is not available to the general public.

Accounting environment facing internal users.   Managers are free to develop any accounting information that is necessary to satisfy their decision-making needs, constrained only by cost considerations and technological limitations. Managerial accounting helps managers to focus on problem situations and solutions, and managers must often use accounting information in conjunction with other information (i.e., the economic outlook for growth or technological changes in products) to make sound business decisions.

Most businesses share similar objectives, which may be defined in terms of profits, providing a common purpose for the development of fairly standard managerial accounting procedures. It is not uncommon for different companies to have similar payroll systems, inventory control systems, and other accounting systems. Managerial accounting courses cover the concepts and techniques that have been developed to deal with common internal accounting problems.

What Information Is Relevant and Feasible?   To illustrate the interplay of external users, managers, and auditors, consider a hypothetical case in which Mr. M (an inexperienced manager of a company) is negotiating for a loan from Ms. B (an inexperienced bank loan officer).

Ms. B: I am in the business of lending money and I really want you as a customer, but first I want you to provide the following information:

1. Financial statements showing the condition of your company and its performance over the last three years.

2. An evaluation of the credit ratings of all your customers.

3. Complete background reports on your employees.

4. A forecast of sales for the next five years.

Mr. M: I don't have all of that information and I believe that some of it is confidential. Anyway, all I have available are my financial statements, your item 1. The rest could be developed, but they are not required by GAAP.

Ms. B: OK, give me your financial statements, but they must be accompanied by a report from an independent auditor. After I have reviewed the statements, we will discuss the other items.

The above conversation illustrates some of the actual concerns that must be faced in the real world of business, giving rise to a demand for standard financial information that is produced by managers and independently evaluated for fairness by an outside party.

Mr. M goes back to his office and calls a certified public accountant (CPA), Ms. C, and relays to her the list of items the banker requested.

Ms. C, who is experienced in negotiations between borrowers and lenders and who makes fairness judgments about financial statements, states that item 1 is normally provided to banks in lending situations and that she, after checking the records of Mr. M's company, could make a statement about the fairness of presentations of the financial statements. Other items could also be provided by M's company, such as a list of customers and a forecast, but because of the expense involved, the CPA is seldom called on to evaluate these less-standardized reports, which are not governed by GAAP. Ms. C also informs Ms. B that item 2 would be costly and perhaps impossible to obtain.

What Ms. C is suggesting is that if GAAP were applied by the company in this situation, then a standard set of financial information that could be evaluated by an independent party would result. Not all of the information desires of the banker will be met by the standardized, audited financial statements. In some cases, it may be too costly or inappropriate for borrowers to provide these additional data. In other cases, unaudited management information such as forecasts may also be provided. While unaudited information not included in the standardized financial statements may be developed if all parties can agree to it, such special information would not fall into the realm of GAAP. Opinions on financial statements by independent auditors, called audit reports, are often requested by banks and are a required part of all financial statements published by companies whose ownership shares (called *stock*) are publicly traded on the U.S. stock exchanges.

As stated earlier, management has access to all sorts of financial information about the entity, including all of the records and outputs of the accounting information system (depicted as circle A in Exhibit 1–1). Much of this information is private or insider information and is not voluntarily revealed to outsiders. Some parties outside the business, such as a banker who is evaluating the company's requests for a loan, may be desirous of all information that will aid in making the decision (depicted as circle B in Exhibit 1–1). A banker desires financial information, such as historical and forecasted financial statements, budgets, feasibility studies, and tax returns, and perhaps other nonfinancial data, such as the backgrounds and health of key employees. The intersection of A and B represents the financial information provided to outsiders.

Where does the outside party get the rest of the desired information? A banker who lends money to a business may have access to economic projections and industry data, but there is always a residual uncertainty, which remains in the realm of professional judgment and creates a risk the bank must bear if it makes the loan. It also must be understood that even formal, audited financial statements are not perfect reflections of the economic reality, and such imperfections can add to the risks of doing business.

In summary, not all financial information available to management is given to or desired by outside decision makers. Of that information requested, a portion is GAAP based and audited, and a portion is not. The future is uncertain, and though much accounting and other information is available, an element of risk will be borne by investors and creditors who buy stock and lend money. Of course, the returns they expect to earn on their investments or loans reflect relative risk, and that is why government-guaranteed bonds generally pay lower interest rates than bonds of corporations.

This textbook focuses most of its attention on financial accounting information for external and internal users—information that is communicated through GAAP-based standard financial statements. Exhibit 1–2 summarizes and compares the external, internal, and governmental user groups.

Forms of Business Entities

Objective 3
The three forms of business entities— proprietorships, partnerships, and corporations.

All business organizations use accounting information as a basis for making decisions. Based on their ownership structure, businesses are classified as *proprietorships, partnerships,* or *corporations.* Although the ownership structure of business organizations may differ, their accounting information processes are similar.

For accounting purposes, a **business entity** is an economic unit separate from its owners, and all business entities have some similar features. In other words, each business entity is viewed as a separate individual, and the accounting for a small business with only a few owners is remarkably similar in many respects to that of a business with thousands of owners. Of course, the scale and degree of complexity vary greatly.

By definition, then, an entity is the unit accounted for on the company's financial accounting reports; and for accounting purposes an entity is always viewed as separate from the owners of the business. This accounting concept of viewing the business as having an existence separate from its owners is known as the business entity concept, separate entity concept, or entity concept.

This textbook concentrates on profit-seeking business entities. Remember, however, that other types of organizations not operated for profit (churches, charities, municipalities, schools, and so on) also use accounting information and function as separate economic entities. Not-for-profit entities are discussed in Appendix D at the end of this text.

In the next section, we discuss three prevalent forms of business organization: proprietorships, partnerships, and corporations. You will see that in terms of accounting they differ mostly in how owners' interests are recorded.

Proprietorships.   A proprietorship is a business owned by one person. Usually proprietorships are small businesses that are managed by their owner, such as a restaurant or a small

EXHIBIT 1–1

Relationships among the Information Sets

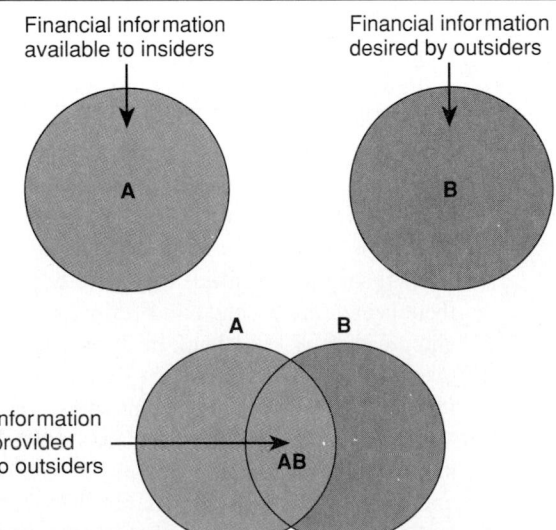

Financial information available to insiders

Financial information desired by outsiders

A

B

A   B

Information provided to outsiders

AB

retail clothing store. However, many proprietors (sole owners) may hire people to help manage their businesses.

Since accounting views all forms of businesses as separate entities, the records of the business resources and activities of the proprietor (owner) must be kept separate from the records of the owner's other resources and activities. For example, if you were the sole owner of a nightclub, a separate golf course business, and personal assets such as a home and car, you would probably have separate accounting records for each business, and you would not mix your golf course records or personal records with those of the nightclub. However, the law does not view a proprietor's several businesses and personal assets as separate, and creditors could possibly claim any and all of the owned assets to cover the debts of any one entity. Thus, creditors of a proprietorship may legally claim the personal resources of the owner or those of other businesses he or she may own. As a result, a proprietor is said to have unlimited liability.

Partnerships.   In a partnership, two or more persons share the ownership interest in a business. Many professionals, such as physicians, lawyers, and accountants, organize their

EXHIBIT 1–2

Comparison of Accounting Information User Groups

| | External Users | | Internal Users |
	Nongovernment	Government	
Who are they?	Investors and creditors, present and potential	Internal Revenue Service (IRS) Securities and Exchange Commission (SEC) Regulatory agencies	Company officers and employees who manage the business
What type of accounting is employed?	Financial accounting	Income tax accounting Other specialized accounting	Managerial accounting
What types of decisions do these users make?	Credit-granting decisions Investment decisions Mergers and acquisitions	Policy decisions concerning taxation and other economic consequences Assessing tax obligations Setting utility rates	Control of operating decisions: Investment decisions Product pricing decisions Salaries and bonuses for managers
What specific accounting information do they receive?	Financial statements published by the entity in periodic reports (including balance sheet, income statement, retained earnings statement, and statement of cash flows)	Special-purpose reports (such as income tax returns) Financial statements of public utilities, banks, etc.	All of those stated at left, plus budgets, cost reports, and many varied types of statements and records with specific details about business activity

practices as partnerships. Each partner has a specified percentage of ownership in the business, which may differ from the interests of the other partners. For example, assume that Smith, Jones, and Colson are partners in a law firm, with Smith owning a 50% interest; Jones, a 30% interest; and Colson, a 20% interest. The partners would use this ratio of partnership interest as the basis for sharing the profits and losses of their business, unless they were to agree to another sharing arrangement.

Like proprietorships, accounting views partnerships as entities separate from their owners. The Smith, Jones, and Colson law firm is the business entity and would be accounted for as such. However, legally, partnerships are like proprietorships in that the business is not viewed separately from its owners, and unlimited liability is conveyed to each of the partners. While some partnership agreements may limit one or more of the partner's liability, at least one partner must be personally liable for the debts of the partnership. Unlimited liability is a major disadvantage of both partnerships and proprietorships. Another unique feature of partnerships is that, in general, they dissolve when someone leaves the partnership or when someone new is admitted into the partnership. Later in this text we delve more deeply into partnership accounting.

Corporations.   In a corporation, ownership interests are represented by shares of stock. Owners of corporate stock are called stockholders or shareholders. The shares of stock, called capital stock or common stock, represent a unit of ownership and may be sold or transferred to new owners at any time.

Corporations are unique in that they are viewed as separate entities for both accounting and legal purposes. Usually owners of corporate stock can sell shares without the approval of other stockholders; and in most cases, stock owners have limited liability in that the most they can lose in the corporation is the amount they originally invest.

A corporation is formed by filing for a corporate charter with the appropriate governmental unit in the state of incorporation. When the application is approved by the state, the corporation becomes a legal entity, ready to issue stock and conduct business in accordance with the terms of the approved corporate charter. The details of corporate accounting are covered in several succeeding chapters of this text.

The United States has more proprietorships than partnerships or corporations, but corporations own most of the business assets and generate most of the sales and income. Also, a corporation may have thousands of different owners, and the ownership may change daily as shares of the corporation's stock are bought and sold among owners through organized trading institutions called stock exchanges.

A corporation whose stock is traded by one or more stock exchanges (such as the New York Stock Exchange, American Stock Exchange, or Pacific Stock Exchange) is referred to as a publicly held company or publicly traded company. Corporations whose stock is not publicly traded are referred to as closely held or privately held companies. An initial public offering (IPO) takes place when a privately held entity issues stock to the general public for the first time. This is called going public.

BUSINESS FORMATION	In this section, we will see how all of the considerations discussed above affect the many decisions that have to be made before a business is organized. Ann, Bill, and Connie are research scientists working for three different companies but with long-standing mutual interests since their college days. While they shared a dream of working together on space technology projects someday, each accepted a job with a different research-oriented organization after graduation. At their 10-year college reunion, they had long conversations about the exciting projects they could undertake. Ann suggested that now was the time to fulfill their dream.

Ann: We can act as independent consultants, but share office space and expertise. If I have a problem on a project, I could call on one of you and vice versa.

Bill: How do we compensate each other for time spent on the other's project? Do we bill each other by the hour?

Connie: What happens if I expand and hire associates? My projects then could grow to such an extent that I could use up all of your time. Besides, some of the projects would have to have security clearance and I don't know if NASA would allow that kind of consultation.

Ann: Yes, and if one of us gets a patent, how do we share the glory and the profits?

Ann, Bill, and Connie are discussing issues at the heart of the motivation for forming a business. As independent agents, Ann, Bill, and Connie could conceivably cooperate to their mutual advantage, but a formal business entity helps to solve the problems that are created when individual self-interest conflicts with the goal of coordinated effort. Obviously, Ann, Bill, and Connie feel that they would be better off sharing each other's expertise, but they are worried that if they operated as independent agents it would be difficult to achieve equitable sharing of efforts and rewards. Also, it would be difficult to control unique information and knowledge that springs from joint efforts. The answer to some of these concerns is found in a business entity. Listen as Ann, Bill, and Connie come to that conclusion themselves.

Connie: As much as I would like to maintain my independence, I can see that what we need is to form either a partnership or a corporation. That way, the company would be the contractor with the government and we could work on the things that each of us does best.

Bill: Wait—you know what a business is like. You've got to go through lawyers and red tape to form one and then you need accountants to keep track of everything. I don't know anything about accounting. What happens if one of us quits or dies? Also, to help us start the business, we probably would have to get bank loans and they would want financial statements. How would these loans affect my own savings if the company can't pay? How do we decide what our salaries would be?

Connie: Let's not go off the deep end. Forming a business solves our big problems. We can work together and share ideas and contract as a group. That's the main thing. So we need to learn some accounting and some principles of business. Look, we are rocket scientists for crying out loud. Business and accounting can't be that hard.

Connie is right. Forming a business solves some very important problems. The fact that millions of business entities exist tells us that many problems are solved this way and that the benefits often exceed the costs.

Accounting is designed to provide the information about a business needed by owners, managers, employees, government agencies, and others in order to make informed decisions. As we will see, accounting issues come up even before the business is formed, and accounting is used in planning and evaluating for ongoing businesses.

Often, those who lend money to a business, called creditors, along with the owners who invest in the business, want to see accounting information that reveals the financial position of the company and its operating results, both of which accounting systems provide. No two accounting information systems are exactly the same, and none addresses all the information needs of outsiders (e.g., creditors) or the concerns expressed by Ann, Bill, and Connie automatically. However, with careful planning, accounting information can help to address the concerns of Ann, Bill, and Connie as well as the needs of creditors and other outside parties.

Choosing the Form of Business Organization

Ann, Bill, and Connie decide to take the plunge and form a business. However, Ann is worried.

Ann: Before we go any further, I think we have to discuss the best way to organize. It seems to me that an equal partnership is the best; that way we all have equal incentives. But I don't really understand what a partnership means in terms of sharing profits and losses.

Bill: Maybe a corporation would be better. I heard that with a corporation our liability would be limited, whatever that means. I don't know whether a corporation or a partnership is best, but I'll tell you what I believe are the characteristics we want. We want a form of business so that we can each invest different amounts, the business can continue if one of us leaves for any reason, and our personal assets can be protected from lawsuits that might result from our business activities.

Ann: And, where we are protected from lawsuits against one of us for something we may have done unrelated to the business, like an auto accident while on vacation.

Connie: Then it seems to me that we want a corporate form of business, but doesn't that involve getting a state charter and that kind of thing? I think that a partnership would be best in that it would signal our customers that we take full responsibility for our actions and, besides, we could get professional insurance to cover any lawsuits. Also, I like the idea of having a say in who the other owners of the business are. I wouldn't want one of you to sell your shares to a stranger.

We can see that Ann, Bill, and Connie are discussing their major concerns about the form of a business organization—concerns that are valid for all types of businesses, from the smallest to the largest.

Exhibit 1–3 compares the three forms of business enterprises—proprietorships, partnerships, and corporations. Note again that legally, proprietorships and partnerships have unlimited owner liability, but accounting considers them as entities separate from their owners. Accounting also views corporations as separate entities, but they have the desirable feature of limiting owner liability. There are other factors besides those noted in Exhibit 1–3 that may need to be considered in selecting the form of business organization. For example, different forms of business may face different income tax laws. These other

EXHIBIT 1–3

Comparison of Forms of Business Entities

	Proprietorship	Partnership	Corporation
Ownership structure	Single owner	Multiple owners, with specified interest in business	Multiple owners, with interest percentages represented by stock holdings
Requirements for transfer of ownership	Approval of proprietor	Usually approval of all partners	Sale of stock
For accounting purposes, the entity to be accounted for	Proprietorship (separate from the proprietor)	Partnership (separate from its partners)	Corporation (separate from its stockholders)
Legal liability from business activities	Unlimited: May result in personal loss	Unlimited: May result in personal loss	Limited: Loss limited to owners' investment in the business entity

factors are considered in more detail in business law courses, income tax accounting courses, and other business courses. Also, not all of the concerns expressed by Ann, Bill, and Connie are addressed by the form of business. For example, their decision to form a corporation or a partnership does not resolve the compensation issue raised by Bill. Specific agreements would have to be made to resolve such issues.

FINANCIAL STATEMENTS

Accounting information is communicated in many different types of statements and reports. However, as noted earlier in the discussion between Mr. M and the banker Ms. B, starting on page 6, external users of accounting data normally rely, to a large extent, on a standard set of financial statements. The standardized statements governed by GAAP include the following:

1. Balance sheet (or position statement).
2. Income statement (or earnings statement).
3. Retained earnings statement.
4. Statement of cash flows.

The remainder of this chapter will introduce you to the nature and purpose of each of these four statements. These four GAAP-governed standardized statements are what auditors must audit for publicly traded companies to comply with SEC regulations.

The Balance Sheet

Objective 4

The three basic categories of a balance sheet— assets, liabilities, and stockholders' equity.

The balance sheet is a "snapshot" of the business's financial position **at a specific date.** Exhibit 1–4 shows how the headings of balance sheets identify the name of the company (Technotic Space Labs), the name of the statement (Balance Sheet), and the specific date of the statement (December 31, 19xx). The following are the three basic categories of resources and obligations reported in a balance sheet:

1. **Assets.** Certain resources controlled by the business.
2. **Liabilities.** Claims by creditors.
3. **Stockholders' (owners') equity.** Claims by owners of the business.

Assets are defined as the future economic benefits controlled by a particular business entity. For example, cash held by a business is an asset that can be used to purchase other assets or pay for services. Land is an asset representing future economic benefits because land may provide a location to conduct future operations. Likewise, a factory or building and its furniture, machinery, and equipment are assets representing future benefits insofar

EXHIBIT 1–4

CORPORATION:

Technotic Space Labs
Balance Sheet
December 31, 19xx

Assets		Liabilities and Stockholders' Equity	
Cash	$ 819,000	Liabilities*	$ 418,000
All other assets*	589,000	Stockholders' equity*	990,000
Total assets	$1,408,000	Total liabilities and stockholders' equity	$1,408,000

*Details are shown later in this chapter.

as they will enable the business to operate and earn income (profits). In addition, if a business did not own assets, it would have to rent them in order to operate. Thus, assets are the pool of economic resources controlled by a business and used in its operations with the intent of generating a larger pool of economic resources.

Most businesses have obligations in the form of claims that outsiders can make on company assets. These obligations, or debts, are called liabilities. Liabilities require that a business transfer assets or something of value to other parties (usually individuals, businesses, and/or governments) in the future. Many different economic activities may result in liabilities, such as borrowing cash from a bank or buying goods or services on account (or on credit). Thus, we can think of liabilities as the specific claims against the assets of a business entity that will require future outflows of assets or other value.

Stockholders' (owners') equity is the owners' claims to the net assets of a business entity. We use "net asset" here because owners' claims have lower priority than creditors' claims. Net assets (assets minus liabilities) equal the owners' claims. These owners' claims are also equal to the sum of (1) the capital the owners originally invested in the business and (2) the net income from business operations that has been retained in the business since its beginning.

Exhibit 1–4 illustrates the stockholders' equity as it is reported in the balance sheet of the corporation Technotic Space Labs. The term stockholders' equity (or shareholders' equity) is normally used for describing the owners' claims in the case of a corporation.

Exhibit 1–5 illustrates how the owners' equity section would appear if Technotic Space Labs were organized as a proprietorship or a partnership. In the proprietorship example, Mr. X is the owner. His claim of $990,000 is indicated under "Owner's equity" in the single item, "X, capital." In the partnership example, the business is owned by three partners, A, B, and C. The claims of the three owner-partners are listed separately under "Owners' equity" with a total also equaling $990,000.

The Balance Sheet Equation. From Exhibits 1–4 and 1–5, you can see that all the assets of a business entity are claimed by two major groups: (1) creditors who have specific claims against the business entity's assets; and (2) owners who have invested in the entity's assets and whose claims equal the total assets minus the creditors' claims. This relationship is expressed in the balance sheet equation:

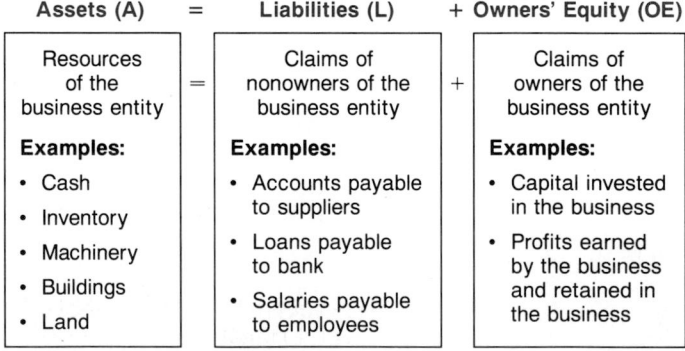

Assets (A)	=	Liabilities (L)	+	Owners' Equity (OE)
Resources of the business entity	=	Claims of nonowners of the business entity	+	Claims of owners of the business entity
Examples:		**Examples:**		**Examples:**
• Cash • Inventory • Machinery • Buildings • Land		• Accounts payable to suppliers • Loans payable to bank • Salaries payable to employees		• Capital invested in the business • Profits earned by the business and retained in the business

For Technotic Space Labs as a corporation, this equation uses the term *stockholders' equity,* and is expressed as:

$$\text{Assets (A)} = \text{Liabilities (L)} + \text{Stockholders' Equity (SE)}$$
$$\$1,408,000 = \$418,000 + \$990,000$$

The balance sheet equation applies to all balance sheets; but, since each business is different, the detailed elements (cash, equipment, inventory, and so on) shown in the balance sheet may differ. Also, just as with all algebraic equalities, the balance sheet equation can

EXHIBIT 1–5

Proprietorship and Partnership Forms of Ownership
PROPRIETORSHIP:

Technotic Space Labs
Balance Sheet
December 31, 19xx

Assets		Liabilities and Owner's Equity	
Cash	$ 819,000	Liabilities.	$ 418,000
All other assets	589,000	Owner's equity:	
		X, capital	990,000
		Total liabilities and	
Total assets	$1,408,000	owner's equity	$1,408,000

PARTNERSHIP:

Technotic Space Labs
Balance Sheet
December 31, 19xx

Assets		Liabilities and Owners' Equity	
Cash	$ 819,000	Liabilities.	$ 418,000
All other assets.	589,000	Owners' equity:	
		A, capital	$ 330,000
		B, capital	330,000
		C, capital	330,000
		Total owners' equity	$ 990,000
		Total liabilities and	
Total assets	$1,408,000	owners' equity	$1,408,000

be manipulated to express different relationships, all of which are equally valid. For example, using the balance sheet numbers of Technotic Space Labs, the balance sheet equation can appear as

1. Assets (A) = Liabilities (L) + Stockholders' Equity (SE)
   $1,408,000 = $418,000 + $990,000

or

2. Assets (A) − Liabilities (L) = Stockholders' Equity (SE)
   $1,408,000 − $418,000 = $990,000

or

3. Assets (A) − Stockholders' Equity (SE) = Liabilities (L)
   $1,408,000 − $990,000 = $418,000

Accounting Transactions and the Balance Sheet. Business activities are the events that alter the assets, liabilities, or owners' equity of the business and its balance sheet. These events are called accounting transactions. Note that only business activities that affect the elements of the accounting equation are accounting transactions. Business activities such as writing a memo or holding a business conference are not accounting transactions in themselves, although they may lead to future accounting transactions.

All accounting transactions can be classified as (1) financing, (2) investing, or (3) operating activities. Financing activities are those accounting transactions related to creditors and owners of the company, such as the borrowing and paying of loans and the sale of stock and payments to stockholders. Investing activities are related to the acquisition and disposal of assets for use in the business. Operating activities are those related to customers, such as sales and payments to employees and other suppliers of goods and services. In Chapter 2, operating activities are introduced.

Objective 5
How accounting transactions affect the balance sheet equation and the balance sheet.

To illustrate how financing and investing activities affect the balance sheet, we return to our research scientists, Ann, Bill, and Connie, who are now entrepreneurs and who have decided to form Technotic Space Labs (TSL) as an equal partnership among the three. We will examine the first nine transactions of Technotic Space Labs (TSL). As you study these nine transactions, continually refer to Exhibit 1–6 which gives the transactions in a spreadsheet analysis format. Note that the balance sheet equality is maintained after the effect of each transaction is recorded on the spreadsheet.

Transaction 1: Financing—Partners contribute cash. On January 10, 19xx, Ann, Bill, and Connie form the TSL partnership by each contributing $330,000. TSL begins its existence with the following balance sheet:

Technotic Space Labs
Balance Sheet
January 10, 19xx

Assets		Owners' Equity	
Cash	$990,000	A, capital	$330,000
		B, capital.	330,000
		C, capital.	330,000
Total assets	$990,000	Total owners' equity	$990,000

Note that both assets and owners' equity equal $990,000, and that the balance sheet is in balance.

Transactions 2 and 3: Financing—Borrowing from the bank; and Investing—Buying land. On January 15, 19xx, TSL borrows $400,000 from a bank (transaction 2). To do this, it gives the bank a note (a promise to pay) stating that in five years TSL will repay the loan. On the same day, TSL uses $100,000 of the $400,000 to buy land for a building site (transaction 3). The bank note increases the asset cash by $400,000 and results in a note payable (a liability) of $400,000—increasing both sides of the balance sheet to $1,390,000. The purchase of the land for $100,000 only affects the asset side of the balance sheet—cash is decreased $100,000, and the new asset, land, $100,000, is added. After transaction 3 the TSL balance sheet appears as shown below:

Technotic Space Labs
Balance Sheet
January 15, 19xx

Assets		Liabilities and Owners' Equity	
Cash	$1,290,000	Liabilities:	
Land	100,000	Notes payable	$ 400,000
		Owners' equity:	
		A, capital	$ 330,000
		B, capital	330,000
		C, capital	330,000
		Total owners' equity	$ 990,000
Total assets	$1,390,000	Total liabilities and owners' equity . . .	$1,390,000

EXHIBIT 1–6

Spreadsheet Analysis of Balance Sheet Equation, Technotic Space Labs

Technotic Space Labs

Trans- action No.	Assets					=	Liabilities		+	Owners' Equity
	Cash	Note Receivable	Lab Equipment	Land	Lab		Accounts Payable	Notes Payable		Total Capital
1	990,000									990,000
2	400,000							400,000		
3	−100,000			100,000						
4	−300,000				300,000					
5	− 6,000	6,000								
6			60,000				60,000			
7	−125,000		125,000							
8			− 2,000				− 2,000			
9	− 40,000						−40,000			
Ending Balances	819,000	6,000	183,000	100,000	300,000		18,000	400,000		990,000
	$1,408,000						$1,408,000			

Using the accounting equation to illustrate the effect that transactions 1–3 have on the balance sheet, we have

Transaction No.	Assets		=	Liabilities	+	Owners' Equity
	Cash	Land		Notes Payable		Total Capital
1	$ 990,000					$990,000
2	400,000			$400,000		
	$1,390,000			$400,000		$990,000
3	− 100,000	$100,000				
	$1,290,000	+	$100,000	=	$400,000	+ $990,000

Transaction 4: Investing—Building a lab. The company hires a contractor to build a lab, which is completed at the end of October 19xx. On November 1, 19xx, it pays $300,000 to the contractor and takes title to the lab facility. The asset cash is reduced $300,000 (to $990,000), and the $300,000 is used to create the asset lab (or building). Many business transactions follow this pattern of decreasing one asset, cash in our example of TSL, and establishing a new asset, such as the lab built by TSL, or increasing an existing asset, for example, by adding an addition to the lab. These transactions do not change the total assets of the business—only the composition of the assets change.

After the November 1 transaction, the accounting equation and the three sections of the balance sheet are as follows:

Assets (A) $1,390,000		= =	Liabilities (L) $400,000		+ +	Owners' Equity (OE) $990,000	
Cash	$ 990,000		Notes payable.	$400,000		A, capital	$330,000
Land	100,000					B, capital	330,000
Lab	300,000					C, capital	330,000
	$1,390,000	=		$400,000	+		$990,000

Transaction 5: Investing—Partner borrows from partnership.   On November 10, Bill borrows $6,000 from the partnership, agreeing to pay it back within 90 days. This transaction allows us to observe the separate entity concept. When one of the owners borrows money from the business, since the business is always viewed as a separate entity apart from its owners, the owners' equity, which is $990,000, is not affected. Instead, the asset cash is reduced by $6,000 and another asset, note receivable, is increased to show the claim of the business against one of its owners. This is an investing activity because the partners invest in this particular asset.

In the case of Bill, the note receivable represents the company's claim to receive cash from Bill in the future. Notes receivable could also result when customers acquire goods by promising to pay cash on some future date and sign a "note" to that effect. After the November 10 transaction, the effect on the balance sheet equation and the balance sheet is as follows:

Assets (A) $1,390,000		= =	Liabilities (L) $400,000		+ +	Owners' Equity (OE) $990,000	
Cash	$ 984,000		Notes payable.	$400,000		A, capital	$330,000
Note receivable . . .	6,000					B, capital	330,000
Land	100,000					C, capital	330,000
Lab	300,000						
	$1,390,000	=		$400,000	+		$990,000

Transaction 6: Investing—Acquire lab equipment.   On November 20, TSL buys lab equipment amounting to $60,000 on open account from Duotech, Inc. This transaction differs from transactions 4 and 5 in that the balance sheet totals change—both assets and liabilities increase $60,000. Transaction 6 is similar to transaction 2 in that the financial size of the business seems to increase by adding more assets and liabilities to the balance sheet. Note, however, that the net assets (assets − liabilities) and owners' equity remain at $990,000. Purchasing equipment on open account, called accounts payable, means that the seller gives the equipment to the company in exchange for its informal promise to pay for the supplies at a later date. Buying on credit is routine for companies with good credit ratings. Usually large businesses have purchasing agents who are authorized to buy items for the business on open account, thereby committing the business to pay for the purchases at a later date.

After transaction 6 is completed, the balance sheet equation and balance sheet totals are as follows:

open account

Assets (A) $1,450,000		=	Liabilities (L) $460,000		+	Owners' Equity (OE) $990,000	
Cash	$ 984,000		Accounts payable	$ 60,000		A, capital	$330,000
Note receivable . . .	6,000		Notes payable.	400,000		B, capital	330,000
Lab equipment	60,000					C, capital	330,000
Land	100,000						
Lab	300,000						
	$1,450,000	=		$460,000	+		$990,000

Transactions 7, 8, and 9: Investing—Buying equipment and returning equipment—and Financing—Paying a debt. On December 3, TSL pays $125,000 for new equipment (transaction 7). Transaction 7 differs from transaction 6 in that TSL uses cash to pay for the equipment instead of credit. As a result, cash is decreased and equipment is increased for the cost of the lab equipment, $125,000.

On December 5, TSL returns $2,000 of the lab equipment bought from Duotech, Inc., on November 20 because it was defective (transaction 8). Duotech gave TSL a credit on account of $2,000. In this transaction, the balance sheet totals are again changed—assets and liabilities are decreased by $2,000. The return of the defective goods reduced both the asset lab equipment and the liability accounts payable by $2,000.

On December 27, TSL paid $40,000 to Duotech (transaction 9). This transaction reduced assets and liabilities, thereby changing some of the balance sheet totals once again. The asset cash and the liability accounts payable are both reduced by $40,000 for the payment to Duotech for equipment purchased earlier on open account. TSL still owes Duotech $18,000 for equipment purchased on account as of the end of 19xx.

After transactions 7, 8, and 9 are completed, the balance sheet equation and balance sheet are

Assets (A) $1,408,000		=	Liabilities (L) $418,000		+	Owners' Equity (OE) $990,000	
Cash	$ 819,000		Accounts payable	$ 18,000		A, capital	$330,000
Note receivable . . .	6,000		Notes payable.	400,000		B, capital	330,000
Lab equipment	183,000					C, capital	330,000
Land	100,000						
Lab	300,000						
	$1,408,000	=		$418,000	+		$990,000

The balance sheet equality is maintained throughout the life of the business. A balance sheet such as the one shown below may be prepared at any time; and as long as all steps are performed to maintain the equality of the balance sheet equation, the balance sheet will balance; that is, assets will always equal liabilities plus owners' equity.

Technotic Space Labs
Balance Sheet
December 31, 19xx

Assets		Liabilities and Owners' Equity	
Cash	$ 819,000	Liabilities:	
Note receivable	6,000	Accounts payable	$ 18,000
Lab equipment	183,000	Notes payable	400,000
Land	100,000	Total liabilities	$ 418,000
Lab	300,000	Owners' equity:	
		A, capital	$ 330,000
		B, capital	330,000
		C, capital	330,000
		Total owners' equity	$ 990,000
Total assets	$1,408,000	Total liabilities and owners' equity	$1,408,000

None of the nine transactions was operating because TSL as of 12/31/xx had engaged in only financing and investing. In Chapter 2 we explore the accounting for operating transactions. Now that we have seen how investing and financing accounting transactions affect the balance sheet, we must introduce the other major financial statements and show how they relate to the balance sheet. The following sections introduce the income statement, the retained earnings statement, and the statement of cash flows.

Basic Financial Statements and Their Relationships

The income statement, also called the statement of operations, earnings statement, and profit and loss statement, reports the results of business operations for a period of time, such as one month, one quarter, or one year. These business operations involve business revenues and business expenses. Revenues represent measures of increases in owners' equity resulting from operating activities, while expenses represent measures of decreases in owners' equity resulting from operating activities. The excess of revenues over expenses represents net income (net profit) as follows:

$$\text{Revenues} - \text{Expenses} = \text{Net Income}$$

Although many consider the balance sheet to be the most fundamental financial statement, the income statement is also very important because it indicates the profitability of the business. As you will learn, if a company repeatedly shows a net loss, when expenses exceed revenues, the company will not be able to survive unless owners or creditors are willing to provide more resources. The following illustrates the basic format (much simplified) of an income statement:

Company Name
Income Statement
For the Period Ended 12/31/xx

Revenues	$145,000
Expenses	(98,000)
Net income	$ 47,000

The retained earnings statement explains the changes that occurred in the retained earnings portion of stockholders' equity during a period of time (one year, for example) due to business operations (net income) and payments made to owners in the form of dividends, which are returns to stockholders for their investment in the business. Retained earnings are only shown in statements prepared by corporations. The following illustrates the basic format (much simplified) of a retained earnings statement:

Company Name
Retained Earnings Statement
For the Period Ended 12/31/xx

Beginning retained earnings.	$ 23,000
Add: Net income.	17,000
Subtract: Dividends	(30,000)
Ending retained earnings	$ 40,000

The statement of cash flows classifies the three major types of business activities—investing, financing, and operating—and shows where the cash comes from during a period, how the cash is used, and the resulting cash balance. While this statement is explained in greater detail in Chapter 14, the development and analysis of cash flows is covered throughout this textbook. The following illustrates the basic format (much simplified) of a statement of cash flows:

Company Name
Statement of Cash Flows
For the Period Ended 12/31/xx

Operating activities:		
Cash from operations		$ 44,000
Investing activities:		
Cash paid for equipment		(22,000)
Financing activities:		
Cash from issuance of a note	$ 10,000	
Cash paid for dividends	(30,000)	(20,000)
Net increase in cash for the period		$ 2,000

Objective 6

The difference between the balance sheet, income statement, retained earnings statement, and statement of cash flows.

To summarize the reporting characteristic of accounting, the balance sheet lists the financial position of the business as of a specific date, while the income statement, retained earnings statement, and statement of cash flows essentially explain how and why balance sheet amounts change from one date to another (e.g., from the beginning of the year to the end of the year). Most large businesses prepare these four financial statements, and they are the most common examples of standardized financial statements. How do the income statement, the retained earnings statement, and the statement of cash flows relate to the balance sheet? You will not be able to fully answer that question until you have studied most of this text, but Exhibit 1–7 shows the most direct ties between the four statements.

• SUMMARY

After studying this chapter, you should be aware of some of the complexities of the accounting environment. We divided the users of accounting information into two major groups: external users and internal users. Within these user groups, the focus was on external users, internal managers, independent auditors, accounting policymakers, and representatives of government—all playing the roles of either senders or receivers of accounting information.

EXHIBIT 1–7

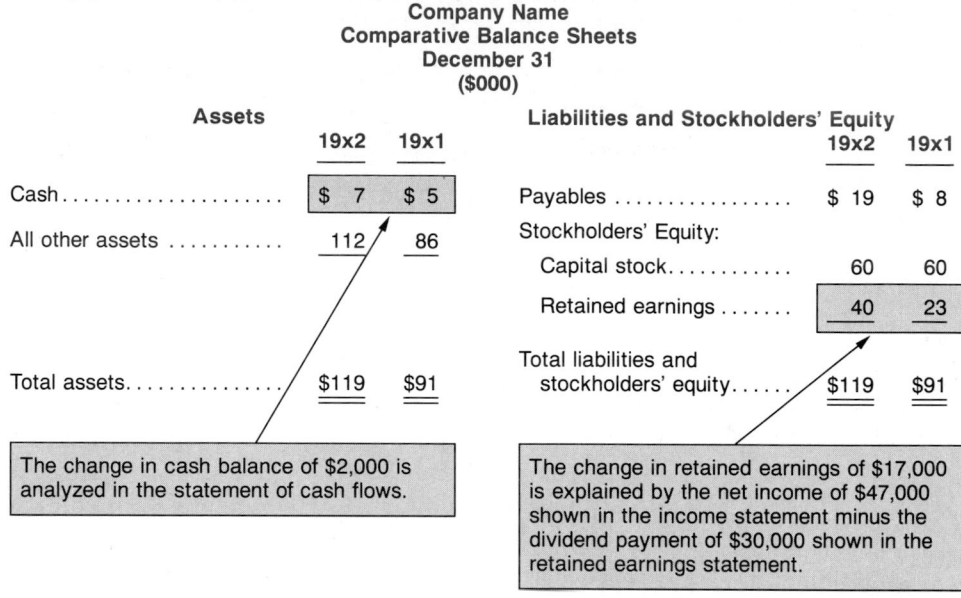

Company Name
Comparative Balance Sheets
December 31
($000)

Assets	19x2	19x1		Liabilities and Stockholders' Equity	19x2	19x1
Cash......................	$ 7	$ 5		Payables	$ 19	$ 8
All other assets	112	86		Stockholders' Equity:		
				Capital stock...........	60	60
				Retained earnings	40	23
Total assets..............	$119	$91		Total liabilities and stockholders' equity......	$119	$91

The change in cash balance of $2,000 is analyzed in the statement of cash flows.

The change in retained earnings of $17,000 is explained by the net income of $47,000 shown in the income statement minus the dividend payment of $30,000 shown in the retained earnings statement.

We focused on business entities that produce accounting information: proprietorships, partnerships, and corporations. Through the use of financial statements, accounting information communicates in words and numbers the results of economic activities. While these financial statements are the primary source of accounting information for external users, we will see in later chapters that many decisions of internal users are also based on these statements.

The interrelationship of the four financial statements—balance sheet, income statement, statement of retained earnings, and statement of cash flows—was introduced. The balance sheet provides the financial position of the business as of a specific date, while the income statement, retained earnings statement, and statement of cash flows essentially explain how and why certain key balance sheet amounts change from one date to another.

In this chapter we concentrated on the balance sheet and the balance sheet equation, which is the foundation of the accounting process. You learned the components of the balance sheet and how it communicates the financial position of the business. Financing and investing transactions, with the aid of a spreadsheet analysis, were examined in relation to the balance sheet equation and the balance sheet. The unbreakable rule of always maintaining the balance sheet equality of assets equaling liabilities plus owners' equity was repeatedly illustrated.

Accounting involves the process of providing information on economic activities that will be useful in the decision making of external and internal accounting information users. As you learn more about the strengths and weaknesses of accounting, you will gain a better understanding of why accounting is often called the *language of business*.

• DEMONSTRATION EXERCISE

On April 1, 19xx, its first day of operations, the Gold Advertising Agency, Inc., had the following transactions:

a. Sold 100 shares of capital stock for $25,000 cash.
b. Purchased supplies to be used in the agency for $500 on account.

c. Paid the April and May rent of $4,800 in advance for office space.

d. Advanced J. J. Gold $5,000, accepting a note from J. J. Gold.

e. Purchased land for $10,000 cash and a $50,000 note.

Construct the end of the day (April 1, 19xx) balance sheet with the aid of the spreadsheet analysis format. (Refer to Exhibit 1–6.)

Solution:

Gold Advertising Agency, Inc.

Date of Event	Assets					=	Liabilities		+	Stockholders' Equity
	Cash	Note Receivable	Supplies	Prepaid Rent	Land		Accounts Payable	Notes Payable		Capital Stock
4/1/xx a.m.										
a.	25,000									25,000
b.			500				500			
c.	− 4,800			4,800						
d.	− 5,000	5,000								
e.	−10,000				60,000			50,000		
4/1/xx p.m.	5,200	5,000	500	4,800	60,000		500	50,000		25,000

Gold Advertising Agency, Inc.
Balance Sheet
April 1, 19xx

Assets		Liabilities and Stockholders' Equity	
Cash	$ 5,200	Liabilities:	
Note receivable	5,000	Accounts payable	$ 500
Supplies	500	Notes payable	50,000
Prepaid rent	4,800	Total liabilities	$50,500
Land	60,000	Stockholders' equity:	
		Capital stock.	$25,000
		Total stockholders' equity	$25,000
Total assets	$75,500	Total liabilities and stockholders' equity.	$75,500

Organizations Involved in Policymaking

Objective 7
The organizations involved in accounting policymaking and how they serve the external, internal, and governmental user groups.

In accounting, as in other systems of our economy and society, organizations exist that perform important policy services for special groups of individuals. Exhibit 1A–1 lists nine accounting organizations and the accounting users they represent. Study this exhibit before reading the discussion that follows.

The American Accounting Association (AAA), organized in the early 1900s, indirectly represents the interest of all parties in the accounting environment—external users, internal users, auditors, and policymakers. The AAA is made up primarily of university and college accounting educators, many with backgrounds in various aspects of accounting practice. Although the AAA cannot directly set policies, it provides indirect input to the policymaking processes of the Financial Accounting Standards Board (FASB) and other groups. Many members of the AAA hold influential positions, including one membership on the seven-member board of the FASB. In many direct and indirect ways, committees of the AAA have significantly influenced the development of accounting as we know it today.

The American Institute of Certified Public Accountants (AICPA) was originally organized in 1887 and has been the organization of practicing Certified Public Accountants (CPAs) since its beginning. An important function of the AICPA is to monitor the certification process of CPAs, which is conducted on a state-by-state basis. Upon completion of the CPA requirements, students of accounting are employed in (1) public accounting, which includes independent auditing, tax accounting, and consulting services; (2) private or industrial accounting; and (3) governmental and other not-for-profit accounting.

To guide auditors, the AICPA establishes generally accepted auditing standards (GAAS)—a set of rules and guidelines for auditing financial statements. In addition, the AICPA has been involved in establishing accounting policies that affect GAAP by defining the most appropriate accounting methods to be applied to certain special industries. These guidelines provide direction to both auditors and managers.

EXHIBIT 1A–1

Organizations Representing Accounting User Groups

Organization	Users Represented
American Accounting Association (AAA)	External users Internal users Policymakers Auditors
American Institute of Certified Public Accountants (AICPA)	Managers (internal users) Auditors Policymakers
Financial Executives Institute (FEI)	Managers (internal users)
Financial Accounting Standards Board (FASB)	Policymakers
Government Accounting Office (GAO) and other governmental agencies	Governmental users
Internal Revenue Service (IRS)	Governmental users
International Accounting Standards Committee (IASC)	Professional associations worldwide
National Association of Accountants (NAA)	Managers (internal users)
Securities and Exchange Commission (SEC)	Policymakers Governmental users

The AICPA provides its 250,000 members with a monthly publication, *The Journal of Accountancy.* This publication has been reporting current accounting events and issues of interest to CPAs since 1905.

The accounting organizations that specialize in representing the view of managers are the Financial Executives Institute (FEI) and the Institute of Management Accountants (IMA). The FEI is a national organization that includes in its membership the chief financial officers and other financial executives of many publicly traded corporations. The various committees of the FEI follow accounting developments and contact policymakers to express the position of its members. The IMA is also a national organization, and its membership consists of controllers, chief accounting officers, treasurers, accounting managers, and holders of other accounting-related positions. Both the FEI and the IMA have over 100,000 members each and publish monthly journals that report on current developments.

Accounting policymakers essentially look after the interests of the external users who are not otherwise represented by influential accounting organizations. In order of importance, the organizations that directly or indirectly influence policymaking by determining the nature and content of the financial statements of publicly traded companies are

1. The Financial Accounting Standards Board (FASB).
2. The Securities and Exchange Commission (SEC).
3. The American Institute of Certified Public Accountants (AICPA).
4. The International Accounting Standards Committee (IASC).

In the United States, the Financial Accounting Standards Board (FASB) is an independent, private organization that consists of seven full-time board members plus a full-time research staff. The board members are generally selected from backgrounds in auditing, corporate management, financial analysis, and education. The FASB is the primary organization responsible for establishing GAAP and setting accounting policy.

The Securities and Exchange Commission (SEC) is a branch of the federal government with legal authority to establish accounting policies for publicly traded companies. However, since 1939, the SEC has delegated the primary responsibility for policymaking to the private sector currently represented by the FASB. The SEC does influence the nature and content of GAAP, but the most significant accounting pronouncements are currently issued through the FASB.

Between 1939 and 1973, before the creation of the FASB, the AICPA had the primary responsibility for setting accounting policy. Today, as stated above, the AICPA defines appropriate methods for certain special industries and has primary responsibility for the development of generally accepted auditing standards (GAAS).

The International Accounting Standards Committee (IASC) is the primary body that establishes international accounting standards. The IASC responds to the financial information needs of multinational corporations and the international investment communities. Established in 1973 by associations of professional accountants in nine countries, the IASC is now supported by professional organizations in over 70 countries. It has issued over 30 nonbinding standards thus far and most of these standards have found general acceptance in the United States, Canada, the United Kingdom, France, and Japan. It is expected that as the world's markets become more interconnected, financial standards will be harmonized more and more and organizations such as IASC will play a greater role.

• KEY TERMS

Accounting. An information process that communicates the results of economic activities and states in ways that are useful to decision makers.

Accounting transactions. Business activities or events that affect the assets, liabilities, and owners' equity of the business and its balance sheet.

Assets. Economic resources that a business owns or controls; future economic benefits controlled by a particular business entity as a result of past economic activities.

Audit reports. Opinions on financial statements by independent auditors.

Balance sheet. Lists all of the company's assets, liabilities, and ownership interests at a specific point in time; also called position statement or statement of financial position. If the balance sheet contains data for more than one point in time, it is called a comparative balance sheet.

Balance sheet equation. Assets equal liabilities plus owners' equity.

Business entity. Economic unit separate from its owners; the business unit accounted for on the company's financial statements; viewed as separate from the owners of the business; also called the business entity, separate entity, or entity concept.

Capital stock. A unit of ownership in a corporation; also called common stock.

Closely held company. Corporation whose stock is not publicly traded; also called privately held company.

Corporation. Business whose ownership interests are represented by shares of stock called common stock or capital stock; owners of stock (stockholders or shareholders) have limited liability.

Creditors. Those who lend money to the business.

Dividends. Payments to stockholders as a return on their investments. A distribution of the net income, which reduces retained earnings.

Expenses. Measures of decreases in owners' equity resulting from operating activities.

External users. All individuals and other entities that are not managers employed by the business entity who have an interest in the company's financial affairs; also called outsiders.

Financial accounting. Accounting information provided to external users in the form of financial statements.

Financial statements. Standardized financial reports on the money measurements of a specific business entity.

Financing activities. Accounting transactions related to creditors, debtors, and owners of the company.

General-purpose reports. Financial statements that are given to outside parties and that are prepared according to GAAP.

Generally accepted accounting principles (GAAP). A set of rules or guidelines used to prepare financial statements.

Governmental users. Governmental entities that often request specific accounting information they need, such as the Internal Revenue Service (IRS) and the Securities and Exchange Commission (SEC).

Harmonization. The process of making fundamentally similar the accounting principles and practices of different countries with the goal of greater comparability of financial reports.

Income statement. Reports the results of business operations for a period of time such as a year; indicates the profitability of the business; also called statement of operations, earnings statement, or profit and loss statement.

Internal Revenue Service (IRS). A governmental agency that requires special-purpose reports indicating the amount of federal income taxes owed by the business.

Internal users. Managers of a business.

Investing activities. Accounting transactions related to the acquisition and disposal of long-term assets used in the business.

Liabilities. Claims by outsiders to receive cash or other assets from the business at some future date.

Managerial accounting. Accounting information used by internal managers to plan and operate the business.

Net assets. Assets minus liabilities; the owners' claims against the business.

Net income. Results when a business is able to sell its goods and/or services for more than they cost the company; also called net profit or earnings.

Open account. A purchase for credit rather than cash; also called buying on credit.

Operating activities. Accounting transactions related to customers and suppliers of products and services; transactions that are intended to affect income and are of interest to the business for income measurement purposes.

Owners' equity. The owners' claims to the net assets of a business entity; shown in the balance sheet of a proprietorship as owner's equity, of a partnership as owners' equity or partners' equity, and of a corporation as stockholders' equity.

Partnership. Noncorporate business owned by two or more owners.

Proprietorship. Noncorporate business owned by one person.

Publicly held company. Company (corporation) whose stock is traded by one or more stock exchanges; also called publicly traded company.

Retained earnings statement. Report explaining changes that occurred in retained earnings during a period of time (one year, for example) due to business operations and dividends payments made to owners.

Revenues. Measures of increases in owners' equity resulting from operating activities.

Securities and Exchange Commission (SEC). A governmental unit that regulates stock exchanges and corporations whose securities are traded thereon.

Statement of cash flows. Classifies investing, financing, and operating activities—showing where the cash came from during a period, how the cash was used, and the resulting cash balance.

Stock exchanges. Organized trading institutions where shares of stock can be bought and sold.

Stockholders. Owners of corporate stock; also called shareholders.

Stockholders' equity. See owners' equity. Also called shareholders' equity.

· Appendix Key Terms

American Accounting Association (AAA). Professional organization representing the interests of external users, internal users, auditors, and policymakers.

American Institute of Certified Public Accountants (AICPA). Professional organization of Certified Public Accountants (CPAs) representing auditors and other CPAs.

Financial Accounting Standards Board (FASB). Independent, private organization that is primarily responsible for establishing GAAP and setting accounting policy.

Financial Executives Institute (FEI). Professional organization representing the viewpoint of managers.

Generally accepted auditing standards (GAAS). A set of rules or guidelines for auditing financial statements.

International Accounting Standards Committee (IASC). The primary body that recommends international accounting standards.

Institute of Management Accountants (IMA). Professional organization representing managers.

• SYNONYMS

Balance sheet; position statement; statement of financial position.

Balance sheet equation; accounting equation.

Business entity; business entity concept; separate entity concept; entity concept.

Capital stock; common stock.

Income; profit.

Income statement; statement of operations; earnings statement; profit and loss statement.

Merchandise; inventory.

Net income; net profit; earnings.

Open account; buying on credit.

Publicly held company; publicly traded company.

Retained earnings; retained income; retained surplus.

Stockholders; shareholders.

• QUESTIONS

1. Define accounting.
2. Who are the external users of accounting?
3. Who are internal users?
4. Describe the responsibilities of internal users. What are the difficulties encountered in carrying out these responsibilities?
5. Name two of the governmental users of accounting.
6. What are the primary types of decisions involving accounting data made by external users?
7. What kinds of decisions involving accounting data are made by internal users?
8. What kinds of decisions involving accounting data are made by governmental users?
9. What are the three forms of businesses?
10. How do proprietorships differ from partnerships?
11. How do corporations differ from partnerships?
12. What is the difference between closely held companies and publicly traded companies?
13. What is a balance sheet?
14. What are the definitions of assets, liabilities, and owners' equity?
15. What is the balance sheet equation and why must it balance?
16. What are the primary examples of accounting reports?
17. Explain how the other financial statements relate to the balance sheet.
18. Describe the three categories into which all accounting transactions can be placed.
19. Describe two transactions that increase the total assets on the balance sheet.
20. Describe a transaction that does not change the total assets on the balance sheet.

• Appendix Questions

21. What are the accounting organizations representing the interests of internal users?
22. What are the accounting organizations representing the interests of auditors?
23. What are the accounting organizations representing the interests of external users?
24. Who determines generally accepted accounting principles (GAAP)?
25. Who determines generally accepted auditing standards (GAAS)?
26. Your friend is a law student who is interested in learning about the legal structure of accounting. He wants to know who makes accounting rules that govern the financial reports of publicly owned companies. Also, he has noticed articles that refer to generally accepted accounting principles and would like to know what these are and who establishes these principles. Explain to your friend what you know about the answers to his questions.

• EXERCISES

E 1–1

Accounting Users

L.O.1, 2*

1. The complex accounting environment consists of the following users:
   a. Senders and receivers.
   b. Investors, stockholders, bankers, and managers.
   c. Governmental, external, and internal.
   d. Internal and external.
2. Policymakers—
   a. Determine the accounting rules and procedures necessary to provide managers, external users, and auditors with meaningful information.
   b. Attempt to provide external users with as little information as possible.
   c. Include only the SEC and IRS.
   d. Report on the fairness of a company's financial reports.
3. Managerial accounting—
   a. Must follow GAAP.
   b. Provides more timely and detailed information than that provided to external users.
   c. Methods are identical no matter what purpose a company or an individual is pursuing.
   d. All of the above.
4. Governmental users—
   a. Can be viewed as a special class of external users, since many governmental agencies have the power to require any specific accounting information they need.
   b. Include only the IRS and SEC.
   c. Operate in a relatively simple environment that is void of ambiguity.
   d. Request information for no specific purpose.

E 1–2

Forms of Business

L.O.3

1. In a proprietorship—
   a. One person is the owner.
   b. The owner has unlimited liability.
   c. The business is viewed as a separate entity by accountants.
   d. All of the above.
2. A partnership—
   a. Is owned by two or more individuals or entities with unlimited liability.
   b. Is viewed as the favorable form of business by manufacturing companies.
   c. Divides its income equally among partners no matter how the ownership interests are contributed.
   d. All of the above.
3. In a corporation—
   a. Ownership is represented by shares of stock.
   b. One or more individuals or entities can be the owners.
   c. Owners' liability is limited to the amount originally invested.
   d. All of the above.
4. In comparing legal views with accounting treatments—
   a. Corporations are viewed as separate entities for legal purposes only.
   b. Partnerships are viewed as separate entities for both legal and accounting purposes.
   c. Proprietorships are viewed as separate entities for accounting purposes but not for legal purposes.
   d. All of the above.

E 1–3

Characteristics of Accounting

L.O.4

1. In accounting, money amounts—
   a. Measure the economic resources or assets of the business.
   b. Measure the cash held by the business.
   c. Measure the net income or performance of the business.
   d. Help to communicate past, present, and future business activities.
   e. All of the above.

---

*L.O. refers to the learning objectives given at the beginning of each chapter.

2. The change statements explain changes in a company's position from one date to another. The change statements include—
   a. Income statement, statement of cash flows, and retained earnings statement.
   b. Balance sheet, earnings statement, and statement of cash flows.
   c. Income statement, position statement, and statement of cash flows.
   d. Income statement, balance sheet, and retained earnings statement.

E 1–4
Balance Sheet Preparation
L.O.4, 6

Lawrence Pool Installation, Inc., has the following items on June 30, 19xx:

Accounts receivable	$27,000
Accounts payable	13,000
Cash	7,000
Capital stock	75,000
Equipment.	85,000
Land	20,000
Notes payable	12,000
Salaries payable	15,000
Retained earnings	24,000

Required:
Prepare the June 30, 19xx, balance sheet.

E 1–5
Balance Sheet Preparation
L.O.4, 6

Carpet Cleaners, Inc., has the following items on September 30, 19xx:

Accounts receivable	$ 7,800
Accounts payable	5,890
Cash	15,400
Capital stock	25,000
Equipment.	30,600
Notes payable	10,000
Retained earnings	11,105
Salaries payable	4,575
Supplies	2,770

Required:
Prepare the September 30, 19xx, balance sheet.

E 1–6
Comparison of Different Forms of Owners' Equity
L.O.4

Net assets (assets less liabilities) for Blackford Lumber equal $81,375 on December 31, 19xx. Prepare the owners' equity section of the balance sheet for that date assuming

1. The business is owned by John Blackford only.
2. The business is owned equally by brothers John and Rick Blackford and their sister Kate Merrill.
3. The business is incorporated and has capital stock of $50,000.

E 1–7
Balance Sheet Equation and Balance Sheet Preparation
L.O.4, 6

The following items make up the complete balance sheet of the Tres Hombres Company on June 30, 19xx:

Accounts receivable	$ 38,542
Accounts payable	21,856
Buildings and equipment	187,693
Cash	17,214
Supplies	49,047
Notes payable.	105,356
Retained earnings	?
Salaries payable.	25,070
Land	73,000
Capital stock	150,000

Required:
Prepare the June 30, 19xx, balance sheet.

E 1–8
Balance Sheet
Equation and Balance
Sheet Preparation
L.O.4, 6

The following items make up the complete balance sheet of the Python Company on September 30, 19xx:

Basko, capital	$205,000
Frich, capital	210,000
Wilson, capital	215,000
Accounts receivable	43,867
Notes payable.	118,680
Cash	?
Machinery and equipment.	197,542
Salaries payable.	12,943
Land and building	347,108
Supplies	112,587
Income taxes payable	8,761
Accounts payable	13,056

Required:
1. Compute the September 30, 19xx, cash on hand.
2. Prepare the September 30, 19xx, balance sheet.

E 1–9
Balance Sheet Equation
L.O.4, 6

Assume that Gerry Lobo is the sole proprietor of a computer software business. His balance sheet on December 31, 19x1, was:

Software Styles
Balance Sheet
December 31, 19x1

Assets		**Liabilities and Owner's Equity**	
Cash	$ 2,000	Liabilities:	
Supplies	8,000	Accounts payable	$ 7,000
Land	20,000	Notes payable	60,000
Building	48,000	Total liabilities	67,000
		Owner's equity:	
		Lobo, capital.	$11,000
		Total owner's equity. . . .	$11,000
		Total liabilities and	
Total assets	$78,000	owner's equity	$78,000

On January 19, 19x2, a fire destroyed the facilities of Software Styles. The proprietor's capital account had not changed during January and had a balance of $11,000 at the date of the fire. At the date of the fire, the creditors said that the business owed them $10,000 for accounts payable and $60,000 for the note. All cash is held by First National Bank in Lobo's checking account, which was $3,000 at the time of the fire. The insurance company agreed to pay for the lost assets. What was the amount of assets lost at the date of the fire? (Hint: Do not include land in the loss.)

E 1–10
Balance Sheet Equation
L.O.4, 6

1. If a company has total stockholders' equity of $8,900, then—
   a. A total of $8,900 in capital stock was issued by the company.
   b. The business has total assets of $8,900.
   c. Net income less dividends for the period was $8,900.
   d. Total assets exceed total liabilities by $8,900.
2. If assets are $4,000—
   a. Stockholders' equity must be $4,000.
   b. Liabilities must be $4,000.

   c. Stockholders' equity plus liabilities must be $4,000.

   d. None of the above.

  3. When 5,000 shares of stock are issued for $10,000 cash at the start of a corporation—

   a. The stockholders are considered to be creditors of the corporation.

   b. All stockholders must own the same percentage interest in the corporation.

   c. The value of each share is $2 and may be sold back to the corporation at any time for that amount.

   d. The loss of the stockholders is limited to $10,000.

  4. Assets of a business are—

   a. Things the business uses to operate.

   b. Future economic benefits controlled by the business as a result of past transactions.

   c. Things legally owned by a business that do not have a balance due remaining to be paid on them.

   d. Things provided by the owners of a business who hold stock.

  5. The balance sheet equation may **not** be stated as—

   a. Liabilities = Assets − Owners' Equity.

   b. Owners' Equity + Liabilities = Assets.

   c. Assets − Liabilities = Owners' Equity.

   d. Assets = Liabilities − Owners' Equity.

E 1–11

Balance Sheet Equation and Business Transactions

L.O.5

Analyze the following transactions and complete the form below by stating the amount of the increase or decrease and what component(s) of each balance sheet element is affected:

Example: Sold stock to three investors for $180,000.

 a. Purchased office supplies for $600 cash.

 b. Purchased land for $25,000 cash.

 c. Borrowed $50,000 from the local bank.

 d. Loaned a needy employee $20,000 cash.

 e. Paid the insurance premium for the next 12 months, $12,000.

 f. Purchased $1,000 of additional supplies on account.

 g. Purchased a building for $100,000 cash.

 h. Paid $300 to the supplies vendor and returned $500 of damaged supplies.

	Assets	=	Liabilities	+	Stockholders' Equity
Example:	+180,000 Cash				+180,000 Capital stock
a.					
b.					
c.					
d.					
e.					
f.					
g.					
h.					

Demonstrate that the balance sheet equation remains in balance.

· Appendix Exercise ————————————————————————

E 1–12

Policymaking Organizations

L.O.7

1. The set of rules and guidelines for auditing financial statements are—

 a. GAAP.

 b. GAAS.

 c. GAAP and GAAS.

 d. FASB and AICPA rules.

2. The policymaking organization with primary responsibility for establishing generally accepted accounting principles is—
   a. The Securities and Exchange Commission.
   b. The Internal Revenue Service.
   c. The Financial Accounting Standards Board.
   d. The American Institute of Certified Public Accountants.
3. The accounting organizations that exist to represent managers are—
   a. The Financial Accounting Standards Board and the American Accounting Association.
   b. The AICPA and the SEC.
   c. The Internal Revenue Service and the Government Accounting Office.
   d. The Institute of Management Accountants and the Financial Executives Institute.
4. The set of rules and guidelines for preparing financial statements are—
   a. GAAP.
   b. GAAS.
   c. GAAP and GAAS.
   d. FASB rules.

• PROBLEMS

P 1–1
Forms of Business Organizations
L.O.3

James Jones is thinking of acquiring a franchise for the New World Basketball Conference. Since you have had some business courses, he asks you for your advice. Jones asks you about the different forms of business organizations, since he is not sure whether to have the team set up as a proprietorship, a partnership, or a corporation. The franchise will cost about $3 million to get started.

Required:
Write a paragraph on the advantages and disadvantages of the different forms of business organizations and make a recommendation to James Jones.

P 1–2
Comparison of the Three Forms of Business Organizations
L.O.3

Mason Smith has a number of business investments. He is the sole proprietor of a grocery store, a partner in a hardware store, and a stockholder in a local chemical company. He also owns a summer home, a permanent residence, and several vehicles. The total value of assets owned by Smith is estimated at $4 million. Write a paragraph to answer each of the following **independent** questions concerning Mason Smith:

1. Smith's banker has asked for financial statements for the grocery store and the hardware store businesses. Smith is unsure how to provide this information since he only owns part of the hardware store. How should these businesses be reported to Smith's banker?
2. A customer decides to sue for $2 million in damages due to faulty products purchased from the hardware store. Smith's ownership capital in the hardware store is only $500,000. How much might Smith lose if the customer wins the lawsuit?
3. The chemical company is sued by the Environmental Protection Agency for illegal dumping and is expected to have to pay $10 million. Smith paid $100,000 for his stock in the company. The chemical company has total stockholders' equity of $5 million, and total assets of only $8 million. How much does Smith stand to lose from this lawsuit?
4. Smith used a check from the grocery store's checking account to pay bills owed by the hardware store operations. What accounting assumptions, if any, are violated by such behavior?

P 1–3
Decision Making and Forms of Business Organizations
L.O.3

Jackson's General Store is 100% owned by Maureen Jackson. The general store has earned large profits in recent years, and Jackson is considering buying an interest in another business. Two attractive alternatives available to Jackson are described below.

Alternative 1:
The El Doughno Bakery is currently owned by two brothers. The bakery is going to expand to a second location in hopes of doubling the business and the profits. To do so, the brothers are looking for a new partner to contribute $100,000 cash in exchange for a 50% partnership interest.

Alternative 2:

The Taco fast-food restaurant is owned by five stockholders. The restaurant is going to expand the size of its present location in an effort to provide more seating space for customers. The expansion is expected to cost $100,000 and will be financed by the sale of stock to a new stockholder. The new stockholder would then have one-sixth of the total stock of Taco.

Jackson is not certain which alternative to choose. Both alternatives are expected to return about the same amount of profits to Jackson in the near future. Jackson is interested in your advice.

Required:

Write A concise paragraph in answer of each of the following questions:

1. What kind of decision is Jackson making?
2. What kind of user of accounting information would we call Jackson in this specific decision?
3. What are the potential advantages of each alternative that you see?
4. What important difference should Jackson be aware of in the organizational structure of the two businesses?
5. What effect, if any, will the acquisition of either alternative have on the accounting system for Jackson's General Store? Explain your answer.

P 1–4

Event Analysis and Balance Sheet Preparation

L.O.5, 6

The following balance sheet items pertaining to the Landis Corporation on December 31, 19x1, are listed in alphabetical order:

Accounts payable	$ 58,000
Building	147,000
Cash.	38,000
Equipment	240,000
Supplies	71,000
Land.	62,000
Notes payable	75,000
Other liabilities	88,000
Accounts receivable	43,000
Retained earnings.	? *80000*
Capital stock	300,000

During January 19x2, the following events occurred:

a. Acquired supplies on account, $19,000.
b. Borrowed $50,000 cash from the bank signing a note.
c. Paid $28,000 cash on note payable.
d. Collected $23,000 on accounts receivable.
e. Issued Landis stock for $75,000 cash.
f. Paid $48,000 on accounts payable.

Required:

1. Prepare a spreadsheet analysis as illustrated in Exhibit 1–6, placing the beginning balances given in the balance sheet data of December 31, 19x1, on the first line of the spreadsheet. Fill in the missing amount for retained earnings as of December 31, 19x1.
2. Complete the spreadsheet analysis to account for the six events noted in the problem for January 19x2. Indicate the new balances for each balance sheet item after considering these six events.
3. Prepare the January 31, 19x2, balance sheet based on the spreadsheet analysis.

P 1–5

Event Analysis and Balance Sheet Preparation

L.O.5, 6

The Butler Corporation was formed in September 19xx. The following transactions occurred during the first three months:

19xx

Sept. 1   Sold stock to stockholders for $1.5 million in cash.
       10   Acquired land and building for $1.2 million cash.
       30   Borrowed $800,000 cash from the bank.

Oct. 12   Purchased equipment costing $750,000, paying $250,000 cash. The balance due in 90 days was represented by a note signed by Butler.

  26   Purchased supplies costing $85,000 on open account.

Nov. 10   An officer of Butler Corporation borrowed $5,000 from the corporation, signing a 90-day note.

  16   Returned supplies purchased in October costing $7,000 for credit on account.

  17   Paid $45,000 cash on account for the supplies purchased. The balance was to be paid in December.

  29   Paid cash of $150,000 on note signed October 12.

Required:

1. Prepare a spreadsheet analysis as illustrated in Exhibit 1–6 for Butler Corporation for the first three months of business.
2. Prepare the November 30, 19xx, balance sheet.

P 1–6
Balance Sheet
Preparation
L.O.6

Bill and Sally Foster operate the Captain's Table Restaurant, and each has one-half the owners' equity. At June 30, 19x1, the restaurant has equipment and furnishings for which they paid on June 20, $38,000, and eight months' rent has been paid in advance on the building at $2,400 per month. The food and supplies on hand cost $1,200 and the restaurant's checking account has $8,700 in it. An additional $200 is kept in the cash register at the restaurant. Suppliers are owed $1,100 and the restaurant still owes $15,000 on the note payable used to finance the equipment and furnishings.

Required:
Prepare a balance sheet for the Captain's Table Restaurant at June 30, 19x1.

P 1–7
Balance Sheet Analysis
L.O.5, 6

Valley Fashions, a sole proprietorship owned by J. Klein, started business on January 1, 19x1, with the following balance sheet:

Valley Fashions
Balance Sheet
January 1, 19x1

Cash	5,000	Accounts payable	11,000
Supplies	28,000	Long-term note payable . . .	12,000
Store equipment	17,000	Mortgage payable	82,000
Building	92,000	Total liabilities	105,000
Land	15,000	J. Klein, capital.	52,000
Total	157,000	Total	157,000

During 19x1, sales were very good. Two sales clerks were hired and advertisements were run in the newspaper and on TV. Klein invested an additional $40,000 to refurbish the building, upgrade the store equipment, and expand storage space. At the end of 19x1 Klein drew up the balance sheet shown below:

Valley Fashions
Balance Sheet
December 31, 19x1

Cash	4,000	Accounts payable	62,000
Accounts receivable	12,000	Long-term note payable . . .	12,000
Supplies	66,000	Mortgage payable	82,000
Store equipment	27,000	Total liabilities	156,000
Building	122,000	J. Klein, capital.	90,000
Land	15,000		
Total	246,000	Total	246,000

Required:
Klein is very happy with the first-year results since the assets of the business have increased by more than 50% and net assets have increased by $38,000. Comment on the performance of Valley Fashions for 19x1.

P 1–8

Income Statement and
Statement of Cash Flows

L.O.6

The following items relate to National Corporation's fiscal year ended December 31, 19x1 (in thousands):

Sales revenue	$440.0
Interest expense	15.7
Salaries expense	163.3
Rent expense.	47.0
Selling and administrative expense	25.1
Income tax expense.	72.2
Cash from operations	138.2
Cash paid to acquire factory building	69.1
Cash from sale of stock	31.4
Cash paid for dividends	94.2

Required:
1. Prepare an income statement for the year ended December 31, 19x1.
2. Prepare a statement of cash flows for the year ended December 31, 19x1.

P 1–9

Assets, Liabilities, and
Stockholders' Equity

L.O.4

Listed below are the descriptions of several items that pertain to the financial affairs of the Delta Company for January 19x1, its first month of operations:

a. Amount of loans on 1/15/x1 that must be paid back during January 19x2.
b. Cost of the Delta Company's warehouse paid on 1/20/x1.
c. Cost of unused supplies kept for use in the office.
d. Amount owed to suppliers of inventory at 1/31/x1.
e. Cash in the checking account at 1/31/x1.
f. Amount of money paid for stock by the owners as of 1/31/x1.
g. Amount owed at 1/31/x1 to suppliers.
h. Amount paid for office furniture on 1/29/x1.
i. Amount of sales planned for each line of product carried for February 19x1.

Required:
1. Indicate the balance sheet category to which each item belongs.
2. As what form of business entity is Delta organized? How do you know?

• CASES

C 1–1

Asset and Liability
Valuation

L.O.4

James Jones and four other stockholders each contributed $500,000 to form a new WBC basketball team. The franchise was acquired on January 1, 19xx, at the cost of $2 million, of which $400,000 was paid immediately. A note was signed with the WBC league officials for the balance scheduled to be paid at the beginning of each of the next four years ($400,000 per year). The team signed up eight players resulting in a total annual salary commitment of $2 million. Also, the team paid a total of $1.5 million as signing bonuses to the top four players to get them to sign with the team. Prior to the start of the season, Jones' team, the Mildcats, reported the following balance sheet:

Mildcats, Inc.
Balance Sheet
September 30, 19xx

Assets		Liabilities and Stockholders' Equity	
Cash	$ 400,000	Liabilities:	
Equipment	200,000	Player contracts payable	$2,000,000
Player contracts . . . . ,	3,500,000	Total liabilities	$2,000,000
Franchise	400,000	Stockholders' equity:	
		Capital stock.	$2,500,000
		Total stockholders' equity	$2,500,000
Total assets	$4,500,000	Total liabilities and stockholders equity	$4,500,000

Required:

1. Critically evaluate the balance sheet as reported.
2. Indicate any items you feel should be eliminated, revised, or added.
3. What accounting concepts did you use to help you answer part 2 above?

C 1–2
Financial Statement
Disclosure
L.O.6

A standard set of financial statements includes change statements that provide details on cash and retained earnings: the statement of cash flows and the statement of retained earnings. Write a short analysis of why you believe these amounts are the ones detailed. Why, for example, is there not also a statement of machinery and equipment? (Hint: Consider the relative importance that different balance sheet amounts have for decision makers.)

C 1–3
Internal Users versus
External Users
L.O.2

All major corporations record their operating assets for financial accounting purposes at their original (historical) costs. Several of these corporations, however, keep track of these same assets' current appraisal values (which may be higher than cost) for managerial decision-making purposes. Comment on this inconsistent practice from the view of the accounting profession.

• Evaluating Financial Statements

C 1–4
Financial Statement
Examination—
Ralston Purina
L.O.4

Examine the annual report for Ralston Purina that is provided in Appendix E at the end of this textbook and give the amounts from the Consolidated Balance Sheet as of September 30, 1992:

1. Cash.
2. Notes payable.
3. Land.
4. Inventories.
5. Machinery and equipment.
6. Long-term debt.
7. Dividends payable.
8. Retained earnings.

C 1–5

Balance Sheet Preparation—IBM

L.O.4, 6

International Business Machines Corporation (IBM) reported the following items in a recent annual report (in millions):

Accounts payable	$ 1,970
Cash	755
Capital stock	?
Loans payable	1,410
Notes and accounts receivable	9,971
Plant and other property	21,268
Other assets.	25,820
Other liabilities.	20,060
Retained earnings	28,053
Total assets	?
Total liabilities	?
Total stockholders' equity	34,374

Required:

1. Prepare a balance sheet using the above information for IBM.
2. Does the company have enough cash to pay the accounts payable? How will they pay these obligations?

C 1–6

Balance Sheet Preparation and Analysis—McDonald's

L.O.4–6

The following summarized balance sheet is for McDonald's Corporation, the nation's leading fast-food chain, at the end of a recent year.

**McDonald's Corporation
Balance Sheet
December 31
(in millions)**

Assets		Liabilities and Stockholders' Equity	
Cash and receivables	$ 364	Liabilities:	
Supplies	38	Accounts payable	$ 461
Investments	182	Taxes and other liabilities	789
Property and equipment	4,878	Bonds payable	2,131
Intangible assets	232	Security deposits by franchisers	81
Other assets	275	Total liabilities	$3,462
		Stockholders' equity:	
		Capital stock.	$ 130
		Retained earnings	2,377
		Total stockholders' equity	$2,507
		Total liabilities and	
Total assets	$5,969	stockholders' equity.	$5,969

The liability identified as *Security deposits by franchisers* represents advance payments for services to be received in the future by franchisers who are planning to open new McDonald's restaurants. In the month after this balance sheet was reported, assume that McDonald's received additional cash security deposits from future McDonald's restaurant owners of $25 million. At the same time McDonald's purchased new equipment costing $70 million by signing a long-term note for $50 million and paying the other $20 million in cash. Assume no other transactions have occurred since the reported balance sheet.

Required:
1. Prepare the revised balance sheet for McDonald's to reflect the impact of the investing and financing activity described in the problem.
2. Are the shareholders of McDonald's Corporation any better off now than they were at the time the original balance sheet was reported? Briefly explain your answer.

C 1–7
Accounting Equation—
Ralston Purina
L.O.5

Refer to the 1992 Ralston Purina Company annual report (Appendix E) and show that the following are true:

1. $\dfrac{\text{Change in assets}}{\text{from 1991–1992}} = \dfrac{\text{Change in liabilities}}{\text{from 1991–1992}} + \dfrac{\text{Change in stockholders' equity}}{\text{from 1991–1992}}$

2. $\begin{array}{c}\text{Change in Retained} \\ \text{Earnings from} \\ 1991\text{–}1992\end{array} = \begin{array}{c}\text{Net income} \\ \text{from income} \\ \text{statement}\end{array} - \begin{array}{c}\text{Dividends and other adjustments from} \\ \text{Statement of Shareholders'} \\ \text{Equity}\end{array}$

3. $\begin{array}{c}\text{Change in cash + Marketable securities} \\ \text{(Ralston's definition of cash)}\end{array} = \begin{array}{l}\text{Net cash flow from operations (+ or −)} \\ \text{Net cash flow from investing activities (+ or −)} \\ \text{Net cash flow from financing activities (+ or −)} \\ \text{Effect of exchange rate on cash}\end{array}$

· Appendix Cases

C 1–8
Accounting
Environment—
the Role of GAAP
L.O.7

General Motors Corporation has reporting responsibilities to many different groups and individuals including the SEC, the IRS, General Motors' current and future stockholders, and the financial institutions that may lend them money in the future.

Required:
Write a concise answer to each of the following questions:

1. What is the role of financial statements based on generally accepted accounting principles in meeting these reporting responsibilities?
2. What decision-making information does each of these groups likely need that is not provided in GAAP financial statements? How do these decision makers go about getting this other information?

C 1–9
The Role of
International Standards
L.O.7

Assume the following scenario: Northwest Airlines is in need of a large amount of cash and is negotiating with Royal Dutch Airlines (KLM) of the Netherlands for the following series of relationships.

1. Northwest would get $400,000,000 from KLM for 20% ownership.
2. Northwest would get $200,000,000 from KLM in the form of a two-year loan.
3. Northwest would get $100,000,000 from KLM for one-half share of NW's London and Paris airport operations. Profits would be shared equally.

Required:
Write a concise statement of how harmonization of accounting standards might affect these negotiations.

2

The Relationship between the Balance Sheet and the Income Statement

Today's business environment is very challenging due to such factors as the increasing complexity of financial transactions, rapidly changing technology and the impact of globalization. All of our professionals must have objectivity and integrity as well as a knowledge of business processes to be successful.

Eugene M. Freedman
Coopers & Lybrand

· Learning Objectives

After studying Chapter 2, you should understand

1. The concepts involved in analyzing balance sheet equation transactions, p. 42.
2. The nature of operating, financing, and investing activities, pp. 42–43.
3. Revenue and expense definitions, pp. 43–45.
4. The complete balance sheet equation, pp. 45–47.
5. How to analyze the operating activities of a corporation, pp. 47–49.
6. Revenue and expense recognition, pp. 48–49.
7. The matching principle, p. 49.
8. Why adjustments are necessary, pp. 53–55.
9. The distinction between the accrual basis and the cash basis of accounting, pp. 55–57.
10. The purpose of the income statement and its relationship to the balance sheet, pp. 58–59.

The knowledge you acquired in Chapter 1 is background to help you understand accounting and its function in our society. You also were introduced to some basic relationships
found in financial statements, especially the balance sheet equation, which will be of
importance to you throughout your study of accounting.

Objective 1

*The concepts involved in
analyzing balance sheet
equation transactions.*

In Chapter 1 you were told that a transaction must always keep the equation in balance.
When an event changes the dollar amount of one side of the balance sheet equation, the
event must also change the other side of the equation by the same dollar amount. This dual
effect is the basis for the more complete version of the accounting equation, which you
will begin to study in this chapter.

The balance sheet equation introduced in Chapter 1 was

$$\text{Assets (A)} = \text{Liabilities (L)} + \text{Owners' Equity (OE)}$$

The term owners' equity in the equation is a broad term used to describe the owners' interests in the business. Except for the appendix to Chapter 11, the remainder of this textbook
will focus on corporations, whose owners are called stockholders or shareholders. Therefore, our balance sheet equation will contain the term stockholders' equity as follows:

$$\text{Assets (A)} = \text{Liabilities (L)} + \text{Stockholders' Equity (SE)}$$

Since the organization of corporations differs from the organization of proprietorships and
partnerships, accounting for stockholders' equity is unique in some respects. However,
most of the discussion in this and other chapters applies also to proprietorships and
partnerships.

This chapter discusses the concepts involved in analyzing transactions, the complete
balance sheet equation, and a more in-depth coverage of analyzing the financing, investing, and operating activities of a corporation. After following the effects of transactions
for a corporation for an operating period, the chapter concludes with an analysis of the
resulting financial statements and their meaning. It is crucial, for a thorough appreciation
of accounting, that the goal of analysis and decision making always be kept in mind. Accounting theory, methods, statements, and policymaking bodies would be meaningless if
no relevant information were produced.

**THE COMPLETE
BALANCE SHEET
EQUATION—
ADDING
REVENUES,
EXPENSES, AND
RETAINED
EARNINGS**

Objective 2

*The nature of financing,
investing, and operating
activities.*

Analyzing and recording transactions requires the recognition of changes that business
transactions cause in the balance sheet. In the accounting process, these changes involve the
double effect of increasing and decreasing dollar amounts according to the equality that
was explained earlier. Several possible combinations of increases and decreases are illustrated in Exhibit 2–1.

Earlier, we learned that all accounting transactions affect the dollar amount assigned to
some combination of assets, liabilities, and stockholders' equity, even though the totals for
any or all of these categories do not necessarily change. We also saw examples of financing and investing transactions and how they affected the balance sheet. In this chapter, we
expand our analysis of transactions to include operating activities. First we expand our
definitions of each of these terms:

1. Financing activities are those transactions involved with owners and creditors
   such as issuance of stock, sale of bonds, borrowing from banks and other
   institutions, payment of dividends to owners, repayment of loans, and so on.
   Financing activities bring in the financial resources (usually cash) that are
   needed.

2. Investing activities are those transactions that involve the acquisition or sale of
   productive assets, such as plant, equipment, land, and other assets that are not

EXHIBIT 2–1

Possible Combinations of Effects of Transactions on the Balance Sheet Equation

Type of Dual Effect	Balance Sheet Equation Effects				
	A	=	L	+	SE
1. Only assets change:					
Increase one asset	+$100				
Decrease another asset	− 100				
2. Only liabilities change:					
Increase one liability			+$250		
Decrease another liability			− 250		
3. Increase in assets:					
Increase an asset.	+$380				
Increase a liability or stockholders' equity			+$380	or	+$380
4. Decrease in assets:					
Decrease an asset	−$420				
Decrease a liability or stockholders' equity.			−$420	or	−$420
5. Other "complex changes," such as					
Decrease one asset and.	−$ 50				
Increase another asset	+ 100				
Increase a liability or stockholders' equity			+$ 50	or	+$ 50

completely consumed in the current period or offered for sale in the ordinary course of operations. Investments bring in the specific assets a business needs.

3. Operating activities are those transactions related to providing goods and services to customers, including sales to customers, receipts from customers, payments to suppliers, payments for taxes, payments for wages, the consumption of supplies, the using up of productive assets, and similar transactions.

Objective 3
Revenue and
expense definition.

Proper accounting for operating activities requires an understanding of revenues and expenses, and how the income statement illustrated in Chapter 1 is related to the changes in the balance sheet. The transactions illustrated in Chapter 1 were all the result of financing and investing activities; none pertained to operations. Operating transactions give rise to revenues and expenses and are intended to result in an increase in the net assets (assets minus liabilities) of the company although management's plans are not always successfully accomplished. Consider the following definitions of revenues and expenses:

Revenues are increases in net assets (defined as assets minus liabilities) that result from providing goods or services to customers. Revenues usually result in an increase in cash or accounts receivable, which are promises of cash from customers.

Expenses are the decreases in net assets that occur in order to earn revenues. Expenses usually result in decreases in assets or increases in liabilities to workers, called wages payable, suppliers, called accounts payable, and others such as taxing authorities and creditors.

These definitions enable us to think of revenues as the rewards of operations in the form of increases in net assets, and expenses as the cost of achieving the rewards. If a business is profitable, it will have net income (often called **net profits or earnings**). All of these terms are used when revenues exceed expenses during a period of time, resulting in an increase in net assets due to operating transactions. A net loss indicates the opposite; that is, expenses exceeded revenues. The increase in net assets from profitable operations is reflected in the balance sheet by increasing stockholders' equity. The stockholders' equity account that is increased along with the increase in the net assets is called retained earnings. To illustrate how the balance sheet reflects profitable operations, consider the examples that follow and their related effect on the balance sheet equation of the Z Company. For illustration purposes, the following initial balance sheet amounts are assumed: Assets = $12,000; Liabilities = $4,000; and Stockholders' Equity = $8,000.

Revenues

A revenue transaction is an operating transaction with an outside entity that increases net assets. For instance, if Z Company sells a service to a customer and receives $1,000 in cash, that one transaction increases net assets by $1,000 as shown in the following analysis.

Z Company

	Assets	=	Liabilities	+	Stockholders' Equity
Initial balance	$12,000	=	$4,000	+	$8,000
Operating transaction:					
Revenue—Sale for cash . . .	**+ 1,000**				**+ 1,000**
New balance	$13,000	=	$4,000	+	$9,000

Expenses

The expense from this transaction results when, for instance, cash of $800 is paid to the employee providing the service, thereby decreasing net assets:

Z Company

	Assets	=	Liabilities	+	Stockholders' Equity
Initial balance	$12,000	=	$4,000	+	$8,000
Operating transaction:					
Revenue	+ 1,000				+ 1,000
Expense—Wages.	**− 800**				**− 800**
New balance	$12,200	=	$4,000	+	$8,200

Note that the two operating transactions are shown separately with two separate effects, one increasing net assets ($1,000) and the other decreasing net assets ($800). Their combined effect results in an increase of $200 in net assets and an equal increase in stockholders' equity.

Retained Earnings

Retained earnings is a category of stockholders' equity that captures revenue and expense effects and, as we will see below, also dividend effects. Let us expand the balance sheet equation and assume that the initial $8,000 stockholders' equity consists of $5,000 paid-in capital and $3,000 retained earnings.

Z Company

	Assets	=	Liabilities	+	Paid-in Capital	+	Retained Earnings
					Stockholders' Equity		
Initial balance	$12,000	=	$4,000	+	$5,000		$3,000
Operating transaction:							
Revenue	+ 1,000						+ 1,000
Expense	− 800						− 800
New balance	$12,200	=	$4,000	+	$5,000	+	$3,200

dividends

The retained earnings classification of stockholders' equity also captures the effects of paying owners a return on their investment; that is, dividends. In our example, assume that Z Company pays dividends of $100 to owners.

Z Company

	Assets	=	Liabilities	+	Paid-in Capital	+	Retained Earnings
Initial balance	$12,000	=	$4,000	+	$5,000		$3,000
Operating transaction:							
Revenue	+ 1,000						+ 1,000
Expense	− 800						− 800
Financing transaction:							
Dividends	− 100						− 100
New balance	$12,100	=	$4,000	+	$5,000	+	$3,100

Objective 4

The complete balance sheet equation.

In studying the expanded balance sheet equation given above, note the following:

1. Stockholders' equity consists of
   a. Paid-in capital (the amount paid by owners for stock).
   b. Retained earnings.

2. Retained earnings consists of the cumulative (since the beginning of the entity) net effect on stockholders' equity of revenues, expenses, and dividends:
   a. Revenues (R) add to retained earnings.
   b. Expenses (E) reduce retained earnings.
   c. Dividends (D) reduce retained earnings, but dividends are not expenses or operating activities.

Now we can further expand the balance sheet equation:

$$\text{Assets} = \text{Liabilities} + \text{Stockholders' Equity}$$

$$\text{Assets} = \text{Liabilities} + \text{Paid-in Capital} + \text{Retained Earnings}$$

$$\text{Assets} = \text{Liabilities} + \text{Paid-in Capital} + \text{Revenues} - \text{Expenses} - \text{Dividends}$$

or

$$A = L + SE$$

$$A = L + PIC + RE$$

$$A = L + PIC + (R - E - D)$$

The following diagram shows the relationship between the balance sheet equation, the operating activities that generate income (revenues and expenses), and dividend payments to stockholders. (Remember that dividend payments are not expenses or operating activities.) Look first at the right-hand column under RE. The excess of revenues over expenses increased retained earnings by $200. This same $200 is shown as an increase in net assets in the left-hand column under A = L. Now go to the right-hand column again and see that the owners were paid a cash dividend of $100. Go back to the left-hand column and note that net assets decreased $100 as a result of the payment of dividends. Note again that the same net money amounts are added and subtracted on both sides of the balance sheet equation.

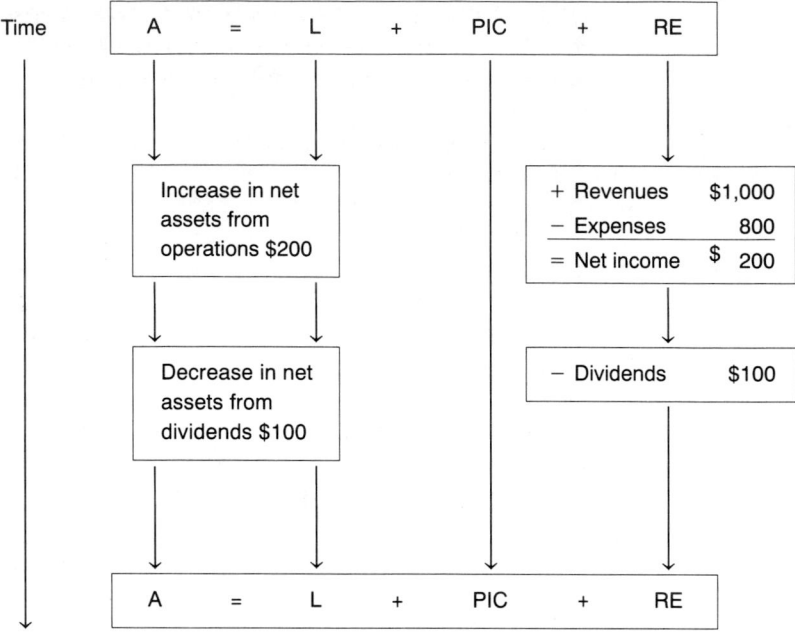

You now can relate the above diagram to Exhibit 2–1, which gave five possible combinations of transactions. The cumulative effect of the $200 increase in net income under RE and the increase in net assets of $200 belong to group 3—increase in assets and increase in stockholders' equity. The dividend decrease under RE of $100 and the decrease in net assets of $100 belong to group 4—decrease in assets and decrease in stockholders' equity. Cash dividends are payments to stockholders that reduce assets and also reduce retained earnings, thus keeping the balance sheet equation in balance.

Noncash Operating Transactions

Revenue and expense transactions do not necessarily involve cash. To illustrate how cash flows and revenues and expenses may differ, consider the following examples:

	Effects of Transactions on the Balance Sheet Equation				
	A	=	L	+	SE
Example 1					
In year 1: Perform service for promise to receive cash and bill customer for $12 "receivable"	+$12 receivable				+$12 revenue
In year 2: Collect receivable in cash . .	−$12 receivable + 12 cash				
Example 2					
In year 1: Collect $15 cash from customer for services to be performed later. . . .	+$15 cash		+$15 customer advances		
In year 2: Perform service for customer			−$15 customer advances		+$15 revenue

In the first example, the revenue transaction increases retained earnings and an asset. When the customer later pays for the service, one asset (receivable) is decreased while another (cash) is increased by the same amount, $12. No revenue is reported simply from the collection of the receivable.

In the second revenue example, in year 1 a customer gave the company $15 for services to be performed in year 2. At the time the company received the cash advance, the asset cash increased; and because the company had not yet performed the service, an unearned revenue (called customer advances) in the liability section of the balance sheet was increased (you will learn more about this later). In year 2, when the service is performed, revenue is recorded as shown in example 2 by decreasing the liability and increasing retained earnings. In both examples, revenue is reported at a different point in time than when cash is received. Revenue need not be accompanied by cash and does not necessarily represent increases in cash when reported.

Since expenses result from an outflow of net assets, we can also reflect expenses with many different types of balance sheet effects, including asset decreases or liability increases. Note the following two examples:

	Effects of Transactions on the Balance Sheet Equation				
	A	=	L	+	SE
1. An expense that decreases an asset	−$8 stamps				−$8 expense
2. An expense that increases a liability			+$9 advertising payable		−$9 expense

The first expense might be the result of using $8 worth of postage stamps from those stamps on hand. The asset stamps would be decreased by $8, and postage expense would decrease stockholders' equity by $8. The second example might occur when a newspaper advertisement is purchased on account. A liability, advertising payable, would be increased by $9, and advertising expense would decrease stockholders' equity by $9. In both of these examples, the items go directly to expense because we assume their benefits are used up immediately and no future benefits remain. Both examples also involve outflows of net assets that do not simultaneously affect cash, illustrating that expenses and cash consumption are not synonymous.

More on Operating Activities

Objective 5
How to analyze the operating activities of a corporation.

As we previously stated, operating transactions are those related to customers and suppliers of goods and services used in the pursuit of profits. Revenues and expenses result from operating transactions that increase or decrease net assets. For instance, consider the following four operating transactions:

1. Cash sales $70
2. Cash expenses   60
3. Purchase of merchandise on credit   30
4. Payment of accounts payable.   20

All are operating transactions but not all represent revenues or expenses; that is, not all have an effect on net assets. Consider the following assumed balance sheet amounts for Robotics Company.

	Assets	=	Liabilities	+	Paid-in Capital	+	Retained Earnings
Initial balances	$100	=	$20	+	$30	+	$ 50

If we reformulate the equation to emphasize net assets, we get

	Assets	−	Liabilities	=	Paid-in Capital	+	Retained Earnings
Initial balances	$100	−	$20	=	$30	+	$ 50
	Net assets ($80)			=	Stockholders' equity ($80)		

Now, let us analyze the effects of each transaction.

	Assets	−	Liabilities	=	Paid-in Capital	+	Retained Earnings
Initial balances	$100	−	$20	=	$30	+	$ 50
Transaction 1:							
Cash sales	+ 70						+ 70
Balance after sales . . .	$170	−	$20	=	$30	+	$120
	Net assets ($150)			=	Stockholders' equity ($150)		

The increase in retained earnings is a revenue because the operating transaction increased net assets.

Transaction 2, the payment of expenses, is also an operating transaction that changes net assets, in this case reducing net assets by $60 as follows:

	Assets	−	Liabilities	=	Paid-in Capital	+	Retained Earnings
Balance after sales	$170	−	$20	=	$30	+	$120
Transaction 2:							
Cash expenses	− 60						− 60
Balance	$110	−	$20	=	$30	+	$ 60
	Net assets ($90)			=	Stockholders' equity ($90)		

Therefore, the $60 entry is an expense because it is an operating transaction that reduces net assets, and it is reflected with a negative retained earnings effect.

However, not all operating transactions affect net assets; therefore, not all operating transactions are classified as revenues or expenses. For instance, transactions 3 and 4 are operating in that they reflect dealings with suppliers, but as you see below, these transactions have no effect on net assets or on retained earnings.

	Assets	−	Liabilities	=	Paid-in Capital	+	Retained Earnings
Balance after transactions 1 and 2 . . .	$110	−	$20	=	$30	+	$ 60
Transaction 3:							
Purchase on credit.	+ 30		+ 30				
Transaction 4:							
Payment of accounts payable	− 20		− 20				
Balance	$120	−	$30	=	$30	+	$ 60
	Net assets ($90)			=	Stockholders' equity ($90)		

Objective 6
Revenue and expense
recognition.

Recognition of Revenues and Expenses.   When the impact of revenue or expense transactions is recorded (as in the examples illustrated above for transactions 1 and 2), it is said to be recognized. In accounting, to **recognize** simply means to record the effect of an event. Revenue and expense recognition is governed by certain accounting concepts.

Before revenues and expenses can be recognized in the accounting records, they must meet the following criteria:

1. Revenues must be realized or realizable.
2. Revenues must be earned.
3. Expenses representing the outflow of net assets required to earn the revenue must be objectively measurable.

The realization of revenues occurs when the resulting inflow of net assets is in the form of cash or some other item that may be converted to a known amount of cash, usually as a promise from a customer to pay cash within some period of time, called accounts receivable. When the selling company receives cash or something else of value, the revenue is **realized**. When accounts receivable are created, the revenue is considered to be **realizable** until cash or something else of value is collected.

The realization principle requires that revenues be **earned** before they are recorded. This principle is followed around the world. In virtually all countries, revenues are considered to be earned when the business has provided the necessary goods or services that give rise to the revenues. For example, when a business delivers merchandise or provides services to customers, the business is generally considered to have *earned* revenue. As a result, the seller recognizes revenues normally at the time (1) the seller has performed the service and/or delivered the product and (2) the seller has received something of value that has been realized or is realizable.

Expenses are the outflows of net assets given up or consumed by the business to produce revenue. Expenses are often determined along with revenues, since revenues seldom occur without accompanying sacrifices or efforts that are necessary to earn revenues.

Objective 7
The matching principle.

The matching principle involves the process of relating the benefits from operations (revenues) with the efforts or costs of achieving those benefits (expenses) during an accounting period. The matching process addresses the question, What net assets are given up (consumed) by the business to obtain the recorded revenues? Net income is the difference between the revenues and expenses from profit-seeking activities for a period. You will learn more about the matching principle later.

In the next section you see how financing, investing, and operating transactions affect the various balance sheet categories for a company that starts operations and experiences all three types of transactions during the accounting period.

• COMPREHENSIVE EXAMPLE: TWIN PINES LABORATORIES

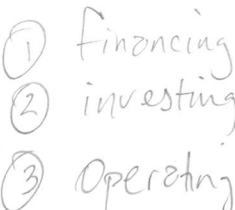

We will examine a series of economic activities that would commonly occur during the initial stages of a corporation's life. Our corporation—Twin Pines Laboratories—was organized as a testing laboratory specializing in technical aerospace instrumentation problems. We will emphasize (1) the nature of the transaction—financing, investing, or operating; (2) the effect on the balance sheet equation; and (3) the specific increases and decreases in the balance sheet categories that result. As you study each of the following six business transactions of Twin Pines Laboratories, refer to Exhibit 2–2, the spreadsheet analysis for transactions 1 through 6. Later we will analyze transactions 7 through 22 plus adjustments at December 31 to complete the accounting period.

Transaction 1: Financing Activity—Issuance of Stock.   On June 10, 19x1, Twin Pines Laboratories issued 2,500 shares of stock to each of four stockholders—a total of 10,000 shares. Each stockholder contributed $50,000—a total initial capital investment of $200,000. Both assets (cash) and stockholders' equity (capital stock) increased $200,000.

Transaction 2: Operating Activity—Renting Facilities and Equipment.   On June 15, 19x1, Twin Pines rented for a year (July 1, 19x1 to June 30, 19x2) office and laboratory facilities for $120,000 and equipment for $50,000—a total of $170,000. This transaction

EXHIBIT 2–2

Spreadsheet Analysis of Transactions 1 through 6, Twin Pines Laboratories

Twin Pines Laboratories

| Date of Event | Trans-action No. | Assets | | | | = | Liabilities | | + | Stockholders' Equity |
		Cash	Supplies	Prepaid Rent	Land		Accounts Payable	Notes Payable		Capital Stock
6/10/x1	1	200,000								200,000
6/15/x1	2	−170,000		170,000						
6/21/x1	3				2,500		2,500			
6/25/x1	4		25,000				25,000			
6/29/x1	5	− 2,500					− 2,500			
6/30/x1	6	80,000						80,000		
6/30/x1		107,500	25,000	170,000	2,500		25,000	80,000		200,000

$305,000 $305,000

Assets, $305,000 = Liabilities, $105,000 + Stockholders' equity, $200,000

involves the exchange of one asset—cash—for a new asset—prepaid rent. The asset cash is decreased by $170,000, a new asset prepaid rent is increased by $170,000, leaving the balance sheet equation in balance. Prepaid rent represents objectively measurable future benefits controlled by the business for a one-year period.

Transaction 3: Investing Activity—Purchasing Land. Businesses often increase their assets by increasing their liabilities. For example, on June 21, 19x1, Twin Pines purchased a plot of land to be used for a site for a storage facility for $2,500 to be paid within 30 days. This transaction created a $2,500 liability called accounts payable and a $2,500 asset called land. Note that net assets (assets minus liabilities) stayed the same; therefore, stockholders' equity remained unchanged at $200,000.

Transaction 4: Operating Activity—Purchasing Supplies on Account. On June 25, 19x1, Twin Pines purchased laboratory supplies for $25,000 from Hooker Supplies to be paid in 30 days. A new asset, supplies, was created for $25,000; and the liability, accounts payable, increased $25,000 (to $27,500).

Transaction 5: Operating Activity—Paying on Accounts Payable. On June 29, 19x1, Twin Pines paid $2,500 for the land. The payment decreased the asset cash $2,500 and decreased the liability accounts payable $2,500.

Transaction 6: Financing Activity—Borrowing from a Bank. On June 30, 19x1, the day before beginning its lab operations, Twin Pines borrowed $80,000 from State Bank, signing a two-year note payable on June 30, 19x3. The asset cash increased $80,000 (to $107,500), and a new $80,000 liability, notes payable, was created.

Exhibit 2–3 shows the balance sheets of Twin Pines on June 10, 19x1, and June 30, 19x1. As you review the spreadsheet in Exhibit 2–2 and the balance sheets in Exhibit 2–3, note that transactions 2 through 6 did not change the initial net asset position of Twin Pines and did not result in profits for its owners. No changes in net assets were made

EXHIBIT 2–3

Comparison of Twin Pines Laboratories Balance Sheets, June 10, 19x1, and June 30, 19x1

Twin Pines Laboratories
Balance Sheet
June 10, 19x1

Assets		Stockholders' Equity	
Cash	$200,000	Capital stock.	$200,000
Total assets	$200,000	Total stockholders' equity	$200,000

Twin Pines Laboratories
Balance Sheet
June 30, 19x1

Assets		Liabilities and Stockholders' Equity	
Cash	$107,500	Liabilities:	
Supplies	25,000	Accounts payable	$ 25,000
Prepaid rent	170,000	Notes payable	80,000
Land	2,500	Total liabilities	$105,000
		Stockholders' equity:	
		Capital stock.	200,000
Total assets	$305,000	Total liabilities and stockholders' equity.	$305,000

despite the fact that the amount of total assets and total liabilities changed several times. To date, no profit was made by Twin Pines because no revenues or expenses have been recorded.

We now resume our example of Twin Pines Laboratories, which worked on a number of projects for three different customers between July 1, 19x1, and December 31, 19x1. The transactions that follow pertain to these three projects during that period. The numbering of these transactions begins with transaction 7, continuing on from transactions 1 through 6.

Date	Transaction No.	Transaction
19x1		
July 15	7	Purchased $30,000 of supplies on open account.
20	8	Billed client A for project Z-2, $45,000 due in 30 days.
21	9	Billed client B for project Z-X, $80,000 due in 30 days.
26	10	Paid $35,000 on accounts payable.
27	11	Received $50,000 from client B on accounts receivable.
30	12	Paid salaries, $65,000.

The effect of these transactions on the balance sheet equation is illustrated in the spreadsheet analysis in Exhibit 2–4. Notice that for transaction 8 (July 20, 19x1), revenue was recognized at the time the client was billed $45,000, the agreed-upon price for hiring Twin Pines to do the project identified as Z-2. Twin Pines does not have to wait until cash is received to recognize revenue, since the inflow of assets is assumed to be measurable (equal to $45,000), realizable (collectible from client A), and earned (Twin Pines had

EXHIBIT 2–4

Spreadsheet Analysis of Transactions 7 through 12, Twin Pines Laboratories

Twin Pines Laboratories

Date of Event	Trans-action No.	Assets					=	Liabilities		+	Stockholders' Equity		
		Cash	Accounts Receivable	Supplies	Prepaid Rent	Land		Accounts Payable	Notes Payable	Capital Stock	Retained Earnings		
											Revenues	Expenses
7/1/x1	Bal.	107,500		25,000	170,000	2,500		25,000	80,000	200,000		
7/15/x1	7			30,000				30,000				
7/20/x1	8		45,000								45,000	
7/21/x1	9		80,000								80,000	
7/26/x1	10	− 35,000						−35,000				
7/27/x1	11	50,000	−50,000									
7/30/x1	12	− 65,000										−65,000
											125,000	−65,000
7/31/x1	Bal.	57,500	75,000	55,000	170,000	2,500		20,000	80,000	200,000	60,000	

$360,000 $360,000

Assets, $360,000 = Liabilities, $100,000 + Stockholders' equity, $260,000

completed the work required on project Z-2). As a result, the billing of $45,000 on
July 20, 19x1, and $80,000 on July 21, 19x1, gives rise to revenue, while the collection of
cash on July 27, 19x1 simply reduces the asset accounts receivable and increases the
asset cash.

Notice also that the balance sheet equation totals given in Exhibit 2–4 maintain the
equality, Assets = Liabilities + Paid-in Capital (Capital Stock) + Retained Earnings,
after each transaction. The balance sheet for July 31, 19x1, is as follows:

Twin Pines Laboratories
Balance Sheet
July 31, 19x1

Assets		**Liabilities and Stockholders' Equity**	
Cash	$ 57,500	Liabilities:	
Accounts receivable	75,000	Accounts payable	$ 20,000
Supplies	55,000	Notes payable	80,000
Prepaid rent	170,000	Total liabilities	$100,000
Land	2,500		
		Stockholders' equity:	
		Capital stock.	$200,000
		Retained earnings	60,000
		Total stockholders' equity	$260,000
		Total liabilities and	
Total assets	$360,000	stockholders' equity.	$360,000

Continuing with the activities of Twin Pines for 19x1, the following transactions occurred:

Date	Transaction No.	Transaction
19x1		
Aug. 1	13	Received $40,000 on accounts receivable.
29	14	Billed clients A and C $120,000 for projects completed to date.
Sept. 15	15	Received $100,000 on accounts receivable.
20	16	Paid salaries, $105,000.
Oct. 20	17	Purchased supplies of $75,000 on account.
31	18	Billed clients A, B, and C $195,000 for projects completed to date.
Nov. 15	19	Received $230,000 on accounts receivable.
28	20	Paid $80,000 on accounts payable.
Dec. 15	21	Paid salaries, $150,000.
30	22	Billed clients A, B, and C $185,000 for projects completed to date.

The results of transactions 13 through 22 are summarized in Exhibit 2–5. Since the balance in retained earnings was $0 on July 1, 19x1, and is reported at $305,000 on December 31, 19x1 (Exhibit 2–5), the change in retained earnings resulting from operating activities for the last six months of 19x1 appears to be $305,000. This amount represents net income after the results of transactions with outside parties, but adjustments are needed in order to determine net income.

Adjustments to the Balance Sheet

When the bank loaned Twin Pines $80,000 on June 30, 19x1 (transaction 6), Twin Pines agreed to present to the bank a formal balance sheet as of December 31, 19x1. The preliminary balances in Exhibit 2–5 are summarized in the following balance sheet of December 31, 19x1:

Twin Pines Laboratories
Preliminary Balance Sheet
December 31, 19x1

Assets		**Liabilities and Stockholders' Equity**	
Cash	$ 92,500	Liabilities:	
Accounts receivable	205,000	Accounts payable	$ 15,000
Supplies	130,000	Notes payable	80,000
Prepaid rent	170,000	Total liabilities	$ 95,000
Land	2,500	Stockholders' equity:	
		Capital stock	$200,000
		Retained earnings	305,000
		Total stockholders' equity	$505,000
		Total liabilities and	
Total assets	$600,000	stockholders' equity	$600,000

Objective 8
Why adjustments are necessary.

If you compare this balance sheet with the second balance sheet in Exhibit 2–3, you will note that both balance sheets show the item "Prepaid rent, $170,000." Now look at the dates of both balance sheets. The second balance sheet in Exhibit 2–3 is dated June 30, 19x1; the balance sheet above is dated December 31, 19x1. Six months have passed since

EXHIBIT 2–5

Spreadsheet Analysis of Transactions 13–22, Twin Pines Laboratories

Twin Pines Laboratories

Date of Event	Trans-action No.	Assets					=	Liabilities		+	Stockholders' Equity	
											Retained Earnings	
		Cash	Accounts Receivable	Supplies	Prepaid Rent	Land		Accounts Payable	Notes Payable	Capital Stock	Revenues	Expenses
7/31/x1	Bal.	57,500	75,000	55,000	170,000	2,500		20,000	80,000	200,000	125,000	− 65,000
8/1/x1	13	40,000	− 40,000									
8/29/x1	14		120,000								120,000	
9/15/x1	15	100,000	−100,000									
9/20/x1	16	−105,000										−105,000
10/20/x1	17			75,000				75,000				
10/31/x1	18		195,000								195,000	
11/15/x1	19	230,000	−230,000									
11/28/x1	20	− 80,000						−80,000				
12/15/x1	21	−150,000										−150,000
12/30/x1	22		185,000								185,000	
											625,000	−320,000
Preliminary balance, 12/31/x1	Bal.	92,500	205,000	130,000	170,000	2,500		15,000	80,000	200,000	305,000	

$600,000 $600,000

Assets, $600,000 = Liabilities, $95,000 + Stockholders' equity, $505,000

Twin Pines prepaid one year's rent for its office and laboratory facilities and equipment. Obviously, the asset, prepaid rent, can no longer be valued at $170,000. You must decrease the asset by $85,000 (six months' rent) and increase the expense under retained earnings by $85,000. This leaves a remaining asset value of $85,000 for the next six months' rent (January 1, 19x2, to June 30, 19x2). This is called an adjustment because it adjusts the records to reflect certain operating effects. These adjustments, which account for activities and transactions that do not directly involve outside parties, are explained in the paragraphs that follow.

All the transactions we have considered before the prepaid rent discussion above have been external transactions. External transactions are triggered by economic events with outside parties. Usually external transactions are accompanied by source documents, such as sales invoices, purchase orders, checks, and shipping receipts. These transactions involve an exchange between two parties, each of which is looking out for its own best interest. This is called an arm's length transaction and it is generally considered that the exchange will be at the fair market value of the item. If this were not so, one of the parties would not agree to the exchange and there would not be a transaction.

The adjustment we must make for prepaid rent is called an internal transaction. Internal transactions are not directly triggered by economic events with outside parties or evidenced by source documents from outside parties. Accountants identify internal transactions by examining the preliminary balances at the end of an accounting period and record the effect needed to state correctly the assets, liabilities, and stockholders' equity of the business.

Some adjustments may be identified by looking at the preliminary balances of the balance sheet and thinking about the definitions of the balance sheet elements—as we did with the prepaid rent of Twin Pines. Other adjustments call for additional information and special procedures. You will learn more about adjustments in Chapter 4.

When we determined that the prepaid rent of Twin Pines was half used up on December 31, 19x1, we reduced the asset, prepaid rent, by one half and we increased expenses shown in retained earnings—to keep the balance sheet equation in balance. We used the matching principle because we were matching the rent expense with the related period of benefit (July 1, 19x1, to December 31, 19x1). If we waited until 19x2 to adjust the prepaid rent, the entire $170,000 would become an expense in 19x2 and nothing would have been expensed in 19x1.

We will also make adjustments for three other items that created expenses that must be matched to the revenues reported in 19x1:

- Interest payable for use of $80,000 borrowed on June 30, 19x1, for a six-month period is $4,000 according to the terms of the loan.
- Salaries for work performed by lab technicians since the last payday of $47,000 have not been paid.
- The consumption of supplies during the period of $102,000 is explained below.

To properly state the balance sheet of Twin Pines on December 31, 19x1 the following four adjustments (labeled *a*, *b*, *c*, and *d*) must be made on December 31, 19x1:

Adjustment Reference	Adjustments (internal transactions)
a.	Decrease the asset prepaid rent by $85,000 for one-half year's use of facilities and equipment; decrease retained earnings $85,000 for rent expense.
b.	Increase the liability interest payable by $4,000 for interest owed to date; decrease retained earnings $4,000 for interest expense.
c.	Increase the liability salaries payable by $47,000 for unpaid salaries earned to date; decrease retained earnings $47,000 for salary expense.
d.	Decrease the asset supplies for the amount of supplies used during the period. A count of supplies on hand at the end of 19x1 revealed that $28,000 in supplies remained to be used in future periods. This means that $102,000 of supplies were consumed and should be shown as a reduction of the asset supplies and as an expense.

interest payable
+ interest expense

The spreadsheet analysis shown in Exhibit 2–6 summarizes all of the activities and adjustments for Twin Pines from June 10, 19x1, to December 31, 19x1, the first six months of the company's operations. The resulting balance sheet is shown in Exhibit 2–7.

Objective 9
The distinction between the accrual basis and the cash basis of accounting.

The adjustments that were made above for Twin Pines' first six-month period of operations were necessary according to generally accepted accounting principles (GAAP) and are the result of the accrual basis of accounting. The accrual basis of accounting states that revenues must be recorded when they are earned and expenses must be recorded in the periods that the efforts to achieve income occurred. Thus, if a sale of merchandise is made in December 19x1 but cash is not collected until early 19x2, accrual accounting would recognize the revenue in 19x1, along with the expenses associated with the sale. The asset, accounts receivable, is increased, indicating that the money is owed to the business, and a revenue item under retained earnings is increased for an equal dollar figure.

EXHIBIT 2–6

Spreadsheet Analysis of All Transactions for 6/10 through 12/31/x1, Twin Pines Laboratories

Twin Pines Laboratories

Date of Event	Cash	Accounts Receivable	Supplies	Prepaid Rent	Land	Accounts Payable	Notes Payable	Interest Payable	Salaries Payable	Capital Stock	Retained Earnings	Explanation
			Assets			=	Liabilities			+	Stockholders' Equity	
6/10/x1	200,000									200,000		Initial balance
6/15/x1	−170,000			170,000								Prepay rent
6/21/x1					2,500	2,500						Purchase land
6/25/x1			25,000			25,000						Purchase supplies
6/29/x1	− 2,500					− 2,500						Pay for land
6/30/x1	80,000						80,000					Borrow cash
7/15/x1			30,000			30,000						Purchase supplies
7/20/x1		45,000									45,000 (R)	Project revenue
7/21/x1		80,000									80,000 (R)	Project revenue
7/26/x1	− 35,000					−35,000						Pay for supplies
7/27/x1	50,000	− 50,000										Collect cash
7/30/x1	− 65,000										− 65,000 (E)	Salaries expense
8/1/x1	40,000	− 40,000										Collect cash
8/29/x1		120,000									120,000 (R)	Project revenue
9/15/x1	100,000	−100,000										Collect cash
9/20/x1	−105,000										−105,000 (E)	Salaries expense
10/20/x1			75,000			75,000						Purchase supplies
10/31/x1		195,000									195,000 (R)	Project revenue
11/15/x1	230,000	−230,000										Collect cash
11/28/x1	− 80,000					−80,000						Pay for supplies
12/15/x1	−150,000										−150,000 (E)	Salaries expense
12/30/x1		185,000									185,000 (R)	Project revenue
a.				− 85,000							− 85,000 (E)	Rent expense—facilities and equipment
b.								4,000			− 4,000 (E)	Interest expense
c.									47,000		− 47,000 (E)	Salaries expense
d.			−102,000								−102,000 (E)	Supplies expense
Balances, 12/31/x1	92,500	205,000	28,000	85,000	2,500	15,000	80,000	4,000	47,000	200,000	67,000	

$413,000 $413,000

Assets, $413,000 = Liabilities, $146,000 + Stockholders' equity, $267,000

EXHIBIT 2–7

Balance Sheet of Twin Pines Laboratories at December 31, 19x1

Twin Pines Laboratories
Balance Sheet
December 31, 19x1

Assets		Liabilities and Stockholders' Equity	
Cash	$ 92,500	Liabilities:	
Accounts receivable	205,000	Accounts payable	$ 15,000
Supplies	28,000	Notes payable	80,000
Prepaid rent	85,000	Interest payable	4,000
Land	2,500	Salaries payable	47,000
		Total liabilities	$146,000
		Stockholders' equity:	
		Capital stock	$200,000
		Retained earnings	67,000
		Total stockholders' equity	$267,000
		Total liabilities and	
Total assets	$413,000	stockholders' equity	$413,000

If the sale is not recorded until the business collects the cash, the business would be using the cash basis of accounting. The cash basis of accounting is not generally accepted for financial reporting purposes; however, the cash basis is sometimes used for income tax accounting purposes.

Notice how the accrual basis of accounting is used in the Twin Pines example. The revenues and expenses are recognized or recorded as shown in the spreadsheet analysis, and revenue and expense recognition does not require the inflow or outflow of cash. When Twin Pines completes the projects, the amount of the cash to be received for the projects is recorded as accounts receivable and revenue is recorded in stockholders' equity. Likewise, Twin Pines recognizes expenses for supplies used and year-end unpaid salaries that are not accompanied by cash payments; these are recorded as decreases in the asset supplies and increases in the liability salaries payable, and in keeping with the double-entry accounting system, equal amounts of expense are recorded in the stockholders' equity section. None of these changes would be recorded on a strict cash basis of accounting according to which revenues are recognized only when cash is received from customers and expenses are recognized only when cash is paid to suppliers, employees, and others.

As a final note, we should realize that many end-of-period adjustments are made automatically in computerized information systems. The timing and amount of many adjustments, including adjustments to record interest, unpaid wages, and reductions in prepaid expenses and supplies, can be anticipated at the time of the original transaction. As a result, these adjustments can be programmed into the computer at the date of the original transaction and made automatically at the end of the accounting period.

Income Statement

The revenues and expenses identified in the "Retained Earnings" column of the spreadsheet analysis in Exhibit 2–6 represent the benefits (revenues) and costs (expenses) of the first six months of laboratory operations for Twin Pines. Since financial statement users

Objective 10
The purpose of the
income statement and
its relationship to
the balance sheet.

are very concerned with the operating performance of a business, operating results are reported in a separate financial statement called the income statement.

The formal income statement provides a more convenient summary of the operating activities than the spreadsheet analysis. The income statement of Twin Pines for the six months ended December 31, 19x1, would be:

Twin Pines Laboratories
Income Statement
For the Six Months Ended December 31, 19x1

Project revenues		$625,000
Less expenses:		
Salary expense	$367,000	
Supplies expense	102,000	
Rent expense	85,000	
Interest expense	4,000	
Total expenses		558,000
Net income		$ 67,000

Note that the income statement does not report the effects of financing or investing activities (e.g., borrowing money or buying land) that occurred during the six-month period.

The income statement and the balance sheet are both widely used formal financial statements. While the balance sheet provides a snapshot of the financial position of a business at a point in time, the income statement describes the operating transactions called revenues and expenses that were experienced over a period of time.

Exhibit 2–8 shows the relationship of the income statement and the balance sheet for Twin Pines for the period July 1, 19x1, to December 31, 19x1, in which only operating transactions took place. You can see that the $67,000 increase in net assets from the profitable operations is matched in the balance sheet equation by an increase of $67,000 in the stockholders' equity heading "Retained Earnings." Hence, the increase in retained earnings

EXHIBIT 2–8

Relationship of Net Income to Change in Net Assets and Retained Earnings

Twin Pines Laboratories
($000)

	Net Assets			=	Stockholders' Equity			
	Assets	−	Liabilities	=	Capital Stock	+	Retained Earnings	
	305	−	105	=	200	+	0	
Net assets (A − L), 7/1/x1		200				200		Total stockholders' equity, 7/1/x1
Operating activities		+ 67				+ 67		Operating activities
Net assets (A − L), 12/31/x1		267		=		267		Total stockholders' equity, 12/31/x1
	413	−	146	=	200	+	67	
	Assets	−	Liabilities	=	Capital stock	+	Retained earnings	

represents the increase in net assets from profit-seeking transactions that have been retained in the business for future use. In this example, we have no dividends, which decrease both net assets and retained earnings. In the Twin Pines example, the increase in net assets from $200,000 on July 1 to $267,000 on December 31 is the basis for the $67,000 amount in retained earnings.

Cash Flow Analysis
of Twin Pines
Laboratories' Results

Consider the following conversation between the president of Twin Pines Labs (a biochemist) and his chief accountant, which took place after the president received the financial statements, the balance sheet in Exhibit 2–7, and the income statement shown above.

President: I want to fully understand the meaning of these financial statements, the real economic results for the period. How did each kind of activity affect our cash and net income?

Accountant: OK, first let's talk about the three major categories of activities: financing, investing, and operating. Under financing, we issued stock and got a bank loan. Those transactions increased our total assets by $280,000.

President: Yes, but your balance sheet here shows assets of $413,000.

Accountant: Well, we also generated assets by earning net income of $67,000, and, in essence, by borrowing from our workers and suppliers another $66,000. Notice that we show three liabilities other than the note—accounts payable of $15,000, interest payable of $4,000, and salaries payable of $47,000. Each of these amounts is still owed.

President: Didn't we have any investing transactions?

Accountant: Not much, only the purchase of the land. It didn't affect net income, but we paid $2,500 in cash. All of the rest is rented. Our operating activities resulted in net income of $67,000 but we had a negative cash flow from operations—mostly because we still have $205,000 of accounts receivable owed us by customers and we prepaid rent of $85,000 which will not be expensed until next period.

President: With all those liabilities, how capable are we of paying them off? I only see cash of $92,500.

Accountant: Keep in mind we have a healthy $205,000 in receivables from customers, which should come in soon. So, our ability to pay is very good.

This conversation, though a bit rambling, is an example of the task accountants have in translating their statements into a language that is understood by nonaccountants.

Now consider a more rigorous analysis of the transactions from June 10 to December 31 that affected Twin Pines' cash. There were two financing transactions, which had the following effects on cash:

Financing Activity	Cash Effect
Issued stock for cash	+$200,000
Borrowed from bank	+ 80,000
Cash from financing activities	+$280,000

Note that income was not affected by these transactions, but cash increased by $280,000. The only investing activity during the period was the purchase of the land for $2,500 on credit and the subsequent payment of that amount:

Investing Activity	Cash Effect
Purchased land on credit	$ 0
Paid the liability for land	− 2,500
Cash used by investing activities	−$ 2,500

Operating activity involved transactions with several external parties—customers, owners of rented building and equipment, suppliers, and workers, and several adjustments related to supplies consumed, unpaid salaries, recognition of prepaid rent used, and unpaid interest.

Operating Activity	Cash Effect
Sales on credit	$ 0
Received cash from customers.	+ 420,000
Payment for rental of building and equipment	− 170,000
Adjustment to record rent expense	0
Purchased supplies on credit.	0
Payment to suppliers	− 115,000
Adjustment to record supplies used	0
Payment of salaries	− 320,000
Adjustment for unpaid salaries	0
Adjustment for unpaid interest	0
Cash used by operating activities.	−$185,000

Note that although net income is $67,000, the cash from operating activities was a negative $185,000.

Putting all three activities together gives a summary cash flow analysis:

	Cash Effect
Beginning cash amount	$ 0
Financing activities	+ 280,000
Investing activities	− 2,500
Operating activities	− 185,000
Ending cash amount, 12/31/x1	$ 92,500

This type of analysis will be covered in detail in Chapter 14. •

Listen in on the following conversation between a slightly frustrated accounting student, Kevin, and his tutor, Marie, a senior who has just accepted a position with a very prestigious CPA firm.

Kevin: I followed everything OK with the balance sheet. There are assets, liabilities, and owners' equity. So the money amounts for assets always equal the amounts for liabilities plus owners' equity. But the income statement and retained earnings blow me away. I don't get the connection.

Marie: Look, there are two ways for money to come into a company. The first is financing, in which you sell stock or borrow money. If you sell $100 in stock your first balance sheet has an asset, cash, of $100 and owners' equity, common stock, of $100. (She begins to write the balance sheet equation on the blackboard.)

Kevin: Right. That's the part I understand.

Marie: Hold on, there's another way of getting money into the company, and that's operations. For instance, say you sell a service, like getting $50 for tutoring someone in accounting, ha ha.

Kevin: That'll be the day. OK, so cash increases by $50, and that's where I lose it.

Marie: Remember, the balance sheet equation has got to balance after every transaction. So you increase cash by $50 and increase owners' equity by $50 and call it sales. So you have ... (Marie puts the following on the blackboard)

Assets		=	Liabilities		+	Stockholders' Equity	
Cash	$150			$0		Common stock	$100
						Sales.	50
Total assets . . .	$150		Total liabilities	$0		Total stockholders' equity	$150

Kevin: OK, but what about an expense of doing business, say paying a telephone bill of $20? I know it reduces cash by $20, but what else? Does it reduce sales by $20?

Marie: No, but you use another category called expenses. Then the balance sheet equation looks like this:

Assets		=	Liabilities		+	Stockholders' Equity	
Cash	$130			$0		Common stock	$100
						Sales.	50
						Expenses.	(20)
Total assets . . .	$130		Total liabilities	$0		Total stockholders' equity	$130

Kevin: OK, I see that, but what is retained earnings and what do you show on the income statement?

Marie: The income statement is a report that shows sales minus expenses and net income, which in this case is $50 − $20 = $30, as follows:

Sales	$50
Expenses	20
Net income	$30

Retained earnings is the balance sheet amount that shows the accumulated net income of the business since it started minus any dividend amounts paid to owners since it started. If we pay $10 to the owner, we reduce cash by $10 and we reduce retained earnings by $10.

Kevin: Hold it; that's where I get lost. I don't see retained earnings on the balance sheet.

Marie: OK, let's list the final balance sheet amounts and you'll see that retained earnings is just the net of the net income and the dividend.

Assets		=	Liabilities		+	Stockholders' Equity	
Cash	$120			$0		Common stock	$100
						Retained earnings . . .	20
Total assets . . .	$120		Total liabilities	$0		Total stockholders' equity	$120

Kevin: What happened to sales and expenses?

Marie: In this case retained earnings takes the amount of the sales of $50 minus the expense of $20 and the dividend of $10, which equals $20. The final balance sheet does not show the individual revenue, expense, and dividend components, but only the retained earnings balance. So at the end of the period this company has $120 in cash, which they got by selling stock for $100 and by earning $30 in net income, but they paid $10 in dividends and therefore retained only $20 of net income in the business. So you see, a business gets its money from financing activities and from operations. Another thing: The dividend is part of the financing activities. So financing activities netted $90 and operations netted $30, and that's how we got our cash balance of $120.

Kevin: I think I've got it.

• SUMMARY

This chapter illustrates that many aspects of accounting work together to provide external and internal users with financial statements—particularly the balance sheet and income statement. Again, as in Chapter 1, the balance sheet equation is highlighted as a major foundation of accounting. Just looking at the following complete balance sheet equation used by corporations should remind you of the contents of this chapter.

$$\text{Assets} = \text{Liabilities} + \text{Stockholders' Equity} \tag{1}$$

$$\text{Assets} = \text{Liabilities} + \text{Paid-in Capital} + \text{Retained Earnings} \tag{2}$$

$$\text{Assets} = \text{Liabilities} + \text{Paid-in Capital} + \text{Revenues} - \text{Expenses} - \text{Dividends} \tag{3}$$

Before you analyze balance sheet equation transactions, you should understand some of the basic concepts and principles underlying the accounting model. In this chapter, we discussed how revenue recognition, the matching principle, and the accrual basis of accounting help us measure the assets, liabilities, and stockholders' equity (including revenues and expenses) of the business entity. These concepts will be further illustrated in the next two chapters.

From formula 2 you know that the stockholders' equity of a corporation contains paid-in capital (capital stock), which was invested by the stockholders, and retained earnings, which is further divided in formula 3 into revenues, expenses, and dividends.

If you change the first formula, you can see how the residual interest of the stockholders is equal to the net assets (assets minus liabilities) of the business:

$$\text{Assets} - \text{Liabilities} = \text{Stockholders' Equity}$$

$$\text{Net Assets} = \text{Stockholders' Equity}$$

From this last formula, you should try to understand that when operating transactions provide revenues, the result is an increase in net assets. Alternatively, when operating transactions cause net assets to decrease (i.e., assets are being used up or liabilities are being increased), the result is *expenses*. Because revenues and expenses are a part of retained earnings, you can see how revenues add to retained earnings and expenses reduce retained earnings. In this way, you can describe the operating activities of a business in terms of their effect on the balance sheet equation. Dividends also reduce retained earnings, but dividends are unique in that they are not expenses or operating activities. Dividends return some of the profits of the business to the stockholders.

The chapter concluded with the income statement—a summary of the operating activities of a business. The income statement shows how operating activities affect retained earnings. Throughout the chapter, the financing and investing activities of a business were contrasted with the operating activities of a business. The overall picture of accounting relationships presented in this chapter will provide an important background for the chapters that follow.

• DEMONSTRATION EXERCISE

WFT Tax Services, Inc., has the following balance sheet at December 31, 19x1:

WFT Tax Services, Inc.
Balance Sheet
December 31, 19x1

Assets		Liabilities and Stockholders' Equity	
Cash	$ 4,100	Liabilities:	
Accounts receivable	1,650	Accounts payable	$ 1,200
Note receivable	2,000	Total liabilities	$ 1,200
Prepaid rent	3,600		
Prepaid insurance	1,800	Stockholders' equity:	
		Capital stock.	$10,000
		Retained earnings	1,950
		Total stockholders' equity	$11,950
		Total liabilities and	
Total assets	$13,150	stockholders' equity.	$13,150

The following information pertains to January 19x2:

1. Recorded cash sales of $3,515 and credit sales of $5,210. Also collected $4,950 from customers' accounts during the month.
2. Purchased supplies of $560 for cash to be completely consumed during January.
3. Paid tax preparers' salaries of $4,960.
4. Paid the January utility bill of $650 and the telephone bill of $324.
5. Prepaid rent represents three months' rent, January through March.
6. Prepaid insurance represents three months' insurance, January through March.
7. Interest revenue on the note receivable for the month of January is $30.
8. Unpaid salaries earned through the end of January amount to $575.

Using the spreadsheet analysis format, record the above transactions and prepare an income statement and a balance sheet.

Solution:

WFT Tax Services, Inc.

	Assets						=	Liabilities	+	Stockholders' Equity	
Event	Cash	Accounts Receivable	Note Receivable	Interest Receivable	Prepaid Rent	Prepaid Insurance	Accounts Payable	Salaries Payable	Capital Stock	Retained Earnings
1/1/x1	4,100	1,650	2,000		3,600	1,800	1,200		10,000	1,950
1	3,515	5,210								8,725
	4,950	−4,950								
2	− 560									− 560
3	−4,960									−4,960
4	− 974									− 650
										− 324
5					−1,200					−1,200
6						− 600				− 600
7				30						30
8								575		− 575
1/31/x1	6,071	1,910	2,000	30	2,400	1,200	1,200	575	10,000	1,836

13,611

WFT Tax Services, Inc.
Income Statement
For the Month Ended January 31, 19x2

Revenues:

Preparation revenue	$8,725	
Interest revenue	30	
Total revenues		$8,755

Expenses:

Salaries expense	$5,535	
Supplies expense	560	
Rent expense	1,200	
Insurance expense	600	
Utilities expense	650	
Communications expense	324	
Total expenses		8,869
Net loss		$ (114)

WFT Tax Services, Inc.
Balance Sheet
January 31, 19x2

Assets:		Liabilities:	
Cash	$ 6,071	Accounts payable	$ 1,200
Accounts receivable	1,910	Salaries payable	575
Note receivable	2,000	Total liabilities	$ 1,775
Interest receivable	30	Stockholders' equity:	
Prepaid rent	2,400	Capital stock	$10,000
Prepaid insurance	1,200	Retained earnings	1,836
		Total stockholders' equity	$11,836
		Total liabilities and	
Total assets	$13,611	stockholders' equity	$13,611

• KEY TERMS

Accounts receivable. A promise from a customer to pay cash sometime in the near future.

Accrual basis of accounting. An accounting method used for financial statements prepared in accordance with GAAP. Revenues are recorded when earned and expenses in the periods when the efforts to achieve income occur and not necessarily when cash flows.

Adjustments. Internal transactions of the business recorded at period end when receivables and payables and previously unrecognized revenues and expenses are recognized.

Arm's length transaction. An exchange between independent parties at fair value of the item(s) exchanged.

Cash basis of accounting. The method of accounting in which revenues and expenses are not recognized until cash is received or paid; this method is not generally accepted for financial reporting purposes.

Expenses. Measures of decreases in owners' equity resulting from operating activities. Decreases in net assets that occur in order to earn revenues.

External transactions. Transactions triggered by economic events with outside parties; these events affect the assets, liabilities, and stockholders' equity of the business.

Income statement. Financial statement used to evaluate the operating performance, revenues, and expenses of a business for a period of time.

Internal transactions. Adjustments needed to state correctly the assets, liabilities, and stockholders' equity of the business.

Matching principle. Concept employed by accountants to relate the benefits from operations (revenues) with the efforts or costs (expenses) of achieving these benefits during the accounting period.

Net loss. The excess of expenses over revenues for a period.

Paid-in capital. The amount paid by owners for stock.

Realization. The process by which revenue generates an inflow of cash or other item that can be converted into cash, at which time the revenue is said to be realized.

Recognition. The process of formally incorporating an item into the financial statements as an asset, liability, revenue, expense, or the like; to recognize means to record.

Retained earnings. The cumulative net effect on stockholders' equity of revenues, expenses, and dividends from all prior periods.

Revenues. Measures of increases in owners' equity resulting from operating activities. Operating transactions resulting in net asset increases or inflows, measured at fair market value. Revenues increase stockholders' equity.

Stockholders' equity. Paid-in capital (capital stock) plus retained earnings.

• SYNONYMS

Adjustments; internal transactions.

Capital stock; paid-in capital; stock.

Income statement; earnings statement.

Net income; net profit; earnings.

Recognize; record.

Revenues; sales.

Stockholders' equity; owners' equity.

• QUESTIONS

1. What are the components of stockholders' equity in the most detailed balance sheet equation?
2. How do increases in revenues affect stockholders' equity? Net assets?
3. How do increases in expenses affect stockholders' equity? Net assets?
4. What does the dual effect of transactions on the balance sheet require when a transaction has the effect of decreasing total assets by $100?
5. What are financing activities?
6. What are investing activities?
7. What are operating activities?
8. Give two examples of financing activities that increase assets.
9. Give two examples of investing activities and tell what their effect is on total assets.
10. Give two operating activities and explain their effect on total assets and net assets.
11. What are revenues? Give an example and discuss its cash flow effects.
12. What are expenses? Give an example and discuss its cash flow effects.
13. When are revenues recorded?
14. Describe how revenues and expenses affect the balance sheet equation.
15. Who receives dividends? Out of what category are dividends paid?
16. Differentiate between operating and nonoperating transactions.
17. How do internal transactions, or adjustments, differ from external transactions?

18. How is the matching process related to the accrual basis of accounting?
19. How does the cash basis of accounting differ from the accrual basis of accounting?
20. Discuss why the information found on an income statement cannot be obtained from a balance sheet and a statement of cash flows.

• EXERCISES

E 2–1
Comprehensive
L.O.1, 6, 7, 9

1. Revenue recognition requires that—
   a. The revenues must be earned.
   b. The revenues are received in cash or some other asset, such as an account receivable, that can be converted to cash.
   c. The revenues must be realized or realizable.
   d. All of the above.
   e. None of the above.
2. The matching principle—
   a. Involves analysis of which costs are used up (consumed) in the process of earning the revenues reported for the period.
   b. Compares the cash received with the cash paid for goods and services.
   c. Calls for the measurement of net assets given up to obtain the net assets received or receivable from operating transactions.
   d. All of the above.
   e. Only (*a*) and (*c*) are correct.
3. Which of the following is accounted for differently under the cash and accrual bases of accounting?
   a. Receive cash from sale of merchandise to customer.
   b. Pay for services received.
   c. Prepay rent for two years.
   d. Pay salaries in cash.
   e. None of the above.
4. What tasks are required at the end of an accounting period in order to achieve the accrual basis of accounting?
   a. Investing activities.
   b. Dividend decisions.
   c. Adjustments (internal transactions).
   d. Financing activities.
   e. All of the above.
5. In the balance sheet equation, an increase in an asset—
   a. May be accompanied by an increase in a liability.
   b. May be accompanied by a decrease in an asset.
   c. May be accompanied by an increase in revenues.
   d. May be accompanied by an increase in paid-in capital.
   e. All of the above.

E 2–2
Types of Business Transactions
L.O.2

The following business transactions occurred during the current accounting period:

a. Sold additional stock to shareholders for cash.
b. Purchased office supplies.
c. Purchased new showcases for displaying merchandise to customers.
d. Borrowed cash from bank by signing a note due in monthly installments over the next three years.
e. Purchased a delivery van for cash.
f. Provided a service on account.
g. Collected cash from customers owing money on their accounts.

Required:
Indicate whether each of the transactions described above is an operating, financing, or investing activity.

E 2–3
Asset and Liability
Recognition
L.O.1, 6

In each of the items below, determine if an asset, liability, or stockholders' equity should be recognized. If so, describe the elements of the balance sheet that are affected and the amount.

a. A famous actor contracts to be the company spokesperson for future compensation payments.
b. A landlord is paid $2,000 for the next quarter's rent.
c. First National Bank lends the company $50,000.
d. A malpractice suit is brought against a doctor. The outcome amount is unknown.
e. Shares of capital stock are sold to investors for $44,000.

E 2–4
Stockholders' Equity
L.O.1, 4

On April 1, 19xx, Bumbling, Inc., declares bankruptcy and reports the following balance sheet:

Bumbling, Inc.
Balance Sheet
April 1, 19xx

Assets		Liabilities and Stockholders' Equity	
Cash	$ 412	Liabilities:	
Accounts receivable	15,770	Accounts payable	$ 4,822
Supplies	914	Notes payable	10,000
		Total liabilities	$14,822
		Stockholders' equity:	
		Capital stock	$ 5,000
		Retained earnings	(2,726)
		Total stockholders' equity	$ 2,274
		Total liabilities and	
Total assets	$17,096	stockholders' equity	$17,096

Required:
Determine the stockholders' interest in this company and write a paragraph explaining what this amount relates to.

E 2–5
Balance Sheet Elements
L.O.1, 4

Classify the following items as to whether they are assets (A), liabilities (L), or stockholders' equity (SE). If they are part of SE, tell whether they are stock (S), revenues (R), expenses (E), or dividends (D).

_____	*a.* Notes receivable.		_____	*h.* Consulting fees.
_____	*b.* Cash.		_____	*i.* Salaries expense.
_____	*c.* Land.		_____	*j.* Interest payable.
_____	*d.* Supplies.		_____	*k.* Accounts receivable.
_____	*e.* Capital stock.		_____	*l.* Accounts payable.
_____	*f.* Dividends payable.		_____	*m.* Dividends.
_____	*g.* Unearned revenue.			

E 2–6
Determining Retained
Earnings
L.O.1, 4

On January 1, 19xx, FBON, Inc., had a $400,000 balance in Retained Earnings. During 19xx, FBON earned income of $50,000 and declared and paid dividends of $20,000. Also, FBON received cash of $15,000 as an additional investment in stock by its owners. Determine the balance of Retained Earnings on December 31, 19xx.

E 2–7
Balance Sheet Equation
L.O.1, 4

The following information was taken from the financial statements of Aeroquip Corporation:

Total assets at 12/31/x2	$1,700,000
Net income of 19x2	70,000
Total liabilities at 12/31/x1	720,000
Total liabilities at 12/31/x2	650,000
Total assets at 12/31/x1	1,600,000

Required:
What was the apparent amount received by Aeroquip during 19x2 from the sale of Aeroquip stock? No dividends were declared or paid during the year.

E 2–8
Balance Sheet Equation
L.O.1, 4

The following information is available for the Trying Corporation:

Total assets at 12/31/x2	$250,000
Total liabilities at 12/31/x2	80,000
Dividends paid during 19x2	11,000
Total assets at 12/31/x1	200,000
Net income for 19x2	31,000

No Trying Corporation stock was bought or sold during 19x2.

Required:
Compute the amount of total liabilities on December 31, 19x1.

E 2–9
Balance Sheet Equation
L.O.1, 4

Fill in the missing number.

Cash	$ 5,625
Supplies	915
Accounts receivable	18,746
Equipment	20,000
Land	25,000
Accounts payable	4,669
Notes payable	10,000
Capital stock	50,000
Retained earnings	?

E 2–10
Balance Sheet
L.O.1, 4

Prepare a balance sheet for the DRB Engineering Corporation as of November 30, 19xx, from the following information:

Cash	$ 16,200
Prepaid Rent	25,000
Supplies	5,800
Equipment	140,000
Accounts Receivable	91,500
Accounts Payable	?
Notes Payable	80,000
Capital Stock	120,000
Retained Earnings	41,750

E 2–11
*Operating, Investing,
and Financing Activities*
L.O.2

Baker, Inc., entered into a number of transactions, described below. You are to indicate whether each of these transactions is an operating (O), a financing (F), or an investing (I) activity. Note that some transactions may have more than one purpose.

_____ *a.* Sold Baker capital stock to stockholders for cash.
_____ *b.* Sold a service to customers on open account.
_____ *c.* Purchased equipment for cash. *noncurrent*
_____ *d.* Borrowed cash from bank by signing a note payable.
_____ *e.* Provided services to customers for cash.
_____ *f.* Purchased supplies for cash from suppliers.
_____ *g.* Acquired land in exchange for stock. *I, F*
_____ *h.* Recorded unpaid salaries payable at the end of the accounting period.
_____ *i.* Recorded interest payable on bank loans.

E 2–12
Events or Adjustments
L.O.2, 6, 8

Able Corporation entered into a number of transactions, described below. Indicate whether these are transactions with outsiders (T) or adjustments (A) and whether they are investing (I), financing (F), or operating (O) activities.

_____ *a.* Recorded salaries payable at the end of the accounting period.
_____ *b.* Paid accounts payable with cash.
_____ *c.* Borrowed cash from the bank.
_____ *d.* Sold a service on open account.
_____ *e.* Recorded interest payable.
_____ *f.* Recorded rent expense by reducing the asset prepaid rent.
_____ *g.* Received cash for services to be provided by Able next accounting period.
_____ *h.* Issued Able capital stock to stockholders.
_____ *i.* Paid cash dividends to stockholders.

E 2–13
Matching Principle
L.O.6, 7

At month's end, Katie's Answering Service has the following items:

a. Supplies at the beginning of the month were $500. During the month, Katie's purchased $925 supplies; $315 is now on hand.
b. At the beginning of the month, Katie's paid $52,000 cash to Shosing Realtors for four months' rent.
c. Switchboard operators have earned $5,300 during the month, of which $5,000 has been paid in cash.

Required:
Determine the amount to be recognized as revenue or expense for the month for each item.

E 2–14
Income Statement
L.O.10

Prepare an income statement for Schafer Electronics Corporation for the quarter ending March 31, 19xx, from the following information:

Interest Revenue	$ 5,000
Rent Expense	18,000
Salaries Expense	32,000
Supplies Expense	2,100
Advertising Expense	12,000
Utilities Expense	10,000
Insurance Expense	6,000
Service Revenue	81,000

E 2–15
Comprehensive
L.O.2, 4, 5

1. Retained Earnings—
   a. Is net income for the year minus expenses for the year.
   b. Is cumulative net income minus cumulative expenses minus cumulative dividends.
   c. Appears on the income statement.
   d. Is an asset.
   e. None of the above.

2. The income statement—
   a. Lists all assets owned by the company.
   b. Shows assets minus liabilities.
   c. Is part of the balance sheet.
   d. Shows the results of operations for a period.
   e. None of the above.
3. The balance sheet equation—
   a. Is in balance only at the beginning and end of the period.
   b. Is Assets + Liabilities = Owners' Equity.
   c. Reports on sales and expenses.
   d. Is sales minus expenses minus dividends equals net income.
   e. None of the above.
4. Operating transactions include—
   a. Sale of common stock.
   b. Borrowing from a bank.
   c. Performance of a service for cash.
   d. Paying dividends.
   e. None of the above.
5. Financing transactions include—
   a. Purchasing a building.
   b. Paying rent.
   c. Collecting a receivable.
   d. Borrowing from a bank.
   e. None of the above.

• PROBLEMS

P 2–1
Comprehensive
L.O.1, 3, 6, 7, 8

For each statement below, identify the name of the principle or term described.

1. The process accountants go through to relate the benefits from operations with the efforts or costs of achieving these benefits.
2. Holds that revenue should be recognized in the period earned rather than when cash is received.
3. Triggered by economic events with outside parties.
4. Operating transactions resulting in net asset increases or inflows.
5. Formally incorporating an item into the financial statements as a component of assets, liabilities, and stockholders' equity.
6. Excess of revenues over expenses.

P 2–2
Asset Valuation
L.O.1

In some transactions it appears as though the value of assets given equals the value of assets received. In other transactions they do not seem to be equal. Consider the following transactions:

a. Company X provides a service to a customer for $1,000 cash and incurs $500 in expenses.
b. Company B sells land valued at $10,000 to Company J in exchange for Company J stock with a market value of $10,000.

Required:
Write a paragraph answering each of the following questions.
1. Are both transactions based on fair values?
2. Are both transactions considered arm's length?
3. In transaction (a) above, what is the fair value of the service?

P 2–3
Balance Sheet Equation;
Net Assets from
Operations
L.O.4, 5

Assume the following balance sheet data are taken from three different companies after considering all transactions and adjustments (including stock and dividend transactions):

	Company A	Company B	Company C
Balance sheet data:			
Total assets, 1/1/xx	$100,000	$720,000	$380,000
Total assets, 12/31/xx	250,000	680,000	390,000
Total liabilities, 1/1/xx	60,000	530,000	100,000
Total liabilities, 12/31/xx	130,000	450,000	140,000
Additional facts:			
Capital stock sold for cash in 19xx	50,000	50,000	40,000
Dividends declared and paid in cash in 19xx.	10,000	20,000	0

Required:
Compute the increase or decrease in net assets for 19xx attributable to the operations (net income) of each company.

P 2–4
Balance Sheet Equation;
Net Income and Net Loss
L.O.4, 10

Assume the following balance sheet data are the same for four different companies after considering all transactions and adjustments (including stock and dividend transactions):

	Total Assets	Total Liabilities
Beginning of the year.	$ 85,000	$20,000
End of the year	100,000	10,000

Additional information that is already included in the amounts reported above for each company is as follows:

Company A: The company did not issue any additional stock and did not declare any dividends.

Company B: The company did not issue any additional stock but declared and paid dividends of $11,000.

Company C: The company issued $28,000 of additional stock but did not declare any dividends.

Company D: The company issued $10,000 of additional stock and declared dividends of $18,000.

Required:
On the basis of the above data, calculate the net income or net loss of each company for the year.

P 2–5
Transaction Analysis
L.O.1, 7

During the month of September 19x1, the Winwood Realty Corporation completed the following transactions:

a. Purchased office supplies for inventory on account.
b. Paid rent for October.
c. Issued additional capital stock, receiving cash.
d. Recorded salaries paid to employees during the month.
e. Paid various office expenses incurred during September.
f. Earned service revenue, receiving cash.
g. Paid the amount owed to the vendor for the office supplies purchased in (*a*) above.
h. Used half of the supplies purchased in (*a*) above.
i. Declared and paid cash dividends to stockholders.
j. Paid interest due for September for a note payable to the bank.

Required:
Indicate the effect of each transaction on the balance sheet equation by the appropriate number from the following list:

1. Increase in one asset, decrease in another asset.
2. Increase in an asset, increase in a liability.
3. Increase in an asset, increase in stockholders' equity.
4. Decrease in an asset, decrease in a liability.
5. Decrease in an asset, decrease in stockholders' equity.

P 2–6

Preparing Financial Statements
L.O.3, 6, 10

On January 2, 19x5, your first day on the job as accountant for Young Corporation, you are given the following list of balance sheet and income statement items. You are told that all appropriate adjustments have been made as of December 31, 19x4, and that no transactions occurred on January 1.

Accounts payable	$ 22
Prepaid expenses	9
Service revenue received in advance	13
Supplies	46
Capital stock	90
Advertising expense	18
Sales revenue	296
Cash	15
Rent expense—facilities	49
Prepaid rent—facilities	72
Utilities expense	7
Salaries expense	163
Supplies expense	54
Notes payable	74
Accounts receivable	36
Retained earnings, 12/31/x3	13
Land	39

Assume that all of the balances given in the data above are normal and correct.

Required:
1. Prepare an income statement for 19x4.
2. Compute the amount to be reported in retained earnings as of December 31, 19x4.
3. Prepare a balance sheet as of December 31, 19x4.

P 2–7
Event Analysis
L.O.4–8, 10

The Duotech Corporation reported the following balance sheet data at the end of 19x1:

Duotech Corporation
Balance Sheet
December 31, 19x1
(in millions)

Assets		Liabilities and Stockholders' Equity	
Cash	$ 19	Liabilities:	
Accounts receivable	22	Accounts payable	$ 20
Prepaid expenses	15	Income taxes payable.	9
Supplies.	31	Notes payable	75
Building	177	Total liabilities	$104
Land	20	Stockholders' equity:	
		Capital stock.	$160
		Retained earnings	20
		Total stockholders' equity	$180
Total assets	$284	Total liabilities and stockholders' equity	$284

The following transactions (in millions) occurred during January 19x2:

a. Collected accounts receivable of $17.
b. Sold a service for $60 on account.
c. Purchased supplies costing $20 on account.
d. Paid income taxes payable of $9.
e. Paid accounts payable of $18.
f. Paid selling and administrative expenses of $5. *Salaries for employees*
g. Collected accounts receivable of $35.

During January, Duotech used $8 of the prepaid expenses. At January 31, $29 in supplies were still on hand. *rent paid ahead of time*

Required:

1. Using a spreadsheet analysis like that illustrated in Exhibit 2-6 (page 56), prepare a summary of the January transactions for Duotech.
2. Prepare an income statement for January 19x2 and the January 31, 19x2, balance sheet.

P 2–8
Event Analysis
L.O.4–8, 10

Technavest, Inc., began operations in 19x1. During 19x1, the following transactions occurred (all amounts are in thousands):

19x1
Oct. 12 Sold Technavest stock for $200 cash.
      15 Purchased supplies for $80 on open account.
      23 Rented facilities and equipment for one year starting November 1, 19x1, for $24 cash.
      28 Purchased postage stamps for $8 cash.
Nov. 1 Opened for business.
      15 Provided services for $38 on credit.
      20 Borrowed $50 from bank for a two-year note.
      22 Paid cash of $16 on accounts payable.
      28 Collected cash of $32 on accounts receivable.
      30 Paid salaries of $40 in cash.
Dec. 5 Provided services for $89 on credit.
      16 Paid advertising bill of $2 in cash.
      18 Provided services for $115 on credit.
      19 Paid salaries of $106 in cash.
      22 Collected $150 on accounts receivable.
      23 Paid accounts payable of $40 in cash.
      25 Closed for holidays until the next year.

Additional Data:

As of the end of the year, the following adjustments were needed:

a. Recognize rent expense.
b. Recognize unpaid salaries of $30.
c. Recognize unpaid interest on note of $1.
d. Recognize unused postage stamps on hand at year-end of $5.
e. Recognize unused supplies of $32.

Required:

1. Using a spreadsheet analysis like the one illustrated in Exhibit 2–6 (page 56), prepare a summary of the transactions described in the problem.
2. Prepare an income statement for 19x1 and a balance sheet for Technavest at December 31, 19x1.

P 2–9
Event Analysis
L.O.4–8, 10

The Dual Peaks Corporation started business in 19x1. The following transactions occurred:

19x1
Mar. 1   Sold Dual Peaks stock for $600,000 in cash.
      15   Purchased land for $75,000 cash.
      15   Rented a building by signing a one-year lease. Paid $84,000 for the first year's rent to begin May 1, 19x1.
      23   Paid $35,000 for the rental of equipment for seven months starting May 1, 19x1.
      31   Hired two managers to run business at an annual salary of $90,000 each, first payments to be made on May 30.
      31   Borrowed $30,000 from the local bank.
Apr. 10   Paid $16,000 cash for radio advertisements in April and May announcing grand opening.
      15   Acquired $39,000 of supplies on open account.
      24   Purchased another company's stock as an investment for $100,000.
May   1   Provided services for $38,500 cash.
      16   Provided services for $89,600 on account.
      20   Paid $15,000 cash on accounts payable.
      28   Provided services for $65,900 on open account.
      30   Collected cash of $63,000 on accounts receivable.
      30   Paid wages and salaries of $62,000.

Additional Data:

a. Interest payable on the bank borrowing amounted to $690 as of the end of May.
b. One month's rent on the building and the equipment had expired by the end of May.
c. Supplies of $20,000 were on hand at May 31.

Required:

1. Using a spreadsheet analysis like the one illustrated in Exhibit 2–6 (page 56), prepare a summary of the transactions described in the problem.
2. Prepare an income statement for the three months of business and a balance sheet at May 31, 19x1.

P 2–10
Event Analysis—
General Dynamics
L.O.4–8, 10

General Dynamics manufactures many different products, including F-16 fighter jets, Tomahawk antiship cruise missiles, M1A1 Abrams Army Tanks, and Trident and Seawolf class submarines. The following balance sheet data are summarized from a recent December 31 annual report.

General Dynamics
Balance Sheet
December 31
(in millions)

Assets		Liabilities and Stockholders' Equity	
Cash	$ 195	Liabilities:	
Receivables	1,948	Current liabilities	$ 820
Supplies.	380	Long-term liabilities	2,468
Property, plant, and equipment	1,364	Total liabilities	$3,288
Other assets	665	Stockholders' equity:	
		Paid-in capital	$ 80
		Retained earnings	1,184
		Total stockholders' equity	$1,264
Total assets	$4,552	Total liabilities and stockholders' equity. . .	$4,552

Assume that the following items summarize the operations during January following the balance sheet data above (amounts in millions):

a. Had sales of $2,000 on account and consumed supplies of $300.
b. Collected $2,548 cash from the U.S. government on accounts receivable.
c. Used up equipment costing $44 during the month of January (record as an expense).
d. Paid salaries of $757 in January.
e. Paid accounts payable of $163 in January.
f. Paid other current liabilities of $650 in January.
g. Prepaid expenses for rent of $42, included in "Other Assets," expired during the month of January.
h. Recorded unpaid salaries at the end of January for $187.
i. Recorded previously unrecorded current liabilities (primarily for interest expense and income tax expense) at the end of January for $456.
j. Dividends of $200 were paid in cash during January.

Required:
1. Using a spreadsheet analysis like the one illustrated in Exhibit 2–6 (page 56), fill in the beginning balances from the December 31 balance sheet and then prepare a summary of the effect of the data items above from January on the balance sheet equation. Compute ending balances in all balance sheet columns in the spreadsheet.
2. Prepare the January income statement and retained earnings statement, and the balance sheet as of January 31.

P 2–11
Financial Statement Adjustments
L.O.7, 8, 10

The following financial statements were prepared by the Farber Company's accounting clerk:

Farber Company
Balance Sheet
December 31, 19x1

Assets		Liabilities and Stockholders' Equity	
Cash	$ 8,500	Liabilities:	
Accounts receivable	14,080	Accounts payable	$12,160
Supplies	5,710	Revenue received in advance	1,200
Prepaid insurance	3,620	Note payable.	22,540
Building	45,900	Total liabilities	$35,900
Land	20,000		
		Stockholders' equity:	
		Capital stock.	$22,000
		Retained earnings	39,910
		Total stockholders' equity	$61,910
Total assets	$97,810	Total liabilities and stockholders' equity . .	$97,810

Farber Company
Income Statement
For Year Ended December 31, 19x1

Revenues		$184,350
Expenses:		
Selling and administrative	$129,180	
Salaries	42,160	
Total expenses		171,340
Net income		$ 13,010

In discussing these statements with the president of the company you learn that the following items have not been recorded:

a. Interest payable on the note for the year is $2,200.
b. The prepaid insurance was for a two-year policy and one year of it has expired.
c. Supplies of $3,000 remain in the supplies storeroom.
d. Three new trucks were ordered on January 1, 19x2, to be delivered in April at a cost of $22,000 each.
e. Salaries payable for work performed since the December 21, 19x1, payday amount to $1,800.
f. One half the revenue received in advance has been earned.

Required:
1. Discuss the adjustments indicated by the additional information supplied by the president.
2. Prepare a revised balance sheet and a revised income statement for Farber Company.

P 2–12
Balance Sheet Equation:
Revenues and Expenses
L.O.4, 10

Assume the following amounts are taken from the financial statements of three different companies:

	Co. A	Co. B	Co. C
Total assets, 1/1/xx	$440,000	$560,000	$668,000
Total assets, 12/31/xx	490,000	654,000	568,000
Total liabilities, 1/1/xx	250,000	203,000	316,000
Total liabilities, 12/31/xx	280,000	230,000	?
Total stockholders' equity, 1/1/xx	190,000	?	352,000
Total stockholders' equity, 12/31/xx	?	424,000	326,000

Required:
1. Company A had revenues for 19xx of $412,000, expenses of $397,000 and did not pay any dividends. What amount of capital stock was sold in 19xx?
2. Company B had revenues for 19xx of $748,000, sold $25,000 worth of stock, and paid $12,000 in dividends. What were expenses in 19xx?
3. Company C sold $20,000 worth of stock, paid no dividends, and had $593,000 in expenses in 19xx. What were revenues in 19xx?

P 2–13
Preparation of Financial
Statements
L.O.9, 10

PC Service, Inc., started business in early 19x1. The corporation initially raised capital by selling $100,000 in stock to a group of 10 investors. The managers then signed a one-year lease on a retail building to begin on March 1, 19x1, for $4,000 per month. They paid a year's rent in advance. Supplies were purchased and operations were started on March 1, 19x1. Sales were made on account to 17 customers during March. At the end of March, the firm had $34,700 in cash and owed a bank $10,000 on a note taken out on March 15. Full payment had been received from all customers except for the most recent sale of $12,000. In addition, $1,000 in down payments had been received from customers waiting for a new unit that would be available in June. Supplies of $58,500 are on hand on which a $25,000 payment is still owed to the supplier. Sales totaled $102,000 for the month. Salaries, advertising, supplies, and utilities totaled $84,800, all of which were paid in cash. Interest of $50 is owed to the bank for the note.

Required:
1. Prepare a balance sheet at March 31, 19x1, for PC Service, Inc.
2. Prepare an income statement for the month ended March 31, 19x1.
3. What would sales revenue be under the cash basis of accounting?

P 2–14
Revenue/Expense
Recognition
L.O.6

Arnwood Engineering is a design-consultant company. The following transactions occurred during the month of December 19x1:

a. Received $20,000 as a down payment on a project to be started and completed the next summer.
b. Purchased on account $5,000 of special supplies for January 19x2 work.
c. Paid $17,000 to the staff for December employment.
d. Advanced $6,000 to salespersons for sales commissions expected to be earned on January 19x2 sales.
e. Received $12,000 from Buck Company in payment for a project to be started and completed during 19x2.
f. Paid $27,000 to a consulting engineer who had worked on a project completed in November, 19x1.
g. Received $44,000 payment on account for projects completed before December 1.

Required:
For each item listed, indicate whether the amount of any inflow should be recognized as a revenue in the financial statements for the year ended December 31, 19x1, and whether the amount of any outflow should be recognized as an expense. If the amount should not be recognized, state what else must occur for the revenue or expense to be recognized.

P 2–15
Balance Sheet and
Income Statement
L.O.10

F&M, Inc., a landscaping business, started operations early in July of 19x1. Construct a balance sheet and an income statement at July 31, 19x1, based on the following transactions.

a. Issued stock for $10,000 cash.
b. Borrowed $5,000 from a bank.
c. Provided landscaping services for $6,000 cash during the period.
d. Paid $300 for telephone service for the period.
e. Paid $2,000 in salaries during the period.
f. Paid dividends of $1,000 to owners.
g. Purchased land for $4,000.

• CASES

C 2–1
Measuring Balance
Sheet Elements
L.O.1

You have been hired by a bank to examine the balance sheet of a potential borrower. The balance sheet contains the following items (in millions):

Assets:

Prepaid advertising	$ 1
Land (at estimated fair market value)	15
Famous paintings (at original cost)	35
Estimated value of managerial talent	5
Vacant building (at estimated selling price)	46
Investment in stocks (at cost, market value equals $10) . . .	8

Liabilities:

Cash in bank	2
Notes payable	10
Wages payable	11
Taxes payable	6

Required:
Identify any items that appear to be incorrectly stated from an accounting point of view and indicate the correct treatment in each instance. Write a paragraph on what information you as a potential lender would like to know about each item.

C 2–2
Comparison of
Financial Statements
L.O.10

Discussions occasionally occur in accounting circles about which financial statement is the most useful. Of the four standard statements, select the financial statement you feel is the most useful, and outline the arguments supporting your choice.

C 2–3
Balance Sheet Equation
L.O.1

A newly formed company found itself without much cash in the early days of the business. Therefore, it decided to pay its workers partly with cash and partly with stock in the company. The workers could then sell some of the stock to others if they needed the cash.

Required:
Write concise answers to the following questions:

1. What was the effect on the balance sheet of the August 19x1 payroll, which paid $8,000 to employees in cash and issued $8,000 in stock to employees for employee wages?
2. What was the effect on the balance sheet of the sale by the employees of $4,000 of this stock to other investors?

• Evaluating Financial Statements

C 2–4
Retained Earnings—
Warner-Lambert
L.O.4

Warner-Lambert is a major worldwide company specializing in the development, production, and marketing of health care and consumer products. These products range from prescription and non-prescription pharmaceuticals to chewing gums, razors and blades, and home aquarium products. Warner-Lambert reported the following information in a published statement of consolidated retained earnings (in thousands):

	Year Ended December 31	
	Year 2	Year 1
Retained earnings at beginning of year	$1,456,062	$?
Net income (loss)	?	223,887
Dividends declared	117,248	118,003
Retained earnings at end of year.	1,023,218	?

Required:
Fill in the missing information and discuss the relationship between the retained earnings balance and the net income amount.

C 2–5
Income Statement
Preparation—
General Mills
L.O.10

The following information is taken from an annual report of General Mills, a major competitor in consumer foods, restaurants, and specialty retailing with such familiar products as Cheerios and Hamburger Helper and the Red Lobster restaurant chain (in millions):

Cash	$ 56.4
Land	100.9
Interest expense.	38.8
Miscellaneous expenses	113.1
Notes payable.	4.7
Retained earnings	812.9
Sales	4,586.6
Selling, general, and administrative expenses	4,109.6

Required:
Prepare General Mills' income statement for the year ended May 25, 19x6. What effect does net income have on the balance sheet?

C 2–6
Income Statment—
Ralston Purina
L.O.4, 10

Examine the 1992 annual report for Ralston Purina Company provided in Appendix E at the end of this book.

Required:
1. Fill in the following amounts from the financial statements for the year ended September 30, 1992. What effect does net income have on retained earnings and net assets?
    a. Interest expense.
    b. Cost of products sold.
    c. Income tax expense.
    d. Net sales.
    e. Net income.
    f. Selling; general and administrative expense.
    g. Dividends.
    h. Advertising and promotion expense.
2. List Ralston Purina's exact titles for the four major financial statements.

C 2–7
Recognition of
Revenue—Dow Jones
& Company
L.O.6

Shown below is a condensed version of a recent income statement from Dow Jones & Company, a financial news service firm that publishes, among other things, *The Wall Street Journal.*

Dow Jones & Company
Statement of Income
For the Year Ended Dec. 31
(in thousands)

Revenues:

Advertising	$429,052
Circulation	193,930
Other	107,691
Total revenues	$730,673

Expenses:

News, production, and royalty	$214,495
Selling, administrative, and general	192,060
Newsprint	95,750
Postage	51,121
Depreciation	27,805
Total expenses	$581,231
Operating income	$149,442
Other income	7,113
Net income before taxes	$156,555
Income tax expense	68,452
Net income	$ 88,103

Required:
Write one short paragraph in answer to each of the following questions:

1. How do you think Dow Jones determines when advertising revenues are recognized?
2. How do you think Dow Jones determines when subscription (circulation) revenues are recognized?
3. When would you recognize revenues on a trial subscription in which customers get two weeks of papers and pay for them only if they continue?

C 2–8
Revenue Recognition
L.O.3, 6, 8

A major problem in the economic development of the economy of the new Russian republic is the nonconvertibility of the ruble; that is, rubles cannot be taken out of Russia and converted into other currencies such as dollars. Therefore, in order to get something of value out of a Russian business venture, some companies use a barter system. The following is a case in which bartering is used and specific accounting issues come to the fore. American Energy Corporation (AEC) designed a refinery for a Russian oil producer, Russia Petro, Ltd. (RP), at a fee equivalent to $10,000,000. In payment, RP delivered crude oil with a market value of $10,000,000 to AEC's Rotterdam facilities. Consider the following specific events:

Jan. 2   AEC signs the contract to design the refinery.
Nov. 1   AEC delivers and RP accepts the completed plans.
Nov. 10   An RP supertanker departs Russia in route to Rotterdam with $10,000,000 worth of crude oil.
Dec. 1   The crude oil is delivered and accepted by AEC in Rotterdam.

AEC incurred $6,000,000 in costs for design personnel and all supporting activities related to the RP project.

Required:
Write a short analysis of how AEC should recognize revenues and match expenses in this situation.

3

Introduction to the Accounting Cycle

Business ethics is not by any means a purely business matter. The tap root of ethical behavior, in an individual sense, comes from values training and cultural inculcation, the origins of which are outside the business world—in the larger environment.

Shaun F. O'Malley
Price Waterhouse

· Learning Objectives

After studying Chapter 3, you should understand

1. The debit-credit convention, pp. 84–87.

2. How to analyze transactions (cycle step 1) and record them (cycle step 2) in the debit-credit format of the formal accounting system, pp. 91–92.

3. The relation between the journal and the ledger (cycle step 3), pp. 92–96.

4. The role of the trial balance as a check on the debit-credit convention and as a tool to help prepare adjustments (cycle step 4) and financial statements (cycle step 5), pp. 100–101.

5. How adjustments, based on past and/or expected future transactions, are recorded at the end of an accounting period (cycle step 4 developed further in Chapter 4), pp. 101–6.

6. The role of matching and revenue recognition in helping to guide the end-of-period adjusting entries, pp. 101–2.

7. The difference between the cash basis and the accrual basis of accounting, and the principles of the accrual model, pp. 108–9.

8. The concepts of historical cost, objectivity, and materiality, pp. 109–10.

In Chapter 2, you learned how the financing, investing, and operating activities of a business affect the complete balance sheet equation. After this initial sequence of financing and investing activities, there is a continuous mix of all three types of activities. As the operations of the business occur, the need for financing (e.g., borrowing) and investing (e.g., purchasing equipment) activities also occur. Thus, all three business activities occur on an ongoing basis. Accounting must provide an organized method of processing the results of operating, financing, and investing activities so that financial reporting can occur on a timely basis for managers and owners to evaluate the results of past transactions. In this chapter, the system used by accountants to report quickly and efficiently on the results of the many business transactions is illustrated.

Before you can process accounting information, you must understand the accounting system of debits and credits explained in the first section of this chapter. Then you will be ready for an overview of the accounting cycle—six steps that end with the preparation of financial statements. This chapter explains the first three accounting cycle steps in detail and introduces the other steps, which are explained more fully in Chapter 4. These accounting cycle steps are integrated in an example of the financing, investing, and operating activities of a service corporation. It is important to keep in mind that the accounting system explained in Chapters 3 and 4 is simply a more efficient way of summarizing large numbers of transactions than that illustrated in Chapters 1 and 2. While these formal steps of the accounting cycle will replace the less formal spreadsheet analysis illustrated in Chapters 1 and 2, they will accomplish the same purpose: to capture and report the effects of business transactions in the financial statements.

Chapter 3 illustrates how most accounting systems actually translate financing, investing, and operating transactions into accounting information. After studying the basic flow of transactions to financial statements, you will be introduced to some of the methods used to analyze the financial results reported in the statements. A discussion of accrual accounting concludes the chapter.

THE ROLE OF DEBITS, CREDITS, AND T ACCOUNTS

In Chapters 1 and 2, we used spreadsheet analysis to show how transactions affect the complete balance sheet equation. The columns of the spreadsheet referred to the assets, liabilities, and stockholders' equity of the business, with increases in any of these columns reported as positive numbers and decreases as negative numbers. In this chapter and hereafter we refer to each column as an account, such as the Cash account or the Land account. These accounts will report all of the activities that increase or decrease the account balance in a ledger account. Formal ledger accounts, illustrated later in this chapter, are often depicted as T accounts. A T account is so named because it looks like a capital T. The use of plus and minus notations in the columns of the spreadsheet is now replaced by left-side or right-side entries to these T accounts. All left-side entries to any T account are referred to as debits (abbreviated **Dr.**) and all right-side entries to any T account are referred to as credits (abbreviated **Cr.**). Therefore:

$$\text{Debit} = \text{Dr.} = \text{Left-side entry}$$

$$\text{Credit} = \text{Cr.} = \text{Right-side entry}$$

and the T account would appear as follows:

Title of Account (e.g., Cash)

Debit (left) entries	Credit (right) entries

An account balance is the difference between the sum of the debits and the sum of the credits in each ledger, or T, account. The assets are designed to have debit balances, while liabilities and stockholders' equity have credit balances. Since Assets = Liabilities + Stockholders' Equity, we can say that the sum of the debit balances equals the sum of the credit balances.

Now consider the diagram in Exhibit 3–1, which relates the spreadsheet format used in Chapters 1 and 2 with the T account format. We can see how having asset accounts with debit balances and liabilities and stockholders' equity accounts with credit balances enables us to have Assets = Liabilities + Stockholders' Equity and, at the same time, have

EXHIBIT 3–1

Relation between Spreadsheet and T Accounts

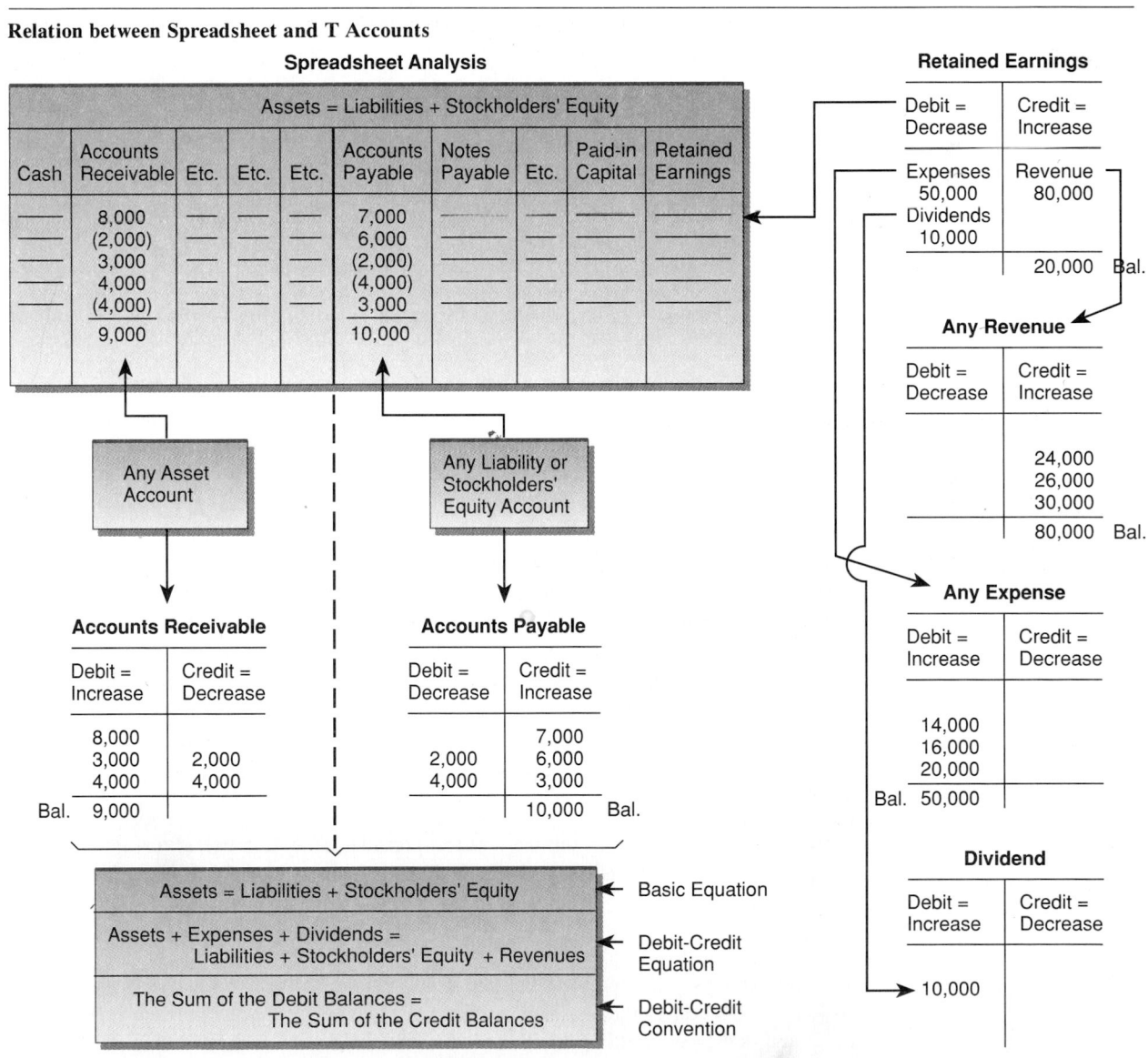

the sum of the debit balances equal the sum of the credit balances. This is accomplished by requiring debits and credits to have the opposite effects on assets than they have on liabilities and stockholders' equity. This opposite effect may be illustrated as follows:

1. First, review the equation for how the balance in any account is determined:

Any Account	Equation						
	Beginning Balance	+ Increases	− Decreases	=	Ending Balance
(e.g., Accounts Receivable). . . .	$8,000	+ $7,000	− $6,000	=	$9,000

2. Now illustrate the equation so that debits (Dr.) and credits (Cr.) have the opposite effects on assets than they have on Liabilities and Stockholders' Equity accounts, as follows:

	Equation						
	Beginning Balance	+ Increases	− Decreases	=	Ending Balance
Any asset (e.g., Accounts Receivable). . . .	Dr. $8,000	+ Dr. $7,000	− Cr. $6,000	=	Dr. $9,000
Any liability or stockholders' equity (e.g., Accounts Payable)	Cr. $7,000	+ Cr. $9,000	− Dr. $6,000	=	Cr. $10,000

The use of T accounts and debits and credits also pertains to revenues and expenses, which are now viewed as a separate set of T accounts. When combined, the revenue and expense T accounts represent the Retained Earnings T account, as depicted in Exhibit 3–1. The normal account balance for Retained Earnings is a credit like any other liability or stockholders' equity account. Since revenues increase retained earnings, revenue accounts normally have credit (right-side) balances, as noted with the $80,000 in credits in Exhibit 3–1. The balances in the expense accounts or the Dividend account are normally debits because they reduce retained earnings. The system of using debits and credits in T accounts, as summarized in Exhibit 3–1, enables us to add to the rule, Assets = Liabilities + Stockholders' Equity + Revenues − Expenses − Dividends (or Assets + Expenses + Dividends = Liabilities + Stockholders' Equity + Revenues), a second important rule:

For All Transactions, the Debits Must Equal the Credits.

This rule will be used throughout the text and provides us with a useful test to determine whether the accounting system is in balance since the sum of all debit balances must equal the sum of all credit balances at all times.

How Debits and Credits Are Used in Recording Transactions

The development of the complete balance sheet equation given in Chapter 2 is repeated below. The equation elements are illustrated as T account titles to indicate how the increases and decreases in all of the individual accounts (e.g., Cash) for each element of the equation (e.g., Assets) are recorded.

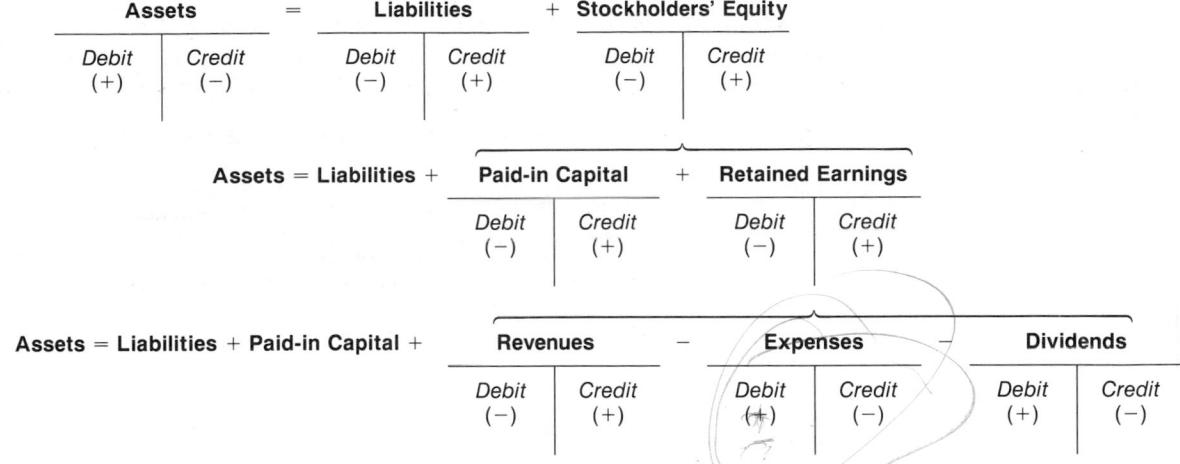

The increases and decreases of accounts illustrated above can now be translated into the following rules:

1. Increases in assets are debits, and decreases in assets are credits.
2. Decreases in liabilities and stockholders' equity are debits, and increases in liabilities and stockholders' equity are credits.
3. Since increases in revenues increase retained earnings, increases in revenues are credits, and decreases in revenues are debits.
4. Since increases in expenses and dividends decrease retained earnings, increases in expenses and dividends are debits, and decreases in expenses and dividends are credits.

The balance sheet equality is maintained after each transaction so that Assets = Liabilities + Stockholders' Equity. This system of recording transactions in accounts in such a way that **the sum of the debits for each transaction equals the sum of the credits** is known as the double-entry system.

BUSINESS AND OPERATING CYCLES

The business entity has an infinite life and is a continuous stream of operating, financing, and investing activities. These activities can be viewed as consisting of two types of cycles, **operating cycles** and **business cycles.** An operating cycle is a period of time needed to convert cash to goods and/or services and back to cash. A business cycle encompasses many operating cycles, and represents the time needed to convert cash to productive resources and back to cash. Consider the depiction in Exhibit 3–2. The inner circle represents the operating cycle of the business. This process of converting cash to goods or services back to cash occurs *many times each year* in most businesses. For example, a retailer may buy merchandise from suppliers, and sell it on account for $800. Once the $800 cash is collected and the cost to sell the goods, such as commissions and the cost of the merchandise, has been paid the operating cycle is complete.

The business cycle is a broader concept and takes longer to complete. The entity usually begins by obtaining financing from the issuance of stock and/or debt. The cash proceeds are then normally invested in productive assets such as buildings, machinery, equipment, vehicles, furniture, and so on. These assets are all eventually consumed in the normal course of business, some over 1 or 2 years (such as carpeting for a showroom), others over 40 or 50 years (such as a building). The process of converting

EXHIBIT 3–2

**Operating and
Business Cycles**

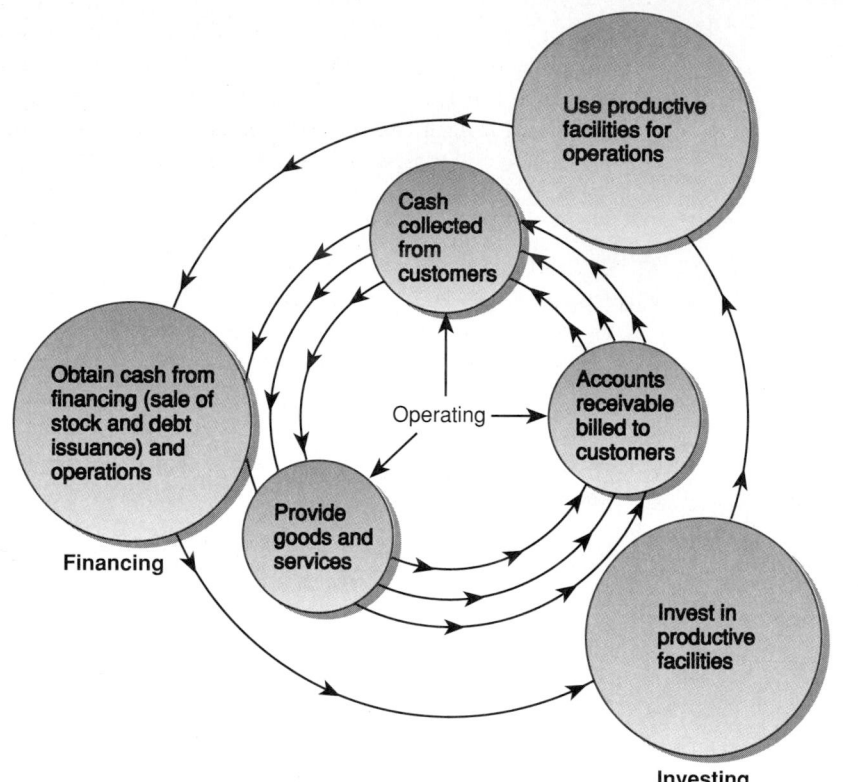

Operating cycle = Inner circle
               = Time to complete one cycle measured in days or months (i.e., 60 days)
Business cycle = Time to complete one cycle of outer circle, measured in years (i.e., 20 years, life
               of plant assets)

these productive assets back to cash is subtle, and very long in duration when compared with the operating cycle.

In most businesses, neither the operating cycle nor the business cycle ever end. Except in the case of bankruptcy or other terminations of business activities, a business goes on indefinitely. The perpetual nature of most business entities gives rise to the going concern assumption (or **concept**) underlying accounting. Simply stated, the going concern assumption is that the business will remain in business indefinitely.

Another concept that results from the continuous nature of business activity is the periodicity concept, which requires that the entity report financial statements to external decision makers on a timely basis even though cycles are incomplete. Consequently the financial statements are reported in their entirety at least annually for virtually all business entities, with some financial data provided by most companies on a quarterly basis. Of course, for internal decision making, financial data are usually reported more often, with some financial data provided on a daily basis (i.e., current cash balance). However, **annual reports** represent the primary financial statement data prepared for external decision makers by nearly all entities.

As noted in Chapter 2, accrual accounting is used as the basis for financial statements. Accrual accounting is in contrast to cash-based accounting, and permits financial statements to measure the position of the business and its periodic performance (i.e., net income) despite the incomplete nature of operating and business cycles. Accrual accounting is used as the basis of financial statements for publicly owned corporations in the United States and all industrialized nations. A formal comparison of cash- versus accrual-based accounting is provided later in this chapter. The formal accounting cycle examined next, like the informal accounting cycle introduced in Chapters 1 and 2, is based on accrual accounting. It illustrates how the business activities are summarized and converted to **periodic financial statements** of a **going concern** using **accrual accounting.**

OVERVIEW OF THE ACCOUNTING CYCLE

The accounting cycle is the systematic sequence of steps or operations that are required to be performed in order to prepare periodic financial statements. In Chapters 1 and 2, we illustrated an informal cycle used to produce these financial statements. In Chapters 3 and 4, we introduce the formal accounting cycle, which consists of the following six steps:

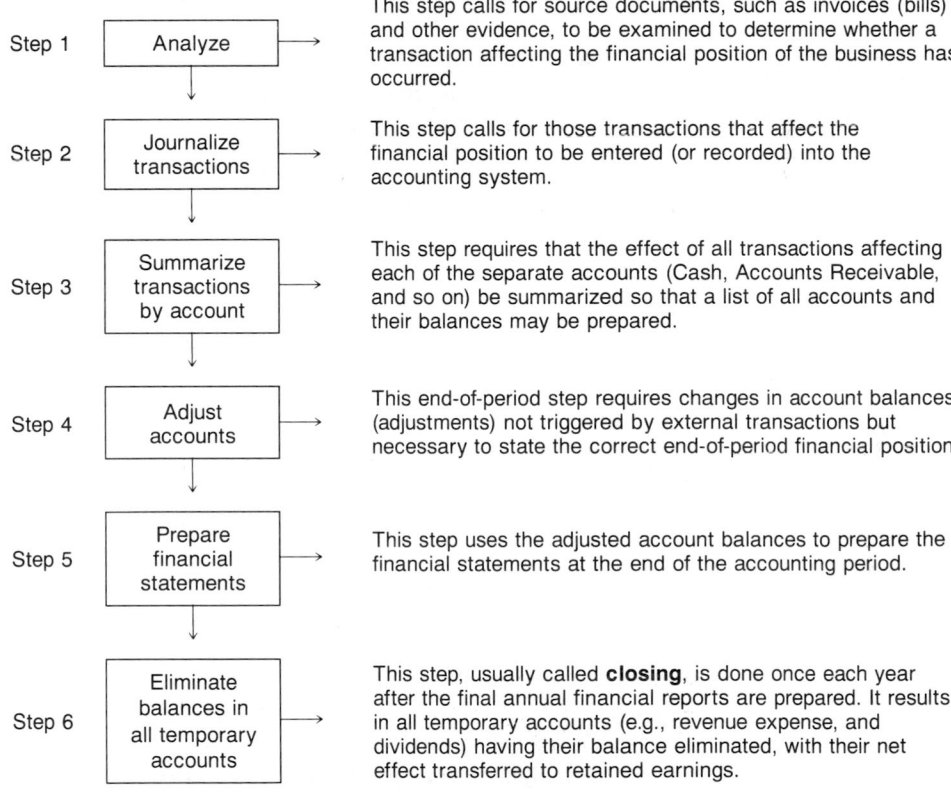

Step 1 — Analyze → This step calls for source documents, such as invoices (bills) and other evidence, to be examined to determine whether a transaction affecting the financial position of the business has occurred.

Step 2 — Journalize transactions → This step calls for those transactions that affect the financial position to be entered (or recorded) into the accounting system.

Step 3 — Summarize transactions by account → This step requires that the effect of all transactions affecting each of the separate accounts (Cash, Accounts Receivable, and so on) be summarized so that a list of all accounts and their balances may be prepared.

Step 4 — Adjust accounts → This end-of-period step requires changes in account balances (adjustments) not triggered by external transactions but necessary to state the correct end-of-period financial position.

Step 5 — Prepare financial statements → This step uses the adjusted account balances to prepare the financial statements at the end of the accounting period.

Step 6 — Eliminate balances in all temporary accounts → This step, usually called **closing**, is done once each year after the final annual financial reports are prepared. It results in all temporary accounts (e.g., revenue expense, and dividends) having their balance eliminated, with their net effect transferred to retained earnings.

Steps 1, 2, and 3 of the accounting cycle are used to summarize all the transactions of a business—financing, investing, and operating—and are explained in this chapter. You were introduced to step 4—adjusting the accounts—in Chapter 2. More is said about the adjustment process later in this chapter and again in Chapter 4. Step 5 is illustrated in this chapter and reviewed in Chapter 4 where step 6 is introduced.

ANALYZING TRANSACTIONS (ACCOUNTING CYCLE STEP 1)

Analyzing source documents and other evidence of external transactions—step 1 in the accounting cycle—is the key to accurately recording accounting information. Source documents are records usually retained in business files that provide evidence about the transactions that have actually occurred. Examples of source documents are sales receipts, invoices for merchandise purchased, utility bills, and so on. Other evidence, such as contracts with suppliers and employees, is also used to interpret transactions.

Since analyzing begins with recognizing the effects each transaction has on the assets, liabilities, and stockholders' equity of a business, it helps to understand the debit-credit relationships explained earlier in the chapter. To help familiarize you with these fundamentals, we follow a simple business through a series of transactions and observe the effect of these transactions on T accounts and formal ledger accounts. In this section, we begin with financing and investing activities. In studying each transaction, ask yourself the following three questions:

1. To what specific type of asset, liability, or stockholders' equity account (including the categories paid-in capital, retained earnings, revenues, expenses, and dividends) does the transaction belong?
2. Did the transaction increase or decrease the affected accounts?
3. Should the individual accounts affected be debited or credited?

Examples of Analyzing   To illustrate cycle step 1, we will begin to describe a business situation and follow it through to illustrate the complete six-step accounting cycle. Fitness Clinic, Inc., was organized as a service business providing individual and class instruction in physical fitness. Since the Fitness Clinic is a corporation, stockholders are the owners of the business.

Transaction 1: Financing Obtained.   On December 28, 19x1, Fitness Clinic began operations with $100,000 cash received from the sale of stock to three stockholders, Jim, Jay, and Janet.

Analysis of transaction 1.   Two accounts are affected—Cash (asset) and Capital Stock (stockholders' equity). Cash is increased (debited), and Capital Stock is increased (credited). The Cash and Capital Stock T accounts are affected as follows:

Cash		Capital Stock	
Debit = Increase	Credit = Decrease	Debit = Decrease	Credit = Increase
19x1 Dec. 28 (1) 100,000			19x1 Dec. 28 (1) 100,000

Note that the date and transaction number are given to the left of the dollar amount to aid in our discussion. Dollar signs are not used in T accounts.

Transaction 2: Rental of Building and Office Equipment.   On December 31, 19x1, Fitness Clinic paid $20,000 for two months' advance rental of a building and office equipment. This payment represents an asset, usually called "prepaid rent," because it provides future benefits controlled by Fitness Clinic.

Analysis of transaction 2.   Two accounts are affected—Cash (asset) and Prepaid Rent (asset). The asset cash is decreased (credited) and the asset prepaid rent is increased (debited). After transactions 1 and 2, the T accounts appear as follows:

Cash		Prepaid Rent	
Debit = Increase	Credit = Decrease	Debit = Increase	Credit = Decrease
19x1 Dec. 28 (1) 100,000	19x1 Dec. 31 (2) 20,000	19x1 Dec. 31 (2) 20,000	
Bal. Dec. 31 80,000			

Capital Stock

Debit = Decrease	Credit = Increase
	19x1
	Dec. 28 (1) 100,000

Note that the Cash account now has both a debit of $100,000, representing an increase, and a credit of $20,000, representing a decrease. The difference between debits and credits in any individual account at any point in time is called the account balance. For the Cash account, the balance is a debit balance of $80,000 after the second entry.

Every account has a balance at all times (even though the balance might not always be shown in manual systems). The accounting system of recording increases and decreases is arranged so that each type of account (e.g., asset accounts) has either a debit or a credit as its normal balance. Account groups with normal debit balances are assets, expenses, and dividends; account groups with normal credit balances are liabilities, paid-in capital (capital stock), retained earnings, and revenues. Knowing the normal balance of an account is necessary if you are to follow the examples in this text.

JOURNALIZING TRANSACTIONS (ACCOUNTING CYCLE STEP 2)

In the examples above, we illustrated how T accounts give a status report on how the results of transactions affected the balance in each asset, liability, or stockholders' equity account. A ledger is a complete set of the T accounts that form the basic structure of the formal accounting system. This is why T accounts are also called ledger accounts. Another important record used in an accounting system, however, is the journal. A **journal** is a chronological record where each accounting transaction is recorded in the order of the date that it occurred so that all of the accounts affected by a specific transaction, along with their respective debit or credit impact, are listed in one place. This record is called the **journal**, which is also known as the book of original entry.

The general journal is the most common and basic journal used by companies. The term *general journal* will be used in this textbook; however, the word *journal* used alone will also be used to refer to the general journal.

A journal entry (or **general journal entry**) is a complete record of an accounting transaction that lists all affected accounts and their respective debit or credit amounts. For each journal entry, the debits must equal the credits. For example, transaction 1 of the Fitness Clinic increased the asset account Cash by $100,000 (debit) and increased the stockholders' equity Capital Stock account by $100,000 (credit). Both the debit and credit effects of this transaction are shown in the following informal journal entry:

Objective 2

How to analyze transactions (cycle step 1) and record them (cycle step 2) in the debit-credit format of the formal accounting system.

Date	Accounts	Debit	Credit
19x1			
Dec. 28	Cash (A)*.	100,000	
	Capital Stock (SE).		100,000
	To record the issuance of capital stock.		

*We are using the abbreviations "A" for assets, "L" for liabilities, "SE" for stockholders' equity other than revenues and expenses, "R" for revenues, and "E" for expenses to help familiarize you with the account categories that are affected by journal entries.

A more formal format for journal entries is as follows:

GENERAL JOURNAL					J1
Date		Account Titles and Explanation	Ref.	Debit	Credit
19x1 Dec.	28	Cash (A)	111	100,000	
		Capital Stock (SE)	311		100,000
		To record the issuance of capital stock.			

Note that in the above journal entry, the debit entry is written first. Then the credit entry is indented below the debit entry. This entry format is conventional and we use it throughout the text. "J1" is the page number of the journal, and "Ref." refers to the number assigned to each ledger account in that journal entry. Journal entries are recorded for each transaction in the order in which they occur (chronological order).

Complex Entries

As we illustrated in Chapter 2, sometimes events impact more than two accounts at once. For example, if Fitness Clinic purchased a building that cost $250,000 by paying $25,000 in cash and signing a note for $225,000, the informal journal entry would be:

		Debit	Credit
Date xx	Building (A)	250,000	
	Cash (A)		25,000
	Note Payable (L)		225,000
	To acquire a building.		

The sum of the debits must always equal the sum of the credits for each entry, whether it has two or more accounts involved.

THE RELATIONSHIP BETWEEN THE JOURNAL AND LEDGER ACCOUNTS

As explained earlier, the informal T account is used for instructional purposes to represent the formal ledger account. While both account representations have a title, debit and credit columns, and a balance, the formal ledger account allows for more detail and the orderly handling of more transactions.

Exhibit 3–3 illustrates formal ledger accounts for Fitness Clinic's Cash, Prepaid Rent, and Capital Stock T accounts. Note that in the formal ledger accounts (1) running balances are maintained after every entry; (2) in the Cash and Prepaid Rent asset accounts, the normal account balance is a debit, and any credit balances would be put in parentheses; and (3) in the Capital Stock stockholders' equity account, the normal account balance is a credit, and any debit balances would be put in parentheses.

Recall that a ledger is a file that contains all the accounts used in an accounting system. Small companies often use only one file, called a general ledger. Larger companies often use several subfiles, called subsidiary ledgers. Subsidiary ledgers are further explained in Chapter 5. When the term *ledger* is used alone in this textbook, the reference is to the general ledger.

Accounts within a ledger are organized as they appear in the financial statements—asset accounts, liability accounts, and stockholders' equity accounts, as well as revenue, expense, and dividend accounts. Depending on the detail required, each group of ledger accounts is assigned a multidigit number (e.g., assets to the 100s, liabilities to the 200s),

EXHIBIT 3–3

Formal Ledger Accounts

GENERAL LEDGER						

Cash   Account No. 111

Date		Explanation	Ref.	Debit	Credit	Balance Debit (Credit)
19x1 Dec.	28	Issuance of capital stock	J1	100,000		100,000
	31	Prepayment of rent	J1		20,000	80,000

Prepaid Rent   Account No. 131

Date		Explanation	Ref.	Debit	Credit	Balance Debit (Credit)
19x1 Dec.	31	Prepayment of rent	J1	20,000		20,000

Capital Stock   Account No. 311

Date		Explanation	Ref.	Debit	Credit	Balance (Debit) Credit
19x1 Dec.	28	Issuance of capital stock	J1		100,000	100,000

with individual accounts numbered within the range of the multidigit series for its group. For example, each asset can be assigned a three-digit number ranging from 100 to 199 or a four-digit number from 1000 to 1999. To locate a particular account and its number, companies prepare a list of account titles for each major balance sheet category. This list is called a chart of accounts (see Exhibit 3–4). We will be using the account titles shown in Exhibit 3–4 and many others throughout this textbook. The account numbers following the account titles are used in the reference ("Ref.") column of the journal (illustrated earlier) to facilitate cross-referencing between the journal and ledger. Likewise, the reference column in the ledger (see Exhibit 3–3) cross-references the page of the journal that contains the complete transaction from which the ledger entry came.

Current and Noncurrent Accounts

Balance sheet accounts for assets and liabilities are frequently grouped into current and noncurrent categories. A current asset is one that is expected to be used up or converted to cash within one year or within the operating cycle, whichever is longer. A current liability is one that is expected to require cash or other assets to be used within one year or within the operating cycle, whichever is longer. Another way to say this is that the items represented by the money amounts in current assets (e.g., accounts receivable) and current liabilities (e.g., accounts payable) will "turn over" in less than one year; therefore, their amounts are considered current. Balance sheets that separate current assets and liabilities from noncurrent assets and liabilities are called classified balance sheets. The assets and liabilities listed in Exhibit 3–4 that are marked with an asterisk (*) are normally identified as current accounts in classified balance sheets.

EXHIBIT 3–4

**Chart of Accounts
Example**

Chart of Accounts

Account Titles	Account Nos.
Assets	100–199
Cash*	111
Accounts Receivable*	121
Prepaid Rent*	131
Supplies Inventory*	141
Land	151
Buildings	161
Equipment	162
Liabilities	200–299
Accounts Payable*	211
Salaries Payable*	212
Income Taxes Payable*	215
Notes Payable*	217
Bonds Payable	250
Stockholders' equity	300–399
Capital Stock	311
Retained Earnings	331
Revenues	400–499
Consulting Fees	411
Service Revenue	421
Interest Revenue	441
Miscellaneous Revenue	491
Expenses	500–599
Salaries Expense	511
Commissions Expense	512
Travel and Entertainment Expense	513
Advertising Expense	521
Rent Expense	531
Office Supplies Expense	541
Utilities Expense	551
Communications Expense	552
Laundry Service Expense	553
Income Tax Expense	591
Dividends (or Dividends Declared)[†]	615

*Normally identified as current in classified balance sheet.

[†]Remember that Dividends Declared is a separate type of account that does not enter into the measurement of net income but does reduce retained earnings.

**Posting to the Ledger
(Cycle Step 3)**

Periodically the debit-credit effects of each journal entry are recorded in the separate ledger accounts through a procedure called posting. This posting from the journal to the ledger is usually done each day or after each journal page is complete in manual systems, and is done automatically as journal entries are made in computerized systems. The "Ref."

column is completed as each entry is posted. Fitness Clinic's transactions 1 and 2 affected three accounts—Cash, Prepaid Rent, and Capital Stock. The debits and credits shown in the journal must be posted to the ledger accounts indicated. The journal entry for transaction 1 is posted to the Cash and Capital Stock ledger accounts as follows:

Objective 3
The relation between the journal and the ledger (cycle step 3).

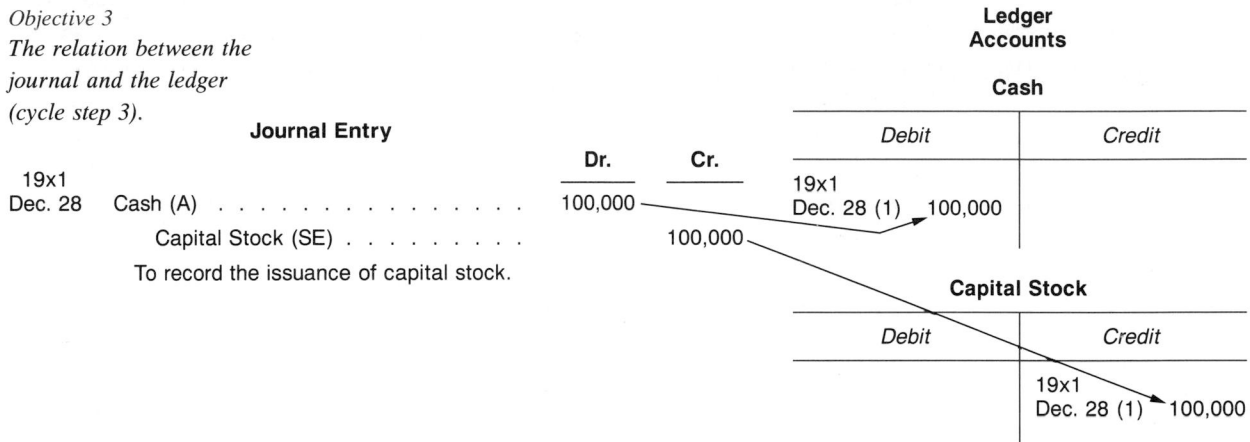

Note that the $100,000 Cash debit in the journal entry is posted as a debit to the Cash account, and the $100,000 Capital Stock credit in the journal entry is posted as a credit to the Capital Stock account. Thus, posting is used to transfer the debit and credit effects of the activities of a business (financing, investing, and operating) from a chronological record (journal) to individual records (ledger accounts).

The journal entry for transaction 2 is posted as follows:

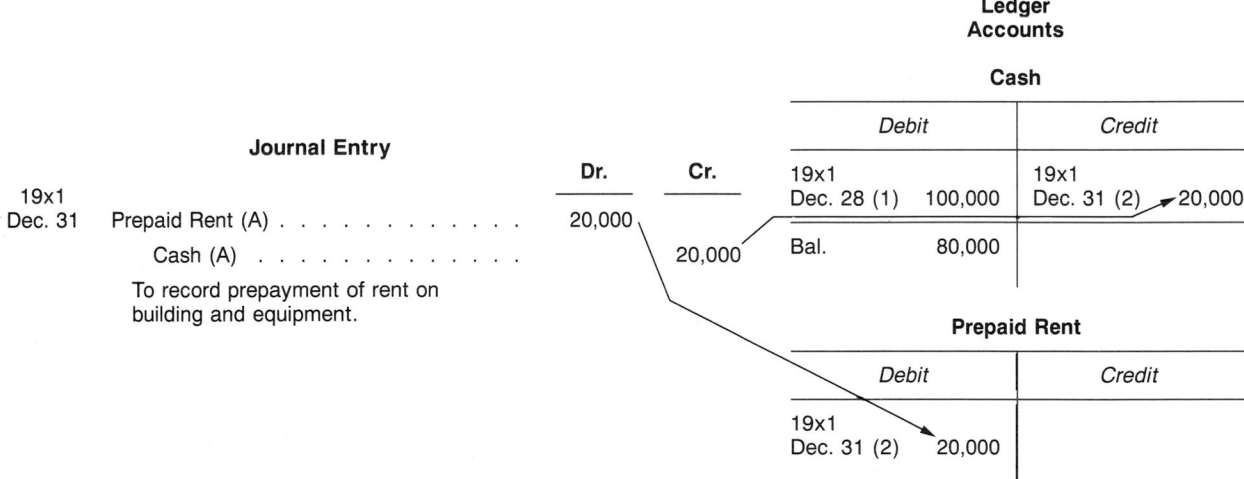

The $20,000 debit for Prepaid Rent in the journal entry is debited to the Prepaid Rent account, and the $20,000 credit for Cash in the journal entry is credited to the Cash account. The balance in the Cash account is now $80,000.

Exhibit 3–5 illustrates the more detailed version of posting from the *formal* journal to the *formal* ledger accounts, and shows the cross-referencing that exists between the journal and the ledger accounts.

EXHIBIT 3–5

Posting from the Journal to the Ledger

GENERAL JOURNAL   J1

Date		Acct. Titles/Explanation	Ref.	Debit	Credit
19x1 Dec.	28	Cash (A)	111	100,000	
		Capital Stock (SE)	311		100,000
		To record the issuance of capital stock.			
	31	Prepaid Rent (A)	131	20,000	
		Cash (A)	111		20,000
		To record prepayment of rent on building and equipment.			

GENERAL LEDGER

Cash   Account No. 111

Date		Explanation	Ref.	Debit	Credit	Balance Debit (Credit)
19x1 Dec.	28	Issuance of capital stock	J1	100,000		100,000
	31	Prepayment of rent	J1		20,000	80,000

Prepaid Rent   Account No. 131

Date		Explanation	Ref.	Debit	Credit	Balance Debit (Credit)
19x1 Dec.	31	Prepayment of rent	J1	20,000		20,000

Capital Stock   Account No. 311

Date		Explanation	Ref.	Debit	Credit	Balance (Debit) Credit
19x1 Dec.	28	Issuance of capital stock	J1		100,000	100,000

ACCOUNTING DURING AN OPERATING PERIOD (ACCOUNTING CYCLE STEPS 1, 2, 3, AND 4)

Recall that the accountant's basic measure of profitability is net income, which is

$$\text{Revenues} - \text{Expenses} = \text{Net Income}$$

Another way of stating net income is:

$$\frac{\text{Net Assets Generated}}{\text{by Operations}} - \frac{\text{Net Assets Consumed}}{\text{by Operations}} = \text{Net Income}$$

Also, recall that net income is added to the retained earnings balance at the end of each period and, after deducting the dividends declared (announced dividends) for the period, provides the ending retained earnings needed to balance the balance sheet equation (Assets = Liabilities + Stockholders' Equity) as follows:

Retained earnings, beginning of the period	$ xxx
+ Net income (or subtract net loss)	xxx
− Dividends declared	(xxx)
Retained earnings, end of the period	$ xxx

Temporary and Permanent Accounts

Because revenue and expense accounts are used to accumulate the effects of operating transactions for a period of time only, they are called temporary accounts or **nominal accounts.** They are temporary because after a specified period of time, their balances are transferred to the retained earnings account (called *closing*). Retained earnings, like all balance sheet accounts, is a permanent account, which records the cumulative effect of revenues and expenses from all prior accounting periods. Dividends is also a temporary account that is closed to retained earnings. In Chapter 4, we will explain this closing process and show how it is that revenue, expense, and dividend accounts begin each new accounting period with no balances.

Recording Transactions during an Operating Period (Accounting Cycle Steps 1, 2, and 3)

To illustrate how accountants measure net income, we return to the Fitness Clinic example. As you recall, on December 28, 19x1, the stockholders of Fitness Clinic invested $100,000 cash in the corporation—a financing transaction. Then on December 31, 19x1, rent ($20,000) was prepaid for two months to provide Fitness Clinic with a place to conduct its operations.

In January 19x2, Fitness Clinic began its instruction in physical fitness. The following entries occurred during January:

Date	Entry No.	Description of Entry	Amount
19x2			
Jan. 14	3	Salaries paid in cash	$ 10,000
22	4	Salaries paid in cash	15,000
27	5	Utilities paid in cash	3,000
29	6	Laundry services paid in cash	7,000
30	7	Service revenue collected in cash	100,000
30	8	Borrowed cash from bank	35,000
30	9	Purchased equipment for cash	110,000
31	10	Unpaid salaries	5,000
31	11	Consumed one month's prepaid rent during January	10,000
31	12	Declared and paid dividends	5,000
31	13	Determined income taxes for the month	10,000

Each transaction (entries 3–9 and 12 above) and each adjustment (entries 10, 11, and 13 above) triggers a journal entry, the debits and credits of which are posted to ledger accounts. To help you understand the types of transactions, we have grouped them into operating activities, financing activities, and an investing activity.

Operating Activities. Most transactions of a business involve operating activities. A company's major sources and uses of cash usually involve its customers and the suppliers of goods and services used by the company; that is, from the operating activities of the company. You will see that Fitness Clinic has both cash and noncash operating transactions that must be fully understood if the results of its operations are to be properly interpreted.

Cash expenses. During the month of January 19x2, the journal of Fitness Clinic showed that the following cash expenses (transactions 3–6) were incurred:

		GENERAL JOURNAL			J2
Entry No.	Date	Account Titles and Explanation	Ref.	Debit	Credit
	19x2 Jan.				
3	14	Salaries Expense (E)	511	10,000	
		Cash (A)	111		10,000
		To record salaries paid.			
4	22	Salaries Expense (E)	511	15,000	
		Cash (A)	111		15,000
		To record salaries paid.			
5	27	Utilities Expense (E)	551	3,000	
		Cash (A)	111		3,000
		To record utilities paid.			
6	29	Laundry Service Expense (E)	553	7,000	
		Cash (A)	111		7,000
		To record laundry service paid.			

Each transaction is supported by a source document—employees' timecards, utility bills, and laundry bills. All entries that record cash expenses depict the same basic kind of transaction. The company uses cash, and the credits to the Cash account record this fact. The debits to expense accounts represent the offsetting reductions in stockholders' equity (Retained Earnings).

Service revenue. Transaction 7—receipt of service revenue—occurred when the clients of Fitness Clinic paid for fitness instruction. Revenue is recognized (recorded) because the payments have been *earned* and the benefits are *realized* or are *realizable* by Fitness Clinic. These recognition criteria are followed by virtually all industrial nations. The source documents for these revenues are copies of the receipts given to customers. As indicated in the journal below, Cash is increased by the debit entry, and Service Revenue is increased by the credit entry. If payment is received *before* it has been earned, the credit entry would be recorded in a liability account, often called "Advances from Customers" or "Unearned Revenue." Later, once these advances are earned, the liability is reduced with a debit and revenue is increased with a credit.

		GENERAL JOURNAL			J2
Entry No.	Date	Account Titles and Explanation	Ref.	Debit	Credit
7	19x2 Jan. 30	Cash (A)	111	100,000	
		Service Revenue (R)	421		100,000
		To record service revenue.			

Financing Activities. As is often the case with a new business, additional sources of funds are needed if the business is expanding. On January 30, 19x2, Fitness Clinic borrowed $35,000 by signing a note with its bank. Fitness Clinic also declared and paid a cash dividend of $5,000 to its stockholders. The journal entries for these two financing activities are:

		GENERAL JOURNAL			J3
Entry No.	Date	Account Titles and Explanation	Ref.	Debit	Credit
8	19x2 Jan. 30	Cash (A)	111	35,000	
		Notes Payable (L)	217		35,000
		To record cash borrowed from the bank.			
12	31	Dividends (SE)	615	5,000	
		Cash (A)	111		5,000
		To record dividends declared and paid to stockholders.			

This first entry records the increase in cash by the debit to the Cash account, and the credit to Notes Payable records the increase in the obligation to the creditor. The second entry records a decrease in retained earnings (stockholders' equity) with the debit to Dividends and the decrease in cash by the credit to the Cash account. If the dividends had been declared but not paid, a liability account, Dividends Payable, would have been credited since dividends are a legal obligation once declared.

Investing Activity. Most businesses invest some of their funds in income-producing assets that will be used over several periods. Fitness Clinic purchased equipment on January 30, 19x2, as indicated by the following journal entry:

		GENERAL JOURNAL			J3
Entry No.	Date	Account Titles and Explanation	Ref.	Debit	Credit
9	19x2 Jan. 30	Equipment (A)	162	110,000	
		Cash (A)	111		110,000
		To record purchase of equipment for cash.			

This entry shows that an asset acquisition is recorded with a debit entry, and the corresponding reduction of the asset cash is recorded with a credit.

Trial Balance

Objective 4
The role of the trial balance as a check on the debit-credit convention and as a tool to help prepare adjustments (cycle step 4) and financial statements (cycle step 5).

When the rule of debit and credit is applied to all transactions, the summary results of all account balances will have equal debits and credits. This can be tested by a trial balance. A trial balance is a list of all account balances with separate columns for debit and credit balances. Since debits must equal credits, the totals of both columns should always be identical. After the first three steps of the accounting cycle have been completed for a period of time, a trial balance is often prepared prior to performing step 4, the adjusting process. While the trial balance is not necessary, it often helps evaluate what adjusting entries need to be made. Note that a trial balance may be taken at any time. A trial balance is simply a list of all accounts and their balances. Different names for trial balances are used to help describe at what stage in the cycle the trial balance is taken. An unadjusted trial balance, such as the one shown in Exhibit 3–6 for Fitness Clinic, Inc., indicates that adjustments (cycle step 4) have not been made. An adjusted trial balance indicates that cycle step 4 has been completed.

At the end of January, Jim, Jay, and Janet, the owners of Fitness Clinic's stock, were examining the information in the unadjusted trial balance in Exhibit 3–6 when the following discussion took place.

Jim: Well, based on this trial balance our accountant prepared, it looks like we could have paid ourselves a bigger dividend.

Jay: Yes. If I remember my introductory accounting correctly, I figure that net income for January was $65,000! (Jay shows the following computations.)

Services	$100,000
Salaries	− 25,000
Utilities	− 3,000
Laundry	− 7,000
Net Income	$ 65,000

Janet: (Studying Jay's computations): Wait a minute; that doesn't seem right to me. Haven't we forgotten something?

Jim: I can't imagine what. All our bills are paid and we accounted for all the transactions of the business in the journal—I looked it over to make sure that our accountant didn't forget anything.

Jay: What could be missing, Janet?

Janet: I know—the asset "prepaid rent" is overstated! We paid $20,000 for two months' rent on January 1. Since it's now the end of January, we don't have an asset worth $20,000 any longer!

Jim: She's right, Jay! How could we have overlooked that?

Jay: Oh yes, now I remember; that's one of those things that need an adjustable entry.

Janet: You mean *adjusting* entry. And you're right, it is an entry that has not yet been recorded.

Jay: I remember my professor saying that accountants had to look at the trial balance at the end of an accounting period and determine what adjustments were necessary to properly report all assets and liabilities at that date.

Jim: Hey! That must be why the accountant labeled this the "unadjusted trial balance"!

Janet: (Smiling cynically): Very good, Jim! Maybe we'd better get an adjusted trial balance before we try to measure income for January.

EXHIBIT 3–6

Unadjusted Trial Balance

Fitness Clinic, Inc.
Unadjusted Trial Balance
January 31, 19x2

	Debits	Credits
Cash	$ 65,000	
Prepaid Rent.	20,000	
Equipment	110,000	
Notes Payable		$ 35,000
Capital Stock		100,000
Service Revenue		100,000
Salaries Expense.	25,000	
Utilities Expense	3,000	
Laundry Service Expense	7,000	
Dividends	5,000	
Totals	$235,000	$235,000

Introduction to Adjusting Entries (Accounting Cycle Step 4)

Objective 5

How adjustments, based on past and/or expected future transactions, are recorded at the end of an accounting cycle period (cycle step 4, developed further in Chapter 4).

When the unadjusted trial balance does not accurately reflect the assets and liabilities of the business, it is necessary to record periodic adjusting entries. Adjusting entries are journal entries used to record internal transactions at the end of an accounting period. Most internal transactions (or adjusting entries) stem from transactions with outside parties that have occurred before the end of an accounting period or will occur after the end of an accounting period. Fitness Clinic has three such adjusting entries—unpaid salaries, consumption of a prepayment (rent), and unpaid taxes.

Unpaid Salaries. When employees have worked but have not yet been paid at the end of an accounting period, an adjusting entry is necessary. These unpaid salaries are a liability because they represent future claims, which will call for cash outflows by Fitness Clinic. The following entry is required:

		GENERAL JOURNAL			J3
Entry No.	Date	Account Titles and Explanation	Ref.	Debit	Credit
10	19x2 Jan. 31	Salaries Expense (E)	511	5,000	
		Salaries Payable (L)	212		5,000
		To record unpaid salaries.			

Objective 6

The role of matching and revenue recognition in helping to guide the end-of-period adjusting entries.

This adjusting entry (like many others) is based on the *matching concept* discussed in Chapter 2. The debit to Salary Expense is a reduction in stockholders' equity, and the credit to Salaries Payable is an increase in a liability. Because the actual payment of these salaries will occur in the future (February), this demonstrates how adjusting entries can match expenses (salaries) with revenues before assets (cash) are used to pay for the expenses. This adjustment also reports a new liability account, Salaries Payable, which will appear in the adjusted trial balance and in the January 31 balance sheet.

Consumption of a Prepayment.   Another type of adjusting entry motivated by matching is required to account for prepaid rent, which was paid in an earlier transaction (in December) to cover expenses for January and February of 19x2 and is partially consumed in January.

GENERAL JOURNAL					J3
Entry No.	Date	Account Titles and Explanation	Ref.	Debit	Credit
11	19x2 Jan. 31	Rent Expense (E)	531	10,000	
		Prepaid Rent (A)	131		10,000
		To record January rent.			

An expense represents the consumption of an asset or the incurrence of an obligation that will consume an asset at a later date. In this case, the asset, Prepaid Rent, is being consumed (reduced); thus the credit entry reducing the asset account.

Unpaid Taxes.   On January 31, 19x2, after examining its revenues and expenses, Fitness Clinic determined that it would owe the federal government $10,000 for income taxes. The adjusting entry to match this expense with January's revenues is

GENERAL JOURNAL					J3
Entry No.	Date	Account Titles and Explanation	Ref.	Debit	Credit
13	19x2 Jan. 31	Income Tax Expense (E)	591	10,000	
		Income Taxes Payable (L)	215		10,000
		To record income taxes owed for January.			

The ledger in Exhibit 3–7 indicates the accounts affected by all 13 of Fitness Clinic's journal entries after posting. Note that the source of the posted amount is indicated by inserting the journal page in the "Ref." column of each account.

After posting the January transactions, adjusting entries to the ledger, and determining the balances of the accounts, the adjusted trial balance illustrated in Exhibit 3–8 can be constructed by listing all the account titles and their debit and credit balances in a two-column schedule. You will learn more about adjusting entries and trial balances in Chapter 4.

Financial Statements Preparation (Accounting Cycle Step 5)

Once the adjusted trial balance is prepared, step 4 of the cycle is complete and financial statements (step 5 of the cycle) may be prepared just as it was in Chapter 2. The order for preparing the financial statements is important. The balance sheet cannot be prepared before the income statement and retained earnings statement because (1) net income must be computed in order to know how much to add to retained earnings; and (2) the new retained earnings balance—after adding net income (or deducting net loss) and deducting dividends (if any)—is needed to make the balance sheet balance. Exhibit 3–9 shows these

EXHIBIT 3–7

Ledger Accounts of Fitness Clinic, Inc., on January 31, 19x2

GENERAL LEDGER

Cash   Account No. 111

Date		Explanation	Ref.	Debit	Credit	Balance Debit (Credit)
19x1 Dec.	28	Issuance of capital stock	J1	100,000		100,000
	31	Prepayment of rent	J1		20,000	80,000
19x2 Jan.	14	Salaries paid	J2		10,000	70,000
	22	Salaries paid	J2		15,000	55,000
	27	Utilities paid	J2		3,000	52,000
	29	Laundry services paid	J2		7,000	45,000
	30	Service revenue	J2	100,000		145,000
	30	Proceeds from note	J3	35,000		180,000
	30	Equipment purchase	J3		110,000	70,000
	31	Dividends paid	J3		5,000	65,000

Prepaid Rent   Account No. 131

Date		Explanation	Ref.	Debit	Credit	Balance Debit (Credit)
19x1 Dec.	31	Prepayment of rent	J1	20,000		20,000
19x1 Jan.	31	January rent expense	J3		10,000	10,000

Equipment   Account No. 162

Date		Explanation	Ref.	Debit	Credit	Balance Debit (Credit)
19x2 Jan.	30	Equipment purchase	J3	110,000		110,000

Salaries Payable   Account No. 212

Date		Explanation	Ref.	Debit	Credit	Balance (Debit) Credit
19x2 Jan.	31	Unpaid salaries	J3		5,000	5,000

Income Taxes Payable   Account No. 215

Date		Explanation	Ref.	Debit	Credit	Balance (Debit) Credit
19x2 Jan.	31	Jan. income taxes owed	J3		10,000	10,000

EXHIBIT 3–7 (*continued*)

Notes Payable   Account No. 217

Date		Explanation	Ref.	Debit	Credit	Balance (Debit) Credit
19x2 Jan.	30	Bank note	J3	35,000	35,000	35,000

Capital Stock   Account No. 311

Date		Explanation	Ref.	Debit	Credit	Balance (Debit) Credit
19x1 Dec.	28	Issuance of capital stock	J1		100,000	100,000

Service Revenue   Account No. 421

Date		Explanation	Ref.	Debit	Credit	Balance (Debit) Credit
19x2 Jan.	30	Service revenue	J2		100,000	100,000

Salaries Expense   Account No. 511

Date		Explanation	Ref.	Debit	Credit	Balance Debit (Credit)
19x2 Jan.	14	Salaries paid	J2	10,000		10,000
	22	Salaries paid	J2	15,000		25,000
	31	Unpaid salaries	J3	5,000		30,000

Rent Expense   Account No. 531

Date		Explanation	Ref.	Debit	Credit	Balance Debit (Credit)
19x2 Jan.	31	January rent expense	J3	10,000		10,000

Utilities Expense   Account No. 551

Date		Explanation	Ref.	Debit	Credit	Balance Debit (Credit)
19x2 Jan.	27	Payment of utilities	J2	3,000		3,000

EXHIBIT 3–7 (*concluded*)

Laundry Service Expense						Account No. 553
Date		Explanation	Ref.	Debit	Credit	Balance Debit (Credit)
19x2 Jan.	20	Payment of laundry bill	J2	7,000		7,000

Income Tax Expense						Account No. 591
Date		Explanation	Ref.	Debit	Credit	Balance Debit (Credit)
19x2 Jan.	31	January income taxes	J3	10,000		10,000

Dividends						Account No. 615
Date		Explanation	Ref.	Debit	Credit	Balance Debit (Credit)
19x2 Jan.	31	Dividends paid	J3	5,000		5,000

EXHIBIT 3–8

Adjusted Trial Balance

Fitness Clinic, Inc.
Adjusted Trial Balance
January 31, 19x2

	Debits	Credits
Cash	$ 65,000	
Prepaid Rent	10,000	
Equipment	110,000	
Salaries Payable		$ 5,000
Income Taxes Payable		10,000
Notes Payable		35,000
Capital Stock		100,000
Service Revenue		100,000
Salaries Expense	30,000	
Rent Expense	10,000	
Utilities Expense	3,000	
Laundry Service Expense	7,000	
Income Tax Expense	10,000	
Dividends	5,000	
Totals	$250,000	$250,000

three statements for Fitness Clinic, Inc., which are prepared in order by taking the appropriate account balances from the adjusted trial balance in Exhibit 3–8. The income statement accounts listed in the trial balance are included in the income statement; the net income from the income statement along with the dividends account are included in the retained earnings statement; and the ending balance from the retained earnings statement along with all of the asset, liability, and stockholders' equity account balances from the

EXHIBIT 3–9

Income Statement, Retained Earnings Statement, and Comparative Balance Sheets

Fitness Clinic, Inc.
Income Statement
For the Month Ended January 31, 19x2

Service revenue		$100,000
Expenses:		
Salaries expense	$30,000	
Rent expense	10,000	
Utilities expense	3,000	
Laundry service expense	7,000	
Total expenses (excluding income tax)		50,000
Net income before taxes		$ 50,000
Income tax expense		10,000
Net income		$ 40,000

Fitness Clinic, Inc.
Retained Earnings Statement
For the Month Ended January 31, 19x2

Retained earnings, December 31, 19x1	$ 0
Net income for January	40,000
Dividends	(5,000)
Retained earnings, January 31, 19x2	$35,000

Fitness Clinic, Inc.
Comparative Balance Sheets

Assets	December 31, 19x1	January 31, 19x2	**Liabilities and Stockholders' Equity**	December 31, 19x1	January 31, 19x2
Current assets:			Current liabilities:		
Cash	$ 80,000	$ 65,000	Salaries payable . . .	$ 0	$ 5,000
Prepaid rent	20,000	10,000	Notes payable	0	35,000
Total current assets.	$100,000	$ 75,000	Income taxes payable	0	10,000
Noncurrent assets:			Total current liabilities. . . .	$ 0	$ 50,000
Equipment	0	$110,000	Stockholders' equity:		
Total noncurrent assets.	0	$110,000	Capital stock.	$100,000	$100,000
			Retained earnings . .	0	35,000
			Total stockholders' equity	$100,000	$135,000
Total assets	$100,000	$185,000	Total liabilities and stockholders' equity. .	$100,000	$185,000

adjusted trial balance are in the January 31 balance sheet. Note that although the revenue, expense, and dividends accounts all affect the balance sheet in some way, they are never listed in the balance sheet as separate accounts.

Analyzing the Effects of an Operating Period

In the Fitness Clinic example, the transactions recorded during its operating period changed the company's assets, liabilities, and stockholders' equity. Cash decreased, prepaid rent decreased, equipment increased, liabilities increased, capital stock remained unchanged, and retained earnings increased. The changing state of assets, liabilities, and stockholders' equity is illustrated in the comparative balance sheets in Exhibit 3–9. Note that cash has a net decrease of $15,000; prepaid rent decreased by $10,000; equipment has an increase of $110,000; liabilities increased by $50,000; and the stockholders' residual interest increased by a net of $35,000, the amount of net income less dividends. Finally, note that the increase in net assets ($135,000 − $100,000 = $35,000) equals the increase in retained earnings, which is net income less dividends ($40,000 − $5,000 = $35,000).

Operating and Nonoperating Cash Flows. Decision makers are always interested in the status of a business's cash flow—the amount of cash flowing into the business and the amount of cash flowing out. Exhibit 3–10 analyzes Fitness Clinic's cash flow from all sources. Because all sales (service revenues) were for cash in January, sales provided $100,000 in positive cash flows. Remember that income statements represent more than

EXHIBIT 3–10

Comparison of Operating and Nonoperating Cash Flows, Fitness Clinic, Inc.

Income Statement		January 19x2 Cash Flow	Explanation for Cash Flow Effects
			Cash Flow Analysis
Revenue:			**Operating transactions:**
Service revenue	$100,000	$ 100,000	All sales were received in cash.
Expenses:			
Salary expense	30,000	25,000	$5,000 is to be paid in February.
Utilities expense	3,000	3,000	All utilities are paid in cash.
Rent expense	10,000	0	$10,000 was prepaid in December.
Laundry expense.	7,000	7,000	All laundry services were paid for in cash.
Income tax expense	10,000	0	$10,000 is to be paid in February.
Net income	$ 40,000	$ 65,000	Cash flow from **operations.** (The difference of $25,000 between net income and cash flow from operations occurs because certain expenses did not require a cash outflow in January.)
			Financing transactions:
		$ 35,000	Note is to be paid off in the future.
		(5,000)	Cash dividends were paid to owners.
		$ 30,000	Increase in cash from **financing** activities.
			Investing transactions:
		$(110,000)	Cash was paid for equipment.
		$(110,000)	Decrease in cash from **investing** activities.
		$ (15,000)	Overall cash decrease. (See balance sheets in Exhibit 3–9.)

just the cash flow of a business; they reflect the flow of net assets. Not all the expenses for the month of January 19x2 required cash payment. The rent was actually paid in December 19x1 (the previous period), but $10,000 of the original payment was consumed in January. The salaries still owed to employees at January 31 will be paid in February, but the $5,000 of salaries are shown in the January income statement because the value of the employees' services was consumed in January. The $10,000 of income tax expense is recognized in January because the $10,000 is related to January's income, but the tax obligation required no cash flow in January. Since Fitness Clinic only paid $35,000 in cash for expenses, the difference between the $100,000 cash from sales and the $35,000 cash paid for expenses resulted in $65,000 positive cash flow provided by operations.

In January 19x2, Fitness Clinic borrowed $35,000, paid dividends of $5,000 (financing activities), and purchased equipment for $110,000 (investing activity). Thus, the total inflow of cash totaled $100,000 (from operations $65,000 plus borrowing of $35,000), but the outflow of cash totaled $115,000 (for equipment purchase of $110,000 plus dividends of $5,000) and exceeded the inflow of cash by $15,000. Thus, cash reported in the comparative balance sheets in Exhibit 3–9 decreased by $15,000, from $80,000 to $65,000.

ACCRUAL VERSUS CASH BASIS OF ACCOUNTING

In Chapter 2, you learned that financial statements for businesses are based on the *accrual basis of accounting*. **Accrual accounting** is the approach to accounting that allows recording of the effects of transactions in the period in which economic events take place even if cash flow from the transactions takes place in another period. In accrual accounting, revenues are recorded when earned and expenses are recorded to reflect the costs of obtaining the reported revenues. Because of accrual accounting, the income statement for a period of time will rarely equal the cash flow from operations (as illustrated in Exhibit 3–10).

Objective 7
The difference between the cash basis and the accrual basis of accounting.

Accrual accounting permits revenues to be recorded before or after cash is collected and expenses to be recorded before or after bills are paid. Note that in an accrual system a cash outflow is called an expenditure, while an expense is the use of an asset or incurrence of an obligation in order to obtain revenue. Consider the following comparison between the cash basis and accrual basis of accounting:

	Journal Entries					
	Cash Basis			**Accrual Basis**		
Event	**Accounts**	**Dr.**	**Cr.**	**Accounts**	**Dr.**	**Cr.**
1. Buy merchandise for $50	Merchandise Expense (E)	50		Merchandise (A)	50	
	Cash (A)		50	Cash (A)		50
2. Sell merchandise costing $50 for $100 on account	No entry			Accounts Receivable (A)	100	
				Sales (R)		100
	No entry			Merchandise Expense (E)	50	
				Merchandise (A)		50
3. Receive $100 cash on account	Cash (A)	100		Cash (A)	100	
	Revenue (R)		100	Accounts Receivable (A)		100
4. Receive a bill for newspaper advertising $30	No entry			Advertising Expense (E)	30	
				Accounts Payable (L)		30
5. Pay for advertising $30 cash	Advertising Expense (E)	30		Accounts Payable (L)	30	
	Cash (A)		30	Cash (A)		30

The pure cash basis of accounting only records inflows and outflows of cash, with revenues not recorded until cash is received and expenses not recorded until cash is paid. The difference between the cash basis and accrual basis is largely one of timing in that they recognize revenues and expenses at different points in time, often in different accounting periods (e.g., different years).[1]

Accrual accounting calls for the recognition of expenses in the period in which their economic benefits are received regardless of when cash is paid. Also, accrual accounting normally calls for the recognition of revenues in the period in which a sale is made, or a service rendered, even though cash might not be received until the following period. Often this results in a receivable being recorded for a sales transaction and a liability being recorded for an expense transaction, as we saw in our examples.

Throughout this textbook, the principles of accrual accounting govern recognition decisions for balance sheet and income statement purposes. Of course, many business decisions are also concerned with cash flow and cash position. Because of this need for cash-based data, GAAP also requires a statement of cash flows to accompany the accrual-based statements.

Other Accounting Characteristics and Assumptions

Objective 8
The concepts of historical cost, objectivity, and materiality.

In this chapter we have considered several basic accounting concepts: revenue recognition; matching; going concern; periodicity. These concepts, along with certain qualitative characteristics and assumptions, provide direction to accountants and are often generally referred to as **accounting principles.** They all play a role in determining whether financial statements are prepared in accordance with generally accepted accounting principles.

In recording the transactions in cycle steps 1 through 3 for the Fitness Clinic example, we were employing both the *historical cost assumption* and the qualitative characteristics of *objectivity* or *verifiability*. These features help to enhance the consistent qualities of the data found in financial statements. The historical cost assumption calls for all transactions to be recorded at their original (historical) transacted amounts. This use of historical cost is based on the assumption that the values of the recorded items will not change over time.[2] This prohibits companies from arbitrarily changing the values of their assets, liabilities, or stockholders' equity accounts. For example, if Fitness Clinic's capital stock, which originally sold for $100,000, later had a market value of $200,000, the historical cost assumption would prohibit Fitness Clinic from changing the historical value to the market value. Note that the historical cost assumption is the primary basis for all financial statements around the world. Whenever a departure from historical cost is used, most countries require that the departure be disclosed or explained in the notes accompanying the financial statements. In Japan and Switzerland such departures are very unusual. However, in most countries, including the United States, some departures from historical cost are required in certain circumstances. Some examples will be covered in later chapters.

One of the reasons accountants have adopted the historical cost assumption is because the historical amounts of transactions are objectively measurable and independently verifiable. The objectivity quality (or **verifiability quality**) suggests that the data recorded in cycle steps 1 through 4 and reported in the financial statements be based on objective or verifiable evidence. If, for example, 20 people were asked to determine the market value

---

[1]Note that over the life of the firm the measurement of net income on a cash basis will be the same as on an accrual basis once the balance in all noncash assets and all liabilities becomes zero. This may be seen in the simple example provided here. There are no balances left in any of the assets or liabilities in this illustration (other than cash), and the ending cash balance of $20 equals the net income on both the cash basis and the accrual basis. Of course, in real cases it is doubtful that all noncash asset and liability balances will ever be zero at the same time.

[2]The historical cost assumption is also sometimes thought of as the stable dollar assumption since it assumes that the value of the measurement unit (the dollar) does not change over time.

of a plot of land in the heart of a city, their answers would probably vary considerably, making the market value of the land an unverifiable (or subjective) measure. However, if asked to determine the historical cost of the same land, their answers would likely be the same (providing they could locate the original purchase or sales documents). Because accountants place such a high value on the quality of objective or verifiable measurements, financial statements are based on historical costs, which are considered to be more objective or verifiable than other measures.

The fact that historical cost may vary considerably from fair economic value is somewhat reduced by the going concern assumption. Recall that the going concern assumption predicts that all incomplete business cycles will eventually be completed. If an asset such as equipment has a historical value of $50,000 and a current fair economic value of $75,000, it results in a temporary undervaluation in the current balance sheet. However, since the equipment will eventually be converted back to cash from its use in producing goods and/or from its eventual sale, the use of historical cost versus current fair value will not alter the eventual cash results. Once the cycle is completed, the method previously used to value the incomplete cycles is irrelevant as far as the actual cash results are concerned.

Another underlying principle in accounting is the materiality principle. The materiality principle requires the accounting information system to report all material events and transactions affecting the business entity. What is a material amount? While this question is not specifically answered in a measurable way, the accounting literature defines a **material amount** as **an amount that would probably affect the decision of a knowledgeable user** of accounting information.

Consider the following conversation between the stockholders of Fitness Clinic.

Janet: Hey! Jay—Jim, our accountant just showed me the gas and electric bill from Consolidated Utilities. He said the January bill for $3,000 was based on an estimate, and it only covered up to January 27. The February bill was based on an actual meter reading, and it came to $6,000 for the period January 27 to February 27!

Jim: That's outrageous! $6,000 for one month!

Jay: It probably means their $3,000 estimated bill for January was too low. I knew we were running up the bills, leaving the windows open in the middle of the winter.

Janet: Yes, but our clients are roasting without it, and we can't shut the heat off or the showers freeze up.

Jay: Hey, does that mean the January income statement we gave the bank was wrong? Did we lie about our profits?

Jim: On no! Are we going to be in trouble over this?

Janet: Just relax a minute. If we take the average of these two bills, it comes to $4,500 per month. That means our expenses for January were understated by about $1,500 ($4,500 versus $3,000). I'm not sure if a $1,500 difference in a $40,000 reported net income is material.

Jay: Wait. Don't forget that by understating our expenses we *overstated* our taxes, so the effect on net income would be even less than $1,500 on an aftertax basis.

Jim: I suggest that we tell the bank anyway. They could probably tell us whether it would be material or not since they are the ones who wanted to see our income statement.

As this example points out, determining what is a material amount is not always easy. You should note that applying the materiality principle prohibits one dollar amount from being identified for all situations. For example, a material dollar amount for Ford Motor Company would be much larger than a material amount for your corner drugstore. While materiality is a somewhat abstract principle, it is an important feature of GAAP financial statements. Financial statement users may assume that there are no material omissions or misstatements if the statements are prepared in conformance with GAAP.

• SUMMARY

The formal accounting cycle may be described as the following six-step process:

Step	Description	Chapter Location
1	Analyze transactions/events	Chapter 3
2	Journalize transactions	Chapter 3
3	Post journal entries to ledger	Chapter 3
4	Prepare adjusting entries and post to ledger	Chapters 3 and 4
5	Prepare financial statements from ledger account balances	Chapters 3 and 4
6	Close temporary accounts	Chapter 4

The example of the Fitness Clinic illustrated steps 1 through 5 for the first month of its operations. The financial statements prepared from cycle steps 1 through 5 provided the balance sheet and income statement based on accrual accounting. The differences between cash and accrual accounting for Fitness Clinic were reconciled in a cash flow analysis. The subsequent discussion of cash-based versus accrual-based accounting illustrated that the central difference is the timing with which events are recognized and recorded.

The chapter also introduced several important accounting concepts, including

- Business cycles.
- Operating cycles.
- Going concern assumption.
- Periodicity (time period).
- Historical cost assumption.
- Objectivity (verifiability).
- Materiality.

These concepts help explain the framework of existing accounting principles and practices that make up generally accepted accounting principles (GAAP).

• DEMONSTRATION EXERCISE

Financial Planners, Inc., (FPI) began operations on February 1, 19x1, with the following transactions:

a. Sold capital stock for $50,000.
b. Paid $9,000 for three months' office rent plus another $2,400 for the security deposit. Also paid $500 for one month's rent of office equipment.

During the month of February, FPI also had the following activity:

c. Recorded consulting fees earned of $12,000. Received $4,500 in cash, and the remaining was recorded on account. (Hint: Accounts Receivable is recorded.)
d. Purchased office supplies to be used during the month for $190 cash.
e. Paid salaries of $6,000 and commissions of $3,000 in cash.
f. Received and paid the utility bill of $130 and the telephone bill of $312.
g. Paid entertainment expense of $950 in cash.
h. Recorded the invoice for an introductory ad in *The Wall Street Journal*. The ad, which appeared in February, cost $750, and payment is not due until next month.
i. At the end of the month, FPI purchased office furniture and equipment for $5,670 on account.

Required:
1. Record the above transactions and the adjusting entry required for rent in general journal form including explanations. Post the entries to the appropriate T accounts using the chart of accounts given in Exhibit 3–4, page 94.

2. Prepare a month-end income statement, and post net income or net loss to the Retained Earnings account.
3. Prepare a February 28, 19x1, balance sheet.

Solution:

GENERAL JOURNAL					J1
Date		Account Titles and Explanation	Ref.	Debit	Credit
19x1 Feb.	1	Cash (A)	111	50,000	
		Capital Stock (SE)	311		50,000
		To record issuance of stock.			
	1	Prepaid Rent (A)	131	9,500	
		Security Deposit (A)	171	2,400	
		Cash (A)	111		11,900
		To record prepayment of rent.			
During Feb.		Cash (A)	111	4,500	
		Accounts Receivable (A)	121	7,500	
		Consulting Fees (R)	411		12,000
		To record revenue for the month.			
		Office Supplies Expense (E)	541	190	
		Cash (A)	111		190
		To record purchase of supplies.			
		Salaries Expense (E)	511	6,000	
		Commissions Expense (E)	512	3,000	
		Cash (A)	111		9,000
		To record salaries and commissions for the month.			
		Utilities Expense (E)	551	130	
		Communications Expense (E)	552	312	
		Cash (A)	111		442
		To record expense for the month.			
		Travel and Entertainment Expense (E)	513	950	
		Cash (A)	111		950
		To record expense for the month.			
		Advertising Expense (E)	521	750	
		Accounts Payable (L)	211		750
		To record invoice for *The Wall Street Journal* ad.			
19x1 Feb.	28	Equipment (A)	162	5,670	
		Accounts Payable (L)	211		5,670
		To record purchase of equipment and furniture.			
	28	Rent Expense (E)	531	3,500	
		Prepaid Rent (A)	131		3,500
		To adjust for February rent.			

	Cash		111
(a)	50,000	(b)	11,900
(c)	4,500	(d)	190
		(e)	9,000
		(f)	442
		(g)	950
Bal.	32,018		

	Accounts Receivable		121
(c)	7,500		
Bal.	7,500		

	Prepaid Rent		131
(b)	9,500	(j)	3,500
Bal.	6,000		

	Equipment		162
(i)	5,670		
Bal.	5,670		

	Security Deposit		171
(b)	2,400		
Bal.	2,400		

	Accounts Payable		211
		(h)	750
		(i)	5,670
		Bal.	6,420

	Capital Stock		311
		(a)	50,000
		Bal.	50,000

	Consulting Fees		411
		(c)	12,000

	Salaries Expense		511
(e)	6,000		

	Commissions Expense		512
(e)	3,000		

	Travel and Entertainment Expense		513
(g)	950		

	Advertising Expense		521
(h)	750		

	Rent Expense		531
(j)	3,500		

	Office Supplies Expense		541
(d)	190		

	Utilities Expense		551
(f)	130		

	Communications Expense		552
(f)	312		

Financial Planners, Inc.
Income Statement
For the Month Ended February 28, 19x1

Revenue:

Consulting fees $12,000

Expenses:

Salaries expense	$6,000	
Commissions expense	3,000	
Travel and entertainment expense	950	
Advertising expense	750	
Rent expense	3,500	
Office supplies expense	190	
Utilities expense	130	
Communications expense	312	
Total expenses		14,832
Net income (loss)		$ (2,832)

	Retained Earnings	331
	2,832	
Bal.	2,832	

Financial Planners, Inc.
Balance Sheet
February 28, 19x1

Assets		Liabilities and Stockholders' Equity	
Current assets:		Liabilities:	
Cash	$32,018	Accounts payable	$ 6,420
Accounts receivable	7,500	Total liabilities	$ 6,420
Prepaid rent	6,000	Stockholders' equity:	
Total current assets	$45,518	Capital stock	$50,000
Noncurrent assets:		Retained earnings	(2,832)
Office equipment and		Total stockholders' equity	$47,168
furniture	$ 5,670		
Security deposit	2,400		
Total noncurrent assets	$ 8,070		
Total assets	$53,588	Total liabilities and stockholders' equity . .	$53,588

• KEY TERMS

Account. Provides a separate record for each asset, liability, and stockholders' equity item on the balance sheet and each temporary account such as revenue, expense, and dividends. Indicates increases and decreases based on debit and credit rules. Informal T account is used for instructional purposes, while the formal ledger account is used for both instructional purposes and actual accounting systems.

Account balance. Difference between debits and credits in any individual account at any point in time.

Accounting cycle. Six accounting steps that begin with analyzing transactions and end with closing journal entries.

Accrual accounting. The approach to accounting that allows recording of the effects of transactions in the period in which economic events take place even if cash flow from the transactions is at another point in time. In accrual accounting, revenues are recorded when revenue is earned and expenses are recorded when the effort to produce revenue is expended; contrasts with cash basis of accounting. Accrual accounting is the same as accrual basis of accounting in the Chapter 2 list of key terms.

Adjusted trial balance. The end-of-period trial balance taken after cycle step 4.

Adjusting entries. Journal entries used to record internal transactions at the end of an accounting period.

Business cycle. The period of time it takes to convert cash to productive facilities and/or resources and back to cash. Usually not determinable in a going concern.

Chart of accounts. List of account titles and account identification numbers used by a business in its accounting system.

Classified balance sheet. A balance sheet that shows current and noncurrent classifications for assets and liabilities.

Credit. Right side of account or journal entry.

Current asset. An asset that is expected to be consumed or converted to cash in its entirety within one year or operating cycle, whichever is longer.

Current liability. A liability that is expected to utilize cash or other current assets within one year or operating cycle, whichever is longer.

Debit. Left side of an account or journal entry.

Double-entry system. System whereby each transaction affects two or more accounts and where the total debits equal the total credits for each transaction.

Expenditure. An outflow of cash for the acquisition of a product, the receiving of service, or the reduction of an obligation.

General journal. Chronological record that records accounting transactions in the order of the date they occur so that all debits and credits for all transactions are listed in one medium of original entry; also called journal.

General ledger. A collection of all ledger accounts.

Going concern assumption. The business entity is assumed to have an indefinite life; therefore, financial statements are based on the principle of continuous life; also called going concern concept.

Historical cost assumption. The requirement that all transactions be recorded at their original (historical) transacted amounts.

Journal entry. Record of the effects of an accounting transaction with equal debit and credit effects; also called general journal entry.

Ledger. A file that contains all of the accounts used in an accounting system; also called general ledger.

Ledger account. A formal record of all increases and decreases in an account from which an account balance can be obtained at any time. See T account.

Material amount. A material amount is one that would probably affect the decision of a knowledgeable user of accounting data.

Materiality principle. The requirement that the accounting system and resulting financial statements reveal all material events or transactions affecting the business.

Normal balance. The side of the account (debit or credit) on which the increases are recorded. Assets, expenses, and dividends have normal debit balances, while liabilities and paid-in capital, retained earnings, and revenues have normal credit balances.

Objectivity. A preferred quality of accounting information. Accountants require that data recorded in the accounting records be based on objective or verifiable information.

Operating cycle. The period of time needed to convert cash to goods and/or services and back to cash. Usually several operating cycles occur within a year.

Periodicity concept. States that although business activity is continuous, financial statements divide this continuous flow into uniform time periods.

Permanent accounts. Accounts that appear on the balance sheet—assets and liabilities, and those stockholders' equity accounts that are not closed to Retained Earnings; also called real accounts.

Posting. Recording, transferring, or copying of the debit and credit dollar amounts from the journal into the appropriate ledger accounts.

Source documents. Records usually retained in business files that provide evidence about external transactions that have occurred.

Subsidiary ledgers. Subfiles providing detail for specific general ledger accounts.

T account. An informal record of all increases and decreases in an account from which balances may be determined. See ledger account.

Temporary accounts. The accounts that are closed to Retained Earnings, including revenue, expense, and dividend accounts; also called nominal accounts.

Trial balance. A list of account balances with columns for debit and credit balances used to show that the balance sheet equation remains in balance through equal debits and credits.

Unadjusted trial balance. Trial balance prepared before the adjustments (cycle step 4) have been made.

• SYNONYMS

Complex entry; compound entry.

Expenditure; cash payment.

Journal; general journal.

Ledger; general ledger.

Ledger account; T account.

Net income; profit; earnings.

Objectivity; verifiability.

Permanent accounts; real accounts; balance sheet accounts.

Temporary accounts; nominal accounts; income statement and dividend accounts.

• QUESTIONS

1. What is the main purpose of the double-entry system in accounting and what role do debits and credits play in it?
2. How do debits affect assets? Liabilities? Stockholders' equity?
3. How do credits affect assets? Liabilities? Stockholders' equity?
4. What is the effect of debits and credits on revenues? Expenses? Retained earnings?
5. If revenues increase retained earnings and retained earnings normally has a credit balance, then what kind of balance will revenues normally have? How are revenues increased?
6. If expenses decrease Retained Earnings and Retained Earnings normally has a credit balance, then what is the normal balance for expense accounts? How are expenses decreased?
7. What is an account? A ledger account? A T account?
8. Describe the information contained in a formal ledger account.
9. How is a trial balance used, and how is it different from a balance sheet?
10. What is a journal? Describe the data that are entered into a journal entry. What role does the chart of accounts play in journalizing?
11. What triggers the need to record a journal entry?

12. Describe the process of posting. How often does posting take place?
13. What is a trial balance taken after the first three cycle steps called? What types of accounts does it consist of at this stage?
14. What does cycle step 4 accomplish?
15. How does matching affect cycle step 4?
16. Explain why the adjusting entries, all recorded at the end of an accounting period, are sometimes referred to as internal transactions. To what two types of external transactions are these adjustments related?
17. What is the trial balance called when prepared after cycle step 4?
18. Give an example of a journal entry describing an operating transaction.
19. Give an example of a journal entry describing a financing transaction.
20. Give an example of a complex journal entry for an investing transaction.
21. Give an example of an adjusting journal entry for an operating account. What original transaction does this adjusting entry refer to?
22. Which statement contains permanent accounts?
23. Which statement contains only temporary account balances? Where is the net effect of the temporary account balances of prior accounting periods reported?
24. Give journal entry examples of the following effects:
    a. Increase an asset and increase a liability.
    b. Increase an asset and increase stockholders' equity.
    c. Decrease an asset and decrease a liability.
    d. Increase one asset and decrease another asset.
    e. Increase a liability and decrease stockholders' equity.
25. When looking at the results of operations, what does the income statement show?
26. Why is net cash flow different from net asset flow?
27. What is accrual accounting? How does it differ from cash accounting?
28. What is the periodicity concept?
29. Differentiate between expenditures and expenses.
30. State the balance sheet classification of each of the following accounts (asset, liability, or stockholders' equity):
    a. Rent Expense.
    b. Prepaid Rent.
    c. Equipment.
    d. Accounts Payable.
    e. Retained Earnings.
    f. Salaries Payable.
31. Explain how the historical cost is related to the quality of objectivity.
32. Explain the materiality principle and define a material amount.

• EXERCISES

E 3–1

Describing Accounts
L.O.1, 2, 3

Listed below are some of the ledger accounts of the Johnson Corporation. Identify each account as either an asset, liability, or stockholders' equity account and tell if the account normally carries a debit or credit balance. If the account is a stockholders' equity account, describe the type of account (paid-in capital, revenue, expense, etc.).

a. Cash.   k. Communications Expense.
b. Accounts Receivable.   l. Consulting Fees.
c. Salaries Payable.   m. Unearned Consulting Fees.
d. Capital Stock.   n. Accounts Payable.
e. Prepaid Insurance.   o. Land.
f. Insurance Expense.   p. Notes Payable.
g. Interest Revenue.   q. Prepaid Rent.
h. Dividends.   r. Retained Earnings.
i. Bonds Payable.   s. Building.
j. Machinery and Equipment.   t. Supplies.

E 3–2
Journal Entries and Accounts—Multiple Choice
L.O.1, 2

1. Which group of accounts contains only those that normally have a debit balance?
   a. Accounts Receivable, Retained Earnings, and Equipment.
   b. Bond Investment, Cash, and Capital Stock.
   c. Prepaid Insurance, Equipment, and Interest Expense.
   d. Note Receivable, Salaries Payable, and Communications Expense.
   e. None of the above.

2. Which group of accounts contains only those that normally have a credit balance?
   a. Consulting Fees, Land, and Supplies.
   b. Capital Stock, Accounts Payable, and Taxes Payable.
   c. Interest Revenue, Land, and Furniture and Fixtures.
   d. Notes Payable, Retained Earnings, and Communications Expense.
   e. None of the above.

3. Hien Condiments, Inc., purchases manufacturing equipment by issuing a short-term note for $45,000. Which journal entry is used to record this transaction?
   a. Debit Notes Payable and credit Equipment for $45,000.
   b. Debit Equipment and credit Cash for $45,000.
   c. Debit Equipment and credit Notes Payable for $45,000.
   d. Debit Inventory and credit Notes Payable for $45,000.

4. Which of the following entries increases total assets?
   a. Debit Cash and credit Accounts Payable.
   b. Debit Equipment and credit Notes Payable.
   c. Debit Cash and credit Capital Stock.
   d. All of the above.
   e. None of the above.

5. Which of the following transactions increases net assets (stockholders' equity)?
   a. Buy land for cash (one half) and notes payable (one half).
   b. Borrow cash from bank in exchange for a note.
   c. Buy new equipment for cash.
   d. Sell merchandise to a customer for a profit.
   e. None of the above.

6. Which of the transactions in question 5 above are financing or investing activities?
   a. a and c only.
   b. b and d only.
   c. a, b, and c only.
   d. a and b only.
   e. None of the above.

E 3–3
Effects of Transactions
L.O.1, 2

Listed below are various transactions for the Byrne Company that occurred during 19xx. At the time the journal entries for these transactions were made, did the respective transactions **increase**, **decrease**, or cause **no change** in (1) the current cash balance and (2) the current period net income under the accrual basis of accounting? Remember, a transaction's effect on cash may differ from its effect on net income.

a. Declaration and payment of a cash dividend.
b. Sale of services on credit.
c. Issuance of a $10,000 note in return for cash.
d. Payment of an accounts payable on a purchase made in the current period.
e. Payment of 19xx rent on a building.
f. Payment of salaries.

E 3–4
Preparing Journal Entries
L.O.1, 2

Prepare the journal entries in general journal form that the Sullivan Company would record for the following events during 19xx:

a. Purchased $400 of supplies on account on January 27.
b. Prepaid two months' rent of $5,000 in cash on February 1.
c. Provided $3,900 of services on account on May 31.
d. Issued additional capital stock for $10,000 on July 31.

E 3–5
Preparing Journal Entries
L.O.1, 2

Listed below is a series of transactions for the King Company that occurred in 19x2.

19x2

Jan. 1   Paid $12,000 for 19x2 rent of office space.

Feb. 3   Purchased sewing machines at a total cost of $8,000; paid cash of $4,000 with the balance due on March 10, 19x2.

Mar. 5   Paid the outstanding balance on the sewing machines purchased on February 3.

Mar. 20 Collected $9,500 cash for credit sales recorded during 19x1.

Nov. 1   Paid $7,000 cash for a fire and theft insurance policy covering 19x3 and 19x4.

Dec. 31 Declared and paid a cash dividend of $10,000.

31   Recorded rent expense for the year.

credit ppd ins

Required:

Prepare the journal entries in journal form for the above transactions.

E 3–6
Preparing Journal Entries
L.O.1, 2

For transactions *a–f* below, give the appropriate journal entries in informal journal form as illustrated on page 91, for the Miser Company.

a. Issued shares of capital stock to investors in exchange for $40,000 cash.

b. Purchased a piece of equipment for $50,000, for which Miser paid $30,000 cash and the remainder in the form of a long-term note.

c. Purchased supplies (an asset) on credit for $5,000.

d. Paid the $5,000 owed in transaction *c.*

e. Prepaid an insurance policy for $1,000 cash. Coverage begins next year.

f. Used up $600 of the supplies purchased in transaction *c.*

E 3–7
Preparing Journal Entries
L.O.1, 2

Consider the following selected business transactions of the Rocky Mountain Real Estate Company in September 19xx. Assume monthly statements are prepared.

19xx

Sept. 1   Performed rental management services for apartment building for $4,000, of which $1,500 was collected in cash at the time the services were performed and the remainder was billed with payment expected in October.

9   Cash amounting to $75 was stolen from the company's cash drawer. The company's insurance does not cover this type of loss.

10   Declared and paid a cash dividend of $10,000 on the company's capital stock.

15   Paid $2,300 for 19xx taxes on business property. This amount was previously recorded on August 31, 19xx, with the following entry:

Property Tax Expense	2,300	
Property Taxes Payable		2,300

19   Purchased three company cars at a total cost of $35,000. Paid $10,000 in cash and signed a $25,000, one-year, 10% note for the balance.

30   Utilities expense for the main office amounts to $5,000 for the month of September; $2,900 was paid on September 30, and $2,100 remains unpaid.

30   Real estate brokers working for the company earned commissions of $25,000 during September, of which only $10,000 had been previously paid before today.

30   Estimated income tax for September is $9,500. No income tax was paid during the month.

Required:

Prepare journal entries in journal form to record the above transactions using appropriate revenue, expense, asset, liability, and stockholders' equity accounts. Prepare entries only for the transactions indicated on the dates indicated.

E 3–8
Journal Entries and
Effect on Financial
Statements
L.O.1, 2, 4

ABC Corporation was formed on January 1, 19xx. Assume that the following three transactions are the **only** transactions in which ABC was involved during 19xx:

a. Three investors contributed $10,000 each in return for the issuance of 100 shares of capital stock to each investor.
b. ABC Corporation incurred operating expenses of $8,500, $7,000 of which were paid in cash.
c. ABC Corporation earned revenues of $22,000, $15,000 of which were received in cash.

Required:
1. Prepare journal entries for the above transactions to record their proper effects.
2. Prepare the December 31, 19xx, balance sheet. What is the total dollar value of assets?
3. Compute the correct net income figure for ABC for 19xx using the accrual basis of accounting.

E 3–9
Trial Balance
Preparation
L.O.4

Richmond Electronics general ledger consists of the following accounts on March 31, 19xx:

Accounts Receivable	$ 18,000
Accounts Payable	12,000
Building	50,000
Capital Stock.	30,000
Cash	7,000
Communications Expense	10,000
Interest Payable	1,500
Land	15,000
Notes Payable	20,000
Retained Earnings	5,500
Salaries Expense	60,000
Salaries Payable	6,000
Service Revenue	100,000
Supplies Expense	15,000

Required:
Prepare the March 31, 19xx, trial balance. Assume that all accounts carry their normal balances.

E 3–10
Trial Balance
Preparation
L.O.4

The general ledger for Kasar, Inc., consists of the following accounts on December 31, 19xx:

	Normal (not normal)
Accounts Receivable	$ 9,500
Accounts Payable	12,700
Building	80,000
Capital Stock.	150,000
Cash	?
Communications Expense	5,000
Income Tax Expense	760
Income Taxes Payable	760
Interest Receivable	800
Interest Revenue	800
Land	60,000
Note Receivable	10,000
Rent Expense	6,000
Retained Earnings	(5,000)
Salaries Expense	30,000
Salaries Payable	5,000

RE   20,000
       (5,000)
       (4,000)

	Normal (not normal)
√ Service Revenue	55,000
√ Supplies Expense.	10,000
√ ×Supplies Inventory	2,000
√ Utilities Expense	1,000

Required:

Prepare the December 31, 19xx, trial balance, filling in the missing amount. Unless otherwise indicated, assume that all accounts carry their normal balances.

E 3–11
Determining Retained Earnings Account Balance
L.O.4

On January 1, 19xx, the Sky-High Company had a $20,000 credit balance in its Retained Earnings account. During 19xx, the Sky-High Company incurred a net loss of $5,000, declared and paid cash dividends of $4,000, and issued 1,000 new shares of stock for $3,500 cash. Compute the balance in the Retained Earnings account for the Sky-High Company on December 31, 19xx.

E 3–12
Cycle Steps 1 and 2
L.O.1, 2

Record the following transactions in the journal on January 1, 19xx, assuming monthly statements are prepared.

a. Paid $20,000 cash for five months' rent of equipment.
b. Agreed to pay a new manager, hired January 1, $6,000 per month on the first day of each month starting February 1.
c. Purchased supplies (an asset) for $750 cash.
d. Borrowed $10,000 cash by signing a note at the bank.

E 3–13
Cycle Steps 3 and 4
L.O.2, 3, 4

1. Consider the transactions in Exercise 3-12 above, and post their effects to the appropriate ledger accounts.
2. Prepare any necessary adjusting entries at January 31, 19xx, suggested by the operating transactions in Exercise 3-12.

E 3–14
Adjusted Trial Balance
L.O.4

The income statement accounts prepared as of December 31, 19xx, the end of Howley Company's fiscal year, contain the following balances:

	Debits	Credits
Service Fees.		$9,000
Rent Expense	$ 500	
Salaries Expense	2,600	
Supplies Expense	200	
Advertising Expense	300	
Income Tax Expense	540	

Included in other accounts are Dividends Declared and Paid of $1,000 and Retained Earnings of $12,500.

Required:

1. Prepare an income statement for the year ending December 31, 19xx.
2. Prepare a retained earnings statement for the year ending December 31, 19xx.

E 3–15
Multiple Choice
L.O.3, 7

1. The accounting cycle—
   a. Includes analyzing source documents, entering transactions, and posting.
   b. Includes preparing trial balances.
   c. Includes adjusting entries, closing temporary accounts, and preparing financial statements.
   d. All of the above.
2. Posting, one of the mechanical steps in the accounting cycle, is done to—
   a. Tie the transactions entered in the journal to the individual accounts in the general ledger.
   b. Create more clerical work.
   c. Prepare the accounts for the closing process.
   d. Analyze the source documents received from external users.

3. During its first year of operations, Sperry paid its employees $10,000 but owed its employees an additional $2,000. Assuming the accrual basis of accounting is used, the amount Sperry will recognize as salary expense at year-end on its income statement is—
   a. $10,000.
   b. $8,000.
   c. $20,000.
   d. $12,000.

4. Accountants recognizing transactions and amounts in one period even though the cash consequences may occur in different periods describes—
   a. Financial accounting.
   b. Cash basis of accounting.
   c. Accrual basis of accounting.
   d. Managerial accounting.

E 3–16
Accounting Principles
L.O.7

1. The going concern assumption—
   a. Means a business has a life as long as its owners.
   b. Suggests that there is no end point in the life of a business.
   c. Requires that financial statements be prepared periodically.
   d. All of the above.
   e. None of the above.

2. The use of historical costs—
   a. Requires adjustments for periodic changes in the value of assets and liabilities.
   b. Is the basis for financial statements prepared in conformance with GAAP.
   c. Differs from the original transacted amounts used to record the events of the business.
   d. All of the above.
   e. None of the above.

3. A material amount is—
   a. $1,000,000 or more.
   b. $500,000 or more.
   c. $250,000 or more.
   d. Not defined in money amounts, but is relative to the size of the business.
   e. None of the above.

4. Objectivity—
   a. Requires transactions to be recorded at amounts that are verifiable.
   b. Requires the use of historical costs or market value, whichever is more objective.
   c. Requires that no subjective judgments be used to record events or transactions.
   d. All of the above.
   e. None of the above.

5. Periodic financial statements must be prepared—
   a. At least once each year.
   b. At the end of the business operations.
   c. Whenever someone asks for them.
   d. Weekly, monthly, quarterly, and annually.
   e. None of the above.

E 3–17
True or False Questions
L.O.2, 3, 4, 7

Use T or F to indicate whether the following statements are true or false:

_____ 1. Periodicity is required because of the going concern assumption.
_____ 2. The historical cost principle is more consistent with the objectivity principle than a fair market value principle.
_____ 3. Matching requires first knowing the costs of the period and then finding their benefits.
_____ 4. The double-entry system requires exactly two accounts to be affected by each transaction.
_____ 5. The double-entry system requires that the total debits equal the total credits for each transaction.
_____ 6. A material omission could be so small that you would not have changed your decision had you known about it.

———   7. Asset accounts are all permanent accounts.
———   8. Revenue accounts are all permanent accounts.
———   9. Total debits must always equal total credits.
——— 10. Debit means increase and credit means decrease.

E 3–18
Annual Report—
Ralston Purina
L.O.4

Consider the 1989 Ralston Purina annual report reproduced in Appendix E at the end of this text. From the Consolidated Statement of Earnings, identify the following amounts for fiscal 1989.

1. Net sales.
2. Total costs and expenses.
3. Income taxes.
4. Net earnings.

• PROBLEMS

P 3–1
Balance Sheet Equation
L.O.1, 2

National Stock Investments (NSI) begins business on January 1, 19xx, by receiving $1 million from owners for capital stock and borrowing $500,000 from the local bank. During January, additional transactions were:

Transaction	Date	Explanation	Amount
a.	Jan. 1	Paid for January and February rent	$ 10,000
b.	4	Purchased office supplies (an asset) on account	2,500
c.	10	Earned and collected sales commissions	100,000
d.	15	Paid salaries for January 1–15	35,000
e.	30	Paid telephone and other utility bills for January	3,100
f.	31	Earned and collected sales commissions	94,000
g.	31	Issued a note to purchase land for use as the site of an office building	100,000
h.	31	Paid salaries for January 16–31	40,000
i.	31	Made necessary adjusting entries for rent and office supplies.	

At month-end, $500 of office supplies were on hand. All sales commissions and purchases are on a cash basis.

Required:
1. Analyze each transaction in terms of debits and credits by filling out the following schedule. (Show revenues and expenses as changes in stockholders' equity.)

Transaction	Assets	=	Liabilities	+	Stockholders' Equity
Issued stock	Dr. $1,000,000				Cr. $1,000,000
Borrowed funds	Dr. 500,000		Cr. $500,000		
a.					
b.					
c.					
d.					
e.					
f.					
g.					
h.					
i.					

2. Prove the balance sheet equation remains in balance.

P 3–2
Recording and Reporting
L.O.2, 3

Refer to the NSI transactions in Problem 3–1. In journal form, prepare the journal entries for each transaction using the appropriate revenue and expense accounts. Post the entries to the appropriate T accounts and construct the month-end income statement. Prepare the January 31, 19xx, balance sheet.

P 3–3
Transaction Analysis
L.O.1, 2

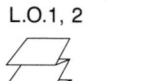

For each of the following transactions identify the account titles that would be debited and credited and the effect on the **total assets** reported on the balance sheet [increase (+), decrease (−), or no effect (NE)]. Assume monthly statements are prepared.

a. The recording of an invoice for new equipment; payment to be made later.
b. The entry to record the payment of the monthly utility bill not previously accrued.
c. The entry to record the advance payment for four months' rent.
d. The recording of tornado loss on a building (not covered by insurance).
e. The month-end adjusting entry made to record accrued interest.
f. Declaration and payment of a dividend on the same day.

P 3–4
Journalizing and Posting
L.O.1, 2, 3

Audit, Inc., started business on April 1, 19x1, and had the following transactions during its first month of operations. Assume monthly statements are prepared.

a. Sold stock for $40,000, 50% each to A. Andersen and C. Lybrand.
b. Acquired equipment from P. Mitchell Company with an invoice price of $12,500; $3,000 was paid in cash, and $9,500 is to be paid in one month.
c. Purchased office supplies (an asset) for cash from T. Ross Company for $400.
d. Paid $1,800 salaries to A. Young for April in cash.
e. Received $22,000 in cash for services rendered but not yet recorded.

Required:
1. Prepare the journal entries in journal form for the above transactions.
2. Set up the necessary ledger accounts and post the effects of the above entries into the appropriate ledger accounts.

P 3–5
Comprehensive
L.O.1–6

Meyers Cleaning Service, Inc., has the following transactions during its first quarter of operations, which ended on June 30, 19xx:

a. Sold capital stock of $30,000 to investors.
b. Paid cash of $3,000 for three months' rent of office space. Rent is expensed when paid.
c. Paid $15,000 for rental of cleaning equipment to June 30.
d. Purchased $5,000 cleaning supplies for cash; used $3,000 during the quarter.
e. Paid $1,000 for bonding (insurance) of employees for six months, covering April through September.
f. Recorded cleaning service revenue of $42,000 for the period; $16,000 was received in cash, and the remainder on account.
g. Paid $12,000 in wages for cleaning employees and $4,000 in supervisor's salary.
h. Paid cash of $716 for advertising between April 1 and June 30.
i. Received utility bill for $1,189 for the period (but did not pay it until July).
j. Received $17,000 from customers on account.
k. Recorded income tax expense for the period of $560, to be paid in July.

Required:
1. Record the above transactions and any necessary adjusting entries in journal form and post to the appropriate ledger accounts.
2. Prepare an adjusted trial balance as of June 30.
3. Prepare an income statement and a retained earnings statement for the quarter ending June 30.
4. Prepare the June 30, 19xx, balance sheet.

P 3–6

T Account Balances

L.O.1, 4

Consider the following T accounts of the newly formed company, Alice's Decorating Service:

Cash		Accounts Receivable		Supplies Inventory	
55,000	28,000	32,000	14,000	900	650
10,000	4,000				
14,000	950				
	450				
	200				

Prepaid Rent		Accounts Payable		Notes Payable	
4,000	2,000	450	900		10,000

Capital Stock		Service Revenue		Salaries Expense	
	55,000		32,000	4,000	
				7,000	
				9,800	
				7,200	

Rent Expense		Utilities Expense		Supplies Expense	
2,000		950		650	
		200			

Required:

1. Compute the balance in each account as illustrated in Exhibit 3–1 and prepare a trial balance at September 30, 19xx.
2. Prepare the income statement and retained earnings statement.
3. Prepare the September 30, 19xx, balance sheet.

P 3–7
Preparing Financial Statements
L.O.4

Amalgamated Financial has the following adjusted trial balance at December 31, 19xx:

Amalgamated Financial
Adjusted Trial Balance
December 31, 19xx

	Debits	Credits
Cash	$ 6,300	
Accounts Receivable	45,900	
Note Receivable	8,000	
Supplies.	400	
Prepaid Insurance	1,200	
Accounts Payable		$ 2,600
Income Taxes Payable		5,132
Capital Stock		20,000
Retained Earnings		13,540
Consulting Fees		105,700
Interest Revenue		960
Salaries Expense	72,000	
Supplies Expense	4,100	
Insurance Expense.	1,200	
Utilities Expense	3,700	
Income Tax Expense	5,132	
Totals.	$147,932	$147,932

Required:
Construct an income statement and retained earnings statement for the year and a year-end balance sheet.

P 3–8
Preparing Financial Statements
L.O.4

Consider the following adjusted trial balance for Genovesee's, Inc.:

Genovesee's, Inc.
Adjusted Trial Balance
December 31, 19xx

	Debits	Credits
Cash	$ 1,400	
Accounts Receivable	22,500	
Supplies	225	
Prepaid Rent	20,000	
Prepaid Insurance.	6,250	
Accounts Payable.		$ 3,000
Capital Stock.		20,000
Retained Earnings		?
Advertising Fees		58,000
Salaries Expense	25,000	
Travel and Entertainment Expense	4,200	
Telephone Expense	800	
Rent Expense	10,000	
Insurance Expense	1,250	
Supplies Expense.	500	
Utilities Expense	650	
Totals	$92,775	?

Required:

1. Prepare the income statement and then compute the ending Retained Earnings balance for the year ended December 31, 19xx.
2. Prepare the December 31, 19xx, balance sheet.

P 3–9
Preparing Financial Statements
L.O.4

The adjusted trial balance with the accounts in alphabetical order, of the Midland Goods Company at June 30, 19x2, is shown below.

Midland Goods Company
Adjusted Trial Balance
June 30, 19x2

	Debits	Credits
Accounts Payable		$ 2,350
Accounts Receivable	$ 18,300	
Advertising Expense	5,000	
Capital Stock		40,000
Cash	1,200	
Selling Expenses.	142,600	
Dividends (declared and paid)	11,000	
Equipment.	49,600	
Income Tax Expense	15,000	
Income Taxes Payable		11,600
Interest Receivable.	1,100	
Interest Revenue		5,800
Inventory	21,000	
Note Receivable	50,000	
Miscellaneous Expenses	8,100	
Rent Revenue		18,510
Retained Earnings, 7/1/x1		55,390
Sales Revenue—Cash		93,000
Sales Revenue—Credit		98,500
Unearned Rent.		9,750
Utilities Expense	12,000	
Totals.	$334,900	$334,900

Required:

1. Prepare Midland's income statement and a retained earnings statement for the year.
2. Prepare the June 30, 19x2, balance sheet. Note that the retained earnings balance is from last year.

P 3–10
Adjusted Trial Balance
L.O.1, 4

T accounts with their balances for the Super Company at the end of its fiscal year on December 31, 19xx, immediately following the posting of transactions and adjustments were as follows:

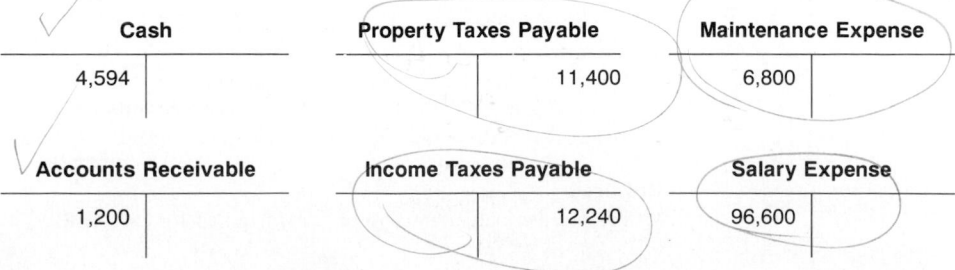

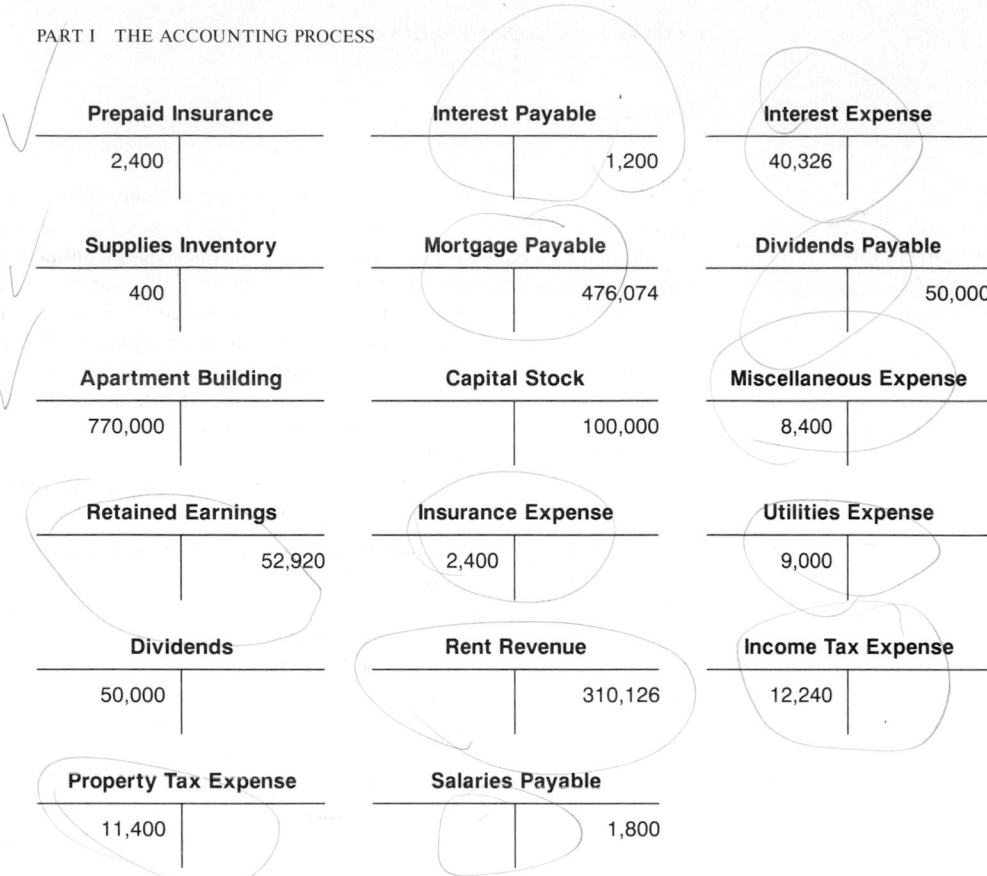

Prepaid Insurance		Interest Payable		Interest Expense	
2,400			1,200	40,326	

Supplies Inventory		Mortgage Payable		Dividends Payable	
400			476,074		50,000

Apartment Building		Capital Stock		Miscellaneous Expense	
770,000			100,000	8,400	

Retained Earnings		Insurance Expense		Utilities Expense	
	52,920	2,400		9,000	

Dividends		Rent Revenue		Income Tax Expense	
50,000			310,126	12,240	

Property Tax Expense		Salaries Payable	
11,400			1,800

Required:

Prepare an adjusted trial balance.

P 3–11
Preparing Financial Statements
L.O.4

Refer to Problem 3-10 and the Super Company.

Required:

1. Prepare an income statement and retained earnings statement for the year ended December 31, 19xx.
2. Prepare the December 31, 19xx, balance sheet.

P 3–12
Preparing Journal Entries and Analyzing Their Effects
L.O.1, 2, 3

The following lettered transactions present summary information for the Typo Services Company for the fiscal year ending December 31, 19x2:

a. Typo collected cash of $27,000 for typing services performed: $4,000 of the fees collected were for services performed in 19x1, and $2,000 of the fees earned in 19x2 remained uncollected on December 31, 19x2.

b. The company paid office salaries of $9,000. However, the last payroll payment for fiscal year 19x2 was made on December 21, 19x2; salaries amounting to $450 were earned during the period December 22 through December 31, 19x2. No salaries for 19x1 remained unpaid at December 31, 19x1.

c. At the end of 19x2, Typo purchased typewriters, for which it paid $1,200 in cash and also issued a $1,200 note.

d. Typo paid a total of $4,100 for office rent in 19x2. This amount includes $300 for December 19x1 rent, which was unpaid on January 1, 19x2.

e. The company paid $910 for utility and telephone bills for 19x2. The electricity bill for December 19x2, amounting to $55, remained unpaid at December 31, 19x2.

Required:

1. Prepare the journal entry (or entries) required for each lettered item. Show calculations.

2. Indicate the effect of each item listed above on the company's assets, liabilities, and net income at December 31, 19x2. Also indicate the dollar amount of each effect.

P 3–13
Multiple Choice
(Challenging)
L.O.3–6

1. At the end of its accounting period, June 30, 19x0, Fulton Company owed $3,000 for property taxes, of which only $1,000 had been accrued before year-end adjusting entries were made. The adjusting entry required to be made on June 30, 19x0, would result in
    a. $2,000 debited to an expense account and credited to an asset account.
    b. $2,000 debited to a liability account and credited to an expense account.
    c. $3,000 debited to an expense account and credited to a liability account.
    d. $2,000 debited to an expense account and credited to a liability account.
    e. $1,000 debited to a liability account and credited to an expense account.

2. The Supplies Expense account of Nova Company showed a balance of $15,000 at December 31, 19x9 (the end of its first annual accounting period), representing the cost of all supplies purchased during the year. The company used supplies costing $9,000 during the year and at the end of the year actual supplies on hand amounted to $6,000. The adjusting entry required to reflect the above information would do the following to the accounting equation:
    a. Increase assets and decrease stockholders' equity.
    b. Increase assets and increase liabilities.
    c. Increase assets and increase stockholders' equity.
    d. Decrease assets and decrease liabilities.
    e. Decrease assets and decrease stockholders' equity.

3. Which of the following is not an application of accrual accounting?
    a. Recording advertising fees earned at the time cash payment is received, which is two months after the work was performed.
    b. Recording telephone expense when the monthly bill is received.
    c. Recording advertising fees as earned at the time the work is done.
    d. Adjusting unearned advertising fees to the proper balance at the end of the accounting period.
    e. None of the above.

4. Which of the following errors, each considered individually, would cause the trial balance totals to be unequal?
    a. A fee of $150 earned and due from a client was neither debited to accounts receivable nor credited to a revenue account because the cash had not been received.
    b. A payment of $340 for equipment was posted as a debit for $300 to equipment and a credit of $340 to cash.
    c. A receipt of $80 from an account receivable was journalized and posted as a debit of $80 to cash and a credit of $80 to sales.
    d. A credit of $100 to accounts receivable was posted to sales. The debit was properly posted to cash.
    e. None of the above.

P 3–14
Multiple Choice
(Challenging)
L.O.4, 5, 6

1. The beginning balance in accounts receivable was $10,000. During the year cash collections from customers on accounts receivable totaled $350,000. The ending balance in accounts receivable was $70,000. What were sales on account during this year?
    a. $360,000.
    b. $420,000.
    c. $350,000.
    d. $410,000.
    e. None of the above.

2. The beginning cash balance was $20,000 more than the ending cash balance. If there were no financing activities during the year, and if investing activities during the year used $80,000 in cash, what was cash from operating activities during the year?
    a. $60,000 cash from operations.
    b. −$20,000 cash from operations.
    c. $100,000 cash from operations.
    d. −$60,000 cash from operations.

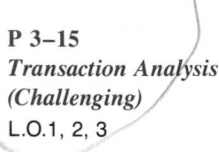

3. At the end of 19x4 Mason Company owed $8,000 in wages payable after adjustments. The balance in the wages payable account prior to adjustments was $2,000. The adjusting entry required for wages at the end of 19x4 must have been—
   a. A debit of $8,000 to wage expense.
   b. A credit of $6,000 to wage expense.
   c. A debit of $6,000 to wage expense.
   d. A credit of $8,000 to wage expense.

4. Which of the following is **not** an application of accrual accounting?
   a. Recording of wage expense at the time wages are paid each month-end.
   b. Recording of service revenue when customer has paid half of the cost for services to be provided the next month.
   c. Recording of rent expense at the end of the period by reducing the asset "prepaid rent."
   d. Recording of service revenue when customer has paid cash for services upon their being rendered.
   e. None of the above.

5. Which of the following errors, considered separately, would cause the trial balance to be out of balance?
   a. Debit cash and credit sales revenue for $450 paid by a customer on an account receivable.
   b. Debit equipment and credit cash for $500 of purchase of supplies inventory.
   c. Credit accounts payable $50 for a sale of services to a customer for $80 cash. (Debit was $80 to cash.)
   d. Credit accounts receivable $100 for cash received as a down payment for future services that will cost $200. (Debit was to cash for $100.)
   e. None of the above.

P 3–15
Transaction Analysis
(Challenging)
L.O.1, 2, 3

A-1 Travel, Inc., starts the current year 19x2 with the following balance sheet:

A-1 Travel, Inc.
Balance Sheet
December 31, 19x1

Assets		Liabilities and Stockholders' Equity	
Current assets:		Liabilities:	
Cash	$ 100,000	Accounts payable	$ 75,000
Accounts receivable	200,000	Salaries payable	15,000
Prepaid rent (for 10 months)	175,000	Total liabilities	$ 90,000
Total current assets	$ 475,000	Stockholders' equity:	
Noncurrent assets:		Capital stock	$1,200,000
Land	1,500,000	Retained earnings	685,000
		Total stockholders' equity	$1,885,000
		Total liabilities and	
Total assets	$1,975,000	stockholders' equity	$1,975,000

During January 19x2, A-1 had operating, financing, and investing transactions with the following summary results. Assume monthly statements are prepared.

a. Sales totaled $1,800,000, and accounts receivable had an ending balance of $400,000.
b. Expenses, including rent expense, totaled $1,300,000, and accounts payable and salaries payable had ending balances of $90,000 and $5,000, respectively. No rent was paid in January.
c. Office equipment was purchased and received on January 31, 19x2, for $29,000. A $29,000 note due on February 15, 19x2, was given in exchange for the equipment.
d. A-1 borrowed $250,000 on January 31, 19x2, to be paid back to the bank on June 30, 19x2.

Required:
1. In journal form, prepare the journal entries suggested by the above transactions. Post the transactions to the proper ledger or T accounts. (Hint: Set up T accounts for each balance sheet account and compute the missing data needed to balance.)

2. Analyze the effects of transactions described in *a*, *b*, *c*, and *d* by completing the following schedule:

Transaction	Asset Effect	Income Statement Effect	Cash Flow Effect
Example	−$1,000	−$1,000	No effect

P 3–16

Trial Balance, Financial Statements, and Operating Analysis (Challenging)

L.O.4, 7

Refer to the A-1 Travel, Inc., facts in the preceding problem.

Required:

1. Prepare the income statement for the month and the January 31, 19x1, balance sheet. Ignore income taxes.
2. Analyze the cash flow during the month. Do so by looking at all of the debits and credits in the cash ledger (or T) account and identifying each item as a *source* or a *use* of cash from operating, financing, and investing activities in the following format:

A-1 Travel, Inc.
Statement of Cash Flows
For the Month Ended January 31, 19x2

Operating activities:

Investing activities:

Financing activities:

Change in cash flow:

P 3–17

Cash and Accrual Accounting (Challenging)

L.O.7

Complete the table below for the effects of the following selected transactions from Clay's Ceramics Company. For both the cash basis of accounting and the accrual basis of accounting, indicate whether the Cash account and net income are increased (I), decreased (D), or not affected (NA).

a. Paid for the next three years' rent, $24,000.
b. Purchased office equipment for cash, $15,000.
c. Recorded end-of-period salaries to be paid next period, $10,000.
d. Paid for advertising in the local paper, $1,065 cash.
e. Received cash from a customer for a previous credit sale, $5,600.
f. Paid salaries earned last year, $8,000. — already earned
g. Recorded cash sales, $3,000.
h. One year's prepaid rent has expired, $8,000.
i. Purchased office supplies (an asset), $875 cash.
j. Paid the monthly utility bill, $660 cash.

Example: Sold services on credit, $50,000.

	Cash Basis of Accounting		Accrual Basis of Accounting	
	Cash Account	**Net Income**	**Cash Account**	**Net Income**
Example:	NA	NA	NA	I
a.				
b.				
c.				
d.				
e.				
f.				
g.				
h.				
i.				
j.				

P 3–18
Cash Flow versus
Accrual Accounting
L.O.7

George Johnson started a ticket sales business in the London theater district at the age of 18. George purchased tickets from theaters for popular upcoming plays. As the dates of the performance approached, the plays would be sold out well in advance. Visitors to London wishing to see plays that were otherwise sold out would go to entrepreneurs like George willing to pay more than the original cost (face value) for these "hot" tickets. The concierges at most of the hotels in the theater district would direct guests to people like George, who would set up their businesses (consisting of a briefcase filled with tickets) at specific locations (street corners) at specific times (e.g., 3 to 7 P.M. daily).

George started out slowly but quickly learned the ropes. With 180 pounds sterling in savings he started out in 19x2 purchasing 10 tickets to a 19x3 performance of *Miss Saigon*. George sold the tickets on January 10, 19x3, the night of the performance, for 1,000 pounds sterling. Assume that no other transactions occurred for 19x2 and 19x3.

Required:
1. Prepare annual income statements for George Johnson for 19x2 and 19x3 on an accrual basis.
2. Prepare annual cash flow statements for George Johnson for 19x2 and 19x3 summarizing cash-in and cash-out.
3. Do cash outflows always precede the accrual measurement of income? Explain.
4. Do cash inflows always follow the accrual measurement of income? Explain.
5. What is the difference between net cash flows and net income over the two-year period 19x2–19x3? Will this difference generally hold in other cases?

P 3–19
Adjusting Entries
L.O.5, 6

Several internal transactions of the Robar Company require adjusting entries at the end of the current accounting period, December 31, 19x1. The details of these transactions are the following:

a. $13,000 is owed to employees for work performed during the last week of 19x1.
b. $4,000 of the Supplies Inventory (an asset) was used during the current period.
c. $2,200 of Prepaid Insurance expired during the current period.
d. $8,000 is owed for income taxes on 19x1 income.
e. $200 interest is owed on a note held by the bank.
f. $800 of Prepaid Rent expired during the current period.

Required:
1. Prepare adjusting journal entries to record the above internal transactions.
2. Set up the necessary ledger accounts and post the entries to the accounts.

P 3–20
Analysis of T Accounts
(Challenging)
L.O.1, 5, 6

The accountant for New Process, Inc., has lost some of the details of the firm's accounting information for the month of February 19x1.

Missing Amount	What Is Known
a. Collections of Accounts Receivable	Beg. Balance of Accounts Receivable $13,200. Sales on account $65,000. End. Balance of Accounts Receivable $10,500.
b. Purchases of Supplies Inventory	Beg. Balance of Supplies $1,800. Supplies Expense $10,000. End. Balance of Supplies $2,500.
c. Beginning Balance in Prepaid Rent	End. Balance in Prepaid Rent $1,200. Rent Expense $6,200. Cash paid for rent $7,000.
d. Ending Balance in Salaries Payable	Beg. Balance in Salaries Payable $5,500. Salaries Expense $32,000. Cash paid for salaries $29,300.
e. Amount borrowed from the bank during the month	Beg. Balance in Note Payable $10,000. Payments made on principal $6,000. End. Balance in Note Payable $8,000.

Required:
Use your understanding of how transactions affect ledger accounts to help the accountant determine the missing amounts.

P 3–21
Finding Trial
Balance Errors
L.O.4

Xebec Company prepared the following adjusted trial balance at December 31 of their first year of operations. All accounts have normal balances and all amounts are correct.

	Debit	Credit
Accounts Payable		$ 26,000
Accounts Receivable	$ 28,000	
Advertising Expense	12,000	
Capital Stock		250,000
Cash	45,000	
Equipment.	180,000	
Income Tax Expense	4,500	
Income Tax Payable	4,500	
Insurance Expense.	3,800	
Interest Revenue		1,600
Land	70,000	
Note Payable		20,000
Prepaid Insurance		1,800
Rent Expense	22,000	
Retained Earnings		0
Salaries Expense	85,000	
Salaries Payable		5,000
Service Revenue		180,000
Supplies Expense	28,000	
Supplies Inventory		4,000
Utilities Expense	3,000	
	$485,800	$488,400

Required:
1. Locate the errors that have caused the trial balance to be out of balance.
2. Prepare a corrected adjusted trial balance in proper format.

P 3–22
Recording from
Source Documents
(Challenging)
L.O.1, 2

The following source documents support the day's transactions for Better Computer Services, Inc.:

a. Services Invoice for J. Brown:

Programming services	$12,000
Computer installation	3,000
Cleaning printer	45
Total	$15,045
Less: Cash received	0
Total on account	$15,045

b. Sales and Services Invoice for T. Jones:

Programming services	$11,000
Software	900
Total	$11,900
Less: Cash received	1,000
Total on account	$10,900

c. *Electric Bill* for the current month (unpaid):

Total due . . . . $ 723

d. *Telephone Bill* for the current month (paid by check):

Total paid . . . . $ 437

e. *Packing Slip* in office furniture that arrived today:

3 Desks ($400 each) . . . . $ 1,200

2 Tables ($150 each)   300

Total due on account . . . . $ 1,500

f. *Purchase Invoice* for delivery truck picked up at the dealer today:

Delivery truck $36,000

Dealer preparation   500

Total $36,500

Less: Cash down payment   5,000

Total financed $31,500

g. *Checks* received from customers on their accounts:

F. Smith . . . . $ 600

M. Green   400

Required:

Analyze the source documents and prepare the journal entries necessary to record the effect of each transaction.

P 3–23
Trial Balance Errors (Challenging)
L.O.4

Federation, Inc., prepared the following adjusted trial balance at December 31, 19x1, and is concerned that it does not balance:

	Debit	Credit
Cash.	$ 124,000	
Accounts Receivable	65,900	
Prepaid Rent	41,000	
Supplies Inventory.	19,500	
Building	420,000	
Land.	365,000	
Accounts Payable.		$ 65,500
Notes Payable		145,000
Income Taxes Payable.		10,500
Salaries Payable		11,400
Capital Stock		580,000
Retained Earnings.		203,000
Service Revenues		318,000
Advertising Expense.	35,000	
Salaries Expense	137,400	
Rent Expense.	52,000	
Supplies Expense	65,000	
Income Tax Expense	10,500	
	$1,335,300	$1,333,400

The auditors have discovered the following errors that were made in posting the firm's journal entries:

a. A $1,000 debit to Cash was posted correctly but the credit to Accounts Receivable was posted for $100.

b. A $3,200 credit to Cash was posted correctly but the debit to Prepaid Rent was posted for $2,200.

c. A $2,000 debit to Accounts Receivable was posted correctly but the credit to Service Revenue was not posted.

d. A $5,000 debit to Accounts Payable and $5,000 credit to Cash were not posted.

e. A $600 credit to Cash was posted correctly but the $600 debit was incorrectly posted to Salaries Payable rather than Salaries Expense.

Required:

Prepare a memo to the manager of Federation explaining the errors you discovered based on the facts provided. Include a numerical summary.

• CASES

C 3–1
Accrual Accounting
L.O.7

Robin Matthews started an office machine repair business on January 1, 19x1, with cash of $1,000 and use of a building for six months without rental payments (however, rent of $400 per month will be charged from July 1, 19x1, to December 31, 19x1). The ordinary rental cost of this building is $200 per month. Robin has decided not to pay herself a salary for the first six months of operations and to live on $1,000 a month that she will withdraw from her personal savings.

Ms. Matthews makes the following estimates of operating activity for the four quarters of 19x1:

	Quarter			
Estimates	**1**	**2**	**3**	**4**
Revenues:				
Repair revenues (customers have 30 days to pay)*	$8,000	$10,000	$11,000	$12,000
Expenses (all cash):				
Supplies	$1,000	$ 1,000	$ 1,000	$ 1,000
Utilities	2,500	2,500	2,500	2,500
Rent—equipment	2,000	2,000	2,000	2,000
Rent—building	0	0	1,200	1,200
Salary	0	0	3,000	3,000
Total payments	$5,500	$ 5,500	$ 9,700	$ 9,700

*Assume that Accounts Receivable balance at quarter-end is 20% of sales for the quarter.

Required:

Robin comes to you for financial advice. She asks:

1. Am I going to make a profit this year?
2. Will I have to borrow money to stay in business?

Using your knowledge of accrual accounting, write a report that answers the above questions. List any assumptions you need to make to complete your analysis.

C 3–2
Cash versus
Accrual Accounting
L.O.7

To compare the cash basis of accounting to accrual accounting, consider the following simple business situation. Assume that revenues are reported at the time of sale and that expenses are matched against sales. Further, assume no costs other than the product costs given below.

On September 1, 1985, Susan Upton returned to school for her senior year. As a business student, she had worked hard to learn the ways of being an entrepreneur, and she hoped to go into business for herself upon graduation. She knew a former sorority sister who had started a T-shirt–printing business in town after graduation and was succeeding. Susan visited her and got her to print 100 T-shirts for Susan with a Business School logo on the front for $1,000, to be paid within one week. Susan picked up the T-shirts on September 2 and took them up to school, where she proceeded to sell $800 worth for $1,200 to her friends and acquaintances, none of whom had any cash at the time of the sale. The lack of cash sales didn't deter Susan since she knew most of her customers and would see them throughout the term. She went home on September 2 feeling richer even though she had no money in her pocketbook.

On September 3 classes began. Susan ran into all of her customers in the halls, and collected all $1,200 owed her in cash during the course of the day. On her way back to her apartment that night, she stopped and paid her account at the T-shirt shop, giving her former sorority sister $1,000 in cash. While she hadn't brought the remaining $200 worth of T-shirts to school that day, a lot of people were asking if they could get one, and she had promised to bring them the next day.

On September 4 the last $200 worth of T-shirts went fast. Susan sold them for $300 to the first customers offering cash. Although this ended Susan's T-shirt venture for the term, it boosted her confidence that she would have a successful career after graduation.

Required:
1. For each of the three days, September 2, 3, and 4, prepare an accrual-based income statement for Susan Upton's T-shirt venture.
2. For each of the three days, September 2, 3, and 4, prepare a cash flow statement for Susan that summarizes (a) the cash taken in and (b) the cash paid out.
3. What is the total accrual-based income over the life of this venture? Are there any incomplete operating or business cycles in this venture?
4. What is the total cash flow over the life of this venture?
5. What is the relation between accrual income measures and cash flow measures over the life of any business venture?

· Evaluating Financial Statements ———————————————

C 3–3
Preparing a Balance Sheet—R. J. Reynolds Industries, Inc.
L.O.4

R. J. Reynolds Industries, Inc., one of the world's leading consumer products businesses, with interests in Nabisco Brands, Kentucky Fried Chicken, and others, had the following balance sheet accounts and account balances (amounts are in millions) on December 31, 1985:

Accounts and notes receivable	$1,944
Accounts payable	3,060
Capital stock	2,026
Cash	589
Current portion of long-term debt	172
Income taxes accrued	232
Inventories	3,209
Long-term debt	4,857
Notes payable	666
Other long-term assets	5,593
Other long-term liabilities	1,560
Prepaid expenses	136
Property, plant, and equipment	5,459
Retained earnings	4,357

Required:
Prepare the classified December 31, 1985, balance sheet. Be sure to categorize the assets and liabilities into current and noncurrent.

C 3–4
Transaction Analysis—Reebok International Ltd.
L.O.2, 3

Selected accounts and account balances (amounts in thousands) from the December 31, 19x6, balance sheet of Reebok International Ltd., a leading producer of apparel and shoes are as follows:

Accounts Receivable	$120,075
Accounts Payable	67,865
Capital Stock	119,961
Cash	66,077
Notes Payable	22,111
Prepaid Selling Expenses (Short-Term)	2,324

During January 19x7, the following transactions occurred:

a. Issued 100,000 additional shares of capital stock for $3 per share.
b. Recorded sales of $87,546,000. Total selling expenses amounted to $43,773,000. Two thirds of the sales were on credit; the remainder for cash. Three fourths of the selling expenses were paid in cash.
c. Paid $500,000 to the local bank on a note payable plus an additional $60,000 for interest.
d. Received $97,053,000 from customers on accounts.

Required:
Record the above transactions in journal form and post to the appropriate ledger accounts. (Round all amounts to the nearest thousand.)

C 3–5
Balance Sheet Preparation—AMR Corporation
L.O.4

On December 31 of a recent year, AMR Corporation, consisting primarily of American Airlines, reported the following balance sheet data (in millions):

Retained earnings	$1,368
Current liabilities	1,985
Flight equipment	?
Cash and securities	?
Long-term obligations under capital leases	1,183
Other long-term obligations	622
Accounts receivable	690
Deposits for purchase of flight equipment	145*
Inventories and other current assets	336
Total current assets	2,109
Property and facilities	907
Long-term investments and other assets	677
Capital stock	1,141
Long-term debt	1,229

*This is not considered a current asset by AMR Corporation.

Required:
Place the information provided into a classified balance sheet and solve for the amounts of the missing information.

4

Completion of the Accounting Cycle

An auditor is continually confronted with temptation. We want our clients to succeed. We want them to like us, to retain us as auditors and refer us to others. Such temptation challenges our integrity and our obligations to conscientiously serve the interests of the public. Our own morality and the very future of the public accounting profession require that we resist such temptation.

Edward M. Parks
Plante & Moran

· Learning Objectives

After studying Chapter 4, you should understand

1. How the accounting concepts of revenue recognition, matching, and periodicity relate to adjusting entries, pp. 142–45.

2. The way the adjusting entries (in cycle step 4) place the account balances on an accrual basis so that financial statements may be prepared, pp. 147–52.

3. The relation between adjusting journal entries, ledger balances, and unadjusted and adjusted trial balances, pp. 153–56.

4. How the worksheet is used to summarize cycle steps 1 through 5, pp. 157–59.

5. How the formal closing process wipes the slate clean in the temporary accounts (revenues, expenses, and dividends) for the start of a new period and includes the last period's results in retained earnings, pp. 160–62.

6. How to correct the current period's errors, pp. 162–63.

7. How reversing entries are used (Appendix 4A), pp. 178–79.

8. How the income statement and balance sheet can be converted to common-size statements by using percentages of total revenues or total assets (Appendix 4B), pp. 180–81.

In Chapter 3 you learned about the first three steps in the formal accounting cycle: (1) analysis of transactions; (2) journalizing; and (3) posting to the ledger. In addition, steps 4 (adjusting) and 5 (financial statement preparation) were introduced, with the help of the unadjusted and adjusted trial balances. Chapter 4 continues our examination of the formal accounting cycle, taking a closer look at steps 4 and 5, introducing step 6 (the closing process) and the post-closing trial balance. In addition, you will be introduced to a new version of an accounting worksheet, much different from the spreadsheet analysis used in the first two chapters. You will learn about the linkages between the worksheet and the formal journal and ledger, with emphasis on how adjusting entries and their effects on the financial statements are shown in the worksheet. Other topics in the chapter include the correction of current period errors, reversing entries (Appendix 4A), and a simple analysis of financial statements (Appendix 4B).

REVIEW OF THE ACCOUNTING CYCLE

The six steps of the accounting cycle were introduced in Chapter 3. The key tasks of these six accounting cycle steps are as follows:

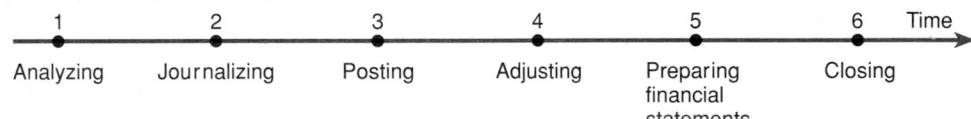

The first three accounting steps (analyzing transactions, journalizing or entering transactions into the journal, and posting from the journal to the ledger accounts) are triggered by evidence (invoices, checks, and so on) of transactions with external parties. Accounting cycle step 4—making the necessary adjusting entries—results from internal transactions usually documented by internally generated schedules of depreciation, schedules of interest, payroll records, and the like. From the adjusted trial balance following step 4, the financial statements of step 5 are prepared. Closing—accounting cycle step 6—is the most mechanical step, in that all temporary account balances are merely transferred to Retained Earnings, as we shall see later in this chapter. Steps 4 and 6 both involve making journal entries and, therefore, include journalizing and posting. A more detailed depiction of the accounting cycle would be as follows:

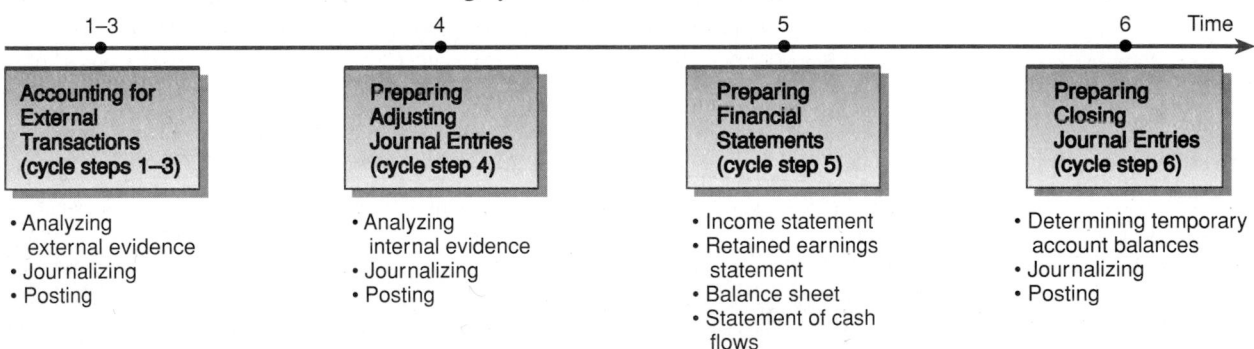

The time period covered by the accounting cycle varies depending on the length of time between financial statements. When preparing annual financial statements, the accounting cycle lasts one year. Companies also use monthly and quarterly accounting cycles. Business transactions—the raw inputs to the accounting system—occur intermittently throughout the accounting period.

Transactions occur in response to economic decisions and processes that are not necessarily related to standard time periods such as three months (a quarter) or a calendar year. For example, a payroll may be paid on December 28, but the accounting period ends on December 31; or a yearly insurance premium paid on November 18 may provide coverage that straddles two accounting periods. Because the periodicity concept calls for periodic financial statements that might not be of the same period as all of the business transactions, accountants must use accrual accounting to convert the business transactions to the uniform intervals of time covered by the financial statements. Periodicity is accomplished with the guidance of revenue recognition and matching discussed in earlier chapters.

Individual transactions trigger the analyzing, journalizing, and posting steps (steps 1, 2, and 3) of the accounting cycle. Posting to ledger accounts may take place at the same time as the transactions, or transactions may be accumulated and totals posted after a period of time (e.g., as each journal page is filled, or at the end of each day). In any event, steps 1, 2, and 3 of the accounting cycle are recorded as the underlying business transactions actually occur. At the same time, the needs of decision makers for timely information require that the accounting cycle summarizes the economic effects as of a specific date and for a distinct time period. As shown in the following diagram, the last three accounting cycle steps—adjusting, preparing financial statements, and closing—are end-of-period steps designed to facilitate these information requirements.

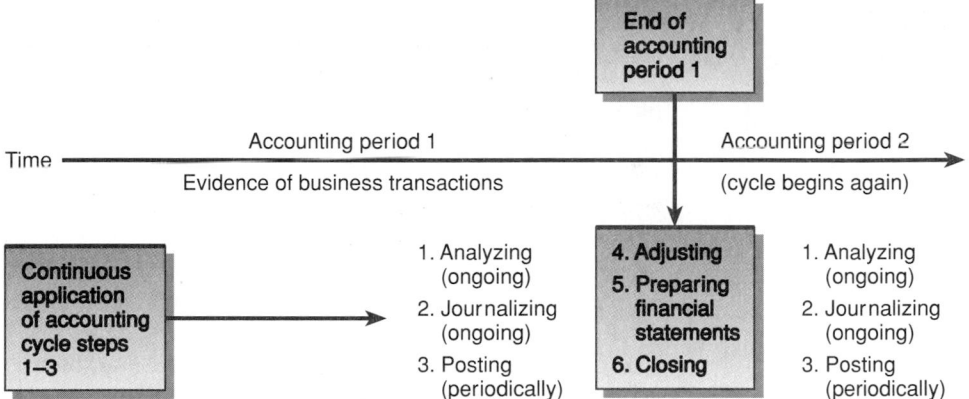

Depending on the size of the corporation, the six accounting cycle steps are based on hundreds, thousands, or possibly millions of specific accounting transactions. Summarization is necessary if all of the data are to be converted into meaningful financial statements. Balance sheets, income statements, and other financial statements should be viewed as informative summaries that communicate a company's economic conditions and flows.

ADJUSTING ENTRIES (ACCOUNTING CYCLE STEP 4)

As you know from Chapters 2 and 3, accountants use accrual accounting because (1) both cash and noncash transactions affect the economic status of a company and (2) periodic information is needed on the economic effects of a company's transactions. To comply with the accrual accounting concept, accountants prepare adjusting entries at the end of each accounting period. These adjusting entries reflect any changes in the economic status of the business that have not already been accounted for by the entries that were recorded during the accounting period. Thus, adjusting entries are period-end journal entries used to update accounts so that the financial statements report the correct balances in assets, liabilities, and shareholders' equity at the end of the period, as well as revenues and expenses for the period in conformance with the accrual concept.

The adjusting entries that must be recorded at the end of the accounting period can be grouped into two major categories: (1) *period-end allocations,* involving the updating of existing account balances that originated from *past transactions*, and (2) *period-end accruals,* involving business activities that will require known *future transactions* that have not yet been recorded. We will see that in the former case (allocations) the adjustments do not usually require new account titles to be developed, whereas with accruals we often need to develop new accounts to record the necessary adjusting entries. This section discusses period-end allocations and accruals, and gives an example of recording the period-end allocations and accruals of a service organization.

Adjusting-Entries—
Period-End Allocations

Period-end allocations involve adjustments to account balances from original transactions whose current and/or future periods' effect on expenses and/or revenues have not yet been recorded.[1] Allocation-type adjustments are typically made to unearned (prepaid) revenue accounts, such as the subscription example given below, and to prepaid expense accounts, such as the prepaid rent transaction explained in Chapter 3. Long-term assets, such as buildings and equipment, and short-term assets, such as prepaid insurance and supplies, also belong to the prepayments group, and their costs incurred in past transactions are allocated to current and future periods of benefit. When economic value still exists in an asset on hand at the end of a period, some portion of the original cost must remain as an asset. Note that the term *deferred* (meaning "delayed") is often used to further describe assets and liabilities affected by allocation-type adjustments. Therefore, **deferred assets** are often delayed expenses, whereas **deferred liabilities** are often delayed revenues, and allocation-type adjusting entries are often made when these deferred amounts are ready to be released (no longer need to be delayed) for purposes of measuring the current period's income. In this text, we will most frequently refer to this process as allocation.

Objective 1
How the accounting concepts of revenue recognition, matching, and periodicity relate to adjusting entries.

The following example of an end-of-period adjusting entry for a magazine advance subscription demonstrates the allocation procedure for a past transaction originally recorded as a liability—delayed revenue—when cash in advance was received. On January 1, 19x1, a publisher receives $600 cash for a three-year subscription to one of its publications. This original transaction will affect more than one accounting period. What are the income statement and balance sheet effects of this $600 in years 1, 2, and 3?

Although cash of $600 is received in year 1, all three years are involved in the revenue-generating process. Since the revenue is not earned until the magazines are delivered to the customers and the deliveries will occur over three years, revenue must be recognized over three years. If the full $600 cannot be recognized as revenue in year 1, how is it accounted for? Exhibit 4–1 illustrates the alternative methods of handling the $600 such that each accounting period—year 1, year 2, and year 3—shows the revenue earned.

Note that in accounting alternative 1, the cash collected in advance (January 1, 19x1) was debited to Cash and credited to Subscriptions Revenue, an income statement account. Since the cash collection was initially recorded by increasing Cash and increasing Subscriptions Revenue, an adjusting entry is needed at year-end to reduce revenue and recognize a $400 liability—Unearned Subscriptions Revenue—for the $400 to be earned in years 2 and 3. The $400 is a liability at the end of year 1 because the revenue is not *earned* until the publications are delivered in years 2 and 3. Thus, the adjusting entry is needed to allocate the original $600 to the three accounting periods of benefit and recognize the $400 obligation to the subscriber at the end of the first accounting period. In alternative 2, however, the initial entry records a liability—Unearned Subscriptions Revenue—which now requires an end-of-period adjustment to reduce the liability and record the $200 revenue that has been earned by the end of the first year (December 31, 19x1). Which alternative is correct? Alternative 2 may be more correct on January 1, 19x1, because no revenue has been earned as of that date. In practice, we may find both approaches being used. However, looking at the income statement and balance sheet effects reported at the end of each year in Exhibit 4–1, you can see that the results of both alternatives are the same. A

[1] The allocation-type adjusting entries spread these amounts out over their current and future periods of benefit because of the requirement that expenses be **matched** with related revenues and the requirement of **periodicity**, which demands financial statements at regular intervals.

EXHIBIT 4–1

Alternative Methods of Recording Revenue Earned

Date	Purpose of Entry	Accounting Alternative No. 1		Accounting Alternative No. 2	
		DEO	*CRED*		
1/1/x1	Cash transaction — To record receipt of cash.	Cash (A). . . . . 600 Subscriptions Revenue (R). . . .	600	Cash (A). . . . . 600 Unearned Subscriptions Revenue (L).	600
12/31/x1	Adjusting entry — To allocate revenue between years 1, 2, and 3.	Subscriptions Revenue (R). . . . . . 400 Unearned Subscriptions Revenue (L).	400	Unearned Subscriptions Revenue (L). . . . . 200 Subscriptions Revenue (R). . . .	200
	Income statement effect Balance sheet effect	Revenue = $200 Liability = $400		Revenue = $200 Liability = $400	
12/31/x2	Adjusting entry — To recognize revenue in year 2.	Unearned Subscriptions Revenue (L). . . . . 200 Subscriptions Revenue (R). . . .	200	Unearned Subscriptions Revenue (L). . . . . 200 Subscriptions Revenue (R). . . .	200
	Income statement effect Balance sheet effect	Revenue = $200 Liability = $200		Revenue = $200 Liability = $200	
12/31/x3	Adjusting entry — To recognize revenue in year 3.	Unearned Subscriptions Revenue (L). . . . . 200 Subscriptions Revenue (R). . . .	200	Unearned Subscriptions Revenue (L). . . . . 200 Subscriptions Revenue (R). . . .	200
	Income statement effect Balance sheet effect	Revenue = $200 Liability = $ 0		Revenue = $200 Liability = $ 0	

business should adopt one method and use it consistently. As long as the end-of-period adjustments are made correctly, the results will always be the same.

Many current-period transactions will create the need for end-of-period adjusting entries to allocate the recorded amounts to the current period and future periods. Notice that this first type of adjusting entry that allocates existing amounts reported in balance sheet accounts to current and future periods *usually* will not require new balance sheet accounts to be established.

Adjusting Entries—
Period-End Accruals

Period-end accruals include (*a*) accrued revenues and (*b*) accrued expenses that are related to past and/or future transactions with outside parties. The word *accrue* means to record amounts of revenue or expense that have accumulated over the current period, but have not yet been accounted for in an accounting entry. Thus, accrued revenues and expenses have accumulated or accrued during the current accounting period and, therefore, must be recorded at the end of the period by way of adjusting entries. When the accrued revenues or expenses are recorded, a corresponding balance sheet account such as a receivable or payable is also recorded. An example of an accrued revenue is interest revenue that has been earned but is unrecorded at period end. For example, on October 1, 19x1, a company deposits $10,000 in an investment account that earns 12% annual interest with payments at the end of each six-month period. At December 31, 19x1, three months' interest ($10,000 × .12 × 3/12 = $300) has been earned on this account but no cash has been received. The following adjusting entry would be made:

```
19x1
Dec. 31   Interest Receivable (A). . . . . . . . . . . . . . . . . . . . . .   300
               Interest Revenue (R). . . . . . . . . . . . . . . . . . . . . . .          300
          To record interest accrued at year-end ($10,000 × .12 × 3/12).
```

The balance sheet account, Interest Receivable, would not be required were it not for this accrual-type adjusting entry. If interest revenue were only recognized (recorded) when cash was received (as in the cash basis of accounting), then only the cash and interest revenue accounts would be needed.

If we assume that a check for six months' interest ($600) is received on March 31, 19x2, the following entry would be made to record the receipt of cash:

```
19x2
Mar. 31   Cash (A) . . . . . . . . . . . . . . . . . . . . . . . . . . . .   600
               Interest Receivable (A). . . . . . . . . . . . . . . . . . . . .          300
               Interest Revenue (R). . . . . . . . . . . . . . . . . . . . . .          300
          To record the receipt of six months' interest on the investment account.
```

Why do we want to show $300 interest revenue in 19x1 instead of all $600 interest in 19x2? The **revenue recognition concept** applies here, stating that the revenue should be reported in the period in which it is both earned and either realized or realizable. The revenue recognition concept provides accountants with guidance in answering the important question, When should revenue be reported? We will face many examples where this concept is employed as we move through the text.

A common example of accrued expenses is services performed by employees that are unpaid at the time the accounting period ends. For example, assume that a company pays its employees $1,500 per week ($300 per day) each Friday and that the end of the company's accounting period—December 31, 19x1—falls on a Wednesday. As a result, on December 31, 19x1, three days of employees' salaries ($900) are due that have not been shown as an expense for the accounting period ending December 31, 19x1. This type of adjusting entry, one based on a transaction yet to be recorded, is necessary for recording the expense and obligation that exist on December 31, 19x1. The year-end adjusting entry for this accrued expense would be recorded as follows:

```
19x1
Dec. 31   Salaries Expense (E) . . . . . . . . . . . . . . . . . . . . . .        900
              Salaries Payable (L) . . . . . . . . . . . . . . . . . . . . .                900
          To accrue three days' unpaid salaries at year-end.
```

Notice that this accrual establishes an additional liability account balance for Salaries Payable. Without this year-end adjustment the balance in Salaries Payable would have been zero, and it may have been excluded from the unadjusted trial balance. This is why many accrual-type adjusting entries appear to require additional balance sheet accounts to be reported.

Next assume that on January 2, 19x2, when the actual payroll of $1,500 is paid, the following entry is made:

```
19x2
Jan. 2    Salaries Expense (E) . . . . . . . . . . . . . . . . . . . . .      600
          Salaries Payable (L) . . . . . . . . . . . . . . . . . . . . . .    900
              Cash (A) . . . . . . . . . . . . . . . . . . . . . . . . .             1,500
          To record the payroll for the week ending January 2, 19x2.
```

This entry debits Salaries Expense for two days' payroll pertaining to 19x2 ($600) but not yet recorded, and debits Salaries Payable for the three days' payroll ($900) recorded as an expense in 19x1 by way of an end-of-period accrual-type adjusting entry. The entire payroll for the week ($1,500) is then credited to Cash. The January 2 entry eliminates the balance in the Salaries Payable account.

The guiding accounting concept for this and many other accrued expenses recorded by period-end adjusting entries is the **matching principle.** The matching principle (or **matching concept**) tells accountants to record expenses in that period in which the related benefits (revenues) are recorded, thus fully matching costs (expenses) with benefits (revenues) so that the periodic accrual accounting measurements of net income will accurately portray the performance of the company for the stated time period. In the above case, we assume that on January 2, 19x2, $900 of salaries were paid for work performed in 19x1 that benefited 19x1 revenues. If the employees had not worked the last three days in 19x1, we might have expected 19x1 revenues to be less. Therefore, matching requires that these salaries for the last three days of 19x1 be charged against 19x1 revenues and not expensed in 19x2, when the salaries are actually paid.

Remember that in an accrual accounting system, cash flow does not necessarily coincide with the amounts shown on the income statement. Thus, at the end of an accounting period, to achieve account balances in conformance with accrual accounting, previously unrecorded assets, revenues, liabilities, and expenses must be recorded, and often revenue-related and expense-related items must be allocated between two or more accounting periods.

Example of a Company's Adjusting Entries

On December 1, 19x1, Legislative Minds, Incorporated, (LMI) was organized by three former members of Congress (Larry, Maureen, and Ian) for the purpose of providing lobbying services for special-interest groups. The initial financing and investing activities necessary to begin operations occurred in December. On January 2, 19x2, the operating activities of LMI began. The owners wanted financial statements prepared at the end of the company's first month of operation, January 31, 19x2.

Ian, who had taken a bit of accounting, prepared the unadjusted trial balance (after cycle steps 1 through 3) illustrated in Exhibit 4–2 at the end of January and distributed copies to Larry and Maureen at their regular weekly meeting on February 2, 19x2. The following discussion took place.

EXHIBIT 4–2

Unadjusted Trial Balance

Legislative Minds, Incorporated
Unadjusted Trial Balance
January 31, 19x2

	Unadjusted Trial Balance		Income Statement*	
	Debits	Credits	Debits	Credits
Cash	$ 1,260			
Accounts Receivable	12,150			
Note Receivable	4,800			
Office Supplies	1,200			
Prepaid Rent	24,000			
Prepaid Insurance	12,000			
Office Equipment	3,000			
Trademark	12,000			
Accounts Payable		$ 4,560		
Capital Stock		40,000		
Consulting Fees		61,000		$61,000
Salaries Expense	27,000		$27,000	
Travel and Entertainment Expense	6,000		6,000	
Communications Expense	1,300		1,300	
Utilities Expense	450		450	
Postage Expense	400		400	
Totals	$105,560	$105,560	$35,150	$61,000
Net income (?)			25,850	
Totals			$61,000	$61,000

*Note: This is **not** the appropriate place to prepare an income statement, as the discussion in the LMI example points out.

Larry: Well, it looks like we're off to a great start. If I can have my share of the $25,850 in net income for January soon, I may buy that new car I've been thinking about. Let's pay ourselves a dividend to celebrate.

Maureen: How can we do that, Larry? We only have about $1,200 in cash. How can net income be so good with so little cash left?

Ian: Wait a minute, you guys. I'm not so sure we should be talking about paying any big dividends just yet. I've prepared this statement based on what I could remember from my accounting class and with the help of my old textbook, but I know it's not exactly complete. First of all, I know that one of the reasons we have any cash at all in this trial balance is that a new client came in last week and gave me some cash for consulting services that we haven't yet provided. Although I included it in the revenue account, Consulting Fees, I know we haven't earned it yet.

Maureen: Great! Then it's worse than I thought, since net income is overstated and we wouldn't have as much as $1,260 cash were it not for this last new client. How can this be?

Ian: Well, remember that measuring net income isn't the same as measuring cash, Maureen. Some of the revenues that we've received in cash have been put back into the business to pay for rent, insurance, and so on. Prepayments for future expenses have already been made for February and beyond in some cases, so we have something of real value here. Also, we've spent a lot on developing our trademark so that everyone around Washington will recognize our logo, and that will hopefully have long-term benefits.

Larry: It's not as bad as it looks, Maureen. I know one client who owes us $5,000. He said he'll deliver the check to me tonight at our church meeting. That will bring in some cash.

Maureen: So, how much of a dividend can we pay ourselves anyway? What is our real net income for January and how much can we declare as a dividend without hampering our operations?

Ian: You know, those questions are really important and yet difficult to answer, Maureen. I may be in over my head with this accounting stuff. I'm thinking we should probably get some professional help.

Larry: I agree. That's a good idea. We've got to be able to answer Maureen's questions sooner or later, and the sooner the better. How can we make good business decisions if we don't know how much net income we've earned? We'll never be able to make a sound dividend decision unless we have confidence in how well we've done.

Ian: OK. Let's postpone deciding about any dividend until I get some help with some of the adjustments that need to be made to this trial balance. I'll hire a real sharp accountant to help us out. I don't know what the final net income number will be, Maureen, but I expect it to be less than $25,000 for sure. What's the next topic on our agenda? . . .

The conversation between Larry, Maureen, and Ian points out the importance of accurate accrual accounting records to provide the basis for business decisions. The end-of-period adjustment process, guided by the important concepts of revenue recognition and matching (as well as other guiding concepts introduced later in the text) provide an important step in preparing financial statements that can be used as a basis for business decisions. For example, every business needs to know the answers to fundamental questions, such as, How is the business doing this period? When the accrual accounting process is not complete, measures of periodic net income and other basic business information cannot be determined.

Let's turn now to the period-end adjustment process that is being directed by the accountant Ian hired. In the following paragraphs you will learn how LMI's accountant performed the necessary adjustments so that the financial statements as of January 31, 19x2, would give an accurate economic picture of LMI.

Exhibit 4–2 provides LMI's unadjusted trial balance as of January 31, 19x2. (You should ignore the shaded income statement columns in Exhibit 4–2 since they are not appropriate to use with an unadjusted trial balance.) We will examine several of the elements of LMI's unadjusted trial balance and describe the types of adjusting entries necessary to comply with the objectives of accrual accounting. The adjustments have been divided into the two main categories discussed above—period-end allocations and period-end accruals.

Objective 2

The way the adjusting entries (in cycle step 4) place the account balances on an accrual basis so that financial statements may be prepared.

Examples of Period-End Allocations. As stated earlier, period-end allocations involve (*a*) unearned revenues that affect the current and/or future accounting periods and (*b*) prepayments that affect the current and/or future accounting periods. LMI's unearned revenue—Unearned Consulting Fees—is discussed first, followed by LMI's prepayments, including transactions related to Prepaid Rent, Prepaid Insurance, Depreciation and Amortization, and Office Supplies. These allocations requiring end-of-period adjusting entries are often identified by evaluating the account balances listed in the unadjusted trial balance and asking the question, **Are there any amounts included in the account balances that should not be there as of the end of the period?**

Unearned consulting fees (unearned revenue). In LMI's unadjusted trial balance given in Exhibit 4–2, a balance of $61,000 is shown in the Consulting Fees revenue account. This balance resulted from transactions recorded by debits to Cash for cash fees, debits to

Accounts Receivable for fees earned but not yet paid, and credits to Consulting Fees. Assume that $2,000 of the amount now recorded as Consulting Fees represents a client's prepayment for services that have not yet been performed. This amount should be transferred from the Consulting Fees revenue account to a new liability account, which could be called Unearned Consulting Fees. This $2,000 liability is an obligation of the company because the client is entitled to future services or the client may demand a return of the prepayment. To report the $2,000 unearned revenue, the Consulting Fees revenue account is debited to reduce the recognized revenue for the period, and the Unearned Consulting Fees liability account is credited to reflect the company's obligation to provide the service in the future. Thus, the adjusting entry on January 31, 19x2, is:

a.   19x2
      Jan. 31   Consulting Fees (R)   2,000

                    Unearned Consulting Fees (L)   2,000

                 To allocate $2,000 of the fees collected in January to
                 future periods.

If LMI had not expected the $2,000 cash payment earned in January when it was received, it could have been recorded as a liability at that time.

Prepaid rent (short-term prepayment). On January 2, 19x2, LMI paid $24,000 for the rent on office space from January 2 through March 31. Thus, on January 2, $24,000 is recorded in the Prepaid Rent account to represent advance payment of three months' rent. The following adjusting journal entry is necessary on January 31 because one month's portion of the economic value of the prepayment has been consumed:

b.   19x2
      Jan. 31   Rent Expense (E)   8,000

                 Prepaid Rent (A)   8,000

                 To record one month's rent expense.

The entry reduces the current asset, Prepaid Rent, with a credit and reduces stockholders' equity with a debit to the Rent Expense account. This is an example of an adjusting entry that allocates a prepayment by transferring an amount from an asset account to an expense account.

Exhibit 4–3 shows the flow of costs from Prepaid Rent, a current asset category on January 2, 19x2, to the income statement expense category over the three-month period. Allocations such as these are common adjustments. As you will see, the same basic process applies to other prepayments as well as to long-term assets.

Prepaid insurance (short-term prepayment). When insurance premiums are paid in advance, adjusting entries are needed to record that some of the insurance protection has been consumed. LMI's yearly insurance premium of $12,000 was paid on January 2, 19x2. At that time, the Prepaid Insurance asset account was debited $12,000 and Cash was credited $12,000. By January 31, LMI had consumed one-twelfth ($\frac{1}{12}$) of the insurance protection, or $1,000, and the following adjusting entry is necessary:

c.   19x2
      Jan. 31   Insurance Expense (E)   1,000

                 Prepaid Insurance (A)   1,000

                 To record one month's premium as insurance expense.

This leaves $11,000 in the current asset Prepaid Insurance to be expensed in future months.

Office supplies (short-term prepayment). Office supplies are usually purchased in quantity and used as the need arises. The amount used in a given period is charged to Office Supplies Expense. The exact amount charged is usually determined by counting

EXHIBIT 4–3

**Allocations of
Prepaid Rent**

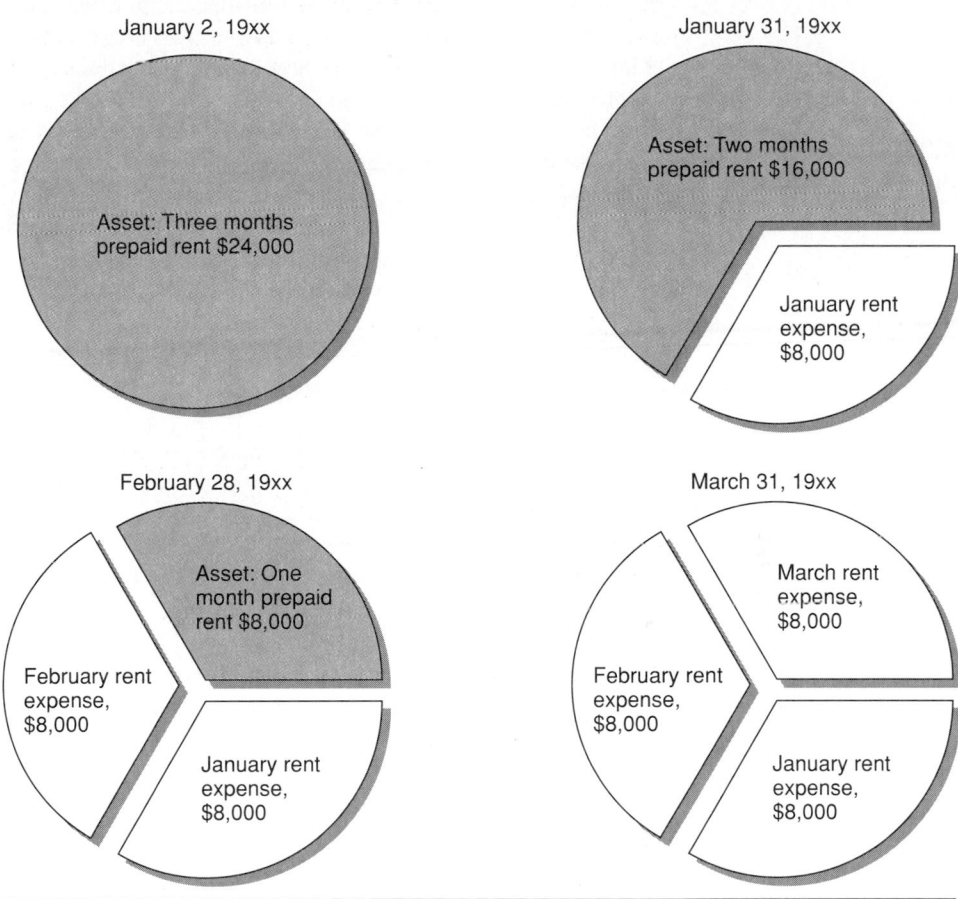

the amount of the supplies and subtracting the ending amount of supplies on hand from the total of the beginning balance and the amount purchased during the current period. This method is easier than keeping track of the exact usage of supplies on a day-to-day basis. For example, LMI has supplies costing $300 on hand at January 31, 19x2. The $1,200 shown in the unadjusted trial balance of Exhibit 4–2 represents the amount of supplies available—the cost of the beginning supplies inventory plus supplies purchases for the month.

Cost of supplies available for use	$1,200
Less ending inventory on 1/31/x2	300
Cost of supplies used in January	$ 900

The $300 represents the amount left on January 31, 19x2, and available for use in future periods. Thus, $900 must be charged to January's Office Supplies Expense, as follows:

Debit credit

d.	19x2		
	Jan. 31	Office Supplies Expense (E)	900
		Office Supplies (A)	900
		To record cost of supplies used in January.	

Depreciation and amortization (long-term prepayments). Closely related to the adjusting entries for the current assets is the allocation of the cost of a noncurrent asset. When an asset costing a material amount has a useful economic life exceeding one year, its cost is put into a noncurrent asset account. Such assets are expensed over their useful life. Immaterial assets with long lives, such as a $2 wastebasket, are expensed when purchased since the cost of accounting for such assets would exceed the value of the information. LMI has two material long-term assets that were partially consumed during January—office equipment and trademark. The trademark account represents costs incurred to develop the "mark" or business logo. These costs are normally amortized over the period of expected benefit, but never in excess of 40 years.

When tangible assets with physical form, such as office equipment, are expensed or written off over time, the term *depreciation* is used. When intangible assets representing future benefits (which often exist only as legal documents), such as patents, copyrights, and trademarks or tradenames, are expensed or written off over time, the term *amortization* is used.

Depreciation and amortization are processes that allocate original costs of noncurrent assets used by operating activities over the periods benefited by their use. These processes have the same purpose as other allocations of prepaid expenses—the costs of the assets used by operating activities must be allocated (matched) to the periods that benefit from their use. For example, LMI purchased $3,000 of office equipment on January 2, 19x2, and assigned the office equipment an estimated useful life of 60 months. Assuming that all of the equipment's value will be consumed during the next 60 months (i.e., the office equipment will have no value at the end of the 60 months), 1/60 of the cost of the asset is allocated to each month as depreciation expense. The entry to record this depreciation expense adjustment is

e.   19x2
   Jan. 31   Depreciation Expense—Office Equipment (E)   50
                     Accumulated Depreciation—Office Equipment (XA)*   50
               To record depreciation of office equipment for January.
   *(XA) is the symbol for a contra asset to be discussed below.

What is the Accumulated Depreciation account, and why is it used instead of crediting the Office Equipment account directly? The Accumulated Depreciation account is called a contra account because its balance (a credit in the case of depreciation) is subtracted from the debit balance of the related asset being depreciated.The asset account, Office Equipment in this case, maintains a debit balance of $3,000 equal to its original, or "historical," cost until the asset is fully used or sold. The contra asset account's credit balance will be increased (by $50 each month) over the life of the asset in order to report the portion of the asset's original cost that has been expensed. The difference in the debit asset balance less credit contra asset balance should always be a net debit, and is referred to as the net book value of the asset or the **net asset.** As a result of this process, readers of the ledger balances will always know (1) the original cost of the long-term asset; (2) the depreciation expense on the asset for the current period; and (3) the total depreciation taken to date. To illustrate how this information is communicated, assume that the ledger balances for the office equipment and the accumulated depreciation are reported in the LMI balance sheets at the following dates:

	1/31/19x2	2/28/19x2	12/31/19x2
Office equipment	$3,000	$3,000	$3,000
Less: Accumulated depreciation.	50*	100	600
Net office equipment.	$2,950	$2,900	$2,400

*$3,000/60 = $50 per month

Note that the change in the Accumulated Depreciation account from the end of January to the end of February tells us the depreciation expense for the month of February ($100 − $50 = $50/month). This also suggests that depreciation expense for January was $50, and that each month depreciation expense was $50 since the year-end balance in Accumulated Depreciation of $600 is equal to 12 months at $50 per month.

At the end of the 60-month period, when the asset is no longer in use and is disposed of, the asset's debit balance, $3,000 in the case of the office equipment, will equal the credit balance in the accumulated depreciation account, and the net asset balance will be zero. At this time, the following entry would be made to eliminate the fully depreciated asset from the books:

Accumulated Depreciation—Office Equipment (XA)	3,000	
Office Equipment (A)		3,000

To eliminate the asset and contra asset account for fully depreciated
office equipment.

In the United States, GAAP does not permit long-lived depreciable assets to be adjusted upward if they increase in value. The historical cost principle does not allow such revaluations for U.S. firms. However, in France and Sweden such revaluations are commonly found. And in the United Kingdom some firms have revalued their depreciable assets in some cases. The adherence to historical cost for depreciable assets is not uniformly applied around the world.

The amortization of the **trademark** follows the same basic pattern as depreciation. The original cost is allocated to the periods benefiting from the use of the asset. However, contra accounts are not normally used when recording amortization of intangible assets such as trademarks.

Assume that LMI has estimated the useful life of the $12,000 trademark to be five years (60 months) from January 1, 19x2. The entry to record the appropriate adjustment is

f.   19x2

Jan. 31 Amortization Expense (E)	200	
Trademark (A)		200

To record amortization of trademark for January: $12,000 × 1/60.

The Trademark account balance and balance sheet disclosures for January 31, 19x2, and June 30, 19x4, are as follows:

Date	Original Cost	Amortization Taken to Date	Trademark Account Balance	Amortization Expense for the Month
1/31/x2	$12,000	$ 200	$11,800	$200
6/30/x4	12,000	6,000	6,000	200

Balance sheet disclosures:

Noncurrent Assets	1/31/x2	6/30/x4
Trademark.	$11,800	$6,000

Note that, in contrast to depreciation, because no contra account is used, only the net book value is shown on the balance sheet.

Examples of Period-End Accruals.   Period-end accruals, as explained earlier, involve (*a*) accrued revenues in the form of receivables and (*b*) accrued expenses in the form of payables. These are revenues and expenses that have accumulated but have not been recorded. LMI has two period-end accruals or balance sheet items that have not been recorded as of January 31, 19x2—interest receivable and salaries payable. Note that an accrued revenue usually results in a debit to an asset account and a credit to a revenue account; an accrued expense usually results in a debit to an expense account and a credit to a liability account. Accruals that require end-of-period adjustments are often identified by asking the question, Are there any unrecorded receivables or unrecorded payables that are not in the unadjusted trial balance but should be there?

Interest receivable (accrued asset).   On January 2, 19x2, LMI loaned $4,800 to one of its owners and received a one-year note with an annual interest rate of 16%. LMI, therefore, has earned $64 interest income by January 31, 19x2 ($4,800 at 16% for one month). This accrued receivable is recorded as follows:

[handwritten note in margin: Interest Revenue]

g.   19x2
Jan. 31   Interest Receivable (A)   64
             Interest Revenue (R).   64
       To accrue interest receivable on note: $4,800 × .16 × 1/12.

Note that this entry records a new asset that did not previously exist in the unadjusted trial balance. Since interest is earned as time passes, no interest had been earned on January 2, and therefore the recording of the interest receivable waited until the end of the period. This Interest Receivable item will remain on LMI's books and will be increased by other month-end accruals until the entire $4,800 plus all interest is received from the maker of the note. When payment is received, Cash would be debited for the amount received, Note Receivable would be credited for the $4,800 principal amount, and Interest Receivable would be credited for the interest. Because the asset has been earned as of January 31, stockholders' equity must be increased by means of the credit to Interest Revenue. The $64 revenue will be shown on LMI's income statement for the month of January 19x2.

Salaries payable (accrued liability).   Because LMI does not pay its employees until February 11, LMI has an unpaid payroll amount on January 31. The accrued salaries expense must be shown in the income statement, and if we assume that amount is $2,115, the following debit to Salaries Expense and credit to (accrued) Salaries Payable is made:

h.   19x2
Jan. 31   Salaries Expense (E)   2,115
             Salaries Payable (L).   2,115
       To accrue salaries unpaid at January 31, 19x2.

Salaries Payable represents an obligation to employees that will be paid at the next payday, at which time the liability will be debited and Cash credited.

Income taxes payable (accrued liability).   LMI must also record its income tax expense for the period. This is an accrual because it represents an unpaid obligation and expense that has not yet been recorded by period-end, thus requiring an adjusting entry. The entry, assuming a $2,330 income tax, is

i.   19x2
Jan. 31   Income Tax Expense (E).   2,330
             Income Taxes Payable (L)   2,330
       To accrue income taxes for January.

LMI's adjusting entries are now completed. In the sections that follow you will learn how LMI's accountant uses the unadjusted trial balance amounts plus these adjusting entry amounts to prepare its financial statements.

RELATIONSHIP OF JOURNAL AND LEDGER TO UNADJUSTED AND ADJUSTED TRIAL BALANCES

Objective 3

The relation between adjusting journal entries, ledger balances, and unadjusted and adjusted trial balances.

LMI's accountant, you will recall, started with Ian's unadjusted trial balance (Exhibit 4–2) from LMI's ledger accounts before making the necessary adjustments. After the accountant completed the journal entries *a* through *i*, these entries were posted to the ledger accounts. New ledger accounts were established for the new accounts required by the adjustments. Remember that adjusting entries **must** be journalized in the journal and posted to the ledger accounts, just as are all the transactions made during the month.

When the LMI accountant had finished journalizing and posting the adjusting entries to the ledger accounts, the accountant prepared a new trial balance from the ledger. Since all the necessary adjustments have now been made, this new trial balance is called the adjusted trial balance.

Exhibit 4–4 summarizes the effects that the adjusting entries *a* through *i* have on the existing accounts and newly generated accounts. Note that several new accounts have been added to the adjusted trial balance. Several new balance sheet accounts, designated as having a balance of "None" in LMI's unadjusted trial balance reported in Exhibit 4–4, have been added to the list of accounts because they were affected by adjusting entries but had no balances until that time. This schedule is not a substitute for the formal journalizing and posting of the adjusting entries that the LMI accountant has already performed. In fact, the schedule can be made before the adjusting entries are journalized and posted to the ledger accounts, but the adjusting entries will become part of the company's records by journalizing and posting these entries to the ledger. You will see later in this chapter how this schedule becomes part of a worksheet, which is an organizing tool accountants use at the end of the accounting period.

RELATIONSHIP OF ADJUSTED TRIAL BALANCE, INCOME STATEMENT, RETAINED EARNINGS STATEMENT, AND BALANCE SHEET

The adjusted trial balance has all the components needed to construct the period-end income statement, retained earnings statement, and balance sheet, as illustrated in Chapter 3. To illustrate this process once again, the adjusted trial balance given in Exhibit 4–4 is repeated at the left of Exhibits 4–5 and 4–6. Exhibit 4–5 shows how the adjusted trial balance is used to prepare an income statement and a retained earnings statement, and Exhibit 4–6 shows how the adjusted trial balance is used to prepare a balance sheet. Refer to these two exhibits as you study the paragraphs that follow.

The format of LMI's income statement in Exhibit 4–5 shows two major sections—"Revenue" and "Expenses"—plus a section titled "Other revenue." The "Other revenue" section can contain miscellaneous revenues and expenses that do not result from the main business activity of the company. When other revenues and expenses are insignificant in amount, companies include them under a miscellaneous or catchall category in the major section of their income statement.

In Chapter 3, you learned how both the permanent (balance sheet) accounts and temporary (income statement) accounts are listed in the unadjusted and the adjusted trial balances. In Exhibit 4–5, you can follow the arrows from the temporary accounts of LMI's adjusted trial balance to the components of LMI's income statement.

As you can see from studying the arrows from LMI's adjusted trial balance to LMI's balance sheet in Exhibit 4–6, both permanent account balances and the effects of temporary account balances (by means of the Retained Earnings account) are represented in the balance sheet. Note that all account balances, other than those shown in the income statement, are listed in the balance sheet as assets, liabilities, or stockholders' equity. For LMI,

EXHIBIT 4–4

Flow of Information from Unadjusted Trial Balance to Adjusted Trial Balance

Legislative Minds, Incorporated
Trial Balances
For the Month Ended January 31, 19x2

Account Titles	Unadjusted Trial Balance Debit	Unadjusted Trial Balance Credit	Adjustments Debit	Adjustments Credit	Adjusted Trial Balance Debit	Adjusted Trial Balance Credit
Cash	1,260				1,260	
Accounts Receivable	12,150				12,150	
Note Receivable	4,800				4,800	
Interest Receivable	None		(g) 64		64	
Office Supplies.	1,200			(d) 900	300	
Prepaid Rent.	24,000			(b) 8,000	16,000	
Prepaid Insurance	12,000			(c) 1,000	11,000	
Office Equipment.	3,000				3,000	
Accumulated Depreciation— Office Equipment.		None		(e) 50		50
Trademark.	12,000			(f) 200	11,800	
Accounts Payable		4,560				4,560
Unearned Consulting Fees.				(a) 2,000		2,000
Salaries Payable				(h) 2,115		2,115
Income Taxes Payable				(i) 2,330		2,330
Capital Stock		40,000				40,000
Retained Earnings, 1/1/x2.		None				0
Consulting Fees		61,000	(a) 2,000			59,000
Salaries Expense.	27,000		(h) 2,115		29,115	
Travel and Entertainment Expense . . .	6,000				6,000	
Communications Expense	1,300				1,300	
Utilities Expense	450				450	
Postage Expense.	400				400	
Totals	105,560	105,560				
Rent Expense			(b) 8,000		8,000	
Insurance Expense			(c) 1,000		1,000	
Office Supplies Expense			(d) 900		900	
Depreciation Expense— Office Equipment.			(e) 50		50	
Amortization Expense.			(f) 200		200	
Interest Revenue				(g) 64		64
Income Tax Expense			(i) 2,330		2,330	
Totals			16,659	16,659	110,119	110,119

net income, which is the net of the income statement accounts, is then added to the beginning Retained Earnings account balance to arrive at the ending balance sheet total for retained earnings. As we discussed in Chapter 3, dividend declarations also create a temporary account that is closed to Retained Earnings. In the current example, LMI declared no dividends.

EXHIBIT 4–5

Adjusted Trial Balance and the Income Statement and Retained Earnings Statement

Legislative Minds, Incorporated
Adjusted Trial Balance
January 31, 19x2

	Debits	Credits
Cash	$ 1,260	
Accounts Receivable	12,150	
Note Receivable	4,800	
Interest Receivable	64	
Office Supplies	300	
Prepaid Rent	16,000	
Prepaid Insurance	11,000	
Office Equipment	3,000	
Accumulated Depreciation—Office Equipment		$ 50
Trademark	11,800	
Accounts Payable		4,560
Unearned Consulting Fees		2,000
Salaries Payable		2,115
Income Taxes Payable		2,330
Capital Stock		40,000
Retained Earnings, 1/1/x2		0
Consulting Fees		59,000
Salaries Expense	29,115	
Travel and Entertainment Expense	6,000	
Communications Expense	1,300	
Utilities Expense	450	
Postage Expense	400	
Rent Expense	8,000	
Insurance Expense	1,000	
Office Supplies Expense	900	
Depreciation Expense—Office Equipment	50	
Amortization Expense	200	
Interest Revenue		64
Income Tax Expense	2,330	
Totals	$110,119	$110,119

Legislative Minds, Inc.
Income Statement
For the Month Ended January 31, 19x2

Revenue:		
Consulting fees		$59,000
Expenses:		
Salaries expense	$29,115	
Travel and entertainment expense	6,000	
Communications expense	1,300	
Utilities expense	450	
Postage expense	400	
Rent expense	8,000	
Insurance expense	1,000	
Office supplies expense	900	
Depreciation expense—office equipment	50	
Amortization expense	200	
Total expenses		$47,415
Income before other revenue		$11,585
Other revenue:		
Interest revenue		64
Net income before taxes		$11,649
Income tax expense		2,330
Net income		$ 9,319

Legislative Minds, Inc.
Retained Earnings Statement
For the Month Ended January 31, 19x2

Retained earnings, January 1, 19x2		$ 0
Add: Net income		9,319
Less: Dividends		0
Retained earnings, January 31, 19x2		$ 9,319

EXHIBIT 4–6

Adjusted Trial Balance and Balance Sheet

Legislative Minds, Incorporated
Adjusted Trial Balance
January 31, 19x2

	Debits	Credits
Cash	$ 1,260	
Accounts Receivable	12,150	
Note Receivable	4,300	
Interest Receivable	64	
Office Supplies	300	
Prepaid Rent	16,000	
Prepaid Insurance	11,000	
Office Equipment	3,000	
Accumulated Depreciation—Office Equipment		$ 50
Trademark	11,800	
Accounts Payable		4,560
Unearned Consulting Fees		2,000
Salaries Payable		2,115
Income Taxes Payable		2,330
Capital Stock		40,000
Retained Earnings, 1/1/x2	0	
Consulting Fees		59,000
Salaries Expense	29,115	
Travel and Entertainment Expense	6,000	
Communications Expense	1,300	
Utility Expense	450	
Postage Expense	400	
Rent Expense	8,000	
Insurance Expense	1,000	
Office Supplies Expense	900	
Depreciation Expense—Office Equipment	50	
Amortization Expense	200	
Interest Revenue		64
Income Tax Expense	2,330	
Totals	$110,119	$110,119

Legislative Minds, Inc.
Balance Sheet
January 31, 19x2

Assets

Current assets:

Cash		$ 1,260
Accounts receivable		12,150
Note receivable		4,800
Interest receivable		64
Office supplies		300
Prepaid rent		16,000
Prepaid insurance		11,000
Total current assets		$45,574

Noncurrent assets:

Office equipment	$ 3,000	
Less: Accumulated depreciation	50	
Trademark		11,800
Total noncurrent assets		$14,750
Total assets		$60,324

Liabilities and Stockholders' Equity

Current liabilities:

Accounts payable		$ 4,560
Unearned consulting fees		2,000
Salaries payable		2,115
Income taxes payable		2,330
Total liabilities		$11,005

Stockholders' equity:

Capital stock		$40,000
Retained earnings		9,319
Total stockholders' equity		$49,319
Total liabilities and stockholders' equity . .		$60,324

LMI's balance sheet classifies assets and liabilities as current and noncurrent. A **current asset** is one that is expected to be consumed or converted to cash in its entirety within one year or the company's operating cycle, whichever is longer. A **current liability** is expected to utilize cash or other current assets within one year or the company's operating cycle, whichever is longer.

LMI's office equipment is classified as a noncurrent asset because, although part of the equipment is consumed through depreciation, the equipment will not be entirely consumed during the following year. The unearned consulting fees are classified as a current liability because the company expects that cash and other current assets will be consumed in providing services to customers in the next year and that the revenue will be recognized within a one-year period.

THE WORKSHEET: AN ACCOUNTING TOOL

Objective 4

How the worksheet is used to summarize cycle steps 1 through 5.

Most businesses have the need to examine their financial statement performance many times throughout the year. This requires preparing steps 4 and 5 of the cycle—adjusting entries and financial statements. However, businesses may not wish to record the adjustments *formally* in their journal and ledger each time they want to examine a balance sheet or an income statement. To facilitate preparation of financial statements (cycle step 5) (whether or not adjusting entries are formally journalized and posted to the ledger), accountants often use a worksheet. The worksheet is a convenient tool for preparing steps 4 and 5 of the cycle from an unadjusted trial balance prepared after steps 1, 2, and 3. In Exhibits 4–5 and 4–6 we illustrated how the January 31, 19x2, financial statements were prepared from the information in the adjusted trial balance. Exhibit 4–7 illustrates this same statement preparation process in a 12-column worksheet format. This worksheet summarizes the results of steps 1 through 5 of the accounting cycle and contains the following accounting data:

Columns	Data	Relation to Cycle Steps
1–2	Unadjusted trial balance	After steps 1–3
3–4	Adjusting entries.	Step 4
5–6	Adjusted trial balance	After step 4
7–8	Income statement	Part 1 of step 5
9–10	Retained earnings statement	Part 2 of step 5
11–12	Balance sheet	Part 3 of step 5

The adjusting entries in columns 3 and 4 explain the differences between the unadjusted trial balance (columns 1 and 2) and the adjusted trial balance (columns 5 and 6) since the balances in each account are simply summed across. The income statement is prepared in columns 7 and 8 with the debit of $9,319 at the bottom of column 7 (entry *j*) needed to balance columns 7 and 8 representing net income. The credit side of entry *j* for $9,319 is carried to column 10 and added to retained earnings. (If there were dividends for LMI, the balance would be carried across from column 1 to column 9, resulting in a deduction from retained earnings.) The debit of $9,319 for entry *k* at the bottom of column 9 needed to balance columns 9 and 10 is the sum of beginning retained earnings ($0 credit) plus net income ($9,319 credit) less dividends ($0 debit). This credit side of entry *k* is equal to the ending retained earnings balance and is carried to column 12 in the balance sheet as retained earnings. The mechanics of the worksheet in Exhibit 4–7 are only a

EXHIBIT 4–7

Preparing a Worksheet

Legislative Minds, Incorporated
Worksheet
For the Month Ended January 31, 19x2

Account Titles	Unadjusted Trial Balance		Adjustments	
	(1) Debit	(2) Credit	(3) Debit	(4) Credit
Cash	1,260			
Accounts Receivable	12,150			
Note Receivable	4,800			
Interest Receivable			(g) 64	
Office Supplies	1,200			(d) 900
Prepaid Rent	24,000			(b) 8,000
Prepaid Insurance	12,000			(c) 1,000
Office Equipment	3,000			
Accumulated Depreciation—Office Equipment				(e) 50
Trademark	12,000			(f) 200
Accounts Payable		4,560		
Unearned Consulting Fees				(a) 2,000
Salaries Payable				(h) 2,115
Income Taxes Payable				(i) 2,330
Capital Stock		40,000		
Retained Earnings, 1/1/x2		0		
Consulting Fees		61,000	(a) 2,000	
Salaries Expense	27,000		(h) 2,115	
Travel and Entertainment Expense	6,000			
Communications Expense	1,300			
Utilities Expense	450			
Postage Expense	400			
Rent Expense			(b) 8,000	
Insurance Expense			(c) 1,000	
Office Supplies Expense			(d) 900	
Depreciation Expense—Office Equipment			(e) 50	
Amortization Expense			(f) 200	
Interest Revenue				(g) 64
Income Tax Expense			(i) 2,330	
	105,560	105,560	16,659	16,659
Net income				
Retained Earnings, 1/31/x2				
Totals				

Adjusted Trial Balance		Income Statement		Retained Earnings Statement		Balance Sheet	
(5) Debit	(6) Credit	(7) Debit	(8) Credit	(9) Debit	(10) Credit	(11) Debit	(12) Credit
1,260						1,260	
12,150						12,150	
4,800						4,800	
64						64	
300						300	
16,000						16,000	
11,000						11,000	
3,000						3,000	
	50						50
11,800						11,800	
	4,560						4,560
	2,000						2,000
	2,115						2,115
	2,330						2,330
	40,000						40,000
	0				0		
	59,000		59,000				
29,115		29,115					
6,000		6,000					
1,300		1,300					
450		450					
400		400					
8,000		8,000					
1,000		1,000					
900		900					
50		50					
200		200					
	64		64				
		47,415	59,064				
2,330		2,330					
110,119	110,119	49,745	59,064				
		(j) 9,319			(j) 9,319		
				(k) 9,319			(k) 9,319
		59,064	59,064	9,319	9,319	60,374	60,374

slightly different way of preparing financial statements from the method illustrated in Exhibits 4–5 and 4–6. The resulting statements are, of course, the same. The worksheet is a commonly used tool in accounting, especially for preparing statements over periods of less than one year.[2]

CLOSING ENTRIES (ACCOUNTING CYCLE STEP 6)

The final step in the accounting cycle is closing the books for the period. Closing the books requires the recording and posting of closing entries, which eliminate the balance in all income statement and dividend accounts. This step is not performed unless it is the last time that net income will be computed for the period—normally only once a year. In other words, if the first five cycle steps, which include the measurement of net income, are being made for purposes of evaluating the monthly or quarterly performance of the business, closing entries would not be required. To close the books for LMI at the end of January would result in formally eliminating the balances in all income statement accounts and starting February with a set of income statement accounts with no balances. This would not permit a measure of two-month (January/February) or annual (19x2) net income by using the income statement accounts. As a result, closing entries to "wipe the slate clean" in the (temporary) income statement accounts are normally journalized and posted only once each year. This closing process is often aided by the use of a new temporary account, Income Summary, which is only used at the time of closing to facilitate both closing and income measurement. Although LMI would not ordinarily close its books at the end of one month, we will use the adjusted trial balance in Exhibit 4–7 (also found in Exhibits 4–5 and 4–6) to illustrate the closing process. Since only the temporary (non–balance sheet) accounts are closed, let us consider the adjusted balances in these accounts. Their pre-closing T account balances, along with the closing entries, and post-closing T account balances for LMI's temporary accounts are illustrated in Exhibit 4–8. Notice that the closing entries simply force the post-closing balances in all temporary accounts to be zero (a clean slate) for next period and record their effect in the Income Summary account (a very temporary account), which is then itself closed to the Retained Earnings account. The closing of the books on January 31, 19x2, will prohibit us from going back and changing the revenue and expense accounts from January, since their net income effect is in retained earnings once February begins.

Objective 5
How the formal closing process wipes the slate clean in the temporary accounts for the start of a new period and includes the last period's results in retained earnings.

POST-CLOSING TRIAL BALANCE AND NEW ACCOUNTING CYCLE

Exhibits 4–6 and 4–7 both illustrated how the balances of the permanent accounts become the balance sheet items. Assume that LMI's accountant has completed the LMI income statement and balance sheet, has closed the temporary accounts, and is now ready for the new accounting period. To test for posting errors in account balances, on January 31, 19x2, LMI's accountant takes a post-closing trial balance. The post-closing trial balance, illustrated in Exhibit 4–9, is a listing of all account balances just as the other trial balances were. However, after closing only the permanent balance sheet accounts are left with a balance.

Remember that all trial balances are internal documents used to help check completeness and accuracy. The unadjusted trial balance is prepared before the company has made its adjustments; the adjusted trial balance is prepared after the adjustments have been made; and the post-closing trial balance is prepared after the closing entries have been made and before a new accounting period begins.

---

[2]There are other versions of worksheets used in practice which have more or fewer columns. For example, the retained earnings columns are sometimes omitted (see demonstration exercise on page 174). Remember that the worksheet is simply a tool to help you prepare the financial statements—any form will do.

EXHIBIT 4–8

Closing Entries (Step 6)

Pre-Closing Ledger Balances Temporary Accounts

Closing Journal Entries

Post-Closing Ledger Balances Temporary Accounts

Consulting Fees

| | 59,000 |

Interest Revenue

| | 64 |

Salaries Expense

| 29,115 | |

Travel and Entertainment Expense

| 6,000 | |

Communications Expense

| 1,300 | |

Utilities Expense

| 450 | |

Postage Expense

| 400 | |

Rent Expense

| 8,000 | |

Insurance Expense

| 1,000 | |

Office Supplies Expense

| 900 | |

Depreciation Expense

| 50 | |

Amortization Expense

| 200 | |

Income Tax Expense

| 2,330 | |

Closing Journal Entries

(*l*)	Consulting Fees	59,000	
	Interest Revenue	64	
	Income Summary.		59,064
	To close revenue accounts.		
(*m*)	Income Summary.	49,745	
	Salaries Expense.		29,115
	Travel and Entertainment Expense		6,000
	Communications Expense		1,300
	Utilities Expense		450
	Postage Expense.		400
	Rent Expense		8,000
	Insurance Expense		1,000
	Office Supplies Expense		900
	Depreciation Expense.		50
	Amortization Expense.		200
	Income Tax Expense		2,330
	To close expense accounts.		
(*n*)	Income Summary.	9,319	
	Retained Earnings		9,319
	To close income summary account.		

Post-Closing Ledger Balances Temporary Accounts

Consulting Fees

| (*l*) | 59,000 | | 59,000 |
| | | Bal. | –0– |

Interest Revenue

| (*l*) | 64 | | 64 |
| | | Bal. | –0– |

Salaries Expense

| | 29,115 | (*m*) | 29,115 |
| Bal. | –0– | | |

Travel and Entertainment Expense

| | 6,000 | (*m*) | 6,000 |
| Bal. | –0– | | |

Communications Expense

| | 1,300 | (*m*) | 1,300 |
| Bal. | –0– | | |

Utilities Expense

| | 450 | (*m*) | 450 |
| Bal. | –0– | | |

Postage Expense

| | 400 | (*m*) | 400 |
| Bal. | –0– | | |

Rent Expense

| | 8,000 | (*m*) | 8,000 |
| Bal. | –0– | | |

Insurance Expense

| | 1,000 | (*m*) | 1,000 |
| Bal. | –0– | | |

Office Supplies Expense

| | 900 | (*m*) | 900 |
| Bal. | –0– | | |

Depreciation Expense

| | 50 | (*m*) | 50 |
| Bal. | –0– | | |

Amortization Expense

| | 200 | (*m*) | 200 |
| Bal. | –0– | | |

Income Tax Expense

| | 2,330 | (*m*) | 2,330 |
| Bal. | –0– | | |

Income Summary

(*m*)	49,745	(*l*)	59,064
(*n*)	9,319	.	9,319
		Bal.	–0–

Retained Earnings

			–0–
	–0–		
		(*n*)	9,319
		Bal.	9,319

Dividends

| | –0– | | –0– |

EXHIBIT 4–9

**Post-Closing
Trial Balance**

**Legislative Minds, Incorporated
Post-Closing Trial Balance
January 31, 19x2**

	Debits	Credits
Cash	$ 1,260	
Accounts Receivable	12,150	
Note Receivable	4,800	
Interest Receivable	64	
Office Supplies	300	
Prepaid Rent	16,000	
Prepaid Insurance	11,000	
Office Equipment	3,000	
Accumulated Depreciation—		
Office Equipment		$ 50
Trademark	11,800	
Accounts Payable		4,560
Unearned Consulting Fees		2,000
Salaries Payable		2,115
Income Taxes Payable		2,330
Capital Stock		40,000
Retained Earnings		9,319
Totals	$60,374	$60,374

CORRECTION OF CURRENT PERIOD ERRORS

Objective 6
How to correct the current period's errors.

During an accounting period, errors may be made in recording and posting accounting entries. The most common errors involve improper amounts and improper classifications. Of course, when such errors are detected, they must be corrected. When this correction process is performed in the same period in which the error occurs, the process is considered routine. For instance, assume that on October 15, 19x1, a company purchases land for $10,000 and erroneously debits Administrative Expense instead of Land and correctly credits Cash. If that error is detected at the end of the period (December 31, 19x1, in this case), the accountant would correct the error by debiting Land and crediting Administrative Expense, giving both accounts their appropriate balances.

Incorrect entry:

19x1			
Oct. 15	Administrative Expense (E)	10,000	
	Cash (A)		10,000
	To record purchase of land.		

Correcting entry:

19x1			
Dec. 31	Land (A)	10,000	
	Administrative Expense (E)		10,000
	To correct October 15, 19x1, entry.		

If such an error were left uncorrected, it would cause erroneous balances in several accounts that flow to the financial statements. In our example, net income, land (noncurrent assets), and retained earnings would all be understated in the year of the error. Also, unless corrected, both land and retained earnings would be understated in subsequent years.

Although this type of correction changes account balances, you must not consider a correction to be the same as an adjusting entry. For example, compare the correcting entry above to an adjusting entry to record depreciation expense. The depreciation adjustment is necessary because a portion of the economic life of an asset is consumed during the period. Although this adjusting entry is made at the end of the period and is similar in appearance to the correcting entry shown above, the adjusting entry does not correct an error but updates the accounts.

REVIEW OF THE COMPLETE ACCOUNTING CYCLE

To review the complete six-step process examined in Chapters 3 and 4, let us consider a new example. (For those who wish to skip this review, turn to the chapter summary on page 171.)

Trans Company was organized on January 1, 19x1, for the purpose of providing transportation. Data *in summary form* from the first year's operations are given below (all amounts are in thousands of dollars):

a. Transportation revenue earned from services performed on account, $2,500.

b. Cash receipts for the year:

Jan. 10	From stockholders for shares of stock	$5,000
June 30	From bank loan	2,000
Jan. 1–Dec. 31	From customers representing collections on account.	1,850
		$8,850

c. Purchased autos costing $2,000 total on February 1 for no down payment. These autos were expected to have a 10-year life and no value at the end of 10 years. The autos were acquired with a loan from the dealer, and were to be paid for in 50 equal monthly interest-free payments of $40 each.

d. Cash disbursements for the year:

Jan. 1	For purchase of land	$1,000
July 1	For advertising (3 years paid in advance)	3,540
Dec. 30	For dividends	100
	For interest on notes payable	5
Jan. 1–Dec. 31	For gasoline	250
Jan. 30–Dec. 15	For wages	1,200
Jan. 30–Dec. 31	For repairs	125
Mar. 1–Dec. 1	For auto payments.	400
		$6,620

e. Unpaid wages as of December 31 are $100.

f. Unpaid gasoline invoices as of December 31 are $60.

g. Accrued interest payable as of December 31 is $5.

The analysis of transactions, journal entries, and ledger account balances for the first three cycle steps pertain to the transactions summarized in items *a* through *d* of our example. Items *e*, *f*, and *g* are accrual type adjusting entries that would pertain to cycle step 4.

The following summary journal entries, ledger accounts, and unadjusted trial balance would result from the first three cycle steps:

Journal Entries (summarizing all transactions for the year):

Reference	Accounts	Debit	Credit
a.	Accounts Receivable (A)	2,500	
	Service Revenue (R)		2,500
	To record sale on account.		
b.	Cash (A).	8,850	
	Capital Stock (SE)		5,000
	Notes Payable (L).		2,000
	Accounts Receivable (A)		1,850
	To record cash receipts for year.		
c.	Automobiles (A)	2,000	
	Auto Loan Payable (L)		2,000
	To record autos purchased with loan.		
d.	Land (A).	1,000	
	Prepaid Advertising (A)	3,540	
	Dividends (D).	100	
	Interest Expense (E)	5	
	Gasoline Expense (E)	250	
	Wages Expense (E).	1,200	
	Repairs Expense (E)	125	
	Auto Loan Payable (L)	400	
	Cash (A).		6,620
	To record cash disbursements for year.		

Ledger Account Balances:

Assets:

Cash			
(b)	8,850	(c)	6,620
Bal.	2,230		

Accounts Receivable			
(a)	2,500	(b)	1,850
Bal.	650		

Prepaid Advertising		
(d)	3,540	
Bal.	3,540	

Autos		
(c)	2,000	
Bal.	2,000	

Land		
(d)	1,000	
Bal.	1,000	

Liabilities:

Auto Loan Payable			
(d)	400	(c)	2,000
		Bal.	1,600

Notes Payable		
	(b)	2,000
	Bal.	2,000

Stockholders' Equity:

Capital Stock		
	(b)	5,000
	Bal.	5,000

Service Revenue		
	(a)	2,500
	Bal.	2,500

Interest Expense		
(d)	5	
Bal.	5	

Gasoline Expense		
(b)	250	
Bal.	250	

Wages Expense		
(d)	1,200	
Bal.	1,200	

Repairs Expense		
(d)	125	
Bal.	125	

Dividends		
(d)	100	
Bal.	100	

Trans Company
Unadjusted Trial Balance
December 31, 19x1
(in thousands)

	Debits	Credits
Cash	$ 2,230	
Accounts Receivable	650	
Prepaid Advertising	3,540	
Autos	2,000	
Land	1,000	
Auto Loan Payable		$ 1,600
Notes Payable		2,000
Capital Stock		5,000
Service Revenue		2,500
Interest Expense	5	
Gasoline Expense	250	
Wages Expense	1,200	
Repairs Expense	125	
Dividends	100	
Totals	$11,100	$11,100

After the first three cycle steps are complete, the unadjusted trial balance (above) can be used to help identify any adjustments needed to complete cycle step 4.

Accrual-type adjustments are required for data items *e, f,* and *g* in this example. The year-end adjusting entries would be:

e.   19x1
     Dec. 31   Wages Expense (E)   100
              Wages Payable (L)   100
              To accrue earned but unpaid wages at year-end.

f.   Dec. 31   Gasoline Expense (E)   60
              Accounts Payable (L)   60
              To accrue gasoline invoices unpaid as of year-end.

g.   Dec. 31   Interest Expense (F)   5
              Interest Payable (L)   5
              To accrue interest on bank note unpaid as of year-end.

Notice that each of these accrual-type adjusting entries require a previously unreported liability account (not found in the unadjusted trial balance) to be established.

We can examine the unadjusted trial balance and ask the following question: Are there any amounts listed as assets or liabilities that no longer represent assets or liabilities? Cash and accounts receivable are properly stated assets; however, prepaid advertising and autos are both overstated since some of their value has been consumed. The advertising was paid on July 1 for three years; therefore, 6 out of 36 months, or one sixth of this amount has expired. The following allocation-type adjusting entry would be recorded at year-end:

h.   19x1
     Dec. 31   Advertising Expense (E)   590
              Prepaid Advertising (A)   590
              To allocate one sixth of prepaid advertising to expense.

The autos were acquired on February 1 and have been in use for 11 months. They are expected to last 10 years, or 120 months, so 11/120 of their cost should be allocated to expense in 19x1. This allocation-type adjusting entry would be recorded as follows:

i.   19x1
    Dec. 31   Depreciation Expense (E)   183
                Accumulated Depreciation (XA).   183
                To record 11 months of depreciation expense on autos.

Examination of the unadjusted trial balance does not suggest any further adjusting entries for period-ending allocations or accruals in this example.

After posting, cycle step 4, we will be ready to prepare the adjusted trial balance and the three financial statements that are prepared from the listed account balances. To illustrate the recording and posting of adjustments *e* through *i* and the resulting financial statements, we provide the worksheet in Exhibit 4–10. From this worksheet, we can examine the results of cycle steps 1 through 3 in the first two columns and the effect of the adjustments made in cycle step 4 (columns 3 and 4) on the adjusted ledger balances (columns 5 and 6), from which the income statement (columns 7 and 8), retained earnings statement (columns 9 and 10) and balance sheet (columns 11 and 12) are prepared.

The formal closing entries to eliminate all balances in these nominal accounts for 19x1 and close their net effect to retained earnings would be recorded in journal form as follows:

j.   19x1
    Dec. 31   Service Revenue   2,500
                Income Summary   2,500
                To close revenue account.

k.   Dec. 31   Income Summary   2,518
                Interest Expense   10
                Gasoline Expense.   310
                Wages Expense.   1,300
                Repair Expense.   125
                Advertising Expense.   590
                Depreciation Expense   183
                To close expense accounts.

l.   Dec. 31   Retained Earnings (Deficit).   18
                Income Summary   18
                To close Income Summary account.

m. Dec. 31   Retained Earnings (Deficit).   100
                Dividends   100
                To close Dividends account.

EXHIBIT 4–10

Trans Company Worksheet

Trans Company
Worksheet
For the Year Ended December 31, 19x1

Account Titles	Unadjusted Trial Balance		Adjustments	
	(1) Debit	(2) Credit	(3) Debit	(4) Credit
Cash	2,230			
Accounts Receivable	650			
Prepaid Advertising	3,540			(h) 590
Autos	2,000			
Land	1,000			
Auto Loan Payable		1,600		
Note Payable		2,000		
Capital Stock		5,000		
Service Revenue		2,500		
Interest Expense	5		(g) 5	
Gasoline Expense	250		(f) 60	
Wages Expense	1,200		(e) 100	
Repair Expense	125			
Dividends	100			
	11,100	11,100		
Advertising Expense			(h) 590	
Depreciation Expense			(i) 183	
Accumulated Depreciation—Autos				(i) 183
Wages Payable				(e) 100
Accounts Payable				(f) 60
Interest Payable				(g) 5
			938	938
Net Income or Loss				
Retained Earnings (or Deficit)				
Totals				

Adjusted Trial Balance		Income Statement		Retained Earnings Statement		Balance Sheet	
(5) Debit	(6) Credit	(7) Debit	(8) Credit	(9) Debit	(10) Credit	(11) Debit	(12) Credit
2,230						2,230	
650						650	
2,950						2,950	
2,000						2,000	
1,000						1,000	
	1,600						1,600
	2,000						2,000
	5,000						5,000
	2,500		2,500				
10		10					
310		310					
1,300		1,300					
125		125					
100				100			
590		590					
183		183					
	183						183
	100						100
	60						60
	5						5
11,448	11,448	2,518	2,500				
			(*l*) 18	(*l*) 18			
		2,518	2,518	118	0		
					118	118	
				118	118	8,948	8,948

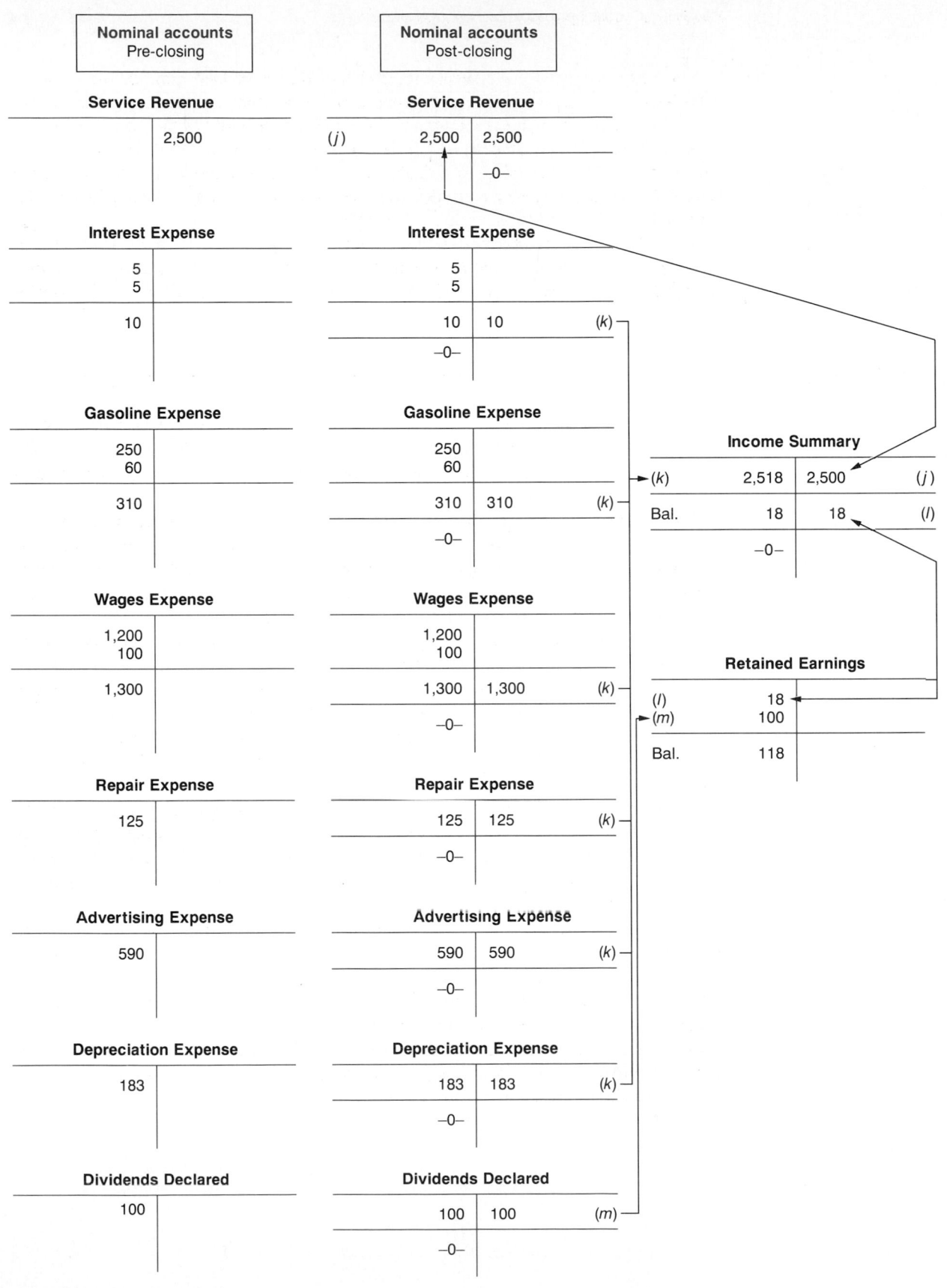

Since expenses exceeded revenues in 19x1 by $18, the retained earnings would have a debit balance and would be labeled retained deficit when formally reported in the balance sheet. It would not be unusual for companies to experience losses in the early years of operations. While Trans Company did declare and pay $100 of dividends in 19x1, further increasing the retained deficit to a $118 debit balance, such dividend payments are not typical. Some state laws would prohibit payment of a dividend if a retained deficit results. This will be discussed in more detail in Chapter 11.

The post-closing trial balance and formal balance sheet that results for Trans Company at the end of 19x1 are provided in Exhibit 4–11. You should study this complete example carefully to review the six steps of the accounting cycle and the role of the accounting worksheet.

• SUMMARY

This chapter concentrated on the final steps in the accounting cycle, which occur at the end of the accounting period—adjusting, preparing financial statements, and closing. The adjusting step was emphasized because adjusting entries are so pivotal in preparing accurate accrual-based financial statements.

Adjustments are necessary because frequently balances in existing accounts must be modified and new accounts often must be created. Entries that involve revenue-related and expense-related account balances affecting more than one period must be spread among accounting periods. Unrecorded accrued revenues and expenses that have accumulated during the accounting period must be recorded as adjusting entries.

After the adjusting journal entries are journalized and posted to the ledger accounts, the adjusted trial balance is prepared. The adjusted trial balance has all the components needed to construct the period-end income statement, retained earnings statement, and balance sheet. All accounts on an adjusted trial balance affect some balance sheet category. The net effect of the income statement accounts becomes part of retained earnings, a permanent account; and all of the permanent accounts go directly into the body of the balance sheet.

In this chapter you learned how accountants prepare a worksheet to aid them in evaluating the financial position of the business. The first five steps in the accounting cycle are summarized in the elements of the worksheet, which is an informal representation of the accounting cycle. The worksheet shows the flow of data from the unadjusted trial balance to the financial statements.

The accounting cycle is completed with closing entries that return all temporary (income statement and dividend) accounts to zero in preparation for the next accounting period. The closing process is done with the aid of the Income Summary account, and the balance in Income Summary, representing the net income or net loss for the period, is transferred to the Retained Earnings account.

Since errors are sometimes made during the recording and posting of transactions, the correction process is explained. You must not confuse the correction process with the adjustment process in which no actual errors are made.

EXHIBIT 4–11

**Trial Balance and
Balance Sheet at
December 31, 19x1,
Trans Company**

Trans Company
Post-Closing Trial Balance
December 31, 19x1
(in thousands)

	Debits	Credits
Cash	$2,230	
Accounts Receivable	650	
Prepaid Advertising	2,950	
Autos	2,000	
Accumulated Depreciation—Autos		$ 183
Land	1,000	
Accounts Payable		60
Wages Payable		100
Auto Loan Payable		1,600
Interest Payable		5
Note Payable		2,000
Capital Stock		5,000
Retained Earnings	118	
Totals	$8,948	$8,948

Trans Company
Balance Sheet
December 31, 19x1
(in thousands)

Assets

Current assets:		
Cash	$2,230	
Accounts receivable	650	
Prepaid advertising	2,950	
Total current assets		$5,830
Noncurrent assets:		
Autos	$2,000	
Less: Accumulated depreciation	183	$1,817
Land		1,000
Total noncurrent assets		$2,817
Total assets		$8,647

Liabilities and Stockholders' Equity

Current liabilities:		
Accounts payable	$ 60	
Wages payable	100	
Interest payable	5	$ 165
Noncurrent liabilities:		
Auto loan payable	$1,600	
Notes payable	2,000	3,600
Total liabilities		$3,765
Stockholders' equity:		
Capital stock	$5,000	
Retained deficit	(118)	
Total stockholders' equity		4,882
Total liabilities and stockholders' equity		$8,647

• DEMONSTRATION EXERCISE

At the end of March 19x1, its second month of operations, Financial Planners, Inc., (FPI) had the following trial balance:

Financial Planners, Inc.
Trial Balance
March 31, 19x1

	Debits	Credits
Cash	$32,778	
Accounts Receivable	12,940	
Office Supplies	350	
Prepaid Rent	4,800	
Prepaid Insurance	3,600	
Security Deposit	2,400	
Office Equipment	5,670	
Accounts Payable		$ 4,500
Capital Stock		50,000
Retained Earnings	2,832	
Consulting Fees		32,000
Salaries Expense	12,000	
Commissions Expense	5,000	
Travel and Entertainment Expense	2,650	
Advertising Expense	715	
Communications Expense	580	
Utilities Expense	185	
Totals	$86,500	$86,500

The following end-of-month data is also available:

a. Prepaid rent of $1,600 is applicable to the month of March.
b. Depreciation for the month on the furniture and equipment is $95.
c. The insurance policy purchased at the beginning of the month is for 12 months.
d. Salaries and commissions earned at the end of the month but not yet paid amount to $1,325 and $900, respectively.
e. Consulting fees of $3,500 that were received but not yet earned have been recorded in Consulting Fees.
f. Office supplies on hand at the end of the month amount to $140.
g. FPI uses a 10% tax rate.

Required:
Prepare FPI's—

1. Complete worksheet for the month.
2. Adjusting journal entries in journal form.
3. Income statement for the month and its March 31 balance sheet.
4. Closing entries for the end of the period.

Solution:

Financial Planners, Inc.
Worksheet
For the Month Ended March 31, 19x1

Account Titles	Unadjusted Trial Balance (1) Debit	Unadjusted Trial Balance (2) Credit	Adjustments (3) Debit	Adjustments (4) Credit	Adjusted Trial Balance (5) Debit	Adjusted Trial Balance (6) Credit	Income Statement (7) Debit	Income Statement (8) Credit	Balance Sheet (9) Debit	Balance Sheet (10) Credit
Cash	32,778				32,778				32,778	
Accounts Receivable	12,940				12,940				12,940	
Office Supplies	350			(f) 210	140				140	
Prepaid Rent	4,800			(a) 1,600	3,200				3,200	
Prepaid Insurance	3,600			(c) 300	3,300				3,300	
Security Deposit	2,400				2,400				2,400	
Office Equipment	5,670				5,670				5,670	
Accumulated Depreciation— Office Equipment				(b) 95		95				95
Accounts Payable		4,500				4,500				4,500
Salaries Payable				(d) 1,325		1,325				1,325
Commissions Payable				(d) 900		900				900
Unearned Consulting Fees				(e) 3,500		3,500				3,500
Income Taxes Payable				(g) 294		294				294
Capital Stock		50,000				50,000				50,000
Retained Deficit, 3/1/x1	2,832				2,832				(h) 186	
Consulting Fees		32,000	(e) 3,500			28,500		28,500		
Salaries Expense	12,000		(d) 1,325		13,325		13,325			
Commissions Expense	5,000		(d) 900		5,900		5,900			
Travel and Entertainment Expense	2,650				2,650		2,650			
Advertising Expense	715				715		715			
Communications Expense	580				580		580			
Utilities Expense	105				185		185			
Rent Expense			(a) 1,600		1,600		1,600			
Depreciation Expense— Office Equipment			(b) 95		95		95			
Insurance Expense			(c) 300		300		300			
Office Supplies Expense			(f) 210		210		210			
							25,560	28,500		
Income Tax Expense			(g) 294		294		294			
	86,500	86,500	8,224	8,224	89,114	89,114				
Net income							(h) 2,646			
Totals							28,500	28,500	60,614	60,614

(h) $2,646 net income added to beginning retained deficit of $(2,832) to obtain ending retained deficit of $(186).

GENERAL JOURNAL					J9
Date		Account Titles and Explanation	Ref.	Debit	Credit
Adjusting entries:					
19x1 Mar.	31	Rent Expense (E)		1,600	
		Prepaid Rent (A)			1,600
		To adjust for March rent expense.			
	31	Depreciation Expense—			
		Equipment (E)		95	
		Accumulated Depreciation—			
		Equipment (XA)			95
		To record depreciation expense.			
	31	Insurance Expense (E)		300	
		Prepaid Insurance (A)			300
		To adjust for insurance expense.			
	31	Salaries Expense (E)		1,325	
		Commissions Expense (E)		900	
		Salaries Payable (L)			1,325
		Commissions Payable (L)			900
		To accrue unpaid salaries and			
		commissions.			
	31	Consulting Fees (R)		3,500	
		Unearned Consulting Fees (L)			3,500
		To adjust for fees received for services			
		not yet performed.			
	31	Office Supplies Expense (E)		210	
		Office Supplies (A)			210
		To adjust for expense of office supplies			
		used during the month.			
	31	Income Tax Expense (E)		294	
		Income Taxes Payable (L)			294
		To accrue income taxes for March.			

Financial Planners, Inc.
Income Statement
For the Month Ended March 31, 19x1

Revenue:

Consulting fees $28,500

Expenses:

Salaries expense	$13,325	
Commissions expense	5,900	
Travel and entertainment expense.	2,650	
Rent expense.	1,600	
Insurance expense.	300	
Depreciation expense—		
office equipment.	95	
Office supplies expense	210	
Utilities expense.	185	
Communications expense	580	
Advertising expense	715	

Total expenses   25,560

Net income before taxes . . . . $ 2,940

Income tax expense   294

Net income . . . . $ 2,646

Financial Planners, Inc.
Balance Sheet
March 31, 19x1

Assets		**Liabilities and Stockholders' Equity**	
Current assets:		Liabilities:	
Cash	$32,778	Accounts payable	$ 4,500
Accounts receivable	12,940	Salaries payable	1,325
Office supplies	140	Commissions payable.	900
Prepaid rent	3,200	Unearned consulting fees	3,500
Prepaid insurance	3,300	Income taxes payable.	294
Total current assets.	$52,358	Total liabilities	$10,510
Noncurrent assets:		Stockholders' equity:	
Security deposit	$ 2,400	Capital stock.	$50,000
Office equipment	5,670	Retained deficit	(186)
Less: Accumulated depreciation—			
office equipment	95		
Total noncurrent assets	$ 7,975	Total stockholders' equity	$49,814
Total assets	$60,333	Total liabilities and stockholders' equity . .	$60,333

GENERAL JOURNAL				J10
Date	Account Titles and Explanation	Ref.	Debit	Credit
Closing entries:				
19x1 Mar. 31	Consulting Fees (R)		28,500	
	Income Summary (SE)			28,500
	To close revenue account.			
31	Income Summary (SE)		25,854	
	Salaries Expense (E)			13,325
	Commissions Expense (E)			5,900
	Travel and Entertainment Expense (E)			2,650
	Advertising Expense (E)			715
	Communications Expense (E)			580
	Utilities Expense (E)			185
	Rent Expense (E)			1,600
	Depreciation Expense—Office			
	Equipment (E)			95
	Insurance Expense (E)			300
	Office Supplies Expense (E)			210
	Income Tax Expense (E)			294
	To close expense accounts.			
31	Income Summary (SE)		2,646	
	Retained Earnings (SE)			2,646
	To close the Income Summary account.			

Reversing Entries

From the discussion on adjusting entries earlier in the chapter, you learned that certain amounts must be accrued at the end of the accounting period to reflect receivables, liabilities, revenues, and expenses correctly. For example, LMI made the following end-of-period adjusting entry for accrued salaries.

```
19x2
Jan. 31   Salaries Expense (E) . . . . . . . . . . . . . . . . . . . . . .   2,115
               Salaries Payable (L) . . . . . . . . . . . . . . . . . . . .          2,115
                  To accrue month-end unpaid salaries.
```

This entry affects the two ledger accounts as follows:

Salaries Expense						Account No. 511
Date		Explanation	Ref.	Debit	Credit	Balance Debit (Credit)
19x2 Jan.	14	Payroll	J2	14,000		14,000
	28	Payroll	J4	13,000		27,000
	31	Adjusting	J5	2,115		29,115
	31	Close account	J6		29,115	0

Salaries Payable						Account No. 212
Date		Explanation	Ref.	Debit	Credit	Balance (Debit) Credit
19x2						
Jan.	31	Adjusting	J5		2,115	2,115

The $2,115 in the liability account, Salaries Payable, would normally be eliminated at the next payroll date. For example, if LMI has a $15,000 total payroll on February 11, 19x2, the following journal entry would be made:

```
19x2
Feb. 11   Salaries Expense (E) . . . . . . . . . . . . . . . . . . . . .   12,885
               Salaries Payable (L). . . . . . . . . . . . . . . . . . . . .    2,115
                  Cash (A). . . . . . . . . . . . . . . . . . . . . . . . .           15,000
                  To record February 11, 19x2, payroll.
```

This entry eliminates the $2,115 balance in Salaries Payable and records a $12,885 Salaries Expense for work performed in February. The person in charge of recording the payroll must be aware that $2,115 has previously been accrued or else the February payroll expense will be overstated.

Objective 7
How reversing entries are used.

The potential confusion and the need to remember to reflect the accrual when the next payroll is processed can be removed by using a reversing entry. A reversing entry is made at the beginning of each new accounting period to eliminate the effects of any previous accrual entries. This process allows the payroll journal entry to be simplified to its familiar form—a debit to Salaries Expense and a credit to Cash. In the LMI case, a reversing entry may be made relating to the payroll. The reversing entry along with the subsequent payroll entry would be as follows:

19x2		
Feb. 1 Salaries Payable (L)	2,115	
Salaries Expense (E)		2,115
To reverse January 31, 19x2, accrual.		
11 Salaries Expense (E)	15,000	
Cash (A)		15,000
To record February 11, 19x2, payroll.		

After these two entries are posted to the ledger, the balance in Salaries Payable is once again zero, and the amount of Salaries Expense at February 11 is again $12,885. This is the same result that was achieved without reversing entries.

Salaries Payable   Account No. 212

Date		Explanation	Ref.	Debit	Credit	Balance (Debit) Credit
19x2 Jan.	31	Adjusting	J5		2,115	2,115
Feb.	1	Reversal	J7	2,115		0

Salaries Expense   Account No. 511

Date		Explanation	Ref.	Debit	Credit	Balance Debit (Credit)
19x2 Jan.	14	Payroll	J2	14,000		14,000
	28	Payroll	J4	13,000		27,000
	31	Adjusting	J5	2,115		29,115
	31	Close account	J6		29,115	0
Feb.	1	Reversal	J7		2,115	(2,115)
	11	Payroll	J8	15,000		12,885

Keep this critical point in mind when thinking about reversing entries: Using reversing entries will not alter the amounts reported on the financial statements. Also, not all adjusting entries can be reversed. Only those entries that require a related entry in the next period can be reversed. Finally, since reversing entries are not necessary, they are often not used.

—————— APPENDIX • 4B ————————————————————————————————————

Introducing a Simple Analysis of Financial Statements

After studying the beginning history of the Fitness Clinic in Chapter 3, you learned that income statements are tools for analyzing the operating results of a company and that this shows how net assets flow from operating activities. In this appendix we continue to explore how financial statements are analyzed and used in business decisions.

The financial statements generated by the accounting cycle are themselves an analysis of the financial condition of a business. For example, the balance sheet in Exhibit 4–6 has a fairly standardized format, with assets divided into current and noncurrent portions and with certain accounts shown separately and other accounts combined. Income statements, too, organize the information in such a way that certain activities are highlighted and the net result, net income, is given prominence as the "bottom line" amount.

If the basic financial statements are an analysis in themselves, is any further analysis necessary? The answer is yes, because different types of comparison across time or across businesses often require some simplifying transformation of the amounts that appear in financial statements.

One of the most basic ways to help analyze financial statement data is to eliminate the size effect of the reported amounts. To look beyond the dollar measures for year-to-year or company-to-company comparisons, analysts frequently state dollar amounts as percentages. Dollar amounts in balance sheets are usually expressed as a percentage of total assets. Dollar amounts in the income statement are usually expressed as a percentage of sales or total revenues. When balance sheets or other financial statements are stated as percentages, they are referred to as common-size statements.

To illustrate this form of analysis, consider a bank loan officer who is trying to decide whether to give a loan to LMI at the end of January. One key element in loan evaluations is the liquidity of the borrower, which is a measure of a business's ability to pay its current liabilities with cash or other current assets soon expected to be converted to cash. LMI reported the following balance sheet data as of the end of January 19x2, stated in terms of both dollars and percentages:

Cash	$ 1,260	2.1%
Accounts receivable	12,150	20.1
Notes receivable	4,800	8.0
Other current assets	27,364	45.3
Total current assets	$45,574	75.5%
Noncurrent assets	14,750	24.5
Total assets	$60,324	100.0%
Total liabilities	$11,005	18.2%
Total stockholders' equity	49,319	81.8
Total liabilities and stockholders' equity	$60,324	100.0%

LMI has only 2.1% of its assets in cash at the end of January, but its current assets, cash and those assets to be converted into cash or to be used up in the next year or operating cycle whichever is longer, represent 75.5% of its assets.

Objective 8
How the income statement and balance sheet can be converted to common-size statements by using percentages of total revenues or total assets.

This relationship of cash to other assets is important in analyzing whether too little or too much cash is maintained. Idle cash earns no return, and good cash management involves keeping idle cash to a minimum.

The proportion of current to noncurrent assets varies with the economic characteristics of an industry. LMI has no inventory and has a modest accounts receivable, which would point to current assets being a smaller percentage of total assets than they would be in an industry with different characteristics. But LMI rents its facilities, and, therefore, its noncurrent assets are very low.

The amount of a company's liability balance relative to its stockholders' equity is also considered of critical importance in evaluating financial health. If a company has a relatively large percentage of debt outstanding relative to stockholders' equity, the company's ability to borrow additional funds may be questioned. The liabilities of LMI are rather small in relation to the total stockholders' equity. This does not necessarily mean that LMI would be considered a good credit risk by bankers.

The relationship of items in LMI's income statement are of interest to management and to outside parties. One way of viewing the income statement that makes it more comparable to that of other companies and other periods is to show all major categories as percentages of total revenues. LMI had total revenues of $59,064 and net income of $9,319 or 15.8% of total revenues ($9,319/$59,064).

Exhibit 4B–1 shows all income statement categories in terms of percentage of total revenues. The major expense categories are salaries, 49.3%; rent, 13.5%; travel and entertainment, 10.2%; income taxes, 3.9%; insurance, 1.7%; office supplies, 1.5%; and all other, 4.1%. These common-size statements help make comparisons within a given business over several accounting periods, or across businesses at a point in time.

All individuals interested in a company may use accounting information to analyze the company's financial results and compare the company with similar companies. Potential and present stockholders, bankers, suppliers, and others must make decisions that require an analysis of financial statements. This subject is explored in greater detail in later chapters.

• KEY TERMS

Adjusted trial balance. Trial balance after all the necessary adjustments have been made.

Adjusting entries. Period-end journal entries used to update accounts and construct financial statements that reflect all of a company's significant economic transactions in conformance with the accrual concept.

Amortization. Process that allocates original costs of intangible noncurrent assets consumed by operating activities over the periods benefited by their consumption.

Contra account. An account whose balance is subtracted from another account to get the net effect or book value. Accumulated Depreciation is an example of a contra account.

Correction process. Process used to correct errors; not to be confused with the adjusting process.

Depreciation. Process that allocates original costs of tangible noncurrent assets consumed by operating activities over the periods benefited by their consumption.

Intangible assets. Assets representing rights that have future benefits such as patents, or copyrights, or trademarks and tradenames.

Net book value of an asset. Asset's original cost less the total amount written off to date, often the original cost minus accumulated depreciation for buildings, plant, and equipment.

EXHIBIT 4B–1

**Income Statement
Showing Percentage
of Total Revenues**

**Legislative Minds, Incorporated
Income Statement
For the Month Ended January 31, 19x2**

	Dollar Amount	Percentage of Total Revenues
Revenue:		
Consulting fees.	$59,000	99.9
Expenses:		
Salaries expense.	$29,115	49.3
Travel and entertainment expense	6,000	10.2
Communications expense	1,300	2.2
Utilities expense	450	0.8
Postage expense.	400	0.7
Rent expense	8,000	13.5
Insurance expense.	1,000	1.7
Office supplies expense.	900	1.5
Depreciation expense—office equipment	50	0.1
Amortization expense.	200	0.3
Total expenses.	$47,415	80.3
Income before other revenue.	$11,585	19.6
Other revenue:		
Interest revenue	64	0.1
Net income before taxes	$11,649	19.7
Income tax expense	2,330	3.9
Net income	$ 9,319	15.8

Period-end accruals. Adjusting entries to record revenues, expenses, receivables, and payables that have accumulated during the accounting period but have not as yet been recorded.

Period-end allocations. Adjusting entries that involve (*a*) revenue-related and (*b*) expense-related account balances that affect more than one period and therefore must be spread among accounting periods.

Post-closing trial balance. Gives the period-end account balances after all temporary accounts have been closed to retained earnings.

Retained deficit. A negative retained earnings balance or a debit balance in the cumulative sum of periodic net income less net losses and dividends.

Tangible assets. Assets with physical form such as land, buildings, and equipment.

Worksheet. Tool used by accountants to show the flow of account balances from an unadjusted trial balance to the financial statements; provides an overview of the end-of-period accounting cycle steps of adjusting and preparing financial statements.

• **Appendix Key Terms** ———————————————

Common-size statements. Dollar amounts of a company's financial statements expressed in percentage form.

Liquidity. A business's ability to meet current obligations by means of available cash and other assets that can be converted to cash or used as cash.

Reversing entry. Entry made at the beginning of a new accounting period to eliminate the effects of a previous accrual entry; these entries do not affect the income statement amounts or the period-end balance sheet amounts.

• SYNONYMS

Accounting cycle; accounting period.

Adjusting entries; period-end accruals and allocations.

Allocation; depreciation; amortization.

Post-closing trial balance; after-closing trial balance.

Tangible asset; physical asset.

• QUESTIONS

1. Describe the six steps of the accounting cycle. Discuss the timing of each step in the accounting period.
2. Which steps of the accounting cycle occur only at the end of a company's accounting period? Why?
3. Describe the two major categories of adjusting entries.
4. Give two examples of period-end allocations.
5. Give two examples of period-end accruals.
6. How does the unadjusted trial balance differ from the adjusted trial balance?
7. What question is answered by allocation-type adjusting entries? What question is answered by accrual-type adjusting entries?
8. Consider the adjusting entry to record unpaid salaries. Is this entry based on the concept of revenue recognition or matching? Why?
9. What is a worksheet? What is its purpose?
10. Explain the relation between the 12 worksheet columns and the first five steps of the accounting cycle.
11. What cycle steps included in the worksheet must be formally performed elsewhere in records of the company to generate the same financial statement results reported in the worksheet?
12. What financial statements can be provided from a worksheet prepared at the end of the accounting period?
13. When does the closing process occur?
14. What accounts are affected by the closing process?
15. What is the purpose of the Income Summary account and in which step of the accounting cycle is it employed?
16. In what permanent account is the effect of net income or loss from all periods reported?
17. Define the correction process. Are correcting entries the same as adjusting entries?
18. Give two examples of when correcting entries are necessary.
19. What is the effect on the balance sheet when the JMK Company erroneously records the same payment of an account payable twice? Only one check was written.

• Appendix Questions

20. What is a reversing entry? What is its purpose?
21. Describe a situation in which a reversing entry is used.
22. Describe two percentage relationships that can be used to analyze financial statements.

• EXERCISES

E 4–1

Effect of Adjusting Entries on Balance Sheet

L.O.3

Garnet Corporation recorded the following adjusting entries at the end of 19x3:

a.	Rent Expense (E)	1,500	
	Prepaid Rent (A)		1,500
b.	Unearned Revenue (L)	3,000	
	Service Revenue (R)		3,000

Required:
Explain the impact of each adjusting entry on the year-end balance sheet amounts for assets, liabilities, and stockholders' equity (after closing revenues and expenses to retained earnings).

E 4–2

Effect of Adjusting Entries on Balance Sheet

L.O.3

Arnett Corporation recorded the following adjusting entries at the end of 19x4:

a.	Advertising Expense (E)	4,000	
	Prepaid Advertising (A)		4,000
b.	Wage Expense (E)	3,000	
	Accrued Wages Payable (L)		3,000
c.	Interest Receivable (A)	1,000	
	Interest Income (R)		1,000

Required:
Explain the impact of each adjusting entry of the year-end balance sheet amounts for assets, liabilities, and stockholders' equity (after closing).

E 4–3

Adjusting Entries

L.O.1, 2

Beltway Corporation noted that the following items required adjusting entries at the end of 19x4:

a. Cash of $3,000 for services not yet performed was recorded as service revenue in 19x4.
b. Wages of $4,800 for work performed in 19x4 had not yet been paid to hourly employees.
c. Utilities of $2,000 for power used in 19x4 had not yet been billed to or paid for by Beltway.

Required:
Record the adjusting entries for these items.

E 4–4

Adjusting Entries

L.O.1, 2

Meltway Corporation noted that the following items required adjusting entries at the end of 19x5:

a. A cash payment of $60,000 was recorded as a debit to prepaid rent on July 1, 19x5 for rental equipment for the next 18 months.
b. Cash of $90,000 was received on October 1, 19x5, from customers for heating systems maintenance contracts that called for inspections once a month by Meltway over the next 15 months. Unearned Service Revenue was credited at that time.
c. Services performed during the last week of 19x5 but not yet billed to customers amounted to $8,000. The wages of the service employees for this work, $2,500, would not be paid until 19x6.

Required:
Record the adjusting journal entries for these items.

E 4–5

Recording Earned Revenue

L.O.1

In May, cash of $15,000 was collected in advance on magazine subscriptions and credited to the Unearned Subscriptions account. Of this $15,000, $9,000 was earned by delivery of magazines in June. Prepare the June 30 journal entry needed to record revenue earned. What was the cash flow related to this entry?

E 4–6
*Determining Rent
Payment (Challenging)*
L.O.1

Company Z debits all rent payments for the facilities it uses to the Prepaid Rent account. On January 1, 19xx, the Prepaid Rent account had a $2,000 debit balance. The income statement for the first six months of 19xx showed $1,500 of rent expense, and the June 30, 19xx, balance sheet showed prepaid rent of $800. Compute the amount of cash paid by Company Z for rent in the first six months of 19xx. What is the difference between rent expense and cash paid to the landlord? Explain your answer.

E 4–7
*Determining Insurance
Expense*
L.O.1

On September 30, 19xx, the Joy Company recorded the $8,000 payment for a two-year insurance policy as a prepaid asset. The company's fiscal year ends on December 31. Journalize the amount the Joy Company would record as insurance expense for 19xx.

E 4–8
Depreciation
L.O.1

On April 1, 19xx, Birdwatchers, Inc., has a balance of $45,000 in its Equipment account and a balance of $7,600 in its Accumulated Depreciation—Equipment account. Depreciation expense for the quarter ending June 30, 19xx, is $3,800. Record the adjusting journal entry made at the end of the quarter and show the balance sheet presentation related to equipment for Birdwatchers, assuming no equipment was purchased or sold during the quarter.

E 4–9
*Determining Supplies
Purchased and
Consumed (Challenging)*
L.O.1

During 19x1, the Whitney Corporation purchased $12,150 of office supplies and recorded the purchases in the Office Supplies account. On January 1, 19x1, the corporation had a balance of $600 in the Office Supplies account. On December 31, 19x1, the corporation had $400 of office supplies on hand.

During the next year 19x2, Whitney used $6,100 of supplies and had $850 of office supplies on hand at the end of the year. (Hint: Use a T account to answer the questions.)

Required:
1. Determine the amount of supplies used during 19x1 and the amount of supplies purchased during 19x2.
2. Prepare the adjusting journal entries in informal journal form that the Whitney Corporation made to record the supplies used during 19x1 and 19x2.

E 4–10
*Alternative Recording
Methods*
L.O.1

Patrick's Toy Shop prepaid $2,400 for three months' rent on January 1, 19xx. Prepare the journal entries Patrick would make on January 1 and January 31 regarding rent, using two different methods:

a. Rent Expense is initially debited for $2,400.
b. Prepaid Rent is initially debited for $2,400.

E 4–11
*Determining Accrued
Salaries*
L.O.1

A salesperson started working at Super Sam's Discount Store on August 1, 19x1, at a salary of $700 per month. The salesperson quit working at the store on January 15, 19x2. Super Sam's pays its salespeople on the 15th of each month for work done through that date. Determine the amount of salaries expense and prepare the journal entries that Super Sam's should record for this salesperson for each monthly payment plus any adjusting entries at December 31, 19x1. Include the final payment of January 15, 19x2. Assume each month has 30 days.

E 4–12
*Journal Entries and
Analyzing Their Effects*
L.O.1

For the following transactions (1) record the journal entry or adjusting entry and (2) indicate the impact on net income and cash (I = increase; D = decrease; NE = no effect):

a. Recorded sales of $6,000 on open account.
b. Purchased supplies of $3,000 for cash.
c. Accrued income taxes of $800 as a year-end adjustment.
d. Recorded depreciation for the year of $1,200.
e. Received $1,500 for services to be performed next year.
f. Paid salaries of $14,000 in cash.

g. Recorded cash sales of $3,000.
h. Paid $8,000 cash for January and February rent on January 1, 19xx. Recorded January rent expense at this time.
i. Purchased a piece of office equipment for $2,000 cash.
j. Accrued $1,600 salaries at month-end.
k. Paid the monthly telephone bill of $400 in cash.
l. Received proceeds from a note receivable of $20,000 plus $1,000 of interest.
m. Paid a two-year insurance premium of $36,000 in advance.
n. Paid utilities for the month of $900 in cash.
o. Recorded monthly insurance expense paid for in *m* above.

E 4–13
Adjusting Entries
L.O.1

For the following transactions, record (1) the journal entry made; and (2) the effect and amount of the entry on net income, total assets, and cash.

a. Cash of $200 had been received last year for services performed during the current year. (Record entry for the current year only.)
b. During the last month of the year, $900 cash is received for services to be performed next year.
c. Interest for the year of $4,800 on a note payable is recorded but not yet paid.
d. Of the amount charged to Rent Expense during the year, $1,500 applies to the following year.

E 4–14
Effect of Adjusting Entry Errors
L.O.1, 8

At the end of 19x1, the Lawrence Company had balances as shown in column 1 below. If correct adjusting entries had been made, the adjusted balances would be as shown in column 2.

		(1) Amount per Books	(2) Correct Amount
a.	Office Supplies	$500	$350
b.	Prepaid Insurance	300	450
c.	Unearned Revenue	700	580
d.	Salaries Payable	500	300
e.	Income Taxes Payable (the taxes were paid in January)	500	775

Assume that the adjusting entries for 19x1 were not made. Record the necessary adjusting entries, and state the effect of each omission on 19x1 net income, using the following symbols:

Symbols	Effect
O	Overstatement
U	Understatement
N	No effect

E 4–15
Error Correction
L.O.6

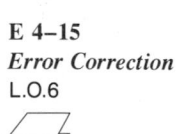

While preparing to close its year-end books, Insiders, Inc., discovers the following errors:

a. Depreciation expense of $5,200 for the year was charged to Travel and Entertainment Expense.
b. Salaries at the end of the year for $13,300 were accrued to the Notes Payable account.
c. An invoice received for $10,000 of supplies purchased on account during the year was recorded under Salaries Payable. When the invoice was paid, Accounts Payable was debited.

Required:
Show the incorrect journal entries that were initially made and the correct journal entries that should have been made. Prepare the journal entries to correct the errors.

E 4–16
Error Correction
L.O.6

In posting transactions for the month, the bookkeeper for Star Jewelry Company made the errors described below. For each error, indicate the amount by which the month-end trial balance totals would be out of balance because of that transaction. Also indicate whether the total for the debit or the credit column would be excessive. Consider each transaction independently.

Example: A debit to Cash of $88 was posted as $888. (The credit was properly posted.)
Answer: $800 excess debit to Cash.

a. A debit of $250 to Supplies Inventory was posted as $520. (The credit was properly posted.)
b. An entry debiting Salary Expense and crediting Cash for $300 was not posted.
c. A credit of $80 to Accounts Payable was not posted. (The debit was properly posted.)
d. A credit of $100 to Accounts Receivable was posted to Sales. (The debit was properly posted.)
e. A debit of $410 to Equipment was posted twice. (The credit was properly posted.)

E 4–17
Mutliple Choice
L.O.3, 5

1. For the year ended December 31, 19x1, Murphy Corporation has net income of $74,500. The entry to close this amount to the balance sheet is—
   a. Debit net income and credit income summary.
   b. Debit retained earnings and credit net income.
   c. Debit income summary and credit retained earnings.
   d. Debit income summary and credit various revenue and expense accounts.
   e. None of the above.
2. At the end of 19x2, Jeffries Company had total expenses of $82,875, total revenues of $95,325, total dividends of $4,000, and a pre-closing retained earnings balance of $158,000. The ending retained earnings balance should be—
   a. $166,450.
   b. $141,550.
   c. $174,450.
   d. $149,550.
   e. None of the above.
3. Bests Foods contracted for $240,000 of newspaper advertising equal to 240 full-page ads to be used as desired over a two-year period beginning July 1, 19x1. At the end of 19x1, a total of 40 full-page ads had been run and another 10 had been slated to be run the first week of 19x2. The balance in prepaid advertising at the end of 19x1 should be—
   a. $0.
   b. $180,000.
   c. $190,000.
   d. $200,000.
   e. None of the above.
4. Closing entries—
   a. Must be formally posted to the ledger accounts.
   b. Are recorded every time a worksheet is prepared.
   c. Eliminate the balance in all nominal accounts.
   d. Only a and c are correct.
   e. All of the above.
5. Z Company's year-end unadjusted trial balance reported retained earnings of $492,000. Dividends of $10,000 were declared and paid during the year. The year-end balance sheet reported retained earnings of $526,000. Net income for the year must have been—
   a. $24,000.
   b. $34,000.
   c. $54,000.
   d. $10,000.
   e. None of the above.

E 4–18
Ralston Purina Annual Report
L.O.1

Consider the Ralston Purina annual report reproduced in Appendix E at the back of this text.

Required:
1. From the Consolidated Statement of Earnings and the Consolidated Balance Sheet, identify the following amounts:
   a. Net earnings, fiscal 1992.
   b. Retained earnings, September 30, 1991.
   c. Retained earnings, September 30, 1992.
2. Compute the amount of dividends declared during fiscal 1992 using the following relationship:

> Retained earnings, beginning of period
> Plus: Net earnings for period
> Less: Dividends declared for period
> Equals: Retained earnings, end of period

E 4–19
Recording and Analysis of Entries
L.O.2

The following independent transactions pertain to the operations of a management consulting company with a December 31 year-end.

a. Purchased $18,000 of office furniture for cash of $3,000 and a note of $15,000.
b. Borrowed $2,000 to be repaid next year.
c. Received $17,000 cash from the maturity value of an interest-bearing investment that had cost $15,500 earlier this year. Interest had not been accrued.
d. Recorded credit sales of $8,000.
e. Paid invoice of $15,000 on accounts due.

Required:
1. Record the necessary entries for *a* through *e* above.
2. Indicate the impact on *net income* and cash for items *a* through *e* above.
3. For each item *a* through *e* above indicate whether it represents an operating (O), financing (F), or investing (I) activity—or some combination of these.

E 4–20
Multiple Choice
L.O.1, 3

1. If X Company debits an expense account instead of the Land account when purchasing land, this error will—
   a. Overstate expenses.
   b. Understate retained earnings.
   c. Understate assets.
   d. All of the above.
   e. None of the above.
2. If, at the end of an accounting period, Z Company computes its depreciation for the period to be $15,000, they should—
   a. Debit the asset and credit Retained Earnings $15,000.
   b. Debit Depreciation Expense and credit Accumulated Depreciation $15,000.
   c. Debit Accumulated Depreciation and credit Depreciation Expense $15,000.
   d. Debit Retained Earnings and credit the asset $15,000.
   e. None of the above.
3. Z Company records $2,000 of wages payable on the last day of the accounting period.
   a. This is an allocation-type adjusting entry.
   b. This is an external transaction.
   c. This is an accrual-type adjusting entry.
   d. This is a simple payment of wages in cash.
   e. None of the above.

4. Which of the following adjusting entries addresses the question, What accounts are not included as assets and/or liabilities in the unadjusted trial balance but are assets and/or liabilities?
   a. Adjusting for interest payable.
   b. Adjusting for accumulated depreciation.
   c. Adjusting for amortization of a trademark.
   d. Adjusting for part of a long-term prepaid asset.
   e. None of the above.

· Appendix Exercises

E 4–21
Reversing Entries
L.O.7

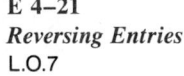

On December 31, 19x1, the year-end unpaid salaries of Miller, Inc., amounted to $15,964. On January 7, 19x2, Miller pays $32,500 to its employees. Record the 19x1 year-end adjusting entry, and the reversing entry and entry to record the payment to employees made in 19x2.

E 4–22
Common-Size Income Statement
L.O.8

BES, Inc., has the following excerpt from its adjusted trial balance on December 31, 19xx:

	Debits	Credits
Sales Revenue		$92,400
Salaries Expense	$53,000	
Communications Expense	4,830	
Utilities Expense	3,600	
Rent Expense	12,000	
Insurance Expense	1,800	
Depreciation Expense	2,100	
Advertising Expense	900	
Interest Expense	500	
Totals	$78,730	$92,400

Required:
Prepare a year-end income statement including each item's percentage of total revenue, thus converting it to a common-size income statement. State percentages to the nearest tenth (.xxx = x.x%).

• PROBLEMS

P 4–1
*Preparing Closing
Entries and the
Financial Statements*
L.O.2, 3

The Erie Company's adjusted trial balance for the year ended December 31, 19x1, appears below. The accounts are listed in alphabetical order.

Erie Company
Adjusted Trial Balance
December 31, 19x1

	Debits	Credits
Accounts Payable		$ 37,210
Accounts Receivable.	$ 53,000	
Accumulated Depreciation—Buildings		30,000
Accumulated Depreciation—Equipment		36,000
Buildings	170,000	
Capital Stock		130,000
Cash	58,710	
Communications Expense	1,450	
Delivery Expense	1,800	
Depreciation Expense—Buildings and Equipment	13,000	
Equipment	90,000	
Income Tax Expense.	12,960	
Income Taxes Payable		10,960
Insurance Expense	1,500	
Interest Expense	29,700	
Interest Revenue		6,500
Investments, Short-Term	45,000	
Land.	55,000	
Notes Payable, Long-Term		235,000
Notes Receivable, Short-Term.	10,000	
Patents and Trademarks	50,000	
Prepaid Insurance	8,000	
Property Taxes Expense	9,000	
Property Tax Payable		15,000
Retained Earnings, 1/1/x1		33,000
Salaries Expense	60,100	
Salaries Payable		10,000
Service Revenue		154,750
Supplies	28,100	
Utilities Expense	1,100	
Totals	$698,420	$698,420

Required:
1. Using the accounts listed in the trial balance, prepare an income statement and a retained earnings statement for the year ended December 31, 19x1.
2. Prepare the December 31, 19x1, classified balance sheet for Erie. Remember to include current and noncurrent assets and liabilities.
3. Prepare the closing entries for Erie as of December 31, 19x1.

P 4–2

Adjusting Entries

L.O.2

Preview Properties is a real estate company with the following transactions for 19xx:

19xx

July 1 Prepayment of rent of $2,400 for two years is recorded in the Prepaid Rent account.

Sept. 30 Prepayment of insurance of $1,800 for one year is recorded in the Insurance Expense account.

Dec. 31 The company pays its employees on Fridays. The year 19xx ends on Wednesday when $2,500 is owed to employees for work performed. No entry has been made.

31 Depreciation of $3,000 on office equipment for 19xx is unrecorded.

31 A major sale was completed on December 29, 19xx, for $60,000. The salesperson's commission is $6,000. The sale was made on account and has not been recorded. The commission also has not been recorded or paid.

Required:

Record all necessary journal entries including adjusting entries at period-end based on the above facts.

P 4–3

Adjusting Entries

L.O.2

The fiscal year of the Blaze Corporation ends on December 31. Examination of the accounting records and related documents of the company on December 31, 19x1, provides the following information that should be considered for adjusting entries:

a. The company paid a $2,100 fire insurance premium covering the period from July 1, 19x1, through January 31, 19x2. The payment was recorded as follows:

Insurance Expense	2,100	
Cash		2,100

b. On October 1, 19x1, the company paid $2,400 to rent a machine for the six-month period ending March 31, 19x2. At the time of payment, Prepaid Rent was debited.

c. The bookkeeper recorded a $3,000 payment to rent a building for November 19x1 as a debit to Prepaid Insurance and a credit to Cash.

d. The company used a Supplies Inventory account to record purchases of supplies during the year. The balance in this account on January 1, 19x1, was $1,200. During the year, supplies were purchased in the amount of $6,000. On December 31, 19x1, an inventory count showed that supplies on hand amounted to $1,500.

e. On December 31, 19x1, the bookkeeper determined that employees had earned $12,090 in salaries that had not yet been paid.

Required:

Based on the above information, prepare in general journal form the adjusting or correcting journal entries required on December 31, 19x1. Assume that Blaze Corporation has not made any adjusting entries during 19x1.

P 4–4
Adjusting Entries
L.O.1–4

Smintog Company has the following unadjusted trial balance at December 31, 19xx:

Smintog Company
Unadjusted Trial Balance
December 31, 19xx

	Debits	Credits
Cash	$ 1,000	
Accounts Receivable	500	
Prepaid Rent	3,000	
Supplies	600	
Equipment	4,000	
Accumulated Depreciation—Equipment		$ 800
Accounts Payable		400
Notes Payable		2,000
Capital Stock		4,000
Retained Earnings		500
Service Revenue		1,000
Sales Revenue		3,500
Salaries Expense	1,300	
Supplies Expense	1,800	
Totals	$12,200	$12,200

The following information is available at year-end:

a. Prepaid rent at December 31, 19xx, is $1,000.
b. The equipment has a useful life of 20 years, with no residual value. Unrecorded depreciation for the year is $200.
c. Supplies inventory remaining at December 31, 19xx, is actually $900.
d. Employees' salaries of $400 incurred at the end of 19xx were neither paid nor recorded.
e. Of the $1,000 of service revenue recorded, $500 was for deposits paid to Smintog from customers for services not performed as of December 31, 19xx.

Required:
Give the adjusting journal entries in general journal form for the Smintog Company using the unadjusted trial balance and the additional information.

P 4–5

Preparing a Worksheet

L.O.1, 2, 4

Edston's Plastics Company, Inc., has the following unadjusted trial balance at December 31, 19x1:

Edston's Plastics Company, Inc.
Unadjusted Trial Balance
December 31, 19x1

	Debits	Credits
Cash	$ 5,300	
Supplies Inventory	600	
Accounts Receivable	18,000	
Note Receivable	6,000	
Prepaid Rent	2,400	
Equipment	22,800	
Accumulated Depreciation—Equipment		$ 3,200
Accounts Payable		5,200
Notes Payable		15,000
Capital Stock		20,000
Retained Earnings		7,450
Sales Revenue		27,800
Rent Expense	2,400	
Salaries Expense	19,000	
Maintenance Expense	1,400	
Utilities Expense	750	
Totals	$78,650	$78,650

The following information is available at month-end:

a. Depreciation on the equipment for the month is $150.
b. Interest on the note receivable is $70 for the month.
c. Interest on the note payable is $225 for the month.
d. An inventory of supplies on hand shows $450 on December 31, 19x1.
e. Unpaid salaries at month-end are $1,850.
f. An unpaid and unrecorded invoice of $230 for maintenance services received was discovered in the December 31 mail.

Required:

Construct a partial worksheet with the following columns and record the above information into the worksheet:

Unadjusted Trial Balance		Adjustments		Adjusted Trial Balance	
Debit	Credit	Debit	Credit	Debit	Credit

P 4–6
Preparing a Worksheet,
Optional Closing
Entries, and Financial
Statements
L.O.2–4

The unadjusted trial balance and the adjusted trial balance of the Super Shape Health Club are shown below as of the end of the fiscal year December 31, 19xx:

	Unadjusted Trial Balance		Adjusted Trial Balance	
	Debits	Credits	Debits	Credits
Cash	$ 3,020		$ 3,020	
Accounts Receivable	2,200		2,200	
Prepaid Rent.	1,250			
Office Supplies.	160		50	
Exercise Equipment.	23,170		23,170	
Accumulated Depreciation—Exercise Equipment.		$ 4,230		$ 6,680
Salaries Payable		100		345
Interest Payable				500
Income Taxes Payable				2,275
Unearned Membership Fees		900		470
Notes Payable		4,000		4,000
Capital Stock		1,000		1,000
Retained Earnings, 1/1/xx.		1,955		1,955
Membership Fees Earned		41,420		41,850
Interest Expense			500	
Office Supplies Expense	95		205	
Rent Expense	2,750		4,000	
Salaries Expense.	20,960		21,205	
Depreciation Expense—Exercise Equipment			2,450	
Income Tax Expense			2,275	
Totals	$53,605	$53,605	$59,075	$59,075

Required:
1. Prepare the complete worksheet for Super Shape Health Club.
2. Prepare a balance sheet and an income statement.
3. (Optional) Prepare the closing entries for Super Shape Health Club at December 31, 19xx.

(Note: Our solution uses a 10-column worksheet like that illustrated on page 174 in the demonstration exercise. You may also use a 12-column worksheet like that illustrated in Exhibit 4–7.)

P 4–7
Preparing a Worksheet and Closing Entries
L.O.3–5

Bart Computer Repairs, Inc., has the following unadjusted trial balance on December 31, 19x1:

Bart Computer Repairs, Inc.
Unadjusted Trial Balance
December 31, 19x1

	Debits	Credits
Cash	$ 8,000	
Accounts Receivable	6,000	
Office Supplies	1,000	
Building	50,000	
Land	12,000	
Accounts Payable		$ 8,500
Notes Payable		35,500
Capital Stock		7,000
Retained Earnings, 1/1/x1		6,900
Service Revenue		50,000
Salaries Expense	18,000	
Rent Expense	8,400	
Office Supplies Expense	1,500	
Utilities Expense	3,000	
Totals	$107,900	$107,900

The following information is available at year-end:

a. Sales on credit of $700 in the last week of December were not recorded because although the work has been completed, no invoices would be mailed until January 3.
b. All office supply purchases are recorded in Office Supply Expense. An inventory taken on December 31 revealed that $1,200 of office supplies are on hand.
c. The building is being depreciated over 20 years at $2,500 per year. No entry has been made for 19x1.
d. The $8,400 of rent expense includes all of 19x1 rent plus a prepayment of the rent for January and February 19x2. The monthly rental fee has remained unchanged during the year.
e. Employees have earned $2,000 for the last week of December but have not yet been paid.
f. Interest owed but not yet recorded on the note payable is $500.
g. The company, using a 20% tax rate, determined income tax expense to be $3,240.

Required:
1. Prepare a worksheet for Bart Computer Repairs, Inc. (Note: Our solution uses a 10-column worksheet like that on page 174 in the demonstration exercise. You may also use a 12-column worksheet like that in Exhibit 4–7.)
2. Prepare the closing entries in general journal form for the year-end.

P 4–8
Transactions, Partial
Worksheet, and Closing
Entries
L.O.1, 2, 4, 5

The balance sheet for Saturn Dry Cleaning at the end of its latest fiscal year appears as follows:

Saturn Dry Cleaning, Inc.
Balance Sheet
August 31, 19xx

Assets		Liabilities and Stockholders' Equity	
Current assets:		**Liabilities:**	
Cash	$ 3,200	Accounts payable	$ 1,940
Accounts receivable	900	Total liabilities	$ 1,940
Supplies	1,600		
Total current assets.	$ 5,700	**Stockholders' equity:**	
		Capital stock.	$ 4,000
Noncurrent assets:		Retained earnings	8,360
Equipment	$10,200	Total stockholders' equity	$12,360
Less: Accumulated depreciation	1,600		
Total noncurrent assets	$ 8,600	Total liabilities and stockholders'	
Total assets	$14,300	equity	$14,300

Business transactions during the accounting period for the month of September 19xx are summarized as follows:

a. Paid rent for the month of $360 in cash.
b. Purchased $100 supplies on account. Recorded as an asset, supplies.
c. Received $3,600 from cash customers for dry cleaning sales.
d. Paid $1,620 on outstanding accounts payable for expenses incurred during August 19xx.
e. Charged $1,180 to customers for dry cleaning sales on account.
f. Paid the following expenses incurred in September in cash:

Salaries expense	$1,280
Utilities expense.	450
Miscellaneous expense.	540

g. Received $775 from customers for services performed before September.
h. Determined by taking an inventory that supplies amounting to $30 were used during the month.
i. Estimated $170 of depreciation on the equipment for the month.
j. Declared and paid cash dividends to stockholders of $500.

Required:
1. Prepare the journal entries in general journal form for the above transactions. All adjustments are included in the above items. Post the journal entries to the appropriate T accounts.
2. Prepare the adjusted trial balance columns, the income statement columns, and the balance sheet columns of a worksheet for Saturn.
3. Prepare and post the closing entries in journal form.

P 4–9
Effects of Errors
L.O.6

At the end of January 19xx, before adjusting entries for the month, the following accounts had balances as shown in column 1 below. If correct adjusting entries had been made, the adjusted balance in the accounts would be as shown in column 2. Assume that adjusting entries were not made. Indicate the effect (understated, overstated, or no effect) and the amount in dollars of the effect of each omission on January net income.

		(1) Amount per Books	(2) Correct Amount
a.	Interest Payable	$ 130	$ 400
b.	Accounts Receivable	2,100	3,300
c.	Dividends Declared and Paid	0	1,000
d.	Prepaid Rent	750	600
e.	Accumulated Depreciation	1,700	2,100
f.	Prepaid Insurance	600	375
g.	Income Tax Expense	900	1,150
h.	Supplies	600	700

P 4–10
Effects of Errors
L.O.6

During August 19xx, the accountant for Wacko Party Stores, Inc., made the accounting errors listed below. Wacko prepared annual financial statements on August 31, 19xx. Assume that you are an auditor for Wacko. Your supervisor has asked you to write a memo indicating the impact of each of the items noted below on (1) net income; (2) total assets; (3) total liabilities; and (4) stockholders' equity. Prepare a well-organized memo to explain the effects of each error clearly. Assume that net income for the year ending August 31, 19xx, has been closed to Retained Earnings.

a. Failure to record the sale of land for cash. The selling price of the land was $5,000 more than it originally cost.
b. Dividends declared and paid in August were not recorded.
c. Store supplies purchased on credit and used up during August were not recorded. The supplies have not yet been paid for.
d. Cash receipt of $10,000 for the issuance of 100 shares of stock was not recorded.
e. One-year insurance premium for $2,000 was paid on August 1, 19xx. The full amount was debited to Prepaid Insurance, and no adjustment has been made.
f. September rent was paid in August and recorded as a debit to Rent Expense and a credit to Cash when paid.

P 4–11
Adjusting Entries and Financial Statements
L.O.2, 3

Fasco Motors, Inc., started business on December 1, 19x1, with the following balance sheet before operations commenced:

Fasco Motors, Inc.
Balance Sheet
December 1, 19x1

Assets		Liabilities and Stockholders' Equity	
Current assets:		**Liabilities:**	
Cash	$ 2,700	Accounts payable	$ 4,200
Supplies	1,600	Notes payable	5,000
Total current assets	$ 4,300	Total liabilities	$ 9,200
Noncurrent assets:		**Stockholders' equity:**	
Equipment	$ 9,900	Capital stock	$20,000
Land	15,000	Total stockholders' equity	$20,000
Total noncurrent assets	$24,900	**Total liabilities and**	
Total assets	$29,200	stockholders' equity	$29,200

During the period from December 1, 19x1, to December 31, 19x1, the following transactions occurred:

a. Paid rent of $2,100 in cash for December 19x1 and January 19x2.

b. Sales of $24,000 were made, all in cash.

c. Salaries amounted to $3,800 paid in cash and $200 payable at year-end.

d. Borrowed $10,000 on a 90-day note to be paid back plus interest of $900 on March 15, 19x2.

e. The December telephone bill of $320 was received but not yet paid on December 31, 19x1.

f. Equipment is being depreciated over three years. One thirty-sixth of the cost is to be depreciated in December.

Required:

1. Prepare a summary journal entry for each of the above to reflect both the original entry and/or the year-end adjusting entry.

2. Prepare the income statement for the month and the December 31, 19x1, balance sheet in good form.

P 4–12
Multiple Choice
(Challenging)
L.O.2–4

1. The only transactions affecting the Accounts Receivable account of the Horton Company during 19x9 were credit sales and payments by credit customers. The ending balance of Accounts Receivable on December 31, 19x9, was $100,000. During 19x9 there were $65,000 in credit sales and the company received $84,000 in payments from customers applicable to their outstanding balances. The beginning balance of Accounts Receivable on January 1, 19x9, was—
   a. $19,000.
   b. $35,000.
   c. $81,000.
   d. $84,000.
   e. $119,000.

2. A post-closing trial balance would consist only of the following:
   a. Assets and liabilities.
   b. Real accounts.
   c. Assets, liabilities, capital stock, and dividends.
   d. Nominal accounts.
   e. Two of the above.

3. Haneco paid $3,600 on August 1, 19x8, for a four-year fire and theft insurance policy; on February 1, 19x9, Haneco paid $2,520 for a three-year auto insurance policy. The Prepaid Insurance account should have a balance of the following amount on September 30, 19x0, the end of Haneco's accounting year:
   a. $1,740.
   b. $2,335.
   c. $2,770.
   d. $3,350.
   e. $3,835.

4. Refer to question 3 above. Determine the amount of insurance expense for Haneco for the year ended September 30, 19x9:
   a. $1,460.
   b. $1,610.
   c. $1,740.
   d. $2,520.
   e. $4,510.

5. All of the following statements are true about the accounting worksheets illustrated in the chapter *except:*
   a. Even though adjusting entries are reflected on the worksheet, adjusting journal entries must be made in the journal to record the information in the formal accounting records.
   b. The Cash balance reported in the "Adjusted Trial Balance" columns of the worksheet is equal to the Cash balance reported in the "Balance Sheet" columns of the worksheet.
   c. The worksheet is basically an accounting tool designed to aid in the preparation of financial statements.

d. The balance sheet columns of the worksheet will not balance without being adjusted for the net income or net loss amount for the period.

e. If expenses exceed revenues during the period, the debit column of the "Income Statement" columns is increased by the amount by which expenses exceed revenues.

P 4–13
Multiple Choice
L.O.2, 3, 6

1. The accounting records of the Alton Company reflected the following information for its accounting year ended December 31, 19x9 (its first year of business):

Sales revenue (20% on credit)	$200,000
Rent paid to the landlord during 19x9 ($2,000 of this amount was paid during 19x9 for January 19x0 rent)	26,000
Office expenses (all paid by cash).	25,000
Selling expense (all paid by cash)	35,000
Depreciation	15,000
Wages paid during 19x9 (not included in office or selling expenses above)	35,000
Accrued wages payable at 12/31/x9.	5,000
Prepaid insurance at 12/31/x9	4,000

Based on the above data the net income for 19x9 on the accrual basis of accounting was—
a. $21,000.
b. $24,000.
c. $60,000.
d. $61,000.
e. $64,000.

2. On May 1, 19x0, the Ace Rental Company collected $2,800 rent for the four-month period ended August 31, 19x0. The amount collected was debited to Cash and credited to Rent Collected in Advance. The company's accounting year ends on July 31. Adjusting entries on July 31, 19x0, that related to this transaction included the following:
a. A credit to Rent Revenue for $700.
b. A debit to Rent Collected in Advance for $700.
c. A debit to Rent Expense for $700.
d. A debit to Prepaid Rent for $2,100.
e. A debit to Rent Collected in Advance for $2,100.

3. On September 30, 19x0, Fox Company paid $8,100 rent for the next nine months on the building it occupies. The company had an opening balance of $1,600 in Prepaid Rent on January 1, 19x0, and made seven monthly payments of $800 each for rent during the period March 1 through September 30, 19x0. The amount of rent expense incurred by the company during the fiscal year ending December 31, 19x0, is—
a. $7,200.
b. $8,300.
c. $9,900.
d. $13,700.
e. $15,300.

4. The Higgins Company annual accounting period ends on December 31. On July 1, 19x0, Higgins purchased for $1,200 a fire insurance policy for the period 7/1/x0–6/30/x1, and on that date the bookkeeper recorded the following entry *twice*:

Prepaid Insurance	1,200	
Cash		1,200

As a result of this error, which of the following is true *at the time the entry* was made?
a. Total assets were overstated.
b. Total liabilities were understated.
c. Net income was understated.
d. Stockholders' equity was understated.
e. Stockholders' equity was unchanged.

5. At the end of the accounting year, Alden Company's accountant made the following entry:

Unearned Fees (L)	2,500	
Fees Earned (A)		2,500

Which one of the following descriptions best applies to this entry?

a. The entry converts a liability (which was incurred when cash was collected for services to be performed) into revenue (which was earned by performance of the services).

b. The entry involves a debit to a liability account and a credit to a receivable account.

c. The entry involves a combination of debit and credit entries that makes no sense.

d. The entry establishes a receivable for fees that have been earned but not yet collected.

e. The entry reflects the fact that the customer has not yet paid the company for services that the company has performed for the customer.

P 4–14
Analysis of T Accounts
(Challenging)
L.O.1–3

The accountant for Wood Products, Inc., lost the details of some of the firm's accounting entries that were made during 19x1. All cash payments are debited to asset accounts (e.g., Prepaid Rent, Prepaid Insurance, Supplies Inventory) and adjusted to expense at year-end.

Missing Amount	What is Known
a. Ending balance in Supplies Inventory	Beginning balance in Supplies Inventory, $1,300 Supplies purchased in 19x1, $14,000 Adjusting entry debit to Supplies Inventory Expense, $14,400
b. Salaries Expense for 19x1	Beginning balance in Salaries Payable, $5,000 Cash paid for salaries, $57,000 Ending balance in Salaries Payable, $8,000
c. Rent Expense for 19x1	Beginning balance in Prepaid Rent, $800 Cash paid for prepaid rent, $6,000 Ending balance in Prepaid Rent, $1,400
d. Insurance Expense for 19x1	Beginning balance in Prepaid Insurance, $600 Cash paid for insurance policy, $3,600 Ending balance in Prepaid Insurance, $900
e. Sales for 19x1	Beginning balance in Accounts Receivable, $10,000 Ending balance in Accounts Receivable, $9,000 Beginning balance in Revenue Received in Advance, $0 Ending balance in Revenue Received in Advance, $2,000 Total cash received from customers in 19x1, $216,000

Required:

Use your understanding of how normal journal entries and adjusting journal entries affect ledger accounts to provide the missing information. (Hint: Set up T accounts to help solve for missing amounts.)

P 4–15
Effects of Errors
L.O.3

The following accounting errors were made by the Maple Leaf Corporation during 19x1. Assume that the financial statements have been prepared for 19x1 and that net income has been closed to retained earnings. Indicate the impact of each error on net income, total assets, total liabilities, and stockholders' equity using the following symbols:

Symbol	Effect
O	Overstatement
U	Understatement
NE	No effect

Note: Four responses are necessary for each error.

a. The adjusting entry for the expiration of $2,000 of Prepaid Rent was not made.
b. The adjusting entry for $5,000 of Accrued Salaries Payable was not made.
c. A $10,000 cash purchase of office machinery was incorrectly recorded as a debit to Supplies Expense.
d. A $932 payment on Accounts Payable was incorrectly recorded as a credit to Cash and a debit to Accounts Payable of $923.
e. November credit sales of $13,000 were incorrectly recorded at $1,300.

P 4–16
Comprehensive
(Challenging)
L.O.1–3, review of
Chapter 3

Amanda and Matthew Darling both have had experience with large public relations companies and are now in the first month of operations with their own company, AMD, Inc. The following transactions have taken place during January 19x1:

a. The owners purchased 10,000 shares of capital stock for $5 per share.
b. Borrowed $20,000 from the First Dallas National Bank to be paid back in July of 19x1. Monthly interest expense of $180 will be paid on the fifth of the next month.
c. Prepaid office rent for January, February, and March with a $3,000 cash payment. In addition, office equipment was rented for $750 per month, and the payment for January was made on January 2.
d. Sold services of $30,000, of which $20,000 was received in cash and the remainder is to be received from customers by February 10.
e. Paid the January telephone bill of $500 and utility bill of $190 in cash.
f. Salaries of $500 per week were paid on Friday of each week. January 31 was a Tuesday, and no entry has been made for the two unpaid workdays. So far, $2,000 cash for salaries has been paid.
g. Office supplies of $1,000 were acquired for cash on January 1, and $200 remained in stock on January 31.
h. Office furniture and equipment, purchased for $18,000, was delivered on January 1. The office equipment is expected to be used over a 10-year period and to have no residual value. Monthly depreciation expense is $150. No cash was paid in January. The invoice has a February 15, 19x1, due date.

Required:
1. Prepare in journal form the journal entries for the above transactions and the January 31 adjustments. Post the entries to the appropriate ledger accounts.
2. Prepare an adjusted trial balance for January 31, 19x1.
3. Prepare the income statement for the month and the balance sheet at January 31, 19x1.
4. (Optional) Discuss AMD's sources and uses of cash. Compare them to the revenues and expenses reported in the income statement, noting differences between revenues versus cash inflows as well as expenses versus cash outflows.

P 4–17
Review of Cash to
Accrual Basis
(Challenging)
L.O.2

Saunders Engineering, Inc., has been in business several years and has prepared its most current comparative balance sheet for December 31, 19x1 and 19x2.

Saunders Engineering, Inc.
Comparative Balance Sheet

	12/31/x2	12/31/x1
Assets		
Current assets:		
Cash	$35,300	$ 5,100
Accounts receivable.	28,300	31,200
Note receivable.	0	8,000
Interest receivable.	0	800
Total current assets	$63,600	$45,100
Noncurrent assets:		
Equipment	$45,000	$40,000
Less: Accumulated depreciation.	36,000	24,000
Total noncurrent assets	$ 9,000	$16,000
Total assets	$72,600	$61,100
Liabilities and Stockholders' Equity		
Liabilities:		
Accounts payable.	$ 1,000	$ 800
Notes payable	0	20,000
Interest payable.	0	1,800
Salaries payable	1,890	2,250
Total liabilities	$ 2,890	$24,850
Stockholders' equity:		
Capital stock	$50,000	$30,000
Retained earnings.	19,710	6,250
Total stockholders' equity	$69,710	$36,250
Total liabilities and stockholders' equity	$72,600	$61,100

The following is a summary of transactions that took place during the year 19x2:

Payments:
a. Purchased equipment. . . . . $ 5,000
b. Paid salaries 76,000
c. Paid property taxes 9,200
d. Paid dividends. 5,000
e. Paid utility bill 1,100
f. Paid note and interest 21,800
g. Paid on accounts payable. 10,500

Receipts:
h. Collected cash from customers 130,000
i. Sold stock. 20,000
j. Collected interest on note receivable 800
k. Collected on note receivable 8,000

Required:

Construct an accrual-based income statement for 19x2 based on the above information. (Hint: Make up a set of T accounts as needed, starting with balance sheet accounts and their beginning and ending balances. Post summary entries for items *a–k* first.)

• Appendix Problems

P 4–18
Common-Size Income Statement, Balance Sheet
L.O.8

Refer to the August 31, 19xx, balance sheet information given in Problem 4–8 for Saturn Dry Cleaning, Inc.

Required:

Prepare a common-size balance sheet using percentages of total assets rounded to one decimal place (.xxx = x.x%).

P 4–19
Common-Size Income Statement, Balance Sheet
L.O.8

Refer to the unadjusted trial balance given in Problem 4–7 for Bart Computer Repairs, Inc. Assume there are no adjustments required for Bart.

Required:

1. Prepare a common-size income statement for 19x1 showing each item as a percent of revenues. Show percentages to one decimal place (x.x%).
2. Compute the new retained earnings balance at December 31, 19x1, and prepare a common-size balance sheet at this date.

P 4–20
Common-Size Income Statement, Balance Sheet, Reversing Entry
L.O.5, 6, 8

Refer to the adjusted trial balance information given for Super Shape Health Club in Problem 4–6.

Required:

1. Prepare a common-size income statement showing each item's percentage to total revenues. Show percentages to one decimal place (x.x%).
2. Prepare the December 31, 19xx, balance sheet.
3. Prepare the post-closing trial balance.
4. Prepare in general journal form the reversing entry for accrued salaries.

P 4–21
Adjusting (and Optional Reversing) Entries
L.O.2, 7

The following internal transactions of the International Corporation require adjusting entries at December 31, 19x1:

a. A balance of $19,000 is in the firm's Prepaid Insurance account. One half of this amount expired during the current period and the other half will expire at December 31, 19x2.
b. $1,100 of unrecorded interest on a $10,000 Note Payable is owed at December 31, 19x1. The interest will be paid in full on February 1, 19x2.
c. $15,000 of the $46,000 Supplies Inventory remains unused.
d. $34,000 of salaries are owed to employees for work done during the current period. The next scheduled payday is January 10, 19x2.
e. $600 of a total $900 in unrecorded service revenue has been earned on Contract #5263. The contract will be completed and the total revenues collected on January 3, 19x2.
f. $38,000 in income tax expense will be due on 19x1 income. The tax will be paid on March 1, 19x2, when the firm files its tax return.

Required:

1. Prepare adjusting entries for the above-listed internal transactions.
2. (Optional) Identify the adjusting entries above that could be reversed to save bookkeeping effort later in 19x2. Prepare those reversing entries.

P 4–22
Adjusting (and Optional Reversing) Entries
L.O.2, 7

The following internal transactions of American Services, Inc., require adjusting entries at December 31, 19x1:

a. $1,200 of supplies, used during the current period, remain in Supplies Inventory.
b. Depreciation for the period on the building is $27,000.
c. Interest of $480 has been earned on a Note Receivable the firm holds. The interest will be received in full on June 1, 19x2.

d. $18,000 remains in the Prepaid Rent account. All of it has expired except for two months of rent at $1,500 per month, which will expire in 19x2.

e. Commissions earned during 19x1 but not yet paid to employees amount to $11,000. These will be paid on January 30, 19x2, along with those commissions earned in January 19x2.

f. Of the $640,000 paid by customers and recorded as service revenue during 19x1 only $635,000 has been earned. The remaining $5,000 will be earned in 19x2.

Required:

1. Prepare adjusting entries for the above-listed internal transactions.
2. (Optional) Identify the adjusting entries above that could be reversed to save bookkeeping effort later in 19x2. Prepare those reversing entries.

• CASES

C 4–1
Accrual versus Cash Accounting
L.O.1, 3

Company A and Company B are identical in every way except for their accounting methods. One uses the cash basis and the other uses the accrual basis. Both started business on January 1, 19x1, and both had identical transactions. Consider the before-closing trial balances of each as of the end of 19x1.

	Company A		Company B	
	Debits	Credits	Debits	Credits
Cash.	$ 80,000		$ 80,000	
Accounts Receivable.	20,000			
Prepaid Rent	5,000			
Prepaid Insurance	3,000			
Land.	40,000		40,000	
Buildings and Equipment	50,000		50,000	
Accumulated Depreciation—Buildings and Equipment		$ 5,000		
Accounts Payable		12,000		
Salaries Payable		8,000		
Capital Stock		158,000		$158,000
Sales.		130,000		110,000
Rent Expense.	10,000		15,000	
Insurance Expense	5,000		8,000	
Salaries Expense	45,000		37,000	
Depreciation Expense—Buildings and Equipment	5,000			
Other Expenses	50,000		38,000	
Totals	$313,000	$313,000	$268,000	$268,000

Required:

As a newly hired bank loan analyst, you have been asked by your boss to write a memo discussing the differences and similarities in the accounting treatments of these two companies on an item-by-item basis. You are also asked to identify the strengths and weaknesses of each system in terms of communicating the economic status of each company and its operating results.

• Evaluating Financial Statements

C 4–2
*Adjusting Journal
Entries—Detroit Edison
Company*
L.O.2

The Detroit Edison Company services a 7,600-square-mile area providing over half of Michigan's population with electric and steam energy. Assume that Detroit Edison has the following transactions (in thousands) during 19x5:

a. Depreciation for the year of $218,500.
b. Records rent expense of $900 that was prepaid in 19x4.
c. Accrued $100 interest owed on a note payable.
d. Salaries earned but not yet paid are $142.
e. Accrues income tax for the year of $50,989.

Required:
Record the above transactions in general journal form.

C 4–3
*Preparation of Balance
Sheet—Molson
Companies Limited*
L.O.2

The following information is taken from the 19x5 annual report of Molson Companies, a Canadian corporation comprised of three principal businesses, Molson Breweries of Canada Limited, Diversey Corporation, and Beaver Lumber Company Limited. All amounts are in thousands.

	May 31	
	19x5	19x4
Accounts payable	$236,176	$216,476
Accounts receivable	191,537	174,104
Capital stock	64,565	63,168
Cash	?	112,064
Dividends payable	5,730	5,713
Equipment	406,912	377,842
Inventories	214,892	200,910
Notes payable, long-term	238,777	237,999
Notes payable, short-term	75,460	69,389
Other long-term assets	121,836	104,028
Other long-term liabilities	72,574	48,974
Prepaid assets, short-term	28,747	17,741
Retained earnings	337,606	?
Taxes payable	3,014	25,289

Required:
Prepare the classified comparative balance sheets for the Molson Companies Limited. Assume dividends are paid once each year. What was the fiscal 19x5 net income?

C 4–4
Adjustments—Hershey
Foods Corporation
L.O.1, 2

Consider the following data taken from Hershey Foods Corporation's 19x7 financial statements:

Income statement data:

Sales	$2,433,793
Costs and expenses	2,139,680
Interest expense	24,711
Income tax expense	121,231
Net income	148,171

Data on liabilities:

Current liabilities:

Accounts payable	$ 130,415
Accrued liabilities:	
Payroll	47,459
Advertising	31,144
Other	42,888
Accrued income taxes	16,414
Short-term notes	31,449
Total current liabilities	$ 299,769
Long-term liabilities	349,230

Memo:

Dividends declared in 19x7	$ 51,467

Required:

Give the best answer to the following multiple-choice questions.

1. Hershey's income tax expense—
   a. Is less than the amount currently owed to the government for income taxes.
   b. Is equal to the amount currently owed to the government for income taxes.
   c. Results in an accrued liability because a portion of 19x7 tax obligation is unpaid at year-end.
   d. Has no effect on the balance sheet items listed above.
2. The accrued liabilities shown in Hershey's balance sheet—
   a. Were closed to the Income Summary account.
   b. Must be reversed in January 19x8.
   c. Represent expenses that will affect the 19x8 income statement.
   d. Were recorded in adjusting entries at year-end.
3. Hershey's net income amount—
   a. Represents cash inflow from customers minus any accounts receivable balance at year-end.
   b. Increased retained earnings more than dividends decreased retained earnings.
   c. Decreased retained earnings more than dividends increased retained earnings.
   d. Has no effect on the balance sheet accounts.

C 4–5
Analysis of Results
(Challenging)
L.O.3

Tax Advice Corporation (TAC) reported the following partial comparative balance sheet data at the end of 19x5:

Partial Balance Sheet Data
($000)

	December 31	
	19x5	**19x4**
Accounts receivable (asset)	$2,940	$2,620
Prepaid rents (asset)	615	750
Prepaid service revenue (liability).	730	850

During 19x5, TAC reported service revenue (its only revenue account) of $18,000,000. Accounts receivable, which only pertain to service customers, were decreased by $16,000,000 during 19x5 for payments received on customer accounts. All of the prepaid service revenue from 19x4 was earned during 19x5. Also, all of the prepaid rent from 19x4 was expensed during 19x5, with total rent expense for 19x5 reported at $2,820,000. All rent must be paid in advance.

Required:
(Hint: Use T accounts to help answer these questions.)
1. How much of the 19x5 service revenue was paid for in cash during 19x5? How much of the 19x5 service revenue was on open customer accounts?
2. How much cash was paid for rent during 19x5?
3. What is the difference between total cash flows from these two items (service revenue, rent expense) and their income statement amounts?

One of the most
valuable characteristics
(if not the most valuable)
is your reputation, your
integrity. You do not acquire
this suddenly, but earn it
and keep it over your
lifetime. It is one of the
characteristics that will
weigh heavily in the
promotability of a person.

Eugene H. Flegm
General Motors Corporation

P·A·R·T

II

*Accounting for Major
Business Transactions*

FINANCIAL STATEMENT COMPONENTS EMPHASIZED IN CHAPTER 5

Hi-Tech Corporation
Balance Sheet For December 31, 1994

	1994	1993
Current assets:		
Cash	$ xxx	$ xxx
Accounts receivable.	**xxx**	**xxx**
Allowance for bad debts.	**(xx)**	**(xx)**
Merchandise inventory.	**xxx**	**xxx**
Total current assets.	$ xxx	$ xxx
Noncurrent assets:		
Total noncurrent assets	$ xxx	$ xxx
Total assets	$ xxx	$ xxx
Current liabilities:		
Accounts payable	**$ xxx**	**$ xxx**
Notes payable.	**xx**	**xx**
Total current liabilities.	$ xxx	$ xxx
Noncurrent liabilities:		
Total noncurrent liabilities	xx	xx
Stockholders' equity:		
Total stockholders' equity	$ xxx	$ xxx
Total liabilities and stockholders' equity	$ xxxx	$ xxxx

Hi-Tech Corporation
Income Statement For 1994

	1994	1993
Sales	**$ xxx**	**$ xxx**
Less: Sales returns and allowances	**(xx)**	**(xx)**
Sales discount	**(xx)**	**(xx)**
Net sales	**$ xxx**	**$ xxx**
Cost of goods sold	**xxx**	**xxx**
Gross margin	**$ xxx**	**$ xxx**
Bad debts expense	**xx**	**xx**
Total expenses.	$ xxx	$ xxx
Net income	$ xx	$ xx

Hi-Tech Corporation
Cash Flow Statement For 1994

	1994	1993
Operating activities		
Receipts from customers	**$ xxx**	**$ xxx**
Payments to suppliers.	**(xxx)**	**(xxx)**
Payments for salaries.	(xxx)	(xxx)
Cash used in operating activities	$ xxx	$ xxx
Investing activities	$ xxx	$ xxx
Financing activities	$ xxxx	$ xxxx
Net change in cash	$ xx	$ xx

5

Accounting for Merchandising Operations—Planning, Purchases, and Sales

Reasonable people—particularly corporate managers and independent auditors—will occasionally disagree over whether the selection or application of a given accounting principle is appropriate. But there should never be a case where what is marginally permissible under the accounting rules prevails over what is ethical in a general sense.

> Dominic A. Tarantino
> Price Waterhouse and
> AICPA

· Learning Objectives

After studying Chapter 5, you should understand

1. The importance of preparing a business plan during the preoperating phase of a business, pp. 213–17.
2. How to account for merchandise inventory—net purchases, cost of goods available for sale, and cost of goods sold, pp. 219–25.
3. How to account for sales revenue, p. 226.
4. The relationship between accounts receivable and bad debts, pp. 226–28.
5. How to account for sales returns and allowances, p. 228.
6. How to account for sales discounts pp. 228–29.
7. Accounting for nonmerchandise-related transactions, pp. 229–30.
8. How to prepare a worksheet and financial statements for a merchandising company, pp. 230–31.
9. How to analyze the effects of a merchandising company's operations, pp. 231–37.
10. Accounting for bad debts, credit card sales, and installment sales (Appendix), pp. 240–46.

Accounting information is a major input for the decision-making process. It helps to explain past performance and enables management to plan for the future. Decision makers outside the business need accounting information for purposes such as investing, lending, regulating, merging, and taxing. Decision makers inside the business use accounting information in investing, financing, and planning and controlling the operations of the business. By following a new business from its inception through an accounting cycle, you will learn how those responsible for planning, financing, and controlling operations create and use accounting systems. This chapter illustrates how an accounting system evolves in response to the needs of both internal and external decision makers.

The emphasis in this chapter is on a merchandising business—a business that buys items from suppliers (wholesalers and manufacturers) and sells them to customers. The distinguishing characteristic of a merchandising company is that a physical product acquired from a supplier is involved. Although the chapter discussion is in a merchandising context, many of the major issues pertain to all types of businesses.

The merchandising company we use as an example in this chapter is a retail computer supply store. You will learn the importance of accurate accounting for merchandise inventory and sales revenue in planning and controlling operations. The chapter concludes with an analysis of the first-quarter operations. The appendix discusses accounting for bad debts in detail, as well as credit card sales and installment sales.

USE OF ACCOUNTING INFORMATION BY ENTREPRENEURS

Usually when people first conceive of a business venture, they have some idea of their goals, where they will obtain their resources, and how they plan to operate their business. Goals may vary from maximizing profits to fulfilling a lifetime desire to own a business. Resources may include personal and creative skills, cash in a savings account, other personal assets, and various sources of credit. Plans may be sketchy, such as "purchase merchandise from manufacturers and sell this merchandise to a retail market," or plans may be elaborate, including detailed statistical analysis with specific operating, marketing, and financing strategies. The goals, resources, and plans are as varied as the people who become entrepreneurs (i.e., people who organize, manage, and assume the risks of a business).

In addition to goals, resources, and plans, a successful business must have a system that will help entrepreneurs organize their thoughts and visualize the probable effect of alternative courses of action. Accounting systems work well in this capacity for a wide variety of business settings. They are designed to measure the progress of a business venture and thus provide a useful structure for business decisions. Forward-looking data can be obtained from a well-structured accounting system, allowing decision makers to forecast the financial consequences of alternative business actions before the actions take place.

Before a business venture can begin, entrepreneurs must look to the future. A crucial step is to visualize the possible outcomes of the business effort. What will the company's status be after operating for a week, a month, or a year? To answer this question, decision makers must imagine future income statements and balance sheets when they plan operations, and they must also foresee the company's possible assets and obligations at future dates.

An accounting system can provide estimates of the possible outcomes that management can expect in the future. These estimates are in the form of projected (forecasted) balance sheets, which provide possible financial states in the future, and projected (forecasted) income statements, which visualize the possible results of future operations. Projected balance sheets and income statements need not be different in format from the statements you have studied in the previous chapters. However, the data used to prepare the statements are derived from a combination of past events and estimates of future events.

Estimating future events for the operations of a business is beneficial in executing the plans of a business organization. Also, the information that accounting systems provide is valuable in guiding the actions of members of the business organization. Some of the questions the accounting system can help answer are, When should inventory be ordered? Are costs within reasonable bounds? Are customers paying invoices in a timely fashion? Are new sources of financing needed?

In this chapter you will follow the exploits of two young entrepreneurs from the initiation of their merchandising business through their first operating period. The section that follows shows how accounting aids in the preoperating and initial operating phases of a business. Subsequent sections illustrate how accounting is used in other phases of business activity.

Preoperating Phase of a Business

Mary and Brad are recent college graduates with strong computer skills. They were both "bitten by the computer bug" early in life and developed compulsive study habits that involved solitary work with their computers as companions. Although Mary and Brad were successful students, their education was rather narrow and did not include any business courses.

A mutual friend introduced Mary to Brad at a computer software fair. They became good friends and had long conversations about computers and their future careers. Soon Mary and Brad realized that their skills and personal compatibility could be the ingredients of a computer-related business venture. They believed that small businesses needed not only the software available from many sources but also the personal instruction and attention their expertise in computers could provide. The two friends decided that a computer supply store with a knowledgeable staff catering to small businesses would be successful because the sales personnel they had dealt with in the large chain stores were either not knowledgeable in computers or were unfriendly to customers.

Objective 1
The importance of preparing a business plan during the preoperating phase of a merchandising business.

In early December 19x1, Mary and Brad incorporated their venture as Byte-Size, Inc. Operations were scheduled to begin on January 2, 19x2. Mary and Brad prepared a planning document they called *First Quarter 19x2*. They each planned to purchase $11,000 of Byte-Size stock, and they estimated their merchandise sales at $125,000 for the first quarter. Their lack of business and accounting knowledge is clearly evident in their planning document, shown in Exhibit 5–1.

Mary and Brad soon realized that their planning of Byte-Size left much to be desired and that their document was not very helpful in actually planning their business operations. They knew that often cash would have to be paid in advance. For example, the landlord of the building they were to rent demanded up-front payments for a security deposit and rent; and their primary supplier, Computech, Inc., required payment for purchases within 20 days of delivery. Since Byte-Size would obviously not sell all of its merchandise in 20 days, some of the company's money would be tied up in merchandise.

EXHIBIT 5–1

The First-Quarter Planning Document

Byte-Size, Inc. First Quarter 19x2		
Starting cash		$ 22,000
Expected sales		+ 125,000
Expected payments:		
Merchandise.	$100,000	
Other.	10,000	− 110,000
Ending cash.		$ 37,000

Mary and Brad also knew they would have to provide credit for some of their customers, but they were only vaguely aware of the advantages and disadvantages of customer credit. Although customer credit would generate more sales, there was the chance of not collecting the full amount that was owed to them.

Now Mary and Brad began to understand that their future success as entrepreneurs depended on many decisions and economic events, some of which were not within their control. Also, they realized that all of the hundreds of events involved in running a business affect the ongoing financial status of the business. Thus, for their business to remain financially solvent throughout a period, Mary and Brad knew they must be able to meet ongoing obligations. Our two aspiring entrepreneurs realized they needed a system that would help them see the probable outcomes of their expected actions.

What should these future business leaders do now? After pondering this for a while, Mary and Brad decided they needed advice from someone knowledgeable in business who could forecast the outcomes of their business venture. Brad's father was an accountant, but Brad had never been interested in his father's profession. In fact, Brad was not really sure what accountants did. However, since his father's advice would be free, Brad invited Mary to his hometown to talk to his father.

Brad's father was surprised that his son, who in the past had no interest in business, was now planning to be an entrepreneur. After listening to their story, Brad's father said, "Your goals and basic strategy seem sound enough, but you are in dire need of a comprehensive business plan and a system of record-keeping." Brad's father continued: "Go to the business school at your university and hire a graduate student. They are often looking for part-time work, and they are not expensive. I'll review the work to be sure everything is in order."

Constructing a
Business Plan for a
Merchandising
Business

Mary and Brad took the advice of Brad's father and hired Frank McDonald-Mellon, or FM, an accounting doctoral student who had worked as a CPA for several years. FM began by giving Mary and Brad the rudiments of an accounting vocabulary in the form of a review of the first four chapters of a financial accounting textbook. He explained terms such as assets, liabilities, stockholders' equity, revenues, expenses, transactions, journal entries, ledger accounts, and financial statements. Soon Mary and Brad realized that their original planning document was of little help because it did not reflect the many transactions and relationships found in an actual business. After providing an introduction to accounting and business terminology, FM studied the needs of Byte-Size and constructed a projected balance sheet and income statement based on assumptions of Byte-Size's first quarter of operations.

To project a quarter-ending balance sheet and income statement, FM listed Byte-Size's starting cash, the timing of its initial cash payments, its expected cash inflow from sales and cash outflows for merchandise, and various other expenditures. Then he traced the expected journal entries to the period-end financial statements. FM discovered that based on the assumed timing of the transactions, the projected cash balance would be inadequate, and a cash shortage would occur during the quarter if the planned operations actually took place.

To ensure continued operations, Byte-Size needed additional capital of at least $20,000. Under the assumption that Byte-Size could borrow $20,000 and repayment of the loan could be delayed for at least three months, FM traced the effects of this additional cash on the projected financial statements. These forward-looking financial statements became the business plan for Byte-Size shown in Exhibit 5–2.

Note that three items occur in Byte-Size's projected statements that were not in the statements of service companies—merchandise inventory (an asset in the balance sheet), cost of goods sold, and gross margin (both found in the income statement). Merchandise inventory (or **inventory**) is an asset equal to the cost of merchandise on hand ready for sale. Cost of goods sold is an expense representing the cost of merchandise sold to customers during the period. Gross margin (sometimes called **gross profit**) is a subtotal on the income statement computed as sales less cost of goods sold. Generally, each item held for sale has a selling price that is a certain percentage higher than its cost; this is called the markup. If a computer retailer purchases a unit for $1,000 and marks it up for sale to $1,500, the markup is $500 or 50%. Gross margin for a period is based on the sum of all the markups on all units sold during the period. Merchandise inventory and cost of goods sold are discussed in detail in a following section titled "Accounting for Merchandise Inventory."

Projected financial statements such as Byte-Size's projected balance sheet, income statement, and cash flow statement given in Exhibit 5–2 are good planning tools. These projected statements are also useful at the end of a period when actual performance is compared with projections. In the paragraphs that follow we review the accounting concepts and techniques used to convert actual transactions into financial statements. Later, you will learn how to compare actual results to projected statements.

Use of the Plan to Acquire Financing.   FM told them, "It won't work without more cash up front. A bank will not give you the loan without a solid assurance of repayment, and you have no track record as successful business people. It's a good plan but you need somebody to back up the loan, a cosigner. You know the old story: They want to lend to people who don't need it." Neither Brad nor Mary smiled. "Anyway," continued FM, "after

EXHIBIT 5–2

First Quarter 19x2 Business Plan for Byte-Size, Inc.

Byte-Size, Inc.
Projected Balance Sheet
March 31, 19x2

Assets		Liabilities and Stockholders' Equity	
Current assets:		Liabilities:	
Cash	$ 9,200	Accounts payable	$ 2,000
Accounts receivable	20,000	Notes payable	20,000
Security deposit	4,500	Interest payable	750
Merchandise inventory	22,500	Total liabilities	$22,750
Total current assets	$56,200	Stockholders' equity:	
Noncurrent assets:		Capital stock	$22,000
Computer	$ 5,000	Retained earnings	16,450
		Total stockholders' equity	$38,450
		Total liabilities and	
Total assets	$61,200	stockholders' equity	$61,200

Byte-Size, Inc.
Projected Income Statement
First Quarter 19x2

Sales		$125,000
Cost of goods sold		93,750
Gross margin		$ 31,250
Salaries	$6,400	
Other expenses	8,400	14,800
Net income		$ 16,450

EXHIBIT 5–2 (*concluded*)

Byte-Size, Inc.
Projected Cash Flow Statement
From Inception to March 31, 19x2

Operating activities:	
Receipts from customers	$ 105,000
Payments to suppliers	(114,250)
Payments for rent	(9,000)
Payments for utilities	(900)
Payments for salaries	(6,400)
Payments for office supplies	(850)
Payments for insurance	(1,400)
Cash to be used in operating activities	$ (27,800)
Investing activities:	
Payment for computer	$ (5,000)
Cash to be used in investing activities	$ (5,000)
Financing activities:	
Receipt from sale of stock	$ 22,000
Receipt from bank loan	20,000
Cash to be provided by financing activities	$ 42,000
Projected 3/31/x2 cash balance	$ 9,200

Assumptions upon which projections are based:

Purchases on credit	$ 116,250
Cash payments to suppliers for first quarter: January, $52,000; February, $40,250; and March, $22,000, with $2,000 still outstanding at end of quarter (March 31, 19x2).	
Sales	125,000
Cash collections from customers for first quarter sales: January, $25,000; February, $35,000; March, $45,000, with $20,000 still outstanding at end of quarter (March 31, 19x2).	
Cost of merchandise sold	93,750
Security deposit payment for rented building	4,500
Rent payments	4,500
Utility payments	900
Salary payments	6,400
Proceeds from bank loan	20,000
Interest accrued on loan	750
Office supplies purchase	850
Insurance premiums payment	1,400
Computer purchase	5,000

you show them some profitable operations, the banks will look at the risks differently." Brad took the plan to his father, who agreed to cosign the note. Shortly after Byte-Size constructed its comprehensive business plan, a tangible benefit resulted. On December 30, 19x1, Mary and Brad took their business plan to a local bank and were able to negotiate a 15%, $20,000 loan due on June 30, 19x2. In explaining why she approved the loan, the banker said she was particularly interested in Byte-Size's projected liquidity (ability to have enough cash to meet obligations) as shown by the company's projected current ratio and quick ratio. From the expression on Mary and Brad's faces, the banker realized that they did not understand the terms *current ratio* and *quick ratio,* so she gave the following explanation:

Current ratio is the ratio of current assets to current liabilities, or

$$\frac{\text{Current assets}}{\text{Current liabilities}} = \text{Current ratio}$$

Higher ratios are viewed as signs of higher liquidity. Byte-Size projected current assets of $56,200 and current liabilities of $22,750:

$$\frac{\$56,200}{\$22,750} = \text{Current ratio of 2.47 to 1}$$

The banker told Mary and Brad that she always reviewed current ratio carefully for short-term loans, and she thought Byte-Size had a reasonable current ratio.

Quick ratio is the ratio of quick assets which are cash, receivables, and marketable securities, to current liabilities, or

$$\frac{\text{Quick assets}}{\text{Current liabilities}} = \text{Quick ratio}$$

Usually high quick ratios are considered indicators of quick convertibility to cash. Byte-Size projected quick assets of $29,200 and current liabilities of $22,750:

$$\frac{\$29,200}{\$22,750} = \text{Quick ratio of 1.28 to 1}$$

The banker told Mary and Brad that the quick ratio was a more stringent indicator of liquidity. She added that she also considered the projected quick ratio of Byte-Size to be reasonable.

"I'm really impressed with your plan, and heaven knows that we need more knowledgeable people running computer software outlets, but either you have to put up more cash of your own or you need to get a cosigner for the loan. After being assured that Brad's father would back up the loan, the banker emphasized that she approved the loan primarily because the business idea seemed to make good economic sense, the assumptions seemed valid, and the business plan reflected good planning. The $20,000 loan now gave Byte-Size the financial cushion that FM had said was needed.

Accounting for Preoperating Transactions

On December 28, Mary and Brad purchased the Byte Size, Inc., capital stock for a total of $22,000. On December 30, they signed the bank note for $20,000 and received the cash. They also made three cash expenditures related to rent of their building and to acquire merchandise inventory. The five initial transactions in December 19x1 are as follows:

Date	Description of Transaction
19x1	
Dec. 28	Issued stock for $22,000 cash.
28	Paid security deposit on their rented building, $4,500 cash.
28	Paid three months' rent (January, February, and March) for the building, $4,500 cash.
30	Signed bank note for $20,000, at an annual interest rate of 15%.
30	Purchased a local bookstore's computer software inventory for $8,500.

Exhibit 5–3 shows Byte-Size's initial journal entries and the resulting December 31, 19x1, balance sheet.

EXHIBIT 5–3

Initial Journal Entries and Balance Sheet of Byte-Size

_	GENERAL JOURNAL				J1
Date	Account Titles and Explanation	Ref.	Debit	Credit	
19x1 Dec. 28	Cash (A)	111	22,000		
	Capital Stock (SE)	311		22,000	
	To record initial investment.				
28	Security Deposit (A)	171	4,500		
	Cash (A)	111		4,500	
	To record deposit on rented building.				
28	Prepaid Rent (A)	131	4,500		
	Cash (A)	111		4,500	
	To record prepayment of three months' rent.				
30	Cash (A)	111	20,000		
	Note Payable (L)	217		20,000	
	To record 15% loan, with principal and interest due June 30, 19x2.				
30	Merchandise Inventory (A)	142	8,500		
	Cash (A)	111		8,500	
	To record acquisition of merchandise from ABC Discount Stores.				

Byte-Size, Inc.
Balance Sheet
December 31, 19x1

Assets		Liabilities and Stockholders' Equity	
Cash	$24,500	Liabilities:	
Merchandise inventory . . .	8,500	Note payable	$20,000
Security deposit	4,500	Total liabilities	$20,000
Prepaid rent	4,500	Stockholders' equity:	
		Capital stock	$22,000
		Total liabilities and	
Total assets	$42,000	stockholders' equity	$42,000

The next section discusses the typical accounting decisions that must be made for a merchandising business. As you follow the history of Byte-Size, you will learn the first law of business—not everything goes according to plan. Many unexpected events confront businesses, and Byte-Size is no exception. At the end of the first quarter, we will compare Byte-Size's actual operations with their business plan and indicate how Mary and Brad can intelligently plan the operations of their next period.

ACCOUNTING FOR MERCHANDISE INVENTORY

A merchandising business usually has its merchandise on hand ready to be sold. As mentioned earlier, items held for sale are called *merchandise inventory*. The method of handling merchandise ready for sale varies with the type of merchandising company. For example, the merchandise inventory of a supermarket is on open shelves, and customers

Objective 2

How to account for merchandise inventory — net purchases, cost of goods available for sale, and cost of goods sold.

have direct access to the specific items they want to purchase. However, in a carpet store, customers usually select carpets from small samples, while the actual merchandise is either in a warehouse ready for delivery or must be ordered from a carpet manufacturer. On the other hand, mail-order merchandising operations use catalogs to promote their products, so the customer does not see the actual item purchased until it arrives by mail or delivery service. Some mail-order companies do not own a stock of merchandise but order from their suppliers only what is needed for specific customer orders, and the supplier ships the merchandise directly to the customer. Regardless of how the merchandise company provides its merchandise for sale, the basic accounting procedures illustrated in this chapter apply to all merchandising companies.

Byte-Size purchases its inventory from suppliers. Some of the inventory is on display in the front of the store. The excess inventory is stored in a storage area at the back of the store. At any financial statement date, the cost of the merchandise still on hand appears on the balance sheet as an asset, merchandise inventory, and the cost of the merchandise sold to customers during a period appears on the income statement as an expense, cost of goods sold.

The simplest flow of merchandise inventory for an accounting period is

Starting amount:	Beginning inventory.	$ xxx
Additions:	Net purchases	xxx
Subtotal:	Cost of goods available for sale	$ xxx
Deduction:	Ending inventory (asset on the balance sheet)	(xxx)
Amount sold:	Cost of goods sold (expense on the income statement)	$ xxx

Net purchases is computed as follows:

Gross purchases − invoice prices of merchandise acquired			$xxx
Less:	Purchase returns and allowances for damaged or unwanted items . .	$(xx)	
	Purchase discounts for prompt payment	(xx)	(xx)
Plus:	Freight-in		xx
Net purchases.			$xxx

Usually the merchandising company (the purchaser) pays the freight for merchandise shipped from suppliers. The freight cost is called freight-in and is added to arrive at net purchases as shown above. Freight is sometimes paid by the shipper, as you will learn later.

This section concentrates on an inventory process called the periodic inventory method of determining cost of goods sold. This method requires a physical count of the units of inventory on hand *periodically* to measure the value of the ending inventory and cost of goods sold. The units on hand are multiplied by the cost per unit to determine the ending inventory. Then, cost of goods sold is computed using the calculation illustrated above. (Chapter 6 discusses the perpetual inventory method—a method that keeps a continuous record of cost of inventory items on hand and cost of goods sold.)

To understand the periodic inventory system, study the relationship of the three formulas below, which gives you another way of thinking of the relationships in the schedules above. Formula 1 states that to determine the cost of goods sold, you subtract the ending inventory from the cost of goods available for sale. Formula 2 states that to determine the cost of goods available for sale, you add net purchases to the beginning inventory.

Formula 3 states that to determine net purchases, you subtract (*a*) purchase returns and allowances and (*b*) purchase discounts from gross purchases, and then add freight-in.

Formula 1: Cost of goods sold $=$ Cost of goods available for sale $-$ Ending inventory

Formula 2: Cost of goods available for sale $=$ Beginning inventory $+$ Net purchases

Formula 3: Net purchases $=$ Gross purchases (invoice prices of purchases acquired) $-$ Purchase returns and allowances $-$ Purchase discounts $+$ Freight-in

In the periodic inventory method, the balance sheet account, Merchandise Inventory, is not affected until the end of the accounting period. Separate accounts are used for Purchases, Purchase Returns and Allowances, Purchase Discounts, and Freight-In, none of which appear on the financial statements. We will see shortly that all of the balances in these accounts flow into either inventory or cost of goods sold.

To understand formula 1, you must understand the terms in formulas 2 and 3. For this reason, we subdivide this section into determining net purchases, determining cost of goods available for sale, and determining cost of goods sold. Refer frequently to these three formulas as you study the paragraphs below.

Determining
Net Purchases

Net purchases (formula 3) is the total of gross purchases (invoice prices of merchandise acquired) minus purchase returns and allowances, minus purchase discounts, and plus freight-in. To determine the net purchases for an accounting period, you must understand gross purchases, purchase returns and allowances, purchase discounts, and freight-in.

Gross Purchases. The total invoice price of all merchandise purchases without regard to discounts, returns, or allowances is called gross purchases. To record gross purchases, a Purchases account is used. Only merchandise bought for resale is recorded in the Purchases account.

During the first quarter in 19x2, Byte-Size received invoices totaling $145,500 for merchandise received from suppliers. These purchases were recorded at various times throughout the quarter and are recorded in the following summary entry:

(1) Purchases (A)   145,500
      Accounts Payable (L)   145,500

Some of the entries shown in this chapter are summary entries. They represent the effects of many separate entries made at different times throughout the quarter. Thus, no dates are given, and the explanation line is omitted. For convenience in referencing, from this point on, we have numbered all of Byte-Size's journal entries.

Purchase Returns and Allowances. Because of defects or errors, not all merchandise received from suppliers is acceptable. Therefore, allowances are often made by the supplier for merchandise defects. If a defect is serious, the merchandise may be returned for full credit. If a defect is minor, the purchaser may decide to keep the merchandise providing the supplier agrees to reduce the price or amount owed. The term purchase returns and allowances includes merchandise returned for credit and merchandise on which allowances have been made for defects.

Byte-Size returned one shipment of diskettes for $2,600 credit and received a $600 credit for defective paper that would have to be sold at a reduced price. These credits are recorded in the Purchase Returns and Allowances account, a contra asset account (XA), as follows:

(2)   Accounts Payable (L)   2,600

      Purchase Returns and Allowances (XA).   2,600

    To record return of defective diskettes.

(3)   Accounts Payable (L)   600

      Purchase Returns and Allowances (XA).   600

    To record allowance for inferior paper.

A contra account, you recall from Chapter 4, is an account whose balance is subtracted from another account to get the net amount. In this case the contra account will be subtracted from gross purchases to determine net purchases.[1]

Purchase Discounts.   Some suppliers give discounts to customers when bills are paid promptly. These discounts are called purchase discounts and reduce the buyer's cost of merchandise. Since discounts are a reduction of the purchase price, the Purchase Discounts account is a contra asset (XA) account.

During the first quarter of 19x2, Byte-Size paid invoices for purchases totaling $110,000. No discounts were offered on invoices totaling $70,000, and payment was recorded as follows:

(4)   Accounts Payable (L)   70,000

      Cash (A).   70,000

Discounts were offered and taken on $40,000, and such payments are summarized as follows:

(5)   Accounts Payable (L)   40,000

      Cash (A).   39,200

      Purchase Discounts (XA)   800

When a supplier offers discounts, they are usually stated on the invoice with a special designation such as 2/10, n/30, which means that a 2% discount may be taken if the invoice is paid within 10 days; and if the invoice is not paid in 10 days, the total amount would be due within 30 days. Thus, if a company chooses not to take the discount, payment will usually be made at the latest possible date, allowing the company to retain its cash as long as possible.

Is it a good business decision to take a discount when it is offered? The answer to this question depends, of course, on the terms of the discount. During the period shown in transaction 5, Byte-Size saved $800 by paying the invoice 20 days before the 30-day deadline. Since the use of money is often measured by its annual interest rate, let us determine the annual interest rate represented by 2% for 20 days. Two percent is to 20 days the same as the annual interest rate is to 360 days, or $.02/20 = x/360$, $x = .001(360)$, $x = 0.36$, or

---

[1]We classify purchases as an asset account and therefore Purchase Returns and Allowances and Purchase Discounts discussed below are contra asset accounts. If purchases were classified as an expense account because it ultimately flows into Cost of Goods Sold then it would be classified as a contra expense account. The justification for classifying purchases as an asset is that it flows directly into inventory, which is an asset.

36%. You can also compute the annual interest rate by multiplying 2% times 18 periods of 20 days each ($360 \div 20 = 18$). A 36% yearly interest rate is an extremely high rate of interest. Remember Byte-Size is only paying 15% on its borrowed funds. This high annual interest percentage for cash discounts is not only a recognition for quick payment of the invoice but also a marketing device used by suppliers to attract customers.

In entry 5 above, we illustrated the gross method of recording purchase discounts. This method initially records purchases at their total invoice amount and only records the discount when and if it is taken. However, the actual cost of the merchandise was the total price less the discount taken. It is up to Byte-Size to decide whether the discount will be taken.

An alternative to the gross method that enables businesses to keep track of discounts not taken is called the net method, which starts by recording purchases net of possible discounts. Then if the purchases are paid within the discount period, no adjustments are needed. The following table of journal entries compares how a $500 invoice with terms of 2/10, n/30 is recorded using the net method and the gross method when it is paid within the discount period and when it is paid after the discount period:

Journal Entry	Net Method Paid		Gross Method Paid	
	Within Discount Period	After Discount Period	Within Discount Period	After Discount Period
Recording purchase:				
Purchases (A)	490	490	500	500
Accounts Payable (L)	490	490	500	500
Recording payment:				
Accounts Payable (L)	490	490	500	500
Discounts Lost (E)		10		
Purchase Discounts (XA)			10	
Cash (A)	490	500	490	500

When discounts are not taken, the net method records the lost discount amount as an expense. Only the net cost of the merchandise flows to the Merchandise Inventory and Cost of Goods Sold accounts. In all circumstances, therefore, under the net method, the gross cost less discounts go to Merchandise Inventory and Cost of Goods Sold, and any lost discounts are recorded as a separate expense in the income statement. This method makes management aware of lost discounts that become material. On the other hand, under the gross method, the cost of inventory depends on the decision whether or not to take a discount. If a discount is taken, the inventory costs go down; if the discount is not taken, inventory costs are higher.

Freight-In. In addition to purchases, returns and allowances, and discounts, another common component of net purchases is freight-in paid by the buyer. These freight charges are accounted for in an account titled **Freight-In.**

During the first quarter, Byte-Size paid $1,264 for incoming freight, as shown in the following summary entry:

(6) Freight-In (A)   1,264
       Cash (A)   1,264

Freight-In is a common account used by merchandising companies since companies usually pay the freight on the merchandise they buy for resale.

Determining Cost of Goods Available for Sale

The cost of goods available for sale during an accounting period (formula 2, page 220) is the beginning inventory plus net purchases. We have discussed how accountants record purchase returns and allowances, discounts and freight-in. Now we will see how beginning inventory becomes a component of cost of goods available.

Beginning Inventory. During December, before Byte-Size opened its doors, Mary and Brad purchased the discontinued software line of a local bookstore. Included with the $8,500 invoice from the bookstore was a list of the items purchased and their cost. For Byte-Size—a new business—this was their beginning inventory for the first quarter of 19x2. During the first quarter, Byte-Size purchased more merchandise and sold some merchandise. At the end of the first quarter, then, the ending inventory contained the merchandise that remained after selling items from the beginning inventory and from the purchases made during the quarter. In an ongoing business, the ending inventory of an accounting period becomes the beginning inventory of the next accounting period.

Byte-Size's Cost of Goods Available for Sale. Now that you understand the nature of gross purchases, purchase returns and allowances, purchase discounts, beginning inventory, freight-in, and net purchases, you are ready to determine Byte-Size's cost of goods available for sale.

Using the cost figures given for Byte-Size earlier in the chapter, cost of goods available for sale for the first quarter of operations can be summarized as follows:

Beginning inventory			$ 8,500
Purchases (gross)		$145,500	
Less: Purchase returns and allowances	$(3,200)		
Purchase discounts	(800)	(4,000)	
Add: Freight-in		1,264	
Net purchases			142,764
Cost of goods available for sale			$151,264

Determining Cost of Goods Sold

The cost of goods sold (formula 1, page 220) is the cost of goods available for sale minus the ending inventory. Since you know how to determine the cost of goods available for sale, you have only to learn how accountants determine ending inventory.

Ending Inventory. In a periodic inventory system such as that used by Byte-Size, a physical count of the inventory on hand is taken at the end of an accounting period, and the cost of the actual units on hand is the amount recognized as the inventory balance on the period-end balance sheet. This **ending inventory** is the merchandise that *remains* available for sale at the end of an accounting period, the beginning inventory for the next period.

Byte-Size determined the dollar amount of its ending inventory on March 31, 19x2, by counting the merchandise displayed in the store and in storage. Then the number of units of the different inventory items was multiplied by the net cost per item after subtracting allowances and discounts from purchase cost.

We will assume that Byte-Size's ending inventory balance determined by the above procedure is $54,000. To determine cost of goods sold for the period, Byte-Size uses the cost of goods available for sale, $151,264, minus the ending inventory balance, $54,000. To record cost of goods sold, two adjusting entries are needed.

The first adjusting entry establishes a preliminary Cost of Goods Sold amount with a journal entry that eliminates the balances in all the other inventory-related accounts. Thus, the net of all the related account balances are put into the Cost of Goods Sold account. This is accomplished by the following journal entry:

(7)	Cost of Goods Sold (E)	151,264	
	Purchase Returns and Allowances (XA)	3,200	
	Purchase Discounts (XA)	800	
	Merchandise Inventory (beginning) (A)		8,500
	Purchases (A)		145,500
	Freight-In (A)		1,264

To transfer the beginning inventory and the other accounts that relate to net purchases to Cost of Goods Sold.

The $151,264 is *not* the final cost of goods sold. Another adjustment is needed to debit Merchandise Inventory for the cost of merchandise on hand at the end of the period and to reduce Cost of Goods Sold by the same amount, thus establishing the correct inventory balance in Merchandise Inventory, which will be carried to the next period.

(8)	Merchandise Inventory (ending) (A)	54,000	
	Cost of Goods Sold (E)		54,000

To establish the ending inventory.

The following shows how the two entries[2] result in the final Cost of Goods Sold amount:

Beginning inventory	$ 8,500
Net purchases	142,764
Cost of goods available for sale	$151,264
Ending inventory	54,000
Cost of goods sold	$ 97,264

Exhibit 5–4 shows how entries 7 and 8 relating to ending inventory affect Byte-Size's accounts. Five items make up the $151,264 debit to Cost of Goods Sold: the beginning amount in Merchandise Inventory, Purchases, Purchase Returns and Allowances, Freight-In, and Purchase Discounts. This $151,264 is the cost of goods available for sale discussed earlier. The credit to Cost of Goods Sold of $54,000 comes from entry 8, the amount of the Merchandise Inventory's ending balance.

---

[2]Cost of goods sold could also be recorded in one entry as follows:

Cost of Goods Sold (E)	97,264	
Inventory (A)	45,500	
Purchase Returns and Allowances (XA)	3,200	
Purchase Discounts (XA)	800	
Purchases (A)		145,500
Freight-in (A)		1,264

Note that the $45,500 represents the increase in the inventory balance from the beginning to the end of the period.

EXHIBIT 5–4

Byte-Size's Accounts Related to Inventory

Merchandise Inventory

Beg. bal.	8,500	(7)	8,500
(8)	54,000		
Bal.	54,000		

To the balance sheet

Purchases

(1)	145,500	(7)	145,500
			–0–

Purchase Returns and Allowances (XA)

(7)	3,200	(2)	2,600
		(3)	600
			–0–

Cost of Goods Sold

(7)	151,264	(8)	54,000
Bal.	97,264		

Closed to Income Summary

Purchase Discounts

(7)	800	(5)	800
			–0–

Freight-In

(6)	1,264	(7)	1,264
			–0–

These accounts have zero balances after adjustment of inventory and recording of cost of goods sold.

ACCOUNTING FOR SALES

Objective 3
How to account for sales revenue.

To account for the first-quarter sales of Byte-Size, Mary and Brad began by learning how to recognize and record a sale. Since Byte-Size offered credit to customers, Mary and Brad had to learn from their accountant, FM, how to account for accounts receivable and for customers who did not pay what was owed. Knowing that Byte-Size would have some sales returns and allowances, FM also taught Mary and Brad the method accountants use to record (1) sales returns and allowances and (2) sales discounts given to customers for prompt payment.

Revenue Recognition

Although Mary and Brad knew that they must record their sales revenue for the first quarter of 19x2, they were not sure (1) when a sales transaction was considered completed, (2) what was the appropriate time to record a sale, and (3) how to determine the amount of each sale. So FM gave them the following sales recognition criteria saying that when all four criteria were met, a sale could be recorded.

1. Delivery of merchandise—the point at which the buyer takes responsibility for the item.
2. Measurement of the selling price—the point at which the selling price is known by both parties.
3. Receipt of cash or a valid receivable or other asset—the point at which something of known value is being transferred to the seller.
4. Reasonable determination of all relevant costs—the point at which no material uncertainties exist about the cost of the item to the seller.

These specific criteria for a merchandising company are applications of the revenue recognition criteria we discussed in Chapter 2—that revenues must be realized or realizable, that revenues must be earned, and that related expenses must be objectively measurable.

For a merchandising company such as Byte-Size, these four criteria are usually all met on the date the customer takes possession of the merchandise. FM instructed Mary and Brad to record credit and cash sales as follows (we are using summary entries):

(9) Accounts Receivable (A)	124,450	
Sales (R)		124,450
(10) Cash (A)	9,300	
Sales (R)		9,300

As you will see in the following sections, special considerations are sometimes made for uncollectible receivables, sales returns and allowances, and sales discounts. These considerations can affect the amounts actually collected from customers.

Accounts Receivable and Bad Debts

Objective 4
The relationship between accounts receivable and bad debts.

Companies usually have many credit customers who owe the company for outstanding invoices. Companies expect that most of their customers will pay their bills within a normal period, but some customers will be delinquent, while others will default and never pay. Defaulted invoices are called bad debts (or **uncollectible accounts**). The procedures discussed below are aimed at recording the net receivables at an amount equal to expected cash flows from customers.

To minimize bad debts, companies begin by carefully checking the creditworthiness of potential credit customers. Once credit is extended, a systematic approach should be taken to follow up on late accounts. Then, if necessary, appropriate collection procedures must be initiated for delinquent payers. However, even the best-conceived and best-operated system of credit granting and follow-up will not eliminate all problems.

As with all business situations, companies must watch out for the "point of overkill," because the cost of a credit-granting system can exceed its expected benefits. An extremely tight credit policy could actually screen out a significant number of reasonably safe customers, and a too-aggressive collection process could drive away customers who would have paid anyway and perhaps become repeat customers. Regardless of the credit policy employed by a company, inevitably some potentially good customers will be lost or not accepted, and some bad customers will be granted credit.

Accountants have developed procedures to estimate and account for the many combinations of results that occur in dealing with credit customers. The following example from Byte-Size and the appendix at the end of this chapter illustrate the most important of these procedures.

On March 31, 19x2, Byte-Size had been in operation for three months, and no specific invoices had been determined uncollectible. However, Mary read in a trade journal (*Software Retailing*) that about 2% of all small retailer credit sales were ultimately "written off as bad debts." In talking with FM, Mary learned that this phrase meant that when customers could not be made to pay their obligations, the accounts receivable amounts were removed from the company's books by journal entries and usually never collected.

Mary was concerned about the possibility of bad debts. She wondered if the bad debts should be anticipated or whether all accounts receivable amounts should be recognized as assets until proven to be uncollectible? Mary knew that an asset such as accounts receivable represented economic value in the form of expected cash inflow. To Mary, it was apparent that if the book value of the receivable exceeds the expected cash inflow, the receivable should be reduced. Then the receivable would be properly valued and the negative impact of expected bad debts would be matched to the period of sale.

FM explained to Mary that if Byte-Size uses 2% of the first quarter's credit sales ($124,450 × .02) as its best estimate of future bad debts related to first-quarter sales, the following adjusting entry would be made at the end of the quarter:

(11)	19x1			
	Mar. 31	Bad Debts Expense (E)	2,489	
		Allowance for Bad Debts (XA)		2,489
		To record estimated uncollectible accounts.		

The Allowance for Bad Debts account is a contra asset account to the Accounts Receivable account representing an estimate of uncollectible accounts receivable. The balance in this contra account is subtracted from the balance in accounts receivable in the balance sheet to arrive at the net receivable, which is the amount expected to be received from credit customers, net of bad debts, for all outstanding receivables as of the balance sheet date.

To understand how the Allowance for Bad Debts contra account is used, you must realize that a business keeps a record of each individual customer's receivable balance. This is called a *subsidiary record,* and all individual customers' outstanding amounts are kept in a subsidiary ledger. The total of all balances in the subsidiary ledger is represented in the general ledger with one account called the control account (or primary account). We are concerned here with the Accounts Receivable control account in the general ledger. The appendix to this chapter and the appendix to Chapter 7 provide more detail on the use of control accounts and subsidiary ledgers.

Adjusting entry 11 reduces net income and net accounts receivable, but no subsidiary account for individual customers is affected by this entry. Remember that at this time it is not known which customers will not pay their bills. The 2% used above is an overall estimate of bad debts, that may or may not turn out to be accurate. Neither the subsidiary customer balances nor the Accounts Receivable control account is affected by the adjustment, and both remain equal to each other at all times.

When specific invoices are proven to be uncollectible, the following entry, referred to as a **write-off entry,** is made:

Allowance for Bad Debts (XA)	xxx	
Accounts Receivable (A)		xxx
To write off uncollectible accounts.		

It is at this time that the specific customer invoice is removed from the Accounts Receivable control account and the related subsidiary ledger account.

Throughout the accounting period, the amount of the Allowance for Bad Debts account fluctuates as specific bad debts are recognized. However, the Bad Debts expense account is recorded only in the period-end adjusting entry. The appendix at the end of the chapter gives more detail about accounting for bad debts.

Sales Returns and Allowances

Objective 5
How to account for sales returns and allowances.

After customers take possession of purchased goods, the merchandise may be returned if it is damaged, inferior, or unwanted. Customers do not have an absolute right to return purchased items, but most merchandisers allow some returns. Sometimes the merchandiser gives the customer a reduction in price if the merchandise is damaged and the customer decides to keep it. The term sales returns and allowances refers to the merchandise returned by customers or the reduction in sales price given to customers due to unsatisfactory merchandise.

To keep track of returned or damaged merchandise, a company records the amounts in a contra revenue account called *Sales Returns and Allowances.* Byte-Size allowed a credit customer to return some damaged diskettes for full credit. The entry to show this return is:

(12)	19x1			
	Mar. 3	Sales Returns and Allowances (XR)	4,125	
		Accounts Receivable (A).		4,125
		To record receipt of merchandise returned by a customer.		

Note that the original sale for the diskettes was a credit sale. If the customer had paid cash for the diskettes, then the customer would have received cash or credit toward the reduction in cost of a future purchase.

The Sales Returns and Allowances account is a contra revenue account because it is treated as a reduction in sales and its balance is subtracted from gross sales in arriving at net sales on the income statement.

Sales Discounts

Objective 6
How to account for sales discounts.

Just as purchase discounts discussed earlier in the chapter reduce net purchases, sales discounts, which are shown as reductions in total or gross sales for the period, are reductions given to customers for prompt payment. Byte-Size offers its customers credit terms of 1/10, n/30 (1% of invoiced amount can be deducted if customer pays within 10 days of invoice date or the total invoice price is due within 30 days of invoice date).[3]

During the first quarter of 19x2, Byte-Size collected cash from its credit customers on invoices totaling $96,300. Of the $96,300, receipts on $54,200 of original sales were

---

[3]Note again that this gives customers a strong incentive to make early payments. The annual rate could be computed in the same way as shown on page 221 for purchase discounts: $0.01/20 = x/360$, $x = 0.0005(360)$, $x = .18$. An annual return of 18% may be considered a good return on funds by customers.

reduced by the 1% sales discount. The summary journal entries for these two transactions are

(13)	Cash (A)	53,658	
	Sales Discounts (XR)	542	
	Accounts Receivable (A)		54,200
	To record receipts on which 1% discounts were taken.		
(14)	Cash (A)	42,100	
	Accounts Receivable (A)		42,100
	To record receipts on which discounts were not taken.		

The Sales Discounts account is a contra revenue account to the Sales account and is shown as such on the income statement. Thus, to determine net sales, both sales returns and allowances and sales discounts are subtracted from gross sales.

The above example uses the gross method of recording sales and sales discounts. Just as purchase discounts can be recorded using the net method, sales can also be recognized using the net method. The net method initially records the sales at their cash equivalent value assuming the discounts will be taken. When the customer pays within the discount period, no reference to a Sales Discounts account is required. If, however, payment is made after the discount period, the account Sales Discounts Not Taken is credited. The following journal entries would be made by Byte-Size if the net method were used. These entries are alternatives to entries 9, 13, and 14, respectively.

Accounts Receivable (A)	123,206	
Sales (R)		123,206
To record credit sales net of discount: $124,450 − (.01)($124,450)		
Cash (A)	53,658	
Accounts Receivable (A)		53,658
To record collections of credit sales net of discount taken.		
Cash (A)	42,100	
Sales Discounts Not Taken (R)		421
Accounts Receivable (A)		41,679
To record collections of credit sales for which discounts were not taken.		

On the income statement, the sales discounts not taken would appear under the "Other revenue" section. Most companies do not use the net method because it highlights something that is usually immaterial.

ACCOUNTING FOR TRANSACTIONS NOT RELATED TO INVENTORY AND SALES

Objective 7
Accounting for nonmerchandise-related transactions.

Byte-Size had the following transactions during its first quarter that were not related to inventory and sales:

Date	Transaction No.	Description	Amount
19x2			
Jan. 2	15	Purchased six-month insurance policy	$1,500
4	16	Purchased office supplies	300
5	17	Purchased computer for office use (five-year life, no estimated salvage value)	9,000
Various dates	18	Paid salaries for January–March	6,400
Mar. 25	19	Paid utilities for January–March	300

EXHIBIT 5–5

Journalizing Byte-Size's
Transactions Not
Related to Inventory
and Sales

	Date	Account Titles and Explanation	Ref.	Debit	Credit
		GENERAL JOURNAL			J3
(15)	19x2 Jan. 2	Prepaid Insurance (A)	143	1,500	
		Cash (A)	111		1,500
		To record prepayment of insurance for six months.			
(16)	4	Supplies (A)	132	300	
		Cash (A)	111		300
		To record purchase of office supplies.			
(17)	5	Equipment (A)	151	9,000	
		Cash (A)	111		9,000
		To record purchase of computer for office use.			
(18)	Various	Salaries Expense (E)	521	6,400	
		Cash (A)	111		6,400
		To record January–March salaries paid.			
(19)	Mar. 25	Utilities Expense (E)	522	300	
		Cash (A)	111		300
		To record January–March utilities expense.			

The journal entries for these transactions are given in Exhibit 5–5. Since we have used transactions similar to these in previous chapters, you should have no difficulty in understanding them.

At the end of the first quarter, Byte-Size must make adjusting entries for the following accruals and allocations:

Transaction No.	Transactions Requiring Adjusting Entries
20	Three months of rent expense, $4,500. (Recall that this amount was prepaid in December 19x1.)
21	One half of insurance premium paid January 2 (transaction 15), $750, expired.
22	Of $300 supplies purchased January 4 (transaction 16), only $75 remain. The supplies used ($225) are expensed.
23	Three months' depreciation for computer purchased on January 5 (transaction 17) is $450 ($9,000/60 months $\times$ 3 months).
24	Three months' interest on note due June 30, 19x2, is $750 ($20,000 $\times$ 0.15 $\times$ $^3/_{12}$).

Objective 8
How to prepare a
worksheet for a
merchandising company.

Exhibit 5–6 gives the journal entries for these adjustments. Remember that adjusting entries 7, 8, and 11 were covered previously. The resulting adjusted account balances before closing are shown in T accounts in Exhibit 5–7. Exhibit 5–8 (page 234) shows a worksheet for Byte-Size that includes all of the transactions you have studied.

EXHIBIT 5–6

**Journal Entries
for Byte-Size's
Adjusting Entries**

		GENERAL JOURNAL			J4
	Date	Account Titles and Explanation	Ref.	Debit	Credit
(20)	19x2 Mar. 31	Rent Expense (E)	523	4,500	
		Prepaid Rent (A)	142		4,500
		To adjust January–March rent expense.			
(21)	31	Insurance Expense (E)	524	750	
		Prepaid Insurance (A)	143		750
		To adjust January–March insurance expense.			
(22)	31	Office Supplies Expense (E)	525	225	
		Supplies (A)	132		225
		To adjust office supplies used during the January–March period.			
(23)	31	Depreciation Expense— Equipment (E)	526	450	
		Accumulated Depreciation— Equipment (XA).	156		450
		To record depreciation expense on office equipment for January– March period.			
(24)	31	Interest Expense (E).	527	750	
		Interest Payable (L)	222		750
		To record January–March interest expense on the outstanding note.			

**ANALYSIS OF THE
EFFECTS OF
BYTE-SIZE'S
OPERATIONS**

*Objective 9
How to analyze the effects
of a merchandising
company's operations.*

Now that Byte-Size has been in operation for three months, the time has come to compare the actual financial statements of Byte-Size on March 31, 19x2, with the projected statements in the business plan prepared by FM at the beginning of the period. Exhibit 5–9 shows that **some** variations exist. Are the variations from the projected statements in the business plan good or bad? This question requires careful analysis.

The first thing you should know is that variations from plans normally occur, and these variations in and of themselves do not indicate a poor planning process. As a tool of analysis, accounting helps interpret the results of operations and aids in revising plans for the future. When you view the results of the first three months of Bite-Size's operations along with their original projections, you note that Byte-Size was fairly accurate in projecting sales and cost of goods sold; therefore, the actual gross margin was close to the projection. Also, other expenses were considerably less than projected resulting in greater net income than expected.

Byte-Size's projected and actual balance sheets show two significant differences. Merchandise Inventory and Accounts Payable are both much larger than expected. Now think about the relationship of these two accounts. Inventory was purchased on credit, thereby increasing Accounts Payable. What does this mean for short-term liquidity? If the Accounts Payable at March 31 must be paid before cash can be collected from customers,

EXHIBIT 5–7

Byte-Size's Account Activity in T Accounts

Cash			
Bal.	24,500	(4)	70,000
(10)	9,300	(5)	39,200
(13)	53,658	(6)	1,264
(14)	42,100	(15)	1,500
		(16)	300
		(17)	9,000
		(18)	6,400
		(19)	300
Bal.	1,594		

Accounts Receivable			
(9)	124,450	(12)	4,125
		(13)	54,200
		(14)	42,100
Bal.	24,025		

Allowance for Bad Debts			
		(11)	2,489
		Bal.	2,489

Merchandise Inventory			
Bal.	8,500	(7)	8,500
(8)	54,000		
Bal.	54,000		

Purchases			
(1)	145,500	(7)	145,500
Bal.	–0–		

Purchase Returns and Allowances			
(7)	3,200	(2)	2,600
		(3)	600
		Bal.	–0–

Purchase Discounts			
(7)	800	(5)	800
		Bal.	–0–

Freight-In			
(6)	1,264	(7)	1,264
Bal.	–0–		

Supplies			
(16)	300	(22)	225
Bal.	75		

Security Deposit			
Bal.	4,500		

Prepaid Rent			
Bal.	4,500	(20)	4,500
Bal.	–0–		

Prepaid Insurance			
(15)	1,500	(21)	750
Bal.	750		

Equipment			
(17)	9,000		
Bal.	9,000		

Accumulated Depreciation— Equipment			
		(23)	450
		Bal.	450

EXHIBIT 5–7 (*concluded*)

Accounts Payable			
(2)	2,600	(1)	145,500
(3)	600		
(4)	70,000		
(5)	40,000		
		Bal.	32,300

Note Payable			
		Bal.	20,000

Interest Payable			
		(24)	750
		Bal.	750

Capital Stock			
		Bal.	22,000

Sales			
		(9)	124,450
		(10)	9,300
		Bal.	133,750

Sales Returns and Allowances			
(12)	4,125		

Sales Discounts			
(13)	542		

Cost of Goods Sold			
(7)	151,264	(8)	54,000
Bal.	97,264		

Salaries Expense			
(18)	6,400		

Utilities Expense			
(19)	300		

Rent Expense			
(20)	4,500		

Insurance Expense			
(21)	750		

Supplies Expense			
(22)	225		

Depreciation Expense—Equipment			
(23)	450		

Interest Expense			
(24)	750		

Bad Debts Expense			
(11)	2,489		

EXHIBIT 5–8

Worksheet for Byte-Size, Inc.

Byte-Size, Inc.
Worksheet
For the Quarter Ended March 31, 19x2

Account Titles	Unadjusted Trial Balance (1) Debit	(2) Credit	Adjustments (3) Debit	(4) Credit	Adjusted Trial Balance (5) Debit	(6) Credit	Income Statement (7) Debit	(8) Credit	Balance Sheet (9) Debit	(10) Credit
Cash	1,549				1,594				1,594	
Accounts Receivable	24,025				24,025				24,025	
Allowance for Bad Debts				(11) 2,489		2,489				2,489
Merchandise Inventory	8,500		(8) 54,000	(7) 8,500	54,000				54,000	
Purchases	145,500			(7) 145,500						
Purchase Returns and Allowances		3,200	(7) 3,200							
Purchase Discounts		800	(7) 800							
Freight-In	1,264			(7) 1,264						
Supplies	300			(22) 225	75				75	
Security Deposit	4,500				4,500				4,500	
Prepaid Rent	4,500			(20) 4,500						
Prepaid Insurance	1,500			(21) 750	750				750	
Equipment	9,000				9,000				9,000	
Accum. Depreciation—Equipment				(23) 450		450				450
Accounts Payable		32,300				32,300				32,300
Note Payable		20,000				20,000				20,000
Interest Payable				(24) 750		750				750
Capital Stock		22,000				22,000				22,000
Sales		133,750				133,750		133,750		
Sales Returns and Allowances	4,125				4,125		4,125			
Sales Discounts	542				542		542			
Salaries Expense	6,400				6,400		6,400			
Utilities Expense	300				300		300			
Cost of Goods Sold			(7) 151,264	(8) 54,000	97,264		97,264			
Rent Expense			(20) 4,500		4,500		4,500			
Insurance Expense			(21) 750		750		750			
Supplies Expense			(22) 225		225		225			
Depreciation Expense—Equipment			(23) 450		450		450			
Interest Expense			(24) 750		750		750			
Bad Debts Expense			(11) 2,489		2,489		2,489			
Totals	212,050	212,050	218,428	218,428	211,739	211,739	117,795	133,750	93,944	77,989
Net income/Retained earnings							15,955			15,955
Totals							133,750	133,750	93,944	93,944

EXHIBIT 5–9

Simple Financial Statement Analysis

Byte-Size, Inc.
Balance Sheet Analysis
March 31, 19x2

	Actual	Business Plan	Variance (Actual − Plan)
Assets			
Current assets:			
Cash	$ 1,594	$ 9,200	−$ 7,606
Accounts receivable	24,025	20,000	+ 1,536
Allowance for bad debts	(2,489)		
Merchandise inventory	54,000	22,500	+ 31,500
Office supplies	75		+ 75
Security deposit	4,500	4,500	0
Prepaid insurance	750		+ 750
Total current assets	$82,455	$56,200	+$26,255
Noncurrent assets:			
Office equipment	$ 9,000		
Less: Accumulated depreciation	(450)		
Total noncurrent assets	$ 8,550	$ 5,000	+$ 3,550
Total assets	$91,005	$61,200	+$29,805
Liabilities and Stockholders' Equity			
Liabilities:			
Accounts payable	$32,300	$ 2,000	+$30,300
Note payable	20,000	20,000	0
Interest payable	750	750	0
Total liabilities	$53,050	$22,750	+$30,300
Stockholders' equity:			
Capital stock	$22,000	$22,000	$ 0
Retained earnings	15,955	16,450	− 495
Total stockholders' equity	$37,955	$38,450	−$ 495
Total liabilities and stockholders' equity	$91,005	$61,200	+$29,805

Byte-Size may need to find a new source of financing. Also, the cash balance is less than first projected, primarily because the cost of the computer and payments for inventory are greater than expected.

Byte-Size must carefully plan for the next period. A new loan or more capital from the two owners may be necessary. The first quarter's experience and the analysis of results show that the plan for the next quarter must consider the high level of investment in inventory that was underestimated in the original plan. Thus, Mary and Brad must seriously question the need for so much inventory on hand. If they decide that such a high level of inventory is necessary, they should consider investing more of their money or borrowing more money. Also Mary and Brad must make a cash flow forecast including due dates on loans.

EXHIBIT 5–9 (*concluded*)

Byte-Size, Inc.
Income Statement Analysis
For the Quarter Ended March 31, 19x2

	Actual	Business Plan	Unexpected Net Income Effect
Sales	$ 133,750		
Less: Sales returns and allowances.	4,125		
Sales discounts	542		
Net sales	$ 129,083	$ 125,000	+$4,083
Cost of goods sold	97,264	93,750	− 3,514
Gross margin	$ 31,819	$ 31,250	+$ 569
Expenses:			
Salaries expense	$ 6,400	$ 6,400	$ 0
Bad debt expense	2,489		− 2,489
Rent expense	4,500	4,500	0
Utilities expense	300	900	+ 600
Other expense	2,175	3,000	+ 825
Total expenses	$ 15,864	$ 14,800	−$1,064
Net income	$ 15,955	$ 16,450	−$ 495

Byte-Size, Inc.
Comparison of Actual and Projected Cash Flows
From Inception to March 31, 19x2

	Actual	Business Plan	Unexpected Cash Flow Effect
Operating activities:			
Receipts from customers	$ 105,058	$ 105,000	+$ 58
Payments to suppliers.	(118,964)	(114,250)	− 4,714
Payments for rent	(9,000)	(9,000)	0
Payments for utilities	(300)	(900)	+ 600
Payments for salaries	(6,400)	(6,400)	0
Payments for office supplies	(300)	(850)	+ 550
Payments for insurance	(1,500)	(1,400)	− 100
Cash used in operating activities	$ (31,406)	$ (27,800)	−$3,606
Investing activities:			
Payment for computer.	$ (9,000)	$ (5,000)	−$4,000
Cash used in investing activities	$ (9,000)	$ (5,000)	−$4,000
Financing activities:			
Receipt from sale of stock	22,000	22,000	0
Receipt from bank loan	20,000	20,000	0
Cash provided by financing activities . .	$ 42,000	$ 42,000	$ 0
3/31/x2 cash balance.	$ 1,594	$ 9,200	−$7,606

To summarize this analysis of Byte-Size's first quarter of operations, we can conclude that the business is profitable, but it has a problem with short-term liquidity.

How would Byte-Size, Inc.'s financial statements be different in other countries? There are interesting differences in the terminology and principles that are used in accounting around the world. For instance, in France and the United Kingdom, the balance sheet would not be classified in order of liquidity as is the Byte-Size balance sheet in Exhibit 5–9. Notice that current assets are shown in one section and long-term assets in another. Also, within each section, assets are listed in order of liquidity—that is, closeness to cash. For example, Cash is shown before Accounts receivable, which in turn is shown before Inventory, and so forth. If Byte-Size operated in the United Kingdom the income statement would lead off with *Turnover,* the word used in place of *Sales.* Another terminology difference between U.S. and British statements is that the word *Stocks* is used instead of *Inventory.* As we explore accounting issues in greater detail in the chapters that follow, we will also highlight other differences and similarities in accounting terminology, principles, and measurement among the major economic powers of the world.

SUMMARY

This chapter begins by discussing the need for an accounting system when planning and operating a merchandising business. Compared to a service business, a merchandising business possesses unique accounting and operating problems relating to inventory. By following Byte-Size, Inc., from the planning stage to the operating stage and then analyzing its operations, the important accounting questions related to inventories were introduced.

In planning operations, merchandising managers must make crucial decisions about the nature and amounts of inventory to be purchased and maintained. This leads to questions of financing inventory purchases and the appropriate accounting for inventory. Inventory costs flow to cost of goods sold, an expense on the income statement, and merchandise inventory, a current asset account on the balance sheet. Understanding the formulas for cost of goods sold, cost of goods available for sale, and net purchases is necessary to see the relationship between ending inventory, beginning inventory, freight-in, gross purchases, purchase returns and allowances, and purchase discounts.

Since merchandising businesses buy merchandise for resale to customers, accounting for sales must be understood before a business can accurately determine its net income. You must know when to recognize a sale, the appropriate time to record a sale, and the correct amount of a sale. Many sales are on credit, and credit sales involve accounts receivables and bad debts. Recording an expense and a reduction in the book value of accounts receivable for estimated bad debts is an application of the matching concept where all related expenses are matched to the period in which revenue is recognized. Some sales are returned, which involve sales returns and allowances. When discounts are allowed, accounting must provide for them. All of these items were discussed in this chapter.

This chapter concludes by using the output of the accounting system to analyze the operations of a merchandising company. As a tool of analysis, accounting not only records the history of a company but also helps in guiding its future. As you continue to study each chapter in this textbook, your appreciation for the effectiveness of the accounting system in planning and controlling businesses will increase.

• DEMONSTRATION EXERCISE

The following information is taken from the accounting records of the Sell-It-Now Company for the end of the second quarter of 19xx:

Beginning inventory	$ 24,000
Purchases	145,000
Discounts taken on merchandise purchased	980
Merchandise returned to supplier because of damage or inferior quality	3,700
Freight costs incurred in bringing merchandise to the store	6,400
Ending inventory	18,300
Sales (gross)	268,000
Discounts taken by customers	3,900
Merchandise returned by customers	6,225
Freight costs incurred in delivering merchandise to customers	2,850
Invoice No. 217 determined to be uncollectible	425

Required:

1. Determine net sales for the quarter.
2. Determine cost of goods sold associated with those sales.
3. Determine bad debt expense for the period if Sell-It-Now estimates bad debts to be 2% of *net* sales. All sales are made on credit. Prepare the journal entry to record bad debt expense.
4. Prepare the journal entry that Sell-It-Now would make to write off invoice No. 217 on June 30, 19xx.
5. (Appendix) Prepare the journal (or entries) that the company would make if on October 15, 19xx, payment for invoice No. 217 was unexpectedly received.

Solution:

1. Net sales for the period:

Sales		$268,000
Less: Sales returns and allowances	$ 6,225	
Sales discounts	3,900	10,125
Net sales		$257,875

2. Cost of goods sold for the period:

Beginning inventory		$ 24,000
Purchases	$145,000	
Less: Purchases discounts	980	
Purchase returns and allowances	3,700	140,320
Plus: Freight-in		6,400
Net purchases		$146,720
Cost of goods available for sale		$170,720
Ending inventory		18,300
Cost of goods sold		$152,420

3. Estimate of bad debts for the period:

Net sales.	$257,875
Estimate percentage.	× .02
	$ 5,158

19xx			
June 30	Bad Debt Expense (E).	5,158	
	Allowance for Bad Debts (XA)		5,158
	To record estimate for uncollectible accounts.		

4.	19xx		
	June 30 Allowance for Bad Debts (XA)	425	
	Accounts Receivable (A).		425
	To write off invoice No. 217.		

5.	19xx		
	Oct. 15 Accounts Receivable (A).	425	
	Allowance for Bad Debts (XA)		425
	To reestablish previously written off account.		
	Cash (A)	425	
	Accounts Receivable (A).		425
	To record receipt of payment on invoice No. 217.		

Bad Debt E

Allowance for Bad debt (XA)   DR   CR
   Accts receivable (A)   425

                                             425

Bad Debts, Credit Card Sales, and Installment Sales

Objective 10
Accounting for bad debts,
credit card sales, and
installment sales.

This appendix continues the discussion of accounting for bad debts that began in the chapter. You will learn how a business estimates the amount of bad debts to be recognized, how to write off a bad debt, and how to record a collection of an account previously written off. The appendix ends with a section on accounting for credit card sales and installment sales.

ACCOUNTING FOR BAD DEBTS

In most businesses, the timing of cash inflows depends to a large extent on the contractual arrangements made with customers and others who ultimately pay cash into the business. In a standard credit sales transaction, the customer takes possession of the goods or receives the benefits of services and promises to pay the invoice price in the future. This contractual arrangement is not the same as receiving cash at the time of the sale; however, usually the time between the sale and receiving the cash is short.

When a credit sale is made, the business uses a current asset account called *Accounts Receivable* to carry the amount owed by customers between the point of sale and the receipt of cash. The Accounts Receivable account represents the total money amount of all outstanding invoices; however, the future economic benefit to be received by the company depends on the willingness and ability of customers to meet their obligations. The probability of collecting all receivables is usually less than 100%. Some risks always exist with outstanding receivables. Notes receivable and other receivables not necessarily related to sales also involve the risk of noncollection. How should we account for the risks inherent in such situations? This question is answered in the section that follows.

Estimating Bad Debts

Accountants make provision for the risks of not collecting accounts receivables by estimating the amount of bad debts a company may incur and showing these estimates as a contra account to the Accounts Receivable account. Then, accounts receivable is shown on the balance sheet as net of the estimated uncollectible bad debts.

Several methods are used by accountants to estimate bad debts. In this section we discuss the two methods used most often—the accounts receivable aging method and the percentage-of-sales method.

For our example, we are using Overnight Express, Incorporated (OEI). OEI began business operations on October 1, 19x1. It has many cash customers for whom OEI sends small individual shipments and a smaller number of commercial customers for whom it sends large shipments. OEI mails invoices to its commercial customers. For the fourth quarter of 19x1, OEI has the following sales experience:

Cash sales.	$1,100,000
Credit sales	2,800,000
Cash collections from credit customers	2,426,000

Aging of Accounts Receivable. As you can see in Exhibit 5A–1, OEI keeps two complementary records of its accounts receivable—the general ledger Accounts Receivable account and a subsidiary ledger. The balance of the Accounts Receivable account in the general ledger equals the total outstanding invoices of the separate customer accounts in the subsidiary ledger. As mentioned in the chapter, the general ledger account is often called the *control* or *primary account*. The subsidiary ledger allows management to keep track of each customer and each invoice issued to each customer.

EXHIBIT 5A–1

	Control Account from the General Ledger		Subsidiary Customer Accounts

Accounts Receivable

Credit sales	2,800,000	Collections	2,426,000
Balance	374,000		

Air Products, Inc.	
14,000	1,000
10,000	

Allcomp, Inc.	
8,000	2,000
6,000	

•
•
•

Other subsidiary accounts for individual customers (not shown in this example).

•
•
•

Young Supply	
21,000	16,500
4,500	

$374,000 =   Total of all customer
             subsidiary ledger
             balances

Accountants make an analysis of the outstanding invoices, and they determine the probability of noncollection. This analysis (1) gives the company an opportunity to follow up on slow-paying customers and (2) provides the needed allowance for bad debts to be included in the balance sheet. The net book value of the receivable shown in the balance sheet should be the total amount that the company expects to collect. Matching calls for the current period to absorb the expense associated with any losses expected from noncollection.

One way that accountants estimate the uncollectibles is by making an aging schedule that lists an outstanding invoice or group of invoices by age and gives the probability of collection based on the number of days outstanding. Exhibit 5A–2 shows the aging schedule for OEI.

EXHIBIT 5A–2

**Accounts Receivable
Aging Schedule for OEI**

**Overnight Express, Incorporated
Accounts Receivable Aging Schedule
Outstanding Invoices at December 31, 19x1**

Invoice No.	Date Issued	Amount	Age in Days	Percent Probability of Noncollection	Expected Bad Debt Amount
1002	9/15/x1	$ 18,000	107	50%	$ 9,000
2076	9/30/x1	47,500	87	40	19,000
3026	10/15/x1	30,000	77	40	12,000
4053	10/31/x1	22,500	62	40	9,000
5037	11/15/x1	24,000	46	25	6,000
6021	11/30/x1	12,000	31	25	3,000
7011	12/15/x1	20,000	16	10	2,000
8001–8086 . . .	All after 12/15/x1	200,000	1–15	1	2,000
		$374,000			$62,000

All of the invoices listed in OEI's aging schedule in Exhibit 5A–2 have some probability of not being collected, but OEI does not know which of these invoices will not be collected. Note that on December 31, invoice No. 1002 issued on September 15 has an estimated 50% chance of not being collected, which means that the expected future value is one half of the invoice amount.

Such probabilities as shown in Exhibit 5A–2 are based on the company's experience and/or on industry statistics. If in OEI's case these probabilities are accurate, $62,000 of the outstanding invoices on December 31, 19x1, will not be collected. This amount is the loss in economic benefits that can be expected if the probabilities of noncollection are accurate.

To provide for bad debts, OEI's accountant would make the following adjusting entry to record the expense and a reduction in the book value of the Accounts Receivable account:

```
19x1
Dec. 31   Bad Debts Expense (E) . . . . . . . . . . . . . . . . . . . .   62,000
              Allowance for Bad Debts (XA) . . . . . . . . . . . . . . .            62,000
                  To record estimated uncollectible accounts.
```

Remember, this is OEI's first year of operations. Accounting for bad debts on an ongoing basis is shown below.

Percentage-of-Sales Method. As an alternative to the aging method, uncollectibles can be estimated by the percentage-of-sales method. This method charges a percentage of credit sales for the period to Bad Debts Expense. For example, the industry average of uncollectible accounts for OEI is 2% of credit sales. The adjusting entry for OEI would be:

```
19x1
Dec. 31   Bad Debts Expense (E) . . . . . . . . . . . . . . . . . . . .   56,000
              Allowance for Bad Debts (XA) . . . . . . . . . . . . . . .            56,000
                  To record estimated uncollectible accounts ($2,800,000 × .02).
```

The percentage could also be applied to net credit sales; that is, sales minus sales returns and allowances and sales discounts.

To summarize, the aging method calls for an analysis of outstanding invoices and results in an estimate of the uncollectible amount. The balance in the Allowance for Bad Debts account is made to equal this estimate by means of the adjusting entry, which debits Bad Debts Expense and credits Allowance for Bad Debts. The method gives a balance in the allowance account, which is the company's best estimate of uncollectible accounts. Alternatively, under the percentage-of-sales method, Bad Debt Expense is estimated and debited for the estimated amount (a percentage of net credit sales) and the allowance account is credited for the same amount. The aging method is more balance sheet–oriented, resulting in a best estimate of uncollectibles in the allowance account balance. The percentage-of-sales method is more income statement–oriented because the bad debt expense is estimated without regard to the resulting balance in the allowance account.

Writing Off Bad Debts and Accounting for Bad Debts Expense in a Subsequent Accounting Period

An invoice is determined to be uncollectible when a customer declares bankruptcy, dies, disappears without a trace, or is in some other way unable to pay. Assume that on January 2, 19x2, before any new credit sales are recorded, OEI determined invoice No. 1002 to be uncollectible. To write off this bad debt, OEI reduces the Accounts Receivable balance by $18,000, as follows:

```
19x2
Jan.  2   Allowance for Bad Debts (XA) . . . . . . . . . . . . . . . . .   18,000
              Accounts Receivable (A) . . . . . . . . . . . . . . . . . .            18,000
                  To record write-off of invoice No. 1002.
```

The net book value of the accounts receivable is not affected by this entry, and net income is not directly reduced. Under the allowance method, the book value of the receivable and net income are directly affected only at period-end when the adjusting entry is made to record the bad debts expense.

You should note that the write-off of a specific customer's account must also be recorded in the customer's record in the subsidiary ledger so that the balance in the general ledger Accounts Receivable account and the total of the customer balances in the subsidiary ledger are equal. The effects of entries to record bad debts expense and to write off an account are as follows (assuming the aging method was used to estimate bad debts):

Date	Outstanding Invoices	−	Allowance for Bad Debts	=	Net Book Value of Accounts Receivable
12/31/x1 (before write-off) . . .	$374,000	−	$62,000	=	$312,000
1/2/x2 (after write-off)	$356,000	−	$44,000	=	$312,000

Note also that the balance in the Allowance for Bad Debts is reduced from $62,000 to $44,000, and this reduction may affect the period-end adjustment for 19x2. For example, if the aging analysis of outstanding invoices on March 31, 19x2, shows expected bad debts of $120,000 and the Allowance for Bad Debts remains at $44,000 at the end of the quarter, an adjustment of $76,000 would be necessary to establish the proper balance in the allowance account. The journal entry for this would be:

```
19x2
Mar. 31   Bad Debts Expense (E) . . . . . . . . . . . . . . . . . . . . .   76,000
              Allowance for Bad Debts (XA) . . . . . . . . . . . . . . .            76,000
                  To record estimated uncollectible accounts.
```

Collection of a
Previously Written Off
Invoice

An invoice is written off when it is deemed uncollectible, but sometimes cash is collected on that invoice at a later date. When this occurs, the proper procedure is to reestablish the written off amount and then record the collection of cash in the usual manner. Assume that during 19x2, OEI wrote off an invoice as follows:

```
19x2
May 15    Allowance for Bad Debts (XA). . . . . . . . . . . . . . . . .    980
              Accounts Receivable (A) . . . . . . . . . . . . . . . . .          980
          To record write-off of invoice.
```

On July 2, a check is received for $980 from the errant customer, and the following entries are made:

```
19x2
July   2    Accounts Receivable (A) . . . . . . . . . . . . . . . . . .    980
              Allowance for Bad Debts (XA) . . . . . . . . . . . . . .          980
            To record reinstatement of invoice previously written off.
            Cash (A) . . . . . . . . . . . . . . . . . . . . . . . . .    980
              Accounts Receivable (A) . . . . . . . . . . . . . . . . .          980
            To record receipt of payment on account.
```

Notice that these entries have no direct effect on net income. The period-end adjusting entries establish the bad debt expense, which depends on the estimates of uncollectibility and the existing balance in the allowance for bad debts under the aging method.

CREDIT CARD SALES

Many retail businesses use bank cards such as Visa or MasterCard as their primary means of selling on credit. This relieves the retailer from the risk of noncollection because the credit card company assumes the risk. The credit card company charges the retail business a percentage of the original sales price as compensation for assuming this risk and providing the collection service.

Since the credit card company assumes the risk and bills the customer, the retailer's accounting effort and clerical activity are much reduced. Exhibit 5A–3 shows the relationship of retailer and customer with and without credit cards.

The enormous popularity of retailer arrangements with credit card companies is testimony that these credit cards involve economic efficiencies. Generally, credit card companies are efficient at evaluating creditworthiness, collection, and recordkeeping.

Customers also find using national credit cards convenient. Carrying one or two of the major credit cards reduces the need for holding cash, and paying bills can be done with one or two checks rather than many checks to individual retailers.

The following example illustrates the retailer's accounting for a credit card sale: On March 1, 19x1, Otis, Inc., sold a spreadsheet program to Ms. Stockman for $450 by means of Americard, which charges Otis, Inc., a 4% fee on the sales price. The entries to record the sale and collection were as follows:

```
19x1
Mar.   1    Accounts Receivable, Americard (A). . . . . . . . . . . . . .    432
            Credit Card Fee Expense (E) . . . . . . . . . . . . . . . . .     18
              Sales (R) . . . . . . . . . . . . . . . . . . . . . . . .          450
            To record sale on credit card basis.
Apr.   1    Cash (A) . . . . . . . . . . . . . . . . . . . . . . . . . .    432
              Accounts Receivable, Americard (A) . . . . . . . . . . . .          432
            To record collection of account.
```

EXHIBIT 5A–3

Retail/Credit Customer Relationship with and without Credit Cards

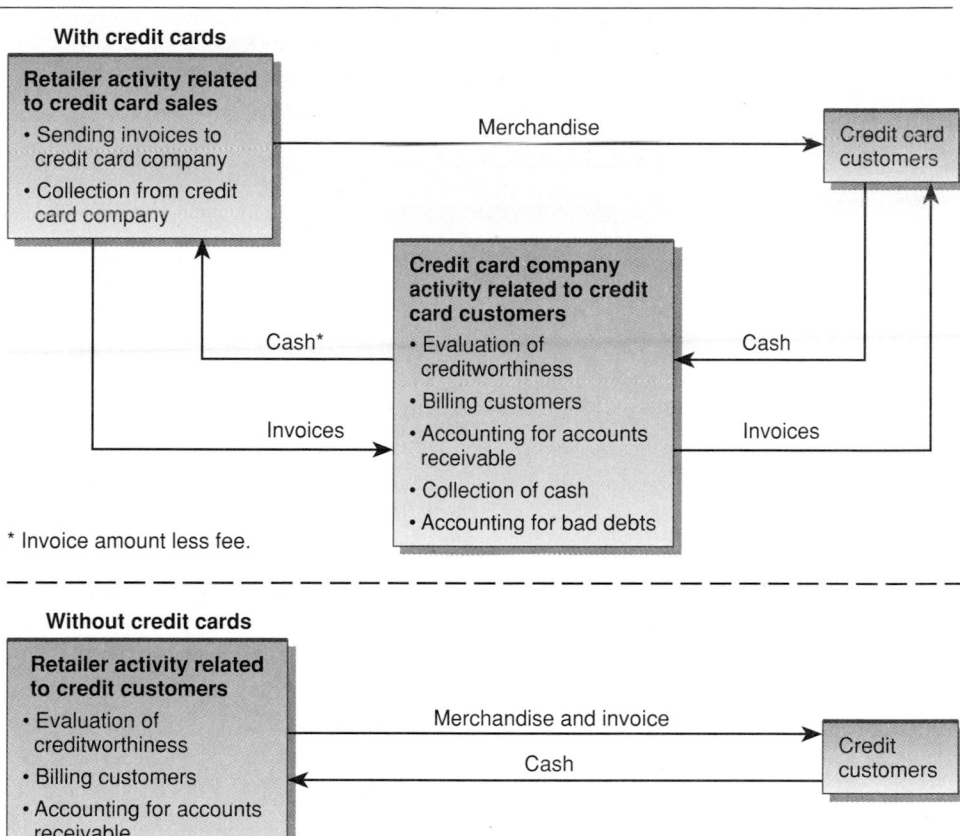

* Invoice amount less fee.

Otis could have recorded the gross amount of receivables, but this would have made the accrual of the credit card fee expense at the end of the accounting period necessary. For example, assume that Otis, Inc., has credit card sales of $100,000 through Americard in 19x1 and collected $90,000 of the sales by the end of the period. The following entries summarize the accounting if the gross receivables amount is recorded:

During 19x1	Accounts Receivable, Americard (A)	100,000	
	Sales (R)		100,000
	To record gross sales made on a credit card basis.		
	Cash (A)	86,400	
	Credit Card Fee Expense (E)	3,600	
	Accounts Receivable, Americard (A).		90,000
	To record collection of account from Americard.		
Dec. 31	Credit Card Fee Expense (E)	400	
	Allowance for Credit Card Fee (XA)		400
	To record accrual of credit card fee attributed to sales for which payment has not yet been received from Americard.		

```
      19x2
      Jan. 15    Cash (A) . . . . . . . . . . . . . . . . . . . . . . . . . . . .    9,600
                    Allowance for Credit Card Fee (XA) . . . . . . . . . . . . . .     400
                        Accounts Receivable, Americard (A) . . . . . . . . . . . .          10,000
                    To record collection of cash from Americard.
```

The balance sheet at December 31, 19x1, would show the net receivable ($10,000 − $400) from Americard as a current asset.

INSTALLMENT SALES

Not all receivables are paid in one payment. Retailers, such as Sears Roebuck, have billions of dollars in installment sales that involve payment over several months or years with interest charges being added on the unpaid balance. Because these payment periods are usually considered to be within the operating cycle of the retailer, installment sales receivables are usually classified as current assets, even if they extend beyond one year. The tax considerations and specific accounting procedures applicable to installment sales are covered in intermediate or advanced courses in accounting.

• KEY TERMS

Allowance for Bad Debts. Contra asset account to the Accounts Receivable account that represents the estimation of uncollectible accounts receivable.

Bad debts. Invoices that have been determined to be uncollectible; also called uncollectible accounts.

Beginning inventory. Cost of goods available for sale at the beginning of the operating period; ending inventory of previous accounting period.

Control account. Ledger account that reflects the total of all subsidiary accounts.

Cost of goods available for sale. Total cost of all merchandise held for sale during the period; beginning inventory plus net purchases plus freight-in.

Cost of goods sold. Cost of merchandise sold to customers during the period; cost of goods available for sale minus ending inventory.

Current ratio. Ratio of current assets to current liabilities.

Ending inventory. Merchandise that remains available for sale at the end of an accounting period, becomes the beginning inventory for the next period.

Entrepreneur. One who organizes, manages, and assumes the risks of a business venture.

Freight-in. Cost of delivering the merchandise from supplier to the purchaser; part of cost of net purchases.

Gross margin. Sales less cost of goods sold; also called gross profit.

Gross method. Initial recording of sales or purchases at their total invoice amount without regard to potential discounts, returns, or allowances.

Gross purchases. Total invoice price of all merchandise purchases without regard to potential discounts, returns, and allowances.

Gross sales. Total invoice price of sales.

Liquidity. Ability to have cash or equivalent needed to meet obligations.

Markup. The difference between the cost of an item of merchandise and its selling price, often expressed as a percentage of cost.

Merchandising business. A business that buys items from suppliers and sells them to customers.

Merchandise inventory. Cost of merchandise on hand ready for sale; also called inventory.

Net method. Initial recording of sales or purchases net of their expected discounts, returns, and allowances.

Net purchases. Gross purchases minus purchase returns, allowances, and purchase discounts, and plus freight-in.

Net sales. Gross sales minus discounts, returns, and allowances.

Periodic inventory method. Method involving a physical count of units of inventory on hand at the end of a period and multiplying the units by the cost per unit based on the cost of goods available and the total units available for the period.

Projected (forecasted) balance sheets. Forecasted balance sheets based on hypothetical transactions.

Projected (forecasted) income statements. Forecasted income statements based on hypothetical transactions.

Purchase discounts. Discounts given by some suppliers to customers when bills are paid promptly.

Purchase returns and allowances. Credit given for returned merchandise; allowances made for defective merchandise.

Quick ratio. Ratio of quick assets, such as cash and receivables, to current liabilities.

Sales criteria. The four criteria that are used to determine if a sale should be recorded: delivery of merchandise, measurement of selling price, receipt of cash or a valid receivable or other asset, and reasonable determination of all relevant costs.

Sales discounts. Reduction in sales price given to customers for prompt payment.

Sales returns and allowances. Merchandise returned by customers for which credit is given, or the reduction in sales price given to customers due to defects in merchandise.

Subsidiary ledger. Individual accounts that have a control account in the general ledger, such as individual customer accounts receivable.

Write-off entry. Entry to eliminate a specific customer receivable from the accounting records.

· Appendix Key Terms

Aging schedule. List of outstanding invoices and their probability of collection based on the length of time the invoice has been outstanding.

Installment sales. Sales of merchandise that involve payment over several months or years with interest charges added on the unpaid balance.

Percentage-of-sales method. Method of estimating bad debts based on a percentage of credit sales.

· SYNONYMS

Allowance for Bad Debts; Allowance for Uncollectibles; Allowance for Doubtful Accounts.

Bad debts; uncollectibles.

Control account; primary account.

Gross profit; gross margin.

Merchandise inventory; inventory.

Pro forma; projected.

· QUESTIONS

1. Explain how a merchandising business differs from a service business.
2. Describe the process entrepreneurs go through to set up their businesses. Why go through this process?
3. What are projected financial statements? How do they differ from the statements generated by an accounting cycle?

4. In drawing up a plan, what items must be considered for a merchandising concern?
5. How does the preoperating phase differ from the operating phase of a business?
6. Describe the periodic inventory method.
7. Explain the costs included in the goods available for sale amount for a period. Explain the subcomponents of each cost.
8. Describe the gross and net methods for recording purchase discounts and sales discounts.
9. How is cost of goods sold determined? Differentiate between cost of goods sold and cost of goods available for sale.
10. Define sales and the four criteria evaluated to determine whether a sale is made.
11. How are the projected financial statements made at the beginning of an accounting period used at the end of the accounting period?
12. Explain how accounts receivable are created. Will all accounts receivable be collected?
13. Define sales discounts and sales returns and allowances.

• Appendix Questions

14. Give two reasons why accountants analyze their outstanding accounts receivable for uncollectible accounts.
15. There are several ways to estimate bad debt expense. Describe two of the methods.
16. The Brody Company writes off a $5,400 invoice to J. Jones as uncollectible in 19x1. In 19x2, after winning the lottery, Jones decides to pay the invoice. What is the balance sheet effect of the entries the Brody Company records on its books when the payment is received?
17. Differentiate between the accounting treatment for a credit sale and treatment for a credit card sale.
18. What are installment sales?

• EXERCISES

E 5–1
Determining Beginning Inventory
L.O.2

Renner Company has net sales of $240,000 and a gross margin of $60,000. Determine the beginning inventory of merchandise if net purchases are $170,000 and year-end inventory is $40,000.

E 5–2
Determining Cash Payments to Suppliers
L.O.2

From the beginning to the end of January, the Merchandise Inventory account balance increased by $8,000 and the Accounts Payable account balance decreased by $4,000. Cost of goods sold during January was $44,000. All inventory purchases were made on open account, and no merchandise was returned to suppliers. Determine the amount of cash paid to suppliers of inventory during January.

E 5–3
Determining Purchases
L.O.2

On April 1, 19x1, Geriatrics Supply, Inc., had $412,000 of merchandise in beginning inventory. On March 31, 19x2, ending inventory was $394,000. Cost of goods sold was $1,529,000 for the year. During the year, GSI took discounts of $15,200 and returned $8,315 of merchandise. Determine gross purchases for the fiscal year ending March 31, 19x2.

E 5–4
Recording Purchases
L.O.2

The following transactions are taken from the accounting records of Charles Plumbing Supplies, which records its merchandise inventory using the periodic inventory method:

Apr. 6 Purchase $25,000 of merchandise; terms 1/10, n/30, invoice No. 113.
     8 Purchase $12,800 of additional merchandise; terms 2/10, n/20, invoice No. 21693.
    10 Returned $900 of merchandise on invoice No. 21693 because of defects.
    15 Paid invoice No. 113.
    27 Paid invoice No. 21693.

Required:
Record the above transactions in general journal form using

1. The net method.
2. The gross method.

E 5–5
Determining Cost of Goods Sold
L.O.2

Cost goods sold = cost available – ending inventory

Andrew's Country Store has the following information regarding its merchandise on December 31, 19xx, its year-end:

31,000 + 465,900

Beginning inventory	$ 31,000
Ending inventory	39,600
Freight-in	4,350
Purchases	465,900
Purchases discounts	2,525
Purchase returns and allowances.	6,750

Required:
Prepare the adjusting entries at year-end to record cost of goods sold for the year.

E 5–6
Determining Cost of Goods Sold
L.O.2

Cannon, Inc., used the periodic inventory method. Prior to year-end adjusting entries, the following account balances were reported in the trial balance:

Purchases	$176,545 dr.
Freight-In.	17,100 dr.
Sales Returns and Allowances	10,800 dr.
Purchase Returns and Allowances	21,400 cr.
Discounts Lost	9,500 dr.
Inventory, 1/1/xx	45,000 dr.
Inventory, 12/31/xx	40,000 dr.

Required:
Compute the cost of goods sold for the year.

E 5–7
Sales, Sales Discounts, and Sales Returns and Allowances
L.O.3, 5, 6

Computer Parts, Inc., (CPI) has the following transactions relating to sales:

a. Sales of $36,000 on credit; terms 1/10, n/30.
b. Cash sales of $8,000.
c. Return of defective merchandise with a gross amount sold in *a* of $1,800.
d. Received payment within the discount period for $12,000 of the merchandise sold in *a*.
e. Received payment for $10,000 of the merchandise sold in *a* after the discount period expired.

Required:
1. Record the above transactions in journal form assuming that CPI uses the net method to record its sales discounts.
2. Record the above transactions in journal form assuming that CPI uses the gross method to record its sales discounts.

E 5–8
Determining Sales Revenue
L.O.3

The Jewel Corporation sells all merchandise on a credit basis. On January 1, 19x1, the Accounts Receivable account balance was $200,000. Cash received from customers in 19x1 was $470,000, of which $35,000 was advance payments on merchandise to be delivered in February 19x2. The Accounts Receivable account balance on December 31, 19x1, was $300,000. Compute the amount the Jewel Corporation should record as Sales Revenue for 19x1.

E 5–9
Determining Credit Sales and Bad Debts
L.O.3–6

Forward Auto Supply has the following information at its April 30 month-end:

Cash sales.	$ 92,100
Cash collections on account	239,700
Sales discounts.	1,250
Sales returns and allowances	3,100
Accounts receivable, 4/1	61,000
Accounts receivable 4/30	53,700

Returns and allowances were from credit customers. All sales are recorded using the gross method. No accounts receivable were written off during the year. Bad debts computed using the percentage-of-sales method is estimated at 1% of net credit sales.

Required:
1. Determine net credit sales for the month.
2. Prepare the adjusting journal entry to record estimated bad debts expense for April.

E 5–10
Accounts Receivable and
Bad Debts
L.O.4

Nelson's trial balance before adjustments on December 31, 19xx, included the following accounts and balances:

	Debits	Credits
Accounts Receivable	$60,000	
Allowance for Bad Debts		$ 3,000
Sales Revenue		600,000

The company makes all sales on account. Using the aging method, the company estimates that $4,000 would be uncollectible. Accounts Receivable had a balance of $70,000 on January 1, 19xx, and the company wrote off specific bad accounts during 19xx in the amount of $5,500 which is reflected in the above account balances.

Required:
1. Prepare the summary journal entries for the 19xx transactions that resulted in the above trial balance amounts.
2. Prepare the necessary adjusting journal entry (or entries) at December 31, 19xx, for the Nelson Company related to the above information.
3. Show how accounts receivable should be presented on Nelson's balance sheet at December 31, 19xx.

· Appendix Exercises

E 5–11
Accounts Receivable
Related Transactions
L.O.3, 4, 6, 10

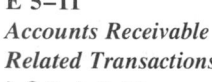

Record the following transactions for World-Wide Toys, Inc.:

Oct. 16   Sold on account $64,500 of merchandise to Toys-R-Them; terms 2/10, n/30, invoice No. 31562. Sales discounts are recorded using the net method.
   21   Wrote off as uncollectible invoice No. 16786 for $8,134 (net).
   25   Received payment in full of invoice No. 31562.
   30   Received $6,249 in payment of invoice No. 09553 which had previously been written off.
   31   An aging of accounts receivable reveals $43,126 worth of accounts as uncollectible. The allowance account before adjustments has a $200 debit balance. Record the adjusting journal entry.

E 5–12
Bad Debts
L.O.4, 10

1. DRB Engineering had credit sales of $1,067,000 during 19xx. Prior experience has revealed 1% of these sales will be uncollectible. Bad debt expense for 19xx is—
   a. $21,340.
   b. $106,700.
   c. $10,670.
   d. None of the above.
2. Giles, Inc., has the following sales: cash sales, $68,000; credit sales, $740,500; credit card sales, $410,800. Giles estimates bad debts to be 1.5% of credit sales. Bad debts expense for the period is—
   a. $77,269.50.
   b. $11,107.50.
   c. $22,215.00.
   d. $18,289.50.

3. Baker Company had a beginning Allowance for Uncollectibles balance of $7,500 credit at January 1, 19xx, and an ending credit balance of $8,900 at December 31, 19xx. Bad debts expense for 19xx was $19,700. The write-offs of bad debts during 19xx totaled—
    a. $21,100.
    b. $19,700.
    c. $18,300.
    d. $8,900.

4. The Konrad News Agency has the following account balances before adjusting entries:

Accounts Receivable.	$430,000 dr.
Allowance for Uncollectibles . . .	3,260 cr.

From an analysis of the customers' accounts using the aging method, it is determined $14,200 will be uncollectible. Bad debt expense for the period is—
    a. $4,300.
    b. $17,460.
    c. $43,000.
    d. $10,940.

E 5–13
Bad Debts
L.O.4, 5, 10

Village Depot, Inc., showed the following normal balances in its accounts prior to recording bad debt expense:

Gross Sales	$185,000
Operating Expenses	93,500
Sales Returns and Allowances.	14,000
Income Tax Expense	12,500
Cost of Goods Sold.	52,800
Allowance for Bad Debts	1,200

Forty percent of Village Depot's gross sales were on credit, and 55% of sales returns and allowances related to credit sales. The company uses the percentage of net credit sales method to estimate bad debt losses. Prepare the journal entry Village Depot would make to record its bad debt expense if the company estimates an expected loss rate on net credit sales of 7%.

E 5–14
Aging Accounts Receivable
L.O.10

Gorton's Jewelers, Inc., uses the aging of accounts receivable method to estimate its uncollectible accounts. Gorton's bookkeeper has compiled the following information from the company's accounts receivable subsidiary ledger:

Days Outstanding	Total of Invoices	Estimated Uncollectible Percentage
0–30 . . .	$115,000	10
31–60 . . .	90,000	15
61–90 . . .	48,000	25
91–120 . . .	15,500	50
121 + ...	1,000	80

On December 31, 19xx, the Allowance for Bad Debts account has a debit balance of $1,050.

Required:
Prepare the journal entry Gorton's would make to record its bad debts expense for 19xx.

E 5–15
Credit Card Sales
L.O.10

During 19xx, Carson's Fitness Center had total sales of $1,450,000. Customers used a major credit card on 30% of those sales. The credit card company charges a 1.5% fee. Record the journal entries Carson's would make to record the credit card sales and receipt of cash from the credit card company on those sales.

E 5–16
Comprehensive
L.O.1, 4, 9, 10

1. A merchandising business—
   a. Usually manufactures the items it sells.
   b. Purchases the items it sells.
   c. Sells to cash customers only.
   d. Carries no inventory.
   e. None of the above.

2. A comprehensive business plan—
   a. Is based on historic events and transactions.
   b. Focuses on financing activities.
   c. Includes assumptions about future sales, expenses and financing.
   d. Is created by an outside party such as a bank.
   e. None of the above.

3. Cost of goods sold—
   a. Is an asset.
   b. Is a liability.
   c. Is a revenue item.
   d. Is the cost of inventory available for sale.
   e. None of the above.

4. Cost of goods available for sale—
   a. Appears on the balance sheet.
   b. Represents the cost of inventory that could have been sold during the period.
   c. Represents the cost of the inventory sold during the period.
   d. Is equal to net purchases.
   e. None of the above.

5. Freight-in—
   a. Is an expense.
   b. Is a revenue item.
   c. Appears on the balance sheet.
   d. Is increased by purchase discounts.
   e. None of the above.

6. When projecting cash flows—
   a. Credit sales and collections is not important.
   b. The timing of cash payments on accounts payable is not important.
   c. Assumed financing activities are important.
   d. The choice of the net or the gross method of recording purchases is critical.
   e. None of the above.

7. The balance in the Accounts Receivable account at period-end—
   a. Is equal to the total of the subsidiary accounts receivable ledger account balances.
   b. Is equal to the total invoices outstanding minus the balance in Allowance for Bad Debts.
   c. Is not affected by cash collections.
   d. Is not affected by write-offs of bad debts.
   e. None of the above.

8. Holding everything else constant the Allowance for Bad Debts balance at period-end—
   a. Is not affected by the choice of the aging or the percentage-of-sales method.
   b. Will be higher for companies with less risky customers.
   c. Is equal to the total of all outstanding invoices.
   d. Is equal to the invoices written off during the period.
   e. None of the above.

9. When a customer pays a previously written off invoice—
   a. The accounts receivable balance is not affected.
   b. Cash is not affected.
   c. The total of the subsidiary accounts receivable ledger will not equal the accounts receivable control account balance.
   d. An income statement account is directly affected.
   e. None of the above.

10. If a retailer makes a credit card sale—
    a. Net income is increased by the total sales price.
    b. Net income is not affected until the retailer receives cash.
    c. The customer pays the retailer.
    d. The service fee reduces the retailer's net income for the period.
    e. None of the above.

• PROBLEMS

P 5–1
*Purchases, Sales, and
the Income Statement*
L.O.2, 3, 7

The Maize-N-Blue Shop, Inc., had the following transactions during August 19xx:

a. Bought $25,000 worth of "M" shirts. Paid $10,000 in cash, the remainder on account.
b. Total cash sales for the month were $40,000.
c. Paid monthly salaries to employees of $5,000.
d. Paid $12,000 on account to supplier of shirts.
e. Incurred $4,000 of miscellaneous operating expenses. Paid $2,500 in cash with remainder on account.

Additional Information:
a. Assume that all the shirts purchased were sold and that the shirts are the only product sold by the shop. All sales are for cash. There was no beginning inventory.
b. Interest expense on a note payable was $1,000 for the month of August.

Required:
1. Record the journal entries in journal form for the above transactions.
2. Prepare the income statement for the Maize-N-Blue Shop, Inc., for the month of August.

Purchases
Inventory (A)   25,000
*   Cash (A)   /*

P 5–2
Preparation of Financial Statements
L.O.8

The adjusted trial balance for the Tinker Corporation at April 30, 19x2 (the end of its fiscal year) is shown below. The accounts are given in alphabetical order. Closing entries have not been made.

Tinker Corporation
Adjusted Trial Balance
April 30, 19x2

	Debits	Credits
Accounts Payable		$ 45,000
Accounts Receivable.	$ 103,400	
Accumulated Depreciation—Store Equipment		15,000
Accumulated Depreciation—Office Equipment		1,000
Administrative Salaries Expense	42,500	
Advertising Expense	50,000	
Cash	47,000	
Cost of Goods Sold	604,000	
Capital Stock		312,000
Depreciation Expense—Store Equipment	3,750	
Depreciation Expense—Office Equipment	250	
Income Tax Expense	34,500	
Income Taxes Payable		7,500
Insurance Expense	4,500	
Interest Expense	14,000	
Interest Revenue		3,250
Merchandise Inventory	377,500	
Miscellaneous Selling Expenses	2,500	
Miscellaneous General and Administrative Expenses	750	
Notes Payable, Long Term		25,000
Note Receivable, Long Term	16,000	
Office Equipment	4,000	
Retained Earnings, 5/1/x1		115,900
Sales Returns and Allowances	2,000	
Sales Revenues		905,000
Salaries Expense	89,000	
Store Equipment	37,500	
Salaries Payable		3,500
Totals	$1,433,150	$1,433,150

Required:
Using the above adjusted trial balance prepare an income statement and a balance sheet as would be required at April 30, 19x2.

P 5–3
*Determining Cost of
Goods Sold and
Preparing Financial
Statements*
L.O.2, 8

The following trial balance was taken from the accounts of the Holmes Company at the end of its fiscal year. All adjusting entries have been made except for those to determine cost of goods sold. No closing entries have been made.

**Holmes Company
Trial Balance
December 31, 19xx**

	Debits	Credits
Cash	$ 3,350	
Accounts Receivable	5,720	
Allowance for Doubtful Accounts		$ 260
Merchandise Inventory 1/1/xx	20,760	
Purchases	112,650	
Purchase Returns and Allowances		680
Purchase Discounts		1,830
Freight-In.	670	
Store Supplies	575	
Office Supplies	180	
Prepaid Insurance.	935	
Store Equipment	19,410	
Accumulated Depreciation—Store Equipment		3,120
Office Equipment	4,210	
Accumulated Depreciation—Office Equipment		1,130
Accounts Payable.		895
Salaries Payable		4,600
Capital Stock.		20,000
Retained Earnings, 1/1/xx		4,585
Sales		200,195
Sales Returns and Allowances	510	
Sales Discounts	1,430	
Salaries Expense	31,950	
Rent Expense	9,000	
Bad Debt Expense	260	
Store Supplies Expense	3,550	
Depreciation Expense—Store Equipment	2,240	
Office Supplies Expense.	840	
Depreciation Expense—Office Equipment	520	
Insurance Expense	935	
Communications Expense	2,500	
Utilities Expense	6,700	
Advertising Expense.	8,400	
Totals	$237,295	$237,295

A year-end physical inventory determined that the ending merchandise inventory is $18,650.

Required:
1. Prepare in journal form the adjusting journal entries to determine cost of goods sold for the year and establish the December 31, 19xx, ending inventory balance.
2. Prepare an income statement for the year and a December 31, 19xx, balance sheet.

P 5–4
Preparing Adjusting Entries
L.O.4, 7

On December 31, 19x5 (Perlick Corporation's year-end), the following balances appeared in the accounts of the Perlick Corporation's unadjusted trial balance:

Perlick Corporation
Unadjusted Trial Balance
December 31, 19x5

	Debits	Credits
Cash	$ 15,970	
Accounts Receivable	23,100	
Allowance for Doubtful Accounts		$ 200
Merchandise Inventory. . . . . _	6,300	
Prepaid Insurance.	3,360	
Note Receivable	10,000	
Equipment	86,600	
Accumulated Depreciation—Equipment		28,000
Accounts Payable.		5,650
Notes Payable		8,000
Capital Stock.		80,000
Retained Earnings, 1/1/x5		15,735
Sales Revenue—Credit		45,900
Sales Revenue—Cash.		11,300
Cost of Goods Sold	37,180	
Rent Expense	5,500	
Salaries Expense	6,775	
Totals	$194,785	$194,785

Examination of the records and related documents provides the following additional information that should be considered for adjusting entries:

a. The Prepaid Insurance account is comprised of a $3,360 payment made on April 30, 19x5, for a two-year building insurance policy.
b. Perlick's credit manager estimates that the average expected loss rate for bad debt losses due to uncollectible accounts is 1% of 19x5 credit sales. It has also been determined that two individual customers' accounts totaling $375 will never be collected and should be written off. The company uses the percentage-of-sales method to record bad debt expense and estimates 19x5 bad debt expense to be $459.
c. The note receivable arose when the corporation loaned one of its employees $10,000 on August 1, 19x5. Both the $10,000 principal amount and interest are due on July 31, 19x7. Interest for 19x5 is $500.
d. The equipment was purchased on January 1, 19x1, at a total cost of $86,600 and is estimated to have a 12-year useful life to the company and a $2,600 residual value. Depreciation for 19x5 is $7,000.
e. Interest owed but not paid on the note payable is $800. Principal plus interest will be paid in 19x6.

Required:
Based on the above data, prepare the adjusting entries in journal form required on December 31, 19x5. New accounts may be needed.

P 5–5
Worksheet and Financial Statements
L.O.8

Taking the information from Problem 5-4, prepare a worksheet, income statement, and balance sheet.

P 5–6
Bad Debts
L.O.4

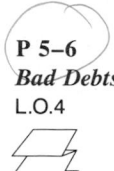

The Wolverine Corporation's unadjusted trial balance at December 31, 19xx, shows a debit balance of $200,000 for Accounts Receivable. The Allowance for Bad Debts has a debit balance of $5,000. Net credit sales for the year were $2 million. The corporation uses the percentage-of-net-credit-sales method to record bad debts, and estimates 1% of net credit sales or $20,000 of those sales to be uncollectible.

Required:
1. Determine the bad debts expense for the Wolverine Corporation for 19xx.
2. Determine the balance in the Allowance for Bad Debts account for the Wolverine Corporation at December 31, 19xx, after adjusting entries.

P 5–7
Recording Purchases and Sales
L.O.2–6

The following transactions took place during the month of June 19xx for the Zach Company:

a. Purchased merchandise on account, $6,000; terms 2/10, n/30. All purchases are recorded using the gross method.
b. Purchased merchandise on account, $4,000; terms 1/15, n/45.
c. Purchased merchandise on account, $1,000; terms 2/10, n/30.
d. Purchased merchandise for cash, $1,500.
e. Purchased merchandise on account, $3,000; terms 1/10, n/30.
f. Made a sale on account, $1,000. All sales are made on terms of 1/10, n/30 and are recorded using the gross method.
g. Made a sale for cash, $200.
h. Because the customer had filed for bankruptcy, determined that an account receivable in the amount of $600 was uncollectible and wrote the account off.
i. Returned $300 of the merchandise purchased in item *e*.
j. Made a sale on account, $3,000.
k. Made a sale on account, $4,000.
l. Paid for the merchandise in item *a* within the discount period.
m. Paid for the merchandise in item *b* but **not** within the discount period.
n. Collected on the sale referred to in item *f* within the discount period.
o. Recorded additional cash sales for the month, $3,200.
p. Recorded additional credit sales for the month, $29,000.
q. Recorded additional credit purchases for the month of $15,000. No discount terms were offered.
r. Paid for the merchandise referred to in items *e* and *i* within the discount period.
s. The customer who purchased merchandise in item *k* returned half of the order due to a mistake on the part of Zach Company.
t. Received payment for merchandise referred to in items *k* and *s* within the discount period.
u. Bad debt expense for the month is estimated to be $150.

Required:
Prepare in general journal form the journal entries for the above transactions.

A | R (A)   A B D (XA)   B D E (E)

2,000,000   5,000 | 29,000   20,000

200,000 | 15,000

P 5–8
Posting Journal Entries and Preparing Financial Statements
L.O.7, 8

On June 1, 19xx, Robins Merchandising, Inc., has the following trial balance:

Robins Merchandising, Inc.
Trial Balance
June 1, 19xx

	Debits	Credits
Cash	$ 9,000	
Accounts Receivable	20,000	
Allowance for Bad Debts		$ 1,000
Merchandise Inventory	18,000	
Accounts Payable		12,000
Capital Stock		20,000
Retained Earnings		14,000
Totals	$47,000	$47,000

Transactions and other information for June:

a.	Credit sales	$400,000
b.	Cash collections	395,000
c.	Credit purchases	270,000
d.	Payments to suppliers	275,000
e.	Payments for salaries	65,000
f.	Unpaid salaries at June 30	8,000
g.	Payments for other expenses	48,000
h.	Cost of goods sold	256,000
	Merchandise inventory at June 30	32,000
i.	Bad debts expense	4,000

Required:
1. Open T accounts for the above accounts with the balances provided. Post the transactions to the appropriate accounts opening any new ones as needed.
2. Foot the T accounts to the final month-end balances. Prepare the adjusting journal entry to determine cost of goods sold and post to the appropriate accounts.
3. Prepare a month-end income statement and the June 30, 19xx, balance sheet.

P 5–9
Filling in the Missing Data
L.O.2, 3, 7

Given below are various balance sheet accounts, income statement accounts, and other data for the Dolesky Corporation. Some amounts for accounts listed have been deliberately omitted. Not all accounts of the corporation are listed.

Selected Balance Sheet Accounts

	December 31, 19x2 Debits	Credits	December 31, 19x1 Debits	Credits
Cash	$82,000		$78,000	
Accounts Receivable	?		26,000	
Supplies Inventory	3,000		2,500	
Merchandise Inventory	45,000		50,000	
Equipment	40,000		40,000	
Accumulated Depreciation—Equipment		$16,000		$12,000
Income Taxes Payable		4,200		10,000
Retained Earnings		?		39,000

Selected Income Statement Accounts
For the Year Ended

	12/31/x2	12/31/x1
Sales	$108,000	$99,000
Cost of Goods Sold	?	44,000
Supplies Expense.	1,200	1,000
Net Income	20,000	16,000

Additional information for 19x2:

a. Credit sales $29,000

b. Purchases of inventory   27,000

c. Collections on accounts receivable   18,000

d. Dividends declared and paid by Dolesky.   4,000

e. Supplies are recorded as an asset when purchased.

Required:

Using the information provided above, compute the following amounts for the Dolesky Corporation for 19x2:

1. Cost of goods sold for 19x2.
2. Depreciation expense for 19x2. No assets were purchased or sold during the year.
3. Accounts receivable at December 31, 19x2.
4. Cash sales for 19x2.
5. Purchases of supplies for 19x2.
6. Retained earnings at December 31, 19x2.

P 5–10
*Accounts Receivable
(Challenging)*
L.O.2–4

Selected information at the conclusion of three consecutive years of operations of Floate Company follows:

	12/31/x3	12/31/x2	12/31/x1
Accounts receivable	$ 500	$ 500	$400
Allowance for bad debts	?	30	40
Inventory, beginning balance.	?	70	60
Inventory, ending balance	?	?	70
Purchases (net)	?	810	?
Cost of goods available for sale	870	?	710
Sales	3,000	2,500	?
Cost of goods sold	810	790	?
Bad debts expense.	24	17	20

The following additional information is available:

a. The balance in the Allowance for Bad Debts account was $38 at the beginning of 19x1.

b. Actual accounts receivable written off during these years were as follows:

19x1	. . . . .	?
19x2	. . . . .	?
19x3	. . . . .	$14

c. All sales are made on credit.

d. Bad debt expense is estimated at 1% of sales in 19x1.

Required:

Analyze the various accounts and determine the following:

1. Cost of goods sold for 19x1.
2. Cost of goods available for sale for 19x2.
3. Ending inventory balance for 19x2 and 19x3.
4. Purchases for 19x1 and 19x3.
5. Sales for 19x1.
6. Accounts receivable written off in 19x1 and 19x2.
7. Allowance for bad debts at 12/31/x3.
8. Cash collected on accounts receivable for 19x2 and 19x3.

P 5–11
Sales and Cost
of Goods Sold
L.O.2, 3, 5, 6

The Joel Company uses the periodic method of recording its purchases of merchandise. The company's adjusted trial balance as of December 31, 19x2 (its fiscal year-end), appears below.

Joel Company
Adjusted Trial Balance
December 31, 19x2

	Debits	Credits
Cash	$ 63,200	
Accounts Receivable	10,000	
Allowance for Uncollectible Accounts		$ 2,200
Merchandise Inventory, 1/1/x2	40,000	
Purchases	110,000	
Purchase Returns and Allowances		2,000
Freight-In.	1,000	
Store Equipment	60,000	
Accumulated Depreciation—Store Equipment		24,000
Accounts Payable.		16,000
Income Taxes Payable.		6,000
Capital Stock.		80,000
Retained Earnings, 1/1/x2		18,000
Sales		204,000
Sales Returns and Allowances	4,000	
Administrative Expense	43,000	
Depreciation Expense	6,000	
Discounts Lost	4,000	
Income Tax Expense	6,000	
Dividends Declared and Paid.	5,000	
Totals	$352,200	$352,200

A physical inventory count at December 31, 19x2, showed that the company's inventory on hand was $32,000.

Required

1. Analyze the above information and compute the following:
   a. Net sales.
   b. Net purchases.
   c. Cost of goods sold.
   d. Gross margin.
2. Prepare in journal form the adjusting entries to record the cost of goods sold for the period.
3. Prepare in journal form the closing entries and compute the retained earnings balance for the Joel Company on December 31, 19x2.

P 5–12
Sales
(Challenging)
L.O.2–6

The Washington Company was formed on July 1, 19x1. It decided to use the periodic inventory system, offer terms of 2/10, n/30 on credit sales, record sales revenue under the net method, and close its books annually on June 30. During its first year of operations, the following selected transactions occurred:

a. Sales for cash, $10,000.
b. Sales on credit, $120,000 gross price.
c. Allowances of $6,000 (gross price) were granted to credit customers who complained within the discount period about receiving damaged goods.
d. Returns of goods within the discount period by credit customers, $8,500 gross price.
e. The gross invoice amount for collections from credit customers was $73,800. All credit customers took discounts.
f. The credit manager estimated bad debts losses to be 2% of net credit sales for the year or $2,068.
g. Purchased $85,000 of merchandise, with no discount terms being offered.
h. A physical inventory indicated that $12,000 of inventory was on hand at June 30, 19x2.

Required:
Based on the above information, compute the following amounts for the company's first year of operation:

1. Sales discounts taken on cash collections from credit customers.
2. Net sales revenue.
3. Gross margin on sales.
4. Net accounts receivable in the balance sheet at June 30, 19x2.

P 5–13
Operating Analysis
L.O.1, 9

1. Projected or forecasted financial statements are used—
   a. Before operations begin.
   b. To provide insights to the future and visualize the possible results of future operations.
   c. When negotiating for financing.
   d. All of the above.

Use the following data for questions 2 and 3.
   Selected account balances from the Wolverine Company's general ledger are as follows:

Accounts Payable.	$ 8,000
Accounts Receivable	45,000
Cash	15,600
Income Taxes Payable.	5,000
Inventory.	34,000
Notes Payable (due in 9 months)	30,000
Prepaid Rent	14,000
Salaries Payable	22,500
Supplies	3,000

2. Wolverine's current ratio is (round to two decimal places)—
   a. 1.44.
   b. 1.95.
   c. 1.70.
   d. .93.
3. Wolverine's quick ratio is (round to two decimal places)—
   a. 1.44.
   b. .93.
   c. .75.
   d. 1.70.

4. Accountants compare projected financial statements with actual financial statements to—
   a. Interpret the results of operations.
   b. Determine if potential problems exist.
   c. Revise plans for the future.
   d. All of the above.
   e. None of the above.

P 5–14
Receivables and Bad Debt Analysis
L.O.4

The Balance Corporation reported $35,850,000 in credit sales during 19x7. Credit receivables written off as uncollectible during 19x7 amounted to $360,000. Bad debt expense for 19x7 was 1% (0.01) of credit sales for 19x7. The following balance sheet data were reported by Balance at the end of 19x7 (after adjusting entries):

Partial Balance Sheet Data

	December 31	
	19x7	19x6
Accounts receivable	$2,700,000	$2,500,000
Less: Allowance for bad debts	160,000	150,000
Net accounts receivable	$2,540,000	$2,350,000

Required:
1. Reconstruct the journal entry (or entries) to record the estimate for bad debt expense for 19x7.
2. Reconstruct the journal entry (or entries) to record write-offs for 19x7.

P 5–15
Analysis of Balance Sheet Results (Challenging)
L.O.9

The following comparative balance sheet data were available for the Westend Corporation as of the end of 19x5:

Westend Corporation
Balance Sheet
December 31, 19x5
(in millions)

Assets	19x5	19x4	Liabilities	19x5	19x4
Cash	$ 3	$ 2	Accounts payable (Inventory only)	$ 10	$ 19
Accounts receivable	18	15	Notes payable.	55	50
Inventory	47	50	Sales revenue received in advance	15	11
Equipment (net)	89	95	General expenses payable	18	12
Land	40	40	Total liabilities.	$ 98	$ 92
Buildings	136	120	**Stockholders' Equity**		
Accumulated depreciation—buildings . . .	(72)	(74)	Capital stock	125	125
			Retained earnings	38	31
Total assets	$261	$248	Total liabilities and stockholders' equity . .	$261	$248

Additional information ($000,000):

Dividends declared and paid to Westend's stockholders	$ 12
Cash payments on accounts payable during 19x5.	103
Cash collected on accounts receivable during 19x5	148
Cost of building sold during 19x5	18
Accumulated depreciation on buildings sold during 19x5	5
Gain on sale of building sold in 19x5.	7
Cost of equipment purchased during 19x5	6

Required:

Answer the following questions concerning Westend Corporation. (Hint: Set up T accounts to help solve for the missing information.)

1. How much depreciation expense was taken in 19x5 on equipment? No equipment was sold during 19x5.
2. What was Westend's net income for 19x5?
3. If total sales revenue reported for 19x5 was $170 million, what was the amount of 19x5 sales revenue from cash (versus credit) sales during 19x5? (Note that all $11 million of Sales Revenue Received in Advance from 19x4 was earned during 19x5. Also, there were no sales returns or refunds of any kind.)
4. How much inventory was acquired during 19x5?
5. What was the cost of inventory sold during 19x5?
6. Cash payments for general expenses during 19x5 were $60 million. What was the amount of general expense reported in the 19x5 income statement?

P 5–16
Analysis of Balance Sheet Results (Challenging)
L.O.9

Consider the following comparative balance sheet data (in millions) for American Brands, Inc., maker of tobacco products (Lucky Strike, Pall Mall), distilled spirits (Jim Beam, Gilbey's Gin), Titleist golf balls, Master locks, and many other consumer products:

	As of December 31	
Selected Balance Sheet Data	**19x7**	**19x6**
Assets:		
Accounts Receivable.	$1,128	$ 692
Less allowance for uncollectibles	39	26
Accounts Receivable—Net	$1,089	$ 666
Inventories	1,693	1,264
Property plant and equipment.	1,840	1,385
Less accumulated depreciation	775	640
Net property plant and equipment	$1,065	$ 745
Other assets	209	105
Liabilities:		
Accounts payable (all pertaining to inventory).	$ 316	$ 256
Accrued taxes payable.	923	607
Long-term debt	1,631	671

The following additional data are assumed to be from either the income statement or the cash flow statement (in millions):

Cash received for plant and equipment sold during 19x7	$ 17
Loss on sale of plant and equipment sold in 19x7	20
Depreciation expense for 19x7	141
Taxes paid in cash during 19x7	349
Additional cash borrowed long-term during 19x7.	1,482
Other expenses for 19x7	950
Cash payments for inventory during 19x7.	10,870
Bad debt expense for 19x7	118
Recoveries of prior year's write-offs during 19x7.	3
Credit sales from 19x7	13,110

Additional assumptions:

a. All inventory is purchased on account.

b. Other assets are all for prepaid expenses.

c. Other expenses are all from expired prepaid expenses.

Required:

1. What was cost of goods sold for 19x7?

2. What were write-offs of bad debts for 19x7? 108

3. How much cash was collected on accounts receivable during 19x7? 12,569

4. How much cash was paid for prepaid expenses in 19x7? (Hint: Assume that all *Other Assets* were prepaid expenses and that all *Other Expenses* were first recorded as *Other Assets*.)

5. What was 19x7 income tax expense?

6. How much long-term debt was retired in 19x7?

· APPENDIX PROBLEMS

P 5–17
Accounts Receivable
L.O.4, 10

Zeron Nursery Company had the following before adjusting trial balance items at year-end on December 31, 19x1 (all accounts carry their normal balances):

Cash.	$ 180,000
Accounts Receivable	2,200,000
Allowance for Uncollectibles	228,000
Sales	10,500,000
Sales Returns and Allowances	300,000

Required:

1. Prepare adjusting journal entries for Zeron related to bad debts if —

a. Two percent of net sales is used to estimate uncollectibles.

b. The aging of Accounts Receivables method is used, and it is estimated that $380,000 of accounts receivable will not be collected.

2. Prepare the entries needed on January 25, 19x2, for the collection of a $12,800 account written off on December 1, 19x1.

P 5–18
Aging of Accounts Receivable
L.O.10

The Winston Company's accounting department has compiled the following information as of December 30, 19xx, from its accounts receivable subsidiary ledger:

Month Issued	Total of Outstanding Invoices	Estimated Uncollectible Percentage
Dec.	$410,000	10%
Nov.	106,000	15
Oct.	62,000	25
Sept.	15,000	40
Aug.	16,000	
July	5,400	
June	2,300	
May	1,100	60
Apr.	0	
Mar.	4,200	
Feb.	0	
Jan.	10,000	

Winston writes all invoices off that are over a year old. The company uses the percentages shown to estimate its bad debt expense.

At December 31, 19xx, the Accounts Receivable account has a debit balance of $632,000; the Allowance for Bad Debts account also has a debit balance of $1,350 before adjustments.

Required:
1. Prepare a schedule showing the aging of Winston's Accounts Receivable account.
2. Prepare the journal entry to record bad debt expense for the year.
3. Show the balance sheet presentation of accounts receivable on December 31, 19xx.

P 5–19
Receivables and Bad Debts Analysis (Challenging)
L.O.10

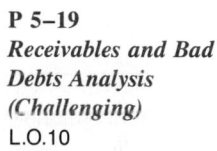

Bradley Corporation is a wholesaler doing business with a group of retail stores in the Los Angeles area on a credit basis. Bradley reported the following balance sheet data (after adjustment) as of the end of 19x4.

	December 31	
	19x4	**19x3**
Accounts Receivable—Retailers	$5,275,100	$2,967,800
Less: Allowance for bad debts	126,100	228,950
Net Accounts Receivable	$5,149,000	$2,738,850

Bradley estimates bad debt expenses at one half of 1% (.005) of credit sales. All sales are on credit. Bradley has experienced significant increases in sales during the past few years, as noted in the following summary:

	For the Year		
	19x4	**19x3**	**19x2**
Credit sales (in millions)	$40.85	$32.70	$26.35

Required:
1. Reconstruct the adjusting journal entry that was recorded at the end of 19x4 to reflect the year-end estimate for bad debt expense.
2. Assume there are no collections on accounts once they are written off. What was the amount of write-offs recorded by Bradley during 19x4?
3. What was the amount of cash collected on accounts receivable during 19x4?
4. As a banker who has made large loans to Bradley, you are responsible for evaluating Bradley's credit position. Do you feel Bradley's creditworthiness is improving or worsening? Answer "improving" or "worsening" and give support for your answer based **only** on the data provided—**do not** assume any additional facts.

P 5–20
Comprehensive
L.O.2, 3, 10

Salem Electronics, Inc., is a retailer of one brand of personal computers and has the following history of transactions during the first month of operations:

Feb. 1 Sold common stock for $200,000.

1 Leased a store and a warehouse for $10,000 a month and paid $30,000 in advance for the first three months.

3 Purchased 100 units of inventory at $800 per unit. Terms were 2/10, net/30. Salem uses the net method to record purchases.

13 Paid accounts payable for the February 3 purchase net of discount.

24 Purchased 50 units under the same terms and for the same price as before.

25 Returned two items from the February 24 purchase because of defects and was given full credit.

Various dates During the month total sales were 110 items at $1,200 per unit. Credit sales were for 60 units and the rest were for cash. Cash collected from credit customers amounted to $52,000. Other expenses paid during the month were

Telephone	$ 1,800
Rented Equipment	3,500
Salaries	25,000
Insurance	1,100
Miscellaneous	2,400

Month-end Thirty-eight units of inventory were still on hand at the end of the month. Salem's management expects that 2% of credit sales will be lost to bad debts.

Required:

Record all journal entries including any necessary adjusting and closing entries. Prepare the Salem's balance sheet, income statement, and statement of cash flows.

• CASES

C 5–1

Inventory and Cost of Goods Sold

L.O.2, 7

Plastic Made, Inc., started business this year to purchase high-quality kitchen containers from several manufacturers for sale by mail order directly to customers. Now that the first year of operations is over, the accountant is trying to decide the best way to construct an income statement. The following facts are applicable to the first year:

Beginning inventory	$ 0
Invoices received for merchandise purchased during the year.	800,000
Damaged merchandise returned to the manufacturer.	12,000
Invoices paid during the year on credit purchases	750,000
Freight-in paid by Plastic Made, Inc.	2,500
Freight paid by manufacturer	1,200
Inventory of merchandise on hand at year-end	30,000
Cost of supplies used in warehouse maintenance	500
Cost of wages for warehouseperson	22,000
Property taxes on merchandise	3,000
Cost of shipping to customers.	4,000

Required:

1. Calculate and discuss how cost of goods sold is determined.
2. Write a short analysis of why certain items are not included in cost of goods sold, and explain what effect they have on net income.

C 5–2

Preparing an Income Statement—Monsanto Company

L.O.8

The following selected information appears in a published annual report of the Monsanto Company, which provides a diverse product line ranging from chemical and agricultural products to low-calorie sweeteners and synthetic fibers (all amounts in millions):

Accounts payable	$ 522
Amortization expense.	88
Cash	195
Cost of goods sold	4,841
Income tax expense	170
Interest expense	178
Interest revenue	63
Inventories.	1,097
Land	101
Marketing and administrative expenses	919
Net sales	6,747
Other revenue	23
Technological expenses.	548

There are several formats for income statements; two are shown below.

Format A:

Net sales	$xxx
Cost of goods sold	xxx
Gross margin	$ xx
Expenses	xx
Income from operations	$ xx
Other:	
Interest revenue (or expense)	xx
Miscellaneous revenue (or expense)	(xx)
Net income before taxes	$ xx
Income tax expense	xx
Net income	$ xx

Format B:

Revenues:	
Net sales	$xxx
Other revenue	xx
Total revenues	$xxx
Expenses:	
Cost of goods sold	$xxx
Detailed expenses	xx
Miscellaneous expenses.	xx
Total expenses	$xxx
Net income before taxes	$ xx
Income tax expense	xx
Net income	$ xx

Required:

Prepare Monsanto's income statement for each of the above formats. Write a paragraph about the differences in information transmitted by each.

C 5–3
Cash Flow and Net Income
L.O.9

On November 10, 19x1, you, as a business consultant for MD Pizza, are present at the following conversation between two partners of a chain of pizza stores who are trying to decide whether they should expand, starting January 1, 19x2, into a college town 50 miles west of their current region, which currently includes 20 locations and a fleet of 40 delivery trucks.

"We need a loan to get started. Trucks are going to cost $200,000 and equipment $50,000. Leases on 10 locations, another $10,000 down. We have to lease the warehouse with a $5,000 deposit, and I project negative cash flow from operations of $10,000 for each of the first six months and breaking even for the second six months. That's another $60,000 we need plus interest on the amount borrowed at 10% minimum," said one partner.

"Without this new operation, we will probably have net income next year of about $600,000. If we go into it you mean we're going to have close to zero?" asked the other partner.

Required:

In a short memo explain to the partners the difference between cash flow and net income and discuss the effect of each item mentioned in the conversation above on both cash flow and net income. Assume that after starting operations all transactions are on a cash basis and that inventory levels for the new operations stay about the same at $200,000. Assume also that the company borrows the amount needed for the initial cash outflow and that any other cash deficiencies will be contributed by the partners. Assume that trucks and equipment have five-year lives with no salvage value.

C 5–4
Inventory Transactions and Liquidity Analysis
L.O.2, 9

Bradford, Inc., reported the following items on its comparative balance sheet at December 31, 19x6:

	December 31	
	19x6	**19x5**
Inventory.	$ 96,214,000	$53,999,000
Accounts Payable.	$108,419,000	$86,000,000

All inventory was purchased on credit and cost of goods sold for the year was $1,284,000,000.

Required:
1. How much cash was paid for inventory during 19x6? (Hint: Use T accounts to solve this case.)
2. Write a concise analysis that answers the following questions: How much of the inventory buildup (increase) required cash outflow? Did the company's liquidity improve or worsen because of its inventory acquisition and payment activities?

· APPENDIX CASE

C 5–5
Accounts Receivable and Bad Debts—General Mills, Inc.
L.O.4

General Mills, a major competitor in consumer foods, restaurants, and specialty retailing with such popular items as Cheerios, Wheaties, and the Red Lobster restaurant chain, has the following information from an annual report:

**General Mills, Inc., and Subsidiaries
Excerpt from Balance Sheet
(in millions)**

	5/25/x1	5/26/x2
Accounts receivable	$220.0	$284.5
Allowance for doubtful accounts	6.3	4.0

Assume that General Mills writes off $4.2 million of accounts during the fiscal year 19x2 and that it uses the percentage-of-sales method to estimate bad debts. Write a short report explaining the effect that writing off bad debts has on cash flows, net income, and net assets.

Diamond Corporation
Income Statement
For 1994

	1994	1993
Revenues		
Total revenues	$ xx,xxx	$ xx,xxx
Expenses		
Cost of goods sold	**xx,xxx**	**xx,xxx**

Diamond Corporation
Balance Sheet
12/31/94

	1994	1993
Current assets		
Inventory at FIFO cost	**$xx,xxx**	**$xx,xxx**
Less allowance to reduce inventory to market	**(xx)**	**(xx)**
Inventory at LCM	**$xx,xxx**	**$xx,xxx**
Noncurrent assets		
Total noncurrent assets	xx,xxx	xx,xxx
Current liabilities		
Total current liabilities	xx,xxx	xx,xxx
Noncurrent liabilities		
Total noncurrent liabilities	xx,xxx	xx,xxx
Stockholders' equity		
Total stockholders' equity	xx,xxx	xx,xxx

Diamond Corporation
Cash Flow Statement
For 1994

	1994	1993
Operating activities		
Cash paid to suppliers	**$xx,xxx**	**$xx,xxx**
Investing activities		
Cash for investments	(xx,xxx)	(xx,xxx)
Financing activities		
Cash from financing	xx,xxx	xx,xxx

**FINANCIAL
STATEMENT
COMPONENTS
EMPHASIZED IN
CHAPTER 6**

6

Inventory

Very little is black and white. Is inventory salable and at what price? Is a receivable collectable just because the debtor is still in business? Asset valuation is an issue of being true to yourself first and then carrying that answer through to your reporting responsibilities.

Richard R. Current
The Shane Group, Inc.

· Learning Objectives

After studying Chapter 6, you should understand

1. The decision that managers must make in choosing between the periodic inventory system and the perpetual inventory system, pp. 274–75.

2. The four cost flow methods—specific identification (SI); first-in, first-out (FIFO); last-in, first-out (LIFO); and weighted average (WA)—and how they are used in periodic inventory systems, pp. 278–82.

3. The lower-of-cost-or-market measurement test, pp. 283–85.

4. The impact of inventory errors, pp. 284–86.

5. How to analyze inventory changes, pp. 286–89.

6. How to measure the cost of ending inventory using LIFO, FIFO, and moving average (MA) methods in a perpetual system (Appendix 6A), pp. 292–94.

7. The fundamentals of the retail method of estimating inventory value (Appendix 6B), pp. 296–98.

8. LIFO reserves and LIFO liquidation (Appendix 6C), pp. 299–300.

Along with investments in plant, property, and equipment, many businesses invest a large portion of their resources in inventories. The term *inventory* is used (1) to refer to a specific physical item of merchandise, (2) to identify a general category of merchandise, and (3) to refer to all merchandise that is included as an asset. Inventories are considered current assets since they will usually be converted to cash in less than one year (or, by definition, within the operating cycle).

Inventory consists of merchandise that is produced or obtained to be sold in the regular course of business for the purpose of making a profit. Companies can earn a profit from selling inventory because they add form, place, and/or time utility to the merchandise making it worth more to the buyer than the merchandise cost the seller. For example, a retail furniture store buys furniture from various parts of the world and provides place utility (through its retail location) and time utility (having the goods available when the customer wants them).

This chapter begins with a discussion of how managerial decisions affect the inventory costs reported in the financial statements. The chapter also shows you how to analyze the inventory and cost-of-goods-sold figures on comparative financial statements, and concludes with three appendixes that provide additional inventory information.

IMPORTANCE OF INVENTORY

The efficient use of inventory has a significant effect on the performance of a business. For most merchandising and manufacturing businesses, inventory is the lifeblood of profitable business operations. (Although we do not discuss manufacturing companies in this textbook, manufacturing companies produce products that are sold to merchandising companies and other customers.)

Controlling the amount of inventory a business has on hand involves detailed planning. Merchandise that remains in inventory for long periods of time is not earning a return. In fact, merchandise that remains in inventory is costly to the business and results in (1) increased financing costs when merchandise is purchased with borrowed funds, (2) storage costs for space that could be available for other business operations, (3) increased administrative costs to safeguard and keep track of the merchandise, and (4) the risk that inventory will become obsolete. On the other hand, sales may be lost if sufficient inventory is not on hand.

In the remainder of this chapter, you will learn some of the decisions that merchandising managers must make pertaining to inventory measurement. These decisions include

1. Selection of an inventory system.
2. Defining components of cost and measuring quantities.
3. Selection of an inventory costing method.
4. Testing inventory cost relative to market value (lower of cost or market).

The alternative choices examined in these sections are all within the framework of generally accepted accounting principles (GAAP), even though selection of alternative choices may lead to significant differences in inventory measurements and operating income, as you will learn.

SELECTION OF AN INVENTORY SYSTEM

Two types of inventory systems available to merchandising and manufacturing companies are the periodic inventory system and the perpetual inventory system. An **inventory system** enables the business to measure the cost of inventory on hand (the asset account) and the cost of inventory sold (the expense account). Recall that the **periodic inventory system** illustrated in Chapter 5 provides measures of ending inventory and cost of goods sold only (periodically) when a physical inventory count is taken and the ending inventory cost is computed. The set of accounts in a periodic system enables the following computations to be made periodically:

Beginning inventory	$xxx	(from last period's physical count)
+ Net purchases (computation below)	+ xxx	(from the purchases accounts)
Cost of goods available for sale	$xxx	
− Ending Inventory (asset)	− xxx	(from this period's physical count)
Cost of goods sold (expense)	$xxx	

The net purchases amount is computed from the following ledger accounts:

		Normal Balance
Purchases	$xxx	Debit
− Purchase returns and allowances (if any)	− xx	Credit
− Purchase discounts (if any)	− xx	Credit
+ Freight-in (if any)	+ xx	Debit
Net purchases	$xxx	Debit

The periodic system was used by Byte-Size, Inc., in Chapter 5.[1]

The perpetual inventory system also permits the business to obtain a measure of ending inventory and cost of goods sold. However, the perpetual system does not use the purchases accounts to record acquisitions of inventory. Instead, in the perpetual inventory system records are kept so that the balance in Inventory and Cost of Goods Sold are continuously (perpetually) updated each time merchandise is purchased or sold. Rather than waiting until the end of an accounting period to measure Inventory and Cost of Goods Sold, these two accounts are updated on an ongoing basis. For example, consider the following comparisons for the purchase of $700 of merchandise inventory:

Entry to Purchase Merchandise

In a Periodic System			In a Perpetual System		
Purchases (A).	700		Inventory (A)	700	
Accounts Payable (L) . . .		700	Accounts Payable (L) . . .		700

The asset, inventory, is directly increased at the time merchandise is purchased in the perpetual system. Similarly, inventory is decreased and cost of goods sold is increased directly when merchandise is sold. Assume that merchandise costing $500 is sold for $800. The following comparison may be made:

Entries to Sell Merchandise

In a Periodic System			In a Perpetual System		
Accounts Receivable (A)	800		Accounts Receivable (A). . . .	800	
Sales (R)		800	Sales (R)		800
(no entry)			Cost of Goods Sold (E)	500	
			Inventory (A)		500

---

[1] You may wish to examine the periodic inventory system illustrated on pages 218–25 if you need to review this material.

Objective 1
The decision that managers must make in choosing between the periodic inventory system and the perpetual inventory system.

The periodic system does not record the outflow of inventory or cost of goods sold until the end of the accounting period. The perpetual system records the outflow of inventory at the time goods are sold, thus providing an up-to-date balance in inventory and cost of goods sold at all times. In a manual accounting system the continuous recording of additions (for purchases) and deletions (for sales) from each inventory item would make the perpetual system costly to use. However, with the increased usage of fast, high-powered computerized systems, more and more companies are using the perpetual system for inventories. Perpetual systems help reduce the chances of lost sales because of stockouts. Since perpetual systems tell managers how many units of each product are on hand at all times, it is easier to know when to reorder each product. It is also easier to prevent quantities of each product from becoming too large or too small in a perpetual system. Even department stores and grocery stores, which carry hundreds of different low-cost items, now use perpetual systems, many involving wands or electronic reading devices that scan sales tickets or bar coded labels to reduce the inventory quantity of each specific item of merchandise instantly as it is sold. (See Chapter 7 Appendix B for more details.)

There are advantages and disadvantages to both perpetual and periodic systems. In general, periodic systems are simpler and less costly, while perpetual systems are somewhat more complex and more costly. However, even these generalizations may not always be true, and each specific situation should be evaluated to decide which system is most appropriate.

The journal entries and information provided by the periodic and perpetual systems are summarized in Exhibit 6–1. Note, however, that both systems **will not usually provide the same results for the ending asset value and for cost of goods sold.** Only under the FIFO costing method will perpetual and periodic systems provide the same results, as will be illustrated in the next section of the chapter. You should carefully examine the similarities and differences in the two systems illustrated in Exhibit 6–1.

MEASUREMENT OF INVENTORY QUANTITY AND COST

Costing inventory requires two pieces of information: (1) the number of units or other measure of inventory quantities (e.g., pounds, feet, and so on); and (2) the cost per unit. Below we consider these two components in order.

Inventory Quantity

An inventory count must be taken at least once each year. This counting, called a physical inventory count, or simply "taking inventory," is required for both perpetual and periodic systems. In a periodic system it is needed to measure the ending inventory cost. In a perpetual system it is used to check on the accuracy of the perpetual records, thereby helping management estimate losses due to theft, spoilage, breakage, and so on. Taking a physical count requires special care for three types of inventory:

1. Inventory in transit.
2. Goods out on consignment.
3. Special-order goods.

When taking the physical inventory count, the inventory should normally include all merchandise owned by the business but not yet sold. This includes sales of inventory in transit when the legal title to inventory has not passed to the buyer/customer. The seller's invoice usually indicates when the title of the goods passes to the buyer. For example, an invoice marked FOB shipping point indicates that the goods are free on board (FOB) to the seller's point of shipment only—the title passes to the buyer as goods leave the seller's location,

EXHIBIT 6–1

Accounting Entries for Periodic and Perpetual Accounting Systems

A. Comparison of Journal Entries to Record Events Concerning Inventory

Events	Periodic		Perpetual	
1. Buy goods on open account, terms 2/10, net 30.	**Purchases (A)** . . . . 600 Accounts Payable (L)	600	**Inventory (A)** . . . . 600 Accounts Payable (L)	600
2. Pay for freight on purchase of goods.	**Freight-In (A)** . . . . 60 Cash (A)	60	**Inventory (A)** . . . . 60 Cash (A)	60
3. Return 10% of goods purchased in (1) above.	Accounts Payable (L) . . . . . . 60 **Purchase Returns (XA)** . .	60	Accounts Payable (L) . . . . 60 **Inventory (A)**	60
4. Pay for 50% of goods purchased in (1) above within discount period.	Accounts Payable (L) . . . . . . 300 Cash (A) . . . . **Purchase Discounts (XA)** .	294 6	Accounts Payable (L) . . . . 300 Cash (A) . . . . **Inventory (A)**	294 6
5. Pay for 40% of goods purchased in (1) above after discount period.	Accounts Payable (L) . . . . . . 240 Cash (A)	240	Accounts Payable (L) . . . . 240 Cash (A)	240
6. Sell goods costing $410 for $700 cash.	Cash (A) . . . . 700 Sales (R)	700	Cash (A) . . . . 700 Sales (R) . . . . **Cost of Goods Sold (E)** . . . . . 410 **Inventory (A)**	700 410

B. Ledger Balances before Adjusting and Closing Entries

Periodic		Perpetual	
Inventory (beginning)	$ 0	Inventory (ending)	$184 Debit*
Purchases	600 Debit	Cost of Goods Sold	410 Debit
Freight-In	60 Debit		
Purchase Returns	60 Credit		
Purchase Discounts	6 Credit		

C. Adjusting and Closing Entries

	Periodic		Perpetual	
1. To adjust.	**Inventory (ending) (A)** . . . . . **184** **Cost of Goods Sold (E)** . . . . **410** Purchase Returns (XA) . . . . . 60 Purchase Discounts (XA) . . . . 6 Inventory (beginning) (A) . . Purchases (A) . . . . Freight-In (A)	 0 600 60	No entry.	
2. To close.	Income Summary . . . . 410 Cost of Goods Sold (E) . . .	410	Income Summary . . . . 410 Cost of Goods Sold (E)	410

D. Ledger Balances after Adjusting and Closing

Periodic		Perpetual	
Inventory	$184 Debit	Inventory	$184 Debit

*This balance is found as follows:

	Inventory		
(1)	600	(3)	60
(2)	60	(4)	6
		(6)	410
	184		

and the buyer pays the freight from the point of shipment. FOB destination indicates that the goods are free on board (FOB) to the buyer's location. Title passes to the buyer as the goods are received at the buyer's location, and the seller pays the freight charges up to the point where the buyer takes delivery and title.

FOB shipping point and FOB destination are not the only possible inventory-in-transit situations. Title to inventory can pass to the buyer at any point agreed to by both buyer and seller.

Goods out on consignment are owned by a company but held by some agent of the company at another location for possible sale to customers. For example, farm equipment is usually owned by the manufacturer but held on consignment by farm implement sales agents in farming communities. The equipment is part of the manufacturer's inventory until sold by the agent.

When a customer places a special order for merchandise, the company usually assumes that it has made a sale as soon as the merchandise is ready to be delivered. If the special-order goods are on hand at the end of an accounting period waiting to be delivered to the customer, the company usually records the goods as a sale, and the item is not included in the company's inventory even though the company still has possession of the goods.

Inventory Cost

The identification of inventory cost is guided by a concept that applies to all assets. Inventory costs should include **all costs necessary to place the inventory into its intended useful state.** Application of the concept often requires professional judgment.

Costs that are assigned to units of inventory are called product costs. For a manufacturing company, accountants must use judgment to determine the product costs per unit for materials, direct labor, and other production costs. For a merchandising company, product costs usually consist of the invoice cost of merchandise, plus freight-in, and less any discounts for timely payment and for purchase returns and allowances.

While other costs may be included in merchandise inventory, in practice accountants rarely include them. Packaging costs, such as shopping bags, and assembly costs, such as costs for assembling bikes, could be assigned to merchandise inventory. However, most merchandisers expense these costs as *period costs* rather than include them in inventory as product costs. Period costs, also called **revenue expenditures,** are costs incurred to generate revenue and are expensed in the period in which they occur (not assigned to inventory).

Because companies often purchase identical inventory items at different prices during the accounting period, accountants must use one of four alternative cost flow methods to measure the dollar value of inventory. These four methods, illustrated next, are specific identification (SI); first-in, first-out (FIFO); last-in, first-out (LIFO); and weighted average (WA). Note that these four cost flow methods are used to measure ending inventory and cost of goods sold.

Selection of an Inventory Cost Flow Method: Periodic Inventory Systems

Accounting systems assign costs to inventories using the four common cost flow methods. If the cost of merchandise does not change over time, all four cost flow methods will result in the same measures of cost of goods sold and ending inventory. However, because the cost of most inventory items changes over time, the question that must be answered is, What unit costs should be assigned to the inventory units sold and what unit costs should be assigned to the inventory units remaining on hand at year-end?

When different batches of inventory are purchased (or manufactured) at different costs, some systematic cost flow method must be used to assign the actual unit costs paid to both the units sold and the units remaining at the end of the period. The method used to assign costs to units sold and units on hand does **not** need to be the same as the actual physical flow of goods and rarely is in practice. **However,** as illustrated below, **the total cost of all of the inventory available must equal the costs assigned (allocated) to the units sold (cost of goods sold) plus the costs assigned to the units remaining on hand (ending inventory) no matter which cost flow method is used.**

The four cost flow methods *describing* cost of goods sold are defined as follows:

1. Specific identification (SI).   In the SI method, the actual cost of each specifically identified unit sold is charged to cost of goods sold. This method would be useful for inventories that are valuable and somewhat unique, such as precious jewels or automobiles. Specific identification is the only inventory costing method that values each unit of inventory at its actual cost. All other costing methods are based on *assumed* cost flows.

2. First-in, first-out (FIFO).   The FIFO method assumes that the "first goods in" (beginning inventory, then the first purchases) are the first goods sold. The FIFO method assigns the actual cost of the "first goods in" to cost of goods sold. FIFO could be used for all inventories with large quantities, such as hand tools or small appliances, chemicals, tires, and so on.

3. Last-in, first-out (LIFO).   The LIFO method assumes that "the last goods in" (most recent purchases) are the first goods sold. LIFO assigns the actual cost of the "last goods in" to cost of goods sold. Like FIFO, LIFO can be used for large quantities of like items such as appliances, auto parts, paint, and so on. LIFO generally does not follow the physical flow of goods.

4. Weighted average (WA).   The WA method measures the cost of the units sold (as well as the ending inventory) using the weighted average cost of all prior purchases. The weighted average cost is computed by taking the cost of goods available for sale and dividing by the number of units available for sale (beginning inventory plus purchases). This computation weights the cost of each batch of inventory purchased or made in proportion to the quantity purchased. For example, 100 units at a cost of $5 each (total $500) plus 200 units at a cost of $4.25 each (total $850) results in a weighted average cost of $4.50 [($500 + $850)/(100 + 200)]. The weighted average method applies the same average cost to goods on hand and to goods sold, thus smoothing out the effects of changes in inventory costs.

Jack and Maryann were both future accounting students at the University. They were hired by the Student Lounge to sell school supplies in the Lounge, which was owned by a local bookstore. Since this was a new venture for both the Lounge and the two students, they were not sure how to begin. Let's listen in on their conversation in April 19x1, their first year at the University.

Jack: Well, at least we have some kind of job to help us finance our courses that we'll be taking in the spring term.

Maryann: Yeah, but I'm not sure I know enough to develop an accounting system for these supplies we're supposed to sell.

Jack: Don't worry. The accounting professor we're going to have said to just keep track of our purchases and sales and by the end of spring term we'll know all we need to know about how to account for them.

Jack and Maryann are about to learn how to account for inventory for the Student Lounge. To illustrate the information needed and how it is used to cost out the ending inventory and measure cost of sales, we will focus on one of the items sold by the Lounge, a new erasable ink pen.

Objective 2
The four cost flow
methods—specific
identification (SI); first-in,
first-out (FIFO); last-in,
first-out (LIFO); and
weighted average—and
how they are used in
periodic inventory systems.

To illustrate the four cost flow methods, assume that during 19x1 the Student Lounge began selling a new erasable ink pen. The purchases and sales of the pens during 19x1 are given below. Note that parentheses are used around the sales figures to remind you that these figures represent decreases in inventory.

	Units	Unit Cost	Total Cost	Total Sales Revenue
Beginning inventory	0	$0	$ 0	
Purchase, 5/1	40	6	240	
Sales, 5/1 to 8/30 at $8 each	(20)			$ 160
Purchase, 8/30	290	7	2,030	
Sales, 9/1 to 9/30 at $10 each	(245)			2,450
Purchase, 9/30	20	9	180	
Sales, 10/1 to 12/31 at $11 each	(35)			385
Units on hand at end of period	50			
Cost of goods available for sale			$2,450	
Sales revenue				$2,995

From the purchases and sales data we can see that 350 units were purchased (40 + 290 + 20) for $2,450, and that 300 units were sold (20 + 245 + 35) for $2,995, leaving 50 units in inventory. Now we address the question, How much did we make on the sale of 300 units?

The specific identification method would not be appropriate for erasable ink pens, which are low-value items with no specifically identifiable features. The other three methods would all be appropriate for costing something like erasable ink pens. The FIFO method assumes that the first items placed into inventory are the first items to be sold. The FIFO measure for cost of goods sold and ending inventory would be computed as follows:

FIFO cost of goods sold—Compute cost of the 300 units sold.
Remember, FIFO means that the earliest purchases are in cost of goods sold.

Units	×	Unit cost	=	Total cost
40	×	$6	=	$ 240
260*	×	$7	=	1,820
300				$2,060

*From the purchase of 290 units on 8/30.

FIFO ending inventory—50 units remaining.
FIFO means that the most recent purchases are in inventory.

Units	×	Unit cost	=	Total cost
20	×	$9	=	$180
30*	×	$7	=	210
50				$390

*From the purchase of 290 units on 8/30.

Since cost of goods sold plus ending inventory cost must always equal cost of goods available for sale ($2,450 in this example), **both** computations illustrated above are not required. For example, given ending FIFO inventory of $390, we know from the following that cost of goods sold must be $2,060:

Beginning inventory	$ 0	
+Net purchases.	+ 2,450	
Cost of goods available for sale	$2,450	
−Ending inventory (FIFO)	− 390	(computed above)
Cost of goods sold.	$2,060	(forced or computed as above)

Unlike FIFO, LIFO assumes that the last items placed in inventory are the first items sold, despite the fact that in most cases this is not physically possible. The LIFO cost of ending inventory and cost of goods sold for the Student Lounge data given above would be computed as follows:

LIFO ending inventory—50 units remaining.

LIFO means oldest purchases are in inventory.

Units	×	Unit cost	=	Total cost
40	×	$6	=	$240
10*	×	$7	=	70
50				$310

*From the purchase of 290 units.

LIFO cost of goods sold—Compute cost of the 300 units sold.
Remember, LIFO means the most recent purchases are in cost of goods sold.

Cost of goods available for sale	$2,450	
−Ending inventory (LIFO)	− 310	(computed above)
Cost of goods sold.	$2,140	(forced)

The **weighted average cost** for the Student Lounge example is computed to be $7 per unit, as follows:

$$\frac{\text{Cost of goods available}}{\text{Total units available}} = \frac{\$2,450}{350} = \$7.00$$
$$\text{(beginning inventory + purchases)}$$

Therefore, ending inventory is $350 (50 units × $7) and cost of goods sold is $2,100 (300 × $7) using the weighted average method. Be careful to note that, in this first illustration (summarized in Exhibit 6–2), cost of goods available for sale is the **same** for FIFO, LIFO, and WA **because there is no beginning inventory,** since it is the first period of operations. Later, when we illustrate the next period's results for the Student Lounge, you will see how each method results in a different (1) **beginning inventory;** (2) **cost of goods available for sale;** and (3) **ending inventory,** which is normally the case.

Gross margin is the dollar difference between net sales and cost of goods sold. The measurements of Student Lounge's ending inventory, cost of goods sold, and gross margin for 19x1 under the **assumed** cost flows—FIFO, LIFO, and WA—are compared in Exhibit 6–2. Remember that you do not actually have to sell the pens on a FIFO basis to use

EXHIBIT 6–2

Student Lounge
Comparison of FIFO,
LIFO, and WA for 19x1

	19x1		
	FIFO	**LIFO**	**WA**
Sales revenue	$2,995	$2,995	$2,995
Cost of goods sold:			
Beginning inventory	$ 0	$ 0	$ 0
Purchases:			
40 @ $6.	$ 240	$ 240	$ 240
290 @ $7.	2,030	2,030	2,030
20 @ $9.	180	180	180
Cost of goods available for sale	$2,450	$2,450	$2,450
Less ending inventory (50 units):			
20 @ $9 and 30 @ $7	390		
40 @ $6 and 10 @ $7		310	
50 @ $7*			350
Cost of goods sold	$2,060	$2,140	$2,100
Gross margin	$ 935	$ 855	$ 895

*$2,450/350 units = $7 per unit weighted average cost.

the FIFO cost flow method. Thus, the actual flow of the products need not be the same as the cost flows except when using the SI method. As a result, FIFO, LIFO, and WA are called cost flow assumptions.

Nature of Cost Flow Differences. Notice that the value of the Ending Inventory as reported in the balance sheet at the end of 19x1 and the amount of Cost of Goods Sold reported in the income statement of 19x1 will differ depending on which cost flow assumption is used. In the Student Lounge example, LIFO results in the lowest ending inventory value ($310) and the lowest gross margin ($855) but the highest cost of goods sold ($2,140), while FIFO results in the highest ending inventory value ($390) and the highest gross margin ($935) but the lowest cost of goods sold ($2,060).

In periods of increasing inventory costs, LIFO will generally result in the highest cost of goods sold and, therefore, the lowest net income and ending inventory value. Keep in mind, however, that the Student Lounge is really no better off using one cost flow assumption instead of another! The economic facts—the purchases and the sales—are constant, and the **cost flow assumption only affects the timing of when specific inventory costs are assigned to cost of goods sold.**

Jack and Maryann looked at the alternative results summarized in Exhibit 6–2 at the end of 19x1. The following conversation took place:

Jack: Well, we've got to decide which one of these cost flow assumptions to use.

Maryann: It looks like we are stuck with a periodic inventory system, which is good, actually, since it's so easy to use. Can you imagine keeping perpetual records for all these items?

Jack: Right! We could make a career out of this part-time job that way. Say, it looks to me like LIFO will give us the worst results since ending inventory is only $310 and cost of goods sold is the highest ($2,140). Maybe we should use it so students don't feel like we're ripping them off.

Maryann: Yes, but why not show the best results so we can ask for a raise? You know we're not exactly getting rich running this supply center. FIFO seems to make more profit since inventory is the highest while cost of goods sold is the lowest.

Jack: Yeah, but don't forget—the Student Lounge has to file a tax return and pay taxes on its profits, so FIFO means paying more income tax too. That will actually result in less cash on hand to give us a raise or a year end bonus.

The discussion between Jack and Maryann is one that has occurred many times in new businesses trying to decide which cost flow assumption to use. Does it really matter? Let's see what happens the following year. Assume that in 19x2, the Student Lounge had the following purchases and sales of erasable ink pens:

	Units	Unit Cost	Total Cost	Total Sales Revenue
Beginning inventory (from 12/31/x1)	50	?	?	
Sales, 1/1 to 3/31 @ $12	(40)			$ 480
Purchase, 4/1	100	$10	$1,000	
Sales, 4/1, to 9/30 @ $12	(110)			1,320
Units on hand at end of period	0			
				$1,800

By September 30, 19x2, all pens were sold, and the Student Lounge decided to discontinue the pens. The results shown in Exhibit 6–3 reflect the three alternative cost flow assumptions for 19x2, and for the years 19x1 and 19x2 combined.

Note that the **total cost of goods sold for the pens for the two years is the same for all three cost flow methods.** As a result, the total gross margin from the pens for the two years is the same—$1,345 for each cost flow method. However, the timing of when costs flow into income and when profit is recognized is different for each of the three cost flow assumptions. Thus, the Student Lounge example illustrates that total gross margin over the life of a business will be the same no matter which cost flow method is used. At the same time, the year-to-year measures of assets, expenses, and profits will normally differ between alternative methods.

Importance of Alternative Inventory Methods. Given the examples above, how should a company select a cost flow method? LIFO states the asset, inventory, at older costs but matches current costs against income. FIFO reports the asset at current costs but matches older costs against income. Under present accounting rules, no choice is available that would report both the asset and the cost of goods sold at the current cost of inventory when price changes occur.

From an economic standpoint, perhaps the method of inventory measurement that companies should use for financial reporting is the same method they use for income tax reporting. The tax laws are written in such a way that LIFO may be used for tax reporting purposes only if it is also being used for financial reporting purposes. This prevents companies experiencing increasing costs from showing high profits for financial reporting purposes (from using FIFO, for example) and lower profits for tax purposes by using LIFO. As a result, most companies experiencing rising costs (such as Student Lounge) should use the LIFO inventory method for financial reporting purposes so that they may currently minimize taxable income and income tax expense.

EXHIBIT 6–3

Cost Flow Assumptions of Student Lounge for 19x2 and Cost of Goods Sold for 19x1 and 19x2

		19x2		
	Units	FIFO	LIFO	WA
Sales revenue for 19x2.		$1,800	$1,800	$1,800
Cost of goods sold:				
Beginning inventory	50	$ 390	$ 310	$ 350
Purchases (net)	100	1,000	1,000	1,000
Cost of goods available for sale	150	$1,390	$1,310	$1,350
Ending inventory	0	0	0	0
Cost of goods sold.	150	$1,390	$1,310	$1,350
Gross margin for 19x2		$ 410	$ 490	$ 450
Total cost of goods sold:				
From 19x1 (see Exhibit 6–2)		$2,060	$2,140	$2,100
From 19x2 (see above).		1,390	1,310	1,350
		$3,450	$3,450	$3,450
Total gross margin:				
From 19x1 (see Exhibit 6–2)		$ 935	$ 855	$ 895
From 19x2 (see above).		410	490	450
		$1,345	$1,345	$1,345

In the Student Lounge example, taxes would be lower in 19x1 under LIFO, which reports the lowest gross margin ($855). This temporary tax savings in 19x1 will eventually be offset, but at least temporarily the lower taxes will save the business cash, leaving more cash to invest or otherwise use to earn additional profits. In summary, while LIFO will generally provide the lowest net income for companies with increasing inventory costs, it will also result in lower income taxes and, therefore, cash savings available for use by the business. Since most companies have experienced increasing inventory costs over the past 20 years or so, it is not surprising that LIFO is one of the most popular inventory methods among large publicly owned companies.[2] LIFO's real cash savings from reduced income taxes provide a greater benefit than the higher accrual net income that could be reported under FIFO or other alternatives. However, because managers' compensation is normally based in part on accounting income, managers may have financial incentives to use FIFO even when LIFO might reduce corporate income taxes. Because of this potential conflict of interests it is not uncommon to find companies paying bonuses based on FIFO measures of income, but using LIFO for reporting purposes.

The LIFO periodic method provides the greatest amount of flexibility in measuring inventory and cost of goods sold. Since LIFO values inventory at costs that frequently differ from their current costs by a material amount, the release of these inventory costs from the sale of LIFO layers (that is, the sale of units valued at older LIFO costs) can greatly increase profits. The sale of LIFO layers, called **LIFO liquidations,** is achieved by letting

[2]See *Accounting Trends and Techniques: 1992* (New York: AICPA, 1992), p. 142. About 60% of the firms surveyed used LIFO for some portion of their inventories. However, only one third of the sampled firms used LIFO for over 50% of their inventory.

inventory quantities decrease so that older LIFO costs are assigned to units of current sales. In this way, the LIFO periodic method provides managers with a means of manipulating income. Appendix 6C describes how financial statement readers can detect whether current income has been effected by such LIFO liquidations.

While LIFO is popular in the United States because of its tax benefits and its potential to manipulate income, some countries, such as Australia, do not allow LIFO. Also, the International Accounting Standards Committee (IASC) once proposed to eliminate the LIFO method as an inventory costing alternative. LIFO is not as popular in the United Kingdom as it is in the United States, in part because it can facilitate income manipulation in periods of increasing unit costs of inventory. In Japan, the weighted average method is the predominant method used.

Inventory Cost Flow Methods: Perpetual Inventory Systems

The four inventory cost flow methods that are used in periodic systems are also used in perpetual systems. LIFO and WA will normally result in different inventory and cost of goods sold measures for perpetual and periodic systems. On the other hand, **SI and FIFO yield the same results in both perpetual and periodic systems.** In a perpetual system, the WA method is called moving average (MA) method because a new weighted average is computed each time goods are purchased.

Detailed examples of the LIFO, FIFO, and WA cost flow methods applied to the perpetual system using the Student Lounge data are provided in Appendix 6A.

Consistency and Inventory Measurement

One of the primary principles of accounting is the consistency principle, which means that accounting methods should be applied on a consistent basis from year to year whenever possible. When a company makes a change in the basis used to prepare its financial statements, the effect of the change must be adequately disclosed to financial statement users.

The consistency principle also suggests that a company should use the same inventory cost flow method each year. When reasonable justification results in changes in inventory cost flow methods, the effect of the change on the ending inventory and the net income must be fully disclosed in financial statements.

TESTING INVENTORY COST RELATIVE TO MARKET VALUE (LOWER OF COST OR MARKET)

Often in accounting **conservative measurement procedures are used to recognize (record) all possible losses and costs as soon as they become apparent but to recognize (record) gains or profits only after they are clearly realized or realizable.** One of the areas in which these conservative rules apply is inventory measurement. Once a company has determined its inventory cost using one of the cost flow methods, the company must further determine if the market value of the inventory is below cost. When market value is below cost, the inventory must be written down to the market value according to the lower-of-cost-or-market (LCM) valuation method. Note that if inventory that had a cost greater than market value were not written down to market, it would result in a loss when sold in future periods. The LCM method is applied to inventory in all industrialized nations, making it the predominant practice worldwide.

To compare the actual cost of inventory to market values, companies use the current cost to replace the existing inventory at the end of the period—called the inventory's current replacement cost. If the current replacement cost of the inventory on hand at the end of the year is less than its original cost, then an adjusting entry (LCM adjustment) such as the following is required:

19xx		
Dec. 31	Cost of Goods Sold (E) xxx	
	Merchandise Inventory (A)	xxx

To record write-down of inventory to its current replacement cost.

To illustrate, in anticipation of the coming school year, Byte-Size acquired 1,000 units of Bus Ad software for $15 per unit in September 19xx. The company expected the software to be a big seller at $25 each, but a new product, Spreadsheet III, turned out to be the most popular item in 19xx. By the end of 19xx, Byte-Size still had 500 unsold units of Bus Ad with a cost of $7,500 (500 × $15) in inventory. The replacement cost of the Bus Ad at the end of 19xx was $10 per unit and was not expected to increase in the near future. Byte-Size was in the following position at the end of 19xx:

Item	Quantity	FIFO Cost	Replacement Cost	Lower of Cost or Market
Bus Ad Software	500	$7,500	$5,000	$5,000

The entry at the end of 19xx would be

```
19xx
Dec. 31   Cost of Goods Sold (E) . . . . . . . . . . . . . . . . . . .   2,500
              Merchandise Inventory (A) . . . . . . . . . . . . . . . . . . .           2,500
          To record write-down of inventory.
```

Objective 3
The lower-of-cost-or-market measurement test.

The LCM method should be applied to inventory at the end of each accounting period. LCM may be applied to each type of inventory item separately, to each category of inventory item, or to inventory in total.

For example, assume that Byte-Size has only two categories of inventory on hand at the end of 19xx (see Exhibit 6–4). Note that the item-by-item basis of LCM shown in the exhibit results in the lowest possible LCM inventory measurement. This will always be true when the item-by-item basis is used.

Normally, the group-of-items basis and the total-inventory basis of applying LCM will generate different results, as illustrated in Exhibit 6–4. In Exhibit 6–4, LCM on the total-all-items basis ($33,805) is equal to FIFO cost. LCM on the group basis ($33,435) and item-by-item basis ($30,755) are both less than FIFO cost and would require an adjusting entry similar to that illustrated above.

Inventory Errors

It is not uncommon to have some errors in inventory quantities and/or costs in companies that handle large quantities of many different types of merchandise. The physical count taken at the end of the accounting period and the costing of the quantities on hand will often locate these errors.

Objective 4
The impact of inventory errors.

When errors are made and identified in the same accounting period, correcting entries are used to correct the books. For example, assume that Byte-Size took a physical count at the end of 19x3 and found 65 units of HPEE calculators on hand. The perpetual records revealed that 80 units at $30 each should have been on hand. The 15 missing units could have been lost, damaged and thrown out, or stolen by employees or customers. In any case, the inventory must be written down to reflect the actual number of units on hand. The following error correction would be made:

```
19x3
Dec. 31   Cost of Goods Sold (E) . . . . . . . . . . . . . . . . . . .   450
              Inventory (A) . . . . . . . . . . . . . . . . . . . . . . . . .           450
          To write down the loss of 15 calculators.
```

Most inventory errors are discovered in the same period that they occur as long as accurate physical counts are taken and costing the quantities is done correctly.

Inventory errors that effect more than one year are normally **counterbalancing errors,** also called **self-correcting errors.** In most cases these errors will correct themselves the next year. To illustrate a counterbalancing error, assume that Byte-Size also had a printer inventory, and that at the end of 19x4 it made an error in the physical count of this inventory, reporting 120 units (printers) on hand at $1,500 each instead of 102 units on hand

EXHIBIT 6–4

LCM Method As Used by Byte-Size

	Quantity	FIFO Cost	Replacement Cost	LCM Basis Item-by-Item LCM	LCM Basis Group-of-Items LCM	LCM Basis Total-All-Items LCM
				Comparison for individual LCM		
Software						
Bus Ad	500	$ 7,500	$ 5,000	$ 5,000		
Load Star	300	6,000	7,500	6,000		
Spreadsheet III	190	4,180	4,370	4,180		
Terminal Talk.	350	6,300	7,525	6,300		
Total software group		$23,980	$24,395	$21,480	$23,980	
				Comparison for group LCM		
Calculators:						
CASSEO	90	$ 4,500	$ 4,680	$ 4,500		
TEEYE	75	3,375	3,150	3,150		
HPEE	65	1,950	1,625	1,625		
Total calculators		$ 9,825	$ 9,455	$ 9,275	$ 9,455	
				For group LCM		
Grand total		$33,805	$33,850	$30,755	$33,435	$33,805
				Comparison for total inventory LCM		

at $1,500 each. Assume that Byte-Size uses a periodic inventory system and that the cost of printers available for sale in 19x4 was $975,000. Further assume that net printer purchases for 19x5 were 500 units at $1,500 each ($750,000), and that the ending printer inventory count at the end of 19x5 correctly reported 115 units on hand at $1,500 each. The following analysis shows that the incorrect results for 19x4 are offset in 19x5, so that the sum of the two years' incorrect results equals the sum of the two years' correct results:

	Incorrect Results 19x4	Incorrect Results 19x5	Correct Results 19x4	Correct Results 19x5
Beginning Inventory	$ 0	$180,000	$ 0	$153,000
+Purchases (net)	975,000	750,000	975,000	750,000
Cost of Goods available	**$975,000**	$930,000	**$975,000**	$903,000
−Ending Inventory.	180,000*	**172,500**	153,000[†]	**172,500**
Cost of Goods Sold	$795,000	$757,500	$822,000	$730,500
Total Cost of Sales: 19x4 + 19x5		**$1,552,500**		**$1,552,500**

*120 units at $1,500 each.
[†]102 units at $1,500 each.

The inventory reported in the December 31, 19x5, balance sheet is the same ($172,500) in both cases, and the total amount of expense (cost of goods sold) over the two-year period is also the same ($1,552,500)! While not all inventory errors are counterbalancing, most errors not found in the period they originate (i.e., 19x4 in the example above) will automatically correct themselves in the following period.

ANALYSIS OF INVENTORY CHANGES

So far this chapter has illustrated the alternative ways a company may elect to measure, record, and report its inventory. Like many other chapters, the illustrations of inventory systems and costing methods use more information than we normally find in a set of published financial statements. This section of the chapter attempts to explain what inventory data are normally provided in financial statements and illustrates how we can analyze these inventory data to obtain information not specifically reported in the statements.

Assume that you are looking over a company's annual report. What information related to inventory is available in the financial statements? The following data should be available from the company's comparative balance sheets and income statement in virtually every case:

Balance sheet data:
- Beginning inventory balance (= last year's ending inventory balance).
- Ending inventory balance.
- Beginning accounts payable balance (= last year's ending balance).
- Ending accounts payable balance.

Income statement data:
- Cost of goods sold for the current period.

Note that in analyzing financial statements, the above data should be available regardless of whether a perpetual or periodic system is employed, since both systems must report ending inventory and cost of goods sold each period. *In fact, it is not possible to determine whether a perpetual or a periodic system is in use by looking at the published financial statements.*

While the financial statements do not normally tell us (1) the amount of inventory purchased (or made) during the year, or (2) the payments made to inventory suppliers, these data may be of interest to us. By understanding the interrelationship between the accounts used to measure and record inventory, as illustrated in the chapter, we will be able to estimate these two pieces of information, as well as others. First, let's summarize what we learned in the chapter concerning the general types of business transactions that result in increases or decreases in Inventory, Accounts Payable, and Cost of Goods Sold:

Objective 5
How to analyze inventory changes.

1. Inventory is increased and Accounts Payable is increased when merchandise is acquired on account.
2. Inventory is decreased and Cost of Goods Sold is increased when merchandise is sold.
3. Accounts Payable is decreased and Cash is decreased when payment is made for merchandise acquisitions on account.

Note that these generalizations may not always be true. For instance, the Inventory account is not increased when purchases are made in a periodic system; instead, the Purchases account is increased. However, in looking back in time and analyzing the past financial statements of a company, we will see that *these generalizations are always appropriate.* Based on the effects of the three transactions summarized above and the financial statement balances in Inventory, Accounts Payable, and Cost of Goods Sold, the interrelationship between these three accounts is summarized in Exhibit 6–5.

EXHIBIT 6–5

Relationship to Accounts Payable, Cost of Goods Sold, and Cash to Merchandise Inventory

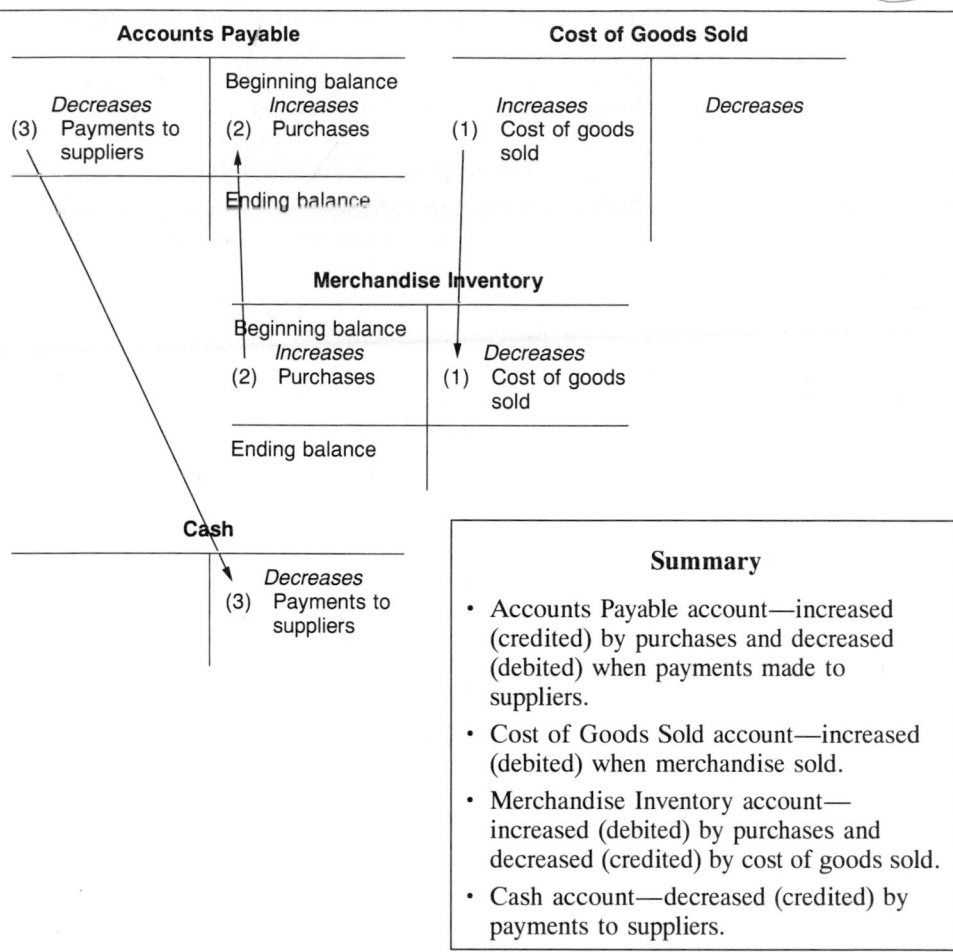

Accounts Payable

Decreases	Beginning balance *Increases*
(3) Payments to suppliers	(2) Purchases
	Ending balance

Cost of Goods Sold

| *Increases* | *Decreases* |
| (1) Cost of goods sold | |

Merchandise Inventory

Beginning balance *Increases*	*Decreases*
(2) Purchases	(1) Cost of goods sold
Ending balance	

Cash

| | *Decreases* |
| | (3) Payments to suppliers |

Summary

- Accounts Payable account—increased (credited) by purchases and decreased (debited) when payments made to suppliers.
- Cost of Goods Sold account—increased (debited) when merchandise sold.
- Merchandise Inventory account—increased (debited) by purchases and decreased (credited) by cost of goods sold.
- Cash account—decreased (credited) by payments to suppliers.

The following example illustrates how to determine (1) the amount of inventory purchased during the year and (2) the payments made to the suppliers. To begin, assume that the following facts are obtained from the two-year comparative balance sheets and income statement of the Arens Corporation, as shown below in T account form.

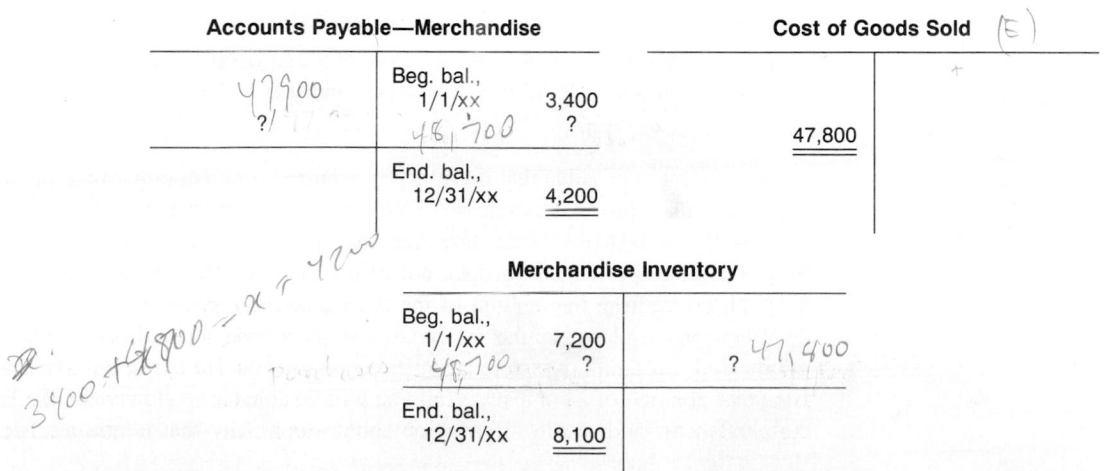

Accounts Payable—Merchandise

	Beg. bal., 1/1/xx	3,400
		?
	End. bal., 12/31/xx	4,200

Cost of Goods Sold

| 47,800 | |

Merchandise Inventory

Beg. bal., 1/1/xx	7,200	
	?	
End. bal., 12/31/xx	8,100	

By using the following steps we will insert the missing information into the above accounts to arrive at the information given in Exhibit 6–6.

Step 1. The $47,800 debit (increase) to Cost of Goods Sold must also decrease (credit) the Merchandise Inventory account (see Exhibit 6–6). (This is the same as entry 1 in Exhibit 6–5.)

Step 2. By decreasing Merchandise Inventory $47,800, we must increase inventory by $48,700 to explain the $900 increase in the Merchandise Inventory balance. The following formula can be used to determine the amount of merchandise inventory purchases that should be placed on the debit side of Merchandise Inventory:

$$\begin{array}{ccccccc} \text{Ending} & & \text{Beginning} & & \text{Cost of} & & \text{Merchandise} \\ \text{inventory} & - & \text{inventory} & + & \text{goods} & = & \text{inventory} \\ \text{balance} & & \text{balance} & & \text{sold} & & \text{purchases} \\ \$8,100 & - & \$7,200 & + & \$47,800 & = & \$48,700 \end{array}$$

Now, we have answered the first question, How much inventory did Arens purchase during the year? Next, the amount of inventory purchases—$48,700—is inserted as a credit in the Accounts Payable account as shown in Exhibit 6–6 because we assume all purchases are made on credit. (This is entry 2 in Exhibit 6–5.)

Step 3. Since we know that $48,700 merchandise was purchased during the year and have inserted this amount in Accounts Payable, we are ready to answer the second question: How much did Arens pay suppliers during the year? This amount can be determined from the following formula:

$$\begin{array}{ccccccc} \text{Beginning} & & \text{Merchandise} & & \text{Ending Accounts} & & \text{Amount paid} \\ \text{Accounts} & + & \text{inventory} & - & \text{Payable} & = & \text{on Accounts} \\ \text{Payable} & & \text{purchases} & & \text{balance} & & \text{Payable} \\ \text{balance} & & & & & & \\ \$3,400 & + & \$48,700 & - & \$4,200 & = & \$47,900 \end{array}$$

Accounts Payable can be forced to balance by decreasing (debiting) the Accounts Payable account $47,900 and decreasing (crediting) Cash as shown in Exhibit 6–6. (This is entry 3 in Exhibit 6–5.)

Note that it is possible that inventory is acquired for cash rather than on account. To the extent that there are cash purchases, both the increases and decreases to Accounts Payable are equally overstated. Notice, however, that this offsetting error created by the assumption of only credit purchases does **not** affect the accuracy of your answer to the second question concerning the amount of the payments to suppliers.

When you understand the interrelationships between inventory changes and cost of goods sold, accounts payable, and other accounts, you are better equipped to evaluate the financial position of a company. And you will be able to "read between the lines" of financial statements and obtain information about a company that is not specifically reported.

EXHIBIT 6–6

Determining Purchases and Accounts Payable for Year

Accounts Payable		
		3,400
Step 3 47,900	Step 2	48,700
		4,200

Cost of Goods Sold	
Step 1 47,800	

Merchandise Inventory		
		7,200
Step 2	48,700	Step 1 47,800
		8,100

Cash	
	Step 3 47,900

Summary

Merchandise purchased during year:
$8,100 - \$7,200 + \$47,800 = \$48,700$
Payments made on account:
$3,400 + \$48,700 - \$4,200 = \$47,900$

• **SUMMARY**

This chapter began with a discussion of the four measurement decisions that managers must make pertaining to inventory. The four inventory measurement decisions examined in the chapter are

1. Selection of an inventory system:
   a. Periodic system.
   b. Perpetual system.

2. Identification of inventory costs:
   a. Taking a physical inventory.

3. Selection of a cost flow method:
   a. Specific identification (SI) method.
   b. First-in, first-out (FIFO) method.
   c. Last-in, first-out (LIFO) method.
   d. Weighted average (WA) method (or moving average method).

4. Testing inventory cost relative to market value (lower of cost or market):
   a. Item-by-item basis.
   b. Group-of-items basis.
   c. Total-all-items basis.

To the extent that these alternative inventory measurement decisions simply result in alternative ways to allocate inventory costs to cost of goods sold, the selection of a measurement system will not have any *direct* economic consequences on the firm. While the different measurement methods (e.g., SI, FIFO, LIFO, and WA) will result in different asset and net income figures in any given period, over the life of the firm they will all generate the same total income. These different inventory measurement methods essentially allocate a given pool of inventory dollars (equal to the total actual cost of inventory) to income at different points in time. As a result, the alternative inventory measurements may be viewed as being different in the timing of their release of inventory costs to periodic earnings.

The major exception to this general evaluation of "what's going on" with alternative inventory measurements stems from the *indirect* income tax consequences resulting from the use of the LIFO method. Using LIFO rather than some other method in periods of increasing inventory costs will generally result in the real economic benefit of lower income taxes, all else being equal. Also, since management compensation systems are often based on accounting income, the selection of an inventory measurement system could indirectly effect the amount of managements' salaries and bonuses.

The lower-of-cost-or-market (LCM) test was illustrated after the coverage of cost flow methods. It should be noted, however, that the LCM test is a required aspect of inventory measurement, not an option. The impact of inventory errors was also illustrated in the chapter, with examples explaining the effect of errors on financial statements. The chapter concluded with an analysis of inventory changes. This showed you how to use information from comparative statements to determine new information—the amount of inventory purchased during the year and the amount paid to suppliers.

• DEMONSTRATION EXERCISE

The A. J. Company had the following activity during the year:

Date	Transaction	Units	Unit Cost	Unit Selling Price
1/1	Beginning inventory	1,000	$2.00	
3/31	Purchase No. 1	2,000	2.75	
6/30	Sale No. 1	2,500		5.50
8/25	Purchase No. 2	2,000	3.50	
11/15	Sales No. 2	2,250		7.00

Selling price is always 200% of the most recent purchase cost per unit.

Required:
Calculate the total sales, cost of goods sold, and gross margin based on

1. LIFO periodic.
2. Weighted average periodic.
3. FIFO periodic.

Total Sales = 4,750

Solution:
Total sales of 4,750 units:

Sale	Units	×	Selling Price	=	Total Sales
No. 1	2,500	×	$5.50	=	$13,750
No. 2	2,250	×	7.00	=	15,750
	4,750				$29,500

Cost of goods sold (4,750 total units sold):

LIFO periodic:

Units	×	Unit Cost	=	Total Cost	
2,000	×	$3.50	=	$ 7,000	
2,000	×	2.75	=	5,500	
750	×	2.00	=	1,500	
4,750				$14,000	Cost of Goods Sold

Weighted average periodic:

$$\frac{[(1,000 \times \$2.00) + (2,000 \times \$2.75) + (2,000 \times \$3.50)]}{5,000 \text{ units}} = \$2.90/\text{unit}$$

$$4,750 \times \$2.90 = \underline{\$13,775} \quad \text{Cost of Goods Sold}$$

FIFO periodic:

Units	×	Unit Cost	=	Total Cost	
1,000	×	$2.00	=	$ 2,000	
2,000	×	2.75	=	5,500	
1,750	×	3.50	=	6,125	
4,750				$13,625	Cost of Goods Sold

Gross margin summary:

	LIFO	WA	FIFO
Sales	$29,500	$29,500	$29,500
Cost of goods sold	14,000	13,775	13,625
Gross margin.	$15,500	$15,725	$15,875

Cost Flow Methods — Perpetual Inventory System

The Student Lounge example that we analyzed in the chapter used the periodic inventory system. In this appendix, the Student Lounge example is presented as using the perpetual system. This will illustrate how the cost flow computations of the perpetual inventory system are affected by the **pattern of purchases and sales.**

Consider once again the purchases and sales data in the Student Lounge example on page 278. Notice that the sales data were only used to compute total sales in the earlier examples. Since the periodic system only computes cost of goods sold at the end of the accounting period, there is no need to record the cost for each sale. However, the perpetual system records the cost of each sale and the reduction in inventory that results from each sale as follows:

Accounts Receivable (A)	xxx	
Sales (R)		xxx
To record sales on credit.		
Cost of Goods Sold (E)	yyy	
Merchandise Inventory (A)		yyy
To record the cost of sales.		

The cost to be recorded at the time of sales depends on the cost flow method used by the company.

LIFO PERPETUAL COST FLOW METHOD

Using the LIFO perpetual cost flow method for the Student Lounge data on page 278, the following computation schedule illustrates how to determine the costs for reducing inventory and increasing Cost of Goods Sold at the time of each (summary) sales entry.

LIFO Perpetual Record Merchandise Inventory—Erasable Pens			
Description and Computation	Units	Unit Cost	Total Cost
Beginning balance	0	$0	$ 0
Purchase 5/1	40	6	240
Sold 20 units costing $6 = $120	(20)	(6)	(120)
Balance: From 5/1, 20 @ $6 = $120	20	6	$ 120
Purchase, 8/30	290	7	2,030
Sold 245 units costing $7 = $1,715	(245)	(7)	(1,715)
Balance: From 5/1, 20 @ $6 = $120			
From 8/30, 45 @ $7 = $315			
65 $435	65	mixed	$ 435
Purchase, 9/30	20	9	180
Sold 35 units costing: 20 @ $9 = $180			
15 @ $7 = 105			
35 $285	(35)	(mixed)	(285)
Balance: From 5/1, 20 @ $6 = $120			
From 8/30, 30 @ $7 = 210			
50 $330	50		$ 330

The entries to record the purchases and summary entries for all sales made between purchases are:

Date	Accounts	Dr.	Cr.
May 1	Inventory (A).	240	
	Accounts Payable (L).		240
May 2– Aug. 30	Cost of Goods Sold (E) . . . . Inventory (A).	120	120
Aug. 30	Inventory (A). . . . . Accounts Payable (L).	2,030	2,030
Aug. 31– Sept. 30	Cost of Goods Sold (E) . . . . Inventory (A).	1,715	1,715
Sept. 30	Inventory (A). . . . . Accounts Payable (L).	180	180
Oct. 1– Dec. 31	Cost of Goods Sold (E) . . . . Inventory (A).	285	285

The inventory T account would show the following:

Inventory—Erasable Pens

Bal.	0			
5/1	240	5/1 to 8/30	120	
8/30	2,030	9/1 to 9/30	1,715	
9/30	180	10/1 to 12/31	285	
12/31 Bal.	330			

MOVING AVERAGE COST FLOW METHOD

In the perpetual system, the moving average method requires that a new average inventory cost be computed *after each purchase*. The following computation schedule illustrates the moving average calculation procedures for the Student Lounge example. The ending balance of 50 units at $7.41 each (rounded) would result in a $371 ending inventory value.

Inventory—Erasable Pens

	Units	Computation of Average Unit Cost	Unit Cost	Total Cost
Beginning balance	0	—	$0.00	$ 0
Purchase, 5/1	40	Not needed	6.00	$ 240
Sales, 20 units	(20)	—	6.00	(120)
Balance.	20		6.00	$ 120
Purchase, 8/30	290		7.00	2,030
Balance.	310	$2,150/310 =	6.94	$2,150
Sold, 245 units	(245)		6.94	(1,700)
Balance.	65		6.94	$ 450
Purchase, 9/30	20		9.00	180
Balance.	85	$630/85 =	7.41	$ 630
Sold, 35 units	(35)		7.41	(259)
Balance.	50		7.41	$ 371

Objective 6

How to measure the cost of ending inventory using LIFO, FIFO, and moving average (MA) methods in a perpetual system.

Recall that **FIFO perpetual is the same as FIFO periodic in all cases.** As a result, using the FIFO computations from the chapter (page 278), the following summarizes the results of the alternative methods for 19x1:

Inventory Method	Ending Inventory		Cost of Goods Sold	
	Periodic (in chapter)	Perpetual (in appendix)	Periodic (in chapter)	Perpetual (in appendix)
FIFO	$390	$390	$2,060	$2,060
LIFO	310	330	2,140	2,120
WA/MA	350	371	2,100	2,079

· DEMONSTRATION EXERCISE

The A.J. Company had the following activity during the year:

Date	Transaction	Units	Unit Cost	Unit Selling Price
1/1	Beginning inventory	1,000	$2.00	
3/31	Purchase No. 1	2,000	2.75	
6/30	Sale No. 1.	2,500		5.50
8/25	Purchase No. 2	2,000	3.50	
11/15	Sale No. 2.	2,250		7.00

Selling price is always 200% of the most recent purchase cost per unit.

Required:

Calculate the total sales, cost of goods sold, and gross margin based on:

1. LIFO perpetual.
2. Moving average perpetual.
3. FIFO perpetual.

Solution:

Total sales:

Sale	Units	×	Selling Price	=	Total Sales
No. 1	2,500	×	$5.50	=	$13,750
No. 2	2,250	×	7.00	=	15,750
	4,750				$29,500

Cost of goods sold (4,750 total units sold):

LIFO perpetual:

	Units	×	Unit Cost			=	Total Cost	
Sale No. 1:	2,000	×	$2.75	=	$5,500			
	500	×	2.00	=	1,000		$ 6,500	
Sale No. 2:	2,000	×	$3.50	=	$7,000			
	250	×	2.00	=	500		7,500	
	4,750						$14,000	C/G/S

Moving average:

Sale No. 1:

$$\frac{[(1,000 \times \$2.00) + (2,000 \times \$2.75)]}{3,000 \text{ units}} = \$2.50$$

Sale No. 2:

$$\frac{[(500 \times \$2.50) + (2,000 \times \$3.50)]}{2,500 \text{ units}} = \$3.30$$

Total cost of goods sold under MA method:

Units	×	Unit Cost	=	Total Cost
2,500	×	$2.50	=	$ 6,250
2,250	×	3.30	=	7,425
4,750				$13,675 C/G/S

FIFO perpetual:

	Units	×	Unit Cost		=	Total Cost
Sale No. 1:	1,000	×	$2.00	=	$2,000	
	1,500	×	2.75	=	4,125	$ 6,125
Sale No. 2:	500	×	$2.75	=	$1,375	
	1,750	×	3.50	=	6,125	7,500
	4,750					$13,625 C/G/S

Gross Margin Summary	LIFO	MA	FIFO
Sales	$29,500	$29,500	$29,500
Cost of goods sold	14,000	13,675	13,625
Gross margin.	$15,500	$15,825	$15,875

Inventory Estimation Methods

The major drawback of the periodic inventory method is that the cost of goods sold (and gross margin) cannot be computed without knowing the ending inventory. Interim financial statements, that is, statements prepared for periods of less than a year, cannot be prepared without a measure of ending inventory and cost of goods sold. Thus, managers are unable to evaluate how well the business is doing until the end of the accounting period when a physical inventory is taken. To illustrate, consider the following data normally known in a periodic system:

Sales (known from sales register).	$180,000
Cost of goods sold:	
Beginning inventory (known from last year's ending inventory)	$ 22,000
Add: Purchases (net) (known from balances in purchases accounts)	196,000
Cost of goods available for sale.	$218,000
Less: Ending inventory.	?
Cost of goods sold	$?
Gross margin	$?

Once the ending inventory is known, cost of goods sold and gross margin may easily be computed. However, since it is costly and time consuming to take a physical inventory during the accounting period, accountants have developed various methods to estimate the inventory balance at any point in time. This makes it possible for managers to evaluate performance without waiting for a physical inventory. In this appendix you will learn about the retail inventory estimation method.

RETAIL INVENTORY METHOD

If the relationship between retail prices and costs is not fixed, retailers may still estimate their inventory balance (and resulting cost of goods sold) by keeping track of the relationship between cost (amount retailer pays for merchandise) and retail prices (amount retailer sells the merchandise for). The retail (selling) price is normally marked or ticketed on each item. The retail inventory method requires records to keep track of

1. Beginning inventory at cost and retail value.
2. Purchases at cost and at retail.

Combined with information about total sales (at retail prices), the above information enables retailers to estimate inventory value at any point in time. The ending inventory estimated using the retail inventory method can also be compared with the actual physical count of inventory at year-end to estimate inventory losses due to theft, disasters, and so on, for a period of time.

To illustrate the retail method, assume Prostyle Shoes reported sales in January of $740. In addition, the following information was available at the end of January 19xx:

	Cost Price	Retail Selling Price
Beginning inventory, 1/1/xx	$286	$ 305
Purchases (net)	544	695
Goods available for sale	$830	$1,000
Cost as a percent of retail: $830/$1,000 = 83% = 0.83		

Objective 7
The fundamentals of the retail method of estimating inventory value.

The relationship in this example—called a cost ratio—indicates that on average costs are equal to 83% of selling prices. The ending inventory at **retail** selling prices is found by taking the retail value of goods available for sale ($1,000) less net sales ($740), or $260. The ending inventory **at cost** is then estimated by multiplying the ending inventory at retail by the cost ratio ($260 × 0.83 = $215.80). This computation and the resulting estimate of profit for the month of January may be illustrated as follows:

	Cost Price	Retail Selling Price	
Beginning inventory, 1/1/xx.	$286	$ 305	Cost ratio:
Purchases (net)	544	695	
Goods available for sale	$830	$1,000	$\frac{\$830}{\$1,000} = 0.83$
Less net sales		− 740	
Ending inventory at retail prices		$ 260	
Cost ratio.		× .83	
Estimated ending inventory at cost prices		$215.80 = $216 rounded	

Estimated Profit—January

Sales (net)		$740
Cost of goods sold:		
Beginning inventory	$286	
Purchases (net)	544	
Cost of goods available for sale	$830	
Estimated ending inventory (from above)	216	
Cost of goods sold.		614
Gross margin		$126

This example illustrates the basic approach of the retail inventory method. Additional details can be included in retail estimation systems that add to both the complexity of the calculations and the accuracy of the resulting estimates of ending inventory. These estimation methods are accurate to the point where they are acceptable as a basis for financial statements as well as income tax returns. The additional complexities and other variations of the retail method are covered in detail in most intermediate accounting texts.

APPENDIX • 6C

LIFO Reserves and LIFO Liquidation

Many companies using the LIFO inventory method for reporting purposes also keep records on a FIFO basis. These companies frequently use FIFO for internal reports throughout the year (due to simplicity and lower cost) and convert to LIFO at year-end using LIFO inventory estimation procedures.[3] This conversion to LIFO (from FIFO) at year-end is normally accomplished with the following type of adjusting entry:

19xx		
Dec. 31　Cost of Goods Sold (E)	xxx	
LIFO Reserve (XA)		xxx
To convert FIFO inventory to LIFO value.		

This adjusting entry increases expenses (cost of goods sold), and decreases assets (inventory) and net income. The LIFO Reserve account is a contra asset to merchandise inventory, and is shown as follows:

Partial Balance Sheet

[handwritten: FIFO > LIFO Inventory]

Accounts receivable (net)		$187,550
Merchandise inventory (at FIFO)	$386,200	
Less: LIFO reserve	41,000	
Merchandise inventory (at LIFO)		345,200

---

[3]These procedures go beyond the scope of this text but are covered in detail in most intermediate accounting texts.

Since the LIFO value of inventory is less than FIFO the contra asset balance should be a credit. The LIFO reserve reports the **cumulative difference** between LIFO and FIFO inventory value from all prior periods. The credit balance in the reserve is a measure of the cumulative impact of price increases on inventory over time. However, it is possible for this reserve to experience a decrease (debit) in any given year. The two factors that could cause the year-end adjusting entry to decrease the reserve balance (make it a smaller credit balance) are

Objective 8
LIFO reserves and LIFO liquidation.

1. **A decrease** in inventory costs (costs for the period declined).
2. Sales of inventory in excess of units purchased or made in the current period. This causes a reduction in inventory quantities during the year below the beginning inventory quantity (forcing the sales to be costed out at costs of prior years) called a **LIFO liquidation.**

The following T accounts explain how these factors could cause the LIFO reserve account either to increase or decrease from year to year:

Merchandise Inventory (FIFO)			LIFO Reserve	
Beginning balance at FIFO				Beginning balance
Increases Purchases at FIFO	*Decreases* Cost of goods sold at FIFO		*Decreases* 1. Inventory costs decrease during the year. 2. Liquidation from sales of beginning inventory at prior years' LIFO costs.	*Increases* 1. Inventory costs increase during the year.
Ending balance at FIFO				Ending balance

To illustrate, assume that Technavest Corporation had the following balances at the end of 19xx *prior to adjustment* of the LIFO reserve:

Merchandise Inventory (FIFO)				LIFO Reserve	
19xx Jan. 1	380,000 993,200	*C.O.G.S.* 987,000	*5200*	19xx Jan. 1	46,200
Dec. 31	386,200				

The beginning balance in the LIFO reserve account ($46,200) represents the accumulated differences between FIFO and LIFO from all prior periods. If Technavest had always used FIFO instead of LIFO to measure inventory, the net asset Merchandise Inventory would have been reported as $380,000 on January 1, 19xx, or $46,200 larger than the LIFO value of $333,800 ($380,000 FIFO cost less $46,200 LIFO reserve balance). To offset this larger asset value the total amount of inventory costs charged to cost of goods sold in all prior years would have been $46,200 less had FIFO been used in all prior periods.

If Technavest experienced no price changes and no reductions in beginning inventory levels during 19xx, then no adjusting entry to the LIFO reserve account would be necessary at the end of 19xx. Technavest would report inventory of $340,000 ($386,200 less LIFO reserve of $46,200) in the 19xx balance sheet and cost of goods sold of $987,000 (the decrease to inventory) in the 19xx income statement. Instead, assume that Technavest experienced a $5,200 decrease in its LIFO reserve during 19xx due to decreasing inventory costs during 19xx.[4] The following year-end adjusting entry would be made:

```
19xx
Dec. 31   LIFO Reserve (XA) . . . . . . . . . . . . . . . . . . .    5,200
              Cost of Goods Sold (E) . . . . . . . . . . . . . . . . . .              5,200
          To convert FIFO inventory to LIFO value.
```

After this entry, the following account balances would be reported:

Balance Sheet Accounts

	12/31/xx	1/1/xx
Merchandise inventory (FIFO)	$386,200	$380,000
LIFO reserve.	(41,000)	(46,200)
Inventory (LIFO)	$345,200	$333,800

Income Statement

Cost of goods sold (LIFO) ($987,000 − $5,200)	$981,800

The adjusting entry to the LIFO reserve for the 19xx cost decreases resulted in a $5,200 increase to assets and a $5,200 decrease in cost of goods sold. Adjustments to the LIFO reserve are normally made at the end of each accounting period when reports are prepared. This liquidation of a portion of the LIFO reserve is permanent. Future period price increases will increase the LIFO reserve, while future period price decreases and/or LIFO liquidations will decrease the LIFO reserve.

DEMONSTRATION EXERCISE

Jipper Corporation reported the following data in its 19x9 balance sheet (in $000):

	19x9	19x8
Inventory (at FIFO cost)	$258,730	$285,317
Less: LIFO reserve	95,817	84,317
Inventory (at LIFO cost)	$162,913	$201,000

Required:
1. Did inventory costs increase or decrease in 19x9?
2. What was the 19x9 year-end adjustment to the LIFO reserve assuming there were no LIFO liquidations?
3. What was the 19x9 year-end adjustment to the LIFO reserve assuming there was a $6,000,000 LIFO liquidation in 19x9?

Solution:
1. Inventory costs **increased** because the LIFO reserve increased. Note that although total inventory value declined, this was due to lower inventory **quantities**, not lower costs. The only way the LIFO reserve can increase is as a result of cost increases.

---

[4] An explanation of the accounting procedures used to arrive at this estimated price decrease of $5,200 is beyond the scope of this textbook. These procedures are discussed in intermediate accounting texts.

2. The year-end adjusting entry would have been

Cost of Goods Sold (E)   11,500,000
    LIFO Reserve (XA)   11,500,000
  To increase LIFO reserve.

The T account analysis is

LIFO Reserve

	84,317,000	Given 12/31/x8 balance
	11,500,000	Adjusting entry (plug)
	95,817,000	Given 12/31/x9 balance

3. If a $6,000,000 LIFO liquidation occurred in 19x9, the year-end adjustments would have been

LIFO Reserve (XA)   6,000,000
    Cost of Goods Sold (E)   6,000,000
  To record liquidation of LIFO inventory layers.
Cost of Goods Sold (E)   17,500,000
    LIFO Reserve (XA)   17,500,000
  To increase LIFO reserve.

The T account analysis is

LIFO Reserve

Given 19x9 liquidation	6,000,000	84,317,000	Given 12/31/x8 balance
		17,500,000	Adjusting entry (plug)
		95,817,000	Given 12/31/x9 balance

• KEY TERMS

Consistency principle. Principle stating that accounting methods should be applied on a consistent basis from year to year whenever possible.

Cost flow assumptions. Another term to describe cost flow methods—LIFO, FIFO, and weighted average; term *assumption* used because the actual physical flow of goods need not be the same as the cost flow method used; only affects the timing of when specific inventory costs are transferred to cost of goods sold.

Counterbalancing error. Inventory error that corrects itself the next year; also called self-correcting error.

Current replacement cost. The current cost to replace existing inventory.

First-in, first-out (FIFO). Cost flow method that *assumes* that the "first goods in" were the first goods sold and assigns the actual cost of the "first goods in" to cost of goods sold.

FOB destination. Goods are free on board (FOB) to the buyer's location; the seller pays the freight charges up to the point where the buyer takes delivery and title passes to the buyer.

FOB shipping point. Goods are free on board (FOB) to the seller's point of shipment only—title passes to the buyer as goods leave the seller's location, and the buyer pays the freight from the point of shipment.

Goods out on consignment. Goods owned by company but held by some agent of the company at another location for possible sale to customers.

Gross margin. Net sales less cost of goods sold; also called gross profit.

Inventory. Merchandise that is produced or obtained to be sold in the regular course of business for the purpose of making a profit.

Inventory in transit. Inventory that is between the seller and buyer but legally owned by one or the other, depending on shipping terms.

Last-in, first-out (LIFO). Cost flow assumption that *assumes* that "the last goods in" (most recent purchases) were the first goods sold and assigns the actual cost of the "last goods in" to cost of goods sold.

Lower-of-cost-or-market (LCM) valuation method. Method used to write inventory down to its market value when the current replacement cost of the inventory is less than its original cost.

Moving average (MA). A cost flow assumption used in a perpetual inventory system; new weighted average is computed each time goods are purchased.

Period costs. Costs incurred to generate revenue; expensed in the period they occur (not assigned to inventory); also called revenue expenditures.

Perpetual inventory system. System that continuously updates the records for the quantity and cost of each type of item in inventory; the Merchandise Inventory account is increased when companies purchase merchandise and decreased when companies sell merchandise.

Physical inventory count. Count of actual inventory on hand; necessary in a periodic inventory system to determine cost of goods sold and ending inventory; necessary in a perpetual inventory system to ensure against errors.

Product costs. Costs assigned to units of inventory.

Special-order goods. Goods special ordered for a customer; if special-order goods are on hand at the end of an accounting period waiting to be delivered to customer, company usually records the goods as a sale, and the goods are not included in the company's inventory even though company still has possession of goods.

Specific identification (SI). Cost flow method in which actual cost of each specifically identified unit sold is charged to cost of goods sold when units are actually sold. This is the only cost flow method that matches actual costs with the actual physical flow of goods.

Weighted average (WA). Cost flow assumption that measures the cost of the units sold using the weighted average cost of all purchases.

· APPENDIX KEY TERMS

Cost ratio. Relationship of an inventory item's cost to its selling price.

Interim financial statements. Statements prepared during the accounting period on a monthly or quarterly basis.

LIFO Reserve. A contra asset account that reduces inventory from FIFO value to LIFO value; reports the cumulative difference from all prior years between the FIFO and LIFO inventory values.

Retail inventory method. Inventory estimation method based on the relationship between retail prices and costs.

· SYNONYMS

Current cost; replacement cost; current replacement cost.

Counterbalancing error; self-correcting error.

Gross margin; gross profit.

Interim financial statements; monthly statements; quarterly statements.

Period cost; revenue expenditure.

Perpetual system; real-time system.

Physical inventory; actual inventory count.

Shrinkage; loss from theft and/or damaged goods.

• QUESTIONS ───

1. What are three costs incurred by keeping inventory too long?
2. What are the two types of inventory systems?
3. What are the attributes of a periodic system?
4. What are the attributes of a perpetual system?
5. What are the advantages and disadvantages of a perpetual system?
6. Which inventory system requires a physical count of inventory at least once a year?
7. When does title to goods pass to the buyer?
8. What does the term *FOB destination* mean?
9. What is the effect on the income statement if a seller records the transfer of title to goods too soon? (Assume goods are sold at a profit.)
10. What are goods out on consignment and how do they affect inventory ameasurement?
11. What are special-order goods and how do they affect inventory measurement?
12. What are self-correcting errors?
13. What is the effect on earnings when ending inventory is overstated?
14. What costs are to be included in the asset inventory?
15. What are four common cost flow methods?
16. Which cost flow method is the only one that is always consistent with the actual physical flow of goods?
17. Which cost flow method results in the lowest earnings in periods of increasing inventory unit costs?
18. Which cost flow method results in the highest earnings in periods of decreasing inventory unit costs?
19. Over the life of a business, which cost flow method will result in the highest gross profits assuming increasing unit costs? Assuming decreasing unit costs?
20. For tax purposes, which inventory cost flow should be used in periods of increasing inventory unit costs? Why?
21. When and how does the lower-of-cost-or-market (LCM) method require a change in the inventory measurement?
22. How is market value measured in the LCM method?
23. Identify three ways that the LCM test may be applied to an inventory made up of many different types of merchandise.

• APPENDIX QUESTIONS ──────────────────────────────────

24. Which cost flow methods will provide the same inventory measurements in both perpetual and periodic systems? Why?
25. Which cost flow methods will provide different inventory measurements in a perpetual system than in a periodic system? Why?
26. What information is needed to estimate inventory using the retail method?
27. What is a LIFO Reserve account? How is it used?

• EXERCISES

E 6–1
Perpetual/Periodic
Recording
L.O.1

The following events of TOK Corporation, which records its purchases at their gross invoice amount, occurred during June of 19xx:

19xx
June 3   Purchased $45,000 of merchandise on open account from Vendor, Inc.; terms 2/15, n/30.
      10   Paid $17,920 to Max Corporation for goods billed for $18,350, taking a $430 purchase discount.
      12   Sold merchandise costing $40,000 to a client for $50,000 cash.
      15   Paid $1,795 in freight bills for merchandise acquired.
      17   Returned $7,000 of merchandise to Vendor, Inc., and paid balance of June 3 purchase in cash.
      25   Acquired $39,500 in merchandise from XYZ, Inc.; terms 2/15, n/30.
      28   Some of the merchandise sold on June 12 was returned for a full refund of the $5,000 selling price. The goods were expected to be resold.

Required:
1. Record these events assuming a periodic inventory system is used.
2. Record these events assuming a perpetual inventory system is used.

E 6–2
Perpetual/Periodic
Recording
L.O.1

The following events occurred during July 19x5 for the Beat Corporation, which records its purchases at their gross invoice amount:

19xx
July 1   Purchased merchandise inventory on open account for $63,000, terms 2/10, n/30.
      6   Purchased merchandise inventory on open account for $87,000, terms 2/15, n/30.
      8   Returned $6,000 of July 1 purchase and paid the balance in cash.
      10   Sold merchandise costing $50,000 for $95,000 on open account.
      12   Purchased merchandise inventory on open account for $57,500, terms 2/10, n/30.
      15   Received and paid freight bills of $1,640 in cash for merchandise purchased earlier on open account.
      20   Paid for July 6 purchase in cash.
      23   Returned $15,000 of July 12 purchase.
      27   Paid balance due on July 12 purchase.
      30   Half of merchandise sold on July 10 was returned for credit, and payment was received for the balance due.

Required:
1. Record these events assuming a periodic inventory system is used.
2. Record these events assuming a perpetual inventory system is used.

E 6–3
FIFO Periodic
L.O.2

Printer Supplies, Inc., which sells bottles of ink, had the following transactions in January related to the ink:

Jan. 1   Beginning inventory of 100 bottles and total cost of $600.
      8   Purchased 400 bottles at a cost of $8 each.
      22   Sold 450 bottles at $15 each.
      30   Counted ending inventory of 50 bottles.

Printer Supplies uses a periodic inventory system and FIFO inventory costing method.

Required:
Compute the cost of the ending inventory and cost of goods sold.

E 6–4
LIFO Periodic
L.O.2

The following data are from the ledger of the Rose Company for 19xx:

Date	Transaction	Units	Unit Cost	Total Cost
1/1	Beginning inventory	200	$6.00	$1,200
2/10	Purchase.	600	7.00	4,200
4/15	Sale	400	—	—
6/30	Purchase.	100	8.00	800
8/16	Sale	400	—	—
10/31	Purchase.	300	8.50	2,550

Required:
Using a periodic inventory system and LIFO, determine the cost of the ending inventory and the cost of goods sold for 19xx.

E 6–5
LIFO Periodic
L.O.2

The following table reflects inventory activity for Theisman Surgical Supplies, Inc., during 19xx:

Date	Transaction	Units	Unit Cost
1/1	Beginning inventory	400	$1.00
2/15	Purchase	200	1.25
6/30	Sale	300	—
9/20	Purchase	300	1.50
11/30	Sale	500	—
12/15	Purchase	100	1.75

Total sales for the year were $1,500.

Required:
Determine the cost of the ending inventory, cost of goods sold, and gross margin during 19xx if the company uses LIFO and a periodic inventory system.

E 6–6
Inventory Costing Methods/Periodic
L.O.2

The following information applies to the Ross Appliance Shop during 19xx:

Date	Transaction	Units	Unit Selling Price	Units	Unit Cost
1/1	Beginning inventory.			200	$20
1/27	Sold	120	$32		
4/15	Purchase			190	22
7/16	Sold	140	35		
9/12	Purchase			160	24
11/20	Sold	180	36		
12/29	Purchase			110	25

Required:
Determine the ending inventory (units and dollar amounts), cost of goods sold, and gross margin at December 31, 19xx, under each of the following inventory costing methods using a periodic inventory system:

1. FIFO.
2. LIFO.
3. WA.

E 6–7
Inventory Costing
Methods/Periodic
L.O.2

The inventory records for the Hope Company for January 19xx are as follows:

Date	Transaction	Units	Unit Cost	Unit Selling Price
1/1	Beginning inventory	100	$25	
1/6	Purchase.	25	26	
1/10	Purchase.	30	27	
1/17	Sold	45		$50
1/23	Purchase.	20	27	
1/28	Sold	10		52

Required:
1. Assuming that the Hope Company uses the periodic inventory method applied on a LIFO basis, determine the costs assigned to the ending inventory on January 31, 19xx.
2. Assume that the Hope Company uses the periodic inventory system and the specific identification inventory costing method. All of the items sold on January 17 came from beginning inventory, and all of the items sold on January 28 came from the January 10 purchase. Based on these assumptions, determine the gross margin for January 19xx.
3. Assuming that the Hope Company uses the periodic inventory system applied on a WA basis, determine the cost of goods sold (rounded to the nearest whole dollar) for January 19xx. Round unit costs to three decimal places ($x.xxx).

E 6–8
Inventory Costing
Methods/Periodic
L.O.2

The following data are available for the Stockout Company at the end of 19xx:

Date	Transaction	Units	Unit Cost	Total Cost
1/1	Beginning inventory	80	$10	$ 800
3/10	Purchase.	100	9	900
6/26	Purchase.	50	11	550
9/5	Purchase.	60	10	600
11/15	Purchase.	40	13	520
12/31	Purchase.	70	14	980
		400		$4,350

The physical inventory count at year-end revealed 120 units on hand. Stockout uses a periodic inventory system.

Required:
1. Compute cost of goods sold for 19xx:
   a. Using the FIFO cost method.
   b. Using the LIFO cost method.
   c. Using the WA cost method.
2. Which method will result in the highest net income for 19xx?

E 6–9
Lower-of-Cost-or-Market
Method
L.O.3

Whembly Corporation reported the following balances as of the end of 19xx:

Inventory at FIFO cost.	$ 475,620
Cost of Goods Sold	9,857,340

The market value (replacement cost) of Whembly's inventory at the end of 19xx is $457,500. Whembly uses the lower-of-cost-or-market method.

Required:
1. What should Whembly report as the balance sheet value of inventory at the end of 19xx?
2. What should Whembly report as cost of goods sold for 19xx? Prepare the journal entry to record the LCM value.

E 6–10
LCM Test
L.O.3

The records of Nancy's Exterior Decorating, Inc., provide the following data relating to inventories for the years 19x6 and 19x7:

	Inventory (in thousands)		
	12/31/x7	12/31/x6	1/1/x6
At average cost	$145	$123	$112
At lower of average cost or market	135	110	112

Required:
1. What should be reported as ending inventory at the end of 19x6?
2. What should be reported as ending inventory at the end of 19x7?

E 6–11
Inventory Errors
L.O.4

Answer the following independent questions, selecting the appropriate choice in each case.

1. The ending inventory mistakenly included goods that had been sold to a customer, therefore—
   a. Net income is overstated and assets are understated.
   b. Net income is understated and assets are overstated.
   c. Both net income and assets are overstated.
   d. Both net income and assets are understated.
2. A purchase of 1,000 units of merchandise on open account was somehow recorded twice in the company's periodic inventory system. As a result—
   a. The ending inventory is overstated.
   b. Cost of goods sold is understated.
   c. Cost of goods sold is overstated.
   d. The ending inventory is understated.
3. A quantity of inventory out on consignment was omitted from ending inventory. As a result—
   a. There is no error.
   b. The ending inventory is understated.
   c. Profits are understated.
   d. Both *b* and *c* are correct.
   e. None of the above.
4. A company using a periodic system was billed twice for the same inventory purchase, and paid both bills by mistake. As a result—
   a. Inventory is overstated and receivables from vendor is understated.
   b. Cost of goods sold is overstated and receivables from vendor is understated.
   c. Net income is overstated and receivables from vendor is understated.
   d. Accounts payable is overstated and receivables from vendor is understated.
5. A company using a perpetual system was billed twice for the same purchase, and paid both bills by mistake. As a result—
   a. Inventory is overstated and receivables from vendor is understated.
   b. Cost of goods sold is overstated and receivables from vendor is understated.
   c. Net income is overstated and receivables from vendor is understated.
   d. Accounts payable is overstated and receivables from vendor is understated.

E 6–12
Correcting Inventory
L.O.4

Consider the following transactions for Whiz Company:

a. Whiz Company recorded the following entry on July 1, 19xx:

Merchandise Inventory	42,500	
Accounts Payable		42,500

The invoice for this purchase was actually for $24,500. Record the correcting journal entry.

b. Whiz Company recorded the following entries on September 10, 19xx:

Accounts Receivable	25,000	
Sales		25,000
Cost of Goods Sold	15,000	
Merchandise Inventory		15,000

The merchandise recorded as sold was actually only sent to a distributor of Whiz Company for possible sale to customers. These goods are out on consignment and still belong to Whiz. Record the correcting entries.

E 6–13
Cost Flows
L.O.2

1. Acquisition cost for a heavily used raw material changes frequently. The book value of the inventory of this material at year-end will be the same if perpetual records are kept as it would be under a periodic inventory method only if the book value is computed under the—
   a. Average cost method.
   b. First-in, first-out method.
   c. Last-in, first-out method.
   d. None of the above.

2. DEK Corporation's inventory cost on its statement of financial position would have been lower using FIFO than if LIFO had been used. Assuming no beginning inventory, in what direction did the cost of purchases move during the period?
   a. Up (increasing).
   b. Down (decreasing).
   c. Very constant.
   d. Cannot be determined.

3. In the periodic inventory method, which of the following generally would not be separately accounted for in the computation of cost of goods sold?
   a. Delivery charges on the sale of inventory.
   b. Cash (purchase) discounts on merchandise purchased during the period.
   c. Purchase returns and allowances on merchandise acquired during the period.
   d. Cost of freight-in for merchandise purchased during the period.

4. Which method of inventory pricing best approximates specific identification of the actual flow of costs and units in most perishable goods merchandising situations?
   a. Weighted average cost.
   b. FIFO.
   c. LIFO.
   d. All of the above.

E 6–14
Analysis of Inventory
(Challenging)
L.O.4, 5

1. If ending inventory of 19x5 is overstated, then the net income for 19x5 will—
   a. Be overstated.
   b. Be understated.
   c. Not be affected.
   d. Offset the error.
   e. None of the above.

2. B Company had cost of goods sold of $43,000 during the period. The balance in the accounts payable for merchandise *increased* $5,000 during the period. Inventory, all of which is acquired on account, had an ending balance of $60,000. Cash payments for inventory acquired on account totaled $50,000 during the period. What was the beginning balance in inventory?
   a. $72,000.
   b. $53,000.
   c. $48,000.
   d. $43,000.
   e. $67,000.

3. Suppose that D Corporation purchased 400 units of inventory on January 1, 19x5, for $700 per unit. The ending inventory consisted of 150 units, and sales for the period amounted to 410 units. If D Corp. uses FIFO perpetual and the total ending inventory cost is equal to the total beginning inventory cost, what is cost of goods sold for the period?
   a. $280,000.
   b. $385,000.
   c. $175,000.
   d. Cannot be determined based on above data.
   e. None of the above.

4. An understatement of $3,500 in inventory at the end of 19x3 would—
   a. Have no effect on net income of 19x3.
   b. Overstate the beginning inventory of 19x4.
   c. Overstate net income in 19x3.
   d. Overstate cost of goods sold for 19x4.
   e. None of the above.

E 6–15
Evaluating Inventory Changes
L.O.5

Gulford Corporation reported the following data in its 19x2 annual report:

	19x2	19x1
Balance sheet data:		
Inventory	$187,600	$173,500
Accounts payable	67,450	73,900
Income statement data:		
Cost of goods sold	763,500	691,890

Assume that Gulford purchases all inventory on account, and the Accounts Payable account is used only for purchases of inventory.

Required:
1. Compute net purchases for Gulford Corporation for 19x2.
2. Compute the amount of cash payments made during 19x2 on Accounts Payable.

· APPENDIX EXERCISES

E 6–16
LIFO Perpetual
(Appendix 6A)
L.O.6

The following table reflects inventory activity for Theisman Surgical Supplies, Inc., during 19xx:

Date	Transaction	Units	Unit Cost
1/1	Beginning inventory	400	$1.00
2/15	Purchase	200	1.25
6/30	Sale	300	—
9/20	Purchase	300	1.50
11/30	Sale	500	—
12/15	Purchase	100	1.75

Total sales for the year were $1,500.

Required:
Determine the cost of the ending inventory, cost of goods sold, and gross margin during 19xx if the company uses LIFO and a perpetual inventory system.

E 6–17
Inventory Costing Methods/Perpetual
(Appendix 6A)
L.O.6

The following information applies to the Ross Appliance Shop during 19xx:

Date	Transaction	Units	Unit Selling Price	Units	Unit Cost
1/1	Beginning inventory.			200	$20
1/27	Sale	120	$32		
4/15	Purchase			190	22
7/16	Sale	140	35		
9/12	Purchase			160	24
11/20	Sale	180	36		
12/29	Purchase			110	25

Required:

Determine the ending inventory (units and dollar amounts), cost of goods sold, and gross margin at December 31, 19xx, under each of the following inventory costing methods using a perpetual inventory system. Round unit costs to three decimal places ($x.xxx).

1. FIFO.
2. LIFO.
3. MA.

E 6–18
*Inventory Costing
Methods/Perpetual
(Appendix 6A)*
L.O.6

The inventory records for the Hope Company for January 19xx are as follows:

Date	Transaction	Units	Unit Cost	Unit Selling Price
1/1	Beginning inventory	100	$25	
1/6	Purchase.	25	26	
1/10	Purchase.	30	27	
1/17	Sold	45		$50
1/23	Purchase.	20	27	
1/28	Sold	10		52

Required:

1. Assuming that the Hope Company uses the perpetual inventory method applied on a LIFO basis, determine the costs assigned to the ending inventory on January 31, 19xx.
2. Assume that the Hope Company uses the perpetual inventory system and the specific identification inventory costing method. All of the items sold on January 17 came from beginning inventory, and all of the items sold on January 28 came from the January 10 purchase. Based on these assumptions, determine the gross profit for January 19xx.

E 6–19
*Moving Average
Method/Perpetual
(Appendix 6A)*
L.O.6

XYZ Company buys and sells grommets, using a perpetual system with the moving average inventory costing method. It had the following transactions in September:

Sept. 1   Beginning inventory 200 grommets; total cost $500.
       5   Purchased 200 grommets at $3 each.
      14   Sold 350 grommets at $5 each.
      28   Purchased 50 grommets at $3.25 each.

Required:

1. Prepare a perpetual inventory record on a MA basis for the month of September assuming no other transactions are made.
2. Compute cost of goods sold for September and cost of the ending inventory as of September 30.

E 6–20
*Retail Inventory Method
(Appendix 6B)*
L.O.7

Gerry's Department Store uses the retail method to value its inventory. The following data are available:

	Cost	Retail
Beginning inventory	$ 40,000	$ 70,000
Purchases.	292,000	397,000
Sales		390,000

Required:

Estimate the ending inventory cost, cost of goods sold, and gross profit. (Round the cost ratio to two decimal places.)

E 6–21
LIFO Reserve
(Appendix 6C)
L.O.8

Majors, Inc., reported the following preliminary account balances at the end of 19xx before adjustments:

	Preliminary Balance
Inventory (FIFO).	$196,250 dr.
LIFO Reserve	34,100 cr.
Cost of Goods Sold	515,840 dr.

Inventory costs increased rapidly during 19xx, with the resulting difference between FIFO and LIFO inventory value increasing by $14,300 for 19xx.

Required:
1. Record the 19xx year-end adjusting entry to the LIFO Reserve account.
2. Compute the amount to be reported for inventory and for cost of goods sold in Majors's 19xx financial statement (assuming no other adjustments to either account).

• PROBLEMS

P 6–1
Inventory Costing
L.O.2

Jacobs Corporation experienced the following inventory activity during the first four months of 19xx.

Date	Transaction	Units	Unit Cost	Unit Selling Price
1/1	Beginning inventory	60	$100	
1/19	Purchase.	100	120	
2/20	Sold	75		$240
3/23	Purchase.	180	130	
4/24	Sold	120		260

At the end of April, Jacobs decided to cut selling prices in order to try to improve profits. The results for the next four months were

Date	Transaction	Units	Unit Cost	Unit Selling Price
5/3	Purchase.	200	$140	
6/1	Sold	220		$210
6/5	Purchase.	380	150	
7/18	Sold	360		225
8/4	Purchase.	500	150	
8/29	Sold	460		225

Required:
1. Assume that Jacobs uses the FIFO periodic inventory method. Compute ending inventory, cost of goods sold, and gross margin for each of the two separate four-month periods. (In other words, treat each four-month period like a separate year.)
2. Repeat requirement 1 using the LIFO periodic inventory method.
3. Compare your answers to parts 1 and 2 above. Did the cut in selling prices work as hoped? Is the effect of the price cut greater than the difference between LIFO and FIFO?

P 6–2
Comparison of Periodic/Perpetual Journal Entries
L.O.1

The following transactions involving the Fashion Friend Department Store were selected from the records of July 19xx:

a. Purchased merchandise on credit at an invoice cost of $2,300 with terms 2/10, n/30.
b. Returned damaged goods purchased in *a* with an invoice cost of $200 to the vendor. Fashion Friend received a credit against its outstanding account balance.
c. Sold merchandise for cash, $800, and on credit, $1,900. The inventory for this sale had a cost of $1,700. Fashion Friend's terms on credit sales are 2/10, n/30.
d. Paid invoice for the inventory purchases in *a* after the discount period.
e. Received payment from customer for sale made in *c* within the discount period.

Required:
Record all necessary entries that would be made for each transaction under a periodic inventory system and a perpetual inventory system. Use the gross method for sales and purchase discounts.

P 6–3
Recording in a Periodic System
L.O.1

During May 19xx, the following transactions occurred regarding Day Company's inventory:

19xx

May 2 Acquired on account $18,700 of merchandise inventory delivered by Rush Trucking whose freight bill for $600 was paid in cash by Day. The terms of the purchase were 2/10, n/30.
6 Sold merchandise costing $15,000 to a customer for $23,500 on open account; terms 2/10, n/30.
8 Acquired $26,000 in merchandise; terms 2/10, n/30, FOB destination. The freight bill was $500.
9 Returned $2,000 of merchandise acquired on May 2 for credit and paid the balance due.
12 Sold merchandise costing $8,000 to a customer for $13,200 on open account; terms 2/10, n/30.
14 Collected cash from customer for May 6 sale.
23 Purchased merchandise on open account costing $17,000; terms 2/10, n/30. The freight bill of $480, FOB shipping point, was paid in cash.
25 Returned $4,000 worth of merchandise acquired May 8 for credit and received an allowance of $1,200 for damaged goods that were not returned by Day. Paid the balance of the May 8 purchase in cash.

Required:
1. Record all necessary entries assuming Day Company uses a periodic inventory system and records sales and purchase discounts taken in separate accounts.
2. Identify one advantage and one disadvantage of periodic systems.

P 6–4
Recording in a Perpetual System
L.O.1

Consider the facts in Problem 6–3 for Day Company.

Required:
1. Record the events, assuming Day Company uses a perpetual inventory system.
2. Identify one advantage and one disadvantage of perpetual systems.

P 6–5
Inventory Cost Flows
L.O.2

The following information is taken from the records of Merkel Retail Store for the month of January 19x2.

Jan. 1 Beginning inventory is 150 units at $20 each.
5 Purchase 2,000 units at $18 each.
19 Sell 1,800 units.
25 Purchase 500 units at $22.70 each.
30 Sell 450 units.
31 Ending inventory is 400 units.

Merkel uses the periodic inventory system.

Required:
Compute the cost of the ending inventory and cost of goods sold for the following cost flow alternatives:

1. FIFO.
2. LIFO.
3. Weighted average.

P 6–6
Inventory Costing Methods/Periodic/ Perpetual (Challenging)
L.O.2

The following information applies to Widgets, Inc., for 19xx:

Inventory of Item X	Units	Unit Price
Beginning inventory, 1/1.	200	$3.00
Purchase, 2/10.	600	3.50
Sale, 4/15	400	—
Purchase, 6/30.	100	4.00
Sale, 8/16	400	—
Purchase, 10/31	300	4.25

Required:
1. Using a periodic inventory system and LIFO, determine—
   a. The cost of goods available for sale in 19xx.
   b. The cost of goods sold in 19xx.
2. Using a periodic inventory system and FIFO, determine the cost of goods sold during 19xx.
3. In 19xx, does using FIFO instead of LIFO result in a higher or lower balance in ending inventory? By what amount?
4. (Optional) Using a perpetual inventory system and LIFO, determine the ending inventory cost and cost of goods sold for item X. (Relates to Appendix 6A.)

P 6–7
Inventory Costing Methods/Periodic
L.O.2

The following information relates to inventory purchases and sales of the Caribbean Company for May 19xx.

Date	Transaction	Units	Unit Cost	Selling Price per Unit
5/1	Beginning inventory	150	$6	
5/9	Purchase.	130	7	
5/12	Sale	140		$20
5/17	Purchase.	200	8	
5/21	Sale	130		20

Required:
Calculate the following amounts:

1. Number of units in ending inventory on May 31.
2. Cost of goods available for sale during May.
3. FIFO (periodic) cost of goods sold for May.
4. FIFO (periodic) ending inventory at May 31.
5. FIFO (periodic) gross margin for May.
6. WA (periodic) cost of goods sold for May.
7. WA (periodic) ending inventory at May 31.
8. Specific identification ending inventory at May 31. (Assume that the May 12 sale was made from units in beginning inventory and that the May 21 sale was made from units purchased on May 17.)

P 6–8
Inventory Costing
Methods (Challenging)
L.O.2

The Martin Corporation reported the following inventory data for 19x1:

Beginning inventory	20 units costing $9 each
Purchases during the year:	
February 28.	40 units @ $13 each
June 13.	60 units @ $11 each
September 24	40 units @ $ 9 each
November 5.	25 units @ $ 7 each

Required:
1. Compute the total cost of the remaining 55 units in the ending inventory using the following methods. (Hint: Will you use the periodic or perpetual inventory system?)
   a. The LIFO method.
   b. The FIFO method.
   c. The WA method.
2. Answer the following questions:
   a. Which method would result in the lowest net income? Why?
   b. Which method would result in the most current inventory value at the end of the year?
   c. Which method would result in the best "matching" of revenues and expenses for the current year?

P 6–9
Lower-of-Cost-or-Market
Method
L.O.3

The following inventory data are taken from the records of the Palmrose Floors Corporation at December 31, 19xx:

	Quantity in Square Yards	Total FIFO Cost	Total Replacement Cost
Indoor/outdoor carpets:			
Sil No. 87	9,817	$98,170	$100,250
Dray No. 76	6,215	79,420	80,690
Gard No. 97	1,940	31,500	27,150
		209,090	*208,090*
Plush carpets:			
CC No. 452	1,830	15,790	14,650
Milih No. 841.	3,205	29,750	31,490
Welb No. 543	2,906	18,725	18,100
		64265	*64240*
		273,355	*272,330*

Required:
1. Compute the ending inventory value for 19xx using the LCM method applied on an item-by-item basis.
2. Repeat part 1 above using the group-of-items basis.
3. Repeat part 1 above using the total-all-items basis.

P 6–10
LCM Tests
L.O.3

The following data relate to the ending inventory of the Somer Store:

Inventory Classification	Quantity	Cost per Unit FIFO	Cost per Unit Market
Rubber boats:			
5 person	200	$150.00	$175.00
4 person	100	125.00	110.00
Golf clubs:			
Irons	150	40.00	37.50
Woods	100	25.00	30.00
Fishing gear:			
Reels	60	12.50	14.00
Rods	40	5.00	4.00

Required:

You have been asked to advise Somer's management on how to apply the lower-of-cost-or-market method, which has not previously been used by Somer. Write a memo explaining the alternative applications and make a recommendation based on the facts of this problem.

P 6–11
Multiple Choice (Challenging)
L.O.2–5

1. As the new accountant for the Adams Company, you are asked to estimate the effect of shifting from LIFO to FIFO for costing its inventory. The following data are available at December 31, 19xx:

Sales revenue	$700,000
Beginning inventory at 1/1 (LIFO)	10,000
Purchases	400,000
Ending inventory at 12/31	
LIFO	40,000
FIFO	45,000

If the changes were made from LIFO to FIFO at December 31, 19xx—

a. Gross profit for 19xx would increase by $5,000, relative to the amount of gross profit that would result if LIFO were continued.

b. Gross profit for 19xx would not be different from the amount that would result if LIFO were continued.

c. Cost of goods available for sale for 19xx would decrease by $5,000, relative to the amount of cost of goods available for sale if LIFO were continued.

d. Cost of goods sold for 19xx would be $410,000, and gross profit would be $290,000.

e. Sales for 19xx would decrease.

2. When the owner of the Cornerstone Gift Shop arrived at work on Monday morning, October 15, 19xx, she discovered that merchandise had been stolen during the weekend. The following data are available from the accounting records for the accounting year, which began January 1, 19xx, and from a physical count of merchandise inventory taken on the morning of October 15:

Sales for the period 1/1–10/14	$209,800
Beginning inventory, 1/1	13,950
Purchases for the period 1/1–10/14	131,300
Cost of inventory remaining on hand 10/15	13,640
Average gross profit rate	45%

The cost of the inventory stolen during the weekend would be estimated to be—

a. $13,640.

b. $16,220.

c. $29,860.

d. $37,200.

e. $50,840.

3. An examination of the accounting records of the Plagens Company was performed during January 19x3 concerning information reported for the year ended December 31, 19x2. The company uses the periodic inventory system. The following transactions occurred around the end of 19x2:

1. An invoice for $8,900, terms FOB shipping point, was recorded by Plagens as a purchase on December 30, 19x2; the goods were included in determining the December 31 inventory. Documentation reveals the goods were shipped by the supplier on January 2, 19x3, and received by Plagens on January 3, 19x3.

2. Merchandise costing $7,400 was recorded as a purchase on January 6, 19x3, when the invoice was received by Plagens; the goods were *not* included in determining the December 31 inventory. The invoice stated terms FOB shipping point. The goods were shipped by the supplier on December 31, 19x2, and were received by Plagens on January 2, 19x3.

3. An invoice for $16,500 in merchandise was recorded by Plagens as a purchase on December 29, 19x2; terms were FOB destination. The goods were included in determining the December 31 inventory, although they were not received by Plagens until January 2, 19x3.

The net effect the above transactions is to—

a. Understate 19x2 cost of goods sold by $18,000.

b. Overstate inventory at 12/31/x2 by $25,400.

c. Understate total assets at 12/31/x2 by $7,400.

d. Overstate 19x3 net income by $32,800.

e. Overstate inventory at 12/31/x2 by $7,400.

4. Holland Shoes sells three types of wooden shoes. Total inventory amounts, stated at original cost and replacement cost, for the shoes at December 31, 19x2, follow:

Type of Shoe	Cost	Replacement Cost
Functional	$2,000	$ 900
Cushioned	3,000	2,700
Deluxe	6,000	7,500

Holland normally values its inventory at lower-of-cost-or-market applied on an individual item basis. By how much would the valuation of the inventory differ if "lower-of-cost-or market" were applied on a total inventory basis, instead of on the individual item basis?

a. $1,500 higher.

b. $100 higher.

c. $1,400 lower.

d. $1,400 higher.

e. $1,500 lower.

P 6–12
Inventory Errors
L.O.4

As a new auditor on the audit engagement of SFI, you have recently discovered the following errors concerning inventory measurement in its periodic inventory system for the year ending December 31, 19x8:

a. The 19x6 ending inventory was understated $92,000.

b. Inventory costing $40,000 was assumed to be out on consignment as of the end of 19x7 when it had actually been sold in 19x7. The sale was recorded as revenue in 19x7. The $40,000 was not included in the 19x8 ending inventory.

c. Merchandise costing $51,000 was correctly included in the 19x7 ending inventory based on the physical count but was not recorded as a purchase until January 19x8.

d. Merchandise was recorded as a purchase in December 19x8 for $60,000 but the goods were not received until January 19x9. The goods were shipped on January 1, 19x9, by the vendor. The ending physical inventory count did not include this merchandise.

Required:

Write a memo to the SFI management that explains the effects, if any, each of the four items *a* to *d* above has on the 19x8 net income, 19x8 net purchases, and the 19x8 ending inventory value, indicating the overstatement or understatement effect and the amount for each.

P 6–13
Inventory
Errors/Periodic
L.O.4

The Gamma Corporation is a December 31, year-end company. At the end of the year before the books were finally closed, their internal auditor discovered the following errors, which had occurred during the year, and noted the entry that should have been made in each case.

Erroneous Entry			Entry That Should Have Been Made		
1. Purchases	5,250		Purchases	2,550	
Accounts Payable		5,250	Accounts Payable		2,550
2. Accounts Payable	3,100		Accounts Payable	5,100	
Purchase Returns		3,100	Purchase Returns		5,100
3. Accounts Payable	16,500		Accounts Payable	18,000	
Cash		16,500	Purchase Discounts		1,500
			Cash		16,500
4. Purchases	18,700		Purchases	18,700	
Freight-In	1,200		Accounts Payable		18,700
Accounts Payable		19,900			
5. Advertising Expense	1,340		Purchases	1,340	
Accounts Payable		1,340	Accounts Payable		1,340

Required:

Record the entries to correct each of these five errors separately.

P 6–14
Impact of Inventory
Errors (Challenging)
L.O.4

The Major Value Pak Corporation reported the following data in its 19x2 annual report (in millions):

Excerpt from Balance Sheet
At December 31

	19x2	19x1
Inventory	$167	$159

Excerpt from Income Statement

For the Year Ended
December 31

	19x2	19x1
Net income	$31	$28

Assume that in 19x3, it was discovered that a clerical error was made in valuing the 19x1 ending inventory, and the correct value should have been $164 million instead of $159 million. Assume the tax rate for 19x1 and 19x2 is 40%.

Required:

1. By how much are assets overstated or understated at the end of 19x1?
2. By how much is net income overstated or understated for 19x1?
3. By how much are assets overstated or understated at the end of 19x2?
4. By how much is net income overstated or understated for 19x2?

P 6–15
Evaluating Inventory
Changes (Challenging)
L.O.5

During 19xx, the Railsback Company sold merchandise costing $876,300 for $2,387,500. The Merchandise Inventory increased by $37,200 during 19xx to a year-end balance of $239,800. Accounts Payable decreased by $8,950 during 19xx to a year-end balance of $114,000. All purchases and sales are made on account. Accounts Receivable increased by $14,900 during 19xx to a year-end balance of $154,000.

Required:
1. Compute Railsback's net purchases for 19xx.
2. Compute cash payments made on Accounts Payable during 19xx assuming only merchandise inventory affects the Accounts Payable balance.
3. Compute the cash receipts from customers during 19xx assuming Accounts Receivable are only for customer credit sales.

P 6–16
Evaluating Inventory
Changes (Challenging)
L.O.5

During the past year, Siller Corporation sold merchandise on open account that had cost $1,857,000 to customers for $3,225,000. From its beginning balance of $650,000, the Merchandise Inventory increased by $53,650 during the year. The balance in Accounts Payable decreased by $45,820 during the year to a year-end balance of $387,200. Assume all purchases and sales are made on account. Accounts Receivable decreased by $21,500 during the year to a year-end balance of $487,630.

Required:
1. Compute Siller's inventory additions (purchases) for the year.
2. Compute cash payments on accounts payable during the year (assume accounts payable are all for inventory purchases only).
3. Compute the cash collected from customers during the year (assume accounts receivable are only for customers' sales).

· APPENDIX PROBLEMS

P 6–17
Inventory Costing
Methods/Perpetual
(Appendix 6A)
L.O.6

Consider the data in Problem 6–7. Assume the Caribbean Company uses the perpetual inventory system.

Required:
Calculate the following:

1. LIFO cost of goods sold for May.
2. LIFO cost of ending inventory at May 31.
3. FIFO cost of goods sold for May.
4. FIFO cost of ending inventory at May 31.

P 6–18
Inventory
Costing/Perpetual
(Appendix 6A)
L.O.6

Refer to the data given for the Jacobs Corporation in Problem 6–1.

Required:
1. Assume Jacobs uses the FIFO perpetual inventory method. Compute ending inventory, cost of goods sold, and gross margin for each of the two separate four-month periods.
2. Repeat requirement 1 above using the LIFO perpetual inventory method.

P 6–19
Retail Inventory Method
(Appendix 6B)
L.O.7

The Retail Sales Company uses the retail inventory method to value its merchandise inventory. The following information is available:

	Cost	Retail
Beginning inventory.	$139,780	$ 247,120
Purchases	996,320	1,720,880
Freight-in	42,750	
Purchase returns	(7,650)	(16,000)
Sales		1,703,000

Required:
1. What is the ending inventory at retail?
2. What is the cost to retail ratio?
3. What is the estimate of ending inventory and cost of goods sold?

P 6–20
Retail Inventory Method
(Appendix 6B)
L.O.7

Flasks Department Store values its inventory using the retail method. The following data are available at January 31, 19x2:

	Cost/Price	Retail Selling Price
Inventory, 2/1/x1	$ 54,800	$ 65,200
Purchases	479,700	608,625
Purchase returns	(14,500)	(23,825)
Sales		587,930
Sales returns		(16,250)

Required:
Based on the data provided, compute the estimated cost of Flasks' ending inventory, cost of goods sold, and gross margin using the retail inventory estimation method.

P 6–21
LIFO Reserves
(Appendix 6C)
(Challenging)
L.O.8

The Balance Corporation reported the following data at December 31, 19x2:

	19x2	19x1
Inventory (FIFO).	$17,600	$16,900
Less LIFO reserve	2,850	3,150
Inventory (LIFO).	$14,750	$13,750

During 19x2, Balance discontinued several of its major lines of inventory, replacing them with newer, more efficient product lines. This change created LIFO liquidations that reduced the December 31, 19x1, LIFO reserve balance by $1,850. Balance has a tax rate of 40% on all income and reported net income of $3,440 in 19x2. Cost of goods sold for 19x2 was $83,200.

Required:
1. Did the cost of Balance's inventory acquired during 19x2 increase, decrease, or remain the same?
2. What was the 19x2 tax effect of the LIFO liquidations? (Indicate increase or decrease and amount.) In other words, how much more or less tax was paid in 19x2 because of the LIFO liquidations?
3. If the FIFO inventory method had been used during 19x2, what would cost of goods sold have been for 19x2? (Do not consider prior years, only 19x2.)

P 6–22
LIFO Reserves
(Appendix 6C)
(Challenging)
L.O.8

The following data pertain to Airy, Inc., as of December 31, 19x2:

	19x2	19x1
Balance sheet data:		
Inventory (FIFO value)	$10,000	$8,965
Less LIFO reserve	3,000	1,390
Inventory (LIFO value)	$ 7,000	$7,575
Other data:		
19x2 cost of goods sold (under LIFO)	$18,000	
19x2 tax rate	40%	
19x2 net income	2,250	

The LIFO reserve ($3,000 in 19x2) is the cumulative difference between the LIFO and FIFO inventory value over all prior years. The change in the LIFO reserve ($3,000 − $1,390) is the difference between LIFO and FIFO inventory values during 19x2. Since the reserve increased in 19x2, the difference between LIFO and FIFO became greater in 19x2.

Required:
1. What would the 19x2 cost of goods sold have been if the FIFO inventory method had been used in 19x2? (Do not consider prior years, only 19x2.)
2. What was the apparent 19x2 income tax savings attributable to the LIFO inventory method in comparison to the FIFO method?

P 6–23
LIFO Reserves/LIFO Liquidation (Appendix 6C)
L.O.8

The Taxing Corporation reported the following data in its 19x2 annual report:

	19x2	19x1
Balance sheet data:		
Inventory (FIFO)	$ 765,806	$ 820,000
Less LIFO reserve	188,506	159,400
Inventory (LIFO)	$ 577,300	$ 660,600
Other data:		
Cost of goods sold (LIFO)	$10,954,000	$9,857,000

During 19x2, Taxing had LIFO liquidations of $40,000 from the elimination of one of its product lines.

Required:
1. Did Taxing's inventory costs increase or decrease during 19x2? By how much?
2. What would have been reported for cost of goods sold in 19x2 if Taxing had not liquidated LIFO inventory and if no cost increases or decreases had occurred?

• CASES

C 6–1
Inventory Systems
L.O.1

The Barnes Hardware Store has three stores in the area. The stores all carry the same items. About 50% of all merchandise carried has a cost of less than $5 per unit, with most of these low-priced items being carried in large quantities to avoid stockouts. The low-priced items represent about 60% of sales dollars. About 40% of all merchandise carried costs between $5 and $100 per unit, with the other 10% of the merchandise costing over $100 per unit. The mid-priced items account for 20% of sales dollars, while the high-priced merchandise accounts for the other 20% of sales dollars.

Barnes is currently using a periodic inventory system, but a computer salesperson has suggested that with some new sales register equipment and some computer support a perpetual system could be installed at a cost of about $250,000—a one-time cost. Barnes has annual sales of about $12 million and is presently carrying about $3 million in inventory.

Required:
As a friend of the owners of Barnes, you have been asked to advise them on whether or not to buy the new system. Write a short report explaining:
1. The advantages and disadvantages of the present system.
2. The potential advantages and disadvantages of the proposed system.
3. What other information there is that Barnes might try to obtain to help make the right decision.

C 6–2
Inventory Systems/Cost Flow Methods
L.O.2

Mason Jewelers has been in business for less than a year and is about to prepare its financial statements for the first time. Mason carries many standard items such as watches, gold chains, and so on that are not unique. They also carry some unique items such as valuable stones and gems that are priced and stored separately. The prices of most items have increased by over 10% during the past year, and Mason has replaced much of its original inventory several times at higher prices each time.

Mr. Mason, the owner, knows very little about accounting but has heard that different inventory methods can affect the amount of profit reported. Mason Jewelers has a $200,000 bank loan that is reviewed by the bank each year based on Mason's financial statements. Mr. Mason wants to put his best foot forward and report a healthy financial result to his bankers from the first year of operations. Also, he is considering an additional loan of $100,000 to expand his inventory. Mason Jewelers is expected to be in a 30% tax bracket this year.

Required:

1. Which inventory system or systems would you advise Mr. Mason to use? Explain your selections.
2. Assuming Mr. Mason wants to maximize net income in the first year, which method should he use?
3. Assuming Mr. Mason wants to maximize cash flow in the first year, which method should he use?
4. Which method should Mason's bank prefer? Why?

C 6–3
Inventory Cost Flow Choice
L.O.2

The Byte-Size Company has just finished its first year of operations. Its managers, Brad and Mary, were trying to decide which inventory method to use. Brad had made the following calculations:

Assume that inventory was computed based on the following:

	LIFO	FIFO	Weighted Average
Ending Inventory	$1,755	$1,880	$1,800
Cost of Goods Sold	9,650	9,525	9,605

Brad favors using the LIFO method because it results in the highest cost of goods sold and, therefore, the lowest taxable income. He argues this will save cash needed to pay taxes without making Byte-Size worse off. Mary favors using FIFO because it reports the highest net income. Besides, Mary argues, LIFO will only require more taxes to be paid in future periods to offset the lower taxes now, so the company cannot be much better off. Brad and Mary both seem committed to their positions.

LIFO   COGS greater

Required:

1. If you assumed that the inventory costs of Byte-Size are expected to increase each year in the future, which method would you favor? Explain your answer.   *FIFO*
2. If you assumed that the inventory costs are expected to decrease each year in the future, which method would you favor? Explain.   *FIFO   COGS greater*
3. Identify any flaws in Brad's or Mary's arguments.
4. What reason can you give to help explain why all companies do not use LIFO?

C 6–4
Cash Flow Choice and Purchase Decision
L.O.2

Raven Corporation started a new division of the business in 19x2 to acquire from wholesalers and sell to retail customers unfinished wooden kitchen sets. During the first year of operations, Raven made the following purchases:

Date (19x2)	Units	Unit Cost	Total Cost
January 19	1,200	$180	$216,000
May 23	400	230	92,000
June 15	1,200	240	288,000
Sept. 1.	600	260	156,000
Nov. 15	800	270	216,000
	4,200		$968,000

During 19x2 Raven sold 2,800 units for $900,000, with sales units increasing steadily throughout the year as people across the country heard of the economical high-quality product from satisfied customers. Sales are expected to be brisk in 19x3, and management is considering purchasing an additional 2,000 units in December of 19x2 from the supplier at a unit price of $270. The supplier's costs have been increasing rapidly, and further cost increases are expected in 19x3. The offer for 2,000 units at $270 each will expire December 24, 19x2. No payments are required until April of 19x3 if the special offer is accepted by Raven.

Raven is a calendar year-end company. The wooden furniture division must decide which cost flow method will be used to cost out the sales in 19x2 and future years. Expenses other than for merchandise amounted to $128,000 in 19x2. Raven's year-end cash position is very low, but the bank has offered to extend additional credit to Raven. The income tax rate for 19x2 is 35%.

Required:
1. Ignore for a moment the offer to purchase an additional 2,000 units. Assuming Raven uses the periodic inventory system in the wooden furniture division, which cost flow method would you recommend for Raven? Explain.
2. Now consider the special purchase offer of 2,000 units for $270 each. Should Raven accept this offer? What affect would this decision have on your recommendation of a cost flow method?
3. Assume that Raven is going to acquire the additional 2,000 units. Further assume that the option to accept the special purchase offer has been extended until January 10, 19x3 (instead of December 24, 19x2). When would you make the purchase? Explain your choice.
4. Assume that Raven decides to accept the special purchase offer in 19x2 and elects the LIFO method. Describe the effect on 19x2 net income and the effect on cash at year-end. (Assume taxes must be paid in cash at year-end.)
5. Assume that Raven declines the special purchase offer and elects the FIFO cost flow method. Describe the effect on 19x2 net income and the effect on cash at year-end. (Assume that taxes must be paid in cash at year-end.)

C 6–5
LIFO Cost Flow and Taxes (Challenging)
L.O.2

Northern Power Company operates as an electric utility in northern Michigan. Its chief source of energy is coal, which provides fuel to power plants at six locations. The plants normally carry a minimum inventory of 6,000 tons of coal each during the winter months.

A coal miners' strike during 19x5 is having a serious effect on Northern's operating results. Because Northern uses the LIFO periodic method and has a December 31 year-end, its year-end inventory is usually large and costed at very low (old) prices. For example, at the end of 19x4 Northern reported inventory of 42,000 tons: 40,000 tons at an average of $50 per ton from purchases that had occurred 5 to 10 years earlier, and 2,000 tons from 19x4 purchases at $100 per ton. During 19x5, because of the strike, coal supplies are limited and Northern's cost per ton has reached $120.

The coal shortage has caused Northern's 19x5 year-end coal inventory to drop 32,000 tons to 10,000 tons. This, in turn, has caused Northern's profits to soar since low-cost coal inventory (including 26,000 tons at $50 per ton) from prior years (i.e., "LIFO layers") are being expensed against current revenues. The current revenue rates, set by the State Regulatory Commission (SRC), are based on coal costs of about $120 per ton. Because of the higher profits, the SRC is thinking about forcing Northern to give its customers a temporary rate reduction on electric bills in early 19x6. Also, because of the higher profits, 19x5 income taxes were about $400,000 higher than normal.

Required:
1. Northern is putting together a response to the SRC's proposal for a rate reduction. Identify any points you feel support Northern's case for no rate cuts.
2. Northern is developing a petition to the federal and state income tax authorities asking them to allow Northern to charge operations with coal at a cost of $120 per ton in computing taxable income. Northern would like your help in identifying factors supporting their argument. Northern plans to return its coal inventory to normal levels (about 40,000 tons) as soon as the strike is over.
3. Assume that Northern wins its appeals for no rate reduction and for the use of the current $120 per ton cost in computing taxable income. **Before** Northern replaces the shortfall in the coal inventory (about 30,000 tons below normal levels at the end of 19x5), what will be the effect of the coal shortage on Northern's cash position? (Assume that utility bills are paid in cash by customers each month.) What will be the effect on Northern's cash position after it replaces the shortfall in the coal inventory?

C 6–6
Economic Effects
of LIFO
L.O.2

The Star Share Corporation has been experiencing increasing inventory costs for years. Because of a conservative management team, however, Star Share has always used the FIFO inventory method. You have recently been promoted to chief financial officer (CFO) of the corporation, resulting in a large raise, a bonus based on net income, and a stock option plan. As one of your first projects, you investigate what would happen to Star Share if they changed to the LIFO inventory method. Your analysis provides the following results (amounts are in millions):

	Assumption	
	Continue to Use FIFO Method	Switch to LIFO Method
Ending inventory (asset)	$ 435	$ 390
Cost of goods sold	3,850	3,895
Tax payments on income	76.5	61.2
Net income.	148.5	118.8
Dividends to stockholders	80	80

Required:
Do you decide to switch to LIFO? Explain your decision, but confine your explanation to an evaluation of the cash flow effects of these alternatives.

· EVALUATING FINANCIAL STATEMENTS

C 6–7
Evaluating Inventory
Changes—Dow
Chemical Company
L.O.5

The following data are taken from a recent annual report of the Dow Chemical Company (in millions):

Balance Sheet

	19x2	19x1		19x2	19x1
Assets:			Liabilities:		
Cash.	$ 19	$ 12	Accounts payable. . . .	$947	$1,056
.					
.					
.					
Inventories	1,927	1,961			

Other data:

	19x2	19x1
Cost of goods sold	$9,516	$9,446

Assume that Dow's cost of goods sold consists only of inventory costs, and that all inventory is purchased on account.

Required:
1. How much inventory was acquired by Dow during 19x2?
2. How much cash was paid on accounts payable during 19x2?

· APPENDIX CASES

C 6–8
LIFO: Perpetual or
Periodic (Appendix 6A)
L.O.6

The Spear Company has been using the LIFO periodic inventory system for many years. The management is pleased with LIFO because of its tax savings feature. Spear has experienced cost increases in all inventory items each year, and had a balance in its LIFO Reserve account of $447,350 as of 19x3.

During 19x4, management asks you to explain whether LIFO perpetual offers any advantages over LIFO periodic. A business acquaintance of Spear's president claims that with LIFO perpetual he is able to achieve tax savings **and** increased profits when needed. Apparently, the increased profits stem from the timing of purchases in such a way that older (lower) LIFO prices are sometimes charged to cost of goods sold, resulting in larger profits.

To help explain how this might work, consider using the following example of one of Spear's main inventory items for the month of January 19x4:

	Units	Unit Cost	Total
Beginning LIFO inventory:			
From 19x8	50	$ 80	$4,000
From 19x0	40	100	4,000
	90		$8,000
Purchases 19x4:			
1/15/x4	45	160	$7,200
1/22/x4	60	162	$9,720
Sales 19x4:			
1/5/x4	10 units		
1/12/x4	35		
1/19/x4	20		
1/25/x4	35		
	100 units		

Required:
1. Explain to Spear's president how LIFO perpetual can result in higher profits than LIFO periodic.
2. Is it possible for LIFO perpetual to provide higher profits *and* greater tax savings than LIFO periodic?
3. Some people argue that LIFO perpetual results in *more taxes* than almost any other method (including FIFO) in years when older, lower cost units are charged to cost of goods sold (e.g., when units costing $80 from 19x8 or $100 from 19x0 are sold in the example above). They say that this offsets the tax benefits of earlier years, making LIFO (or LIFO perpetual) a more costly inventory method with no real cash savings. The president asks for your comments on this potential criticism.

C 6–9
Inventory Estimation Methods (Appendix 6B)
L.O.7

The Arbor Luggage Company had a fire in its warehouse on December 15, 19x2, that destroyed all of its inventory. The company needs to determine how much inventory was in the warehouse at the time of the fire in order to file a claim with its insurance company. Fortunately, the accounting records are thought to be accurate and up to date, with purchases of merchandise inventory recorded up to the time of the fire. Unfortunately, the company does not have a perpetual inventory system and does not know the amount of inventory that was in the warehouse at the time of the fire. The last physical count of the warehouse inventory took place on December 31, 19x1.

Required:
1. What accounting method might be available to help Arbor Luggage estimate the warehouse inventory lost in the fire?
2. Identify the accounting information required in order to make the estimate and how it would be used to estimate the lost inventory.

C 6–10
LIFO Reserve—General Motors (Appendix 6C) (Challenging)
L.O.8

General Motors Corporation uses the lower-of-cost-or-market (LCM) inventory method, where "cost" is based primarily on the LIFO method for domestic (U.S.) inventories. The following data were reconstructed from GM's 19x8 footnote disclosures.

	($ in millions)	
	19x8	**19x7**
Inventory at FIFO	$10,509.6	$10,299.6
LIFO reserve	2,525.3	2,359.9
Inventory at LIFO	$ 7,984.3	$ 7,939.7

GM reported no LIFO liquidations in 19x8.

Required:
1. What was the effect on GM's 19x8 pre-tax income from using LIFO rather than FIFO for 19x8? (Do **not** include the effect from before 19x8.)
2. What happened to GM's inventory costs during 19x8? Did costs increase, decrease, remain about the same, or can you not determine this from the data given?
3. What is your estimate of the current cost of GM's 19x8 ending inventory?
4. GM's 19x8 return on asset ratio is computed as ($ in millions):

$$\frac{\text{19x8 Net income}}{\text{Average total assets}} = \frac{\$4,856.3}{\$164,063.1} = 2.96\%$$

What would happen to GM's 19x8 return on assets ratio if GM had used FIFO in 19x8 and all prior years? Assume the tax rate for all years is 30%.

White Corporation
Balance Sheet 12/31/94

	1994	1993
Current assets:		
Cash	$ xxx	$ xxx
Accounts receivable	xxx	xxx
Allowance for bad debt	(xx)	(xx)
Merchandise inventory	xxx	xxx
Notes receivable	xxx	xxx
Total current assets.	$ xxx	$ xxx
Noncurrent assets:		
Total noncurrent assets	$ xxx	$ xxx
Total assets	$ xxx	$ xxx
Current liabilities:		
Total current liabilities.	$ xxx	$ xxx
Noncurrent liabilities:		
Total noncurrent liabilities	$ xx	$ xx
Stockholders' equity:		
Total stockholders' equity	$ xxx	$ xxx
Total liabilities and stockholders' equity	$x,xxx	$x,xxx

White Corporation
Income Statement For 1994

	1994	1993
Sales	$ xxx	$ xxx
Cost of goods sold	xxx	xxx
Gross margin	$ xxx	$ xxx
Other revenue—interest	xx	xx
Expenses		
Total expenses.	$ xxx	$ xxx
Net income	$ xx	$ xx

White Corporation
Cash Flow Statement For 1994

	1994	1993
Operating activities		
Receipts from customers	$ xxx	$ xxx
Payments to suppliers.	(xxx)	(xxx)
Payments for interest	(xxx)	(xxx)
Cash used in operating activities	$ xxx	$ xxx
Investing activities	$ xxx	$ xxx
Financing activities		
Receipts from sale of stock	$x,xxx	$x,xxx
Receipts from bank loan.	xxx	
Cash used in financing activities	$x,xxx	$x,xxx
Net change in cash	$ xx	$ xx

FINANCIAL
STATEMENT
COMPONENTS
EMPHASIZED IN
CHAPTER 7

7

Internal Controls, Cash, and Notes Receivable

Management has the obligation to safeguard assets and to assure that accounting information is accurate. The chapter begins with a discussion of the procedures businesses adopt to safeguard assets and follows with a discussion of accounting for cash and notes receivable.

Cash is the most flexible and most widely accepted asset. It is used in all kinds of transactions as a medium of exchange. The flow of cash in and out of the business provides the momentum that enables the business to continue its operations. Owners, customers, and creditors bring cash into the business, and cash flows out of the business to owners in the form of dividends, to suppliers for products and services, and to creditors in payment of obligations. Employees, governments, and many others have cash transactions with businesses. Another current asset that is often associated with cash is short-term investment in marketable securities. This topic is covered in Chapter 12 along with other investments.

Even when a transaction with an outside party does not immediately involve cash, it usually affects the company's cash flow sooner or later. For example, purchases and sales on credit eventually involve cash flow. Successful business operations depend on successful management of the company's cash.

In Chapter 5, you were introduced to the importance of credit sales and accounts receivable in businesses. This chapter continues the discussion on accounting for receivables by explaining how companies account for notes receivable. A note is a formal contract issued by the debtor as evidence of an obligation to pay a specific amount to the creditor at a specific time. Sometimes customers convert their accounts receivable into a note. The discussion on notes receivable includes discounting a note receivable at a bank. Appendix 7A gives additional information on special accounting journals and control accounts. Appendix 7B introduces some basic features of electronic data processing of accounting information.

INTERNAL CONTROL

What Are Internal Controls?

Every business has objectives and is organized in ways expected to help achieve those objectives. Internal control is the process by which an entity's management reasonably assures that objectives are met.[1] Such objectives can relate to competitiveness, customer satisfaction, quality, reliability of accounting numbers and reports, appropriate use of resources, compliance with laws and regulations, and many other interconnected goals. In its broadest sense, internal control can be viewed as the process that helps management achieve all of these goals. The major components of internal control are (1) integrity, ethical values, and competence; (2) management environment and leadership style; (3) objectives; (4) risk; (5) information systems; (6) control procedures; (7) communication; (8) management of change; and (9) monitoring. In our introduction to this topic, we will concentrate on examples dealing with safeguarding certain assets and maintaining the integrity of the accounting numbers and reports.

People are at the heart of any internal control effort. If objectives are to be achieved, ways must be fashioned to help people understand, communicate, and perform in a coordinated and consistent manner. As with all human endeavor the starting point is the understanding of responsibilities and authority. Most internal control problems come from human failings, such as lack of integrity of management, unclear business philosophy, and lack of integration and communication of objectives. Often, as business conditions change these weaknesses become pronounced, putting undue pressure on subordinates.

---

[1]The discussion in this and the following paragraph is based on *Internal Control-Integrated Framework* (Exposure Draft, March 12, 1991), Committee of Sponsoring Organizations of the Treadway Commission, New York.

Consider the following conversation between the controller (Bonnie) of Fashions, Inc., and the manager (Jack) of one of its local department stores, who has just been promoted directly from a position in fashion design and buying.

Controller: Jack, we are instituting a new plan of internal control for all of our stores and I'm here to answer any of your general questions.

Store Manager: Remember, Bonnie, I know nothing about accounting. Give me a simple definition of internal control. Is it kind of like intestinal fortitude? Ha, Ha.

Controller: Control is a term we use for a system to help assure us that the assets of the company are safeguarded, that all transactions are authorized, and that policies are followed and stuff like that. What I have brought with me is a checklist of things to be concerned about and a short write-up on implementing each item on that list. First we want you and your top people to read the write-ups, and next month one of my people will come in to help with specifics.

Store Manager: Wait a minute. My people are honest, and I keep a pretty close eye on everything. Isn't that enough?

Controller: I agree that most of our people are honest—the vast majority are—but remember that a person's situation may change, and sometimes we, as managers, don't understand the pressure some of the staff may be under. Temptation can overcome even those we trust.

Store Manager: OK, give me a concrete example of what we're talking about.

Controller: Think of a basic transaction type like purchasing and think of all the opportunities there are for losses. The ordering process, for instance. Here we want separation of duties so that one person can't both perpetrate and hide an irregularity. So we want to make sure we have policies about authorizations of a purchase, ordering, taking custody of the merchandise, paying the bills, recording of the transactions, and so on. In general we don't want the same people doing all of those duties.

Store Manager: I see, but that might be a problem because we don't have that many different people to spread the duties out to.

Controller: Well, we have ways of judging just how fine the separation has to be. In some cases duties can be combined but never all of them. Going on with this type of transaction, in addition to separation of duties we would want to safeguard the inventory once we take possession, which means restricting access to the inventory itself and to the records of inventories. Also, authority and responsibility for inventory must be assigned to certain people so that there is no question as to who makes access decisions. Another general procedure we think is valuable is a system of reconciliations where we would count the inventory and make sure that the ending amount ties to the amount acquired less sales, tying accounts payable to the statement of our supplier and that kind of thing.

Store Manager: OK. I get the picture. What's in that ominous looking folder there?

Controller: This contains checklists for internal controls issues for all major types of transactions like sales, purchasing, cash receipts and payments, and production.

After reading the above narrative, you might conclude that internal controls seem like just good common sense. That is true, but as with our store manager, a trusting manager will not focus on all the potential problem areas, and therefore careful study and continuous oversight is needed. Of course managers would like to prevent all errors and irregularities from ever occurring but, practically, the goal in most settings is to reduce the amounts of losses to a minimum and to increase the probability of detection of those that do occur.

The extent of the internal controls necessary to protect the operations of a business depends on the size and function of the business. In Chapter 5, you followed two entrepreneurs as they established their business goals, obtained resources, and developed plans for the operation of Byte-Size, Inc. With the help of a graduate accounting student,

Byte-Size established an accounting system that enabled it to monitor operations and determine possible corrective action for their cash flow problem. As an enterprise grows, it must add internal controls to protect its assets and accounting data and to make sure its employees operate efficiently and comply with prescribed managerial policies.

The first topic in this section discusses the general principles of internal control. Then you will learn some of the procedures companies use to establish controls over assets and accounting data. An explanation of the cost-benefit evaluation of controls concludes this section.

Before studying the topics that follow, you must remember that competent, honest employees are the foundation of all successful internal controls. No matter how well a system is designed, it will fail if the people charged with its operations do not perform adequately. Great care should be taken in screening new personnel, providing thorough employee training, placing employees in positions commensurate with their capabilities and interests, and providing feedback on employee performance.

General Principles of Internal Control

Prior to establishing internal controls, a business must have an effective organizational plan or structure designed by management according to the goals and functions of the business. The type of organizational plan used by a business depends on many factors, such as size of the business, philosophy of management, and so on. For example, Byte-Size, Inc., (our Chapter 5 example) is a small business with only the owners, Mary and Brad, working in the business. Byte-Size, therefore, would have a simple organizational plan, perhaps just an agreement about how they would share the work and responsibilities. However, as the company grows and adds new employees, it must develop a more elaborate organizational plan. The internal controls the company builds into its organizational plan should be based on the following general principles:

Objective 1

The five general principles of internal control.

1. **Authorization and responsibility.** Top management must authorize the lines of authority in the organization and determine the responsibilities of each employee. In addition, each employee in authority is responsible for his or her decisions and actions, and the performance of subordinates must be authorized by a supervisor.

2. **Separation of duties (division of work).** Separation of duties discourages employee theft and fraud. In addition, the work of one employee can provide an internal check on the work by another employee, thus helping to avoid honest mistakes.

3. **Protection of assets.** Physical assets should be covered by insurance to ensure they will be replaced if a casualty occurs. To ensure against theft, employees in important asset-responsible positions should be rotated periodically, and employees handling cash should be bonded. Bonding is a type of insurance policy taken out on certain employees that will pay the company damages if an employee misappropriates assets. The actual control of cash is discussed later in this chapter.

4. **Mechanical and electronic devices.** Various devices such as computers, cash registers, check protectors, and time clocks are valuable aids for internal control.

5. **Accounting system procedures.** Many different procedures can be used to ensure that the accounting system provides internal controls over the recording of transactions pertaining to assets, liabilities, revenues, and expenses. Some of the procedures used to protect the accounting system are discussed in the following subsection on internal control procedures.

These five general principles emphasize the importance of internal control. In fact, to protect stockholders of publicly owned corporations, in 1977 the federal government established the Foreign Corrupt Practices Act. Although it was originally established to prevent bribes of foreign officials by employees of publicly traded U.S. corporations, the act requires the management of the corporation to assume the responsibility of maintaining accurate accounting records and a system of internal control over these records.

Accounting Control Procedures

Objective 2
The internal control procedures used to safeguard assets and ensure the accuracy and reliability of accounting data.

Accounting controls are the technical procedures of an accounting information system that are designed to ensure that (1) relevant transactions are recorded, (2) the financial statements are sound, and (3) the company's assets are protected. Since the primary duty of such internal controls is the safeguarding of assets and the accuracy and reliability of accounting data, the paragraphs that follow discuss these two topics in turn.

Safeguarding Assets. The following controls show specific approaches to the general goals discussed earlier.

1. **Separation of physical asset control from asset recordkeeping.** In Chapter 6, you learned the importance of inventory. Unfortunately, the theft of inventory by employees is a serious problem in many companies. Thus, internal controls should be established so that the same employee does not control the company's physical assets and keep the records for these assets. Cash, the most liquid of assets, is covered in detail in a separate section of this chapter. Much of that discussion deals with controls over cash.

2. **Periodic comparison of actual assets on hand with amount reported in the records.** The use of the physical inventory count studied in Chapter 6 is an important element of internal control. At least once a year a physical inventory count should be taken. The need for an asset count also applies to plant, property, and equipment items. Theft of small items, such as hand tools, is difficult to detect, but procedures that limit access and assign responsibility can discourage theft. For example, if a foreman knows that a detailed accounting of all hand tools in a department is necessary, he or she will devise methods to control access to the hand tools. Later in this chapter, under bank reconciliation procedures, we emphasize the importance of comparing actual cash on hand and in banks with cash records.

3. **Proof that a liability exists before payment is made.** The general principle of separation of duties is also effective in controlling theft associated with payments to suppliers, for example, the employee who receives merchandise should not authorize payment for the merchandise. Also, an invoice to a supplier should not be authorized for payment unless a purchase order (a document authorizing the purchase of the merchandise) and a receiving report (a document prepared when merchandise is received) are attached to the invoice.

Ensuring the Accuracy and Reliability of Accounting Data. The accuracy and reliability of accounting data begins with authorized transactions. Again, some of the general internal control measures mentioned earlier are useful to ensure that the accounting data is accurate and reliable. In addition, companies can use various other procedures, such as the following.

1. **Accuracy of source documents.** Since external transactions originate with source documents (checks, invoices, purchase orders, and shipping and receiving reports), these documents should be prenumbered to discourage tampering. Companies also use other methods to promote and/or detect authenticity and accuracy of the documents, such as requiring employee signatures on various documents to indicate that the figures have been checked.

2. **Accuracy of recordkeeping.** Several procedures can be used to check the recordkeeping of employees. A valuable procedure is to separate recording duties so that related transactions are not recorded by one employee. In Chapter 5, you were introduced to subsidiary ledgers and the relationship of subsidiary ledgers to the general ledger. In addition to providing the company with necessary and detailed information, subsidiary ledgers can promote separation of duties and double checks for the account balances.

3. **Special journals.** Special journals are books of original entry designed to process a class of repetitive transactions efficiently. They add efficiency in some applications and provide an opportunity to implement internal controls. Companies commonly keep special journals for sales, purchases, cash receipts, and cash disbursements. Thus, the sales transactions are entered only in the sales journal, the purchases transactions in the purchases journal, and so on. If scale of operations permits, separation of duties is possible by assigning different people to each journal. Appendix 7A illustrates the use of special journals and ledger control accounts.

Accounting systems that use special journals still need a general journal. Companies always have some transactions that occur infrequently or do not fall into the common categories represented by the special journals. For example, an unusual transaction such as the purchase of land for common stock would be recorded in the general journal. The separation of groups of transactions into special journals creates a more efficient method of recording transactions and provides more control over accounting procedures. In manual accounting systems, special journals also lead to more efficient posting of transaction information to the ledger accounts.

4. **Regular evaluations of recordkeeping.** Every internal control system must include regular recordkeeping evaluations to make sure that all the appropriate control techniques are installed and followed. Owners of small businesses usually are personally involved in maintaining controls and evaluating the company's internal control system. Larger businesses often have internal auditing departments ensuring that internal controls are performing as designed.

In many large corporations the internal audit department is required to perform two types of audits—operational audits and financial audits. An operational audit focuses on management controls and how well various levels of management are performing under these controls, and helps to evaluate efficiency. The financial audit tests for conformance to accounting procedures and indicates to management that the controls in the accounting system are functioning as designed and the system is providing reliable information.[2]

Cost-Benefit
Evaluation of Internal
Controls

Objective 3
The cost-benefit evaluation
of accounting control.

An accounting system is subject to the same cost-benefit evaluation as any other business function. Companies must judge the costs of changing accounting systems and implementing controls against the benefits. Certain costs may increase when companies (1) increase the amount of accounting information recorded and reported, (2) increase the speed with which this information is available, and (3) add internal controls to protect the accounting system, but such changes lead to reduced theft and waste, and greater customer satisfaction. Weighing costs and benefits is at the core of management decisions including those related to controls.

For example, assume that a restaurant has one waiter who prepares the guest checks and also collects the money from the customers. Principles of good internal control would suggest these duties be separated. Thus, to avoid potential problems, the restaurant owner could hire a cashier so that the waiter would prepare prenumbered guest checks, and the cashier would collect the money and retain the guest check. At the end of the day, the amount of money collected should equal the total amount of the guest checks. Any unaccounted guest check numbers could be investigated.

The separation of duties suggested above usually improves the accuracy of the accounting information and discourages dishonesty. Note, however, that if the restaurant owner

---

[2]In addition to the internal audit, the books and records of many companies are subject to external audits, as introduced in Chapter 1. An **external audit** is a review by an outside independent auditor who is not an employee of the company. These audits are conducted by firms of certified public accountants and are part of the controls exercised by parties external to the company's management, such as stockholders and bankers.

hires a cashier, the cost of running the business may increase. The restaurant owner must weigh the cost of adding this internal control against the benefit that would be received. Often a manager finds that it is difficult to place a specific dollar value on such a potential change.

CASH

Cash is a word that we normally use in our everyday life when referring to coins and currency. Generally, we call it money. In accounting, cash includes more than coins and currency; it also includes amounts on deposit such as checking accounts, and checks and money orders made out to the business. Accountants define cash as the money that a business has on hand or has a right to and easy access to, such as money orders, checks, and balances in checking accounts.

Cash is the most current and the most liquid of assets. It can be used immediately for many purposes in and out of business. Whereas other business assets, such as raw materials, computers, delivery trucks, and buildings, have more specific uses, cash is acceptable as the general medium of exchange. Cash is flexible; it can be used to rent or purchase any number of products and services.

Checks written on a checking account are considered the same as cash payments. Checking accounts are called demand deposits because the depositor has free access to the cash without advance notification to the bank. If a bank requires notification before a business can use the money, these accounts are called time deposits and usually they earn interest. Because the business may not have immediate access to time deposits, they are not as liquid as cash and are classified as investments.

In addition to time deposits, short-term and long-term investments with withdrawal restrictions should not be classified as cash. Also, if a loan contract with a bank requires that the borrower deposit specific sums (called compensating balances) in a noninterest-earning account or an account that earns less than the market rate of interest, this minimum balance is classified as an investment or restricted cash, since the money is not freely available to the depositor. Usually, these compensating balances must be maintained as long as the loan is outstanding.

In Japan, where companies often have very close relationships with banks, the practice of demanding compensating balances during the term of a loan is prevalent. For instance, a company may borrow for one year 100,000,000 yen and pay 10,000,000 yen as interest. Part of the loan agreement may have the company leave 20,000,000 yen in the bank in an account that earns no interest. In such a case the real interest rate on the loan would not be 10% but 12.5% because although the company pays 10,000,000 yen per year, it has access to only 80,000,000 yen; thus the real annual interest rate is .125 (10,000,000/80,000,000 = .125.) In the United States, the amount of such compensating balances would not be shown as cash on the balance sheet. In Japan, the compensating balance is shown as part of cash.

In contrast to investments, cash is completely liquid, and unless otherwise specifically stated in a contract, all business debts can be paid in cash. Businesses use cash to pay their employees, taxes, and dividends to stockholders. Customers use cash to pay for a company's services and products. Cash can be used immediately for legitimate business purposes, and it can be used just as easily for unauthorized purposes.

The flexibility of cash disappears once it is used to purchase another asset such as a piece of equipment or a building because the asset purchased may not be easily sold and turned back into cash. For example, if a company purchases a factory building to manufacture its products rather than subcontract the products from another company, the company has committed funds hoping to increase its efficiency in the long term. At the same time, however, future cash decisions have been restricted. The company also assumes that spending the cash for the building will increase the future flow of cash into the business, but it takes time for such returns to be earned.

The Balance Sheet Presentation of Cash

Nothing is simple in today's world: Not even the way the word *cash* is used in financial reporting. To this point in the text, in most of our examples we have used *cash* in its simple sense. When we have debited and credited cash it was to record the inflows and outflows of currency or to record the receipt of checks made out to the business or made out by the business to a payee. We did hint at a more complex view of cash in our introduction to the Statement of Cash Flow when we used the term *cash equivalents,* and more will be said about that in Chapter 14. In this chapter we will focus on the accounting for cash in the sense of determining the proper balance of this asset, which includes amounts of currency, checks made out to the business, and balances in unconstrained bank accounts, commonly called checking accounts.

One major stumbling block to understanding financial statements is that the same word is often used in different ways in different aspects of accounting. Consider the following excerpts from published balance sheets:

The Standard Register Company

Current assets:	(dollars in thousands)
Cash.	$ 3,470

Apple Computer, Inc.

Current assets:	(dollars in thousands)
Cash and cash equivalents	$374,682

IPCO Corporation

Current assets:	(dollars in thousands)
Cash and cash equivalents—unrestricted	$ 10,157
Cash—restricted	7,689

Premier Industrial Corporation

Current assets:	
Cash (including temporary investments of $40,503)	$ 48,767

As can be seen from these excerpts the word *cash* is used in different ways and in combination with other words on published financial statements. Moreover, the usage has changed over time. The following analysis, taken from *Accounting Trends and Techniques,*[3] shows how the reporting of cash has evolved in recent years.

How Cash Is Disclosed on Balance Sheets	Number of Companies Reporting	
	1990	1987
Cash alone	123	215
Cash and cash equivalents	401	197
Cash combined with marketable securities	73	189
No cash shown	3	0
Total number of companies in sample	600	600

Keep in mind that balance sheets are summaries of detailed accounting records that include many ledger accounts, so the *Cash and Cash Equivalents* on the balance sheet does not imply that there is only one ledger account with that title. In most cases balances under such captions are sums from several accounts. We will concentrate on the accounts that relate to the most liquid and unconstrained asset, which we commonly term *cash*.

---

[3] *Accounting Trends and Techniques: 1991* (New York: AICPA).

Cash Flow
Management

One of management's greatest responsibilities is controlling cash flows. This section begins with the importance of cash flow management. Then a discussion of cash flow control continues the coverage of protection of assets begun earlier in the chapter. Before we delve into the specifics of managing cash and accounting for cash transactions, consider the following conversation between Bonnie (recall she is the controller of Fashions, Inc., in our introduction to internal controls on page 329), and Jack (the store manager).

> **Controller:** Another major area we need to work on is cash management. We want all of our people to adopt the philosophy that too much cash is bad.
>
> **Store Manager:** Oh yeah, empty your pockets. I'll take all you have.
>
> **Controller:** Ha, Ha. Very funny. But in a way that proves my point. Cash is so liquid that it creates a control problem, especially if it's in currency. In addition, it doesn't earn us a return if it's idle.
>
> **Store Manager:** Sure, so we deposit it in the bank on a daily basis.
>
> **Controller:** Right, but ordinary checking, while safeguarding the asset, doesn't usually earn any interest. We want to establish procedures that safeguard the asset, maintain minimum necessary balances in noninterest-earning accounts, and have the maximum return on all of our resources.
>
> **Store Manager:** We need to be a bit flexible. We can't work with zero in our checking accounts.
>
> **Controller:** You're correct, but we want to always work toward minimizing the amount and also be able to pay obligations as they come due, and that means paying a lot more attention to the timing of payments. For example, your store's weekly payroll runs about $18,000, right? You issue those checks on Friday and they clear the banks on Monday. We want to put the money in the checking account at the latest time the bank will allow to cover the checks. Now some of our stores are keeping the payroll amount for a whole week before the checks are issued. Our investment people could be earning interest for all that time. Multiply that lost interest by our 30 stores for several weeks a year, and we're talking about a lot of lost revenues.

Objective 4
*Cash flow management
and cash control.*

You should be familiar with the importance of timing cash flows. As you recall, Byte-Size, Inc., of Chapter 5 had a cash flow problem. Even though the entrepreneurs followed their accountant's advice and borrowed money before they began their business, an analysis of the company's operations after three months showed that Byte-Size's liquidity problem had not been completely solved. A severe cash shortage was likely without more financing.

Small companies are not the only ones where cash is of major concern. In any one period, a large company may have millions of dollars of cash inflows and outflows while the company's cash balance may be a relatively small amount. The timing of these cash inflows and outflows is one of the most important and difficult functions of managers.

Managers must time the inflow of cash so that enough cash is available to pay the company's obligations as they occur. If management fails to keep enough cash flowing in to meet the company's obligations, a serious situation can develop. Many companies have gone bankrupt because their cash flow was poorly timed and inadequate. Management also must not have too much cash on hand, because idle cash is not productive. Thus, the goal is to have just enough cash on hand to meet company obligations and also have a small cash cushion for emergencies.

Cash Control

You learned from the discussion on internal control that safeguarding assets is an important function of management. Because of the relative ease with which cash can be used for unintended purposes, special precautions must be taken to safeguard cash. Some of these precautions have been discussed earlier in the chapter. Additional procedures for ensuring the safety of cash are discussed in the paragraphs that follow.

Prudent cash control usually includes the following precautions:

1. Employees who handle cash should not record cash transactions.
2. Employees who handle cash receipts should not handle cash payments.
3. Significant amounts of cash should not be held as currency but should be deposited in the bank intact each day.
4. All cash disbursements should be made by check and approved by someone who is separate from the functions of check writing and signing.
5. Prenumbered checks should be used for disbursements except for small amounts, for which a petty cash imprest system (to be defined later in the chapter) should be used.
6. Periodic bank reconciliations are prepared by employees who do not handle cash or record cash transactions.

You will notice that most of these safeguards, and many other safeguards used by companies, are designed to isolate functions so that no employee can misuse cash without the collusion of one or more other employees. The following example illustrates the importance of separation of duties pertaining to the handling of cash.

Employee A handles the receipt of money (currency, not checks) from customers and also records and deposits the money in the bank. Upon receipt of a $300 currency payment from customer X, employee A pockets the money and does not record the receipt until customer Y makes a payment of at least $300 in currency, at which time customer X's payment is recorded. Customer Y's payment is not recorded until customer Z pays, and so on. In this way, employee A has effectively taken $300 from the company by delaying the date when cash receipts are recorded and deposited. This activity is called lapping because the cash receipts of one customer are applied to the receivables of another customer. The separation of duties would force employee A to find other dishonest co-workers to help perpetrate and conceal the crime.

The above example is simplified to illustrate the importance of separation of duties. It would be more difficult for employee A to appropriate the money if checks made out to the company were involved. The endorsing of the checks may not be too difficult, but employee A would have to convert the checks into cash, for example, by establishing a bogus checking account.

The use of checks provides a method of internal control both to the business and the customer. The paragraphs that follow discuss checking accounts, bank statements, reconciliation of checking accounts, and the control of petty cash, a fund many companies use for small incidental expenses.

Checking Accounts.   In most companies, the inflow of cash is in the form of checks. Checks made out to the company, money orders, and currency are usually deposited in a bank checking account. Often a company will keep several checking accounts at one or more banks. One checking account might be used exclusively for payroll and another might be used to pay suppliers. Such specialized checking accounts provide safeguards against misappropriation of funds.

The procedure of opening a company checking account is similar to opening a personal checking account. The employees authorized to sign checks must sign a bank signature card so that the bank can validate the check signatures if necessary. Banks generally provide printed deposit tickets and serially numbered checks printed with the company's name, address, and identification number. The company's identification number and the bank's identification number are printed in magnetic ink so that the checks can be processed by computer.

The company keeps a record of the checks written, deposits made, and the balance left in the checking account. Small businesses often use their check stubs as a record; large businesses enter this information directly into their computerized accounting system. No matter how cash is recorded, the company must reconcile the balance shown in its records with the balance in the bank's records.

The company's records and the bank's records register the same transactions and could, if it were not for timing differences, be viewed as mirror images of one another. You recall from Chapter 3 that increases in the Cash account are recorded as debits and decreases as credits, and that at any point in time the company can determine the balance in the Cash account. When the company deposits cash in its checking account, the company becomes a creditor of the bank, because the balance in the company's checking account is an obligation of the bank. The deposit increases (credits) the bank's demand deposit liability.[4] Cleared checks, withdrawals, and service charges are decreases (debits) in the bank's demand deposit liability. Thus, to the bank, the company is a depositor and a creditor because the balance in the company's checking account is an obligation of the bank.

Bank Statements. Periodically, usually monthly, the bank sends the company a bank statement. The bank statement is a document that shows the beginning and ending balances in the checking account and gives details of the deposits, withdrawals, bank service charges, and other activities. Exhibit 7–1 illustrates one form of bank statement. You will note that letter codes are listed at the bottom of the statement. The explanation of these common letter codes follows.

1. EC—error correction. When the bank makes an arithmetic error and corrects the error, the symbol EC follows the correction.

2. SC—service charge. A service charge is the bank's fee for services involved in maintaining a checking account. The service charge can be based on the number of transactions (checks cleared, deposits made, and so on), and often the average balance in the account has an effect on the amount of the charge. Sometimes a bank will waive service charges for customers with large average balances because the banks can earn revenue on these funds.

3. OD—overdrafts. An overdraft occurs when a combination of checks written and service charges incurred exceeds the amount on deposit. When the company has an overdraft, does it have a negative asset or a positive liability? Such credit balances are reported as current liabilities on the company's balance sheet because the deficiency must be made up by a payment or a cash deposit to the bank.

4. NSF—nonsufficient funds (not sufficient funds). A nonsufficient funds (NSF) check is a check deposited in the company's checking account but not honored by the check writer's bank because the balance in the check writer's checking account is insufficient to cover the check. Some banks charge the depositor of the NSF check a small "charge-back" fee. The maker of the NSF check is always charged a fee for checks returned. Exhibit 7–2 illustrates a chain of events resulting from NSF checks. In this example, the depositor of the NSF check was not charged a fee.

Company A in Exhibit 7–2 pays an invoice with check No. 802 for $1,500 to Company B; however, Company A's checking account balance is only $950. Both Company A and Company B have checking accounts at First Bank. Company B deposits Company A's check. When First Bank processes the deposit and Company A's checking account does not have $1,500 to cover the check, Company A is charged a $50 penalty for the NSF check. Company A then cancels check No. 802 and records the penalty as a miscellaneous expense or as part of the monthly service charge. Company B is notified that

---

[4]A cleared check is one that has been processed by the bank and deducted from the checking account balance.

EXHIBIT 7–1

Bank Statement

Ameritex Bank
100 Main Street
Gainesville, TN 99999-0870

Statement Date: 10/31/xx
Account Number: 110-7777-6

Arrow, Inc.
579 Broadway Drive
Gainesville, TN 99999-0880

Summary for the Month:

Previous balance	$ 1,080
2 deposits totaling	20,500
33 checks or withdrawals	(21,080)
SC	(25)
Current balance	$ 475

Detail of Transactions:

Deposits			Checks (Withdrawals)		
Date	*Amount*		*Date*	*Check No.*	*Amount*
10/22/xx	$ 8,500		10/1/xx	1124	$ 82
10/30/xx	12,000		10/16/xx	1155	197
Total	$20,500		·	·	·
			·	·	·
			·	·	·
			10/28/xx	1197	600
			Total		$21,080

Explanation of Symbols

EC	Error Correction	OD	Overdraft	MC	Miscellaneous Charges
SC	Service Charge	NSF	Not Sufficient Funds	IN	Interest Earned

Company A's NSF check was returned. After these transactions, if no other cash has been paid or received, Company A has $900 in its checking account. Company A must still pay Company B for the invoice.

5. MC— miscellaneous charges.   Miscellaneous charges are fees charged by a bank for stopping payment on checks, printing checks for customers, and other miscellaneous services. Such charges are recorded by the depositor as service charges.

6. IN— interest.   Banks sometimes pay interest on the cash balances in checking accounts. This interest is reported on the bank statement and calls for the depositor to make a journal entry to increase Cash and record Interest Revenue.

Objective 5
Cash reconciliation.

Reconciliation of Checking Accounts.   If you have a checking account, you know that time lags occur between the time (1) you write a check and the bank reduces your balance, (2) you make a deposit and the bank records the deposit, and (3) the bank subtracts service charges from your checking account and you are notified of the deduction on your

EXHIBIT 7–2

Example of NSF Check Transaction

Company A		Company B	
Writes check No. 802 for $1,500:		**Receives check No. 802 for $1,500:**	
Accounts Payable (L)	1,500	Cash (A)	1,500
Cash (A)	1,500	Accounts Receivable (A)	1,500

First Bank

Deposited check returned to Company A's account as an NSF check; amount of check subtracted from Company B's account.

Company A		Company B	
Cancels check No. 802 and records penalty:		**Gets notice of NSF check:**	
Cash (A)	1,500	Accounts Receivable (A)	1,500
Accounts Payable (L)	1,500	Cash (A)	1,500
Service Charge (E)	50		
Cash (A)	50		

monthly bank statement. These time lags are the primary reason that your personal checking account balance does not always agree with the balance on your bank statement. In addition to timing differences, discrepancies also occur due to errors.

When the company receives its bank statement, the company must compare and reconcile the bank's records with the company's records. Since the bank and the company maintain separate records, the bank reconciliation acts as an independent check of the cash balance. The following steps are common in reconciling a bank statement:

1. Check the beginning balance on the bank statement to make sure it is the ending balance of the previous month's statement.

2. Compare the company's deposits made to the bank this month plus any deposits in transit at the end of last month against the deposits shown on the bank statement. If the company shows more deposits than the bank, check to see whether any deposits are in transit. Deposits in transit are deposits recorded in the company's records as of the bank statement date but not reflected in the current bank statement. These money amounts are legitimately recognized as cash by the depositor.

3. Compare the checks returned (cleared) by the bank with the record of checks written and with any outstanding checks at the end of the previous month to determine which checks have cleared the bank. Outstanding checks are checks that have been written and recorded by the company but have not cleared the bank at the time the bank statement is prepared. Also compare the amount on the check with the amount reported on the bank statement.

4. Check the bank statement for any increases (such as interest or the collection of a note receivable by the bank) and decreases (such as service charges or NSF checks) that are reported on the bank statement but have not been accounted for in the company's checking account record.

After performing steps 1 through 4, all the necessary amounts are known to explain the differences between the cash balance and the bank statement balance. Such an explanation or listing of differences is called a reconciliation.

Checking account reconciliation — a simple example. The following example begins with the transactions recorded in a company's Cash account and follows the procedure a company uses to check the account against the bank statement.

Arrow, Inc., has a Cash account with the following transactions close to the end of the month:

Cash						Account No. 111
Date		Description	Ref.	Debit	Credit	Balance Debit (Credit)
19x1 Oct.	1	Beginning Balance				1,400
	28	Check No. 1197	J5		600	500
	29	Check No. 1198 *Outstanding*	J5		150	350
	30	Deposit	J6	100		450

On October 31, First Bank sends Arrow a bank statement that shows a $475 balance after deduction of a service charge of $25. Also, the bank statement does not show either that check No. 1198 has cleared the bank or that the October 30 deposit has been received. Since the bank shows a $475 balance and Arrow shows $450, obviously neither $475 nor $450 can be the correct balance.

We must (1) determine the correct balance and (2) record any necessary adjustments to Arrow's records. Study Exhibit 7–3 as you follow Arrow's reconciliation procedure.

Arrow's ledger account balance of $450 and First Bank's statement balance of $475 are shown in the two bars at the left of the exhibit. Since First Bank has already taken the $25 service charge from its balance, Arrow must make the following entry to record the service charge shown in Exhibit 7–3.

```
19xx
Oct. 31   Service Charge Expense (E) . . . . . . . . . . . . . . . . . . . . . . . .   25
               Cash (A) . . . . . . . . . . . . . . . . . . . . . . . . . . . . .        25
          To record service charge for October.
```

As you can see in Exhibit 7–3, after the recording of the $25 service charge the company ledger balance is $425. No other entries are necessary on Arrow's books.

First Bank shows a balance of $475, but the bank has not yet recorded the October 30 deposit of $100 and the October 29 check No. 1198 for $150. The bank will increase its obligation to Arrow by $100 when it records the October 30 deposit and decrease the obligation by $150 when check No. 1198 clears. Both transactions will be reflected on the next bank statement. Since Arrow's deposits and checks are recorded correctly no adjusting entries are required.

• COMPREHENSIVE EXAMPLE

Now let's look at a more comprehensive example. The business of Depositor, Inc., began on January 1, 19xx, with a deposit of $100,000 at First Bank. Depositor's cash transactions for January are shown in Exhibit 7–4. First Bank records the January deposits, cleared checks, and service charges, which result in the bank statement shown in Exhibit 7–5.

EXHIBIT 7–3

Reconciliation Process

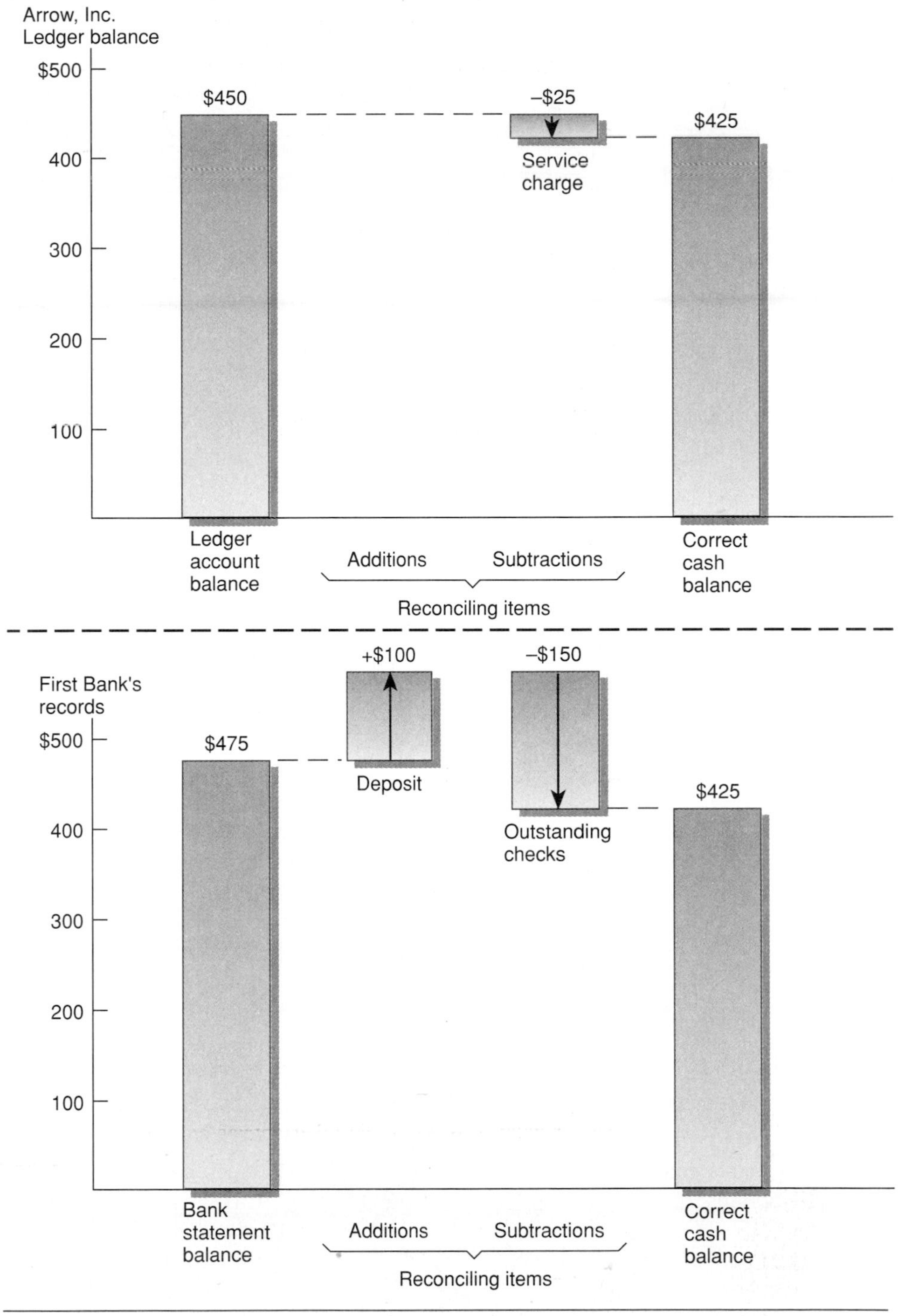

Arrow, Inc.
Ledger balance

$500

−$25
Service charge

$450

400

300

200

100

Ledger account balance

Additions   Subtractions

Reconciling items

$425

Correct cash balance

First Bank's records

$500

$475

+$100
Deposit

−$150
Outstanding checks

$425

400

300

200

100

Bank statement balance

Additions   Subtractions

Reconciling items

Correct cash balance

EXHIBIT 7–4

January Cash Transactions of Depositor, Inc.

Cash						Account No. 111
Date		Description	Ref.	Debit	Credit	Balance Debit (Credit)
19xx Jan.	1	Deposit		100,000		100,000
	2	Checks written			8,960	91,040
	4	Deposit		4,956		95,996
	6	Checks written			17,451	78,545
	7	Deposit		9,267		87,812
	8	Deposit		15,116		102,928
	10	Checks written			33,470	69,458
	13	Deposit		9,513		78,971
	17	Deposit		16,397		95,368
	19	Deposit		17,725		113,093
	20	Checks written			15,692	97,401
	25	Deposit		25,137		122,538
	26	Checks written			12,168	110,370
	30	Deposit		23,240		133,610
	31	Deposit		25,360		158,970
	31	Checks written			16,584	142,386
Totals				246,711	104,325	

Note that the balance in Depositor's Cash account (Exhibit 7–4) is $14,751 more than First Bank's balance ($142,386 − $127,635 = $14,751). This difference is made up of (1) deposits in transit of $48,600, which is the difference between total deposits of $246,711 and deposits recorded by the bank of $198,111; (2) outstanding checks of $34,334, which is the difference between total checks written of $104,325 and checks cleared of $69,991; (3) an unrecorded service charge of $135; (4) a check-printing charge of $125; and (5) an NSF check of $225.

The bank reconciliation of Depositor's records and First Bank's records is shown below:

Depositor, Inc.
Bank Reconciliation
January 31, 19xx

Balance per statement from First Bank.	$127,635	Balance per Depositor's Cash account	$142,386
Add:		Deduct:	
Deposits in transit	48,600	Service charge.	(135)
Deduct:		Check-printing charge.	(125)
Outstanding checks.	(34,334)	NSF check, customer No. 213	(225)
Adjusted bank balance	$141,901	Adjusted Cash account balance	$141,901

EXHIBIT 7–5

First Bank's January Transactions of Depositor, Inc.

First Bank
200 Main Street
White Cloud, MN 00000-1111

Statement Date: 1/31/xx
Account Number: 1360 000 000

Depositor, Inc.
17 Industrial Drive
White Cloud, MN 00000-1111

Summary for the Month:

Previous balance	$ 0
8 deposits totaling	198,111
33 checks or withdrawals	(69,991)
NSF	(225)
MC *misc*	(125)
SC	(135)
Current balance	$127,635

Detail of Transactions:

Deposits		Checks (Withdrawals)		
Date	*Amount*	*Date*	*Check No.*	*Amount*
1/2/xx	$100,000	1/6/xx	10001	$ 4,000
1/6/xx	4,956	1/6/xx	10002	10,000
1/8/xx	9,267	1/7/xx	10003	2,140
1/10/xx	15,116	.	.	.
1/14/xx	9,513	.	.	.
1/18/xx	16,397	.	.	.
1/21/xx	17,725	1/31/xx	10046	1,340
1/26/xx	25,137	1/31/xx	10049	692
	$198,111	Total		$69,991

Explanation of Symbols

EC	Error Correction	OD	Overdraft	MC	Miscellaneous Charges
SC	Service Charge	NSF	Not Sufficient Funds	IN	Interest Earned

(handwritten margin notes: 48,600 / 34,334 / 135 / 125 / 225)

The journal entries Depositor, Inc., makes to record the service charge, check-printing charge, and reestablishment of the account receivable (the NSF check) are as follows:

19xx			
Jan. 31	Service Charge Expense (E)	135	
	Miscellaneous Expenses (E)	125	
	Cash (A)		260
	To record bank service charge and check-printing charge.		
	Accounts Receivable (A)	225	
	Cash (A)		225
	To record NSF check returned by the bank.		

The Cash account has a debit balance representing an asset that is available for use in the business. After recording the above entries, the ending cash balance of $141,901 will appear on the balance sheet as a current asset. To summarize the effects of all January transactions, consider a summary of Depositor's cash transactions in the following T account.

Cash

Beg. bal.	0	Checks written	104,325
Deposits	246,711	Service charge	135
		Check-printing	
		charge	125
		NSF check	225
End. bal.	141,901		

Objective 6
A petty cash imprest system.

Petty Cash.   A business has many miscellaneous uses for small amounts of cash, such as paying cab fares, postage, coffee supplies, delivery charges, and tips. It would be cumbersome and expensive to write checks to pay for these small items, but control and orderly recordkeeping are still necessary.

A petty cash imprest system allows for a fund of ready cash, usually a small amount of cash, while at the same time assuring systematic accountability. The fund begins with a stated amount (which can be increased or decreased as the need demands). As the fund is used, from time to time it is replenished to its original amount.

The petty cash imprest system calls for recordkeeping by the custodian of the fund. Usually, the petty cash is kept in a cash box. As money is used, it is replaced by a signed receipt stating who received the money and how it was spent.

When cash is initially given to the custodian, the Petty Cash account is debited and the Cash account is credited for the amount of the check, and the Petty Cash account balance remains at that amount. As the cash in the fund is used up, no entries are made in the Petty Cash account; but when the fund is replenished with a check, expense accounts representing the cash spent from the fund are debited and the Cash account is credited. Note that the Petty Cash account balance does not change.

Exhibit 7–6 illustrates the following example of establishing and using a petty cash fund. Study this exhibit as you read the example.

Joseph Karnes is the office manager of a business that initiates a petty cash system on July 1 by cashing a company check for $500. The following entry is made:

19xx
July 1   Petty Cash (A)   500
              Cash (A)   500
          To record establishment of petty cash system.

During July, Mr. Karnes disburses the following funds:

Date	Transaction
19xx	
July 2	Paid $90 for stamps (circle 2, Exhibit 7–6).
13	Paid $80 for cab fares for overtime workers (circle 3, Exhibit 7–6).
22	Paid $75 for flowers sent to an ill employee (circle 4, Exhibit 7–6).
30	Paid $145 for dinners for overtime workers (circle 5, Exhibit 7–6).

EXHIBIT 7–6

Example of a $500 Petty Cash Fund (Currency plus Receipts)

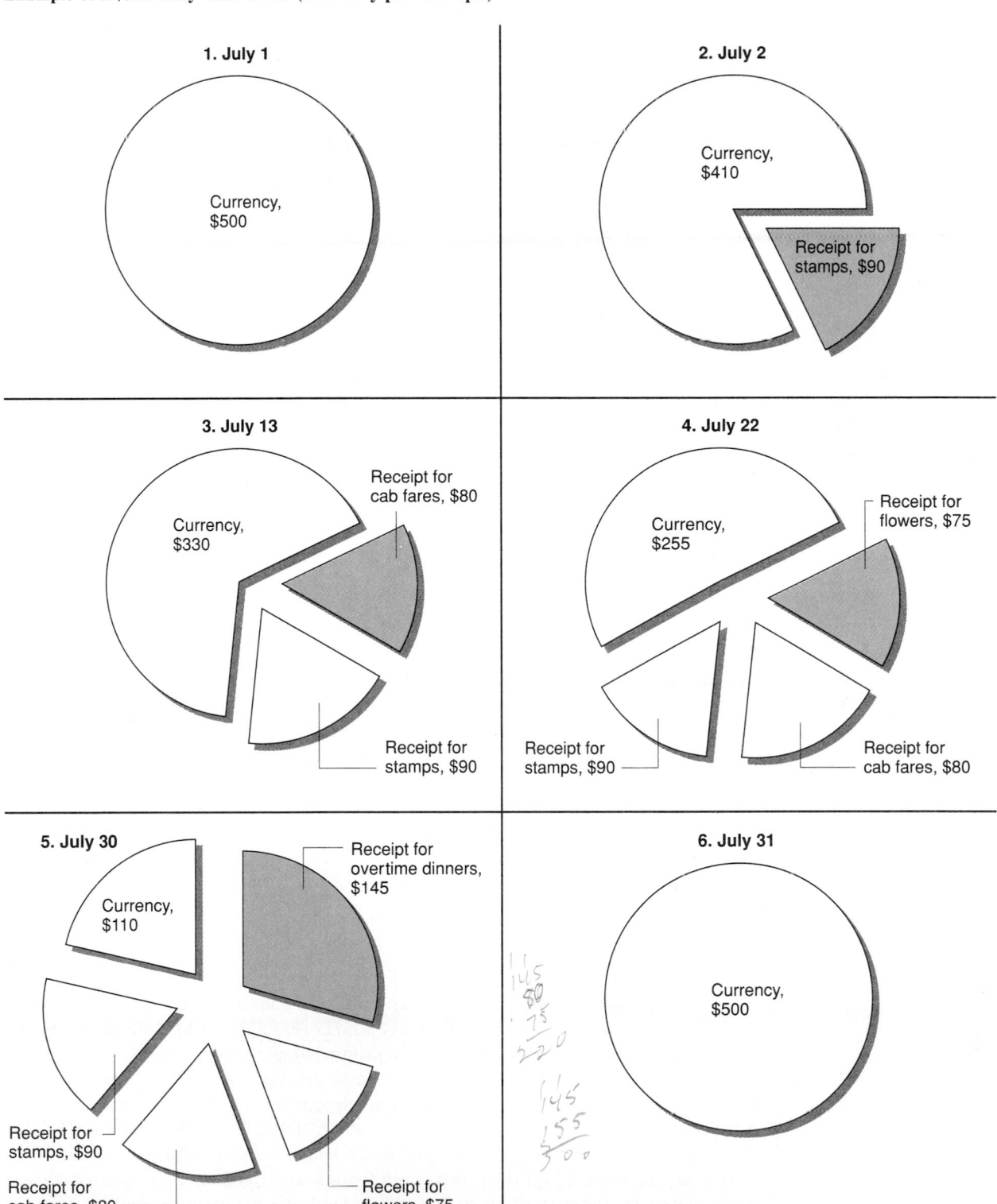

The receipt for each payment was kept in the cash box. On July 31, Mr. Karnes counted the remaining cash in the fund at $110. The following journal entry was made to replenish the fund:

```
19xx
July 31    Postage Expense (E). . . . . . . . . . . . . . . . . . . . . . .    90
           Miscellaneous Expense (E) . . . . . . . . . . . . . . . . . . .   300
               Cash (A) . . . . . . . . . . . . . . . . . . . . . . . . .              390
           To record replenishment of petty cash fund.
```

The Petty Cash account balance remains at $500 and is not affected by disbursements or replenishments. Circle 6 of Exhibit 7–6 shows the petty cash fund replenished to $500—which is the same beginning amount of the fund shown in circle 1.

Shortages and overages can occur in the petty cash fund due to oversight and error, such as the failure to get a receipt for a cash payment for cab fare. For instance, if the currency in Mr. Karnes's petty cash fund equaled only $105 on July 31 and receipts added up to $390, a $5 shortage would be charged to Miscellaneous Expense, as follows:

```
19xx
July 31    Postage Expense (E). . . . . . . . . . . . . . . . . . . . . . .    90
           Miscellaneous Expense (E) . . . . . . . . . . . . . . . . . . .   305
               Cash (A) . . . . . . . . . . . . . . . . . . . . . . . . .              395
           To record replenishment of petty cash fund.
```

Of course, material discrepancies should be investigated. If the discrepancies are immaterial, the Miscellaneous Expense account can be used to expense the difference. However, if a company wants to keep track of the discrepancies that occur, a Cash Over and Short account can be used. Some companies, such as grocery stores, department stores, and banks, use the Cash Over and Short account because they have a greater chance of day-to-day discrepancies.

The petty cash fund can also be increased or decreased. To increase the fund, the fund custodian requests cash in excess of the sum of receipts. If Mr. Karnes decided to reduce the $500 petty cash fund to $250, he would turn in all his receipts and request a check to bring the petty cash fund up to $250 rather than $500. The journal entry to do this is

```
19xx
July 31    Postage Expense (E). . . . . . . . . . . . . . . . . . . . . . .    90
           Miscellaneous Expense (E) . . . . . . . . . . . . . . . . . . .   300
               Petty Cash (A) . . . . . . . . . . . . . . . . . . . . . . .            250
               Cash (A) . . . . . . . . . . . . . . . . . . . . . . . . .              140
           To record replenishment of petty cash fund and to reduce the fund
           from $500 to $250.
```

You should note that the petty cash fund has its own system of internal control. One person is responsible for the fund. When the fund needs replenishing, the total amount of receipts (each of which is signed by the party who is issued the cash) in the cash box and the cash left in the cash box should equal the original amount of the fund. This is checked by another person who writes the check to replenish the fund and voids the receipts so they cannot be used again. It is a good practice to replenish the fund at the end of each period in order that all expenses be properly recorded and matched. This also allows for a determination that actual cash on hand is equal to the ledger account balance.

Because the balance kept in the petty cash fund is small, you rarely see petty cash as a separate item on the balance sheet. Usually, individual cash accounts such as Cash in Bank No. 1, Cash in Bank No. 2, Petty Cash, and similar unrestricted amounts of cash are combined and shown as one line item, Cash, on the balance sheet.

NOTES RECEIVABLE

In Chapter 5, we defined accounts receivable as the asset representing the customer's obligation between the sale and the receipt of cash. Thus, when a customer owes an outstanding invoice that the company expects to collect within a short period of time, the amount of the invoice is included in the accounts receivable asset on the balance sheet. The invoice is a document that indicates general contractual terms between a vendor and a customer. Generally, the printed form states what is expected of customers who purchase goods or services from the vendor. Because the customers accept the product or service, it is expected that they will comply with the terms of the invoice.

In contrast to accounts receivable, a note receivable represents a more formal contractual relationship evidenced by a document that is "custom-made" for a specific party. When a debtor of the business signs a document promising payment to the business of a specific amount at a specific time, the document signed is a formal contract called a promissory note, or **note.** It stipulates the terms governing cash payments, including dates, amounts to be paid, and perhaps interest rates.

You may wonder why a company uses a formal note. Formal notes give a clear legal status and interpretation to the understanding between the creditor (the payee), the person or entity to whom the note is issued, and the debtor (the maker). All important terms are stipulated in the note and understood by all parties involved. Also, if cash is needed a note can often be turned into cash easily by means of bank discounting, which will be described later in this chapter. Upon examining the note, the following facts should always be determinable even though some of them are not explicitly stated:

Term	Meaning
Principal amount	Amount lent or borrowed.
Maturity date	Date that the debtor is required to make the final payment on the note.
Maturity amount	Amount to be paid at the maturity date.
Interest	Amount the debtor pays for use of the money, which is the excess of the total payments to the creditor over the principal amount; Principal × Interest rate × Time period money is used = Interest.
Interest rate	Annual percentage that when applied to the principal for the time period(s) yields the interest amount.

What is the difference between notes receivable and accounts receivable? In some respects, all of the above facts given for a note can also be determined for an account receivable. Although often interest is not charged on ordinary accounts receivable, some companies do charge interest when payment is delayed beyond 30 days. Both notes receivable and accounts receivable are contracts, but notes have more formality, with the basic facts written on a legal document that is signed by both the debtor and creditor. However, an ordinary sales agreement evidenced by an invoice is generally as enforceable as a note. Thus, when a seller has evidence that a debtor has taken possession of a product or has been rendered a service, the law views the debtor as legally bound to pay the invoice amount to the seller. A note, however, is direct evidence of the debtor's obligations, and no other evidence is usually needed to establish the debtor's legal obligation.

What follows is a discussion on how to compute interest, which is followed in turn by a discussion of the accounting for a note receivable and the accounting for a dishonored note. The last topic in this section explains how a company discounts a note receivable at a bank in order to convert the note to cash before the note's maturity date.

Computation of Interest

As stated earlier, interest is computed by applying an interest rate to an outstanding amount for the period involved. In this text, we use annual interest rates, but, as we will see, interest is frequently earned for only a portion of a year. When a note is outstanding for a portion of a year, the applicable fraction must be used in computing interest. No fixed rules exist on how to determine this proportion, and companies differ in the methods they use. To see the effects of different methods, consider the following example.

A company has a $1,000 principal amount note with a 10% annual interest rate that is outstanding from July 1 through December 31. How much interest is applicable to July? For a full year the interest for the note would be $100, because the annual interest rate is 10%. Since July 1 to December 31 is one-half year, the interest for the six months is $50; and since July is one sixth of the half year, the interest for July would be $8.33 ($\frac{1}{6} \times \frac{1}{2} \times .10 \times \$1,000$, or $50 divided by 6).

You can also figure interest on a proportion of a year by using a daily basis. If the year has 365 days, based on a yearly 10% interest and 365 days in a year, each day would have $0.274 of interest ($\frac{1}{365} \times .10 \times \$1,000$). Therefore, interest for the month of July (31 days) would be $8.49 ($\frac{31}{365} \times .10 \times \$1,000$).

As you can see, the method chosen to determine the interest amount—monthly basis versus daily basis—results in minor differences in the interest amount. In this text, we assume that each month has 30 days and receives one twelfth of the annual interest. Therefore, a six-month note receives one half of the annual interest, a 90-day note receives one fourth, a 60-day note receives one sixth, and so on. Thus, we assume that each year has 360 days; therefore, the computation of interest for July on the $1,000, 10% note above could be done as follows: $1,000 $\times$ .10 $\times$ $\frac{1}{12}$ = $8.33.

Accounting for a Note Receivable

Objective 7
Accounting for notes receivable.

To illustrate how to account for a note receivable, the following example is given. This particular example is used because it contains a situation frequently encountered in the business world.

Electrostat, Inc., owes Express Overnight, Inc., (EOI) $50,000 for an outstanding invoice (No. 1278). When the invoice comes due, Electrostat cannot make the $50,000 payment. On January 1, 19xx, EOI decides to accept Electrostat's one-year promissory note, which calls for a December 31, 19xx, payment of $57,500. No interest rate is given on the note, but you can compute the rate by means of the following known relationships:

Analysis of Note Receivable from Electrostat

Principal amount:	$50,000 (the invoice amount).
Maturity amount:	$57,500 (the amount to be paid at maturity).
Maturity date:	December 31, 19xx.
Interest:	$7,500 ($57,500 − $50,000).
Interest rate:	15% ($7,500 ÷ $50,000).

EOI records the following entries for the note:

```
19xx
Jan.  1    Notes Receivable (A) . . . . . . . . . . . . . . . . . . . .    50,000
              Accounts Receivable (A) . . . . . . . . . . . . . . . .              50,000
           To record acceptance of note in place of accounts receivable.

Dec. 31    Cash (A) . . . . . . . . . . . . . . . . . . . . . . . . .    57,500
              Interest Income (R) . . . . . . . . . . . . . . . . . .               7,500
              Notes Receivable (A) . . . . . . . . . . . . . . . . .              50,000
           To record receipt of note payment.
```

The time line shown in Exhibit 7–7 is helpful in studying the relationships created by the note. Since the note begins with a principal of $50,000 and at the end of the year has a maturity amount of $57,500, the interest for the year is $7,500.

EXHIBIT 7–7

Notes Receivable: Principal and Maturity Amounts

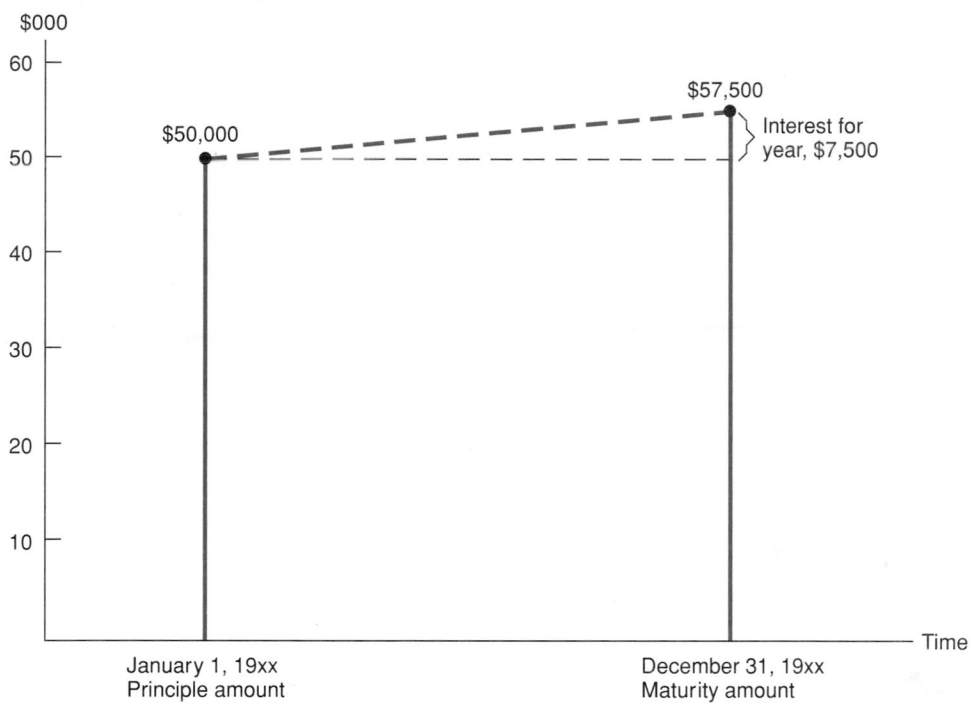

The interest of $7,500 earned during the one-year period represents the increase in the net assets of EOI that results from this transaction. You can verify the $7,500 interest amount by multiplying $50,000 by the 15% interest rate determined earlier, which gives $7,500.

Now let's change the EOI example so that the interest earned straddles two accounting periods. Assume that EOI ends its accounting period on June 30 and that the other facts relating to the note are the same as above. EOI would make the following entries:

```
19xx
Jan.  1   Notes Receivable (A) . . . . . . . . . . . . . . . . . . . . . .   50,000
              Accounts Receivable (A). . . . . . . . . . . . . . . . . .              50,000
          To record acceptance of note in place of accounts receivable.

June 30   Interest Receivable (A). . . . . . . . . . . . . . . . . . . .    3,750
              Interest Income (R) . . . . . . . . . . . . . . . . . . . .              3,750
          To record interest earned to date.

Dec. 31   Cash (A) . . . . . . . . . . . . . . . . . . . . . . . . . . .   57,500
              Notes Receivable (A) . . . . . . . . . . . . . . . . . . .              50,000
              Interest Receivable (A). . . . . . . . . . . . . . . . . .               3,750
              Interest Income (R) . . . . . . . . . . . . . . . . . . . .               3,750
          To record receipt of note payment.
```

The balance sheet presentation at June 30, 19xx, shows the $50,000 principal in the Notes Receivable account and the $3,750 accrued interest in the Interest Receivable account. When only one account, Notes Receivable, is used, it includes both principal and interest.

Express Overnight, Inc.
Partial Balance Sheet
June 30, 19xx

Current assets:		
Cash		$xx,xxx
Accounts receivable.	$xx,xxx	
Less: Allowance for bad debts	x,xxx	xx,xxx
Notes receivable		$50,000
Interest receivable		3,750
Total current assets		$xx,xxx

The reason we record the $3,750 is based on the revenue recognition concept. By June 30, EOI has earned interest because the debtor has held EOI's money for six months and there is a legitimate claim.

Accounting for a Dishonored Note

In the above discussion, we assume that Electrostat will honor its note. However, notes are not always honored at maturity. When a customer does not honor a note at maturity, the company has several options: (1) legal action to collect the amount, (2) renegotiation of the note, or (3) forgiveness of the debt and/or write-off of the receivable.

Before expensive legal action is taken, the company will usually discuss the matter with the debtor and attempt to develop an arrangement for payment. If that appears fruitless, then the company could initiate legal proceedings to force payment, if in fact the debtor has the assets to pay all or a part of the amount due. In either case, the note remains on the books of the creditor until it is collected or until it is determined that it will not be collected. Sometimes a past due debtor will eventually pay even though there has been a default at the maturity date. Creditors who believe that with more time the payment will be made could issue a new note to replace the old note in an amount equal to the old principal plus the earned but unpaid interest. Study the following example.

Good Guy, Inc., accepted a 12%, 60-day note on August 1, 19xx, from a customer, G. Holliday, for a $9,000 outstanding invoice that was not paid on its due date. The following entries were made by Good Guy to (1) record the note and (2) issue a new note when the original note was dishonored:

19xx				
Aug. 1	Notes Receivable (A)		9,000	
	Accounts Receivable (A)			9,000
	To record the receipt of a 12%, 60-day note for invoice No. 11078.			
Sept. 30	Notes Receivable (A)		9,180	
	Notes Receivable (A)			9,000
	Interest Income (R)			180
	To record the receipt of a 12%, 60-day note to replace former note (G. Holliday).			

As you can see, the new note has been increased by $180, which is the interest earned to date on the note ($9,000 × .12 × $^{60}/_{360}$). Good Guy, Inc., will attempt to collect the receivable in the normal manner; and in the event of noncollection and no chance of collection, the $9,180 receivable will be written off.

If the new note is dishonored and no further attempt is made to collect, Good Guy would write off the note as follows.

12/1	Loss on Dishonored Note (E)	9,180	
	Notes Receivable (A).		9,180
	To record the write-off of a dishonored note.		

Another approach to the write-off of the note would be to return the amount to Accounts Receivable and then to write it off as a normal bad debt. (See Chapter 5 for a discussion of the accounting methods used.)

12/1	Interest Income (R).	180	
	Accounts Receivable (A)	9,000	
	Notes Receivable (A).		9,180
	To record the dishonored note of G. Holliday, to eliminate previously recorded interest income, and to recognize the balance as an accounts receivable.		
12/1	Allowance for Bad Debts (XA).	9,000	
	Accounts Receivable (A)		9,000
	To write off the uncollectible account of G. Holliday.		

Decreasing the allowance account creates the need for a larger bad debts expense accrual at year-end, resulting in the same income statement effect as the write-off of the note shown above. One reason for using the accounts receivable and allowance for bad debts would be to have those involved with credit sales be informed that the customer has defaulted, in case future questions are asked about the customer's creditworthiness.

Discounting a Note Receivable at a Bank

If a company needs cash and holds a note, the company (the payee) can endorse the note and sell it to a bank before the note matures. This transaction is called discounting because the bank deducts the interest it charges in advance and thus discounts the note. The amount of the discount depends on the maturity value of the note, the bank's discount rate, and the time period to maturity. The company receives the proceeds of the note from the bank—the maturity value of the note less the bank's fee for discounting.

If the maker of a discounted note defaults, the payee usually remains liable to pay the bank when the note matures. The note is then discounted with recourse. Recourse means that the ultimate risk of default is not passed on to the bank. The bank merely advances funds to the payee and earns a financing fee on the advanced amount. The following diagrams illustrate the events that occur when a note is discounted.

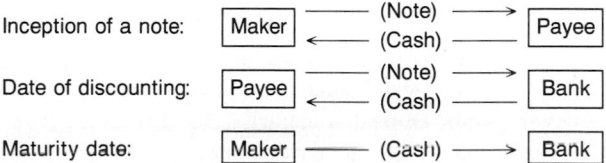

The bank earns money on this transaction by means of the discount rate applied to the maturity value of the note. An example of a discounted note follows.

On January 1, 19x1, Maker, Inc., issues a 10%, $10,000 principal amount note with a maturity date of December 31. The payee of the note is Payee, Inc. On July 1, 19x1, Payee discounts the note at a local bank, and the discount rate is 20%. The key to understanding this transaction is knowing the meaning of the 20% discount rate.

The bank wants to earn a fee equal to 20% per year on the maturity value of a discounted note for the amount of time it will hold the note. The maturity value of a note is the principal plus unpaid interest at maturity. In this example, the maturity value is $11,000 [computed: $10,000 + ($10,000 × .10)], and the proceeds to be paid to Payee on July 1 are computed as follows:

Maturity amount	$11,000
20% for one-half year left until maturity	× .10
Discounting fee.	$ 1,100
Proceeds ($11,000 − $1,100)	$ 9,900

Payee, therefore, receives $9,900 from the bank on July 1. The bank now has the right to collect the $11,000 from Maker on December 31. Payee makes the following entries to record the transactions related to the note:

19xx			
Jan. 1	Notes Receivable (A)	10,000	
	Cash (A) or Accounts Receivable (A)		10,000
	To record receipt of note.		
July 1	Cash (A)	9,900	
	Financing Expense (E)	100	
	Notes Receivable Discounted (XA)		10,000
	To record discounting of note.		
Dec. 31	Notes Receivable Discounted (XA)	10,000	
	Notes Receivable (A)		10,000
	To record elimination of note when it is paid to the bank.		

The financing expense recorded above could be recorded as interest expense. However, by using financing expense, accountants indicate the results from netting the discounting fee charged by the bank, which in this example is $1,100, and the interest that would have been earned if the note had been held by Payee for the entire year, $1,000.

As a contra account to Notes Receivable, Notes Receivable Discounted is used when the bank has recourse to the payee in the event that the maker of the note defaults. By using the contra account, the book value of the note is reduced to zero, but the original note receivable is maintained as a reminder that a real liability will result if the payee defaults. Such a situation results in a contingent liability, which means that an accounting liability may result if another specific event(s) occurs. Contingent liabilities are discussed in Chapter 9.

If the $10,000 note were discounted without recourse, then Payee would have credited Notes Receivable on July 1 because no contingency would exist. In this example, we assume that Maker is notified of the bank discounting the note and knows that the bank must be paid at maturity. Sometimes the maker is not notified and pays the payee at maturity. Then, the payee must forward the maturity amount to the bank.

Why Should I Discount a Note?

In order to understand the business reasons for discounting a note, listen to the following conversation between José the owner of a natural foods store, Frodo's Feast, and his uncle, Manuel, who is a banker and who is trying to give him advice about a cash flow problem.

José: Uncle, my business is fine but I made a big mistake taking a 60-day note for the $100,000 purchase made by that cafeteria chain, Castles. I know that the amount is pretty safe, they are a strong company, and I'm earning good interest, but it's tying up all my cash.

Manuel: Listen, José, there is a way to get your money now.

José: I can't go to Castles. A deal is a deal; and anyway, if they had the cash they would have paid in the first place.

Manuel: What I mean is that you can discount the note at a bank and get your cash now. Of course, there is a fee. We poor bankers have to make a living too.

José: OK, I give you the note and you give me $100,000. Sounds great, but what about the interest?

Manuel: Of course, if you tie up my cash, I get the interest, just like before, when you got the interest. Now, this is how it goes. I compute a net amount that you will get based on a percentage that I want to make on the maturity amount. I subtract the fee and give you the net.

José: What if Castle doesn't pay?

Manuel: Well, then you owe me the maturity amount. I can't lose unless you go under too. Look at it this way: You'll be no worse off than you are now, but you'll get the cash now, and pay a modest fee to keep your poor old uncle and aunt from the poor house. All kidding aside, this kind of deal, where I have recourse against you if the maker defaults, keeps the fee down because my risk is reduced by having both Frodo's and Castles to back up the maturity amount.

Discounted Notes that Are Dishonored. It is possible that the discounted note with recourse will not be paid by Maker at maturity. If such a default occurs, Payee would become liable to pay the bank the full $11,000 on December 31. Payee then records this payment as follows:

```
19x1
Dec. 31   Notes Receivable Discounted (XA) . . . . . . . . . . . . .   10,000
          Notes Receivable (A) . . . . . . . . . . . . . . . . . . .    1,000
              Cash (A) . . . . . . . . . . . . . . . . . . . . . . .            11,000
          To record payment to the bank for a discounted note that the
          maker dishonored.
```

Maker is now obligated to pay Payee for the full maturity value of the note, which is the amount paid to the bank by Payee upon default. What remains on Payee's books is a receivable of $11,000, which will be eliminated as follows if cash is received from Maker.

```
19x2
Jan.  5   Cash (A) . . . . . . . . . . . . . . . . . . . . . . . . .   11,000
              Notes Receivable (A) . . . . . . . . . . . . . . . . .            11,000
          To record receipt of note payment.
```

The effects of the above note transactions on the balance sheet and income statement follow.

Payee, Inc.

| Date | Transaction | Balance Sheet Effects | | Income Statement Effects |
		Cash	Notes Receivable	
19x1				
Jan. 1	Receipt of note	$(10,000)	$ 10,000	$ 0
July 1	Discounting of note	9,900	(10,000)	(100)
Dec. 31	Dishonoring of note	(11,000)	11,000	0
19x2				
Jan. 5	Receipt of cash for note	11,000	(11,000)	0
	Net effect.	$ (100)	$ 0	$(100)

The net effect on cash is equal to the net effect on the income statement: Cash was reduced by $100, and income was reduced by $100. If this note had not been discounted and had been paid at maturity, the following effects would have resulted:

Payee, Inc.

Date	Transaction	Cash	Notes Receivable	Income Statement Effects
19x1				
Jan. 1	Receipt of note	$(10,000)	$ 10,000	$ 0
Dec. 31	Receipt of cash for note	11,000	(10,000)	1,000
	Net effect.	$ 1,000	$ 0	$1,000

When Payee discounted the note, it had an expense of $100. This is the net of the interest to be paid by Maker ($1,000) and the discounting fee earned by the bank ($1,100). Remember that it is possible for the discounting fee to be less than the interest earned at the time of discounting on the note, in which case Interest Income is credited and net income is increased.

• SUMMARY

This chapter began with a definition of internal control. You then learned general principles of effective accounting control: authorization and responsibility, separation of duties, protection of assets, and accounting system procedures. Because of the importance of internal control procedures, these procedures were discussed in detail. You were cautioned to remember that the management principle of measuring costs of any operation against its benefits also pertained to internal control.

Since cash is a cornerstone of successful business operations, an entire section in the chapter was devoted to cash. Because of its liquidity, considerable space was devoted to cash control, which involves checking accounts, bank statements, reconciliation of checking accounts, and the control of petty cash. The overlap between general internal controls and specific accounting internal controls—including cash control—was clearly evident by the frequent repetition in accounting internal control procedures of the importance of separation of duties.

The chapter concluded with an introduction to notes receivable, including interest computation and accounting for notes receivable and dishonored notes. You learned about discounting a note at a bank and how to record transactions pertaining to this procedure. The underlying importance of cash flow to successful business operations again becomes evident when companies find it necessary to turn a note receivable into a cash receipt before maturity.

• DEMONSTRATION EXERCISE

The following selected transactions are from the records of Acro Services, Inc., for 19xx:

19xx
Feb. 19 Monthly bank statement is received. A check from C. Jones, a customer, for $1,700 has been returned NSF, and a bank service charge for $84 appears on the statement.
Apr. 7 Request for $243 to reimburse the $300 petty cash fund is received. The following receipts are attached: $75 postage, $68 office supplies, and $95 delivery charges, which are charged to miscellaneous expense.
June 1 Accepted a $35,000, 8%, 60-day note from customer, L. Zekan.

19xx

July 31 Received payment on note from L. Zekan.

Oct. 31 Discounted with recourse a $20,000, 12%, six-month note due on November 30, 19xx, at 24% at the local bank.

Dec. 1 Received notice from the local bank that the discounted note was not paid.

Required:

Prepare the journal entries in general journal form that Acro would have made for the above transactions. This is Acro's first year of operations, and December 31 is its year-end.

Solution:

GENERAL JOURNAL					J10
Date		Account Titles and Explanation	Ref.	Debit	Credit
19xx Feb.	19	Accounts Receivable (A)		1,700	
		Cash (A)			1,700
		To record customer's NSF check returned by the bank.			
		Service Charge Expense (E)		84	
		Cash (A)			84
		To record bank service charge for the month.			
Apr.	7	Postage Expense (E)		75	
		Office Supplies Expense (E)		68	
		Miscellaneous Expense (E)		100	
		Cash (A)			243
		To record replenishment of petty cash fund including a $5 shortage in Miscellaneous Expense.			
June	1	Notes Receivable (A)		35,000	
		Accounts Receivable (A)			35,000
		To record a 60-day, 8% note from customer.			
July	31	Cash (A)		35,467	
		Notes Receivable (A)			35,000
		Interest Income (R)			467
		To record payment received on note.			
Oct.	31	Cash (A)		20,776	
		Interest Income (R)			776
		Notes Receivable Discounted (XA)			20,000
		To record discounted note: Maturity = Principal ($20,000) + Interest ($20,000 × .12 × $^{6}/_{12}$ = 1,200) = $21,200. Proceeds = Maturity ($21,200) − Discount fee ($21,200 × .24 × $^{1}/_{12}$) = $20,776.			
Dec.	1	Notes Receivable Discounted (XA)		20,000	
		Notes Receivable (A)		1,200	
		Cash (A)			21,200
		To record payment to bank on defaulted note.			

Special Accounting Journals and Control Accounts

Objective 8
Special journals and control accounts.

Prior to the availability of computers and electronic data processing, most companies used some form of a manual or mechanical system to record business transactions. Although computers are used in most businesses today, some small companies still use the manual system of accounting. By using the special journals and control accounts discussed in this appendix, manual systems can handle large volumes of transactions efficiently and provide useful information to management. Many computer systems also use versions of the journals discussed in this appendix.

The typical small retail business uses the following special journals: sales, cash receipts, purchases, and cash disbursements. All accounting systems also have a general journal because, as was stated in the chapter, not all transactions will fit into the structure of the special journals.

The names of the special journals are self-explanatory. The sales journal records credit sales. The cash receipts journal records all cash receipts from cash sales, credit customers, and other sources (such as bank loans). The purchases journal records purchases of merchandise inventory, supplies, and any other items purchased on credit. The cash disbursements journal records all checks written to pay suppliers, employees, and others.

Each special journal contains a series of columns into which transactions are entered. A "key" column records the common account feature of all the transactions entered into that journal. In the cash receipts journal, the key column is the Cash Dr. column. A transaction should not be entered into a special journal unless part of the transaction is recorded in the key column. Also, a separate column is established for each other account that requires frequent entries. For example, in the cash receipts journal, an Accounts Receivable Cr. column is required because much of the cash collected is from customers paying on account.

Along with the columns frequently used, most special journals have a general-purpose column where an account that is not included among the special columns can be identified and the amount entered. This column usually is called the Other Debits column or Other Credits column.

In this discussion on special journals, our example is the Wilco Company, a retailer of luggage and gifts. In addition to its cash sales, Wilco provides its own credit sales program to approved customers—the company does not accept other credit cards. Wilco uses four special journals—sales, cash receipts, purchases, and cash disbursements. The relationship of the subsidiary ledgers with the four journals is also explained. For illustration purposes, we examine only a limited number of transactions for Wilco during the month.

SALES JOURNAL

All credit sales are entered into the sales journal. Exhibit 7A–1 contains the sales journal for the Wilco Company. The columns of the sales journal include the following: Date; Customer; Ref.; Invoice No.; and Sales Cr., Accounts Receivable Dr. Since the amount of the sale and the amount of the accounts receivable are the same, only one amount column is necessary. All credit sales are entered into the journal in the numerical order of the invoices. Study the entry for invoice No. 1343. In addition to the date, the invoice number, and the amount, the customer's name (Rachel Allen, in this case) is inserted.

Periodically the amount column is totaled and the sales journal is posted. The sales journal is posted in two stages. First the $10,885 total of the Sales Cr., Accounts

EXHIBIT 7A–1

Wilco Company's
Sales Journal

							SALES JOURNAL			S1
Date			Customer		Ref.	Invoice No.	Sales Cr., Accounts Receivable Dr.
19xx Aug.	1	Rachel Allen	√	1343	450
	6	Jean Coll	√	1344	1,260
	13	Allo Corporation	√	1345	8,625
	29	Richard Smith	√	1346	550
					10,885
					(411) (121)

Receivable Dr. column is posted to the Sales account and the Accounts Receivable account. To indicate that posting is done, the account numbers are inserted in parentheses below the total of $10,885. The individual invoices are then posted to the customers' accounts in the subsidiary ledger and check marks inserted in the Ref. column to indicate that posting is complete.

**CASH RECEIPTS
JOURNAL**

Any cash received by Wilco is recorded in the cash receipts journal. The columns of the cash receipts journal include the following: Date, Name (cash source), Invoice No., Ref., Cash Dr., Accounts Receivable Cr., Sales Cr., and Other Credits. Payments from customers and cash sales make up an important part of any company's receipts, which is the reason for the associated special columns in the cash receipts journal. The Other Credits column is used for occasional cash receipts that are not collections on account or sales, such as a refund from a utility company for overpayment of a previous bill. The Wilco Company cash receipts journal is shown in Exhibit 7A–2.

The posting of the cash receipts journal is very similar to the sales journal. Rather than posting one column to two separate accounts, however, you must verify that debits equal credits in the cash receipts journal. After the columns are totaled, the Cash Dr. column should equal the sum of the Accounts Receivable Cr., Sales Cr., and Other Credits columns. By its nature, the Other Credits column cannot be posted in total. Each entry must be posted and the appropriate account number inserted in the column to indicate that posting is complete. If the debits do not equal credits, the mistake(s) must be discovered and corrected. Then the column totals are posted to the general ledger and account numbers inserted in the columns to indicate that posting is complete. If a customer makes a payment on his/her account, that payment must be posted to the subsidiary ledger to update the customer's account. When that posting is completed, a check mark is inserted in the column. If no subsidiary ledger is involved in the transaction, the Ref. column will remain blank.

As we discussed in Chapter 5, managers know the total amount of accounts receivables by referring to the Accounts Receivable control account (general ledger account that provides a summary total of underlying subsidiary accounts). They know the amount owed by each individual customer by referring to the subsidiary ledger. Exhibit 7A–2 illustrates Wilco's Accounts Receivable control account and the supporting subsidiary accounts, and their relationship with the sales journal and cash receipts journal. Note that the total of

EXHIBIT 7A–2

Wilco Company's Cash Receipts Journal, Accounts Receivable Control, and Subsidiary Ledger Accounts

									Other Credits (Debits)	
Date		Name	Invoice No.	Ref.	Cash Dr.	Accounts Receivable Cr.	Sales Cr.		Amount	Account
19xx Aug.	3	Cash sales			6,217		6,217			
	5	R. Smith	1285	✓	1,250	1,250				
	13	Cash sales			4,217		4,217			
	17	R. Allen	1343	✓	450	450				
	17	Electric Co.			45				45	561
	29	Cash sales			8,915		8,915			
					21,094	1,700	19,349		45	
					(101)	(121)	(411)			

CASH RECEIPTS JOURNAL — CR8

GENERAL LEDGER

Accounts Receivable   121

Beg. bal.	3,210	Cr.8	1,700
S1	10,885		
End. bal.	12,395		

ACCOUNTS RECEIVABLE SUBSIDIARY LEDGER

Allen, Rachel

S1	450	Cr.8	450
End. bal.	–0–		

Allo Corporation

Beg. bal.	1,320		
S1	8,625		
End. bal.	9,945		

Coll, Jean

S1	1,260		

Exton Corporation

Beg. bal.	640		

Smith, Richard

Beg. bal.	1,250	Cr.8	1,250
S1	550		
End. bal.	550		

the subsidiary accounts receivable [Allen ($0) + Allo ($9,945) + Coll ($1,260) + Exton ($640) + Smith ($550)] equals the Accounts Receivable ledger (control) account of $12,395.

In addition to the Accounts Receivable control account, many other general ledger accounts may be supported by subsidiary accounts. Among them are Accounts Payable,

Notes Receivable, Merchandise, Equipment, and Loans Payable. The techniques for operating such accounts are essentially the same as those illustrated for the accounts receivable subsidiary ledger.

**PURCHASES
JOURNAL**

Exhibit 7A–3, p. 360, illustrates the purchases journal the Wilco Company uses, where all its credit purchases are entered. Since this journal includes all purchases made on credit, the key column of this journal is the Accounts Payable Cr. column. The Merchandise Inventory Dr. and Supplies Dr. columns are the other columns included since they are frequently used. The remaining columns include the following: Date, Supplier, Invoice No., Ref., and Other Debits. This last column will handle those occasional purchases that are not for merchandise or supplies.

Again, the posting of this journal is very similar to the procedure used for the cash receipts journal. The columns must be footed and debits must equal credits. Wilco then posts the column totals to the appropriate accounts and inserts the account numbers to indicate that posting is complete. The other debits are posted individually. For example, Wilco's bookkeeper will credit $19,297 to Accounts Payable for the total purchases made on credit for the period. Wilco also uses a subsidiary ledger to detail its Accounts Payable control account. The suppliers' individual accounts are credited to update the balances owed to those suppliers. Check marks in the Ref. column indicate posting to the subsidiary ledger is complete.

**CASH
DISBURSEMENTS
JOURNAL**

Exhibit 7A–4, p. 360, illustrates the Wilco Company's cash disbursements journal. As the name implies, the key column for this journal is the Cash Cr. column. For Wilco, debits to Accounts Payable and Salaries Payable are frequently made and these become the special columns in this journal. Additional columns of the cash disbursements journal include the following: Date, Payee, Check No., Ref., and Other Debits. Again, the Other Debits column is for transactions that do not fit in the specific account columns. Notice that the disbursements are entered into the journal in numerical order by check number. This sequential ordering is for control purposes to ensure against unrecorded disbursements.

The procedure for posting follows that used for the cash receipts and purchases journals. Columns are totaled; debits must equal credits. Posting to the general ledger is indicated by account numbers and posting to any subsidiary ledgers by check marks.

APPENDIX • 7B

Electronic Data Processing

In this section, we will concentrate on illustrating the advantages of computers in the accounting system rather than how computers work, since most of you are familiar with computer systems. Consider the following features of a system:

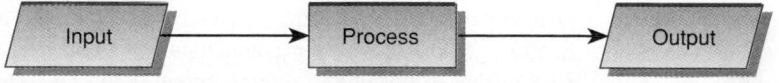

This general pattern applies to all kinds of systems; for example, in manufacturing where the inputs are raw materials, the process is the work of applying labor and equipment to materials, and the output is the finished product.

EXHIBIT 7A–3

Wilco Company's Purchases Journal

			Invoice No.	Ref.	Accounts Payable Cr.	Merchandise Inventory Dr.	Supplies Dr.	Other Debits (Credits)	
Date		Supplier						Amount	Account
PURCHASES JOURNAL									P6
19xx Aug.	3	Acme Leather	32756	√	11,450	11,000	450		
	16	Botts Gifts	A625	√	2,310	2,310			
	19	DS Displays	963	√	4,210			4,210	171
	30	Tay Paper	2336	√	1,327		1,327		
					19,297	13,310	1,777	4,210	
					(211)	(131)	(141)		

EXHIBIT 7A–4

Wilco Company's Cash Disbursements Journal

			Check No.	Ref.	Cash Cr.	Accounts Payable Dr.	Salaries Payable Dr.	Other Debits (Credits)	
Date		Payee						Amount	Account
CASH DISBURSEMENTS JOURNAL									CD9
19xx Aug.	4	Tay Paper	2735	√	650	650			
	14	Acme Leather	2736	√	14,803	14,803			
	18	K. Ball	2737		785		785		
	18	N. Alto	2738		639		639		
	23	Electric Co.	2739		410			410	561
	29	Daily News	2740		450			450	543
	31	K. Ball	2741		830		830		
	31	N. Alto	2742		684		684		
	31	C. Lerch	2743		214		214		
					19,465	15,453	3,152	860	
					(101)	(211)	(221)		

The electronic data processing system has the same basic structure with the final output being information and each step involving electronic devices to capture, process, and communicate the information.

Data input is accomplished in all sorts of ways, but in all cases some change in the business occurs; for instance, inventory is increased or decreased, and that change is entered by a person, or even automatically in some cases. The process would then update files related to inventory, and the output could be a check written to suppliers, an updated inventory report, or any other report of which inventory is a component. For instance, the income statement and balance sheet are affected by all the inventory transactions of a period, and therefore the system has to keep track of all changes. Electronic output in the case of inventories could involve access to current balances by a production manager who needs to know how many specific items are available in order to schedule production.

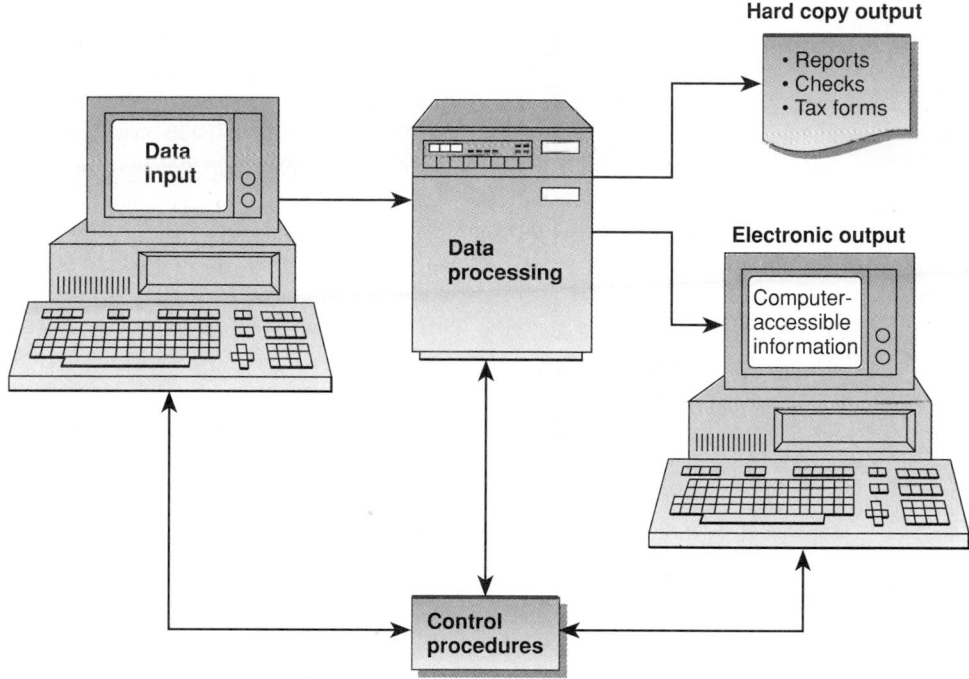

Because information is so crucial to organizational success, the concept of control of information is as important as control of any other resource. The above diagram shows that control functions are integrated into electronic data processing systems, where a key objective is to make sure that access to the system is proper and authorized.

The widespread use of computers has resulted in significant changes in the gathering and processing of accounting data in accounting systems. Computers have increased the amount and kind of data that can be recorded, summarized, and analyzed for management's use. Also, the computer's capacity for massive storage and rapid calculation has resulted in quicker processing of transactions. As a result, managers are asking for more timely information than ever before. Although the cost per unit of processing the information has gone down, some contend that the increase in total volume has driven overall costs up. In any event, new opportunities for increased efficiency have certainly been created, but new challenges for controlling business operations have also been created.

Since not all the decision-making information that managers need is financial, the accounting system is only part of the overall information system used to run a company. Managers must consider the financial and nonfinancial results of management action, and the accounting data must be carefully coordinated with the company's overall data information system.

Computerized processing is a blend of people, machine, programs, and procedures designed to add efficiency and effectiveness to the accounting system. The computer revolution provides several important advantages for the accounting process:

Objective 9
The advantages of electronic data processing.

1. **Quick processing**—especially for large-volume jobs, such as invoices and payrolls.
2. **Timeliness of reports**—accounts can be updated instantaneously.
3. **Analysis**—results and forecasts of business operations can be prepared and compared immediately.

4. **Reducing certain risks**—credit cards can be authorized via telecommunications, for example.

5. **Increased accuracy**—computers seldom make computational or clerical errors.

Data can be entered into the computerized accounting system in batches or on a real-time basis. In a batch system, entries are collected for some period of time and entered into the computer periodically—daily or weekly. When a transaction is entered into the computer in a real-time system, it is immediately posted to the general and subsidiary ledger accounts and incorporated into reports. One entry in the system transfers data to several places and into various reports.

Whereas a computerized system can work with one entry, manual systems often involve multiple entries requiring one entry in the general ledger accounts and another entry in the subsidiary accounts; and if the same information is needed for another report (such as for inventory records) a third entry is likely to be made. These multiple entries make the collecting of information costly and increase the chance for errors. In the computerized system, both the cost and number of error possibilities should decrease.

Although fewer clerical errors may occur in the computerized system, the errors that do occur may be difficult to track. The paper flow that characterizes manual systems makes tracing errors to sources relatively easy. The electronic trail in computer systems is elusive, and special control procedures are needed before such systems are auditable.

The speed of computerized data gathering and accounting entry processing is evident when you compare the computerized systems commonly used today in large grocery and retail stores with the method used in small retail businesses. In a small business, a sale is usually rung up on a cash register. The register clerk enters the price of each item purchased. Often a code is also entered that identifies the department that sold the item. The register can accumulate not only the customer's total purchase but also the total daily sales for each department and the entire store. At the end of the day, the results of the day's activities are printed out on a tape produced by the cash register. This tape contains the information that accountants enter into the accounting journals. For example, assume that the tape for July 21, 19xx, showed the following information:

Department sales:	
Hardware	$1,026
Paint	3,079
Clothing	2,973
Sundries	375
Total department sales	$7,453
Sales tax	373
Total cash collected	$7,826

Accountants enter the above information into the journals, either at the end of that day or at some later time. The entry in the general journal is

19xx			
July 21	Cash (A)	7,826	
	Hardware Sales (R)		1,026
	Paint Sales (R)		3,079
	Clothing Sales (R)		2,973
	Sundries Sales (R)		375
	Sales Taxes Payable (L)		373
	To record cash register sales.		

In addition to the sales transaction, the store must also account for the cost of the inventory sold, and it must have procedures to reorder necessary inventory.

Companies using modern electronic data processing systems design their computerized accounting system so that sales data immediately enters the entire accounting system. In addition, significantly more information is obtained at the time of the sale.

For example, in a retail business with a modern electronic data processing system, the register clerk records most of the purchased products by entering the product's Uniform Product Code (UPC) directly into the computer (see Exhibit 7B–1). The computer to which the cash register is attached enters the appropriate prices, identifies the department that is making the sale, totals the sale, calculates the sales tax, and totals the amount owed by the customer. When the product has no UPC, the register clerk must use the cash register keys to enter the product's inventory number, and the computer completes the operation. Now the computer has the same information about the sale that was in the cash register totals of the previous example. In addition, as soon as the register clerk enters the product's UPC or inventory number, the computer inputs the data into the accounting system. Thus, entries into the accounting system are made almost instantaneously instead of waiting until the end of the day or some future time.

Computerized accounting systems also supply information valuable for inventory management. When a product's UPC or inventory number is entered into the computer, it automatically keeps track of the products that are sold. As a result, managers can prepare reports indicating which products must be ordered from the warehouse or purchased from suppliers.

EXHIBIT 7B–1

Computerized Cash Register System

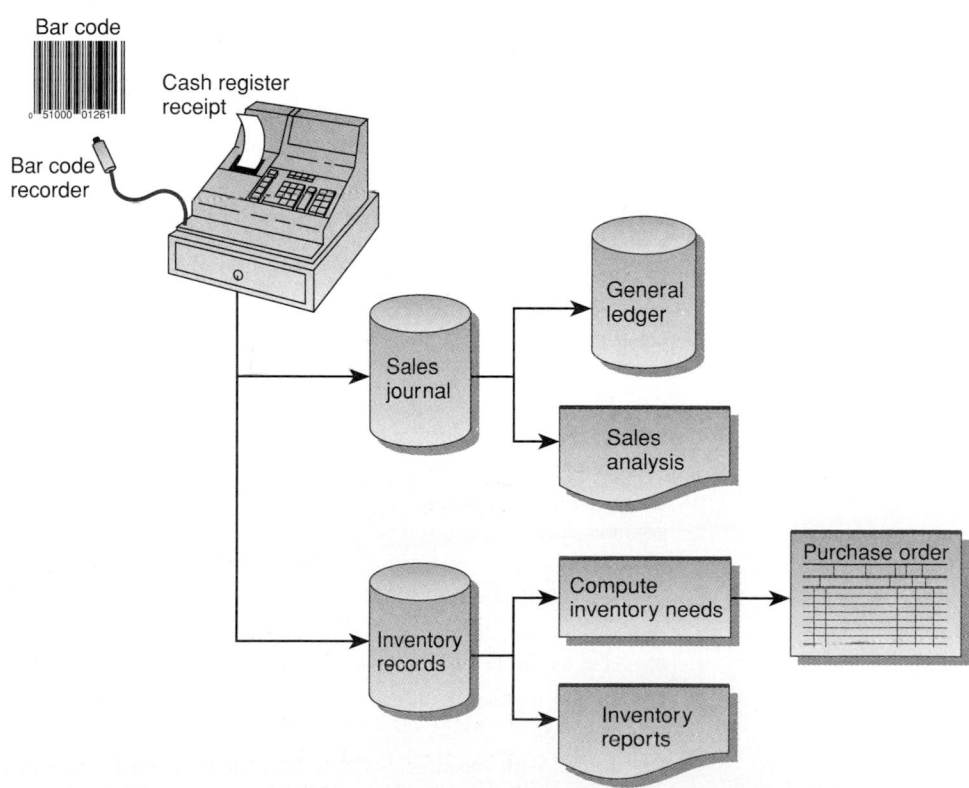

Exhibit 7B–1 shows how the computerized cash register system begins with a UPC and puts out recorded information into a sales journal and inventory records. The sales journal in the exhibit is a subsidiary journal mentioned earlier in the chapter and discussed in detail in Appendix 7A.

As is true with all business decisions, a careful analysis of the costs and benefits of adopting new technology is imperative. Given the current level of competition, businesses simply must explore all avenues of reducing costs and increasing efficiency. Because of the economies of scale, large and complex entities are utilizing more and more sophisticated electronic data processing systems, but smaller entities are also benefiting greatly from the improvements in power and flexibility of the small-scale systems currently available.

Although the introduction of electronic data processing has made possible the gathering of more decision-making information at relatively low cost, electronic data processing has some problems. The ease with which data can be recorded, transferred, and analyzed increases the need for special internal controls. For example, in a computer environment, separation of duties involves such steps as authorization of program changes and the use of different programmers for various elements of the accounting system. Security steps include passwords, identification numbers, machine-readable codes, and automatic limits on certain transactions.

• KEY TERMS

Accounting controls. The technical procedures designed to ensure the integrity of recorded transactions and financial statements and to protect assets.

Bank reconciliation. Process by which a company's Cash account is compared with the bank statement to ensure against errors in the company's records and the bank's records.

Bank statement. A document prepared periodically by the bank that shows the beginning and ending balances in the checking account and gives details of deposits, withdrawals, service charges, and other activities.

Bonding. Type of insurance policy taken out on certain employees that will pay the company damages if an employee misappropriates assets.

Cash. Money the bank will accept for deposit in checking accounts (coins, currency, checks written to depositor, traveler's checks, money orders) and demand deposits that are available to the business without restrictions; banks do not accept postage stamps, postdated checks, or notes receivable for deposit.

Cash control. Steps taken to safeguard the cash asset from dishonest employees and other persons who may have access to the company's cash.

Checking account. A demand deposit at a bank in which checks made out to the company and any money orders or currency are deposited and from which checks are written; also called a demand deposit account.

Compensating balances. Sums required by a bank loan contract to be deposited in a noninterest-earning account or an account that earns less than the market rate of interest.

Demand deposits. Checking accounts in which the depositor has free access to the cash without advance notification to the bank.

Deposits in transit. Deposits recorded in the company's records as of the bank statement date but not reflected in the current bank statement.

Discounted without recourse. Payee is not liable to pay the bank if the maker of a discounted note defaults.

Discounted with recourse. If the maker of a discounted note defaults, payee remains liable to pay the bank when the note matures.

Discounting. Transaction by which a business endorses a note and sells it to a bank before the note matures.

Financial audit. An audit that tests for conformance to accounting procedures and assures management that the controls in the accounting system are functioning as designed and the system is providing reliable information.

Interest. The amount paid for the use of money; the excess of the total paid back to the creditor over the principal.

Interest rate. Annual percentage that when applied to the principal of the note for the time period yields the interest amount.

Internal auditing department. Department in a corporation that ensures that internal controls are performing as designed.

Internal control. The process by which an entity's management reasonably ensures that objectives are met.

Lapping. A form of theft in which an employee takes the cash paid by one customer and then applies the payment of another customer to the accounts receivable of the first customer.

Maker. Person or entity that issues a note; the debtor.

Maturity amount. Amount to be paid at maturity date.

Maturity date. Date when the debtor is required to make the final payment on a note.

Miscellaneous charges. Charges made by the bank to the depositor for services such as stopping payment on checks, printing checks, and so on.

Nonsufficient funds (NSF) check. Check deposited in the company's checking account but not honored by the check writer's bank because the balance in the writer's checking account is insufficient to cover the check; also known as not sufficient funds.

Operational audit. An audit focusing on management controls and how well various levels of management performs under these controls.

Outstanding checks. Checks that have been written and recorded by the company but have not cleared the bank at the time the bank statement is prepared.

Overdraft. Occurs when the company has written checks for more money than is in the company's checking account.

Payee. Person or entity to whom a note is issued; known as the creditor.

Petty cash imprest system. Method that allows for a fund of ready cash while at the same time assuring systematic accountability.

Principal amount. Amount lent or borrowed.

Proceeds. Amount received by a company that discounts a note—maturity value of the note less the bank's fee for discounting.

Promissory note. Formal contract between a debtor and a creditor that stipulates the terms governing cash payments including dates, amounts to be paid, and perhaps interest rates; commonly called a note.

Service charge. The fee charged by the bank for services for maintaining a checking account.

Special journals. Books of original entry designed to process a class of repetitive transactions efficiently.

Time deposits. Accounts on deposit at a financial institution that require notification before the business can use the money.

· Appendix Key Terms

Batch system. Process by which entries are collected for some period of time and entered into the computer periodically—daily or weekly; compare to real-time system.

Cash disbursements journal. Special journal used to record all checks written to pay suppliers, employees, and others.

Cash receipts journal. Special journal used to record all cash receipts from cash sales, credit customers, and other sources.

Control account. General ledger account that provides a summary total of underlying subsidiary accounts.

Purchases journal. Special journal used to record purchases of merchandise inventory, supplies, and other items purchased on credit.

Real-time system. A computer accounting system in which transactions are posted immediately to the general and subsidiary ledger accounts and into various other reports and records.

Sales journal. Special journal used to record credit sales.

• SYNONYMS

Checking accounts; demand deposits.

Defaulted; dishonored.

Draft; check.

Maker; issuer of note; debtor on a note.

Not sufficient funds; insufficient funds; NSF.

Overdraft; overdrawn.

Payee; recipient; creditor.

Principal; face value.

Promissory note; note.

• QUESTIONS

1. Briefly describe why a company should provide an internal control system. Differentiate between internal controls that are related to the firm's accounting system and other internal administrative controls.
2. Describe three reasons why internal controls are used.
3. Internal controls are based on five principles. Describe in detail three of those principles.
4. Before a company installs or adds to its internal control system, the costs of the system are weighed against its benefits. Explain some of the costs and benefits of an internal control system.
5. Explain the concept of separation of duties and describe how this concept applies to the various functions associated with the recording and handling of cash in a business.
6. An employee who opens mail from customers is also assigned to maintain petty cash, prepare bank deposits, and prepare journal entries in the cash receipts journal. What are the dangers inherent in this situation from a cash control point of view?
7. If you were responsible for the operations of a school cafeteria, what controls would you establish for the handling of the cash paid by customers?
8. Define cash. How is it different from any other asset?
9. What types of cash may not be included in a company's balance sheet category cash?
10. Virtually all companies use checking accounts or demand deposits. Define a checking account and explain why it is used.
11. Because of the nature of cash, steps should be taken to control it. Describe these steps.
12. Companies prepare bank reconciliations for what reason(s)?
13. The Sedley Company is preparing its bank reconciliation statement for the month of November 19xx. What type of item would the company add to the "Balance per Bank Statement" as part of the process of determining the "Adjusted Bank Balance"? What types of items would be subtracted?
14. Describe and explain six different items that may appear on a bank statement.

15. Define a petty cash imprest system. Why is it used?
16. Define four terms used in describing a note.
17. Why would a company discount a note? Describe the discounting process.
18. On June 30, customer S. Merrill issues you a $2,000, 12%, 60-day note in payment on her account. On August 31, Merrill defaults on the note. On September 30, you receive a check for $2,040 from Merrill. Explain the nature of the asset you hold from Merrill on June 30 and August 31.
19. Assume that you discount a note with recourse and the maker defaults. What responsibilities do you have to the bank where you discounted the note? Does your answer differ if the note was discounted without recourse?

· Appendix Questions

20. Describe the advantages of using special journals.
21. What types of transactions are entered in the sales journal, the cash receipts journal, the purchases journal, and the cash disbursements journal?
22. How do special journals aid in establishing controls?
23. Describe an electronic cash register system in terms of its hardware and software components.

· EXERCISES

E 7–1

Accounting Controls

L.O.1, 2, 9

1. Internal controls are—
   a. Methods used to safeguard assets.
   b. Procedures a company uses to keep its employees in check.
   c. Operational efficiency and adherence to managerial policies.
   d. Plans, methods, and measures a company uses to safeguard its assets, check the accuracy and reliability of its accounting data, promote operational efficiency, and encourage adherence to prescribed policies.
2. Accounting controls are designed to ensure—
   a. That transactions are executed in accordance with management's authorization.
   b. That transactions are recorded as necessary.
   c. That access to assets are permitted only according to management's authorization.
   d. That comparison of the accounting records with the existing assets is performed and differences are corrected.
   e. All of the above.
3. As a company grows, a larger, more elaborate organizational plan is usually developed. This plan includes an internal control system based on some general principles including—
   a. Equality of assets and liabilities plus owners' equity; debits equal credits.
   b. Authorization and responsibility, protection of assets, separation of duties, and accounting system procedures.
   c. Execution of transactions in accordance with management's authorization, access to assets in accordance with management's authorization, and recording of transactions as necessary.
   d. Separation of physical asset control and recordkeeping, periodic comparison of actual assets with reported assets, and proof of liability existence.
4. Using a computerized accounting system provides several advantages over using a manual system. The advantages include—
   a. Increased efficiency through a reduction in the work force.
   b. Opportunity for risk reduction, increased accuracy, and quick processing for large-volume jobs, thus providing reports and analysis on a timely basis.
   c. Elimination of number of journals that must be kept.
   d. All of the above.
   e. None of the above.

E 7–2
Bank Statement Reconciliation
L.O.5

Given the following facts, prepare a bank reconciliation and determine the actual cash balance of the Simson Company. (Assume this is the only relevant information.)

Balance per bank statement	$10,000
Checks written by Simson	27,000
Checks clearing the bank	26,500
Deposits by Simson	12,000
Deposits recorded by the bank	11,750
Bank service charges	300
Check written and accidentally recorded twice by Simson	575

E 7–3
Bank Statement Reconciliation
L.O.5

Consider the following items in connection with a bank reconciliation:

a. The bank made an error on one of the company's checks by entering $100 on the records instead of $1,000.
b. A service charge of $322 appears on the bank statement.
c. An $8,539 deposit in transit does not appear on the bank statement.
d. Eight of the company's checks totaling $22,765 are still outstanding and do not appear on the statement.
e. A check from a customer, R. Dunne, for $579 was returned to the depositor's bank NSF.

Required:
If you start your reconciliation with the amount per the bank statement, what would you do with each of the above items to reconcile the company's (depositor's) Cash account balance and the bank statement balance?

E 7–4
Bank Statement Reconciliation
L.O.5

Each item in a bank reconciliation has one of the following effects:

1. Increase bank balance.
2. Increase book balance.
3. Decrease bank balance.
4. Decrease book balance.

Required:
Identify which type of effect each of the following items would have:

1. Error in the total on our deposit ticket noted by the bank in favor of the bank (for example, total was overstated).
2. Interest on checking account balance.
3. Checks that have been written but have yet to clear the bank.
4. Deposit in transit.
5. Bank service charge.
6. NSF checks.

E 7–5
Petty Cash
L.O.6

Sue Coy of Great Ideas Advertising Agency was looking for an easier system to handle transactions of small amounts of cash where use of a check was inconvenient. A $100 petty cash system was established on September 1, 19xx, and shows the following on October 4, 19xx:

Receipt for postage	$24.16
Receipt for office supplies	38.21
Receipt for miscellaneous items.	17.92
Cash on hand.	20.86

Required:
Prepare the journal entries to record the establishment and the replenishment of the fund.

E 7–6
Petty Cash
L.O.6

Prepare the journal entries to record the following:

Feb. 1 Establish a $250 petty cash fund.
     15 Replenish fund. Cash on hand totaled $75.36. Receipts for the following included

Stamps	$65.00
Flowers	49.50
Office supplies	39.56
Lunch for client.	20.58

     28 Replenish fund and increase it to $500. Cash on hand totaled $86.21. Receipts for the following included

Stamps	$66.00
Office supplies	79.21
Door lock	15.45

E 7–7
Petty Cash
L.O.6

In examining the $2,000 petty cash fund of Future Sound, Inc., you discover the following data:

Receipts	Amount
13—Cab fares	$ 506
18—Postage charges	230
1—Umbrella	26
21—UPS bills	770
1—Pocket calculator	84
14—Batteries for warehouse lights	20
2—Adding machine tapes	36
	$1,672
Over and short	(72)
Cash and bills	400
	$2,000

All items costing less than $200 are expensed. (Hint: Use miscellaneous expense for items that do not seem to fit in a major category.)

Required:
Record the entry or entries necessary to replenish the petty cash fund.

E 7–8
Balance Sheet
Classifications
L.O.4, 6

Explain how each of the following should be reported on a balance sheet:

a. An IOU signed by an employee that promises to repay petty cash for $15 she took to pay for lunch when she had forgotten her money.
b. The amount in a checking account (demand deposit).
c. A money order made out to the company in payment of an invoice.
d. A $50,000 money market certificate in a local savings and loan. The money is available at any time with the payment of a penalty of one quarter's interest.
e. U.S. postal stamps in the amount of $3,000.

E 7–9
Interest Computation
L.O.7

Compute interest for the following notes. Consider each note separately.

a. Interest for 45 days on a $5,000, 8%, 60-day note.
b. One month of interest on a $25,000, 12%, one-year note.
c. Total interest on a $16,000, 11%, 45-day note.
d. One year's interest on a $50,000, 10%, three-year note.

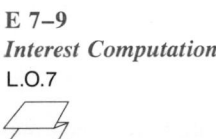

E 7–10
Notes Receivable
Related Transactions
L.O.7

Record the following transactions for the Easy-Money Corporation:

Feb.   1   Accepted a $15,000, 16%, 90-day note from Cye Lablanski for an outstanding invoice.
Mar. 15   Recorded receipt of quarterly interest payment of $900 from Joe Burroughs.
May   2   Recorded receipt of note payment from Lablanski at maturity.

E 7–11
Notes Receivable
L.O.7

The notes receivable subsidiary ledger of Scholten Enterprises, Inc., contains the following:

> $ 10,000, 10%, 30-day note
> 150,000, 14%, 60-day note
> 45,000, 8%, 90-day note
> 300,000, 7%, 120-day note
> 250,000, 18.5%, 180-day note

Required:
Prepare the journal entries to

1. Record the above notes. Assume that each involves a cash payment by Scholten.
2. Record the receipt of principal and interest on each note. Assume that all transactions occur in the same fiscal year.

E 7–12
Recording of Interest
L.O.7

Jay Smithers, accounting clerk for Top Secret, Inc., has been asked to record receipt of principal and interest on the following notes:

a. $26,000, 12%, 60-day note; half of total interest has previously been accrued.
b. $64,000, 18% note dated April 15; payment received September 1 of the same year.
c. $39,000, 6%, 30-day note.
d. $100,000, 13%, 45-day note; 15 days have previously been accrued.

Required:
Record the receipt of the principal and interest on the above notes. Assume that each month has 30 days.

E 7–13
Discounting a Note
L.O.7

Columbo Dairy holds the following note:

Face amount.	$10,000
Annual interest rate.	12%
Term	90 days
Date of note	3/10/x1

The note is discounted at a bank on 4/1/x1 at a discount rate of 10%. The discounting contract is "with recourse."

Required:
What were the proceeds from the bank? Assume each month has 30 days.

E 7–14
Discounting a Note
L.O.7

On January 1, 19xx, Playthings, Inc., accepts an 11%, six-month note from a customer for $5,000, with principal and interest due on July 1, 19xx. Due to a cash shortage, Playthings decides to sell the note to Huckster Bank. On May 1, 19xx, Huckster discounts the note with recourse at a 20% annual discount rate.

Required:
Determine how much Huckster must pay for the note.

E 7–15
Discounting a Note
L.O.7

On March 1, 19xx, Bob sold Sue a new stereo system for $3,000 and received a 12%, six-month note receivable. On June 1, 19xx, he discounted it at the bank at 15%.

Required:
1. Prepare the journal entry to reflect the June 1, 19xx, transaction assuming that the note was discounted with recourse.
2. Discuss why discounting a note can create a contingent liability.

E 7–16
Dishonored Note
L.O.7

Stark Company discounted, with recourse, Burke's $44,000 note at the local bank. The note had a maturity value of $46,000. Burke defaulted on the note.

Required:
1. Record the journal entries Stark made on the date of default and six months later when a $48,500 check was received from Burke in repayment of the note. (Note that more interest is paid for the period between maturity and payment date.)
2. What journal entries would Stark have made on those dates if the note had been discounted without recourse?

E 7–17
Multiple Choice
L.O.1–7

1. Internal controls help to—
   a. Minimize employee turnover.
   b. Maximize customer dissatisfaction.
   c. Minimize losses from errors and irregularities.
   d. Maximize market share.
   e. None of the above.
2. Separation of duties—
   a. Is aimed primarily at efficiency.
   b. Encourages theft and fraud.
   c. Cannot be used in an electronic data processing system.
   d. Is the same as the entity concept.
   e. None of the above.
3. Cash—
   a. Is synonymous with currency in most businesses.
   b. Includes receivables when there is a high probability of collection.
   c. Is the sum of the money that a company has easy access to reduced by the amounts currently payable.
   d. Includes balances in unrestricted checking accounts.
   e. None of the above.
4. A checking account balance for a business—
   a. Is always equal to the balance in the business's Cash ledger account.
   b. Excludes petty cash.
   c. Is not currency and is therefore not cash.
   d. Increases by an adjusting entry when there are outstanding checks.
   e. None of the above.
5. Positive cash balances in noninterest-bearing checking accounts—
   a. Are of no value to the business.
   b. Are a legal requirement.
   c. Should be minimized.
   d. Are current liabilities of the business.
   e. None of the above.
6. The reconciliation of a bank statement—
   a. Often results in a journal entry to record service charges.
   b. Is necessary only when the cash balance on the business's books is larger than the balance on the bank statement.
   c. Should be ignored if the differences are not very large.
   d. Is carried out by bank personnel.
   e. None of the above.
7. Petty cash—
   a. Is never held in the form of currency.
   b. Is usually in the form of a checking account balance.
   c. Is a current liability on the balance sheet.
   d. Is an expense.
   e. None of the above.
8. The principal amount of a note—
   a. Increases as interest compounds.
   b. Decreases as interest is paid.

   c. Stays constant until part or all of the note is paid off.
   d. Is not recorded until maturity.
   e. None of the above.
 9. A note receivable balance—
   a. Appears on the balance sheet as a current or long-term asset.
   b. Appears on the balance sheet as a current or long-term liability.
   c. Appears on the income statement as interest revenue.
   d. Appears on the income statement as interest expense.
   e. None of the above.
10. When a note is discounted at a bank—
   a. The maker receives the proceeds.
   b. The maker may be contingently liable if there is a default.
   c. The payee receives the proceeds.
   d. The payee continues to receive the interest payments on the note.
   e. None of the above.

· **Appendix Exercises** ───────────────────────────────────────

E 7–18
Multiple Choice
L.O.8, 9

1. Special journals
   a. Are not part of the formal records of the business.
   b. Help make manual systems more efficient.
   c. Require separation of duties.
   d. Eliminate the need for the general ledger.
   e. None of the above.
2. Electronic data processing—
   a. Eliminates human errrors.
   b. Can be justified only if it costs less than a manual system.
   c. Will usually reduce mechanical errors.
   d. Will usually reduce costs but increase mechanical errors.
   e. None of the above.

E 7–19
Special Journals
L.O.8

Describe the special journals in which each of the following items would be recorded:

a. Monthly payroll.
b. Payment received from a credit customer.
c. Cash sale.
d. Credit sale.
e. Invoice for merchandise purchased on account.
f. Deductions from employee paychecks.
g. Cash receipt from customer for prepaid subscriptions.
h. Payment to replenish petty cash fund.

E 7–20
Control Accounts
L.O.8

Warehouse Foods Company has a balance of $36,900 in its Accounts Receivable control account. This account is supported by the following subsidiary ledger:

Customer	May 1 Amount
T. Berry	$ 9,000
F. Channing. . . .	6,400
R. Nixon	3,550
B. Scott	4,000
G. Smith	3,700
F. Stone	5,600
L. Wilson	4,650
Total	$36,900

During the month of May 19xx, Warehouse had the following activity related to its Accounts Receivable account:

Customer	Sales	Receipts
T. Berry	$5,550	$13,000
F. Channing	0	4,000
R. Nixon	2,700	3,200
B. Scott	0	4,000
F. Stone	1,550	5,000
L. Wilson	1,200	0

Required:

Compute the ending balance in the Accounts Receivable account. Post the above transactions to the subsidiary ledger and prepare a schedule showing the ending balances in each customer's account.

• PROBLEMS

P 7–1
Petty Cash
L.O.6

The P&G Company created a $350 petty cash fund for its accounting department on July 1, 19xx. During the following two months, the fund made the following payments:

Last-minute purchase of mailing labels	$68
Dinner for overtime workers	56
Postage stamps	44
Cab fare for out-of-town visitor to the department manager	72

Cash on hand at August 29, 19xx, is $108.

Required:

1. Prepare the journal entry to create the fund on July 1, 19xx.
2. Prepare the journal entry for the replenishment of the fund on August 29, 19xx.

P 7–2
Bank Reconciliation
L.O.5

The Chung Company reported the following data related to its cash transactions for the month of March 19xx:

Balance per bank statement at the close of business, 3/31/xx	$40,000
Bank statement service charge for March 19xx.	20
Collection of note by bank—reported on March bank statement.	2,000
Deposit in transit, 3/31/xx	6,000
Outstanding checks, 3/31/xx	8,000
NSF check from J. Smith, a customer, returned by the bank with the March statement	250

Required:

1. Determine the amount of cash that should appear on the company's balance sheet as of March 31, 19xx.
2. Record the journal entries in general journal form for the NSF check, the note collection, and the service charge.
3. What journal entry is required to record the $6,000 deposit in transit?

P 7–3
Bank Statement
Reconciliation
L.O.5

Katydid Enterprises' bank statement for the month ended July 31, 19xx, gave the following information:

Beginning balance, July 1	$3,500
Deposits during July	2,645
Checks cleared during July	3,217
NSF check (R. Maki)	63
Bank service charge	25
Ending balance, July 31.	2,840

Katydid's general ledger Cash account for July showed the following:

Beginning balance, July 1	$3,500
Deposits made.	2,800
Checks written.	3,300
Ending balance, July 31.	3,000

There were no deposits in transit or checks outstanding as of June 30, 19xx. However, there were outstanding checks and deposits in transit as of July 31, 19xx.

Required:
Reconcile the bank statement and prepare any journal entries Katydid Enterprises would need to make.

P 7–4
Bank Statement
Reconciliation
L.O.5

The trial balance of the North Sales Company shows a balance of $8,000 in the Cash account at December 31, 19xx. The bank statement received after the trial balance was prepared indicates the following:

a. A check written for $89 in payment of an advertising bill for that amount was erroneously recorded on the company's books as $98.
b. The bank deducted $30 for collection and service charges that have not been entered on the company's books.
c. A deposit for $243 that the company made in late December did not appear on the bank statement.
d. The bank collected a note receivable for the company in the total amount of $1,750 including $50 of interest; the company did not know that the bank made this collection until the bank statement was received.
e. The bank statement included a check written by North Star Salt Corporation that was charged against North Sales Company's account.

Required:
1. Prepare the appropriate journal entries that North Sales Company would make to record the above.
2. What action, if any, would North Sales Company take for the items that did not require a journal entry to be made?

P 7–5
Bank Statement
Reconciliation
L.O.5

You are the independent auditor for Systat Software, Inc., and you are currently comparing the cash balance as of December 31, 19xx, with the most recent bank statement, dated December 31, 19xx. You are given the following summary information for the year from Systat's accountant:

Beginning cash balance, 1/1/xx.	$ 85,500
Deposits during 19xx	1,400,000
Checks written during 19xx.	(1,350,000)
Service charges for first 11 months of 19xx.	(2,750)
Ending cash balance, 12/31/xx	$ 132,750

You reconcile the bank statement and discover the following:

a. The service charge for December is $280, which was not recorded on Systat's books.
b. Eight checks totaling $9,000 and two checks totaling $3,500 written by Systat in November are still outstanding.
c. One check written in November to an advertising company for $10,800 was recorded as $1,080 in November, and it was included in the current bank statement at the correct amount. The original entry was

```
19xx
Nov. 30   Advertising Expense . . . . . . . . . . . . . . . . . . . . . .   1,080
              Cash . . . . . . . . . . . . . . . . . . . . . . . .                 1,080
```

d. Checks and cash totaling $8,750 were deposited after the bank closed on December 31, 19xx, and did not show up on the current bank statement.

Required:
1. What is the correct cash balance at December 31, 19xx?
2. What cash-related journal entries, if any, are necessary on Systat's books at December 31, 19xx?

P 7–6
*Bank Statement
Reconciliation
(Challenging)*
L.O.5

Greedy Corporation deposits all receipts intact each day and pays all debts by check. On July 31 of the current year, the balance of its Cash account was $2,105. However, the bank statement of that date showed a balance of $5,586. The following information is available from the records:

a. The June 30 bank reconciliation showed seven checks outstanding:

Check No.	Amount
764	$ 882
801	1,156
802	90
804	150
805	705
806	65
808	1,010

Of these checks, No. 764 and No. 808 were not returned with the July 31 bank statement.
b. July checks written but not returned with the bank statement totaled $2,859.
c. While comparing returned checks to the cash payments records, it was found that check No. 894 issued to the electric company and debited to Utilities Expense had been written for $908 and had cleared the bank at that amount but had been recorded on the books at $980.
d. The following items were returned with the bank statement:
    1. Notification that a check for $260 written by a customer, Darwin Company, on their account, had been returned NSF.
    2. Bank service charge for the month totaled $22.
e. The bank statement also contained a notification that the bank had deposited $641 to Greedy's account. This amount was net of the bank's collection fee of $15 and resulted from a transfer of 931 Canadian dollars from a Canadian bank. This transfer was in settlement of a $662 receivable balance in the account of Windsor Bros. Ltd., a Canadian firm. This arrangement is the normal method of doing business between Windsor Bros. and Greedy. Greedy applies any gains or losses on currency conversion to Miscellaneous Income or Expense. The $15 bank service fee is **not** included in the $22 of bank service charges for the month.
f. The bank erroneously cleared check No. 814 at $762. It had been written for $765 and was properly recorded in Greedy's records.
g. The July 31 deposit amounted to $1,704. This deposit had not been made in time to be included in the bank's records for July.

Required:
1. Prepare the July 31 bank reconciliation.
2. Prepare all journal entries required as a result of the reconciliation.

P 7–7
Interest
L.O.7

Star Equipment Company, which is in the business of designing, manufacturing, and selling equipment to move materials, accepts the following notes at the beginning of September:

> *a.* $ 25,000, 8%, 180-day note
> *b.*   50,000, 10%, 90-day note
> *c.*   60,000, 12%, 120-day note
> *d.*   100,000, 15%, 1-year note

Required:
Determine Star Equipment's interest income for the month of September.

P 7–8
Notes Receivable
(Challenging)
L.O.7

Boxton, Inc., custom-builds yachts and allows customers to delay payment for various periods. During the current year Boxton sold the following yachts, for which the customer signed the following notes:

Yacht	Delivery Date	Maturity Date of Note	Maturity Amount of Note	Selling Price of Yacht	Cost of Yacht
13-A	1/31/x1	1/31/x2	$ 77,000	$ 70,000	$ 50,000
17-C	6/30/x1	6/30/x2	154,000	*10% interest* 140,000	104,000
101-B	9/30/x1	9/30/x2	220,000	200,000	180,000

Required:
1. What was the annual interest rate on the notes? Explain.
2. What effect did these sales and notes have on the revenue of Boxton for the year ended December 31, 19x1? (Assume 30-day months for interest computation purposes.) Explain.
3. How would your answer to 2 above change if the yachts had been sold for cash?

P 7–9
Discounting a Note
L.O.7

On December 1, 19x1, Utopia sold $3,000 worth of merchandise to Moore in exchange for a $3,000, 12%, four-month note. The principal and interest on the note are payable on March 31, 19x2. Utopia's fiscal year ends on December 31.

Required:
Assume that each month has 30 days.
1. On March 1, 19x2, Utopia discounts the note with recourse at a 20% discount rate at the First State Bank. Determine how much in proceeds Utopia will get from the discounting.
2. Record all of Utopia's entries for 19x1 and 19x2 related to the note.
3. Assume that Moore pays off the note to the bank on March 31, 19x2. Prepare all necessary journal entries for Utopia on the date of payment.
4. Discuss why a bank charges a fee to discount a note.

P 7–10
Notes Receivable
L.O.7

A summary of the activity in the Accounts Receivable and Notes Receivable accounts of HiTech Consultants for 19xx appears below:

Accounts Receivable

Balance, 1/1/xx	$ 762,000
Credit sales for 19xx	12,050,000
Cash collections for 19xx	(10,660,000)
Acceptance of notes for two separate invoices.	(430,000)
Default by maker of discounted note	199,500
Balance, 12/31/xx	$ 1,921,500

Notes Receivable

Balance, 1/1/xx	$ 0
Acceptance of notes for accounts receivable	430,000
Collection of Note No. 1	(240,000)
Default of discounted Note No. 2	(190,000)
Balance, 12/31/xx	$ 0

Notes Receivable Discounted

Balance, 1/1/xx	$ 0
Discounting of Note No. 2	190,000
Default of discounted Note No. 2	(190,000)
Balance, 12/31/xx	$ 0

(handwritten margin notes): Record Interest after already considered receiv. Credit it the rest record the rest as interest income (credit)

The two notes have the following features:

(handwritten margin notes): Feb 15. Brooks note accrued $80 4080 x 12% x 45/360 due interest on interest + 61 → new int income

	Principal	Interest	Maturity Amount	Proceeds from Discounting
Note No. 1	$240,000	$12,000	$252,000	$ 0
Note No. 2	190,000	9,500	199,500	185,000

Required:
Show all journal entries in general journal form related to the above notes.

P 7–11
Notes Receivable Transactions and Discounting
L.O.7

Kaline Company has the following transactions affecting Notes Receivable during its first two years of operations:

19x1

(handwritten: 4 mos. due Feb 15)

Oct. 15 Made a sale to Caldwell Corporation and accepted a $2,000, 12%, 120-day note.
Nov. 1 Accepted a $3,600, 10%, 90-day note from S. Shelata in place of an accounts receivable. *(Feb.1)*
 1 Accepted a $4,000, 12%, 60-day note from Brooks Company in place of an accounts receivable.
Dec. 1 The Brooks Company note was discounted with recourse at the bank at 14%.
 31 Accrued interest receivable was recorded for all notes receivable.

(handwritten margin: N/R/D debit to return N/R. No bank deal. Now we interest won't cash)

19x2

Jan. 1 Received notification from the bank that the Brooks Company note had been dishonored. Kaline paid the bank.
Feb. 1 Collected the Shelata, Inc., note.
 15 Collected the Caldwell Corporation note.
 15 Collected the Brooks Company note along with interest for the entire period it had been outstanding.

Required:
Prepare all journal entries in general journal form for the above events. Round all computations to the nearest dollar. Assume that each month has 30 days.

P 7–12
Notes Receivable Transactions and Discounting (Challenging)
L.O.7

Benefit-for-Life, Inc., has the following transactions for the period:

a. Made a sale on account, $3,000; terms 1/10, n/30. All sales are recorded using the gross method.
b. Made a sale on account, $2,000; terms 1/10, n/30.
c. Made a sale accepting a 12%, 90-day note for $8,000 in payment.
d. Made a sale accepting a 10%, 120-day note for $6,000 in payment.
e. Accepted a 60-day, 15% note for a customer's account receivable in the amount of $4,000.

f. Collected the account receivable in *a* within the discount period.

g. Discounted at the bank the note referred to in *c* 60 days before maturity, at 15%, without recourse.

h. Discounted at the bank the note referred to in *d* 90 days before maturity at 16%, with recourse.

i. Collected the receivable referred to in *b* after the discount period expired.

j. Received notice from the bank that the note in *h* was dishonored. Paid the bank in full and reestablished the note on the books.

k. Collected the note referred to in *e*.

l. Collected the note referred to in *j* with no additional interest.

Required:

Prepare the journal entries in general journal form required for the above transactions.

P 7–13
Notes Receivable and Discounting (Challenging)
L.O.7

Plymouth Manufacturing has a large number of notes receivable and, accordingly, maintains a subsidiary ledger for them. You have recently been hired as an accounting clerk and have been assigned the maintenance of this ledger. You are told that there are "problems" with the ledger and that it does not balance with the general ledger control account Notes Receivable.

During your first month on the job, the following transactions and additional information come to your attention:

a. The subsidiary ledger as of the beginning of the month that had been maintained by the previous clerk is shown below.

Maker	Amount	Face Terms
Bird Company.	$ 4,000	11%, 90 days
Birr, Inc.	6,000	10%, 6 months
Floate, Inc.	1,000	14%, 90 days
Gregory Supply Company	7,500	12%, 60 days
Holmes Industries	12,000	12%, 90 days
Krissie Manufacturing	3,000	11%, 120 days
Paula's Kitchen Supply	9,000	10%, 30 days
Ray Farmer Building Company	11,000	14%, 120 days
Topsy Turvy Amusements	2,000	14%, 6 months
Zach Company	5,000	15%, 1 year
Total	$60,500	

The balance in the general ledger control account of $63,710 is inaccurate at the beginning of the month because of *b*, *c*, and *d* below.

b. The general ledger account balance includes a credit for $150 arising from the collection of a note in the previous month. This amount arose when a $3,000, 10%, six-month note from Spencer Company was collected and the previous accounting clerk credited the entire proceeds to Notes Receivable.

c. One of the items in the general ledger account balance is the 12%, 90-day note from Holmes Industries recorded at its maturity value of $12,360 with the $360 having been credited to Interest Income. The previous accounting clerk frequently used this procedure for familiar customers who were known to be excellent about paying.

d. In the previous month the Bird Company's $4,000, 11% note was mistakenly recorded by a debit to Notes Receivable and a credit to Cash for $7,000.

e. The following new notes were created during the month from sales:

Maker	Face Amount	Terms
Fox Company.	$2,500	14%, 90 days
Zach Company	8,000	12%, 6 months
Gregory Supply	4,000	13%, 90 days
Bird Company.	6,000	13%, 90 days

f. A 10%, 60-day note with face value of $3,000 was accepted in payment for an account receivable from Car-Mac Industries.

g. The following new notes were collected during the month along with interest:

Paula's Kitchen Supply note of $9,000

Birr, Inc., note of $6,000

h. To generate cash for a payroll, the $7,500 Gregory Supply Company note was discounted, without recourse, at the bank at 16% 30 days before maturity.

Required:
1. Make all necessary entries related to the above items.
2. Prepare a schedule of the notes outstanding that agrees with the appropriate balance in the general ledger. (Assume that interest is *not* accrued each month.)

• Appendix Problems

P 7–14
Special Journals
(Appendix 7A)
L.O.8

The following transactions were taken from accounting records of Mott, Inc., for July 1, 19xx:

a. Received $1,600 from customer M. Logan, invoice No. 2333.
b. Paid Office Realty, Inc., $24,000 for six months' rent of office space.
c. Created a $200 petty cash fund.
d. Recorded weekly payroll to the following: A. Bird, $600; C. Sullivan, $900; D. Devol, $500; and P. Ross, $1,100.
e. Received payment from Comtype on invoice No. 2230, $1,000 less 2% discount. Comtype uses the gross method.
f. Paid Jenkins Glassworks $500 on invoice No. 216899.
g. Received payments on $10,000 note from G. Hanks plus $1,000 interest.
h. Received a $50 refund from the local utility company, Electric Works.
i. Paid monthly communications bill for $1,445 to On-Site Phone Company.
j. Paid $140 to American Company for renewal of annual magazine subscriptions.
k. Paid Schaffer Music Company $320 on invoice No. 11111.
l. Recorded cash sales of $3,600 for the day.

You have been called on to demonstrate the timesaving features of special journals.

Required:
1. Construct a cash receipts journal and a cash payments journal and record the entries above. Use account names for other debits and credits. Mott begins the month with check No. 107 and issues all checks consecutively.
2. Explain what the timesaving features are of the special journals.
3. Are there any other characteristics of special journals that make them desirable?

P 7–15
Control Accounts
(Appendix 7A)
L.O.8

Polo Fabrics, Inc., sells high-quality fabrics to customers throughout the United States. Invoices are sent for each shipment. One major customer was sent its shipments in May 19xx, and the following special journal transactions were recorded for the customer:

Excerpt from Sales Journal

Date	Customer	Invoice No.	Sales Cr. Accounts Receivable Dr.
5/2	Utah Shirts, Inc.	5-08	$18,000
5/8	Utah Shirts, Inc.	5-11	67,000
5/16	Utah Shirts, Inc.	5-24	13,800
5/30	Utah Shirts, Inc.	5-30	44,150

Excerpt from Cash Receipts Journal

Date	Invoice Name	No.	Cash	Accounts Receivable	Sales	Other Credit (Debit) Amount	Account
5/7	Utah Shirt	4-11	$55,000	$55,000			
	Utah Shirt	4-15	43,500	43,500			
5/29	Utah Shirt	5-08	18,000	18,000			
	Utah Shirt	5-11	67,000	67,000			

Required:
1. Assuming that invoice No. 4-11 and invoice No. 4-15 were the only outstanding invoices for Utah Shirts at the beginning of May, construct a subsidiary ledger account for Utah Shirts, Inc., for the May transactions.
2. What is the relationship of the Sales account and the Accounts Receivable control account to the subsidiary ledger accounts? How do each affect the financial statements?

P 7–16
Special Journals and
Control Accounts
(Appendix 7A)
L.O.8

Consider the following sales and purchases transactions for the first day of operations of TCI Company:

a. Sold $10,000 of merchandise to C. Steinacker on account. No terms were given.
b. Purchased $6,000 of merchandise from R. Ford on account.
c. Sold $7,000 of merchandise to T. Jones on account.
d. Purchased $900 of office supplies on account from Marsh's Office Supply Store.
e. Sold $200 of merchandise to M. Hambo for cash.
f. Purchased $4,000 of office furniture on account from Marsh's Office Supply Store.
g. Purchased merchandise worth $800 for cash.
h. Purchased $690 of merchandise on account of F. Stahl.

TCI posts from the special journal daily.

Required:
1. Record the above transactions, if appropriate, in either the sales or purchases journal.
2. Open and post the transactions to the appropriate general and subsidiary ledger T accounts as necessary at the end of the first day.

• CASES

C 7–1
Control Systems
L.O.2, 4

Burns Computer Supplies sells products for cash and on credit. Betty Burns has instituted a flow of duties chart that she believes provides good control over cash transactions (see Exhibit 7C–1).

EXHIBIT 7C–1

Flow of Duties Chart

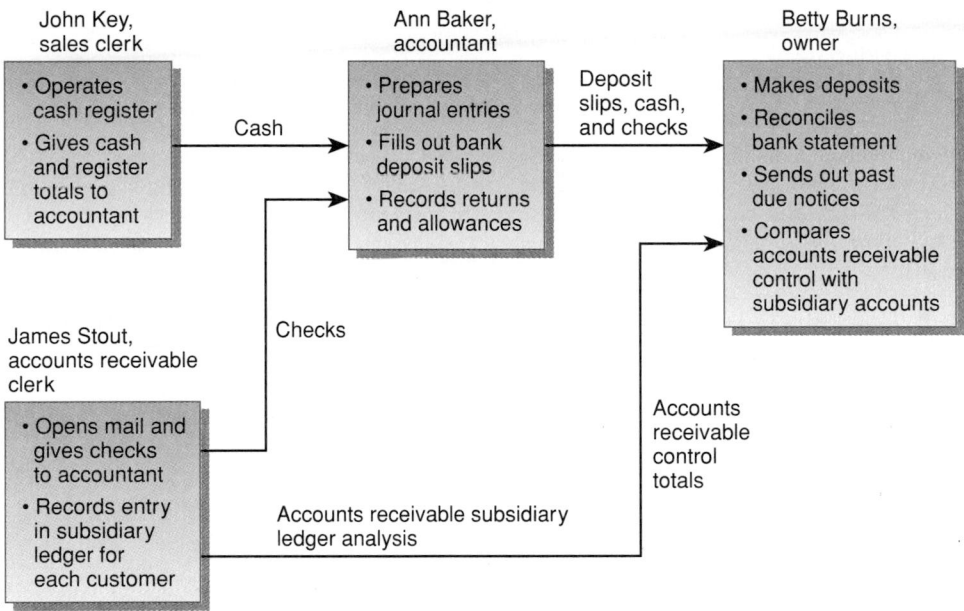

Ann Baker is in grave financial straights and has concocted the following fraudulent scheme. She plans to

a. Record a fictitious return of damaged merchandise from a customer who has actually paid an invoice amount (say, $500).
b. Pocket cash equal to the fictitious return of damaged merchandise.

Her logic is that Betty Burns will rely on the subsidiary ledger to check on unpaid invoices, but her scheme will circumvent this check because the subsidiary ledger will show the invoice paid.

Required:
1. Will the scheme work? Why or why not?
2. How would you improve the control system, and why?

C 7–2
Definition of Cash
L.O.4

Environmental Impact Company has a Cash balance on its balance sheet of $38,500 at year-end. An examination of the transactions in the classification reveals the following:

Balance in Cash-in-Bank account	$10,500
Petty cash balance	500
Marketable securities market value	15,000
Savings account—36-month certificate, penalty for early withdrawal	7,500
Noninterest-earning bank account that must be maintained under a loan agreement with the bank	5,000
Total cash balance	$38,500

Required:
As Environmental's auditor, you are to explain the nature of cash and comment on the appropriate treatment of each item shown above as a component of cash.

C 7–3
Bank Statement Reconciliation and Cash Control
L.O.4, 5

While reviewing the bank statement of your company you find a $10,000 difference between the deposits on the bank statement and the deposits on the company's record. You note a specific $10,000 deposit on the company's records that was not shown on the bank statement. At the end of the next month you find that the $10,000 deposit was actually made at the middle of the month.

Required:
Does this set of facts indicate a cash control problem? What steps would you take?

C 7–4
Petty Cash and Control
L.O.1, 2, 4, 8

You are about to organize your own consulting firm. You need to establish a petty cash fund of $500.

Required:
Discuss what types of needs you might have for petty cash, how you would keep record of the petty cash transactions, and any concerns you might have for controlling petty cash.

C 7–5
Discounting of Note and Liquidity Analysis
L.O.7

The following is an excerpt from a recent annual report of Clark Equipment Company and consolidated subsidiaries. Clark Equipment Company is an international manufacturer of heavy equipment including forklifts, endloaders, and other construction and manufacturing equipment.

	December 31	
	19x7	**19x6**
Current assets (in thousands):		
Cash	$115,599	$58,484
Accounts and notes receivable (less allowance for doubtful accounts of $4.3 million for each year)	63,044	34,819

Assume that the above balances were prepared before adjusting for the following hypothetical transaction:

On December 31, 19x7, Clark discounted with recourse a 10%, 12-month, $15 million note due June 30, 19x8. The bank requires a 15% annual discount rate. No interest has been accrued or received to date.

Required:
1. How much will the bank pay for the note?
2. How would Clark's balance sheet be affected by the discounting? Has Clark improved its liquidity by means of the discounting?

C 7–6

Notes Receivable and
Business Decisions

L.O.7

West Coast Instruments, Inc., (WCI) is a producer of electronic equipment. One of its very important suppliers, Bently Plastics, Inc., (BP) has requested that WCI lend it $2,000,000 on a six-month note at 18% interest in order that BP expand its manufacturing facilities. The expansion would be devoted to supplying WCI exclusively. BP proposes the following schedule:

5/15	BP issues a note to WCI.	$2,000,000
11/15	BP pays off the note plus interest.	2,180,000

WCI's president makes the following statement about the matter to his vice-president of finance: "Given we definitely want BP to expand to ensure our supply, why don't we go ahead and lend the money? That way we will earn the interest." His vice-president replies: "We need all of our available cash for our own expansion. We would have to borrow ourselves if we give them the loan." The president then says: "Couldn't we lend the money and then discount the note and still have use of the cash? Work up the numbers for me as soon as possible." The vice-president responds: "OK, but keep in mind that when you discount a note at a bank they charge a substantial discount rate, and we would be contingently liable if the maker defaults."

Required:

1. Show the journal entries necessary on WCI's books if they lend the money to BP and BP pays on time.
2. Show the journal entries necessary on WCI's books if it lends the money to BP and then immediately discounts the note at a bank at a 20% discount rate, with recourse. Assume the note is paid on time.
3. Under what conditions do you think lending money to a supplier makes good business sense?
4. Does it make good business sense to discount a note at a bank if, as is the case here, the discount fee is more than the interest that would have been earned on the note?

Rabic Inc.
Income Statement
For the Years Ending December 31

	1994	1993
Revenues		
Total revenues	$ xxx	$ xxx
Expenses		
Depreciation expense	**xxx**	**xxx**
Amortization expense	**xx**	**xx**
Depletion expense.	**xx**	**xx**

Rabic Inc.
Balance Sheet
As of December 31

	1994	1993
Current assets		
Total current assets.	$ xxx	$ xxx
Noncurrent assets		
Plant, property, and equipment.	**x,xxx**	**x,xxx**
Less accumulated depreciation	**(x,xxx)**	**(x,xxx)**
Net plant assets.	**$ x,xxx**	**$ x,xxx**
Natural resources (net)	**xxx**	**xxx**
Franchise rights (net)	**xxx**	**xxx**
Goodwill (net).	**xx**	**xx**
Current liabilities		
Total current liabilities.	xxx	xxx
Noncurrent liabilities		
Total noncurrent liabilities	xxx	xxx
Stockholders' equity		
Total stockholders' equity	xxx	xxx

Rabic Inc.
Cash Flow Statement
For the Years Ending December 31

	1994	1993
Operating activities		
Cash from operations	$ xxx	$ xxx
Investing activities		
Investment in equipment.	**(x,xxx)**	**(xxx)**
Sale of old equipment	**xx**	**xxx**
Financing activities		
Cash from financing	xxx	xxx

FINANCIAL
STATEMENT
COMPONENTS
EMPHASIZED IN
CHAPTER 8

8

Long-Term Assets

Expensing versus capitalization of items. Many nonaccounting managers push for expensing in good times and capitalizing in bad times.

Ronald L. Leach
Eaton Corporation

· Learning Objectives

After studying Chapter 8, you should understand

1. How to measure the acquisition costs of intangible assets, including group asset purchases, pp. 387–89.

2. Four depreciation methods—straight-line, units-of-output, sum-of-the-years'-digits, and declining-balance, pp. 391–94.

3. How to determine depreciation for partial years, and how to make revisions in depreciation estimates, pp. 397–98.

4. How to account for costs capitalized or expensed subsequent to acquisition, pp. 399–401.

5. How to record disposals of tangible assets at net book value, disposals involving gains or losses, and disposals of fully depreciated assets, pp. 402–3.

6. The importance of evaluating changes in plant assets, pp. 404–7.

7. Accounting for long-term intangible assets, pp. 408–11.

8. Accounting for asset exchanges (Appendix 8A), pp. 414–16.

9. Accounting for natural resources (Appendix 8B), pp. 417–19.

In earlier chapters you learned that a company's assets (1) arise from past transactions, (2) are controlled by the company, and (3) have measurable future benefits beyond the current accounting period. Both tangible and intangible assets have these characteristics. The difference between these two types of assets is the nature of their future benefits.

Tangible assets are long-term assets having a physical form, such as buildings and equipment. Tangible assets normally represent a much larger dollar investment than intangible assets. Tangible assets are sometimes divided into two categories: (1) those that will be used up in the normal course of business; and (2) those that will not be consumed by business operations. The first category is often called wasting assets (or **productive assets** or **consumable assets**), and consists of the following types of tangible assets:

1a. Buildings (also called *Plant*).
1b. Equipment and machinery.
1c. Furniture and fixtures.
1d. Natural resources (minerals, oil, and so on).

Tangible assets that will not be consumed in the business are generally limited to land (or "property"), which will benefit future operations of the business for an indefinite time period. It is not uncommon to see land reported along with buildings, machinery, and equipment as a single amount in published balance sheets, and referred to by such captions as "plant, property and equipment," "plant assets," or some other similar terminology.

Intangible assets are resources with no physical substance, such as patents or copyrights. Intangible assets along with wasting tangible assets do not last indefinitely, but are consumed through the normal course of business operations. The accrual accounting model requires that the cost of these long-term tangible and intangible assets be charged (expensed) against revenues over the periods of benefit. This process of assigning the cost of a long-term asset such as a piece of equipment to the years in which it will benefit the operations is generally referred to as **cost allocation,** which is any system of assigning costs to accounting periods. More specifically, for tangible assets the cost allocation process is called depreciation or depletion, while for intangible assets it is called amortization. Both depreciation and amortization are simply systematic cost allocation methods of expensing the cost of long-term tangible and intangible assets to the income statements of the periods benefiting from their use.

Tangible assets have value to a business because of what they are and what they are capable of doing or providing—a value based on the asset's physical capability to provide benefits. The value of **intangible assets** to a business stems from what they **represent**. Most intangible assets consist of legal contracts or documents that entitle a business to certain rights representing future benefits. For example, a patent is a legal document that entitles a specified business to the exclusive rights to an invention or process for a specific period of time. The patent itself is merely a paper document; however, the patent represents rights that may be very important to the business.

In this chapter we examine the following life cycle of long-term tangible assets:

1. Acquisition of long-term tangible assets.
2. Depreciation or depletion of long-term tangible assets—allocation of costs to periods of benefit.
3. Costs subsequent to acquisition—additions to long-term tangible assets.
4. Disposal of long-term tangible assets.

The discussion on the life cycle of long-term tangible assets is followed by an evaluation of changes in these assets. We conclude the chapter with a discussion of accounting for intangible assets. Two appendixes at the end of the chapter cover asset exchanges and natural resources.

Long-term tangible assets used in a company's production process represent one of the major investments of resources for most product-oriented businesses. Along with inventory, long-term tangible assets represent the primary operating assets of most business entities.

ACQUISITION OF LONG-TERM TANGIBLE ASSETS	The acquisition cost of all assets is the **current fair market value of the assets given or received, whichever is more objectively measurable.** In most cases fair market value is based on the amount of cash given or borrowed, and is readily measurable. However, when assets are acquired without an exchange of cash, fair value may be ambiguous. For example, if land were acquired in exchange for legal services or for used equipment, fair value could be difficult to measure objectively. In all asset acquisitions we must use the fair value of the assets given or received, whichever is the most objectively measurable at the time of the transaction. Applications of these guidelines for asset measurement may call for judgment on the part of the accountant and will not always lead to a clear or obvious solution to asset measurement problems.

Costs Included in the Original Cost of an Asset

Objective 1
How to measure the acquisition costs of tangible assets, including group asset purchases.

What is the total cost to be included in recording an asset? **The asset's recorded value should include all costs necessary to acquire the asset and to place the asset into its intended useful state.** For example, the cost to insure a new casting machine while it is in-transit to the buyer's plant would be included in the cost of the machine. However, insurance on the machine once it is placed into use would be charged to the period covered as insurance expense. When costs are added to an asset account, the costs are said to be capitalized, since they add to the assets of the business. When costs are not capitalized, they are expensed (or "charged") to the current period. The two examples of capitalized costs that follow are (1) capitalization of costs necessary for placing an asset into its intended useful state and (2) capitalization of interest costs.

Capitalization of Costs Necessary to Place an Asset into Its Intended Useful State. Assume that Delta Corporation purchased land on which Delta intended to build a factory. However, before Delta could begin construction of the factory, it had to remove an old barn and prepare the building site. The events that follow occurred shortly after the $75,000 land purchase.

Delta paid a salvage company $2,000 to tear down the old barn and sold the wood for $2,200. To prepare the land for a building site, Delta paid $3,400 to have the land cleared and graded. The net cost of these three activities was $3,200 ($2,000 − $2,200 + $3,400). This cost should be added to the value of the Land account (capitalized) rather than expensed because these activities were necessary to prepare the land for its intended purpose.

Interest Capitalization.   Another component of an asset's cost may be interest incurred on borrowings. GAAP requires interest to be included as a cost of major long-term assets that require an extended length of time to prepare them for their intended purpose. Assets such as a new plant or warehouse require a construction period during which interest costs are to be included as a cost of the asset. Interest costs are included as a cost of constructed assets regardless of whether self-constructed or constructed by an outside contractor/builder. The amount of interest to be included in the asset's cost depends on the accumulated cost of the asset throughout the construction period and the length of the construction period.[1]

---

[1]This procedure is explained in some detail in *FASB Statement No. 34,* "Capitalization of Interest Cost" (Norwalk, Conn.: FASB, 1979). Note that if interest to be capitalized is not material in amount, capitalization may be ignored.

EXHIBIT 8–1

Disclosure of Capitalization of Interest

The Dow Chemical Company

Excerpt from footnotes:

Interest cost reported in income statement (in millions)

	19x3	19x2
Total interest incurred on debt	$478	$579
Less: interest capitalized	− 47	− 65
Net interest expense	$431	$514

Analysis of impact of interest capitalization (in millions)

	19x3	19x2
Reported net income	$334	$399
Capitalized interest as a percentage of reported net income	14.1%	16.3%

Exhibit 8–1 shows the disclosure for interest capitalization reported by Dow Chemical Company in a recent annual report. The top of Exhibit 8–1 provides the footnote explanation of the total amount of interest for each year (i.e., $478 million for 19x3); the amount of interest capitalized, or added to Dow's assets (i.e., $47 million in 19x3); and, the net amount of interest expensed each year (i.e., $478 − $47 = $431 million expensed in 19x3). In the lower part of Exhibit 8–1 we compute capitalized interest as a percent of reported net income to determine whether interest capitalization has a material effect on income. In 19x3, the interest capitalized by Dow ($47 million) was equal to about 14.1% of reported net income ($47/$334). In 19x2, the amount was 16.3% of net income. While the amount of interest capitalized by a company is usually only a small fraction of its total interest costs for the period, its effect on net income is sometimes significant.

Group Purchases

The purchasing of assets as a group instead of in separate transactions creates special measurement problems. To illustrate, assume that Campus Rentals, Inc., acquired three houses from another rental agency for a package price of $380,000. The three houses were to be renovated and rented as student housing. The following information is available:

House Address	Square Feet	Property Tax Assessment Value
1181 Summit Street	2,816	$121,600
2247 Hill Street	1,408	76,000
1818 Olivia Street	2,176	106,400
	6,400	$304,000

Note that the assessed value does not depend entirely on floor space. However, either the square feet or assessed value measures could be used to assign the total cost to the three separate properties. If we assume that the square footage of floor space determined the fair value of the three houses, the $380,000 total cost could be assigned (allocated) to the three houses as follows:

House	Square Feet	Percent of Total Square Feet	×	Amount to be Allocated	=	Allocated Cost per House
Summit.	2,816	.44 (2,816/6,400)		$380,000		$167,200
Hill.	1,408	.22 (1,408/6,400)		380,000		83,600
Olivia	2,176	.34 (2,176/6,400)		380,000		129,200
	6,400	1.00 (6,400/6,400)		380,000		$380,000

The selection of the "most appropriate" basis for allocating the total cost of a **group purchase** (also called a basket purchase) can have a significant affect on the recorded cost of the individual assets. Since by definition the term *allocation* identifies an arbitrary process, obviously there is no single correct way to allocate any such cost.

DEPRECIATION OF LONG-TERM TANGIBLE ASSETS

Productive assets such as plant, equipment, machinery, vehicles, and warehouses are tangible long-term assets representing future benefits to the business. However, in time, the operations of the business will "use up" or consume the future benefits of these tangible assets. As a result, the original cost of tangible assets minus their expected resale value when fully used (called residual value or **salvage value**) must be systematically expensed over their expected useful lives. Depreciation expense is the amount that is charged to current income to reflect the portion of the asset's benefit used during that period. The difference between an asset's original cost and its estimated salvage value is called its depreciable base. A portion of the depreciable base is allocated to income each period over the asset's estimated useful life, which is the length of time the asset is expected to be used by the business.

Recall from Chapters 3 and 4 that the adjusting entry to record periodic depreciation expense is

```
19x2
Dec. 31   Depreciation Expense (E) . . . . . . . . . . . . . . . .      100,000
                  Accumulated Depreciation (XA) . . . . . . . . . . . . .              100,000
```

 Depreciation expense reduces net income, but has **no** direct effect on cash flow. The cash outflow would normally occur when the depreciable asset is purchased. Depreciation expense (along with amortization expense for intangibles and depletion expense for natural resources) always represents an expense that does **not** use cash. This is why the statement of cash flows normally adds depreciation expense to net income in measuring the "cash flow from operations."[2] The account used to offset depreciation expense is a contra asset account, accumulated depreciation, which accumulates depreciation expense from all periods and is reported in the balance sheet as follows:

Partial Balance Sheet

	December 31	
	19x2	19x1
Machinery	$900,000	$900,000
Less Accumulated Depreciation	200,000	100,000
Net Book Value—Machinery	$700,000	$800,000

---

[2]The Ralston Purina Annual Report in Appendix E illustrates this point on page 922. Also, this point is further explained in Chapter 14 on the statement of cash flows.

The difference between the original cost of depreciable assets and their accumulated depreciation is the assets' net book value (or just **book value**). Sometimes only the net book value of "plant assets" is reported in the balance sheet, with details about the cost of the assets and their accumulated depreciation reported in the footnotes following the financial statements.

The alternative depreciation methods commonly used in practice are considered in the following sections, along with illustrations of how to determine a partial year's depreciation and how to account for depreciation expense when either the original estimated life or original estimated salvage value are revised.

Alternative
Depreciation

Generally accepted accounting principles (GAAP) allow several methods of systematically depreciating (allocating) the depreciable base of an asset over its periods of benefit. These different methods permit businesses some flexibility in deciding how fast the depreciable base of an asset is assigned to the periods of benefit. To illustrate how this selection might be made, let's listen in on a conversation between Brad and Mary that occurred during the first year of operations of Byte-Size.

Brad: You know, we really need to decide what depreciation method we are going to use for our equipment, Mary. I don't know if we should use straight-line or some other method.

Mary: Well, what difference will it make, Brad?

Brad: Straight-line will spread out or "allocate" the cost evenly over the life of the equipment, while the more rapid depreciation methods allocate more of the cost in the early years of use and less in later years. It is kind of like this. (Brad sketches the following graph to show depreciation expense.)

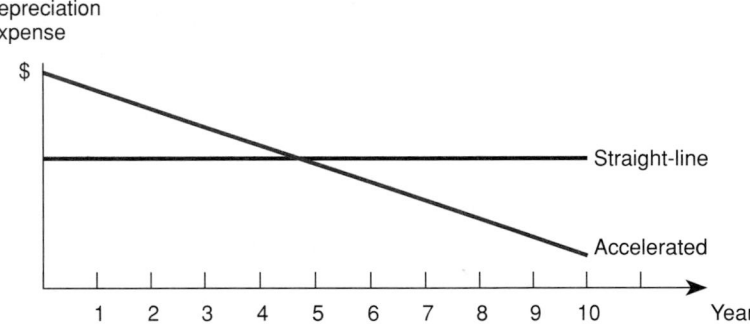

Mary: Is the total depreciation taken over the life of the equipment any different for one method or the other?

Brad: No, they are the same in total.

Mary: So an accelerated method will result in more expense in the first few years of use than straight-line. Why should we consider doing that?

Brad: Well, what if a change in technology occurs? Our equipment may be less useful in the latter part of its useful life, therefore it might make sense to have less depreciation expense later on.

Mary: Yes, but the bank may feel better about lending us money if our expenses were lower in the first few years of our business. Lower expenses would make it easier for us to show a profit.

Brad: You know, since we don't need to use the same method for income tax purposes that we decide to use for financial reporting purposes, it really doesn't matter too much what method we decide on. The depreciation method that we choose for financial reporting purposes will not affect our cash flow.

Mary: Yes, but I wonder if the bank knows that? They aren't going to ask us for our tax return—only for the financial statements. I say we use the straight line. Besides being simple to use, it will improve our first few income statements compared to what they would report under some accelerated method.

The discussion between Brad and Mary points to some common questions and concerns in the choice of a depreciation method. Before we consider these issues in more detail, let us consider an example of each of the following types of depreciation methods allowed within GAAP:

Objective 2

Four depreciation methods—straight-line, units of output, sum-of-the-years'-digits, and declining-balance.

1. Straight-line depreciation.
2. Units-of-output depreciation.
3. Accelerated depreciation:
   a. Sum-of-the-years'-digits depreciation.
   b. Declining-balance depreciation.

Straight-Line Depreciation. The example given in Exhibit 8–2, and examples illustrated earlier in the book, have all been based on straight-line depreciation. The straight-line depreciation method assumes that assets are equally useful over all time periods of use. Thus, a $50,000 asset with a two-year useful life and a $10,000 residual value would be depreciated (expensed) equally over the two years of use, or $20,000 depreciation expense per year.

Straight-line depreciation is the most common method used for preparing financial statements. You can use the following formula to measure straight-line annual depreciation:

$$\begin{matrix} \text{Straight-line annual} \\ \text{depreciation} \\ \text{expense} \end{matrix} = \frac{\text{Cost} - \text{Residual (salvage) value}}{\text{Number of years of useful life}}$$

Exhibit 8–2 shows the straight-line depreciation for the $50,000 asset described above.

Units-of-Output Depreciation. The units-of-output depreciation method records depreciation expense based on the amount of use an asset receives during the period. For example, assume a machine costs $50,000, has a $10,000 residual value, and has an estimated useful life of 10,000 hours of running time. If the machine is used for

EXHIBIT 8–2

Straight-Line Depreciation

**Depreciation Schedule
Calculation: Straight Line**

$$\frac{\$50,000 - \$10,000}{2 \text{ years}} = \$20,000 \text{ per year}$$

Date and Period	Cost	−	Accumulated Depreciation	=	Book Value	Depreciation Expense
1/1/x1	$50,000		$ 0		$50,000	
19x1						$20,000
12/31/x1	50,000		20,000		30,000	
19x2						20,000
12/31/x2	50,000		40,000		10,000	

6,000 hours in year 1 and 4,000 hours in year 2, depreciation amounts for each unit would be computed using the following equation:

$$\text{Units-of-output depreciation expense (per unit)} = \frac{\text{Cost} - \text{Residual (salvage) value}}{\text{Number of ``units'' in useful life}}$$

Exhibit 8–3 shows the units-of-output depreciation schedule for the $50,000 machine.

Accelerated Depreciation. Although depreciation is the allocation of an asset's original cost to the periods that benefit from the asset's use, each period will not always receive equal benefit from the use of an asset. Often the asset's early years will provide more benefits than the later years.

When assets provide more benefits in earlier periods than in later periods, an accelerated depreciation schedule may be justified. Accelerated depreciation is a general term to describe depreciation methods that give higher depreciation expense amounts to the early years of the asset's useful life than are given to the asset's later years. Two accelerated depreciation methods are discussed in the paragraphs that follow: declining-balance depreciation and sum-of-the-years'-digits depreciation.

Declining-balance depreciation. To help you understand the declining-balance method of depreciation, we begin with an example of the straight-line depreciation method. Assume that Arrow, Inc., purchases a delivery truck on January 1, 19x1, for $50,000. The truck has an estimated useful life of five years and an estimated residual value of $10,000. Straight-line depreciation would, therefore, be $8,000 per year, computed as follows:

Straight-Line Depreciation Computation

Cost	$50,000
Less: residual value	− 10,000
Depreciable base	$40,000

$$\frac{\$40,000}{5 \text{ years}} = \$8,000 \text{ per year straight-line depreciation expense}$$

EXHIBIT 8–3

Units-of-Output Depreciation

**Depreciation Schedule
Calculation: Units-of-Output**

$$\text{Hourly depreciation expense} = \frac{\$50,000 - \$10,000}{10,000 \text{ hours}} = \$4 \text{ per hour}$$

Year 1:	6,000 hours × $4 = $24,000
Year 2:	4,000 hours × $4 = 16,000
	10,000 hours $40,000

Date and Period	Cost	−	Accumulated Depreciation	=	Book Value	Depreciation Expense
1/1/x1	$50,000		$ 0		$50,000	
19x1						$24,000
12/31/x1	50,000		24,000		26,000	
19x2						16,000
12/31/x2	50,000		40,000		10,000	

When the declining-balance depreciation method is used, the amount of depreciation expense is accelerated. To accomplish this acceleration, more than 100% of the straight-line depreciation rate is applied to the declining book value of the depreciable asset. The formula for declining-balance depreciation is

$$\begin{array}{c}\text{Asset book value at} \\ \text{beginning of year}\end{array} \times \begin{array}{c}\text{Multiple of the} \\ \text{straight-line rate}\end{array} = \begin{array}{c}\text{Declining-balance} \\ \text{depreciation expense}\end{array}$$

Using Arrow's delivery truck as an example, we will illustrate a depreciation schedule for 150% of the straight-line rate. The straight-line depreciation rate, stated as a percentage of the cost of the truck, is 20% (100%/5-year life = 20% per year = .20 or 20%). Therefore, the **150% declining-balance method** would use a 30% rate (150% × 20% = 1.50 × .20 = .30) and a **200% declining-balance method** (or **double-declining balance method**) would use a 40% rate (200% × 20% = .40) for this example.

The depreciation schedule for the truck using 150% declining-balance depreciation is given in Exhibit 8–4. Note that in declining-balance depreciation, the residual value is ignored in computing annual depreciation expense and **not** considered until the end of the asset's useful life. Also, depreciation expense is always a **constant percent** (30% in this example) of the declining book value. After five years the book value in this example happens to be $8,403 ($50,000 cost less $41,597 accumulated depreciation). The final year's depreciation expense is sometimes "forced" to achieve the desired residual value. For example, if Arrow recorded $2,005 depreciation expense in year 5 instead of $3,602 as scheduled, the book value at the end of year 5 would equal $10,000, the estimated residual value. This alternative approach for the final year of use is illustrated in the Exhibit 8–4 footnote.

Sum-of-the-years'-digits depreciation. The sum-of-the-years'-digits (SYD) depreciation method also provides an accelerated schedule of depreciation. However, unlike the declining-balance method, this method considers the estimated residual value of the asset as did the straight-line and units-of-output methods. To use the SYD method, you must

---

EXHIBIT 8–4

Declining-Balance Depreciation	**Depreciation Schedule Calculation: 150% Declining Balance**

Straight-line rate = 100%/5 years = 20% per year = .20

150% declining balance = .20 × 1.50 = .30, or 30%

Year	Book Value at Beginning of the Year	×	150% of the Straight-Line Rate	=	Depreciation Expense Current Year	Accumulated Depreciation Balance
1	$50,000		30% (.30)		$15,000	$15,000
2	35,000		30% (.30)		10,500	25,500
3	24,500		30% (.30)		7,350	32,850
4	17,150		30% (.30)		5,145	37,995
5*	12,005		30% (.30)		3,602	41,597
Total					$41,597	

Alternatively:

5.	$12,005		Forced		$ 2,005	$40,000
					$40,000	

compute the sum of the number of years of useful life and use this sum as a denominator for each year. For Arrow's delivery truck, which has a five-year life, the sum would be $5 + 4 + 3 + 2 + 1 = 15$. The more general formula for an asset with an n-year life is

$$\text{Formula for determining the sum of a series of numbers} = \frac{n(n + 1)}{2}$$

$$\text{The sum of the series } 1\text{--}5 = \frac{5(5 + 1)}{2} = 15$$

The formula for computing the depreciation expense for the period using the SYD method is

$$\frac{\text{Asset's}}{\text{depreciable base}} \times \frac{\text{Remaining number of years of asset's life}}{\text{Sum-of-the-years'-digits}} = \frac{\text{SYD depreciation}}{\text{expense for the period}}$$

The depreciable base, which in our example is $40,000, is then multiplied by the fraction of the first year's digit, in this case five years over the total sum of the years, or 15. The first year's depreciation for an asset with a depreciable base of $40,000 \times 5/15 = \$13,333$. Exhibit 8–5 shows the sum-of-the-years'-digits depreciation schedule for Arrow's truck.

Exhibit 8–6 uses the $50,000 truck example and compares the effects of straight-line depreciation, 150% declining-balance depreciation, and sum-of-the-years'-digits depreciation. Both of the accelerated methods provide more depreciation expense than the straight-line method in the first two years of use and less in the last two years of use, as graphically illustrated at the bottom of Exhibit 8–6.

DEPRECIATION, TAXES, AND CASH FLOW

The depreciation methods illustrated in the previous section of this chapter are all acceptable for financial reporting purposes. The straight-line method is the most common and is used by about 93% of publicly traded corporations for financial reporting purposes.[3] However, most companies use an accelerated method of depreciation for income tax reporting purposes. Tax laws normally allow companies to depreciate long-term tangible assets over a shorter period than their estimated economic life and at an accelerated rate. Since companies normally wish to reduce taxable income for income tax reporting purposes, they often take a different depreciation expense deduction for tax purposes than that reported in the financial statements.

EXHIBIT 8–5

Sum-of-the-Years'-Digits Depreciation	Year	Depreciable Base	×	Sum-of-the-Years'-Digits Rate	=	Depreciation Expense Current Year	Accumulated Depreciation Balance
	1	$40,000	×	5/15		$13,333	$13,333
	2	40,000	×	4/15		10,667	24,000
	3	40,000	×	3/15		8,000	32,000
	4	40,000	×	2/15		5,333	37,333
	5	40,000	×	1/15		2,667	40,000
	Total			15/15		$40,000	

---

[3] See *Accounting Trends and Techniques: 1992* (New York: AICPA, 1992), p. 304.

EXHIBIT 8–6

Comparison of Straight-Line, 150% Declining-Balance, and Sum-of-the-Years'-Digits Depreciation

Asset's original cost: $50,000
Useful life: 5 years
Salvage value: $10,000

Year	Straight-Line	Accelerated Methods 150% Declining-Balance	Accelerated Methods Sum-of-the-Years'-Digits
1	$ 8,000	$15,000	$13,333
2	8,000	10,500 26,667	10,667
3	8,000	7,350	8,000
4	8,000	5,145	5,333
5	8,000	2,005 (forced)	2,667
Total . . .	$40,000	$40,000	$40,000

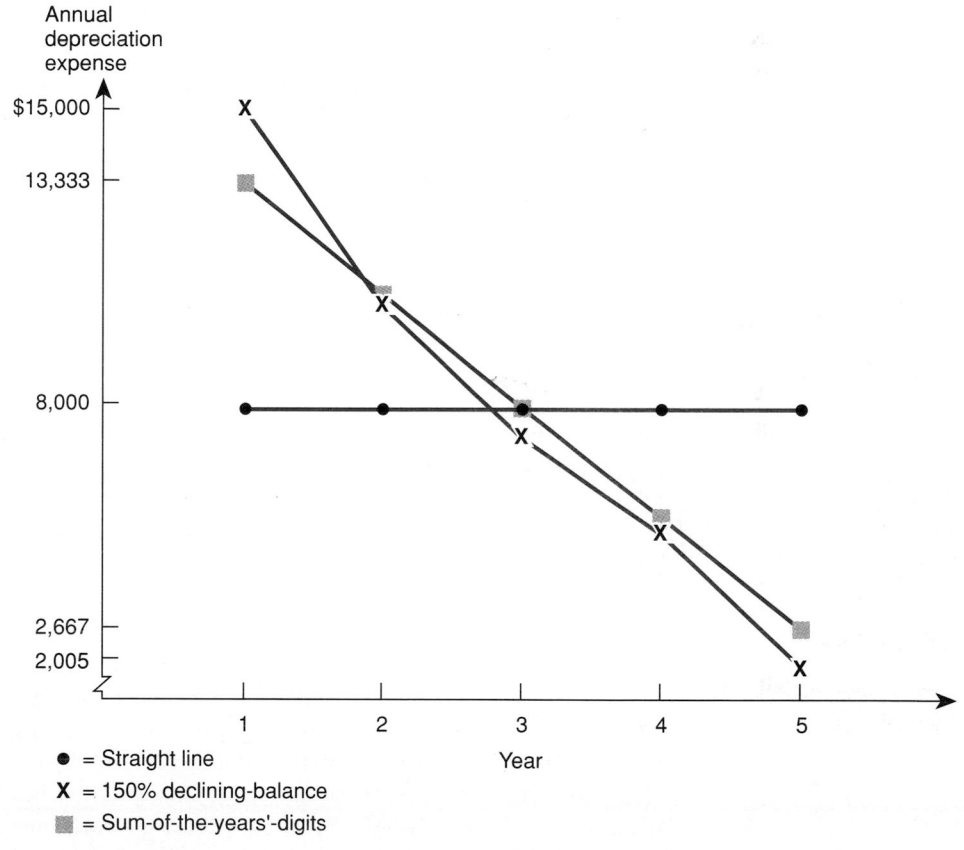

● = Straight line
X = 150% declining-balance
▩ = Sum-of-the-years'-digits

To illustrate the difference between book and tax depreciation, assume that Legislative Minds, Inc., (LMI) acquired computer equipment on January 1, 19x1, for $800,000 cash. The equipment has an estimated useful life of eight years and no salvage value. LMI uses straight-line depreciation for book purposes, but the tax laws allow the following six-year depreciation schedule:

Year of Use	Percentage of Cost to Be Depreciated
1.	20.00%
2.	32.00
3.	19.20
4.	11.52
5.	11.52
6.	5.76
	100.00%

The difference between book depreciation expense and tax depreciation expense over the life of the asset is zero, as illustrated in the following schedule:

Year	Computation of Income Tax Depreciation Expense		Straight-Line Book Depreciation Expense		Tax Expense over (under) Book Expense
1	$800,000 × .2000 = $160,000	−	$100,000	=	$ 60,000
2	800,000 × .3200 = 256,000	−	100,000	=	156,000
3	800,000 × .1920 = 153,600	−	100,000	=	53,600
4	800,000 × .1152 = 92,160	−	100,000	=	(7,840)
5	800,000 × .1152 = 92,160	−	100,000	=	(7,840)
6	800,000 × .0576 = 46,080	−	100,000	=	(53,920)
7	None 0	−	100,000		(100,000)
8	None 0	−	100,000		(100,000)
	$800,000	−	$800,000		$ 0

Notice that the depreciation expense allowed for both income tax purposes and book purposes is limited to the price paid for the equipment—$800,000. The cash outflow of $800,000 on January 1, 19x1, is offset by different patterns of depreciation expense, but total depreciation expense is $800,000 for both book and tax purposes.

Why should LMI use the accelerated method for tax purposes if it results in the same total depreciation expense? The answer to this question lies in the fact that money has "time value." In other words, $1 of cash today is worth more than $1 in five years, because it can be used to earn more cash in the five-year period. Assuming that tax rates do not change, LMI will ultimately pay the same amount of total tax whether it uses straight-line or the allowable accelerated method of depreciation. However, by using the accelerated method, LMI has more cash in the near term, which it can use to earn additional cash to help pay future taxes!

The LMI example helps explain why companies use accelerated depreciation for income tax purposes, while often using straight-line depreciation for financial reporting purposes. The relation between depreciation, income taxes, and cash flows may be summarized by the following statements:

1. A cash outflow normally occurs when a depreciable asset is acquired.
2. Recording depreciation expense does **not** involve a cash outflow, because depreciation is a noncash expense that reduces income and reduces long-term tangible assets (by increasing accumulated depreciation—a contra asset) but does **not** reduce cash.
3. Over the depreciable asset's life, **total** depreciation expense will be the same for all depreciation methods.
4. For income tax purposes, accelerated depreciation methods are preferred because they result in tax savings in the early years of an asset's life. These early tax savings mean less cash is required to pay taxes, making more cash available for investing or operating activities.

Keeping these key facts in mind will keep you from becoming confused about decisions concerning depreciable assets. We discuss how such book and tax differences are accounted for in Chapter 9.

Partial Year's Depreciation

Objective 3
How to determine
depreciation for partial
years . . .

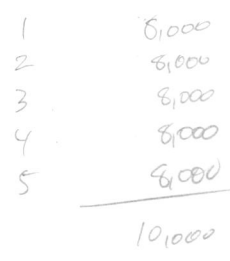

How is depreciation expense computed for assets acquired during an accounting period rather than at the start of a year? Although many options are available, the two methods most often used to determine depreciation for assets acquired during a period are

1. Round purchase date to **nearest month** and prorate depreciation for number of months used.
2. Use one half of a year's depreciation on all assets acquired or sold during the year (known as the half-year convention).

To illustrate these two methods, assume a company purchases a truck for $50,000 on May 7, 19x1, with an estimated life of five years and an estimated residual value of $10,000. Using the nearest-month approach, eight months' depreciation (May to December) would be taken in 19x1. Referring to the annual amounts reported in Exhibit 8–6, the depreciation amounts for the first two years (19x1 and 19x2) for each of the three alternatives using the nearest-month approach and the half-year convention would be as shown in Exhibit 8–7. A careful study of Exhibit 8–7 will indicate the differences in the results of the nearest-month approach and the half-year convention.

In future examples and problems, you should assume that unless otherwise stated, monthly depreciation is taken for asset acquisitions and asset disposal or retirements that do not occur at the beginning or end of a year. If assets are purchased at the beginning of the year or sold at the end of the year, use a full year's depreciation.

Group Depreciation of Tangible Assets

Some low-cost assets providing benefits for long time periods are expensed as purchased. Most companies have policies indicating the minimum dollar amount an asset must cost before it is capitalized and depreciated. It is not unusual to see large corporations expense all asset purchases below $200 to $500.

In some cases even minor assets should be capitalized and expensed over their useful lives. When needed to depreciate large numbers of minor assets, such as power hand tools, accountants often use the group depreciation method. Under this method, large quantities of similar assets are capitalized as purchased and then depreciated on a group basis rather than individually. A fixed percentage of the total value of the group of assets is then taken as depreciation expense each year. In some companies group depreciation methods are also used to account for most or all depreciable assets, and not just minor assets. Group depreciation procedures are illustrated in most intermediate accounting texts.

EXHIBIT 8–7

Comparison of Nearest-Month Approach and Half-Year Convention

Nearest-Month Approach

Year	Straight-Line	150% Declining-Balance	Sum-of-the-Years'-Digits
		Alternative Methods	
19x1	$8,000 × 8/12 = $5,333	$50,000 × .30 × 8/12 = $10,000	$40,000 × 5/15 × 8/12 = $ 8,889
19x2	$8,000	$40,000 × .30 = $12,000*	$40,000 × 5/15 × 4/12 = $ 4,444
			$40,000 × 4/15 × 8/12 = 7,111
			$11,555

*Note the second (and subsequent) year's depreciation expense may also be computed the long way as follows:

$$\$50,000 \times .30 \times 4/12 = \$ 5,000$$
$$+\ 35,000 \times .30 \times 8/12 = \underline{\ \ 7,000}$$
$$\$12,000$$

Half-Year Convention

Year	Straight-Line	150% Declining-Balance	Sum-of-the-Years'-Digits
		Alternative Methods	
19x1	$8,000 × 1/2 = $4,000	$50,000 × .30 × 1/2 = $ 7,500	$40,000 × 5/15 × 1/2 = $ 6,667
19x2	$8,000	$42,500 × .30 = $12,750	$40,000 × 5/15 × 1/2 = $ 6,667
			$40,000 × 4/15 × 1/2 = 5,333
			$12,000

Revisions in
Depreciation Estimates

*Objective 3
. . . and how to make
revisions in depreciation
estimates.*

Since depreciation is based on **estimates** of the asset's useful life and residual value at the date of acquisition, what happens when these **estimates** are no longer appropriate? To illustrate, assume that the Student Lounge acquired a new refrigeration unit for selling soda and juice, paying $46,000 cash on January 1, 19x1. At first the cooler is expected to have a useful life of four years and a residual value of $2,000. The annual straight-line depreciation expense for the cooler is computed as follows:

$$\text{Cost} \quad - \text{ Residual value} = \text{Depreciable base}$$
$$\$46,000 - \quad \$2,000 \quad = \quad \$44,000$$

$$\frac{\$44,000}{4 \text{ years}} = \underline{\$11,000} \text{ per year depreciation expense}$$

Depreciation expense of $11,000 is recorded at the end of 19x1 and the end of 19x2. However, **during** 19x3, the Lounge decides that the cooler will last five years instead of four and will have a residual value of $3,000 rather than $2,000. The book value at the **beginning** of 19x3 (year 3) is as follows:

Cooler cost	$46,000
Less: Accumulated depreciation	22,000
Book value	$24,000

No matter when changes are made in depreciation estimates, the new estimates must be applied to the remaining book value **as of the beginning of the year of the change.** The book value of the cooler at the beginning of 19x3 is $24,000. Therefore, the new depreciation rate for the last three years of the asset's useful life is calculated as follows:

Remaining book value, 1/1/x3	$24,000
Less new estimated residual value	− 3,000
Remaining depreciable base.	$21,000
Divided by remaining life	÷ 3 years
New depreciation rate.	$ 7,000 depreciation expense per year

Student Lounge will use the annual depreciation expense of $7,000 per year for 19x3, 19x4, and 19x5, the remainder of the cooler's useful life. A complete depreciation schedule for the five-year life of the cooler is

As of	Depreciation Expense	Accumulated Depreciation	Net Book Value
1/1/x1	$ 0	$ 0	$46,000
12/31/x1	11,000	11,000	35,000
12/31/x2	11,000	22,000	24,000
12/31/x3	7,000	29,000	17,000
12/31/x4	7,000	36,000	10,000
12/31/x5	7,000	43,000	3,000 *residual value*
Total	$43,000		

Remember that this procedure for changes in either useful life, residual value, or both will **affect current and future years only.** No adjustments are made to prior years' depreciation amounts for changes in estimates.

COSTS SUBSEQUENT TO ACQUISITION

After tangible assets are acquired and placed into use, additional expenditures often occur. The accountant must determine whether these costs are *capital expenditures* or *periodic expenses.* Capital expenditures are costs that provide future benefits to the asset either by extending its useful life or by continuing its productive capacity or efficiency. If an additional outlay does not meet the conditions of a capital expenditure, it is charged to income as a **period cost** or revenue expenditure in the period it is incurred. Capital expenditures may be recorded as separate new assets or as additions to the original cost of existing assets.

Typical types of capital expenditures include

Objective 4
How to account for costs capitalized or expensed subsequent to acquisition.

1. **Betterments** and **improvements** (e.g., partitions added to a building to improve customer traffic flow).
2. **Additions** (e.g., a 10-foot extension of the rear of a building for more inventory storage).
3. **Unexpected replacements** and **renewals** (e.g., a new roof on a two-year-old building).

Typical types of periodic expenses include

1. **Repairs** (e.g., replacement of broken tiles in floor).
2. **Maintenance** (e.g., the cleaning of windows twice each year).
3. **Expected replacements** and **renewals** (e.g., carpeting for a customer entryway).

The most troublesome costs subsequent to acquisition are probably replacements and renewals. When these costs are **expected** to occur accountants normally expense them as routine costs. For example, tuning an engine, replacing spark plugs, replacing factory light bulbs, painting, and carpeting are examples of replacements and renewals that are expected to occur and are normally treated as periodic expenses.

Costs that significantly extend the life, productive capacity, or efficiency of an existing asset should be capitalized and depreciated over the remaining life of the asset. Also, unexpected replacements and renewals are usually capitalized. Because of the conservative nature of accounting, when a question exists whether an item should be capitalized or expensed, the item is often expensed.

Capitalization of
Subsequent Costs

When costly renewals or replacements are not expected to occur, their costs are normally capitalized as an additional cost of the asset. The capitalization of these subsequent asset costs involves increasing the recorded amount of the tangible asset, which in turn increases the amount of periodic depreciation expense. The following example illustrates this procedure.

Assume that Legislative Minds, Inc., (LMI) owns a communications satellite for its long-distance data transmissions. On February 10, 19x5, the satellite, which originally cost $3 million, developed an unexpected malfunction. The net book value at the start of 19x5 was $2 million, with the remaining life estimated at 10 years and no residual value. A NASA space shuttle replaced the defective elements of the satellite on March 23, 19x5, at a cost of $800,000. This unexpected replacement cost is a capitalizable cost to LMI because it improved the productive capacity of the satellite from being nonproductive to being productive once again, as originally intended. If the replacement did not extend the original useful life of the satellite and if LMI uses straight-line depreciation to the nearest month, the following entries are recorded for 19x5:

19x5				
Mar. 23	Communication Satellite (A)		800,000	
	Cash (or Accounts Payable—NASA)			800,000
	To record cost of unexpected replacement.			
Dec. 31	Depreciation Expense (E)		261,538	
	Accumulated Depreciation—Satellite (XA)			261,538
	$2,000,000 ÷ 120 months × 3 months = $50,000 plus ($2,000,000 − $50,000 + $800,000) ÷ 117 months × 9 months = $211,538.			

Since the $800,000 unexpected replacement cost was necessary for reestablishing the usefulness of the satellite, it is added to the $1,950,000 remaining asset book value that is to be depreciated over the next 117 months.[4] Alternatively, if the replacement had been expected, such as for maintenance on the satellite, the entire $800,000 cost would be expensed on March 23, 19x5, and annual depreciation would remain at $200,000 per year.

When costs incurred after the acquisition of an asset have short lives and/or are relatively immaterial, they are often considered periodic expenses. Alternatively, subsequent

---

[4]Note that several other possible solutions could also be acceptable for accounting for these facts. For example, the $800,000 repair cost could be depreciated for one-half year in 19x5 instead of nine months. Also, the depreciation expense for the period the satellite was not working could be recorded as a loss instead of depreciation expense. As long as these alternatives do not result in material differences in operating results, they are all reasonable and acceptable.

EXHIBIT 8–8

Subsequent Costs

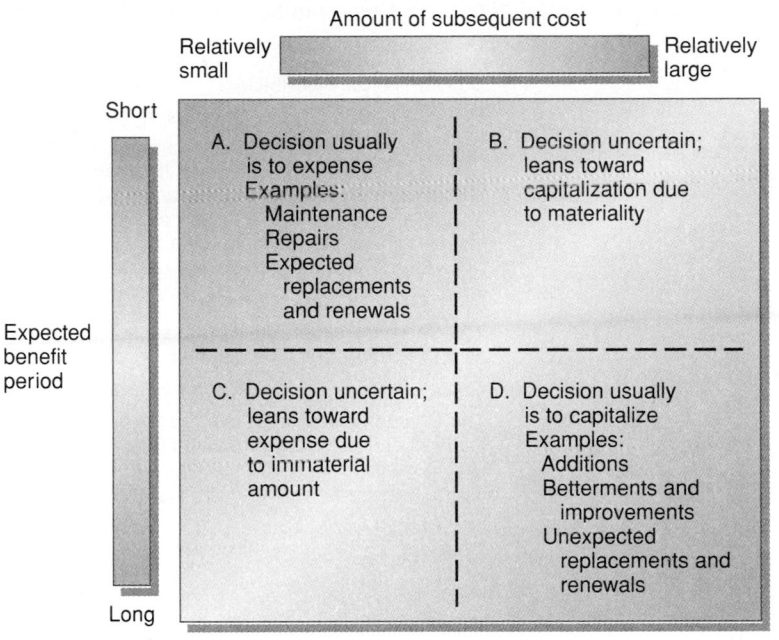

Amount of subsequent cost

Relatively small — Relatively large

Expected benefit period — Short / Long

A. Decision usually is to expense
   Examples:
      Maintenance
      Repairs
      Expected replacements and renewals

B. Decision uncertain; leans toward capitalization due to materiality

C. Decision uncertain; leans toward expense due to immaterial amount

D. Decision usually is to capitalize
   Examples:
      Additions
      Betterments and improvements
      Unexpected replacements and renewals

costs that have long lives or are relatively material in amount are usually capitalized. Exhibit 8–8 provides a decision table to aid in the evaluation of subsequent costs. Note that the table only examines four extreme situations. In practice, the cost and period of future benefit are not always easily classified as small and large or short and long. Some cases are more common and easier to decide than others, especially when the cost and useful life are both large and long or small and short as in cells A and D. The difficult decisions are those depicted in cells B and C and near the center intersection.

The annual report of Atwood Oceanics, Inc., and Subsidiaries, reproduced in Exhibit 8–9 gives an example of a cost like that shown in cell B of Exhibit 8–8. Under the heading "Deferred costs and expenses," the Atwood report explains that its vessels are brought into port about every two years for routine maintenance during drydocking. While two years is a fairly short benefit period, the costs must be relatively large (material) because Atwood expenses these costs "over the period to the next scheduled drydocking (normally two years)" rather than expensing the entire cost in the year of drydocking.

Lease Assets

Companies sometimes acquire assets and the financing of the assets in a single transaction. These are normally called leases. Leases that are essentially **purchases** of long-term assets with financing are called *capital leases,* or *financing leases.* These capital leases (asset purchases) are treated the same as other assets, with buildings, machinery, equipment, and other capital lease assets recorded as long-term assets and depreciated or amortized over the expected period of future benefits. The financing (borrowing) is accounted for like any other interest-bearing debt, in accordance with the terms of the debt contract. In essence, long-term assets acquired in a capital lease transaction are treated like other long-term assets. Chapter 10, Appendix B, discusses capital leases in more detail.

EXHIBIT 8–9

Annual Report Example

Atwood Oceanics, Inc., and Subsidiaries

Excerpt from footnotes to consolidated financial statements

(1) SUMMARY OF SIGNIFICANT ACCOUNTING POLICIES

Depreciation, maintenance and retirement policies—

Depreciation is provided on the straight-line method over the estimated useful lives of the various classifications of assets. Estimated useful lives are ten to twelve years for drilling vessels and equipment, three years for drill pipe and three to ten years for other equipment. Maintenance, repairs and minor replacements are charged against income as incurred; major replacements and betterments are capitalized and depreciated over the remaining useful life of the asset as determined upon completion of the work.

Deferred costs and expenses—

The Company defers the cost of scheduled drydocking and the cost is charged to expense over the period to the next scheduled drydocking (normally two years).

Capitalization of interest during construction—

The Company capitalizes, as cost of drilling vessels and equipment, the interest costs incurred during the construction period on funds borrowed to finance the construction of drilling vessels.

Errors in Accounting for Asset Costs after Acquisition

From discussions in earlier chapters, you should understand the importance of **accurately** recording costs incurred after the acquisition of assets. The incorrect expensing of a capital expenditure as a revenue expenditure results in (1) understating the net income of the current period because the expense is too high; (2) a fully expensed asset with no depreciation expense left for future periods, resulting in an overstated future net income; and (3) understating the current and future years' assets because no assets are recorded. Thus, this type of error can seriously affect the measurement of periodic net income and results in the mismatching of costs with their periods of benefit. To report a company's financial condition accurately, you must apply the guidelines for capital and revenue expenditures in an appropriate and consistent way.

DISPOSAL OF LONG-TERM TANGIBLE ASSETS

When a company disposes of tangible assets, all related account balances are updated and eliminated as of the date of the asset disposal. In addition, any proceeds from the sale of the asset increase the company's assets (cash). The difference between the sale proceeds and the eliminated account balances is either a gain or a loss.

In the paragraphs that follow, examples are given for asset disposals at net book value, disposals involving gains or losses, and disposals of fully depreciated assets. In all of these examples, we assume that the **book value of the assets has been adjusted to the date of disposal.**

Disposals at Net Book Value

Objective 5
How to record disposals of tangible assets at net book value, disposals involving gains or losses, and disposals of fully depreciated assets.

Assume that LMI sold 15 fully depreciated microcomputers on January 1, 19x5, for $9,000. Originally, the computers cost $3,500 each. They had an estimated residual value of $600 each (or, 15 × $600 = $9,000 total) and were fully depreciated as of December 31, 19x4. The relevant account balances just before recording the sale were:

Microcomputers (15)		Accumulated Depreciation— Microcomputers (15)	
52,500			43,500

The entry to record the sale of the 15 microcomputers is:

```
19x5
Jan. 1   Cash (A). . . . . . . . . . . . . . . . . . . . . . . . . .        9,000
             Accumulated Depreciation—Microcomputers (XA) . . . . . . . . .   43,500
                 Microcomputers (A) . . . . . . . . . . . . . . . . . . . .           52,500
                 To record sale of 15 microcomputers at net book value.
```

Note that this entry records the inflows and outflows of net assets at the time of exchange. The outflows (assets given up) are recorded by eliminating the balances in all accounts pertaining to the microcomputers (the asset and the accumulated depreciation accounts). The inflows are recorded by an increase in cash, the asset received in the transaction. In this example, the net book value of the assets given up ($52,500 asset less $43,500 contra asset equals $9,000 net book value) and the asset received (cash, $9,000) are equal; therefore, the disposal of the computers did not result in a gain or loss.

Disposals Involving Gains or Losses

When the net book value of assets given up differs from the fair market value of the assets received in the exchange, a gain or loss occurs. In the computer example given above, we can assume that because an outside party was willing to pay $9,000 for the 15 used computers, the fair market value of the computers happened to equal their book value at January 1, 19x5. The following examples illustrate the more typical cases where book value differs from fair value at the time of disposal.

Proceeds in Excess of Net Book Value.   To illustrate a gain on the disposal of assets, assume now that LMI sold the 15 micros on January 1, 19x5, for $12,000 instead of $9,000. The following entry would be recorded:

```
19x5
Jan. 1   Cash (A). . . . . . . . . . . . . . . . . . . . . . . . . .      $12,000
             Accumulated Depreciation—Microcomputers (XA) . . . . . . . . .   43,500
                 Microcomputers (A) . . . . . . . . . . . . . . . . . . . .           52,500
    Revenue →    Gain on Sale of Computers (R). . . . . . . . . . . . . .              3,000
                 To record sale of microcomputers.
```

Whenever the value of the assets received (cash of $12,000 in this case) is greater than the net book value of the assets disposed of, a gain will result. This situation occurs because the depreciation (cost allocation) process is *not* a valuation process. In other words, depreciation is not intended to reflect the change in an asset's market value. Depreciation is simply a way of assigning the asset's depreciable base (*original* cost less salvage value) to the years of benefit. Therefore, it is very unusual for the net book value to equal market value for depreciable assets during their useful life. And, at the end of the asset's useful life it is also common to have the salvage value (an amount that is based on an *estimate* at the time of purchase) not equal the market value, since there is normally much uncertainty about the value of fully depreciated assets.

Proceeds Less than Book Value.   To illustrate a loss on the disposal of an asset, refer again to the LMI example. Assume now that the computers are sold for $5,000 on January 1, 19x5. The following entry would be recorded:

```
19x5
Jan. 1   Cash (A). . . . . . . . . . . . . . . . . . . . . . . . . .        5,000
             Accumulated Depreciation—Microcomputers (XA) . . . . . . . . .   43,500
    Expense →   Loss on Sale of Computers (E) . . . . . . . . . . . . . .      4,000
                 Microcomputers (A) . . . . . . . . . . . . . . . . . . . .           52,500
                 To record sale of microcomputers.
```

Whenever the value of assets received is less than the net book value of the assets disposed of, a loss will result.

ANALYSIS OF CHANGES IN LONG-TERM ASSETS

In previous chapters you were introduced to the importance of knowing how to evaluate a company's financial reports. Understanding the relationship between the long-term asset accounts (e.g., asset and accumulated depreciation) and other account balances is also useful in financial report analysis. Often this knowledge can be used to obtain information about the acquisitions and disposals of long-term assets that is not explicitly reported in the financial statements.

The relationship between long-term accounts and other accounts can best be understood by examining the reasons for changes in the account balances. For example, consider the following accounts associated with a tangible asset:

Balance Sheet Accounts:

Plant and Equipment		Accumulated Depreciation— Plant and Equipment	
Beg. bal.			Beg. bal.
Increases	*Decreases*	*Decreases*	*Increases*
(1) Buy new assets	(3) Sell or retire old assets	(3) Sell or retire old assets	(2) Depreciation expense on assets
End. bal.			End. bal.

Income Statement Account:

Depreciation Expense	
Increases	
(2) Annual depreciation expense	

To illustrate the three types of changes that effect these T accounts, assume the following three entries:

(1)	Plant and Equipment (A).	40,000	
	Cash (A).		40,000
	To record acquisition of new assets.		

(2)	Depreciation Expense (E)	8,000	
	Accumulated Depreciation—Plant and Equipment (XA)		8,000
	To record annual depreciation expense on plant assets.		

(3)	Cash (A).	400	
	Accumulated Depreciation—Plant Equipment (XA)	9,000	
	Plant and Equipment (A).		9,200
	Gain on Sale of Plant Equipment (R)		200
	To record sale of assets.		

The published financial statements do not always provide information on the purchase and sale of plant assets (1 and 3 above); however, major purchases (1 above) are often reported in the statement of cash flows as an investing activity of the company.

Objective 6
The importance of evaluating changes in plant assets.

To illustrate how you might use your understanding of these relationships, assume that LMI reported the following data:

	19x7	19x6
From balance sheet data:		
Equipment (at cost)	$12,000	$14,000
Accumulated depreciation—equipment.	(7,500)	(8,000)
From income statement or statement of cash flows data:		
Depreciation expense—equipment.	600	550
From statement of cash flows data:		
Investment in equipment	850	320

Using T accounts to evaluate the changes in equipment for 19x7, the following data are known:

	Equipment				Accumulated Depreciation— Equipment	
Bal.	14,000				8,000	Bal.
(1)	850		?	?	600	(2)
Bal.	12,000				7,500	Bal.

The amounts in the above T accounts represent

1.   Purchases of equipment given in statement of cash flows.
2.   Depreciation expense given in income statement.
Bal. Beginning and ending balances given in the balance sheet.

The credit to Equipment that is needed to balance the account is $2,850 ($14,000 + $850 − $12,000). Also, the debit to Accumulated Depreciation—Equipment must be $1,100 ($8,000 + $600 − $7,500). Apparently, LMI sold equipment that had cost $2,850 with accumulated depreciation of $1,100 taken prior to the sale. The known elements of the entry to record this sale are the following:

(3)	Cash (A)	?	
	Accumulated Depreciation—Equipment (XA)	1,100	
	Gain or Loss on Sale of Equipment (R or E)	?	?
	Equipment (A)		2,850
	To record sale of equipment.		

Investors may be interested in the additional insight that LMI sold equipment that was less than 50% depreciated. This could indicate new technology in their manufacturing process, or perhaps equipment purchases that were not well planned in some prior year. In any case, understanding the relationship between long-term assets and other accounts is useful in acquiring data on asset disposals that might not be detailed in the financial statements.

Using the Analysis of Long-Term Assets

The analysis of changes in long-term assets illustrated above can be useful for evaluating and comparing financial statements. Before Brad and Mary gave the Byte-Size financial statements to their banker, for comparison purposes they decided to see how similar companies were reporting long-term assets. From the recent year-end financial statements of a competitor, Computrak, Inc., they obtained the following financial statement data:

From Computrak's Balance Sheet:

	19x3	19x2
Equipment (at cost)	$20,500	$20,000
Accumulated depreciation—equipment	(8,250)	(8,000)
Net equipment	$12,250	$12,000

From Computrak's Statement of Cash Flows:

Depreciation expense—equipment (added back to net income to get cash flows from operating activities)	$ 2,050	$ 2,000
Cash used for investment in equipment	$ 5,000	0
Cash from the sale of equipment	$ 3,500	0

Let us listen to Brad and Mary as they evaluate these financial statement results.

Brad: (looking over Computrak's financial report): Hey, Mary, we should look at how Computrak accounts for their equipment to see if our estimates of useful life and our method of depreciation are in line with our competitor's.

Mary: Good idea. Let's see what they're using for the useful life of their equipment. I'm not sure how long our useful life should be.

Brad: How can we do that? In their footnotes to their financial statements it only says they're using straight-line depreciation. They don't say anything about useful life.

Mary: Brad, you might be good at the technical part of accounting, but you didn't get much out of the analysis part of the course. Look at the depreciation expense compared to the cost of the equipment and it will give you some idea.

Brad (looking at the balance sheet): Well, the change in accumulated depreciation is $8,250 − $8,000, or $250, so it appears that their equipment will last about 82 years. (Brad has divided the $20,500 cost at 12/31/x3 by the $250 change in accumulated depreciation.)

Mary: That's good, Brad, but 82 years seem a bit unreasonable. Also, you can't be sure that the change in accumulated depreciation between 19x2 and 19x3 is the total depreciation expense for 19x3. What if they sold some equipment during 19x3?

Brad: Well, how can we tell? It appears to me that they bought $500 of new equipment during 19x3, because the "equipment (at cost)" went from $20,000 to $20,500.

Mary: That doesn't prove that they didn't sell anything, Brad. They could have simply bought $500 more than what they sold. Look, if $250 was the annual depreciation expense, and Computrak uses straight-line depreciation, the 12/31/x2 balance of $8,000 in accumulated depreciation would suggest that they've been in business about 33 years. (Mary divides $8,250 by $250 for Brad to see).

Brad: That can't be right then. I know Computrak has been in business for five years. Too bad they don't report depreciation expense as a separate expense in their income statement. What good is this analysis Mary?

Mary: Brad, just be patient. You can usually find the depreciation expense amount in the statement of cash flows—it is usually added back to net income to get "cash from operations" because it is an expense deducted to compute net income that does **not** use cash. The cash flow statement will also usually tell you about cash used for purchases of long-term assets as well as the cash received from the sale of long-term assets. Let's look. (Mary flips to Computrak's cash flow statement.)

Brad: You're right, Mary. This says that the 19x3 depreciation expense was $2,050. How can that be?

Mary: Look, Brad, just take all the information you have now and put it into the following structure:

Equipment (at cost)			Accumulated Depreciation		

Beg. bal.
Acquisitions
		Sold
		  equipment
			Depreciation taken
			  on sold equipment
					Beg. bal.
					Depreciation
					  expense

End. bal.					End. bal.

Brad: OK, let's see. From the balance sheet and the cash flow statement, we know the following data:

Equipment (at cost)				Accumulated Depreciation		
(12/31/x2)	20,000				8,000	(12/31/x2)
(Acquired)	5,000	(Sold?)	(Sold?)		2,050	(Depr. exp.)
(12/31/x3)	20,500				8,250	(12/31/x3)

Mary: Now plug in the missing amounts needed to make the accounts balance.

Brad: Oh, I see; like so. . . .

Equipment (at cost)				Accumulated Depreciation	
	20,000				8,000
	5,000	4,500		1,800	2,050
	20,500				8,250

Mary: Right. Now we can see that they sold equipment with an original cost of $4,500 and accumulated depreciation of $1,800 during 19x3. The cash flow statement says they received $3,500 from the sale of equipment, so their journal entry to record the sale must have been like so. . . .

Accumulated Depreciation	1,800	
Cash	3,500	
Equipment (at cost)		4,500
Gain on Sale.		800

Brad: That's good Mary. But what about the life of their equipment? We still don't have an estimate.

Mary: That's easy, Brad. Let's take the depreciation expense from 19x2, $2,000, and divide it into the original cost of $20,000. That's 10 years as an estimated total life. Now, we can check it by dividing $2,000 into the accumulated depreciation at 12/31/x2 of $8,000—that's four years already used as of the end of the *last year*. You said they've been in business five years, so that seems to check out OK, Brad. I'd say 10 years is a good estimate of what they're using as a useful life for their equipment.

Brad: Nice work, Mary! We were guessing about a seven-year life for our equipment. I know we have the same sort of equipment, too. I suggest we also use a 10-year life.

Mary: I agree. It will make our measure of income more comparable to that of our main competitor. The bank shouldn't complain about that.

Brad: Absolutely not, expecially once you show them your supporting analysis of the competition, Mary. This is really good work!

This vignette helps us to understand how financial statement analysis can be used as a basis for business decisions. This type of analysis can help financial statement users compare and evaluate the financial statements of similar companies for a wide variety of decision-making purposes, including performance evaluation and investment or credit-granting decisions regarding plant and equipment.

INTANGIBLE ASSETS

As noted earlier, the value of intangibles stems from the rights they provide rather than their physical form. Most intangibles are legal documents whose physical form is merely paper. However, the rights that intangibles document may be extremely important assets of a business. Intangible assets are often classified as identifiable and unidentifiable intangibles.

Objective 7
Accounting for long-term
intangible assets.

Identifiable intangibles are separate and specifically identifiable items, while unidentifiable intangibles are **not** separate or observable assets. Examples of identifiable and unidentifiable intangibles follow.

Identifiable intangibles:

Patents

Copyrights

Trademarks and brand names

Franchises and licenses

Research and development (R&D)

Computer software development

Organization costs

Unidentifiable intangibles:

Goodwill

These identifiable and unidentifiable intangibles are discussed in this section.

As was described earlier in this chapter, the costs of all intangibles are allocated (expensed) to the income statement of the benefit period by **amortization.** Amortization expense for intangible assets is essentially the same as depreciation expense for tangible assets. **Intangibles must be amortized over a period of 40 years, their economic useful life, or legal life, whichever is less.**[5]

Accounting for
Identifiable Intangibles

Accounting for the life cycle of intangibles is very similar to the accounting for tangible assets, discussed in the first part of this chapter. Intangibles are recorded at the cost necessary to obtain them. The cost of intangibles is often small, consisting primarily of legal fees and perhaps the cost of a prototype or sample of the item to which the intangible pertains (e.g., patented invention).

Amortization of intangible assets is on a straight-line basis in virtually all cases, and contra asset accounts are usually not used. If an intangible asset cost $36,000 and has an estimated useful life of 18 years, the following entry is made each year for 18 years:

Amortization Expense (E)   2,000
    Intangible Asset (A)   2,000
        $36,000/18 years = $2,000 per year amortization expense.

The paragraphs that follow discuss most common identifiable intangibles, including patents, copyrights, trademarks and brand names, franchises and licenses, research and development (R&D) costs, computer software development costs, and organization costs.

Patents.   The federal government grants patents to the inventor of a new product or process. Patents entitle the inventor to the exclusive right to use the product or process, or to sell it to others for their use, for a 17-year period. Because patents often deal with products or processes that are subject to rapid technological change, their useful lives may often be less than their 17-year legal life.

The recorded cost of a patent is limited to its legal costs plus the actual cost of developing the prototype. If patents are purchased from their inventor, they are recorded at the price paid for the patent. The legal costs of successfully defending patent rights in court are capitalized as part of the patents. However, if the defense of a patent fails, the patent is worthless and written off as a loss.

---

[5]See *APB Opinion No. 17,* "Intangible Assets" (New York: AICPA, 1970).

Copyrights. The federal government grants copyrights for literary or artistic works. When copyrights are granted to a business, the rights are for a 75-year period; when granted to an individual, the rights are for the life of the creator plus 50 years. The cost of developing copyrighted material is usually small; however, copyrights purchased from their creator may be costly. The useful lives of most copyrights are much less than their legal lives.

Trademarks and Brand Names. Words, symbols, or designs used to identify and distinguish a product or group of products are called trademarks and brand names. They are registered with the federal government and do not expire. The cost of developing trademarks or brand names at the time they are registered is usually insignificant, resulting in a relatively low asset value. However, for successful products, such as Coca-Cola or Chevrolet, these symbols or names can be valuable. No legal limit exists for the life of trademarks and brand names; therefore, their costs should be amortized over the lesser of 40 years or their expected economic life (as with all other intangibles).

Franchises and Licenses. Franchises and licenses are rights granted by a government or a private enterprise to distribute, sell, service, or otherwise handle a specified line of goods and/or services. Governmental units grant licenses to drive automobiles, sell liquor, fish, hunt, and so on. Private businesses grant franchises for Taco Bell restaurants, Days Inn motels, National Football League teams, and so on. The length of the rights granted by the license or franchise depends on the terms stipulated in each agreement. The cost of the license or franchise agreement should be recorded as an asset and amortized over its economic life, but not in excess of 40 years.

Research and Development (R&D) Costs. Research and development (R&D) costs are incurred in searching for new knowledge (research) that may be used to create new products or to improve old products or services (development). Some industries, such as the aerospace, computer, and ethical drug industries, undergo rapid change and spend considerable amounts on R&D activities to maintain their competitive advantage.

For the past two decades, accounting for R&D costs has been a controversial topic. The key issue is the uncertain and unmeasurable nature of the future benefits expected from the current period's R&D activity. Often judgment plays a crucial role in deciding whether any given expenditure or R&D project has future benefits (revenue), thus making the difference between either capitalization or expensing huge amounts. To avoid these measurement problems, the FASB has decided that all routine R&D costs should be expensed as incurred.[6] As a result, even though some R&D activity seems to represent an intangible asset with future economic benefits, R&D costs are not normally capitalized as intangible assets. In most countries the treatment of R&D is the same as in the United States. However, in Spain and in Hong Kong, R&D need not be expensed, but can be capitalized and amortized over future periods.

Computer Software Development. Many small companies are in the business of developing computer software. Because the costs of developing the computer programs (the intangible assets) represent a major part of the "assets" of many software developers, the FASB has established separate guidelines for these businesses.[7] Software developers are required to expense all R&D costs until the "technological feasibility" of the software

---

[6]See *FASB Statement No. 2,* "Accounting for Research and Development Costs" (Norwalk, Conn.: FASB, 1974).

[7]*FASB Statement No. 86,* "Accounting for the Cost of Computer Software to Be Sold, Leased or Otherwise Marketed" (Norwalk, Conn.: FASB, 1985).

product has been established. The detailed guidelines for determining exactly when technological feasibility of a product occurs (covered in more detail in *FASB Statement No. 86*) is ultimately dependent on professional judgment. After technological feasibility of a software product has been established, development costs are capitalized as assets. These capitalized costs are amortized over 40 years or the estimated product life, whichever is shorter.

Organization Costs.   The costs incurred in establishing a business are called organization costs. They are normally capitalized as an intangible asset. These costs include expenditures for legal fees and the filing fees necessary for filing for incorporation (or partnership papers, and so on) and for doing business in a state or states; license fees; accounting fees for developing a recordkeeping system; computer software fees for developing an information processing system; cost of the initial stock offering (if a corporation); and other similar costs involved in preparation for business operations.

In theory, organization costs are either expenses or permanent assets. Thus, at the time the costs are incurred, they could have future benefit or have no future benefit. However, since organization costs are the costs of starting the business and a business is expected to continue indefinitely, it is unlikely that you would expect these costs to benefit only a portion of the life of the business. As a result, you might argue for either permanent (life of the business) capitalization or immediate expensing of such costs.

In practice, organization costs are normally capitalized and expensed (amortized) over a five-year period. This is the usual income tax treatment of these costs, and companies normally follow this same procedure for financial reporting purposes. In any case, GAAP requires all intangibles to be amortized over time spans no longer than 40 years.

Accounting for Unidentifiable Intangibles: Goodwill

The primary unidentifiable intangible asset is goodwill. Since goodwill can have many possible characteristics, it is considered a complex and unusual asset to record. Goodwill can include a superior management talent, business location, product reputation, customer loyalty, and future earnings potential. All of these attributes can result in unrecorded assets that lead to future benefits for the business. It is considered an unidentifiable intangible because its makeup is too complex to be attributed to any one of the many attributes that represent goodwill. As a result, goodwill is defined as representing the otherwise unrecorded assets of the business.

Goodwill is one of the possible reasons for the difference between the book value of the firm's net assets, as measured under GAAP, and the market value of the firm's net assets, as measured by the market price of its shares of stock in the case of a publicly owned corporation. The difference between a firm's book value and its market value may be attributable to the following two elements.

1. Goodwill: the market value of the unrecorded net assets of the firm (e.g., the human assets of the firm).
2. Asset revaluations: the difference between the reported book value of the firm's net assets and their current fair market value.

Although the market value of a publicly traded firm is readily available, accounting under U.S. GAAP does not permit firms to record their own goodwill or to revalue their assets.[8] Generally accepted accounting principles hold that goodwill **must be purchased from an outside party to be recorded as an asset.** The purchase transaction satisfies the need for objective, verifiable measurement of an asset's value that would be absent for

---

[8]Interestingly, a number of other countries, including the United Kingdom, France, and Sweden, allow revaluation of plant assets to their current value.

goodwill not purchased. Thus, goodwill is recorded only when one company purchases another company. Recorded goodwill is amortized over 40 years or the expected period of economic benefit, whichever is less.

The following information about Graphic Corporation on December 31, 19x1, illustrates how goodwill is measured and recorded:

Graphic Corporation
Balance Sheet Data
December 31, 19x1

Recorded Items on Books	Estimated Market Value	Recorded Book Value
Assets (various)	$560,000	$490,000
Liabilities (various)	200,000	200,000
Net assets	$360,000	$290,000

Note that the recorded or "identifiable," net assets have a book value of $290,000 as of December 31, 19x1, and an estimated $360,000 fair market value. Assume that Baird Corporation is able to purchase Graphic's net assets for $400,000 cash on January 1, 19x2. For accounting purposes, **goodwill is measured as the excess of the price paid over the fair market value of the *identifiable* net assets acquired.** In this case, goodwill is $40,000 ($400,000 − $360,000) and would be recorded on Baird's books as follows:

```
19x2
Jan.  1   Various Assets (A) . . . . . . . . . . . . . . . . . . . . .   560,000
          Goodwill (A) . . . . . . . . . . . . . . . . . . . . . . .    40,000
              Various Liabilities (L) . . . . . . . . . . . . . . . . . . .          200,000
              Cash (A)  . . . . . . . . . . . . . . . . . . . . . . .          400,000
          To record the purchase of Graphic Corporation.
```

Note that Graphic's book values are not used by Baird Corporation in recording the purchase. Assuming a 40-year amortization period, Baird would record the following entry each year-end:

```
19x2
Dec. 31   Amortization Expense—Goodwill (E) . . . . . . . . . . . . . . .    1,000
              Goodwill (A) . . . . . . . . . . . . . . . . . . . . . . .            1,000
          To record annual amortization of goodwill.
```

From the above transaction, we can see why it is appropriate to define goodwill as the unrecorded assets of a business. Apparently, Baird was willing to pay $40,000 more than the fair market value of Graphic's **identifiable** net assets because of Graphic's **unrecorded** assets.

Companies such as Baird Corporation can use many ways to estimate the amount of unrecorded assets of an investment like Graphic Corporation. However, for accounting purposes, goodwill is always measured as the difference between the purchase price and the fair market value of the net assets acquired.

• SUMMARY

This chapter introduced you to the life cycle of long-term assets, which involves their acquisition, depreciation, costs subsequent to acquisition, and disposal. Long-term asset acquisition cost includes all costs necessary for placing the asset into its intended state.

The depreciation of tangible assets includes determining the asset's depreciable base and choosing a depreciation method. In this chapter we discussed straight-line depreciation, units-of-output depreciation, and two accelerated depreciation methods, declining-balance and sum-of-the-years'-digits. Tangible asset depreciation also involves accounting for partial year depreciation as well as making revisions in depreciation estimates.

When additional expenditures occur after long-term tangible assets are acquired and placed into use, accountants must determine whether these costs should be capitalized or expensed. In general, costs that provide future benefits to the asset are capitalized; other costs are expensed.

When a company disposes of a long-term asset, the company updates the asset's depreciation or amortization expense and eliminates all amounts related to the asset from its books. Examples were given in the chapter of disposals at net book value, disposals involving gains or losses, and disposals of fully depreciated assets.

You know from previous chapters that one of the goals of studying this textbook is to learn how to evaluate a company's financial statements. This chapter included a section on financial statement evaluation as it pertains to changes in long-term assets. This form of financial statements analysis can often result in additional information not explicitly reported in the financial statements.

The last section of the chapter examined the identifiable intangibles (patents, copyrights, trademarks and trade names, franchises and licenses, R&D, computer software development, and organization costs) and goodwill. While a few unique features apply to intangibles, most procedures used to account for the life cycle of intangibles—from acquisition to disposal—are similar to those for long-term tangible assets.

Two appendixes follow this summary. They provide information on accounting for asset exchanges and natural resources. You will find this additional information helpful in establishing a complete picture of what accountants include in accounting for long-term assets.

• DEMONSTRATION EXERCISE

Linear Graphics, Inc., purchased a new graphics printer on January 1, 19x1, for $75,000 with an estimated life of four years and a $15,000 residual value. It is also estimated that the printer will be used by the company for a total of 30,000 hours. During 19x1, the printer was used for 12,570 hours, and during 19x2 for 8,620 hours.

Required:
Compute depreciation expense for 19x1 and 19x2 using the following depreciation methods.

a. Straight-line.
b. Units-of-output.
c. Sum-of-the-years'-digits.
d. 150% declining-balance.

Solution:

Year	Straight-Line	Units-of-Output	Sum-of-the-Years'-Digits	150% Declining-Balance
19x1.	$15,000	$25,140	$24,000	$28,125
19x2.	15,000	17,240	18,000	17,578

Computations:
Straight-line depreciation method:

$$\frac{\$75,000 - \$15,000}{4 \text{ years}} = \$15,000 \text{ depreciation expense per year}$$

Units-of-output depreciation method:

$$\frac{\$75,000 - \$15,000}{30,000 \text{ hours}} = \$2 \text{ depreciation expense per hour}$$

19x1: $12,570 \times \$2 = \$25,140$

19x2: $8,620 \times \$2 = \$17,240$

Sum-of-the-years'-digits depreciation method:

Denominator $= 1 + 2 + 3 + 4 = 10$

19x1: $(\$75,000 - \$15,000) \times 4/10 = \$24,000$

19x2: $(\$75,000 - \$15,000) \times 3/10 = \$18,000$

150% declining-balance depreciation method:

Rate: Straight-line rate $\times$ 150% = 150% declining-balance rate

$.25 \times 1.5 = 37.5\%$ or $.375$

19x1: $\$75,000 \times .375 = \$28,125$

19x2: $(\$75,000 - \$28,125) \times .375 = \$17,578$

Asset Exchanges

Sometimes companies exchange long-term assets for other assets before the original assets have been fully depreciated. When this occurs, accountants record the exchange in a manner similar to the disposal of assets that are **not** fully depreciated. The assets given up are recorded as outflows, the assets acquired are recorded as inflows, and any differences are recorded as gains or losses on the exchange. This general method of accounting for exchanges, called the **fair value method** (or the **fair market value method**), is the first topic discussed in this appendix.

Although the fair value method of recording asset exchanges is appropriate for most asset exchanges, this appendix also discusses two exceptions: (1) the exchange treatment due to income tax laws and (2) the special accounting rule for certain exchanges involving similar assets.

FAIR VALUE METHOD OF RECORDING ASSET EXCHANGES

The fair value method of recording exchanges treats the assets given up as outflows and the assets acquired as inflows. To illustrate, assume Baker Construction Company owned a grader originally costing $45,000 that had $26,000 recorded accumulated depreciation (net book value is $19,000) as of December 31, 19x1. On December 31, 19x1, Baker traded the grader for a new semitractor that would move machinery from one job to another. The semitractor had a fair market value (or cash price) of $88,000 and an expected useful life of five years (no scrap value). Baker acquired the semi by paying $70,000 cash plus the old grader. The fair value of the assets given and received is computed as follows:

Fair Value of Assets Received		Fair Value of Assets Given	
Semi	$88,000 (cash price)	Cash	$70,000
		Grader	18,000*
			$88,000

*Cash value of semi	$88,000
Less cash paid by Baker.	− 70,000
Fair value of used grader	$18,000

The gain or loss on the transaction is computed by taking the difference between the fair market value and the book value of the assets given in the exchange (the same as in the asset disposals illustrated earlier), as follows:

*Objective 8
Accounting for asset exchanges.*

Assets Given	Fair Value of Assets Given	−	Less Book Value of Assets Given	=	Gain or (Loss) on Exchange
Cash.	$70,000		$70,000		$ 0
Grader	18,000		19,000		(1,000)
Total	$88,000		$89,000		$(1,000)

The book value of the grader ($19,000) was $1,000 more than the fair market value of the grader, resulting in a loss on the exchange. The entry to record this asset exchange is

19x1			
Dec. 31	Equipment—Semitractor (A)	88,000	
	Accumulated Depreciation—Grader (XA).	26,000	
	Loss on Exchange (E)	1,000	
	Equipment—Grader (A)		45,000
	Cash (A)		70,000
	To record the exchange of a grader for a new semi.		

Notice that the fair market values of the assets received are known in the example above, since the semitractor's cash price was given as $88,000. This made it fairly easy to compute the apparent fair market value of the used grader because **the fair value of assets given and received must be equal in any arm's-length transaction.**[9] Sometimes, the fair market value of the asset received (the new asset) and the fair market value of the asset given (the used equipment) are both unknown, making it difficult to record the exchange transaction. Often the income tax method, described below, is used to record such exchange transactions.

INCOME TAX METHOD

Because of the difficulty in measuring the fair value of the assets given or received in many exchange transactions, the income tax laws normally require special treatment for asset exchanges. In general, **tax laws do not recognize gains or losses on the exchange of assets.** For tax purposes, any gain or loss is deducted or added to the book value of the newly acquired asset. To illustrate, in the semitractor example Baker Construction would record the following:

19x1			
Dec. 31	Equipment—Semitractor (A)	89,000	
	Accumulated Depreciation—Grader (XA).	26,000*	
	Equipment—Grader (A)		45,000*
	Cash (A)		70,000*
	To record the exchange for tax purposes.		

Note that the figures marked with an asterisk (*) are the same as in the previous entry, which recorded the exchange using the fair market value method. These components of the entry, which record the outflow of the old asset and the cash flow effect must always be the same no matter which method is used. To change these figures would be to change the economic facts of the situation. Since the grader no longer is Baker's asset, Baker must eliminate the original cost of the grader ($45,000) and its accumulated depreciation to date ($26,000). Also, the cash outflow must be recorded since it is the amount paid by Baker.

Note, however, that for the new asset, the income tax method results in a different asset value than the fair market value method. For tax purposes, Baker shows no loss, but the company will record depreciation expense of $89,000 over the life of the semi (assuming no scrap value), resulting in total changes to income of $89,000. For financial reporting purposes, Baker should use the fair market value method, which results in a $1,000 loss plus $88,000 depreciation expense over the life of the asset. Both methods result in total charges to earnings of $89,000.

---

[9]In other words, there is no reason to believe that the semi dealer would accept less than $88,000 in value for the semi from Baker Construction.

SPECIAL EXCHANGE CASE

The accounting policymakers have ruled that a special gain recognition formula must be used that defers recognition of any resulting gain for asset exchanges when

1. Similar productive assets are exchanged.
2. A gain would result using the fair market value.
3. Both assets given and received have the ability to generate future earnings.[10]

Only when these three conditions are present can companies use the special measurement method. Thus, many asset exchanges would not be affected by the special case procedures, and the fair market value method would be used for financial reporting purposes. Since gains and losses are normally not recorded for tax purposes, the special procedures do not apply to income tax reporting.

• Demonstration Exercise

Andrew's Body Shop purchased a paint machine on March 31, 19x1, for $14,780. The machine had a salvage value of $500 and an expected life of seven years. Straight-line depreciation on a monthly basis was used in allocating the machine's cost over its useful life. On July 20, 19x5, J. Andrew sold the machine.

Required:
1. Assuming that depreciation expense has been correctly recorded as of December 31, 19x4, record depreciation expense to date of disposal using the nearest-month approach.
2. Record the journal entry if the machine is
   a. Sold for cash equal to its net book value.
   b. Sold for $4,800 cash.
   c. Sold for $7,200 cash.
   d. Exchanged for a different type of equipment valued at $18,900; $12,500 in cash is also given for the new equipment. Use the fair value method to record this exchange.

Solution:

1. $\dfrac{\$14,780 - \$500}{7 \times 12 \text{ months}} = \$170$ depreciation per month

$\$170 \times 7$ months $= \$1,190$ depreciation expense for December 31, 19x4, to July 20, 19x5

19x5			
July 20	Depreciation Expense	1,190	
	Accumulated Depreciation—Equipment		1,190
	To record depreciation to date of disposal.		

2. Accumulated depreciation:

19x1:	9 × $170 =	$1,530
19x2:	12 × 170 =	2,040
19x3:	12 × 170 =	2,040
19x4:	12 × 170 =	2,040
19x5:	7 × 170 =	1,190
		$8,840

---

[10]For an explanation of this procedure, see *APB Opinion No. 29,* "Accounting for Nonmonetary Transactions" (New York: AICPA, 1973).

a. Cash (A)   5,940
    Accumulated Depreciation—Equipment (XA)   8,840
        Equipment (A)   14,780
    To record disposal of equipment at NBV.

b. Cash (A)   4,800
    Accumulated Depreciation—Equipment (XA)   8,840
    Loss on Sale of Equipment (E)   1,140
        Equipment (A)   14,780
    To record disposal of equipment at less than NBV.

c. Cash (A)   7,200
    Accumulated Depreciation—Equipment (XA)   8,840
        Equipment (A)   14,780
        Gain on Sale of Equipment (R)   1,260
    To record disposal of equipment for more than NBV.

d. Equipment (A)   18,900
    Accumulated Depreciation—Equipment (XA)   8,840
        Equipment (A)   14,780
        Cash (A)   12,500
        Gain on Exchange (R)   460
    To record exchange of equipment.

APPENDIX • 8B

Accounting for Natural Resources

Natural resources include iron ore, crude oil, natural gas, and timberlands. Like plant, equipment, furniture, and so on, natural resources are wasting assets; however, in several respects they are different. Instead of being purchased, natural resources are usually discovered. As a result, their cost does not represent their fair market value at time of acquisition but is usually far less than their fair value. For example, suppose that a company spends $25,000 to search for natural gas that is worth $1 million at the date of discovery. The cost of the resources is recorded as $25,000. Normal practice is that the profit of $975,000 is recognized only when the resource is sold for $1 million.

Accounting for natural resources involves recording their depletion, recording changes in estimated amounts of natural resources, treating asset costs associated with extracting natural resources, and understanding statutory depletion rates. These topics are discussed in this appendix.

DEPLETION OF NATURAL RESOURCES

Objective 9
Accounting for natural resources.

The recorded cost of natural resources consists of the costs necessary and reasonable to purchase (or discover) the natural resources. Once extracted, natural resources are either sold to another company for further processing or they are processed further by the company that extracted them. In either case, the natural resources normally are reclassified from the asset Natural Resources to the asset Inventory once they are extracted. They remain in Inventory until they are expensed as cost of goods sold once a sale has occurred. The entries that follow record a discovery of oil in early 19x1, and the depletion (extraction) of the oil during 19x1 and 19x2, which transfers the recorded value of the natural resources from the long-term asset Oil Reserves to Oil Inventory. Note that depletion is an allocation process similar to depreciation and amortization in that it assigns the cost of a long-term asset to Inventory, which is in turn expensed as goods are sold. To illustrate, assume that North Sea, Inc., spent $1 million in 19x1 on an oil discovery that was estimated to contain 500,000 barrels of oil. North Sea extracted 100,000 barrels of oil in 19x1 and 140,000 barrels in 19x2. The following entries are made to record the discovery and extraction of the oil:

19x1			
Jan. 1 to May 1	Oil Reserves (A).	1,000,000	
	Cash (A)		1,000,000
	To summarize all discovery costs during 19x1.		

Depletion computation:

$$\frac{\text{Cost}}{\text{Barrels}} = \frac{\$1\ \text{million}}{500,000} = \$2\ \text{cost per barrel}$$

Dec. 31	Oil Inventory (A).	200,000	
	Oil Reserves (A).		200,000
	To record depletion for oil extracted during 19x1: 100,000 barrels × $2 per barrel depletion.		
19x2			
Dec. 31	Oil Inventory (A).	280,000	
	Oil Reserves (A).		280,000
	To record depletion for oil extracted during 19x2: 140,000 barrels × $2 per barrel depletion.		

The recording of depletion may be offset by either a credit to the Oil Reserves asset account or by a credit to the contra asset account Accumulated Depletion—Oil Reserves, which is similar to accumulated depreciation. Most companies directly reduce depletable assets, as in the entries above.

CHANGES IN ESTIMATED AMOUNTS OF RESOURCES

The estimated quantity of natural resources is similar to the estimated life of a building or machine in that the estimate may change over time. The accounting procedure to record these **changes in estimates** is the same as that used for long-term assets.

To illustrate a common occurrence of changes in the estimated amount of natural resources, assume that at the start of 19x3 a new geological survey is conducted by North Sea, Inc. Before the survey, the estimated undepleted oil reserve is 260,000 barrels [500,000 − (100,000 + 140,000)]. After the survey, it is estimated that 320,000 barrels remain to be extracted. To determine the new depletion rate, the remaining net book value of the asset **at the beginning of the period of change** is depleted over the new estimated number of barrels remaining to be depleted as of the beginning of the period, as follows:

Revised depletion rate:

$$\frac{\text{Remaining cost}}{\substack{\text{New estimate of}\\\text{remaining quantity}}} = \frac{(\$1,000,000 - \$200,000 - \$280,000)}{320,000\ \text{barrels}} = \frac{\$1.625\ \text{cost}}{\text{per barrel}}$$

If we assume that 150,000 barrels were extracted during 19x3, the appropriate entry is;

```
19x3
Dec. 31    Oil Inventory (A). . . . . . . . . . . . . . . . . . . . . . . .    243,750
               Oil Reserves (A). . . . . . . . . . . . . . . . . . . . .                243,750
           To record depletion of oil extracted during 19x3:
           150,000 barrels at $1.625 each.
```

ASSET COSTS ASSOCIATED WITH RESOURCES

Often assets acquired for purposes of extracting resources have little or no value once the resources are completely extracted. Examples of such assets include a shed or house constructed as a base camp for harvesting lumber in a remote forest or an oil-drilling platform constructed in the North Sea. These assets should be depreciated over their expected economic life or the expected time required to extract the resources, whichever is the shorter period. Generally, once the resources are extracted, such assets provide no future benefits, and therefore they should be fully depreciated. The amount to be depreciated includes the cost of these assets less any residual value expected when the natural resources are fully extracted.

STATUTORY DEPLETION RATES

For income tax purposes, the amount of depletion expense allowed in a period is normally based on the sales of the resources during the period multiplied by a legally set percentage called the statutory depletion rate. The statutory depletion rate varies depending on the type of natural resources being extracted. As a result, depletion for tax purposes is not based on the actual cost of the resources.

As designed by Congress, this tax law provides an incentive for business to explore for additional natural resources. In general, the more scarce the natural resource, the higher the statutory depletion rate. Since the tax depletion amounts are more than the depletion taken for financial reporting purposes, the statutory depletion percentages result in a greater allowable deduction for tax purposes than the actual depletion recorded in the financial statements.

• KEY TERMS

Accelerated depreciation. Any depreciation method that results in higher depreciation expense in the early years of the asset's useful life than in the asset's later years.

Accumulated depreciation. The cumulative amount of depreciation expense taken in the current and prior periods; reported on the balance sheet as a contra asset.

Acquisition cost. Current fair market value of the assets given or received, whichever is more objectively measurable; should include all costs necessary to acquire the asset and place it into its intended useful state.

Amortization. Allocation process similar to depreciation used for intangible assets.

Basket purchase. Group purchase of assets.

Capital expenditures. Costs that provide future benefits and are, therefore, recorded as assets (or additions to existing assets).

Capitalized. Said of costs: recorded as an asset (as opposed to an expense).

Copyright. Intangible asset granted by the federal government for literary or artistic works.

Declining-balance depreciation method. An accelerated depreciation method.

Depreciable base. The portion of an asset's cost that is expected to be depreciated (consumed) over the asset's useful life.

Depreciation. Allocation process that systematically assigns the cost of a tangible asset to the income statements during the asset's useful life.

Depreciation expense. Amount of an asset's cost expensed to current income.

Franchises and licenses. Rights granted by a government or a private enterprise to distribute, sell, service, or otherwise handle a specified line of goods and/or services.

Goodwill. The otherwise unrecorded assets of a business; the difference between the price paid and the fair market value of the identifiable assets acquired.

Group depreciation method. Depreciation method according to which large quantities of similar assets are depreciated as a group rather than individually.

Half-year convention. Taking one half of a year's depreciation expense on all assets purchased and sold during the year.

Identifiable intangibles. Assets that are separate and specifically identifiable items, such as patents, copyrights, and trademarks.

Intangible assets. Long-term resources with no physical substance, such as patents. Their value to the business stems from the rights they represent rather than their physical form.

Net book value. For a depreciable asset, this is the asset's cost less its accumulated depreciation; also called book value.

Organization costs. Costs incurred in getting a business started.

Patent. An intangible asset that entitles a specified entity to the exclusive rights to some invention or process.

Research and development (R&D) costs. Costs incurred in searching for new knowledge that may be used to create or improve new products or services.

Residual value. Asset's estimated market value at the end of its period of use; also called salvage value or scrap value.

Revenue expenditure. An expenditure that is expensed, or charged against revenues, in the current period; also called period expense.

Straight-line depreciation method. Method of depreciation that assumes that assets are equally useful over all time periods of use.

Sum-of-the-years'-digits (SYD) depreciation method. An accelerated depreciation method.

Tangible assets. Long-term assets that have physical substance (such as equipment) representing future benefits.

Trademarks and brand names. Words, symbols, or designs used to identify and distinguish a product or group of products; also called brand names.

Unidentifiable intangibles. Intangible assets that are not separate or observable (principally goodwill).

Units-of-output depreciation method. Method that records depreciation expense based on the amount of use an asset receives during the period.

Useful life. Length of time an asset is expected to be used by a business in the capacity for which it is purchased.

Wasting assets. Tangible assets whose benefits are essentially consumed or used up over time.

· Appendix Key Terms

Depletion. Allocation process, similar to depreciation, used for natural resources.

Statutory depletion rate. The legally set percentage of sales allowed as depletion expense for natural resources for income tax purposes.

· SYNONYMS

Assets; capitalized costs.

Basket purchase; group purchase.

Book value; net book value.

Building; plant; physical plant; facilities.

Current cost; replacement cost.

Expensed; charged.

Fair value; fair market value.

Long-term assets; noncurrent assets.

Natural resources; wasting assets.

Productive assets; wasting assets; consumable assets.

Residual value; salvage value; scrap value.

Revenue expenditure; period expense; expense.

• QUESTIONS

1. Identify two categories of long-term assets that differ based on their physical substance.
2. Identify two types of tangible assets. How do they differ?
3. What is the major category of tangible assets?
4. How is the acquisition cost of an asset measured?
5. What types of costs may be capitalized as the cost of an asset?
6. Is interest cost a capitalizable cost? Explain.
7. How are costs measured when assets are purchased as a group?
8. What is depreciation? Depreciation expense? Accumulated depreciation?
9. What is the "depreciable base" of an asset?
10. Describe four alternative depreciation methods.
11. What is the basis of allocation in the straight-line method?
12. How does the declining-balance method differ from the other methods?
13. What is the formula for the sum-of-the-years'-digits method?
14. What is the half-year convention, and how is it applied in computing depreciation expense?
15. Which depreciation method is the best to use for financial reporting purposes?
16. What happens if the actual life of an asset turns out to be longer or shorter than originally estimated?
17. Should companies have fully depreciated assets in use in their businesses?
18. Explain the difference between a capital expenditure and a revenue expenditure.
19. What costs are capitalized subsequent to the acquisition of an asset? Why?
20. What subsequent costs are expensed as incurred? Why?
21. What is the impact of expensing a subsequent cost that should have been capitalized?
22. What happens when assets are sold for more or less than their book value?
23. When assets are no longer in use, how are they treated?
24. What are intangible assets?
25. What are the two main categories of intangible assets?
26. Define four identifiable intangible assets and explain how each is amortized.
27. What are organizational costs and how are they amortized?
28. Define goodwill. When and how is goodwill measured in accounting?
29. Can any company report goodwill? Explain.

• Appendix Questions

30. When one asset is exchanged for another asset and cash is also paid, how is the gain or loss determined in the fair value method?
31. For income tax purposes, what is the value of a new asset acquired in exchange for an old asset plus cash?
32. When are special rules required for recording asset exchanges?
33. What are natural resources, and how is their cost measurement different from that of most other assets?
34. How is depletion measured for financial reporting purposes?
35. What are statutory depletion rates?

• EXERCISES

E 8–1
Acquisition Cost
L.O.1

Mark's Meat acquired a new meat locker on January 1, 19x4. The locker had a list price of $65,000, but the seller offered a 2% discount if the full amount was paid in cash within 10 days of the sale. The bill to have the freight company pick up the locker and deliver it came to $1,200. A salvage company removed the old meat locker at a cost of $1,950. The wiring and installation of the new locker cost $2,250 cash. Mark's accountant returned from vacation on January 15 and sent a check dated January 10 for $63,700 for the locker the next day, hoping the discount would be allowed. The refrigeration unit failed in the first week the locker was used due to a wiring problem, and $1,590 of meat was spoiled. The wiring problem was corrected by the contracting company at its expense, but the loss of the meat was not covered by the contractor. Mark received a bill for $1,300 from the company that had sold them the meat locker. This bill has not been paid.

Required:
1. Determine the acquisition cost of the meat locker.
2. Record the acquisition assuming that all costs were paid in cash except as noted.

E 8–2
Acquisition Cost
L.O.1

Life Line Insurance acquired a 15-acre parcel of land in 19x4 on which to build a new office building. A house valued at $250,000 was located on the land, along with some wooden sheds used to store farm equipment. Life Line paid $500,000 cash and also gave a $3 million note payable over the next 10 years with 10% annual interest on the unpaid balance.

At a cost of $96,000 cash Life Line demolished the house and sheds. They sold the salvageable contents of the house for $39,000 cash. They put in a road to facilitate construction at a cost of $200,000 cash. They paid a contractor $2 million cash plus a mortgage note of $13 million for the construction of the office building. The mortgage required 10% annual interest.

Required:
Record the transactions as required using a separate account for Land and for Building.

E 8–3
Group Purchase
L.O.1

Rent-a-Clunk purchased five used cars from U-Rent for $20,000 total. The following data were available from U-Rent at the time of the purchase:

Vehicle	Original Cost	Book Value
Tempo	$10,900	$ 2,500
Topaz	11,650	3,000
Cougar.	16,980	3,500
T-Bird	15,550	3,500
Econoline.	14,200	4,000
Total.	$69,280	$16,500

Required:
1. Which value is more appropriate for allocation purposes, original cost or book value?
2. Record the value of each vehicle, assigning the $20,000 cost on the basis of their original cost. (Round all answers to the nearest dollar.)

E 8–4
Depreciation Methods
L.O.2

On January 1, 19x1, the Tavares Company bought a record-making machine for $72,000. This machine had an expected useful life of 10 years with an estimated residual value of $8,000. The machine was expected to be able to produce 40,000 records during its life.

Required:
1. Compute the 19x1 depreciation expense on the machine using the sum-of-the-years'-digits depreciation method. (Round to nearest dollar.)
2. The machine actually produced 12,000 records in 19x1. Compute the 19x1 depreciation expense on the machine using the units-of-output depreciation method.

E 8–5
Depreciation Methods
L.O.2

Go Blue, Inc., purchased a machine on January 1, 19x1, for $55,000. The machine has an estimated residual value of $5,000 and a useful life of five years. The company uses the 200% declining-balance depreciation method.

Required:
1. Compute the amount Go Blue will record for depreciation on the machine in 19x2.
2. Compute the depreciation expense for 19x2 if Go Blue uses the straight-line method or the sum-of-the-years'-digits method rather than the declining-balance method.

E 8–6
Depreciation Methods
and Change in Estimate
L.O.2, 3

Spud's Lounge purchased a dishwashing machine with an estimated 10-year useful life for $26,000. The estimated residual value is $2,000, and the accumulated depreciation at the end of year 5 for the machine is $12,000. It is now the beginning of year 6, and Spud has reevaluated the estimated total useful life to be 13 years. Assume that the straight-line method is used. Compute the depreciation expense for year 6.

E 8–7
Change in Estimate
L.O.3

On January 1, 19x1, Boose, Inc., purchased furniture for $218,000. The furniture was expected to last five years and to have a residual value of $18,000. Late in 19x4, Boose revised its estimate of the salvage value from $18,000 to $40,000. Boose uses straight-line depreciation.

Required:
Compute the depreciation expense for 19x1 and for 19x4.

E 8–8
Half-Year Convention
L.O.3

The Using Corporation acquired a machine on May 1, 19x1, at a cost of $78,000. The machine had an estimated useful life of 10 years and an estimated salvage value of $3,000. The half-year convention is used by the corporation.

Required:
Compute (rounding all answers to the nearest dollar) the depreciation expense for the second year of use (19x2) assuming:

1. The straight-line method is used.
2. The 175% declining-balance method is used.
3. The sum-of-the-years'-digits method is used.

E 8–9
Half-Year Convention
L.O.3

Lily Lumber reported the following activities during 19x5 concerning its depreciable assets.

Feb.   1   A power saw having a net book value on January 1, 19x5, of $4,800 and annual (straight-line) depreciation of $1,200 per year was sold for $4,500 cash. The saw had originally cost $12,000.

Mar.   1   A new power saw was acquired for $15,800 cash. It has an expected useful life of eight years and no salvage value. The 200% declining-balance method will be used.

July   15   A new forklift truck costing $23,000 and having an expected life of 60,000 hours of use and no scrap value was acquired for cash. The truck was used 500 hours in 19x5.

Oct.   31   A new warehouse was placed in service today. The new storage facility cost $125,000 cash and is expected to last 30 years and have no scrap value. Sum-of-the-years'-digits depreciation will be used.

Required:
Using the half-year convention, record all of the journal entries for 19x5 needed in order to account for the four events described in the exercise, including any adjusting entries for recording depreciation. (Round all computations to nearest dollar.)

E 8–10
Nearest-Month
Depreciation
L.O.3

Janet's Jet Travel Service reported the following activities during 19x9 concerning depreciable assets.

Feb.   15   Purchased a new high-speed printer for $4,980 cash. The useful life is five years and the estimated scrap value is $480. The 150% declining-balance method is used.

May   20   Sold for $3,000 cash a used computer whose January 1, 19x9, net book value was $3,200. The computer, which had originally cost $10,000, was being depreciated on a straight-line basis at the rate of $900 per year.

Nov. 18   Purchased a new delivery car for $15,000 cash. The car is expected to be used 60,000 miles and to have a scrap value of $3,000. The car had been driven 2,150 miles by year-end.

Dec. 1   Purchased a new communications system for $23,600 cash. The system, which will be depreciated using the sum-of-the-years'-digits method, should last 8 years and have a salvage value of $1,600.

Required:

Using the nearest-month approach, record all of the journal entries for 19x9 to account for the four events described in the exercise, including any adjusting journal entries to record depreciation. (Round all computations to nearest dollar.)

E 8–11
Depreciation and Taxes
L.O.2

Argo Corporation purchased equipment costing $85,000 on January 1, 19x1, for cash. The estimated useful life was four years and the estimated salvage value was $5,000. The tax rate is fixed at 30%.

Required:

1. What is the total depreciation expense over the life of the asset that may be taken for tax purposes?
2. What is the total depreciation expense over the life of the asset that may be taken for book purposes?
3. How much less income tax expense will Argo pay over the asset's life in comparison with the income taxes it would have paid if it had not purchased the equipment?

E 8–12
Subsequent Costs/Basket Purchase
L.O.1, 4

The Colette Corporation purchased a factory building and the land it was on for $210,000. At that time, the land had an appraised value of $100,000, and the building had an appraised value of $150,000. Colette then put a new roof on the factory building at a cost of $10,000. Compute the total amount debited to the Factory Building account.

E 8–13
Subsequent Costs
L.O.4

For each of the events described below, indicate whether the cost should be capitalized or expensed. Assume the company involved has total assets of $1,500,000 and average net income of $50,000.

a. Built an addition to the warehouse, adding 2,000 square feet at a cost of $23,000.
b. Paid $280 to have windows in rented office building cleaned.
c. Added partitions to sales showroom for privacy in client meetings at a cost of $2,300.
d. Painted interior of showroom at a cost of $295 for the third time in two years due to heavy traffic.
e. Replaced chipped tiles in showroom floor at a cost of $675.
f. Replaced dead tree outside showroom at a cost of $600. This was the only loss from the 10 trees planted five years earlier during landscaping renovations.

E 8–14
Subsequent Costs
L.O.4

The Gabel Cable TV Company invested $2,500,000 in a cable broadcasting system in January of 19x1. The new system was expected to handle all cable transmissions for eight years and was being depreciated on a straight-line basis (assuming no salvage value). In May 19x3, a severe thunderstorm destroyed a key component of the transmission system. The replacement, which cost Gabel $635,000, was not insured. Although the replacement did not add to the useful life of the system, it was necessary in order for the system to be used, and it was installed on May 31, 19x3.

Required:

Record the journal entry to account for the replacement component, and record the journal entries to account for depreciation expense in 19x3 and 19x4. You should compute depreciation to the nearest month. (Round all computations to nearest dollar.)

E 8–15
Disposal of Assets
L.O.5

Zeron Company owns a drill press. The press originally cost $35,000 and had a 10-year useful life with a $5,000 residual value. At December 31, 19x5, the drill press had accumulated depreciation (after all adjusting entries) of $12,000. Zeron uses straight-line depreciation to the nearest month.

Required:

1. How old was the machine at December 31, 19x5?
2. If the drill press were sold on March 31, 19x6, for $17,000 cash, what would be the journal entry (entries) on that date?

E 8–16
Disposal of Assets
L.O.5

On January 1, 19x1, Berry Corporation sold equipment that had originally cost $50,000 and had accumulated depreciation of $22,000 for $12,000 and a one-year note receivable. The note had a face value of $16,000 and paid interest of $3,000 at the end of one year.

Required:
Record the sale of the old equipment

1. Using the above facts.
2. Using the above facts, except that $10,000 cash was received rather than $12,000.
3. Using the above facts, except that $14,500 cash was received rather than $12,000.
4. Assuming that the equipment was scrapped rather than sold.

E 8–17
Patents
L.O.7

On January 14, 19xx, Johnson, Inc., filed a lawsuit against Jayco for a patent violation, arguing that Jayco was using a patented process owned by Johnson to produce its products. Johnson spent $578,000 in legal fees to defend its exclusive right to the patented process.

Required:
1. Assume the lawsuit was successful for Johnson. How should Johnson treat the legal fees?
2. Assume the lawsuit was **not** successful. What should Johnson record regarding the legal fees? The patent?

E 8–18
Goodwill
L.O.7

Baker Corporation acquired a small tool and die company for $480,000 on December 31, 19x1. The tool and die company reported the following data:

	Book Values	Estimated Market Values
Recorded assets	$450,000	$550,000
Recorded liabilities . . .	150,000	150,000
Net assets recorded . .	$300,000	$400,000

Baker amortizes goodwill over 40 years.

Required:
1. Compute the goodwill, if any, included in this purchase.
2. Record the amortization of goodwill for 19x2 for Baker.

E 8–19
Intangibles
L.O.7

Select the best alternative for each of the following multiple-choice questions or statements.

1. The XYZ Company reported an asset, Patents, $38,000—
   a. The patents which were licensed by the federal government.
   b. Which represented the unamortized legal fees plus the cost of developing prototypes.
   c. Which would be amortized over no more than 17 years.
   d. All of the above are correct.
   e. None of the above is correct.
2. Research and development costs—
   a. Are costs of searching for new knowledge.
   b. Are costs of creating new products.
   c. Are very important activities in some industries leading to new products but are still not allowed to be recorded as assets in most cases.
   d. All of the above are correct.
   e. None of the above are correct.
3. In practice, organization costs—
   a. Are expensed as incurred.
   b. Are capitalized as a permanent asset.
   c. Are capitalized and amortized over 40 years.
   d. Are capitalized and amortized over five years.
   e. None of the above.

4. Copyrights granted to a business are—
   a. Granted by the federal government for a 75-year period of time.
   b. Amortized over not more than 40 years.
   c. Granted for original works of art and music.
   d. All of the above are correct.
   e. None of the above are correct.
5. On January 12, 19x5, XYZ Corporation paid legal fees of $35,000 to successfully defend its patent, which had a net book value of $5,000 and a remaining legal life of eight years at that time.
   a. The $35,000 should be capitalized as an asset in 19x5.
   b. The $35,000 should be expensed in 19x5.
   c. The amortization should be $625 per year for 19x5 and thereafter.
   d. Amortization expense for 19x5 should be $2,500.
   e. None of the above.

E 8–20
Depreciation, Amortization, and Depletion Expense
L.O.2, 5, 7, 9

For each of the following unrelated situations, calculate the annual depreciation, depletion, or amortization expense for the Andrews Company for its fiscal year ended December 31, 19x5.

1. A five-year-old patent was purchased for $480,000 on January 1, 19x5. The patent will probably be useful commercially for 12 more years.
   a. $12,000.
   b. $28,235.
   c. $40,000.
   d. $24,000.
2. Various building fixtures costing $56,000 were constructed and permanently installed on January 1, 19x5, in a building being rented from another company. The useful life of the fixtures was estimated to be 15 years, and the residual value was estimated to be $6,000. The rental agreement ends in eight years. The rental agreement contained no provision for the removal of fixtures.
   a. $3,333.
   b. $7,000.
   c. $3,733.
   d. $6,250.
3. On January 1, 19x3, the company purchased a machine at a cost of $25,000. The machine was estimated to have a useful life of four years, after which it could be sold for $1,000. The company is using the sum-of-the-years'-digits method to record depreciation on the machine.
   a. $5,000.
   b. $4,800.
   c. $2,400.
   d. $7,500.
4. On January 1, 19x4, the company purchased a building for $100,000. The company is using the 200% declining-balance method to record depreciation and estimates that the building has a $20,000 residual value. Depreciation expense on the building for 19x4 was $10,000.
   a. $18,000.
   b. $10,000.
   c. $9,000.
   d. $7,000.
5. (Appendix 8B) The company purchased a mining site for $290,000 on June 15, 19x5, containing an estimated 1 million tons of coal. Before starting mining operations, the company paid $5,000 in legal fees to acquire proper title. The company estimates that it can sell the mining site for $15,000 after all the coal has been extracted. During 19x5, 85,000 tons of coal were extracted and sold.
   a. $25,075.
   b. $24,650.
   c. $23,375.
   d. $23,800.

E 8–21

Accounting Policies—
Ralston Purina
L.O.2, 4, 5, 7

Consider the Ralston Purina Company's (RPC's) annual report in Appendix E at the end of the text. Refer to the first page of footnotes, "Summary of Accounting Policies," in answering the following questions.

Required:

1. What is RPC's policy on costs subsequent to acquisition?
2. Where are gains or losses on the disposal of properties reported?
3. What is the method and useful life used for depreciable assets?
4. What is the method and useful life used for intangible assets?

E 8–22

Assets Disposals—
Ralston Purina
L.O.5, 6

Consider the Ralston Purina Company's (RPC's) annual report in Appendix E. Refer to the footnote, "Analysis of Balance Sheet Changes" (page 932). RPC disposed of some property during fiscal 1992. From RPC's Cash Flow Statement, we know the cash proceeds of the property disposals were $62.0 million.

Required:

1. Compute the gain or loss (pretax) on the disposals for fiscal 1992.
2. What was the percentage of depreciation taken on these disposed-of assets prior to their sale?

• Appendix Exercises

E 8–23

Assets Exchanges
(Appendix 8A)
L.O.8

On January 1, 19xx, Danko, Inc., traded in a used truck in exchange for a new truck. The old truck cost $28,000 and had a net book value of $9,000 on the date of exchange. The new truck had a "list" price of $40,000 but could be purchased for $35,000 cash. Danko gave the old truck plus $27,000 cash in exchange for the new truck.

Required:

1. Record the exchange using the fair value method.
2. Record the exchange using the tax method.
3. Does this exchange qualify as a "special case" exchange? Explain.

E 8–24

Asset Exchanges
(Appendix 8A)
L.O.8

Waite, Inc., acquired land from Bolding Corporation in exchange for 1,000 units of Waite's inventory. The inventory had cost Waite $76,800 to manufacture during the current year and had a regular selling price of $140 per unit. The land had been on Bolding's books at an original cost of $60,000 and was recently appraised at a value of $135,000 by an independent real estate agent.

Required:

Using the fair value method, answer the following questions:

1. What is the cost of the land to be recorded by Waite?
2. What is the cost of the inventory to be recorded on Bolding's books?
3. Is there a gain to be recorded by Bolding on this transaction? If so, how much is it?
4. Record the entry to acquire the land on Waite's books.

E 8–25

Natural Resources
(Appendix 8B)
L.O.9

The North Shore Corporation spent $1,680,000 cash in 19x8 to discover 480,000 barrels of crude oil. During the remainder of 19x8, they extracted 80,000 barrels and sold them to a processing company for $5.50 per barrel. During 19x9 North Shore extracted 200,000 barrels of crude oil and sold them to a processing company for $6 per barrel. Extraction costs were $0.02 per barrel in both 19x8 and 19x9.

Required:

1. Record the discovery costs and the depletion for 19x8 and 19x9.
2. What was the gross profit on sales in 19x8? 19x9?

• PROBLEMS

P 8–1
Basket Acquisition Cost
L.O.1

On January 19, 19x5, Tristar Airlines acquired three passenger aircraft from Midnorth Airways for $45 million in cash. The three aircraft were renovated, repaired, painted, and placed into service on June 30, 19x5. The following data are available regarding these aircraft:

	(dollars in millions)		
	B747	**B757**	**DC9**
Current replacement cost new.	$33.0	$29.0	$23.0
Age at date of purchase	7 years	5 years	3 years
Appraisal value	$16.0	$16.0	$18.0
Cost to renovate, repair, and paint.	$ 2.5	$ 2.0	$ 1.0
Estimated remaining service life at January 19, 19x5 . . .	10 years	12 years	15 years
Estimated salvage value	$ 2.0	$ 1.4	$ 0.7

Required:
1. Measure the acquisition cost of each plane.
2. Record the acquisition on Tristar's books.
3. Record the costs for renovation, repair, and painting on Tristar's books. Assume that cash was used for payment.
4. Record depreciation expense for 19x5 and 19x6 using the straight-line method.

P 8–2
Acquisition Costs
L.O.1

Elton Corporation incurred the following costs in the process of buying new cutting equipment for its furniture manufacturing plants:

Invoice cost of cutting machines	$137,500
Installation labor	250
Installation materials	475
Freight charges for delivery	4,380
Insurance costs	2,000
Special cutting bands for machine	17,000
Supervisor's salary for day machines installed	200
Sales tax on machine (5%)	6,875
Sales tax on special cutting bands (5%)	850
Cost of materials used while adjusting machines	770

The installation labor was based on the actual cost of Elton's workers who installed the machinery. The freight charges were for both railroad fees ($2,300) and trucking fees ($2,080) using Elton's own trucks. Insurance costs were for a one-year insurance policy sold by the manufacturer to take effect on the first day of operation. The cutting bands were only useful in conjunction with the cutting machines, which could not be operated without the bands. The manufacturer offered a 4% discount on the invoice price of the cutting machines if paid within 30 days of delivery. Elton did not pay within the 30-day period.

Required:
1. Determine the cost of the cutting machines.
2. Record the appropriate entries to account for all of the costs noted in the problem.

P 8–3
Acquisition Cost Allocation
L.O.1

On May 1, 19x1, Danco, Inc., purchased a 10-acre parcel of land for $150,000 to be used as a future building site. On June 10, 19x4, Danco sold five acres of the land for $200,000 cash and constructed a warehouse on the remaining five acres at a cost of $180,000 cash.

Required:
1. What are some of the additional facts that you might like to know in order to record the sale on June 10, 19x4? Why?

2. Record the above facts assuming no additional information.
3. Explain how you decided to allocate the $150,000 original land cost to the two five-acre parcels on June 10, 19x4. Why did you choose this method?

P 8–4
Asset Acquisition/
Basket Purchase
L.O.1

The Lime Tree Complex purchased three houses from Campus Realtors for a total price of $450,000. The three houses were to be made into apartments for student rentals. The following data were available concerning the three houses:

Unit	Square Feet of Floor Space	Assessed Value	Campus Realtors Book Value
A	3,496	$ 90,000	$120,000
B	2,944	70,000	90,000
C	2,760	60,000	100,000
Total	9,200	$220,000	$310,000

All three houses were between three and five years old. Unit A was assessed last year at $90,000, while units B and C were assessed this year. The assessed value is estimated to be 50% of the market value of each house. The current replacement cost of similar quality houses in the area is about $52 per square foot. All three houses are in excellent locations and should be easy to rent. The rental fee will be based on the size of the apartment units, since all will be similarly equipped.

Required:
1. Assume no goodwill exists in the purchase by Lime Tree. Allocate the $450,000 purchase price to the three units on the basis you believe is most equitable.
2. Explain why you did not choose the alternative methods for allocating the $450,000 cost.
3. (Optional) Assume that Lime Tree sells unit A for $195,000 the day after its purchase from Campus Realtors. Does this affect your allocation method? Explain.
4. (Optional) Record the sale of unit A for $195,000 cash by Lime Tree the day after it is purchased from Campus Realtors.

P 8–5
Depreciation Methods
L.O.2

On January 1, 19x1, Daydreamer Corporation purchased a "sleep" machine for $112,000. The estimated useful life is five years, and the residual value is $20,000. The estimated productive output is 50,000 hours of use. Daydreamer's fiscal year ends December 31.

or. cost 112,000
Life 5yrs
salvage 20,000

Required:
1. Using the sum-of-the-years'-digits method, compute depreciation expense for 19x1 and 19x2 and the machine's book value at December 31, 19x2.
2. During 19x1, the machine was used for 12,000 hours. Compute the 19x1 depreciation expense using the units-of-output method.
3. Using the 150% declining-balance method, compute the 19x1 and 19x2 depreciation expenses and the machine's book value at the end of both fiscal years.

P 8–6
Depreciation Methods
L.O.2

On January 1, 19x1, the Salinsky Company purchased a machine for $10,000. The machine has a 20-year life and no residual value. It is estimated the machine will be used 40,000 hours. During 19x1 and 19x2, the machine was used 3,000 and 2,500 hours, respectively. The company has a December 31 year-end and uses a monthly depreciation measurement.

Required:
Determine the depreciation expense amounts for 19x1 and 19x2 using the following depreciation methods (round answers to nearest dollar):

1. Straight-line.
2. Sum-of-the-years'-digits.
3. 200% declining-balance.
4. Units-of-output.

P 8–7
Depreciation Methods/
Nearest-Month Approach
L.O.2, 3

An asset that cost $50,000 with a $5,000 residual value and a five-year life was purchased on April 1, 19x1, by JKA Corporation. The company uses the nearest-month approach to record depreciation expense.

Required:

Compute depreciation expense for the fiscal years ended December 31, 19x1 and 19x2, using the following depreciation methods:

1. Straight-line.
2. Sum-of-the-years'-digits.
3. 200% declining-balance.

P 8–8
Depreciation Methods/
Half-Year Convention
L.O.2, 3

The Tooz Company installed a machine in its factory at a total cost of $15,800. Its useful life was estimated at five years or 50,000 units of product. The residual value is estimated to be $600. Production was 11,000 units for the first year of operation; 13,000 units for the second year; and 9,000 units for the third year. Tooz Company uses the half-year convention for measuring depreciation expense.

Required:

Compute the depreciation expense for the first three years of the machine's use under the following depreciation methods:

1. Straight-line.
2. Units-of-output. (Round to nearest cent per unit.)
3. Sum-of-the-years'-digits. (Round to nearest dollar.)
4. 200% declining-balance. (Round to nearest dollar.)

P 8–9
Depreciation Methods/
Partial Years
L.O.2, 3

On May 15, 19x4, Mastco, Inc., acquired a new furnace for its glazing operations. The furnace cost $35,650. Freight costs amounted to $760 and the installation of the furnace cost $590. The estimated salvage value of the furnace in seven years is $2,000. The furnace is expected to be useful for 14,000 hours of glazing. It was used for 1,200 hours during 19x4 and 2,000 hours during 19x5.

Required:

Record the depreciation expense for 19x4 and 19x5 using the following alternative methods:

1. Straight-line, computed to closest month.
2. Sum-of-the-years'-digits, computed using the half-year convention.
3. 150% declining-balance, computed to the closest month (round rate to four decimals).
4. Units-of-output.

P 8–10
Depreciation and Taxes
L.O.2

Ladro Corporation reports income *before* considering depreciation expense and taxes of $200,000 every year. Ladro acquired depreciable assets at a cost of $250,000 on January 1, 19x1. The assets have a useful life of six years and no salvage value. The income tax rate is 34% every year.

Required:

1. Assume that Ladro uses the straight-line method for its books, but, for income tax purposes, Ladro depreciates the assets over five years as follows: 30% (year 1); 25% (year 2); 20% (year 3); 15% (year 4); 10% (year 5). Compute the tax savings or the additional taxes each year from 19x1 to 19x6 compared with the straight-line method.
2. Explain why Ladro should not use straight-line depreciation for income tax purposes too.

P 8–11
Depreciation and Taxes
(Challenging)
L.O.2

Wayco, Inc., is considering applying the following depreciation schedules to a $100,000 asset acquired on January 1, 19x1, and expected to have a five-year useful life and no salvage value.

Year	Schedule 1	Schedule 2
1	30%	20%
2	25	20
3	20	20
4	15	20
5	10	20
	100%	100%

Required:
1. Compute depreciation expense for each of the five years for each schedule.
2. Assume net income before taxes and depreciation expense is $65,000 each year, and the tax rate is 40%. Compute net income for 19x1 and 19x2 under each alternative.
3. Assume cash flow from operations before considering taxes and depreciation expense is $55,000 in 19x1 and $60,000 in 19x2. Taxes must be paid in cash each year. Compute cash flow from operations after taxes and depreciation expense for 19x1 and 19x2.

P 8–12
Change in Estimate
L.O.3

Paymor Corporation purchased equipment on January 1, 19x1, for $86,600. The equipment was expected to have a 15-year life and $3,600 residual value. Paymor uses straight-line depreciation. On December 31, 19x5 (the fifth year of use), the technology for this equipment changed significantly, and the estimated useful life was decreased from 15 years to 8 years with no change in residual value.

Required: (Round to nearest dollar.)

1. Record depreciation expense for 19x1.
2. Record depreciation expense for 19x5 and 19x6.

P 8–13
Change in Estimate
L.O.3

Welden, Inc., discovered in 19x8 that it had been using fully depreciated equipment throughout the year and that the equipment was expected to be useful for at least three more years (after 19x8) with no residual value. The original cost of $480,000 had been fully depreciated over 12 years on a straight-line basis by the end of 19x7.

Required:
1. What should have been done prior to 19x8?
2. Assume that this situation was discovered before the books were closed for 19x7. What should Welden have depreciated for 19x7? For 19x8?
3. How could Welden prevent this situation from occurring in the future?

P 8–14
Errors in Recording Plant and Equipment (Challenging)
L.O.1

On May 20, 19xx, Bradley Corporation purchased land for $450,000 cash for a future building site. The following additional costs were incurred during 19xx and added to the Land and Buildings account on Bradley's books:

Date	Item	Amount
19xx		
June 10	Paid for cutting trees	$ 7,850
15	Sold cut trees to local sawmill	(3,500)
22	Destroyed old barn on land	8,300
23	Sold old barn's wood to furniture company	(6,750)
30	Paid for grading of land and excavation of building site	15,000
July 10	Paid for paved road to building site	110,000
18	Paid first payment to construction company	1,300,000
23	Paid for insurance to cover building during construction period	13,000
Aug. 31	Paid for final payment on building	700,000
31	Paid interest on money borrowed to pay construction company initial payment	48,000
Sept. 30	Paid agency for grand opening fees including prizes given to public, promotions, etc.	19,500
	Balance: Land and buildings	$2,211,400

Bradley plans to depreciate this amount over 50 years on a straight-line basis.

Required:
1. Identify any errors made by Bradley in recording the transactions described above.
2. Determine the appropriate balances to be recorded in the following accounts: Land, Roadway, Buildings.
3. Prepare the necessary entries to correct the records of Bradley. Do not record any depreciation for 19xx.

P 8–15
Disposal of Assets
L.O.5

On September 14, 19x7, the Pullman Corporation disposed of two pieces of machinery from its office equipment division. The first machine had cost $28,750 on January 1, 19x1. It was originally expected to have a 10-year useful life and no scrap value. The machine was being depreciated using the 200% declining-balance method computed by the half-year convention. The machine was sold to a competitor for $8,300 cash.

The second machine was acquired on May 3, 19x1, at a cost of $33,700. It had an estimated useful life of eight years and an estimated residual value of $2,500. The second machine was being depreciated on a straight-line basis computed to the nearest month. It was sold for $7,500 cash.

Required: (Round to nearest dollar.)

1. Compute the gain or loss from the sale of each machine separately.
2. Record the entries to dispose of the two machines.

P 8–16
Depreciation, Depletion, and Disposal of Assets (Challenging)
L.O.2–5, 9

Below is a schedule of selected account balances taken from the Apollo Corporation's adjusted trial balance at December 31, 19x8. The corporation's fiscal year ends on December 31.

	Debits	Credits
Delivery Truck.	$ 10,000	
Accumulated Depreciation—Delivery Truck		$ 6,000
Machine A	50,000	
Accumulated Depreciation—Machine A		40,000
Machine B	60,000	
Accumulated Depreciation—Machine B		24,000
Machine C	78,000	
Accumulated Depreciation—Machine C		59,200
Building	200,000	
Accumulated Depreciation—Building.		62,182
Land.	100,000	
Mining Properties	150,000	
Accumulated Depletion—Mining Properties		50,000

During 19x9, the following transactions occurred related to the above accounts:

19x9

Jan. 1 Made substantial improvements, costing $45,000, to Machine C. Machine C was purchased on January 1, 19x1, for $78,000 and has been depreciated on a straight-line basis. On January 1, 19x1, the corporation estimated that the machine had a useful life of 10 years and a residual value of $4,000. The corporation estimates that the improvements increased the machine's total useful life to 12 years and residual value to $13,000.

Feb. 1 Sold the delivery truck for $4,100 cash. The depreciation expense of $300 for the month of January on the truck has not yet been recorded.

Mar. 1 Machine A was destroyed by fire. The insurance proceeds amounted to $4,000. Depreciation expense on this item for January 1, 19x9, through March 1, 19x9, has not been recorded yet and amounts to $400.

May 1 Paid $400 cash for routine repairs to the machines.

Dec. 31 Made the adjusting entry for depletion of mining properties, which were originally acquired for $150,000. The corporation estimates that the properties will produce a total of 150,000 tons of ore during their useful life. During 19x9, 10,000 tons of ore were produced.

      31 Made the adjusting entry for Machine B. Machine B was purchased on January 1, 19x8, at a cost of $60,000. The corporation is using the 200% declining-balance depreciation method to record depreciation on the machine and estimates that the machine has a $5,000 residual value.

Dec. 31   Made the adjusting entry to record depreciation on the building. The building was purchased on January 1, 19x7, and has a 10-year useful life with a $20,000 residual value. The corporation is using the sum-of-the-years'-digits depreciation method to record depreciation.

     31   Made the adjusting entry to record depreciation for Machine C.

Required:

Prepare the journal entries in general journal form for the above transactions.

P 8–17
Subsequent Costs
L.O.4

The Marccoor Corporation recorded a number of events during 19xx that are being disputed by the company's auditors. The central question in each case is whether or not a capital expenditure took place.

Event A: Marecoor paid $156,000 in legal fees to *successfully* defend its right to the exclusive use of a patented product for data transmission.

Event B: Land held as a future building site was originally zoned for commercial use until a citizens group successfully had it rezoned in 19xx for residential use only. Marecoor sued the local zoning board to reverse their decision or pay damages but was not successful. Legal fees were $100,000.

Event C: Marecoor replaced the carpet and repainted two floors of its 10-story office building at a cost of $425,000. This process occurs about once every five years.

Required:

Indicate whether or not these items are capital expenditures. Record the entries to account for the costs in each event.

P 8–18
Subsequent Costs
L.O.4

For each of the situations described below, determine whether the expenditure involved should be capitalized or expensed and give the reason for your decision. Assume the assets of each company are about $1,500,000.

1. Apex Company had a car drive into the storefront on Main Street. The uninsured damage to the front of the building (doors, glass, brick, and so on) cost Apex $2,965 to fix. *Expense*

2. In 19x3, Meal Furniture Store painted the exterior of its showroom facilities, for only the third time in the company's 100-year history, at a cost of $3,215. The building was originally a red brick structure. *Expense*

3. Arthur Marwick has two floors at the top of the World Center Building. The carpet has just been replaced at a cost of $60,000 to help celebrate 50 years of practice as a local CPA firm. *E*

4. The Main Front Bookstore recently put a new roof on its building at a cost of $15,000. The old roof had been repaired several times in each of the last five years and was no longer worth repairing.

5. *Betterment* The Barnes Ace Hardware Store recently spent $6,950 to landscape its store and parking lot area as their part of a major local beautification project in Hill City.

6. Ace Moving and Storage had to pay $3,000 to replace engines on two moving vans. Both vans had been purchased just 15 months earlier, and the replacements were not covered by warranty. This was the earliest such replacement in the company's history. *unexpected*

P 8–19
Multiple Choice
(Challenging)
L.O.1–4

1. The Lionel Corporation purchased a new machine on October 31, 19x1. A $250 cash down payment was made and three monthly installments of $800 each will be made beginning on November 30, 19x1. If Lionel had purchased the machine for cash, it would have paid $2,500. Lionel paid no installation charges under the monthly payment plan but a $50 installation charge would have been incurred with a cash purchase. The amount to be capitalized as the cost of the machine on October 31, 19x1 would be—

   a. $2,700.
   b. $2,650.
   c. $2,550.
   d. $2,500.
   e. $300.

2. In order to increase its parking area, the County Fair Shopping Center acquired adjoining land for $40,000 and a building located on the land for $15,000. The cost of razing the building and leveling the land to prepare the site for a parking lot was $1,500. Which account should be debited for the $1,500?

   a. Parking Lot.
   b. Construction Expense.
   c. Accumulated Depreciation—Parking Lot.
   d. Depreciation Expense.
   e. None of the above.

3. The Gladwin Construction Company bought a piece of construction machinery on January 2, 19x0, for $24,000. In addition, freight costs of $1,500 were paid by Gladwin. The company estimates the useful life of the machine to be five years and that it will have a residual value of $3,000. The company's annual accounting period ends on December 31. The amount of depreciation expense on the machine for **19x1** under the 200% declining-balance method of depreciation would be—

   a. $5,400.
   b. $5,760.
   c. $6,120.
   d. $10,200.
   e. None of the above.

4. The Krieger Company purchased a tooling machine on January 1, 19x1, for $50,000. The machine was being depreciated using the straight-line method over an estimated useful life of 20 years, with no residual value. On January 1, 19x1, when the machine had been in use for 10 years, Krieger paid $10,000 to overhaul the machine. As a result of the improvement, the Company estimated that the useful life of the machine would be extended an additional five years. What depreciation expense should be recorded for the machine in 19x1 using the straight-line method?

   a. $2,000.
   b. $2,333.
   c. $2,500.
   d. $7,000.
   e. None of the above.

P 8–20
Goodwill
L.O.7

Sunoma Wines acquired the net assets of Hill Round Ltd. for $1,580,000 cash on January 1, 19xx. The following information was available for Hill Round on the date of purchase:

	Fair Market Value	Book Value
Cash.	$ 115,000	$ 115,000
Inventory	285,000	120,000
Land.	1,295,000	485,000
Buildings	460,000	340,000
Total assets	$2,155,000	$1,060,000
Liabilities	750,000	750,000
Net assets	$1,405,000	$ 310,000

Sunoma estimates that all intangible assets will have a 25-year economic life and uses straight-line amortization for all intangibles.

Required:

1. Compute the amount of goodwill purchased by Sunoma.
2. Record the purchase of Hill Round on Sunoma's books on January 1, 19xx.
3. Record amortization of goodwill by Sunoma on December 31, 19xx.

P 8–21
Goodwill
L.O.7

Gulf-Eastern Industries exchanged one of its communication satellites for a 100% interest in WAVO Radio Station. The following data are available about the exchange:

Satellite

	Book Value	Estimated Fair Market Value
Cost	$3,900,000	
Accumulated depreciation	820,000	
Net	$3,080,000	$4,300,000

WAVO Radio Station

	Book Value	Estimated Fair Market Value
Assets	$1,850,000	$3,980,000
Liabilities	790,000	790,000
Net assets	$1,060,000	$3,190,000

Assume that both WAVO Radio owners and Gulf-Eastern management agree that the fair market value (cash-equivalent price) of the satellite—Sitcom I—is $4.3 million. Also, both parties agree that WAVO Radio has future earnings potential that is not reflected in the recorded assets of WAVO.

Required:
1. What is the apparent amount of goodwill, if any, that Gulf-Eastern seems willing to pay for when buying WAVO Radio?
2. At what value should the investment in WAVO be recorded?
3. Assume that the net assets acquired by Gulf-Eastern have a fair value of $4.3 million. Record the exchange on Gulf-Eastern's books. Use a single asset account, "Investment in WAVO," to record the inflow of assets in this exchange.

P 8–22
Analysis of Plant Assets
L.O.6

Jay-Kay Products acquired equipment costing $48,000 in 19x2 and recorded depreciation expense on equipment of $26,000 for the year. The following balance sheet data were reported at the end of 19x2:

	December 31	
	19x2	19x1
Equipment (at cost)	$498,650	$487,500
Accumulated depreciation—equipment	130,000	115,950
Net book value—equipment	$368,650	$371,550

The sale of used equipment during the year produced a gain of $2,850.

Required:
1. Compute the original cost of the used equipment sold in 19x2.
2. Compute the accumulated depreciation on the used equipment sold in 19x2.
3. Record the sale of used equipment.

P 8–23
Analysis of Plant Assets
L.O.6

Assume that your examination of the Armco Steel's 19x2 annual report revealed the following facts (in millions):

	December 31	
	19x2	19x1
Machinery (at cost)	$28	$29
Accumulated depreciation—machinery	10	9

During 19x2, Armco purchased $3 million in new machinery and sold used machinery at a loss of $2 million. Depreciation expense on machinery for 19x2 was $2 million.

Required:
1. Compute the original cost of the used machinery sold at a loss.
2. Compute the amount of accumulated depreciation on the used machinery sold at a loss.
3. Record the sale of used machinery.
4. What percent of the used machinery had been depreciated before the sale?

P 8–24
Analysis of Plant Assets
(Challenging)
L.O.6

The following information for the machinery and equipment of the Bardsley Corporation was taken from its 19x5 annual report:

	December 31		
	19x3	19x4	19x5
Machinery at cost net of accumulated depreciation	$2,875	$2,327	$2,756

	For the Year Ended December 31		
	19x3	19x4	19x5
Depreciation expense	$300	$315	$330

During 19x4, no acquisition of machinery occurred, but some machinery was sold by Bardsley for cash at a gain of $37. No machinery was sold in 19x5, but some new machinery was acquired for cash.

Required:
1. How much cash was provided by the sale of machinery in 19x4?
2. How much cash was used to acquire machinery in 19x5?

• Appendix Problems

P 8–25
Asset Exchanges
(Appendix 8A)
L.O.8

Barnett Company acquired a four-color printing press from Mr. Graves who was going out of business. The press had cost Mr. Graves $170,000 five years earlier. The current replacement cost of the press was $360,000. A printing industry publication listed the estimated market value of the press (and others like it) at $200,000. Barnett Company gave Mr. Graves a two-year $100,000 note that paid 10% interest each year, plus 2,000 shares of Barnett stock that were selling for $55 per share on the date of the exchange. Barnett stock was selling for $58 per share by the end of the accounting period. Use the fair value method to respond to the requirements below.

Required:
1. What is the cost to be reported by Barnett at the date of the transaction?
2. Record the entry to account for the purchase of the press using the fair value method.
3. Assume now that no market price was available for Barnett's stock during the year of the purchase. What value would be assigned to the press at the date of purchase?

P 8–26
Asset Exchange
(Appendix 8A)
L.O.8

Partners Pizza acquired a new delivery truck on July 1, 19x7, at a cost of $7,350 cash plus its old truck. The old truck had been acquired for $7,000 cash on July 1, 19x3, and was being depreciated on a straight-line basis using the half-year convention and assuming no scrap value. The estimated useful life of a delivery truck is five years. One of the delivery persons who worked for Partners offered to buy the truck for $900 cash. However, the new truck dealer wanted $8,500 cash for the new truck without the old truck as a trade-in, so Partners took the trade-in value of the old truck.

Required:
1. What is the fair value of the new truck?
2. Record the depreciation on the old truck to June 30, 19x7, for the year 19x7.
3. Record the asset exchange on July 1, 19x7, using the fair value method.

4. Record depreciation expense on the new truck for 19x7 using straight-line depreciation assuming no salvage value.
5. Repeat requirement 3 above using the income tax accounting method.

P 8–27
Natural Resources
(Appendix 8B)
L.O.9

The Big Dig Mining Company negotiated a rental agreement with the government of Ziembaro to extract copper ore from government coastal property for an eight-year period. The copper ore mining rights cost Big Dig $2,260,000 cash. The following additional facts were provided to you by Big Dig at the end of 19x1, the year the rental agreement was negotiated:

Cost of mining roads	$ 5,100,000
Cost of mining equipment and buildings	$ 9,440,000
Estimated physical life of equipment and buildings	15 years
Estimated tons of copper ore to be extracted	20,000,000 tons
Estimated maximum copper ore extraction possible per year starting in 19x2	2,000,000 tons

Because of the political climate in Ziembaro, the rental agreement, which expires at the end of 19x8, is not expected to be renewable. Also, because of the remote location of the mines, all of the equipment must be abandoned upon termination of the mining operations.

In 19x2, Big Dig extracted and sold 2,000,000 tons of copper ore at a selling price of $50 per ton.

Required:
1. Compute the depletion rate per ton of copper ore.
2. Record depletion for 19x2.
3. Assume mining and processing costs are $3.25 per ton during 19x2. Compute the total inventory cost of the copper ore sold in 19x2 and the gross profit on sales.

P 8–28
Depletion/Change in
Estimate (Appendix 8B)
(Challenging)
L.O.9

The Voldez Oil Corporation discovered 25 million barrels of oil in 19x1 in the Gulf of Alaska. The total cost of the discovery, including drilling costs, platforms, and so on, amounted to $18 million. During 19x1, Voldez extracted 8 million barrels of oil, which were sold to Standard of California for $120 million.

Required:
1. Compute the depletion rate per barrel and in total for 19x1 for Voldez Oil.
2. Assume the statutory depletion rate for tax purposes is 29% of sales dollars. Compute the tax depletion for 19x1. How much more depletion can Voldez Oil report in 19x1 for tax purposes compared to the financial reports?
3. Assume that in 19x2 Voldez extracted another 10 million barrels of oil. Then, in early 19x3, a new survey reported that the estimated remaining amount of unextracted oil was 15 million barrels. Two million barrels had been extracted in 19x3 **prior** to this survey, and another 8 million barrels were extracted in 19x3 after the survey. What is the new depletion rate as a result of this change in estimate? What is the amount of depletion to be reported in 19x3 by Voldez Oil?

• CASES

C 8–1
Depreciation
L.O.2, 3

Rawlings, Inc., acquired equipment on June 15, 19x1, at a cost of $140,000. The equipment was expected to last 10 years and have a $20,000 residual value. Rawlings used straight-line depreciation, resulting in $12,000 depreciation per year. Rawlings took one-half year's depreciation ($6,000) in 19x1. On September 30, 19x7, Rawlings sold the equipment for $70,000 cash to Wilson Corporation. Rawlings took $6,000 depreciation expense on the equipment for 19x7 in accordance with the half-year convention and recorded the following entry at the time of sale:

19x7			
Sept. 30	Cash	70,000	
	Accumulated Depreciation	72,000	
	Equipment		140,000
	Gain on Sale of Equipment		2,000

Rawlings' auditor is contending that Rawlings never specified it was using the half-year convention, and that nine months of depreciation (or $9,000) should have been taken in 19x7. This would have turned the $2,000 gain into a $1,000 loss.

Required:
1. Are the numbers in the case correct?
2. Assume the numerical data provided are all correct. Is the auditor's position correct or not?
3. If Rawlings refused to go along with the auditor, how much more income before tax would be reported in 19x7?
4. Is your answer to part 3 peculiar to this case or does it apply in general?
5. What additional information could be viewed to help solve this dispute, assuming that Rawlings had been in business for many years?

C 8–2
Goodwill
L.O.7

Consider the facts in Problem 8-4 concerning the basket purchase of three houses by Lime Tree Complex. Is there any goodwill in this transaction? Explain your position referring to the definition of goodwill.

C 8–3
Acquisition Costs
L.O.1

West Corporation acquired the following assets from Baiman, Inc., on January 1, 19xx, at a total cost of $2,875,000:

- Land (corner lot at Stadium and Main, Atherton, Ohio).
- Building (brick construction, built 25 years ago, 4 stories).
- Equipment (average remaining life, six years).

The book values of these assets on Baiman's books at the date of purchase were

	Book Values
Land.	$ 75,000
Building (net)	1,080,000
Equipment (net)	620,000
Total	$1,775,000

On January 10, 19xx, before West did anything with the idle Baiman facilities, the equipment was sold to Jarrell Corporation for $750,000.

Required:
1. How might West assign the $2,875,000 purchase price to the three different assets?
2. What method of asset valuation would be most appropriate for West if any value desired were available?
3. What is the gain or loss, if any, that you think should be recorded on January 10, 19xx, by West from the sale of the equipment?
4. If Baiman had sold the equipment directly to Jarrell, what would be your estimate of the selling price of the equipment?

C 8–4
Subsequent Costs
L.O.4

L & M Real Estate owns four furnished rental houses in Chelsea near Community University. The following expenditures took place in 19x5 concerning these rental properties:

Property 1:
   Interior painting, $780.
   Replace rear door, $650.
   Replace screens and storms, $800.
   Replace some furniture, $1,360.

Property 2:
   Replace carpeting in living room and stairs, $1,650.
   Replace some furniture, $760.

Property 3:
   Resurface gravel driveway, $435.
   Paint exterior, $1,290.
   Replace furniture in kitchen, $1,500.

Property 4:
   Paint interior, $695.
   Paint exterior, $1,150.
   Replace sliding glass door, $520.

Required:

Determine which expenditures should be expensed in 19x5 and which should be capitalized. Give the reason for each of your decisions.

C 8–5
Subsequent Costs
L.O.4

The Briarwood Mall is a major shopping center located on a 30-acre site near Centerville. The complex has just undergone a major renovation to celebrate its 25th anniversary of being in business. The following expenditures were incurred during the renovation.

Item	Cost	Estimated Useful Life
1. Landscaping	$120,000	15 years
2. Parking lot light fixtures	180,000	20 years
3. New high-intensity bulbs in all fixtures	15,000	18 months
4. Repair parking lot surface holes.	95,000	5 years
5. Sealant to parking lot surface.	32,000	2 years
6. Repaint exterior of buildings	63,000	4 years
7. Repaint interior of mall.	79,000	3 years
8. New interior benches for seating	125,000	8 years

The net book value of the mall before renovations was $5,600,000.

Required:

1. Explain which items you believe should be capitalized as assets and which items you believe should be expensed. In each case, explain the reason(s) supporting your decisions.
2. Which decision in your answer above are you least confident about? What factors might support an alternative treatment of these costs?

C 8–6
Depreciation and Taxes
L.O.2

Wellman Corporation acquired new lab equipment on January 1, 19x3, at a cost of $520,000. The equipment is expected to have a 10-year life and a $20,000 salvage value. Wellman reports income before taxes and before depreciation expense of $250,000 in 19x3 and $300,000 in 19x4. The income tax rate is 34% and taxes must be paid in cash.

Required:

1. Which of the following depreciation methods will result in the lowest income tax payments for 19x3 and 19x4 combined?
   a. Straight-line.
   b. 150% declining-balance.
   c. Sum-of-the-years'-digits.
2. Which depreciation method results in the highest net income for 19x3 and 19x4 combined?
3. Assuming you are Wellman's chief accountant, which method would you advise them to use? Explain your choice.

C 8–7
Depreciation and Taxes
L.O.2

The Lakeland Corporation has been in business for less than one year. The owner, Mr. Griffin, has been asked by his accountant to select a depreciation method for financial reporting purposes. The accountant told Mr. Griffin that he was going to use the most accelerated method possible for income tax purposes, with most major assets to be depreciated over 18 years even though they are expected to be useful for 60 years or more. The accountant has told Griffin that selection of a method for financial reporting purposes will affect earnings, with straight-line resulting in the highest profits.

Lakeland's profits before income taxes and depreciation for the initial year of operations was about $170,000. The depreciation expense taken for tax purposes was $410,000. The range of possible depreciation expense measures for financial reporting purposes is $70,000 to $240,000.

Mr. Griffin is totally confused by these alternatives and, given all the conflicting information, uncertain of the accountant's ethics. He knows you are an accounting major, and at a recent dinner party with your family (friends of Griffin's) he asked you the following questions.

1. What should be Lakeland's profit objective for income tax purposes?
2. What should be Lakeland's profit objective for financial reporting purposes?
3. How much better off will Lakeland be if I elect to use the $70,000 depreciation expense method for financial reporting purposes? How much more cash will Lakeland have using one versus the other?
4. Is my accountant violating any accounting principles or procedures?

Write up a response to the four questions posed to you by Mr. Griffin.

• Evaluating Financial Statements

C 8–8
Change in Estimates— GM (Challenging)
L.O.3

General Motors Corporation leases automobiles to customers through its many GM dealerships. These automobiles are reported as assets on GM's books and are depreciated over their estimated useful lives. In 19x7, GM reported net income of $3,550.9 million compared to 19x6 income of $2,994.7 million, or a 20.5% increase in 19x7. However, in its financial statement footnotes, GM revealed the following information:

> In the first quarter of 19x7, (GM) revised the rates of depreciation on automobiles... (leased) to retail customers.... These revisions had the effect of increasing (GM's) 19x7 net income by $254.7 million.

GM also noted the following change in the estimated life of its plant and equipment:

> In the third quarter of 19x7, (GM) revised the estimated service lives of its plants and equipment and special tools [effective] January 1, 19x7. These revisions... had the effect of reducing 19x7 depreciation and amortization (expense) by $1,236.6 million.

Assume that the effect of the second change on GM's 19x7 net income was $816.1 million [$1,236.6 × (1 − tax rate) = $1,236.6 × .66].

Required:
1. In what direction was the change in the life of leased automobiles?
2. In what direction was the change in the life of plants, equipment, and special tools?
3. What would GM have reported as net income in 19x7 if these changes in estimates had not been made? What would have been the percentage change in 19x7 net income over 19x6 net income?
4. Was GM correct in making a change in estimate in the third quarter but carrying the effect of the change back to the beginning of 19x7, the year of change?

C 8–9
*Annual Report
Analysis—IBM*
L.O.6

The following balance sheet data were reported by International Business Machines Corporation (IBM) in a recent annual report (in millions of dollars):

	19x6	19x5
Plant, machines, and property.	$38,121	$34,483
Less: Accumulated depreciation	16,853	14,803
Net book value	$21,268	$19,680

Assume that from the other financial statement data you learn that IBM recorded depreciation expense of $3,316 million and that they sold machines with a net book value of $647 million during 19x6?

Required:
What is the apparent amount of additional investment in plant, machines, and property during 19x6?

C 8–10
*Annual Report
Analysis—
General Electric*
L.O.6

A recent annual report for General Electric Corporation (GE) reported the following balance sheet data:

**Property, Plant, and Equipment
December 31
(in millions)**

	19x6	19x5
Land	$ 271	$ 178
Buildings	4,087	3,449
Machinery and equipment.	12,061	10,218
Other plant assets	1,955	1,861
Total original cost	$18,374	$15,706
Less:		
Accumulated depreciation balance at January 1	$ 7,806	$ 7,089
Current year expense	1,460	1,249
Asset disposals	(733)	(532)
Balance at December 31	$ 8,533	$ 7,806
Net book value	$ 9,841	$ 7,900

During 19x6, GE acquired $3,680 million in property, plant, and equipment. This included $1,638 million in assets acquired through their purchase of RCA in 19x6.

Required:
1. What was the apparent original cost of assets disposed of during 19x6 by GE?
2. What was the approximate percentage of depreciation taken on assets disposed of during 19x6 prior to their disposal?

C 8–11
*Analysis of
Intangibles—
Ralston Purina*
L.O.2, 6, 7

Consider the Ralston Purina Company's (RPC's) annual report in Appendix E at the back of the text. Refer to the two footnotes, "Supplemental Balance Sheet Information" and "Analysis of Balance Sheet Changes" along with the combined amount of "depreciation and amortization" reported in the fiscal 1992 Statement of Cash Flows.

Required:
1. How much was amortization expense for fiscal 1992? (Hint: use T accounts.)
2. How much was depreciation expense for fiscal 1992?
3. What was the cost of intangibles acquired during fiscal 1992? (Hint: use T accounts.)

Massey Corporation
Balance Sheet For 12/31/94

	1994	1993
Current assets:		
Total current assets.	$ xxx	$ xxx
Noncurrent assets:		
Total noncurrent assets	$ xxx	$ xxx
Total assets	$ xxx	$ xxx
Current liabilities:		
Accounts payable	**$ xxx**	**$ xxx**
Salaries payable.	**xxx**	**xxx**
Notes payable.	**xx**	**xx**
Taxes payable.	**xx**	**xx**
Total current liabilities.	**$ xxx**	**$ xxx**
Noncurrent liabilities:		
Total noncurrent liabilities	xx	xx
Stockholders' equity:		
Total stockholders' equity	xxx	xxx
Total liabilities and stockholders' equity	$ xxxx	$ xxxx

Massey Corporation
Income Statement For 1994

	1994	1993
Net sales	$ xxx	$ xxx
Cost of goods sold	xxx	xxx
Gross margin	$ xxx	$ xxx
Expenses		
Interest expense.	**xx**	**xx**
Total expenses	$ xxx	$ xxx
Net income	$ xx	$ xx

Massey Corporation
Cash Flow Statement For 1994

	1994	1993
Operating activities		
Payments for interest	**(xx)**	**(xx)**
Cash used in operating activities	$ xxx	$ xxx
Investing activities		
Cash used in investing activities	$ (xxx)	$ (xxx)
Financing activities		
Issuance of note.	**xxx**	
Cash paid in maturity of note	**(xxx)**	**(xxx)**
Cash used in financing activities	$ xxxx	$ xxxx
Net change in cash	$ xx	$ xx

FINANCIAL STATEMENT COMPONENTS EMPHASIZED IN CHAPTER 9

9

Current Liabilities and Payroll

A particularly troublesome situation to me would be knowledge of an environmental exposure that is neither quantified nor otherwise apparent. In today's over-reactionary and over-regulated environment, premature disclosure could severely and unnecessarily damage the company; but what if someone was harmed by delay?

Richard R. Current
The Shane Group, Inc.

· Learning Objectives

After studying Chapter 9, you should understand

1. Accounting for definitely determinable liabilities, which include accounts payable, short-term notes payable, dividends payable, and the current portion of long-term debt, pp. 444–54.

2. Accounting for estimated liabilities, which include income taxes, property taxes, vacation pay, and warranties, pp. 453–60.

3. Accounting for contingent liabilities, pp. 460–63.

4. The importance of a payroll system to a company, pp. 463–64.

5. The effect of payroll deductions and employer taxes, pp. 464–67.

6. The nature of deferred income taxes (Appendix) pp. 470–72.

7. The financial statement effects of deferred income taxes (Appendix), pp. 472–73.

Liabilities were defined in Chapter 1 as claims by outsiders to receive cash, other assets, or services from the business at some future date. These claims require future sacrifice and arise from past transactions. In Chapter 2, you learned that liabilities are debts of the business that are recorded in the accounting records. Another way of saying the same thing is that liabilities are the obligations of the business to deliver assets or perform services to which money amounts can be assigned.

If at the balance sheet date, a liability is such that the cash, goods, or services owed are to be paid, provided, or performed within one year or one operating cycle, whichever is longer, the liability is current or short term; otherwise, the liability is noncurrent or long term. This chapter focuses on current liabilities. Noncurrent or long-term liabilities are discussed in Chapter 10.

The key to determining whether a liability is short term or long term is the expected timing of the flow of assets or services that are required to eliminate the obligation. Current liabilities can arise from transactions with suppliers, banks, employees, governments, and many other entities. Most current liabilities are paid off in a routine, ongoing manner. Suppliers' invoices usually call for payment within a month of receipt; payrolls are paid weekly, semimonthly, or monthly; taxes have defined payment dates; notes usually have fixed interest and principal payment dates. And long-term liabilities become short term when payment is scheduled within a year or operating cycle, whichever is longer, of the balance sheet date. Not all countries define long and short term in the same way. In Spain, for instance, short term is used for maturities of up to eighteen months, and in Germany long term is used for four years and over.

Appendix E of this book shows the current liabilities in an annual report of Ralston Purina Company. Although this represents typical current liability disclosure, it demonstrates that a great deal of variation exists in the terminology used to describe current liabilities. The word *payable* is often used as in "Accounts payable"; the word *accrued* is also used as in "Accrued liabilities." While no formal rules exist governing such terminology, accruals usually represent the results of adjusting entries that record payables at year-end. For some current liabilities, neither term is used, as in "Income taxes" in the "Current liabilities" section of Ralston's balance sheet.

In this chapter we categorize current liabilities as (1) definitely determinable current liabilities, (2) estimated liabilities, and (3) contingent liabilities. Although liabilities related to payroll are definitely determinable, we discuss them separately, in the Payroll Accounting section, because in most businesses payroll is a major expense that generates several liabilities. The appendix to the chapter discusses deferred income taxes, which are created when income tax expense for a period does not equal the income tax obligation to the government for that period.

DEFINITELY DETERMINABLE CURRENT LIABILITIES

Objective 1
Accounting for definitely determinable liabilities.

Do All Liabilities Appear on the Balance Sheet?

A definitely determinable current liability is an existing current liability of a precisely measurable amount. The definitely determinable current liabilities discussed in this section are accounts payable, short-term notes payable, dividends payable, and the current portion of long-term debt. Later in the chapter, we discuss other liabilities that exist but whose amounts must be estimated. We also discuss several situations in which a liability may result if certain future events take place.

Before looking at specifics, consider the following dialog as an introduction to the concept of definitely determinable liabilities.

Two friends, a bank president and a CPA partner, are having lunch and engaging in their usual kidding about each other's professions; but in this case there is a serious theme that is a good introduction to accounting for liabilities.

Banker: Look, I lend money to companies and I rely on their financial statements, particularly the reported liabilities, because if I give them the loan, that loan will show up there on the right side of their balance sheet (It *is* the right side, correct?) along with all the rest of the debts. The more creditors the borrower has the higher my risks of not being paid back.

Accountant: OK; so what's the problem? If there is one thing we beancounters are good at it's coming up with a pretty reliable number for liabilities.

Banker: I agree with that, for the liabilities you actually put on the balance sheet, like accounts payable, salaries payable, notes payable, and all that. What I worry about are the quote liabilities unquote that you don't necessarily show. For instance, I gave a $4 million, one-year loan to a seemingly healthy company last year. It turns out that they were being sued by the government for a toxic waste spill and that it could possibly take $30 million to clean it up. Now, that amount was *not* on the balance sheet even though the spill took place before the year-end.

Accountant: Listen, I don't know about that case specifically, but this is in general how I would approach such a situation. At the balance sheet date, if an event has taken place that has created a definite liability, like unpaid salary or borrowing, I would record it. If an event like a toxic spill had taken place that might create a liability in the future, whether I record it or not depends on the probability of the future actions, like the outcome of lawsuits. We have rules about how we determine the probabilities.

Banker: So you are admitting that it could be okay for this potential liability not to be on the balance sheet?

Accountant: It depends on the probabilities involved. When we are 100% sure that an obligation exists we record it even if we have to estimate the amount, as is often the case for taxes. If we are not sure, but something has happened already that makes it probable that there will be an obligation, we will estimate it and record and/or disclose something in the notes to the financials according to our rules.

Banker: Look, wouldn't it be better to show the worst-case scenario? It is what I don't know that can hurt me, and if it's not shown on the balance sheet, how do you expect me to know about it?

Accountant: The accounting rules aim at giving a realistic picture of the business. Nobody would ever get a loan if we always looked at the most negative possibilities. Then we'd both be out of business. I'll bet you the price of lunch that if your people looked closely at the notes to that balance sheet they would find that something was mentioned about the problems of that toxic spill.

Banker: Maybe, but that's not the same as being shown on the balance sheet.

This conversation touches on many issues we will formally cover in the sections that follow, and it focuses on the fact that accountants must use professional judgment in all aspects of their job, even in determining whether or not a liability exists.

Accounts Payable

Accounts payable is a current liability used to record the purchase of goods and services on credit. For example, when a purchaser receives goods shipped on open account from suppliers, the transaction causes an entry of the following kind to be recorded on the customer's books:

```
19xx
Apr.  1   Purchases (A) . . . . . . . . . . . . . . . . . . . . . . . .  1,000
              Accounts Payable (L)  . . . . . . . . . . . . . . . . . . . .       1,000
          To record purchase of merchandise on account.
```

When classified under Accounts Payable, the obligation usually will be paid off soon with no interest charged on the outstanding amount, although cash discounts are often given for early payment. (See Chapter 5 for a discussion of cash discounts.) If payment were made on the liability recorded above and no discount were taken, the following entry would be recorded:

```
19xx
Apr. 15   Accounts Payable (L) . . . . . . . . . . . . . . . . . . . . . .    1,000
              Cash (A) . . . . . . . . . . . . . . . . . . . . . . . . .             1,000
          To record payment of invoice dated April 1.
```

The balance sheet of a company shows the total liabilities to be paid. The accounts payable amount is based on the assumption that the company normally expects to pay all invoice amounts less the discounts expected to be taken. Companies do not make an estimation of nonpayment for accounts payable such as the estimation of noncollection for accounts receivable. If the entity is a going concern (i.e., expected to stay in business for the foreseeable future), the accountant assumes that all debts will be paid according to the contractual terms. Creditors have the legal right to payment, and it is reasonable to assume that they will pursue that right to receive payment even to the point of forcing the sale of the debtor's assets, if need be.

Interest—Simple and Compound

Consider the following simple borrowing transaction by Borrower Corporation.

Borrows	Pays
$10,000	$11,000
1/1/x1	12/31/x1

What do you believe determined the $11,000 payback? The difference between the amount received upon borrowing and the amount paid back is the interest on the loan. Interest is determined by multiplying the amount borrowed (principal) by the interest rate (a percentage applied to principal). The formula for computing interest is

$$(\text{Interest per period}) = (\text{Principal})(\text{Interest rate})(\text{Number of periods})$$

Applying the specific amounts from the case of Borrower Corporation to the above formula we get

$$\$1,000 = (\$10,000)(.10)(1)$$

How was the interest rate determined? In this case we know that if we start with a liability of $10,000 (the principal) and we pay back $11,000 (the maturity amount) in one year, interest equals $1,000. The interest amount for a period divided by the principal at the beginning of the period is the interest rate for the period; that is, $1,000 divided by $10,000 = 10\%$.

If we change our example to a two-period example we can make a distinction between two types of interest: simple and compound. Consider the following transaction, again at a 10% interest rate:

Method 1		Method 2	
Borrows	**Pays**	**Borrows**	**Pays**
$10,000	$12,000	$10,000	$12,100
1/1/x1 12/31/x1 12/31/x2		1/1/x1 12/31/x1 12/31/x2	

Why is the total interest under method 1 less than under method 2? In this case the total interest for the two-year period is $2,000 for method 1 and $2,100 for method 2, computed as follows:

		Simple Interest Computation	Compound Interest Computation
1/1/x1	Principal at 1/1/x1	$10,000	$10,000
	Interest for year 1 at 10%	1,000	1,000
	Balance owed at 12/31/x1	11,000	11,000
	Interest for year 2 at 10%	1,000	1,100
	Total maturity amount	$12,000	$12,100

Method 1 demonstrates what is called simple interest for which the interest earned in the first period is ignored in the computation of the interest for the second period; that is, we simply multiply the initial principal by the stated interest to get the interest for any period. Method 2 is an example of a compound interest calculation where the interest in the first period is added to the principal for the next period's computation of interest. Note that under simple interest all periods have the same interest amount; namely, [(initial principal) × (interest rate)]. Under compound interest each period has a different interest amount. Year 1 has $1,000, the same as under simple interest, but year 2 has $1,100, computed as follows: [(initial principal plus unpaid interest to date) × (interest rate)]. Throughout this text we assume compound interest. Unless otherwise stated, interest is compounded annually. Compound interest will be covered more thoroughly in Chapter 10.

Short-Term Notes Payable

A short-term note payable is a liability with many of the same attributes as accounts payable except that a note is a formal contract of indebtedness between a debtor (the **maker** of the note) and a creditor (the **payee** of the note). Short-term notes are usually interest bearing, but they can also be noninterest bearing. The paragraphs that follow discuss two forms of the same contractual relationship: interest-bearing short-term notes and noninterest-bearing short-term notes.

Interest-Bearing Short-Term Notes.   An interest-bearing short-term note issued to a creditor by a debtor specifies the principal amount of the note (i.e., the initial amount borrowed), the interest rate, and the maturity date. Exhibit 9–1 gives the general format of an interest-bearing short-term note. To illustrate a short-term interest-bearing (and, later, noninterest-bearing) note, we will follow the transactions of Jetstar Labs, Inc.

EXHIBIT 9–1

Interest-Bearing Short-Term Note

```
_____(Location)_____          _____(Date)_____

_____(Maker of note)_____  promises to pay  _____(Payee)_____

on _____(Due date)_____      $ ____(Principal)____      plus

interest at _____(Interest rate)_____  percent per annum.


                              _____(Signature)_____
```

On November 1, 19x1, Jetstar Labs, Inc., (which has a December 31 year-end) borrowed $100,000 from National Bank and signed a six-month note (see Exhibit 9–2) at an annual interest rate of 12%. Often, in this text and in the real world, the terms *annual interest rate* and *interest rate* are used interchangeably. Unless stated otherwise, assume that *interest rate* means annual interest rate. The principal and interest are to be paid on May 1, 19x2. The initial liability of Jetstar is the face amount or principal of the note, $100,000. The additional liability for interest is recorded at year-end in a separate account called Interest Payable. The total amount paid at maturity is $106,000, which is the principal plus interest for the six-month period. The interest accrued at year-end is recorded by means of an adjusting entry and represents two months' interest on the $100,000 principal. The journal entries to record the note on Jetstar's books, the accrued interest, and the payment of the note at maturity are

19x1			
Nov. 1	Cash (A)	100,000	
	Short-Term Notes Payable (L).		100,000
	To record 12%, six-month note.		
Dec. 31	Interest Expense (E)	2,000	
	Interest Payable (L)		2,000
	To record interest for two-month period:		
	$100,000 \times .12 \times {}^2\!/_{12} = \$2,000.$		
19x2			
May 1	Interest Expense (E).	4,000	
	Interest Payable (L)	2,000	
	Short-Term Notes Payable (L).	100,000	
	Cash (A)		106,000
	To record payment of principal plus interest and record interest		
	expense for four-month period in 19x2.		

The entries above indicate that at December 31, 19x1, Jetstar was liable for the $100,000 principal plus $2,000 interest, or $102,000.

At December 31, 19x1, does Jetstar owe $102,000 or is this merely an accounting representation of an economic abstraction? This question is difficult to answer because the note contract indicates that principal plus interest is due on the maturity date; it does not say how much Jetstar legally owes on December 31, 19x1. Accountants, however, are in the business of communicating economic substance rather than legal form; and standard

EXHIBIT 9–2

Jetstar Labs, Inc., Note

Jackson, Wyoming   November 1, 19x1
Jetstar Labs, Inc., promises to pay National Bank on May 1, 19x2, one hundred thousand dollars ($100,000) plus interest at twelve (12) percent per annum.
J. R. Jet
——————————————————
J. R. Jet, President

accounting principles state that interest accrues under the assumption that each month covered by the note gets the same benefit from a short-term loan. If the note were to be paid off early, for example on December 31, the $102,000 is a reasonable approximation of what National Bank would accept. However, unless specified in the contract, the bank is not obligated to accept the early payment, and certainly it cannot force the debtor to make an early payment.

By means of the analysis of Exhibit 9–3, we will now review the fundamental concept of the effects of interest accumulated on the total liability related to the obligation.

At the date the note is issued, the principal of $100,000 (the amount of cash received) is the liability balance. Interest accumulates evenly throughout the term of the note. At 12/31/x1, $2,000 of interest has accumulated, so the total obligation related to the note is $102,000. At 5/1/x2, the maturity date, another $4,000 of interest has accumulated, giving a total liability related to the note of $106,000, and this is the cash payment to the maker of the note. Therefore total interest is the total *cash out* of $106,000 *minus* the total

EXHIBIT 9–3

Cash Flow and Interest Accumulation on a Note

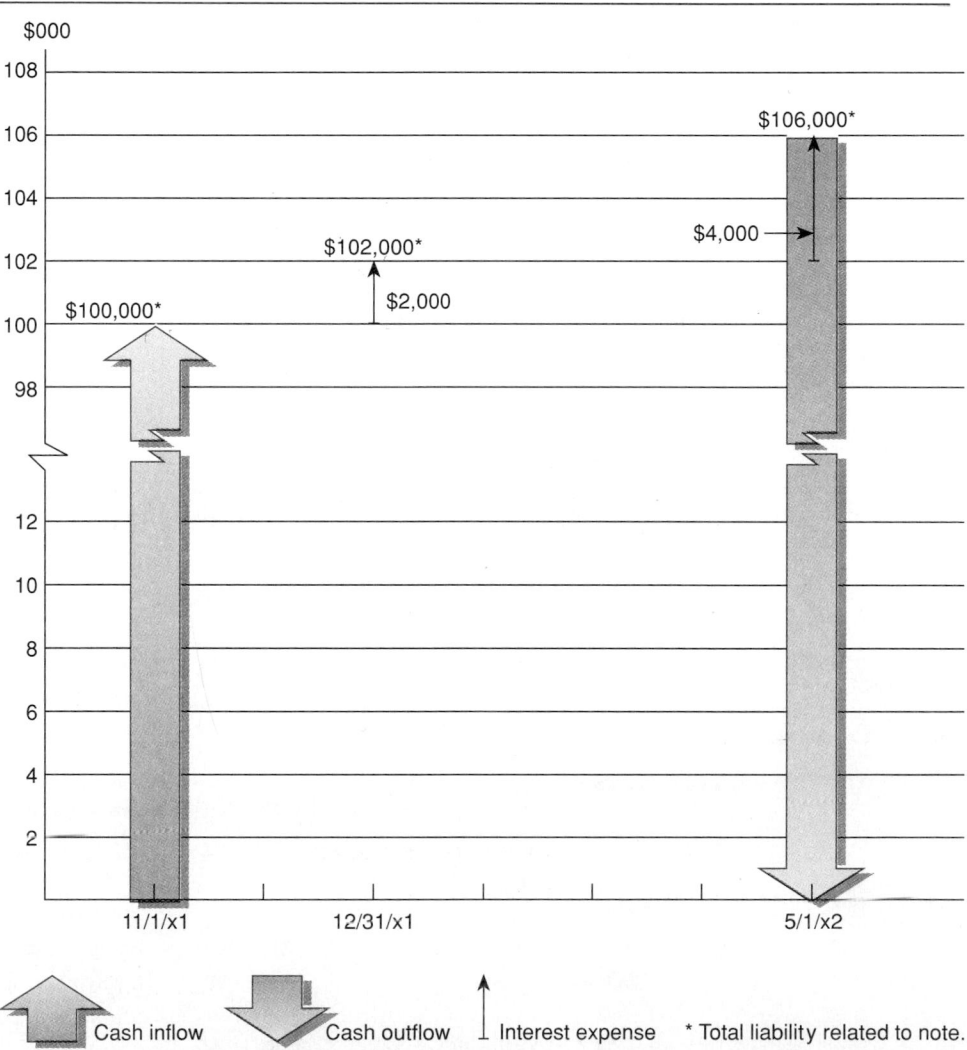

Cash inflow   Cash outflow   Interest expense   * Total liability related to note.

cash in of $100,000, or $6,000. The $6,000 is recognized as interest expense over two periods; 19x1 gets $2,000 and 19x2 gets $4,000.

Noninterest-Bearing Short-Term Notes. A noninterest-bearing short-term note does not specify an interest rate, and its maturity value is the face value of the note. To refer to a note as noninterest-bearing does not mean that interest is not a factor. Interest is **imputed,** that is, taken into consideration, whenever it is a real factor in determining the total cash inflow and the total cash outflow from a borrowing or lending transaction of any kind. Imputed interest is the interest that is related to a note or other financial instrument when there is no overt mention of an interest factor on the instrument. For example, on November 1, 19x1, Jetstar could have promised to pay National Bank $106,000 on May 1, 19x2. Although the face value of the note is $106,000, Jetstar does not receive $106,000 from the bank. Instead, interest is taken into consideration, and Jetstar receives an amount less than $106,000, depending on the "implied" interest rate. Assume that Jetstar receives $100,000; the $6,000 difference between what is received and paid in this noninterest-bearing note is the bank's interest charge for the use of the $100,000. Although the interest rate is not specified, the interest of $6,000 on the $100,000 borrowed is for one half of a year, and the interest rate is seen to be 12%. This interest rate is then used to make the interest calculations.

The journal entries to record the noninterest-bearing note are:

```
19x1
Nov.  1    Cash (A) . . . . . . . . . . . . . . . . . .     100,000
           Discount on Notes Payable (XL) . . . . . . . . . . . .       6,000
                Short-Term Notes Payable (L). . . . . . . . . . . .               106,000
           To record noninterest-bearing note.

Dec. 31    Interest Expense (E) . . . . . . . . . . . . . . . . .       2,000
                Discount on Notes Payable (XL) . . . . . . . . . . . .               2,000
           To record interest for two-month period:
           $100,000 × .12 × ²/₁₂ = $2,000.

19x2
May   1    Interest Expense (E) . . . . . . . . . . . . . . . . .       4,000
           Short-Term Notes Payable (L). . . . . . . . . . . . . .     106,000
                Discount on Notes Payable (XL) . . . . . . . . . . . .               4,000
                Cash (A) . . . . . . . . . . . . . . . . . . . .               106,000
           To record payment of principal plus interest and record interest
           expense for four-month period.
```

Note that the economic substance of the noninterest-bearing note is no different than that of an interest-bearing note. Compare the balance sheet and income statement disclosures of the two types of note:

Interest-Bearing:

Jetstar Labs, Inc.
Partial Balance Sheet
December 31, 19x1

Current liabilities:

Notes payable.	$100,000
Interest payable	2,000
	$102,000

Noninterest-Bearing:

Jetstar Labs, Inc.
Partial Balance Sheet
December 31, 19x1

Current liabilities:

Notes payable	$106,000
Discount on notes payable	(4,000)
	$102,000

Jetstar Labs, Inc. Partial Income Statement For the Year Ended December 31, 19x1		Jetstar Labs, Inc. Partial Income Statement For the Year Ended December 31, 19x1	
Expenses:		Expenses:	
Interest expense.	$ 2,000	Interest expense	$ 2,000

The account, Discount on Notes Payable, is a contra account (one that is subtracted from another account—Notes Payable, in this case). Since the noninterest-bearing note has the maturity value stated on the note, that amount is often recorded as notes payable, but the contra account is used to reduce the liability to its appropriate balance.

Dividends Payable

A corporation's board of directors has the right to decide whether or not to distribute earnings to its stockholders in the form of cash dividends and must decide on the amount to be paid on outstanding stock. Once cash dividends are declared, they become definite obligations of the company. As an obligation, declared cash dividends are recorded as a current liability. If no dividends are declared, no obligation exists, and no liability is recorded.

Time usually elapses between the declaration date and the payment date of cash dividends, and the establishment of the liability on the declaration date recognizes that the company owes money to the stockholders at that point. For example, if on December 15, 19x1, Los Alamos, Inc., has 1 million common shares outstanding and declares a $0.25 per share dividend to be paid on January 15, 19x2, the journal entries for the declaration and payment are

```
19x1
Dec. 15    Dividends (SE) . . . . . . . . . . . . . . . . . . . .    250,000
                Dividends Payable (L) . . . . . . . . . . . . . . .              250,000
           To record declaration of dividend:
           1,000,000 × $0.25 = $250,000.


19x2
Jan. 15    Dividends Payable (L) . . . . . . . . . . . . . . . . .    250,000
                Cash (A) . . . . . . . . . . . . . . . . . . . . .              250,000
           To record payment of dividend.
```

When dividends are discussed in detail in Chapter 11, you will learn that not all forms of dividends and other disbursements to stockholders have such clear-cut accounting treatment.

Current Portion of Long-Term Debt

As stated at the beginning of this chapter, long-term liabilities are those liabilities that are not expected to be paid to creditors within one year or one operating cycle, whichever is longer. However, the current portion of a long-term debt is classified on the balance sheet as a current liability. For example, assume that a company borrows $300,000 and signs a three-year note on December 31, 19x1, to be paid in three payments, on December 31 of 19x2, 19x3, and 19x4, plus 10% annual interest on the unpaid balance. Exhibit 9–4 shows the relationship of cash in, cash out, interest, and the liability balances on each date after each payment. Again, the total interest is the total cash out of $360,000 minus the total cash in of $300,000 or $60,000 allocated to 19x2, 19x3, and 19x4 ($30,000, $20,000, and $10,000, respectively). The following series of journal entries are recorded:

```
19x1
Dec. 31    Cash (A) . . . . . . . . . . . . . . . . . . . . . . .    300,000
                Notes Payable (L) . . . . . . . . . . . . . . . . .              300,000
           To record 10%, three-year note.
```

EXHIBIT 9–4

Cash Flows and Interest Amounts on a Long-Term Note

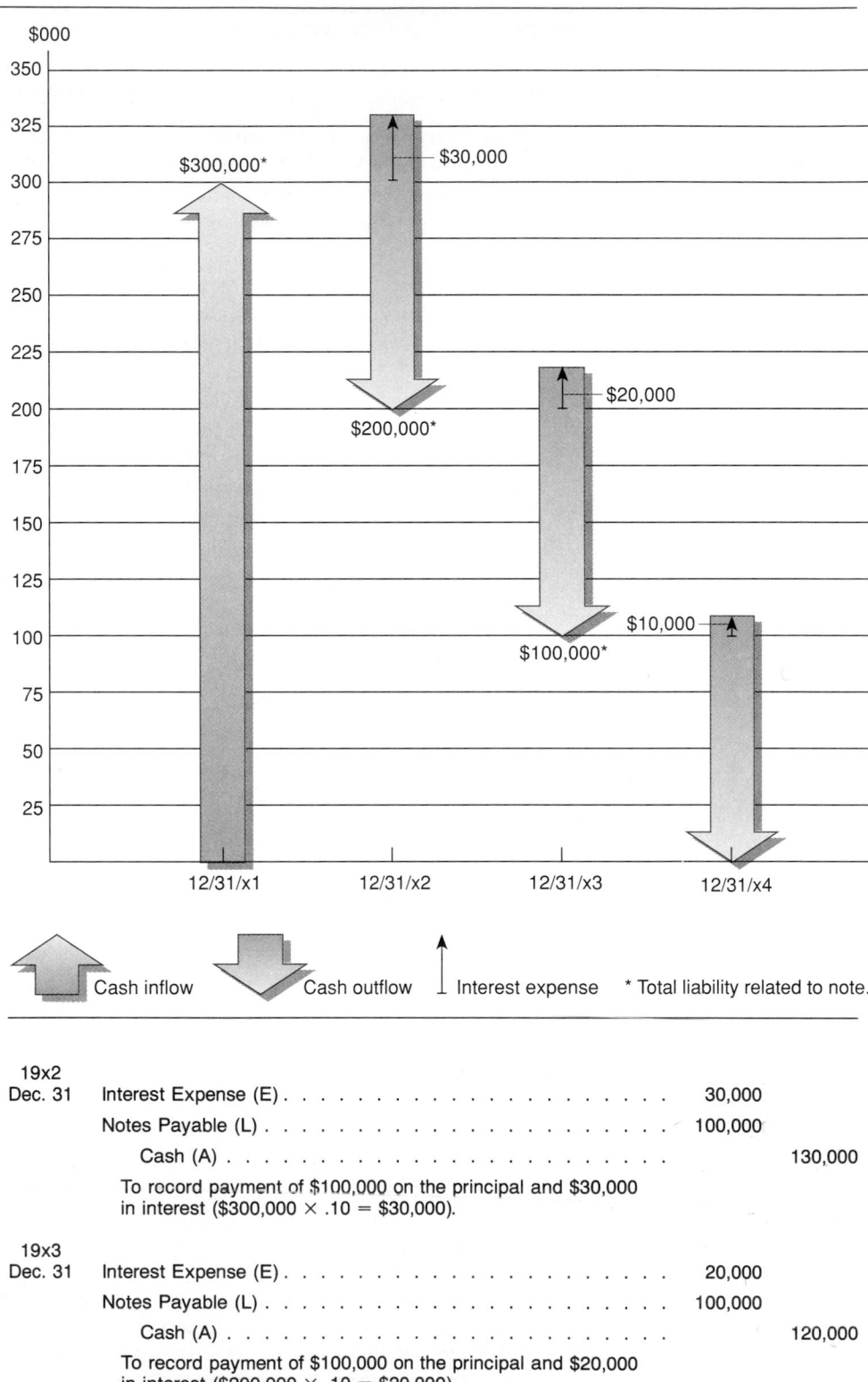

19x2
Dec. 31   Interest Expense (E)   30,000
            Notes Payable (L)   100,000
               Cash (A)   130,000
            To record payment of $100,000 on the principal and $30,000
            in interest ($300,000 × .10 = $30,000).

19x3
Dec. 31   Interest Expense (E)   20,000
            Notes Payable (L)   100,000
               Cash (A)   120,000
            To record payment of $100,000 on the principal and $20,000
            in interest ($200,000 × .10 = $20,000).

19x4

Dec. 31   Interest Expense (E) 10,000

         Notes Payable (L) 100,000

            Cash (A) 110,000

         To record payment of $100,000 on the principal and $10,000
in interest ($100,000 × .10 = $10,000).

The following table shows how the current liability and long-term liability of this $300,000 note is related to its total liability during the three-year period from December 31, 19x1, to December 31, 19x4:

| | | | Balance Sheet Classification | | |
| | | | | | |
Date	Total Liability	=	Current Liability*	+	Long-Term Liability†
12/31/x1	$300,000		$100,000		$200,000
12/31/x2	200,000		100,000		100,000
12/31/x3	100,000		100,000		0
12/31/x4	0		0		0

*To be paid within one year or one operating cycle if longer.
†To be paid after one year or one operating cycle if longer.

It is important to see that in this case no interest is accrued at year-end, either because no time has elapsed (as on December 31, 19x1) or because the interest has been paid up-to-date (as is the case on December 31, 19x2, 19x3, and 19x4). Also, because interest is paid each year, there is no compounding of interest even though this note extends beyond one year. Although it is expected that the interest amounts will be paid as scheduled, no liability exists for interest until time has elapsed.

ESTIMATED LIABILITIES

Not all liability amounts are known with certainty at financial statement dates. When a company has a liability with a reasonable basis for estimating or measuring the amount that must be paid, the company makes the estimate and records the liability; these are estimated liabilities. Liabilities are commonly estimated for income taxes, property taxes, vacation pay, warranties, and many other obligations for which precise amounts are not known.

Income Taxes

Federal, state, and local governments levy income taxes on a business's taxable income. Businesses compute their income tax obligations on income tax forms that include the tax versions of revenues and expenses, called *taxable revenue* and *deductions*, respectively. The rules for determining taxable revenues and tax deductions often differ from the rules for inclusion of revenues and expenses on income statements. In this subsection, we examine the current liability created by the income tax obligation. The appendix to this chapter discusses the accounting treatment for differences between accounting and tax measurements of pre-tax income.

Objective 2
Accounting for estimated liabilities, which include income taxes, property taxes, vacation pay, and warranties.

Why doesn't a company know its exact income tax obligation at the balance sheet date of each accounting period? Because of the complexity of the tax law, the time needed to complete the tax return for one year usually extends far into the next year. For this reason, the tax obligation shown on income statements may be different from the final tax obligation. By the filing deadline, the company often pays an estimated amount and files for an extension, which allows the company to delay submitting its final tax return for several months after the normal tax deadline. Thus, the Income Tax Payable account shown on many balance sheets is an estimate based on knowledge as of the date the balance sheet is prepared. Such an estimate creates a current liability that will be paid later and that will probably be adjusted further when the final tax filing is made.

Consider the following example of cash payments and accruals for Universal Alliance, Inc.:

19x1

Dec. 31 Income Tax Expense (E)   720,000

Income Taxes Payable (L)   720,000

To record estimated tax expense for 19x1.

19x2

Apr. 15 Income Taxes Payable (L)   720,000

Cash (A)   720,000

To record cash payment of estimate when filing for
an extension.

July 1 Income Tax Expense (E)   40,000

Cash (A)   40,000

To record the payment of $40,000 on the final filing of
19x1 income tax return, representing additional tax of
$39,000 plus a $1,000 interest charge.

Note that the tax expense for 19x1 was underestimated by $39,000, and the government charges interest of $1,000 on the underestimated amount. Changes in estimates such as this are usually recorded as expense in the period the company makes the final determination of the correct amount. For Universal Alliance, the $720,000 estimated tax expense was recorded in 19x1, and the additional $40,000 expense from 19x1 was recorded in 19x2. This agrees with the general principle that changes in estimates are reported in the current period, or current and future periods only. The $1,000 interest could be charged to Interest Expense rather than Income Tax Expense.

Most companies pay income taxes during the year; therefore, the liability balance at year-end does not equal the total obligation for taxes for the entire year. To illustrate the procedure companies generally use to record taxes, assume that Print, Inc., has a 30% tax rate. The schedule that follows summarizes Print's activity for each quarter in the 19x1 operating year by listing its net income before taxes (NIBT), tax expense, taxable income, tax payments, and current liability at quarter-end.

	NIBT	Tax Expense	Taxable Income	Payment to Government	Current Liability at Quarter-End
3/31/x1	$ 300,000	$ 90,000	$ 300,000	$ 0	$90,000
4/15/x1				90,000	
6/30/x1	300,000	90,000	300,000	0	90,000
7/15/x1				90,000	
9/30/x1	300,000	90,000	300,000	0	90,000
10/15/x1				90,000	
12/31/x1	300,000	90,000	300,000	0	90,000
1/15/x2				90,000	
Total	$1,200,000	$360,000	$1,200,000	$360,000	

Note that in this example even if tax expense exactly equals tax liability at each quarter-end balance sheet date, we still have a current liability at the balance sheet date because the actual payment to the government comes after the end of the accounting period.

The summary journal entries made in 19x1 for Print's 19x1 taxes are

Income Tax Expense (E)	360,000	
Income Taxes Payable (L)		360,000
To record four quarters of tax expense.		
Income Taxes Payable (L)	270,000	
Cash (A)		270,000
To record payment of taxes to the government at the end of quarters 1, 2, and 3.		

The Income Taxes Payable account balance of $90,000 is a current liability for the unpaid taxes at the balance sheet date, December 31, 19x1.

Estimated Property Tax
    For many local governments, such as cities and counties, the property tax is a major source of tax revenue. Property taxes are usually based on a stated percentage of assessed values of real property (land and building) and personal property (property, other than real property, such as furniture, automobiles, jewelry, inventory, and sometimes owned stocks and bonds issued by other companies). Businesses must pay property taxes just as individuals, and the differences in the time periods covered by the property tax bill and the business's fiscal periods often lead to the necessity of estimates.

The following example illustrates how companies use estimates for property taxes. Motion Electric, Inc., a corporation located in Arbor City with a December 31 year-end, began business operations on January 1, 19x1. On September 1 of each year, Arbor City sends out property tax bills (due September 30) for the period January 1 through December 31 of that year. Motion Electric estimates that property taxes for 19x1 will total $60,000. Since Motion Electric prepares quarterly financial statements, it estimated its property tax for quarters 1 and 2 and made the following journal entries on March 31 and June 30:

19x1			
Mar. 31	Property Tax Expense (E)	15,000	
	Property Taxes Payable (L).		15,000
	To record estimated property tax for the first quarter.		
June 30	Property Tax Expense (E)	15,000	
	Property Taxes Payable (L).		15,000
	To record estimated property tax for the second quarter.		

The diagram and bar chart in Exhibit 9–5 illustrate Motion Electric's accounting for property tax. To study Exhibit 9–5, begin with the horizontal axis on the diagram and bar chart that show the four quarters of 19x1. In the diagram, the heavy dot represents the cumulative property tax expense, and the square represents the cumulative cash paid. The $15,000 located at the heavy dot above quarter 1 in the diagram indicates that Motion Electric recognized this $15,000 as an expense and as a current liability. The square on the horizontal axis above quarter 1 indicates that the cash paid to March 31 is zero. The $15,000 is also shown in the bar chart above quarter 1. The June 30 entry is indicated in the diagram and bar chart in the same manner as the March 31 entry. Since Motion Electric has not paid any cash on June 30, the square in the diagram is at zero; however, the

EXHIBIT 9–5

Relationship among Property Tax Cash Flow, Expense, Liability, and Prepayments

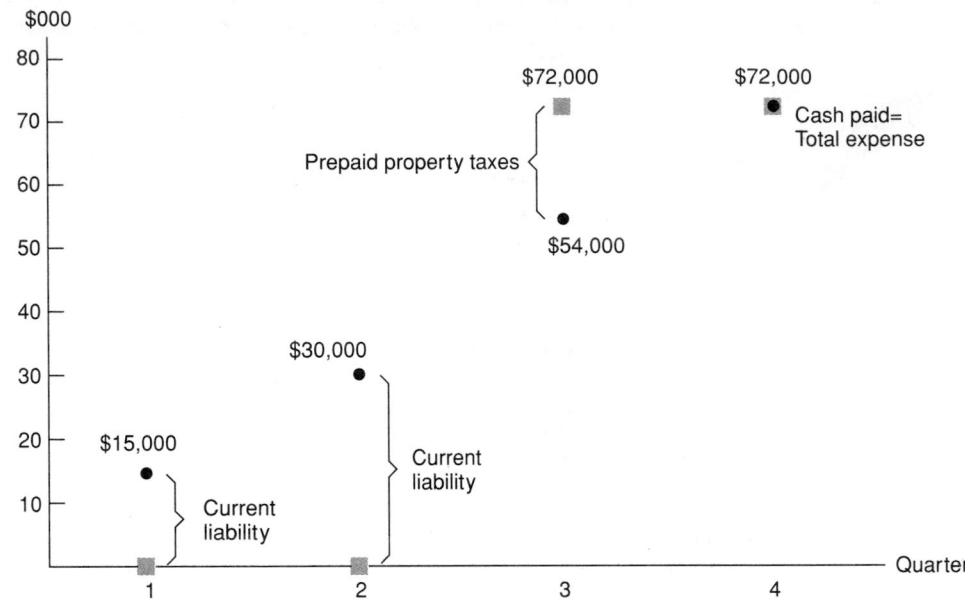

● Cumulative expense.

■ Cumulative cash paid.

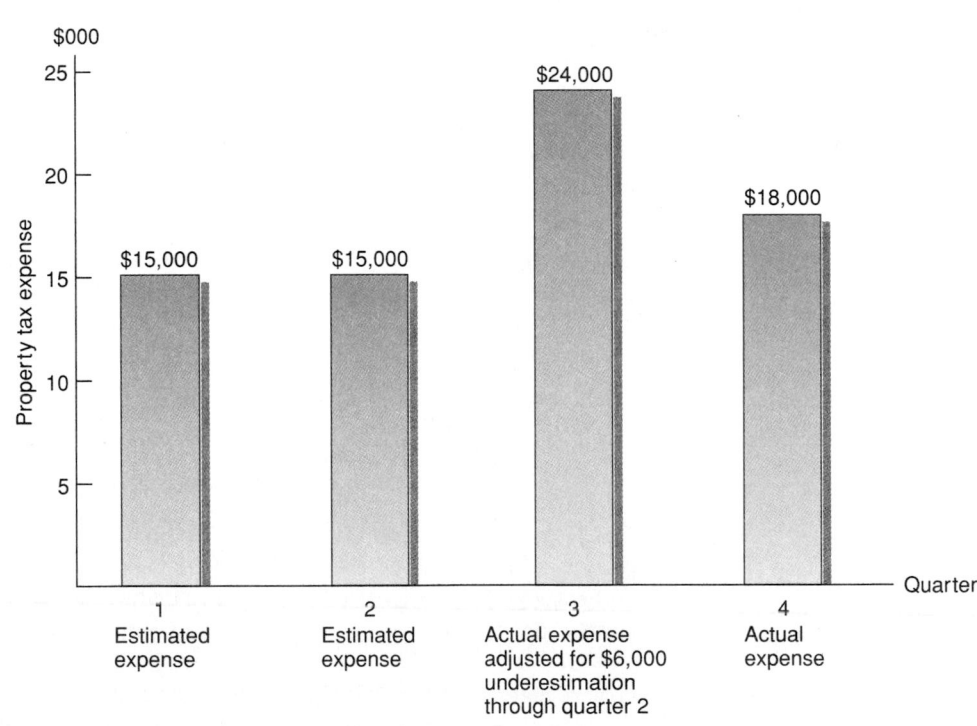

cumulative expense is increased to $30,000, as indicated by the heavy dot, and the current liability has grown to $30,000.

On September 30, 19x1, Motion Electric paid the $72,000 property tax bill and made the following entry:

```
19x1
Sept. 30    Property Tax Expense (E) . . . . . . . . . . . . . . . . .     24,000
            Property Taxes Payable (L) . . . . . . . . . . . . . . .       30,000
            Prepaid Property Taxes (A) . . . . . . . . . . . . . . .       18,000
                Cash (A). . . . . . . . . . . . . . . . . . . . . .                    72,000
            To record payment of 19x1 property tax bill.
```

Above quarter 3 in the diagram of Exhibit 9–5, the square indicating cumulative cash paid has moved to $72,000. The heavy dot indicating cumulative expense has moved to $54,000. The increase from $30,000 cumulated expense to $54,000 is explained in the bar chart above quarter 3. When Motion Electric estimated its yearly property tax at $60,000, $15,000 was allotted to each quarter. Since receiving the $72,000 tax bill, Motion Electric knows that each quarter should have been allotted $18,000 ($72,000 ÷ 4 quarters = $18,000 per quarter); thus, expense through quarter 2 was underestimated by $6,000. When this $6,000 underestimate is added to the $30,000 already expensed plus the $18,000 for quarter 3, the cumulative expense through quarter 3 is $54,000. Since Motion Electric paid the entire $72,000 on September 30, the $18,000 allotted to quarter 4 is initially a prepaid asset.

At year-end Motion Electric records the following journal entry for the fourth quarter:

```
19x1
Dec. 31     Property Tax Expense (E) . . . . . . . . . . . . . . . . .     18,000
                Prepaid Property Taxes (A) . . . . . . . . . . . . . .                 18,000
            To allocate prepaid property tax to the fourth quarter.
```

The final $18,000 expense entry on December 31, 19x1, eliminates the prepayment. Above quarter 4 in the diagram, the cumulative expense equals the cash paid for the year (the heavy dot is inside the square), and no liability or expense remains on the books at the end of quarter 4.

Vacation Pay

Some businesses allow employees to accumulate, rather than use, vacation time. The amount of time employees have earned and not taken at the end of an accounting period is vacation liability and represents an obligation of the business.[1] Usually, the fiscal period in which the vacation is earned absorbs the expense associated with paying employees for time off. Any unclaimed vacation pay at period end is accounted for by an accrual entry based on an estimate of the cost of providing the vacation time in the future.

Assume that a company has an employee who earns one day of vacation for each full month worked and that the employee's salary is $100 per day in 19x1 and 19x2. The employee took no vacation in 19x1 and worked all 12 months. During January 19x2, the employee took all 12 days of vacation accumulated through December 31, 19x1. The journal entries to account for the 19x1 vacation pay are as follows:

```
19x1
Dec. 31     Vacation Expense (E) . . . . . . . . . . . . . . . . . . . .     1,200
                Estimated Vacation Liability (L) . . . . . . . . . . . . . . .             1,200
            To record unused vacation for 19x1:
            12 months × 1 day of vacation × $100 = $1,200.
```

---

[1] See *FASB Statement No. 43*, "Accounting for Compensated Absences" (Norwalk, Conn.: FASB, 1980), for more details.

```
19x2
January    Estimated Vacation Liability (L) . . . . . . . . . . . . . . . . .    1,200
                 Salaries Payable (L) [or Cash (A)] . . . . . . . . . . . . . .              1,200
           To record vacation taken: 12 days × $100 = $1,200.
```

Note that 19x2 is not charged with vacation expense for vacation earned in 19x1. Year 1 was charged with 12 months' salary expense (months worked in year 1) and 12 days' vacation expense (vacation earned in year 1 but taken in year 2). This is an application of the matching principle, according to which the period that received the benefit is charged with the resulting expense. Of course, at the end of year 2, any outstanding vacation time earned in 19x2 by that date would be accounted for in the manner shown above.

Warranties

Many businesses guarantee their products against defects for a certain period of time after the sale. The expected costs of honoring warranty commitments should be assigned to the period in which the revenue for the sale of the warranted item is earned. Again, the objective is to match the expense with the period of benefit, and it is assumed that offering warranties enhances sales. Thus, the period of sale should absorb the expected warranty expense.

To record estimates of outstanding warranty commitments at the end of each accounting period, adjusting entries are used. Because the actual expenditures are usually different from the estimates, subsequent periods' income statements must absorb the difference between the estimated and the actual amounts.

Assume that Orange Computer, Inc., begins to manufacture and sell printers for microcomputers during May 19x1 and stops manufacturing the printers in 19x2 with no sales after December 31, 19x2. No warranty expenditures are expected after December 31, 19x3. At December 31, 19x3, the following facts and estimates are known:

	19x1	19x2	19x3
Sales.	$18,000,000	$20,000,000	$　　0
Total estimated warranty cost for annual sales . . .	2% of sales (= $360,000)	2% of sales (= $400,000)	$　　0
Actual warranty costs incurred during the year . . .	$　　　0	$　410,000	$390,000

On December 31, 19x1, Orange Computer made the following entry:

```
19x1
Dec. 31    Warranty Expense (E) . . . . . . . . . . . . . . . . . . . .    360,000
                 Warranty Payable (L) . . . . . . . . . . . . . . . . . . .              360,000
           To record estimated warranty costs at 2% of sales.
```

During 19x2, Orange Computer made the following summary entry for amounts expended on warranty activities:

```
During
19x2       Warranty Payable (L) . . . . . . . . . . . . . . . . . . . .    410,000
                 Cash, Supplies, Wages Payable, etc. . . . . . . . . . . .              410,000
           To record settlements of warranty claims.
```

Since Orange Computer spent $410,000 for warranty activities during 19x2, Warranty Payable has a $50,000 debit balance before adjustment on December 31, 19x2; that is, the net of the beginning credit balance of $360,000 and the debit of $410,000 is a debit of

$50,000. The entry to record the adjustment for the warranty expense at December 31, 19x2, is the following:

```
19x2
Dec. 31    Warranty Expense (E) . . . . . . . . . . . . . . . . . .    400,000
                Warranty Payable (L) . . . . . . . . . . . . . . . . .              400,000
                To record estimated warranty costs associated with
                19x2 sales: $20,000,000 × .02.
```

The following T account depicts the 19x1 and 19x2 activity:

Warranty Payable

		19x1	
		Dec. 31	360,000
		19x2	
19x2	410,000	Dec. 31	400,000
		Bal.	350,000

During 19x3, the company paid out $390,000 in warranties and made the following entry:

```
During
19x3    Warranty Payable (L) . . . . . . . . . . . . . . . . . . .    350,000
        Warranty Expense (E) . . . . . . . . . . . . . . . . . .     40,000
                Cash, Supplies, Wages Payable, etc. . . . . . . . . . . . .              390,000
                To record settlements of warranty claims.
```

The Warranty Payable account as of December 31, 19x3, is as follows:

Warranty Payable

		19x1	
		Dec. 31	360,000
		19x2	
19x2	410,000	Dec. 31	400,000
		Bal.	350,000
19x3	350,000		
		Bal.	0

Let's review the economic flows, expenses, and liabilities related to Orange's warranty commitments. In 19x1, Orange Computer had no outflows related to warranties, but it recognized $360,000 in warranties expense and, therefore, $360,000 in the current liability Warranty Payable. In 19x2, Orange Computer had outflows of $410,000 related to actual warranty claims. These claims could have stemmed from sales made in either 19x1 or 19x2 or both. At December 31, 19x2, Orange Computer must recognize a liability equal to the best estimate of the future outflows for warranties. If we assume that 2% of sales is still the best estimate of warranty costs at the end of 19x2, then $400,000 should be recorded as warranty expense for 19x2, leaving a liability of $350,000 for estimated future claims. The cumulative estimated warranty commitment to date of $760,000 (2% of cumulative sales of $38 million) minus the cumulative warranty payments to date of $410,000 equals the current Warranty Payable at December 31, 19x2, of $350,000.

Exhibit 9–6 shows the three-year history of Orange Computer's warranty obligation. The heavy dot in the exhibit represents the cumulative warranty expense (the total recognized expense for the current and previous periods), and the square represents the cumulative outflows (the total cash payments and other outputs related to warranties of the product for the current and previous periods). As indicated on December 31, 19x1, the current liability is $360,000, because the expense charged to date exceeds the payments to date (indicated by the square above 12/31/x1 on the time line) by that amount. On December 31, 19x2, the current liability is $350,000 because new sales have increased the cumulative expense to date to $760,000 (indicated by the heavy dot above 12/31/x2 on the time line) and the cumulative payments to date (indicated by the square above 12/31/x2) amount to only $410,000. On December 31, 19x3, because the printer line has been discontinued and because it is assumed that no further warranties are in effect, the total payments to date equal the total obligation estimated for the printers sold (indicated by the heavy dot inside the square above 12/31/x3 on the time line), and no liability remains. The bar chart shows the warranty expense charged each year. Note that year 3, in which no sales of printers were made, is charged with $40,000 of warranty expense. Again, this is an application of the general principle that the current year absorbs the effects of previous inaccuracies in estimates. Total cumulative expense over the three years for warranties exactly equals $800,000, which is the total amount of payments made to settle warranty claims.

CONTINGENT LIABILITIES

Objective 3
Accounting for contingent liabilities.

Contingent liabilities occur when a company does not actually have a current obligation but a real possibility exists that an obligation will develop based on the resolution of a past event. Review the discussion on page 444, "Do all liabilities appear on the balance sheet?" as an introduction to the following material on contingent liabilities.

A chemical company has a toxic spill, and some of the surrounding farmland may have been affected. However, the company disputes all claims made by the owners of the farmland, and a $30 million lawsuit ensues. At year-end, the lawsuit is yet to be resolved. Should the accountant for the chemical company record a liability because of this contingency (the possibility of a future payment or sacrifice because of a past event)? The answer depends on the probability that a payment will be required. In this case, assume that the chemical company loses the suit in 19x2, and a judgment of $12 million is made on June 30, 19x2. Of course, the outcome was unknown on December 31, 19x1. Let's review the facts by means of the following time line:

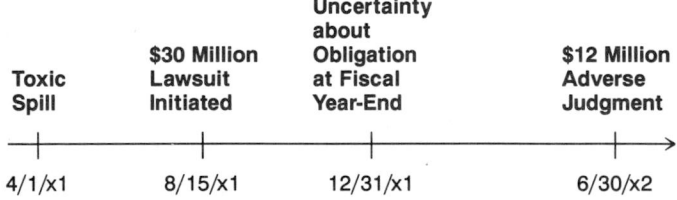

If at December 31, 19x1, the attorney for the company believed that an adverse judgment was **probable** and that the best estimate of the amount the company would be required to pay was $10 million, the following entries would have been made:

```
19x1
Dec. 31   Loss—Toxic Spill (E) . . . . . . . . . . . . . . . . .   10,000,000
                Estimated Lawsuit Liability (L) . . . . . . . . . . .              10,000,000
          To record the probable loss resulting from a toxic spill.
```

EXHIBIT 9–6

Relationship between Orange Computer's Warranty Expense, Cash Payments, and Warranty Payable

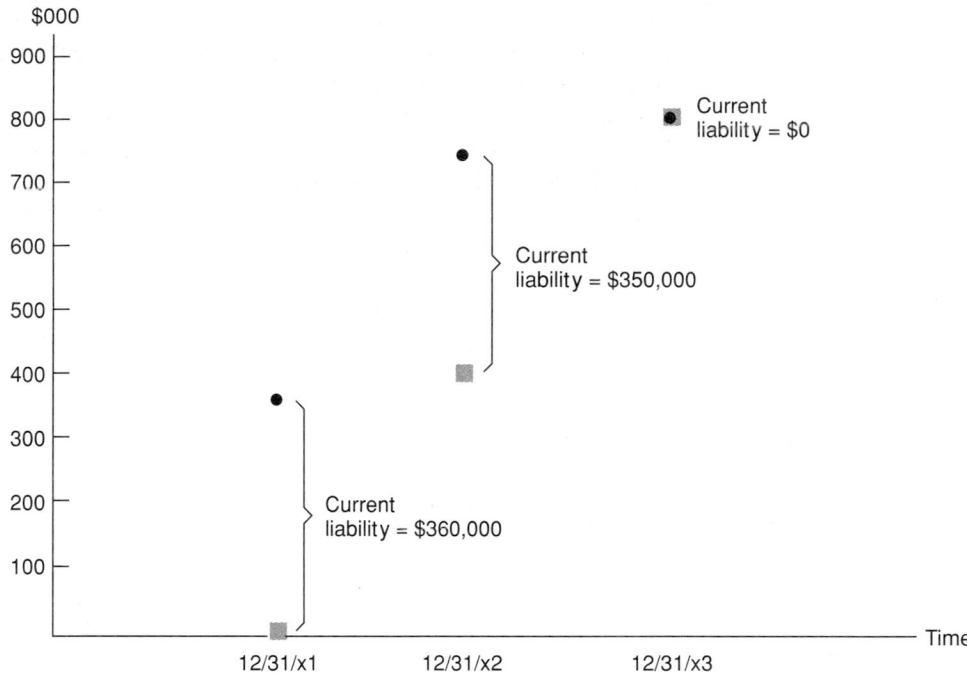

● Cumulative expense.
▨ Cumulative cash paid.

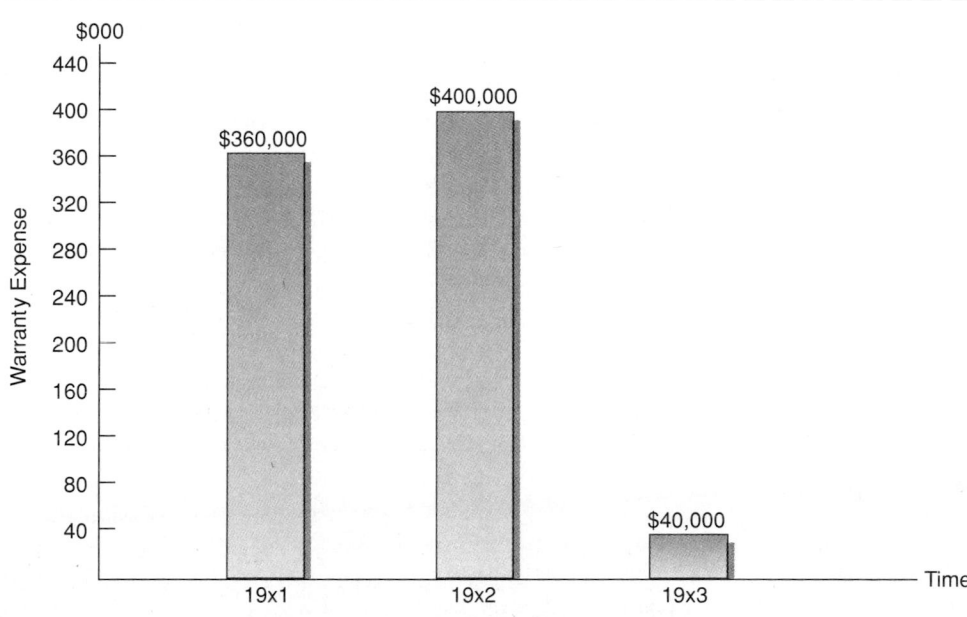

```
19x2
June 30   Loss—Toxic Spill (E)  . . . . . . . . . . . . . . . . .      2,000,000
          Estimated Lawsuit Liability (L)  . . . . . . . . . . . .     10,000,000
              Cash (A) . . . . . . . . . . . . . . . . . . . .                       12,000,000
          To record settlement of lawsuit.
```

Note that the chemical company did not record an amount at the time of the spill because at that time the company did not believe it was liable. Since the company believed that by year-end $10 million would probably have to be paid, the estimated liability was recorded even though it was possible that the verdict would be favorable, and no payment would be made. Although a contingency was created at the time of the spill, an estimated liability was recorded only when the payment was deemed **probable** and a **reasonable estimate** could be made of the amount.

In the case of contingent liabilities, specific terms are used to designate likelihoods, *remote, reasonably possible,* and *probable.*[2] Each likelihood leads to a different accounting action, as can be seen in the following table:

Likelihood	Likelihood of Future Event	Action
Remote	Slight	None
Reasonably possible	More than remote and less than probable	Disclose in a note to the balance sheet.
Probable	Likely	If the amount can be reasonably estimated, record the liability. If not reasonably estimable, disclose in a note to the balance sheet.

Common practice includes warranties in estimated liabilities even though they seem to meet the definition of contingencies that are probable; that is, although they are probable they do not require a payment unless the future event of the need for repairs occurs. This text reflects the common practice of recording warranties as estimated liabilities.

Another type of contingency exists when a company may have to pay a third party if another party does not perform according to a contract. In this contingency, the money amounts may be known, but the unanswered question is whether a payment will be necessary. For example, assume that Company A guarantees the debt of one of its suppliers, Company B. Company A may have made this guarantee so that Company B could secure a bank loan to finance the facilities needed to manufacture a product for Company A. Because it is important to Company A that Company B get the loan, Company A is willing to guarantee that default by Company B will be reimbursed by Company A. In such a case, Company A is said to be contingently liable in the event of Company B's default. A similar situation is created when a company discounts a note with recourse. If the maker defaults, the payee who discounted the note must pay (see Chapter 7). When the amounts involved are significant, these contingencies are usually reported in a footnote to the balance sheet.

The excerpts from several financial statements appear in Exhibit 9–7. The Allis Chalmers and Warner-Lambert excerpts illustrate a common type of contingent liability. The companies state that certain contingencies exist but that management and legal counsel do not believe that the resolutions of these contingencies will materially affect the financial statements. The Owens-Illinois example is more precise in that a specific reason

---

[2]*FASB Statement No. 5,* "Accounting for Contingencies" (Norwalk, Conn.: FASB, 1975).

EXHIBIT 9–7

Examples of Annual Report Disclosures of Contingent Liabilities

Allis Chalmers

Excerpt from footnotes:

Commitments and Contingent Liabilities
There are various lawsuits pending against the Company and its subsidiaries arising in the normal course of business. Management believes, based on the opinion of counsel, that final disposition of these actions will not have a materially adverse effect on financial position or results of operations.

Warner-Lambert Company

Excerpt from footnotes:

NOTE 11
Contingencies
Various claims, suits and complaints, such as those involving government regulations, patents and trademarks and product liability claims, arise in the ordinary course of Warner-Lambert's business. In the opinion of Warner-Lambert, all such pending matters are without merit or are of such kind or involve such amounts, as would not have a material adverse effect on the consolidated operating results or financial position of Warner-Lambert if disposed of unfavorably.

Owens-Illinois

Excerpt from footnotes:

Contingencies. Owens-Illinois was contingently liable at December 31, 1985, under guarantees of loans and other obligations in the principal amount of $29.5 million....The Company is one of a number of defendants (typically ten to twenty) in a substantial number of lawsuits by persons alleging personal injury as a result of exposure to dust from asbestos fibers.

and amount are stated. Remember that these disclosures are in notes to the financial statements and are not necessarily recorded as liabilities. They represent unresolved matters that may require the recording of measurable liabilities in the future.

PAYROLL ACCOUNTING

Objective 4
The importance of a payroll system to a company.

In most companies, the payroll (salaries and wages) is a recurring and important function. The company's unpaid salaries and wages at the end of an accounting period are shown as current liabilities on the balance sheet. Since most companies withhold taxes, insurance, and other amounts from an employee's paycheck, these withholdings, or payroll deductions, create current liabilities owed to many different entities and are also shown on the balance sheet if they are unpaid at the end of an accounting period.

A company usually follows a routine process or system to prepare its payroll. The size of the company and its individual needs dictate the type of system used. Payroll systems range from the simple manual system used for four or five employees to the sophisticated data processing system used by large companies with thousands of employees. This section begins with a brief introduction to the payroll system. Discussions on social security taxes, federal and state income tax withholding, other payroll deductions, and unemployment taxes follow.

Payroll System

The payroll process has received much attention because of its importance and the relatively large money amounts involved. Companies must maintain accurate employee records on the employee's date of employment, name, address, pay rate, age, number of dependents for personal income tax withholding purposes, hours worked, vacation time allowed and taken, and much more.

Payroll systems must also be controlled so that companies can prevent payroll fraud. Internal control methods are designed to prevent the issuing of payroll checks to nonexistent workers and the payment of incorrect amounts. Controlling payroll fraud requires an integration of efforts and records across several departments of a business.

Exhibit 9–8 illustrates some of the main features of a factory assembly payroll system in which information is accessible electronically by various departments. Notice the separation of duties between the departments. In the example shown in Exhibit 9–8, the stored Personnel Database may be accessed by more than one department for various purposes. For instance, the accounting department needs some of the information to process the payroll. This accessibility creates both new control problems and opportunities to solve old control problems.

The preparation of payroll checks and maintenance of the payroll records shown in Exhibit 9–8 includes keeping track of deductions made from employees' pay such as those made for social security taxes, federal and state income taxes, insurance premiums, pension contributions, and so on. Employers must also pay certain payroll taxes, such as social security, federal unemployment taxes, state unemployment taxes, and workmen's accident compensation taxes. Thus, you should remember that in addition to acting as collection agents for social security taxes and income taxes, employers must pay certain payroll taxes based on the gross earnings of employees.

The following summarizes the payroll responsibilities of employees and employers often found in practice:

Employee Responsibilities (withholdings from employees' pay)	Employer Responsibilities (paid by employer)
FICA (social security)	Wages
Federal income taxes	FICA (social security)
State income taxes	Federal unemployment taxes
Local income taxes	State unemployment taxes
Other:	Other:
Pension	Pension
Insurance	Insurance
Credit union	Vacation
Union dues	

Not all payrolls contain all of these items. We will give examples of each major item in the following sections.

FICA (Social Security) Taxes

Objective 5
The effect of payroll deductions and employer taxes.

One of the largest social programs administered by the federal government is the system of retirement, disability, hospitalization, and survivors' benefits called the *social security system.* Both employer and employee contribute to social security in the form of taxes applied to wages up to a certain maximum amount each year for each employee. At this writing, the tax rate levied under the Federal Insurance Contributions Act (FICA) is .0765. The monies withheld from the employee's paycheck and an equal amount paid by the employer are called social security taxes or **FICA taxes,** with the employer acting as the collection agent.

To illustrate the payment of FICA taxes, consider an employee, Jennifer Smith, whose gross wages are $3,000 in January 19x1. Assuming that the FICA rate for year 19x1 is 7%, the employee's net pay would be reduced by $210 ($3,000 × .07). At the same time,

EXHIBIT 9–8

**Payroll System
for Factory
Assembly Workers**

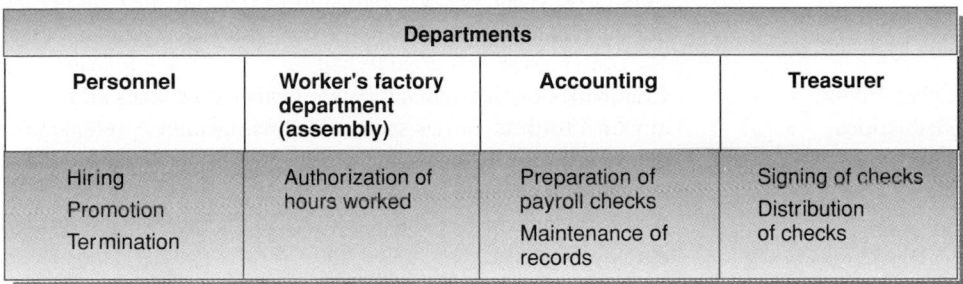

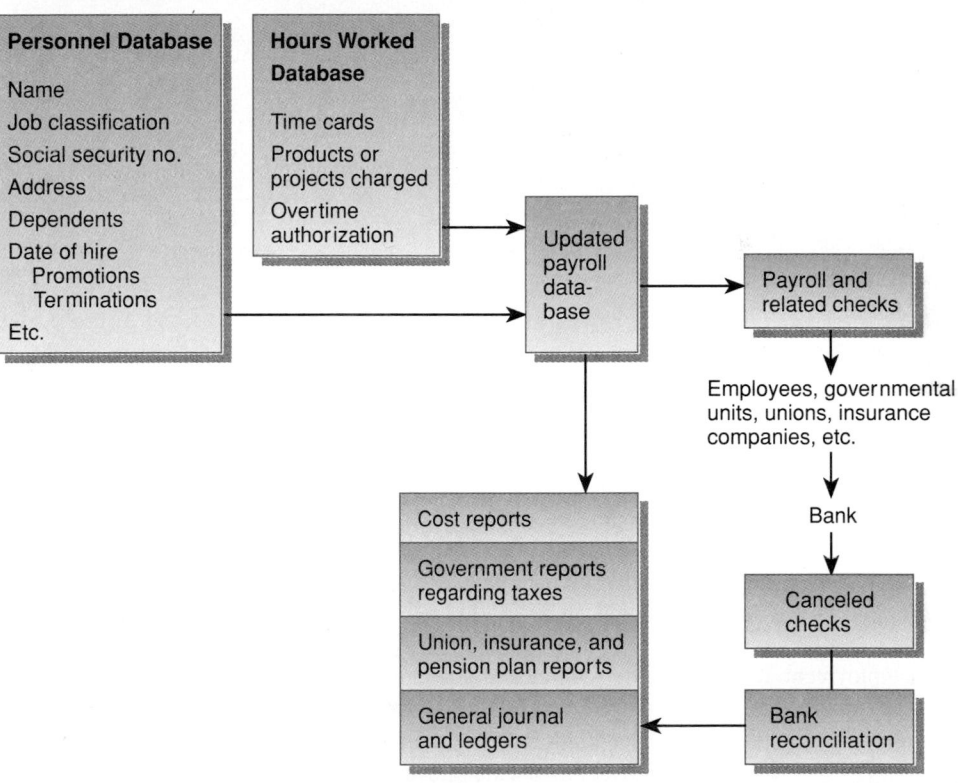

the employer would be responsible for an additional $210, the employer's FICA tax. The employer now owes the Social Security Administration $420, of which half is a payroll deduction and half is an expense to the employer.

Federal and State
Income Tax
Withholding

Each employee must file a W-4 form (an Employee's Withholding Exemption Certificate) establishing the employee's exemptions and thereby the income tax withholding amount. The employer is responsible for withholding the appropriate amount of federal income tax. Most states and some cities require similar procedures to determine the appropriate amount of state and city income taxes to be withheld.

To illustrate, consider again the employee with a gross wage of $3,000 and total FICA tax of $420. Assume that the amounts to be withheld for federal and state income taxes are $600 and $120, respectively. The employer withholds from the employee's wages $210 FICA tax plus $600 federal income tax plus $120 state income tax, a total of $930. The employer matches the employee's $210 FICA tax and sends the government $420, which is applied to the employee's FICA account. In addition, the employer must send $600 to the Internal Revenue Service and $120 to the state income tax authority. The employer does not contribute to the employee's state and federal income taxes.

Other Payroll Deductions

Companies often withhold amounts other than taxes from employee's pay and remit these amounts to third parties such as unions, insurance companies, savings plans, and pension plans. Assume the employee discussed above participates in an insurance plan that costs the employee $85 per month and a retirement plan that costs $105 per month, both of which are matched by the employer. The table below summarizes the computation of this employee's net pay:

Jennifer Smith
Payroll Computation for January 19x1

Gross pay		$3,000
Withholdings:		
FICA	$210	
Federal income tax	600	
State income tax	120	
Insurance	85	
Pension	105	
Total withholding		1,120
Net pay		$1,880

As you can see, a considerable difference exists between Jennifer's gross pay and net pay. Jennifer's "take-home" pay is only 62.7% of her gross pay. The 37.3% difference is owed by the employer to various agencies. Remember that each employee's situation is different, and that this is but one example.

Unemployment Taxes

The federal and state governments have a joint program to fund benefits paid to unemployed workers. The Federal Unemployment Tax Act (FUTA) imposes a tax on wages paid by employers. The amount levied is 6.2% of the first $7,000 of the wages of each employee. States are allowed to levy up to 5.4% to be paid to the state, leaving only .8% payable to the federal government. The state varies the amount of tax each employer must pay, depending on the employer's claim experience. Employers with more employee unemployment claims pay a higher rate than those with fewer claims.

To illustrate, assume that Jennifer Smith's wages are subject to a .8% FUTA tax and a 3% state unemployment tax and that the employer matches Jennifer Smith's pension and insurance payments. The complete payroll computation for Jennifer Smith is as follows:

Schedule of Current Liabilities Related to Jennifer Smith's January 19x1 Wage

	Employee's Portion	Employer's Portion	Total Liability to Third Parties
Payee:			
Federal government:			
FICA	$ 210	$210	$ 420
Income tax.	600		600
FUTA		24	24
State government:			
Income tax.	120		120
Unemployment		90	90
Other agencies:			
Pension	105	105	210
Insurance	85	85	170
Total	$1,120	$514	$1,634

The journal entry that records Salary Expense, deductions, and net pay of $1,880 is as follows:

```
19x1
Jan. 31   Salaries Expense (E). . . . . . . . . . . . . . . . . . . . . . . .   3,000
              FICA Payable (L) . . . . . . . . . . . . . . . . . . . . . .           210
              Federal Income Tax Withholding Payable (L) . . . . . . . . . .         600
              State Income Tax Withholding Payable (L) . . . . . . . . . . .         120
              Pension Contribution Payable (L) . . . . . . . . . . . . . . .         105
              Insurance Premium Payable (L) . . . . . . . . . . . . . . . .           85
              Cash (A) . . . . . . . . . . . . . . . . . . . . . . . . . .        1,880
          To record Jennifer Smith's wages.
```

The journal entry that records the employer's portion of the payroll liabilities is the following:

```
19x1
Jan. 31   Payroll Expense (E) . . . . . . . . . . . . . . . . . . . . . . .     514
              FICA Payable (L) . . . . . . . . . . . . . . . . . . . . . .           210
              FUTA Payable (L) . . . . . . . . . . . . . . . . . . . . . .            24
              State Unemployment Tax Payable (L) . . . . . . . . . . . . .            90
              Pension Contribution Payable (L) . . . . . . . . . . . . . . .         105
              Insurance Premium Payable (L) . . . . . . . . . . . . . . . .           85
          To record employer's payroll-related expenses.
```

Salaries Expense includes Jennifer Smith's $3,000 gross pay, and Payroll Expense includes the $514 of various payments to be made to the government and other agencies, which are the employer's responsibility. Note that the employee's portion ($1,120) is called withholdings and that the employer merely acts as an agent of the employee in making these payments. In the normal course of business, an employer would usually issue checks for the amounts withheld for all employees and the employer's portion during the month following the payroll payment.

SUMMARY

This chapter deals primarily with the business transactions that create short-term obligations. Some of the transactions involve liabilities with known money amounts and payment dates (definitely determinable current liabilities), such as invoices from suppliers, notes, dividends, and the current portion of long-term debt. Other transactions require estimations (estimated liabilities), such as income taxes, property taxes, vacation pay, and warranties. Sometimes a past event creates the need to disclose a potential obligation even though no payment may actually become necessary (contingent liabilities). Such contingencies are recorded if a loss is probable and a reasonable estimate can be made of the amounts involved.

The payroll process involves maintaining accurate employee records and a control system that will prevent payroll fraud. Payrolls create current liabilities for unpaid salaries and for payments that the employer makes to third parties such as government agencies, insurance companies, unions, and so on. Withholdings from employees' wages for income taxes, FICA taxes, insurance, unions, and several others are deductions from gross pay that are subsequently transmitted to the third parties. Some of the payroll-related liabilities are for costs borne solely by the employer, such as certain insurance payments and unemployment taxes.

In this chapter the focus was on current or short-term liabilities. Chapter 10 discusses noncurrent or long-term liabilities. Remember that the key to determining whether a liability is short term or long term is the expected timing of the flow of assets or services that are required to eliminate the obligation.

• DEMONSTRATION EXERCISE

Selected transactions from the fiscal year 19x1 for Kangaroo Electronics (KE) follow:

19x1

Jan.   14   Received $4,300 of merchandise inventory on account. KE uses the perpetual inventory system. No discount is given.

Mar. 30   Borrowed $5,000 from the local bank for one year at 8% interest.

May   15   Declared a $0.10 dividend on the 100,000 outstanding shares of common stock to be paid on June 1.

June   1   Paid cash dividend.

June 15   Filed the previous year's income tax return, which reported taxes of $54,000 owed to the government. On April 15, KE had paid $56,000, which had been fully accrued on December 31 of the previous year, and filed for an extension.

Aug. 15   Recorded August 15 payroll. Gross pay for all employees is $15,900. Deductions from employees included: $1,113 for FICA, $950 for federal income tax, $576 for state income tax, and $200 for insurance premiums. KE's expenses related to the payroll include matching amounts for FICA and insurance, $600 for retirement benefits, and $636 for FUTA.

Dec. 15   The property tax bill is received for $88,000 for 19x1. For the first three quarters, KE estimated the annual property tax to be $80,000. The bill is paid on December 24.

       31   Employees' unused vacation time amounts to $2,380.

       31   KE estimates that warranty payments on the current year's sales will equal 2.5% of total sales of $5,670,000.

       31   Recorded interest expense on the March 30 note.

Required:

Record in general journal form the journal entry for each of these transactions.

Solution:

		GENERAL JOURNAL			
Date		Account Titles and Explanation	Ref.	Debit	Credit
19x1 Jan.	14	Inventory (A)		4,300	
		Accounts Payable (L)			4,300
		To record merchandise purchased.			
Mar.	30	Cash (A)		5,000	
		Notes Payable (L)			5,000
		To record bank loan.			
April	15	Tax Payable		56,000	
		Cash			56,000
		To record payment of tax.			
May	15	Dividends (SE)		10,000	
		Dividends Payable (L)			10,000
		To record dividends declared.			
June	1	Dividends Payable		10,000	
		Cash			10,000
		To record dividend payment.			
June	15	Income Tax Receivable (A)		2,000	
		Income Tax Expense (E)			2,000
		To record overpayment to government of income taxes.			
Aug.	15	Salaries Expense (E)		15,900	
		Payroll Expense (E)		2,549	
		FICA Payable (L)			2,226
		Federal Income Tax Withholding Payable (L)			950
		State Income Tax Withholding Payable (L)			576
		FUTA Payable (L)			636
		Pension Contribution Payable (L)			600
		Insurance Premium Payable (L)			400
		Cash (A)			13,061
		To record payroll.			
Dec.	24	Property Tax Expense (E)		28,000	
		Property Taxes Payable (L)		60,000	
		Cash (A)			88,000
		To record payment of property tax bill.			
	31	Vacation Expense (E)		2,380	
		Estimated Vacation Liability (L)			2,380
		To record unused vacation for the year.			
	31	Warranty Expense (E)		141,750	
		Estimated Warranty Liability (L)			141,750
		To record estimated warranty costs.			
	31	Interest Expense (E)		300	
		Interest Payable (L)			300
		To record interest expense on the bank loan: ($5,000 × .08 × 9/12).			

More on Income Taxes

Objective 6
The nature of deferred
income taxes.

Because tax laws often are aimed at affecting business policies, the net income before taxes (NIBT), which is based on accounting principles and methods, and the taxable income, which is based on IRS regulations, often differ. Some differences are permanent in that an amount that appears as a revenue or expense on the income statement never affects the tax return, and other differences are temporary with the difference reversing over time.

In this appendix, we look closely at differences between accounting (book) items and tax return items, which often result in a new type of liability being recorded. The liability is titled **deferred taxes,** and it represents the differences between the amount charged to income tax expense and the sum of the amounts already paid and currently payable to the government through the current period.

Temporary differences are differences between the tax basis and the book basis of certain items that reverse over time. For example, accountants often depreciate assets over estimated useful lives on a straight-line basis, while using accelerated schedules for tax purposes. The government allows faster depreciation for tax purposes in order to encourage investment in plant and equipment. If different schedules for depreciation are adopted for book and tax purposes, different tax amounts for book and tax purposes will result.

Accounting for taxes varies greatly throughout the world. In addition to the United States, several countries recognize deferred taxes, such as the United Kingdom, Canada, and the Netherlands. However, in several major countries, such as Germany and Japan, it makes little real difference whether or not deferred taxes are recognized, because there is little difference in book and tax accounting. In Germany, for instance, in order to get the most favorable tax benefits the company must conform its financial statements to the tax requirements.

ACCOUNTING FOR TEMPORARY DIFFERENCES

To become familiar with the basics of the current principles governing income tax accounting,[3] we will follow the simple example of Depo, Inc., for its 19x1, 19x2, and 19x3 taxable years. This is merely an introduction to a very complex area of accounting, but a careful analysis of the Depo case will give you a foundation for an understanding of the income tax reporting practices of corporations. First, you must appreciate the contrasts between the "books" of the corporation (i.e., the formal accounting records and statements) and the income tax return. Exhibit 9A–1 shows excerpts from Depo's income statements and tax returns for 19x1, 19x2, and 19x3. Although, several types of business events can create book/tax differences, we will concentrate on the depreciation differences in our coverage.

---

[3]*FASB Statement No. 96,* "Accounting for Income Taxes" (Norwalk, Conn.: FASB, 1987).

EXHIBIT 9A–1

Comparison of Depo, Inc.'s Books and Tax Return	**Depo, Inc.** **For the Years Ended December 31** **(in thousands)**			

Depo, Inc.
For the Years Ended December 31
(in thousands)

	19x1	19x2	19x3	Total 19x1–x3
Excerpt from Income Statement:				
Income before depreciation expense.	$200	$200	$200	$600
Depreciation expense	40	40	40	120
Net income before taxes (NIBT)	$160	$160	$160	$480
Income tax expense (at 30%).	48	48	48	144
Excerpt from Tax Return:				
Taxable income before depreciation	$200	$200	$200	$600
Depreciation deduction	80	40	0	120
Taxable income.	$120	$160	$200	$480
Current tax obligation (at 30%)	36	48	60	144

Deferred Tax Liability   In Exhibit 9A–1, consider the **net income before taxes** versus the **taxable income** amounts and the **income tax expense** versus the **current tax obligation** amounts. What causes the differences? To answer this question we must know more about the asset being depreciated by Depo, which is given in the following schedule:

Data on Depo's Depreciable Equipment

Purchased on January 1, 19x1	$120,000
Estimated useful life	3 years
Estimated salvage value	$0
Applicable tax rate for all years	30%
Method of depreciation used for books	straight-line over 3 years
Method of depreciation used for tax	accelerated over 2 years

	19x1	19x2	19x3	Total
Depreciation expense per books (in thousands).	$40	$40	$40	$120
Depreciation deduction per tax return (in thousands)	80	40	–0–	120

Depo's differing depreciation schedules for books and tax return creates **temporary differences,** which are defined as differences between the book carrying amounts and the tax bases of assets and liabilities that will affect the tax return in the future. The book carrying amount (book basis) is the purchase price of $120,000 minus the depreciation expense charge through the current balance sheet date (accumulated depreciation) or the asset's net book value as discussed in Chapter 8. The tax basis is the purchase price minus the depreciation deduction taken to date on tax returns. Depo's equipment has the following history:

	(in thousands)		
	19x1	19x2	19x3
Books:			
Original purchase price	$120	$120	$120
Cumulative depreciation expense to date	40	80	120
Year-end book carrying amount (book basis) . .	$ 80	$ 40	$ 0
Tax:			
Original purchase price	$120	$120	$120
Cumulative depreciation deduction to date . . .	80	120	120
Tax basis	$ 40	$ 0	$ 0

Consider the $40,000 difference between the book carrying amount and the tax basis on December 31, 19x1. This is a temporary difference because the cumulative difference in depreciation for book and tax purposes reverses and is eliminated by the end of the equipment's useful life. For tax purposes, in 19x1 there was a deduction of $80,000, leaving only $40,000 to be deducted in future years. For book purposes, the opposite is true; $80,000 remains to be charged in future years after year 19x1.

Objective 7
The financial statement effects of deferred income taxes.

How do the temporary differences affect the financial statements? Refer to Exhibit 9A–1. Depreciation for books and tax, while both adding to $120,000 over three years, are different each year. The current tax obligation is 30% of taxable income each year, while tax expense is 30% of NIBT each year. In 19x1 $36,000 is due the government for taxes but $48,000 is charged to tax expense. The $12,000 difference is 30% of the temporary difference between book and tax bases of the asset being depreciated; that is ($80,000 − $40,000) × 30% = $12,000. The following schedule gives the computation of deferred tax liability for each year:

	(in thousands)		
	19x1	19x2	19x3
Book basis	$80	$40	$0
Tax basis	40	0	0
Cumulative temporary difference	$40	$40	$0
Deferred tax liability at 30%	12	12	0

The deferred tax liability then is the cumulative temporary difference at the balance sheet date multiplied by the current tax rate.

In 19x1 the tax expense is $48,000, $36,000 of which is currently payable and $12,000 is deferred; that is, payable in the future. The liability account Deferred Tax Liability is, therefore, increased by $12,000 in 19x1. Because the cumulative temporary difference remains at $40,000 at December 31, 19x2, no change is made to the Deferred Tax Liability account. At December 31, 19x3, the cumulative temporary difference is zero; and, therefore, the deferred tax liability is zero also. The journal entries to accomplish proper reporting are as follows (in thousands):

Account Title	December 31, 19x1		December 31, 19x2		December 31, 19x3	
	Debit	**Credit**	**Debit**	**Credit**	**Debit**	**Credit**
Income Tax Expense (E) . . .	48		48		48	
Deferred Tax Liability (L) . . .		12		0	12	
Income Taxes Payable (L) . .		36		48		60

The sum of the tax currently payable ($36,000 at December 31, 19x1) and the increase in deferred tax liability ($12,000 at December 31, 19x1) equals the total tax expense for 19x1. For 19x2, there is no change in the deferred tax liability; therefore, the tax currently payable is equal to the expense for the year. The tax payable at December 31, 19x3, is $60,000, but the expense is $48,000. The $12,000 difference is the reversal of the amount deferred in 19x1.

The balance sheet classification of deferred tax liability is a noncurrent liability at December 31, 19x1, and a current liability on December 31, 19x2. The current/noncurrent designation depends on when the temporary differences reverse. Exhibit 9A–2 depicts the reversal of a temporary difference.

Deferred Tax Assets

Our example concentrated on a temporary difference created by using accelerated depreciation for income tax purposes versus straight-line depreciation for book purposes. Such a difference creates a deferred tax liability in the early years that reverses in the later years. Temporary differences can create *deferred tax assets* as well as liabilities.

A deferred tax asset is created when the cumulative temporary difference is associated with an initial excess of tax currently payable to the government over the tax expense reported on the income statement. An example of an event that creates this situation is warranty costs. While GAAP allows for warranty costs to be estimated and accrued, thus matching revenues and expenses, the tax laws permit warranty costs to be deducted from revenues only when actual warranty expenditures are made. The procedures for determining and recording deferred tax assets are similar to those described for deferred tax liabilities, but there are limitations and complexities involved that are beyond the scope of this text.

ACCOUNTING FOR OTHER BOOK/TAX DIFFERENCES

Without considering temporary differences, book net income before taxes (NIBT) may not equal taxable income because certain items that appear on the income statement may not appear on the tax return. An example of such a difference is interest on municipal bonds, which is revenue for book purposes that is never taxed. Jefferson Investment, Inc., has two sources of revenue, real estate commissions and municipal bond interest, resulting in the following summarized partial income statement:

Jefferson Investment, Inc.
Summarized Partial Income Statement
For the Year Ended December 31, 19xx

Revenues:		
Real estate commissions.	$100,000	
Municipal bond interest.	50,000	$150,000
Expenses		80,000
Net income before taxes		$ 70,000

EXHIBIT 9A–2

Reversal of Temporary Differences

Temporary differences

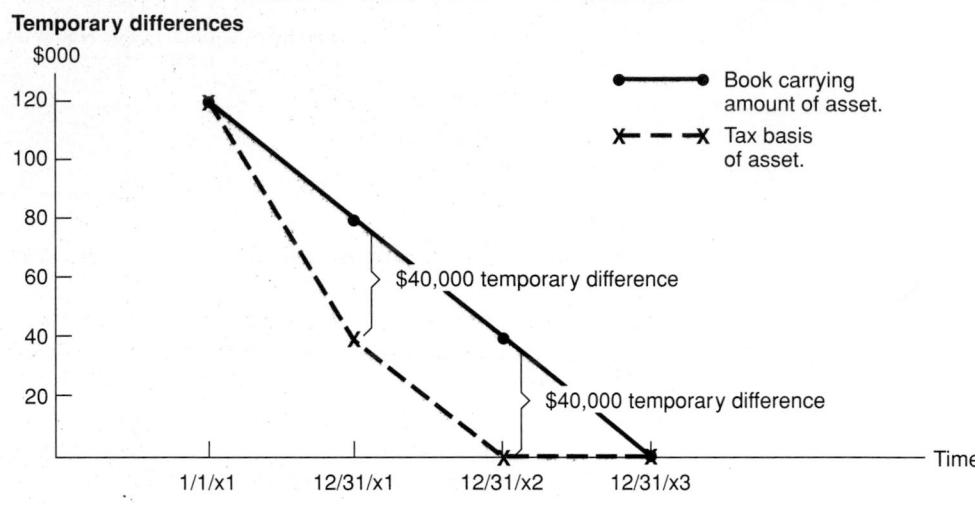

Comparison of depreciation expense and depreciation deductions

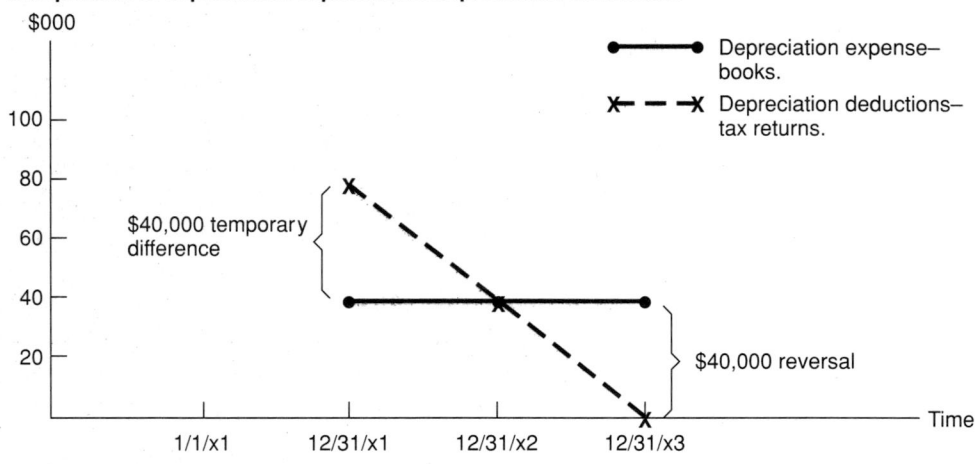

Deferred liability account balances

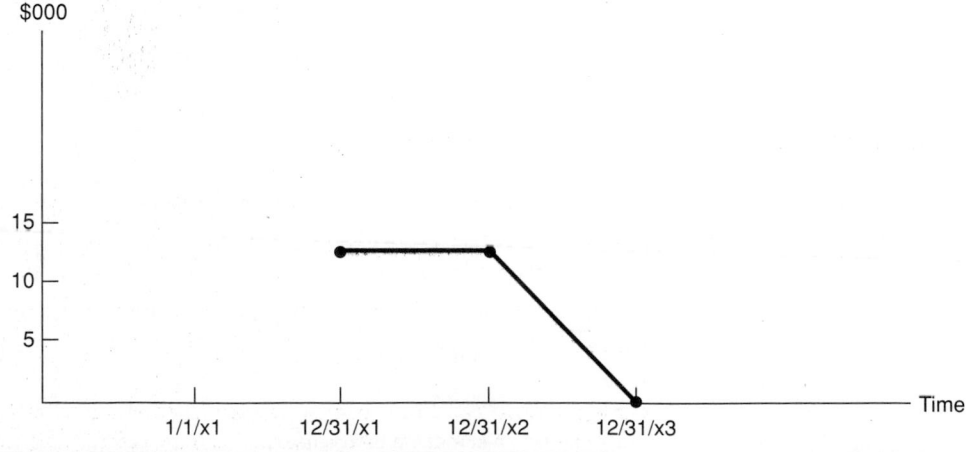

If the applicable tax rate is 30%, how much should be recognized as tax expense for the period? To answer this you must examine Jefferson Investment, Inc.'s tax return.

Jefferson Investment, Inc.
Summary of Tax Return

Taxable revenue	$100,000
Deductions	80,000
Taxable income	$ 20,000
Tax rate	.30
Tax obligation	$ 6,000

Jefferson will record only $6,000 tax expense on net income before taxes (NIBT) of $70,000 because the $50,000 of municipal interest will never be taxed. Such a difference between taxable income and NIBT changes the percentage relationship of tax expense to NIBT. Normally, you would expect tax expense to be 30% (or whatever the tax rate is for the period) of NIBT; but in this case it turns out to be less than 10% ($6,000/$70,000). The journal entry to record tax expense is as follows:

```
19xx
Dec. 31   Income Tax Expense (E) . . . . . . . . . . . . . . . . . . . .   6,000
              Income Taxes Payable (L) . . . . . . . . . . . . . . . . .          6,000
          To record tax obligation for the period.
```

The resulting summarized income statement would be

Jefferson Investment, Inc.
Summarized Income Statement
For the Year Ended December 31, 19xx

Revenues:		
Real estate	$100,000	
Municipal bond interest	50,000	$150,000
Expenses		80,000
Net income before taxes		$ 70,000
Tax expense		6,000
Net income		$ 64,000

Accounting for income taxes can be a complicated topic. A more complete treatment of this subject can be found in a more advanced accounting text.

• KEY TERMS

Accounts payable. A current liability used to record the purchase of goods and services on credit.

Cash dividends. Earnings distributed to stockholders; corporation's board of directors declares cash dividends and the amount to be paid on outstanding stock becomes a legal obligation.

Compound interest. Interest earned both on the principal and on accrued interest.

Contingency. A situation that creates a possibility for a liability to be created because of a past event.

Contingent liabilities. Occur when a company does not actually have a current obligation but a real possibility exists that an obligation will develop based on the resolution of a past event.

Current liabilities. Liabilities that are due within one year or one operating cycle, whichever is longer.

Declaration date. Point in time when the board of directors declares a dividend to stockholders and a current liability is established.

Definitely determinable current liability. An existing current liability of a precisely measurable amount.

Estimated liability. An existing liability for which the amount is not precisely known but for which a reasonable estimate can be made.

Federal Insurance Contributions Act (FICA). Law setting up the social security program, which is a system of retirement, disability, hospitalization, and survivors' benefits.

Federal Unemployment Tax Act (FUTA). Law that set up the joint program between federal and state governments to fund benefits for unemployed workers through taxation of employers.

Imputed interest. The interest that is related to a note or other financial instrument when there is no overt mention of an interest factor on the instrument.

Income taxes. Taxes levied by federal, state, and local governments against a business's taxable income and against employees' earnings.

Interest-bearing short-term note. A short-term note that specifies the principal amount of the note, the interest rate, and the maturity date.

Long-term liabilities. Liabilities that are not expected to be paid to creditors within one year or one operating cycle, whichever is longer.

Noninterest-bearing short-term note. A short-term note not specifying an interest rate, whose maturity value is the face value of the note.

Payment date. Date on which dividends are paid in cash.

Payroll deductions. Amounts withheld from employees' earnings by the employer for income taxes, FICA taxes, and other purposes.

Property taxes. Major source of tax revenue for local governments; usually based on a stated percentage of assessed values of real property (land and buildings) and personal property (property other than real property, such as furniture, automobiles, jewelry, inventory, and sometimes stocks and bonds).

Short-term note payable. A liability with many of the same attributes as accounts payable except that a note is a formal contract of indebtedness between a debtor (the **maker** of the note) and a creditor (the **payee** of the note). It can be either interest-bearing or noninterest-bearing.

Simple interest. Interest earned only on the unpaid principal.

Social security taxes. Taxes levied under the Federal Insurance Contributions Act; a portion is paid by employees and the other portion paid by the employer. Also called FICA taxes.

Vacation liability. Cost of vacation earned by employees but not taken at the end of an accounting period; represents an obligation of the business that must be recognized in the period in which it is earned, thus creating a current liability on the books.

Warranty commitments. Obligations created when businesses guarantee their products against defects for a certain period of time after the sale.

· Appendix Key Terms

Book carrying amount. Amount of an asset or liability on the accounting records.

Deferred tax asset. Created when the cumulative temporary difference is associated with an initial excess of tax currently payable to the government over the tax expense reported on the income statement.

Deferred tax liability. A liability created when the income tax expense for a period exceeds the income tax burden for the period.

Tax basis. Amount of an asset or liability on the tax records.

Temporary difference. The differences between the book carrying amounts and the tax bases of assets and liabilities that will affect the tax return in the future.

• SYNONYMS

Beancounters; accountants, used affectionately.

Principal; amount borrowed or loaned.

Net pay; take-home pay.

Payable; accrued.

Social security tax; FICA tax.

Taxes currently payable; current tax obligation.

Tax expense; tax provision.

Timing difference; temporary difference.

Warranty; guarantee.

Withholding; payroll deductions.

• QUESTIONS

1. Define current liabilities.
2. Why does a company not record an estimate for the possibility of nonpayment of accounts payable?
3. Define five parts of a promissory note.
4. Dividends are paid to a company's stockholders. What do the dividends represent to those stockholders? What comparable payments are made to creditors?
5. Describe the two significant dates involved in the issuance of dividends and what each date means.
6. Why are accountants concerned with determining when long-term notes become short term?
7. Distinguish between definitely determinable current liabilities and estimated liabilities. Describe four different types of estimated liabilities.
8. Why is it necessary to estimate income taxes? Property taxes?
9. What is the purpose of accruing vacation pay?
10. What must the accountant be concerned with in order to estimate warranty liability for the year?
11. In what ways do contingent liabilities differ from definitely determinable and estimated liabilities?
12. Describe how contingent liabilities are treated in the financial statements.
13. How is a contingent liability disclosed in financial statements?
14. Why are organizations so concerned with their payroll systems?
15. Describe the different departments' responsibilities in the payroll system.
16. Describe three employer expenses associated with payroll.
17. Describe four items deducted from an employee's pay and explain how they are treated by the employer.

• Appendix Questions

18. Define temporary differences.
19. Contrast book carrying amount and tax basis of a depreciable asset.
20. Over the life of the business, what are the effects of temporary differences? Why?
21. Contrast deferred tax liability and taxes payable.
22. How would you decide on the balance sheet classification of a deferred tax liability account?

• EXERCISES

E 9–1
Accounts Payable
L.O.1

Prepare the journal entries related to the following events for Sapak Forestry. Sapak uses the periodic inventory system and the net method for recording purchases.

a. Received goods from Supplier A on February 10 for $10,000. Terms are 2/10, n/30. Paid for goods on February 20.

b. Purchased supplies on account for $550 on February 20. Terms are 2/10, n/30, but Sapak did not pay the supplies until after the discount period expired.

E 9–2
Note Payable
L.O.1

The Graham Company issued a 10%, two-year note payable to the Friendly Bank for a $60,000 loan of cash on October 1, 19xx.

Required:

1. Prepare in general journal form the entry Graham Company recorded on October 1, 19xx.
2. Prepare in general journal form the adjusting journal entry recorded by the Graham Company on December 31, 19xx (its fiscal year-end).

E 9–3
Noninterest-Bearing Note Payable
L.O.1

Needs-the-Money, Inc., issued a one-year noninterest-bearing note for $35,000 cash on September 1, 19x1. The implied interest rate on the note is equal to 10%. Prepare the journal entries on September 1, 19x1, December 31, 19x1, and September 1, 19x2, related to interest expense.

E 9–4
Dividends
L.O.1

On March 15, 19xx, National Motors Company declared a $0.15 dividend on each of its 500,000 shares of common stock, to be paid on May 15, 19xx. In general journal form, record the journal entries made on the declaration and payment dates.

E 9–5
Long-Term Interest-Bearing Note and Reclassification to Current
L.O.1

On October 1, 19x1, Datanow Company took out a $500,000, 12%, four-year note with $125,000 due on September 30 of each year of the note. Interest is paid on September 30 of each year. Datanow's fiscal year ends on December 31 of each year.

Required:
Prepare in journal form all journal entries related to the note over the four years.

E 9–6
Income Taxes
L.O.2

Rent-It-All Company estimates its 19x1 income taxes to be $125,000 when it closes its books for the fiscal year ending December 31, 19x1. When Rent-It-All prepares its income tax return and files it on March 31, 19x2, the actual income tax due and paid to the government is $132,000.

Required:
Prepare the journal entries related to the income taxes.

E 9–7
Property Taxes
L.O.2

On January 1, 19xx, Flights on the Wing, Inc., estimates its property tax for 19xx to be $60,000 and uses that estimate in preparing its quarterly financial statements. On September 15, Flights receives its tax bill, which it pays immediately for $52,000.

Required:
Record all journal entries during the year related to property taxes.

E 9–8
Vacation Pay
L.O.2

Mabel's Furniture Company accrued vacation pay at December 31, 19x1 and 19x2, of $760 and $940, respectively. Mabel's paid $570 of the 19x1 accrued vacation pay in 19x2.

Required:

1. In general journal form, prepare the journal entries Mabel's Furniture Company makes related to accrued vacation pay during 19x1 and 19x2.
2. Determine the liability related to vacation pay on December 31, 19x2.

E 9–9
Warranties
L.O.2

Breitmeyer's Micro, Inc., a producer of the latest in high-tech microwave ovens, has sales of $2,796,400 during 19x1, its first year of operations. Breitmeyer's estimates the warranty work required to be 3% of sales. During 19x2, warranty expenditures were $56,000, and sales were $3,209,000. There were no warranty expenditures during 19x1.

Required:

1. In general journal form, record the journal entry Breitmeyer's made at December 31, 19x1, its fiscal year-end.
2. Record any journal entries related to warranties during 19x2.
3. Discuss why the matching concept is a key factor in accounting for warranties.

E 9–10
Contingent Liabilities
L.O.3

On September 30, 19x1, Chemicals, Inc's corporate executives know of a pending lawsuit filed on June 20, 19x1, by one of its former employees on the grounds of known dangerous working conditions. The lawsuit has been filed for $750,000, but the corporate legal department believes it will be settled for $100,000.

Required:

1. Prepare any necessary journal entries at the September 30 year-end.
2. Prepare the footnote disclosures that Chemicals would show in its 19x1 annual report.
3. If on August 14, 19x2, the lawsuit is settled for $150,000, what journal entry would Chemicals make on that date?

E 9–11
Payroll
L.O.5

Carol's Country Crafts (CCC) pays its employees twice a month. The August 15 payroll includes $1,527 paid to employees and withholdings of $145 for FICA, $132 for federal income tax, $97 for state income tax, and $200 for direct deposit in the local credit union. CCC is also responsible for FICA of $145, FUTA of $50, and health insurance premiums of $130.

Required:

Prepare the journal entries in general journal form CCC makes for the August 15 payroll.

E 9–12
Payroll
L.O.5

Anita's Fine Confections has gross pay for the payroll period ending April 30, 19xx, of $146,200. The FICA rate is 7.51% for both Anita and her employees. Federal income tax and state income tax withholdings amounted to $7,850 and $5,699, respectively. Retirement benefits of $2,000 and health insurance benefits of $3,600 were paid completely by the employer. Anita must also pay FUTA at a rate of .4% and state unemployment tax at a rate of .35%. All employees are below the applicable maximum wages for FICA, FUTA, and SUTA.

Required:

1. Prepare the journal entries to record the above payroll.
2. Discuss why income taxes withheld are considered liabilities of the company.

E 9–13
Accounts Payable,
Dividends, and
Warranties
L.O.1, 2

1. During June 19x7, Tri-State Furniture Company pays $16,892 to suppliers, purchases $19,236 of goods on account, and has an ending balance in its Accounts Payable account of $4,816. The account's beginning balance is—
   a. $7,160.
   b. $2,344.
   c. $2,472.
   d. $7,288.
2. On December 31, the end of the first year of operations of Conte, Inc., the board of directors declared a $0.35 dividend on each of its 250,000 shares of outstanding common stock. No other dividends were declared during the year. Total dividends paid during the year were—
   a. $87,500.
   b. $0.

   c. $125,000.

   d. $85,700.

 3. Terres Company, a leading seller of computer software, guarantees its products for one year from date of purchase. During 19x6, Terres has sales of $15,875,500 and expects to pay 2% on the warranties. During 19x6 Terres pays $530,000 on warranty repairs. The beginning balance in the Warranty Payable account is $641,000. The ending balance in the account is—

   a. $317,510.

   b. $269,755.

   c. $853,490.

   d. $428,510.

E 9–14

Multiple Choice

L.O.1–5

 1. Interest—

   a. Is the fee charged when notes are defaulted.

   b. Is the fee charged for the use of money.

   c. Is the maturity value of a note.

   d. Is usually stated on the face of an invoice.

   e. None of the above.

 2. Notes payable and accounts payable are different in that—

   a. Notes are always long term and accounts payable are always short term.

   b. Unlike accounts payable, notes have a determinable maturity amount.

   c. Accounts payable are not legal liabilities.

   d. Accounts payable are estimates.

   e. None of the above.

 3. Contingent liabilities—

   a. Are not recorded until the amount is known with certainty.

   b. Are always current liabilities.

   c. May result in the recording of an estimated liability.

   d. Are not recorded until a lawsuit against a company is decided.

   e. None of the above.

 4. Compound interest—

   a. Is based on the initial amount of the liability.

   b. Is based on the initial amount of the liability plus previously paid interest.

   c. Is not used for notes payable.

   d. Over the life of a note is usually less than simple interest.

   e. None of the above.

 5. The total interest expense over the life of a note—

   a. Equals the total cash paid to the creditor.

   b. Equals the total cash paid to the creditor minus the initial liability.

   c. Equals the total current liability.

   d. Is shown as a current liability on the balance sheet.

   e. None of the above.

 6. The current portion of a long-term liability—

   a. Is classified as long term on the balance sheet.

   b. Is the same as the long-term portion of current debt.

   c. Is an expense.

   d. Is classified as current on the balance sheet.

   e. None of the above.

 7. Income tax payable—

   a. Is always equal to income tax expense.

   b. Is a long-term liability.

   c. Appears on the balance sheet only when tax obligations are underestimated.

   d. Is a contingent liability.

   e. None of the above.

 8. The matching principle—

   a. Requires that vacation pay not be expensed until the vacation time is taken.

   b. Requires that an expense be recorded at the end of a period after which earned vacation time for that period is still outstanding.

      c. Requires that interest be computed on a simple interest basis.

      d. Requires that warranty liabilities be recorded as current.

      e. None of the above.

9. FICA taxes—

      a. Are the responsibility of both the employee and the employer.

      b. Are the responsibility of the employer alone.

      c. Are the responsibility of the employee alone.

      d. Result in expenses only if they are unpaid at year-end.

      e. None of the above.

· Appendix Exercises

E 9–15
Deferred Taxes
L.O.6, 7

Esther's Eatery, which has a calendar fiscal year, purchased kitchen equipment for $70,000. The equipment has a seven-year life and no salvage value. Esther uses straight-line depreciation for book purposes and sum-of-the-years'-digits for tax purposes. This is the only temporary difference. For years 19x1, 19x2, and 19x3, net income before depreciation and taxes is $150,000, $135,000, and $100,000, respectively. The income tax rate is 40%.

Required:

1. Compute the cumulative temporary difference for each of the three years.
2. Prepare the journal entries relating to income tax expense and deferred taxes.

E 9–16
Deferred Taxes
L.O.6, 7

Howell Auto Parts, Inc., has the following information from its books and tax return for the last three years:

	NIBT	Taxable Income
19x1.	$1,400,000	$1,000,000
19x2.	1,900,000	1,500,000
19x3.	1,800,000	1,900,000

Net income before taxes in each year includes $150,000 of interest revenue earned from municipal bonds, which is not considered taxable income. All other differences are created by different depreciation methods used for book and tax purposes. The tax rate is 30%.

Required:

Prepare the journal entries related to income tax expense and deferred taxes.

E 9–17
Multiple Choice
L.O.6, 7

1. Tax expense for the period—

      a. Is always equal to net income before taxes times the tax rate.

      b. Is always equal to the tax payable to the government for the period.

      c. Is always greater than the tax paid to the government for the period.

      d. Is always equal to the net income before taxes times the tax rate if there are no permanent differences.

      e. None of the above.

2. A change in a deferred tax liability—

      a. Is equal to a timing difference.

      b. Is equal to a timing difference times the tax rate.

      c. Is equal to a permanent difference.

      d. Always has a short-term component.

      e. None of the above.

• PROBLEMS

P 9–1
Accounts Payable
L.O.1

Airtex, Inc., a manufacturer of pollution control monitoring equipment with a December 31 fiscal year-end, purchases gauges from one primary supplier, White Supply Company. During 19x1, Airtex had cash flow problems and requested that White allow delay of payment of three invoices. White agreed to delayed payment of the invoices if Airtex signed three three-month notes with 10% annual interest paid as follows:

Invoice Date	Invoice No.	Invoice Amount	Date of Note	Due Date
6/30	1001	$100,000	7/31	10/31
9/1	2107	50,000	10/1	12/31
11/2	3612	36,000	12/1	2/28
		$186,000		

Required:
1. Record Airtex's journal entries for the transactions with White during 19x1. (Assume 30-day months for interest calculations and that Airtex uses the perpetual inventory system.)
2. Describe how current liabilities on the December 31, 19x1, balance sheet are affected by these transactions.

P 9–2
Interest and Recording Notes Payable
L.O.1

Smith Company has to finance the $10,000 purchase of a new generator. First Bank offers the following terms:

Principal	$10,000
Annual interest rate	12%, compounded annually
Payment schedule	Interest and principal at maturity
Maturity date	December 31, 19x2
Inception of note	January 1, 19x1

Second Bank offers the following terms with the same effective interest rate as above:

Maturity amount	$12,544
Payment schedule	$12,544 at maturity
Inception of note	January 1, 19x1
Maturity date	December 31, 19x2

2544 Discount on Note

Required:
1. For each note described above, record all journal entries related to the notes for 19x1 and 19x2, assuming that Smith Company has a December 31 year-end.
2. Which note is "interest-bearing"? What is the annual interest rate for each note?
3. Discuss the following statement: All notes have interest factors, either explicit or implicit, and accounting cannot ignore it.

P 9–3
Short-Term Notes
L.O.1

Clearly Corporation typically arranges short-term financing with its bank in order to provide operating cash as needed. Interest expense is recorded upon payment of the note and at the end of each quarter for financial reporting purposes if this occurs sooner.

During 19xx, Clearly Corporation had the following activity in short-term financing:

19xx
Jan. 15 Borrowed $50,000 at 12% on a 60-day note.
Feb. 28 Borrowed $100,000 at 10% on a six-month note.
Mar. 15 Paid the note of January 15 plus interest.
      30 Accrued interest as required for quarterly statements.

19xx

May	1	Borrowed $100,000 on a 9%, 90-day note.
June	30	Accrued interest as required for quarterly statements.
July	15	Borrowed $50,000 on a 10%, six-month note.
Aug.	1	Paid the note of May 1 plus interest.
	30	Paid the note of February 28 plus interest.
Sept.	30	Accrued interest as required for quarterly statements.
Nov.	1	Borrowed $50,000 on an 8%, 90-day note.
Dec.	31	Accrued interest as required.
	31	Closed the Interest Expense account for the year.

Required:

In general journal form, prepare all journal entries the Clearly Corporation made during 19xx for the above notes. Round all computations to the nearest dollar. Assume that each month has 30 days.

P 9–4
Balance Sheet
Classification
(Challenging)
L.O.1, 2

Lonestar, Inc., shows "Accounts payable . . . . $34,300" on its balance sheet at December 31, 19x1, under the "Current liabilities" section. Upon investigation of the subsidiary records, the following details are revealed about the $34,300 amount:

a. Unpaid invoices for office equipment, supplies, and inventory total $24,800. This includes one invoice of $1,500 for a typewriter that was returned to the vendor because it was not the model ordered. The $24,800 credit is part of the Accounts Payable balance.

b. Estimated income taxes to be received from the federal government are $10,500. This represents the estimated overpayment of the current year's taxes. The $10,500 was debited to Accounts Payable.

c. Notes payable to bank total $20,000. This is the principal amount of a promissory note issued to a bank, which is due on December 31, 19x3. The interest on the note is paid semiannually. The $20,000 is part of the Accounts Payable balance.

Required:

1. Comment on the appropriate balance sheet classification of each item.
2. Make the journal entries necessary for correcting the classifications, if there are any.

P 9–5
Dividends, Property
Taxes, and Contingent
Liabilities
L.O.1, 2

Prepare the journal entry or state why no entry is required for each of the following items. Consider each case separately.

Case 1:

a. December 31, 19x1. The board of directors declares a dividend of $0.50 per share; 250,000 shares of common stock are outstanding.

b. January 30, 19x2. The dividend declared on December 31, 19x1, is paid.

Case 2:

a. March 31, 19x1. One quarter of the year's estimated property taxes of $800,000 is recorded.

b. June 30, 19x1. The second quarter of estimated property taxes is recorded.

c. September 30, 19x1. The tax bill for the calendar year 19x1 is received and paid. The bill is for $780,000.

Case 3:

a. A company is a defendant in a lawsuit alleging patent infringement. The lawsuit is for $300,000, an amount that is material to the company. Management and the company's attorney believe the lawsuit is entirely without merit, and the company will prevail.

b. A company is a defendant in a product liability lawsuit of $1 million. This amount is material to the company, and management and the company's attorneys feel they will lose the case. However, management is reluctant to record the liability, because they intend to fight the case and eventually settle for $500,000 "a few years" away.

c. Same as situation b except the amount is not material, and the court's decision is due within the next 60 days.

P 9–6
Property Taxes
L.O.2

The city of Johnsonville levies a yearly property tax equal to 1% of the fair value of real estate. The payment is due on July 1 of each year for the year then ending, and the tax bill is mailed on June 15. Levity, Inc., is a calendar-year company that has paid the following property tax in the last two years:

Period Covered by Tax	Assessed Fair Value	Tax Paid
7/1/x1–6/30/x2	$10,000,000	$100,000
7/1/x2–6/30/x3	16,000,000	160,000

On December 31, 19x3, Levity estimates that the tax for the July 1, 19x3, to June 30, 19x4, period will be $180,000. The estimate made on December 31, 19x2, was exactly correct.

Required:
1. Record the journal entries made for property tax on December 31, 19x2, and on July 1, 19x3.
2. Record the journal entry made on December 31, 19x3, for property tax.

P 9–7
Vacation Pay
L.O.2

Tysen Produce, Inc., has three employees all of whom earn one day of vacation for each month of employment. The following schedule shows each employee's vacation status for 19x1:

Employee No.	Vacation Days Earned	Vacation Days Taken	Vacation Days Carried Over to 19x2
1	12	0	12
2	6	0	6
3	12	5	7

Tysen has recorded all payroll-related expenses in one account, Salary Expense. The expense amount per day of work recorded for each employer during 19x1 was: employee No. 1, $330; employee No. 2, $230; and employee No. 3, $100. Nothing has been separately recorded for vacations during the current year.

Required:
1. Record the necessary adjustment for vacation time.
2. Discuss the implication of the unused vacation time at December 31 for Tysen financial statements and explain why the adjustment is necessary.

P 9–8
Vacation Pay
(Challenging)
L.O.2

Techtronics, Inc., has five employees who worked for the entire year from January 1, 19x2, to December 31, 19x2. Each employee is entitled to 1 day vacation for each 25 days of work to a maximum of 10 vacation days per year, so that in one year, when an employee works for 250 days (50, 5-day weeks), he or she would be entitled to 10 days of vacation (two 5-day weeks) at full pay. There were no carryovers from 19x1, but in 19x2, the work schedule was so tight that most employees did not take all of their earned vacation. The following schedule shows vacation time earned and taken by each employee:

Employee No.	Weeks Worked	Vacation Weeks Taken	Weekly Pay
1	52	0	$850
2	51	1	700
3	50	2	750
4	52	0	900
5	52	0	800

Required:

1. Ignoring all taxes and withholdings, show any entry necessary at December 31, 19x2, to account for vacation pay. Explain your answer.
2. If all current and carryover vacation time is taken in 19x3 and the weekly pay stays the same, show a summary entry to record wage expense for 19x3. (Again, ignore taxes and withholdings.)

P 9–9
Warranties
L.O.2

In 19x1, Foley, Inc., started manufacturing high-quality video cassette recorders and selling them via mail order. One feature of this product that the company feels will be attractive to the prime market target group is the unlimited returns policy for three years. Under this warranty program, Foley will replace any defective set with a new one. Because of the high quality, Foley expects only a 1% return. During 19x1, no returns were made on the following sales:

Units Sold	Sales Price per Unit	Manufacturing Cost per Unit	Units Replaced	Estimated Handling Cost per Unit Replaced
1,200	$1,350	$650	0	$102

12 units @ 650/unit + (12 × 102)

Required:
Prepare the December 31, 19x1, journal entry and the accounting disclosures in the financial statements (if any) required because of the warranty policy.

P 9–10
Contingent Liabilities
L.O.3

Sunbelt Charters, Inc., operates a small airline that specializes in interisland flights in Hawaii. Sunbelt carries liability insurance of $10 million for injury to passengers, but the insurance contract terms call for Sunbelt to pay the first $100,000 of claims for each incident. During 19x1, two incidents occurred that have not yet been settled.

a. On October 12, 19x1, an overhead compartment door opened on landing and a carry-on bag fell on a passenger causing a head injury. The passenger filed a lawsuit on April 15, 19x1, and Sunbelt's attorney has been instructed to settle out of court. At December 31, 19x1, the attorney has a strong belief that the out-of-court settlement will take place on January 20, 19x1, for $85,000.

b. On November 30, 19x1, four passengers were badly injured upon debarking when the portable ramp collapsed. Lawsuits totaling $1.8 million have been filed against Sunbelt and the airport that owned the ramp. On December 31, Sunbelt's attorneys believe strongly that if the lawsuits were taken to trial, they would result in payment of $1.8 million to the injured passengers, but that Sunbelt should be found innocent while the airport will be found negligent and made to pay the damages.

Required:

1. Discuss the nature of the obligations created by these two incidents. Do they create estimated or contingent liabilities?
2. Describe the accounting treatment of each incident, showing any necessary journal entries at December 31 and describing any financial statement effects.

P 9–11
Payroll
L.O.5

Farmland Products, Inc., has three employees who were paid the following amounts for December 19xx:

Employee No.	Gross Pay	Federal Income Tax Withheld	FICA Tax Withheld (employee's portion)	Insurance Withheld	State Income Tax Withheld
1	$7,000	$2,500	$ 0	$50	$190
2	5,000	1,200	350	50	120
3	2,000	600	140	50	100

In addition to the above items, Farmland initiated a hospitalization plan on December 1, 19xx, which will cost $200 per employee per month for the insurance. The employee pays nothing for this benefit. The payments are made in advance for six-month periods. On December 2, 19xx, Farmland made the following entry for the insurance:

Salaries Expense	3,600	
Cash.		3,600

Required:
1. Record the journal entries for the payroll at December 31, 19xx, and for any necessary adjustments.
2. Discuss how balance sheet classifications are affected by the above transactions.

P 9–12
Payroll
L.O.5

The following payroll data is available for the three employees in the sales department of Malmac Corporation:

Employee	Earnings to Date*	Rate
Cobb, T. R.	$43,360	$2,710 per pay period
Gehrig, H. L.	16,000	$10.00 per hour
Williams, T. S.	22,800	$12.00 per hour

*As of beginning of the current pay period.

During the current period, Gehrig worked 80 hours and Williams worked 77. In addition to FICA, amounts withheld during the period are as follows:

	Cobb	Gehrig	Williams
Federal income taxes	$894.30	$210.00	$250.00
State income taxes	130.00	38.40	44.35
City income taxes.	59.60	17.60	20.30
Health insurance premium	38.00	38.00	13.00
Savings plan	100.00	0	25.00

Assume that FICA taxes are 7% for both the employee and the employer on the first $43,800 of wages earned during the year.

Required (For the current pay period):
1. Prepare a schedule computing for each employee gross pay, individual deductions, and net pay.
2. Prepare the journal entry(entries) to record the payroll, including the employer's portion of FICA taxes.

P 9–13
Short-Term Liabilities and Business Decisions (Challenging)
L.O.1, 2, 5

You are a bank loan officer and a potential client, Professional Financial Services, Inc., (PFS) has applied for a loan of $300,000. The proposed note would be issued on 1/1/x2 to be paid back on 2/1/x2 with interest at 20%. On 12/31/x1, PFS supplies the following information:

1. **Schedule of expected liability balances at the 12/31/x1 year-end:**

   Current liabilities:

Accounts payable	$120,000	(due Jan. 10, 19x2)
Salaries payable	62,000	(due Jan. 6, 19x2)
Notes payable	660,000	(see schedule*)
Interest payable	18,717	(see schedule†)
Total current liabilities.	$860,717	

   ***Schedule of Notes Payable:**

Note	Note Made to	Term of Note	Interest Principal	Rate	Interest Payment
1	Scott Products	10/1/x1 to 4/1/x2	$300,000	15%	4/1/x2
2	First Bank	11/30/x1 to 2/28/x2	200,000	16%	End of each month
3	National Mortgage	9/1/x1 to 2/28/x2	160,000	14%	2/28/x2

   †Schedule of Interest Payable (rounded):

   Note 1 ($300,000) (.15) (3/12) = $11,250
   Note 3 ($160,000) (.14) (4/12) = 7,467
   $18,717

2. **Schedule of expected cash payments for January 19x2:**

Payroll	Jan. 6	$125,000
	Jan. 20	125,000
Accounts payable	Jan. 10	120,000
	Jan. 28	60,000
Notes (interest)	Jan. 31	2,667
Other expenses	Jan. 15	15,000
	Jan. 31	30,000

3. **Schedule of cash receipts for January 19x2:**

From customers	Jan. 10	$150,000
	Jan. 20	50,000
	Jan. 30	50,000
From bank—new note	Jan. 1	300,000

4. **Expected cash balance on 12/31/x1, $130,000.**

Required:

1. Show all of PFS's journal entries for the expected January 19x2 transactions assuming that all payments are made on time and that all receipts are collected as scheduled. (Round all amounts to nearest dollar.)
2. Give your opinion about the banker's decision on granting the loan, backed up by an analysis of cash available to pay off the new note when it is due.

· Appendix Problems

P 9–14
Deferred Taxes
(Challenging)
L.O.6

Zach, Inc., purchased a machine for $80,000. It has an estimated life of five years and a salvage value of $5,000. It will be depreciated by the straight-line method for book purposes and by the sum-of-the-years'-digits method for tax purposes, resulting in depreciation expense as follows:

Year	Straight-Line	Sum-of-the-Years'-Digits
1	$15,000	$25,000
2	15,000	20,000
3	15,000	15,000
4	15,000	10,000
5	15,000	5,000

Income before taxes and depreciation each year is $150,000. A tax rate of 40% should be used for all purposes.

Required:
1. Prepare a schedule that shows
   a. Net income before taxes.
   b. Taxable income for each of the first five years involved.
2. Prepare the journal entries to record the tax liability for years 1, 3, and 5.

P 9–15
Deferred Taxes
L.O.6

Stanley Company has two depreciable assets that create timing differences. Depreciation is recorded on the straight-line basis for book purposes and on an accelerated basis for tax purposes.

Asset No.	Depreciation Expense on Income Statement			Depreciation Expense on Tax Form		
	19x1	19x2	19x3	19x1	19x2	19x3
1	$100,000	$100,000	$100,000	$300,000	$200,000	$100,000
2	0	42,000	42,000	0	90,000	40,000

Stanley's income before depreciation and taxes for 19x1, 19x2, and 19x3 was $420,000, $602,000, and $480,000, respectively. The tax rate for all three years was 30%, and this rate is expected to continue into the future.

Required:
1. Show all journal entries for income taxes for the years 19x1, 19x2, and 19x3.
2. Discuss the balance sheet classification for 19x1 affected by the temporary differences.

· CASES

C 9–1
Contingent Liabilities
L.O.3

Precision Company, Inc., was notified on December 31, 19x1, the end of its fiscal period, that a lawsuit had been initiated against them for $10 million. The lawsuit claims that one of Precision's delivery people drove a truck into a pedestrian walkway and injured two people. The police report noted that the driver claims that the pedestrians were walking against the light. Precision's insurance coverage for such accidents has a limit of $1 million. Precision's attorney expects that an out-of-court settlement will be reached for no more than $1 million, but she cannot rule out the possibility of a larger adverse payment.

Required:
Discuss the accounting issues involved in this case. How should Precision disclose this situation in its financial statements?

· Evaluating Financial Statements

C 9–2
Dividends Payable
L.O.1

During 19x6, General Electric Company declared dividends of $1,081 million. GE reported the following current liabilities in its December 31, 19x6, statement of financial position.

	(in millions) December 31	
	19x6	19x5
Current liabilities:		
Short-term borrowings	$ 1,813	$1,297
Accounts payable	2,594	2,204
Progress collections and price adjustments accrued	2,273	2,257
Dividends payable	287	264
Taxes accrued	1,153	751
Other costs and expenses accrued	3,341	2,146
Current liabilities.	$11,461	$8,919

Required:
Compute the dividends General Electric paid during 19x6 and discuss the effects that dividends have on cash flows and current liabilities.

C 9–3
Contingent Liabilities
L.O.3

E. I. Du Pont de Nemours and Company reports the following in its 19x6 consolidated balance sheet (in millions):

	December 31	
	19x6	19x5
Other liabilities	$1,669	$1,475

The footnotes to the financial statements include this excerpt:

Other Liabilities

	December 31	
	19x6	19x5
Reserves for employee-related costs including coal workers' pneumoconiosis.	$ 814	$ 753
Miscellaneous	855	722
	$1,669	$1,475

Required:
1. Describe the nature of this liability. What does this liability represent?
2. Do you think this liability is current or noncurrent? Why?

C 9–4
*Accounts Payable and
Reclassification of
Long-Term Debt*
L.O.1

The following is an excerpt from the December 31, 19x6, balance sheet of Ford Motor Company and consolidated subsidiaries:

	(in millions)	
	19x6	19x5
Current liabilities:		
Accounts payable:		
Trade.	$5,752.3	$4,751.9
Other.	2,546.1	1,825.6
	$8,298.4	$6,577.5

Required:

1. If 19x6 purchases on trade accounts were $8,000 million, what was the amount of cash paid to trade creditors for the year?
2. Is it possible that any of the $5,752.3 million will not be paid in 19x7? Explain.
3. Assume that $1,500 million of the $2,546.1 million is reclassified long-term debt. What is the justification for classifying the $1,500 million as current?

C 9–5
Contingent Liabilities—
Warranties
L.O.3

Dunn Equipment Co. manufactures lightweight, compact electric motors for industrial customers. For the past several years about 1% of the motors have been returned for full credit because of defects. Dunn allows full credit on returns within a year of sale because the transportation and repair costs on average for repairing the used motors would exceed the manufacturing cost of the new engines. Whenever a customer reports a defect within the warranty period, Dunn's standard accounting is to Debit Sales and Credit Inventory for the cost of the new engine.

Required:

Write a memo to management explaining the proper accounting treatment for such a situation. Give the financial statement effects of your suggested accounting.

C 9–6
Noninterest-Bearing Note
L.O.1

As auditor of Kansas Glass Works, Inc., (KGW) you come upon the following history of a transaction involving the purchase of equipment by means of a six-month noninterest-bearing note, recorded in the journal by KGW's accountant:

5/1/x1	Equipment	80,000	
	Notes Payable		80,000

To record the signing of a noninterest-bearing note with a maturity value of $84,000 for the purchase of equipment costing $80,000.

11/1/x1	Interest Expense	4,800	
	Notes Payable	80,000	
	Cash		84,000
	Gain on Interest.		800

To record interest expense at 12% per annum and the payment of the maturity value of the note.

Upon questioning the accountant, you find the 12% was the interest rate charged by a bank for a loan made during October.

Required:

Criticize the handling of the transactions and tell how you would have recorded them.

C 9–7
Contingency
(Challenging)
L.O.3

In June 19x1, All-Right Rental, Inc., rented a chain saw to a minor who was using his older brother's driver's license as identification. The young man was severely injured while using the saw and initiated a $10 million lawsuit against All-Right on November 15, 19x1. At the end of All-Right's fiscal year, December 31, 19x1, the company's attorney is working on an out-of-court settlement that calls for All-Right to pay $1 million in medical expenses and $2 million in damages. The attorney believes that the plaintiff will not accept the offer and will push ahead with the suit. If a trial ensues, the attorney states, "we will probably lose, and if we do, the minimum we will pay is $4 million; but that payment will not come until 19x3 at the earliest."

Required:

Discuss how the concepts of periodicity, matching, measurement, and objectivity affect the accounting for the above facts and describe what the accounting should be for the All-Right contingency.

C 9–8
Contingency
L.O.3

Read the first paragraph section of the "Commitments and contingencies" note to Ralston Purina Company's annual report in Appendix E. Also review Ralston's balance sheet in Appendix E.

Required:

1. Does Ralston have a contingent liability as of the balance sheet date? Explain.
2. Did Ralston record a liability related to "legal matters" on its balance sheet? Explain.

Somers Corporation
Balance Sheet For 12/31/94

	1994	1993
Current assets:		
Total current assets.	$ xxx	$ xxx
Noncurrent assets:		
Total noncurrent assets	$ xxx	$ xxx
Total assets	$ xxx	$ xxx
Current liabilities:		
Total current liabilities.	$ xxx	$ xxx
Noncurrent liabilities:		
Notes payable.	**xx**	**xx**
Bonds payable	**xx**	**xx**
Leases payable	**xx**	**xx**
Total noncurrent liabilities	**$ xx**	**$ xx**
Stockholders' equity:		
Total stockholders' equity	xxx	xxx
Total liabilities and stockholders' equity	$ xxxx	$ xxxx

Somers Corporation
Income Statement For 1994

	1994	1993
Net sales	$ xxx	$ xxx
Cost of goods sold	xxx	xxx
Gross margin	$ xxx	$ xxx
Expenses		
Interest expense.	**xx**	**xx**
Total expenses	$ xxx	$ xxx
Net income	$ xx	$ xx

Somers Corporation
Cash Flow Statement For 1994

	1994	1993
Operating activities		
Payments for interest	**(xx)**	**(xx)**
Cash used in operating activities	$ xxx	$ xxx
Investing activities		
Cash used in investing activities	$ xxx	$ xxx
Financing activities		
Receipts from sale of bonds	**xxx**	**xxx**
Receipt from bank loan	**xxx**	
Payment to retire debt.	**(xx)**	**(xx)**
Payments to retire stock.	**(xxx)**	**(xxx)**
Cash used in financing activities	$ xxxx	$ xxxx
Net change in cash	$ xx	$ xx

FINANCIAL STATEMENT COMPONENTS EMPHASIZED IN CHAPTER 10

10

Long-Term Liabilities— Notes and Bonds

At a corporation with very high ethical standards, finance management has the advantage of not having to convince top management that ethics are important—at Ford that is a given.

Anthony J. Ridley
Ford Motor Company

· Learning Objectives

After studying Chapter 10, you should understand

1. Debt financing and the importance of risk assessment, pp. 494–96.
2. What all long-term debt has in common, pp. 496–501.
3. Accounting for interest-bearing and noninterest-bearing long-term notes, pp. 502–4.
4. Common features of bond contracts, pp. 504–6.
5. Bonds sold at face value, at discount, and at premium, pp. 506–17.
6. Retirement of bonds, pp. 517–18.
7. Bonds sold between interest dates, pp. 517–20.
8. Bond conversions, p. 518.
9. Bond sinking funds, p. 518.
10. Future values and present values (Appendix 10A), pp. 524–27.
11. Present value computations relating to bonds, leases, and pensions (Appendix 10B) pp. 530–36.

In this chapter the focus is on accounting for long-term debt financing—how accounting is affected by the contractual terms of certain noncurrent liabilities such as notes, bonds, leases, and pensions. As you study the chapter, you will note that a key factor in all decisions on noncurrent liabilities is the effect of interest on cash flow and on the financial statements. Once you understand the effects of interest, you will see that the accounting procedures follow a standard pattern.

Why is interest so important in noncurrent liabilities? Interest is the cost of using borrowed funds. The amount of interest over the entire term of a loan is the total cash outflow minus the total cash inflow related to the loan. The longer the time frame of a liability, the greater is the interest relative to the initial amount of the liability. The chapter begins with a discussion of four examples of loan repayment, illustrating the effect of alternative repayment patterns on the total amount of cash a company pays to the creditor of a long-term liability.

Within the chapter accounting for long-term interest-bearing and noninterest-bearing notes is discussed. Then accounting for bonds is explained. Appendix 10A is concerned with techniques used to compute the time value of money—the future and present values; and Appendix 10B discusses special present value problems for bonds, leases, and pensions. The chapter is organized so that each topic builds on the previous topic. Should you have any difficulty with one topic, restudy it and the previous topics before moving on.

TYPES OF LONG-TERM FINANCING

Objective 1
Debt financing and the importance of risk assessment.

The two common types of long-term financing used by corporations are *debt financing* and *equity financing*. Long-term debt financing is a long-term borrowing from creditors; equity financing is the issuance of capital stock to the stockholders of a business. The providers of debt financing (creditors) and equity financing (stockholders) demand returns. For debt financing, the return is interest; for equity financing, the return is dividends and/or share price appreciation of stock. As you might expect, debt financing and equity financing each have advantages and disadvantages, and the terms of the contracts governing them are quite different.

A major difference between debt financing and equity financing is that interest expense is tax deductible to the business while dividend payments to stockholders are not. For income statement purposes, interest expense reduces net income, because it is deemed a cost of doing business while dividend payments are not part of income measurement, because they are seen as distributions of earnings.

Debt financing creates constraints on a corporation not found in equity financing. Debt interest and principal must be paid according to the contractual terms or creditors can take legal action against the corporation. Often the loans made by creditors are secured by assets that are pledged as collateral on the loan (property pledged by the borrower to protect the lender in case of default). Thus, if bankruptcy occurs, the secured creditors have the right to the value of specific assets before other nonsecured creditors and equity holders are paid.

Long-term creditors often require specific provisions, called covenants, that limit management actions relating to paying dividends or acquiring more loans while their debt is outstanding. For example, a corporation could borrow money from a bank under a long-term note with a covenant requiring the corporation to maintain a specified ratio of total liabilities to total equity (called the *debt-to-equity ratio*). If the debtor were to violate the covenant provision, the bank would be entitled to take certain actions such as demanding immediate repayment of the loan.

Equity owners (stockholders) cannot demand dividend payments, and if the business terminates, they have a lower priority claim on the assets of the business than do creditors.

Also, stockholders may prefer that a company use debt financing rather than equity financing because (1) debt financing does not dilute the stockholders' ownership interests; and (2) if a rate of return in excess of the cost of debt financing is earned, the excess return increases the stockholders' interest. You will learn more about equity financing in Chapter 11.

Remember that debt and equity do not have the same contractual rights. When a business terminates, providers of debt financing and equity financing are categorized as to their order of payment, because the law gives different rights to different parties. In general, creditors have priority over equity holders, but a "pecking order" exists among creditors. Senior debt includes debt secured by mortgages that are pledged to specific assets. Junior debt, often called **unsecured** or **subordinated debt,** relies on the general creditworthiness of the debtor. In liquidation, after the pledged assets are used to pay off secured creditors, if the secured creditors are not fully paid, they have equal claims with the unsecured creditors to the remaining assets. Upon liquidation of a business, stockholders typically are not paid anything until all other claimants are paid in full.

Junk Bonds and High Risk

Consider the following conversation between a young stockbroker, who has just started his first job on Wall Street and his father, who is about to retire.

Father: Junior, my pension plan report says that 20% of the assets in the pension fund are in "unsecured, high-yield, subordinated bonds." Someone at work says that's what they call junk bonds. Should I be worried? I don't like the idea of my pension payments depending on junk or whatever they call it.

Son: In the past few years, a lot of bonds were issued to finance leveraged buyouts (LBOs). That usually involves management's or someone else's arranging for all the stock of a company to be bought, and, as part of the financing, the company often issues these kinds of bonds. So, in essence, the management becomes the owners and the institutions like banks and pension funds get these high-yield, which means paying high rates of interest, debt instruments.

Father: I see, but why are they called junk and why would a pension fund buy them?

Son: Well, they are viewed as more risky than other debt of the issuing company. They usually are subordinated, which means they would have a lower priority of payment in case of bankruptcy. But, they pay high rates of interest, so they are attractive to some investors.

Father: Should I be worried about my pension?

Son: That depends. First, only 20% of the assets of your fund are invested in them. I assume the rest of the assets are less risky. Most people believe that if the economy has a major recession, some of the companies that issued a lot of junk bonds would not be able to meet the heavy interest payments and some could go bankrupt. But, on the other hand, most issues of that type have paid on time and are yielding high returns. What I would suggest, Pop, is that you make sure that at least some of your other personal investments are in less risky assets.

Father: That's good advice, but I think I'll write the trustees of the fund a little note expressing my concern.

Son: You have that right and maybe if enough others do the same, they'll reconsider their investment strategy.

The preceding conversation highlights the trade-off between risk and return that all investors must make. Issuance of risky, high-yield securities such as junk bonds has significant cash flow implications, which must be thoughtfully considered by both the issuers and investors.

In this text we focus on going concerns rather than with terminating businesses, but the priority of rights of the various suppliers of funds affects how many ordinary business transactions are recorded and disclosed. In this chapter and the next one, we will discuss accounting for various types of financing activities.

The next section discusses the common traits, or characteristics, of debt financing of noncurrent liabilities. You will find this section important in providing a background for the remainder of the chapter.

COMMON TRAITS AMONG LONG-TERM DEBT

Objective 2
What all long-term debt has in common.

When a company borrows money by means of long-term liabilities, the bank or lending institution first considers the amount of risk involved in the transaction. Risk is the probability of nonpayment or delay in payment of scheduled cash amounts. Before lending money, banks evaluate risk by checking the creditworthiness of a company and studying its financial statements.

A lender wants to be compensated for (1) the risk of loss in case the borrower does not repay the loan and (2) the time value of money during the time the borrower uses the money. These two factors—risk and time—affect the total cash (principal plus interest) that a debtor returns to a creditor. Therefore, given a certain amount borrowed (principal), the debtor's risk level and the timing of its cash payments determine the total cash returned to its creditor.

To help you understand the effect of timing on the total amount of cash a debtor pays to a creditor, this section discusses four general cases illustrating loan repayment: (1) principal and interest paid back in one lump sum, (2) principal paid back in equal amounts along with interest, (3) equal periodic total payments, and (4) interest paid each year and principal paid at maturity. The same basic interest rate, principal amount, and time period are used in all four cases—a $100,000, 10%, three-year loan. The total interest is always measured as the **total cash outflow minus total cash inflow.** Note, however, that the actual amount of interest (and total cash outflow) varies depending on the repayment schedule called for in each separate case.

Case 1—Debtor Pays Loan and Interest Back in One Lump Sum

A company borrowed $100,000 on January 1, 19x1. In this case assume the company paid the lender the total amount of interest and principal in one payment on December 31, 19x3, as shown in the following time line:

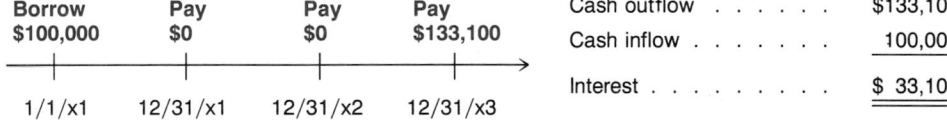

	Borrow **$100,000**	**Pay** **$0**	**Pay** **$0**	**Pay** **$133,100**	Cash outflow	$133,100
Case 1:					Cash inflow	100,000
	1/1/x1	12/31/x1	12/31/x2	12/31/x3	Interest	$ 33,100

On December 31, 19x3, the $33,100 interest the debtor pays back has been **compounded over the three-year period.** Compound interest is interest charged on both the unpaid principal and on any unpaid interest accrued after the inception of the liability. Since the interest rate is 10%, the unpaid amount of interest at the end of the first year is $10,000 ($100,000 × .10 = $10,000), resulting in a $110,000 (principal plus interest) unpaid balance at the beginning of year 2. This $110,000 results in interest of $11,000 for year 2 ($110,000 × .10), and so on. The amortization schedule for this first case over the life of the liability follows:

**Amortization Schedule for Case 1
($100,000, 10%, three-year loan
with lump-sum payment)**

(1) Date	(2) Cash Inflow (outflow)	(3) Interest, 10% of Prior Column 5 Balance	(4) Change in Net Liability	(5) Net Liability (book value of the obligation)
1/1/x1	$ 100,000	$ 0	$ 100,000	$100,000
12/31/x1	0	10,000	10,000	110,000
12/31/x2	0	11,000	11,000	121,000
12/31/x3	0	12,100	12,100	133,100
12/31/x3	(133,100)	0	(133,100)	0
	$ (33,100)	$33,100		

Each column of this amortization schedule communicates important facts about the life of the liability. Column 1 lists the critical dates, beginning with the inception of the $100,000 liability and ending with December 31, 19x3, when the principal plus interest was paid to the creditor. Column 2 shows the cash flows. The net cash flow is negative; $33,100 more cash flowed out than in. Remember, this difference in cash outflows over inflows represents the total interest on the loan. Column 3 shows how the $33,100 of total interest accrued each year. The change in the book value of the liability is shown in Column 4, and the balance at each date is shown in Column 5.

Now study the graphic explanation of Case 1 in Exhibit 10–1. Note that the cash inflow of $100,000 is indicated by the large arrow pointing upward above the 1/1/x1 date on the time axis. On 12/31/x1, the point of the small arrow, representing the net liability balance, is at $110,000. On 12/31/x2, the point of the small arrow is at $121,000. On 12/31/x3, the total obligation grows to $133,100 before the final payment—indicated by the large arrow pointing downward—in which the company paid the loan plus interest, leaving the liability $0. The dollar amounts in Case 1 of Exhibit 10–1 are taken from the amortization schedule of Case 1 given above.

Case 2—Principal Paid Back in Equal Amounts along with Interest

In Case 2, the principal is paid back in equal amounts of $33,333 each period, along with interest of 10% on the reducing unpaid principal, as shown in the following time line:

Borrow $100,000	Pay $43,333	Pay $40,000	Pay $36,667
1/1/x1	12/31/x1	12/31/x2	12/31/x3

Cash outflow $120,000
Cash inflow 100,000
Interest . . . . $ 20,000

EXHIBIT 10–1

Comparison of Different Cash Flow, Interest, and Net Liability Patterns

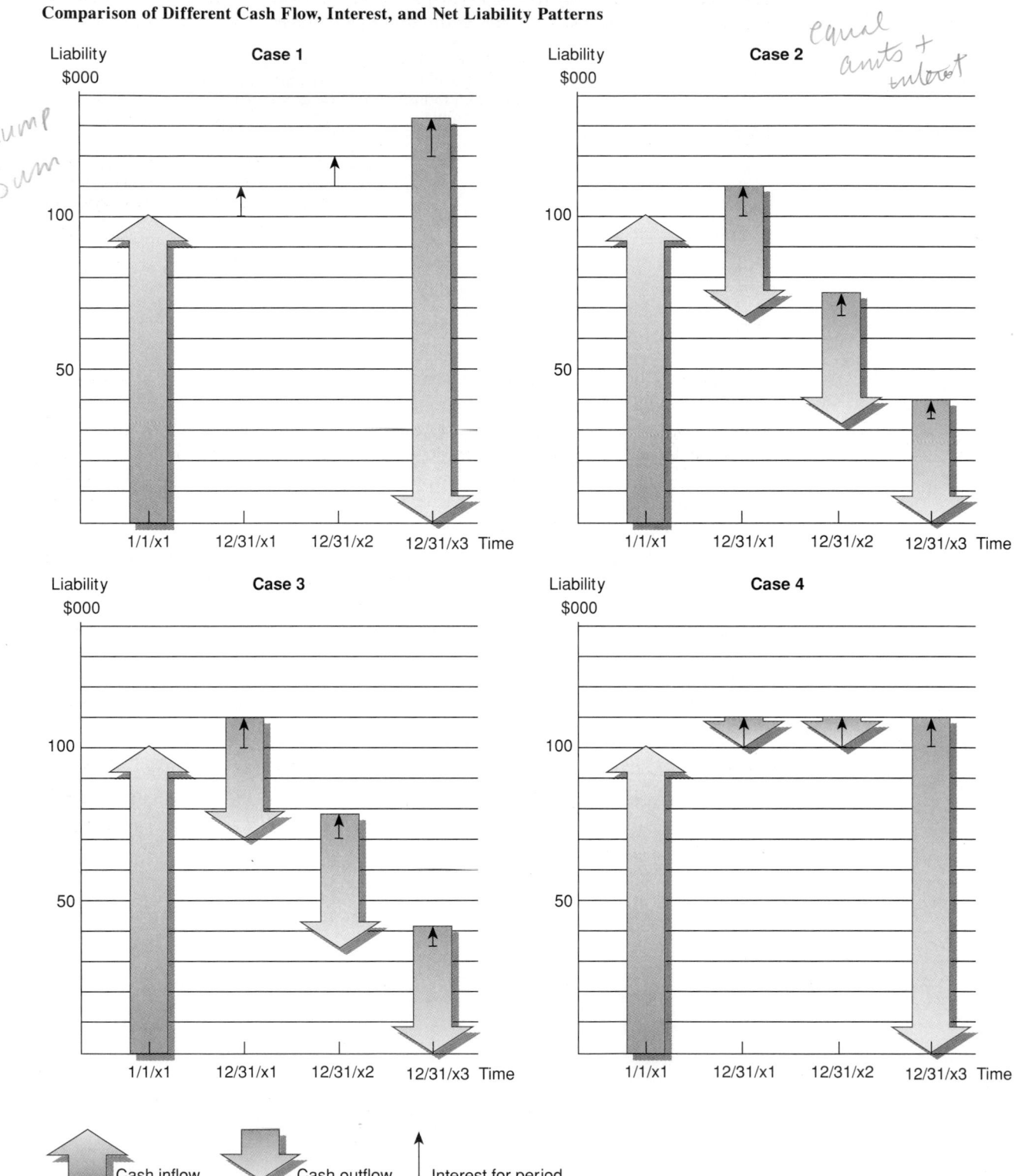

Cash inflow.   Cash outflow.   Interest for period.

At the end of year 1, interest is $10,000 (10% of $100,000). The unpaid balance at the beginning of year 2 is $66,667, and interest for year 2 is, therefore, $6,667, and so on. Again, the events and balances related to the liability can be summarized as follows:

Amortization Schedule for Case 2
($100,000, 10%, three-year loan
with equal principal reductions)

(1) Date	(2) Cash Inflow (outflow)	(3) Interest, 10% of Prior Column 5 Balance	(4) Change in Net Liability	(5) Net Liability (book value of the obligation)
1/1/x1	$100,000	$ 0	$100,000	$100,000
12/31/x1	(43,333)	10,000	(33,333)	66,667
12/31/x2	(40,000)	6,667	(33,333)	33,334
12/31/x3	(36,667)	3,333*	(33,334)	0
	$ (20,000)	$20,000		

*Rounded.

The graphic explanation of Case 2 in Exhibit 10–1 begins with the cash inflow arrow at $100,000 above 1/1/x1 on the time axis. The first payment of $33,333 principal plus $10,000 interest is shown as a total cash outflow of $43,333 above 12/31/x1. The second payment results in an outflow of $33,333 principal plus $6,667 interest above 12/31/x2. The last outflow of cash, shown above 12/31/x3, is $33,334 principal plus $3,333 interest. By comparing Case 2 in Exhibit 10–1 with the above amortization schedule, you can see how the numbers in the amortization schedule are depicted graphically.

Case 3—Equal Principal and Interest Payments

In Case 3, we illustrate a repayment schedule calling for a series of equal payments, which is often referred to as an *annuity* payment schedule. As shown in the following time line, the company pays off its obligation borrowed on January 1, 19x1, with three equal payments of $40,211 at the end of each year, which include the payment of principal and interest.

	Borrow $100,000	Pay $40,211	Pay $40,211	Pay $40,211		Cash outflow	$120,633
Case 3:						Cash inflow	100,000
	1/1/x1	12/31/x1	12/31/x2	12/31/x3		Interest	$ 20,633

Although an annuity repayment schedule holds the payment constant each period, the amounts of interest in the payment decrease each year and the amount of principal reduction increases each period, as summarized in the following amortization schedule:

Amortization Schedule for Case 3
($100,000, 10%, three-year loan
with equal annual payments)

(1) Date	(2) Cash Inflow (outflow)	(3) Interest, 10% of Prior Column 5 Balance	(4) Change in Net Liability	(5) Net Liability (book value of the obligation)
1/1/x1	$100,000	$ 0	$100,000	$100,000
12/31/x1	(40,211)	10,000	(30,211)	69,789
12/31/x2	(40,211)	6,979	(33,232)	36,557
12/31/x3	(40,211)	3,654*	(36,557)	0
	$ (20,633)	$20,633		

*Rounded.

The even payment (annuity) method illustrated in Case 3 is frequently used for term loans of three to five years to finance purchases of automobiles, computers, or equipment. Annuity contracts are also often used over longer time periods (e.g., 30 years) to finance the purchase of houses (home mortgages) or facilities. Appendix 10B shows that the above pattern of payments is also used in leasing contracts with equal payments over several periods.

Now look at the graphic representation of Case 3 in Exhibit 10–1. The cash inflow arrow above 1/1/x1 is again at $100,000. Since the three payments are equal, the three cash outflow arrows are the same size. The dollar amounts for Case 3 in the exhibit again match those in the amortization schedule above.

Case 4—Interest Paid Each Year and Principal Paid at Maturity Date

In Case 4, the company pays its loan obligation with three equal year-end interest payments of $10,000 and at the end of the three-year period it also pays the $100,000 principal, as shown in the following time line:

Case 4:

Borrow $100,000	Pay $10,000	Pay $10,000	Pay $110,000
1/1/x1	12/31/x1	12/31/x2	12/31/x3

Cash outflow	$130,000
Cash inflow	100,000
Interest	$ 30,000

The payment of equal yearly interest makes the following amortization schedule relatively simple:

Amortization Schedule for Case 4
($100,000, 10%, three-year loan with interest paid
annually and a lump-sum principal payment)

(1) Date	(2) Cash Inflow (outflow)	(3) Interest, 10% of Prior Column 5 Balance	(4) Change in Net Liability	(5) Net Liability (book value of the obligation)
1/1/x1	$ 100,000	$ 0	$ 100,000	$100,000
12/31/x1	(10,000)	10,000	—	100,000
12/31/x2	(10,000)	10,000	—	100,000
12/31/x3	(110,000)	10,000	(100,000)	0
	$ (30,000)	$30,000		

This pattern of loan repayment, by which interest is paid each period and the principal is paid at maturity, is often used in bond contracts.

Refer to Case 4 Exhibit 10–1. The cash inflow arrow is again at $100,000 above 1/1/x1 on the time axis. The two cash outflow arrows above 12/31/x1 and 12/31/x2 indicate two payments of $10,000 interest. The cash outflow arrow above 12/31/x3 includes both the yearly interest payment and the principal.

The Common Elements in Long-Term Debt	Even though the contractual terms that determine the repayment schedules of the above cases differ and may each be called by a different name, the following three generalizations can be made:

1. In all cases, the net liability starts out at the amount borrowed, $100,000. This is called the principal.

2. When interest is compounded annually, the interest expense for each period is based on the balance of the liability at the beginning of the period (or the end of the prior period). Note that in all four cases the interest for year 1 is $10,000 (.10 × $100,000). The different cash payments in each case create different beginning-of-the-year net liabilities for years 2 and 3. As a result, interest amounts differ for years 2 and 3.

3. The **net** cash outflow over the life of the liability exactly equals the total cumulative interest for all periods. In all four cases, the principal starts at $100,000, but interest varies from a low of $20,000, in Case 2, to a high of $33,100, in Case 1. The interest differences result from the differing net liability amounts that are outstanding or unpaid at the beginning of each year. In Case 1, both the principal and accumulated interest are outstanding for the entire life of the liability; in Case 2, one third of the principal is paid off each year, quickly reducing the outstanding balance on which interest is computed.

The graphic representations of the four cases in Exhibit 10–1 verify these three generalizations about cash flow, interest, and net liability. Patterns of cash flow and the interest rate determine all other amounts used in accounting for noncurrent liabilities. To the extent that repayment of either principal or interest is delayed, the total cash outflow increases. Given that all cases have the same cash inflow ($100,000 on January 1, 19x1) and the same interest rate (10%), the varying interest for each case is a function of the different timing patterns of cash outflow.

ACCOUNTING FOR LONG-TERM NOTES	As explained in Chapter 7, a promissory note is a formal contract that stipulates the terms governing cash payments including dates, amounts to be paid, and perhaps interest rates. In Chapter 9, you learned that a short-term note can be interest bearing—the face of the note specifies the principal, interest rate, and maturity date—or noninterest bearing—the face of the note does not specify an interest rate, and its maturity value is the face value. The same is true for long-term notes.

Before discussing interest-bearing and noninterest-bearing long-term notes, you should remember from Chapter 9 that both interest-bearing and noninterest-bearing notes charge the debtor interest. The interest rate is not given on the noninterest-bearing note, but the debtor is charged interest and the rate can be determined from the cash flow requirements and dates given on the note. The term *noninterest bearing* is an example of the imprecision in accounting language that has become commonplace. Interest is almost always a factor in accounting for borrowing transactions, and the accountant's challenge is to determine the amount of interest and when and how it should be recognized. Accountants always strive to report the economic substance of transactions. In the case of liabilities, often the legal form of the contract obscures the substance, as illustrated in the wording of a note that seems to imply that there is no interest or that an unrealistically low interest rate is charged for the use of borrowed money.

Interest-Bearing Notes

Accounting for interest-bearing, long-term notes follows the pattern shown in the four cases discussed in the previous section. Interest expense is recorded each period based on the net liability at the beginning of the period and the period of time the liability amount is outstanding. In the four cases, the money was borrowed at the beginning of the first year. In the following example, the money is borrowed during the calendar year.

Company A, a calendar-year company, borrowed $10,000 on October 1, 19x1, to be paid back in 24 months with interest at 12% per year payable at maturity. Because the interest is stated on the face of the note, the rate of interest is called the **face interest rate** or nominal interest rate. The amortization schedule for this note is as follows:

Objective 3
Accounting for interest-bearing and noninterest-bearing long-term notes.

(1) Date	(2) Cash Inflow (outflow)	(3) Interest, 12% of Prior Column 5 Balance	(4) Change in Net Liability	(5) Net Liability (book value of the obligation)
10/1/x1	$ 10,000	$ 0	$ 10,000	$10,000
9/30/x2	—	1,200	1,200	11,200
9/30/x3	(12,544)	1,344	(11,200)	0
	$ (2,544)	$2,544		

Because such a note affects a company's financial position at the date of borrowing and throughout the life of the note, accountants make a series of journal entries. In this example, the fiscal year-end of December 31 does not coincide with the cash flows of October 1, 19x1 and September 30, 19x3. This necessitates accrual entries at December 31, 19x1 and December 31, 19x2, to record the interest for the months that have elapsed.

The following journal entries capture the economic effects of the various phases in the life of the note. Compare the amortization schedule above and the series of journal entries.

```
19x1
Oct.  1   Cash (A). . . . . . . . . . . . . . . . . . . . . . . .   10,000
                Notes Payable (L). . . . . . . . . . . . . . . . . .          10,000
          To record proceeds from note.

Dec. 31   Interest Expense (E) . . . . . . . . . . . . . . . . .      300
                Interest Payable (L) . . . . . . . . . . . . . . . . .            300
          To accrue interest on note:
          3/12 × $10,000 × .12 = 3/12 × $1,200 = $300.

19x2
Dec. 31   Interest Expense (E) . . . . . . . . . . . . . . . . .    1,236
                Interest Payable (L) . . . . . . . . . . . . . . . . .          1,236
          To accrue interest on note:
          9/12 × $10,000 × .12 = 9/12 × $1,200 = $  900
          3/12 × $11,200 × .12 = 3/12 × $1,344 =      336
                                                   $1,236

19x3
Sept. 30  Interest Expense (E) . . . . . . . . . . . . . . . . .    1,008
          Interest Payable (L) . . . . . . . . . . . . . . . . . .    1,536
          Notes Payable (L). . . . . . . . . . . . . . . . . . .   10,000
                Cash (A). . . . . . . . . . . . . . . . . . . . . . .          12,544
          To record the payment of the note at maturity and interest
          from January 1, 19x3, to September 30, 19x3:
          9/12 × $11,200 × .12 = 9/12 × $1,344 = $1,008.
```

Interest expense is recorded each period: $300 in 19x1, $1,236 in 19x2, and $1,008 in 19x3, totaling $2,544, and the computations are given after each journal entry. Notice that even though the total interest of $2,544 is recorded over the life of the note, the precise interest expense for an accounting period was computed according to the months the note was outstanding during that period.

Noninterest-Bearing Notes

The note described in the example above would be a noninterest-bearing note if the maturity amount of $12,544 were described on the note and no mention were made of the interest rate. Remember that if the amount of the original transaction is the same for both interest-bearing and noninterest-bearing notes, the actual economic substance is the same. Thus, a company pays the same amount of interest for a $10,000, 12%, two-year interest-bearing note as it pays for a $12,544 face value, two-year noninterest-bearing note. In both cases the borrower receives $10,000 and repays $12,544 including $2,544 interest.

As discussed in Chapter 9, when an obligation takes the form of a noninterest-bearing note, accountants show the maturity amount of the note reduced by a discount equal to the unrecorded interest to date. The note, therefore, is carried at maturity value, in this case $12,544, with a contra account labeled Discount on Notes Payable used to bring the net book value of the note down to outstanding principal plus accrued and unpaid interest to date. The following entries to record the noninterest-bearing note are different from those for the interest-bearing note above, but they convey the same economic message.

19x1			
Oct. 1	Cash (A)	10,000	
	Discount on Notes Payable (XL)	2,544	
	Notes Payable (L)		12,544
	To record proceeds from note.		
Dec. 31	Interest Expense (E)	300	
	Discount on Notes Payable (XL)		300
	To record interest on note: 3/12 × $10,000 × .12 = 3/12 × **$1,200** = $300.		
19x2			
Dec. 31	Interest Expense (E)	1,236	
	Discount on Notes Payable (XL)		1,236
	To record interest on note: 9/12 × $10,000 × .12 = 9/12 × **$1,200** = $ 900 3/12 × $11,200 × .12 = 3/12 × **$1,344** = 336 $1,236		
19x3			
Sept. 30	Interest Expense (E)	1,008	
	Notes Payable (L)	12,544	
	Discount on Notes Payable (XL)		1,008
	Cash (A)		12,544
	To record the payment of the note at maturity and interest from January 1, 19x3, to September 30, 19x3: 9/12 × $11,200 × .12 = 9/12 × **$1,344** = $1,008.		

When a company uses a noninterest-bearing note, the balance sheet disclosure is different from the disclosure made when a company uses an interest-bearing note. However, in cases of comparable economic substance the **net liability is the same.** As emphasized by the following table, the net liability shown on a balance sheet is not affected by use or nonuse of the contra account, Discount on Notes Payable.

Interest-Bearing Note: No Discount on Notes Payable Account		Noninterest-Bearing Note: Discount on Notes Payable Account	
Excerpt from December 31, 19x1, Balance Sheet		**Excerpt from December 31, 19x1, Balance Sheet**	
Noncurrent liability:		Noncurrent liability:	
Notes payable.	$10,000	Notes payable	$12,544
Interest payable	300	Less discount.	2,244
	$10,300		$10,300
Excerpt from December 31, 19x2, Balance Sheet		**Excerpt from December 31, 19x2, Balance Sheet**	
Current liability:		Current liability:	
Notes payable.	$10,000	Notes payable	$12,544
Interest payable	1,536	Less discount.	1,008
	$11,536		$11,536

Review the noncurrent and current classifications in the above illustration. The note is first classified at December 31, 19x1, as noncurrent, which means that maturity is more than a year off, and is then reclassified as current on December 31, 19x2, when the maturity is less than a year off. Recall that the current/noncurrent balance sheet classification is based on the "one year or operating cycle if longer" rule first introduced in Chapter 3.

ACCOUNTING FOR BONDS

The word bonds describes a whole series of debt contracts with varying terms. In this section, we concentrate on the basic principles for measurement and disclosure of bond liabilities and therefore discuss only a subset of the variations of bonds found in financial markets. This section begins with the characteristics of bonds, followed by discussions on bonds sold at face value, bonds sold at a discount, bonds sold at a premium, bond conversions, bond sinking funds, and bonds sold between interest dates.

Characteristics of Bonds

Corporations, governmental units, charitable organizations, and other entities issue bonds to raise money from the public. Since many potential creditors can be offered bonds, the advantage of bonds over bank loans is that the corporation has a broadly based potential source of capital. Often privately placed debt or notes with individual banks may not provide the magnitude of financing needed by large corporations. Many large corporations find it advantageous to have both private and public debt.

Objective 4
Common features of bond contracts.

Exhibit 10–2 lists the common types of bonds classified according to their security, interest payment, maturity date, and termination characteristics. We discuss these characteristics and their special accounting effects throughout the chapter. Keep in mind that one bond issue may have several of the characteristics listed. For instance, unsecured, coupon, term, convertible bonds are common as well as many other combinations of the characteristics given in Exhibit 10–2.

EXHIBIT 10–2

	Major Characteristics of Bonds	Type of Bond	Explanation of Varying Characteristics
Common Types of Bonds Categorized by Major Characteristics	**Security**	Secured (mortgage) bonds	Bonds are backed by a physical asset as collateral, such as a building.
		Unsecured (debenture)	Bonds are backed only by the bonds credit standing of the company.
	Interest and principal payments	Registered bonds	Names and addresses of bond owners are kept on file with the company or trustee so that interest and principal can be paid directly to the registered owner.
		Coupon (bearer) bonds	Coupons are attached to bonds for each interest payment that state interest amount due and payment date; bondholder endorses coupon when payment is due and presents it to a bank for payment.
	Maturity date	Term bonds	Principal is paid in full on a specified maturity date.
		Serial bonds	Principal is paid on a series of specified future dates.
	Termination	Callable bonds	Bonds can be called in or repurchased by issuer prior to maturity; call price is usually higher than maturity value.
		Convertible bonds	Under specified conditions, bonds can be exchanged for capital stock.
		Redeemable bonds	Under specified conditions, bonds can be presented to the issuer for a specified cash payment.

A survey of the published financial statements of 600 U.S. companies shows the following list of unsecured long-term debt:[1]

Form of Unsecured, Long-Term Debt	Number of Companies	
Notes	418	70%
Debentures	227	38%
Loans	59	10%
Commercial paper	63	11%

Out of the 600 companies sampled, 224 had debentures or unsecured bonds disclosed in their financial statements. Commercial paper consists of notes issued by large corporations. The actual balance sheet usually has one entry titled *Long-term debt,* with the detail shown in a note to the balance sheet, where features such as maturity dates, interest rates, collateral, and so on are given.

Before issuing bonds, a corporation usually must get approval from its board of directors and stockholders—and from the Securities and Exchange Commission if the bonds are to be sold publicly. Then the corporation usually selects a trustee—a bank or trust company—to represent the the interests of the bondholders. For the protection of bondholders, a bond indenture is prepared that describes all rights and obligations of all parties.

---

[1]*Accounting Trends and Techniques: 1992* (New York: AICPA, 1992), p. 199.

Corporations usually issue bonds in a group, called a *bond issue*. The face value or maturity amount of each bond is often $1,000. The term of a bond can vary from 3 years to 30 years. When the bond indenture is prepared for a bond issue, the stated interest rate on the bonds is usually close to the market interest rate. However, since interest rates go up and down as the economy changes, the stated interest rate and the market interest rate are often not the same by the time the bond is sold to the public.

Usually, corporations hire an investment company, or underwriter, to market their bonds. The investment company makes a profit by selling the bonds to the public at a slightly higher price than it pays the corporation and/or by charging the corporation a fee. The purchaser of a bond receives a bond certificate, which states the terms of the bond. A bondholder may not want to keep a bond until it matures, which could be as much as 20 or 30 years after issuance. To facilitate change of bond ownership, some bonds are traded daily on bond markets similar to stock markets. Bond prices are quoted as a percentage of the bond's maturity value. Thus, a $1,000 bond may be sold on any given day at 95, which is 95% of $1,000 or $950, or at 105, which is 105% of $1,000 or $1,050.

Objective 5
Bonds sold at face value, at discount, and at premium.

Assume that on January 1, 19x1, a bondholder acquires a $1,000 face value, 10%, three-year bond for $1,000 cash. The bondholder would receive the following cash payments:

	Interest Payment $100	Interest Payment $100	Interest Payment plus Maturity Amount Payment $1,100
Beginning of year 1	End of year 1	End of year 2	End of year 3

This bond contract calls for equal annual interest payments of $100, and the final payment includes the bond principal. Recall that this is the same pattern we introduced in Case 4 on page 500. Should the bondholder decide to sell the bond, the bond market (potential buyers and sellers of bonds) decides how much to pay for the remaining payments at the date of sale. If the market considers 10% to be the appropriate return for the bond, then buyers should be willing to pay $1,000. If the market determines that something **less than** 10% is an acceptable return for the remaining payments, then more than $1,000 per bond would be paid. When a bond sells for more than face value, it sells at a premium, and this indicates that the stated rate of interest on the bond is above the market rate. When a bond sells for less than face value it sells at a discount, suggesting that the market considers the stated interest rate to be lower than the required rate of interest. The rate of interest required by the market for a particular bond issue at the date of sale is called the **yield rate** or the effective-interest rate.

Bond contracts usually call for semiannual interest payments. The contract of the bond example used above stipulated annual payments. If semiannual payments were stipulated in the contract, the payments would be $50 every six months rather than $100 every year, but the bond would still be a 10% bond. When a $1,000 face value, 10%, three-year bond pays interest semiannually, the interest payments of $50 are computed as follows: $(\frac{1}{2})(10\%)(\$1,000) = \$50$.

Bonds Sold at Face Value

When a bond is sold at face value, the bond is sold for the principal amount, and it yields the interest rate stated on the bond. To illustrate the accounting for these bonds, assume that 100 of Company A's $1,000, 10%, three-year bonds are sold for $1,000 each on January 1, 19x1. As shown in Exhibit 10–3, the cash inflow arrow (broken because of space limitations) is at $100,000, which indicates the company's initial liability is $100,000. Because interest is paid each year, as indicated by the three cash outflow arrows for interest paid,

EXHIBIT 10–3

Patterns of Cash Flows and Amortization Schedule—Bonds Issued at Face Value

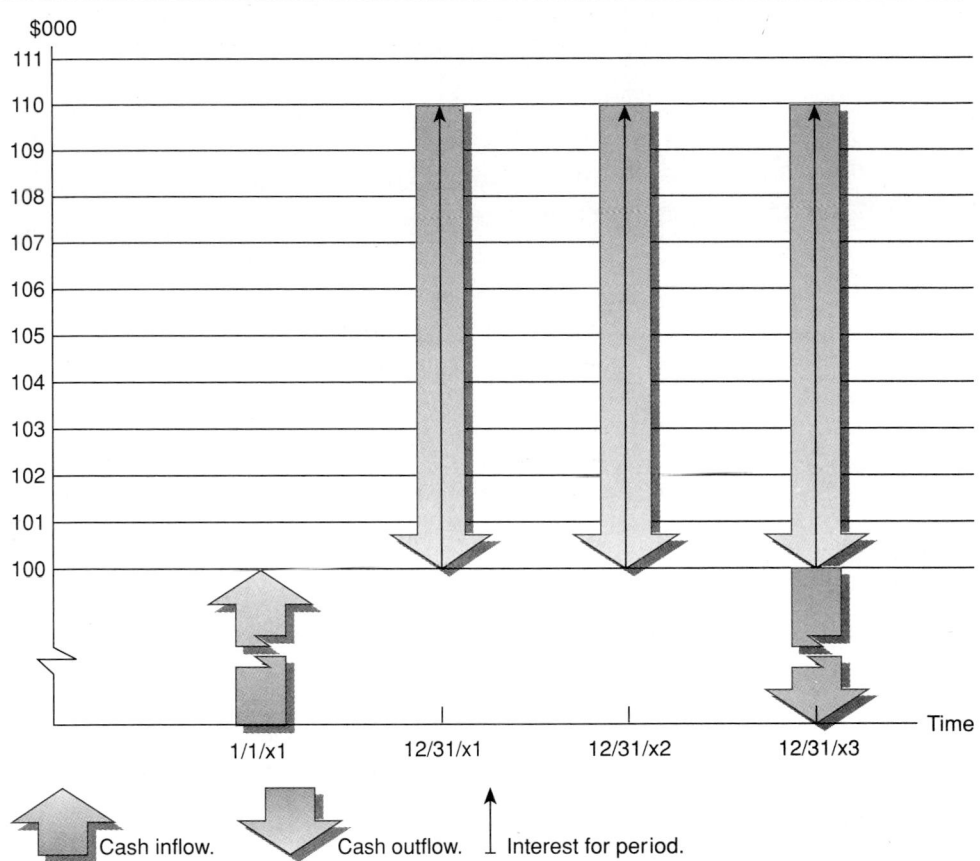

Cash inflow.　Cash outflow.　Interest for period.

Amortization Schedule

Date	Cash Inflow (outflow)	Interest Expense	Change in Net Liability	Net Liability (book value of the obligation)
1/1/x1	$ 100,000	$ 0	$ 100,000	$100,000
12/31/x1	(10,000)	10,000	0	100,000
12/31/x2	(10,000)	10,000	0	100,000
12/31/x3	(10,000)	10,000	0	100,000
12/31/x3	(100,000)	0	(100,000)	0
	$ (30,000)	$30,000		

the liability at the end of each year remains at $100,000 for the entire life of the bond. The last cash outflow arrow indicates the payment, consisting of the $100,000 principal plus the final $10,000 interest payment. The amortization schedule at the bottom of the exhibit also summarizes the relevant money amounts. The journal entries are as follows:

```
19x1
Jan.  1   Cash (A) . . . . . . . . . . . . . . . . . . . . . .   100,000
              Bonds Payable (L). . . . . . . . . . . . . . . . .          100,000
          To record issuance of bonds.
```

Dec. 31	Interest Expense (E)	10,000	
	Cash (A)		10,000
	To record annual interest payment on bonds.		

19x2			
Dec. 31	Interest Expense (E)	10,000	
	Cash (A)		10,000
	To record annual interest payment on bonds.		

19x3			
Dec. 31	Interest Expense (E)	10,000	
	Cash (A)		10,000
	To record last annual interest payment on bonds.		

	Bonds Payable (L)	100,000	
	Cash (A)		100,000
	To record retirement of bonds.		

Total interest expense for any borrowing, including bonds, is always **total cash outflow minus total cash inflow.** For the above bonds, the total interest expense is $130,000 − $100,000 = $30,000, or $10,000 per year, for three years.

Bonds Sold at a Discount

Because bond terms, such as the maturity value, the number of periods, and the timing and amount of interest payments, are fixed, the bond issue price depends upon the effective interest the market establishes for the particular bond issuance. If $100,000 is paid for the bonds with a face value of $100,000 and a stated interest rate of 10%, then exactly 10% is earned each year; that is, 10% × $100,000 = $10,000. Remember that the bond contract is fixed in terms of cash flows to the holder. If bondholders demand less or more than a 10% return, the only way to affect the rate actually earned is to vary the purchase price. Thus, if the market for the bond described above will accept less than a 10% return, it will bid the purchase price of the bonds up above $100,000, thereby reducing the effective interest on the bonds. Alternatively, if the market for the bonds requires more than a 10% return, it will bid the purchase price of the bonds down below $100,000, thus increasing the effective interest on the bonds.[2] Furthermore, the market value of bonds that have already been issued will change as economy-wide changes cause interest rates to fluctuate. As market interest rates go up, bond selling prices go down, and vice versa. Changes in the creditworthiness of bond issuers have similar effects.

If Company A's $100,000 face value, 10%, three-year bonds discussed above were sold for $95,198, the discount would be $4,802, and the net liability or carrying value on the date of sale would be $95,198. The following journal entry records the sale of the bonds.

19x1			
Jan. 1	Cash (A)	95,198	
	Discount on Bonds (XL)	4,802	
	Bonds Payable (L)		100,000
	To record issuance of 10% bonds at an effective-interest rate of 12%.		

---

[2] Note that the total interest on any bond contract is simply the difference between the cash paid and the cash received. As a result, paying less than $100,000 (say, $97,000) for a bond with fixed payments of $10,000 per year "stated" interest plus $100,000 face value at maturity will increase total actual interest by the amount of the discount ($100,000 − $97,000 = $3,000 more interest). For premiums, the effective interest is less than the nominal interest by the amount of the premium paid over the face value.

Balanced Budget WSJ Nov 22 (A 18)

The discount account is a contra account to the long-term liability account, Bonds Payable. The net book value of the liability is the Bonds Payable amount (the maturity value of the bonds outstanding) minus the Discount on Bonds Payable account balance.

How much total interest expense is associated with this bond issue over the life of the issue? Again, total interest expense equals cash outflow minus cash inflow. In this case, $130,000 is the total cash payment to bondholders called for in the bond contracts, and $95,198 is the proceeds from the sale. Total interest expense then is $130,000 minus $95,198, or $34,802 over the life of the issue. This total is composed of (1) $30,000 in nominal interest payments and (2) the $4,802 discount upon issuance. Accountants have developed procedures to record the full $34,802 as an interest expense over the bond issue life. As we will see below, this involves "amortizing" or writing off the discount amount according to a certain schedule causing each year's interest expense for a bond issued at a discount to be the sum of the cash paid and the amortization of the discount for that year. We will discuss two methods accountants use to amortize the bond discount, the straight-line method and the effective-interest method.

Amortization of Discount—Straight-Line Method.   The Discount on Bonds account is a contra account to Bonds Payable that accountants amortize over the life of the bond. The simplest way to amortize the discount is the straight-line method in which equal amounts are amortized each period [$4,802/3 = $1,601 (rounded) each period]. Exhibit 10–4 summarizes the cash flow, interest expense, and net liability amounts for the three-year period. Again, total interest expense of $34,802 for the life of the bonds is equal to the total cash outflow ($130,000) minus total cash inflow ($95,198). Using straight-line amortization, each period is charged with the same amount of interest expense. Interest expense for any period equals the sum of the cash payment for nominal interest and the amortization of discount for the period.

The journal entries at December 31 of each year are

greater

19x1			
Dec. 31	Interest Expense (E)	11,601	
	Discount on Bonds Payable (XL)		1,601
	Cash (A)		10,000
	To record annual interest payment.		
19x2			
Dec. 31	Interest Expense (E)	11,601	
	Discount on Bonds Payable (XL)		1,601
	Cash (A)		10,000
	To record annual interest payment.		
19x3			
Dec. 31	Interest Expense (E)	11,600	
	Discount on Bonds Payable (XL)		1,600
	Cash (A)		10,000
	To record last annual interest payment.		
	Bonds Payable (L)	100,000	
	Cash (A)		100,000
	To record retirement of bonds.		

Amortization of Discount—Effective-Interest Method.   A more precise method of amortizing the discount is called the effective-interest method. Under this method, the interest expense is computed by applying the initial market interest rate to the net liability balance (carrying value) at the beginning of the period.

EXHIBIT 10–4

Patterns of Cash Flows and Amortization Schedule—Bonds Sold at a Discount, Straight-Line Method

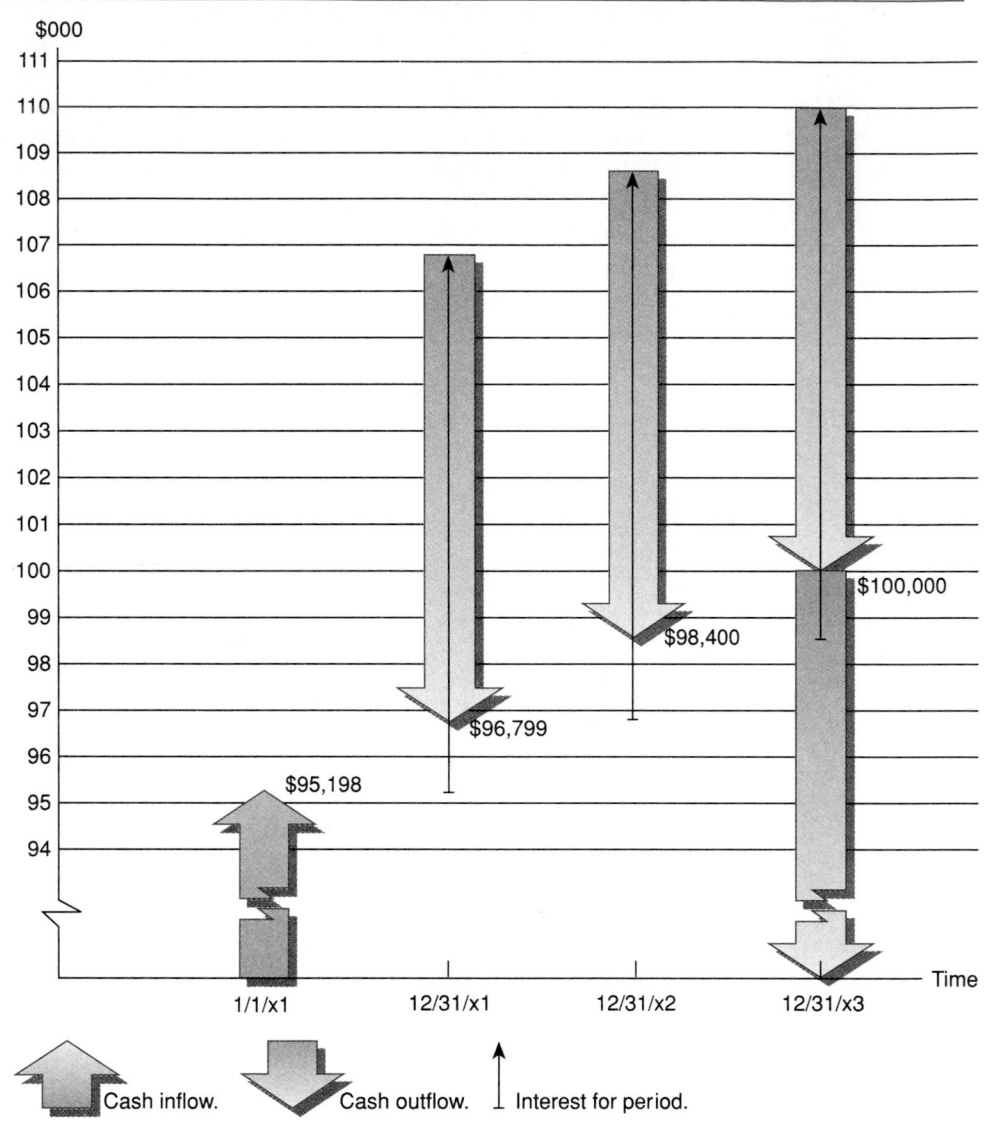

Amortization Schedule—Straight-Line Method

Date	Cash Inflow (outflow)	Interest Expense	Amortization of Discount	Change in Net Liability	Net Liability
1/1/x1	$ 95,198	$ 0	$ 0	$ 95,198	$ 95,198
12/31/x1	(10,000)	11,601	1,601	1,601	96,799
12/31/x2	(10,000)	11,601	1,601	1,601	98,400
12/31/x3	(10,000)	11,600*	1,600	1,600	100,000
12/31/x3	(100,000)	0	0	(100,000)	0
	$ (34,802)	$34,802	$4,802		

*Rounded.

Assume that for Company A, 12% is the **effective-interest rate** at the date of bond issuance. (See Appendix 10B for the method of computing selling prices of bonds given the effective-interest rate.) The interest rate stated on the bond, you recall, is 10%. The bond sold for a discount because the effective-interest rate demanded by the market was higher—12%. Exhibit 10–5 summarizes the patterns of cash flow, interest, and net liability balance that apply to the three years the bonds are outstanding.

Interest expense for any period is the effective-interest rate applied to the beginning-of-the-period net liability balance: 19x1 interest is $95,198 × .12 = $11,424; 19x2 interest is $96,622 × .12 = $11,595; and 19x3 interest is $98,217 × .12 = $11,783 (rounded).[3] The amortization of the discount each year is the difference between the interest expense and the cash payment for nominal interest for the year: 19x1 amortization is $11,424 − $10,000 = $1,424; 19x2 amortization is $11,595 − $10,000 = $1,595; and 19x3 amortization is $11,783 − $10,000 = $1,783.

Again, interest expense of $34,802 for the entire life of the bond issue is total cash outflow ($130,000) minus total cash inflow ($95,198). The net liability or carrying value is the $100,000 face value minus the discount balance, which is gradually amortized over the life of the bond. Interest expense increases because the net liability increases as the discount is amortized.

The journal entries to record the issuance of the bonds, the payment of interest, and the maturity payment are

19x1				
Jan. 1	Cash (A)		95,198	
	Discount on Bonds Payable (XL)		4,802	
	Bonds Payable (L)			100,000
	To record issuance of bonds.			
Dec. 31	Interest Expense (E)		11,424	
	Cash (A)			10,000
	Discount on Bonds Payable (XL)			1,424
	To record annual interest payment and interest expense ($95,198 × .12).			
19x2				
Dec. 31	Interest Expense (E)		11,595	
	Cash (A)			10,000
	Discount on Bonds Payable (XL)			1,595
	To record annual interest payment and interest expense [($95,198 + $1,424) × .12].			
19x3				
Dec. 31	Interest Expense (E)		11,783	
	Cash (A)			10,000
	Discount on Bonds Payable (XL)			1,783
	To record last annual interest payment and interest expense [($95,198 + $1,424 + $1,595) × .12 = $11,783]*			
	Bonds Payable (L)		100,000	
	Cash (A)			100,000
	To record retirement of bonds.			

*Rounded.

---

[3]$98,217 × .12 = $11,786; but we use $11,783 as interest expense to force the net liability to equal $100,000.

EXHIBIT 10–5

Patterns of Cash Flows and Amortization Schedule—Bonds Issued at a Discount, Effective-Interest Method

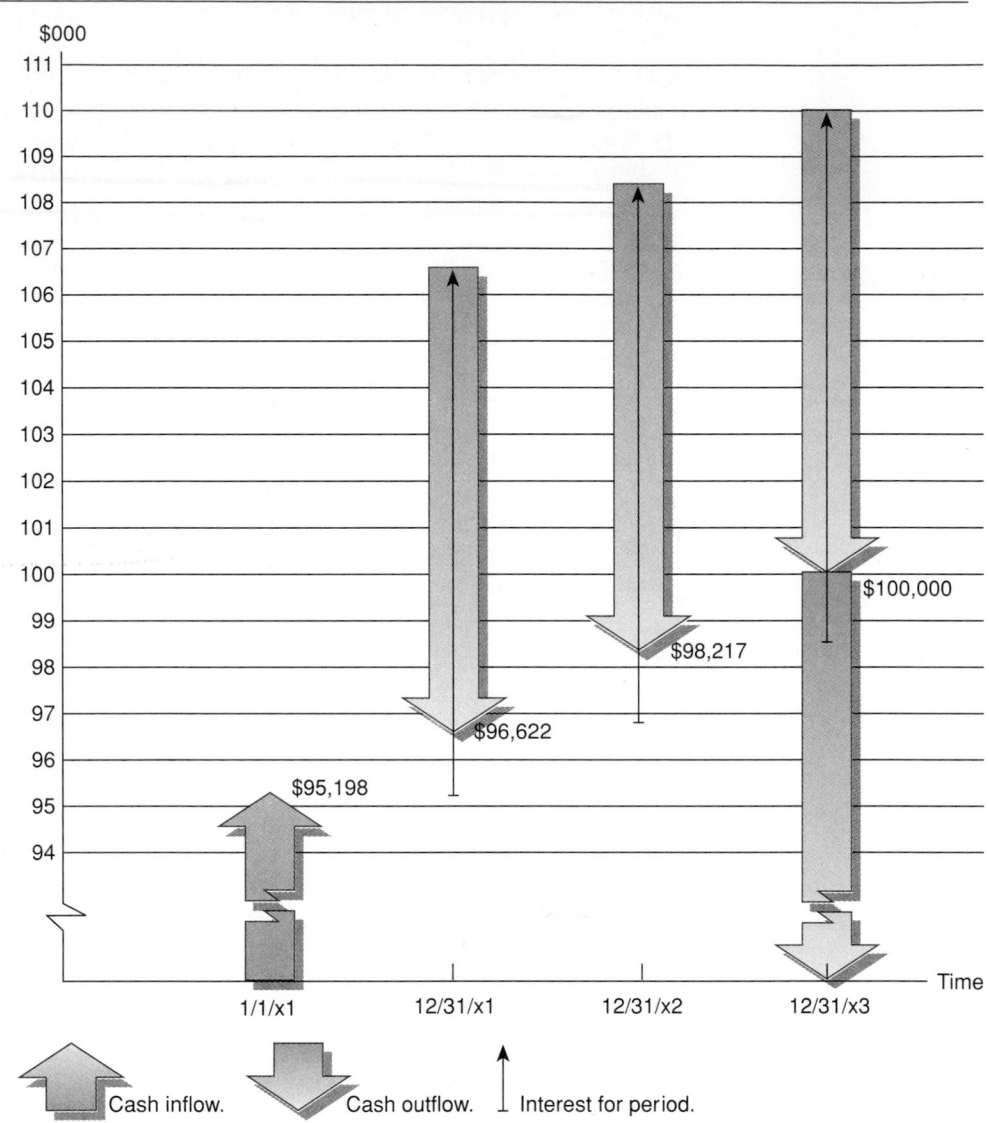

Cash inflow.   Cash outflow.   Interest for period.

Amortization Schedule—Effective-Interest Method

Date	Cash Inflow (outflow)	Interest Expense	Amortization of Discount	Change in Net Liability	Net Liability
1/1/x1	$ 95,198	$ 0	$ 0	$ 95,198	$ 95,198
12/31/x1	(10,000)	11,424	1,424	1,424	96,622
12/31/x2	(10,000)	11,595	1,595	1,595	98,217
12/31/x3	(10,000)	11,783*	1,783	1,783	100,000
12/31/x3	(100,000)	0	0	(100,000)	0
	$ (34,802)	$34,802	$4,802		

*Rounded.

The amortizing of bond discounts is a worldwide practice, with one major exception. In Japan the discount on bonds is not spread out over the life of the bond but is written off as an expense in the year in which the bonds are sold. This, of course, has the effect that Japanese companies with bonds sold at a discount understate their net income. It is extremely important that the following point be clearly understood before moving on: Selling a bond at a discount results in less cash inflow than would be the case if the bond were sold at face value or more; therefore, interest expense over the life of the bond is increased above the total nominal interest payments by the amount of the discount.

Bonds Sold at a Premium

Recall our discussion of bonds sold at a discount. The same logic applies to bonds sold at a premium and techniques for amortizing bond premiums are similar to those used to amortize discounts. Bonds sell at a premium if the interest rate demanded by the market for a particular bond issue is less than the stated interest rate. Amortizing bond premiums has the effect of reducing periodic interest expense below the amount of cash paid for nominal interest.

Going back to our example of Company A's $100,000 maturity, 10%, three-year bonds, assume that the bonds sell for $105,151. Why would the market pay more than face value for bonds (in this case, $5,151 more)? The premium of $5,151 represents the difference between the stated interest payments in the bond contract ($30,000) and the amount of interest required by bondholders for Company A's bonds ($24,849). Note the following cash outflows for this contract:

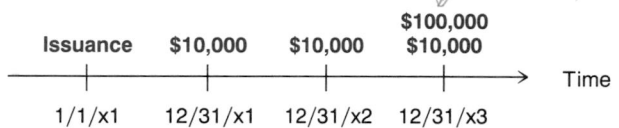

The $105,151 selling price of the bonds above is $5,151 more than the maturity value of the bond. This $5,151 is called the premium on bond payable and is recorded in an adjunct liability account (AL) which is the opposite of a contra account. A contra account such as Discount on Bonds Payable is subtracted from its related primary account. The adjunct account Premium on Bonds Payable is added to the primary account, Bonds Payable. The journal entry to record the sale of the bonds at a premium is as follows:

19x1			
Jan. 1	Cash (A).	105,151	
	Bonds Payable (L)		100,000
	Premium on Bond Payable (AL)		5,151
	To record issuance of 10% bonds at an effective-interest rate of 8%.		

Both the straight-line method and the effective-interest method are also used in the amortization of bonds sold at a premium.

Amortization of Premium—Straight-Line Method.   For bonds sold at a premium, interest expense each period is equal to the cash payment for nominal interest minus the amount of premium amortization. The initial premium on the bonds is amortized in equal amounts over the three-year period, so that the net liability at the date of maturity is $100,000 as shown in Exhibit 10–6.

The journal entries for each payment date are as follows:

19x1			
Dec. 31	Interest Expense (E)	8,283	
	Premium on Bonds Payable (AL)	1,717	
	Cash (A).		10,000
	To record annual interest payment.		

EXHIBIT 10–6

Patterns of Cash Flows and Amortization Schedule—Bonds Sold at a Premium, Straight-Line Method

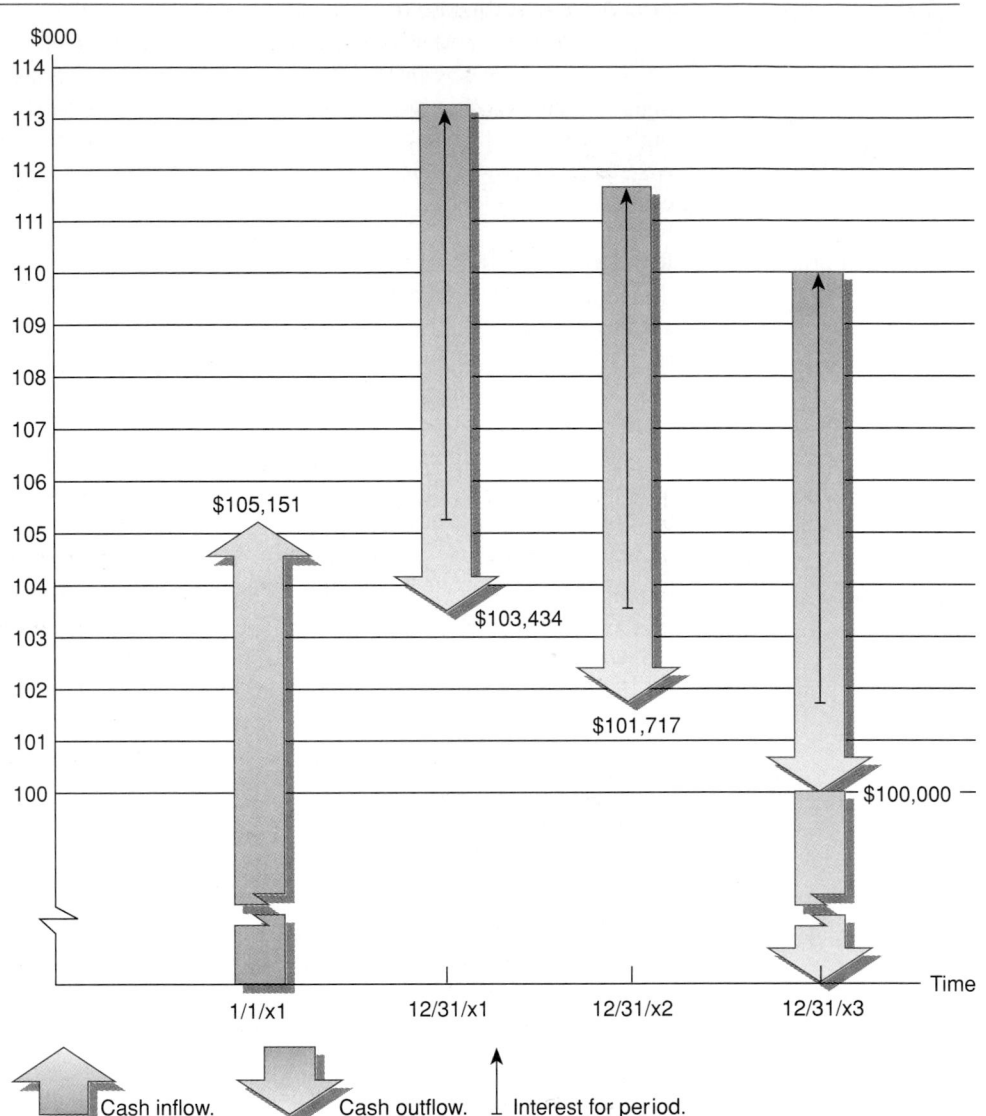

Premium Amortization Schedule—Straight-Line Method

Date	Cash Inflow (outflow)	Interest Expense	Amortization of Premium	Change in Net Liability	Net Liability
1/1/x1	$ 105,151	$ 0	$ 0	$ 105,151	$105,151
12/31/x1	(10,000)	8,283	1,717	(1,717)	103,434
12/31/x2	(10,000)	8,283	1,717	(1,717)	101,717
12/31/x3	(10,000)	8,283	1,717	(1,717)	100,000
12/31/x3	(100,000)	0	0	(100,000)	0
	$ (24,849)	$24,849	$5,151		

19x2			
Dec. 31	Interest Expense (E)	8,283	
	Premium on Bonds Payable (AL)	1,717	
	Cash (A).		10,000
	To record annual interest payment.		
19x3			
Dec. 31	Interest Expense (E)	8,283	
	Premium on Bonds Payable (AL)	1,717	
	Cash (A).		10,000
	To record last annual interest payment.		
	Bonds Payable (L)	100,000	
	Cash (A).		100,000
	To record retirement of bonds.		

Amortization of Premium—Effective-Interest Method. Just as with bond discount, a more precise method of calculating the interest expense is to apply the effective market interest rate to the beginning-of-the-period net liability amount. In this case, the **effective-interest rate** is 8%. (See Appendix 10B for the method of computing bond selling price given the effective-interest rate.) Exhibit 10–7 summarizes the pattern of cash flow, interest, and net liability balance applicable to the three years the bond is outstanding. Just as with bond discounts, the interest expense for a year is the effective-interest rate applied to the beginning-of-the-period net liability balance: 19x1 interest is $105,151 \times .08 = \$8,412$; 19x2 interest is $103,563 \times .08 = \$8,285$; and 19x3 interest is $101,848 \times .08 = \$8,152$ (rounded). The amortization of premium is the cash flow for nominal interest minus the interest expense for each year: 19x1 amortization is $\$10,000 - \$8,412 = \$1,588$; 19x2 amortization is $\$10,000 - \$8,285 = \$1,715$; and 19x3 amortization is $\$10,000 - \$8,152 = \$1,848$.

19x1			
Dec. 31	Interest Expense (E).	8,412	
	Premium on Bonds Payable (AL)	1,588	
	Cash (A)		10,000
	To record annual interest payment.		
19x2			
Dec. 31	Interest Expense (E).	8,285	
	Premium on Bonds Payable (AL)	1,715	
	Cash (A)		10,000
	To record annual interest payment.		
19x3			
Dec. 31	Interest Expense (E).	8,152	
	Premium on Bonds Payable (AL)	1,848	
	Cash (A)		10,000
	To record last annual interest payment.		
	Bonds Payable (L).	100,000	
	Cash (A)		100,000
	To record retirement of bonds.		

EXHIBIT 10–7

Patterns of Cash Flows and Amortization Schedule—Bonds Sold at a Premium, Effective-Interest Method

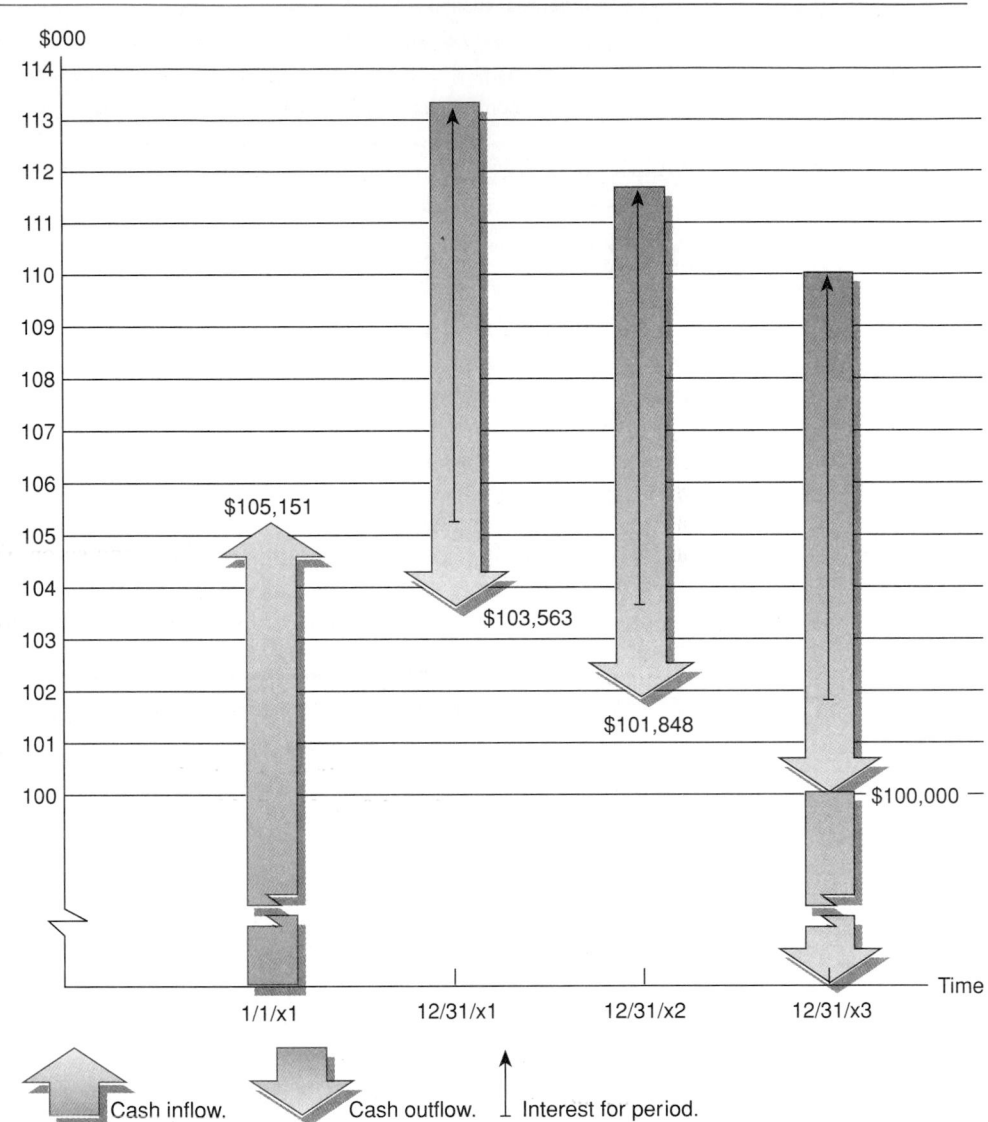

Amortization Schedule

Date	Cash Inflow (outflow)	Interest Expense	Amortization of Premium	Change in Net Liability	Net Liability
1/1/x1	$ 105,151	$ 0	$ 0	$ 105,151	$105,151
12/31/x1	(10,000)	8,412	1,588	(1,588)	103,563
12/31/x2	(10,000)	8,285	1,715	(1,715)	101,848
12/31/x3	(10,000)	8,152	1,848	(1,848)	100,000
12/31/x3	(100,000)	0	0	(100,000)	0
	$ (24,849)	$24,849	$5,151		

Retirement of Bonds

Objective 6
Retirement of bonds.

Bond contracts expire on the maturity date, at which time the face value of the bonds must be paid to the bondholder. If bonds are outstanding until maturity, all premiums and discounts are amortized by the maturity date, the book value of the bonds is equal to the required maturity cash payment, and no gain or loss is realized on the retirement.

Bonds often contain a provision giving the issuer the right to retire or **call** the bonds before maturity at a price specified in the bond contract. If a call provision does not exist, issuers can retire bonds simply by making an open-market purchase. Issuers can also offer new debt contracts to the holders of old bonds. Since several methods exist for bond issuers to retire existing debt and corporations frequently make use of these methods, you may question what would motivate a bond issuer to retire bonds.

The decision to retire bonds is based on the following logic. Outstanding bonds require certain fixed cash outflows over a known period of time in the future, but the early retirement of bonds requires a certain immediate cash outflow. Although the decision to retire bonds early involves many factors that are beyond the scope of this text, the comparisons of the returns expected from alternative uses of cash are important in the decision of whether or not to retire bonds early. If the only alternative use of idle cash is the retirement of bonds, then, of course, retirement would be advantageous. In most cases, positive return opportunities are available for new investments, such as expansion of productive capacity, purchase of equity securities of other corporations, and so on. Often the extinguishment of existing debt or the substitution of new debt for existing debt, perhaps in combination with other financing and investing transactions, is expected to yield the most desirable results.

When bonds are retired early, for whatever reason, the Bonds Payable account balance and any balance in the premium or discount account are eliminated, and a gain or loss is recognized for the difference between the amount paid for the bonds and the net liability or carrying value. For example, if the bonds described in the amortization schedule in Exhibit 10–6 were purchased from bondholders on January 1, 19x3, for $106,000, the following journal entry would be made:

```
19x3
Jan. 1   Loss on Retirement of Bonds (IS). . . . . . . . . . . . . . .      4,283
         Bonds Payable (L) . . . . . . . . . . . . . . . . . . . .    100,000
         Premium on Bonds Payable (AL) . . . . . . . . . . . . .        1,717
            Cash (A). . . . . . . . . . . . . . . . . . . . . . . . .         106,000
         To record retirement of bonds.
```

Note that no interest would be paid for year 3 because the bond liability would have been eliminated on retirement as of the beginning of year 3.

Gains or losses on early retirement of debt of any kind are included on the income statement; and if the aggregate of all such items is material, then the total gains or losses must be shown separately as an extraordinary item. (See Chapter 13 for a discussion of extraordinary items.)

Bonds Sold between Interest Dates

Objective 7
Bonds sold between interest dates.

Even though the bond indenture agreement states the interest periods, such as January through June and July through December, bonds may not always be sold at the beginning of the first interest period. Consider the following bond characteristic:

One thousand $1,000 face value bonds with 12% annual interest paid semiannually (i.e., $60 per bond on June 30 and December 31) starting in year 1.

If instead of being issued on January 1, the bonds are issued on March 1, what happens to the January and February interest? Although the bonds are outstanding for only four months of the first interest period, on June 30, 19x1, the corporation pays the bondholders the nominal interest for the entire six months. Assuming the bonds have an effective-interest rate of 12% (no premium or discount), the purchaser must pay the accrued January and February interest in addition to the face value of the bond. In this case, if the issued bonds have a total face value of $1 million, interest would be added to the selling price and computed as follows: $1 million $\times$ .12 $\times$ $\frac{2}{12}$ = $20,000. The journal entries for the first interest period are as follows:

19x1			
Mar. 1	Cash (A)	1,020,000	
	Bonds Payable (L)		1,000,000
	Interest Payable (L)		20,000
	To record issuance of bonds and cash received for interest.		
June 30	Interest Expense (E)	40,000	
	Interest Payable (L)	20,000	
	Cash (A)		60,000
	To record first interest payment.		

The March 1, 19x1, $20,000 payment by the bondholders for interest is returned to the bondholders on June 30, 19x1, with the remainder of the semiannual interest; and the income statement of the issuer is not affected by the first two months' interest. Note that all bondholders would receive the same interest payment (face value times stated interest rate) regardless of when the bonds were issued during the interest period. Since it is commonplace to issue bonds in large numbers over a period of time, this method avoids the high clerical cost that would be incurred if interest payments to bondholders depended on the date of issuance to each bondholder.

Bond Conversions

Objective 8
Bond conversions.

Some bonds are issued with a provision that the bondholder may convert the bond into capital stock. This convertibility gives the bondholder flexibility in managing investments. Initially, the fixed interest and maturity payments may be desirable for the bondholder, but if bonds have a conversion feature and the value of capital stock goes up relative to the bonds, the bondholder may want to convert bonds into stocks.

At the time the **convertible bonds** are issued, they are accounted for in the same manner as all other bonds, with no recognition of the convertibility feature. When the bonds are converted, the Bonds Payable account and the premium or discount account are eliminated, and the appropriate stock accounts are recorded.

As an example of accounting for convertible bonds, assume that a company issued $1,000 face value bonds that currently have a book value of $1,040 and have all interest recorded to date. Each bond is convertible into 50 shares of capital stock valued at $20.80 per share. The journal entry to record the conversion of one bond is as follows:

Bonds Payable (L)	1,000	
Premium on Bonds Payable (L)	40	
Capital Stock (SE)		1,040
To record conversion of one bond into 50 shares of capital stock.		

Notice that no gain or loss is recorded upon conversion, regardless of the fair values of the stocks or bonds.

Bond Sinking Funds

Objective 9
Bond sinking funds.

When companies issue bonds, there comes a time when plans must be made for the payment of the maturity amounts. Since large cash flows are usually involved, it is often the case that a company will not have enough idle cash to pay the maturity amount. Companies sometimes issue new debt to pay off the old debt, or a bond sinking fund may be established that accumulates the needed funds over the life of the bond issue. A bond sinking fund is money put aside for the purpose of retiring bonds. Usually a bond sinking fund is accumulated because the bond contract calls for annual contributions of certain amounts to be invested annually and allowed to grow for the exclusive purpose of paying bond obligations to the bondholders at maturity. The example that follows illustrates accounting for a bond sinking fund.

Sunshine Flowers has a $100,000, five-year bond issue outstanding. At the end of years 1 through 5, Sunshine Flowers put $16,000 into a bond sinking fund. Management intends to use the proceeds from the fund to pay the maturity amount of the bonds. If the fund earns $2,000 in year 2 and $3,000, $3,500, and $3,800 in the subsequent years, the fund would grow as follows:

	Payments into Fund	Investment Revenue	Sinking Fund Balance
12/31/x1	$16,000	$ 0	$16,000
12/31/x2	16,000	2,000	34,000
12/31/x3	16,000	3,000	53,000
12/31/x4	16,000	3,500	72,500
12/31/x5	16,000	3,800	92,300

Journal entries for the accumulation of the bond sinking fund would be as follows:

```
19x1
Dec. 31   Bond Sinking Fund (A) . . . . . . . . . . . . . . . . . . . .   16,000
              Cash (A) . . . . . . . . . . . . . . . . . . . . . . . . .              16,000
              To record annual payment to fund.

19x2
Dec. 31   Bond Sinking Fund (A) . . . . . . . . . . . . . . . . . . . .    2,000
              Investment Revenue (R) . . . . . . . . . . . . . . . . . .               2,000
              To record interest earned on fund.

     31   Bond Sinking Fund (A) . . . . . . . . . . . . . . . . . . . .   16,000
              Cash (A) . . . . . . . . . . . . . . . . . . . . . . . . .              16,000
              To record annual payment to fund.

19x3
Dec. 31   Bond Sinking Fund (A) . . . . . . . . . . . . . . . . . . . .    3,000
              Investment Revenue (R) . . . . . . . . . . . . . . . . . .               3,000
              To record interest earned on fund.

     31   Bond Sinking Fund (A) . . . . . . . . . . . . . . . . . . . .   16,000
              Cash (A) . . . . . . . . . . . . . . . . . . . . . . . . .              16,000
              To record annual payment to fund.

19x4
Dec. 31   Bond Sinking Fund (A) . . . . . . . . . . . . . . . . . . . .    3,500
              Investment Revenue (R) . . . . . . . . . . . . . . . . . .               3,500
              To record interest earned on fund.

     31   Bond Sinking Fund (A) . . . . . . . . . . . . . . . . . . . .   16,000
              Cash (A) . . . . . . . . . . . . . . . . . . . . . . . . .              16,000
              To record annual payment to fund.

19x5
Dec. 31   Bond Sinking Fund (A) . . . . . . . . . . . . . . . . . . . .    3,800
              Investment Revenue (R) . . . . . . . . . . . . . . . . . .               3,800
              To record interest earned on fund.
```

19x5
Dec. 31   Bond Sinking Fund (A)   16,000
               Cash (A)   16,000
           To record annual payment to fund.

When the bonds are retired, the following entries would be made:

19x5
Dec. 31   Cash (A)   92,300
               Bond Sinking Fund (A)   92,300
           To reclassify sinking fund to cash.

      31   Bonds Payable (L)   100,000
               Cash (A)   100,000
           To record retirement of bonds.

In the case of Sunshine Flowers, the sinking fund balance was less than the amount needed to retire the bonds at maturity. In other cases, companies can have surpluses. Obviously, the bond issuer must pay any deficiency in the sinking fund out of cash and can retain any surplus in the sinking fund as long as all contractual provisions of the bond issue have been met.

• SUMMARY

Corporations use two types of long-term financing—debt financing and equity financing. Debt financing is long-term borrowing. Equity financing is the issuance of stock. This chapter focuses on debt financing that generates long-term (noncurrent) liabilities.

Several types of noncurrent liabilities have common traits. They are governed by contractual terms that determine the pattern of cash (or other asset) flows between the creditor and the debtor. Two important generalizations underlie much of the accounting for long-term liabilities:

1. The total interest on a debt contract is the total cash paid to creditors minus the total cash received from creditors.
2. The interest charge for a period is the effective interest rate times the beginning of the period liability balance.

Notes and bonds are common noncurrent liabilities, and the same basic principles govern each. A note is an obligation to one creditor where the amount borrowed, the amount to be paid back, and the payment dates are all stated in the form of a contract between the debtor and a lending institution or other individual creditor. Bonds are contracts printed in anticipation of offering them for sale to many different creditors, or bondholders. Because bond contracts are made to be sold to many people, the terms such as *interest paid* and *dates of payment* are determined in advance, and the market determines at the date of sale the amount to be paid for the bond. Differences in effective and face interest rates cause bonds to be sold at premiums or discounts, and accounting techniques for amortizing these premiums and discounts allow for an orderly recording of periodic interest.

• DEMONSTRATION EXERCISE

The following transactions relate to a $1 million bond issue by Memory Datalink. The 1,000 bonds are $1,000 face value, 8%, five-year bonds with a maturity date of December 31, 19x5.

a. Sell 500 bonds on January 1, 19x1, for a total of $520,792, yielding a 7% effective-interest rate.

b. Sell remaining 500 bonds on March 31, 19x1, for a total of $510,000, yielding an 8% effective-interest rate.

c. Pay interest on the bonds on June 30, 19x1, and December 31, 19x1.

d. Retire 250 of the bonds sold in *a* on January 1, 19x2, for a total of $252,000.

Required:

Prepare the journal entries to record the above transactions using the effective-interest method to amortize bond discounts and premiums.

Solution:

19x1

Jan. 1	Cash (A)		520,792	
	Bonds Payable (L)			500,000
	Premium on Bonds Payable (AL)			20,792
	To record issuance of 8% bonds at 7% effective-interest rate.			

Mar. 31	Cash (A)		510,000	
	Bonds Payable (L)			500,000
	Interest Payable (L)			10,000
	To record issuance of 8% bonds at an 8% effective-interest rate.			

June 30	Interest Expense (E)		18,228	
	Premium on Bonds Payable (AL)		1,772	
	Cash (A)			20,000
	To record semiannual interest payment and amortization of bond premium for bonds issued 1/1/x1: $20,000 - ($520,792 \times .07 \times 6/12)$.			

30	Interest Expense (E)		10,000	
	Interest Payable (L)		10,000	
	Cash (A)			20,000
	To record semiannual interest payment for bonds issued 3/31/x1.			

Dec. 31	Interest Expense (E)		18,166	
	Premium on Bonds Payable (AL)		1,834	
	Cash (A)			20,000
	To record semiannual interest payment and amortization of bond premium for bonds issued 1/1/x1.			

31	Interest Expense (E)		20,000	
	Cash (A)			20,000
	To record semiannual interest payment for bonds issued 3/31/x1.			

19x4

Jan. 1	Bonds Payable (L)		250,000	
	(Debit) Premium on Bonds Payable (AL)		8,593*	
	Gain on Retirement of Bonds (R)			6,593
	Cash (A)			252,000
	To record retirement of 250 bonds issued 1/1/x1.			

*($20,792 - $1,772 - $1,834) × 1/2.

Future Values and Present Values

A dollar in your hand today is worth more than the promise of receiving a dollar one year in the future. Why? First, the promise of receiving a dollar in a year involves risk—something could happen to the debtor to deprive you of the promised dollar. Second, money has time value, and you could invest the dollar so that in a year its value would grow by the amount of interest earned.

Because money has time value, if someone wants to borrow $100 from you today with a promise to pay it back in one year, you would probably charge interest for the use of the money. In the following time line, the present value of your $100 is $100. However, the future value of your $100 has grown to $110; the $10 difference is the interest.

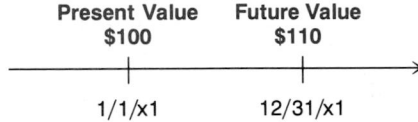

Everything of value commands a price, and owners of valuable items (except perhaps parents) will charge that price for its use. Interest is the price paid for use of money just as rent is the price paid for use of an apartment.

Building on the introduction to interest provided in this chapter, this appendix explains in greater detail how interest affects present and future values.

COMPOUND VERSUS SIMPLE INTEREST

Simple interest is computed by the following formula:

$$\text{Principal} \times \text{Rate} \times \text{Time}$$

If $10,000 is borrowed on January 1, 19x1, at 10% simple interest and paid back on December 31, 19x2, the simple interest is $10,000 × .10 × 2 = $2,000.

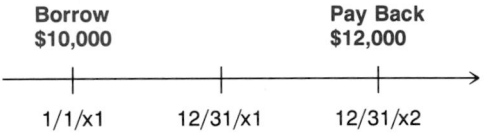

Compound interest uses the time value of money on the entire outstanding amount **including** interest. Thus, **compound interest** is interest charged on both the unpaid principal and any unpaid interest accrued after the inception of the liability. For example, if we change the terms of the $10,000, 10%, two-year loan so that interest compounded annually is paid at maturity, we have the following time line:

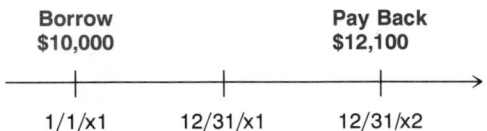

The compound interest amount is computed as follows:

	Amount Outstanding				Interest
Interest—year 1	$10,000	×	.10	=	$1,000
Interest—year 2	11,000	×	.10	=	1,100
Total interest					$2,100

The $100 difference between the $2,000 simple interest illustrated earlier and the $2,100 compound interest is the interest charged on the previous unpaid interest for year 1. The diagram in Exhibit 10A–1 illustrates how the $10,000 borrowed on January 1, 19x1, grows to $12,100 on December 31, 19x2.

EXHIBIT 10A–1

Growth of the Total Amount Outstanding under Compound Interest

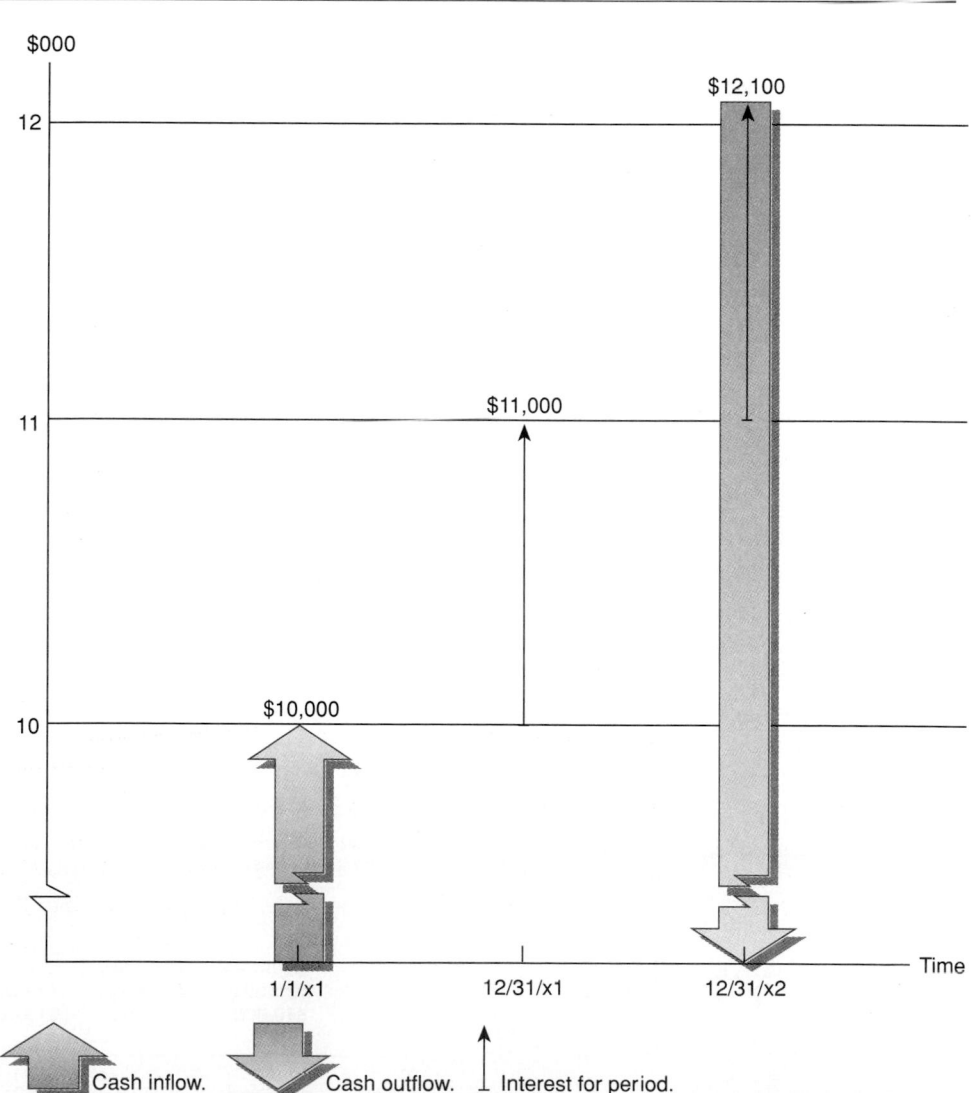

FUTURE VALUES

Future value is the value that an investment today will grow to, by a stated time in the future at a specified interest rate. In this section, you will learn how to compute the future value of a single amount and the future value of an ordinary annuity.

Future Value of a Single Amount

Objective 10
Future values. . . .

If $20,000 is invested on January 1, 19x1, at 10% compound interest, how much will the $20,000 grow to in three years? In other words, what is the maximum that could be withdrawn at the end of three years? The answer is that the $20,000 will grow to its **future value,** which is the sum of the principal and compound interest for the time the investment is held. In the discussion on compound interest, you saw that each year more interest is accumulated, which increases the amount outstanding by more each period.

You can compute the exact amount of future value in several ways. The following table illustrates one method of computing future value:

	Amount Outstanding		Interst Rate		Interest Amount
Interest—year 1	$20,000	×	.10	=	$ 2,000
Interest—year 2	22,000	×	.10	=	2,200
Interest—year 3	24,200	×	.10	=	2,420
Total interest					$ 6,620
Principal					20,000
Future value					$26,620

This type of computation can be time consuming. Therefore, precomputed table factors are available to aid in the computation of compound interest. Table 10A–1 (at the end of this appendix) shows the amount $1 will grow to for different numbers of periods outstanding and different interest rates. In our example, we have three periods at 10% per period. In Table 10A–1 the intersection of the column corresponding to an interest rate of 10% and the row corresponding to three periods (n = 3) gives the appropriate table factor, 1.331. This future value factor is applied to the principal of $20,000 as follows:

$$(\text{Principal})\,(\text{Future value factor}) = \text{Future value}$$

$$(\$20,000)\,(1.331) \quad\quad = \quad \$26,620$$

Future Values of an Ordinary Annuity

Sometimes payments are made in several periodic amounts rather than as a single payment. The same basic pattern is followed for determining the future value of a series of amounts as used to determine the future value of a single amount. For example, assume that payments are made into a fund for $10,000 a year at each year-end for three years and that the fund earns 10% per year. Such patterns of equal amounts separated by equal periods are called annuities.

The following time line shows the equal payments into the fund:

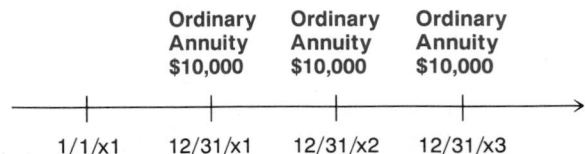

Because money is coming into the fund in the form of an **ordinary annuity,** that is, payments at the end of each period, year 1 has no interest, year 2 earns interest only on the December 31, 19x1, payment, and year 3 earns interest on both the December 31, 19x1 and 19x2, payments, but none on the December 31, 19x3, payment. This is shown in the following table:

	Year 1	Year 2	Year 3	Total
	Interest Earned during			
Annuity payment 1	$0	$1,000	$1,100	$2,100
Annuity payment 2	0	0	1,000	1,000
Annuity payment 3	0	0	0	0
Total	$0	$1,000	$2,100	$3,100

The diagram in Exhibit 10A–2 shows how the payments and compound interest grow to a future amount of $33,100 on December 31, 19x3.

To arrive at the future value of an ordinary annuity, we could make the individual computations or use a table of factors. Table 10A–2 is similar to Table 10A–1 except that Table 10A–2 is for an ordinary annuity of $1. The future value factor for three years and 10%—3.310—is found at the intersection of the 10% interest column and the three-year row. The computation therefore is

$$(\text{Annuity})\,(\text{Future value factor}) = \text{Future value}$$

$$(\$10,000)\,(3.310) \qquad = \qquad \$33,100$$

PRESENT VALUES

Objective 10
. . . and present values.

Sometimes managers know future amounts such as maturity values of bonds and want to compute the present value. This is the "other side of the coin" of the future value concepts and computations discussed above.

If someone promises to pay you $100,000 including principal and interest in three years, what is the present value of the future cash receipt? Or, put differently, what would you pay now for the promise of $100,000 in three years? Study the following time line:

Present Value = ?			Future Value = $100,000
1/1/x1	12/31/x1	12/31/x2	12/31/x3

As you probably have decided for yourself, the answer depends a great deal on interest rate considerations. If you can now earn large returns on invested money, $100,000 three years hence would be worth less than if you can earn only small returns. And, of course, your confidence in the ultimate receipt of the future payment is a crucial consideration also. From the use of future value tables, we know that for any given interest rate the following algebraic relationship exists between present values and future values.

$$\frac{\text{Present value}}{\text{of \$1}} \times \frac{\text{Table factor for}}{\text{future value of \$1}} = \frac{\text{Future value}}{\text{of \$1}}$$

Therefore,

$$\frac{\text{Present value}}{\text{of \$1}} = \frac{\text{Future value of \$1}}{\text{Table factor for future value of \$1}}$$

EXHIBIT 10A–2

**Growth of Investment
by Payments and
Compound Interest**

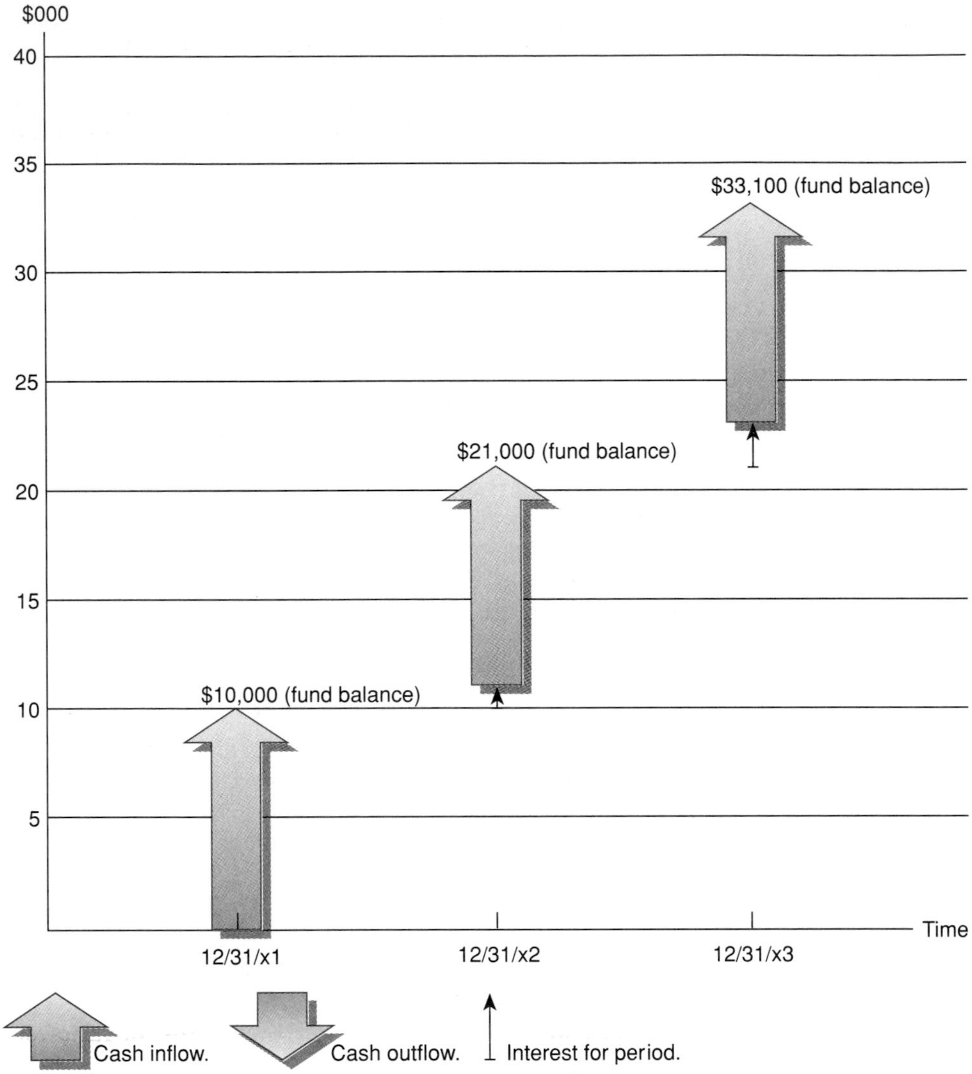

$000

40 ──

35 ──
                                          $33,100 (fund balance)

30 ──

25 ──

20 ──────────────── $21,000 (fund balance) ───────

15 ──

10 ─── $10,000 (fund balance) ─────────────────────

5 ──

                                                          Time
       12/31/x1   12/31/x2   12/31/x3

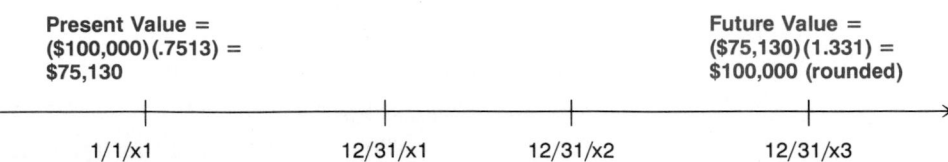

Cash inflow.   Cash outflow.   ⊥ Interest for period.

Hence, the present value factors are the reciprocals of the future value factors. Table 10A–3 shows the present value factors that are the reciprocals of the factors in Table 10A–1. For example, the future value factor for three years at 10% is 1.331. The present value factor for three years at 10% is .7513, and 1/1.331 equals .7513 (rounded).

Going back to our example, the time line is as follows:

Present Value =
($100,000)(.7513) =
$75,130

                                                    Future Value =
                                                    ($75,130)(1.331) =
                                                    $100,000 (rounded)

    1/1/x1   12/31/x1   12/31/x2   12/31/x3

Present Value of an
Ordinary Annuity

Just as the present values of a single future amount must sometimes be computed, often the present value of future annuities must be computed. For example, how much would you have to invest now to withdraw $20,000 at the end of each of the three subsequent years? The time line for this example is as follows:

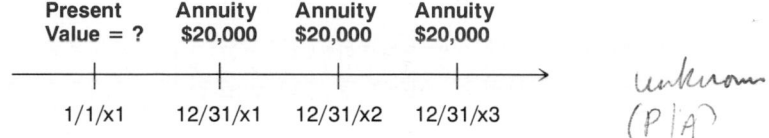

	Present Value = ?	Annuity $20,000	Annuity $20,000	Annuity $20,000
	1/1/x1	12/31/x1	12/31/x2	12/31/x3

To answer this question, you must compute the present value of these amounts. Assuming an 8% interest rate, the present value of each annuity payment is computed separately and added together to sum the total present value as follows:

Present Value of Three Ordinary Annuity Payments

	Future Amount		Table 10A–3 Factor (8%)		Present Value
1 year.	$20,000	×	.9259	=	$18,518
2 years	20,000	×	.8573	=	17,146
3 years	20,000	×	.7938	=	15,876
Total present value					$51,540

Table 10A–4 saves computational time by giving the necessary factors to compute the present value of annuities for different interest rates and time periods. Thus, using the following formula, we can arrive at the same answer as above:

$$(\text{Annuity amount})\,(\text{Table 10A–4 factor}) = \quad \text{Present value}$$

$$(\$20,000)\,(2.5771) \qquad = \$51,540 \text{ (rounded)}$$

Notation Commonly
Used in Future and
Present Value
Computations

We have discussed four tables used for four different but closely related computations. A shorthand notation is used to designate each computation. Note the following relationship with the four tables of factors in Appendix 10A: In Table 10A–1, Future Value of a Single Amount, factors are designated $(F/P, n, i)$, where n is the number of periods and i is the effective-interest rate; in Table 10A–2, Future Value of an Ordinary Annuity, factors are designated $(F/A, n, i)$; in Table 10A–3, Present Value of a Single Amount, factors are designated $(P/F, n, i)$; and in Table 10A–4, Present Value of an Ordinary Annuity, factors are designated $(P/A, n, i)$.

The following is a summary of how to read each notation.

1. $(F/P, n, i)$ reads, "The future value F computed from a known present amount P with n periods and an effective-interest rate of i."

2. $(F/A, n, i)$ reads, "The future value F computed from a known ordinary annuity A with n periods and an effective interest rate of i."

3. $(P/F, n, i)$ reads, "The present value P computed from a known future amount F with n periods and an effective-interest rate of i."

4. $(P/A, n, i)$ reads, "The present value P computed from a known ordinary annuity A with n periods and an effective-interest rate of i."

TABLE 10A–1 Future Value of a Single Amount

n	1%	2%	3%	4%	5%	6%	7%	8%	9%	10%	11%	12%	13%	14%	15%	16%	17%	18%	19%	20%
1	1.0100	1.0200	1.0300	1.0400	1.0500	1.0600	1.0700	1.0800	1.0900	1.1000	1.1100	1.1200	1.1300	1.1400	1.1500	1.1600	1.1700	1.1800	1.1900	1.2000
2	1.0201	1.0404	1.0609	1.0816	1.1025	1.1236	1.1449	1.1664	1.1881	1.2100	1.2321	1.2544	1.2769	1.2996	1.3225	1.3456	1.3689	1.3924	1.4161	1.4400
3	1.0303	1.0612	1.0927	1.1249	1.1576	1.1910	1.2250	1.2597	1.2950	1.3310	1.3676	1.4049	1.4429	1.4815	1.5209	1.5609	1.6016	1.6430	1.6852	1.7280
4	1.0406	1.0824	1.1255	1.1699	1.2155	1.2625	1.3108	1.3605	1.4116	1.4641	1.5181	1.5735	1.6305	1.6890	1.7490	1.8106	1.8739	1.9388	2.0053	2.0736
5	1.0510	1.1041	1.1593	1.2167	1.2763	1.3382	1.4026	1.4693	1.5386	1.6105	1.6851	1.7623	1.8424	1.9254	2.0114	2.1003	2.1924	2.2878	2.3864	2.4883
6	1.0615	1.1262	1.1941	1.2653	1.3401	1.4185	1.5007	1.5869	1.6771	1.7716	1.8704	1.9738	2.0820	2.1950	2.3131	2.4364	2.5652	2.6996	2.8398	2.9860
7	1.0721	1.1487	1.2299	1.3159	1.4071	1.5036	1.6058	1.7138	1.8280	1.9487	2.0762	2.2107	2.3526	2.5023	2.6600	2.8262	3.0012	3.1855	3.3793	3.5832
8	1.0829	1.1717	1.2668	1.3686	1.4775	1.5938	1.7182	1.8509	1.9926	2.1436	2.3045	2.4760	2.6584	2.8526	3.0590	3.2784	3.5115	3.7589	4.0214	4.2998
9	1.0937	1.1951	1.3048	1.4233	1.5513	1.6895	1.8385	1.9990	2.1719	2.3579	2.5580	2.7731	3.0040	3.2520	3.5179	3.8030	4.1084	4.4355	4.7854	5.1598
10	1.1046	1.2190	1.3439	1.4802	1.6289	1.7908	1.9671	2.1589	2.3674	2.5937	2.8394	3.1059	3.3946	3.7072	4.0456	4.4114	4.8068	5.2338	5.6947	6.1917
11	1.1157	1.2434	1.3842	1.5395	1.7103	1.8983	2.1049	2.3316	2.5804	2.8531	3.1518	3.4786	3.8359	4.2262	4.6524	5.1173	5.6240	6.1759	6.7767	7.4301
12	1.1268	1.2682	1.4258	1.6010	1.7959	2.0122	2.2522	2.5182	2.8127	3.1384	3.4984	3.8960	4.3345	4.8179	5.3503	5.9360	6.5801	7.2876	8.0642	8.9161
13	1.1381	1.2936	1.4685	1.6651	1.8856	2.1329	2.4098	2.7196	3.0658	3.4523	3.8833	4.3635	4.8980	5.4924	6.1528	6.8858	7.6987	8.5994	9.5964	10.6993
14	1.1495	1.3195	1.5126	1.7317	1.9799	2.2609	2.5785	2.9372	3.3417	3.7975	4.3104	4.8871	5.5348	6.2614	7.0757	7.9875	9.0075	10.1473	11.4198	12.8392
15	1.1610	1.3459	1.5580	1.8009	2.0789	2.3966	2.7590	3.1722	3.6425	4.1772	4.7846	5.4736	6.2543	7.1379	8.1371	9.2655	10.5387	11.9738	13.5895	15.4070
16	1.1726	1.3728	1.6047	1.8730	2.1829	2.5403	2.9522	3.4259	3.9703	4.5950	5.3109	6.1304	7.0673	8.1373	9.3576	10.7480	12.3303	14.1290	16.1715	18.4884
17	1.1843	1.4002	1.6528	1.9479	2.2920	2.6928	3.1588	3.7000	4.3276	5.0545	5.8951	6.8661	7.9861	9.2765	10.7613	12.4677	14.4265	16.6723	19.2441	22.1861
18	1.1961	1.4282	1.7024	2.0258	2.4066	2.8543	3.3799	3.9960	4.7171	5.5599	6.5435	7.6900	9.0243	10.5752	12.3755	14.4625	16.8790	19.6733	22.9005	26.6233
19	1.2081	1.4568	1.7535	2.1068	2.5269	3.0256	3.6165	4.3157	5.1417	6.1159	7.2633	8.6128	10.1974	12.0557	14.2318	16.7765	19.7484	23.2145	27.2516	31.9480
20	1.2202	1.4859	1.8061	2.1911	2.6533	3.2071	3.8697	4.6609	5.6044	6.7275	8.0623	9.6463	11.5231	13.7435	16.3666	19.4608	23.1056	27.3931	32.4294	38.3376
25	1.2824	1.6406	2.0938	2.6658	3.3864	4.2919	5.4274	6.8485	8.6231	10.8347	13.5854	17.0001	21.2306	26.4620	32.9190	40.8743	50.6579	62.6688	77.3881	95.3963
30	1.3478	1.8114	2.4273	3.2434	4.3219	5.7435	7.6122	10.0626	13.2677	17.4494	22.8922	29.9600	39.1160	50.9503	66.2119	85.8500	111.0650	143.3710	184.6750	237.3760
40	1.4889	2.2080	3.2620	4.8010	7.0400	10.2857	14.9744	21.7244	31.4094	45.2591	65.0006	93.0513	132.7820	188.8840	267.8650	378.7220	533.8690	750.3810	1051.6700	1469.7700

Notation: $(F/P, n, i)$ where F = Future value; P = Present amount; n = Number of periods; and i = Interest rate.

TABLE 10A–2 Future Value of an Ordinary Annuity

n	1%	2%	3%	4%	5%	6%	7%	8%	9%	10%	11%	12%	13%	14%	15%	16%	17%	18%	19%	20%
1	1.0000	1.0000	1.0000	1.0000	1.0000	1.0000	1.0000	1.0000	1.0000	1.0000	1.0000	1.0000	1.0000	1.0000	1.0000	1.0000	1.0000	1.0000	1.0000	1.0000
2	2.0100	2.0200	2.0300	2.0400	2.0500	2.0600	2.0700	2.0800	2.0900	2.1000	2.1100	2.1200	2.1300	2.1400	2.1500	2.1600	2.1700	2.1800	2.1900	2.2000
3	3.0301	3.0604	3.0909	3.1216	3.1525	3.1836	3.2149	3.2464	3.2781	3.3100	3.3421	3.3744	3.4069	3.4396	3.4725	3.5056	3.5389	3.5724	3.6061	3.6400
4	4.0604	4.1216	4.1836	4.2465	4.3101	4.3746	4.4399	4.5061	4.5731	4.6410	4.7097	4.7793	4.8498	4.9211	4.9934	5.0665	5.1405	5.2154	5.2913	5.3680
5	5.1010	5.2040	5.3091	5.4163	5.5256	5.6371	5.7507	5.8666	5.9847	6.1051	6.2278	6.3528	6.4803	6.6101	6.7424	6.8771	7.0144	7.1542	7.2966	7.4416
6	6.1520	6.3081	6.4684	6.6330	6.8019	6.9753	7.1533	7.3359	7.5233	7.7156	7.9129	8.1152	8.3227	8.5355	8.7537	8.9775	9.2068	9.4420	9.6830	9.9299
7	7.2135	7.4343	7.6625	7.8983	8.1420	8.3938	8.6540	8.9228	9.2004	9.4872	9.7833	10.0890	10.4047	10.7305	11.0668	11.4139	11.7720	12.1415	12.5227	12.9159
8	8.2857	8.5830	8.8923	9.2142	9.5491	9.8975	10.2598	10.6366	11.0285	11.4359	11.8594	12.2997	12.7573	13.2328	13.7268	14.2401	14.7733	15.3270	15.9020	16.4991
9	9.3685	9.7546	10.1591	10.5828	11.0266	11.4913	11.9780	12.4876	13.0210	13.5795	14.1640	14.7757	15.4157	16.0853	16.7858	17.5185	18.2847	19.0859	19.9234	20.7989
10	10.4622	10.9497	11.4639	12.0061	12.5779	13.1808	13.8164	14.4866	15.1929	15.9374	16.7220	17.5487	18.4197	19.3373	20.3037	21.3215	22.3931	23.5213	24.7089	25.9587
11	11.5668	12.1687	12.8078	13.4864	14.2068	14.9716	15.7836	16.6455	17.5603	18.5312	19.5614	20.6546	21.8143	23.0445	24.3493	25.7329	27.1999	28.7551	30.4035	32.1504
12	12.6825	13.4121	14.1920	15.0258	15.9171	16.8699	17.8885	18.9771	20.1407	21.3843	22.7132	24.1331	25.6502	27.2707	29.0017	30.8502	32.8239	34.9311	37.1802	39.5805
13	13.8093	14.6803	15.6178	16.6268	17.7130	18.8821	20.1406	21.4953	22.9534	24.5227	26.2116	28.0291	29.9847	32.0887	34.3519	36.7862	39.4040	42.2187	45.2445	48.4966
14	14.9474	15.9739	17.0863	18.2919	19.5986	21.0151	22.5505	24.2149	26.0192	27.9750	30.0949	32.3926	34.8827	37.5811	40.5047	43.6720	47.1027	50.8180	54.8409	59.1959
15	16.0969	17.2934	18.5989	20.0236	21.5786	23.2760	25.1290	27.1521	29.3609	31.7725	34.4054	37.2797	40.4175	43.8424	47.5804	51.6595	56.1101	60.9653	66.2607	72.0351
16	17.2579	18.6393	20.1569	21.8245	23.6575	25.6725	27.8881	30.3243	33.0034	35.9497	39.1899	42.7533	46.6717	50.9804	55.7175	60.9250	66.6488	72.9390	79.8502	87.4421
17	18.4304	20.0121	21.7616	23.6975	25.8404	28.2129	30.8402	33.7502	36.9737	40.5447	44.5008	48.8837	53.7391	59.1176	65.0751	71.6730	78.9792	87.0680	96.0218	105.9306
18	19.6147	21.4123	23.4144	25.6454	28.1324	30.9057	33.9990	37.4502	41.3013	45.5992	50.3959	55.7497	61.7251	68.3941	75.8364	84.1407	93.4056	103.7403	115.2659	128.1167
19	20.8109	22.8406	25.1169	27.6712	30.5390	33.7600	37.3790	41.4463	46.0185	51.1591	56.9395	63.4397	70.7494	78.9692	88.2118	98.6032	110.2846	123.4135	138.1664	154.7400
20	22.0190	24.2974	26.8704	29.7781	33.0660	36.7856	40.9955	45.7620	51.1601	57.2750	64.2028	72.0524	80.9468	91.0249	102.4436	115.3797	130.0329	146.6280	165.4180	186.6880
25	28.2432	32.0303	36.4593	41.6459	47.7271	54.8645	63.2490	73.1059	84.7009	98.3471	114.4133	133.3339	155.6196	181.8708	212.7930	249.2140	292.1049	342.6035	402.0425	471.9811
30	34.7849	40.5681	47.5754	56.0849	66.4388	79.0582	94.4608	113.2832	136.3075	164.4940	199.0209	241.3327	293.1992	356.7868	434.7451	530.3117	647.4391	790.9480	966.7122	1181.8815
40	48.8864	60.4020	75.4013	95.0255	120.7998	154.7620	199.6351	259.0565	337.8824	442.5926	581.8261	767.0914	1013.7043	1342.0251	1779.0903	2360.7573	3134.5218	4163.2130	5529.8289	7343.8577

Notation: $(F/A, n, i)$ where F = Future value; A = Ordinary annuity; n = Number of periods; and i = Interest rate.

TABLE 10A–3   Present Value of a Single Amount

n	1%	2%	3%	4%	5%	6%	7%	8%	9%	10%	11%	12%	13%	14%	15%	16%	17%	18%	19%	20%
1	.9901	.9804	.9709	.9615	.9524	.9434	.9346	.9259	.9174	.9091	.9009	.8929	.8850	.8772	.8696	.8621	.8547	.8475	.8403	.8333
2	.9803	.9612	.9426	.9246	.9070	.8900	.8734	.8573	.8417	.8264	.8116	.7972	.7831	.7695	.7561	.7432	.7305	.7182	.7062	.6944
3	.9706	.9423	.9151	.8890	.8638	.8396	.8163	.7938	.7722	.7513	.7312	.7118	.6931	.6750	.6575	.6407	.6244	.6086	.5934	.5787
4	.9610	.9239	.8885	.8548	.8227	.7921	.7629	.7350	.7084	.6830	.6587	.6355	.6133	.5921	.5718	.5523	.5337	.5158	.4987	.4822
5	.9515	.9057	.8626	.8219	.7835	.7473	.7130	.6806	.6499	.6209	.5934	.5674	.5428	.5194	.4972	.4761	.4561	.4371	.4190	.4019
6	.9420	.8880	.8375	.7903	.7462	.7050	.6663	.6302	.5963	.5645	.5346	.5066	.4803	.4556	.4323	.4104	.3898	.3704	.3521	.3349
7	.9327	.8706	.8131	.7599	.7107	.6651	.6228	.5835	.5470	.5132	.4817	.4524	.4251	.3996	.3759	.3538	.3332	.3139	.2959	.2791
8	.9235	.8535	.7894	.7307	.6768	.6274	.5820	.5403	.5019	.4665	.4339	.4039	.3762	.3506	.3269	.3050	.2848	.2660	.2487	.2326
9	.9143	.8368	.7664	.7026	.6446	.5919	.5439	.5002	.4604	.4241	.3909	.3606	.3329	.3075	.2843	.2630	.2434	.2255	.2090	.1938
10	.9053	.8204	.7441	.6756	.6139	.5584	.5084	.4632	.4224	.3855	.3522	.3220	.2946	.2697	.2472	.2267	.2080	.1911	.1756	.1615
11	.8963	.8043	.7224	.6496	.5847	.5368	.4751	.4289	.3875	.3505	.3173	.2875	.2607	.2366	.2149	.1954	.1778	.1619	.1476	.1346
12	.8874	.7885	.7014	.6246	.5568	.4970	.4440	.3971	.3555	.3186	.2858	.2567	.2307	.2076	.1869	.1685	.1520	.1372	.1240	.1122
13	.8787	.7730	.6810	.6006	.5303	.4688	.4150	.3677	.3262	.2897	.2575	.2292	.2042	.1821	.1625	.1452	.1299	.1163	.1042	.0935
14	.8700	.7579	.6611	.5775	.5051	.4423	.3878	.3405	.2993	.2633	.2320	.2046	.1807	.1597	.1413	.1252	.1110	.0986	.0876	.0779
15	.8614	.7430	.6419	.5553	.4810	.4173	.3625	.3152	.2745	.2394	.2090	.1827	.1599	.1401	.1229	.1079	.0949	.0835	.0736	.0649
16	.8528	.7284	.6232	.5339	.4581	.3936	.3387	.2919	.2519	.2176	.1883	.1631	.1415	.1229	.1069	.0930	.0811	.0708	.0618	.0541
17	.8444	.7142	.6050	.5134	.4363	.3714	.3166	.2703	.2311	.1978	.1696	.1456	.1252	.1078	.0929	.0802	.0693	.0600	.0520	.0451
18	.8360	.7002	.5874	.4936	.4155	.3503	.2959	.2502	.2120	.1799	.1528	.1300	.1108	.0946	.0808	.0691	.0592	.0508	.0437	.0376
19	.8277	.6864	.5703	.4746	.3957	.3305	.2765	.2317	.1945	.1635	.1377	.1161	.0981	.0829	.0703	.0596	.0506	.0431	.0367	.0313
20	.8195	.6730	.5537	.4564	.3769	.3118	.2584	.2145	.1784	.1486	.1240	.1037	.0868	.0728	.0611	.0514	.0433	.0365	.0308	.0261
25	.7798	.6095	.4776	.3751	.2953	.2330	.1842	.1460	.1160	.0923	.0736	.0588	.0471	.0378	.0304	.0245	.0197	.0160	.0129	.0105
30	.7419	.5521	.4120	.3083	.2314	.1741	.1314	.0994	.0754	.0573	.0437	.0334	.0256	.0196	.0151	.0116	.0090	.0070	.0054	.0042
40	.6717	.4529	.3066	.2083	.1420	.0972	.0668	.0460	.0318	.0221	.0154	.0107	.0075	.0053	.0037	.0026	.0019	.0013	.0010	.0007

Notation: $(P/F, n, i)$ where P = Present value; F = Future amount; n = Number of periods; and i = Interest rate.

TABLE 10A–4   Present Value of an Ordinary Annuity

n	1%	2%	3%	4%	5%	6%	7%	8%	9%	10%	11%	12%	13%	14%	15%	16%	17%	18%	19%	20%
1	.9901	.9804	.9709	.9615	.9524	.9434	.9346	.9259	.9174	.9091	.9009	.8929	.8850	.8772	.8696	.8621	.8547	.8475	.8403	.8333
2	1.9704	1.9416	1.9135	1.8861	1.8594	1.8334	1.8080	1.7833	1.7591	1.7355	1.7125	1.6901	1.6681	1.6467	1.6257	1.6052	1.5852	1.5656	1.5465	1.5278
3	2.9410	2.8839	2.8286	2.7751	2.7232	2.6730	2.6243	2.5771	2.5313	2.4869	2.4437	2.4018	2.3612	2.3216	2.2832	2.2459	2.2096	2.1743	2.1399	2.1065
4	3.9020	3.8077	3.7171	3.6299	3.5459	3.4651	3.3872	3.3121	3.2397	3.1699	3.1024	3.0374	2.9745	2.9137	2.8550	2.7982	2.7432	2.6901	2.6386	2.5887
5	4.8534	4.7135	4.5797	4.4518	4.3295	4.2124	4.1002	3.9927	3.8897	3.7908	3.6959	3.6048	3.5172	3.4331	3.3522	3.2743	3.1993	3.1272	3.0576	2.9906
6	5.7955	5.6014	5.4172	5.2421	5.0757	4.9173	4.7666	4.6229	4.4859	4.3553	4.2305	4.1114	3.9976	3.8887	3.7845	3.6847	3.5892	3.4976	3.4098	3.3255
7	6.7282	6.4720	6.2302	6.0021	5.7864	5.5824	5.3893	5.2064	5.0330	4.8684	4.7122	4.5638	4.4226	4.2883	4.1604	4.0386	3.9224	3.8115	3.7057	3.6046
8	7.6517	7.3255	7.0197	6.7327	6.4632	6.2098	5.9713	5.7466	5.5348	5.3349	5.1461	4.9676	4.7988	4.6389	4.4873	4.3436	4.2072	4.0776	3.9544	3.8372
9	8.5660	8.1622	7.7861	7.4353	7.1078	6.8017	6.5152	6.2469	5.9952	5.7590	5.5370	5.3282	5.1317	4.9464	4.7716	4.6065	4.4506	4.3030	4.1633	4.0310
10	9.4713	8.9826	8.5302	8.1109	7.7217	7.3601	7.0236	6.7101	6.4177	6.1446	5.8892	5.6502	5.4262	5.2161	5.0188	4.8332	4.6586	4.4941	4.3389	4.1925
11	10.3676	9.7868	9.2526	8.7605	8.3064	7.8869	7.4987	7.1390	6.8052	6.4951	6.2065	5.9377	5.6869	5.4527	5.2337	5.0286	4.8362	4.6560	4.4865	4.3271
12	11.2551	10.5753	9.9540	9.3851	8.8633	8.3838	7.9427	7.5361	7.1607	6.8137	6.4924	6.1944	5.9177	5.6603	5.4206	5.1971	4.9884	4.7932	4.6105	4.4392
13	12.1338	11.3484	10.6349	9.9857	9.3936	8.8527	8.3577	7.9038	7.4869	7.1034	6.7499	6.4235	6.1218	5.8424	5.5832	5.3423	5.1183	4.9095	4.7147	4.5327
14	13.0037	12.1062	11.2961	10.5631	9.8986	9.2950	8.7455	8.2442	7.7862	7.3667	6.9819	6.6282	6.3025	6.0021	5.7245	5.4675	5.2293	5.0081	4.8023	4.6106
15	13.8651	12.8492	11.9379	11.1184	10.3797	9.7123	9.1079	8.5595	8.0607	7.6061	7.1909	6.8109	6.4624	6.1422	5.8474	5.5755	5.3242	5.0916	4.8759	4.6755
16	14.7179	13.5777	12.5611	11.6523	10.8378	10.1059	9.4467	8.8514	8.3126	7.8237	7.3792	6.9740	6.6039	6.2651	5.9542	5.6685	5.4053	5.1624	4.9377	4.7296
17	15.5623	14.2919	13.1661	12.1657	11.2741	10.4773	9.7632	9.1216	8.5436	8.0216	7.5488	7.1196	6.7291	6.3729	6.0472	5.7487	5.4746	5.2223	4.9897	4.7746
18	16.3983	14.9920	13.7535	12.6593	11.6896	10.8276	10.0591	9.3719	8.7556	8.2014	7.7016	7.2497	6.8399	6.4674	6.1280	5.8179	5.5338	5.2732	5.0333	4.8122
19	17.2260	15.6785	14.3238	13.1339	12.0853	11.1581	10.3356	9.6036	8.9501	8.3649	7.8393	7.3658	6.9380	6.5504	6.1982	5.8775	5.5845	5.3162	5.0701	4.8435
20	18.0456	16.3514	14.8775	13.5903	12.4622	11.4699	10.5940	9.8181	9.1285	8.5136	7.9633	7.4694	7.0248	6.6231	6.2593	5.9288	5.6278	5.3527	5.1009	4.8696
25	22.0232	19.5234	17.4132	15.6221	14.0940	12.7834	11.6536	10.6748	9.8226	9.0770	8.4217	7.8431	7.3300	6.8729	6.4641	6.0971	5.7662	5.4669	5.1951	4.9476
30	25.8077	22.3964	19.6004	17.2920	15.3725	13.7649	12.4090	11.2578	10.2737	9.4269	8.6938	8.0552	7.4957	7.0027	6.5660	6.1772	5.8294	5.5168	5.2347	4.9789
40	32.8347	27.3555	23.1148	19.7928	17.1591	15.0464	13.3317	11.9246	10.7574	9.7791	8.9510	8.2438	7.6344	7.1051	6.6418	6.2335	5.8713	5.5482	5.2582	4.9966

Notation: $(P/A, n, i)$ where P = Present value; A = Ordinary annuity; n = Number of periods; and i = Interest rate.

APPENDIX • 10B

Special Present Value Computations: Bonds, Leases, and Pensions

VALUATION OF BONDS

Objective 11
Present value computations relating to bonds, leases, and pensions.

As discussed in the chapter, a bond is a contract between a debtor (the bond issuer) and a creditor (the bondholder) that promises distinct future cash flows at specific points in time. When a bond is offered to the market, the riskiness of the investment is evaluated by the potential buyers. Riskiness is a function of the probability of default or failure to pay the promised cash payments. For any given bond contract, the higher the perceived risk, the lower the selling price of the bond if all other factors are equal.

The selling price of a bond is the present value of future cash flows. Bonds usually have two types of cash payments: (1) a maturity amount and (2) an annual or semiannual annuity payment for nominal interest.

To illustrate how to determine bond selling prices, the following data for a bond is used:

Issue date:	January 1, 19x1
Maturity date:	December 31, 19x3
Maturity value:	$10,000
Nominal interest rate:	10% per year
Semiannual interest payment dates:	June 30 and December 31

Remember that no matter what the selling price is, this bond will pay the following fixed stream of payments:

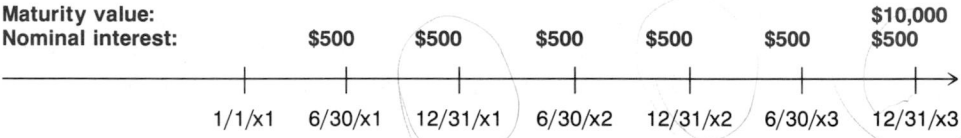

Total cash outflow per bond for the bond issuer is $13,000; that is, six $500 payments plus $10,000 at maturity. What are potential bondholders willing to pay?

Assume that the market demands a 12% per year return on bonds in this risk class. The 12% is this bond's **effective-interest rate.** The selling price, or proceeds, would be the sum of the present values of the annuity amounts and the maturity amount computed at 6% for six payments (half the annual rate and twice the number of years) because the bonds pay interest semiannually. Note that the effective-interest rate is used to value the bonds. The nominal rate merely establishes the cash flows.

$$(P/A, 6, .06)\$500 \quad = (4.9173)\$500 \quad = \$2,459$$
$$(P/F, 6, .06)\$10,000 = (.705)\$10,000 \quad = \$7,050$$
$$\text{Selling price} \ldots \ldots \ldots \ldots \quad \underline{\underline{\$9,509}}$$

Recall from Appendix 10A that the notation $(P/A, n, i)$ reads, "The present value P computed from a known ordinary annuity A with n periods and an effective interest rate of i" and $(P/F, A, i)$ reads, "The present value P computed from a known future amount F with n periods and an effective interest rate of i."

If the bonds paid interest annually and all other terms remained the same, the present values would be based on a 12% effective-interest rate for three periods, which is computed as follows:

Annual Payments

$(P/A, 3, .12)\$1,000 = (2.4018)\$1,000 = \$2,402$

$(P/F, 3, .12)\$10,000 = (.7118)\$10,000 = \underline{7,118}$

Selling price . . . . $\underline{\$9,520}$

In the cases of both semiannual and annual interest payments, this bond sells for a discount, which would be recorded as described earlier in this chapter.

Semiannual and annual payment schedules give slightly different total interest expense amounts because of more frequent compounding for the semiannual payments. Compare the amounts of total interest expense for the three years for each situation below:

Effective Annual Interest Rate	Timing of Payments			
	Semiannual		Annual	
12%	Cash outflow	\$13,000	Cash outflow	\$13,000
	Cash inflow	9,509	Cash inflow	9,520
	Total interest expense	\$ 3,491	Total interest expense	\$ 3,480
8%	Cash outflow	\$13,000	Cash outflow	\$13,000
	Cash inflow	10,524	Cash inflow	10,515
	Total interest expense	\$ 2,476	Total interest expense	\$ 2,485

Note that interest expense is total cash outflow to bondholders minus the cash inflow from the bondholders at issuance. Total nominal interest in all cases is $3,000. Selling the bonds at an effective-interest rate above the nominal interest rate increases the interest expense above $3,000, and selling the bonds at an effective-interest rate below the nominal interest rate decreases the interest expense below $3,000.

LEASES

Leases are contracts that give the lessee (the renter) the right to the use of property, plant, or equipment for a fixed amount of time with a fixed schedule of payments to the lessor (the owner). Consider the following lease contract:

A **lessor** owns an automobile that costs $18,000 on January 1, 19x1, and leases it to the **lessee** for five years, after which the title to the automobile is transferred to the lessee.

Since this lease contract transfers most of the rights and obligations of ownership to the lessee, it is called a capital lease and is recorded as a purchase of equipment by means of long-term borrowing. However, leases in which the lessor, the legal owner, keeps the risks and obligations of ownership are called operating leases, and payments for operating leases are recorded as rent expense. The paragraphs that follow discuss the capital lease of the automobile given in the lease contract example above.

If, in the automobile lease contract, the payments from the lessee to the lessor are equal year-end payments, can we compute the amount of each payment? This is an annuity valuation problem because the payments are equal payments separated by equal periods. If we assume that the lessor wants cash flows sufficient to recapture the $18,000 investment in the automobile plus an annual rate of return of 14%, the Table 10A–4 factors can be used in the following formula to determine the annuity payments:

$$(P/A, 5, .14)\,(\text{Annual lease payment}) = \$18{,}000$$

$$(\text{Annual lease payment}) = \$18{,}000/(P/A, 5, .14)$$

$$= \$18{,}000/3.4331$$

$$= \$5{,}243$$

The five $5,243 annual lease payments, therefore, have a present value of $18,000:

$$(P/A, 5, .14)\,(\$5{,}243) = \$18{,}000$$

$$(3.4331)\,(\$5{,}243) = \$18{,}000$$

Should the automobile be recorded on the lessee's books? A leased asset under the terms described above is recorded as an asset on the lessee's books, and a long-term liability is also recorded. The contract gives the lessee the right to use the automobile for five years and then the title is transferred to the lessee. In substance, that is the same as an outright purchase. The lessor effectively sold the automobile for the present value of the lease payments.

The following schedule summarizes the accounting for such a lease:

Date	Cash Flow	14% Interest	Change in Lease Receivable or Payable	Lease Receivable or Payable
1/1/x1	$ 0	$ 0	$18,000	$18,000
12/31/x1	5,243	2,520	(2,723)	15,277
12/31/x2	5,243	2,139	(3,104)	12,173
12/31/x3	5,243	1,704	(3,539)	8,634
12/31/x4	5,243	1,209	(4,034)	4,600
12/31/x5	5,243	643*	(4,600)	0
	$26,215	$8,215		

*Rounded.

The journal entries to record the lease on the lessor's and lessee's books would be as follows:

Lessor's Books			Lessee's Books		
19x1					
Jan. 1 Lease Receivable (A)	18,000		Leased Auto (A)	18,000	
Automobile (A)		18,000	Lease Payable (L)		18,000
To record lease.			To record lease.		
Dec. 31 Cash (A)	5,243		Interest Expense (E)	2,520	
Lease Receivable (A)		2,723	Lease Payable (L)	2,723	
Interest Revenue (R)		2,520	Cash (A)		5,243
To record receipt of lease payment.			To record payment on lease.		

Lessor's Books			**Lessee's Books**		
19x2					
Dec. 31 Cash (A)	5,243		Interest Expense (E)	2,139	
Lease Receivable (A)		3,104	Lease Payable (L)	3,104	
Interest Revenue (R)		2,139	Cash (A)		5,243
To record receipt of lease payment.			To record payment on lease.		
19x3					
Dec. 31 Cash (A)	5,243		Interest Expense (E)	1,704	
Lease Receivable (A)		3,539	Lease Payable (L)	3,539	
Interest Revenue (R)		1,704	Cash (A)		5,243
To record receipt of lease payment.			To record payment on lease.		
19x4					
Dec. 31 Cash (A)	5,243		Interest Expense (E)	1,209	
Lease Receivable (A)		4,034	Lease Payable (L)	4,034	
Interest Revenue (R)		1,209	Cash (A)		5,243
To record receipt of lease payment.			To record payment on lease.		
19x5					
Dec. 31 Cash (A)	5,243		Interest Expense (E)	643	
Lease Receivable (A)		4,600	Lease Payable (L)	4,600	
Interest Revenue (R)		643	Cash (A)		5,243
To record receipt of lease payment.			To record payment on lease.		

Note that in this case the lessor does not make a profit or gain on the "sale" of the automobile. When the lessor is a manufacturer, there is usually gross profit recognized in the normal way by the recording of sales revenue and cost of goods sold. Sales equal the present value of the future lease payments, and cost of goods sold equals the cost of inventory sold. The lessee would also depreciate the automobile over its useful life in the normal fashion.

The critical issue in accounting for leases is to determine whether the lease is to be accounted for as a capital-type lease (a purchase), as illustrated above, or simply a rental agreement (operating-type lease). To help determine whether or not a lease is a capital lease, the FASB has identified the following four conditions, any one of which causes the lease to be treated as a capital lease by the lessee:[4]

1. Title is transferred to the lessee.
2. The lessee has the option of purchasing the asset in the future at a bargain price (a price below its fair market value).
3. The lease term is 75% or more of the leased property's economic life.
4. The present value of the minimum scheduled lease payments is equal to at least 90% of leased property's fair market value.

These conditions also apply to the lessor; therefore, when a lessee treats a lease as a long-term purchase agreement (a capital lease), the lessor normally treats it as a sale in which financing is provided to facilitate the lessee's purchase. Many variations in lease payments exist, all of which may affect the accounting of lessors and lessees. These topics are covered in detail in intermediate accounting texts.

---

[4]Refer to *FASB Statement No. 13*, "Accounting for Leases" (Norwalk, Conn.: FASB, 1976).

A Conversation about Substance over Form— The Effect of a Lease on the Financial Statements

Jill Petro, the president of Petro Advertisers, is discussing the purchase of a company aircraft with her chief accountant, Bernie Best. Bernie has just concluded his presentation of an analysis of the relative costs of the staff's flying on commercial carriers versus a company-owned jet.

Accountant: J. P., from a pure dollars and cents perspective, it is cheaper to use the airlines, but that doesn't factor in the delay time and customer satisfaction. I look at this as having a customer relations aspect, anyway, so it's hard to quantify the benefits. The bottom line, J. P., is that I recommend the purchase.

President: OK! Review the major costs for me once more.

Accountant: I'll put up slide 1 again.

SLIDE 1
Estimated Yearly Costs of Purchasing and Operating a Surecraft 505.M

Aircraft purchase price.	$5,000,000
Aircraft yearly cost:	
Salaries	150,000
Hanger fees, fuel, insurance, and maintenance . . .	200,000
Depreciation (book)	500,000
Tax savings.	(100,000)
Total yearly cost	$ 750,000
Yearly airline travel to be eliminated.	600,000
Excess yearly cost	$ 150,000

President: I think it would be worth $150,000 in customer relations alone. I know of several cases where we could have landed big accounts if we had that kind of flexibility to bring people together. Now how do we pay for it? Can we lease it and not have to borrow more money?

Accountant: Well, Surecraft has a leasing option, but even if we lease it, we still probably would have to show the liability on the balance sheet, for the amount of the purchase price initially, and of course reduced by the principal payments after that.

President: You mean for one year's rent, don't you?

Accountant: No, for the present value of the required payments under the lease, which in this case equals the total purchase price.

President: You're telling me, that if I rent this plane and have a legal lease contract, your accounting rules would still force me to show a liability, just as if I had borrowed money to purchase it?

Accountant: Listen, J. P., think about it from our bankers' perspective. We sign this noncancellable contract that obliges us to make periodic payments whose present value equals the purchase price, and we use the equipment for its useful life, pay the insurance, and do the maintenance and everything else an owner would do. Does a banker who reads our balance sheet care if it's a loan or a lease?

President: What about taxes? Do they allow us to deduct depreciation as if we had purchased it?

Accountant: For the most part, that's our option and in this case, given the contract Surecraft has offered, I believe we will be able to capitalize and depreciate the aircraft for tax purposes.

President: So, for accounting and tax purposes, you guys just look at it as if it were a purchase. Our bankers won't like that liability, but I guess they'll get used to it.

The above conversation makes two major points. First, the business decision to purchase the aircraft did not depend on a purely quantifiable analysis. As you can see, the purchase option is expected to cost the company $150,000 more than the status quo, but there are other benefits that overcome this. Second, it provides an example of why the economic substance of a contract or transaction is more important than its form. Keep in mind, however, that it is often crucial that the form be completely understood in order that the substance not be overlooked.

PENSIONS

Pension plans are of two major types: (1) defined contribution plans in which certain amounts are contributed to a fund by the employer with no guarantees about future retirement benefits, and (2) defined benefit plans, in which the employer guarantees specific amounts of benefits during retirement. Accounting for defined contribution plans is simple, the contribution to the plan is merely debited to Pension Expense and credited to Cash.

Accounting for defined benefit plans is quite complex, however, and we will only touch on the fundamentals here. The major challenge is determining the expense amounts applicable to any one period. For instance, a plan gives an employee $3,000 at the end of each year of retirement for each year of service. The employee works for five years and is expected to collect five years of pension payments. How much expense is charged to each of the five years of service?

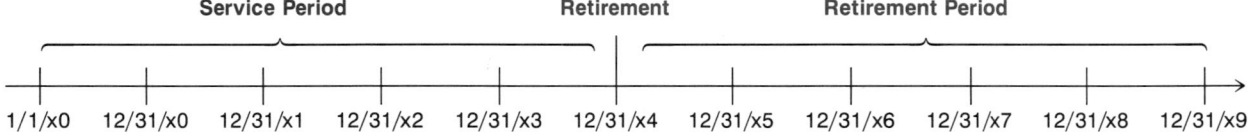

For the first year, what is the employer's obligation at December 31, 19x0? What amount must the employer put aside to provide the employee with retirement benefits in the future? The benefit the employee has earned after working one year is $3,000 for each year of retirement. If we assume a 10% interest rate for all computations, the obligation at December 31, 19x0, is the present value of an annuity of $3,000 per year for five years starting on December 31, 19x5.

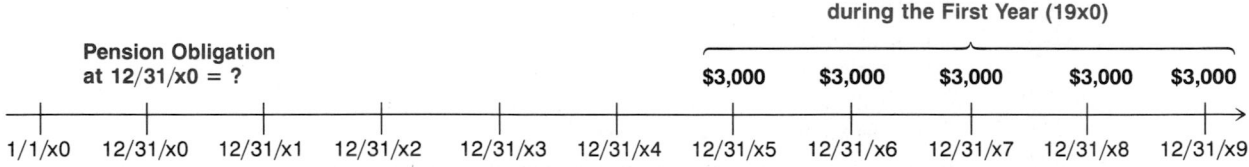

The computation is as follows:

1. $(P/A, 5, .10)\$3,000$ = Present value at 12/31/x4
   $(3.7908)\$3,000 = \$11,372$

2. $(P/F, 4, .10)\$11,372$ = Present value at 12/31/x0
   $(.683)\$11,372 = \$7,767.$

The first part of this two-part computation requires the computation of the present value of the retirement annuity as of the retirement date. This gives the amount needed on December 31, 19x4, to provide withdrawals of $3,000 per year for five years: $(P/A, 5, .10)\$3,000 = \$11,372$. The second part is the computation of the amount at December 31, 19x0, that if invested at compound annual interest of 10% would provide a fund of \$11,372 at December 31, 19x4: $(P/F, 4, .10)\$11,372 = \$7,767$. As depicted in Exhibit 10B–1, the pension obligation is \$7,767 at December 31, 19x0; and if cash is paid, the accounting entry would be as follows:

```
19x0
Dec. 31   Pension Expense (E) . . . . . . . . . . . . . . . . . . . . . .   7,767
               Cash (A) . . . . . . . . . . . . . . . . . . . . . . . . .          7,767
          To record 19x0 pension expense.
```

The year 19x0, therefore, has pension expense of \$7,767. That amount is put into a fund that will grow to \$11,372 by the date of retirement if 10% is earned and compounded. The fund will continue to grow, and \$3,000 per year could be paid to the retiree for five years before the fund would be depleted. Of course, the second, third, fourth, and fifth years would have to be funded in a like manner if the employee is to receive the full pension of \$15,000 per year during retirement, 19x5–19x9.[5]

The actual computations and accounting rules used in pensions are beyond the scope of this text and are covered in intermediate accounting texts.

• KEY TERMS

Bond indenture. Contract that describes all rights and obligations of all parties to the bonds.

Bonds. Any of a series of debt contracts with varying terms, usually involving fixed semiannual or annual interest payments and a fixed maturity amount.

Bond sinking fund. Cash set aside and accumulated over the life of the bond issue to be used to pay off the bonds at maturity.

Compound interest. Interest charged on both the unpaid principal and any unpaid interest accrued after the inception of the liability.

Convertibility. Feature in bonds that allows for the bond to be converted into capital stock.

Covenants. Provisions in loan agreements that govern certain debtor actions and specify conditions under which loans must be repaid before maturity.

Debt financing. Long-term borrowing from creditors.

Discount. Created when a bond sells for less than the face value, suggesting that the market considers the stated interest rate to be lower than the market's required rate of interest.

Effective-interest method. Interest expense for the period is computed by applying the market interest rate to the net liability balance (carrying value) at the beginning of the period.

Effective-interest rate. The rate of return on an investment determined by market forces; also called yield rate.

Equity financing. Issuance of capital stock to the stockholders of a business.

Junior debt. Unsecured or subordinated debt that relies on the general creditworthiness of the debtor; also called unsecured or subordinated debt.

Junk bonds. High-yield, subordinated debentures.

Leveraged buyouts (LBOs). Financing arrangements by which management and/or others gain control of a corporation by means of stock purchases financed by combinations of new investment and the issuance of debt, often in the form of junk bonds.

Nominal interest rate. Interest rate stated on the face of a debt instrument, such as a note or a bond.

---

[5]*FASB Statement No. 87*, "Employer's Accounting for Pensions" (Norwalk, Conn.: FASB, 1985).

EXHIBIT 10B–1

**History of Pension Fund
Needed for 19x1 Service**

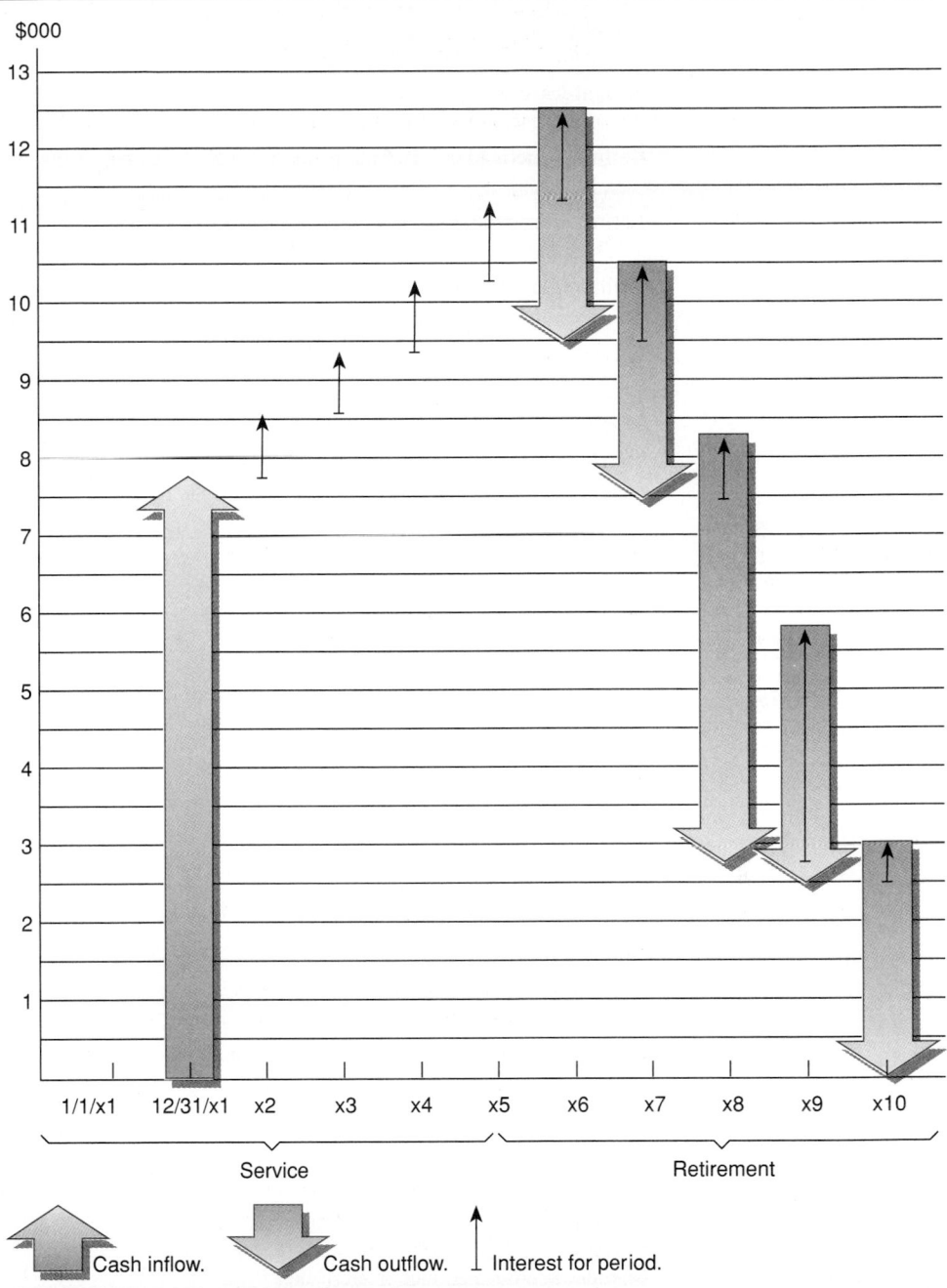

$000

| 1/1/x1 | 12/31/x1 | x2 | x3 | x4 | x5 | x6 | x7 | x8 | x9 | x10 |

Service

Retirement

Cash inflow. Cash outflow. Interest for period.

Premium. Created when a bond sells for more than its face value, indicating that the stated rate of interest on the bond is above the rate required by the market.

Secured. Said of a loan backed by assets that are pledged as collateral.

Senior debt. Liability that is secured by mortgages pledged to specific assets.

Straight-line method. Method used to amortize a bond premium or discount in which equal amounts are amortized each period.

• Appendix Key Terms

Annuities. Payments of equal amounts separated by equal periods of time. Ordinary annuities are paid at the end of each period.

Capital lease. Lease contract that transfers most of the rights and obligations of ownership to the lessee; recorded as purchase of equipment by means of long-term borrowing.

Defined benefit plans. Pension plans in which the employer guarantees specific amounts of benefits.

Defined contribution plans. Pension plans in which certain amounts are contributed with no guarantees about benefits.

Future value. Value that an investment today will grow to in a stated time in the future at a specified interest rate.

Leases. Contracts that give the lessee the right to the use of property, plant, or equipment for a fixed amount of time with a fixed schedule of payments to the lessor (the owner).

Lessee. The renter named in a lease.

Lessor. The owner named in a lease.

Operating leases. Leases in which the lessor, the legal owner, keeps the risks and obligations of ownership.

Present value. The current value of a future payment given an effective-interest rate and a known number of periods.

Proceeds. The net amount received in a bond transaction; the selling price.

• SYNONYMS

Collateral; pledged asset; mortgaged asset; security.

Coupon bonds; bearer bonds.

Covenants; loan provisions.

Creditors; providers of debt financing.

Debt financing; borrowing.

Default; nonrepayment.

Equity financing; stock issuance.

Equityholders; stockholders; equity owners.

Face interest rate; nominal interest rate; coupon rate.

Face value; maturity value.

Junior debt; unsecured debt; subordinated debt.

Long-term; noncurrent

Market interest rate; yield rate; effective-interest rate.

Net liability; carrying value

Nominal interest rate; face interest rate.

Principal; amount borrowed.

Unsecured; debentured; subordinated.

Unsecured bonds; debentures.

• QUESTIONS

1. Differentiate between debt financing and equity financing. How does each group receive a return on its investment?
2. Describe four common cash flow patterns regarding long-term liabilities.
3. What is the difference between an interest-bearing note and a noninterest-bearing note? How are they similar?
4. Describe two different methods of recording a note payable.
5. Define bonds. Describe the differences between what happens when bonds are sold at face value, at a discount, and at a premium.
6. Why do bonds sell in the market for more or less than their face value?
7. What is the market saying when a $1,000, 8%, 10-year bond is sold at 104?
8. Describe the two methods for amortizing a bond discount or a bond premium.
9. What is the difference between an adjunct account and a contra account?
10. Explain the convertibility feature of a bond.
11. Describe the use of a bond sinking fund.
12. Compute the total amount of cash received from the sale of a $1,000, 6%, five-year bond that pays interest semiannually on June 30 and December 31 and is sold on March 1 at 95. Why does this bond sell at a discount?
13. What is an amortization schedule? How does it relate to the account balances?
14. Given that you know the amount borrowed and the date of maturity, does it make a difference in the total cash paid back if the periodic payments of interest are annual or semiannual? Explain.
15. What is the general rule for determining the effective interest expense for an outstanding liability?

· Appendix Questions

16. Differentiate between compound and simple interest.
17. Define the term *annuity*.
18. List the four conditions used to test whether a lease is a capital or an operating lease.
19. What two major types of pensions exist? How are they different?
20. What makes defined benefits plans so complex?
21. Why is the determination of substance over form crucial in accounting for leases?
22. If the future value of an obligation is fixed, how will varying the interest rate affect the present value?

• EXERCISES

E 10–1
Multiple Choice
L.O.1–9

1. Debt and equity financing are different in that—
   a. Debt financing results in payments to outsiders and equity financing does not.
   b. Equity financing adds to the interest burden of the company and debt financing does not.
   c. Interest payments reduce net income and dividend payments do not.
   d. Interest payments are in cash and dividend payments are in stock.
   e. None of the above.
2. What can be said of the priority of payments to creditors and stockholders upon termination of a business?
   a. All stockholders are paid dividends before creditors are paid interest.
   b. Senior debt is paid first, stockholder dividends second, and junior debt last.
   c. The priority depends on the issue date of the stock and the maturity date of the debt.
   d. Debt always has priority over stock.
   e. None of the above.
3. The book value of a liability—
   a. Equals the initial amount borrowed plus all interest paid to date.
   b. Equals the unpaid amount of principal plus the unpaid interest.

    c. Never exceeds the amount of the first principal payment.

    d. Equals the difference between all cash inflow and all cash outflow related to the obligation.

    e. None of the above.

4. Total interest expense over the life of an obligation—

    a. Is affected by the speed of repayment of the principal.

    b. Is unaffected by the speed of the repayment of the principal.

    c. Is recorded as an expense only when the cash payments are made.

    d. Is equal to total cash flow out related to the obligation.

    e. None of the above.

5. Long-term noninterest-bearing notes—

    a. Result in no interest expense to the issuer.

    b. Result in no interest expense to the issuer until the final payment of principal.

    c. Have higher total interest than a comparable interest-bearing note.

    d. Always have a book value equal to the principal.

    e. None of the above.

6. Bonds are sold—

    a. At a discount if the nominal interest rate equals the effective-interest rate.

    b. At a discount if the nominal interest rate exceeds the effective-interest rate.

    c. At a discount if the nominal interest rate is less than the effective-interest rate.

    d. At a discount if the issuer is a relatively risky company.

    e. None of the above.

7. Using the straight-line amortization method for a discount—

    a. Results in total interest expense over the life of the bond being greater than if the effective-interest amortization method is used.

    b. Results in total interest expense over the life of the bond being less than if the effective-interest amortization method is used.

    c. Results in total interest expense over the life of the bond being the same as if the effective-interest amortization method is used.

    d. Is inappropriate for a bond sold at a price below its face value.

    e. None of the above.

8. The effective-interest method of amortizing a bond discount—

    a. Results in equal amounts of interest expense being charged to each period during the life of the bond.

    b. Results in increasing amounts of interest expense being charged to each subsequent period during the life of the bond.

    c. Results in the bonds' payable book value remaining at the maturity value throughout the life of the bond.

    d. Results in less precise interest expense amounts than would be the case under the straight-line method.

    e. None of the above.

9. A premium on a bond—

    a. Results in a contra account being used.

    b. Results in interest expense being greater than if the bond had been sold at a discount.

    c. Is always amortized using the straight-line method.

    d. Results from the nominal interest rate of the bond being less than the effective-interest rate at the date of issue.

    e. None of the above.

10. Bond retirements—

    a. Result in the elimination of all liability balances related to the bond.

    b. May result in gains but never losses.

    c. Result in losses for bonds originally sold at a discount.

    d. Are not allowed if there is any unamortized premium or discount amounts remaining before retirement.

    e. None of the above.

11. A bond sinking fund—
    a. Creates a liability as the fund increases.
    b. Results in expenses equal to contributions to the fund.
    c. Reduces interest expense recorded on the bonds.
    d. Insures that the exact money amount of the principal will be available at maturity.
    e. None of the above.

E 10–2
Common Traits of
Long-Term Liabilities
L.O.2

Jack's Carwash borrows $600,000 at 8% on January 1, 19x1, to be repaid on December 31, 19x4. Consider the following payment terms independently:

a. December 31 year-end payments of $150,000 plus interest on the unpaid balance.
b. Payment of interest only on December 31 of each year and principal on December 31, 19x4.
c. Payment of principal and total interest on December 31, 19x4.
d. Four equal payments of $181,152 on each year-end.

Required:
Prepare an amortization schedule for each of the above payment schemes showing cash inflow and outflow, interest expense for each period, and the net liability at the end of each of the four years. (Round to nearest dollar.)

E 10–3
Long-Term Note Payable
L.O.3

On January 1, 19x1, the Alpha Company negotiated a $200,000 mortgage loan from the Beta Bank. The loan principal and interest are to be repaid in five equal annual installments of $52,760 beginning January 1, 19x2. The loan bears interest at an annual interest rate of 10%. Prepare the journal entries to record the issuance of the note, interest expense, and the five annual installments. Alpha Company's year-end is December 31. (Round to the nearest dollar.)

E 10–4
Interest-Bearing and
Noninterest-Bearing
Notes
L.O.3

The following two notes are issued on January 1, 19x1:

a. $200,000, 10%, two-year note with principal and interest due on December 31, 19x2.
b. $242,000 note due on December 31, 19x2.

The company received $200,000 for each note on January 1, 19x1.

Required:
1. Prepare the journal entries in general journal form to record the issuance of each note, any adjusting entries required, and payment of each note on December 31, 19x2.
2. Show the balance sheet disclosure for each note on December 31, 19x1.

E 10–5
Bond Issuance, Interest,
and Retirement
L.O.5, 6

On January 1, 19x1, the King Corporation issued 7%, 20-year bonds at their face value of $1 million. Interest is payable semiannually on June 30 and December 31.

Required:
Prepare the journal entries in general journal form to record the following:

1. The bond issuance.
2. The first two years of interest payments.
3. Retirement of the bonds at face value at the end of year 20.

E 10–6
Bonds, Discount,
and Straight-Line
Amortization
L.O.5

On January 1, 19x4, the Holst Company issued and sold 600, $1,000 par value, 10%, 10-year bonds when the market interest rate was 8%. The bonds sold for $668,709. Interest is payable each January 1. Holst uses the straight-line amortization method for amortizing bond discount or premium. Show the balance sheet presentation of these bonds on December 31, 19x4. (Round to the nearest dollar.)

E 10–7
Bonds sold at a Discount
L.O.5

Holland Corporation issued $100,000 of five-year bonds with a face value of $1,000 each and 8% interest payable semiannually. The bonds were sold on January 1, 19x1, for $92,278 yielding a 10% effective-interest rate. Compute the total amount of interest expense on these bonds over their five-year life.

E 10–8
Bonds Sold at a Premium
L.O.5

Maker Corporation issued $100,000 in 12% bonds on January 1, 19x1. The bonds pay semiannual interest on June 30 and December 31 each year and were sold for $112,463 for an effective-interest rate of 10%. The bonds mature in 10 years. Compute the interest expense for the first six months of 19x1 using the effective-interest method. (Round to the nearest dollar.)

E 10–9
Bond Conversion
L.O.8

On March 31, 19x4, Turner Electronics converts 100, $1,000 face value bonds with a net book value of $98,800 to 1,000 shares of its capital stock valued at $98.80 per share. The bonds pay 10% semi-annually on June 30 and December 31. Bond interest for the period has not yet been paid but has been accrued to compute the net book value of the bonds.

Required:
Prepare the journal entries to record the interest payment and conversion of the bonds.

E 10–10
Bond Sinking Fund
L.O.9

The Sommers Company established a bond sinking fund to provide funds for the repayment of a $300,000 outstanding bond issue. The bonds mature on December 31, 19x6. The company will make six equal deposits of $43,000 each to the fund each December 31 with the first deposit being made on December 31, 19x1. Deposits to the fund earn interest at a 6% annual interest rate.

Required:
1. Prepare the journal entries in general journal form for the establishment of the fund and the annual payments and interest earned on the fund.
2. Prepare the journal entries in general journal form for the payment of the bonds on December 31, 19x6.
3. Compute total interest earned by the bond sinking fund over the six-year period.

E 10–11
Bond Issuance between Interest Dates
L.O.5, 7

Bozo Corporation issued $100,000 of 12% stated interest, five-year bonds on April 1, 19x5. The bonds pay interest semiannually on June 30 and December 31 and straight-line amortization is used. The total cash received at the date of sale was $103,000.

Required:
1. Show the necessary journal entry (entries) on April 1, 19x5.
2. Show the necessary journal entry (entries) on June 30, 19x5.
3. Show the necessary journal entry (entries) on December 31, 19x5.

E 10–12
Bond Issuance between Interest Dates
L.O.5, 7

On September 1, 19x1, the Yates Company, which has a December 31 year-end, sold 1,000, $10,000, 8%, five-year bonds at face value plus accrued interest. The bonds were dated June 30, 19x1, and interest is payable annually each June 30.

Required:
Prepare the journal entries in general journal form to record the following (round to the nearest dollar):

1. The sale of the bonds on September 1, 19x1.
2. Adjustment on December 31, 19x1.
3. The first interest payment.

E 10–13
Bonds Sold at a Discount
L.O.5

Dorek, Inc., issued $400,000 of ten-year bonds, each with a face value of $10,000 and a coupon interest rate of 10%, payable annually. The bonds all sold on January 1, 19x4, for $316,524, resulting in an effective-interest rate of 14%.

Required (round all answers to dollars):
1. Compute the interest expense to be recorded in 19x4.
2. Compute the total cash interest payments over the life of the bonds.
3. Compute the total interest expense recorded over the life of the bonds.

E 10–14
Coupon versus Effective Interest (Challenging)
L.O.5

Some years ago Brant Corporation issued bonds that would have a maturity value of $100,000 on November 1, 19x6. A portion of the bond amortization table relating to the issue appears below:

Date	Annual Interest Payment	Annual Interest Expense	Premium Amortization	Net Liability
—	—	—	—	—
11/1/x1	—	—	—	$102,195
11/1/x2	$5,000	$4,599	$401	101,794
11/1/x3	5,000	4,581	419	101,375
11/1/x4	5,000	4,562	438	100,937
11/1/x5	5,000	4,531	458	100,479
11/1/x6	5,000	4,521	479	100,000

Required:
1. What was the effective-interest rate on these bonds at issuance?
2. What is the coupon rate of interest on these bonds?
3. Assume the bonds had been issued on November 1, 19x1, for $102,195. What would be the total interest expense over the life of the bond issue? What would be the total cash outflow minus the total cash inflow over the life of the bond issue?

· **Appendix Exercises** ───────────────────────────────

E 10–15
Multiple Choice
L.O.10, 11

1. If you were trying to compute the amount you needed to invest today to pay for a new car three years hence you would have to compute which of the following?
   a. The future value of a known present amount.
   b. The future value of a known ordinary annuity.
   c. The present value of a known future amount.
   d. The present value of a known ordinary annuity.
   e. None of the above.
2. If you were trying to determine how much to put into an investment account now so that you could withdraw $5,000 at the end of each of the next five years you would compute which of the following?
   a. The future value of a known present amount.
   b. The future value of a known ordinary annuity.
   c. The present value of a known future amount.
   d. The present value of a known ordinary annuity.
   e. None of the above.
3. A capital lease usually reflects the following relationship:
   a. The future value of the annual lease payments equals the initial value of the leased asset.
   b. The present value of the annual lease payments equals the initial value of the leased asset.
   c. The initial lease liability on the lessee's books is zero and it grows to equal the initial value of the leased asset at the end of the lease period.
   d. The lessee does not record the leased asset or the lease liability but rather recognizes rent expense each period.
   e. None of the above.
4. A defined benefits pension plan usually—
   a. Results in total pension expense over the service life of the employee equaling the sum of all cash pension payments to the retiree.
   b. Results in total pension expense over the service life of the employee exceeding the sum of all cash pension payments to the retiree.
   c. Results in total pension expense over the service life of the employee being less than the the sum of all cash pension payments to the retiree.
   d. Results in no pension expense being recorded as long as interest is earned by the pension fund.
   e. None of the above.

(FIP, 8,0,06)

E 10–16
Present Values
L.O.10

1. Compute the future values of the following amounts:
   a. $16,000 in eight years at 6% compounded annually.
   b. $25,000 in 10 years at 8% compounded semiannually.
   c. $82,000 in two years at 16% compounded quarterly.
2. Compute the present value (compounded annually) of the following amounts:
   a. $100,000, 6%, five years.
   b. $19,000, 10%, 10 years.
   c. $35,000, 12%, three years.
3. Compute the future value (compounded annually) of the following ordinary annuities:
   a. $6,000, five years, 10%.
   b. $3,000, 10 years, 15%.
   c. $150,000, three years, 12%.
4. Compute the present value (compounded annually) of the following ordinary annuities:
   a. $25,000, 4%, eight years.
   b. $160,000, 10%, five years.
   c. $100,000, 5%, 10 years.

E 10–17
Bond Issuance—
Computing Proceeds
L.O.10, 11

On January 1, 19x6, the King Corporation issued $1 million face value, 7% 10-year bonds. Interest is payable semiannually on June 30 and December 31.

Required:
1. Calculate the proceeds of the bond issue if the market interest rate is 8%.
2. Calculate the proceeds of the bond issue if the market interest rate is 6%.

E 10–18
Computing Bond Proceeds
(Appendix 10B)
L.O.10

On January 1, 19x1, Jaybar Corporation sold 5% bonds with a face value of $100,000. These bonds mature in 20 years, and interest is paid annually on December 31. The bonds were sold to yield 6%.

Required:
1. Compute the proceeds from the sale of Jaybar bonds.
2. Using the effective-interest method of computing interest, how much should be charged (debited) to interest expense in 19x1?

E 10–19
Financing Alternatives
L.O.10, 11

Jacobs Corporation has the option of purchasing a computer system in one of two ways:

1. $118,250 cash now.
2. $17,425 at the end of each of the next 10 years ($0 down), starting one year from now.

Required:
1. Determine which option is the best one to take and explain your choice.
2. Would your answer differ if option 2 required 10 year-end payments of $25,000? Of $11,825? Explain.

E 10–20
Leases
(Challenging)
L.O.10, 11

Baker entered into a lease purchase agreement for a fleet of ships. The ships had a fair market value of $196,360,000 at the date of the lease, were expected to last 20 more years (no scrap value, straight-line depreciation), and the lease called for annual year-end payments of $20 million for the next 20 years. This results in an implicit interest rate of 8%.

Required:
1. Determine the total interest expense over the life of the lease.
2. What would be the balance in the net lease liability at the end of 15 years (after the payment for year 15)? Hint: Calculate the present value of the remaining payments.

E 10–21
Leases
(Challenging)
L.O.10, 11

Bartlett Corporation leased equipment from Henderson, Inc., on January 1, 19x1, by signing a five-year lease contract calling for an $80,000 payment on January 1, 19x1, and five additional annual payments of $100,000 each subsequent December 31. The effective-interest rate in the lease agreement is 10%.

Required:

Compute the total amount of interest expense for Bartlett Corporation over the life of the lease. Hint: Compute the present value of all cash payments and compare that amount to the total cash payments.

• PROBLEMS

P 10–1
Straight-Line and Effective-Interest Amortization Methods
L.O.5

Assume that a company sells the following bonds:

Face value:	$100,000
Stated interest rate:	8%
Interest payment dates:	April 1 and October 1
Date sold:	April 1, 19x1
Term:	Four years

Required:

1. Complete an amortization table using the straight-line method assuming that the bond selling price, $93,533, provides an effective-interest rate of 10%. (Round all calculations to the nearest dollar.)
2. Complete an amortization table using the effective-interest method assuming that the bond selling price, $93,533, provides an effective-interest rate of 10%. (Round all calculations to the nearest dollar.)

P 10–2
Bonds Issued between Interest Dates
L.O.5, 7

The Ogihara Company is authorized to issue 1,000, $1,000, 9%, 10-year bonds. The bonds are dated March 1, 19x1, and interest is payable semiannually on March 1 and September 1. The following transactions occurred regarding the bonds:

19x1
Apr. 1   Sold 500 bonds for $500,000 plus accrued interest.
Sept. 1   Paid the semiannual interest.
Dec. 1   Sold the remaining 500 bonds for $500,000 plus accrued interest.
   31   Accrued interest for the year-end financial statements.
19x2
Mar. 1   Paid the semiannual interest.

Required:

Record the above transactions assuming that premiums and discounts are amortized at each interest payment date and at year-end using the straight-line method. Record all computations to nearest dollar.

P 10–3
Bonds and Discounts
L.O.5

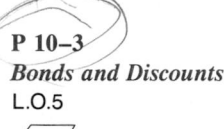

effe

The Brandy Company issued 2,000, $1,000, 8%, 10-year bonds on July 1, 19x1, when the market interest rate was 10%. The proceeds from the issue were $1,750,776. Interest is paid semiannually on June 30 and December 31 of each year, with the first payment being made on December 31, 19x1. The company closes its books on December 31 and recognizes amortization at the time of each interest payment.

Required (round to the nearest dollar):

1. Prepare the journal entry to record the issuance of the bonds on July 1, 19x1.
2. Prepare the journal entries related to the bond issue on December 31, 19x1, and June 30, 19x2, assuming that the company uses the straight-line method for amortization of bond discount or premium.
3. Repeat part 2 using the effective-interest method for amortization of bond discount or premium.

P 10–4
Bonds and Premiums
L.O.5

The Enchilada Corporation issued $100,000 of 10% interest, 20-year bonds on January 1, 19x6. The bonds pay interest semiannually on July 1 and January 1. The bonds were issued for $119,765 to yield an effective-interest rate of 8%. The fiscal year-end is December 31.

Required (round to the nearest dollar):
1. Prepare the entry (entries) to record the issuance of these bonds and to account for their interest for the remainder of 19x6. Use the effective-interest method for amortization of any discount or premium.
2. Compute the total interest expense recorded over the 20-year life of the bond issue.
3. Repeat parts 1 and 2 using the straight-line method for amortization of any discount or premium.

P 10–5
*Bond Discount
and Premium*
L.O.5

The Winston Company sold 50, $1,000, 14% bonds on January 1, 19x1. Interest is payable on June 30 and December 31 of each year. The bonds mature on December 31, 19x4. The company uses the effective-interest amortization method of amortizing bond discount or premium.

Required:
1. Prepare a bond amortization schedule for the four-year period assuming that the proceeds from the bond issue are $53,105. The market interest rate on January 1, 19x1, is 12%. (Round numbers to the nearest dollar.)
2. Prepare a bond amortization schedule for the four-year period assuming that the proceeds from the bond issue are $47,125. The market interest rate on January 1, 19x1, is 16%. (Round numbers to the nearest dollar.)

P 10–6
*Bonds Sold at
a Discount*
L.O.5

Superior Corporation sold a $200,000, 12% bond issue on November 1, 19x1, at 96.5% of maturity value. The bonds were dated November 1, 19x1, and pay interest semiannually on April 30 and October 31. The bonds mature on October 31, 19x5. Superior Corporation uses the straight-line method of amortizing bond discount or premium. Superior's fiscal year ends on December 31.

Required (round to the nearest dollar):
1. Prepare the journal entry to record the sale of the bonds on November 1, 19x1.
2. Prepare the adjusting journal entry required at December 31, 19x1.
3. Show how bonds payable should be reported on the December 31, 19x1, annual financial statement.
4. Prepare the journal entry to record the interest payment on April 30, 19x2.

P 10–7
*Bond Issuance at a
Premium, Interest,
and Retirement*
L.O.5, 6

On January 1, 19x1, the Illini Company issues 10-year bonds of $100,000 at $114,877 for an effective-interest rate of 6%. Interest is payable on December 31 and June 30 at an annual rate of 8%. On July 1, 19x4, the Illini Company reacquires and retires 20% of its own $1,000 bonds at 98. The fiscal period for the Illini Company is the calendar year. The company uses the effective-interest rate method of bond discount or premium amortization.

Required:
1. Prepare the journal entries to record the issuance of the bonds and an amortization schedule through June 30, 19x4.
2. Prepare the journal entries relating to the payment of interest and amortization of discount or premium on December 31, 19x3.
3. Prepare the journal entries to record the reacquisition and retirement of 20% of the bonds on July 1, 19x4.

P 10–8
*Bond Issuance at a
Discount, Interest,
and Retirement
(Challenging)*
L.O.5, 6, 7

Floate Company sold 100 of their $1,000, 8%, 10-year bonds at $87,539, a price that creates an effective interest of 10%. The bonds were sold on January 1, 19x1, with interest payable on June 30 and December 31. The following transactions occurred regarding these bonds:

a. Sale of the bonds on January 1, 19x1.
b. Payment of the semiannual interest and amortization of the discount on June 30, 19x1.
c. Payment of the semiannual interest and amortization of the discount on December 31, 19x1.
d. Assuming that the unamortized discount amounted to $1,862 on December 31, 19x9, after recording the 12/31/x9 payment, make the entry to record the final two interest payments and to retire the bond at maturity.

Required:

Prepare the journal entries in general journal form using the effective-interest method of amortizing the discount for the above transactions. Round all computations to the nearest dollar.

P 10–9
Bond Sale and
Conversion
(Challenging)
L.O.7, 8

Arb Products authorized the issuance of $400,000 of 10-year bonds with a 9% coupon on January 1, 19x0. The bonds pay interest semiannually on June 30 and December 31, and mature on December 31, 19x9. All of the bonds are convertible into common stock of Arb Products after December 31, 19x4, at the rate of 20 shares of Arb no par common for every $1,000 face value bond. Arb common was selling for $35 per share on March 1, 19x0, but by January 31, 19x5, Arb common was trading at $62 per share. On January 31, 19x5, one-half of the bonds were exchanged for 4,000 shares of Arb common stock. Arb uses straight-line amortization for bond discounts or premiums. Accrued interest is paid to the bondholders who convert to common stock up to the date of the exchange.

Required:

1. Record the issuance of these bonds at $404,720 plus accrued interest on March 1, 19x0.
2. Record the interest payments for 19x0.
3. Record the conversion of one-half of the bonds on January 31, 19x5.
4. Record the interest payment for June 30, 19x6, for the remaining one-half of the bonds.

P 10–10
Premium Bonds and
Partial Retirement
L.O.5, 6

Protak Corporation issued $400,000 of five-year bonds on January 1, 19x4. The bonds had a stated interest rate of 10%, paid semiannually, and were sold for $432,458 at a yield of 8%.

Required:

1. Compute the interest expense to be recorded in 19x4.
2. Compute the total cash interest payments over the life of the bonds.
3. Compute the total interest expense recorded over the life of the bonds.
4. Assume that Protak repurchases and retires $100,000 face value of bonds on January 1, 19x5, for $105,000. Record the retirement of these bonds.

P 10–11
Alternative Repayment
Schemes
(Challenging)
L.O.2, 3

On January 1, 19x1, the General Trucking Company borrows $20 million from Union Bank. The loan is at 10% annual interest for four years.

Required:

1. Assume that the loan requires one lump sum payment at 12/31/x4. Prepare an amortization schedule for General Trucking that shows interest expense for each year and in total.
2. Assume that General Trucking agrees to repay the loan with equal principal payments of $5 million each December 31, plus accrued interest for the year. Prepare an amortization schedule that shows interest expense for each year and in total.
3. Assume that General Trucking agrees to repay the $20 million on December 31, 19x4, and accrued interest once each year on December 31. Prepare an amortization schedule that shows interest expense for each year and in total.
4. Assume that General Trucking agrees to repay the loan with four equal payments of $6,309,347. Prepare an amortization schedule that shows interest expense each year and in total.
5. Which repayment scheme calls for the most interest? Why?
6. Which repayment scheme is like a zero coupon (noninterest-bearing) bond or note (also called a deep discount bond/note)? Explain.
7. Which repayment scheme is like a bond sold at face value? Explain.

• Appendix Problems

P 10–12
Bonds—Determining
Proceeds
L.O.5, 10, 11

Determine the proceeds that will be received if bonds are sold under the following circumstances. Prepare the journal entries in general journal form to record these sales:

a. $3 million of 8%, 10-year bonds sold on January 2 with interest payable June 30 and December 31 priced to yield an effective rate of 8%.
b. $3 million of 8%, 10-year bonds sold on January 2 with interest payable June 30 and December 31 priced to yield 12%.

c. $3 million of 12%, 10-year bonds sold on January 2 with interest payable June 30 and December 31 priced to yield 16%.

d. The bonds described in item c priced to yield 10%.

e. $1 million of 12%, 10-year bonds with interest payable June 30 and December 31 issued at face value on March 1.

P 10–13
Present Value
L.O.10

Assume in each of the following cases that the number of years is five and the interest rate is 13%. The following information is also given:

Future value of $1	$1.8424
Present value of $1	0.5428
Future value of a $1 annuity	6.4803
Present value of a $1 annuity. . . .	3.5172

Required:
Compute the following:

1. The amount of each year-end payment required to repay a $5,000 interest-bearing loan.
2. How much a $3,000 deposit will accumulate in five years.
3. How much you should put in the bank on the last day of the next five years to accumulate $4,000 for a trip to Europe when you finish law school.
4. How much cash the bank will give you for a noninterest-bearing note with a face value of $7,000.

P 10–14
Present Value
L.O.10

The state helps a rural county maintain an old bridge and has agreed to pay $6,000 on December 31 of each year for five years toward the expenses. The first payment is to be made on December 31, 19x6. The state wishes to discharge its obligation by paying a single sum to a trust on January 1, 19x6, in lieu of the first payment, due on December 31, 19x6, and all future payments. Calculate the amount the state should pay the trust on January 1, 19x6, assuming the trust earns interest at a rate of 8% compounded annually.

P 10–15
Bonds Present Value Computation (Challenging)
L.O.10, 11

Aerotech reported Bonds Payable on their December 31, 19x6, balance sheet that had a maturity value of $10 million. The bonds mature on December 31, 19x9, and were issued to yield 10%. The bonds pay semiannual interest of $400,000 on June 30 and December 31. Aerotech has a December 31 year-end and uses the effective-interest method for amortization.

Required:
1. What is the net book value of the Bonds Payable in Aerotech's 19x6 annual report?
2. What is the amount of interest expense reported in Aerotech's 19x6 annual report?

P 10–16
Leases (Challenging)
L.O.10, 11

Chattanooga Locomotive, Inc., manufactures locomotives, which it sells to customers using one of two alternative plans:

Plan 1:   Payment of $3 million cash at date of purchase.

Plan 2:   A lease of 10 years with equal annual payments of $488,233 due at the end of each year for 10 years. The title to the locomotive passes to the buyer at the end of the 10-year lease. The implicit interest rate in the lease is 10%.

The expected life of a locomotive is 10 years, and its expected salvage value is zero.

Choo Choo Company leases a locomotive from Chattanooga on January 2, 19x5, using Plan 2. Choo Choo uses straight-line depreciation on all assets.

Required:
1. Record the lease transaction on January 1, 19x5, on Choo Choo's books.
2. Calculate the total expense recorded by Choo Choo for 19x5 in connection with this leased asset and lease obligation.
3. Calculate the total expense recorded by Choo Choo in 19x6 in connection with this leased asset and lease obligation.

P 10–17
Leases
L.O.10, 11

Hauler, Inc., leased 10 tractor trailers from Fuqua Corporation on January 1, 19x1. The fair market value of the trailers was $8.1 million total, and their expected useful life was 12 years with no scrap value. Hauler paid Fuqua $1,605,000 on January 1, 19x1, and agreed to pay an additional $1 million each subsequent January 1 for the next 11 years. The appropriate rate of interest for this lease is 10% for both the lessor and the lessee.

Required:
1. Compute the total amount of interest expense to be paid by Hauler over the life of the lease.
2. Using straight-line depreciation, determine how much total expense Hauler will charge to income in 19x1 for the lease obligation and the leased assets.
3. Compute the net lease liability balance on January 2, 19x6 (the day after the fifth $1 million payment), on Hauler's books.

P 10–18
Leases
L.O.10, 11

Lessee, Inc., agrees to lease a machine from January 1, 19x1. The machine could have been purchased for $2 million cash. The lease is for five years with annual payments of $554,816 due at the end of each of the next five years and the ownership of the machine is transferred to Lessee, Inc., after the final payment. The expected life of the machine for amortization purposes is 10 years. Lessee uses straight-line depreciation on all assets and assumes a zero salvage value. The agreement is a capital lease. Assume a 12% interest factor.

Required:
1. Show all journal entries relating to the leased asset and obligation for the years 19x1 and 19x2 on the books of Lessee, Inc.
2. Show how the asset would be reported on Lessee's balance sheet at the end of 19x2. Explain what the book value represents.

P 10–19
Leases
(Challenging)
L.O.11

BREZ Air Corporation agreed to pay $35,000,000 at the end of each year for the next 20 years in order to acquire two DC10-30 aircraft from Wells Fargo Bank (the lessor). These aircraft have a fair market value of $171,816,750 each at the time the lease is signed. Assume the aircraft will be depreciated over 20 years on a straight-line basis by BREZ, with the aircraft reverting to the lessor after 20 years. This lease is a capital lease for BREZ.

Required:
1. What is the interest rate implied by this lease agreement? (Hint: $(P/A)A = \$171,816,750 \times 2$.)
2. Record the lease at its inception.
3. Compute the balance in the leased assets and lease liability at the end of 10 years.

• CASES ───

C 10–1
Financing Alternatives
(Challenging)
L.O.10, 11

Hatfield Company has to purchase two large generators for its plant on January 1, 19x1. Each generator will cost $500,000. Two alternative payment schemes have been proposed. The first is to borrow $1 million at 12% from a bank with two year-end payments at December 31, 19x1, and December 31, 19x2, equal to one-half of the unpaid principal plus interest for the period. The second is to purchase the generators on time from the manufacturer. The manufacturer's financing plan calls for a down payment of $100,000 per unit plus payments of $200,000 plus interest at 12% for each unit—one payment 12 months and the other 24 months after delivery of the generator. Hatfield Company has a December 31 year-end.

Required:
1. Construct a schedule that shows the cash outflow patterns for each alternative financing method.
2. Discuss the reasons for choosing each method over the other.

C 10–2
Bonds, Analysis
L.O.1, 4, 5

Campbell Company issued $1,000,000 of 10-year, 8% bonds on January 1, 19x1, for $875,480. On the same date, Martin Company issued $1,000,000 of 10-year, 12% bonds for $1,124,720. Both sets of bonds pay interest on June 30 and December 31 of each year, both have similar risk characteristics, and both were issued to yield 10%.

Required:
1. Discuss the factors that must be considered when issuing bonds at a premium and at a discount.
2. Why did Martin receive much higher cash proceeds from their issue when both firms issued the same dollar amount of bonds at the same market rate of interest?
3. Compute the interest expense related to these bonds for each company for 19x1 and 19x2 using the effective-interest method. Why did interest expense in 19x2 increase for Campbell but decrease for Martin?
4. Show the presentation of each bond issue on the two companies' 19x2 balance sheets. Does this presentation accurately reflect the economic substances of these two similar bond issues?

C 10–3
*Comparison of
Financing Methods and
Business Decisions
(Challenging)*
L.O.1, 2

Assume that World Concessions, Inc., (WCI) has the opportunity to operate the main food concession at a world exhibition, which is to run for the two-year period 1/1/x1 through 12/31/x2. The following are the important amounts involved:

Expected cash sales per year.	$6,000,000
Expected cash expenses per year.	$2,500,000
Interest rate for all transactions	10%
Dividend payments	Net income for period

Other information: The Tucson Convention Center owns all of the structures and equipment at the exhibit and it will take possession of all assets on 12/31/x2. WCI has four options: (1) Use its own cash for the initial payment of $5,000,000. (2) Rent the concession assets for a $3,000,000 payment on 12/31/x1 with an option for a second-year rental. (3) Borrow $5,000,000 by signing a two-year note to be paid back in two year-end payments. Each payment reduces the principal by equal amounts and pays interest on the unpaid balance at the beginning of the period. (4) Sign a two-year noncancelable lease agreement with required payments of $2,881,014 on 12/31/x1 and 12/31/x2.

On 1/1/x1 WCI has only one asset, $10,000,000 in a bank account that earns 10%, and it has common stock with a book value of $10,000,000.

Required:

1. Consider the four alternative ways by which WCI can get the right to operate the concession. Use the format below to analyze the balance sheet and income statement effects of WCI's transactions for 19x1. (Hint: The transactions shown here are for Financing Method 1. You may have to modify the format for other methods.)

2. Answer this question: Does the method of financing a particular asset acquisition affect the financial statements?

World Concessions, Inc.
Balance Sheet Analysis
(Financing Method 1)

Bank Account	Concession Assets	Liabilities	Common Stock	Retained Earnings
Beginning balances $	$	$	$	$
Purchase assets				
Sales				
Cash expenses				
Depreciation expense				
Interest revenue				
Dividend				
End balance				

Net income = $ _____

Net assets = $ _____

C 10–4
Riskiness of Collateralized Notes and Debentures
L.O.1, 3, 4

Kingston Ferry Service, Inc., is negotiating for the purchase of two new vessels. Two alternative financing plans are proposed by the corporate treasurer: (1) debenture bonds at an effective-interest rate of 18%, and (2) a note with the vessels used as collateral to be repaid one third each year-end plus interest at an interest rate of 12%.

Required:
Explain why the interest rates of the two alternatives differ, and explain the effect each alternative has on the income statement and balance sheet.

C 10–5
Straight-Line versus Effective-Interest Methods of Discount Amortization
L.O.5

In January Parr Foods, Inc., issued 10-year debenture bonds having total face value of $10,000,000 at a significant discount. The company has a December 31 year-end and pays interest on June 30 and December 31 of each year. The president of the company wants an explanation of the effects on the income statement of the following alternatives: (*a*) amortization of the discount by the effective interest method, and (*b*) amortization of the discount by the straight-line method.

Required:
Write a memo explaining the impact of each alternative on the income statement. Give arguments in favor of each.

C 10–6
Zero Coupon Note
(Challenging)
L.O.3

Consider the following excerpt from a footnote in a recent published annual report:

Note Six: Long-Term Debt

In Millions	May 28, 1989	May 29, 1988
Zero coupon notes, yield 11.14% $555.5 due August 15, 2013	$41.1	$37.6
Zero coupon notes, yield 14⅝% $49.2 due June 30, 1991	36.7	31.9

Zero coupon notes (and bonds) require the debtor to pay back the borrowed amount plus accumulated interest in one lump sum at the maturity date. The reported amounts on the right represent the total obligation (principal plus all interest to date, because no payments have been made) at the end of fiscal 1989 and 1988. The amounts due at maturity ($555.5 million and $49.2 million, respectively) are given after the effective interest dates.

Required:
1. For the first notes (11.14%), what is the total remaining interest expense to be recorded between May 28, 1989, and maturity (August 15, 2013)?
2. For the second notes (14⅝%), what is the apparent compounding period (e.g., quarterly, annually, and semiannually)?
3. For the 14⅝% notes, what was the apparent amount of interest expense for fiscal 1989?

· Appendix Cases

C 10–7
Bonds and Leases
L.O.10, 11

At January 1, 19x3, the long-term liability section of ABC Company balance sheet contained the following items:

Long-Term Liabilities

Bonds payable, 9%, due 19x6	$1,000,000	
Add: Unamortized premium	100,000	$1,100,000
Capitalized lease obligations.		600,000
Deferred income taxes		150,000
Total long-term liabilities.		$1,850,000

Required:
1. Discuss the nature of the cash flows that will be required to satisfy each category of long-term liability on this balance sheet.
2. Explain why the cash received in excess of the face amount to be paid back on the bonds was not recorded as a gain on the sale of the bonds when they were issued in 19x1.
3. On January 15, 19x3, these bonds were selling in the bond market at 97. What economic event would cause the switch from premium to discount? What accounting entry would be required by ABC to account for this economic event?
4. What factors were considered in determining which of ABC's leases would be shown as liabilities?

C 10–8

Present Values and Interest Rates

L.O.10

Consider a case in which two customers, Allen Co. and Baker, Inc., have notes made out to your company with the same required cash flows; that is, five year-end note payments of $5,000 each with an effective-interest rate of 14%. The notes were made on January 1 of the current year. Your company charges 18% to some customers that are considered more risky. Assume that Allen Co. is in strong financial shape and has a reputation of paying on time. It has been discovered that Baker, Inc., on the other hand, is in weak financial shape and has missed payments to other creditors in the past. This was not known when the contract was signed. It is now at the first year-end and the first payments have been received.

Required:

As accountant for your company, you are to write a memo explaining how these receivables are to be valued on the year-end balance sheet and what effect they will have on the income statement.

C 10–9

Noninterest-Bearing Notes and Present Values

L.O.10, 11

Quake Winery purchased a new harvester on September 1, 19x1, and signed a three-year note that calls for one payment three years hence of $266,200, including principal and interest.

Required:

Answer the following questions:

1. If the note does not explicitly state an interest rate, what evidence can be used to determine the purchase price of the equipment and the liability as of the date of purchase?
2. Would changes in the interest rate change the book value of the note and the equipment? Why?
3. Would the income statement be affected by the choice of interest rate? How?

Siller Corporation
Income Statement For 1994

	1994	1993
Net sales	$ xxx	$ xxx
Net sales	xxx	xxx
Cost of goods sold	xxx	xxx
Gross margin	$ xxx	$ xxx
Expenses		
Total expenses	xxx	xxx
Net income	$ xx	$ xx

Siller Corporation
Balance Sheet For 12/31/94

	1994	1993
Current assets:		
Total current assets	$ xxx	$ xxx
Noncurrent assets:		
Organization costs	**xx**	**xx**
Total noncurrent assets	$ xxx	$ xxx
Total assets	$ xxx	$ xxx
Current liabilities:		
Dividends payable	xx	xx
Total current liabilities	$ xxx	$ xxx
Noncurrent liabilities:		
Total noncurrent liabilities	xx	xx
Stockholders' equity:		
Common stock—par.	**$ xxx**	**$ xxx**
Preferred stock—par	**xxx**	**xxx**
Additional paid-in capital		
Common	**xx**	**xx**
Preferred	**xx**	**xx**
Retained earnings.	**xxx**	**xxx**
Treasury stock	**(xx)**	**(xx)**
Total stockholders' equity	**$ xxx**	**$ xxx**
Total liabilities and stockholders' equity	$ xxxx	$ xxxx

Siller Corporation
Cash Flow Statement For 1994

	1994	1993
Operating activities		
Cash used in operating activities	$ xxx	$ xxx
Investing activities		
Cash used in investing activities	$ xxx	$ xxx
Financing activities		
Receipts from sale of stock	**$xxxx**	**$xxxx**
Cash payments for dividends	**(xx)**	**(xx)**
Cash used in financing activities	$ xxxx	$ xxxx
Net change in cash	$ xx	$ xx

FINANCIAL
STATEMENT
COMPONENTS
EMPHASIZED IN
CHAPTER 11

11

Noncorporate and Corporate Business Organizations

All that the auditor must constantly keep in mind is his basic obligation—to maintain strict impartiality in all aspects of audits or other work that involves reporting to third parties, including the general public. This can hardly be considered too onerous or too complex for one who has accepted the responsibilities inherent in the roll of an auditor.

William D. Hall
Arthur Andersen & Co. SC

· Learning Objectives

After studying Chapter 11, you should understand

1. Why people choose different forms of organization for business, pp. 556–59.
2. Accounting for owner's equity in a proprietorship, pp. 560–61.
3. Partnerships—ease of formation, classes of partners, limited life, and mutual agency, pp. 562–63.
4. The special legal features of the corporate form of business organization, pp. 563–65.
5. Accounting for corporate organization costs and issuance of stock, pp. 565–69.
6. The corporate balance sheet presentation of contributed capital, pp. 569–70.
7. Accounting for the reacquisition and retirement of stock, pp. 572–74.
8. Accounting for donated capital, cash dividends, and stock dividends and splits, pp. 574–77.
9. What makes preferred stock different from common stock, pp. 578–79.
10. Some of the accounting challenges created by partnerships (Appendix), pp. 582–94.

This chapter discusses the noncorporate (proprietorships and partnerships) and the corporate (corporations) business organizations. To understand how accounting is affected by the form of business organization, you must first have some knowledge of the fundamental legal and economic factors that have shaped the evolution of those forms. In this chapter you are introduced to many of these issues. The general nature of proprietorships and partnerships and their major underlying accounting concepts are also explained. The appendix to the chapter is an introduction to the accounting for partnerships.

The accounting for the rights and responsibilities of corporate stockholders is discussed in detail in this chapter because accounting reflects these relationships and the transactions that occur between corporations and stockholders. The corporate organization gives business advantages such as the **potential to raise large amounts of capital and to continue in operation when ownership changes.** Stockholders of corporations also have an advantage because they are **not personally responsible for the obligations of the business.** Corporations and stockholders have a legal relationship that is governed by state and federal law. Payments to stockholders, in the form of dividends or upon liquidation, are constrained by the laws of the state in which the corporation is registered. The formal rules that govern the stockholder and the corporation contrast with the ease and informality of asset flow from business to owner found in noncorporate business organizations.

LEGAL AND ACCOUNTING ASPECTS OF NONCORPORATE AND CORPORATE BUSINESSES

Objective 1
Why people choose different forms of organization for business.

The business entity concept is one of the fundamental principles of accounting. Throughout this textbook we have illustrated that in accounting, the business entity is an economic unit separate from its owners.

As you recall from Chapter 1, although accountants view the business as a separate entity, the extent of the legal liability of business owners depends on how the business is organized. For proprietorships (single-owner, noncorporate businesses) and partnerships (multiowner, noncorporate businesses), the owners' legal liability from business activities is unlimited; for corporations the owner has no legal liability and can lose only his or her investment.

In the typical corporate balance sheet (1) assets are listed without reference to their sources, (2) creditors' names do not appear next to liability accounts, and (3) stockholders' equity accounts do not indicate the identities of individual stockholders. Also, in the corporate income statement, no reference is made to how specific stockholders participate in earnings. In a noncorporate business, the basic elements of assets, liabilities, revenues, and expenses in the financial statements are essentially the same as for corporations, but owners have a different legal relationship to the noncorporate business than stockholders have to the corporation. This special legal relationship affects the accounting and reporting for noncorporate businesses, especially owners' equity.

You must distinguish between the legal and accounting aspects of corporate and noncorporate businesses in order to understand the differences between these two forms of business organizations. The assets, liabilities, revenues, and expenses of a corporation are legally separated from stockholders. Thus, creditors of the corporation usually cannot sue stockholders when the company defaults on payment of debts. Also, stockholders usually cannot withdraw assets from the corporation at will. By contrast, the legal view of proprietorships and partnerships does not separate them from their owners. In general, proprietors and partners are responsible for the debts of their businesses and can withdraw assets at will according to prescribed formulas.

As an example, consider two businesses, Corporation A, owned exclusively by Ms. Andrews, and Company B, a proprietorship owned exclusively by Mr. Brown. Both owners contributed $20,000 to start the business. The two businesses are identical in every way except that A is a corporation and B is a proprietorship.[1] The individual balance sheets include the following items:

Corporation A	
Cash	$100,000
Liabilities	80,000
Stockholders' equity	20,000

Company B	
Cash	$100,000
Liabilities	80,000
Brown, capital	20,000

Assume that both businesses lose lawsuits for damages of $300,000 because of defective products. How would the **entity** of each business be viewed from the legal and accounting perspectives? In the corporate organization, Andrews is not at risk of losing any of her personal assets beyond what she has already invested in the corporation ($20,000). Her personal assets are viewed as separate from the obligations of the corporation. From the corporate entity or accounting entity point of view, the lawsuit creates a liability and a reduction of owners' equity, resulting in the following balance sheet for Corporation A, but the liability in no way affects the stockholders' personal obligations.

Corporation A Balance Sheet (after lawsuit)	
Cash	$ 100,000
Liabilities	$ 380,000
Stockholders' equity	(280,000)
Total liabilities and stockholders' equity	$ 100,000

Obviously the corporation cannot pay off the total liability without obtaining more assets by borrowing more money, selling more stock, or generating cash flows from operations. If no additional funds are obtained and bankruptcy is declared, the creditors will not be paid their full amounts, and the stockholder (Andrews) is not liable for the deficiency.

The legal concept of business entity applies differently in the proprietorship, although the balance sheet appears much the same. Because Mr. Brown, as a proprietor, is personally liable for the debts of the business, the law considers the debt of the entity a responsibility of the owner, so the owner must use personal sources to settle the debt. Of course, if Mr. Brown does not have sufficient personal assets, he can declare personal bankruptcy.

From an accounting perspective, the business entity and the owner are kept separate. The accounting records do not mingle personal and business assets and personal assets are not recorded until transferred into the business, as follows:

---

[1]Although in most states it is necessary to have more than one stockholder to form a corporation (usually three or more stockholders are required), for simplicity this case assumes that there is a single stockholder.

1. After the lawsuit liability amount is determined, the business entity is reported as follows:

Company B (after recording loss)	
Cash	$ 100,000
Liabilities.	$ 380,000
Brown, capital	(280,000)
Total liabilities and owner's equity	$ 100,000

Note that the $300,000 loss has reduced "Brown, capital" from a positive $20,000 to a deficit of $280,000. The deficit or negative capital amount of $280,000, which is the $380,000 liability minus the cash in the business, is a legal obligation of the owner. However, from an accounting perspective, the balance sheet shows only business assets and obligations.

2. If Brown were to contribute $300,000 to the business, thus eliminating the $280,000 negative balance and establishing a $20,000 positive balance, the following balance sheet would result:

Company B (after contribution from owner)	
Cash	$ 400,000
Liabilities.	$ 380,000
Brown, capital	20,000
Total liabilities and owner's equity	$ 400,000

Now Company B can pay off the new debt of $300,000 and still be in the same financial position as before the loss. Although the law makes no distinction between the proprietor and the business, accountants do not automatically combine personal and business assets and liabilities. Accounting reports reflect only business assets and liabilities. In the above example, if Brown had not transferred cash into the business, he would still have been responsible for the debt.

To summarize, in corporate accounting the legal and business entity concepts are similar. The stockholders' personal assets and obligations are viewed as completely separate from the corporation. For unincorporated businesses, although the business and personal entities are not merged, the special rights and obligations of owners have some effect on what is reported and how it is reported, and these rights and obligations can lead to real asset flows, such as was the case when Mr. Brown transferred cash into the business to be used to pay off the business's obligation.

TAX AND THE FORM OF THE ORGANIZATION

One very important legal consideration concerning the organizational form of a business is its tax status. Consider the case of Jack Lundlum who has just resigned as a jeweler for a large retailer and is now going to open his own shop to design and manufacture exclusive, custom-made, jewelry. The following is a conversation between Jack and a CPA, who is advising him on his options about the various forms of business.

Jack: There are two main things I'm really concerned about. One is legal liability and the other is taxation of earnings. Can you sketch out my options?

CPA: I agree, those are the critical factors for you. You've got the capital you need, so that's not a problem at this stage, and you are not concerned about continuation of the business if you depart. That leaves taxes and legal liability as major factors. There are three basic categories for tax purposes: (1) unincorporated, which means a proprietorship or a partnership, (2) a C corporation, and (3) an S corporation. In terms of your obligation for business liabilities, there are really two options—to incorporate or not to incorporate.

Jack: Before I get completely confused, let's talk about the liability issue first. If I incorporate, the debts of the corporation are not my personal debts, right? And in a proprietorship or a partnership, the opposite holds; am I correct?

CPA: Right. If you have a partner, he or she shares in the responsibility of the business's debt, and agreements among the partners determine how it is shared. If you don't have a partner, you are fully responsible. With a corporation, all you can lose is your investment.

Jack: You know, maybe I'm worrying for nothing. What can a jeweler be sued for, anyway?

CPA: Well, given the sorry state of our legal system, maybe the pain and suffering caused by your prices. Ha, Ha. Seriously, what if a torch in your workshop injured a worker or a customer slipped on a wet floor?—that sort of thing.

Jack: OK, I think I understand that. What about this business of a C corporation and an S corporation for tax purposes? What's the difference?

CPA: An S corporation gives most of the benefits of the corporate form, but income is taxed as though it were a proprietorship or a partnership; that is, the income is taxable to the owners in proportion to stockholdings, just as in an unincorporated business, even if no dividends are paid to the owners. But when dividends are paid they are not taxed again. In a C corporation, the corporation is considered a taxpayer and pays taxes on income each year, and dividends are taxed to the individual when dividends are paid.

Jack: That doesn't seem fair. That's what they mean by double taxation, right?

CPA: Yes, and a large corporation with many stockholders is stuck with it because they can't elect to be an S corporation. In your case, because you are the primary owner and you don't expect to have many other owners, you will have that option.

Jack: So, in the eyes of the law, a proprietorship or partnership is not a separate entity for liability or tax purposes, an S corporation is viewed as a separate entity for liability purposes but not for taxes, and a C corporation is a separate entity for both liability and tax purposes.

CPA: Very good. Maybe now I should give you my introduction to tax planning.

Jack: No way! I've had enough of this legal mumbo-jumbo. Let's get on with starting the business.

CPA: I know how you feel, but keep in mind that as many small businesses fail for lack of basic business knowledge as for lack of customers.

In the sections that follow, we will discuss the accounting concepts and procedures that are used in accounting for ownership interest in noncorporate and corporate forms of business. Specifics about differences in the taxation of entities can be found in texts on taxation.

NONCORPORATE FORM OF BUSINESS ORGANIZATION

While assets and liabilities are accounted for and reported similarly in noncorporate and corporate balance sheets, major differences occur in the owners' equity accounts. In a proprietorship, owners can withdraw assets and reduce owners' equity at will, and one account is used to represent the overall ownership capital balance. In a corporate business, payments to stockholders are governed by a board of directors elected by stockholders,

Objective 2
Accounting for owner's
equity in a proprietorship.

dividend payments are generally limited to retained earnings, and accountants use different accounts to keep track of the several categories of stockholders' equity.

This section discusses the two noncorporate business forms—proprietorships and partnerships. Under proprietorships, you will learn how to record owner's contributions, earnings, and withdrawals. The discussion on partnerships explains some of the accounting complexities created when a noncorporate business has more than one owner. An appendix introduces some details of partnership accounting.

Proprietorships

To reflect the owner's interest in a proprietorship, accountants use the owner's capital account. All owner contributions (investments) into the business are credited to this capital account; and income, losses, and owner's withdrawals flow in and out of the owner's capital account. For example, M. Maples, M.D., had the following transactions in 19xx:

1. Invested $25,000 in the business January 1, 19xx.
2. Earned $100,000 in fees (all cash).
3. Paid $20,000 for expenses (all cash).
4. Withdrew $95,000 in cash.

The journal entries to record these transactions are as follows:

19xx Jan. 1	Cash (A)	25,000	
	M. Maples, Capital (OE)		25,000
	To record initial investment.		
During 19xx	Cash (A)	100,000	
	Fees Revenue (R)		100,000
	To record cash revenue from services rendered.		
	Expenses (E)	20,000	
	Cash (A)		20,000
	To record the payment for expenses during the year.		
	M. Maples, Drawing (OE)	95,000	
	Cash (A)		95,000
	To record the withdrawal of cash by M. Maples during the year.		
Dec. 31	Fees Revenue (R)	100,000	
	Expenses (E)		20,000
	Income Summary (OE)		80,000
	To close revenue and expenses to Income Summary account.		
	Income Summary (OE)	80,000	
	M. Maples, Capital (OE)		80,000
	To close Income Summary account to permanent capital account.		
	M. Maples, Capital (OE)	95,000	
	M. Maples, Drawing (OE)		95,000
	To close drawing account to permanent capital account.		

Note that the owner's drawing account is not the same as a company's Salaries Expense account. Owners are different from salaried employees because owners have direct access to the assets of the business irrespective of the effort they put into the job. For this reason, the owner's withdrawal of cash is not recorded as an expense of the business. Instead, the payments made to an owner are recorded as withdrawals of capital.

The following statement of owner's equity for M. Maples, M.D., at December 31, 19xx, shows how the various transactions during the year affected the owner's capital account.

M. Maples, M.D.
Statement of Owner's Equity
For the Year Ended December 31, 19xx

M. Maples, capital, January 1, 19xx.	$	0
Plus: Investments		25,000
Net income for year 19xx		80,000
		$105,000
Less: Withdrawals		95,000
M. Maples, capital, December 31, 19xx	$	10,000

The ending balance sheet of M. Maples, M.D., would appear as follows:

M. Maples, M.D.
Balance Sheet
December 31, 19xx

Assets		**Owner's Equity**	
Cash	$10,000	M. Maples, capital	$10,000

Note that in the following T accounts only one capital account, M. Maples, Capital, has a nonzero ending balance.

Cash				**M. Maples, Capital**			
(1)	25,000	(3)	20,000	(7)	95,000	(1)	25,000
(2)	100,000	(4)	95,000			(6)	80,000
	10,000						10,000

M. Maples, Drawing				**Income Summary**			
(4)	95,000	(7)	95,000	(6)	80,000	(5)	80,000
	0						0

Fees Revenue				**Expenses**			
(5)	100,000	(2)	100,000	(3)	20,000	(5)	20,000
			0		0		

Description of numbered entries:
1. The investment transaction is recorded.
2. The revenue transactions are recorded.
3. The expense transactions are recorded.
4. M. Maples withdrawal of $95,000 is recorded.
5. The revenue and expense accounts are closed to the Income Summary account.
6. The Income Summary account is closed to the M. Maples, Capital account.
7. The M. Maples, Drawing account is closed to the M. Maples, Capital account.

Partnerships

Objective 3
Partnerships—ease of
formation, classes of
partners, limited life, and
mutual agency.

As explained in Chapter 1, a noncorporate business with more than one owner is called a *partnership*. The association of individuals as partners creates unique legal rights and obligations resulting in accounting complexities for partnership capital that do not occur in proprietorships. The concept that a proprietorship is legally indistinguishable from the business is relatively simple because the rights and responsibilities of business ownership are under one person's control. In a partnership, however, two or more people have joint ownership, which creates a need for rules to govern the sharing of the joint rights and responsibilities.

A partnership can be created either without a formal agreement among the partners or with a formal agreement. If no formal agreement exists, state laws applicable to partnerships control the legal relationship. The Uniform Partnership Act (UPA) governs the formation, operation, and liquidation of partnerships in most states when no formal agreement exists. When a formal agreement is created, it is called a partnership agreement, or articles of copartnership. The partnership agreement gives the details of the understanding among the partners on the ownership percentages, procedures for asset withdrawals, sharing of profits and losses, and other issues. Specific partnership agreement stipulations may differ from those in the UPA, but the UPA governs in the absence of a partnership agreement.

The paragraphs that follow discuss the ease of partnership formation, classes of partners, limited life of partnerships, and mutual agency.

Ease of Partnership Formation. Partnerships are easy to start. Unlike corporations, usually no legal forms or government approvals are necessary. The legal status of a partnership is established when two or more parties commit resources to a venture and agree to act as partners.

This ease of partnership formation does not mean that complexities cannot occur. Partners must give serious thought to the outcome of many possible events and their implications for the business and the various partners. Even though the formation of a partnership is simple, the smooth operation of a partnership can be extremely difficult unless a partnership clearly stipulates partners' rights and obligations. The appendix to this chapter discusses some of the accounting challenges partnerships create.

Classes of Partners. In all partnerships, there must be at least one partner with unlimited liability. Just as in the case of a sole proprietor, at least one person in an unincorporated business takes full responsibility for the debts of the entity. When the partnership agreement does not specify otherwise, each partner is called a general partner, with unlimited responsibility for the liabilities of the partnership. In states that allow limited partners, the limited partners' responsibilities are no more than the assets that partner contributed to the partnership or some other specific amount.

General partners may be called upon to contribute additional capital if the assets of the partnership are insufficient to pay for legitimate creditor claims. Such contributions create a claim by the contributing partner against other general partners of the partnership. A limited partner, however, would not be required to contribute additional capital. The most a limited partner could lose is the amount previously invested in the partnership or the amount specified.

Limited Life of Partnerships. Unless the partnership agreement states otherwise, a partnership dissolves upon the admission of a new partner or the withdrawal of an old one. The partnership agreement can modify these general conditions. For instance, consider the partnership of David Smith and Carla Jones. If Smith dies, the partnership is dissolved, and the remaining assets of the partnership are divided among Smith's heirs and Jones. If the partnership agreement stipulated that upon a partner's death, a specific person (e.g., Smith's child) would take over the capital amount without interruption, Smith's death would not lead to an ending of the business but merely a name change in the capital accounts.

Often the operation of a business is not disturbed by the legal dissolution of the partnership. It is certainly possible for the business to continue without interruption if the old and new partners cooperate in an orderly transition of ownership. If, on the other hand, the departing partner or the survivors demand specific assets from the business, then operations of the business most likely will be interrupted.

Mutual Agency. All general partners can act as agents for the partnership; that is, they have the legal right to commit partnership assets in transactions with outsiders. The partnership agreement can stipulate restrictions on the agency status of one or more partners. However, in the absence of specific restrictions, all partners are said to have mutual agency, allowing each partner to borrow money, purchase assets, commit to sales contracts, and engage in other transactions in the name of the partnership. While this gives the partnership great flexibility, it also creates a control problem. Because authorization of other partners is not required for a general partner to commit partnership resources, general partners should know and trust one another. Each general partner's business and personal assets can be affected by another partner's decisions. The appendix discusses accounting for partnerships.

CORPORATE FORM OF BUSINESS ORGANIZATION

Accounting for corporate businesses differs in several ways from accounting for noncorporate businesses. The important differences center on the relationship of the entity with its stockholders which is the focus of most of the rest of this chapter. Then we discuss corporate organization costs, the issuance of stock, balance sheet presentation of contributed capital, reacquisition and retirement of stock, donated capital, cash dividends, stock dividends, and special features of preferred stock.

Advantages and Disadvantages of Corporations

Objective 4
The special features of the corporate form of business organization.

To begin, study the following two definitions of a corporation:

- A group of people who get a charter granting them as a body certain of the legal powers, rights, privileges, and liabilities of an individual, distinct from those of the individuals making up the group.[2]
- An association of individuals created by law and existing as an entity with powers and liabilities independent of those of its members.[3]

These definitions highlight two major concepts. First, a corporation is an **association of individuals** that is recognized by law. Second, a corporation has rights and responsibilities **separate** from those of its members. When applied in a business context, these characteristics help explain why corporations are the dominant business form of organization in the United States and control the vast majority of business assets. Because corporations can be associations of large numbers of owners, **large amounts of capital can be generated** allowing corporations to accumulate the necessary assets to operate on a large and often more efficient scale.

The separation of the corporation entity from its owners encourages stockholder investment because the **liability of stockholders is limited.** From the stockholders viewpoint, this is a major advantage of the corporation. Remember, however, that although corporation stockholders are not personally responsible for corporate debts, in case of bankruptcy or poor performance, stockholders could lose all of their investment in the corporation. In general, the losses of stockholders are limited to the amount of their investment.

---

[2]*Webster's New World Dictionary,* 2nd college edition, 1978.

[3]*The Random House College Dictionary,* 1975.

Other advantages of the corporate form of business include the following:

- Ease of transferability of ownership.
- Continuity of existence.
- Separation of management and owners.
- Advantageous tax status.

In contrast to a noncorporate business, a change of stock ownership does not affect the corporation's legal status. The corporation is independent of the specific owners, and there is **continuity of existence** when one owner sells to another. In publicly traded corporations, there is **ease of transferability of ownership** because a market exists where shares can be bought and sold. This ease of ownership transfer is conducive to large-scale investments and operations.

When the shares of a corporation are owned by a small number of stockholders the company is said to be a "closely held" corporation with no public trading of shares. These corporations enjoy the benefit of the corporate form but usually operate on a much smaller scale than large corporations. Privately held corporations far outnumber those corporations that trade on the stock exchanges; of the 3 million corporations in the United States fewer than 1% are publicly traded.

Because stockholders are not necessarily part of management, the **separation of management and owners** makes it possible for corporations to assemble specialized management talent. The stockholders who are willing to take the risks of ownership can indirectly employ managers who have the needed managerial and technical skills but who may not want to assume the investment risk of business ownership. This flexibility of assembling management talent often results in individuals with different preferences and skills contracting with the business entity in a mutually beneficial manner.

The separation of owners and management prevalent in most large corporations can also be a **disadvantage.** Stockholders must make sure that managers operate in the stockholders' best interests. Corporations use many mechanisms to control management actions, starting with the board of directors, who are individuals elected by the stockholders to represent their interests. The board appoints top management and makes major decisions about corporate policy, strategy, compensation, and dividend policy. In addition, the board is responsible for the overall **monitoring** and **control** of management, which involves a relationship with internal and external auditors. The following general hierarchical relationships are common in large corporations:

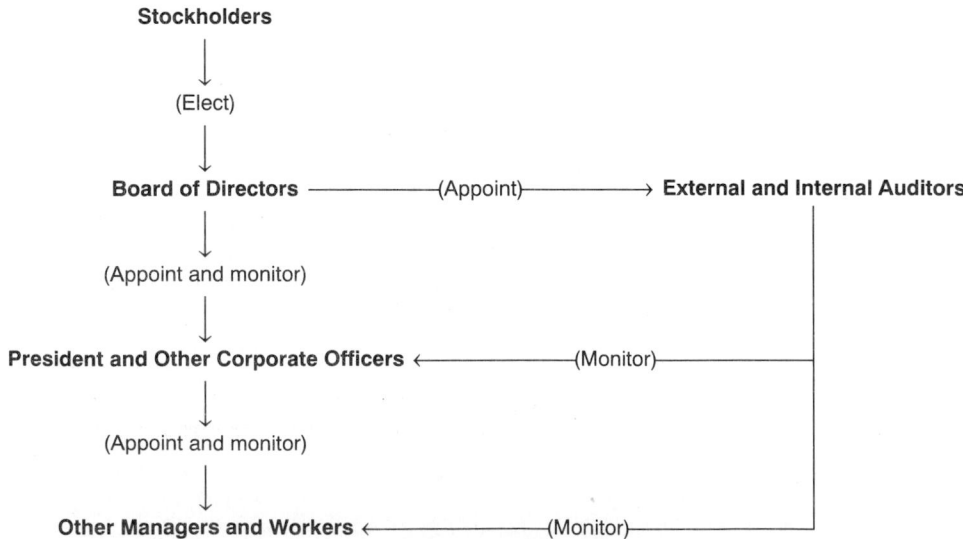

Another disadvantage of publicly traded corporations from management's perspective is the increasing threat of hostile takeovers by outside groups who, if successful, will often replace top management. Seen from another perspective, the threat of hostile takeovers encourage managers to be as efficient as possible.

The corporate system of election, appointment, and monitoring, along with reward structures, is designed to create a consistency of purpose where the goals of the stockholders are fostered by the actions of each member in the corporate hierarchy. Accounting systems designed to successfully accomplish this play a major role in the corporate management process. In addition to the financial accounting systems introduced in this text, corporations also employ managerial accounting systems that provide the information management needs in order to plan, monitor, and control operations.

Another feature of the corporate form is that the government considers it a separate taxable entity, which can give stockholders an advantageous tax status.[4] The profits of the corporation are generally not taxable to the stockholders until funds are distributed in the form of dividends, unlike the income of noncorporate businesses, which is taxable whether or not it is distributed. For small corporate businesses, this separate tax liability could be viewed as a disadvantage because of the added complexity in recordkeeping. Since corporate profits are taxed and dividend distributions to stockholders are taxed again, the possibility of double taxation exists. This creates complexity that may be quite costly, and great care must be taken to minimize the tax burdens of the stockholders.

When individuals in a proprietorship or partnership or individuals thinking about beginning a new business find that the advantages of the corporate business form outweigh the disadvantages, they may decide to apply to a state for a corporate charter. Sometimes incorporators, or promoters, are employed to help organize corporations. These promoters often become owners as well. The efforts of promoters involve developing ideas and plans, attracting potential investors, and drafting a corporate charter or articles of incorporation, which is part of the application necessary to gain a state's permission to form a corporation.

Organization Costs

Objective 5
Accounting for corporate organization costs and issuance of stock.

Lawyers, promoters, and accountants involved in the creation of a business eventually are paid either in shares of corporate stock or in cash after stock has been sold to others. Expenditures incurred in organizing a corporation, such as legal fees, taxes, stock issuance costs, and promotional fees, are generally recorded as an intangible asset account called Organization Costs. For example, assume that a corporate charter was issued to Filex Corporation on January 1, 19xx, and that the first recorded transaction is the following:

19xx			
Jan. 1	Organization Costs (A)	84,000	
	Accounts Payable (L)		84,000
	To record the incurrence of cost during the formation of the corporation.		

Filex may liquidate the accounts payable liability by cash payments or by issuing capital stock. In any event, an intangible asset, Organization Costs, is amortized over some period of time, usually no less than 5 years but never more than 40 years. If Filex decides to amortize the organizational costs over 10 years, the year-end adjusting entry would be

19xx			
Dec. 31	Amortization Expense—Organization Costs (E)	8,400	
	Organization Costs (A)		8,400
	To record the amortization of organization costs.		

---

[4]Refer to the discussion of S and C corporations on p. 559.

Issuance of Stock

Since the issuance of stock is a major source of financing for corporations, we begin with a discussion of the two major types of stock, common stock and preferred stock. Then we cover the concepts of par and stated values and show how stock is recorded and disclosed.

Common Stock.   A major advantage of the corporate business form is that corporations can raise capital from a large number of investors. The primary corporation investors are called common stockholders, and they purchase corporate securities called common stock.

Stockholders who own common stock have the following legal rights:

1. Owners of common shares may vote for the election of members to the board of directors. This voting right is important because the board has the authority to control all major corporate decisions.

2. Common stockholders may have a preemptive right that allows them to maintain a proportionate share of ownership. For example, if a stockholder owns 10% of a corporation's common stock, the stockholder is given the right to purchase 10% of any new stock issuance before the new shares are offered to others.

3. Common stockholders have dividend rights, that is, they share in any distribution of earnings in the form of dividends if the board of directors decides to distribute such dividends.

4. Common stockholders have the **right to the residual assets** (residual asset right) of the corporation upon its liquidation, after all other claims are met.

Preferred Stock.   Another class of stock, preferred stock, carries modifications in the rights discussed for common stock. Preferred stock usually does not carry voting and preemptive rights, and the rights to receive dividends and residual value are usually restricted to stated amounts per share. However, preferred stock carries certain preferences over common stock that makes it attractive to some investors. For example, the preferred stockholder is usually paid a fixed dividend amount per share per period before common stockholders are paid anything. Also, should the business liquidate or terminate, the preferred stockholder receives a fixed amount per share before common stockholders are given any residual. These features make preferred stock less risky than common stock.

A disadvantage of preferred stock is that it has limited "upside" potential. This means that in contrast to common stock, which can increase in value if the corporate fortunes improve, preferred stock is rather limited in its appreciation potential because of the fixed nature of its dividend and liquidation preferences. This limitation of preferred stock can be lessened by convertibility features that allow preferred stock to be traded for common stock. We discuss such features later. Remember that all stocks, including preferred stock, are riskier than debt, which has preference over both common and preferred stock.

Par or Stated Value.   Stock shares are often assigned an amount called par value (also called **stated value**). Common stock par values range from $0.01 to $50 or more per share. Preferred stock usually has $10, $50, or $100 per share par value. If no par value is assigned to the stock, the stock is called no-par stock.

Stock par values have a long history. They were initially required as a minimum investment per share in order to protect creditors of corporations. Although most state laws continue to allow par values, their effectiveness as protection for creditors has always been in doubt. Stock with a par value of $1 may sell for $100 or more. Having a $1 par value may assure creditors that at a minimum of $1 per share was contributed by stockholders, but par value usually has little economic significance.

State laws often require that a **stated value** per share be assigned to no-par stock. However, the stated value also has little economic significance. When a stated value is assigned to no-par stock, the stated value can be no less than the lowest price received from the sale of the no-par stock.

Another term you should become familiar with is legal capital, which usually refers to the amount of par or stated value of all stock outstanding for a corporation. For example, a corporation may have 100,000 shares of $1 par common stock and 10,000 shares of $50 preferred stock outstanding (shares in the hands of owners) which sold for $8 and $55 per share, respectively. The distinction between contributed capital (the total money contributed by owners, which is legal capital plus any money contributed in excess of legal capital) and legal capital is as follows:

			Contributed Capital			
			Legal Capital			
Class of Stock	Number of Shares Outstanding	Selling Price per Share	Par Value per Share	Total Par Value	Contributed Capital in Excess of Par	Total Contributed Capital
Common	100,000	$ 8	$ 1.00	$100,000	$700,000	$ 800,000
Preferred	10,000	55	50.00	500,000	50,000	550,000
				$600,000	$750,000	$1,350,000

Note that the par value of the common stock is far less than its selling price indicating that par value has little economic importance.

Recording Sale of Stock. Corporations usually issue stock for cash, but occasionally they accept other things of value in exchange for shares of stock. Often an attorney, accountant, or promoter will accept shares of stock in lieu of a cash payment for services performed in organizing a corporation. Similarly, partners in a business will often accept shares of stock for the assets they transfer into a newly formed corporation. In the following example, Dynamics Corporation is formed on January 1, 19xx, and issues a total of 17,000 shares of $1 par value stock in exchange for $100,000 cash, an attorney's services valued at $10,000, and a building valued at $60,000. This initial issuance is recorded as follows:

19xx			
Jan. 1	Cash (A).	100,000	
	Organization Costs (A)	10,000	
	Building (A)	60,000	
	Common Stock—Par (SE)		17,000
	Contributed Capital in Excess of Par—Common (SE)		153,000
	To record the issuance of 17,000 shares of common stock with $1 par value.		

The Common Stock—Par account represents the legal capital of the business at the time of the initial issuance. This means that the $17,000 recorded in the Common Stock—Par account has special legal status and must be shown separately in financial statements. If the corporate charter for the corporation in our example did not mention par value for common stock, the no-par stock would be recorded as follows:

19xx			
Jan. 1	Cash (A).	100,000	
	Organization Costs (A)	10,000	
	Building (A)	60,000	
	Common Stock (SE)		170,000
	To record the issuance of 17,000 shares of no-par common stock.		

(CCIEP)

PICIEP

The <u>Contributed Capital in Excess</u> of Par account (sometimes called *Paid-In Capital in Excess of Par*) represents the amount paid by stockholders over the par value. The word premium is sometimes applied to this amount, although the existence or magnitude of such an excess does not necessarily signify relative economic strength. Because the par value per share is set arbitrarily, neither the par nor the excess of par means much by itself. What is of real economic importance is the total amount paid for each share.

The function of par value is more significant in preferred stock where dividend amounts and liquidation values are often stated in terms of par value. For example, on January 1, 19xx, the Essex Corporation issued 10,000 shares of $100 par value preferred stock for $105 per share. Essex recorded this as follows:

```
19xx
Jan. 1   Cash (A). . . . . . . . . . . . . . . . . . . .   1,050,000

            Preferred Stock—Par (SE) . . . . . . . . . . . . .            1,000,000

            Contributed Capital in Excess of
              Par—Preferred Stock (SE) . . . . . . . . . . . . .              50,000
         To record the issuance of 10,000 shares of preferred stock.
```

Preferred stock certificates usually give the par value and the dividend rate, which is often stated as a percentage of par value. If the dividend rate is 10%, then each stockholder receives $10 for each share of $100 par value preferred stock owned each year before any distributions are made to common stockholders.

Stock can also be sold for amounts equal to and less than par value. For example, on January 1, 19xx, Zeron Corporation issued 5,000 shares of $5 par value common stock for $4 per share and recorded the following:

```
19xx
Jan. 1   Cash (A). . . . . . . . . . . . . . . . . . . .     20,000

         Discount on Common Stock (XSE) . . . . . . . . . . . . . . .      5,000

            Common Stock—Par (SE) . . . . . . . . . . . . . . . . .              25,000
         To record issuance of 5,000 shares of common stock
         at $4 per share.
```

Zeron's total contributed capital is only $20,000, but par value is recorded at the legal amount of $25,000. Just as premiums are added to par value to determine total contributed capital, discounts are subtracted from par value to arrive at total contributed capital. The Zeron example is a rare event because issuing stock below par (or stated value) is illegal in some states; and it is often the case that when issuing stock below par is allowed, original stockholders are liable for the discount amount in the event of corporate liquidation. Such an issuance of stock at a discount can negate some of the limited liability advantages of the corporate form of business. In any case, in the rare event it is recorded, the discount account is shown as a contra account to par value on corporate balance sheets.

In the United Kingdom the Share Premium account is credited when stock is issued at an amount in excess of par. The function of this account is very similar to that of Contributed Capital in Excess of Par. In France as many as three separate accounts, called *Premes,* are used, one for cash issues, another for noncash issues, and a third for amounts resulting from mergers.

STOP

Recording Stock Subscriptions.   Corporations sometimes accept promises to pay for stock shares in the form of subscription contracts, by which prospective stockholders enter into an agreement to pay for the stock in installments over some future period of time. Stock is issued only upon final payment of the contract. The end result is the same as an initial cash sale, but because of the time lapse, special accounting treatment is needed.

For example, on January 1, 19xx, Hickman Corporation accepted an $80,000 subscription agreement for 4,000 shares of $2 par value stock to be paid in two installments of $40,000 each on July 1, 19xx, and December 31, 19xx. Hickman recorded the following:

19xx			
Jan. 1	Subscriptions Receivable—Common (A)	80,000	
	Common Stock Subscribed (SE)		8,000
	Contributed Capital in Excess of Par—Common Stock (SE) . .		72,000
	To record subscription agreement for 4,000 shares.		
July 1	Cash (A)	40,000	
	Subscriptions Receivable—Common (A)		40,000
	To record receipt of first installment payment.		
Dec. 31	Cash (A)	40,000	
	Subscriptions Receivable—Common (A)		40,000
	To record receipt of second and final installment payment.		
31	Common Stock Subscribed (SE)	8,000	
	Common Stock—Par (SE)		8,000
	To record the issuance of 4,000 shares of $2 par value common stock.		

In our example, the Common Stock Subscribed account has no balance at year-end and would not appear on the 12/31 balance sheet. When a balance sheet is made before subscribed stock is issued, the Common Stock Subscribed account is shown as stockholders' equity on the balance sheet in the same section as par value. Subscriptions Receivable—Common is a current asset and treated much the same as Accounts Receivable. The Contributed Capital in Excess of Par account is used regardless of whether stock is sold outright or through subscriptions.

Balance Sheet Presentation of Contributed Capital

The balance sheet or a footnote to the balance sheet should indicate the par value of the company's stock and the number of shares authorized, issued, and outstanding. The number of authorized shares is the maximum number of shares allowed to be issued by the corporate charter; the number issued represents the shares sold to owners; and the number outstanding are the shares currently in the hands of owners. These three numbers may be different. All shares authorized may not be issued. Some shares that have been issued may be bought back and held as treasury stock (see page 572) and although treasury shares are considered issued, they would not be considered outstanding.

Exhibit 11–1 shows a corporate annual report disclosure of contributed capital. Note that the par value of Reebok's common stock is listed as $0.01 per share. Compare Reebok's 19x5 total contributed capital of $43,622,000 with its legal capital (par) of $160,000. The average share of common stock was sold by the company for about $2.73 per share, but each share has a par value of only $0.01 per share. Exhibit 11–1 also shows an analysis of the change in Reebok stock from January 1, 19x5, to December 31, 19x5. The 13,053,601 shares previously issued had an average selling price of just over $0.01 per share, while the 2,929,658 shares issued in 19x5 had an average selling price of over $14 per share. Such great differences in the amount per share are not uncommon

Objective 6
The corporate balance sheet presentation of contributed capital.

EXHIBIT 11–1

Example of Annual Report Disclosure of Contributed Capital

Reebok International Ltd. Partial Balance Sheet December 31		
	(000)	
	19x5	**19x4**
Stockholders' equity (Notes 7 and 11): Common stock, par value $0.01 per share; authorized 20,000,000 shares; issued and outstanding 15,983,259 shares in 19x5, 13,053,601 in 19x4	$ 160	$131
Additional paid-in capital	43,462	37

Analysis of Shares Issued in 19x5			
		Rounded	
	Number of Shares Outstanding	**$.01 Par Value**	**Additional Paid-In Capital**
January 1, 19x5	13,053,601	$131,000	$ 37,000
Issued during 19x5.	2,929,658	29,000	43,425,000
December 31, 19x5	15,983,259	$160,000	$43,462,000

when a long period of time separates the two issuances of stock. In the Reebok case, the initial issuance sold for close to par, and the later issuance reflects increased market value.

An important point to remember about shares of stock is that after a corporation issues the shares, they may change hands among investors, but this has no effect on the issuing corporation's accounting for contributed capital. The market value of a share after issuance by a corporation may be greater or less than the initial selling price.

REACQUISITION AND RETIREMENT OF STOCK

A Case of Murky Motivations

In what follows you will eavesdrop on the quarterly meeting of the board of directors of Kenco, Inc., a major manufacturer of turbines, as they discuss their president's plan to reacquire half of the company's stock.

President: Ladies and gentlemen, we have paid our shareholders $0.25 per share for the last 40 quarters. I believe that we have tremendous potential growth in our earnings per share and I believe that the stockholders want more cash flow. So, I propose that we do two things. Buy back and retire half of the outstanding stock and then increase our dividend each quarter for the next eight quarters until we reach $0.50 per share per quarter. We will pay $2 in excess of the current market price of $24 so those interested in immediate cash will be satisfied and then those remaining will be very happy with the increased future dividends and stock value appreciation. Look at Chart 1 to see our projections of the balance sheet effects of the reacquisition assuming everything else remains constant. Note that we will have to use $500 million of cash and securities and a loan of $2.1 billion to make the deal.

Chart 1

	($000)	
	Now	**After Repurchase***
Cash and marketable securities	$1,000,000	$ 500,000
Other assets	4,000,000	4,000,000
	$5,000,000	$4,500,000
Liabilities	$ 500,000	$2,600,000
Common stock (no par)	3,000,000	1,500,000
Retained earnings	1,500,000	400,000
	$5,000,000	$4,500,000

*The journal entry to record the reacquisition and retirement of half of the stock:

	(000)	
Common Stock	1,500,000	
Retained Earnings	1,100,000	
Cash		500,000
Liabilities		2,100,000

Note that retained earnings can be reduced when stock is retired at amounts in excess of the original selling price.

Board member: That really seems to hurt our liquidity with our debt going from $500 million to $2.6 billion. I don't see what we gain by this.

President: Well, we believe that at $24 a share our stock is very much undervalued. If our income increases over the next two years as expected, we believe that the price per share will triple. So buying our own stock is our best investment.

Board member: If that's true, are we hurting ourselves by reducing our future borrowing capacity? We won't be able to build the plant we need to expand our production.

President: No, I don't think so. We could always sell more shares of stock later at the higher price.

Board member: We are reducing our retained earnings by $1.1 billion. Won't that limit future dividends?

President: No, because our projected earnings over the next few years will add considerably to the retained earnings balance.

The preceding conversation hints at the complexity behind many of the buy-backs of stock that have been so prevalent in the stock market of late. What are the president's motivations? Perhaps he or she and management are considering a leveraged buyout, in which a small group borrows money against the assets of the business and buys out all or most of the other shareholders. Or, maybe the president and a group of managers own enough shares to have significant influence in board selection if the total number of shareholders is reduced. Another motivation could be that a hostile takeover, in which an outside party tries to acquire enough shares to get control, is anticipated and, by the borrowing of money and perhaps the elimination of shareholders who might vote against management, the corporation can be made less attractive as a takeover target. Of course, it is also possible that the president is sincerely interested in the welfare of the current shareholders and the competitive position of the company. We leave further discussion of these issues to more advanced accounting and finance texts.

We will now cover the accounting for reacquisitions followed by the accounting for dividends and related issues.

Treasury Stock

Objective 7
Accounting for the reacquisition and retirement of stock.

Although issued stock remains **outstanding** in the hands of owners for long periods of time, sometimes corporations reacquire their shares and reissue them for various purposes. When a company holds reacquired shares, they are called treasury stock (or treasury shares).

If stock is reacquired and retired, the corporation reduces its asset and capital balances permanently. Retirement of stock cancels the shares, and they cannot be reissued. Treasury stock, however, is normally intended for purposes such as employee compensation plans in which shares are issued to employees, and does not involve a permanent reduction in the number of shares outstanding.

Treasury shares held by the issuing corporation have a special status that falls somewhere between issued and unissued shares. Because a corporation cannot own itself, corporate management cannot vote the treasury shares, and the corporation cannot pay itself dividends on the treasury shares it holds. In this sense, treasury shares are similar to unissued shares. Also, treasury shares can be resold without triggering the preemptive right provision that is present in authorized and unissued shares.

Treasury shares are disclosed on the balance sheet as a contra account to all of stockholders' equity. For example, Fuelmakers, Inc., issued all of its 20,000 authorized shares of $1 par value common stock for $5 per share on July 1, 19x1. On December 1, 19x1, Fuelmakers purchased 800 shares of its issued stock on the open market for $6 per share. The journal entries to record these transactions are as follows:

19x1			
July 1	Cash (A).	100,000	
	Common Stock—Par (SE).		20,000
	Contributed Capital in Excess of Par—Common (SE).		80,000
	To record issuance of 20,000 shares of common stock at $5 per share.		
Dec. 1	Treasury Stock—Common (XSE).	4,800	
	Cash (A).		4,800
	To record the acquisition of 800 shares of common stock for $6 per share.		

The December 31, 19x1, balance sheet would include the following stockholders' equity section, assuming net income was $40,000 and no dividends were paid.

Fuelmakers, Inc.
Partial Balance Sheet
December 31, 19x1

Stockholders' equity:

Contributed capital:

Common stock ($1 par) 20,000 shares authorized and issued and 19,200 shares outstanding	$20,000	
Contributed capital in excess of par—common	80,000	$100,000
Retained earnings.		40,000
		$140,000
Less treasury stock at cost—800 shares		(4,800)
Total stockholders' equity.		$135,200

Note the location of the debit balance of $4,800 for treasury stock as contra to all of stockholders' equity. Treasury stock is recorded at cost, which in this case is $4,800, as a contra account to owners' equity. The number of shares authorized and issued are not affected by treasury stock acquisition, but treasury shares do reduce the number of shares outstanding.

Treasury stock can be resold later. No matter what the selling price may be, no gain or loss is recognized on the income statement. Likewise, retained earnings cannot be increased by transactions in a company's own stock; therefore, selling treasury stock for an amount exceeding purchase price does not affect retained earnings. Accountants consider a "gain" on treasury stock sales to be additional contributed capital, much the same as contributed capital in excess of par. For instance, if Fuelmakers sells 400 treasury shares for $8 each ($2 per share more than what they paid for the treasury shares) on January 15, 19x2, the following entry would be recorded:

19x2			
Jan. 15	Cash (A)	3,200	
	Treasury Stock—Common (XSE)		2,400
	Contributed Capital from Treasury Stock Transactions (SE). . . .		800
	To record the sale of 400 shares of treasury stock for $8 per share.		

Treasury stock could be sold for less than the original purchase price. In such cases, the "loss" on the transaction is applied first to any existing credit balance in Contributed Capital from Treasury Stock Transactions. If the "loss" exceeds previous "gains," Retained Earnings or Contributed Capital in Excess of Par may be debited for the excess. For instance, if Fuelmakers sells 200 shares at $3 each on June 12, 19x2, and 200 shares at $2 per share on October 31, 19x2, the $800 balance in Contributed Capital from Treasury Stock Transactions account would first be eliminated and then Retained Earnings would be reduced.

19x2			
June 12	Cash (A)	600	
	Contributed Capital from Treasury Stock Transactions (SE)	600	
	Treasury Stock—Common (XSE)		1,200
	To record the sale of 200 shares of treasury stock for $3 per share.		
Oct. 31	Cash (A)	400	
	Contributed Capital from Treasury Stock Transactions (SE)	200	
	Retained Earnings (SE)	600	
	Treasury Stock—Common (XSE)		1,200
	To record the sale of 200 shares of treasury stock for $2 per share.		

If stock is reacquired for purposes of cancelling the shares, then such a retirement is recorded by debits to Common Stock—Par and Contributed Capital in Excess of Par—Common for the amounts initially paid in. If more is paid upon retirement than was initially paid in, Retained Earnings is debited for the excess. For example, if Fuelmakers, Inc., purchased 1,000 shares at $6.00 per share on December 15, 19x2, the following entry would be made:

19x2			
Dec. 15	Common Stock—Par	1,000	
	Contributed Capital in Excess of Par—Common	4,000	
	Retained Earnings	1,000	
	Cash		6,000
	To record the retirement of 1,000 shares of common stock.		

If the reacquisition was at an amount less than the initial paid-in amount, say $4 per share, then the following entry would be made:

19x2			
Dec. 15	Common Stock—Par	1,000	
	Contributed Capital in Excess of Par—Common	3,000	
	Cash		4,000
	To record the retirement of 1,000 shares of common stock.		

DONATED CAPITAL, DIVIDENDS, AND SPLITS

Donated Capital

*Objective 8
Accounting for donated capital, cash dividends, and stock dividends and splits.*

Sometimes corporations receive assets from outsiders, such as land donated by a municipality as an inducement to open a facility. In cases like these involving no payment of cash or stock, the corporation credits a contributed capital account, Donated Capital, for the fair value of the asset. The balance in the Donated Capital account is an addition to contributed capital along with par value and contributed capital in excess of par. Such contributions have no initial income statement effect. For example, if the Montreux Corporation accepts a building site worth $100,000 from the city of Mount Blanc, the asset Land would be recorded as follows:

19xx			
Jan. 1	Land (A)	100,000	
	Donated Capital (SE)		100,000
	To record receipt of land from the city of Mount Blanc with a fair value of $100,000.		

Because Montreux issued no stock, the city of Mount Blanc has no ownership interest in the company. Of course, Montreux would have an obligation to locate on the Mount Blanc site. If the land is actually worth $100,000 on the date of donation and Montreux can use the land in the same manner as land purchased outright, the financial statements would not distinguish the donated land from other owned land. The Donated Capital balance would stay on the books permanently, even if the land is eventually sold or written off.

You should understand that contributors of capital (whether donated or given in purchase of stock) transfer something of value to the company, usually cash but sometimes other assets. Once the company receives the asset, it is accounted for according to its subsequent use in the business. If a building were donated to a business, the fair value of the building would be recorded as an asset that would be depreciated in the normal fashion.

Cash Dividends

Stockholders invest in corporations to earn a return on their investments. One element of the return on investment is dividend payments. A dividend is a distribution of earnings to stockholders in cash or something else of value. Corporations distribute dividends on a **pro rata** basis; that is, in strict proportion to the number of shares held by the stockholder. For example, if Tymekeep, Inc., has 100,000 shares of common stock issued and outstanding and Ms. Kelp owns 10,000 shares, she will receive 1/10 of total dividend payments. Also, if Tymekeep Inc., has 100,000 shares issued and 10,000 shares are held in treasury, Ms. Kelp's 10,000 shares would give her the right to 1/9 of any dividends distributed, because dividends are paid only on outstanding shares.

The board of directors controls the payment of dividends, and no liability exists for payment of dividends until the board makes a formal **declaration** of dividends. However, the board is constrained in dividend policy in several ways. First, state laws usually limit dividend distributions to the amount of a positive Retained Earnings balance. This usually means that profitable operations must precede dividend payments. Second, even if a corporation has a positive Retained Earnings balance, it still must have assets to distribute, usually cash. As discussed in earlier chapters, profitable operations do not always have cash available. Third, when different classes of stock exist, the corporation must consider dividend preferences. Preferred stock must be paid the proper amount per share before common stock stockholders are paid anything.

Dividend distributions involve a standard series of events:

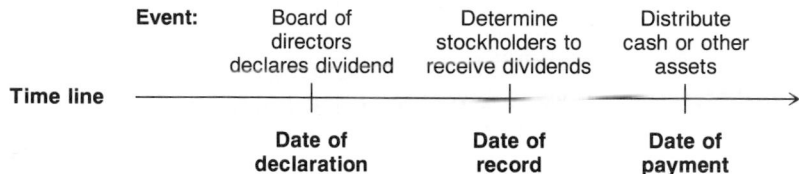

	Event:	Board of directors declares dividend	Determine stockholders to receive dividends	Distribute cash or other assets
Time line				
		Date of declaration	Date of record	Date of payment

As an example, assume that the Wiretron Corporation has the following stockholders' equity:

Wiretron Corporation
Partial Balance Sheet
December 31, 19x1

Stockholders' equity:
  Contributed capital:

Common stock—$2 par, 100,000 shares authorized, issued, and outstanding	$ 200,000	
Contributed capital in excess of par—common.	1,500,000	
Preferred stock—10%, $50 par, 10,000 shares authorized, issued, and outstanding	500,000	$2,200,000
Retained earnings		1,200,000
Total stockholders' equity		$3,400,000

On January 1, 19x2, the board of directors of Wiretron declares a total cash dividend of $250,000 to be paid on January 31, 19x2, to stockholders of record on January 15, 19x2. The board has a policy of paying dividends once a year in this manner. The following series of entries would record the transactions:

19x2				
Jan. 1	Retained Earnings (SE)		250,000	
	Cash Dividends Payable—Common (L)			200,000
	Cash Dividends Payable—Preferred (L)			50,000

To record the declaration of $250,000 in cash dividends to be distributed to preferred stockholders on the basis of 10% of $500,000 or $5 per share and $2 per share to common stockholders.

15	No entry is made on the date of record.		

31	Cash Dividends Payable—Common (L)	200,000	
	Cash Dividends Payable—Preferred (L)	50,000	
	Cash (A)		250,000

To record payment of cash dividends declared on January 1, 19x2.

On the date of declaration, a current liability is recorded because the corporation has an obligation to pay its stockholders once a declaration has been made. For large corporations with thousands of stockholders and active trading of shares, the task of determining the stockholders who are to receive dividends can be a difficult one. For corporations with a small number of shares, it is easier to determine the list of outstanding stockholders. Determining the actual cash recipients does not affect any accounts, and no entry is made on the date of record. The elimination of the liability is recorded on the date of payment.

In the above example, the account Retained Earnings was debited on the declaration date. Often an account titled *Dividends* is debited. This is a temporary account that is closed to retained earnings in the closing entries.

Stock Dividends

As a substitution for or in conjunction with cash dividends, corporations sometimes issue additional shares of stock to existing stockholders. These distributions, called stock dividends, are governed by the preemptive rights of existing stockholders. Therefore, each stockholder would get a pro rata increase in the number of shares owned. Distributing shares rather than cash could be motivated by a desire to issue a dividend at a time of cash shortage. Corporations also issue stock dividends to reduce the market value per share of the outstanding stock.

Small Stock Dividend. If the number of shares distributed is small, for example, less than 20 percent of shares outstanding, the distribution is called a small stock dividend, and Retained Earnings is reduced by the market value of the new shares at the time of the declaration. For instance, assume that on June 30, 19xx, a corporation has 500,000 shares of $1 par value common stock issued and outstanding with a market value of $6 per share and declares a stock dividend to be paid on July 31, 19xx. The number of shares to be distributed pro rata to stockholders of record on July 15, 19xx, is 25,000 shares, or 5% of the outstanding shares. The following journal entries would record the transactions:

19xx				
June 30	Retained Earnings (SE)	150,000	
	Stock Dividend Distributable—Common (SE).		25,000
	Contributed Capital in Excess of Par— Stock Dividend (SE)		125,000
	To record the declaration of a 5% stock dividend (25,000 shares at $6) to stockholders of record on July 15, 19xx.		
July 15	No entry on date of record.		
31	Stock Dividend Distributable—Common (SE).	25,000	
	Common Stock—Par (SE)		25,000
	To record the issuance of 25,000 shares of common stock.		

Note that the Contributed Capital in Excess of Par account is credited for the selling price minus the par value ($150,000 − $25,000).

Accountants do not classify the Stock Dividend Distributable—Common account as a liability but consider it a contributed capital account and list it in the stockholders' equity section of a balance sheet prepared between the declaration and payment dates. Although it is rarely done, the board can rescind stock dividends before the issuance date. This potential recall supports the practice of classifying Stock Dividend Distributable as stockholders' equity rather than as a liability.

Large Stock Dividends and Splits. Distributions of large percentages of stock to existing stockholders are called large stock dividends and stock splits. Accountants view any dividend distribution above 20 to 25% of the shares outstanding as a large stock dividend. These large stock dividends are accounted for by a debit to Retained Earnings for only the par or stated value per share, if any; fair market values are ignored. The credit is to the Common Stock—Par account for large stock dividends. For stock splits, no journal entries are necessary because only the number of shares outstanding and the par value per share, if any, are affected.

Stock splits involve the issuance of new shares at a lower par value to replace the old shares, thus increasing the number of shares outstanding without changing the total dollars of contributed capital. The motivation for a stock split usually relates to a policy of keeping the market price per share within a certain range so that the stock will be more marketable.

The economic effect of a stock split is the same as that of a large or small stock dividend. In all three cases, the individual stockholders each own the same percentage interest in the entity before and after the split or dividend. Neither the total value of the entity nor the individual stockholder's percentage of ownership in the entity change as a result of a split or stock dividend, and net assets (or total stockholders' equity) remains the same.

The following example shows how large stock dividends and splits can affect the corporation's balance sheet and stock prices. Valuedate Corporation has 20,000 shares of $2 par value common stock issued and outstanding on April 1, 19x1, with a market price of $70 per share. A 100% stock dividend would double the number of $2 par value shares outstanding. A 2-for-1 stock split would double the number of shares outstanding and at the same time reduce the par value per share to $1. In both cases, the market would revalue the individual shares, adjusting the price to approximately $35 per share, but the total market value of all shares would be unaffected.

Exhibit 11–2 shows the effects of the 100% stock dividend and the 2-for-1 split on Valuedate Corporation's balance sheet and per share market values. Note that no economic impact occurs in terms of total market value of all shares outstanding. Within the stockholders' equity section of the balance sheet, however, the description of shares outstanding and the par value per share amounts have changed. In the case of a large stock dividend with par value stock, Retained Earnings is reduced by the amount of the credit to the par value account, which is simply the number of shares times the par value.

EXHIBIT 11–2

Comparison of the Effect of Large Stock Dividends and Stock Splits on the Stockholders' Equity Section of the Balance Sheet

Valuedate Corporation

Before Dividend/Split		After 100% Dividend		After 2 for 1 Split	
Stockholders' equity:		Stockholders' equity:		Stockholders' equity:	
Common stock—$2 par, 20,000 shares issued and outstanding	$ 40	Common stock—$2 par, 40,000 shares issued and outstanding	$ 80	Common stock—$1 par, 40,000 shares issued and outstanding	$ 40
Contributed capital in excess of par	85	Contributed capital in excess of par	85	Contributed capital in excess of par	85
	$125		$165		$125
Retained earnings	150	Retained earnings	110	Retained earnings	150
Total stockholders' equity	$275	Total stockholders' equity	$275	Total stockholders' equity	$275

Market value analysis:			Market value analysis:			Market value analysis:		
Shares Outstanding	Market Value per Share	Total Market Value	Shares Outstanding	Market Value per Share	Total Market Value	Shares Outstanding	Market Value per Share	Total Market Value
20,000	$70	$1,400	40,000	$35	$1,400	40,000	$35	$1,400

			Journal entry:			Journal entry:		
			Retained Earnings	40		No entry necessary for a stock split.		
			Common Stock—Par . .		40			
			To record stock dividend.					

Note: Dollars are in thousands.

Special Features of
Preferred Stock

Objective 9
What makes preferred
stock different from
common stock.

Preferred stock may have several contractual stipulations that are not found in common stock. Most preferred stock is cumulative. Thus, dividends not paid in one period accumulate and must be paid in subsequent periods before common stockholders are paid any further dividends.

If cumulative preferred stock dividends are not paid in one year, they accumulate dividends in arrears. For example, if a corporation issues 100,000 shares of $100 par value cumulative 8% preferred stock on January 1, 19x1, and pays no dividends in 19x1 and 19x2, the dividends in arrears as of December 31, 19x2, would be $1.6 million [$10 million × .08 (percent dividend) × 2 (years)]. Before common stockholders could receive any dividends in 19x3, the preferred stockholders would have to receive $1.6 million dividends in arrears plus $800,000 of current preferred dividends applicable to 19x3. Dividends in arrears are not liabilities since no liability exists until dividends are declared. However, once dividends are declared, dividends in arrears have preference and must be paid first.

Sometimes preferred stocks are allowed to participate in cash dividends in excess of the dividend amount stated per share. This is called participating preferred stock. Preferred stock may carry with it a conversion privilege that allows the holder under certain conditions to trade a share of preferred stock, called convertible preferred stock, for a fixed number of common shares. These and many other possible features of preferred stock are discussed in intermediate accounting texts.

Preferred stock contracts often allow the issuing corporation to purchase the preferred stock back from the stockholders by paying a stated amount per share, usually the par value plus a redemption premium. These are known as callable preferred stock. Preferred stock can also be reacquired by making a **tender offer**, which involves offering holders of preferred stock an amount in excess of market value.

Upon issuance, callable preferred stock is accounted for in the same manner as noncallable preferred stock, with Preferred Stock and Contributed Capital in Excess of Par—Preferred being credited for the contributed capital. The entry to record a redemption includes an elimination of the applicable par balance and contributed capital in excess of par balance for the shares redeemed and a credit to Cash. If less is paid to redeem the shares than was received at issuance, a new account, Contributed Capital from Redemption of Preferred Stock, is credited. For example, on January 1, 19xx, the Mirror Corporation has 10,000 shares of $100 par value preferred stock outstanding with contributed capital in excess of par of $100,000, or $10 per share. Assume that all shares of preferred originally sold for $110 per share. On January 10, 19xx, 4,000 shares are purchased on the open market at $105 per share. The journal entry recorded on that date would be as follows:

19xx			
Jan. 10	Preferred Stock (SE)	400,000	
	Contributed Capital in Excess of Par—Preferred (SE)	40,000	
	Contributed Capital from Redemption of Preferred Stock (SE)		20,000
	Cash (A)		420,000
	To record redemption of preferred stock.		

Mirror was able to redeem the stock for $105 per share, or $20,000 less than the original selling price. This excess is credited to a contributed capital account identifying the $20,000 capital as being created by a redemption of preferred stock. If more is paid to redeem the preferred stock than was originally received upon issuance, Retained Earnings is debited for the amount of the excess. In our example, if Mirror had paid $112 per share (instead of $105 per share) to redeem 4,000 shares, the redemption entry would have been

```
19xx
Jan. 10   Preferred Stock (SE) . . . . . . . . . . . . . . . . . . . . .    400,000
          Contributed Capital in Excess of Par—Preferred (SE) . . . . . .     40,000
          Retained Earnings (SE)  . . . . . . . . . . . . . . . . . .          8,000
              Cash (A) . . . . . . . . . . . . . . . . . . . . . . .                     448,000
          To record redemption of preferred stock.
```

In this case the capital in excess of par of $10 per share contributed initially was eliminated, and retained earnings equal to the difference between the original issue price ($110) and the redemption price ($112) of $2 per share was also eliminated.

• SUMMARY

This chapter began with a discussion on how the form of business organization— noncorporate or corporate—affects some aspects of accounting, especially those related to owners' equity. Many other important aspects of accounting are not affected by the form of business organization, such as accounting for most assets, liabilities, revenues, and expenses. Noncorporate businesses are viewed by the law as, in essence, combining the owner and the business for certain purposes. In corporate businesses, the stockholders and the business entity are viewed as separate, both by the law and by accountants.

Corporations provide several advantages over other forms of business. The major advantage for the corporation is the ability to raise large amounts of capital. Limited liability of stockholders, continuity of business, and ease of ownership transfer aid in pooling the financial resources needed for a large business. The economies provided by specialized management not limited to owners also make corporations desirable in today's highly specialized business world.

These and other features of corporations have implications for accounting and business decisions. Balance sheets communicate certain features of stockholder rights, such as the breakdown between par value and contributed capital in excess of par, and the distinctions between common and preferred stock and between contributed capital and retained earnings. Stockholders' equity disclosures make these and other distinctions, some of which are purely legalistic while others are reflective of economic transactions.

Although dividend policy is a very complex issue, accountants must record the effects of dividend declarations and payments. Preferred and common stocks' dividends are controlled by different contractual terms. Several of the common transactions were introduced in this chapter.

• DEMONSTRATION EXERCISE

Flatbush Products, Inc., is formed on September 20, 19x1. The following selected transactions occur during 19x1 and 19x2:

19x1
Sept. 20   Incur $10,000 in legal fees for the organization of the corporation. These fees are paid with 1,000 shares of $10 par value common stock.

30   Issue 10,000 shares of $10 par value common stock for $15 per share and 500 shares of 5%, $100 par value preferred stock for $115 per share.

19x2
Feb. 1   Accept a $36,000 stock subscriptions agreement for 2,000 shares of common stock. One half of the subscriptions are paid for on March 1, and the remainder paid on April 1, when all of the 2,000 shares are issued.

June 30   Purchase 100 shares of previously issued stock at $12 per share. Resell 50 shares on July 15 for $10 per share and another 25 shares on August 31 for $15 per share.

Sept. 30   Declare the preferred stock dividend and a $0.40 per share cash dividend on outstanding common stock of record on October 31. The dividends are to be paid on November 15, 19x2.

Oct. 1   Declare a 10% common stock dividend on outstanding shares with a market value of $18 per share. The dividend is to be issued on November 15 to stockholders of record on October 31.

Dec. 15   Declare a 2-for-1 stock split effective December 31.

     31   The organization costs are amortized over a 20-year period starting January 1, 19x2.

Required:

Prepare the journal entries in general journal form for the above transactions.

Solution:

19x1			
Sept. 20	Organization Costs (A)	10,000	
	Common Stock—Par (SE)		10,000
	To record legal fees for organization.		
30	Cash (A)	150,000	
	Common Stock—Par (SE)		100,000
	Contributed Capital in Excess of Par—Common (SE)		50,000
	To record issuance of 10,000 shares of common stock.		
30	Cash (A)	57,500	
	Preferred Stock (SE)		50,000
	Contributed Capital in Excess of Par—Preferred (SE)		7,500
	To record issuance of 500 shares of preferred stock.		
19x2			
Feb. 1	Subscriptions Receivable—Common (A)	36,000	
	Common Stock Subscribed (SE)		20,000
	Contributed Capital in Excess of Par—		
	Common Stock (SE)		16,000
	To record subscription agreement for 2,000 shares.		
Mar. 1	Cash (A)	18,000	
	Subscriptions Receivable—Common (A)		18,000
	To record receipt of payment on subscription agreement.		
Apr. 1	Cash (A)	18,000	
	Subscriptions Receivable—Common (A)		18,000
	To record receipt of final payment on subscription agreement.		
	Common Stock Subscribed (SE)	20,000	
	Common Stock—Par (SE)		20,000
	To record issuance of 2,000 shares of common stock.		
June 30	Treasury Stock (XSE)	1,200	
	Cash (A)		1,200
	To record purchase of 100 shares at $12 per share of issued stock.		

July 15	Cash (A)	500
	Retained Earnings (SE)	100
	Treasury Stock (XSE)		600

To record sale of 50 shares of treasury stock at $10 per share.

Aug. 31	Cash (A)	375
	Treasury Stock (XSE)		300
	Contributed Capital in Excess of Par—	
	Treasury Stock (SE)		75

To record sale of 25 shares of treasury stock at $15 per share.

Sept. 30	Retained Earnings (SE)	7,690
	Dividends Payable (L)		7,690

To record preferred and common stock dividends declared.

Preferred: 500 shares $\times$ $5 = $2,500.   ~~5% dividend~~

Common: (1,000 + 10,000 + 2,000 − 25) $\times$
$0.40 = $5,190.

Oct. 1	Retained Earnings (SE)	23,355
	Stock Dividend Distributable—Common (SE)		12,975
	Contributed Capital in Excess of Par—	
	Stock Dividend (SE)		10,380

To record declaration of small stock dividend:
12,975 shares $\times$ .10 $\times$ $18 = $23,355.

Nov. 15	Dividends Payable (L)	7,690
	Cash (A)		7,690

To record payment of cash dividends.

Nov. 15	Stock Dividend Distributable—Common (SE)	12,975
	Common Stock—Par (SE)		12,975

To record issuance of 10% stock dividend.

Dec. 15	No journal entry for split.

Dec. 31	Amortization of Organization Costs (E)	500
	Organization Costs (A)		500

To record amortization or organization costs.

Accounting for Partnerships

Objective 10
Some of the accounting challenges created by partnerships.

Proprietorship and partnership accounting differ because of the complexity that multiple ownership creates in terms of rights and duties. Accounting records must reflect legal partnership relationships, especially in the critical area of capital accounts. For example, each partner has a capital account and a drawing account, and the amounts that go into these accounts are strictly governed by the partnership agreement or the Uniform Partnership Act if the partnership agreement is silent or nonexistent. This appendix discusses the accounting for the following critical partnership topics: original investment by partners, partnership profits and losses, return on capital allowance, salaries of partners, financial statements of a partnership, and dissolution of a partnership.

ORIGINAL INVESTMENT BY PARTNERS

The partnership agreement governs the initial dollar amount assigned to each partner's capital contribution as well as the percentages used to distribute subsequent profits and losses of the partnership. For example, the partnership agreement of the ABC Travel Agency, organized on January 1, 19x1, established that partners A, B, and C should make the following contributions:

Partner	Asset Contributed	Agreed-Upon Fair Value
A	Cash.	$10,000
B	Furniture and equipment	8,000
C	Prepaid one year of rent on office space . .	12,000
	Total contribution	$30,000

The journal entry to record the formation of the partnership is

```
19x1
Jan. 1   Cash (A). . . . . . . . . . . . . . . . . . . . . . . . . . . . .   10,000
         Furniture and Equipment (A) . . . . . . . . . . . . . . . . . .    8,000
         Prepaid Rent (A) . . . . . . . . . . . . . . . . . . . . . . . .   12,000
              A, Capital (OE). . . . . . . . . . . . . . . . . . . . . . .          10,000
              B, Capital (OE). . . . . . . . . . . . . . . . . . . . . . .           8,000
              C, Capital (OE). . . . . . . . . . . . . . . . . . . . . . .          12,000
         To record initial investment in partnership.
```

Note that the furniture contributed by B is recorded at a fair value of $8,000 at January 1, 19x1. This furniture may have been purchased previously and used in another business. You may wonder how the $8,000 fair value is established. The $8,000 is not necessarily the original cost or the current book value on B's individual records. The partners simply agreed on the value among themselves.

It is possible that partners could agree to assign capital to owners in some proportion not equal to the actual value of asset contribution. Assume that X, Y, and Z form a partnership. Z has great experience in the industry, and X and Y, who are less knowledgeable, are willing to contribute assets and give Z credit for her experience. The partnership agreement could give each one third of the capital, although the asset contribution comes entirely from X and Y, as follows:

Partner	Asset Contributed	Fair Value of Tangible Assets Contributed	Capital Allocation
X	Cash.	$30,000	$20,000
Y	Equipment	30,000	20,000
Z	None.	0	20,000
		$60,000	$60,000

The journal entry to record the formation of XYZ partnership would be

Cash (A)	30,000	
Equipment (A).	30,000	
X, Capital (OE)		20,000
Y, Capital (OE)		20,000
Z, Capital (OE)		20,000

To record the formation of XYZ partnership.

After the formation of XYZ partnership, each partner has co-ownership of the contributed assets. X's cash and Y's equipment are commingled, and Z has as much right to them as do the others.

PARTNERSHIP PROFITS AND LOSSES

How do the profits and losses affect the capital accounts? The answer depends completely on the partnership agreement, which usually includes a formula for the division of profits and losses. If nothing is stated in the partnership agreement about profits and losses, an equal amount is assigned to each partner. Obviously, such an equal division may not be acceptable when partners make unequal contributions of capital or make unequal efforts in running the business. Several variations of formulas for profit and loss division found in practice will be analyzed. Keep in mind that the partnership agreement can include any formula agreed upon by the partners.

The wording of the partnership agreement is crucial to a partnership, especially on the all-important distribution of profits to partners. Any number of distribution schemes can be devised. This section discusses accounting for partnership earnings under a series of simple assumptions and the four earnings distributions based on the following stated ratios:

1. Equal earnings distribution to each partner.
2. Earnings distribution based on the year's beginning capital balances with no withdrawals.
3. Earnings distribution based on the year's beginning capital balances with withdrawals.
4. Earnings distribution based on average capital balances for the year.

Case 1: Equal Earnings Distribution to Each Partner

The simplest formula for the distribution of earnings is to give each partner equal amounts of earnings. If C contributes $20,000 and D contributes $30,000 on January 1, 19x1, and earnings for years 1 and 2 are $60,000 and $100,000, respectively, the following journal entries summarize the effects of equal distribution of partnership earnings:

```
19x1
Jan.  1   Cash (A) . . . . . . . . . . . . . . . . . . . . . . . .   50,000
              C, Capital (OE) . . . . . . . . . . . . . . . . . .            20,000
              D, Capital (OE) . . . . . . . . . . . . . . . . . .            30,000
          To record the formation of partnership.


Dec. 31   Income Summary (OE). . . . . . . . . . . . . . . . .   60,000
              C, Capital (OE) . . . . . . . . . . . . . . . . . .            30,000
              D, Capital (OE) . . . . . . . . . . . . . . . . . .            30,000
          To close the Income Summary account to the partners'
          capital accounts.


19x2
Dec. 31   Income Summary (OE). . . . . . . . . . . . . . . . .  100,000
              C, Capital (OE) . . . . . . . . . . . . . . . . . .            50,000
              D, Capital (OE) . . . . . . . . . . . . . . . . . .            50,000
          To close the Income Summary account to the partners'
          capital accounts.
```

Case 2: Earnings Distribution Based on Beginning Capital Balances with No Withdrawals

If the partnership agreement states that the beginning capital balance ratio governs the earnings distribution of each period, the following computations would be made for C and D in years 1 and 2:

	19x1 Beginning Balance	Ratio		19x1 Earnings		Distribution of Earnings	19x1 Ending Capital Balance
C, capital.	$20,000	40%	×	$60,000	=	$24,000	$ 44,000
D, capital.	30,000	60	×	60,000	=	36,000	66,000
	$50,000	100%				$60,000	$110,000

	19x2 Beginning Balance	Ratio		19x2 Earnings		Distribution of Earnings	19x2 Ending Capital Balance
C, capital.	$ 44,000	40%	×	$100,000	=	$ 40,000	$ 84,000
D, capital.	66,000	60	×	100,000	=	60,000	126,000
	$110,000	100%				$100,000	$210,000

Journal entries closing the Income Summary to the partners' capital accounts would be made for each year as in Case 1.

Case 3: Earnings Distribution Based on Beginning Capital Balances with Withdrawals

Often partners withdraw cash or other assets from the partnership, thereby reducing their capital balances. This, of course, changes capital ratios. In our example, if C and D withdraw $30,000 and $20,000, respectively, during both 19x1 and 19x2, the following journal entry would be made for the withdrawals:

C, Withdrawals (OE)	30,000	
D, Withdrawals (OE)	20,000	
Cash (A)		50,000

To record withdrawals of money during year by the partners.

Year 1's earnings distribution would not be changed because the beginning balance for 19x1 is not affected by the withdrawal, but year 2's earnings distribution is changed because of the withdrawal's effect on the capital balances of each partner. Study the following tables:

Partner	1/1/x1 Beginning Balance	Ratio		19x1 Earnings	Distribution of Earnings	Capital Balance before Withdrawal	19x1 Withdrawal	19x1 Ending Capital Balance
C, capital	$20,000	40%	×	$60,000	$24,000	$ 44,000	$30,000	$14,000
D, capital	30,000	60	×	60,000	36,000	66,000	20,000	46,000
	$50,000	100%			$60,000	$110,000	$50,000	$60,000

Partner	1/1/x2 Beginning Balance	Ratio		19x2 Earnings	Distribution of Earnings	Capital Balance before Withdrawal	19x2 Withdrawal	19x2 Ending Capital Balance
C, capital	$14,000	23%	×	$100,000	$ 23,000	$ 37,000	$30,000	$ 7,000
D, capital	46,000	77	×	100,000	77,000	123,000	20,000	103,000
	$60,000	100%			$100,000	$160,000	$50,000	$110,000

Again, journal entries closing Income Summary to C's and D's capital accounts would be made at year-end, and the withdrawals would be closed to the capital accounts.

Case 4: Earnings Distribution Based on Average Capital Balances

C and D could decide to distribute earnings on any formula they choose. For example, if the weighted average capital balances are used and 19x1 earnings are not considered until year-end, the computations for 19x1 assuming a withdrawal of $30,000 for C on October 31 would be as follows:

C, Capital Balance		Fraction		Weighted Average Balance
$ 20,000	×	10/12	=	$16,668
(10,000)	×	2/12	=	(1,667)
				$15,001

The beginning capital balance for C is $20,000, the amount contributed at the creation of the partnership, and this balance remains for 10 months. C's withdrawal of $30,000 on October 31, 19x1, reduces the capital balance to a negative $10,000, and the balance remains for two months until December 31, 19x1.

If D withdrew $20,000 on October 31, the following computation of weighted average capital balance would be as follows:

D, Capital Balance		Fraction		Weighted Average Balance
$30,000	×	10/12	=	$25,002
10,000	×	2/12	=	1,667
				$26,669

The earnings distribution would be

Partner	Weighted Average Capital Balance	Ratio		Earnings	Distribution
C	$15,001	36%	×	$60,000	$21,600
D	26,669	64	×	60,000	38,400
	$41,670	100%			$60,000

The ratios are the weighted average capital balance for each partner divided by the weighted average capital of the partnership: for C $15,001/$41,670 = 36% and for D, $26,669/$41,670 = 64%.

RETURN ON CAPITAL ALLOWANCE

Often partners desire a return on their invested amounts before earnings are distributed. When partners are given an allowance for a return or interest on the capital amounts, this reduces the amount to be distributed based on the earnings distribution formula. For example, in the C and D partnership of the previous section, $60,000 was earned in 19x1. If a return on partners' capital balances is allowed, the earnings distribution involves two steps: first, a return is computed for each partner; and second, the residual amount of earnings after subtracting the return on capital is distributed according to the agreed-upon formula.

Assume that (1) C and D agree to a 12% return on average capital balances and (2) the residual amount of earnings after the return on capital is distributed equally. The following schedule shows the computation of income distribution for 19x1:

Partner	12% Return on Weighted Average Capital Balance		Equally Distributed Residual Earnings		Total 19x1 Distribution
C	$1,800	+	$27,500	=	$29,300
D	3,200	+	27,500	=	30,700
	$5,000	+	$55,000	=	$60,000

C's 12% return allowance is based on a $15,001 weighted average capital balance, and D's is based on $26,669 as computed in the previous example. The $27,500 residual earnings distribution to each partner is 50% of the earnings remaining after the allowance of the 12% return.

SALARIES OF PARTNERS

Often partners contribute different levels of service to the business, and this is reflected in differential salary amounts credited to capital accounts before the residual earnings (after the salaries and capital return allowance, if any) are distributed. For example, X and Y agree to share residual earnings equally, but first X is to be credited for $20,000 in salary and Y, $10,000. Assume the following two earnings distribution cases:

Case 1. Earnings before salaries, $100,000.
Case 2. Earnings before salaries, $25,000.

Case 1: Earnings before Salaries, $100,000

In Case 1, X and Y are first credited for their respective salaries, $20,000 and $10,000, which total $30,000. Since the earnings before salaries is $100,000, the residual earnings is $70,000, which is divided equally between X and Y as shown in the following table:

	X	Y	Total
Salary allowance	$20,000	$10,000	$ 30,000
Residual earnings distribution	35,000	35,000	70,000
Distribution	$55,000	$45,000	$100,000

Case 2: Earnings before Salaries, $25,000

In Case 2, the earnings before salary is only $25,000. The salary allowances create a negative residual earnings of $5,000, which must be distributed equally to X and Y. Thus, the total increase in capital accounts is $25,000, but it is distributed as follows:

	X	Y	Total
Salary allowance	$20,000	$10,000	$30,000
Residual earnings distribution . . .	(2,500)	(2,500)	(5,000)
Distribution	$17,500	$ 7,500	$25,000

Although the residual earnings amount is negative, this does not affect the basic form of the entry to close the Income Summary account but does make a considerable difference in the amount credited to each partner's capital.

FINANCIAL STATEMENTS OF A PARTNERSHIP

Partnership financial statements are similar in many ways to those of corporations and proprietorships; however, there are differences in the owners' equity section. A special statement titled **Statement of Partners' Capital** may be shown in addition to the capital accounts given on the balance sheet. The earnings statement often has a section that shows the allocation of net income (loss) to partners. Exhibit 11A-1 highlights the special features of partnership financial statements. Note that there is no income tax expense in PQ's income statement because the partners declare their share of the partnership's income on their own personal income tax returns.

DISSOLUTION OF A PARTNERSHIP

Unless the partnership agreement contains a special provision, the legal status of a partnership changes whenever the identity of the partners changes, for example as the result of the addition of a new partner, withdrawal of a partner, death of a partner, or reduction or increase of the interest of a partner. Often when such a change is made and the business continues, the business routine is uninterrupted. From the legal perspective, however, the old partnership is dissolved, and a new one is created.

EXHIBIT 11A–1

Special Features of Partnership Financial Statements

PQ Partnership
Income Statement
For the Year Ended December 31, 19x1

Fees revenue	$165,000
Expenses:	
Salaries expense	$ 45,400
Rent expense.	24,000
Insurance expense	3,600
Supplies expense	15,600
Utilities expense	18,400
Interest expense	8,000
Total expenses	$115,000
Net income.	$ 50,000

Distribution of income:	
50% to P.	$ 25,000
50% to Q	25,000
Net income.	$ 50,000

PQ Partnership
Statement of Partnership Capital
For the Year Ended December 31, 19x1

	P	Q	Total
Beginning capital, 1/1/x1	$40,000	$40,000	$ 80,000
Add: Net income for the year. . . .	25,000	25,000	50,000
Total available capital.	$65,000	$65,000	$130,000
Less: Withdrawals	5,000	15,000	20,000
Ending capital, 12/31/x1	$60,000	$50,000	$110,000

PQ Partnership
Balance Sheet
December 31, 19x1

Assets		Liabilities and Owners' Equity	
Current assets:		Liabilities:	
Cash.	$ 45,200	Accounts payable	$ 13,200
Accounts receivable.	82,100	Notes payable	80,000
Office supplies	1,200	Salaries payable	12,800
Prepaid rent	8,500	Taxes payable	24,600
Prepaid insurance.	3,600	Total liabilities	$130,600
Total current assets	$140,600		
		Owners' equity:	
		P, capital	$ 60,000
Land.	100,000	Q, capital	50,000
		Total owners' equity	$110,000
Total assets	$240,600	Total liabilities and owners' equity . . .	$240,600

Usually, when a partner is added or withdrawn, assets are added to or taken away from the partnership. In this section we discuss the five major categories of partner changes, shown in the following matrix:

Typical Patterns of Asset Flows		
Addition of a partner	**Case 1** New assets are added to partnership	**Case 2** New assets go to continuing partners
Withdrawal of a partner	**Case 3** Payment is made from partnership assets	**Case 4** Payment is made from partners' personal assets
Addition of a partner and withdrawal of a partner	**Case 5** New assets are given to old withdrawing partner	

Within each major category, several specific cases are discussed.

Adding a New Partner   **Case 1: Assets from New Partner Are Added to the Partnership.** In the first example, Partnership CD, with capital accounts of $100,000 each for C and D, admits a new partner, E, who contributes $100,000 in cash to the partnership.

Old Partnership CD   **New Partnership CDE**
Total Capital = $200,000   **Total Capital = $300,000**

The journal entry to record the admission of E is the following:

```
19x1
Jan. 1   Cash (A). . . . . . . . . . . . . . . . . . . . . . . . . . .   100,000
              E, Capital (OE). . . . . . . . . . . . . . . . . . . . .            100,000
         To record the admission of E to CDE partnership.
```

Note that the entity has grown in size because new assets were added. The partners should prepare a new partnership agreement.

Bonus. Assume that the CD Partnership is such a good business opportunity that E is willing to contribute $100,000 for a 20% interest. The cash goes to the partnership, increasing the net assets and capital by $100,000; and the ending capital of CDE is allocated 40% to C, 40% to D, and 20% to E.

Old Partnership CD   **New Partnership CDE**
Total Capital = $200,000   **Total Capital = $300,000**

The journal entry to record the capital contribution is

```
19x1
Jan. 1   Cash (A). . . . . . . . . . . . . . . . . . . . . . . . . . .   100,000
              C, Capital (OE). . . . . . . . . . . . . . . . . . . . .             20,000
              D, Capital (OE). . . . . . . . . . . . . . . . . . . . .             20,000
              E, Capital (OE). . . . . . . . . . . . . . . . . . . . .             60,000
         To record the admission of E to CDE partnership.
```

This method is called the bonus method because E is willing to pay an amount in excess of the capital credited to him or her, which can be said to be a bonus for the old partners.

In some situations, a partnership may need the talents of a prospective partner enough to offer to pay a bonus to entice him or her into joining the firm. For instance, C and D invite E to become an equal partner for a contribution of only $70,000 in cash. The partnership is $70,000 larger after the admission of E, but C and D have smaller capital balances, as follows:

Old Partnership CD	New Partnership CDE
Total Capital = $200,000	Total Capital = $270,000

In this situation, the bonus of $20,000 goes to E and the transaction is recorded as follows

19x1			
Jan. 1	Cash (A).	70,000	
	C, Capital (OE).	10,000	
	D, Capital (OE).	10,000	
	E, Capital (OE).		90,000
	To record the admission of E to CDE partnership.		

Note that all three partners now have capital of $90,000, or one third of the $270,000 total. Of course, C and D could agree to share the bonus given to E in some other way. It is not necessary that they share it equally.

Case 2: New Assets Go to Continuing Partners.   What if E pays $60,000 personally to both C and D for a one-third share of the partnership?

Old Partnership CD	New Partnership CDE
Total Capital = $200,000	Total Capital = $200,000

The business entity, in this case, has not increased in size because the asset flow was from the new partner to the old partners, bypassing the business completely. The journal entry shows that C's and D's capital accounts are reduced by equal amounts and that E is credited with $66,667 even though the payment to C and D totaled $120,000. The cash received by C and D did not affect the total capital of the partnership.

19x1			
Jan. 1	C, Capital (OE).	33,333	
	D, Capital (OE).	33,334	
	E, Capital (OE).		66,667
	To record the admission of E to CDE partnership.		

Withdrawal of a Partner

When a partner withdraws from a partnership, the remaining partnership legally becomes a new partnership just as when a new partner is admitted. The partnership agreement usually gives details as to the disposition of assets in the case of a withdrawal. A partner has a right to his or her share of the net assets of the partnership, but the book value may be more or less than the fair value of the assets. Consider the MNO partnership with the following balance sheet on January 1, 19x2:

MNO Partnership
Balance Sheet
January 1, 19x2

Assets		Liabilities and Owners' Equity	
Current assets:		Liabilities:	
Cash	$ 20,000	Accounts payable	$ 10,000
Accounts receivable	60,000	Notes payable	50,000
Inventories	100,000	Total liabilities	$ 60,000
Total current assets	$180,000	Owners' equity:	
Noncurrent assets:		M, capital	$120,000
Equipment (net)	$ 40,000	N, capital	120,000
Building (net)	200,000	O, capital	120,000
Total noncurrent assets	$240,000	Total owners' equity	$360,000
Total assets	$420,000	Total liabilities and owners' equity	$420,000

If the partnership agreement allows any partner to withdraw his or her share of assets at any time, some procedure is necessary to appraise the assets for their fair value and then to distribute the fair value according to the formulas prescribed in the partnership agreement. Several variations will be examined.

Case 3: Payment Is Made from Partnership.   On January 1, 19x2, O withdraws from the partnership. The partnership agreement states that a withdrawing partner is entitled to one third of the fair value of the net assets in cash. If M and N want to continue the business, they first must have the net assets appraised and then generate enough cash to pay O. Consider the following appraised values compared with book values:

	Book Value	Appraised Value	Difference
Cash	$ 20,000	$ 20,000	$ 0
Accounts receivable	60,000	55,000	(5,000)
Inventory	100,000	150,000	50,000
Equipment	40,000	60,000	20,000
Building	200,000	225,000	25,000
Accounts payable	(10,000)	(10,000)	0
Notes payable	(50,000)	(50,000)	0
Net assets	$360,000	$450,000	$90,000

The assets of the partnership are first revalued to fair value with the following journal entry:

19x2			
Jan. 1	Inventory (A)	50,000	
	Equipment (A)	20,000	
	Building (A)	25,000	
	Accounts Receivable (A)		5,000
	M, Capital (OE)		30,000
	N, Capital (OE)		30,000
	O, Capital (OE)		30,000
	To record revaluation of MNO partnership.		

Rather than liquidate the business or sell off some of the assets, M and N decide to have the partnership borrow the $150,000 necessary to pay off O:

```
19x2
Jan. 1   Cash (A). . . . . . . . . . . . . . . . . . . . . . . . . .   150,000
             Notes Payable . . . . . . . . . . . . . . . . . . .              150,000
         To record note taken to pay O.

Jan. 1   O, Capital (OE). . . . . . . . . . . . . . . . . . . .   150,000
             Cash (A). . . . . . . . . . . . . . . . . . . . . .              150,000
         To record withdrawal of O from partnership.
```

The following illustrate the changing capital structure of the partnership:

MNO Capital Balance before Restructure, $360,000	MNO Capital Balance after Restructure, $450,000	MN Capital Balance after Withdrawal of O, $300,000

Note that the total capital always equals the net assets of the business. Borrowing the $150,000 does not increase the net assets because the increase in cash is offset by the increase in a liability, notes payable.

Bonuses can be paid to the withdrawing partner, which means the agreement gives a withdrawing partner more assets than his or her capital balance would warrant. This may result from the partnership agreement, or it may be determined that the business would benefit from the departure and a bonus is offered.

Case 4: Payment Is Made from Remaining Partners' Personal Assets.   Consider the KLM partnership where partnership capital is equally divided at $100,000 for each partner. Assume that L sells her share directly to K and M for $120,000. K and M agree the capital of the new partnership would be divided equally between K and M.

Old Partnership KLM Total Capital = $300,000	New Partnership KM Total Capital = $300,000

The fact that L receives $20,000 more than book value is not recorded on the journal of the partnership.

```
19x1
June 30  L, Capital (OE) . . . . . . . . . . . . . . . . . . . .   100,000
             K, Capital (OE) . . . . . . . . . . . . . . . . . . .             50,000
             M, Capital (OE) . . . . . . . . . . . . . . . . . . .             50,000
         To record transfer of L's share of the partnership to K and M.
```

The key to understanding the effect of such transactions on partnerships is the entity concept. In this case, the asset flow circumvented the business entity; therefore, the overall size of the entity stayed the same. The capital account changes reflect the changing ownership of the business entity.

Case 5: New Assets Go to Withdrawing Partner.   Another possibility is for the departing partner to sell his or her share to a new partner; that is, a simultaneous adding and withdrawing of partners. In this case, neither the size of the partnership nor the relative capital balances of the remaining partners changes. For instance, assume that in our KLM example, L sells, with permission of K and M, her one-third share to O for $120,000. Because the partnership does not receive any cash, the following relationship of capital balances applies:

Old Partnership KLM Total Capital = $300,000	New Partnership KMO Total Capital = $300,000

The entry would merely record the fact that L's share is being taken over by O.

```
19x1
June 30    L, Capital (OE) . . . . . . . . . . . . . . . . . . . . . . .    100,000
               O, Capital (OE) . . . . . . . . . . . . . . . . . . . . .              100,000
           To record transfer of L's share of the partnership to O.
```

Various factors could motivate O to pay more or less than book value for the share of the business. As stressed many times, asset book values do not necessarily represent fair values; and when a business is sold in total or in part, the selling parties usually demand fair value.

Liquidation of a Partnership

When partners agree to liquidate or dissolve the partnership, they usually convert all assets to cash, pay off all creditors and then distribute the remaining cash on the basis of balances in the capital accounts. Complexities can arise when partners have negative balances in their capital accounts. The following shows how liquidation normally is recorded; as always, the partnership agreement can stipulate otherwise.

The PQ partnership had the following balance sheet book values before conversion of all assets to cash and the paying off of liabilities. Accounts Receivable yielded $20,000 in cash, and the building was sold for $200,000. The liability amount of $240,000 was paid to creditors.

	Book Value
Cash.	$120,000
Accounts receivable	50,000
Building (net)	400,000
Liabilities	240,000
P, capital	65,000
Q, capital.	265,000

The journal entries to record the sale of assets and payment of the liabilities are as follows:

```
19x1
Sept. 30   Cash (A). . . . . . . . . . . . . . . . . . . . . . . . . . .    220,000
           P, Capital (OE) . . . . . . . . . . . . . . . . . . . . . . .    115,000
           Q, Capital (OE). . . . . . . . . . . . . . . . . . . . . . .    115,000
               Accounts Receivable (A) . . . . . . . . . . . . . . .                50,000
               Building (A) . . . . . . . . . . . . . . . . . . . . . .              400,000
           To record liquidation of partnership's assets and allocation
           of associated losses of $230,000, equally.

           Liabilities . . . . . . . . . . . . . . . . . . . . . . . . . .    240,000
               Cash (A). . . . . . . . . . . . . . . . . . . . . . . . .              240,000
           To record payment of partnership's liabilities.
```

Because the conversion of the assets to cash results in losses totaling $230,000, each partner absorbs $115,000, reducing their capital balances. After posting the journal entries to record the losses, P's and Q's capital accounts would have the following balances:

P, Capital		Q, Capital	
	65,000		265,000
115,000		115,000	
50,000			150,000

Before the partnership is liquidated by means of a payment of the remaining cash to the partners, P must pay $50,000 to the partnership to eliminate the deficit in his account.

```
19x1
Sept. 30   Cash (A) . . . . . . . . . . . . . . . . . . . . . . . . . .      50,000
                P, Capital (OE) . . . . . . . . . . . . . . . . . . . .                50,000
                To record the payment by P of the deficit capital balance.
```

This entry gives P a zero capital balance and the $150,000 of cash is paid to Q.

```
19x1
Sept. 30   Q, Capital (OE) . . . . . . . . . . . . . . . . . . . .     150,000
                Cash (A) . . . . . . . . . . . . . . . . . . . . . .               150,000
                To record the liquidation of the PQ partnership.
```

This example shows a partner's capital account having a debit (negative) balance, which represents an obligation to the remaining partner upon liquidation. During ongoing operations, such negative balances may appear from time to time, and they can be eliminated through profitable operations or additional contributions. This example demonstrates the unlimited liability of general partners to creditors and the possible obligation that results when a partner's capital account is negative.

• KEY TERMS

Authorized shares. Maximum number of shares that the corporate charter allows to be issued.

Callable preferred stock. Preferred stock that allows the issuing corporation to purchase the preferred stock back from stockholders by paying a stated amount per share, usually the par value plus a redemption premium.

Common stock. Corporate securities that carry voting rights, preemptive rights, rights to share in dividends, and rights to the residual assets.

Common stockholders. Investors of corporations who own common stock.

Contributed capital. Total money contributed to the business by the owners.

Convertible preferred stock. Preferred stock that allows the holder under certain conditions to trade a share of preferred stock for a fixed number of common shares.

Corporation. An association of individuals recognized by law that has rights and responsibilities separate from its members.

Cumulative. Characteristic of preferred stock where unpaid dividends accumulate and must be paid in subsequent periods before common stockholders are paid any dividends.

Date of declaration. Date on which dividends are declared.

Date of payment. Date on which payment to stockholders for dividends is made.

Date of record. Date on which determination of which stockholders will receive dividends is made.

Dividend. Distribution of earnings to stockholders in cash or something else of value.

Dividend rights. Stockholders' rights to share in the distributions of earnings in the form of dividends.

Dividends in arrears. Cumulative preferred stock dividends that have not been paid.

Donated Capital. An owners' equity account that is credited when a corporation receives assets that are donated to the corporation; usually this donation is from a government unit that is attempting to encourage a business to locate in its area.

General partners. Owners of a partnership that have unlimited responsibility for the partnership's liabilities.

Hostile takeover. The acquisition by an outside party of enough shares of a corporation to gain control, without the cooperation of management.

Issued. The number of shares that have been sold to owners of a corporation.

Large stock dividends. Issuances of stock (usually 20 to 25 percent of the outstanding stock) to stockholders as dividends.

Legal capital. Amount of par or stated value of stock outstanding.

Leveraged buyout (LBO). A small group arranges a borrowing against the assets of the business and buys out all or most of the other shareholders.

Limited partners. Owners of a partnership whose liability responsibility is limited to the assets contributed to the partnership or some other specific amount.

Mutual agency. Allows each partner to borrow money, purchase assets, commit to sales contracts, and so on, in the name of the partnership without the other partners' consent.

No-par stock. Stock that has no par value assigned to it.

Outstanding. Shares previously issued that are currently held by owners.

Owner's capital account. Account used in a proprietorship or partnership to reflect the owner's interest.

Owner's drawing account. Account used in a proprietorship or partnership to keep track of the owner's withdrawals from the business during the period.

Participating preferred stock. Preferred stock that is allowed to participate with common stock in cash dividends in excess of the dividend amount stated per share.

Partnership. Multiowner, noncorporate business.

Partnership agreement. Formal agreement that lists the rights and responsibilities of partners.

Par value. Arbitrary value per share assigned to a share of stock; also called stated value; usually is the minimum issue price.

Preemptive right. Common stockholders' right to maintain their percentage of ownership.

Preferred stock. Class of stock that carries different rights than common stock, including various preferences.

Premium. Excess paid by stockholders over the stock's par value; also called contributed capital in excess of par.

Proprietorship. Single-owner, noncorporate business.

Residual asset right. Common stockholders' right to the residual assets of a corporation upon liquidation.

Small stock dividends. Issuance to stockholders in the form of a dividend of a small number of shares relative to the total number of outstanding shares (usually less than 20% of outstanding shares of stock).

Statement of owner's equity. Financial statement in a proprietorship and partnership that shows the owner's interest in a business over a period of time.

Stock dividend. Issuance of additional shares of stock to existing stockholders as a substitution for or in conjunction with cash dividends.

Stock splits. Issuances of stock to current stockholders resulting in a reduction in par value per share and a proportionate increase in shares outstanding.

Subscription contracts. Promises to pay the corporation for shares of stock at a future date.

Treasury stock. Shares of previously issued stock reacquired by the company but not retired.

Uniform Partnership Act (UPA). Law that governs the formation, operation, and liquidation of partnerships in most states.

Voting right. Common stockholders' right to elect a board of directors.

• SYNONYMS

Corporate charter; articles of incorporation.

Incorporators; promoters.

Large stock dividend; stock split.

Paid-in capital; contributed capital.

Par value; stated value.

Partnership agreement; articles of copartnership.

Premium; contributed capital in excess of par.

Treasury stock; treasury shares.

• QUESTIONS

1. Define three different forms of business organization and describe the major differences among them.
2. Describe four characteristics of partnerships.
3. Describe the advantages and disadvantages of forming a corporation.
4. Describe the process of forming a corporation.
5. What is common stock? Give four characteristics of common stock.
6. Define preferred stock and list several characteristics. Name two special types of preferred stock.
7. Define par value. Why is it important?
8. How is the accounting treatment different for stock subscriptions versus the issuance of shares of stock for cash?
9. Describe the difference between authorized, issued, and outstanding shares of stock.
10. Define treasury stock. Why would a company repurchase its own stock?
11. If treasury stock is sold for more than it was purchased, what ledger accounts are affected? If it is sold for less than its purchase cost, what accounts are affected?
12. Where does donated capital appear on the balance sheet? Why?
13. What are cash dividends? Why are they issued?
14. In the chapter, three different dates associated with dividends were described. Give those dates and explain why they are important.
15. Define a stock dividend. Differentiate between small and large stock dividends. How does the difference affect the accounting treatment they receive?
16. Illustrate the difference between a large stock dividend and a stock split.

• Appendix Questions

17. Jane, John, and Joe form a partnership by each contributing $50,000. Discuss different ways the first year's profits of $21,000 can be distributed if Jane, John, and Joe withdraw $20,000, $5,000, and $10,000, respectively, on June 30 of the first year.
18. How are the financial statements for a partnership similar to the financial statements for a corporation? How are they different?
19. Describe five different ways the composition of a partnership's ownership can change.

• EXERCISES

E 11–1
Entity Concept
L.O.1

Two businesses identical in every way except that one is a corporation and the other is a partnership find themselves facing the same outcome in a lawsuit—pay the plaintiff $1 million in damages. After completing the appeal process, the damages are reduced to $500,000. Both the corporation and partnership have $300,000 in net assets, and the owners of each business each have $500,000 in personal assets.

Required:
Write a paragraph or two discussing the amount the plaintiff will receive in each case.

E 11–2
Establishment of a
Proprietorship
L.O.2

Harvey James decides to go into business for himself by starting a gourmet catering business. On March 1, 19xx, he contributes the following to the business:

	James's Original Cost	Fair Market Value
Cash	$ 3,000	$ 3,000
Kitchen equipment	10,000	18,000
Serving equipment	1,000	1,900
Paper supplies	750	800
His expert culinary skills		5,000

Required:
Record the journal entry in general journal form that Harvey makes on March 1, 19xx.

E 11–3
Preparing Journal
Entries (proprietorship
versus corporation)
L.O.2, 5

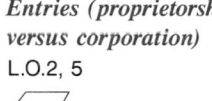

Selected transactions for the Caro Company are as follows:

a. Original investment in the business is $150,000.
b. A salary of $5,000 for the month is paid to the owner (manager of the business).
c. Revenues of $80,000 are earned during the month (all in cash).
d. Expenses (excluding salaries) of $62,000 are incurred on account during the month.
e. Accounts payable paid during the month totaled $56,000.
f. The income for the month is closed to the appropriate owners' equity account. Assume that all appropriate closing entries are made to the Income Summary account.

Required:
1. Prepare the journal entries in general journal form for the above items assuming that Caro is organized as a proprietorship.
2. Prepare the journal entries in general journal form for the above items assuming that Caro is organized as a corporation. The original investment is evidenced by 10,000 shares of $10 par value common stock.

E 11–4
Issuance of Stock
L.O.5

Henry's Fitness Center has the following transactions involving stock issuance:

19xx
Apr. 5   Issues 10,000 shares of $1 par value common stock for $5 per share.
     16   Issues 1,000 shares of $100 par value preferred stock at par.
May 1   Issues an additional 5,000 shares of the common stock for $6 per share to a friend of Henry's.
June 30   Accepts a $20,000 stock subscription for 5,000 shares of common stock. → $5/share
July 31   Receives payment for one half of the stock subscriptions. $1 / par value
Aug. 31   Receives final payment for the stock subscriptions and issues the stock.

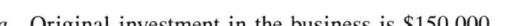

Required:
Record journal entries for the above transactions in general journal form.

E 11–5
Reacquisition of Stock
L.O.7

The Movers Corporation bought 1,000 shares of its previously issued common stock outstanding at $12 per share on October 15, 19x1. On February 21, 19x2, the corporation sold 500 of these shares at $14 per share for cash. On April 14, 19x2, the corporation sold 250 shares at $10 per share for cash. The remaining 250 shares were sold on June 28 at $5 per share for cash.

Required:
Prepare the journal entries in general journal form for the above treasury stock transactions.

E 11–6
Reacquisition of Stock
L.O.7

Guiffre International Corporation had the following transactions during 19xx regarding repurchase of its stock:

19xx
Apr. 20   Repurchases 5,000 shares of $1 par common stock at $7 per share. Guiffre plans to hold the stock for future reissuance.
July 21   Repurchases and retires 3,000 shares of common stock at $4 per share.
Sept. 5   Sells 2,000 shares of treasury stock for $10 per share.
Nov. 30   Sells 1,000 shares of treasury stock for $5.50 per share.

Assume that the stock was originally issued on Jan. 1, 19xx, for $5 per share.

Required:
Prepare the journal entries in general journal form for these transactions.

E 11–7
Cash Dividends
L.O.8

On October 30, 19x5, MasterCraft, Inc., declares a $0.35 cash dividend on its 60,000 shares of common stock to stockholders of record on November 15, 19x5, to be paid on November 30, 19x5. Prepare the journal entries required, if any, on each of the dates.

E 11–8
Stock Dividends
L.O.8

The Banner Corporation had 50,000 shares of $20 par value common stock outstanding at January 1, 19xx. On June 15, 19xx, the board of directors declared a 15% stock dividend on the outstanding common stock. The market value of the stock was $31 per share on June 15, 19xx. The stock was issued on July 30. Prepare Banner's journal entries related to dividends.

E 11–9
Stock Dividends
L.O.8

Swann's Discounters, Inc., has 100,000 shares of $4 par value common stock with a current market value of $10 per share. Consider the following three items independently and prepare the appropriate journal entries for each case:

a. Declares and issues a 5% stock dividend.
b. Declares and issues a 50% stock dividend.
c. Declares and issues a 2-for-1 stock split.

E 11–10
Changes in Stockholders' Equity
L.O.5, 7, 8

Assume the following transactions occur for the General Electric Company, which is involved in technology, services, manufacturing, and other areas. Indicate the effect of each item (increase, decrease, no effect) on total stockholders' equity.

a. Issue 100,000 of additional shares of common stock.
b. Repurchase 1,000 shares of common stock for $43,000.
c. Sale of 25 shares of common stock from J. Blumberg to T. Jones.
d. Sale of 150 shares of treasury stock purchased in *b* for $6,000.
e. Sale of 200 shares of treasury stock purchased in *b* for $9,000.
f. Declare a cash dividend.
g. Declare a 2-for-1 stock split.

E 11–11
Stock Subscriptions
L.O.5

Wiretex, Inc., was organized on April 1, 19x1. One million shares of $3.00 par value common stock were authorized. Two hundred thousand shares were issued for cash at $4.00 per share on 4/1/x1 to A. Hall, and 800,000 shares were subscribed to by two stockholders under the following payment schedule:

Stockholder	Shares	Payments 4/1/x1	10/1/x1	3/31/x2
J. Leno	200,000	$300,000	$300,000	$200,000
J. Carson	600,000	900,000	900,000	600,000

All payments are made on schedule.

Required:
1. Show journal entries at each date.
2. Show how effects of these transactions would be reported on the 12/31/x1 balance sheet.

E 11–12
Multiple Choice
L.O.1–9

1. In terms of responsibility for business obligations, an owner of a business—
    a. Has the same potential liability in a proprietorship as in a corporation.
    b. Is viewed for accounting purposes as part of the business entity.
    c. Is viewed very differently by the law depending on the organizational form of the business.
    d. Has his or her nonbusiness assets more at risk in a corporation than in a proprietorship.
    e. None of the above.
2. A partner—
    a. Can limit his or her business-related liabilities by means of an agreement among the partners.
    b. Cannot limit his or her business-related liabilities without forming a corporation.
    c. Must share any income equally with the other partners.
    d. Cannot be a general partner unless a partnership agreement exists.
    e. None of the above.
3. The tax status of a business—
    a. Is the same under corporate and noncorporate forms.
    b. Is independent of that of the proprietor of a noncorporate business.
    c. Is always improved by the formation as a partnership as opposed to a corporation.
    d. Is governed by the size of the business.
    e. None of the above.
4. In a partnership—
    a. The capital balance for each partner is stable unless new contributions by partners are made.
    b. The capital balance for a particular partner can be affected by the business income and withdrawals of the partner.
    c. The total of all capital balances must remain positive.
    d. Distributions to owners dissolve the partnership.
    e. None of the above.
5. Common stockholders—
    a. Have as one of their rights the right to receive dividend payments after profitable operations.
    b. Have the right to vote on critical operating matters.
    c. Can never receive more dividends per stockholder in a year than preferred stockholders.
    d. Must rely on their representatives on the board of directors to govern company policies in much the same manner as citizens rely on their elected representatives.
    e. None of the above.
6. Preferred stockholders—
    a. Have all the rights of common stockholders plus preferences in terms of dividends and residual values.
    b. Have preference in terms of dividends and residual values.
    c. Always have voting rights.
    d. Have the right to receive annual dividends whenever operations are profitable.
    e. None of the above.
7. The journal entry to record the issuance of common stock must result in the following:
    a. Total contributed capital being equal to total legal capital.
    b. Total par value being equal to total contributed capital.
    c. An increase in Retained Earnings if stock is sold for more than par or stated value.
    d. Total stockholders' equity being equal to or greater than total contributed capital.
    e. None of the above.
8. Treasury stock shares—
    a. Are the shares yet to be issued.
    b. Are the shares that have been repurchased and retired or canceled.
    c. Have no market value.
    d. Are issued but not outstanding shares.
    e. None of the above.

9. If a city donates land to a company—
   a. The land is carried on the balance sheet just as if it had been purchased for cash.
   b. The company has a liability equal to the value of the land.
   c. The city gains ownership interest in the business.
   d. The land has no book value because nothing was paid.
   e. None of the above.
10. The journal entry to record the declaration of a cash dividend—
   a. Reduces net assets.
   b. Reduces contributed capital.
   c. Is made as an adjusting entry at the end of the accounting period.
   d. Is reversed on the payment date.
   e. None of the above.
11. The declaration of a dividend payable in common stock—
   a. Indicates that the company is in a weak cash position.
   b. Cannot affect retained earnings.
   c. Does not require a journal entry.
   d. Creates a liability.
   e. None of the above.

• Appendix Exercises

E 11–13
Establishment of a Partnership and Distribution of Net Income
L.O.10

On August 15, 19x1, Sarah, Sue, and Sally entered into a partnership called SuperFitness Salon. Sarah contributes $10,000. Sue contributes equipment with a fair market value of $5,000, and Sally brings to the partnership her experience as an aerobics instructor. It is decided the partnership will be a 50:25:25 split, respectively, and all profits after salaries will be allocated accordingly. During the first year, which ends on July 31, 19x2, a profit of $12,000 is made. During that same year, Sarah withdraws $5,000, Sue withdraws $2,000, and Sally withdraws nothing but earns a salary of $15,000.

Required:
1. Record the journal entry in general journal form made on August 15, 19x1, to set up the partnership.
2. Record the journal entry in general journal form to allocate the profits and close out the drawing accounts to the capital accounts on July 31, 19x2.

E 11–14
Addition of a New Partner
L.O.10

New Town Relocation Services is a partnership owned by John and Joe with total capital of $150,000, which is shared equally. A new partner, Jim, wants to enter the partnership.

Required:
1. Record the journal entry in general journal form if Jim contributes $75,000 to enter the partnership as an equal partner.
2. Record the journal entry in general journal form if Jim contributes $105,000 to enter the partnership as an equal partner.
3. Record the journal entry in general journal form if Jim contributes $55,000, but he is to be an equal partner in the business.

E 11–15
Withdrawal of a Partner
L.O.10

On April 30, 19x6, Willis decides to withdraw from the Baker, Jones, Willis Surveying Company. On that date the fair market value of the net assets is $540,000. Total book value of the partnership capital is $480,000, which the partners share equally.

Required:
1. Record the journal entry (entries) made if Baker and Jones buy Willis's share of the partnership for fair market value with personal assets. Assume that assets are not revalued on partnership books.
2. If assets of the company are sold and the company liquidated, record the journal entry (entries) for the final payment to owners.

3. Record the journal entry (entries) made if Baker and Jones pay Willis $200,000 to withdraw Willis' personal assets from the partnership. Assume that assets are not revalued on partnership books.
4. Record the journal entry (entries) made if a new partner purchases Willis' share from her for $250,000. Assume that assets are not revalued on partnership books.

E 11–16
Liquidation of a Partnership
L.O.10

The Many Legal Services partnership decides to liquidate on September 30, 19x7. The firm, which shares all profits and losses equally, has the following assets, liabilities, and capital accounts prior to liquidation:

	Book Value	Fair Market Value
Cash	$ 20,000	$20,000
Accounts receivable.	16,000	12,500
Equipment (net).	8,000	2,500
Liabilities.	8,700	8,700
Ross, capital	(22,000)	
Streeter, capital.	57,300	

Required:
1. Determine the book values after conversion of assets to cash and payment of liabilities and record any journal entries in general journal form made in conversion.
2. Record the journal entries made in liquidating the partnership. Assume that an ending deficit in a partner's capital account is paid in cash to the partnership.

E 11–17
Addition of a Partner (Challenging)
L.O.10

The partnership of Jones and Kane had the following summary balance sheet at June 30, 19xx.

Assets	$200,000
Liabilities.	$ 50,000
Jones, capital.	100,000
Kane, capital	50,000
Total liabilities and owners' equity	$200,000

The partners share profits and losses equally.

On June 30, the partners decide to admit Lance to the partnership. Prepare the journal entries in general journal form to record the admission of Lance under the following independent assumptions:

a. Lance will contribute cash of $50,000 for a 25% interest.
b. Lance will contribute cash of $50,000 for a 40% interest.
c. Lance will contribute cash of $50,000 for a 20% interest.
d. Lance will contribute cash of $150,000 for a 50% interest.
e. Lance will give Kane $40,000 for Kane's one-third interest in the existing partnership.
f. Lance will give Jones $80,000 for Jones' two-thirds interest in the existing partnership.
g. Lance will pay Jones and Kane personally $50,000 and $25,000, respectively, for a 30% interest in the newly created partnership.

For *b, c,* and *d,* assume that old partners share the bonus equally.

E 11–18
Distribution of
Partnership Profits
and Losses
(Challenging)
L.O.10

Partners A, B, and C distribute profits and losses as follows: Salaries of $12,000 to A and B and $18,000 to C; a return of 8% on the original investment; and the residual is divided equally. The original cash investments made in 19x1 are A, $60,000; B, $50,000; and C, $40,000.

Net income (loss) for the first four years of operations is as follows:

19x1	$ 66,000
19x2	99,900
19x3	45,000
19x4	(63,000)

Required:
Prepare a schedule computing the amounts allocated to each partner for the first four years of operation.

E 11–19
Multiple Choice
L.O.10

1. Two partners who start with equal contributions and who share profits and losses equally—
   a. Will always have equal balances in their capital accounts.
   b. Will always both be general partners.
   c. Will be limited to equal withdrawals from the business.
   d. Are in no need of a partnership agreement.
   e. None of the above.
2. Upon the admission of a new partner and the departure of an old partner—
   a. The cash paid by the new partner will always increase the assets of the partnership.
   b. The assets of the partnership will not be affected if the cash paid by the new partner is to a departing partner.
   c. The cash paid to the partnership must be equal to or greater than the capital balance of the departing partner.
   d. Some asset, cash or otherwise, must be paid either to the departing partner or to the partnership.
   e. None of the above.

• PROBLEMS

P 11–1
Organization Costs
L.O.5

Derry Corporation was organized on August 10, 19x1. The corporate charter stated that 80,000 shares of $1 par value common stock was authorized. Consider each of the following items independently:

a. 80,000 shares are sold for $4 per share on August 15, 19x1, and $20,000 is paid to organizers of the corporation as compensation for legal and accounting services during the organization period.
b. 75,000 shares are sold for $4 per share, and 5,000 shares are distributed to organizers for promotion, legal, and accounting services during the organization period.

Required:
Prepare the journal entries in general journal form for each case above.

P 11–2
Stock Transactions
L.O.5

Storey Corporation was organized on December 1, 19x1. One hundred twenty thousand shares of $0.25 par value common stock and 10,000 shares of $100 par value preferred stock were authorized. During the month, the following transactions related to stock took place: $0.25

19x1
Dec. 2   Issued 100,000 shares of common stock for $8 per share.
      14   Received subscriptions for 10,000 shares of common stock for $3 per share down payment plus $5.50 per share to be paid on June 30, 19x2.
      16   Issued 10,000 shares of preferred stock for cash of $105 per share.
      20   Issued 5,000 shares of common stock in exchange for the following assets:

	Fair Value
Trucks	$17,000
Computer	10,500
	$27,500

Required:
Prepare the journal entries for the above transactions.

P 11–3
Issuance of Common Stock
L.O.5, 6

Maher Corporation received authorization for 100,000 shares of common stock on September 1, 19x1, and some of the stock is sold on September 10, 19x1. Consider the following items independently.

a. Common stock has a par value of $2 per share, and 50,000 shares sell for $3.50 per share.
b. Common stock has no par value, and 50,000 shares sell for $3.50 per share.
c. Common stock has par value of $2 per share, 50,000 shares sell for $3.50 per share, and 10,000 shares are given to the owner of an office building for purchase of the building. The building had been advertised at a selling price of $40,000.

Required:
1. Show the journal entries for each case.
2. Show the balance sheet disclosure of contributed capital for each case.
3. Explain what the money amount recorded in Owners' Equity means in each case.

P 11–4
Stockholders' Equity Section of Balance Sheet
L.O.6

Good
Equiz question

Strickling Corporation has a fiscal year ending December 31, and on December 31, 19x1, the following information is available.

	Debits	Credits
Retained earnings	$1,150,000	
① Contributed capital in excess of par— common stock		$1,200,000
Treasury stock	215,000	
Common stock—par		2,100,000
Common stock subscribed		125,000
Subscriptions receivable	140,000	
Preferred stock—par		900,000
Discount on preferred stock	100,000	

Can put this first

Required:
Show the stockholders' equity section of Strickling Corporation's balance sheet on December 31, 19x1. Explain how any account not shown in owners' equity would be disclosed.

P 11–5
Stock Subscriptions
L.O.5, 6

Jones, Inc., was authorized to issue 200,000 shares of $0.50 per share par value common stock on January 1, 19x1. One hundred twenty thousand shares were immediately sold for cash for $2 per share, and 40,000 shares were subscribed to at a subscription price of $2.50 per share to be paid in equal payments on June 30, 19x1, and December 31, 19x1. During 19x1, Jones, Inc., had net income of $30,000 and no dividends were paid.

Required:
1. Record all journal entries related to stock for 19x1.
2. Prepare the stockholder's equity section of Jones, Inc., balance sheet on December 31, 19x1.

P 11–6
Treasury Stock
(Challenging)
L.O.6, 7

The stockholders' equity section of the Johnson Corporation appears as follows on the December 31, 19x1, balance sheet:

Stockholders' equity:

Contributed capital:

Common stock, par $1 per share, 2 million shares authorized, 1.5 million shares issued and outstanding	$1,500,000
Contributed capital in excess of par.	3,000,000
Retained earnings	450,000
Total stockholders' equity	$4,950,000

On January 10, 19x2, Johnson Corporation purchased 20,000 shares of common stock on the open market for $4 per share. On October 1, 19x1, 10,000 shares were sold for $5 per share, and on December 15, 19x2, 5,000 shares were sold for $4 per share. At December 31, 19x2, 5,000 shares were still held as treasury stock. Net income for the year was $200,000 and no dividends were declared.

Required:
1. Record all journal entries during 19x2 related to treasury stock.
2. Prepare the stockholders' equity section of Johnson Corporation's balance sheet on December 31, 19x2.

P 11–7
Organization Costs and
Donated Capital
L.O.5, 6, 8

On June 1, 19x1, HiTech, Inc., was issued a corporate charter with authorization of 500,000 shares of no-par common stock. The following transactions took place in the first week following the issuance of the charter:

a. 400,000 shares were issued for cash of $4 per share.
b. $15,000 was paid to the accounting firm that acted as consultant during the organization period.
c. The city of Jacksonville gave the company the title to a parcel of land on which the headquarters of HiTech is to be constructed. The land has an appraised value of $200,000.

At December 31, 19x1, the end of its first fiscal period, HiTech, Inc., reported net income of $120,000 and declared no dividends.

Required:
1. Record journal entries for transactions *a*, *b*, and *c* above.
2. Prepare the stockholders' equity section of the HiTech, Inc., balance sheet on December 31, 19x1.

P 11–8
*Cash Dividends and
Treasury Stock*
L.O.6, 7

On December 31, 19x1, Starke, Inc., reported a retained earnings balance of $1,850,000 and a Contributed Capital in Excess of Par of $750,000. During 19x2, Starke had the following transactions related to its $1 par value stock (50,000 shares of common stock are authorized, issued, and outstanding as of December 31, 19x1):

19x2

June	10	Declared a $.50 per share cash dividend to be paid on July 10, 19x2, to stockholders of record on June 30, 19x2.
July	10	Paid the cash dividend.
	20	Purchased 4,000 treasury shares for $10 per share.
Sept.	20	Sold 2,000 treasury shares for $15 per share.
Dec.	10	Declared a $.50 per share cash dividend to be paid on January 10, 19x3, to stockholders of record on December 31, 19x2.
	31	Closed the Income Summary account and recognized net income of $800,000.

Required:
1. Prepare journal entries in general journal form for the above transactions.
2. Prepare the stockholders' equity section of the balance sheet on December 31, 19x2.

P 11–9
*Stock Dividends
and Balance Sheet
Presentation of
Stockholders' Equity*
L.O.6, 8

The stockholders' equity section of Russell, Inc., on December 31, 19x1, showed 1 million shares of $1 par value common stock issued and outstanding, contributed capital in excess of par of $5 million, and retained earnings of $2.3 million. During 19x2, net income amounted to $650,000.

Although Russell, Inc., generated a considerable amount of cash during 19x2, most of it was used to purchase long-term assets. Management declared a 15% stock dividend on December 10, 19x2, in lieu of a cash dividend to be distributed on January 10, 19x3, to stockholders of record on December 30, 19x2. The stock was selling for $5 per share on the date of declaration.

Required:
1. Prepare all journal entries related to common shares from December 10, 19x2, through January 10, 19x3.
2. Prepare the stockholders' equity section of the balance sheet of Russell, Inc., on December 31, 19x2.

P 11–10
True/False
L.O.1, 5, 7, 8

1. _____ Par value is the same as the current fair market value.
2. _____ Par value is the same as the original selling price.
3. _____ Par value of common stock is always equal to liquidation value.
4. _____ Par value of preferred stock can be equal to liquidation value.
5. _____ Par value of preferred stock always exceeds par value of common stock.
6. _____ Preferred stock dividends have preference over bond interest.
7. _____ Total common stock dividends may exceed total preferred stock dividends.
8. _____ Treasury stock is valued at the fair market value on the balance sheet date.
9. _____ Treasury stock transactions can never result in gains or losses on the income statement.
10. _____ Treasury stock transactions can constrain a company's dividends declarations.
11. _____ Preferred stock always has a maturity date.
12. _____ Preferred stockholders can sue the company for undeclared dividends just as bondholders can sue the company for unpaid interest.
13. _____ Contributed capital is synonymous with par or stated value.
14. _____ Subscriptions receivable is a current asset account.
15. _____ Large stock dividends and stock splits have no effect on contributed capital.

· Appendix Problems

P 11–11
*Establishment of a
Partnership*
L.O.10

Annabel and Beatrice form a partnership in which Annabel contributes cash of $100,000 and Beatrice contributes a proprietorship that has the following trial balance.

	Debits	Credits
Cash	$ 8,000	
Accounts Receivable (net)	26,000	
Inventory.	29,000	
Building and Equipment	58,000	
Accumulated Depreciation		$ 9,000
Accounts Payable.		12,000
Beatrice, Capital		100,000
Totals	$121,000	$121,000

Annabel and Beatrice agree that Beatrice's assets' book values are equal to their fair values. Annabel and Beatrice agree to share the responsibility for the proprietorship's liabilities.

Required:
Make the entries necessary to set up the Annabel and Beatrice partnership.

P 11–12
*Distribution of
Partnership Profits*
L.O.10

The Smith & Brown Group had the following stipulations in its partnership agreement:

- Each partner is allowed 10% return on the beginning capital balances.
- Smith is allowed a salary of $40,000 per year, and Brown is allowed a salary of $30,000 per year.
- The remaining net income or loss after the effect of the return on capital and salary allowance is distributed equally to Smith and Brown.

Smith's beginning capital balance on January 1, 19x2, was $60,000, and Brown's was $50,000. During 19x2, Smith withdrew $35,000, and Brown withdrew $25,000. Net income for 19x2 before allowances for return on capital and salaries was $120,000.

Required:
Prepare a schedule showing how each partner's capital is affected by the above transactions.

P 11–13
*Distribution of
Partnership Profits
(Challenging)*
L.O.10

Schrafts and Lotto invest $140,000 and $100,000, respectively, in a partnership on January 1, 19x1. During 19x1 and 19x2, the partnership has earnings of $80,000 and $120,000, respectively.

Required:
Prepare a schedule showing how each partner's capital is affected under each of the following independent assumptions:

1. The partnership agreement does not mention the distribution of earnings.
2. The partnership agreement calls for a 12% return on beginning capital balance with the remainder of earnings being distributed equally.
3. Earnings and losses are to be shared equally after salary allowances of $60,000 for Schrafts and $20,000 for Lotto.

P 11–14
Establishment of a Partnership (Challenging)
L.O.10

Inkling and Macburg each run separate fast-food businesses. On January 1, 19x1, they agree to form the Burger partnership. The balance sheets of Inkling and Macburg on January 1, 19x1, are as follows:

Inkling's Operations

	Book	Fair Market Value
Cash	$ 8,000	$ 8,000
Accounts receivable (net)	26,000	23,000
Inventory	114,000	130,000
Building and equipment (net). . .	65,000	100,000
Land	10,000	60,000
Total	$223,000	$321,000
Accounts payable	$ 40,000	$ 40,000
Notes payable	10,000	10,000
Owners' equity	173,000	271,000
Total	$223,000	$321,000

Macburg's Operations

	Book	Fair Market Value
Cash	$ 1,000	$ 1,000
Accounts receivable (net) . . .	8,000	8,000
Inventory	42,000	50,000
Total	$51,000	$59,000
Accounts payable	$ 1,500	$ 1,500
Owners' equity	49,500	57,500
Total	$51,000	$59,000

Because Macburg's business seems more dynamic and has more potential, it is decided that Macburg would be given credit for $100,000 in capital over the fair value of Macburg's assets minus liabilities. It is decided that notes payable are not to be transferred to the partnership.

Required:
Record the formation of the Burger partnership.

P 11–15
Withdrawal of a Partner
L.O.10

Hogan and Jones have been partners in Delta Records for several years, and the accounting records show the following account balances at December 31, 19xx. It is believed that the book values and fair values of assets and liabilities are approximately the same.

	Debits	Credits
Cash	$ 18,500	
Accounts Receivable (net)	32,000	
Inventory.	105,000	
Building and Equipment	95,000	
Accounts Payable.		$ 10,000
Notes Payable		7,000
Hogan, Capital		166,500
Jones, Capital		95,000
Hogan, Drawing.	18,000	
Jones, Drawing	10,000	

Jones wants to retire effective December 31, 19xx, and the partners decide on the following terms: Jones will get $10,000 of the cash plus a promissory note from Delta Records for $100,000 to be paid in five annual year-end installments—$20,000 each plus interest at 10%.

Required:
1. Prepare the journal entry in general journal form made by the partnership to record the retirement of Jones.
2. Prepare Delta Records' December 31, 19xx, balance sheet.

P 11–16
Distribution of
Partnership Profits
(Challenging)
L.O.10

The partnership of A, B, and C was formed in 19x1. Initial investments were A, $10,000; B, $20,000; and C, $30,000. Net income over a two-year period is as follows:

19x1	$72,000
19x2	18,000

The partners had withdrawals during this period as follows:

	A	B	C
19x1	$16,000	$20,000	$60,000
19x2	3,000	24,000	7,000

Required:
Prepare a schedule showing the allocations of profits for each year to each partner's capital account under the following independent assumptions:

a. Profits are divided equally.
b. Profits are divided as follows: 37.5% to A; 37.5% to B; and 25% to C.
c. Profits are divided based on the original investments.
d. During 19x1 and 19x2, salaries are assigned to A, B, and C at $10,000, $10,000, and $4,000, respectively. The balance is divided based on original investments.
e. Profits are divided based on the beginning-of-the-year capital balances.

• CASES

C 11–1
Entity Concept
L.O.1

Haney owns two businesses run as proprietorships, an appliance repair shop and a car wash. After hearing the explanation of his rights and responsibilities as a proprietor, Haney asks, "Why should I keep separate accounting records for these two businesses when the law makes no distinction between any of my assets and obligations including those in the business?"

Required:
Draft a response to Haney's question.

C 11–2
Forms of Business
L.O.1, 2, 4

Joe Blunt is a leather craftsman who is going to open a retail store and must decide on the form of business to adopt. He wants to know the legal and accounting differences between the proprietorship and the corporate form of business organizations.

Required:
Write a short response to Mr. Blunt that explains how proprietorships and corporations differ from accounting and legal perspectives.

C 11–3
Issuance of Stocks and
Organization Costs
L.O.5

Lucas, Inc., was organized on January 1, 19x1, with 200,000 shares of $1 par common stock being authorized. The following transactions affecting stock took place during 19x1:

1. On January 1, 19x1, five investors each paid $50,000 for 10,000 shares of stock.
2. On January 1, 19x1, Ms. Spike, the organizer of the corporation, was issued 40,000 shares of common stock for $180,000 in cash. Ms. Spike had incurred $20,000 in legal and other costs during the organization phase. She had paid all costs out of her own pocket, and it was agreed that the "bargain" price she paid for these shares would compensate her for the $20,000.
3. On January 2, 19x1, 50,000 shares were issued to Ms. Spike for a parcel of land she owned. The original cost to her was $200,000.

The following journal entries were made for the above transactions:

a.	Cash	250,000	
	Common Stock—Par		50,000
	Contributed Capital in Excess of Par		200,000
b.	Cash	180,000	
	Common Stock—Par		40,000
	Contributed Capital in Excess of Par		140,000
c.	Land	50,000	
	Common Stock—Par		50,000

Required:
1. Discuss each accounting transaction and show how you would have recorded it.
2. Show how the contributed capital accounts should appear on the 12/31/x1 balance sheet.

C 11–4
Balance Sheet Disclosure
L.O.5, 7

Two stockholders' equity accounts, Treasury Stock and Subscriptions Receivable, have generated considerable controversy in the past because of debate over their proper balance sheet classification. Both accounts have debit balances but are normally located in different sections of the balance sheet. Treasury Stock is normally shown as a contra account to total stockholders' equity and Subscriptions Receivable is normally shown as a current asset.

Required:
1. Discuss the justification for the normal disclosures of these two items.
2. Discuss the possible justification for showing Treasury Stock as an asset and Subscriptions Receivable as a contra stockholders' equity account.

• Appendix Cases ─────────────────────────────────

C 11–5
Allocation of Profits
L.O.10

You overhear the following conversation between your friend, Samantha, and her business partner, Al.

Al: If we form a partnership, we have to share all profits equally, which means that we should contribute the same amounts initially.

Samantha: No, I believe that we must share profits according to our relative capital balances.

Required:
Clarify their misconceptions with a short summary statement of the allowable relationship between capital contributions, capital balances, and profit sharing among partners.

• Evaluating Financial Statements ─────────────────────

C 11–6
Elements of Stockholders' Equity and Rights of Shareholders
L.O.1–4, 6

A corporation may have several categories of stockholders' equity. Each category represents the results of transactions and each in one way or another says something about the rights of stockholders. List the stockholders' equity categories and describe the transactions that affect those categories. Also, discuss the rights of stockholders and tell how some aspect of those rights is related to each category.

C 11–7
Treasury Shares
L.O.7

In a recent annual report, General Motors showed its treasury stock as an asset labeled "Common Stock Held for the Incentive Program" as follows:

General Motors
Consolidated Balance Sheet (excerpt)
(in millions)

Assets:

Current assets:

Cash	$ 369.5
U.S. government and other marketable securities and time deposits— at cost, which approximates market of $5,834.6	5,847.4
Total cash and marketable securities	6,216.9
Accounts and notes receivable—less allowances	6,964.2
Inventories	6,621.5
Prepaid expenses and deferred income taxes	997.2
Total current assets	20,799.8
Equity in net assets of nonconsolidated subsidiaries and associates	4,450.8
Other investments and miscellaneous assets	1,222.5
Common stock held for the Incentive Program (Note 3)	**56.3**

Property:

Real estate, plants, and equipment	37,777.8
Less: accumulated depreciation	20,116.8
Net real estate, plants, and equipment	17,661.0
Special tools	1,504.1
Total property	19,165.1
Total assets	$45,694.5

The following is from Note 3 of GM's balance sheet:

Note 3 (excerpt)

Common stock held for the Incentive Program is stated substantially at cost and used exclusively for payment of Program liabilities (dollar amounts are in millions).

	Shares	Amount
Balance at Jan. 1	592,207	$ 35.2
Acquired during the year	592,680	42.6
Delivered to participants	(358,614)	(21.5)
Balance at Dec. 31	826,273	$ 56.3

Required:

1. Explain the normal balance sheet location of treasury stock.
2. Give the pros and cons of reporting treasury stock as an asset.

C 11–8
*Changes in
Stockholders' Equity
(Challenging)*
L.O.5–7

The following partial owners' equity section of a balance sheet (in thousands) was reported in a recent published annual report.

Preferred stock:

$1 par value, 2,077,189 shares authorized, 421,694 shares outstanding . . . . . . $ 422

Common stock:

$1 par value, 30,000,000 shares authorized, 13,269,650 shares issued   13,270

Capital in excess of par value.   149,472

Retained earnings   522,532

                                                                                     $685,696

Less cost of 209,525 shares of common stock in treasury   8,060

                                                                                     $677,636

The following is an excerpt from a note to the balance sheet:

	Preferred Stock $1 Par Value	Common Stock $1 Par Value	Treasury Stock	
			Shares	**Cost**
Beginning balance	$ 590,528	$13,209,875	(420,021)	$(16,887,000)
Purchase of treasury stock	—	—	(97,000)	(3,727,000)
Conversion and retirements preferred stock and exercise of options.	(168,834)	59,775	307,496	12,554,000
Ending balance	$ 421,694	$13,269,650	(209,525)	$ (8,060,000)

Required:

Study the balance sheet and note excerpt, and write a paragraph explaining how each category (except for retained earnings) was affected by transactions during the year. Be as explicit as possible and state any assumptions you make.

**Barker Corporation
Consolidated Income Statement
For 1994**

	1994	1993
Revenues		
Sales (net)	$ xxx	$ xxx
Dividend income	**xxx**	**xxx**
Investment income—equity investees	**xxx**	**xxx**
Expenses		
Cost of sales	xxx	xxx
Selling, general and administrative	xxx	xxx

**Barker Corporation
Consolidated Balance Sheet
12/31/94**

	1994	1993
Current assets		
Total current assets	$ xxx	$ xxx
Noncurrent assets		
Investments at fair value.	**xxx**	**xxx**
Equity investments in unconsolidated subsidiaries	**xxx**	**xxx**
Current liabilities		
Total current liabilities	xxx	xxx
Noncurrent liabilities		
Total noncurrent liabilities	xxx	xxx
Stockholders' equity		
Total stockholders' equity	xxx	xxx

**Barker Corporation
Consolidated Cash Flow Statement
For 1994**

	1994	1993
Operating activities		
Cash from operations	$ xxx	$ xxx
Investing activities		
Purchase of investments.	**xxx**	**xxx**
Sale of investments	**xxx**	**0**
Financing activities		
Cash from financing	xxx	xxx

**FINANCIAL
STATEMENT
COMPONENTS
EMPHASIZED IN
CHAPTER 12**

12

Investments

One of the most prevalent problems I have noted in the study of financial reports is the amortization period assigned to unidentified "goodwill." The tendency to utilize the maximum allowable period of 40 years is curious given the quality of the asset.

Eugene H. Flegm
General Motors Corporation

· Learning Objectives

After studying Chapter 12, you should understand

1. How to account for trading securities using the fair value method, pp. 616–17.
2. How to account for securities available-for-sale using the fair value method, pp. 617–19.
3. How to account for debt securities held-to-maturity using the amortized cost method, pp. 620–23.
4. The impact of an acquisition using the equity method (used when the investor company has 20% to 50% of the voting stock of the investee company), pp. 625–26.
5. The impact of an acquisition using the consolidation method (used when the investor company owns over 50% of the investee company and controls its operations), pp. 626–36.
6. Additional aspects of consolidation (Appendix 12A), pp. 643–48.
7. Pooling of interests (Appendix 12B), pp. 649–50.

Chapters 10 and 11 discussed the accounting for capital acquired by companies through debt and equity financing. In this chapter you will learn why some companies invest in such assets as bonds or stocks of other businesses. Then the chapter introduces the four methods used to account for investments—fair value, amortized cost, equity, and consolidation. The method a company uses depends on the length of the investment—temporary or long term—and the type of asset acquired and the percentage of the company acquired.

This chapter will help you to understand the nature of different types of investments and to read and evaluate the published financial statements of businesses with significant investment activities.

NATURE AND PURPOSE OF INVESTMENTS

When a company acquires assets with the expectation of receiving interest, dividends, or price appreciation, these assets are called investments. Most business investments are made up of bonds, notes, or stocks of another entity. These investments are also generally referred to as financial instruments. A financial instrument, broadly defined, can be cash, evidence of an ownership interest in an entity (for example, common stock), or any contract that both imposes a contractual obligation to provide cash or other financial considerations on one entity and conveys a contractual right to receive cash or other financial considerations on a second entity (for example, a bond with known cash payment dates). There are numerous financial contracts that fall under the broad definition of financial instruments, including such things as convertible bonds, stock options, "put" options, "call" options, forward contracts, hedges, and interest rate swaps. In this chapter, we do not attempt to define or illustrate all of these financial instruments. Many are so new that the generally accepted accounting principles regarding them are still evolving.[1] We focus instead on the most common forms of investments held by business entities and on current procedures for accounting for them. Note that financial instruments are not the only form of investments. Land, rare works of art, or other valuable assets are sometimes acquired as investments too. Usually, the company's purpose for investing determines the nature of the assets that a company acquires as an investment.

The primary business purposes behind investment activities are

1. To make temporary use of idle cash that the company will need for operating purposes in the not-too-distant future.
2. To make up part of a "savings" program designed to build up a pool of liquid assets for a major purchase (such as a new plant), to refund long-term debt when it matures (a sinking fund), or to accomplish some other long-term objective.
3. To gain a significant investment interest or ownership control in another business entity.

While the last two purposes noted above are long term in nature, the first one has a short-term time horizon. There are numerous ways to categorize investments other than by their purpose or the expected holding period. First of all, most investments in financial instruments may be classified as either debt securities (e.g., notes, bonds, CDs) or equity securities (i.e., any security representing an ownership interest in an enterprise). Furthermore,

---

[1]For a good reference book that defines most financial instruments, see the Coopers & Lybrand publication, *Guide to Financial Instruments* (New York: Coopers & Lybrand, 1988). Note that the FASB has a major project underway to help determine GAAP for financial instruments.

all debt and equity securities may be considered to belong to one of the following classes of investments:

1. **Trading securities:** those debt and equity securities bought and sold with the intention of earning trading profits. A rapid rate of buying and selling is expected for this class of securities (e.g., considerably less than a year).

2. **Available-for-sale securities:** those debt and equity securities which are not classified as trading securities, and those debt securities not being held-to-maturity. These securities may be classified as current or long term depending on management's intention. Voting equity investments of 20% or more are also not considered in the available-for-sale category.

3. **Held-to-maturity securities:** those debt securities purchased with the intention of holding them until they mature.

4. **Voting equity investments:** those investments in voting stock that represent a 20% or greater ownership interest in an investee company.

Exhibit 12–1 summarizes the balance sheet classification and the different accounting methods employed to these four classes of investments.

Replacement of the LCM Method

Until 1993 most investments in equity securities of less than 20-percent interest were accounted for using the **lower-of-cost-or-market (LCM) method.** This method valued the investments at the lesser of their cost or market value at the financial statement date, thereby allowing losses to be recorded for fair values below original cost but not permitting gains to be recorded for fair values above original cost. The LCM method continues to be used in most other countries for valuing temporary investments in marketable securities. However, in 1993 a new accounting pronouncement was issued that requires the **fair value method** of accounting to be used in the U.S. for most investments in debt and equity securities, as noted in Exhibit 12–1. The fair value method, which takes effect in late 1994, essentially requires marketable debt and equity securities to be reported at their current fair market value at the date of the financial statements.[2] In applying the fair value

EXHIBIT 12–1

Investments

Class of Investments	Types of Securities	Balance Sheet Classification	Accounting Method
1. Trading securities	Debt and Equity	Current Assets	Fair value with Gains/Losses to Income
2. Available-for-Sale	Debt and Equity (if less than a 20% voting interest)	Current or Long-term based on intent	Fair value with Gains/Losses to Stockholders' Equity
3. Held-to-Maturity	Debt	Long-term	Amortized Cost
4. Voting Equity Investment	a. Voting interest between 20% and 50% ownership	Long-term	Equity Method
	b. Voting interest over 50% ownership	Not-Observable	Consolidation

[2]Technically, fair value is defined as the amount at which a financial instrument could be exchanged in a current transaction between willing parties, other than in a forced liquidation sale.

method, any unrealized gains or losses that have occurred since the previous statement date are reported in the income statement for "trading securities," or the stockholders' equity section of the balance sheet for securities that are "available-for-sale."[3] These two procedures used to apply the new fair value method are discussed in the following two sections.

Trading Securities

Trading securities are always classified as current assets. They consist of debt and equity securities held principally for purposes of selling them in the near future. These investments are intended to generate profits from expected short-term price changes, but of course may result in losses too. By their definition, trading securities must be highly liquid. As a result, some companies may include trading securities with cash in their balance sheet, and their cash flow statement might also define cash as cash plus trading securities.

Objective 1

How to account for trading securities using the fair value method.

The fair value method of accounting is used to account for trading securities. These investments are recorded at their fair value as of the balance sheet date, with any unrealized gains or losses netted against one another and reported in income.

To illustrate the fair value method for trading securities, assume Griffin Corporation made the following purchases during 19x1:

9/15/x1	Arnett common stock.	$17,350
10/5/x1	Wright bonds (8%)	21,500
12/10/x1	Mowrey preferred stock.	16,750
		$55,600

Griffin classifies these investments as trading securities because it intends to sell them in early 19x2. On December 31, 19x1, the investments had the following fair values based on their year-end market price:

	Original Cost	12/31/x1 Fair Value	Gain (Loss)
Arnett common stock	$17,350	$15,800	$(1,550)
Wright bonds (8%)	21,500	22,000	500
Mowrey preferred stock.	16,750	19,650	2,900
	$55,600	$57,450	$ 1,850

The adjusting entry required at year-end would be:

12/31/x1	Wright Bonds (8%) (A)	500	
	Mowrey Preferred Stock (A).	2,900	
	Arnett Common Stock (A)		1,550
	Unrealized Gain on Trading Securities (R)		1,850

This year-end adjusting entry alters the recorded book values of the trading securities, and when they are sold in 19x2, the difference between their selling price and their December 31, 19x1, fair value will be recorded as a *realized* gain or loss. For example, if Griffin Corp. sells the Arnett stock on January 19, 19x2 for $16,080, the entry would be:

1/19/x2	Cash (A).	16,080	
	Arnett Common Stock (A).		15,800
	Gain on Sale of Stock (R)		280

---

[3]Recall that realized gains and losses result from differences between book value and market value at the date of sale. Unrealized gains and losses occur when book values are increased or decreased without a sale transaction.

Also, assume that on March 31, 19x2, Griffin sells the trading securities in Wright bonds for $21,800 plus accrued interest. Assuming a maturity value of $20,000 and that the interest of 8% per year was paid and recorded to the end of 19x1, the Wright bonds have three months accrued interest at the date of sale or:

$$\$20,000 \times .08 \times 3/12 = \$400 \text{ accrued interest at } 3/31/x2.$$

The entry to record the sale would be:

3/31/x2	Cash (A).	22,200	
	Loss on Sale of Bonds (E)	200	
	Wright Bonds (A)		22,000
	Interest Income (R)		400

Note that bonds are always quoted at a market price excluding accrued interest. The difference between the quoted market price on December 31 ($22,000) and the market price on March 31 ($21,800) is a $200 loss recorded at the time of sale.

Bonds and notes, like equity securities, are reported at their fair value at the financial statement date. Interest income or dividend income is recorded separate from the unrealized gains and losses that result from using fair value accounting. For example, if Griffin Corporation had received $210 in dividends from Mowrey preferred stock on December 15, 19x1, and $400 quarterly interest from the Wright bonds on December 31, 19x1, the entries would have been:

12/15/x1	Cash (A)	210	
	Dividend Income (R)		210
12/31/x1	Cash (A)	400	
	Interest Income (R).		400

These entries would not have an impact on the year-end fair value adjustments illustrated earlier.

What happens if the trading securities are bought and sold before a year-end occurs? In such cases, no *unrealized* gains or losses would be recorded since the securities are no longer on hand at year-end. The *realized* gains or losses on trading securities (not held at year-end) would be reported in the income statement. The realized gains or losses would simply be the difference between the original cost and the selling price of the securities.

Securities Available-for-Sale

Objective 2

How to account for securities available-for-sale using the fair value method.

Debt and equity securities that do not fall into the category of trading securities, and debt securities that are not intended to be held until maturity may be categorized as securities "available-for-sale." This class of investments may be included as either a current asset, a noncurrent asset, or some of both depending on the intention of management.

The fair value method is also used for securities available-for-sale. However, unlike trading securities, the unrealized gains and losses at the balance sheet date are reported as a net amount in a separate component of stockholders' equity until realized (e.g., when the securities are actually sold).

To illustrate, assume the Griffin Corporation acquired the following securities available-for-sale as long-term investments:

Date	Security	Price Paid
9/20/x1	Master preferred stock.	$35,000
10/30/x1	Anderson bonds (6%)	19,000
12/15/x1	Johnson common stock	21,000
		$75,000

Now assume the 19x1 year-end fair values of these securities are as follows:

	Original Cost	12/31/x1 Fair Value	Gain (Loss)
Master preferred stock	$35,000	$36,000	$1,000
Anderson bonds (6%)	19,000	20,000	1,000
Johnson common stock	21,000	23,000	2,000
	$75,000	$79,000	$4,000

The 19x1 year-end adjusting entry would be:

12/31/x1	Master Preferred Stock (A)	1,000	
	Anderson Bonds (6%) (A).	1,000	
	Johnson Common Stock (A)	2,000	
	Unrealized Gains and Losses on Securities (SE)		4,000

Next, assume that on May 10, 19x2, Griffin sells the Master preferred for $37,500 cash. This sale results in a *realized* gain of $2,500 ($37,500 less $35,000 original cost) that must be reported in the income statement. Also, the previous $1,000 unrealized gain must be eliminated from stockholders' equity. The entry to record the sale would be:

5/10/x2	Cash (A).	37,500	
	Unrealized Gains and Losses on Securities (SE)	1,000	
	Master Preferred Stock (A).		36,000
	Realized Gain on Securities (R)		2,500

This entry points out that although the fair value method reports securities at their fair value as of each balance sheet date, a record of their original cost must be maintained in order to measure the realized gain or loss from their ultimate sale. At the time of sale, any previously recorded unrealized gains or losses must be reversed from stockholders' equity in order to report the realized gain or loss. As with trading securities, any dividends or interest on equity or debt securities available-for-sale must be reported in the income statement in the period earned (for interest) or declared (for dividends).

To continue with Griffin's long-term investments, assume the Anderson bonds and Johnson stock remained on hand at the end of 19x2 with the following values:

	Original Cost	12/31/x1 Fair Value	12/31/x2 Fair Value
Anderson bonds (6%)	$19,000	$20,000	$19,500
Johnson common stock	21,000	23,000	25,000
	$40,000	$43,000	$44,500

The adjusting entry required at the end of 19x2 would be

12/31/x2	Johnson Common Stock (A)	2,000	
	Anderson Bonds (6%) (A).		500
	Unrealized Gains and Losses on Securities (SE)		1,500

As a result of this entry, the investments would be reported in the balance sheet at their fair value. The balance in Unrealized Gains and Losses on Securities (SE) would be a credit (gain) of $4,500 at the end of 19x2 after this adjustment. The $4,500 unrealized gain would represent $3,000 in net unrealized gains from the end of 19x1 plus $1,500 in net unrealized gains from the end of 19x2. The T-account activity would be:

Unrealized Gains and Losses on Securities (SE)

Sale 5/10/x2	1,000	4,000	12/31/x1 Adjustment
		1,500	12/31/x2 Adjustment
		4,500	

Note that any *long-term* investments in equity securities that do not represent a voting interest of 20% or more in an investee must be classified as available-for-sale securities with their unrealized gains or losses reported in stockholders' equity. However, long-term investments in debt may be classified as either available-for-sale or held-to-maturity securities depending on management's intentions.

Transfers between investment classes should not be frequent. However, when transfers do take place, the securities are transferred at their fair value at the date of transfer. For additional details on transfers you should refer to a current intermediate accounting text.

A comparison of the fair value method for trading securities versus securities available-for-sale is provided in Exhibit 12–2.[4] The comparison assumes one year-end falls between the date securities are purchased and the date they are sold. For securities available-for-sale more than one year-end may separate the purchase and sale transactions. Note that the key difference is that *unrealized* gains and losses are reported in the income statement each year for trading securities, while the income statement only reports *realized* gains and losses in the year of a sale for securities classified as available-for-sale.

Debt Securities Held-to-Maturity

When companies acquire debt securities with the intention of holding them to maturity, accountants use the amortized cost method and amortize the premium or discount over the remaining life of the security. These **long-term investments are assumed to be held to maturity;** therefore, differences between the price paid and maturity value (discount or premium) should be eliminated (amortized) over the remaining life of the securities.

As illustrated in Chapter 10, the amortization process systematically allocates the discount or premium to the income statement. In the case of the bondholder the discount or premium is eliminated by adding (for a discount) or deducting (for a premium) the periodic amortization to or from the stated (nominal) amount of interest payment. This method is consistent with the fact that bonds purchased at discount provide effective interest **greater** than the stated interest rate on the bond. Alternatively, bonds purchased at a premium provide effective interest **less** than the stated rate.

You should use the effective-interest method (illustrated in Chapter 10) for the amortization of bond premiums and discounts unless no material difference exists between the effective-interest method and the straight-line method. Also, note that for long-term investments in bonds, separate discount or premium accounts are rarely (if ever) used. Investors use the remaining life of the bond from date of purchase as the amortization period for discounts and premiums on long-term bond investments.

[4]For details, see *FASB Statement No. 115,* "Certain Investments in Debt and Equity Securities" (Norwalk, Conn.: FASB, 1993).

EXHIBIT 12–2

Applications of Fair Value Method

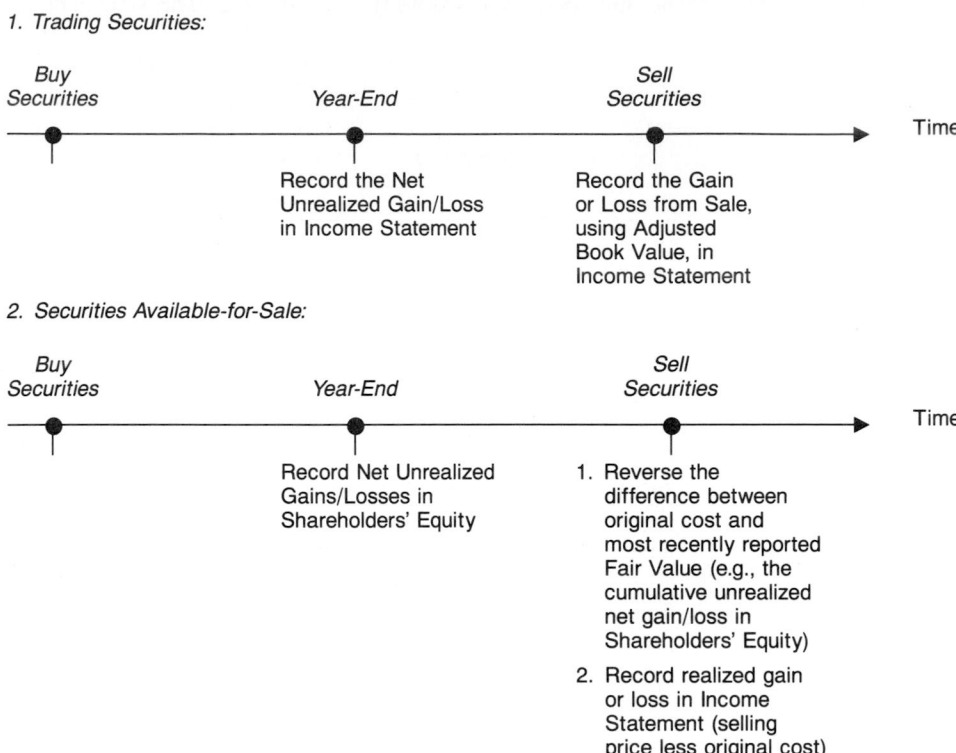

1. *Trading Securities:*

| Buy Securities | Year-End | Sell Securities | Time |

Record the Net Unrealized Gain/Loss in Income Statement

Record the Gain or Loss from Sale, using Adjusted Book Value, in Income Statement

2. *Securities Available-for-Sale:*

| Buy Securities | Year-End | Sell Securities | Time |

Record Net Unrealized Gains/Losses in Shareholders' Equity

1. Reverse the difference between original cost and most recently reported Fair Value (e.g., the cumulative unrealized net gain/loss in Shareholders' Equity)

2. Record realized gain or loss in Income Statement (selling price less original cost)

Objective 3
How to account for debt securities held-to-maturity using the amortized cost method.

To illustrate the amortized cost method, assume that on January 1, 19x1, Alcan Pipe, Inc., purchased 10 bonds with a maturity value of $10,000 each for "94" (94% of their maturity value) or $94,000 total. In other words, $100,000 maturity value bonds sold for a **discount** of $6,000 (or 6% of face value) below their maturity value. Recall from Chapter 10 that bonds sell at a discount when their stated interest rate is less than the current rate required by investors. The bonds mature in five years (December 31, 19x5) and have a stated interest rate of 8% paid semiannually on June 30 and December 31. Assume that the $6,000 total discount on these bonds is amortized on a straight-line basis over the next five years (60 months) at the rate of $100 per month ($6,000/60 months = $100 per month). The entries to record the purchase and the first year's interest payments and discount amortization would be as follows:

19x1

Jan. 1 Bond Investments (A)   94,000
             Cash (A)   94,000
          To record purchase of $100,000 bonds at 94.

June 30 Cash (A)   4,000
             Bond Interest Income (R)   4,000
          To record six months of bond interest.

June 30 Bond Investments (A)   600
             Bond Interest Income (R)   600
          To amortize six months of bond discount.

Dec. 31   Cash (A)   4,000
                   Bond Interest Income (R)   4,000
                   To record six months of bond interest.

Dec. 31   Bond Investments (A)   600
                   Bond Interest Income (R)   600
                   To amortize six months of bond discount.

Exhibit 12–3 gives the complete bond amortization table for the Alcan Pipe bonds. The exhibit illustrates how the book value of the bonds systematically increases to the face value by the date of maturity. Note also that the total interest income reported by the investor over the life of the bonds ($46,000) is equal to the total cash interest payments ($40,000) plus the $6,000 excess of the maturity value received on December 31, 19x5 ($100,000) over the price paid on January 1, 19x1 ($94,000). Hence, the income statement reflects the total difference between the cash received ($140,000) and the cash paid ($94,000) as interest income during the life of the bond investment.

Sale before Maturity.   Assume that Alcan Pipe decided to sell the bonds on August 31, 19x4 (16 months before maturity) for $100,333, which includes $1,333 accrued interest ($100,000 × .08 × 2/12 = $1,333 rounded). If accrued interest is $1,333, then $99,000 of the selling price was for the bonds **without** interest ($100,333 − $1,333). The gain or

---

EXHIBIT 12–3

Amortization Table for a Long-Term Investment in Bonds

Purchase price:	$94,000
Purchase date:	January 1, 19x1
Maturity value:	$100,000
Maturity date:	December 31, 19x5
Nominal annual interest:	$8,000 (8%)
Interest payment dates:	June 30, December 31
Amortization method:	Straight-line

	Semiannual			
Date	Cash Interest (nominal) Received	Amortization of Bond Discount or Premium	Interest Income	Balance in Investment Account
1/1/x1	$ 0	$ 0	$ 0	$ 94,000
6/30/x1	4,000	600	4,600	94,600
12/31/x1	4,000	600	4,600	95,200
6/30/x2	4,000	600	4,600	95,800
12/31/x2	4,000	600	4,600	96,400
6/30/x3	4,000	600	4,600	97,000
12/31/x3	4,000	600	4,600	97,600
6/30/x4	4,000	600	4,600	98,200
12/31/x4	4,000	600	4,600	98,800
6/30/x5	4,000	600	4,600	99,400
12/31/x5	4,000	600	4,600	100,000
	$40,000	$6,000	$46,000	

loss on the sale is the difference between $99,000 paid for the bonds and their book value at date of sale, which is $98,400, computed as follows:

Book value 6/30/x4 (see table in Exhibit 12–2). . .	$98,200
Discount amortization: $100/month for July and August 19x4	200
Book value 8/31/x4	$98,400
Selling price 8/31/x4	$99,000
Book value 8/31/x4	− 98,400
Gain (loss) on sale of bonds	$ 600 gain

The $600 gain is recorded at the time of sale, as follows:

```
19x4
Aug. 31   Interest Receivable (A). . . . . . . . . . . . . . . . . . . . . .     1,333
          Bond Investments (A) . . . . . . . . . . . . . . . . . . . . . .       200
              Bond Interest Income (R). . . . . . . . . . . . . . . . . . .              1,533
          To record two months' interest and discount amortization.

     31   Cash (A) . . . . . . . . . . . . . . . . . . . . . . . . . . . .   100,333
              Bond Investments (A) . . . . . . . . . . . . . . . . . . . .             98,400
              Interest Receivable (A). . . . . . . . . . . . . . . . . . .              1,333
              Gain on Sale of Bonds (R) . . . . . . . . . . . . . . . . .                600
          To record sale of bonds.
```

Purchase between Interest Dates. Now assume that a company purchases bonds between interest dates at a premium. In this example, the company purchases a 9%, $10,000 bond on May 1, 19x6, for $10,800 plus accrued interest. The bond pays semiannual interest of 4.5% ($450) on June 30 and December 31 and matures at the end of 19x7 (20 months). The following entries would be required for 19x6:

```
19x6
May   1   Bond Investments (A) . . . . . . . . . . . . . . . . . . . . .    10,800
          Interest Receivable (A). . . . . . . . . . . . . . . . . . . . .       300
              Cash (A) . . . . . . . . . . . . . . . . . . . . . . . . . .             11,100
          To record purchase of bond plus accrued interest:
          $10,000 × .09 × 4/12 = $300.

June 30   Cash (A) . . . . . . . . . . . . . . . . . . . . . . . . . . . .       450
              Interest Receivable (A). . . . . . . . . . . . . . . . . . .                300
              Interest Income (R) . . . . . . . . . . . . . . . . . . . .                150
          To record receipt of six months' bond interest and two months
          of interest income.

     30   Interest Income (R) . . . . . . . . . . . . . . . . . . . . . .        80
              Bond Investments (A) . . . . . . . . . . . . . . . . . . . .                 80
          To amortize two months' bond premium on a straight-line basis:
          $800/20 months = $40.

Dec. 31   Cash (A) . . . . . . . . . . . . . . . . . . . . . . . . . . .        450
              Interest Income (R) . . . . . . . . . . . . . . . . . . . .                450
          To record receipt of six months' interest.
```

Dec. 31   Interest Income (R)   240

         Bond Investment (A).   240

        To amortize six months' bond premium on a straight-line basis:
        $40 $\times$ 6 = $240.

As noted earlier, the assumption underlying accounting for long-term bond investments is that they will be held until they mature. Therefore, discounts and premiums are always amortized over the remaining life of the bonds. Cash interest, of course, is recorded as received, with the amount of interest income affected by the amortization of discounts or premiums as illustrated above.

Fair Value Accounting Controversy

The advent of fair value accounting for trading securities and securities available-for-sale was stimulated in part by the failures in banks and savings and loans during the late 1980s and early 1990s. These financial institutions were more seriously affected by fair value accounting than other types of businesses because most of their assets (and liabilities) consisted of financial instruments and because their proportion of debt capital to equity capital is very high (e.g., highly "leveraged" enterprises). The debate over fair value accounting was centered on those industries, and carried over to the U.S. Congress where extensive hearings into bank and savings and loan failures were conducted. To illustrate some of the decision-making issues involved in this controversy, let's listen in on a conversation between Larry, Maureen, and Ian, the three owners of Legislative Minds, Inc. (LMI), that occurred in 1991.

Maureen: OK guys, we've got a new client that is willing to pay very well for our lobbying services if we can convince Congress to not require banks to report their assets at fair value.

Ian: Yes, I've been following this controversy in the papers. This is a sticky issue.

Larry: You know, the thing that makes this so controversial is the fact that most banks only have a shareholders' equity equal to about four to five percent of total assets. A typical bank's balance sheet looks like this. (Larry sketches the following on a pad.)

Balance Sheet
(in millions)

Assets:			Liabilities:		
Cash	$	xx	Checking deposits.	$	xx
Loans receivable		xx	Saving deposits		xx
Mortgages.		xx	CDs		xx
Investments		xx	Borrowings		xx
			Total liabilities	$	960
			Stockholders' equity:		
			Stock and retained earnings		40
			Total liabilities and		
Total assets		$1,000	stockholders' equity		$1,000

Maureen: Yep, and that's on a historical cost basis. The controversy over using market values instead of original costs is so important to banks because if the market value of their assets drops by only 5% below historical costs, it would drop their assets to $950 million in Larry's example.

Ian: Yeah, and that's $10 million less than liabilities of $960 million, meaning the stockholders own a bank with negative net worth!

Larry: The banks are afraid that if they are forced to report assets at market value they will frighten the shareholders into thinking their stock is worthless.

Maureen: There may be some truth to that, you know. But worse than that, the banks are terrified that once their depositors find out they have a negative net worth, they'll take their checking, savings, and CDs to some other bank or savings and loan for fear they will not get their money back.

Ian: Of course, that's why we have federal deposit insurance in the United States. The government guarantees that deposits up to something like $100,000 per person will be returned if a bank fails.

Larry: Yeah, but it doesn't exactly make me feel good to have all my cash in a bank with a negative net worth. I'm not sure the banks are right on this issue, Maureen.

Maureen: Listen, Larry, there is a big fee being offered here. It could help us pay off our loan on that communications satellite you talked us into buying. Besides, today's market value is old news by tomorrow. The banks aren't planning to sell all their assets, so why should they have to report them at their market value?

Ian: That's true. Also, it seems like banks should be allowed to report their liabilities at fair value too. What if the decrease in the market value of their assets is less than the decrease in the market value of their liabilities? It seems unfair to only adjust asset values!

Larry: OK, OK; I can find ways to argue for the bank's point of view. But, I'm sure glad I don't own any bank stock myself. They have too much debt and not enough equity for my liking. I guess I'm just not a risk taker.

Maureen: Oh yeah! Then why are you in this high-tech lobbying business?

As we learned in the early part of the chapter, the fair value method is now required for all enterprises with trading securities or securities available-for-sale. While the major impact of this accounting policy is on banks, savings and loans, insurance companies, and other institutions holding significant amounts of financial assets, it pertains to all business enterprises.

EQUITY METHOD

Accountants use the equity method whenever the investor has enough voting stock to **influence the operations of the investee.** Normally, this "influence" includes placing people on the investee's board of directors, hiring top managers, and other actions made possible by exercising ownership voting rights. In practice, such influence is usually assumed to exist if the investor owns between 20 and 50% of the investee's voting stock.[5] When an investor owns over 50% of an investee, the investor has a controlling interest in the investee.

The equity method records the purchase of an investment at the total cost incurred to acquire the securities. Beyond the date of purchase, the **Investments** asset account (also called Equity Investments or Long-Term Investments) is increased for the investor's proportional share of the investee's net income and decreased for dividends received from the investee. These equity procedures result in the investor's increasing its recorded assets and reported net income for its proportional share of the investee's net income regardless of whether the investee paid any dividends to the investor.

---

[5]For more complete details concerning the equity method, see *APB Opinion No. 18,* "The Equity Method of Accounting for Investments in Common Stock" (New York: AICPA, 1971), or most intermediate accounting texts.

Objective 4
The impact of an
acquisition using the
equity method (used when
the investor company has
20% to 50% of the investee
company).

To illustrate the equity method, assume that on January 1, 19x1, Logo Gifts, Inc., acquires a 40% interest in Stadium Foto by purchasing 40% of Stadium's common stock for $60,000 cash. On the date of acquisition, Stadium, the "target" firm, had the following balance sheet data:

Stadium Foto
Summarized Balance Sheet
January 1, 19x1

Assets		Liabilities and Stockholders' Equity	
Current assets:		Liabilities:	
Cash	$ 14,000	Accounts payable	$ 35,000
Accounts receivable	86,000	Notes payable	165,000
Lab supplies	65,000	Total liabilities	$200,000
Total current assets.	$165,000		
Noncurrent assets:		Stockholders' equity:	
Equipment	185,000	Total stockholders' equity	150,000
		Total liabilities and	
Total assets	$350,000	stockholders' equity.	$350,000

Logo's purchase of 40% of Stadium's outstanding common stock for $60,000 cash makes Logo a 40% owner of Stadium Foto. Note that Stadium's stock must be selling at its book value since 40% of Stadium's $150,000 net book value is equal to the $60,000 purchase price. While this is not always the case, in this example Stadium's book value is assumed to equal its market value, and there is no goodwill (refer to Chapter 8, page 410, for a discussion of the measurement of goodwill). Logo records the investment in Stadium using the equity method as follows:

```
19x1
Jan. 1   Equity Investments (A) . . . . . . . . . . . . . . . . . . . . . . .   60,000
             Cash (A). . . . . . . . . . . . . . . . . . . . . . . . . . . . .          60,000
         To record purchase of Stadium's stock.
```

Stadium does not record an entry to reflect the change in its stockholders.

Now assume that Stadium reports a 19x1 net income of $40,000 and pays its stockholders $25,000 in dividends on December 31, 19x1. Logo, a 40% owner, makes the following entries:

```
19x1
Dec. 31   Equity Investments (A). . . . . . . . . . . . . . . . . . . . . .   16,000
              Investment Income (R) . . . . . . . . . . . . . . . . . . . .          16,000
          To record 40% of investee's net income for 19x1.

     31   Cash (A) . . . . . . . . . . . . . . . . . . . . . . . . . . . . .   10,000
              Equity Investments (A) . . . . . . . . . . . . . . . . . . . .          10,000
          To record 40% of investee's dividends.
```

In the first entry, Logo increases its assets and income by $16,000 to reflect Stadium's $40,000 net income in 19x1, 40% of which is Logo's. In the second entry, Logo records the receipt of Stadium's cash dividends. Because these dividends are considered a distribution of Stadium's income, Logo reduces the Investment in Subsidiary asset account and increases the Cash asset account by $10,000, which is Logo's 40% share of Stadium's cash dividends. Note that Logo's $16,000 investment income is **not** affected by the dividend payment and remains at $16,000 with or without cash dividends. The receipt of a cash dividend merely requires a reclassification from the Equity Investments asset account to the Cash asset account. Once the $16,000 Investment Income account is closed out to Retained Earnings, the ending balance sheet effect can be reconciled as follows:

**Net Effects in Balance Sheet Accounts Caused
by Equity Method Following Purchase**

Assets:		Liabilities:	
Cash	+$10,000		
Equity investments . . .	+ 6,000		
		Stockholders' equity:	
		Retained earnings . . .	+$16,000

Exhibit 12–4 gives the Logo and Stadium example illustrating the equity method and shows how the change in the investment is reported in the investor's balance sheet. Note that the balance in the investor's asset equals the investee's net assets (stockholders' equity) times the percent of ownership.

CONSOLIDATION METHOD— CONSOLIDATED FINANCIAL STATEMENTS

The purpose of this introduction to consolidated statements is to explain the fundamental procedures followed by acquiror firms following the acquisition of a **controlling interest** (over 50% of the voting stock) in an investee "target" firm. In other words, how does the acquiror report a target at and after the date of acquisition? Because most large publicly traded companies have "consolidated subsidiaries" (that is, have a controlling interest in one or more acquired targets that continue to operate like separate companies), this basic understanding is important for **reading and interpretating consolidated financial statements.** Also, since the acquisition of a target firm continues to be one of the most material and widely publicized and speculated business transactions, all students of business should have some idea of the major financial statement implications stemming from successful (and failed) takeovers of target firms. The numerous details that go along with consolidating a group of investees controlled by a parent are the primary subject of most advanced accounting texts and are not discussed here.

An investor company with a controlling interest is usually called a parent company, and the investee company is often called a subsidiary or "sub." Although the parent and subsidiary remain as two separate legal entities, they are accounted for, using the consolidation techniques described below, as one economic entity. The owners of the parent company are in control of the resources of the parent and of all its subsidiaries, even though they might not own over 51% of any one subsidiary's stock. Between financial reporting dates, the investor entity will normally account for *all* ownership investments in excess of 20% by using the equity method. However, those investments in excess of a 50% ownership interest must be consolidated for financial reporting purposes using the procedures described in this section of the chapter.[6]

To express the relationship of parent and subsidiary, accountants prepare consolidated financial statements with the aid of a consolidation worksheet to combine the independent financial statements of the parent (investor) and the subsidiary (investee), both of whom remain as separate entities having separate journals, ledgers, and so on. Consolidation

Objective 5
The impact of an acquisition using the consolidation method (used when the investor company owns over 50% of the investee company and controls its operations).

---

[6]This requirement for consolidation is imposed and described in more detail in *Financial Accounting Standards Board Statement No. 94,* "Consolidation of All Majority-Owned Subsidiaries" (Norwalk, Conn.: FASB, 1987), which modifies the basic principles of consolidation as required by *APB Opinion No. 16,* "Business Combinations" (New York: AICPA, 1970).

EXHIBIT 12–4

Equity Method Investments

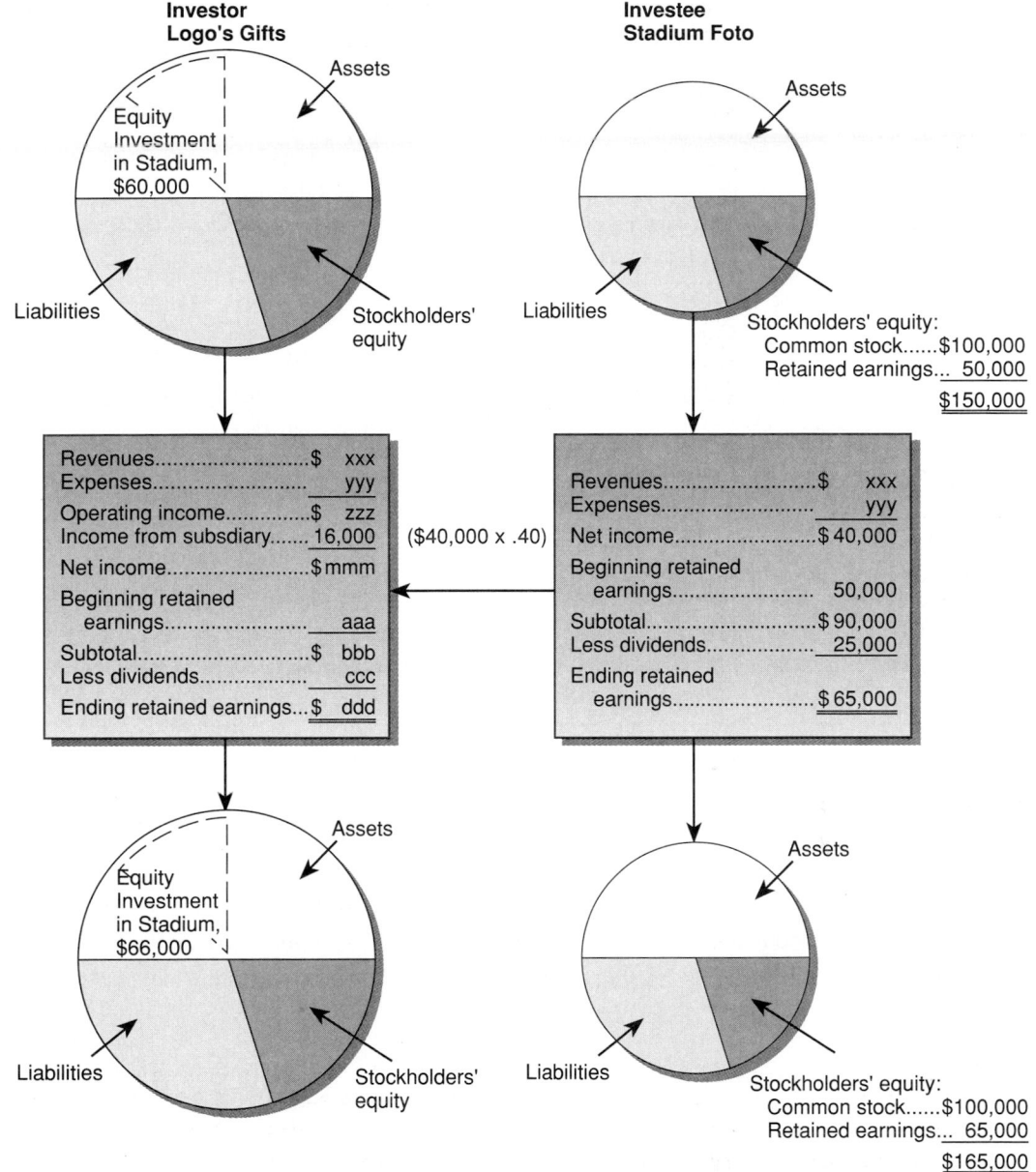

worksheets are not a formal part of the accounting systems of either the parent or subsidiary companies but are schedules that draw data from the separate entities and calculate the adjustments necessary to prepare consolidated financial statements. This separate nature of the parent and subsidiary companies makes it possible for them to report both separately and on a consolidated basis. The investment in the subsidiary appears like an equity investment on the separate books of the parent company just prior to consolidation. Upon consolidation, the single Investment in Subsidiary account used in equity method accounting is eliminated and replaced with all of the specific assets and liabilities of the subsidiary. The purpose of consolidation worksheet entries is to eliminate any duplication that might otherwise result when the financial statements of the parent are added together (combined) with those of the subsidiary. For this reason, consolidation worksheet entries are sometimes referred to as elimination entries.

Simple Situation:
Purchase 100% of
Subsidiary

To illustrate the consolidation process, assume that the book value of acquired net assets equals market value for the purchase of 100% of a subsidiary. This example will enable us to look at the fundamentals of consolidated financial statements needed to understand the financial reports of the thousands of large publicly held companies with consolidated subsidiaries.

Consolidation at Date of Acquisition. Assume that on December 31, 19x1, Big, Inc., acquires a 100% interest in Kidco by purchasing all of Kidco's stock from its owners for $70,000. Just prior to the purchase, the following balance sheet data are available:

Big, Inc.* Balance Sheet December 31, 19x1		Kidco* Balance Sheet December 31, 19x1	
Assets		**Assets**	
Cash	$100,000	Other assets	$100,000
Other assets	500,000		
Total assets	$600,000	Total assets	$100,000
Liabilities and Stockholders' Equity		**Liabilities and Stockholders' Equity**	
Liabilities:		Liabilities:	
All liabilities	$300,000	All liabilities	$ 30,000
Stockholders' equity:		Stockholders' equity:	
Common stock	$200,000	Common stock	$ 50,000
Retained earnings	100,000	Retained earnings	20,000
Total stockholders' equity	$300,000	Total stockholders' equity	$ 70,000
Total liabilities and stockholders' equity	$600,000	Total liabilities and stockholders' equity	$100,000

*The detailed description of the assets and liabilities of the balance sheets is omitted here for simplicity of illustration.

Because this example assumes that Kidco's net book value and net market value are both equal to the $70,000 price paid, there is no goodwill (unrecorded assets) in Kidco at the date of purchase. The purchase by Big should be recorded on its books as follows:

19x1			
Dec. 31	Investment in Kidco (A)	70,000	
	Cash (A)		70,000
	To record purchase of 100% of Kidco stock.		

After Big purchased Kidco, the **unconsolidated** balance sheet of Big and the balance sheet of Kidco would appear as follows:

Big, Inc.	
Unconsolidated Balance Sheet	
December 31, 19x1	
Assets	
Cash	$ 30,000
Investment in Kidco.	70,000
Other assets	500,000
Total assets	$600,000

Liabilities and Stockholders' Equity	
Liabilities:	
All liabilities	$300,000
Stockholders' equity:	
Common stock	$200,000
Retained earnings	100,000
Total stockholders' equity	$300,000
Total liabilities and stockholders' equity . .	$600,000

Kidco (same as above)	
Balance Sheet	
December 31, 19x1	
Assets	
Other assets	$100,000
Total assets	$100,000

Liabilities and Stockholders' Equity	
Liabilities:	
All liabilities	$ 30,000
Stockholders' equity:	
Common stock	$ 50,000
Retained earnings	20,000
Total stockholders' equity	$ 70,000
Total liabilities and stockholders' equity . .	$100,000

Note that Kidco's balance sheet is **not** affected by the purchase since only the names of Kidco's stockholders have changed. Also, at this point the financial statements of Big **look no different than they would if the equity method were used.**

Next, assume that Big wants to prepare a consolidated balance sheet as of December 31, 19x1, the date of acquisition. This requires the following **consolidation worksheet entry:**

Consolidation Worksheet Entry

19x1			
Dec. 31	Common Stock (from Kidco's books)	50,000	
	Retained Earnings (from Kidco's books)	20,000	
	Investment in Kidco (from Big's books)		70,000
	To eliminate intercompany accounts.		

The **worksheet entry** is NOT made in the journal or ledger of Big or Kidco but is only made on a worksheet to facilitate the consolidation of the financial statements. The consolidated worksheet for this case is illustrated in Exhibit 12–5. The debits to the Common Stock and Retained Earnings applied to Kidco's balance sheet should leave these accounts with a zero balance (for consolidation worksheet purposes only). The credit to the Investment in Kidco asset account on Big's balance sheet also leaves it with a zero balance. This consolidation worksheet entry now enables the balance sheets of the two separate companies to be added together (combined) to form a consolidated balance sheet at the end of 19x1. In the worksheet of Exhibit 12–5 this is accomplished by adding across the columns.

The formal consolidated balance sheet of Big, illustrated in Exhibit 12–6, includes all the assets, liabilities, and stockholders' equity of the combined consolidated entity. The consolidation process replaces the single equity method asset account, Investment in Kidco, of $70,000 found on Big's **unconsolidated** balance sheet with all of Kidco's assets ($100,000) and liabilities ($30,000).

Accounting for 100% Owned Subsidiary after Acquisition. To continue the Big and Kidco example, let's examine how Kidco's operations after the date of acquisition affect the consolidation process. Assume that the 19x2 operating results and balance sheet effects

EXHIBIT 12–5

Worksheet for Consolidated Balance Sheet as of Date of Acquisition

	Separate Balance Sheets		Consolidation Worksheet Entries		Big, Inc. Consolidated Balance Sheet 12/31/x1
	Big, Inc.*	Kidco	Debit	Credit	
Assets:					
Cash	30,000				30,000
Investment in Kidco . .	70,000			70,000	
Other assets	500,000	100,000			600,000
Total assets	600,000	100,000			630,000
Liabilities:					
All liabilities	300,000	30,000			330,000
Stockholders' equity:					
Common stock	200,000	50,000	50,000		200,000
Retained earnings . . .	100,000	20,000	20,000		100,000
Total liabilities and stockholders' equity . .	600,000	100,000	70,000	70,000	630,000

*Unconsolidated.

for Big and Kidco are as shown in Exhibit 12–7. Note that in 19x2, Big had a $50,000 operating income from its operations plus $30,000 income from its 100% interest in Kidco's operations — a total of $80,000 net income. The $30,000 net income from Big's investment in Kidco

1. Increased Big's Investment in Kidco balance at December 31, 19x2, by $10,000 (from $70,000 to $80,000) for the portion of Kidco's 19x2 net income that remained in Kidco ($30,000 earnings less $20,000 cash dividends).
2. Increased Big's cash at December 31, 19x2, by $20,000 for the dividends from Kidco.

What effect did the 19x2 income have on Big's *unconsolidated* balance sheet? The $50,000 net income from Big's own operations is assumed to have increased Big's other assets by $50,000.[7] The unconsolidated balance sheet of Big at the end of 19x2 (lower left part of Exhibit 12–7) reports the effects of Big's and Kidco's 19x2 operations. However, Big's income from Kidco's operations are reported as a $30,000 single-line item in Big's unconsolidated 19x2 income statement, and Big's unconsolidated balance sheet shows Kidco's net assets, which are owned by Big, as a single asset of $80,000. Because the equity method reports all of the investee's net assets owned by the investor as a single asset account, and all of the investee's net income owned by the investor as a single-line item in the income statement, **the equity method is sometimes referred to as "one-line consoli-**

---

[7]For illustration purposes, we assume that liabilities remain unchanged for both parent and sub during 19x2. Also we **assume** that the cash dividends are the only source of cash for the parent, Big. These assumptions are not important, but simply help to follow the nature of changes in the balance sheets.

EXHIBIT 12–6

**Consolidated
Balance Sheet**

**Big, Inc.
Consolidated Balance Sheet
December 31, 19x1**

Assets

Cash	$ 30,000
Other assets	600,000
Total assets	$630,000

Liabilities and Stockholders' Equity

Liabilities:	
All liabilities	$330,000
Stockholders' equity:	
Common stock	$200,000
Retained earnings	100,000
Total stockholders' equity	$300,000
Total liabilities and stockholders' equity	$630,000

dation." Big's 19x2 entries to account for Kidco are the same as those used for equity-method investments.

Journal Entries—Big's Books

19x2			
Dec. 31	Investment in Kidco (A)	30,000	
	Income from Kidco (R)		30,000
	To record share of Kidco's 19x2 earnings.		
31	Cash (A)	20,000	
	Investment in Kidco (A)		20,000
	To record share of Kidco's dividends.		

Preparing Big's **consolidated** balance sheet for 19x2 requires the following consolidation worksheet entry:

Consolidation Worksheet Entry

19x2			
Dec. 31	Common Stock (Kidco)	50,000	
	Retained Earnings (Kidco)	30,000	
	Investment in Kidco (Big)		80,000
	To eliminate intercompany accounts for consolidation.		

Exhibit 12–8 shows the complete consolidation worksheet. Note that the total assets for the consolidated company ($710,000) are **not** the same as the sum of the two separate companies' total assets ($680,000 + $110,000 = $790,000). The **net** assets of Kidco ($80,000) at the end of 19x2 are already in Big's **unconsolidated** balance sheet. The consolidation process merely replaces the single equity-method asset of $80,000 (representing Big's share of Kidco's net assets) with all of Kidco's assets ($110,000) and liabilities ($30,000). Also, note that the stockholders' equity in Big's *unconsolidated* balance sheet is the

EXHIBIT 12–7

Effect of Operating Results for 19x2 on Unconsolidated Statements

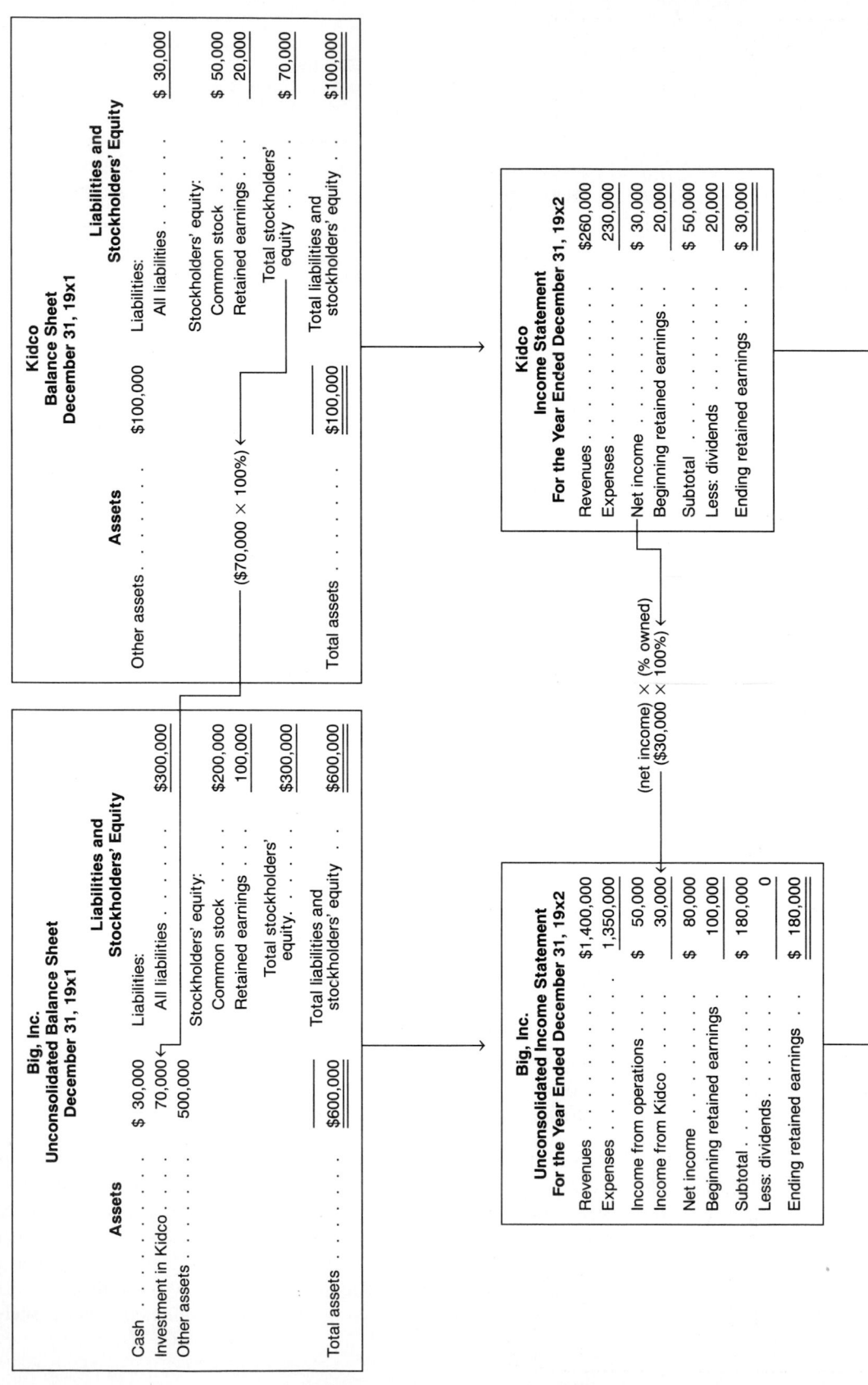

Big, Inc.
Unconsolidated Balance Sheet
December 31, 19x1

Assets		Liabilities and Stockholders' Equity	
Cash	$ 30,000	Liabilities:	
Investment in Kidco	70,000	All liabilities	$300,000
Other assets	500,000	Stockholders' equity:	
		Common stock	$200,000
		Retained earnings	100,000
		Total stockholders' equity . .	$300,000
Total assets	$600,000	Total liabilities and stockholders' equity . .	$600,000

Kidco
Balance Sheet
December 31, 19x1

Assets		Liabilities and Stockholders' Equity	
Other assets	$100,000	Liabilities:	
		All liabilities	$ 30,000
		Stockholders' equity:	
		Common stock	$ 50,000
		Retained earnings	20,000
		Total stockholders' equity . .	$ 70,000
Total assets	$100,000	Total liabilities and stockholders' equity . .	$100,000

($70,000 × 100%)

Big, Inc.
Unconsolidated Income Statement
For the Year Ended December 31, 19x2

Revenues		$1,400,000
Expenses		1,350,000
Income from operations	$ 50,000	
Income from Kidco	30,000	
Net income	$ 80,000	
Beginning retained earnings . .	100,000	
Subtotal	$ 180,000	
Less: dividends	0	
Ending retained earnings . . .	$ 180,000	

(net income) × (% owned)
($30,000 × 100%)

Kidco
Income Statement
For the Year Ended December 31, 19x2

Revenues	$260,000
Expenses	230,000
Net income	$ 30,000
Beginning retained earnings .	20,000
Subtotal	$ 50,000
Less: dividends	20,000
Ending retained earnings .	$ 30,000

Big, Inc.
Unconsolidated Balance Sheet
December 31, 19x2

Assets		Liabilities and Stockholders' Equity	
		Liabilities:	
Cash	$ 50,000*	All liabilities	$300,000
Investment in Kidco	80,000†		
Other assets	550,000‡	Stockholders' equity:	
		Common stock	$200,000
		Retained earnings . . .	180,000
		Total stockholders' equity	$380,000
Total assets	$680,000	Total liabilities and stockholders' equity	$680,000

Kidco
Balance Sheet
December 31, 19x2

Assets		Liabilities and Stockholders' Equity	
		Liabilities:	
Other assets	$110,000	All liabilities	$ 30,000
		Stockholders' equity:	
		Common stock	$ 50,000
		Retained earnings . . .	30,000
	($80,000 × 100%)	Total stockholders' equity	$ 80,000
Total assets	$110,000	Total liabilities and stockholders' equity . . .	$110,000

*$30,000 beginning balance + $20,000 cash dividend from Kidco.
†$70,000 beginning balance + $30,000 Kidco net income − $20,000 cash dividend.
‡$500,000 beginning balance + $50,000 parent's separate net income.

EXHIBIT 12–8

Worksheet for
Consolidated Balance
Sheet as of
December 31, 19x2

	Separate Balance Sheets		Consolidation Worksheet Entries		Big, Inc. Consolidated Balance Sheet 12/31/x2
	Big, Inc.*	Kidco	Debit	Credit	
Assets:					
Cash	50,000				50,000
Investment in Kidco . .	80,000			80,000	
Other assets	550,000	110,000			660,000
Total assets	680,000	110,000			710,000
Liabilities:					
All liabilities	300,000	30,000			330,000
Stockholders' equity:					
Common stock	200,000	50,000	50,000		200,000
Retained earnings . . .	180,000	30,000	30,000		180,000
Total liabilities and stockholders' equity . .	680,000	110,000	80,000	80,000	710,000

*Unconsolidated.

same as the *consolidated* stockholders' equity (stock, $200,000, and retained earnings, $180,000). The consolidation process has no effect on the parent's stockholders' equity.[8]

To prepare a consolidated income statement, you apply the same concepts used to create the consolidated balance sheet—**replace the single account by the detailed accounts.** For Big's consolidated income statement, replace the income from Kidco by all of Kidco's income statement accounts, as follows:

	Unconsolidated Big	+	Kidco	=	Consolidated Big
Revenues.	$1,400,000		$260,000		$1,660,000
Expenses.	− 1,350,000		− 230,000		− 1,580,000
Net income	$ 50,000		$ 30,000		$ 80,000
Income from Kidco	30,000		− 30,000		0
Net income	$ 80,000		$ 0		$ 80,000

The preceding example illustrates the basic principles of consolidation. Its purpose is to provide a fundamental understanding of what it means to report on a consolidated versus an unconsolidated basis. Unconsolidated financial statements report subsidiary investments as a single asset account on the parent company's unconsolidated balance sheet, and a single net revenue or income item on the parent's unconsolidated income statement. This type of presentation in **unconsolidated** financial statements **looks** the same for both equity investments (20 to 50% interest) and subsidiaries where there is a controlling interest (over 50% interest). However, equity investments (those between 20 and 50% ownership) are not subject to the consolidation process.

---

[8]This is the case for all examples used in this text. However, in certain complex situations this assumption may not hold true. Advanced accounting texts address such unusual cases in more detail.

Understanding
Financial Statements

To illustrate the importance of understanding the differences between the equity method of accounting, and consolidated and unconsolidated financial statements, let's listen in on a conversation between the two owners of Byte-Size.

> **Mary:** Well, Brad, what are you doing with all the money you are making from the business? I hope you are putting some away for retirement.
>
> **Brad:** I am, Mary. I have a "self-directed" retirement plan where I can select the types of investments I own. I put most of my investment money into common stocks. Here is a company I'm thinking about buying shares in, for example.
>
> **Mary:** Hm. (Mary looks at the company's balance sheet.) It looks like a very conservative company, Brad. They have about 40% liabilities and 60% stockholders' equity. Not too much long-term debt to pay interest on.
>
> **Brad:** Exactly! I want my retirement investments to be in safe and secure companies.
>
> **Mary:** Hey, wait a minute, Brad. This is an unconsolidated balance sheet! And they show as an asset equity in net assets of First Local Bank! Isn't that the bank that's near bankruptcy?
>
> **Brad:** Let's see that! You're right Mary. That bank has over $500 million in debt and only $2 million in equity. Why do they only report it as an asset of $1.8 million?
>
> **Mary:** Because this is an *unconsolidated* balance sheet, Brad. They only report their share of the *net* assets of the bank as a single asset—as an equity-method investment would be reported. You remember our accounting professor talking about that.
>
> **Brad:** Not really; I must have been sick that day. Let's see, that means.... (Brad computes $1.8 million reported equity in the bank divided by the $2.0 million total equity of the bank.) This company owns about 90% of that troubled bank! That means they are indirectly responsible for about 90% of the bank's $500 million debt. That's about 15 times more debt than they've reported in their unconsolidated balance sheet.
>
> **Mary:** I guess they may not be as conservative as we thought—eh, Brad? Maybe you should look into another company to invest in. That one could be too risky for you.
>
> **Brad:** Yeah, and maybe I'd better check into some of my other investments too. I just might look into some professional investment advice, Mary. You convinced me that I may not be making the best investment decisions.

This discussion between Brad and Mary points out the importance of the difference between consolidated financial statements and their unconsolidated versions, which are based on equity-method accounting. Until Statement of Financial Accounting Standards No. 94 was issued, in 1987, companies were allowed to use the equity method to report the impact of the subsidiaries that operated in lines of business unrelated to those of the parent firm, even when ownership exceeded 50%. This allowed all the auto companies, for example, to report their financing subsidiaries as equity-method investments, producing financial statement results similar to those in the bank example discussed above. Today, all investments over 50% must be consolidated in financial statements labeled "consolidated" according to U.S. GAAP.

Disclosure Implications.   In examining financial statements it is helpful to know the extent to which the reporting entity is made up of equity investments and consolidated subsidiaries. If a reporting entity includes consolidated subsidiaries, the following should hold:

1. The titles to the financial statements should include the word *consolidated*.
2. The footnotes should include the names and/or descriptions of the consolidated subsidiaries. This information would include the percentage of ownership in the consolidated subsidiaries.

If a reporting entity includes equity investments, the following should hold:

1. The income statement should include income from the equity investee(s) as a separate line item to reflect the parent's share in net income from equity (or "unconsolidated") subsidiaries.
2. The balance sheet should include a single asset amount reflecting the parent's share in net assets of the equity investee(s).
3. The footnotes to the financial statements should identify all equity investees and the net asset investment in each.

These features should help you to identify the important components of the reporting entity. A reporting entity with no equity investees or consolidated subsidiaries is generally going to be easier to evaluate than one made up of many equity investees and consolidated subsidiaries, particularly when these investments are in unrelated lines of business. To evaluate reporting entities with stock investments in excess of 20% in other unrelated companies first requires breaking the reporting entity down into components that are similar (for example, electric appliances, aerospace, and so on). Understanding the characteristics of equity investments and consolidated subsidiaries described above is an important first step in evaluating reporting entities with significant investment interests in other companies with unrelated operations.

The U.S. accounting rules illustrated above generally apply to other countries as well. Most industrialized countries employ the equity method for investments representing between 20 and 50 percent of the voting stock, and consolidation for investments in excess of 50 percent ownership. However, in both Japan and Germany there are many exceptions to this general rule. In Japan, for example, if a Japanese company does *not* own over 50 percent of any other company, it does not need to use the equity method for investments between 20 and 50 percent. This situation is very common in Japan, where there are many intercompany investments, but few in excess of 50 percent. The results are that Japanese earnings tend to be significantly understated in many cases. This is one of the reasons why the stock of Japanese companies tends to sell at a higher multiple of their earnings than that of U.S. companies.

There are many other aspects of equity investments and consolidation not illustrated in this chapter. In Appendix 12A we expand on the example above by illustrating two additional common types of consolidations: (1) those in which the subsidiary is less than 100% (but over 50%) owned and there exists a minority interest; and (2) those in which the purchase price does not equal the book value of the subsidiary. In Appendix 12B we explain the difference between the purchase method and the pooling of interests method of accounting for investments in consolidated subsidiaries. These two appendixes may be disregarded by those who are not interested in more details concerning consolidations. Accounting for consolidated investees can be much more complex than we illustrate in this text. Advanced accounting texts cover the subject in much greater detail.

• SUMMARY

In this chapter we examined the fundamental nature of investments in debt and equity securities. For accounting purposes, the primary factors are the term of the investment, either temporary or long term, and the type of investment. Exhibit 12–9 outlines the various types of investments discussed in the chapter and their appropriate accounting method.

Temporary investments may include both trading securities and securities available-for-sale in the form of either debt or equity securities. Since management intends to convert temporary investments to cash in the short term, these investments must be readily

EXHIBIT 12–9

Summary of Investments

Class of Investments	Types of Securities	Correct Accounting Method	Income Statement Effects
Trading Securities (current assets)	Debt and equity	Fair value	Interest and dividend income; unrealized gains/losses; realized gains/losses at point of sale
Available-for-Sale (current or long-term assets)	Debt and equity	Fair value	Interest and dividend income; realized gains/losses at point of sale
Held-to-Maturity (long-term assets)	Debt	Amortized cost	Interest income
Voting Equity Investment (long-term assets)	Voting equity		
	a. 20%–50%	Equity method	Pro rata share of investee's net income added to investor's income
	b. over 50%	Consolidation	Investee's revenues and expenses added to those of investor's; minority interest's pro rata share deducted like a net expense

marketable. Also, they should be low-risk investments since it would be poor management to invest idle cash at a loss. Usually, temporary investments are a minor current asset and are often reported in the balance sheet with cash under the heading "Cash and temporary investments" or some similar title.

Long-term investments are generally more important than temporary investments in terms of both their purpose and relative size. The purpose of long-term investments may be to gain influence in another entity or to build up a liquid asset for future cash needs. If the corporation's goal is to gain influence over another entity, common stock must be purchased; but if the corporation's goal is long-term planning for future cash requirements, any type of marketable security could be purchased.

In order to evaluate the performance of an entity and its subsidiaries, User's of financial statements must understand the fundamentals of alternative accounting methods for investments. For example, an equity investment will report investment income equal to the parent's share of the equity investee's earnings whether or not these earnings are distributed by the investee in the form of dividends. On the other hand, an investment in securities available-for-sale will report investment income equal to the interest earned and/or the dividends declared but will not recognize the investor's share of the investee's net income. If an investor owned an interest in a growth company with rapidly increasing sales and net income but with no dividends, the difference in that investor's net income between a 19% interest and a 21% interest in the growth company's stock could be substantial.

Investors, creditors, managers, and other users must have a basic understanding of the effects of the alternative methods used to account for investments if they are to properly compare and evaluate financial statements of business entities. The alternative methods of accounting for investments introduced in this chapter provide a basis for comparing and evaluating the performance of complex business entities as reported in published financial statements.

• DEMONSTRATION EXERCISE

Bird Corporation, a calendar year company, acquired the following trading securities during 19x5 for cash:

Date Acquired	Security	Original Cost
11/15/x5	Darren Bonds (8%).	$101,000 (plus accrued interest)
12/1/x5	Cathy Common Stock	115,000
12/3/x5	Jess Preferred Stock	88,000
12/15/x5	Chet Common Stock	75,000

The following transactions occurred during 19x5 and 19x6:

1. On December 10, 19x5, Bird Corp. sold all shares of Jess preferred for $95,000 cash.
2. On December 31 the Darren bonds paid interest of $8,000 cash for 19x5. The accrued interest at the date of purchase (11/15/x5) was $7,000.
3. December 31 adjusting entries are recorded as needed. The market values on this date are: Darren bonds $102,500; Cathy common $112,000; Chet common $76,000.
4. On January 19, 19x6, Bird Corp. sold all shares of Chet common for $74,000 cash.

Required:

Record any entries necessary to account for the purchase of these trading securities and any sales or adjustments. Record your entries in chronological order.

Solutions:

11/15/x5	Darren Bonds (8%) (A)	101,000	
	Accrued Interest Receivable (A)	7,000	
	Cash (A)		108,000
12/1/x5	Cathy Common Stock (A).	115,000	
	Cash (A)		115,000
12/3/x5	Jess Preferred Stock (A)	88,000	
	Cash (A)		88,000
12/10/x5	Cash (A)	95,000	
	Jess Preferred Stock (A)		88,000
	Gain on Sale of Investments (R)		7,000
12/15/x5	Chet Common Stock (A)	75,000	
	Cash (A)		75,000
12/31/x5	Cash (A)	8,000	
	Accrued Interest Receivable (A)		7,000
	Interest Income (R).		1,000
12/31/x5	Danen Bonds (8%) (A)	1,500	
	Chet Common Stock (A)	1,000	
	Unrealized Loss on Investments (E)	500	
	Cathy Common Stock (A).		3,000
1/19/x6	Cash (A)	74,000	
	Loss on Sale of Investments (E).		2,000
	Chet Common Stock (A)		76,000

• **DEMONSTRATION EXERCISE** ────────────────────────────────

Dianna, Inc., a calendar year company, acquired the following securities as long-term investments during 19x1:

Date Acquired	Security	Original Cost
3/23/x1	Taylor Common Stock.	$152,000
4/24/x1	Clement Preferred Stock.	128,000
7/31/x1	DVB 6% Bonds.	194,700
		$474,700

The DVB bonds had accrued interest of $7,000 at the date of purchase, and their maturity value is $200,000. They pay interest once a year at December 31 and mature on December 31, 19x5 (53 months from the date of purchase). Dianna, Inc., had no other security transactions during 19x1. At the end of 19x1, the following data were available:

Security	12/31/x1 Fair Value
Taylor Common Stock	$160,000
Clement Preferred Stock	125,000
DVB 6% Bonds	196,000
	$481,000

Required:
1. Assume all three investments are classified by Dianna, Inc., as securities available-for-sale. Record the entries to accounting for these securities.
2. Ignore requirement 1 above. Assume that the two equity securities are classified as available-for-sale and that the DVB bonds are classified as held-to-maturity. Dianna, Inc., uses straight-line amortization for investments in bonds held-to-maturity. Record the necessary entries.
3. If Dianna, Inc., sold all shares of Taylor common stock on November 26, 19x2, for $158,000, what entry would be recorded? Does it matter whether you assume the facts in 1 above versus 2 above?

Solutions:

1. Entries

3/23/x1	Taylor Common Stock (A)	152,000	
	Cash (A)		152,000
4/24/x1	Clement Preferred Stock (A)	128,000	
	Cash (A)		128,000
7/31/x1	DVB 6% Bonds (A)	194,700	
	Accrued Interest Receivable (A).	7,000	
	Cash (A)		201,700
12/31/x1	Cash (A)	12,000	
	Accrued Interest Receivable (A).		7,000
	Interest Income (R)		5,000

12/31/x1	Taylor Common Stock (A)	8,000	
	DVB 6% Bonds (A)	1,300	
	Clement Preferred Stock (A)		3,000
	Unrealized Gains and Losses on Investments (SE) . . .		6,300

2. Entries

3/23/x1	Taylor Common Stock (A)	152,000	
	Cash (A)		152,000
4/24/x1	Clement Preferred Stock (A)	128,000	
	Cash (A)		128,000
7/31/x1	DVB 6% Bonds (A)	194,700	
	Accrued Interest Receivable (A).	7,000	
	Cash (A)		201,700
12/31/x1	Cash (A)	12,000	
	DVB 6% Bonds (A)		500
	Accrued Interest Receivable (A).		7,000
	Interest Income (R)		5,500

(Amortization: $200,000 − 194,700 = $5,300;
$5,300/53 months = $100 per month; 7/31/x1 to
12/31/x1 = 5 months = $500 amortization of bond discount)

12/31/x1	Taylor Common Stock (A)	8,000	
	Clement Preferred Stock (A)		3,000
	Unrealized Gains and Losses on Securities (SE)		5,000

3. Entry

11/28/x2	Cash (A)	158,000	
	Unrealized Gains and Losses on Securities (SE)	8,000	
	Taylor Common Stock (A)		160,000
	Gain on Sale of Investment (R)		6,000

It doesn't matter whether the DVB bonds are considered available-for-sale or held-to-maturity. The sale of Taylor common is the same in either case. The gain of $6,000 is a realized gain based on the difference between fair value at date of sale and original cost: $158,000 − $152,000 = $6,000. The debit to the Unrealized Gains and Losses on Securities (SE) eliminates the previously recorded unrealized gain of $8,000 on Taylor Common.

• **DEMONSTRATION EXERCISE** ─────────────────────────────

Glassel, Inc., has the following information related to its investments in voting equity securities:

	Date Acquired	Original Cost	Percentage Ownership
Lupton, Inc.	1/1/x2	$53,000	40%
Forest Corporation	1/1/x3	22,000	30
Firek, Inc.	1/1/x4	37,000	35

The following information is available for each of the investments' total net income and dividends declared for the years Glassel owned each company.

Year	Lupton, Inc.		Forest Corporation		Firek, Inc.	
	Net Income	Dividends	Net Income	Dividends	Net Income	Dividends
19x2 . . .	$ 70,000	$10,000	N/A	N/A	N/A	N/A
19x3 . . .	90,000	36,000	$10,000	$ 4,000	N/A	N/A
19x4 . . .	100,000	50,000	15,000	16,000	$28,000	$10,000

Required:

1. Prepare the journal entries Glassel would make at December 31, 19x2, through December 31, 19x4, related to the above equity securities.
2. Compute the carrying value of each investment on Glassel's books at December 31, 19x4.
3. Glassel sells its 40% interest in Lupton, Inc., on January 1, 19x5, for $120,000. Prepare the journal entry to record the transaction.

Solutions:

1. During 19x2

Cash (A) 4,000
  Investment—Lupton (A) 4,000

12/31/x2

Investment—Lupton (A) 28,000
  Equity Income (R) 28,000

During 19x3

Cash (A) 15,600
  Investment—Lupton (A) 14,400
  Investment—Forest (A) 1,200

12/31/x3

Investment—Lupton (A) 36,000
Investment—Forest (A) 3,000
  Equity Income (R) 39,000

During 19x4

Cash (A) 28,300
  Investment—Lupton (A) 20,000
  Investment—Forest (A) 4,800
  Investment—Firek (A) 3,500

12/31/x4

Investment—Lupton (A) 40,000
Investment—Forest (A) 4,500
Investment—Firek (A) 9,800
  Equity Income (R) 54,300

2. Investment—Lupton: $118,600
   Investment—Forest: 23,500
   Investment—Firek: 43,300

3. 1/1/x5

Cash (A) 120,000
  Investment—Lupton (A) 118,600
  Realized Gain on Sale (R) 1,400

• DEMONSTRATION EXERCISE

On January 1, 19x4, Paton, Inc., purchased 100% of Sunset Company for $470,000 cash. Immediately prior to the acquisition both entities' balance sheets were:

	Paton, Inc. Balance Sheet 1/1/x4	Sunset Co. Balance Sheet 1/1/x4
Cash.	$ 590,000	$ 62,000
Other assets	3,400,000	658,000
Total assets	$3,990,000	$720,000
Liabilities	$ 960,000	$250,000
Common stock	1,000,000	200,000
Retained earnings	2,030,000	270,000
Total liabilities and stockholders' equity	$3,990,000	$720,000

Required:

1. Prepare the journal entry Paton would make to record the acquisition on January 1, 19x4.
2. Prepare the consolidation worksheet entry at January 1, 19x4.
3. Prepare Paton's January 1, 19x4, consolidated balance sheet.

Solution:

1. Investment in Sunset (A). 470,000

   Cash (A).   470,000

2. Common Stock (Sunset). 200,000

   Retained Earnings (Sunset) 270,000

   Investment in Sunset (Paton).   470,000

3.

Paton, Inc.
Consolidated Balance Sheet
January 1, 19x4

Cash	$ 182,000	Liabilities	$1,210,000
Other assets	4,058,000		
		Stockholders' equity:	
		Common stock	$1,000,000
		Retained earnings	2,030,000
		Total stockholders' equity	$3,030,000
		Total liabilities and	
Total assets	$4,240,000	stockholders' equity	$4,240,000

Additional Aspects of Consolidation

This appendix builds on the example illustrated in the chapter, explaining two additional common aspects encountered in consolidations:

a. What happens if less than 100% of the subsidiary is acquired by the parent as an investment?

b. What happens if the purchase price is greater than the book value of the assets acquired?

If a parent acquires less than 100% of a subsidiary, the stock not owned by the parent is called the **minority interest** in the subsidiary. The minority interest could be between 1% and 50% for a consolidated subsidiary. In the example below we illustrate how the minority interest case is like the example in the chapter in that 100% of the subsidiary's net assets and net income are added into the parent's financial statements. The difference is that the minority interest's share of the net assets is reported like an additional liability in the consolidated balance sheet, and the minority interest's share of net income is reported like an additional expense in the consolidated income statement.

The example that follows will also illustrate how to account for a consolidation when the price paid exceeds the book value of the net assets purchased by the parent. This difference between the value of the net assets on the parent's books and the value of the net assets on the separate books of the subsidiary is not unusual and will require the parent to make adjusting journal entries for this difference in accounting for the net income and net assets of the subsidiary before consolidation takes place.

Objective 6
Additional aspects of
consolidation.

To illustrate these two additional features of consolidated investments, consider again the acquisition of Kidco by Big, Inc., on December 31, 19x1. Now assume Big pays $72,000 cash for a 90% interest in Kidco by acquiring 90% of Kidco's stock in the open market. Just prior to the acquisition, their book values are as follows:

Big, Inc.* Balance Sheet December 31, 19x1		**Kidco** Balance Sheet December 31, 19x1	
Assets		**Assets**	
Cash	$100,000	Other assets	$100,000
Other assets	500,000		
Total assets	$600,000	Total assets	$100,000
Liabilities and Stockholders' Equity		**Liabilities and Stockholders' Equity**	
Liabilities:		Liabilities:	
All liabilities	$300,000	All liabilities	$ 30,000
Stockholders' equity:		Stockholders' equity:	
Common stock	$200,000	Common stock	$ 50,000
Retained earnings	100,000	Retained earnings	20,000
Total stockholders' equity	$300,000	Total stockholders' equity	$ 70,000
Total liabilities and stockholders' equity	$600,000	Total liabilities and stockholders' equity	$100,000

net book value

*The detailed description of the assets and liabilities of the balance sheets are omitted here for simplicity of illustration.

Why would Big pay $72,000 for a 90% interest when 100% of the net book value of Kidco is only $70,000? Two reasons could be that Kidco's net assets are undervalued (book value is less than fair market value) and/or that Kidco has unrecorded assets (goodwill) for which Big is willing to pay.[9]

When a parent acquires a controlling interest in a subsidiary, the parent must determine the fair value of all purchased assets and liabilities. Some of the assets may be carried on the books of the subsidiary at less than current value and some at more. Once the parent has determined the fair value of the recorded assets (and liabilities) of the subsidiary, any excess of the price paid over the fair value of the assets acquired is attributable to goodwill.

In this example assume that Big's purchase price is above Kidco's book value because Big believes (1) Kidco has goodwill and (2) all of Kidco's recorded assets are already recorded at their fair market value. Big views Kidco's **fair market value balance sheet** as follows:

Kidco
Fair Market Value Balance Sheet
December 31, 19x1

Assets		Liabilities and Stockholders' Equity	
Other assets	$100,000	Liabilities:	
Goodwill	10,000	All liabilities	$ 30,000
		Stockholders' equity:	
		Common stock	$ 50,000
		Retained earnings	30,000*
		Total stockholders' equity	$ 80,000
		Total liabilities and	
Total assets	$110,000	stockholders' equity	$110,000

*Includes $10,000 for value of goodwill.

Although Kidco's actual (historical cost) balance sheet does **not** show goodwill (and only has $20,000 retained earnings), Big is willing to pay $72,000 for a 90% interest in Kidco (Kidco's $80,000 assumed net assets × 90% = $72,000) based on **Big's own separate assessment of the value of Kidco.** The journal entry to record the 90% purchase of Kidco would be

Entry in Big's General Journal

19x1				
Dec. 31	Investment in Kidco (A)		72,000	
	Cash (A)			72,000
	To record purchase of 90% of Kidco's stock.			

No entry is made on Kidco's books to reflect goodwill or the purchase by Big. The consolidation worksheet entry to achieve the consolidated balance sheet at the date of purchase would be as follows:

---

[9]Note that most companies' stocks sell in the market in excess of their book value per share because of these two reasons. As a result, it is uncommon to see a company acquired for a price that is at or below book value.

Consolidation Worksheet Entry

19x1
Dec. 31   Common Stock (Kidco) 50,000

Retained Earnings (Kidco) 20,000

Goodwill (New) 9,000

    Investment in Kidco (Big) 72,000

    Minority Interest (New) 7,000

    To eliminate intercompany accounts and record goodwill and
minority interest in the consolidated balance sheet.

Exhibit 12A–1 illustrates the worksheet for the separate and consolidated balance sheets of Big and Kidco at December 31, 19x1. The consolidation worksheet entry eliminates the intercompany accounts:

Common Stock (Kidco)	$50,000
Retained Earnings (Kidco)	20,000
Investment in Kidco (Big)	72,000

The entry establishes two new accounts that did **not** appear in the separate (unconsolidated) financial statements:

An asset—Goodwill	$9,000
A liability—Minority Interest	7,000

The asset account, Goodwill, represents 90% of the goodwill that Big believes exists in Kidco, which is the portion actually paid for by Big.[10] (By paying more than book value for Kidco, Big provided real evidence of the existence of this asset that was not recorded on Kidco's books.) Goodwill will be reported as an asset on Big's consolidated balance sheet. The Minority Interest account represents the 10% of the net assets of Kidco (at their book value) not owned by Big. Since Big will report 100% of the assets of Kidco (including $9,000 of goodwill) in Big's consolidated balance sheet, the credit balance of the Minority Interest account serves like a contra net asset account in reducing the consolidated net assets of Big. The Minority Interest account looks like a liability and is typically reported as a separate item between liabilities and stockholders' equity in consolidated balance sheets. Minority interest should equal the net book value of the subsidiary times the percentage of minority ownership, even when the fair value of the subsidiary exceeds its book value.

Next, assume that the 19x2 operations of Big and Kidco were the same as in the chapter, with Big reporting separate net income of $50,000 and Kidco reporting net income of $30,000 and dividends of $20,000. Recall from Chapter 8 that goodwill must be amortized over no more than 40 years. Assume that Big amortizes goodwill over 20 years in this example. Annual goodwill amortization would be $450 per year ($9,000/20 years = $450 per year). In 19x2, Big records the following journal entries to account for its investment in Kidco:

Entries on Big's Journal

19x2
Dec. 31   Investment in Kidco (A) 27,000

    Income from Kidco (R) 27,000

    To record 90% of Kidco's 19x2 net income ($30,000 × .90).

---

[10]For a review of goodwill, refer to Chapter 8, pp. 410–11.

EXHIBIT 12A–1

Worksheet for
Consolidated
Balance Sheet

	Separate Balance Sheets		Consolidation Worksheet Entries		Big, Inc. Consolidated Balance Sheet
	Big, Inc.*	Kidco	Debit	Credit	12/31/x1
Assets:					
Cash	28,000				28,000
Investment in Kidco . .	72,000			72,000	—
Other assets	500,000	100,000			600,000
Goodwill	—	—	9,000		9,000
Total assets	600,000	100,000			637,000
Liabilities:					
All liabilities	300,000	30,000			330,000
Minority interest	—	—		7,000	7,000
Stockholders' equity:					
Common stock	200,000	50,000	50,000		200,000
Retained earnings . . .	100,000	20,000	20,000		100,000
Total liabilities and stockholders' equity . .	600,000	100,000	79,000	79,000	637,000

*Unconsolidated.

Dec. 31	Cash (A)	18,000	
	Investment in Kidco (A)		18,000
	To record 90% of Kidco's 19x2 dividends ($20,000 × .90).		
31	Income from Kidco (R)	450	
	Investment in Kidco (A)		450
	To amortize 1/20 of 90% of Kidco's goodwill: $9,000/20 years = $450.		

The third entry is an equity method adjustment made by Big because Kidco's net income for 19x2 ($30,000) does not include amortization of Kidco's goodwill. Since goodwill is not recognized on the separate books of Kidco but is recognized by Big in its investment account (as evidenced from Big's payment of $72,000 for a 90% interest), Big must adjust Kidco's net income for the purchased goodwill. Recall that Big's investment in Kidco ($72,000) includes $9,000 for purchased goodwill. To be consistent in its investment account, Big must adjust the 19x2 net income of Kidco for the amortization of the purchased goodwill. The consolidation worksheet entries for the end of 19x2 would be as follows:

Consolidation Worksheet Entry

19x2 Dec. 31	Common Stock (Kidco)	50,000	
	Retained Earnings (Kidco)	30,000	
	Goodwill (New)	8,550	
	Investment in Kidco (Big)		80,550
	Minority Interest (New)		8,000
	To eliminate intercompany accounts and record goodwill and minority interest in the consolidated balance sheet.		

EXHIBIT 12A–2

Worksheet for Consolidated Balance Sheet as of December 31, 19x2

Sheet	Separate Balance Sheets		Consolidation Worksheet Entries		Big, Inc. Consolidated Balance Sheet 12/31/x2
	Big, Inc.*	Kidco	Debit	Credit	
Assets:					
Cash	46,000				46,000
Investment in Kidco . .	80,550			80,550	
Other assets	550,000	110,000			660,000
Goodwill			8,550		8,550
Total assets.	676,550	110,000			714,550
Liabilities:					
All liabilities	300,000	30,000			330,000
Minority interest	—	—		8,000	8,000
Stockholders' equity:					
Common stock	200,000	50,000	50,000		200,000
Retained earnings . . .	176,550	30,000	30,000		176,550
Total liabilities and stockholders' equity . .	676,550	110,000	88,550	88,550	714,550

*Unconsolidated.

Big, Inc.
Consolidated Income Statement
For the Year Ended December 31, 19x2

Revenues		$1,660,000
Expenses (other)		1,580,000
Amortization of goodwill		450
	$	79,550
Less: minority interest		3,000*
Net income	$	76,550

*Kidco's net income	$30,000	
Minority share	× .10	
Minority net income	$ 3,000	

Exhibit 12A–2 provides a complete consolidation worksheet and consolidated income statement for the end of 19x2. Note that although this example illustrates several complexities, the basic principles illustrated earlier in the chapter still apply. The single asset on Big's unconsolidated statements ($80,550 as of the end of 19x2) is being eliminated and replaced with all of Kidco's assets and liabilities, including the unrecorded assets represented by goodwill. Also, Big's stockholders' equity is the same before and after consolidation. Consolidation does not change the substance of the financial reports—only the form of the reports is altered.

• DEMONSTRATION EXERCISE

On January 1, 19x4, Paton, Inc., purchased 80% of Sunset Company for $400,000 cash. Immediately prior to the acquisition both entities' balance sheets were:

	Paton, Inc. Balance Sheet 1/1/x4	Sunset Co. Balance Sheet 1/1/x4
Cash.	$ 590,000	$ 62,000
Other assets	3,400,000	658,000
Total assets	$3,990,000	$720,000
Liabilities	$ 960,000	$250,000
Common stock	1,000,000	200,000
Retained earnings	2,030,000	270,000
Total liabilities and stockholders' equity	$3,990,000	$720,000

The fair market value of Sunset's net identifiable assets equals book value.

Required:
1. Prepare the journal entry Paton would make to record the acquisition on January 1, 19x4.
2. Prepare the consolidation worksheet entry at January 1, 19x4.
3. Prepare Paton's January 1, 19x4, consolidated balance sheet.

Solution:

1. Investment in Sunset (A).   400,000

    Cash (A).   400,000

2. Common Stock (Sunset).   200,000

  Retained Earnings (Sunset)   270,000

  Goodwill (New)   24,000

    Investment in Sunset (Paton).   400,000

    Minority Interest (New)   94,000

3.
Paton, Inc.
Consolidated Balance Sheet
January 1, 19x4

Cash	$ 252,000	Liabilities	$1,210,000
Goodwill	24,000	Minority interest	$ 94,000
Other assets	4,058,000	Stockholders' equity:	
		Common stock	$1,000,000
		Retained earnings	2,030,000
		Total stockholders' equity	$3,030,000
Total assets	$4,334,000	Total liabilities and stockholders' equity.	$4,334,000

Pooling of Interests

The examples illustrated in the chapter and Appendix 12A have all assumed that the parent company was **purchasing** an interest in the subsidiary by paying cash for the stock of the subsidiary. This is the most common form of acquisition, known as the purchase method.

In the purchase method, the parent records the investment at cost. If the cost of the subsidiary is greater than its book value, the recorded value of the subsidiary may be "written up" above its book value in the parent's unconsolidated statements and in the consolidated statements, as illustrated in Appendix 12A. This write-up could result in the addition of "new" asset accounts (such as goodwill) that were not on the subsidiary's books or the revaluation of existing book values reported by the subsidiary. As a result, the parent revalues the assets of the subsidiary at the date of acquisition even though the assets remain at their book values on the subsidiary's books.

Objective 7
Pooling of interests.

In addition to the purchase method of acquisition, an alternative form of acquisition occurs, called pooling of interests. The basic concept supporting the pooling method is that because the two entities are pooling assets and liabilities, revaluation is not necessary. What evidence can support the contention that the two entities are pooling resources rather than one buying the other? The most common indicator is the nature of the exchange transaction. Purchase transactions are primarily for cash, and pooling transactions are primarily exchanges of stock. In general, then, the pooling of interests method is used in cases where 90% or more of the subsidiary is acquired by the exchanging of the stock or other securities of the parent for the subsidiary's stock.[11] The main effect of pooling is the ignoring of the fair value of the (given or received) stock. Accounting for the parent's investment in the subsidiary is based only on the subsidiary's book value. Therefore, the two balance sheets are combined with no adjustments for goodwill or fair values.

If we assumed the same facts as in the example illustrated in the chapter except that (1) the market value of Kidco was something greater than book value and (2) Big had acquired Kidco for Big common stock rather than for cash, then the chapter illustration would be an example of the pooling of interests method. Thus, in *the pooling of interests method, the book values of the subsidiary are added to the book values of the parent in the consolidation process, regardless of whether the fair value of the subsidiary is greater than book value.*

In practice, the use of pooling of interests method is rare because it is difficult to convince 90% of the stockholders of a public company to exchange their stock for the stock (or other securities) of another company. Such acquisitions usually require the agreement of the boards of directors of both companies, which makes the acquisition a "friendly takeover." In recent years, the number of companies using the pooling of interests method of accounting for acquisitions has been about 7% of all companies reporting acquisitions.[12] Cash purchases of securities are much more common than pooling of interests.

In evaluating investments, it is important to know whether the purchase or pooling method is used to account for a company's consolidated subsidiaries. In general, the pooling method results in lower consolidated total assets, which results in a higher return

---

[11]The specific rules governing the use of the pooling method are beyond the scope of this text. These rules and the accounting techniques used to create pooled statements can be found in advanced accounting texts.

[12]See *Accounting Trends & Techniques; 1992* (New York: AICPA, 1992), p. 62.

on assets ratio, all else being equal. The pooling method will also normally result in higher consolidated profits (e.g., no recognition of asset value in excess of their book values) than the purchase method, all else being equal. This also results in a better ratio of net income to net assets (or return on equity) for the pooling method, all else being equal. However, these differences are based strictly on the method of consolidation, and are not real economic differences. As a result, it is necessary for investors to attempt to estimate the differences between the purchase and pooling methods when comparing investment alternatives that use different methods for consolidation purposes.

• KEY TERMS

Amortized cost method. Used when companies acquire long-term investments with stated interest rates and maturity amounts at a premium or a discount and the premium or discount must be amortized over the remaining life of the security.

Available-for-sale securities. Those debt and equity securities which are not classified as trading securities, and those debt securities not being held-to-maturity. These securities may be classified as current or long-term depending on management's intention. They exclude voting equity investments of 20% or more.

Consolidated financial statements. Financial statements that present the parent and subsidiary as one entity.

Consolidation worksheets. Aids that are not a formal part of the separate accounting systems of either the investor or investee companies but are schedules that draw data from the separate entities and calculate the adjustments necessary to prepare consolidated financial statements.

Controlling interest. Occurs when the investor owns over 50% of an investee. Disclosures of investees that are controlled are reported using principles of consolidation.

Elimination entries. Consolidation worksheet entries used to eliminate duplication in the parent's and subsidiary's formal accounting records.

Equity method. Accounting method used for voting equity securities when the investor has enough voting stock to influence the operations of the investee, usually between 20 and 50%.

Fair value. The amount at which a financial instrument could be exchanged in a current transaction between willing parties, other than in a forced liquidation sale. Generally, the current market price, or realizable value.

Financial instruments. These include cash, evidence of ownership interest in an entity, and any contract that both imposes on one entity a contractual obligation to provide cash or other financial consideration and conveys to a second entity a contractual right to receive cash or other financial consideration.

Held-to-maturity securities. Those debt securities purchased with the intention of holding them until they mature.

Investments. Assets acquired by a company with the expectation of receiving interest, dividends, or price appreciation.

Long-term investments. Investments longer than one year.

Lower-of-cost-or-market method. Accounting method used before 1994 for all temporary investments and long-term investments in marketable equity securities of less than a 20% interest.

Marketable equity securities. Stocks publicly traded on stock exchanges.

Nonequity investments. Bonds, notes, and CDs—investments other than voting stocks of publicly traded companies.

Parent. Investor in a subsidiary.

Subsidiary. Investee company.

Temporary investment. Investment that management intends to keep less than one year or operating cycle, whichever is longer.

Trading securities. Those debt and equity securities bought and sold with the intention of earning trading profits. A rapid rate of buying and selling is expected.

Voting equity investments. Those investments in stock that represent a 20% or greater voting ownership interest in an investee company.

· **Appendix Key Terms** ————————————————————————————

Minority Interest account. Similar to an "allowance" account. The minority shareholders' interest in the net assets of the investee firm.

Pooling of interests. Alternative form of recording an acquisition that records the acquired company at book value if 90% or more of the subsidiary is acquired by the exchange of the stock or other securities of the parent for the subsidiary's stock.

Purchase method. Form of recording an acquisition in which the parent pays cash for the subsidiary and records the fair market value of the sub on its books.

· **SYNONYMS** ————————————————————————————————————

Certificates of deposit; CDs.

Corporate notes; commercial paper.

Ease of conversion back to cash; liquidity.

Elimination entries; consolidation worksheet entries.

Equity investee; unconsolidated subsidiary.

Fair value; market value; realizable value.

Investment income; equity investment income; income in unconsolidated subsidiaries.

Parent; investor company.

Subsidiary; sub; investee company.

Temporary investments; investments listed with current assets.

U.S. Treasury notes; T bills.

· **QUESTIONS** ————————————————————————————————————

1. What are the primary business purposes for investments?
2. What is the definition of trading securities?
3. What is the definition of held-to-maturity securities?
4. What is the definition of available-for-sale securities?
5. What accounting method or methods apply to temporary investments in debt and equity securities?
6. What accounting method or methods apply to long-term investments in debt and equity securities?
7. What kinds of investments may result in unrealized gains and/or losses reported in the income statement?
8. What kinds of investments may result in unrealized gains and/or losses that are *not* reported in the income statement? Where are they reported?
9. How can financial statement readers determine the cumulative and current period's net unrealized gains or losses from the year-end portfolio of securities classified as available-for-sale?
10. What method is used to account for long-term investments in bonds?
11. When is the equity method used to account for investments?
12. How do earnings of an equity-method investee affect the earnings of the investor?
13. How do cash dividends received from an equity-method investee affect the earnings of the investor?

14. When is the consolidation method used for investments?
15. What is the impact of subsidiary earnings on the parent's unconsolidated balance sheet and earnings statement?
16. How does the consolidation process eliminate the parent's asset account, Investment in Subsidiary, in order to prepare consolidated financial statements?
17. What is the effect of the consolidation process on the parent's unconsolidated owners' equity section of the balance sheet?
18. What effect does the consolidation process have on the formal journals and ledgers of the parent? The subsidiary?
19. What effect do consolidation worksheet entries have on the formal journals and ledgers of the parent and the subsidiary?

· Appendix Questions

20. When a parent acquires less than a 100% investment in a subsidiary, what new accounts (not found in the separate unconsolidated financial statements of the parent or the subsidiary) are found in the consolidated financial statements? What is the purpose of these accounts?
21. When a parent pays more than book value for a subsidiary, what effect does it have on the subsidiary's separate (unconsolidated) financial statements?
22. What is a pooling of interests?
23. How does the pooling of interests method differ from the purchase method?

· EXERCISES

E 12–1
Temporary Investments in Debt
L.O.1

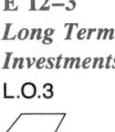

Butler Corporation purchased a U.S. Treasury bill for $97,000 plus accrued interest on July 1, 19x1. The T bill pays semiannual interest at the rate of 8% per year (4% semiannually) on June 30 and December 31. The face (maturity) value of the T bill is $100,000, and the maturity date is December 31, 19x6. Butler holds the T bill until January 31, 19x2, and then sells it for $97,300 plus accrued interest. The fair value of the investment at year-end was $97,400.

Required: (Round to the nearest dollar.)
Record the entries necessary to account for this investment as a trading security on Butler's books from the date of purchase to the date of sale. Assume a December 31 year-end.

E 12–2
Temporary Investments in Debt
L.O.2

Chartex Corporation purchased General Boaters Corporation bonds on May 1, 19x4, for $53,800, plus accrued interest. The bonds have a face value of $50,000 and pay interest at the rate of 9% per year, with semiannual interest payments being made on July 1 and January 1 each year. The bonds mature on January 1, 19x7. Chartex Corporation held the bonds as a temporary investment until March 31, 19x5, when they sold them for $53,900 plus accrued interest. Chartex has a December 31 year-end. The fair value of the bonds at the end of 19x4 was $54,000.

Required: (Round answers to the nearest dollar.)
Record all of the journal entries necessary to account for Chartex's bond investment as a security available-for-sale from the date of purchase to the date of sale.

E 12–3
Long Term Investments
L.O.3

Whalen, Inc., purchased $150,000 face value 8% corporate bonds on May 1, 19x1, for $138,800 cash plus accrued interest. The bonds pay interest semiannually on June 30 and December 31 and mature on December 31, 19x5. Whalen expects to hold these bonds until maturity and uses the amortized cost method with straight-line amortization of the discount. Whalen has a calendar year-end.

Required: (Round answers to the nearest dollar.)
1. Record any necessary journal entries for 19x1 to account for this investment.
2. Prepare the bond amortization table for the remaining life of the bond.

E 12–4
Long Term Investments (Challenging)
L.O.3

Hurd Corporation purchased $200,000 face value 10% bonds on July 1, 19x1, for $212,000. The bonds pay semiannual interest on June 30 and December 31 and mature on December 31, 19x4. Hurd expects to hold these bonds until maturity.

Required: (Round answers to the nearest dollar.)
1. Assuming Hurd uses straight-line amortization on this long-term investment, record the necessary entries for 19x1.
2. Prepare the amortization table for the bonds assuming they are held to maturity.
3. (Optional) Assume that Hurd uses the effective-interest (present value) amortization method as illustrated in Appendix 10B and that the effective annual interest rate is 8%. Record the necessary entries for 19x1 and prepare the amortization table assuming the bonds are held to maturity.

E 12–5
Long-Term Investments (Challenging)
L.O.3

Madden Corporation began investing in high-grade corporate bonds in 19x2 as long-term investments for financing future expansion. On July 1, 19x4, Madden paid $139,798 cash for Star Corporation 10% bonds that had a face value of $150,000 and paid semiannual interest on June 30 and December 31. Madden expects to hold the bonds until they mature on December 31, 19x8.

Required:
1. Prepare a bond amortization table based on straight-line amortization of the bond discount or premium.
2. Record the entries required from the date of purchase to July 1, 19x5.
3. (Optional) Assume the effective interest on the bonds is 12%. Repeat requirements 1 and 2 above using the effective-interest method of amortizing the discount or premium.

E 12–6
Temporary Investments
L.O.1

On June 30, 19x2, Extone Corporation purchased shares of voting stock in the market for $35,000 cash, which was temporarily idle. On September 30, 19x2, these stocks paid $2,800 in cash dividends. At December 31, 19x2, Extone's year-end, the stocks had a market value of $34,000. These are the only temporary investments held by Extone.

Required:
Prepare the journal entries for Extone to account for the investment as trading securities.

E 12–7
Temporary Investments
L.O.2

On September 3, 19x5, Arens, Inc., acquired marketable equity securities for $18,700 cash as a temporary investment. These stocks paid cash dividends of $1,950 on December 30, 19x5. On December 31, 19x5, Arens's year-end, their market value was $17,900. Arens sold these stocks on March 23, 19x6, for $19,000 cash. Arens classified these temporary investments as available-for-sale.

Required:
1. Record the necessary entries on Arens's books.
2. How would the investments be reported in Arens's December 31, 19x5, balance sheet?

E 12–8
Temporary Investments
L.O.2

CENBO, Inc., purchased equity securities of ABC and XYZ during 19x1. All securities were classified as available-for-sale in CENBO's current assets. The numbers of shares, purchase prices, and market prices at December 31, 19x1, are shown below:

Company	Number of Shares	Purchase Price per Share	12/31/x1 Market Price per Share
ABC	1,500	$105	$110
XYZ	400	80	50

During 19x2, CENBO, Inc., sold the 1,500 shares of ABC for $115 per share and purchased 1,000 shares of HIJ for $45 per share cash. The information on the portfolio held at December 31, 19x2, is as follows:

Company	Number of Shares	Purchase Price per Share	12/31/x1 Market Price per Share
XYZ	400	$80	$82
HIJ	1,000	45	30

Required:
Record all journal entries for 19x1 and 19x2 related to marketable equity securities, including any year-end entries that may be necessary.

E 12–9
Temporary Investments
L.O.1

Marsten, Inc., uses idle cash to invest in trading securities as temporary investments during 19x1. At the start of 19x2, Marsten's trading securities were as follows:

| | | Price per Share | |
Stock	Number of Shares	Original	12/31/x1
General Mills	100	$ 45.50	$ 39.75
IBM	100	132.00	109.75
Reebok	250	14.75	15.25

During 19x2, the following events took place (*not* in the order presented):

a. Sold 100 shares of Reebok for $16 per share.
b. Sold 100 shares of IBM for $125 per share.
c. Sold 100 shares of General Mills for $43 per share.
d. Purchased 100 shares of Ford for $52 per share.
e. Purchased 400 shares of Detroit Edison for $17.50 per share.
f. Purchased 200 shares of Apple Computer for $47.50 per share.
g. Received $150 in Ford dividends.
h. Received $185 in IBM dividends.

The market values of stocks held at December 31, 19x2, were as follows:

Reebok	$14.25 per share
Ford	54.00 per share
Detroit Edison	16.00 per share
Apple Computer	49.50 per share

Required:
Record all journal entries for 19x2 related to Marsten's temporary investments in trading securities. Include any year-end adjusting entries that may be necessary for 19x2.

E 12–10
Long-Term Investments
L.O.2

Refer to the facts in exercise 12–9 above. Assume the same facts except that Marsten, Inc., accounts for these investments as long-term securities available-for-sale. Ignore the *19x2* transactions. For *19x1* only reconstruct the year-end adjusting entry. Would your entry have changed if these were short-term investments available-for sale?

E 12–11
Long-Term Stock Investments
L.O.2

Masten, Inc., holds several stocks as long-term investments. Masten did not have any sales or purchases of long-term stock investments during 19x5. At the end of 19x5, the following data were reported:

Stock	Original Cost	12/31/x4 Market Value	12/31/x5 Market Value
Zerox.	$13,850	$14,250	$16,225
Campbell	15,735	14,250	13,975
Rockwell	12,950	10,500	11,115

Required:
Prepare any entries required by Masten, Inc., for 19x5, assuming these stocks are classified as available-for-sale.

E 12–12
*Equity Method
(CPA adapted)*
L.O.4

1. Hysen, Inc., owns 40% of the outstanding stock of Legander Company. During 19x9, Hysen received a $4,000 cash dividend from Legander. What effect did this dividend have on Hysen's 19x9 financial statements?
   a. Increased total assets.
   b. Decreased total assets.
   c. Increased income.
   d. Decreased the investment account.

2. Slayton, Inc., owns a 40% interest in Johnson Corporation. During the calendar year 19x4, Johnson had net income of $100,000 and paid dividends of $10,000. Slayton mistakenly recorded these transactions using the cost method rather than the equity method of accounting. What effect would this have on (1) the Long-Term Investment in Johnson account, (2) net income, and (3) retained earnings, respectively?
   a. Understate 1, overstate 2, overstate 3.
   b. Overstate 1, understate 2, understate 3.
   c. Overstate 1, overstate 2, overstate 3.
   d. Understate 1, understate 2, understate 3.

3. A parent corporation that uses the equity method of accounting for its investment in a 40% owned subsidiary, which earned $20,000 and paid $5,000 in dividends, made the following entries:

Investment in Subsidiary (A)	8,000	
Earnings in Unconsolidated Subsidiary (R)		8,000
Cash (A)	2,000	
Dividend Revenue (R)		2,000

   What effect will these entries have on the parent's balance sheet?
   a. Financial position will be fairly stated.
   b. Investment in subsidiary will be overstated; retained earnings, understated.
   c. Investment in subsidiary will be understated; retained earnings, understated.
   d. Investment in subsidiary will be overstated; retained earnings, overstated.

4. On January 1, 19x6, Schonfeld Corporation acquired, as a long-term investment, a 40% common stock interest in Action Company for $130,000. On that date, Action had net assets of $325,000. During 19x6, Action reported net income of $60,000 and declared and paid cash dividends of $15,000. What is the amount of income that Schonfeld can report from this investment for the calendar year 19x6?
   a. $6,000.
   b. $18,000.
   c. $23,750.
   d. $24,000.

E 12–13
Equity Method
L.O.4

P Company purchased 30% of the outstanding stock of S Company on December 31, 19x1, for $1 million cash. In 19x2, S Company reported net income of $80,000. In 19x2, S Company declared and paid dividends of $10,000.

Required:
1. Record the journal entries P Company makes in recording its interest in S Company.
2. Determine the balance on P's books of its Investment in S Company account at the end of 19x2.

E 12–14
*Fair Value and Equity
Methods*
L.O.1, 2, 4

The following information pertains to the long-term investments of the Lullo Company purchased on January 1, 19x4:

Investment	Number of Shares Purchased	Percentage of Total Outstanding Shares of Company	Cost	Market Price per Share at 12/31/x4	Earnings of Company for 19x4
Maize common stock	10,000	15	$25,000	$2	$75,000
Blue common stock	6,000	30	60,000	9	50,000

Neither Maize nor Blue declared dividends on its common stock in 19x4. Illustrate how these investments would appear in Lullo's December 31, 19x4, balance sheet.

E 12–15
Equity Method
L.O.4

On January 1, 19x1, the Reece Corporation purchased, as a long-term investment, 10,000 shares of the outstanding common stock of the Luke Corporation at $60 per share. Both the Reece Corporation and Luke Corporation fiscal years end on December 31, 19x1. During 19x1, the following events occurred with respect to the Luke Corporation:

Net income reported for 19x1.	$40,000
Dividends declared and paid (per share).	$ .75
Market price per share of common stock on December 31, 19x1	$ 56.00
Number of outstanding shares during all of 19x1 for Luke Corporation	40,000

Required:
1. Prepare the journal entry to record the stock purchase.
2. Prepare the journal entry to recognize the Luke Corporation's net income for 19x1.
3. Prepare the journal entry to record the cash dividend declared and paid by the Luke Corporation.
4. Prepare any required adjusting entries at December 31, 19x1, and compute the ending balance in the asset Investment in Luke.

E 12–16
Long-Term Investments
L.O.2, 4

On January 1, 19xx, the Denver Corporation purchased, as long-term investments, 8% of the voting stock of the Green Corporation for $200,000 and 35% of the voting stock of the Blue Corporation for $400,000. During 19xx, Green Corporation had net income of $80,000 and paid dividends of $50,000. During 19xx, the Blue Corporation had net income of $40,000 and paid dividends of $20,000. The market value at the end of 19xx was equal to original cost for both securities.

Required:
Prepare Denver's journal entry (entries) pertaining to its investments in the Green Corporation and the Blue Corporation.

E 12–17
Methods of Recording Investments
L.O.1–5

Fill in the blanks with the correct method or methods (fair value, amortized cost, equity, or consolidation).

1. Under this method, the purchase of the investments are recorded at cost: _____ .
2. Under this method, it is not appropriate for the investment to be consolidated in preparing the financial statements: _____ .
3. Under this method, year-end adjustments to an asset account are made if the market value of the investment account increased or decreased during the year: _____ .
4. Under this method, the investor recognizes the net income of the investee company multiplied by the investor's ownership percentage in the investee: _____ .

E 12–18
Consolidation
L.O.5

BOT, Inc., acquired 100% of Top Corporation's common stock for $1,500,000 on January 1, 19x1. Top Corporation had the following activity and facts for 19x1.

	1/1/x1
Assets	$2,800,000
Liabilities	1,300,000
Stockholders' equity	1,500,000
19x1 net income.	$ 500,000
19x1 dividends declared and paid on 12/31/x1	200,000

Required:
1. Prepare the journal entries in general journal form that BOT will make during 19x1 regarding its interest in Top Corporation.
2. Prepare the consolidation worksheet entry BOT will make to consolidate Top Corporation at the end of 19x1.

E 12–19
Consolidation at
Acquisition
L.O.5

Bates Corporation acquired 100% of the Terry, Inc., common stock for $148 million cash on January 1, 19x3. The separate balance sheets of the two companies just prior to the purchase by Bates were as follows:

Bates Corporation
Balance Sheet
December 31, 19x2
(in millions)

Assets		Liabilities and Stockholders' Equity	
Cash	$153	Liabilities:	
Accounts receivable	98	Accounts payable	$108
Inventory	86	Notes payable	250
Plant assets (net)	218	Other liabilities	37
Investments	12	Total liabilities	$395
		Stockholders' equity:	
		Common stock	$100
		Retained earnings	72
		Total stockholders' equity	$172
		Total liabilities and	
Total assets	$567	stockholders' equity	$567

Terry, Inc.
Balance Sheet
December 31, 19x2
(in millions)

Assets		Liabilities and Stockholders' Equity	
Cash	$ 11	Liabilities:	
Accounts receivable	101	Accounts payable	$162
Inventory	112	Taxes payable	30
Plant assets (net)	249	Advances from customers	11
Investments	108	Notes payable	230
		Total liabilities	$433
		Stockholders' equity:	
		Common stock	$ 42
		Retained earnings	106
		Total stockholders' equity	$148
		Total liabilities and	
Total assets	$581	stockholders' equity	$581

Required:
1. Record the journal entry to account for the purchase by Bates and the consolidation worksheet entry on January 1, 19x3.
2. Prepare a consolidated balance sheet on January 1, 19x3.

· **Appendix Exercises**

E 12–20
Consolidation—
Minority Interest
L.O.5

Wright, Inc., owns 80% of April Corporation. The following data are available:

Wright, Inc.
Balance Sheets (unconsolidated)
December 31

	19x7	19x6
Assets		
Cash.	$ 196,000	$ 166,000
Investment in April.	504,000	384,000
Other assets	9,800,000	9,450,000
Total assets.	$10,500,000	$10,000,000

Liabilities and Stockholders' Equity

	19x7	19x6
Liabilities	$ 2,700,000	$ 2,700,000
Common stock	2,300,000	2,300,000
Retained earnings	5,500,000	5,000,000
Total liabilities and stockholders' equity	$10,500,000	$10,000,000

April Corporation
Balance Sheets
December 31

	19x7	19x6
Assets (no cash)	$850,000	$700,000

Liabilities and Stockholders' Equity

	19x7	19x6
Liabilities	$220,000	$220,000
Common stock	280,000	280,000
Retained earnings	350,000	200,000
Total liabilities and stockholders' equity	$850,000	$700,000

No dividends were declared by either company in 19x7.

Required:
1. Prepare the consolidation worksheet entry at December 31, 19x7, needed to prepare the consolidated balance sheets.
2. Prepare the consolidated balance sheet for Wright, Inc., as of December 31, 19x7.
3. What was Wright's consolidated net income for 19x7?

E 12–21
Annual Report
Disclosures
L.O.5

Anderson Company discloses the following items on its consolidated income statement:

Total net income.	$12,889,000
Less minority interest	480,000
Consolidated net income	$12,409,000

Required:
1. If the percentage of ownership by Anderson is 60%, what was the subsidiary's separate net income? Show computations.
2. What reference to minority interest would you expect to see on Anderson's consolidated balance sheet?

• PROBLEMS

P 12–1
Temporary Investments
L.O.2

As of December 31, 19x7, Farm Products, Inc., reported the following data for their temporary investments in securities available-for-sale; United Corp. common stock:

Original cost (4/1/x7)	$87,500
Market value (12/31/x7)	$82,600

During 19x8, Farm Products received $2,400 in dividends on these shares. Also, on June 30, 19x8, Farm Products sold all shares of United for $93,000 cash. On December 15, 19x8, Farm Products again acquired United stock for $49,000 cash as securities available-for-sale.

Required:
1. Record dividends for 19x8.
2. Record the sale of stock on June 30, 19x8.
3. Record the purchase of stock on December 15, 19x8.
4. Assume that the total market value of the shares at December 31, 19x8, is $45,000. Record any necessary adjusting entry to account for this fact.
5. Ignore 4 above. Assume instead that the total year-end market value is $49,000. Record any necessary adjusting entry at year-end.
6. Ignore 4 and 5 above. Assume instead that the total year-end market value is $55,000. Record any necessary entry at year-end.

P 12–2
Temporary Investments
L.O.1

The Ski Shop started in business on July 1, 19x3, and has a June 30 year-end. The company invests cash in trading securities. The investment performance over each of the first three years of operations is summarized as follows:

Fiscal Year	Gain (loss) on Sale of Stock	Dividends Declared and Received	June 30 Totals for Stocks on Hand Book Value before Adjustment	June 30 Totals for Stocks on Hand Market Value
19x3–x4 . . .	$ 7,350	$ 650	$ 91,500	$ 89,350
19x4–x5 . . .	(2,100)	1,975	105,600	102,100
19x5–x6 . . .	4,950	860	87,950	91,400

Required:
1. Record the necessary adjusting entries at the end of each of the first three years.
2. Illustrate how the asset account would appear in each of the three year-end balance sheets.
3. Compute the total effect on net income for each year (separately) as a result of the investing activities summarized above.

P 12–3
*Temporary Investments
(Challenging)*
L.O.2

The Wagman Corporation reported the following balance sheet account balances pertaining to their securities available-for-sale on December 31, 19x4. Wagman has no long-term investments in stocks or bonds.

FMC Bonds—face value $100,000, 12% semiannual interest, payable 3/31 and 9/30	$100,000
JRT Common Stock—4,000 shares, original cost $33	132,000
Cort, Inc., Common Stock—5,000 shares, original cost $15	73,950
Accrued Interest Receivable—FMC Bonds	3,000

Wagman uses straight-line amortization on bond discounts and premiums. The following activities took place during 19x5 concerning Wagman's available-for-sale securities:

19x5

Jan.   28   Received cash dividends of $1.25 per share on JRT common.
Feb.   20   Received cash dividends of $0.50 per share on Cort common.
Mar.   31   Received semiannual bond interest on FMC bonds.
Apr.   18   Purchased 5,000 shares of ICC common stock for $25 per share including brokerage fee.
May   5   Sold 2,000 shares of JRT common for $35 per share cash.
June   30   Sold half of the FMC bonds ($50,000 face value) for $54,000 cash.
July   18   Received cash dividends of $0.50 per share on Cort common and $1.25 per share on JRT common.
Aug.   10   Sold 5,000 shares of Cort, Inc., for $13.50 per share cash.
Sept. 30   Received semiannual bond interest on FMC bonds.
Oct.   31   Purchased $75,000 face value TRW bonds for $73,635 plus accrued interest. The bonds mature at the end of 19x8 and bear 10% interest paid semiannually on June 30 and December 31.
Nov.   8   Received an additional 200 shares of JRT common as a result of a 10% stock dividend.
Dec.   31   Dividends declared, but unpaid, at year-end were

> JRT common: $1.25 per share
> ICC common: $1.50 per share

The market values of the stocks and bonds at year-end were

> JRT common: $32.00 per share   FMC bonds $50,000
> ICC common: $24.50 per share   TRW bonds $73,635

Interest was received on the TRW bonds but not on the FMC bonds.

Required:
1. Record the journal entries necessary to account for the transactions and related adjusting entries for the year 19x5 on Wagman's books.
2. Determine the balance in all balance sheet accounts pertaining to Wagman's investments at December 31, 19x5.
3. Determine the total income or loss from Wagman's investment activities to be reported in the 19x5 income statement by source (e.g., interest, dividends, gains and losses on sale of stocks and bonds, unrealized gain or loss).

P 12–4
Bond Investment—
Long Term
L.O.3

On December 31, 19x2, Investor Corporation acquired as a long-term investment $500,000 maturity value bonds of Debt, Inc., for 104.32% of face value. The bonds mature at the end of 19x8 and pay interest on June 30 and December 31 each year at an annual rate of 12%. Investor Corporation's year ends on September 30 each year. Investor uses straight-line amortization on all bond investments.

Required:
1. Record the bond purchase by Investor Corporation.
2. Record the entries for Investor Corporation for 19x3 and 19x4.
3. Assume Investor Corporation sold one half of these bonds on January 1, 19x5, for 104% of maturity value. Record the sale.
4. Assume instead that Investor acquired the bonds as a temporary investment rather than as a long-term investment. Record the entries for 19x3 and 19x4 to account for the bonds.
5. Again assuming that the investment in bonds is temporary, record the sale of one half of the bonds on January 1, 19x5, for 104% of maturity value.

P 12–5
Bond Investment—
Long Term
(Challenging)
L.O.3

On January 1, 19x3, KMI, Inc., acquired GM bonds with a maturity value of $500,000 as a long-term investment. The bonds mature at the end of 19x9 and bear 10% interest paid on a semiannual basis, with payments made each June 30 and December 31. KMI paid $453,525 for the bonds, providing them with an effective interest rate of 12%.

Required: (Round amounts to the nearest dollar.)
1. Record the purchase of the bond by KMI.
2. Record the entries for KMI's bond investment for 19x3 and 19x4. Use straight-line amortization for the bond discount.
3. (Optional) Record the entries for KMI's bond investment for 19x3 and 19x4. Use the effective-interest method to amortize the bond discount.

P 12–6
Long-Term Investments
(Challenging)
L.O.2, 4

On January 2, 19x4, Big Company acquired some of the total 10,000 outstanding voting common shares of Small Corporation as a long-term investment. The annual accounting period of each company is December 31.

The following events occurred:

Alternative 1:
19x4
Jan. 2 Big purchased 1,000 shares of Small stock at $14 per share.
Dec. 15 Small declared a dividend of $1.50 per share, payable January 15, 19x5.
     30 Big learned that Small would report earnings for 19x4 in the amount of $10,000.
     31 The market price of Small's stock was $12 per share.

Alternative 2:
All of the facts are the same as in Alternative 1 except that on January 2, Big purchased 3,000 shares of Small (instead of 1,000 shares).

Required:
Prepare the 19x4 journal entries for the above transactions in general journal form for the Big Company under each alternative. Consider each alternative separately.

P 12–7
Temporary Investments
L.O.1

Harried Corporation purchased the following stocks which it classifies as trading securities:

Date of Purchase	Company	# of Shares	Original Cost per Share
11/1/x4	Motorola	1,000	$92
11/15/x4	Digital	1,000	$38
12/21/x4	IBM	1,000	$42

Harried Corporation had the following subsequent transactions related to its trading securities:
1. On 11/12/x4 Harried sold 500 shares of Motorola for $100 per share.
2. On 12/13/x4 Harried sold 200 shares of Motorola for $102 per share and 800 shares of Digital for $36 per share.
3. On 12/26/x4 Harried sold 100 shares of Motorola for $95 per share, 100 shares of Digital for $40 per share, and 600 shares of IBM for $41 per share.
4. On 12/31/x4, Harried's fiscal year-end, the shares had the following fair values:

Motorola $93/share
Digital $40/share
IBM $38/share

5. On Jan 5, 19x5, Harried sold 100 shares of IBM for $35 per share.

Required:
Record all necessary journal entries for the above transactions.

P 12–8
Comparison of Fair Value and Equity Methods
L.O.2, 4

Serious Corporation acquired a 40% interest in Supplier Company as a long-term investment for $10 million in cash at the end of 19x1. During 19x2 Supplier Company reported net income of $6 million and paid cash dividends of $2 million. Supplier's stock price was unchanged during 19x2.

Required:
1. Report the effects on Serious's assets, liabilities, stockholders' equity, and net income for 19x2 assuming Serious used the fair value method. Ignore income taxes.

2. Repeat requirement 1 above assuming Serious uses the equity method.
3. Repeat requirements 1 and 2 above assuming the facts as given *except* that no cash dividends were paid by Supplier in 19x2.

P 12–9
Long-Term Investments
L.O.2, 4

Rokport, Inc., a calendar year company, acquired 200,000 shares of Raybok stock for $50 per share on January 1, 19x8, as its only long-term investment in stock. The following data concern the Raybok investment for 19x8 and 19x9:

	December 31 Market Price per Share	Reported Net Income (net loss)	Dividends Declared and Paid on 6/30
19x8	$48	$ (5,500,000)	None
19x9	53	15,140,000	$5,000,000

Required:
1. Assume that Raybok had 2 million shares of stock outstanding throughout 19x8 and 19x9. Record any entries needed to account for Rokport's investment in Raybok during 19x8 and 19x9 using the appropriate accounting method.
2. Assume instead that Raybock had 800,000 shares of stock outstanding through 19x8 and 19x9. Record any entries needed to account for Rokport's investment in Raybok during 19x8 and 19x9 using the appropriate accounting method.

P 12–10
Equity Method
L.O.4

On January 2, 19x1, Major Corporation purchased 20,000 shares of Minor Corporation at $30 per share. During 19x1, Minor had net income of $500,000 and declared and paid dividends of $50,000 on July 4. During 19x2, Minor had net income of $400,000 and on July 4 declared and paid dividends of $60,000. On January 2, 19x3, Major sold its investment in Minor at $32 per share.

Required:
Prepare all journal entries Major will make regarding its investment in Minor Corporation assuming that Minor has 50,000 shares of common stock issued and outstanding.

P 12–11
Comparison of Equity and Consolidation Methods (Challenging)
L.O.4, 5

Massive, Inc., acquired a 100% interest in Banker Corporation at the end of 19x1 for $20 million cash. The condensed financial statements of these two companies *just before* the purchase were as follows (in millions):

	Massive	Banker
Total assets (12/31/x1)	$380	$450
Total liabilities (12/31/x1)	190	430
Total stockholders' equity (12/31/x1)	190	20
Reported 19x1 net income	19	2

Required:
1. Assume the purchase is accounted for as an equity investment. Compute Massive's 19x1 return on assets (net income/total assets) and return on equity (net income/total stockholders' equity) before the purchase, based on the available data.
2. Indicate what changes, if any, would occur in the condensed financial statement data *after* the purchase, assuming the equity method is used. Recompute Massive's return on assets and return on equity, based on the available data. (Hint: Banker's 19x1 net income is not added to Massive's because the purchase took place at the end of 19x1 after the income was reported by Banker and purchased by Massive.)
3. Repeat requirement 2 above assuming that Massive prepares consolidated financial statements at the end of 19x1 after purchasing Banker.

P 12–12
Consolidation at Acquisition— 100%
L.O.5

On January 1, 19x2, Giant Corporation acquired a 100% interest in Knat, Inc., by paying $500,000 cash for all of Knat's common stock. The following balance sheet data were available immediately before this acquisition.

Balance Sheet
December 31, 19x1
(in thousands)

	Giant	Knat
Cash	$4,000	$400
Other assets (total)	6,000	200
Liabilities (total).	5,000	100
Stockholders' equity (total).	5,000	500

Required:
1. Prepare the entry to record the purchase of Knat by Giant.
2. Prepare the consolidation worksheet entry at January 1, 19x2, needed to prepare a consolidation balance sheet on that date.
3. Prepare the consolidated balance sheet at January 1, 19x2.

P 12–13
Consolidation at Acquisition— 100% Interest
L.O.5

On June 30, 19x1, Bellows, Inc., acquired a 100% interest in Olson Corporation by paying $900,000 in cash to Olson's shareholders for their stock. The following balance sheet data were prepared by Olson at June 30, 19x1:

Olson Corporation
Balance Sheet

Cash	$ 25,000
Land	200,000
Other assets	975,000
Total assets.	$1,200,000
Liabilities	$ 300,000
Shareholders' equity	900,000
Total liabilities and shareholders' equity	$1,200,000

Bellows reported the following balance on June 30, 19x1, just before the cash purchase of Olson:

Bellows Corporation
Balance Sheet

Cash	$ 2,000,000
Land	5,000,000
Other assets	3,000,000
Total assets.	$10,000,000
Liabilities	$ 6,000,000
Shareholders' equity	4,000,000
Total liabilities and shareholders' equity.	$10,000,000

Required:
1. Prepare the journal entry to record the purchase on June 30, 19x1, on Bellows's books.
2. Prepare the consolidated worksheet entry of June 30, 19x1, needed to prepare the consolidated balance sheet.
3. Prepare the consolidated balance sheet at June 30, 19x1.

P 12–14
Consolidation—
100% Interest
L.O.5

The Major Corporation acquired a 100% interest in Minor, Inc., on January 1, 19x8, by purchasing all of Minor's common stock for $700,000 in cash. The following balance sheet data were available immediately after the purchase:

Balance Sheet
January 1, 19x8
(in thousands)

	Major	Minor
Cash.	$5,000	$200
Investment in Minor	700	0
Other assets (total)	8,300	700
Liabilities (total)	6,000	200
Stockholders' equity (total)	8,000	700

During 19x8, Major reported net income of $1 million, which included $100,000 of income from its investment in Minor. Minor declared and paid dividends of $50,000 in 19x8. Major declared no dividends in 19x8.

Required:
1. Record any entries necessary to account for Major's investment in Minor for 19x8, including the entry to purchase Minor.
2. Assume the liabilities of both Major and Minor were unchanged during 19x8. Prepare a consolidation worksheet for 19x8 including the consolidated balance sheet at December 31, 19x8.

· Appendix Problems

P 12–15
Consolidation at
Acquisition—
90% Interest
L.O.10

Consider the data in Problem 12–13 above for Bellows, Inc. Assume that on June 30, 19x1, Bellows acquired a 90% interest in Olson by paying $810,000 cash for Olson's stock. All other information remains the same as in the earlier problem.

Required:
1. Prepare the journal entry to record the purchase on June 30, 19x1, on Bellows's books.
2. Prepare the consolidation worksheet entry of June 30, 19x1.
3. Prepare a consolidated balance sheet at June 30, 19x1.

P 12–16
Consolidation—
90% Interest
L.O.6

The King Corporation acquired a 90% interest in Jackson, Inc., on May 1, 19x1, purchasing Jackson stock in the open market for $1,800,000 in cash. The following balance sheet data were prepared on May 1, 19x1, immediately after the purchase:

	Jackson	King
Cash	$ 500,000	$1,000,000
Investment in Jackson	0	1,800,000
Other assets	5,000,000	6,000,000
Liabilities	3,500,000	3,000,000
Stockholders' equity	2,000,000	5,800,000

During the remainder of 19x1, Jackson reported net income of $200,000 and declared and paid cash dividends of $100,000 on December 10. King reported net income for the remainder of 19x1 of $500,000, **not** including any income from Jackson. King paid no dividends in 19x1.

Required:
1. Record any journal entries on King's books to account for the purchase and subsequent earnings and dividends of Jackson.
2. Assume that the liabilities of both King and Jackson were unchanged during the remainder of 19x1. Prepare a consolidation worksheet at December 31, 19x1.

3. Prepare a consolidated balance sheet of King and Jackson at December 31, 19x1. Assume no cash inflow from operations for either company.

P 12–17
Consolidation—
80% Interest
L.O.6

On January 1, 19x1, Parent Company acquired an 80% voting stock interest in Kidco. The following data are available immediately after the acquisition:

Balance Sheet Data
January 1, 19x1
(in thousands)

	Parent	Kidco
Cash and other assets	$250	$550
Investment in Kidco.	200	0
Liabilities	50	300
Stockholders' equity	400	250

During 19x1, Parent Company earned income of $125,000 **before** considering income from Kidco, and paid cash dividends of $50,000. Kidco earned income of $60,000 during 19x1, and paid cash dividends of $30,000.

Required:

1. Prepare the consolidation worksheet entry necessary to prepare a consolidated balance sheet on January 1, 19x1.
2. Compute the total owners' equity in the consolidated balance sheet at January 1, 19x1.
3. Assume the total liabilities for both Parent ($50,000) and Kidco ($300,000) are the same on December 31, 19x1, as they were on January 1, 19x1. What would the total assets in the consolidated balance sheet be on December 31, 19x1?
4. Compute consolidated net income for 19x1.
5. What is the balance in Parent Company's asset Investment in Kidco on December 31, 19x1, after adjusting for Kidco's 19x1 earnings but before consolidation?

P 12–18
Consolidation Balance
Sheet—85% Interest
L.O.6

The Bien Hoa Corporation acquired an 85% interest in Soo Lin, Ltd., on January 1, 19x6, for $255 million. At the date of acquisition, after recording the purchase, the following data were available:

Bien Hoa Corporation
Balance Sheet
January 1, 19x6
(in millions)

Assets:		Liabilities.	$370
Investment in Soo Lin.	$255	Stockholders' equity.	415
Other assets	530		
Total assets	$785	Total liabilities and stockholders' equity	$785

Soo Lin, Ltd.
Balance Sheet
January 1, 19x6
(in millions)

Assets	$700	Liabilities.	$400
		Stockholders' equity.	300
Total assets	$700	Total liabilities and stockholders' equity	$700

Required:

1. What is consolidated stockholders' equity on January 1, 19x6?
2. What is minority interest on January 1, 19x6?

3. Assume that the liabilities of both companies remain constant during 19x6. During 19x6, the **separate** net income of Bien Hoa was $120 million, and the separate net income of Soo Lin was $90 million. There were no dividends or stock transactions during 19x6. Prepare the consolidated balance sheet at the end of 19x6.
4. What was consolidated net income for 19x6?

P 12–19
Consolidation and Goodwill—90% Interest (Challenging)
L.O.6

Big, Inc., purchased a 90% interest in Kidco for $630 million cash on January 1, 19x4. The book value and fair market value of Kidco's net assets at the date of acquisition were both equal to $600 million. Immediately after the acquisition the following balance sheet data were available:

**Balance Sheet
January 1, 19x4
(in millions)**

	Big, Inc.	Kidco
Investment in Kidco.	$ 630	$ 0
Other assets	2,000	1,800
Liabilities	1,200	1,200
Stockholders' equity	1,430	600

Required:
1. How much goodwill is included in the $630 million purchase price paid for Kidco?
2. Record the consolidation worksheet entry at the date of purchase to prepare consolidated statements as of January 1, 19x4.
3. Assume that Big, Inc., amortizes goodwill over 30 years. During 19x4, Kidco reported net income of $100 million. Big's **separate** net income (before Kidco's net income is considered) was $150 million for 19x4. Compute the consolidated net income (net of the minority interest's share) for 19x4.

• CASES ──

C 12–1
Investment Methods
L.O.1, 2, 4

Brasco, Inc., acquired an 18% interest in the common stock of Vista Crafts in 19x5 for $1.5 million. Brasco has since managed to place two of its top managers on the board of directors of Vista Crafts.

As of December 15, 19x9, Brasco had experienced below-average sales and profits on its primary operations for the 19x9 calendar year. Brasco had managed to report an increase in earnings in each of the eight years prior to 19x9, but it appeared as though their record of increases would not be achieved in 19x9. Vista Craft had a very good year in 19x9 and was expecting to report record profits. However, Vista's stock price did not change during 19x9.

Required:
1. Assume that you are manager for Brasco and that your annual bonus (which normally makes up about 25% of your total income) is based on the increase in Brasco's bottom-line earnings between this year and the last. What might you do to improve Brasco's 19x9 earnings outlook, despite the late date?
2. Assume that you are a major stockholder in Brasco, and that you are aware of all the facts presented in the case. How would you structure the bonus plan for your top managers to avoid the potential problems of the bonus plan described in 1 above? Be specific, and remember that the bonus should give managers an incentive to increase earnings.

C 12–2
Equity Investments
L.O.4

Flestex Corporation reported the following financial statement data for its equity investments in its 19x9 annual report (in millions):

	19x9	19x8
Balance sheet (noncurrent assets):		
Equity investments in affiliates.	$437	$492
Income statement:		
Equity income and gains (losses) from sale of affiliates (pre-tax)	$171	$ 93

In 19x9, Flestex sold all of its stock in one of its affiliated companies for $167 million cash, resulting in a gain of $49 million before taxes.

Required:
You have been asked to write a memo to your superior evaluating Flestex's equity-method investments. Assume that Flestex originally paid a price for its equity investments equal to book value of the investee companies at the date of purchase. (In other words, Flestex did not pay any premium above the book value of the investees.) Explain any apparent activity in the investment accounts, and include the amount of dividends received by Flestex in 19x9. (Hint: Use a T account to explain the change in the asset account.)

C 12–3
Investments—Ralston Purina Company
L.O.4, 5

Ralston Purina Company includes a number of subsidiaries, as noted in their report in Appendix E at the end of this text. Most of these investments are 100% owned, but some are equity investments in "affiliated companies" and others are less than 100% owned consolidated investments where a minority interest is present. Consider the footnote titled "Supplemental Balance Sheet Information" in answering these questions.

Required:
1. What is the balance in "investments in affiliated companies" at the end of fiscal 1991? 1992?
2. What types of transactions or events could explain the change in "investments in affiliated companies"?
3. What is the balance in "minority interests" at the end of fiscal 1991? 1992?
4. What types of transactions or events could explain the change in minority interests?

· Evaluating Financial Statements

C 12–4
Long-Term Investments— General Motors
L.O.2

Consider the following footnote disclosure from the 19x6 annual report of General Motors. This footnote is describing details of the stockholders' equity section of GM's balance sheet. As noted, the account reflects holding gains or losses from (1) translation of foreign currency (to be discussed in Appendix B) and (2) long-term investments in marketable equity securities (discussed in this chapter).

Excerpt from Footnote 15

(in millions)	19x6	19x5	19x4
Accumulated foreign currency translation and other adjustments:			
Balance at beginning of the year:			
Accumulated foreign currency translation adjustments.	$ (675.0)	$ (789.5)	$ (661.8)
Net unrealized gains on marketable equity securities.	130.0	71.7	91.3
Changes during the year:			
Accumulated foreign currency translation adjustments.	192.2	114.5	(127.7)
Net unrealized gains (losses) on marketable equity securities	30.8	58.3	(19.6)
Balance at end of the year	$ (322.0)	$ (545.0)	$ (717.8)
Total stockholders' equity.	$30,678.0	$29,524.7	$24,214.3

Required:
1. What accounting method is consistent with GAAP for long-term marketable equity securities representing less than a 20% interest in an investee? (Name the method.)

2. GM is using a stockholders' equity account to report unrecognized gains or losses on marketable equity securities. By the end of 19x6, what is the net unrecognized gain or loss? (State the amount and whether it is a gain or a loss.)
3. Name the method apparently being used by GM for valuing its investments in marketable equity securities reported in this footnote.

C 12–5
Investments—
General Electric
L.O.2, 4

General Electric (GE) reported the following footnote data in their 19x6 annual report:

Note 9   Cash and marketable securities

Deposits restricted as to usage and withdrawal or used as partial compensation for short-term borrowing arrangements were not material.

Carrying value of marketable securities was substantially the same as market value at year-end 19x6 and 19x5. Equity securities in the portfolio were carried at a cost of $48 million and $206 million at December 31, 19x6 and 19x5, respectively.

Note 14   Other investments

December 31 (in millions)	19x6	19x5
1. Equity investments	$3,468	$2,604
2. Miscellaneous investments (at cost)[a]		
Government and government-guaranteed securities	177	158
Other	258	344
3. Marketable equity securities	74	81
Less allowance for losses	(63)	(37)
	$3,914	$3,150

[a]Estimated realizable value about the same as cost at year-end.

Note 9 pertains to a current asset account in GE's balance sheet, and note 14 explains part of their long-term Other Investments account in the balance sheet. The balances reported in these two accounts in GE's balance sheets were as follows:

December 31
(in millions)

	19x6	19x5
Marketable securities (note 9).	$ 221	$ 951
Other investments (note 14)	3,914	3,150

After reading the footnote disclosures, answer the following questions:

1. What is the apparent accounting method used for Temporary Investments in Marketable Equity Securities?
2. Are all of GE's temporary investments in marketable securities invested in stocks? If not, what amount is invested in other marketable securities as of the end of 19x6?
3. What is the basis for GE's long-term miscellaneous investments? What is their fair value?
4. Assuming GE invested no additional amounts in equity method investees during 19x6 and received no dividends, what is your estimate of GE's equity income from investees?

C 12–6
Equity Investments—
Ford Motor Company
L.O.4

Ford Motor Company reported the following amounts in a recent annual report:

	19x6	19x5
Balance Sheet–Assets		
Equity in net assets of unconsolidated subsidiaries	$5,088.4	$4,176.4
Income Statement		
Equity in new income of unconsolidated subsidiaries.	816.9	598.1
Statement of Cash Flows		
Purchase of an unconsolidated subsidiary		
(First Nationwide Financial Corporation)	381.7	

Assume there were no other items affecting Ford's balance sheet account other than the dividends Ford received from unconsolidated subsidiaries.

Required:
Compute the dividends received by Ford in 19x6 from its unconsolidated subsidiaries.

C 12–7
Equity Investments—
Ford Motor Company
L.O.4

Ford Motor Company reported the following financial statement data for its equity investments in its 19x8 annual report (in millions):

	19x8	19x7
Balance sheet (noncurrent assets):		
Equity in net assets of affiliated companies.	$2,102.7	$2,001.2
Income statement:		
Equity in net income/(loss) of affiliated companies	$ 147.8	$ (136.6)

Required:
Assume that Ford paid a price equal to book value for these equity investees (affiliates). What were the cash dividends received by Ford Motor from its affiliates in 19x8? (Hint: Use a T account to explain changes in the asset.)

C 12–8
Equity Investments—
USX Corporation
L.O.4

USX Corporation (formerly U.S. Steel) reported the following in their 19x8 annual report (in millions):

	19x8	19x7
Balance sheet (equity investments):		
Investments in partially owned companies and partnerships	$657	$679
Income statement:		
Income (loss) from equity method affiliates	$ 39	$ 13

Required:
Assume USX paid a price equal to book value for its equity investments. What were the apparent dividends received by USX in 19x8 from its equity investments?

C 12–9
Equity versus
Consolidation—
General Electric
(Challenging)
L.O.4, 5

An FASB ruling in 1988 eliminated the use of the equity method of accounting for companies that were over 50% owned by a parent company, requiring consolidation to be used. An example of the impact of this standard is illustrated below.

In 19x6, General Electric reported the following data, which are condensed from their annual report.

**General Electric
Balance Sheet Data
December 31, 19x6
(in millions)**

Assets		Liabilities and Stockholders' Equity	
Equity investments in GE		Liabilities.	$19,482
Financial Service Corp. . .	$ 2,994	Stockholders' equity	15,109
Other assets	31,597	Total liabilities and	
Total assets	$34,591	stockholders' equity	$34,591

**General Electric
Income Statement Data
For the Year Ended December 31, 19x6
(in millions)**

Revenues	$36,221
Expenses	33,033
	$3,188
Equity income from GE Financial Service Corporation	504
Income tax expense	(1,200)
Net income	$ 2,492

Required:

1. Compute GE's return on assets ratio (net income/ending total assets).
2. Compute GE's debt-to-equity ratio (liabilities/stockholders' equity).
3. Now, consider the following data regarding GE Financial Services Corporation (GEFS), a 100% owned subsidiary of GE, which are accounted for in the condensed data above like an equity investment.

**GEFS Balance Sheet Data
(in millions)**

Assets	$53,823
Liabilities	$50,829
Stockholders' equity	$ 2,994
Total	$53,823

Recompute the two ratios required in parts 1 and 2 above by using the GEFS data to prepare fully consolidated financial statement amounts for total assets, total liabilities, and stockholders' equity. Note that consolidated net income will still be $2,492 million.

4. Evaluate the impact of full consolidation versus equity-method accounting on GE's performance ratios.

· **Appendix Case**

C 12–10
*Purchase versus Pooling
Method (Appendix 12 B)*
L.O.7

The directors of Korbet, Inc., are considering a bid for its common stock made by Prentice Corporation. Prentice's 2 million shares of common stock are currently selling for $100 per share, while Korbet's 100,000 shares of common stock are currently selling for $80 per share. Korbet has a net **book value** (net assets) of $6 million as of the end of 19x8. Prentice has made the following offers to Korbet's board for 100% interest in Korbet:

a. 100,000 shares of Prentice in exchange for all 100,000 shares of Korbet; or
b. $9 million cash in exchange for all 100,000 shares of Korbet.

Required:

1. What accounting method would be used if Korbet accepted the first offer?
2. What accounting method would be used if Korbet accepted the second offer?
3. What asset(s) would Prentice report on its unconsolidated financial statements if the first offer were accepted by Korbet?
4. What asset(s) would Prentice report on its unconsolidated financial statements if the second offer were accepted by Korbet?
5. As a director for Korbet, which alternative offer would you prefer? Explain your answer.

I cannot relate to the term "ethical dilemma." Faced with an ethical problem, there is no dilemma—you do what is right. "It's been said that ethical standards, even at their strongest, are always a little gray around the edges. Any code of ethics, in other words, must sometimes deal with situations where there are two—or more— legitimate points of view, and where there is no clear right or wrong answer." (The Ford Corporate Ethics brochure)

Anthony J. Ridley
Ford Motor Company

P·A·R·T

III

Reporting and Evaluating Financial Results

Reynolds, Inc.
Income Statements
For the Years Ending December 31

	1994	1993
Revenues		
Total revenues	$ xxx	$ xxx
Expenses		
Income from continuing operations	**x,xxx**	**x,xxx**
Discontinued operations (net of taxes)	**(xxx)**	**(xxx)**
Extraordinary gain (net of taxes)		**xxx**
Change in accounting method (net of taxes)	**xxx**	
Net income	**$ xxx**	**$ xxx**
Earnings per share:		
Earnings per share from continuing operations	**$ xxx**	**$ xxx**
Discontinued operations per share	**(xx)**	**(xx)**
Extraordinary gain per share		**xx**
Change in accounting method per share	**xx**	
Earnings per share	**$ xxx**	**$ xxx**

FINANCIAL
STATEMENT
COMPONENTS
EMPHASIZED IN
CHAPTER 13

Reynolds, Inc.
Comparative Balance Sheets
As of December 31

	1994	1993
Current assets		
Total current assets.	$ xxx	$ xxx
Noncurrent assets		
Total noncurrent assets	xxx	xxx
Current liabilities		
Total current liabilities.	xxx	xxx
Noncurrent liabilities		
Total noncurrent liabilities	xxx	xxx
Stockholders' equity		
Total stockholders' equity	xxx	xxx

Reynolds, Inc.
Cash Flow Statements
For the Years Ending December 31

	1994	1993
Operating activities		
Cash from operations	$ xxx	$ xxx
Investing activities		
Cash for investments	(xxx)	(xxx)
Financing activities		
Cash from financing	xxx	xxx

13

Understanding the Income and Retained Earnings Statements

In a subsequent year, auditors may discover a material error in the prior year's financial statements for which the auditors had not taken exception because it was unknown. Auditors then are faced with the ethical challenge of either correcting the error by requiring restatement of the prior year's financials, or allowing the error to be reflected in the current year's financials, thereby avoiding potential litigation and confrontation with the client. When faced with this situation, auditors should make the more difficult, but ethical, choice and insist on correction of a material error in the financial statements.

> Robert D. Neary
> Ernst & Young

· Learning Objectives

After studying Chapter 13, you should understand

1. The criteria for recognizing revenues and expenses, pp. 679–80.

2. Accounting for changes in estimates, pp. 680–81.

3. How to differentiate gains and losses from revenues and expenses, pp. 681–82.

4. The nature and purpose of items that receive separate income statement disclosures, including discontinued operations, extraordinary items, and accounting changes, pp. 683–88.

5. The preparation of a retained earnings statement or a statement of changes in stockholders' equity, pp. 688–90.

6. Computation of EPS for a simple capital structure, pp. 690–93.

So far in this textbook, the discussion of specific accounting topics has centered on the balance sheet. Whenever it was appropriate, as we discussed the balance sheet items, we also looked at their impact on the income statement. By now you should understand the important relationship between changes in the balance sheet and their effect on the income statement. For all operating transactions, increases in net assets (total assets less total liabilities) result in increases in income, and decreases in net assets result in expenses or losses and therefore decreases in net income. Thus, net income simply represents the increase in net assets, thereby maintaining the balance sheet equation.

The first section of this chapter reviews the various types of transactions giving rise to revenues, expenses, gains, and losses. These transactions are reported in summary form in the income statement, but they also affect the balance sheet accounts.

The second section of this chapter discusses the statement of changes in stockholders' equity, which examines all balance sheet changes from the viewpoint of the owners. Periodic net income, which is added to the retained earnings balance, explains changes in stockholders' equity from nonowner transactions. To stress this point, some companies use the title **statement of operations** instead of **income statement** or **earnings statement.** The statement of changes in stockholders' equity summarizes balance sheet changes from owner transactions (such as new stock issues and the payment of dividends) and nonowner transactions. We can look at changes in the balance sheet from the owners' point of view in Exhibit 13–1.

In the third section of this chapter you will become familiar with earnings per share (EPS) measurement. Since a company's EPS is often quoted as an indication of the company's financial performance, the information in this section is important.

The focus of this chapter is to discuss and illustrate both routine and unusual operating-related transactions that are reported in the income statement. The objective is to introduce and explain the nature of the various income statement disclosures that could be encountered in reading published, detailed income statements.

EXHIBIT 13–1

**Changes in the
Balance Sheet**

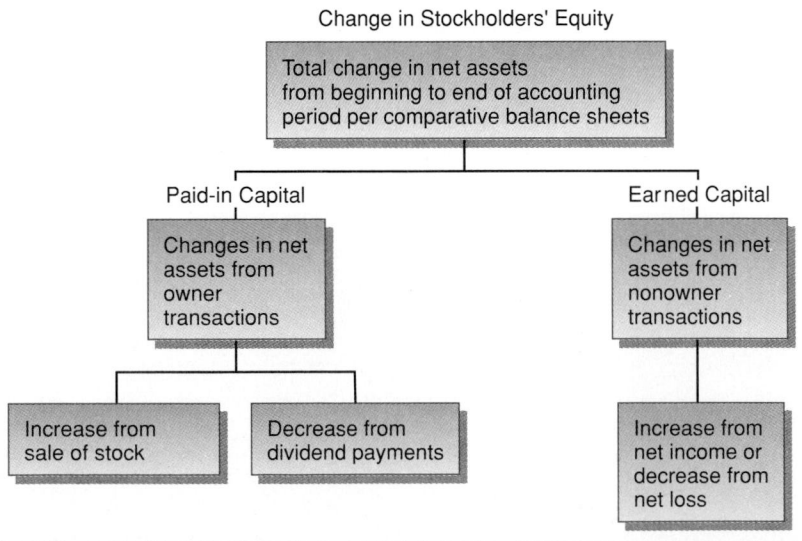

INCOME STATEMENT

The income statement in Exhibit 13–2 is representative of the common operating disclosures made by larger corporations. Note that it presents income statements for the current year and the previous year. Normally, publicly traded companies present income statements for the current year and *two prior years* in order to facilitate comparison and evaluation of a company's operating results. You may wish to refer to the Ralston Purina financial statements in Appendix E to examine actual examples of some of what we discuss in this chapter.

Separate Disclosures

We should keep in mind that one of the most important functions of the income statement is to help users predict the **future** performance of a business. What good is knowing where you have been if it doesn't tell you something about where you might be going next? By providing clear and separate disclosure for all unusual items, past income statements can be relevant for helping users predict future income from operations. Items that are not expected to continue in the future are of less relevance to investors and creditors for predicting the future performance of the business.

In addition to normal operating revenues and expenses, income statements may report on the results of transactions or activities that are not directly related to ongoing operations. These items should receive separate disclosure. Such separately disclosed items would include the following examples, all illustrated in Exhibit 13–3:

Unusual items—categories 3 and 4:

- Gains and losses from the sale of equipment, land, or facilities.
- Losses from write-offs or write-downs of assets (e.g., obsolete inventory).
- Gains or losses from insurance claims.

EXHIBIT 13–2

Common Disclosures Given in an Income Statement

General Electric Motors
Income Statements
For the Years Ending December 31

	19x5	19x4
Revenues:		
Sales revenue	$ 700,000	$ 650,000
Service revenue	250,000	200,000
Interest and dividend income	50,000	50,000
Total revenues	$1,000,000	$ 900,000
Expenses:		
Cost of goods sold	$ 275,000	$ 270,000
Cost of services	70,000	65,000
Selling and advertising expenses	65,000	60,000
Administrative expenses	75,000	70,000
Interest expense	15,000	15,000
Total expenses	$ 500,000	$ 480,000
Income from operations before taxes	$ 500,000	$ 420,000
Provision for income taxes (or income tax expense)	(190,000)	(184,000)
Net income	$ 310,000	$ 236,000

EXHIBIT 13–3

Components of the
Income Statement—
Most Complete Form

General Electric Motors
Income Statements
For the Years Ending December 31

Category of Items		19x8	19x7
1	Revenues:		
	Sales revenue	$ 700,000	$ 650,000
	Service revenue	250,000	200,000
	Interest and dividend income.	50,000	50,000
	Total revenues	$1,000,000	$ 900,000
2	Expenses:		
	Cost of goods sold	$ 275,000	$ 270,000
	Cost of services	70,000	65,000
	Selling and advertising expenses.	65,000	60,000
	Administrative expenses.	75,000	70,000
	Interest expense	15,000	15,000
	Total expenses.	$ 500,000	$ 480,000
3	Gains.	75,000	—
4	Losses	(25,000)	(10,000)
	Income from continuing operations before taxes	$ 550,000	$ 470,000
5	Income tax expense on continuing operations	(200,000)	(180,000)
	Income from continuing operations	$ 350,000	$ 290,000
6	Discontinued operations (net of taxes) . . .	(35,000)	2,000
7	Extraordinary items (net of taxes)	10,000	—
8	Cumulative accounting adjustment (net of taxes).	15,000	—
	Net income	$ 340,000	$ 292,000

Discontinued operations—category 6:

· Operating income/loss from operations that have been discontinued.

· Gain or loss from the sale of the net assets of a discontinued operation (line of business).

Extraordinary items—category 7:

· Gain or loss on the retirement of bonds payable before maturity.

· Gain or loss from an earthquake.

Accounting method change—category 8:

· Cumulative prior years' effect on income of a change in an accounting method.

Exhibit 13–3 illustrates an income statement in its most complete (complex) form to show how each of these items would be separately disclosed. Unusual items (categories 3 and 4 in Exhibit 13–3) are normally disclosed separately and explained in the financial statement footnotes. These unusual gains and losses are, however, included in income from continuing operations. These gains and losses are the net amounts that result from the disposal of used equipment and obsolete inventory and other transactions that are not a normal part of day-to-day business operations.

Category 5 in Exhibit 13–3 represents the income tax expense associated with the items reported in categories 1 through 4. Specific accounting rules require that the last three items (categories 6, 7, and 8) of Exhibit 13–3 be reported as separate items and that the income tax effect be reported with each separate item (i.e., the amount reported for each separate item is net of any taxes).[1] These three items, which are reported separately net of their respective income tax effects, are discussed in some detail later in this chapter.

Before studying these separately disclosed items, let us first review the guiding accounting principles for the measurement and disclosure of normal operating revenues and expenses and changes in accounting estimates.

Revenues and Expenses (categories 1 and 2)

Objective 1
The criteria for recognizing revenues and expenses.

The measurement of revenues and expenses is based on the recognition criteria discussed in Chapters 2 and 3. Because expense recognition is partially dependent on when revenues are recognized, we can think of revenue recognition decisions as coming before expense recognition.

Revenues represent **inflows of net assets.** To be reported in the income statement, revenues must be (1) **measurable**, (2) **realized** or **realizable**, and (3) **earned**. This means that, in the professional judgment of the accountant, the revenues will result in a reasonably measurable amount of economic benefits, usually in the form of cash or receivables (promises to pay cash), and that the efforts to produce these benefits, usually in the form of goods and/or services, have been provided. These criteria are not as objective as most casual users of accounting information believe. Although these three criteria are often satisfied at the point of sale, when goods and/or services are received, this is not always the case. The exact point in time when a business decides to recognize revenue is often one of the most important applications of professional judgment, capable of significantly influencing periodic income measurement.

Revenue can be reported at any point when in the professional judgment of the accountant, the three criteria noted above have been satisfied. For example, some ticket agencies that sell tickets for theater performances or air travel may report revenues from ticket sales even before the services (e.g., air travel) are provided. Also, manufacturers of goods specially designed and produced for a customer may record revenue as soon as production is complete even though the customer has not yet received the goods. There are many examples of companies that report revenues at some point other than when goods and/or services are provided to customers. In each case, the professional judgment is that the three criteria are satisfied at some other point in time.

Expenses represent **outflows of net assets** (e.g., a decrease in an asset like inventory or an increase in a liability like salaries payable). In general, expenses are most often determined by matching, which recognizes those costs that have been incurred in order to obtain the revenues recognized during the period. However, expenses are also recorded as a result of direct expensing and systematic allocations.

Matching occurs when the costs of achieving the recorded revenues are recognized (recorded) as expenses in the same period as their related revenues. Thus, to measure income correctly for the month of May, revenues from the sale of goods in May should be matched with the cost of goods sold, wages necessary to complete the sale, transportation

---

[1]See *APB Opinion No. 20*, "Accounting Changes" (New York: AICPA, 1971), and *APB Opinion No. 30*, "Reporting the Results of Operations" (New York: AICPA, 1973), for details on these disclosure requirements beyond what is discussed later in this chapter.

costs to deliver the goods, and so on. Matching is generally applied to those costs that give rise to revenue, such as inventory use, the wages or salaries directly linked to the sale (e.g., salespersons' commissions), and packaging and delivery costs.

Direct expensing records expenses as they occur, based on the assumption that the revenues associated with these expenses have also been recorded. Examples of direct expense recognition include those costs that are difficult to associate with specific periods of future benefit, such as advertising costs, most research and development costs, and the costs of top administrators' salaries.

To measure periodic net income, some costs require systematic allocation in order to be recognized as expenses. Allocated costs include depreciation of plant and equipment, amortization of intangible assets, and so on. These allocation processes were introduced in Chapter 4 and discussed in detail in Chapter 8. Note that allocated costs normally are recorded at the end of an accounting period by making **adjusting entries to balance sheet accounts.** For example, the expiration of prepaid rent expense, prepaid insurance, and other prepaid expenses are charged to expense through systematic allocations based on the passage of time, use, or some other predetermined basis.

The recording of expenses is based on one of the three processes noted above: (1) matching, (2) direct expensing, or (3) systematic allocation. The timing of when revenues and expenses are reported may vary from company to company. However, once a policy is established for recognizing revenues and expenses, it should be applied consistently from year to year.

Changes in Cost Estimates

Recall from earlier discussions of depreciation expense, bad debt expense, and other allocated and matched costs that the recorded amounts of these expenses are normally based on estimates. For example, depreciation expense **seems to be** the result of an exact process that systematically assigns the cost of depreciable assets to their periods of use. However, to determine an asset's depreciation schedule, the useful life and the salvage value **must be estimated.** Likewise, to match revenues properly with bad debt expense, you must estimate the amount of the current period's credit sales that will not be collected.

Whenever you estimate expenses (or revenues), the passage of time often reveals new information suggesting that your earlier estimates should be revised. For example, you may originally estimate a truck to have a three-year useful life, but after two and one-half years of use, you believe the truck will last four or five years. Chapter 8 illustrated the accounting procedure used for a change in the estimate of an asset's useful life.

The basic method of changing estimates illustrated in Chapter 8 applies to other estimate changes as well. Changes in estimates are accounted for by applying the new estimate to the book value of the item as of the beginning of the period of the estimate change. This charges current and future periods with amounts that are based on current estimates of the benefit period.

Objective 2
Accounting for changes in estimates.

For example, consider a change in an estimate for warranty costs that are normally measured as a percentage of sales. Assume that Byte-Size estimated its warranty expense to be 2% of sales. The balance in the Estimated Warranty Liability account at the beginning of 19x7 was $85,000. During 19x7, sales were $4,850,000. The actual cost of warranty claims made in 19x7 from 19x7 sales and sales of prior years still covered by warranty amounted to $65,000. At the end of 19x7, the following entry was made:

19x7			
Dec. 31	Warranty Expense (E)	97,000	
	Estimated Warranty Liability (L)		97,000
	To record estimated warranty expense on 19x7 sales: $4,850,000 × .02.		

The balance in the Estimated Warranty Liability account at the end of 19x7 is:

Estimated Warranty Liability

	Bal. Jan. 1	85,000
(19x7 actual claims)	(19x7 estimate)	
Jan.–Dec. 65,000	Dec. 31	97,000
	Bal. Dec. 31	117,000

During 19x8, sales were $5 million, and the actual cost of warranty claims made in 19x8 for sales made in 19x8 and prior years was $80,000. Assume that toward the end of 19x8, Byte-Size managers decided that due to the steady increase in the warranty liability balance over the past several years, a more accurate estimate of the warranty cost would be 1.5% of sales. To change the estimate from 2% to 1.5% of sales, you simply apply the new estimate to 19x8 (the entire current year) and future periods. The sales for all of 19x8 times the new estimate results in a year-end adjusting entry of $75,000 (.015 × $5 million), which is recorded as follows:

```
19x8
Dec. 31    Warranty Expense (E) . . . . . . . . . . . . . . . . . . . . .    75,000
                Estimated Warranty Liability (L). . . . . . . . . . . . . .              75,000
           To record estimated warranty expense on 19x8 sales.
```

The balance in the warranty liability at the end of 19x8 would be:

Estimated Warranty Liability

	Bal. Jan. 1	117,000
(19x8 actual claims)	(19x8 estimate)	
Jan.–Dec. 80,000	Dec. 31	75,000
	Bal. Dec. 31	112,000

Note that **changes in estimates do not affect the prior years' results.** On the other hand, a change in estimate made anytime during the current accounting period is applied as if it were made on the **first day of the period.** Accountants apply changes in estimates as of the beginning of the period of the change to allow the new (hopefully improved) estimate to be reflected in the statements for the **entire** period. In the case of Byte-Size, even though management decided toward the end of 19x8 that the estimated warranty cost should be changed, the change was applied to all of 19x8 as if the managers had decided to make this change on the first day of 19x8.

Normally, no disclosure is required in the financial statements when the revenues and expenses of a business are changed due to changes in accounting estimates. However, if a change in estimate has a material impact on the financial statements, the notes to the financial statements should disclose the effect. Exhibit 13–4 gives an example of such a disclosure.

**Unusual Items—
Gains and Losses
(categories 3 and 4)**

Gains and losses (categories 3 and 4 in Exhibit 13–3), sometimes referred to as "unusual items," differ from revenues and expenses in that they are not the normal **operating activities** of the entity. However, most gains and losses result from activities that are peripheral to normal operations, such as when a business restructures its operations to make them more efficient, or when it enters transactions involving investing activities related to future

EXHIBIT 13–4

Annual Report Example of Disclosure of Change in Accounting Estimate

Union Carbide

Excerpt from footnotes:

3. Change in Accounting Estimate

As explained in Note 1, during 1985 Union Carbide revised, retroactive to January 1, 1985, the estimated useful lives used to depreciate the cost of machinery and equipment. The effects of this change in accounting estimate were to increase 1985 depreciation expense by approximately $57 million, and to decrease 1985 net income by approximately $34 million, or $0.16 per share.

Objective 3
How to differentiate gains and losses from revenues and expenses.

operations. Typically, gains occur when a company sells old machinery, buildings, temporary investments, or other assets for more than their book value, thereby resulting in a net increase in net assets. Losses occur when a business sells these types of assets for less than their book value, which results in a net decrease in net assets.

In each period the individual gains and losses are aggregated and their net effect is reported as a separate item within the income from continuing operations section of the income statement, as shown in Exhibit 13–3. Sometimes companies combine gains and losses from separate transactions into a single item on the income statement, such as "Other income" or "Unusual items."

Income Tax Expense—Intraperiod Tax Allocation (category 5)

In the lower portion of the income statement where separately disclosed items are reported (categories 6, 7, and 8 in Exhibit 13–3), each separate item is shown net of its tax effects. This is called intraperiod tax allocation, and requires that the tax effects associated with each special item be reported with the special item. Only the income tax effects associated with income from continuing operations are reported as income tax expense (category 5 in Exhibit 13–3). To charge the continuing operations of the business with the tax effects of all the special items would distort "Income from continuing operations."

To illustrate the effect of intraperiod tax allocation, assume that Byte-Size had a total operating income before income tax expense for 19x5 of $50,000 plus a before-tax extraordinary gain of $10,000. Assume that a flat tax rate of 25% is in effect. The tax expense on operations is $12,500 ($50,000 × .25), and the tax expense on the extraordinary gain is $2,500 ($10,000 × .25), making total income taxes $15,000. The following summary compares the income statement with and without intraperiod tax allocation:

Byte-Size
Income Statement
For the Year Ended December 31, 19x5

	Correct Method: with Intraperiod Tax Allocation	Incorrect Method: without Intraperiod Tax Allocation	
Revenues	$ 490,000	$ 490,000	
Expenses	(440,000)	(440,000)	
Pre-tax operating income	$ 50,000	$ 50,000	
Income tax expense	(12,500)	(15,000)	(overstated)
Income from continuing operations	$ 37,500	$ 35,000	(understated)
Extraordinary gain	7,500	10,000	(overstated)
Net income	$ 45,000	$ 45,000	

Note that the total amount of income taxes and the "bottom line" net income are **not affected** by intraperiod tax allocation, but the subtotals in the income statement are different. With tax allocation, continuing operations are only charged with the $12,500 tax expense related to the $50,000 in pre-tax operating income (based on the assumed uniform tax rate of 25% on all elements of income). The extraordinary gain of $10,000 is reduced by $2,500 for taxes (again, a 25% tax rate), resulting in a net extraordinary gain of $7,500. Without intraperiod tax allocation, the income from continuing operations in this example would be understated by $2,500, and extraordinary gain would be overstated by $2,500.

We should mention two additional aspects of intraperiod tax allocation. First, the tax effects of a special item that results in a loss could be negative, resulting in a tax savings. Second, depending on the specific tax laws, the tax rate applicable to various items may be different from the tax rate on operating income.

Discontinued
Operations
(category 6)

Most large, publicly held companies have multiple business lines. A line of business, or business segment, consists of a "separate major line of business or class of customers."[2] When an entity eliminates one of its business segments, discontinued operations (category 6 in Exhibit 13–3) result. Discontinued operations do **not** include the elimination or phase out of a product line, class of service, or part of a business line.

Companies often discontinue lines of business because they are not profitable. A company with three profitable business lines and one unprofitable line might have higher total future profits if the unprofitable operation is discontinued. However, sometimes plant closings and layoffs associated with discontinued operations may be costly to the company for reasons such as the effect on the company's business reputation.

Objective 4
The nature and purpose of items that receive separate income statement disclosures, including discontinued operations, extraordinary items, and accounting changes.

When a company decides to discontinue a business segment, a separate line item is reported on the income statement. Usually discontinued operations result in two income statement effects:

1. The profit or loss for the current period from the **operating activities** that have been discontinued, net of taxes.
2. The gain or loss from the **sale of the assets** of the discontinued operations, net of taxes.

To illustrate the income statement effects of discontinued operations, assume that KLM, Inc., discontinued its tool and die operations in 19x5, with an operating loss after taxes for 19x5 of $450,000. KLM sold the assets of the tool and die operations in 19x5 at a gain of $250,000 net of taxes. The other 19x5 operations of KLM resulted in after-tax income of $1 million. The partial income statement in Exhibit 13–5 shows how this would be disclosed. Reporting the effects of discontinued operations separately enhances the comparability and consistency of the accounting data and provides relevant data for predicting the future business operating results. When comparative income statements are shown, the

EXHIBIT 13–5

Discontinued Operations	Partial Income Statement		
		19x5	19x4
Income from continuing operations		$1,000,000	$ 900,000
Discontinued operations:			
Operating loss (net of taxes)		(450,000)	(300,000)
Gain on sale of assets (net of taxes).		250,000	—
Net income		$ 800,000	$ 600,000

---

[2]*APB Opinion No. 30.*

data from prior years are restated to separate out the income or loss from the discontinued operations. This is shown in Exhibit 13–5, assuming the operating loss was $300,000 after taxes in 19x4.

Extraordinary Items (category 7)

Objective 4

The nature and purpose of items that receive separate income statement disclosures, including discontinued operations, extraordinary items, and accounting changes.

The second possible category of separately reported items included in the measurement of earnings is extraordinary items, net of taxes (category 7 in Exhibit 13–3). Based on the environment in which the entity operates, an extraordinary item is generally defined as an event that is

1. **Highly** unusual in nature, **and**
2. Not expected to occur again in the foreseeable future.[3]

Most large complex companies will typically have a number of transactions each year that are included in the income statement because they give rise to gains or losses, but that are **not** normal operating activities. These transactions are often referred to as unusual events, a broad category of events that are not directly a part of the business operations. Within this broad category, those unusual events that also meet the two criteria for extraordinary items are reported separately (see category 7 in Exhibit 13–3). Items such as the following are unusual events that **do not** qualify as extraordinary items.

- Write-down or write-off of inventory due to obsolescence or reduced marketability.
- Gains or losses on sale of plant assets.
- Gains or losses on sale of securities.
- Write-offs of large amounts of accounts receivable.
- Losses caused by a strike.[4]

Although these events are somewhat unusual, they are **not extraordinary items** because they do not qualify as being so unusual that a person could not "expect them to occur again in the foreseeable future."[5] The events listed above would typically be reported as gains and losses in the income statement, whereas losses from major earthquakes, hurricanes, floods, and certain other natural disasters would normally qualify as extraordinary items. However, if a company operates in an environment where severe weather, earthquakes, or floods are not extremely uncommon, the general definition above would suggest that losses from these events may not be considered extraordinary. The identification of extraordinary items will necessarily be based on professional judgment because we do not have highly structured guidelines for what qualifies as extraordinary.

In addition to transactions that qualify as extraordinary based on the general definition, one other event has been singled out for separate reporting by makers of accounting rules: gains or losses from the retirement (extinguishment) of long-term debt (bonds payable, notes payable, etc.) before the maturity date.[6] Other than this item, accountants report few items as extraordinary. Thus, income from continuing operations may include the effects of many events that do not appear to be "operating" events but still do not qualify for separate reporting as extraordinary items. For this reason, total revenues less total expenses *before considering gains and losses* (items 3 and 4 in Exhibit 13–3), may be a more useful subtotal for evaluating the *operating performance* of the business.

---

[3]Ibid.

[4]Ibid. par. 23.

[5]Ibid.

[6]*FASB Statement No. 4*, "Reporting Gains and Losses for Extinguishment of Debt" (Norwalk, Conn.: FASB, 1975).

The earnings statement and explanatory footnotes of the Ralston Purina Company shown in Exhibit 13–6 provide a good example of the three separately reported items that we have discussed so far: (1) unusual gains and losses, (2) discontinued operations, and (3) extraordinary items. Note how the separate display permits the reader to estimate that portion of the operating results expected to continue in future periods by eliminating items that are not expected to affect future earnings.

Illustrating Reporting of Accounting Method Changes (category 8)

Objective 4
The nature and purpose of items that receive separate income statement disclosures, including discontinued operations, extraordinary items, and accounting changes.

Accountants prepare financial statements on the basis of many specific accounting methods (sometimes called *accounting principles*). Management selects some of these accounting methods from a number of acceptable alternatives. For example, the method of measuring inventory is selected from a group of acceptable methods such as LIFO, FIFO, and average cost. When a company switches from one generally accepted accounting method to another, the effect of this change must be disclosed.[7]

Accounting for changes in accounting principles involves two steps:

Step 1: Compute the differential effect (if any) on net income of all prior years from using the newly elected method instead of the old (formerly used) method. This difference is called the *cumulative prior years' effect* on net income and measures the difference that would have been reported in net income of all prior years if the new method had been in use since the beginning of the business.

Step 2: Apply the newly elected method to the current and future period's financial statements as if it had been used throughout the current period.

Accountants follow the second step for all changes in accounting methods. Also, the first step is always **measured** (if measurable) the same way, although accountants report this measurement in one of two different ways, using either *current* or *retroactive* recognition, depending on the type of accounting change involved. These two different types of disclosure are explained below.

In most accounting changes, the cumulative prior years' effect from step 1 above is reported as a separate item (net of taxes) in the bottom portion of the income statement, as illustrated in category 8 of Exhibit 13–3. This is known as current treatment since the total of all prior years' effects is reported as a single item in the current year's income statement, and the results of prior years are not adjusted from their original reported amounts. For some accounting changes, accountants use retroactive treatment, which applies the cumulative prior years' effect by restating the results of prior years. This is done by adjusting the beginning retained earnings of the year of the change. The retroactive treatment is generally used when the accounting change seriously limits the comparability of the current year's results with prior years' results. For retroactive treatment the prior years' results are restated.

To illustrate the current and retroactive treatments, assume that during the current year a change in inventory method resulted in an increase in both the beginning asset balance and prior periods' income by $50,000 (assume no tax effect). This is the "cumulative prior years' effect" of step 1 above. To record this change using the **current treatment** (category 8 in the income statement), the following entry would be recorded for the prior years' effect of the change:

Inventory (A) 50,000
    Cumulative Effect of Change in Accounting Method (R)   50,000
  To record change in method of accounting for inventory.

---

[7]Note that companies use separate procedures when switching from an unacceptable (non-GAAP) method to an acceptable one. The procedures are discussed in *APB Opinion No. 20.*

EXHIBIT 13–6

Annual Report Disclosure of Unusual Gains and Losses, Discontinued Operations, and Extraordinary Items

Ralston Purina Company and Subsidiaries
Consolidated Statement of Earnings
Year Ended September 30
(in millions)

	19x6	19x5	19x4
Net sales	$5,514.6	$5,299.4	$4,351.8
Costs and expenses			
Cost of products sold	$3,177.9	$3,229.2	$3,130.5
Selling, general, and administrative	1,094.2	1,033.8	379.5
Advertising	584.6	497.5	395.8
Unusual or nonrecurring items	32.2		38.0
Interest	134.6	111.5	34.8
Investment income	(35.6)	(8.1)	(5.3)
	$4,987.9	$4,863.9	$3,973.3
Earnings from continuing operations before income taxes and extraordinary item	$ 526.7	$ 435.5	$ 378.5
Income taxes	263.1	205.6	167.3
Earnings from continuing operations before extraordinary item	$ 263.6	$ 229.9	$ 211.2
Earnings from discontinued operations		26.5	31.5
Gain on disposal of discontinued operations	148.8		
Earnings before extraordinary item	$ 412.4	$ 256.4	$ 242.7
Extraordinary item—Loss on early retirement of debt	(23.7)		
Net earnings	$ 388.7	$ 256.4	$ 242.7

Partial excerpts from footnotes:

Extraordinary Item

During 19x6, the Company retired, through repurchase and the exercise of redemption provisions under related indentures, approximately $300.8 of its outstanding long-term debt prior to its scheduled maturity. . . . The debt extinguishment results in an extraordinary loss of $23.7 after an income tax benefit of $22.7.

Discontinued Operations

In fiscal 19x6, the Company discontinued its restaurant operations through two separate transactions. In October 19x5, the Company sold its Foodmaker, Inc., restaurant subsidiary. . . . The sales price was $450.0 which consisted primarily of cash. . . . A gain on sale of $148.8 after applicable taxes of $59.2 was recognized. . . .

Sales of the discontinued operations of $564.5 in 19x5 and $628.3 in 19x4 have been excluded from net sales in the consolidated statement of earnings. Earnings of discontinued operations in 19x5 and 19x4 of $26.5 and $31.5, net of income taxes of $19.4 and $27.8, respectively, have been segregated and reported separately from results of continuing operations.

Unusual or Nonrecurring Items

These items represent provisions established (i) in fiscal 19x6 of $32.2 before applicable tax benefits of $7.7 representing the loss on sale of the Company's tuna cannery and related operations in Ecuador and a provision for write-down of tuna boats and related operations and (ii) in fiscal 19x4 for estimated losses of $38.0, before applicable tax benefits of $18.1, related to the closing of the San Diego tuna cannery. These provisions reduced earnings after taxes of $24.5 or $.32 per share in 19x6 and $19.9 or $.22 per share in 19x4.

EXHIBIT 13–7

Reporting Accounting Changes: The Effect on Prior Years' Income

Method A: Current Treatment

Kelly Company
Partial Income Statement
For the Year Ending December 31

	19x7	19x6
Income from continuing operations	$4,897,000	$4,300,000
Discontinued operations (net of taxes)		(350,000)
Extraordinary loss (net of taxes).	(200,000)	
Change in accounting method—prior years' effect (net of taxes) . .	50,000*	
Net income	$4,747,000	$3,950,000

Method B: Retroactive Treatment

Kelly Company
Retained Earnings Statement
For the Year Ending December 31, 19x7

Retained earnings, 1/1/x7	$17,847,000
Change in accounting method (net of taxes)	50,000*
Revised 1/1/x7, balance.	$17,897,000
Net income for 19x7.	4,697,000[†]
Dividends for 19x7	(2,000,000)
Retained earnings, 12/31/x7	$20,594,000

*We assume no taxes on this change.
[†]Net income of $4,747,000 per method A less the $50,000 effect of the accounting change would result in net income per method B of $4,697,000. The $50,000 effect of the accounting change is reported as an adjustment to Retained Earnings in method B.

Note in the above entry that current treatment reports the prior years' effect of an accounting method change as a separate component in the current year's income statement.

As shown in the following entry, **retroactive treatment** directly increases retained earnings for the prior years' effect of the accounting change.

Inventory (A)	50,000	
Retained Earnings (SE)		50,000
To record change in method of accounting for inventory.		

The retroactive treatment is not shown directly on the income statement but appears as an adjustment to the beginning retained earnings balance in the retained earnings statement. Exhibit 13–7 illustrates the current and retroactive treatments.

Whichever treatment is required to record the accounting change, the new accounting method is applied to the current year's financial statements (step 2) to measure net income. The only difference between the current and retroactive treatments is where and how the cumulative prior years' effect (step 1) is disclosed.

Sometimes it is impossible or impractical to measure the cumulative prior years' effect. Then, the new accounting method is applied to the current and future periods only, and no prior years' effect is recorded or reported. Generally, accounting changes are infrequent, and many accounting changes result from changes in accounting rules that eliminate one or more previously acceptable methods. Intermediate accounting textbooks discuss this subject in detail.

The rules governing income statement disclosures in the United States are generally more detailed and specific than in many other countries. The United Kingdom is probably the most similar to the United States in the nature of financial statement reporting requirements for extraordinary items, discontinued operations, and other unusual items. In some countries no rules exist to govern the display of unusual items, and in some countries, such as Italy and Spain the detail provided concerning their effect on current income may be sketchy or nonexistent. Also, tax reports must conform more with financial reporting requirements in some countries, such as Japan, Spain, Germany, and Italy. Because they are interested in reducing their income taxes their financial statements tend to report relatively lower earnings in comparison to U.S. or U.K. reports. These presentation and tax influences contribute to the challenge of comparing the financial reports of corporations from different countries.

RETAINED EARNINGS STATEMENT

The retained earnings statement is sometimes reported as a separate statement, but it may be included as a part of the statement of changes in stockholders' equity. Exhibit 13–8 illustrates a comprehensive example of a retained earnings statement.

Prior Period Adjustments

Objective 5
The preparation of a retained earnings statement. . . .

The beginning **retained earnings** balance captures the effects of net income and dividends for all prior years. This balance is the cumulative earnings amount from all prior years that has not been paid out to stockholders but has been **retained** in the business. If material errors were made in measuring net assets and operating profits in prior years, retained earnings must be corrected by making an adjustment to the beginning balance—a prior period adjustment. For example, assume a $10,000 credit sale from 19x1 was not recorded. The error was discovered on March 23, 19x3, when a customer paid $10,000 for an unrecorded account receivable. The error could be corrected as follows:

```
19x3
Mar. 23   Accounts Receivable (A) . . . . . . . . . . . . . . . . . . . .    10,000
                Retained Earnings (SE)  . . . . . . . . . . . . . . . .              10,000
             To record the credit sale from 19x1.

       23   Cash (A) . . . . . . . . . . . . . . . . . . . . . . . . . . . .    10,000
                Accounts Receivable (A) . . . . . . . . . . . . . . . .              10,000
             To record the collection of the receivable from 19x1.
```

EXHIBIT 13–8

Comprehensive Example of Retained Earnings Statement

Teltex Corporation
Retained Earnings Statement
For the Year Ending December 31, 19x9

Category of Items		
	Retained earnings, 1/1/x9	$4,720,000
1	Prior period adjustment due to errors affecting prior years (net of taxes)	(140,000)
2	Change in accounting method (net of taxes)	(30,000)
	Adjusted retained earnings balance, 1/1/x9	$4,550,000
3	Net income for the period (from the income statement).	325,000
4	Dividends declared for 19x9 (cash and stock dividends)	(120,000)
	Retained earnings, 12/31/x9	$4,755,000

Consider the Teltex example in Exhibit 13–8. A $140,000 error, such as the example discussed above, is reported (net of taxes, if any) as a prior period adjustment, adding to the beginning retained earnings balance in the retained earnings statement (category 1 in Exhibit 13–8). Prior period adjustments are rare, and corrections due to errors of prior periods are seldom observed in actual published financial reports.

In addition to prior period adjustments for errors, the beginning retained earnings balance might be adjusted for accounting changes receiving retroactive treatment (category 2 in Exhibit 13–8). Retained earnings is then increased for net income of the period, or decreased for a net loss (category 3 in Exhibit 13–8). Finally, dividends are deducted from retained earnings (category 4 in Exhibit 13–8) to arrive at the ending retained earnings balance.

STATEMENT OF CHANGES IN STOCKHOLDERS' EQUITY

The statement of changes in stockholders' equity (SCSE) is designed to explain the cause of all changes in stockholders' equity accounts from the beginning to the end of the period. The example in Exhibit 13–9 assumes that (1) $500,000 of no-par common stock was issued by Teltex Corporation during 19x9, (2) **unrealized gains** of $20,000 occurred during the period, and (3) the retained earnings changes are the same as illustrated in Exhibit 13–8.

EXHIBIT 13–9

Example of a Statement of Changes in Stockholders' Equity (SCSE)

Teltex Corporation
Statement of Changes in Stockholders' Equity
For the Year Ended December 31, 19x9

Cause of Change in Net Assets	Stockholders' Equity Accounts			Total Stockholders' Equity
	Retained Earnings	Common Stock (No-Par)	Accumulated Unrealized Gains	
Beginning balances	$4,720,000	$10,000,000	$280,000	$15,000,000
Error correction	(140,000)			(140,000)
Retroactive accounting change	(30,000)			(30,000)
Adjusted balances	$4,550,000	$10,000,000	$280,000	$14,830,000
Net income	325,000			$ 325,000
Unrealized gains			20,000	20,000
Net nonowner transactions				$ 345,000
Balances after nonowner transactions	$4,875,000	$10,000,000	$300,000	$15,175,000
Cash dividends	(120,000)			$ (120,000)
Sale of stock		500,000		500,000
Net owner transactions . . .				$ 380,000
Ending balances	$4,755,000	$10,500,000	$300,000	$15,555,000

Objective 5
The preparation of...a
statement of changes in
stockholders' equity.

Unrealized items typically represent gains or losses on foreign currency translations for foreign operations (see Appendix B at the end of this text for a more complete discussion) or from long-term investments in stocks (as discussed in Chapter 12). Such gains or losses are not reported in net income or retained earnings but are reported as a separate account balance within stockholders' equity.

The SCSE reconciles all changes in stockholders' equity during the period; these changes equal the changes in net assets. As illustrated in Exhibit 13–9, the SCSE divides the change in stockholders' equity, which is always equal to the change in net assets, into three components:

1. Changes due to corrections or restatements (a $170,000 decrease) resulting in an adjusted balance in stockholders' equity of $14,830,000.
2. Changes in net assets from nonowner-related transactions (a $345,000 increase).
3. Changes in net assets from owner-related activities (a $380,000 increase).

The SCSE may also include other accounts not illustrated in Exhibit 13–9, including preferred stock, additional paid-in capital (or "capital in excess of par"), common stock held in the treasury for possible resale, and other shareholders' equity accounts. The Ralston Purina financial statements include an example of the SCSE on page 923 in Appendix E.

The format for the SCSE may vary in practice from that shown in Exhibit 13–9. However, the purpose of the statement is always the same—to explain all of the changes in stockholders' equity. Because of the balance sheet equality (A = L + SE), the changes in stockholders' equity must be equal to the changes in net assets.

The complete SCSE should be reported whenever any significant changes occur in stockholders' equity accounts other than retained earnings. Accountants may use only the retained earnings statement, which is reported in the first column of the SCSE, when retained earnings is the only stockholders' equity account that changed during the period.

EARNINGS PER SHARE

The remainder of this chapter discusses the measurement of earnings per share, the most widely cited piece of accounting data. Earnings per share (EPS) is a basic financial ratio **measuring the periodic earnings of the entity on a "per share of common stock" basis.**

EPS measurements must be reported on the face of the income statement by all publicly traded companies, but EPS need not be reported by private entities. Together with the market price and the dividends per share of common stock, EPS provides stockholders with summarized financial results that are easy to understand and that help them compare the corporation's performance from period to period on a per share basis.

EPS is essentially the net income of the entity divided by the number of outstanding shares of common stock. The objective is to measure the corporation's earnings that are available for the common stockholders. In some cases, this is a fairly simple computation, but the computation may be complicated by a number of factors. The following examples of computing EPS progress from the simplest situation to more complex situations.

Definitions of Simple and Complex Capital Structures

The capital structure of an entity may be described as either simple or complex. A simple capital structure has only one class of voting common stock and no other securities that have the potential to be converted to common stock. A complex capital structure has securities that may be converted to shares of common stock in certain situations. Examples of securities that may be converted to common stock include convertible preferred stock and convertible bonds.[8] In this text we illustrate EPS computations for simple capital structures only. Intermediate and advanced accounting texts cover this topic in greater detail.

Examples of Simple Capital Structure EPS Computations

The three examples of EPS computations that we discuss are example 1, constant shares outstanding; example 2, weighted average shares outstanding; and example 3, preferred stock outstanding. A discussion on the effect of separate disclosures on EPS measurements follows these examples.

Objective 6
Computation of EPS for a simple capital structure.

Constant Shares Outstanding.   Let's begin illustrating EPS computations by assuming a simple capital structure consisting of 400,000 shares of common stock that are issued and outstanding throughout the year. Assume there are no preferred stocks and no convertible securities. Net income for the year is $2 million. The EPS computation for example 1 follows.

Example 1:

$$\text{EPS} = \frac{\text{Net income}}{\text{Number of shares of common stock}}$$

$$\text{EPS} = \frac{\$2,000,000}{400,000} = \underline{\underline{\$5}} \text{ per share}$$

This $5 EPS measure simply means that net income for the year amounted to $5 for every share of stock outstanding. Hence, each share earned $5 of net income.

Weighted Average Shares Outstanding.   What if the number of shares outstanding changes during the year? In such cases, the net income is divided by the weighted average number of shares outstanding during the year. To illustrate, assume the following facts:

Date	Number of Shares Issued	Total Shares Outstanding
1/1/x3.	0	400,000
5/1/x3.	120,000	520,000
11/1/x3.	120,000	640,000
12/31/x3.	0	640,000

Assume that there are no preferred stocks and no convertible securities. The 400,000 shares outstanding at the start of the year increase to 640,000 shares by year-end as a result of the two additional issuances of 120,000 shares each. Earnings for the year are $2 million. Since earnings are assumed to be generated throughout 19x3, the $2 million is divided by the weighted average number of shares of stock outstanding throughout 19x3 to compute EPS. The weighted average number of shares can be

---

[8]Convertible securities are often issued in order to attract new capital to finance expansions or acquisitions. By having the option of changing their investment from, say, debt, which has a stated annual return in the form of interest income, to common stock, investors can maintain a fixed-interest income if the stock price stays flat or falls while receiving potentially high returns if the stock price increases. This option to hold either fixed-interest debt (or fixed-dividend preferred stock) or stock with unlimited potential for increasing in price is attractive to many investors, and explains why convertible securities exist.

computed several ways, but each approach should yield the same answer. Two alternative ways to compute the weighted average shares for the data given above are as follows:

Computation Method A: Cumulative Approach

Balance in Total Number of Shares Outstanding		Fraction of Year (in months) Balance Was Maintained without Change		Weighted Average Number of Shares of Common Stock Outstanding
400,000	×	4/12	=	133,333
520,000	×	6/12	=	260,000
640,000	×	2/12	=	106,667
Weighted average shares				500,000

Computation Method B: Incremental Approach

Source of Layer	Number of Shares in Each Layer	×	Fraction of Year Each Layer Was Outstanding	=	Weighted Average Number of Shares of Common Stock Outstanding
Beginning balance	400,000	×	12/12	=	400,000
May 1 issuance	120,000	×	8/12	=	80,000
November 1 issuance	120,000	×	2/12	=	20,000
Weighted average shares					500,000

Method A will be used in the remainder of the chapter illustrations, but other methods are acceptable. The EPS computation for this second example can now be made given the weighted average number of shares, 500,000, as computed above:

Example 2:

$$EPS = \frac{\text{Net income}}{\text{Weighted average number of shares of common stock}}$$

$$EPS = \frac{\$2,000,000}{500,000} = \underline{\$4} \text{ per share}$$

Preferred Stock Outstanding.   Next, assume the same facts as in example 2 above except that preferred stock is also outstanding and the total preferred stock dividend for 19x3 is $375,000. Since preferred stock dividends must be paid before dividends to common stockholders, they are deducted from net income to compute EPS to common stockholders. The revised EPS computation would be as follows:

Example 3:

$$EPS = \frac{\text{Net income} - \text{Preferred stock dividends}}{\text{Weighted average number of shares of common stock}}$$

$$EPS = \frac{\$2,000,000 - \$375,000}{500,000 \text{ shares}} = \underline{\$3.25} \text{ per share}$$

All three examples of EPS computations examined so far have been for **simple capital structures,** which require only one EPS measurement per year. The practice of subtracting preferred dividends from net income shown in example 3 highlights the goal of EPS disclosure: to communicate the effects of earnings of the period on common stockholders' interests. Conceptually, common stockholders' ability to receive dividends is limited by both earnings and preferred dividend obligations.

Effects of Separate Disclosures. What should be disclosed for EPS when earnings include separate items such as discontinued operations and/or extraordinary items? These separate items normally are provided separate EPS presentation, since stockholders are most interested in the EPS from continuing operations. To illustrate, assume that the $2 million net income in the previous example included an extraordinary loss of $875,000 and a loss from discontinued operations of $750,000. Exhibit 13–10 shows an appropriate EPS presentation of discontinued operations and extraordinary items.

In most instances, the EPS number referred to in the financial news media is EPS from continuing operations. This is the amount of income from ongoing operations that might be expected to continue in future periods. Given investors' interest in the future economic flows of an entity, it is widely assumed that the continuing components of net income are the most relevant for predicting future economic performance.

The reporting of EPS varies considerably around the world. In some countries, such as Italy and Switzerland, no EPS information is required. In other countries, such as the United Kingdom, France, and Australia, the reported EPS figures exclude extraordinary items. Most financial analysts find it useful to compare stock price per share to earnings per share in a ratio commonly known as the **P/E ratio (price/earnings ratio).** In order to compare the P/E ratios of U.S. and foreign corporations, it is important to understand the differences in how the EPS ratio is computed. Adjustments that compensate for different methods of computing EPS are among the many necessary to meaningfully compare the financial statements of U.S. and foreign businesses.

EXHIBIT 13–10

EPS Presentation of Discontinued Operations and Extraordinary Items

Byte-Size
Condensed Income Statement
For the Year Ended December 31, 19x3

Sales	$10,000,000
Cost of sales, taxes, and other expenses (details omitted)	6,375,000
Income from continuing operations	$ 3,625,000
Loss from discontinued operations (net of taxes)	(750,000)
Extraordinary loss (net of taxes)	(875,000)
Net income	$ 2,000,000
Earnings per share of common:	
From continuing operations	$ 6.50*
Discontinued operations	(1.50)†
Extraordinary loss	(1.75)‡
Net income	$ 3.25§

---

*($3,625,000 − $375,000 P.S. dividends)/500,000 shares.
†$750,000/500,000 shares.
‡$875,000/500,000 shares.
§($2,000,000 − $375,000 P.S. dividends)/500,000 shares.

• SUMMARY

This chapter has examined the income statement, retained earnings statement, statement of changes in stockholders' equity, and earnings per share.

In its most complex form, the income statement may include the results of many different types of nonowner transactions giving rise to revenues, expenses, gains, and losses. The format of the income statement is designed to permit readers to separate the strict operating activities of the entity giving rise to revenues and expenses from the other activities resulting in nonoperating gains and losses. Several special classes of transactions require separate disclosure net of taxes, including (1) discontinued operations, (2) extraordinary items, and (3) those changes in accounting methods receiving "current treatment."

The components of the retained earnings statement can include adjustments to the beginning balance for prior period adjustments such as retroactive accounting changes, as well as increases for net income and decreases for dividends. The SCSE is somewhat more comprehensive than a retained earnings statement in that it reconciles all changes in stockholders' equity from both nonowner-related (net income) and owner-related (e.g., dividends, new stock issues, and so on) transactions.

The final segment of the chapter discussed how to measure earnings per share. The chapter illustrated fundamental measurement procedures for simple capital structures. You may wish to examine the consolidated statements of earnings and retained earnings and the related footnotes for the Ralston Purina Company, which are included at the end of the text (Appendix E) for a factual application of the subjects considered in this chapter.

• DEMONSTRATION EXERCISE

Czerkas Industries, Inc., has the following information available at March 31, 19x2, its year-end:

a. Revenues for the period were $4,360,000. Total expenses for the period were $2,875,000.

b. Used equipment was sold for a gain of $40,000.

c. Czerkas recorded a loss of $400,000 from an employee strike that occurred at the beginning of the year.

d. A major line of business was discontinued during the year and its assets sold. During last year, a $200,500 net loss from operations was incurred. The net assets of the discontinued operations were sold for a gain of $100,000.

e. Bonds due to mature in 19x5 were retired early for a $350,000 gain.

f. An accounting method was changed in 19x2. The cumulative effect of this change on income of all prior years (before 19x2) was to increase prior years' income by $240,000 before taxes. The effect of this accounting change in 19x2 has already been included in item a above. This change is to receive retroactive treatment disclosure in the 19x2 financial statements.

g. An error in a prior period's financial statements was discovered. If the error had not been made, reported income before taxes for that period would have been $500,000 less.

h. The income tax rate for income from continuing operations and the prior period error is 30%. For all other items, the income tax rate is 20%.

i. Retained earnings at April 1, 19x1, was $10,280,000. Czerkas Industries declared and paid preferred stock dividends of $100,000 and common stock dividends of $75,000 during the period.

j. On April 1, 19x1, 600,000 shares of common stock were issued and outstanding. An additional 90,000 shares of common stock were sold on November 30, 19x1. The company purchased 60,000 shares of its own common stock on January 31, 19x2.

Required:

1. Prepare the Czerkas Industries, Inc., combined income and retained earnings statement for the year.

2. Prepare the detailed EPS information of Czerkas Industries, Inc., for the period.

Solution:

Requirement 1:

Czerkas Industries, Inc.
Combined Income and Retained Earnings Statement
For the Year Ended March 31, 19x2

Revenues.	$ 4,360,000
Expenses.	(2,875,000)
Gain on sale of equipment	40,000
Loss from employee strike	(400,000)
Income from continuing operations before taxes.	$ 1,125,000
Income tax expense on continuing operations.	337,500
Income from continuing operations	$ 787,500
Discontinued operations:	
Net operating loss (net of taxes).	(160,400)
Gain on sale of assets (net of taxes).	80,000
Extraordinary gain on early debt retirement (net of taxes)	280,000
Net income	$ 987,100
Retained earnings, 4/1/x1	$10,280,000
Prior period adjustment due to error affecting prior year (net of taxes)	(350,000)
Cumulative effect of accounting method change (net of taxes)	192,000
Adjusted retained earnings balance	$10,122,000
Net income	987,100
Dividends declared and paid	(175,000)
Retained earnings, 3/31/x2.	$10,934,100

Requirement 2:

Weighted average number of common stock shares:

Shares Outstanding	×	Period of the year	=	Weighted Average No. Shares Outstanding
600,000	×	8/12	=	400,000
690,000	×	2/12	=	115,000
630,000	×	2/12	=	105,000
Total weighted average number of shares				620,000

EPS computations:

$$\text{Continuing operations} = \frac{\$787{,}500 - \$100{,}000}{620{,}000} = \$1.11$$

$$\text{Discontinued operations} = \frac{\$(80{,}400)}{620{,}000} = \$(0.13)$$

$$\text{Extraordinary gain} = \frac{\$280{,}000}{620{,}000} = \$0.45$$

$$\text{Net income} = \frac{\$987{,}100 - \$100{,}000}{620{,}000} = \$1.43$$

Czerkas Industries, Inc.
EPS Information
For the Year Ended March 31, 19x2

From continuing operations	$ 1.11
From discontinued operations	(0.13)
From extraordinary gain	0.45
Net income	$ 1.43

• KEY TERMS

Business segment. A major line of business or class of customers.

Complex capital structure. A capital structure that includes securities that may be converted to additional shares of common stock in certain situations.

Current treatment. Treatment accorded accounting method changes where the effect of the change is recorded in the current period's income statement.

Direct expensing. Records expenses as they occur based on the assumption that the revenues associated with these expenses have also been recorded.

Discontinued operations. An entity's business segment that has been eliminated, requiring special disclosures in financial statements.

Earnings per share (EPS). Basic financial ratio measuring the periodic earnings of the entity on a "per share of common stock" basis.

Extraordinary items. Based on the environment in which the entity operates, an extraordinary item is both highly unusual in nature and not expected to occur again in the foreseeable future.

Gains. Increases in income attributable to a nonoperating activity.

Intraperiod tax allocation. When reporting special items, this calls for the separate associated tax effects to be reported with the special item rather than on the line with tax expense on continuing operations.

Losses. Decreases in income attributable to a nonoperating activity.

Matching. Occurs when the costs of achieving the recorded revenues are recognized (recorded) as expenses in the same period as their related revenues.

Prior period adjustments. Treatment accorded certain accounting method changes and error corrections that require a restatement of prior years' retained earnings balance.

Retroactive treatment. Treatment accorded certain accounting method changes whereby the cumulative prior years' effect is reported as an adjustment to the beginning retained earnings of the year of the change.

Simple capital structure. A capital structure having only one class of voting common stock and no other securities that have the potential to be converted to common stock.

Systematic allocation. Method of expensing costs. Examples include depreciation and amortization.

Unusual events. Infrequent events not directly related to operations. Extraordinary items are a special category of unusual events.

• SYNONYMS

Accounting methods; accounting principles; accounting procedures.

Direct expensing; period costs.

Discontinued operations; sale of a business segment.

Errors of prior years; prior period adjustments.

Income statement; earnings statement; statement of operations.

Income tax credits; income tax reductions.

Income tax expense; provision for income taxes.

Net income; earnings; net profits.

Statement of changes in stockholders' equity; statement of stockholders' equity; changes in shareholders' equity.

Unusual items; nonoperating gains and losses.

• QUESTIONS

1. What is the relation between net income and the change in the balance sheets from the start of the period to the end of the period?
2. What are the two main categories of transactions that result in changes in net assets? Give an example of each.
3. What criteria are required to recognize revenue?
4. What criteria are required to recognize expenses?
5. Some assets call for estimates in order to be measured. Give two examples.
6. How are changes in estimates accounted for?
7. How do gains and losses differ from revenues and expenses?
8. Where are most gains and losses reported?
9. What is intraperiod tax allocation?
10. What portion of income taxes is reported as income tax expense in the income statement?
11. What are discontinued operations?
12. What is the definition of an extraordinary item?
13. What is the most common example of extraordinary items?
14. How many ways are there to report changes in accounting methods? Explain each.
15. What are prior period adjustments?
16. What is included in the statement of changes in owners' equity (SCSE)?
17. What is EPS?
18. What is the difference between a simple and a complex capital structure?

• EXERCISES

E 13–1
Expense Recognition
L.O.1

For the following list of expenses, indicate which of the following three processes will normally cause the expense to be recognized in income measurement:

Process:
a. Matching.
b. Direct expensing.
c. Systematic allocation.

Expenses:
1. Depreciation—building.
2. Cost of goods sold.
3. Freight-in for merchandise purchases.
4. Freight-out for merchandise sold.
5. Packaging costs for bagging sold merchandise.
6. Advertising for past months' newspaper ads.
7. Office supplies.
8. Amortization of special tools used to service merchandise sold.
9. Research and development.
10. Administrators' salaries.
11. Income taxes.
12. Salespersons' commissions.

E 13–2
Expense Recognition
L.O.1

For each of the following balance sheet accounts, indicate the process by which they would ordinarily become recognized as expenses in the income statement:

Process:
a. Matching against revenue.
b. Direct expensing.
c. Systematic allocation to expense.

Balance Sheet Account:
1. Prepaid insurance for office rent.
2. Inventory—finished products ready for sale.
3. Machinery and equipment for service department.
4. Prepaid advertising.
5. Goodwill.
6. Wages payable—service repair.
7. Consultant's fees payable.
8. Interest payable on long-term note.
9. Natural resources—crude oil.
10. Patents.
11. Prepaid property taxes on office building.
12. Prepaid officers' salaries.

E 13–3
Revenue Recognition
L.O.1

For each situation below, write a note to your supervisor indicating when the earliest acceptable point is for revenue to be recognized. Provide the reasons for your answers. Assume that all companies have December 31 year-ends.

> **Case A:**   A major league baseball franchise sells season tickets each year, with the average number of seats sold by December 31 each year for the forthcoming season equal to 18,000 over the past five years. By December 31, 19x4, the franchise has sold 22,000 season tickets for a total of $17,600,000 cash for the 19x5 season.
>
> **Case B:**   Big Ed's Discount Store has been in business for two years. Ed sells major household appliances to customers in a northeastern city on the following terms: $0 down, 10 equal monthly payments beginning in the fourth month after the month of sale. Ed does a credit check on each customer when they first buy an item, but after the first purchase a repeat customer simply needs to present the invoice from any earlier sale and Ed grants them "instant credit." Ed's sales and accounts receivable balances have grown steadily over the past two years. It is estimated that repossessed appliances account for about 30% to 35% of the first year's sales.

E 13–4
Revenue Recognition
L.O.1

For each situation below, write a memo to your supervisor indicating when the earliest acceptable point is for revenue to be recognized. Provide the reasons for your answers. Assume that the companies have December 31 year-ends.

> **Case A:**   A forthcoming concert at your former school is sold out several weeks beforehand. The promoters collected all $3 million from ticket sales by November 14. All fees, salesagent wages, and commissions had been paid by December 10. The rock star's fee is known in advance (a flat $1 million). The concert dates are January 17 and 18. When can the promoter recognize revenue (and expenses) for this event?
>
> **Case B:**   An exploration firm discovered a large deposit of precious stones on December 13, 19x2. The stones are all of a high grade, and are traded on commodity exchanges throughout the world at prices that have ranged between $1,000 and $1,200 per carat over the past five years. The firm keeps the stones in its inventory until December 28, 19x7, when it sells all of them for $1,020 per carat.

E 13–5
Change in Estimate
L.O.2

The Martin Corporation provides a two-year warranty on all of its products. The actual sales and warranty cost history since the company first offered the warranty in 19x2 has been as follows (in thousands):

	19x6	19x5	19x4	19x3	19x2
Sales.	$7,050	$7,135	$6,820	$6,353	$6,101
Actual cost of warranty repairs	136	122	141	127	143

Martin has been estimating warranty expense at 2.5% of sales each year since 19x2. During 19x7, Martin reported sales of $7,412,000 and incurred actual warranty repair costs of $170,000. Due to the favorable experience, Martin decided to change its estimate of warranty expense to 2% of sales on December 31, 19x7. (Do **not** round answers to nearest thousand.)

Required:
1. What was the balance in the Estimated Warranty Liability account at the start of 19x7?
2. What would be reported as warranty expense for 19x7?
3. What would be the balance in the Estimated Warranty Liability account at the end of 19x7?
4. When and how would the change in estimate affect Martin's financial statements?
5. Would you recommend a warranty expense allowance different than the 2% of sales?

E 13–6
Change in Estimate
L.O.2

The Jackson Corporation purchased equipment at the start of 19x1 at a cost of $157,000. The equipment was expected to last 10 years and to have a salvage value of $12,000. Straight-line depreciation has been used on the equipment.

During 19x6, Jackson's management decided that the equipment would need to be replaced by the end of 19x7 due to obsolescence. The scrap value is still estimated to be $12,000.

Required:
1. What is the book value of the equipment on December 31, 19x5?
2. What should Jackson record for depreciation expense for 19x6?
3. How will this change in estimate be identified by financial statement users?

E 13–7
Multiple Choice
(CPA Adapted)
L.O.1, 3, 4

Select the best answer for each of the following.

1. Expense recognition is based in part on—
   a. Systematic allocations.
   b. Random events.
   c. The reliability of the measurement system.
   d. None of the above.
2. Revenue recognition—
   a. Takes place at the point of sale.
   b. Takes place when goods are received.
   c. May take place only after a purchase order is signed.
   d. Is an objectively determinable point in time requiring little or no judgment.
   e. None of the above.
3. The determination of expenses of an accounting period is based partly on—
   a. Application of the cost principle.
   b. Application of the consistency principle.
   c. Application of the matching principle.
   d. Application of the objectivity principle.
   e. None of the above.
4. A transaction that is material in amount, unusual in nature, but not infrequent in occurrence should be presented separately as—
   a. A component of income from continuing operations, but not net of applicable income taxes.
   b. A component of income from continuing operations, net of applicable income taxes.
   c. An extraordinary item, net of applicable income taxes.
   d. A prior period adjustment, but not net of applicable income taxes.
5. An extraordinary item should be reported separately as a component of income—
   a. Before cumulative effect of accounting changes and after discontinued operations of a segment of a business.
   b. Before cumulative effect of accounting changes and before discontinued operations of a segment of a business.

c. After cumulative effect of accounting changes and after discontinued operations of a segment of a business.

d. After cumulative effect of accounting changes and before discontinued operations of a segment of a business.

E 13–8
Income Statement Preparation
L.O.3, 4

Bartlett Corporation reported the following account balances in the 19x7 pre-closing trial balance (in millions):

Account	Debit (credit)
Cost of Goods Sold	$ 953
Loss on Sale of Factory Equipment	14
Loss on Retirement of Debt.	35
Sales.	(3,106)
Gain on Sale of Assets from Bakery Subsidiary.	(79)
Loss on Operations from Bakery before Discontinuance	15
Gain on Sale of Temporary Investments	(22)
Selling Expenses	786
Administrative Expenses.	857
Interest on Long-Term Debt	32
Dividends Declared by Bartlett	115

Bartlett has an income tax rate of 30% on all items affecting income.

Required:
Prepare Bartlett's 19x7 income statement (in thousands) using proper intraperiod tax allocation.

E 13–9
Income Statement Preparation
L.O.3, 4

Strake, Inc., reported the following account balances (in thousands) at the end of 19x4:

Gain on Sale of Obsolete Inventory	$ 33
Operating Loss from Fabric Division	497
Cost of Goods Sold	14,896
Explosion Loss in Chemical Plant	2,300
Interest Expense	248
Interest Income	169
Sales	35,871
Gain on Sale of Assets from Fabric Division.	630
Loss on Retirement of Debt	220
Selling and Administrative Expenses	8,463

Assume that the appropriate tax rate on all items is 30%. No taxes have been included in the amounts reported above. Do **not** round to the nearest thousand.

Required:
1. Prepare an income statement for 19x4 using proper intraperiod tax allocation.
2. What is your best guess at net income for 19x5?

E 13–10
Income Statement
Preparation
L.O.3, 4

Drake, Inc., reported the following account balances (in thousands) at the end of 19xx:

Sales	$7,837
Cost of Goods Sold.	5,736
Gain on Early Retirement of Debt	347
Fire Loss in Paint Division.	186
Selling and Administrative Expenses	943
Operating Loss from Plastics Division	147
Gain on Sale of Assets from Plastics Division	321
Interest Expense.	129
Loss on Sale of Obsolete Inventory Items	37

Assume that Drake has not considered the tax effect of the data reported above, and that a 30% tax rate is appropriate for all items. Do **not** round to the nearest thousand.

Required:
Prepare an income statement for 19xx using proper intraperiod tax allocation.

E 13–11
Retained Earnings
Statement
L.O.5

Marglett Corporation reported the following balance sheet (in thousands) at December 31, 19x5:

	19x5	19x4
Stockholders' Equity		
Common stock—($1 par)	$ 80	$ 75
Capital in excess of par.	356	290
Retained earnings	228	193
Total stockholders' equity	$664	$558

On April 1, 19x5, Marglett issued 5,000 additional shares of common stock. Marglett paid out $28,000 in cash dividends during 19x5.

Required:
Prepare a retained earnings statement for 19x5.

E 13–12
Statement of Changes
in Stockholders' Equity
L.O.5

The Weltex Corporation began 19x1 with the following stockholders' equity account balances (in thousands):

Common Stock (1,000,000 shares)	$ 8,500
Unrealized Gains and Losses	(267)
Retained Earnings	4,387
Total Stockholders' Equity	$12,620

During 19x1, the following occurred:

a. Declared and paid $400,000 cash dividends to Weltex shareholders.
b. Issued another 200,000 shares of common stock on June 30, 19x1, for $15 per share.
c. Reported net income of $1,430,000 for 19x1.
d. Reported unrealized gains of $48,000.

Required:
Prepare a statement of changes in stockholders' equity for 19x1.

E 13–13
*Statement of Changes
in Stockholders' Equity*
L.O.5

The Marslong Corporation reported the following account balances as of December 31, 19x4 (in thousands):

Common Stock (no par)	$2,675
Unrealized Gains and Losses	143
Retained Earnings	1,431
Total Stockholders' Equity	$4,249

The following occurred during 19x5:

a. Reported net income of $386,000.
b. Declared cash dividends of $128,000.
c. Paid cash dividends of $120,000.
d. Issued 4,500 shares of stock to corporate managers for $72,000 cash.
e. Reported unrealized holding losses of $15,000.

Required:
Prepare a statement of changes in stockholders' equity for 19x5.

E 13–14
EPS Computation
L.O.6

Refer to the data in Exercise 13–11 for the Marglett Corporation.

Required:
Compute EPS for 19x5 for Marglett's stockholders.

E 13–15
EPS Computation
L.O.6

Refer to the data in Exercise 13–12 for Weltex Corporation.

Required:
Compute EPS for Weltex for 19x1.

E 13–16
*Weighted Average
Number of
Shares—EPS*
L.O.6

Owens Engineering, Inc., (OEI) reported earnings of $2,014,000 for the year ending December 31, 19xx. During 19xx, there were several changes in the number of outstanding shares of stock. At the start of 19xx, OEI had 710,000 shares outstanding. On April 30, 19xx, OEI issued 40,000 shares of stock to company officials as a part of their stock incentive plan. On July 1, 19xx, OEI repurchased 50,000 shares of stock in the open market at $24.50 per share. On September 30, 19xx, OEI issued an additional 140,000 shares as partial compensation for the acquisition of Pell Engines Company.

Required:
1. Compute the weighted average number of shares of OEI stock for 19xx.
2. Compute EPS for 19xx (rounded to the nearest cent).

E 13–17
*Weighted Average
Number of Shares*
L.O.6

The Travis Corporation had several changes in its capital structure for the year 19xx, as follows:

Date	Description
1/1	400,000 shares of common stock outstanding
2/28	Issued 25,000 shares of common stock
6/30	Issued 50,000 shares of common stock
9/30	Issued 40,000 shares of preferred stock

Required:
Compute the weighted average number of shares of common stock for 19xx.

E 13–18
EPS Computation
L.O.6

The Eagle Corporation reported net income of $1,987,000 for 19x1. Eagle declared and paid preferred stock dividends of $367,000 and common stock dividends of $285,000 during 19x1. Eagle started 19x1 with 220,000 shares of common stock and sold an additional 60,000 shares on June 30, 19x1.

Required:
Compute Eagle's EPS for 19x1.

• PROBLEMS

P 13–1
Revenue Recognition
L.O.1

The following events occurred during December of 19x1 for the Robinson Corporation, a calendar-year company:

a. Collected cash of $1,800 from a customer on an account receivable. The sale occurred in 19x1.
b. Collected cash of $2,400 from a customer as a deposit for equipment to be delivered and installed by Robinson at the customer's plant in January 19x2.
c. Sold equipment on account to a customer for $8,000. The equipment was installed in December 19x1.
d. Collected cash of $650 from a customer for an account receivable originally recorded in 19x0 and written off as uncollectible early in 19x1.
e. Received a purchase order from a customer for equipment of $18,000 that Robinson has in inventory. The customer plans to install the equipment in January 19x2.

Required:
1. Record the journal entries in general journal form for the above events.
2. For each entry, identify the year in which revenue from the transaction should be recognized in the income statement.
3. What year is revenue recorded for each of these events?
4. Are there any differences between your answers to parts 2 and 3 above? Explain why.

P 13–2
Expense Recognition
L.O.1

The Orbiter Corporation reported the following activities in the last month of 19x0:

a. Paid salaries to top corporate executives of $180,000.
b. Recorded depreciation for the year of $425,000.
c. Recorded reduction in inventory of $487,500 in conjunction with a credit sale to a customer.
d. Recorded purchase on open account of $2,100 in office supplies received on December 31.
e. Paid advertising invoices of $37,800 for newspaper ads from the current month.
f. Recorded accrued interest payable of $8,750 on long-term debt at year-end.
g. Recorded accrued salaries payable of $17,500 at year-end.
h. Purchased $64,000 of machinery with a 10-year economic life for cash.

Required:
1. Record the journal entries in general journal form for the above activities on Orbiter's books.
2. Indicate which year or years each item will be recognized as an expense.
3. Indicate which of the following processes is (or will be) used to recognize the expense for each item recorded in part 1:
   a. Matching.
   b. Direct expensing.
   c. Systematic allocation.

P 13–3
Change in Estimate
L.O.2

Jason Appliances has previously estimated its warranty expense at 2% of annual net sales. The following data are reported at the end of 19x4:

Net sales	$4,000,000
Estimated Warranty Liability account (1/1/x4 balance)	60,000 credit
Payments made during 19x4 for warranty parts and service by Jason . . .	75,000

At the end of 19x4, Jason decides to decrease warranty expense estimates to 1.5% of annual net sales.

Required:
Record the 19x4 warranty expense. What is the Estimated Warranty Liability account balance as of the end of 19x4?

P 13–4
Change in Estimate
L.O.2

The Towers, Inc., owns a hotel that is being depreciated on a straight-line basis. The original esti-mated useful life of the hotel was 50 years, with a $1 million salvage value. The hotel, which origi-nally cost $301 million, had a net book value of $187 million as of December 31, 19x6. During 19x7, certain improvements to the hotel, costing $12 million, were added to the Building account. During 19x7, Towers also revised the expected total useful life from 50 to 60 years, and the salvage value from $1 million to $3 million.

Required:
Record the depreciation expense on the hotel for 19x7.

P 13–5
Change in Estimate
L.O.2

The Whade Corporation purchased equipment at the start of 19x1 at a cost of $400,000. The equip-ment was expected to last five years and had no expected salvage value at the time of the purchase.
The following is the **preliminary** income measurement for Whade for 19x3:

Whade Corporation
Income Statement
For the Year Ending December 31, 19x3

Sales	$4,382,000
Cost of goods sold	(3,845,000)
Gross margin	$ 537,000
Selling and administrative expenses.	(423,000)
Depreciation expense—equipment	(80,000)
Interest expense	(57,000)
Net loss	$ (23,000)

Before the books were closed for 19x3, Whade's management reviewed the equipment and de-cided that the original estimated life of five years was not appropriate, but that an eight-year life was more realistic. Also, Whade's management believes the equipment will have a scrap value of $12,000 instead of zero after it is fully depreciated. Whade uses straight-line depreciation.

Required:
1. Prepare the entry needed to record the change in estimate for 19x3 assuming the books have not yet been closed, but that all adjusting entries have been made.
2. Prepare the revised 19x3 income statement. (Ignore income taxes since Whade makes this change in estimate for financial reporting purposes only.)
3. If Whade's management had made this change in estimate early in 19x4 but before the 19x3 financial statements had been issued to stockholders, how would your answer to part 2 above be different?

P 13–6
*Income Statement
Preparation*
L.O.1, 3, 4

Consider these account balances of the Edge Corporation as of December 31, 19x1:

Salespersons Commissions.	$ 39,000
Sales Returns.	61,000
Depreciation Expense	185,000
Gain on Early Retirement of Debt	120,000
Cost of Goods Sold	5,295,000
Selling and Administrative Expenses.	315,000
Gain on Sale of Assets from Discontinued Operations	395,000
Operating Loss on Operations Discontinued in 19x1	175,000
Sales.	7,532,000
Interest Expense	140,000
Loss on Sale of Discontinued Inventory	77,000
Gain on Sale of Temporary Investments	36,000
Research and Development Expense	93,000

Assume that all items are taxed at the 40% rate and that no income taxes are included in the items listed above.

Required:
Prepare the 19x1 income statement for Edge Corporation using appropriate intraperiod tax allocation.

P 13–7
Income Statement/
Retained Earnings
Statement
L.O.1, 3–5

The following information was summarized from the adjusted trial balance of the Right Company at the end of 19xx:

	Debits	Credits
Sales.		$3,507,000
Cost of Goods Sold	$1,500,000	
Selling Expenses	185,000	
Administrative Expenses	218,000	
Other Gains and Losses		35,000
Discontinued Operations	132,000	
Extraordinary Gain		47,000
Prior Period Adjustment	13,000	
Retained Earnings (1/1/xx balance)		3,840,000
Common Stock (1/1/xx balance)		2,900,000
Dividends Declared—19xx	125,000	
Accounting Change (retroactive treatment)		22,000
Accounting Change (current treatment)	41,000	

Ignore income taxes.

Required:
1. Prepare the 19xx income statement.
2. Prepare the 19xx retained earnings statement.

P 13–8
Income Statement/
Retained Earnings
Statement
L.O.1, 3–5

The following data are from the financial statements of Curry Corporation at December 31, 19xx (its year-end):

p part of normal operations

	Debits	Credits
Gain from sale of land	$	$ 38,000
Prior period adjustment due to error	42,000	
Operating loss on discontinued operations	209,000	
Gain on sale of net assets in discontinued operations		480,000
Income from continuing operations		1,050,000
Change in accounting method	75,000	
Gain from early retirement of debt		79,000
Loss from earthquake	410,000	
Beginning retained earnings		3,565,000
Dividends declared (but unpaid)	50,000	

1/1
to income
from
previous
periods

The change in accounting method is to receive retroactive treatment. None of these data have reported the impact of taxes, which are at a 40% rate.

Required:
Using proper intraperiod tax allocation, prepare a partial income statement beginning with "Income from continuing operations before taxes," and a retained earnings statement.

P 13–9
Income and Retained Earnings Statements
L.O.4, 5

The following year-end balances were taken from the pre-closing trial balance of Trebble, Inc., on December 31, 19x9 (in thousands):

Sales.	$ 577 Cr.
Gain on retirement of debt	32 Cr.
Dividends declared	18 Dr.
Dividend and interest income	26 Cr.
Correction of prior period's error	34 Dr.
Cumulative effect of change in accounting method	12 Dr.
Selling and administrative expenses	108 Dr.
Interest expense.	16 Dr.
Loss from uninsured earthquake damages	60 Dr.
Loss on restructuring of steel operations and closing of one steel plant	14 Dr.
Cost of goods sold.	321 Dr.
Loss on sale of obsolete equipment	7 Dr.
Retained earnings (December 31, 19x8)	1,399 Cr.

The appropriate income tax rate is 30% on all items. Do **not** give answers in thousands of dollars.

Required:
Prepare income and retained earnings statements for 19x9.

P 13–10
Income Statement and Stockholders' Equity
L.O.1, 3–5

Shanklin, Inc., a multisegment San Francisco–based company, experienced the following changes during 19x1:

a. Debt due to mature in 19x2 was retired at a gain of $140,000.
b. Made a change in accounting method calling for retroactive treatment that resulted in a gain of $280,000.
c. Sold obsolete inventory at a loss of $95,500.
d. Incurred $75,000 in damages to several structures due to a minor earthquake registering 5.2 on the Richter scale.
e. Discontinued all retail operations during 19x1. These operations were sold at their market value, which exceeded book value by $650,000. The retail stores had lost $194,000 during 19x1 prior to their closing.
f. Sold securities held for the past 28 years at a gain of $1,850,000. These were the only long-term investments owned by Shanklin.

In addition to these changes, Shanklin reported the following data:

Common stock (no par) (1/1/x1).	6,800,000
Retained earnings (1/1/x1)	4,875,000
Sales	6,730,000
Cost of sales	5,295,000
Selling and administrative expenses	986,000
Interest expense	135,000
Dividends declared and paid.	247,000

In none of the amounts provided above are income taxes included, which are 40% on all items.

Required:
1. Prepare an income statement for 19x1 in good form. Include all items in their appropriate place using proper intraperiod tax allocation.
2. Prepare a retained earnings statement for 19x1.
3. Assume there were 300,000 shares of common stock outstanding during 19x1. Prepare the EPS data to accompany the income statement.

4. What were the changes (increases/decreases) in net assets during 19x1 from
   a. Operations?
   b. Earnings?
   c. All nonowner transactions?

P 13–11
Statement of Changes in Stockholders' Equity
L.O.5

Langstrom Corporation reported the following data (in thousands) at the end of 19x5:

	19x5	19x4
Stockholders' Equity		
Common stock ($2 par)	$ 8,400	$ 8,000
Capital in excess of par	21,000	19,960
Unrealized losses on long-term investments.	(189)	(214)
Retained earnings	13,105	12,732
Total stockholders' equity.	$42,316	$40,478

During 19x5 the following activities took place:

a. Issued 200,000 shares of common stock on May 1, 19x5.
b. Declared and paid cash dividends of $745,000 during 19x5.

Required:
Prepare a statement of changes in stockholders' equity for 19x5.

P 13–12
Reconciling Changes in Stockholders' Equity
L.O.5

During 19x2, the following changes occurred in the balance sheet of Kwicker, Inc.:

Kwicker, Inc.
Balance Sheet
December 31
(in millions)

	19x2	19x1
Assets		
Current assets:		
Cash	$ 2	$ 3
Other current assets	19	17
Total current assets	$21	$20
Noncurrent assets:		
Long-term depreciable assets (net)	$15	$12
Long-term investments	4	5
Total noncurrent assets	$19	$17
Total assets	$40	$37
Liabilities and Stockholders' Equity		
Liabilities:		
Current liabilities	$ 7	$ 6
Long-term liabilities	11	12
Total liabilities	$18	$18
Stockholders' equity:		
Common stock (no par)	$15	$13
Retained earnings	7	6
Total stockholders' equity	$22	$19
Total liabilities and stockholders' equity	$40	$37

During 19x2, Kwicker declared and paid cash dividends of $2 million.

Required:
1. What is the apparent change (increase/decrease) in net assets during 19x2 from nonowner-related transactions?
2. What is the apparent change during 19x2 from owner-related transactions?
3. Determine net income for 19x2.

P 13–13
Discontinued Operations
(Challenging)
L.O.4

In its 19x2 annual report, Multi Corporation disclosed the following results (in thousands):

	19x2	19x1
Sales	$1,826	$1,714
Cost of sales.	(730)	(702)
Depreciation	(112)	(105)
Administrative and other expenses	(701)	(655)
Pre-tax income.	$ 283	$ 252
Income tax expense (30%)	(85)	(76)
Net income	$ 198	$ 176

During 19x3, Multi Corporation discontinued one of its lines of business. The discontinued operation had performed poorly over the past few years with the following **separate** results (in thousands):

	19x3	19x2	19x1
Sales	$145	$ 292	$ 286
Cost of sales.	(77)	(163)	(151)
Depreciation	(13)	(21)	(22)
Administrative and other expenses	(75)	(140)	(135)
Pre-tax loss	$ (20)	$ (32)	$ (22)
Income tax credit (30%).	6	10	7
Net loss	$ (14)	$ (22)	$ (15)

The sale of the net assets of the discontinued operations in September of 19x3 resulted in a pre-tax gain of $100,000. During 19x3, Multi reported the following results (in thousands) **without** considering the discontinued operations:

	19x3
Sales	$1,986
Cost of sales	(835)
Depreciation	(107)
Administrative and other expenses	(697)
Pre-tax income	$ 347

Assume that the appropriate tax rate for all years is 30% and that all amounts are rounded to the nearest thousand.

Required:
1. Prepare the comparative income statements for Multi Corporation for 19x3, 19x2, and 19x1 as they would appear in the 19x3 year-end financial statements.
2. What was the total tax expense for Multi Corporation for the year 19x3?

P 13–14
Accounting Method
Changes (Challenging)
L.O.4

Westwick, Inc., reported the following **preliminary** results for 19x1:

Westwick, Inc.
Combined Statement of Income and Retained Earnings
For the Year Ended December 31, 19x1
(in thousands)

Sales revenues		$12,875
Less:		
Cost of sales	$6,923	
Depreciation expense	743	
Administrative and other expenses	820	8,486
Income before taxes.		$ 4,389
Income tax expense.		1,317
Net income.		$ 3,072
Beginning retained earnings		14,023
		$17,095
Less dividends		2,000
Ending retained earnings		$15,095

Assume that after examining these preliminary figures, Westwick decides to change its inventory accounting method. In computing the effects of this change, Westwick's accountant determined the following:

a. The cumulative effect on all years **prior** to 19x1 is to reduce income by $2,686,000 after considering tax credits of $1,100,000. (The before-tax reduction is $3,786,000.)
b. The effect on 19x1 results would be to increase cost of sales from $6,923,000 to $7,400,000.
c. The appropriate tax rate for 19x1 is 30%.

Required (round all amounts to the nearest thousand):
1. Assume that this accounting method change should receive current treatment (as illustrated in Exhibit 13–7). Prepare the revised 19x1 income and retained earnings statement for Westwick.
2. Assume that this accounting method change should receive retroactive treatment (as illustrated in Exhibit 13–7). Prepare the revised 19x1 income and retained earnings statement for Westwick.
3. What is the total 19x1 tax expense for Westwick from all items including the accounting method change?
4. What was the apparent 19x1 tax savings resulting from this change?

P 13–15
Accounting Method
Change and
Discontinued Operations
(Challenging)
L.O.4

During 19x1, Theta Corporation changed its method of accounting for inventory and also discontinued one of its major lines of business. The effects from these two items were

a. 19x1 cost of goods sold increased by $34 million due to the accounting method change.
b. Net income before taxes for years prior to 19x1 decreased by $127 million due to the accounting method change.
c. Operating losses before taxes in 19x1 from the discontinued operations were $50 million.
d. The net assets of the discontinued operations were sold at a pre-tax gain of $50 million.
e. In 19x1, Theta declared and paid dividends of $45 million.

The preliminary income statement results (in millions) **before** considering the accounting change and **after** eliminating the effects of the discontinued operations were

	19x1
Sales revenue	$1,029
Cost of goods sold	$ 387
Depreciation expense	93
Selling and administrative expense	176
Other expenses	38
Total expenses	$ 694
Pre-tax income from operations	$ 335

The retained earnings balance of Theta at the start of 19x1 was $795 million. The appropriate tax rate for all of Theta's transactions is assumed to be 30%.

Required (round all answers to the nearest million):
1. Assume that the accounting method change is disclosed as a current treatment type of change. Prepare Theta's income statement and retained earnings statement for 19x1.
2. Assume that the accounting method change is disclosed as a retroactive treatment type of change. Prepare Theta's income statement and retained earnings statement for 19x1.
3. What is the total tax expense of Theta for all transactions described in this problem for 19x1.

P 13–16
Special Disclosures
(Challenging)
L.O.3, 4

Fractor Corporation reported several special items in 19x2 in addition to its normal on-going operations. The ongoing operations generated the following results (in millions):

	19x2	19x1
Sales	$661	$602
Less:		
Cost of sales	$279	$263
Selling and administrative expenses	201	189
Depreciation expense	64	57
Other losses (gains)	13	(5)
Total	$557	$504
Pre-tax income from operations	$104	$ 98

In addition to these operating results, you have learned about the following items:

a. Included in other losses (gains) for 19x2 and 19x1 were the following items (in millions):

	19x2	19x1
Write-off of obsolete inventory	$15	
Uninsured fire loss		$ 5
Gain on early debt retirement		(10)
Gain on sale of used assets	(2)	
Total loss (gain)	$13	$ (5)

b. The tax rate on all items is assumed to be fixed at 30%.
c. The discontinued operations of Fractor Corporation generated the following results before taxes (in millions):

	19x2	19x1
Loss from operations	$(10)	$(20)
Gain from sale of assets	30	—
Net	$ 20	$(20)

Note that these results are **not** included in the results from ongoing operations provided above.

d. The company changed an accounting method in 19x2. The cumulative effect of this change on income of all prior years (**before** 19x2) is to increase prior years' income by $40 million **before taxes.** The effect of this accounting change on 19x2 is already included in "Pre-tax income from operations." This change is to receive current treatment disclosure in the 19x2 financial statements.

Required:

1. Prepare the comparative income statements for 19x2 and 19x1 for Fractor Corporation as they should be reported at the end of 19x2 after considering additional items *a* through *d* above. Be sure to employ proper intraperiod tax allocation.
2. Compute the total tax expense for 19x2 from all items included in the income statement in 19x2.

P 13–17
Computing EPS with Preferred Stock
L.O.6

Hay Corporation issued 600,000 shares of common stock when originally organized in 19x1. On July 15, 19x5, Hay issued 400,000 shares of preferred stock, which had no voting rights and was **not** convertible in any way. Hay reported net income during 19x6 of $7,720,000. Hay also declared and paid $1,800,000 cash dividends to common stockholders, and $880,000 cash dividends to preferred stockholders.

Required:
Compute Hay's EPS for 19x6.

P 13–18
EPS with New Shares and Preferred Stock
L.O.6

Danoff, Inc., reported net income of $1,832,000 for 19x7. The following new common stock issues occurred during 19x7:

Jan. 1 1,000,000 common shares outstanding (from prior issuances).
July 31 Issue 120,000 shares of common stock.
Sept. 30 Issue 200,000 shares of common stock.

During 19x7 Danoff declared and paid $380,000 cash dividends to preferred stockholders, and $612,000 cash dividends to common stockholders.

Required:
1. Compute the weighted average number of common shares outstanding during 19x7.
2. Compute EPS on common stock for 19x7.

P 13–19
EPS with New Shares and Preferred Stock
L.O.6

Darren Corporation reported net income for 19x8 of $1,410,000. The following new common stock issues occurred during 19x8:

January 1 450,000 common shares outstanding (from prior issuances).
May 31 Issued 60,000 shares of common stock.
July 31 Issued 90,000 shares of common stock.

During 19x8 Darren declared and paid $365,000 cash dividends to preferred stockholders, and $490,000 cash dividends to common stockholders.

Required:
1. Compute the weighted average number of common shares outstanding during 19x8.
2. Compute EPS on common stock for 19x8.
3. Assume that no new stock was issued in 19x9. Darren paid the same preferred dividends in 19x9, and reported net income of $1,500,000. Compute EPS for 19x9.

P 13–20
EPS: New Common and Preferred Issuances
L.O.6

Edge Corporation began 19x5 with 500,000 shares of common stock and 300,000 shares of preferred stock. On May 31, 19x5, Edge issued 240,000 additional shares of common stock. On June 30, 19x5, Edge issued 300,000 additional shares of preferred stock. The preferred stock pays a $0.75 per share dividend twice each year, on April 1 and October 1. Edge reported net income of $2,819,000 for 19x5. There were no new stock issues in 19x6, when Edge reported net income of $3,083,000.

Required:
Compute EPS on common stock for 19x5 and 19x6.

• CASES

C 13–1
Disclosure
L.O.3, 4

You have recently been hired as a financial advisor to a large corporation. Each of the following items has occurred during the current year. You are asked to write a memo indicating the specific financial statement, if any, in which each would appear, and briefly discuss where and how each item would appear in that statement. State any assumptions made in arriving at your decisions.

a. Loss from tornado damage.
b. Losses from sale of assets of a discontinued segment.
c. Loss on discontinuance of certain operations that are a segment of the entity.
d. Gain on sale of marketable securities properly classified as a current asset.
e. Resignation of the company's president.
f. Write-off of a material amount of intangible assets.

C 13–2
Disclosure
L.O.3, 4

You have recently been hired as a financial advisor to a large corporation. Each of the following items has occurred during the current year. You are asked to write a memo indicating the specific financial statement, if any, in which each would appear, and briefly discuss where and how each item would appear in that statement. State any assumptions made in arriving at your decisions.

a. Gain on sale of fixed assets.
b. Error in recording depreciation for the past three years.
c. Loss on early extinguishment of long-term debt.
d. Write-down of accounts receivable.
e. Change from the FIFO inventory measurement method to LIFO (a current treatment accounting change).
f. Gain on sale of intangible assets.
g. Loss due to the effects of a strike.
h. Loss on disposal of a major segment of an entity—the only segment producing furniture.

C 13–3
Disclosure Decisions
L.O.4

During your first year as staff auditor for a large local CPA firm, you encounter the following difficult situations requiring your judgment as to how they should be disclosed.

a. A company involved in the manufacture of flour had several different operations: growing wheat on company-owned land; storing wheat from its own crops and other companies' crops; milling the wheat into finished products. During the current year, all company land used for growing wheat was sold to another company, along with the equipment used for these operations.
b. During the current period, a company that had previously used the LIFO inventory method changed to FIFO to be consistent with current industry methods.
c. A local farm moved its farming operations to another location up the coast. The costs of this move were high, equal to 50% of revenues for the period. However, the move is expected to improve production for many years.
d. An earthquake damaged the structure of the Bank of Kansas City's main office in downtown Kansas City. The cost to repair the structure will be about 30% of last year's profits. This damage was unusual in that few people actually observed the quake and only a few other companies reported any damage. No one could recall a similar event ever having occurred before in Kansas.

e. During the past period, a client with many foreign operations experienced an unusually large gain from the translation of foreign currency into U.S. currency for financial reporting purposes, five times larger than the largest gain previously reported, and three times larger than all other sources of income for the period.

Required:

Write a memo to your supervisor explaining how you think each of these situations should be reported in the financial statements.

· Evaluating Financial Statements

C 13–4
Annual Report Disclosures— Ralston Purina
L.O.3, 4

Consider the annual report disclosures for Ralston Purina reported in Exhibit 13–6 of the chapter. Answer the following questions:

a. What is the before-tax amount of the "Unusual or nonrecurring items" for 19x6?
b. What is the before-tax amount of the "Gain on disposal of discontinued operations" for 19x6?
c. What is the before-tax amount of the extraordinary loss for 19x6?
d. What was the estimated total "Income taxes" (income tax expense) for Ralston Purina for 19x6 from all components of the earnings statement?
e. What did Ralston Purina probably report for 19x5 "earnings from continuing operations" in 19x5? If this differs from what is reported for 19x5 in 19x6 ($229.9), explain why.

C 13–5
Annual Report Disclosures— Union Carbide
L.O.3, 4

The following data are excerpted from the 19x5 annual report of Union Carbide Corporation (UCC) (amounts are in millions):

**Partial Income Statement
For the Year Ended December 31**

	19x5	19x4
Net sales.	$ 9,003	$9,508
Cost of sales	6,252	6,702
Research and development.	275	265
Selling, administrative, and other expenses.	1,289	1,221
Depreciation	596	507
Interest on debt	292	300
Other expenses (income)	173	(77)
Unusual charges	1,168	—
Income (loss) before income taxes	$(1,042)	$ 590
Income tax credit	441	(227)
Income (loss) of consolidated companies	$ (601)	$ 363

In the financial statement footnotes, Union Carbide disclosed the following details concerning its 19x5 "unusual charges" of $1,168,000.

Excerpt from footnotes:

The following is a summary of the items comprising the 19x5 unusual charges:

Millions of dollars	19x5
Inventory write-downs	$ 78
Fixed asset write-downs, write-offs and related items:	
Net fixed assets	615
Mine development expenses	24
Foreign currency equity adjustment	45
Write-downs of other assets and facility closing costs . . .	202
Staff reduction costs	204
	$1,168

Required:

Consider these data and answer the following questions:

1. Are the "unusual charges" the same thing as extraordinary items?
2. Do any of the unusual charges seem to be items that require separate disclosure as extraordinary items, discontinued operations, or accounting changes?
3. Are the unusual charges stated before tax?
4. What kind of a year did Union Carbide have in 19x5 excluding the unusual items?
5. What would probably happen to earnings in 19x6 and future years if the $1,168,000 in write-downs, write-offs, and so on taken in 19x5 were more than an unusual charge than was actually warranted? In other words, what effect would it have in future periods if inventory (for example) was written down by $78 million when it should have only been written down by say $30 million?

C 13–6
Annual Report Disclosures— General Electric
L.O.3, 4

The following summarized data are abstracted from a recent General Electric (GE) annual report:

**General Electric Company and Consolidated Affiliates
Statement of Earnings
For the Years Ended December 31
(in millions)**

	19x6	19x5
Revenues	$36,725	$29,252
Cost and expenses:		
Cost of goods sold and services sold	$26,187	$20,843
Selling, general, and administrative expense.	5,963	4,594
Interest and other financial charges.	625	361
Unusual items:		
(Gains) from sales of assets	(50)	(518)
Provisions for business restructuring activities	311	447
Special payment to non-exempt and hourly employees . . .		93
Total costs and expenses	$33,036	$25,820
Earnings before income taxes and minority interest.	$ 3,689	$ 3,432
Provision for income taxes.	(1,200)	(1,143)
Minority interest in earnings of consolidated affiliates	3	(12)
Net earnings	$ 2,492	$ 2,277
Net earnings per share (in dollars)	$ 5.46	$ 5.00

In addition, GE reported the following data in its financial statement footnotes:

Excerpt from footnotes:

Regarding Accounting Change

Restatement of prior years' financial statements for the change in method of accounting for oil and gas properties. In 19x6, the Company changed its method of accounting for oil and gas properties from the "full cost" method to the "successful efforts" method.... This change in method must be applied retroactively. Accordingly, previously reported net earnings have been restated downward by $233 million.

Unusual items

Unusual items include pretax gains from certain asset sales and pretax expense provisions for costs of several different types of transactions. Gains from sales of assets which management has determined are not complementary to the Company's future business focus were $50 million in 19x6, and $518 million in 19x5. Total unusual expenses aggregated $311 million in 19x6, and $540 million in 19x5. Details of these unusual gains and expenses follow.

Unusual gains in 19x6 arose from the sale of a small foreign affiliate ($12 million) and adjustments to previous unusual disposition provisions ($38 million).

Unusual costs in 19x6 include the following:
Expense provisions to cover corporate restructuring were $311 million in 19x6. These represent the provisions for expenses of refocusing a wide variety of business and marketing activities and reducing foreign and domestic risk exposures. These provisions include costs of rationalizing and improving a large number of production facilities, rearranging production activities among a number of existing plants, and reorganizing, phasing out or otherwise concluding other activities no longer considered essential to the conduct of the Company's business.

Required:
1. Which type of treatment did GE give its accounting method change, current or retroactive?
2. Where else will the $233 prior years' impact of the change from the full cost method to the successful efforts method be disclosed in GE's financial statements (besides the footnote)?
3. Was the sale of GE's foreign affiliate, reported in the "Unusual items" footnote, a discontinued operation? Explain why you believe it was or was not.
4. Are any of the $311 million costs of restructurings discontinued operation costs? Explain why you believe they are or are not.

C 13–7
Changes in Estimates—
General Motors
(Challenging)
L.O.2

General Motors (GM) has reported a positive trend in earnings on its ($1-2/3 per share par value) common stock. In the past three years, EPS on this stock has been

	1988	1987	1986
EPS on $1-2/3 par value common	$7.17	$5.03	$4.11

Included in GM's 1988 annual report was the following footnote regarding depreciation and amortization of assets.

Depreciation and Amortization
Depreciation is provided based on estimated useful lives of groups of property generally using accelerated methods, which accumulate depreciation of approximately two-thirds of the depreciable cost during the first half of the estimated useful lives.

Expenditures for special tools are amortized over their estimated useful lives. Amortization is applied directly to the asset account. Replacement of special tools for reasons other than changes in products is charged directly to cost of sales.

GMAC provides for depreciation of automobiles and other equipment on operating leases or in company use generally on a straight-line basis.

In the first quarter of 1987, GMAC revised the rates of depreciation for automobiles on operating leases to retail customers to give effect to current experience with respect to the residual values of leased vehicles. These revisions had the effect of increasing GMAC's 1987 net income by $254.7 million, or $0.41 per share of $1-2/3 par value common stock (post-split).

In the third quarter of 1987, the Corporation revised the estimated service lives of its plants and equipment and special tools retroactive to January 1, 1987. These revisions, which were based on

1987 studies of actual useful lives and periods of use, recognized current estimates of service lives of the assets and had the effect of reducing 1987 depreciation and amortization charges by $1,236.6 million or $1.28 per share of $1-2/3 par value common stock (post-split).

Required:

1. Assume that GM made the changes in estimates for assets under "operating leases to retail customers" and "plants and equipment and special tools" for both book and tax (IRS) reporting purposes. Further assume the effective tax rate for GM was 30% in each year. Provide the impact on both *depreciation expense* and *net income* for each change in estimate separately in the schedule below. (Give dollars in millions.)

	1987	
	From Change in Estimate for Operating Leases	**From Change in Estimate for Plants and Equipment and Special Tools**
Effect on depreciation expense (+ or −)	$	$
Effect on net income (+ or −)	$	$

2. Compute the amount of EPS on ($1-2/3 par) common stock that would have been reported in 1987 if these two changes in estimates had not occurred.

3. GM says it "revised the estimated service lives of its plants and equipment and special tools retroactive to January 1, 1987." This retroactive change was made even though it was not decided to change the estimated lives of these assets until the third quarter! Did GM follow GAAP here?

4. Was the change in estimates pertaining to operating leases made *during* the first quarter of 1987 also applied retroactive to January 1, 1987?

Reilly Corporation
Income Statement
For 1994

	1994	1993
Revenues:		
Total revenues	$ xxx	$ xxx
Expenses:		
Total Expenses.	xxx	xxx

Reilly Corporation
Balance Sheet
12/31/94

	1994	1993
Current assets:		
Total current assets.	$ xxx	$ xxx
Noncurrent assets:		
Total noncurrent assets	xxx	xxx
Current liabilities:		
Total current liabilities.	xxx	xxx
Noncurrent liabilities:		
Total noncurrent liabilities	xxx	xxx
Stockholders' equity:		
Total stockholders' equity	xxx	xxx

Reilly Corporation
Statement of Cash Flows
For the Year Ended December 31, 1994
(in $000)

	1994	1993
Cash flows from operating activities:		
Cash received from customers.	**$ x,xxx**	
Cash paid to suppliers of inventory.	**(x,xxx)**	
Cash paid to workers	**(x,xxx)**	
Cash paid to income taxes.	**(x,xxx)**	
Cash paid for interest	**(xxx)**	
Net cash provided by operating activities		**$ xxx**
Cash flows from investing activities:		
Cash paid for purchase of building	**$(x,xxx)**	
Cash paid for purchase of securities	**(xxx)**	
Cash received from disposal of land	**xxx**	
Cash received from disposal of securities	**xxx**	
Net cash used by investing activities.		**$(x,xxx)**
Cash flows from financing activities:		
Cash received from issuing stock	**$ x,xxx**	
Cash paid for dividends	**(xxx)**	
Net cash provided by financing activities.		**x,xxx**
Net increase (decrease) in cash		**$ (xxx)**

FINANCIAL
STATEMENT
COMPONENTS
EMPHASIZED IN
CHAPTER 14

14

Statement of Cash Flows

An auditor is continually confronted with temptation. We want our clients to succeed. We want them to like us, to retain us as auditors and refer us to others. Such temptation challenges our integrity and our obligations to conscientiously serve the interests of the public. Our own morality and the very future of the public accounting profession require that we resist such temptation.

Edward M. Parks
Plante & Moran

· Learning Objectives

After studying Chapter 14, you should understand

1. Why information on operating, financing, and investing cash flows is important to decision makers, p. 720.
2. The format of the statement of cash flows, pp. 720–22.
3. How to analyze the operating, investing, and financing transactions of a company and prepare its statement of cash flows, pp. 726–27.
4. The relationship of balance sheets, income statements, and cash flow statements, pp. 728–33.
5. The effect of noncash transactions on the statement of cash flows, pp. 733–34.
6. The difference between preparing a statement of cash flows with the direct and indirect methods, pp. 734–36.
7. The use of cash flow information in evaluating the performance and prospects of a business, pp. 736–38.
8. The use of a worksheet in preparing a statement of cash flows (Appendix), pp. 743–45.

Objective 1
Why information on operating, financing, and investing cash flows is important to decision makers.

Although the balance sheet, income statement, and statement of retained earnings provide decision makers with useful information, some decisions require information not found in these statements or their accompanying notes. For instance: How much cash did the company's operating activities provide? How much cash did the company use to purchase plant and equipment? How much cash did the company generate from the sale of securities? The answers to such questions are important in appraising a business's viability. The income statement is based on accrual concepts that do not necessarily hinge on whether or not revenues have generated cash or whether or not expenses have consumed cash during a period. The statement of cash flows (SCF), on the other hand, analyzes the effects of cash flow transactions and communicates this information to decision makers.

Although the SCF gives details as to the inflows and outflows of cash in the period just ended and is not a projection of future cash flows, decision makers do use the SCF as a basis for future projections. In order to plan the financing of operations, the paying of obligations, and the providing of adequate returns to investors, managers must project and budget cash flows. Present and potential owners of stock need information on the probable future dividends and the ability of the company to grow through cash reinvestment in operations. In general, a need exists for all types of decision makers to have information about a business's inflows and outflows of cash related to operations, issuance of debt, issuance of stock, investments in assets, dividends, and other types of business transactions.

Chapter 7 introduced you to the accounting definition of cash, defined as money that a business actually has on hand and money that a business has a right and easy access to, such as money orders, checks, and balances in checking accounts. In this chapter we use the term "cash" to mean "cash" plus cash equivalents which are defined as short-term, highly liquid investments such as money market funds, U.S. Treasury bills, and commercial paper. Generally accepted accounting principles (GAAP) exclude equity securities (i.e., investments in the stock of other companies) from the definition of cash equivalent.[1] The SCF explains the change in the sum of cash and cash equivalents by summarizing all of the operating, investing and financing activities that have affected cash plus cash equivalents.

This chapter begins with a study of the format of the SCF. The elements in the SCF will be familiar to you, because they were introduced in Chapters 1 and 2 and because throughout the text we have stressed the three major classes of transactions, operating, investing, and financing. The remainder of the chapter illustrates the analysis of transactions needed to prepare the SCF and emphasizes the relationship of cash flow and accrual-based income statement items.

FORMAT OF THE STATEMENT OF CASH FLOWS

The SCF summarizes the following three major groups of activities affecting cash:

1. Operating activities.
2. Investing activities.
3. Financing activities.

Objective 2
The format of the statement of cash flows.

Each group of activities can result in inflows and outflows of cash, and the SCF is, in essence, a listing of all such flows of cash classified under the three groups of activities.

Exhibit 14–1 illustrates a general format of SCFs and gives some examples of the categories often found in published statements. Note that cash flows can be positive or negative. Each type of transaction listed in the SCF reflects an increase or a decrease of cash. Visualize the typical journal entry related to each type of transaction. Cash received from customers results in debits to Cash. The outflow of cash paid to suppliers results in a

---

[1]*Financial Accounting Standards Board Statement No. 95,* "Statement of Cash Flows" (Norwalk, Conn.: FASB, November 1987).

EXHIBIT 14–1

General Format of
Statement of Cash
Flows—Direct Method

**Corporate Name
Statement of Cash Flows
For the Year Ended (Fiscal Year-End)**

	Increase (decrease)
Cash flows from operating activities:	
Cash received from customers	$ xxx
Cash paid to suppliers of inventory	(xxx)
Cash paid to workers	(xxx)
Cash paid for income taxes.	(xxx)
Cash paid for interest	(xxx)
Net cash flow provided by operating activities	$ xxx
Cash flows from investing activities:	
Cash paid for purchases of land. . . . . $(xx)	
Cash received from sales of investments xx	
Net cash used by investing activities.	(xx)
Cash flows from financing activities:	
Cash received from sale of stock . . . . $ xx	
Cash paid for dividends . . . . (xx)	
Net cash provided by financing activities	xx
Net increase (decrease) in cash	$ xx

credit to Cash, and the parentheses around a figure indicate a negative flow of cash. The format in Exhibit 14–1 is called the *direct method* format because, in the operations section, it lists the amounts received from customers and others and the amounts paid to suppliers and others. An alternative format, introduced later in this chapter, is called the *indirect method* format because it starts with net income and adds and subtracts reconciling items to derive "Net Cash Flow Provided by Operating Activities." Note that the specific items shown in Exhibit 14–1 are examples and are not intended to be comprehensive.

Operating Activities

A common long-term and ongoing goal of businesses is to make profits by providing goods and services to customers. As you recall, the activities necessary to provide goods and services are called operating activities.

Cash provided by operations includes the cash effects of most of the transactions that help determine income. Receipts from customers, payments to suppliers, payments for taxes, and payments for wages are all examples of cash flows related to operations that would be reported in the SCF as operating activities. Payments of interest on loans and receipt of interest and dividends are also considered operating activities. But some income statement transactions are not classified as operating. For instance, sale of a machine at a gain or loss affects net income, but the cash is shown as an investing activity.

Investing Activities

Businesses must put resources to use in order to earn a return for investors. Investing in productive assets, such as plant, equipment, land, and other long-term items, is an important management task. Utilizing idle cash by making loans to others and acquiring securities can be very important in a company's overall profitability, and these also are classified as investing activities.

The statement of cash flows shows the cash results of all investing activities including cash paid for long-term assets, cash received on the disposition of such assets, and cash paid and received for the principal amount of loans made to others. Therefore, the word *investing* is used in a broad way, including the acquisition of long-term assets, as well as the acquisition of securities and the making of loans.

An example of a transaction that might cause confusion is that of a building constructed to be sold but which is rented to another entity for a period before the sale. Production and sale indicate an operating transaction, but holding an asset to generate rent revenue indicates that the asset is an investment. In a case where the most important element is the sale, all cash flows related to the item would be classified as operating. If, in this example, it is determined that the building is going to continue to be rented and not sold, the cash flows related to its acquisition or construction would be classified as investing.

Financing Activities

Before a business can operate or invest, it must obtain financing by means of receipts of cash and perhaps other assets from owners for shares of stock or from borrowing from bondholders and other creditors such as banks. These activities are called financing activities; they are presented in the financing section of the SCF, which shows certain cash flows related to owners and creditors. Many types of financing transactions can occur, including cash inflows from sales of the company's own stocks and bonds and from borrowings and cash outflows such as the repayment of loans, redemption of stock, payment of dividends, and retirement of stock.

Some ambiguities can exist in classifying certain transactions. For example, borrowing activities are considered financing transactions, but the purchase of supplies on credit is an operating transaction. The operating classification also applies to other short-term liability transactions such as those involving salaries payable, taxes payable, and many other payables related to operations.

Exhibit 14–2 gives several examples of how specific transactions are classified on SCFs.

EXHIBIT 14–2

Example of Cash Flow Transactions

Operating Inflows	Operating Outflows
Receipts from customers.	Payments to employees, suppliers, and governments.
Receipts of interest and dividends.	Payments of interest.
Other receipts, such as insurance proceeds, refunds from suppliers, tax refunds, and many others.	Other payments, such as payments for lawsuits, refunds to customers, and many others.

Investing Inflows	Investing Outflows
Receipts from sales of long-term assets, such as property, plant, and equipment, and from sale of investments in equity and debt securities other than cash equivalents.	Payments for long-term assets, such as property, plant, and equipment, and equity and debt securities other than cash equivalents.
Receipts from debtors for the principal amount of loans.	Payments to debtors for principal amounts of loans.
Receipts from selling notes receivables.	

Financing Inflows	Financing Outflows
Receipts from issuance of stock, bonds, and notes.	Payments to stockholders for dividends, retirement of stock, purchase of treasury stock.
Receipts from creditors for the principal amount of loans.	Payments to creditors for the principal amount of loans.

Understanding the
Basics of Cash Flows

In this section we show, by means of a very simple example, the basic relationships between the beginning and ending balance sheets, the income statement, and the statement of cash flows. Later in this chapter we cover a more realistic setting. Consider the following items for Bare Bones, Inc., for the current operating period:

Bare Bones, Inc.
Comparative Balance Sheets
(In thousands)

	Beginning Balance	Ending Balance	Change
Cash.	$10	$17	+$ 7
Land.	0	12	+ 12
Total assets.	$10	$29	+$19
Liabilities	$ 3	$10	+$ 7
Common stock	5	11	+ 6
Retained earnings	2	8	+ 6
Total liabilities and stockholders' equity.	$10	$29	+$19

Transactions (in thousands):

Sales (all cash)	$100
Expenses (all cash)	90
Sale of stock for cash	6
Borrowing of cash from bank	7
Payment of dividends	4
Purchase of land for cash	12

Before we construct a statement of cash flows for Bare Bones, Inc., it is valuable to understand the relationship of change in cash to the change in all other balance sheet accounts.

Recall the basic balance sheet relationship:

$$\text{Assets} = \text{Liabilities} + \text{Stockholders' Equity}$$

Bare Bones, Inc., has the following specific accounts:

$$\text{Cash} + \text{Land} = \text{Liabilities} + \text{Common Stock} + \text{Retained Earnings}$$

An algebraically equivalent equation shows that the cash balance on the previous page is a function of all other balance sheet accounts:

$$\text{Cash} = -\text{Land} + \text{Liabilities} + \text{Common Stock} + \text{Retained Earnings}$$

Further algebraic manipulation tells us that the change (designated Δ) in cash for a period equals the change in all other accounts (in thousands):

$$\Delta\text{Cash} = -\Delta\text{Land} + \Delta\text{Liabilities} + \Delta\text{Common Stock} + \Delta\text{Retained Earnings}$$

$$\$7 \quad = \quad -\$12 \quad + \quad \$7 \quad + \quad \$6 \quad + \quad \$6$$

$$\$7 \quad = \quad \$7$$

Exhibit 14–3 shows how the transactions of Bare Bones, Inc., this period resulted in the positive change in cash of $7,000.

The statement of cash flows describes how operating, investing, and financing transactions changed cash during an accounting period. In the case of Bare Bones, Inc.,

EXHIBIT 14–3

Effects of Bare Bones's Transactions on Cash and Other Accounts (in thousands)

Transactions	Cash	Land	Liabilities	Common Stock	Retained Earnings
Sales	$100				$100
Expenses	(90)				(90)
Sale of common stock	6			$6	
Borrowing of cash	7		$7		
Payment of dividends	(4)				(4)
Purchase of land	(12)	$12	—	—	——
Net change	$ 7 =	−$12 +	$7 +	$6 +	$ 6

EXHIBIT 14–4

Statement of Cash Flows

Bare Bones, Inc.
Statement of Cash Flows
For the Year Ended (fiscal year-end)
(in thousands)

	Increase (decrease)
Cash flows from operating activities:	
Cash received from customers.	$100
Cash paid for expenses.	(90)
Net cash flow provided by operating activities	$ 10
Cash flows from investing activities:	
Cash paid for purchase of land	$ (12)
Net cash used by investing activities	$ (12)
Cash flows from financing activities:	
Cash received from sale of stock.	$ 6
Cash received from borrowing	7
Cash paid for dividends	(4)
Net cash provided by financing activities	$ 9
Net change in cash.	$ 7

categorization of transactions is simple. Note that the numbers in parentheses are negative cash flows (in thousands).

Change in Cash	=	Change in Cash from Operating Transactions	+	Change in Cash from Investing Transactions	+	Change in Cash from Financing Transactions
		Cash from customers $100		Cash paid for purchase of land $(12)		Cash from common stock $6
		Cash paid for expenses (90)				Cash from loan 7
						Cash paid for dividends (4)
$7	=	$ 10	+	$(12)	+	$9

Exhibit 14–4 shows how the various categories of transactions are arranged into a formal statement of cash flows.

In the next section we cover a more complex and complete set of transactions. When necessary, the student should refer back to the Bare Bones example as a general guide.

PREPARING A STATEMENT OF CASH FLOWS	Julie Perez, president of DataCo, Inc., a distributor of computer software, has a problem. It is January 4, 19x3, and although her company has just completed its best year in terms of sales and net income, she is very concerned about liquidity, especially since she has an opportunity to expand into a new region if she moves fast. Her company needs a $2 million, six-month loan, but her banker, Ted Grimley (who has just reviewed the 19x2 income statement and the comparative 19x1 and 19x2 balance sheets shown in Exhibits 14–5 and 14–6) is not impressed with the company's cash-generating ability.
"What Happened to Your Cash?"	

Banker: Julie, what happened to your cash? You started the year with $248,000 and now there's only $34,000. Your income was good, and you even issued stock during the year. Where's your cash flow statement?

Ms. Perez: Listen, Ted, my controller is working on that now. I was in a hurry to talk to you and get the ball rolling on this loan. I'll get it to you as soon as possible. He worked up these preliminary statements for our meeting. I have got to move fast. Is there anything in particular you want more detail on now?

Banker: Let's wait until I have a chance to review the cash flow statement. It will break out the cash flows from operations, financing, and investing activities. As soon as possible of course, we'll need formal statements audited by your CPAs. First things first. The cash flow statement should answer most of my questions.

The banker then gave Ms. Perez a list of other statements that would have to be worked up in addition to complete financial statements, such as projections of cash flows for one year ahead and a detailed statement of what the money would be used for and how it would be repaid. Put yourself in the banker's place. Cash has plummeted by $214,000 even though net income was $2,268,000. Such a discrepancy strikes fear in the heart of a prudent lender. At the end of the chapter we will return to Ms. Perez and her banker, but first we must explore the concepts and methods that underlie DataCo's statement of cash flow. In the sections that follow we will see how a thorough understanding of the cash and accrual effects of each transaction is the key to understanding a cash flow statement.

You can determine the net change in DataCo's cash by computing the difference between the 19x1 cash balance and the 19x2 cash balance shown in DataCo's comparative balance sheets of Exhibit 14–5. DataCo had a net outflow or decrease of $214,000, which is the difference between the $248,000 beginning balance and the $34,000 ending balance. The comparative balance sheets also show the net change in all noncash accounts, but they do not provide an analysis of the operating, investing, and financing cash flow transactions.

Cash flow from operations cannot be determined directly from the income statement because its revenues and expenses are based on accrual accounting, which allows recognition of revenues and expenses regardless of the actual cash effects in the current period. Many transactions other than revenues and expenses affect cash, and the SCF focuses directly on the cash effects of all transactions.

The following section demonstrates how to analyze the operating, investing, and financing transactions of a company. Three additional topics are discussed based on the DataCo example—interest paid and received, noncash transactions, and the indirect method of SCF preparation.

Analysis of Operating Transactions	A very important operating transaction is the receipt of cash from customers, and, in the case of a merchandising concern such as DataCo, the payment of cash to suppliers is

EXHIBIT 14–5

DataCo's Comparative
Balance Sheet

**DataCo, Inc.
Comparative Balance Sheets
(in thousands)**

	December 31	
	19x2	19x1
Assets		
Current assets:		
Cash	$ 34	$ 248
Accounts receivable	2,685	965
Inventory	1,750	1,015
Prepaid insurance	6	12
Marketable securities	250	—
Total current assets.	$4,725	$2,240
Noncurrent assets:		
Land	$ 800	$1,100
Building	4,800	2,700
Accumulated depreciation—building	(1,120)	(850)
Total noncurrent assets	$4,480	$2,950
Total assets	$9,205	$5,190
Liabilities and Stockholders' Equity		
Current liabilities:		
Accounts payable	$ 75	$ 200
Notes payable	460	360
Salaries payable	130	150
Income taxes payable.	168	40
Total current liabilities.	$ 833	$ 750
Noncurrent liabilities:		
Bonds payable	2,200	2,200
Total liabilities	$3,033	$2,950
Stockholders' equity:		
Common stock	$3,664	$1,500
Retained earnings	2,508	740
Total stockholders' equity	$6,172	$2,240
Total liabilities and stockholders' equity	$9,205	$5,190

Objective 3
How to analyze the
operating, investing, and
financing transactions of a
company and prepare its
statement of cash flows.

an operating transaction. We will see that DataCo also made payments of cash for salaries, taxes, and interest, all of which are operating activities.

Cash Received from Customers.   How much cash did DataCo generate from customers during the period? As you have learned, sales to customers in a period are usually not the same as the cash received from customers in the same period because of changes in the balance of the Accounts Receivable account. During 19x2, DataCo had sales on account of $10,870,000 but collected only $9,150,000 cash from customers. Consider the follow-

EXHIBIT 14–6

**DataCo's Income
Statement**

**DataCo, Inc.
Income Statement
For the Year Ended December 31, 19x2
(in thousands)**

Sales		$10,870
Cost of goods sold		5,300
Gross margin		$ 5,570
Expenses:		
Administrative expense	$640	
Marketing expense	660	
Interest expense	220	
Depreciation expense	270	
Total		1,790
Net income before taxes		$ 3,780
Income tax expense		1,512
Net income		$ 2,268

ing journal entries relating to customers during 19x2, and the effect the transactions had on DataCo's cash flow:

Summary Entries		Cash Flow Effect
Accounts Receivable (A)	10,870,000	None
Sales (R)	10,870,000	
Cash (A)	**9,150,000**	**+$9,150,000**
Accounts Receivable (A)	9,150,000	

Recall that **summary entries** like those above indicate that the one entry shown represents the sum of the many entries of its kind actually recorded during the period. Obviously, DataCo had more than one sales transaction during 19x2, but for convenience, we show one summary entry. To follow the relationship of sales and receivables to cash, consider the following T accounts.

Sales

Credit sales	10,870,000

Accounts Receivable

Bal.	965,000	Cash	
Credit sales	10,870,000	collections	9,150,000
Bal.	2,685,000		

Cash

Bal.	248,000		xxx
	xxx		xxx
Receipt of			xxx
cash from			xxx
credit			
customers	9,150,000		
Bal.	34,000		

Objective 4
The relationship of
balance sheets, income
statements, and cash flow
statements.

DataCo's SCF will show the $9,150,000 inflow of cash from customers in the "operating activities" section along with the other operating effects to be discussed below. Exhibit 14–7 shows where the cash flow of $9,150,000 appears on the SCF. As we follow through and develop DataCo's SCF, each new cash flow item will be highlighted until the complete SCF has been prepared. Also note in Exhibit 14–7 that DataCo's net decrease in cash is shown in the last line of its SCF.

Cash Paid to Suppliers.　The "cost of goods sold" item in DataCo's income statement is not the amount of cash flow to suppliers because DataCo purchases its merchandise on credit, and during 19x2, DataCo increased its inventory level by purchasing more than it consumed. Merchandise of $6,035,000 was purchased, but inventory costing only $5,300,000 was sold to customers. Using an analysis of the relevant accounts we can determine that cash payments to suppliers amounted to $6,160,000. The transactions related to inventory and their cash flow effects can be summarized as follows:

Summary Entries			Cash Flow Effect
Inventory (A)	6,035,000		None
Accounts Payable (L)		6,035,000	
Accounts Payable (L)	6,160,000		
Cash (A)		**6,160,000**	**−$6,160,000**
Cost of Goods Sold (E)	5,300,000		None
Inventory (A)		5,300,000	

EXHIBIT 14–7

**Statement of Cash
Flows: Cash Received
from Customers
Highlighted**

**DataCo, Inc.
Partial Statement of Cash Flows
For the Year Ended December 31, 19x2
(in thousands)**

Cash flows from operating activities:		
Cash received from customers	**$9,150**	
Cash paid to suppliers of inventory	(xx)	
Cash paid to workers	(xx)	
Cash paid for income taxes	(xx)	
Cash paid for interest	(xx)	
Net cash provided by operating activities		$ xx
Cash flows from investing activities:		
Cash paid for purchase of building	$ (xx)	
Cash paid for purchase of securities	(xx)	
Cash received from disposal of land	xx	
Cash received from disposal of securities	xx	
Net cash used by investing activities		xx
Cash flows from financing activities:		
Cash received from sale of stock	$ xx	
Cash paid for dividends	(xx)	
Net cash provided by financing activities		xx
Net increase (decrease) in cash		$(214)

The entry to record the purchase of inventory does not reduce cash, and likewise the entry to record the cost of goods sold has no cash effect. Only the payments to suppliers change the cash balance. As you can see, DataCo's cash is decreased by $6,160,000 through payments to suppliers, but its income statement shows an expense of only $5,300,000 for the cost of merchandise actually sold during the period.

Cash Paid for Salaries, Income Taxes, and Interest. DataCo incurred several other expenses during 19x2, but not all had cash flow effects. The following administrative and marketing expenses totaling $1,300,000 are composed of amounts for salaries and insurance:

Summary Entries		Cash Flow Effect
Administrative Expense (E).	640,000	
Marketing Expense (E).	660,000	
Salaries Payable (L)	1,294,000	None
Prepaid Insurance (A)	6,000	
Salaries Payable (L)	1,314,000	
Cash (A)	**1,314,000**	**−$1,314,000**

Cash of $1,314,000 was paid to workers, but only $1,294,000 was charged to expense for the current year. Salaries Payable was reduced by $20,000 during the year because more cash was paid out than was expensed. Refer to the balance sheet in Exhibit 14–5 to confirm that Salaries Payable was reduced by $20,000. Although $6,000 in insurance premiums was expensed in 19x2, no cash was paid for insurance during that year. Insurance premiums were actually paid in the previous year (19x1), and the beginning balance of the asset Prepaid Insurance is being amortized.

Income taxes of $1,384,000 were paid during 19x2, but $1,512,000 was expensed. The difference of $128,000 is the increase in the amount of Income Taxes Payable on the balance sheet during the year.

Summary Entries		Cash Flow Effect
Income Tax Expense (E)	1,512,000	
Income Taxes Payable (L)	1,512,000	None
Income Taxes Payable (L)	1,384,000	
Cash (A)	**1,384,000**	**−$1,384,000**

Interest expense was paid in full to creditors with no amount still outstanding at December 31, 19x2.

Summary Entry		Cash Flow Effect
Interest Expense (E)	220,000	
Cash (A)	**220,000**	**−$220,000**

We can now complete the "operating activities" section of the SCF by putting together all of the cash flow effects from the preceding analysis. As can be seen in Exhibit 14–8, a net of $72,000 cash was provided by operating activities.

EXHIBIT 14–8

Partial Statement of
Cash Flows: Operating
Cash Payments
Highlighted

DataCo, Inc.
Partial Statement of Cash Flows
For the Year Ended December 31, 19x2
(in thousands)

Cash flows from operating activities:

Cash received from customers	$ 9,150	
Cash paid to suppliers of inventory.	**(6,160)**	
Cash paid to workers	**(1,314)**	
Cash paid for income taxes	**(1,384)**	
Cash paid for interest	**(220)**	
Net cash provided by operating activities		**$ 72**

Cash flows from investing activities:

Cash paid for purchase of building	$ (xx)	
Cash paid for purchase of securities	(xx)	
Cash received from disposal of land	xx	
Cash received from disposal of securities	xx	
Net cash used by investing activities		xx

Cash flows from financing activities:

Cash received from sale of stock.	$ xx	
Cash paid for dividends	(xx)	
Net cash provided by financing activities		xx
Net increase (decrease) in cash		$(214)

It is important to compare the net income figure of $2,268,000 with the $72,000 net cash provided by operating activities. Later in the chapter, we will analyze all the differences between net cash provided by operations and the accrual-based income statement amounts. For now, it is sufficient to say that net income is designed to communicate the economic effect of operations, including transactions that do not affect cash such as depreciation, credit sales, and the consumption or sale of inventory. By contrast, cash from operations is exclusively cash flows from operating transactions.

Analysis of Investing
Transactions

Although profits from operations may be the ultimate goal of a business, profits come only after resources are invested in productive assets and projects. Investing transactions involve the dedication of resources to particular return-generating tasks. For instance, the purchase of a factory building for cash is an investing transaction because the building is used to generate profits. Thus, the acquisition of any long-term productive asset is classified as an investing transaction. Also, the sale of such assets often generates cash flows, which are classified as investing transactions.

In addition to the acquisition and sale of long-term productive assets, businesses are involved in other investing transactions. Often businesses purchase securities of other businesses and governments. Businesses also make loans to other entities. Cash flows out when investments are purchased and when loans are made, and cash flows in when investments are sold and when debtors pay back their loans. All cash effects of investing transactions are summarized in the SCF.

Cash Paid for Purchase of Building and Securities. DataCo purchased a building by means of a $1,640,000 cash payment and the issuance of a $460,000 note. The journal entry and cash flow effect of this transaction follow:

Summary Entry		Cash Flow Effect
Buildings (A)	2,100,000	
Cash (A).	1,640,000	−$1,640,000
Notes Payable (L)	460,000	

The entire $2,100,000 is the cost of the buildings, but the cash outflow is only $1,640,000.

DataCo also used cash to acquire securities that will be held as long-term investments:

Summary Entry		Cash Flow Effect
Marketable Securities (A).	600,000	
Cash (A)	600,000	−$600,000

Both the building and securities acquisitions are classified in the SCF as investing activities. Note that if the securities in question were considered cash equivalents (see page 720), then the effect of the transaction would not be shown on the SCF as an investing activity that used cash. Here we are explicitly assuming that the asset Marketable Securities is not a cash equivalent.

Cash Received from the Disposal of Land and Securities. Companies can sell assets such as land, buildings, equipment, and securities to generate positive cash flows. In 19x1, DataCo had two such classes of transactions, the sale of land for $300,000 cash and the sale of some of its investment in marketable securities for $350,000. In both transactions, the amount received equaled the book value of the asset, so no gains or losses were recorded. The journal entries and cash flow effect of these transactions are as follows:

Summary Entries			Cash Flow Effect
Cash (A)	300,000		+$300,000
Land (A)		300,000	
Cash (A)	350,000		+$350,000
Marketable Securities (A).		350,000	

We can now complete the "Cash flows from investing activities" section of DataCo's SCF. This is shown in Exhibit 14–9.

Analysis of Financing Transactions

Businesses must accumulate the necessary funds to carry out operating and investing activities. As you learned in previous chapters, the corporate form of business has many advantages in attracting financing from a wide variety of sources such as common stockholders, preferred stockholders, bondholders, and financial institutions. To obtain funds, businesses must demonstrate that the suppliers of capital have a high probability of earning an adequate return on their money—a return in the form of interest payments and principal payments for creditors and dividend payments and/or appreciation of stock prices for equity holders. The financing section of the SCF helps in making such judgments.

EXHIBIT 14–9

Partial Statement of
Cash Flows: Investing
Activities Highlighted

DataCo, Inc.
Partial Statement of Cash Flows
For the Year Ended December 31, 19x2
(in thousands)

Cash flows from operating activities:		
Cash received from customers	$ 9,150	
Cash paid to suppliers of inventory	(6,160)	
Cash paid to workers	(1,314)	
Cash paid for income taxes	(1,384)	
Cash paid for interest	(220)	
Net cash provided by operating activities		$ 72
Cash flows from investing activities:		
Cash paid for purchase of building	**$(1,640)**	
Cash paid for purchase of securities	**(600)**	
Cash received from disposal of land	**300**	
Cash received from disposal of securities	**350**	
Net cash used by investing activities.		**(1,590)**
Cash flows from financing activities:		
Cash received from sale of stock.	$ xx	
Cash paid for dividends	(xx)	
Net cash provided by financing activities		xx
Net increase (decrease) in cash		$ (214)

Cash Received from the Issuance of Stock.   During 19x2, DataCo sold stock that generated $1,804,000 in positive cash flow, as shown in the following summary entry and cash flow effect:

Summary Entry		Cash Flow Effect
Cash (A)	**1,804,000**	**+$1,804,000**
Common Stock (SE).	1,804,000	

A company could have transactions where the issuance of stock would not result in positive cash flow, such as when stock is issued to pay off a liability or in exchange for assets such as land and buildings. These may be significant events even though no cash changes hands. Later in the chapter you will see how accountants report such noncash transactions along with the SCF.

Dividends Paid.   Financing activities such as the issuance of stocks are usually expected to be followed after a period of profitable operations by dividend payments to stockholders. DataCo declared and paid $500,000 in dividends, which had the following cash flow effect:

Summary Entries			Cash Flow Effect
Retained Earnings (SE)	500,000		
Dividends Payable (L)		500,000	None
Dividends Payable (L)	500,000		
Cash (A)		**500,000**	**−$500,000**

EXHIBIT 14–10

Completed Statement of
Cash Flows: Financing
Activities Highlighted

DataCo, Inc.
Statement of Cash Flows
For the Year Ended December 31, 19x2
(in thousands)

Cash flows from operating activities:		
Cash received from customers	$ 9,150	
Cash paid to suppliers of inventory	(6,160)	
Cash paid to workers	(1,314)	
Cash paid for income taxes	(1,384)	
Cash paid for interest	(220)	
Net cash provided by operating activities		$ 72
Cash flows from investing activities:		
Cash paid for purchase of building	$(1,640)	
Cash paid for purchase of securities	(600)	
Cash received from disposal of land	300	
Cash received from disposal of securities	350	
Net cash used by investing activities		(1,590)
Cash flows from financing activities:		
Cash received from issuing stock	**$ 1,804**	
Cash paid for dividends	**(500)**	
Net cash provided by financing activities		**1,304**
Net increase (decrease) in cash		$ (214)

Often dividends are declared and unpaid at period-end. Remember that the declaration of dividends does not affect cash flow; instead, a credit is made to Dividends Payable. When the company actually pays the dividends to stockholders, cash is of course reduced by the payment amount.

Now that we have analyzed the cash flow effects of all of DataCo's operating, investing, and financing activities, the DataCo SCF is complete, as shown in Exhibit 14–10. The year resulted in a negative cash flow of $214,000—the amount of the change in cash that was determined from DataCo's balance sheet shown in Exhibit 14–5.

Interest Paid
and Received

Note that DataCo shows interest payments as an operating item. This is consistent with current accounting practice. Although a case could be made for classifying interest payments as the result of financing activities and interest received as the result of investing activities, accountants include interest in the operating section of the SCF because accounting policy makers (the FASB) want the operating section of the SCF to include, as far as possible, the cash effects of transactions affecting income.

Noncash Transactions

Objective 5
The effect of noncash
transactions on the
statement of cash flows.

As mentioned earlier, some very significant investing and financing transactions do not affect cash at all or only partly affect cash. For instance, in 19x2, DataCo, Inc., paid off a long-term note with a carrying value of $360,000 by issuing stock. This financing transaction involved no cash. It is not necessary to discuss why the creditor accepted stock instead of demanding cash in payment for the note. Such noncash trades do, in fact, take place from time to time, and the major concern of the accountant is determining the fair value of the items traded. If market values are known (by means of quotations from a stock exchange, for instance), valuation is straightforward. This is not always the case, however, and appraisals may be necessary to determine value. In any event, it is usually possible to establish a fair value for the trade.

Summary Entry		Cash Flow Effect
Notes Payable—Long Term (L) 360,000		None
Common Stock (SE)	360,000	

Such significant noncash transactions must be disclosed in a separate schedule that is shown along with the SCF. DataCo had two noncash trade transactions. In addition to the issuance of stock to pay off the note, a long-term note of $460,000 was used in partial payment of a building, as shown on page 731. Both are shown on the following schedule:

DataCo, Inc.
Statement of Cash Flows
Schedule of Noncash Investing and Financing Activities

Acquisition of building by means of long-term note	$460,000
Stock issued to settle debt	$360,000

Indirect Method

Objective 6
The difference between preparing a statement of cash flows with the direct and indirect methods.

The SCF in Exhibit 14–10 has an operating section that shows the cash received from customers and paid to suppliers of goods and services. This is called the direct method. Another form of analysis, called the indirect method, begins with net income and adds and subtracts noncash income statement items to arrive at net cash provided by operations. The direct method illustrated earlier follows an income statement format by listing the cash from customers followed by the cash paid to suppliers and employees. The indirect method starts with the bottom line of the income statement (net income) or some subtotal near the bottom line such as "income from continuing operations" and deletes revenues and expenses and gains and losses, which do not have a cash flow effect.

The format of the operating section of the SCF using the indirect method is as follows:

Cash flows from operating activities:	
Net income	$ xxx
Adjustments to reconcile net income to net cash provided by operating activity:	
Additions	xxx
Subtractions	(xxx)
Net cash provided by operating activities	$ xxx

In the indirect format we reconcile net income and net cash provided by operating activities. As we will see below, items such as depreciation expense reduce net income but have no effect on cash; and transactions such as paying off accounts payable decrease cash but have no effect on net income. All such reconciling items are analyzed below.

Several operating transactions, such as depreciation expense, have no direct cash flow effect. DataCo's $270,000 depreciation expense was recorded as follows:

Summary Entry		Cash Flow Effect	Net Income Effect	Reconciling Amount
Depreciation Expense (E) 270,000		None	−270,000	+270,000
Accumulated Depreciation (XA)	270,000			

The depreciation entry, therefore, reduced net income by $270,000, but cash was not affected. Therefore, in order to reconcile net income to net cash provided by operating activities, the $270,000 must be added to net income.

Net income includes all sales and not just cash sales. Because credit sales generate accounts receivable, an increase or decrease in accounts receivable during the year would indicate a difference between sales recognized on the accrual basis and cash flow from customers. DataCo's Accounts Receivable account increased $1,720,000 during the year.

Summary Entries			Cash Flow Effect	Net Income Effect	Reconciling Amount
Accounts Receivable (A)	10,870,000		None	+10,870,000	−1,720,000
Sales (R)		10,870,000			
Cash (A)	9,150,000		+9,150,000	None	
Accounts Receivable (A)		9,150,000			

In reconciling net income to net cash provided by operating activities, $1,720,000 must be subtracted from net income.

During 19x2, DataCo's inventory increased by $735,000, which was the result of Data-Co's purchasing more inventory than it sold to customers. In addition the Accounts Payable account decreased by $125,000. Assuming a perpetual inventory system, the following entries summarize this activity:

Summary Entries			Cash Flow Effect	Net Income Effect	Reconciling Amount
Inventory (A)	6,035,000		None	None	−860,000
Accounts Payable (L)		6,035,000			
Accounts Payable (L)	6,160,000		−6,160,000	None	
Cash (A)		6,160,000			
Cost of Goods Sold (E)	5,300,000		None	−5,300,000	
Inventory (A)		5,300,000			

The same type of analysis will show how changes in salaries payable, taxes payable, and prepayments create reconciling items that help to explain the difference between net income and net cash provided by operations.

Summary Entries			Cash Flow Effect	Net Income Effect	Reconciling Amount
Administrative Expenses (E)	640,000		None	−1,300,000	−14,000
Marketing Expenses (E)	660,000				
Salaries Payable (L)		1,294,000			
Prepaid Insurance (A)		6,000			
Salaries Payable (L)	1,314,000		−1,314,000	None	
Cash (A)		1,314,000			
Income Tax Expense (E)	1,512,000		None	−1,512,000	+128,000
Income Taxes Payable (L)		1,512,000			
Income Taxes Payable (L)	1,384,000		−1,384,000	None	
Cash (A)		1,384,000			

Exhibit 14–11 summarizes some of the situations where reconciliation of the net income to net cash is needed if the operating activities in a statement of cash flows is to be shown using the indirect method. Exhibit 14–12 shows how the operating section of DataCo's SCF is prepared using the indirect method.

"This Is What Happened to Our Cash"

Objective 7
The use of cash flow information in evaluating the performance and prospects of a business.

We now return to the negotiations between the banker and Ms. Perez, DataCo's president. As you recall from page 725, the banker asked Ms. Perez, "What happened to your cash?" after he reviewed the preliminary comparative balance sheets and an income statement at their first meeting to discuss a loan. Now it is three days later, and Ms. Perez is armed with two statements of cash flow, one with cash from operations shown using the direct method (our Exhibit 14–10), and the other using the indirect method (Exhibit 14–12). Having reviewed the causes of all cash flows with her controller, she is more confident than ever that her business is sound and worthy of quick action on the loan request. Refer to the exhibits as you read the next section.

Ms. Perez: Let's start with operations. (She points to specific items on the SCF, our Exhibit 14–12.) Our net income was $2,268,000 but most of it came late in the year, 60% in the last quarter, so we built up accounts receivable by $1,720,000 over the previous year. That may look odd, but we have an aggressive marketing effort and credit sales are important to that effort. My people tell me that our current receivables are very sound. We expect to collect all of them within 30 days. The same can be said for our inventory buildup. We added $735,000 to inventories to support our increasing sales. Again, our inventory is all first rate, with increasing fair values. So even though operations show only $72,000 in positive cash flow, our receivables and inventories are of high quality and of real value and their increases account for most of the difference between net income and cash flow from operations.

Banker: I want to talk to your CPA about those two items. If they are as you say, then your actions to increase credit sales and expand inventories probably make good business sense. Are there any other significant items that affected cash?

Ms. Perez: Our financing and investing activities were important and we believe successful. We issued stock for $1,804,000 and we used most of the cash to purchase our new building, for $1,640,000. We increased our investment in securities by $250,000 and the value of that portfolio has grown about 30% since that time.

Banker: Let's review your cash performance. (He refers to the SCF in Exhibit 14–10 and to DataCo's income statement.) You received just over $9 million from customers with sales of just under $11 million. That's where the buildup in receivables came from, and though your cost of goods sold is only $5.3 million, you paid suppliers $6.2 million. Yep, there's no doubt, my people will want to make sure about those receivables and inventory. The rest of it looks good. That building is in a good location with strong real estate values. Now I think I know what happened to your cash.

The above discussion points to the importance of a thorough understanding of the relationship between accrual-based statements such as the income statement and the balance sheet and the non–accrual-based cash flow statement. Sound business decisions can be made only if the perspectives of both are fully understood. It also indicates why both the direct and indirect formats of the SCF are informative in financing decisions.

In most countries financial reports contain analyses that aim at the same basic issues as does the cash flow statement covered in this chapter, but often there are significant differences in definitions and formats. For instance, in France the statement starts with a section on long-term financing and long-term investments followed by an analysis of the change in working capital broken down into operating and nonoperating transactions. Though the French statement does not use cash as the focal point of analysis, it is

EXHIBIT 14–11

Common Adjustments to Net Income—Indirect Method	Items that Appear as Adjustments to Net Income	Explanation of Cash versus Income Statement Effect	Adjustment
	Depreciation, depletion, and amortization	These expense items reduce net income but have no cash effect.	Add back depreciation expense to net income.
	Increase in accounts receivable and accrued receivables	As accounts receivable and accrued receivables increase, net income increases but cash is not affected.	Deduct increase in receivables from net income.
	Decrease in accounts receivable and accrued receivables	A reduction in receivable balances indicates cash receipts but not income recognition.	Add decrease in receivables to net income.
	Increase in inventory	Purchases for the period are not reflected in expenses (cost of goods sold).	Deduct increase in inventory from net income.
	Decrease in inventory	Expenses (cost of goods sold) for the period include items purchased in prior periods.	Add decrease in inventory to net income.
	Increase in prepayments	Payments for certain services exceed related expenses on income statement.	Deduct increase in prepayments from net income.
	Decrease in prepayments	Expenses on income statement exceed related cash payments for services.	Add decrease in prepayments to net income.
	Increase in current liabilities	Expenses exceed related payments to suppliers and others.	Add increase in current liabilities to net income.
	Decrease in current liabilities	Cash payments to suppliers and others exceed related expenses.	Deduct decrease in current liabilities from net income.
	Increase in unearned revenue	Cash receipts from customers exceed amounts recognized as revenue.	Add increase in unearned revenue to net income.
	Decrease in unearned revenue	Revenue recognized exceeds amount of cash receipts from customers.	Deduct decrease in unearned revenue from net income.
	Increase in Deferred Income Tax Liability account	Income tax expense on the income statement exceeds amount currently payable to the government.	Add increase in the Deferred Income Tax Liability account to net income.
	Decrease in Deferred Income Tax Liability account	Amount currently payable to the government exceeds income tax expense for the period.	Deduct decrease in the Deferred Income Tax Liability account from net income.
	Gain on sale of assets	The gain increases net income but the cash effect of the transaction is shown in the investing section.	Deduct the gain from net income.
	Loss on sale of assets	The loss decreases net income but the cash effect of the transaction is shown in the investing section.	Add the loss back to net income.

EXHIBIT 14–12

Statement of Cash Flows: Indirect Method

DataCo, Inc.
Statement of Cash Flows
For the Year Ended December 31, 19x2
(in thousands)

Cash flows from operating activities:			
Net income			$ 2,268
Adjustments to reconcile net income to			
cash provided by operating activities:			
Depreciation		$ 270	
Increase in accounts receivable		(1,720)	
Increase in inventory	$(735)		
Decrease in accounts payable	(125)	(860)	
Decrease in salaries payable.	$ (20)		
Decrease in prepayments	6	(14)	
Increase in income taxes payable		128	(2,196)
Net cash provided by operating activities			$ 72
Cash flows from investing activities:			
Cash paid for purchase of building		$(1,640)	
Cash paid for purchase of securities		(600)	
Cash received from disposal of land		300	
Cash received from disposal of securities		350	
Net cash used by investing activities			(1,590)
Cash flows from financing activities:			
Cash received from issuing stock.		$ 1,804	
Cash paid for dividends		(500)	
Net cash provided by financing activities			1,304
Net increase (decrease) in cash			$ (214)

designed to accomplish the same overall objective as the statement of cash flows; to help the reader understand the effects of significant transactions that are not well explained elsewhere in the financial statements.

• SUMMARY

In evaluating the future of a business, the prospects for future cash flow is almost always crucial. How can decision makers rationally evaluate cash flow prospects? Decision makers can begin by understanding a company's past cash flows. This information is acquired from the statement of cash flow, which reports the cash flows from the operating, investing, and financing activities of a business. The SCF gives information that cannot be found in balance sheets and income statements alone.

The question is, How well can the historical SCF predict future trends? We believe that, although all financial statements are based on historical records, this look into the past, along with sound projections, can give insights into the future.

In this chapter you learned about the general formats of the SCF. Then, by analyzing DataCo, Inc., you were shown how SCFs are constructed. For example, you can prepare the operating section of the SCF either directly, by reviewing the cash received from customers and the cash paid to suppliers and others, or indirectly, beginning with net income and adding or subtracting noncash items to arrive at cash provided by operations. In addition to operations, the SCF emphasizes the other major managerial functions of investing and financing. You were given the concepts and procedures necessary to identify and report the cash flow effects of investing and financing transactions.

An important theme in this chapter is that accrual accounting focuses on income determination and historic cost-based balance sheets, which is crucial to understanding the economic flows and states of an entity. The cash flow statement gives another critical perspective—that of the cash effects of transactions for a period. Neither is the one and only correct approach. They are complementary, providing different insights about a business's activities, current state, and future prospects.

• DEMONSTRATION EXERCISE

Saleco, Inc., has the following December 31, 19x1 and 19x2, balance sheets, 19x2 income statement, and additional information regarding transactions for 19x2.

Saleco, Inc.
Balance Sheet
At December 31

	19x2	19x1
Assets		
Cash	$ 201,400	$ 43,000
Accounts receivable	102,000	42,000
Prepaid rent	1,800	1,200
Plant assets	1,575,000	1,050,000
Less: Accumulated depreciation	(565,000)	(690,000)
Long-term investment, Kalmor stock	400,000	—
Land	500,000	500,000
	$2,215,200	$ 946,200
Liabilities and Stockholders' Equity		
Liabilities:		
Accounts payable	$ 5,500	$ 34,000
Notes payable	600,000	—
Salaries payable	24,000	12,000
Interest payable	10,000	—
Income taxes payable	100,470	—
Total liabilities	$ 739,970	$ 46,000
Stockholders' equity:		
Common stock	$ 300,000	$ 250,000
Contributed capital in excess of par	770,200	320,200
Retained earnings	405,030	330,000
Total stockholders' equity	$1,475,230	$ 900,200
Total liabilities and stockholders' equity	$2,215,200	$ 946,200

Saleco, Inc.
Income Statement
For the Year Ended December 31, 19x2

Revenues:

Sales revenue		$600,000

Expenses:

Depreciation expense	$ 75,000	
Salaries expense	210,000	
Rent expense	12,500	
Interest expense	10,000	
Miscellaneous expense	27,000	
Total expenses		334,500
Operating income		$265,500
Gain on sale of plant assets		30,000
Income before taxes		$295,500
Income tax expense		100,470
Net income		$195,030

Additional data:

a. Plant assets with original cost of $250,000 and accumulated depreciation of $200,000 were sold for $80,000 cash.
b. Dividends declared and paid of $120,000.
c. Issued common stock with a total par value of $50,000 for $500,000 cash.
d. Borrowed $600,000 cash on November 1, 19x2, to be paid back with annual interest of 10% on June 1, 19x3.
e. Sales of $600,000 on credit.
f. Collected $540,000 from credit customers.
g. Incurred salaries expense of $210,000 for the year.
h. Paid $198,000 for salaries.
i. Depreciation expense of $75,000.
j. Purchased plant assets for $775,000 in cash.
k. Incurred miscellaneous expenses of $27,000 on credit.
l. Purchased 5,000 shares of Kalmor Corporation for $400,000 cash.
m. Paid $55,500 of accounts payable.
n. Paid $13,100 for prepaid rent.
o. Incurred rent expense of $12,500.
p. Incurred interest expense of $10,000 on a short-term note of $600,000 acquired on November 1, 19x2.
q. Incurred income tax expense of 34% of income before taxes.

Required:

1. Prepare a statement of cash flows for Saleco for 19x2 using the direct method.
2. Prepare a statement of cash flows for Saleco for 19x2 using the indirect method.

Solution:

Direct Method:

Saleco, Inc.
Statement of Cash Flows
For the Year Ended December 31, 19x2

Cash flows from operating activities:

Cash received from customers	$ 540,000	
Cash paid to suppliers and employees	(266,600)	
Net cash flow from operating activities		$ 273,400

Cash flows from investing activities:

Proceeds from sale of plant assets	$ 80,000	
Payment for purchase of plant assets	(775,000)	
Payment for purchase of Kalmor stock	(400,000)	
Net cash flow from investing activities		(1,095,000)

Cash flows from financing activities:

Net borrowings	$ 600,000	
Proceeds from issuance of stock	500,000	
Dividends paid	(120,000)	
Net cash flow from financing activities		980,000
Net increase in cash		$ 158,400
Cash at beginning of year		43,000
Cash at end of year		$ 201,400

Indirect Method:

Saleco, Inc.
Statement of Cash Flows
For the Year Ended December 31, 19x2

Cash flows from operating activities:			
Net income			$ 195,030
Adjustments to reconcile net income to cash flow from operations:			
Depreciation		$ 75,000	
Gain on sale of plant assets		(30,000)	
Change in current assets and liabilities:			
Increase in accounts receivable		(60,000)	
Increase in prepaid rent		(600)	
Decrease in accounts payable		(28,500)	
Increase in salaries payable		12,000	
Increase in interest and income taxes payable		110,470	
Total adjustments			78,370
Net cash provided by operating activities			$ 273,400
Cash flows from investing activities:			
Proceeds from sale of plant assets		$ 80,000	
Payment for purchase of plant assets		(775,000)	
Payment for purchase of Kalmor stock		(400,000)	
Net cash used by investing activities			(1,095,000)
Cash flows from financing activities:			
Net borrowings		$ 600,000	
Proceeds from issuance of stock		500,000	
Dividends paid		(120,000)	
Net cash provided by financing activities			980,000
Net increase in cash			$ 158,400
Cash at beginning of year			43,000
Cash at end of year			$ 201,400

Worksheet for Statement of Cash Flows

Objective 8

The use of a worksheet in preparing a statement of cash flows.

A working paper technique, called the worksheet method, can be used to help construct an SCF. The same concepts underlie this technique as those discussed in the chapter, and the unique organization on the working paper provides some computational efficiencies.

The working paper in Exhibit 14A–1 uses reconciliations of beginning and ending balance sheet amounts as its major technique. The top half has all the beginning (December 31, 19x1) and ending (December 31, 19x2) balance sheet amounts listed in the first and fourth columns, respectively. The second and third columns reconcile the two balances; that is, the money amounts in those columns show the amounts by which each account increased or decreased during the period. For example, Cash, the object of this analysis, decreased a total of $214,000; therefore, a credit entry is shown in the third column. Accounts Receivable, on the other hand, increased $1,720,000, and this shows in the second column as a debit. Keep in mind that these debit and credit entries are not journal entries but are merely a clerical device for making the worksheet balance. Of course, they do reflect the net debit and credit changes from all the journal entries that affected each account during the period.

The bottom half of the working paper also utilizes the second and third columns to classify the cash flow effects of the changes in account balances in the top half. This classification scheme is the same as the formal SCF illustrated in the chapter: cash from operating activities, cash from investing activities, and cash from financing activities. The object is to describe the net change in cash. For example, find entry 11 in the upper half. It shows that the Land account decreased by $300,000 during the period. This amount shows up in the lower half as an investing activity ("Disposal of land") providing cash of $300,000. Because every entry in the upper half has a counterpart in the lower half, the worksheet is self-balancing.

Although the worksheet format is concise and lends itself to mechanical manipulation, it is only a tool for organization and computation. The real challenge is the mastering of the concepts that allow a cash flow analysis to be prepared from accrual-based records.

We shall reconstruct each working paper entry in terms of its effect on operating, investing, and financing activities. You should first concentrate on the lower half of the working paper and then trace the effect to the upper half.

OPERATING ACTIVITIES

The placement of entry 1 indicates that net income is usually a major source of cash; thus, it is shown as the starting point in the lower part of the worksheet. Find entry 1 in Exhibit 14A–1. Because net income is a major reconciling item between beginning and ending retained earnings, it is shown alone as an increase in retained earnings. Of course, net income does not represent cash flow, so several other balance sheet changes must be analyzed before cash provided by operations is determined.

Entries 2, 7, and 8 are all reconciling items between net income and cash from operating activities, which are added to the net income amount. Depreciation of $270,000 is an expense that did not consume cash in this period. Prepayments of $6,000 were expensed this period but cash flowed in the previous period and the increase in Taxes Payable of $128,000, although expensed this period, will not be paid until 19x3.

Entries 3, 4, 5, and 6 are reconciling items shown as subtractions from net income. Accounts Receivable increased by $1,720,000. This, of course, increased net income but cash

EXHIBIT A14–1

DataCo, Inc.
Working Paper for Statement of Cash Flows
For the Year Ending December 31, 19x2

	12/31/x1	Transactions for Year 2 Debit	Transactions for Year 2 Credit	12/31/x2
Cash	248		(X) 214	34
Accounts Receivable	965	(3) 1,720		2,685
Inventory	1,015	(4) 735		1,750
Prepaid Insurance	12		(7) 6	6
Marketable Securities		(10) 600	(12) 350	250
Building	2,700	(9) 2,100		4,800
Accumulated Depreciation	(850)		(2) 270	(1,120)
Land	1,100		(11) 300	800
Totals	5,190			9,205
Accounts Payable	200	(5) 125		75
Notes Payable	360	(13) 360	(9) 460	460
Salaries Payable	150	(6) 20		130
Taxes Payable	40		(8) 128	168
Bonds Payable	2,200			2,200
Common Stock	1,500		(13) 2,164	3,664
Retained Earnings	740	(14) 500	(1) 2,268	2,508
Totals	5,190	6,160	6,160	9,205

Operating Activities:			
Net Income	(1) 2,268		
Add: Depreciation Expense	(2) 270		
Decrease in Prepayments	(7) 6		
Increase in Taxes Payable	(8) 128		
Subtract:			Net Cash Flow from
Increase in Accounts Receivable		(3) 1,720	Operating Activities
Increase in Inventories		(4) 735	+$72
Decrease in Accounts Payable		(5) 125	
Decrease in Salaries Payable		(6) 20	
Investing Activities:			
Acquisition of Building		(9) 1,640	
Acquisition of Securities		(10) 600	Net Cash Used by
Disposal of Land	(11) 300		Investing Activities
Disposal of Securities	(12) 350		−$1,590
Financing Activities:			
Issuance of Common Stock	(13) 1,804		Net Cash Provided by
Payment of Dividends		(14) 500	Financing Activities
			+$1,304
Decrease in Cash	(X) 214		
Totals	5,340	5,340	

has not yet been received. Inventories increased by $735,000, representing purchases during the year in excess of deliveries to customers. Such purchases are eventually paid for with cash although net income will not be reduced until the merchandise is sold to customers. Accounts Payable decreased by $125,000 by means of cash payments to suppliers, creating a negative cash flow of $125,000 more than is reflected in the expenses shown in the income statement. Likewise, salaries payable decreased by $20,000, reflecting more cash flow to workers than is shown as salary expense. In summary, although net income is shown on the income statement at $2,268,000, operations generated only $72,000 of net cash.

INVESTING ACTIVITIES

Entries 9, 10, 11, and 12 all relate to the cash flow from investing activities. A building costing $2,100,000 was acquired by means of a cash payment of $1,640,000 and a note issuance of $460,000. Securities of $600,000 were acquired using cash. Land and securities were sold for cash of $300,000 and $350,000, respectively. The net effect was $1,590,000 negative cash flow from investing activities.

FINANCING ACTIVITIES

Entries 13 and 14 show cash inflows and outflows from financing activities. Common stock issuance generated $1,804,000 in cash as the result of issuing stock of $2,164,000 for a combination of cash $1,804,000 and the payment of a liability of $360,000. The dividend payment decreased cash and is part of the reconciliation of retained earnings balance. Financing activities, therefore, generated a net positive cash flow of $1,304,000.

The entry marked (X) is shown in the upper half as the cash reconciliation credit and as the balance "Decrease in cash" amount below.

Refer to Exhibit 14–12 earlier in the chapter to see that the formal SCF reflects all the changes analyzed in the working paper in Exhibit 14A–1.

• KEY TERMS

Cash equivalents. Short-term, highly liquid investments that can be converted to cash so quickly as to be considered equivalents of cash. Investments in equity securities are not considered cash equivalents.

Direct method. Method of determining cash from operations by analyzing the cash received from customers and the cash paid to suppliers and others.

Financing activities. Activities that involve receipt or payment of cash or other assets or borrowing from bondholders and other creditors such as banks.

Indirect method. Method of determining cash from operations that begins with net income and adds or subtracts any noncash income statement items to arrive at cash from operations.

Investing activities. Activities involving acquisition and disposal of long-term assets as well as cash paid and received for securities and for the principal amount of loans made to others.

Operating activities. Activities necessary to provide goods and services to customers.

Statement of cash flows (SCF). Financial statement that analyzes the effects of cash flow transactions and gives details as to the inflows and outflows of cash during a period.

• Appendix Key Term

Worksheet method. A working paper method used to help construct an SCF.

• QUESTIONS

1. What information does the statement of cash flows provide that is not provided in the income statement and comparative balance sheets?
2. Define cash equivalents and explain why these are included in analyzing changes in cash from one period to the next.
3. Describe the difference among operating, investing, and financing activities.
4. Why are the receipt and payment of interest considered operating activities?
5. List three types each of operating, investing, and financing inflows and outflows.
6. Which of the three cash flow activities would ordinarily be considered of the greatest long-term importance to the firm?
7. Describe the change in cash in relation to the change in other balance sheet accounts.
8. How are significant investing and financing transactions that do not affect cash, such as the issuance of stock to acquire a building, disclosed in the statement of cash flows?
9. Give three examples of noncash transactions that would be disclosed in the manner described in the answer to the previous question.
10. How does the statement of cash flows differ from the other financial statements?
11. Would it be possible for a firm to report a net loss in its income statement and an increase in cash in its statement of cash flows for the same year? If so, how could this happen?
12. If a deduction for depreciation of assets is not made on the statement of cash flows, as it is on the income statement, when is the deduction for the assets made?
13. Explain the difference between the direct and indirect methods of preparing the statement of cash flows.
14. What advantage does the worksheet method provide in preparing a statement of cash flows?

• EXERCISES

E 14–1
Classifying Transactions
L.O.1

The following selected transactions have been taken from the Western Company. Classify each transaction as to whether it is an operating (O), investing (I), or financing (F) activity:

a. Salaries were paid to employees.
b. Shares of Western's common stock were repurchased and held in treasury.
c. A short-term note receivable was received from a customer.
d. Office supplies were purchased.
e. Land was sold for $100,000 cash.
f. Interest on a long-term note was paid.
g. The principal portion of the long-term note in f was paid.
h. Dividends were declared and paid.

E 14–2
Classifying Transactions
L.O.1

The following transactions from the month of January 19x2, have been taken from the accounting records of Garth Computers, Inc. Classify each transaction as to what amount would appear on the statement of cash flows and where that amount would appear. The direct method was used.

a. A $500,000 long-term note was paid off with $100,000 cash and the issuance of $400,000 in common stock.
b. During the month, merchandise was sold for $60,000 to customers on account. Collections on account amounted to $58,000.
c. Dividends of $20,000 were declared in December 19x1 and paid during January 19x2.
d. Equipment with a net book value of $2,500 was sold for cash at a $300 loss.
e. Temporary marketable equity securities were purchased for $75,000.
f. During the month $40,000 of inventory was purchased on account. Payments to suppliers for the month were $48,000.
g. Interest of $8,000 on short- and long-term notes was paid.
h. A $40,000 settlement from the insurance company was received for a building destroyed by fire last year.

E 14–3
Multiple Choice
L.O.3–5

1. On its statement of cash flows for the period, Donahue, Inc., reports net cash provided by operating activities of $85,000. For the period, Donahue reports depreciation expense of $20,000 and a $6,000 loss on sale of plant equipment. Net income for the period is—
   a. $65,000.
   b. $105,000.
   c. $59,000.
   d. $111,000.

2. On its statement of cash flows for the period, Winfrey, Inc., reports net cash flow from operating activities of $(14,000). The following information is also available: depreciation expense of $10,000; gain on sale of land, $4,000; an increase in accounts receivable, $5,000; and an increase in accounts payable, $2,000. Net income (loss) for the period is—
   a. $(17,000).
   b. $(23,000).
   c. $3,000.
   d. $(3,000).

3. A company purchases a building valued at $150,000 by paying cash of $50,000 and issuing the remainder in common stock. On the statement of cash flows this would appear as a—
   a. $150,000 outflow for financing activities.
   b. $50,000 outflow for investing activities.
   c. $50,000 outflow for financing activities.
   d. $150,000 outflow for investing activities.

4. During the year, Bubbles Company writes off an old invoice for $4,000 as a bad debt. On the statement of cash flows using the direct method for the period this would appear as a—
   a. $4,000 outflow for operating activities.
   b. $4,000 outflow for investing activities.
   c. $4,000 outflow for financing activities.
   d. This item would not appear on the SCF.

E 14–4
Format of Statement of Cash Flows
L.O.2

The following data are summarized from the general ledger Cash account of Fledgling Industries, Inc., for its 19x1 fiscal year, which ended on December 31.

Receipts from customers.	$250,000
Payment for income taxes	8,500
Interest payment on note.	20,000
Proceeds from sale of common stock	100,000
Dividends declared and paid	50,000
Payment to employees.	75,000
Payments to suppliers of inventory	90,000
Proceeds from sale of equipment	28,400
Payment for miscellaneous expenses	22,500
Payment of the long-term note principal	88,000

Required:
Prepare a statement of cash flows in proper format for Fledgling Industries for 19x1.

E 14–5
Effect of Noncash Transactions
L.O.5

Selected investing and financing activities for Fiber Optics, Inc., follow:

a. Declares and pays a $40,000 cash dividend.
b. Purchases a parcel of land for $50,000 and a $400,000 note.
c. Sells a piece of equipment with a net book value of $30,000 for a $4,000 gain. Payment is accepted in the form of $9,000 cash and the remainder in a note.

Required:
Describe how each of the above transactions would be disclosed on Fiber Optics' statement of cash flows or on any supporting schedules.

E 14–6
Effect of Noncash Transactions
L.O.5

Selected information of Niehaus Financing Company for the fiscal year 19x1 is as follows:

a. Purchases a building valued at $750,000 by issuing 15,000 shares of common stock with a per share par value of $10. The current market price of the stock is $50 per share.
b. Pays off a $100,000 short-term note by issuing a $100,000 long-term note.
c. Purchases a $250,000 piece of equipment by paying $50,000 and the remainder in a note.

Required:
Describe how each of the above transactions would be disclosed on Niehaus Financing's statement of cash flows or on any supporting schedules.

E 14–7
Cash Provided by Operating Activities— Direct Method
L.O.3, 4

The following selected information is available for the Salesky Company for the year ended December 31, 19x2 (all amounts in thousands):

	December 31	
	19x2	19x1
Balance sheet data:		
Accounts receivable	$ 50	$52
Inventory	27	31
Prepaid expenses	12	11
Accounts payable	9	11
Salaries payable	14	11
Income taxes payable.	17	19
Income statement data:		
Sales revenue	$400	
Cost of goods sold	136	
Salaries expense.	92	
Depreciation expense	25	
Other expenses	15	
Income tax expense	30	
Loss on sale of building	29	

Additional data:
a. Purchases of inventory during the period totaled $132,000. All purchases are made on credit and the Accounts Payable account is only used for purchases of inventory.
b. All sales were made on credit.

Required:
Prepare the cash provided by operations section of Salesky's statement of cash flows for 19x2 using the direct method.

E 14–8
Cash Provided by Operating Activities— Indirect Method
L.O.6

Refer to the information given in Exercise 14–7. Prepare the cash provided from operations section of Salesky's statement of cash flows using the indirect method.

E 14–9
Statement of Cash Flows—Direct Method (Challenging)
L.O.3, 4

Saunders Engineering, Inc., has been in business several years and has prepared its December 31, 19x2, comparative balance sheet and 19x2 income statement as follows:

Saunders Engineering, Inc.
Comparative Balance Sheet

	12/31/x2	12/31/x1
Assets		
Current assets:		
Cash	$35,300	$ 5,100
Accounts receivable	28,300	31,200
Note receivable	0	8,000
Interest receivable	0	800
Total current assets	$63,600	$45,100
Noncurrent assets:		
Equipment	$45,000	$40,000
Less: Accumulated depreciation	36,000	24,000
Total noncurrent assets	$ 9,000	$16,000
Total assets	$72,600	$61,100
Liabilities and Stockholders' Equity		
Liabilities:		
Accounts payable	$ 1,000	$ 800
Note payable	0	20,000
Interest payable	0	1,800
Salaries payable	1,890	2,250
Total liabilities	$ 2,890	$24,850
Stockholders' equity:		
Capital stock	$50,000	$30,000
Retained earnings	19,710	6,250
Total liabilities and stockholders' equity	$72,600	$61,100

Saunders Engineering, Inc.
Income Statement
For the Year Ended December 31, 19x2

Sales revenue		$127,100
Expenses:		
Salaries expense	$75,640	
Depreciation expense	12,000	
Property tax expense	9,200	
Utilities expense	1,100	
Other expenses	10,700	
Total expenses		108,640
Net income		$ 18,460

The following cash transactions took place during the year:

Payments:

a.	Purchased equipment	$ 5,000
b.	Paid salaries	76,000
c.	Paid property taxes	9,200
d.	Paid dividends	5,000
e.	Paid utility bill	1,100
f.	Paid note and interest	21,800
g.	Paid on accounts payable	10,500

Receipts:

a.	Collected cash from customers	130,000
b.	Sold stock	20,000
c.	Collected interest on note receivable	800
d.	Collected on note receivable previously classified as a long-term loan	8,000

Required:
Prepare Saunders' statement of cash flows for 19x2 using the direct method.

E 14–10
*Statement of Cash
Flows—Indirect Method
(Challenging)*
L.O.6

Refer to the information given in Exercise 14–9.

Required:
Prepare Saunders' statement of cash flows for 19x2 using the indirect method.

E 14–11
*Evaluating Performance
via Statement of
Cash Flows*
L.O.7

Refer to this chapter's Demonstration Exercise and solution. Evaluate Saleco's performance by comparing the balance sheets and income statement with its statement of cash flows.

E 14–12
*Multiple Choice
(Challenging)*
L.O.1–7

1. The net cash flows from operations figure on a statement of cash flows—
   a. Is equal to the net income figure on an income statement.
   b. Is more informative than net income.
   c. Is the net cash effect for all transactions for the period.
   d. Includes cash received from the sale of plant and equipment.
   e. None of the above.
2. A statement of cash flows explains the net change in—
   a. All assets of the business.
   b. The currency, demand deposits, and other items that meet the definition of cash.
   c. Cash plus certain highly liquid investments.
   d. Current assets and liabilities.
   e. None of the above.
3. On the statement of cash flows which of the following groups of transactions would all be classified as financing activity?
   a. Sale of investments, payment of interest, and payment of dividends.
   b. Sale of stock, payment of dividends, and retirement of bonds.

    c. Sale of bonds, payment of bond interest, and receipt from a loan.

    d. Purchase of treasury stock, payment of accounts payable, payment of interest.

    e. None of the above.

4. Determining the total cash paid for wages for a period—

    a. Can be done with knowledge of Wages Payable beginning and ending balances only.

    b. Can be done by analyzing all the entries that affected Wage Expense for the current period.

    c. Can be done with knowledge of the Wages Payable beginning and ending balances and the dollar amount of Wage Expense.

    d. Cannot be done without analyzing all individual payments to wage earners.

    e. None of the above.

5. Which of the following is compatible with an increase, from one period's SCF to the next, in the amount of receipts from customers?

    a. Unchanged cash sales, unchanged credit sales, and an increased Accounts Receivable balance.

    b. Unchanged cash sales, unchanged credit sales, and a decreased Accounts Receivable balance.

    c. Decreased cash sales, decreased credit sales, and an increased Accounts Receivable balance.

    d. No cash sales, unchanged credit sales, and an increased Accounts Receivable balance.

    e. None of the above.

6. Which of the following will not be shown on an SCF with the direct format?

    a. Payments for retirement of stock.

    b. Depreciation.

    c. Receipts from customers.

    d. Payments to suppliers.

    e. None of the above.

7. Which of the following events should be disclosed on the schedule of noncash investing and financing transactions?

    a. Cash received on the sale of a major division of the company.

    b. An unusual increase in inventory balances.

    c. A significant increase in payments for lawsuits.

    d. The liquidation of a major liability by the issuance of stock.

    e. None of the above.

8. Over the life of a depreciable asset purchased for cash—

    a. Total depreciation expense will always equal cash paid for the asset.

    b. Total depreciation expense plus any gain or minus any loss on disposition of the asset will equal the cash paid for the asset.

    c. Total depreciation expense will never equal cash paid for the asset.

    d. Total depreciation expense will always be less than cash paid for the asset.

    e. None of the above.

• **Appendix Exercise** ──

E 14–13

Use of a Worksheet in Preparing a Statement of Cash Flows (Challenging)

L.O.8

Refer to this chapter's Demonstration Exercise. Using the data for Saleco, Inc., prepare the worksheet to aid in completing the 19x2 statement of cash flows for the company.

• PROBLEMS

P 14–1
Indirect Method
L.O.6

The following information is available regarding the current asset and current liability accounts of Searching, Inc. (all carry normal balances and are in thousands):

	December 31	
	19x2	19x1
Cash	$ 120	$ 140
Receivables	975	950
Inventory.	1,960	2,120
Prepaid insurance.	17	21
Accounts payable.	840	805
Revenue received in advance	26	32
Salaries and wages payable	140	115

The following additional data are available (all amounts in thousands):

a. Plant assets, sold at a $300 loss, had originally cost $2,700 and had accumulated depreciation of $1,800 at the time of sale. The sale was for cash.
b. Cash dividends declared in 19x2 were $500.
c. Net income for 19x2 was $495. Depreciation expense was $310 for 19x2, and amortization of intangible assets for 19x2 was $36. Also, cash paid for depreciable equipment in 19x2 amounted to $750.

Required:
1. Compute cash provided by operations for 19x2.
2. Compute the total change (increase or decrease) in cash for 19x2.
3. Compute the cash inflow resulting from the sale of plant assets.

P 14–2
Indirect Method
L.O.6

The following information is available for Taxing Company:

	December 31	
	19x2	19x1
Assets		
Cash	$ 41	$ 31
Accounts receivable	25	18
Inventories.	35	24
Land	70	95
Building, net of depreciation	460	380
Patents, net of amortization	22	17
Total assets	$653	$565

Liabilities and Stockholders' Equity

Liabilities:

Accounts payable	$ 41	$ 60
Salaries payable	10	9
Dividends payable	8	7
Notes payable (long-term)	170	120
Total liabilities	$229	$196

Stockholders' equity:

Common stock, no-par	$280	$260
Retained earnings	144	109
Total stockholders' equity	$424	$369
Total liabilities and stockholders' equity	$653	$565

	For the Year Ended December 31, 19x2
Net income	$ 53
Depreciation of buildings in 19x2	25
Purchase of new building	170
Cash dividends declared in 19x2	18
Gain on sale of buildings (a nonoperating gain included in net income)	10
Purchase of new patent	9

Required:

Using the information presented above, compute cash provided by operations for the year ended December 31, 19x2.

P 14–3
Indirect Method
L.O.6

The following data are taken from the financial statements of Speed Sprocket, Inc. (all accounts carry their normal balances):

Comparative Balance Sheet Data ($000):

	December 31	
	19x2	19x1
Accounts receivable—services	$150	$ 85
Accrued interest receivable	25	30
Plant and equipment (cost)	695	645
Accumulated depreciation	130	145
Accounts payable	71	64
Prepaid service revenue	45	25
Notes payable	120	110

Income Statement Data ($000):

	For the Year Ended December 31, 19x2
Service revenue	$560
Interest revenue	54
Depreciation expense—plant and equipment	28

During 19x2 Speed Sprocket, Inc., acquired new equipment for cash at a cost of $110,000 and also sold some old equipment.

Required:

1. Speed Sprocket, Inc., has no uncollectible accounts. Compute the amount of cash received during 19x2 from customers.
2. Compute the **original cost** and the **accumulated depreciation** on equipment that was disposed of during 19x2.
3. Compute the amount of cash received for interest during 19x2.

P 14–4
Indirect Method
L.O.6

The Bardsley Corporation, a large retail clothing store, reported the following balances in its accounts at December 31, 19x2 (all accounts carry their normal balances and are in thousands):

Sales revenue	$15,700
Interest revenue—customers.	900
Cost of goods sold	7,800
Depreciation expense.	400
Amortization expense.	300
Gain on sale of land held as a long-term investment	120
All other expenses—primarily salaries and wages.	5,500
Net income	$ 2,720

The following balance sheet changes occurred in the current assets and current liabilities during 19x2 (all in thousands):

	December 31 19x2	December 31 19x1	Change Increase (Decrease)
Cash	$ 470	$ 410	$ 60
Receivables	4,974	4,900	74
Inventory	4,551	4,500	51
Other current assets	930	908	22
Accounts payable.	5,102	5,140	(38)
Dividends payable	110	100	10
Other current liabilities	2,940	2,890	50

The following additional data are available (in thousands):

a. Land, sold at a $120 gain had originally cost $4,000. The sale was for cash.
b. Cash dividends declared in 19x2 were $760.

Required:

1. Compute the cash provided by operations for 19x2.
2. Compute the amount of cash paid for dividends in 19x2.
3. Compute the cash inflow resulting from the sale of land.

P 14–5
Indirect Method
(Challenging)
L.O.6

Clark Company is in the process of preparing the annual financial statements on December 31, 19x2, including a statement of cash flows. The balance sheet and income statement have been completed and are summarized below:

Clark Company
Balance Sheet
At December 31

	19x2	19x1
Assets		
Cash	$ 25,500	$ 42,000
Accounts receivable	93,500	75,500
Inventory	63,000	75,000
Prepaid insurance	6,000	15,500
Investments (long-term)	0	25,000
Property, plant, and equipment (net)	180,000	120,000
	$368,000	$353,000
Liabilities and Stockholders' Equity		
Liabilities:		
Accounts payable	$ 38,500	$ 37,400
Accrued salaries payable	6,000	3,500
Notes payable, short-term	38,000	19,100
Mortgage payable (long-term)	80,000	105,000
Total liabilities	$162,500	$165,000
Stockholders' equity:		
Common stock	$120,000	$100,000
Contributed capital in excess of par	26,000	20,000
Retained earnings	59,500	68,000
Total stockholders' equity	$205,500	$188,000
Total liabilities and stockholders' equity	$368,000	$353,000

Clark Company
Income Statement
For the Year Ended December 31, 19x2

Sales		$275,000
Cost of goods sold		218,000
Gross margin		$ 57,000
Expenses:		
Depreciation expense	$20,000	
Other operating expenses	17,000	37,000
Income before taxes		$ 20,000
Income tax expense		6,000
Net income		$ 14,000

Additional data:

a. 200 shares of common stock par value $100 were sold for $130 per share.

b. Dividends of $22,500 were paid on August 30, 19x2.

c. A storage building was purchased for $55,000.

d. The company acquired a machine worth $25,000 in exchange for the General Motors stock being held as an investment. In addition, obsolete equipment that had cost $35,000 and was fully depreciated was scrapped.

Required:

Prepare a statement of cash flows for the Clark Company for the year ended December 31, 19x2, using the indirect method. Use appropriate headings and subheadings.

P 14–6
Statement of Cash Flows—Indirect Method
L.O.6

You are the independent auditor for Rex Tours, Inc., whose fiscal year ended on December 31, 19x3. Your assistant has developed the following analysis to be used for the preparation of Rex Tours's statement of cash flows:

	Increase (decrease)	Details	
Assets:			
Cash and cash equivalents	$ 4,000		
Accounts receivable (net)	7,000	Bad debt expense	$ 3,000
		Accounts receivable increase	10,000
Notes receivable (long-term)	(8,000)	Cash received on loan	8,000
Property, plant, and equipment (net)	12,000	Purchased equipment for cash	16,000
	$15,000	Depreciation expense	4,000
Liabilities:			
Accounts payable and		Accrued expenses	$ 3,000
accrued liabilities	$ 9,000	Accounts payable increase	6,000
Notes payable	(3,000)	Paid off note, 2/25/x3	12,000
		Borrowed cash, 11/15/x3	9,000
Common stock	3,000	Issued stock for cash	3,000
Retained earnings	6,000	Income statement items:	
	$15,000	Sales	$32,000
		Selling and administrative expense	14,000
		Depreciation expense	4,000
		Income tax expense	6,000
		Net income	$ 8,000
		Dividends paid	$ 2,000

Required:
Prepare a statement of cash flows using the indirect method for the operating section.

P 14–7
Statement of Cash Flows—Direct Method (Challenging)
L.O.3, 6

Consider the following income statement, balance sheet, and summary journal entries made for MACC Corporation for the year 19x2 (all in thousands).

MACC Corporation
Income Statement
For the Year Ended December 31, 19x2

Sales	$20,400	
Cost of goods sold	12,240	
Gross margin		$8,160
Operating expenses:		
Salaries and wages	$ 3,500	
Repairs and maintenance	90	
Rent expense	110	
Miscellaneous expense	70	
Depreciation expense	540	
Interest expense	300	
Unrealized loss on temporary investments	20	4,630
Income from operations		$3,530
Gain on sale of long-term assets	$ 200	
Earnings of subsidiary	130	
Interest revenue	40	
Total other revenue		370
Income before taxes		$3,900
Income tax expense		1,326
Net income		$2,574

NOTE: Land with a book value of $410,000 was sold for $610,000.

MACC Corporation
Balance Sheet
At December 31

	19x2	19x1
Assets		
Current assets:		
Cash	$ 2,552	$ 2,332
Accounts receivable	1,420	2,020
Marketable (equity) securities)	738	738
Less: Allowance to reduce to LCM	(82)	(62)
Inventory	1,980	1,120
Accrued interest receivable	10	10
Prepaid miscellaneous expenses	122	72
Total current assets	$ 6,740	$ 6,230
Noncurrent assets:		
Bonds of A Corporation (8%, semiannual payment on 3/31 and 9/30)	$ 500	$ 500
Equity investment in subsidiary—S Corp. (40% owned)	872	742
Machinery and equipment	4,482	3,842
Less: Accumulated depreciation	(1,429)	(1,129)
Buildings and land improvements	7,280	7,280
Less: Accumulated depreciation	(2,650)	(2,410)
Land	2,690	3,100
Total noncurrent assets	$11,745	$11,925
Total assets	$18,485	$18,155

	19x2	19x1

Liabilities and Shareholders' Equity

Current liabilities:

Accounts payable	$ 1,410	$ 510
Salaries and wages payable	120	70
Short-term note payable—suppliers	600	750
Income taxes payable	550	220
Total current liabilities	$ 2,680	$ 1,550

Noncurrent liabilities:

Bonds payable (10%; interest due 6/30 and 12/31)	$ 3,000	$ 3,000
Deferred taxes	1,884	1,208
Total noncurrent liabilities	$ 4,884	$ 4,208

Shareholders' equity:

Common stock	$ 5,050	$ 4,550
Retained earnings	5,871	7,847
Total shareholders' equity	$10,921	$12,397
Total liabilities and shareholders' equity	$18,485	$18,155

Summary entries during the year ($000):

a.	Accounts Receivable	20,400	
	Sales		20,400
b.	Cost of Goods Sold	12,240	
	Inventory		12,240
c.	Inventory	13,100	
	Accounts Payable		13,100
d.	Cash	21,000	
	Accounts Receivable		21,000
e.	Accounts Payable	12,200	
	Cash		12,200
f.	Prepaid Expenses	120	
	Cash		120
g.	Cash	40	
	Interest Revenue		30
	Accrued Interest Receivable		10
h.	Machinery	640	
	Cash		640
i.	Cash	610	
	Land		410
	Gain on Sale		200
j.	Salaries Expense	3,500	
	Salaries and Wages Payable		3,500

k.	Salaries and Wages Payable	3,450	
	Cash		3,450
l.	Cash	400	
	Short-Term Notes Payable		400
m.	Short-Term Notes Payable—Supplies	550	
	Cash		550
n.	Taxes Payable	220	
	Cash		220
o.	Interest Expense	300	
	Cash		300
p.	Cash	500	
	Common Stock		500
q.	Dividends	4,550	
	Cash		4,550
r.	Repairs and Maintenance Expense	90	
	Cash		90
s.	Rent Expense	110	
	Cash		110

Entries at the end of the year ($000):

t.	Unrealized Loss on Short-Term Investments	20	
	Allowance to Reduce Short-Term Investments to Market		20
u.	Miscellaneous Expense	70	
	Prepaid Expenses		70
v.	Accrued Interest Receivable	10	
	Interest Revenue		10
w.	Equity Investment in Subsidiary—S Corporation	130	
	Investment Income		130
x.	Depreciation Expense	300	
	Accumulated Depreciation—Machinery and Equipment		300
y.	Depreciation Expense	240	
	Accumulated Depreciation—Buildings		240
z.	Income Tax Expense	1,326	
	Deferred Taxes		676
	Income Taxes Payable		550
	Cash		100
aa.	Sales	20,400	
	Interest Revenue	40	
	Gain on Sale of Long-Term Assets	200	
	Investment Income	130	
	Income Summary		20,770

bb.	Income Summary	16,260	
	Cost of Goods Sold		12,240
	Salaries Expense		3,500
	Interest Expense		300
	Repairs and Maintenance Expense		90
	Rent Expense		110
	Unrealized Loss on Short-Term Investments		20
cc.	Income Summary	610	
	Depreciation Expense		540
	Miscellaneous Expense		70
dd.	Income Summary	1,326	
	Tax Expense		1,326
ee.	Retained Earnings	1,976	
	Income Summary	2,574	
	Dividends		4,550

Required:

Prepare a statement of cash flows for 19x2 using the direct method.

P 14–8
Statement of Cash Flows—Indirect Method (Challenging)
L.O.6

Refer to the information given in Problem 14–7.

Required:

Prepare a statement of cash flows for 19x2 using the indirect method.

P 14–9
Statement of Cash Flows—Direct Method (Challenging)
L.O.3, 5

SKM, Inc., has the following income statement for 19x2, comparative balance sheets at December 31, 19x2, and 19x2 summary journal entries:

SKM, Inc.
Income Statement
For the Year Ended December 31, 19x2
(in thousands)

Sales		$1,200	
Cost of goods sold		560	
Gross margin		$ 640	
Expenses:			
Salaries and wages expense	$215		
Rent expense	80		
Interest expense	25		
Depreciation expense	60		
Total expenses		380	
Income before taxes		$ 260	
Income tax expense		108	
Net income		$ 152	

SKM, Inc.
Comparative Balance Sheets
December 31
(in thousands)

	19x2	19x1
Assets		
Current assets:		
Cash	$ 125	$131
Accounts receivable (net)	125	40
Inventory	80	50
Total current assets.	$ 330	$221
Noncurrent assets:		
Machinery and equipment	$ 500	$400
Accumulated depreciation	(100)	(40)
Land	80	—
Total noncurrent assets	$ 480	$360
Total assets	$ 810	$581
Liabilities and Stockholders' Equity		
Current liabilities:		
Accounts payable	$ 50	$ 65
Salaries payable	10	10
Income taxes payable.	22	5
Accrued interest	5	—
Total current liabilities.	$ 87	$ 80
Noncurrent liabilities:		
Bonds payable (10%; interest payable 6/30 and 12/31).	$ 150	$150
Long-term note payable	100	—
Total noncurrent liabilities	$ 250	$150
Stockholders' equity:		
Common stock.	$ 200	$200
Retained earnings	273	151
Total stockholders' equity	$ 473	$351
Total liabilities and stockholders' equity	$ 810	$581

NOTE: Machinery and equipment were acquired during 19x2 by the issuance of a $100,000 long-term note (interest payable on January 1 and July 1 at 10%). Land was purchased for $80,000 cash.

Summary journal entries for the year 19x2 are as follows (all amounts in thousands):

a.	Accounts Receivable	1,200	
	Sales		1,200
b.	Cost of Goods Sold.	560	
	Inventory		560
c.	Salaries and Wages Expense	215	
	Salaries Payable		215
d.	Salaries Payable	215	
	Cash		215

e.	Rent Expense	80	
	Cash		80
f.	Interest Expense	25	
	Cash		20
	Accrued Interest		5
g.	Depreciation Expense.	60	
	Accumulated Depreciation		60
h.	Cash	1,115	
	Accounts Receivable		1,115
i.	Inventory	590	
	Accounts Payable		590
j.	Accounts Payable	605	
	Cash		605
k.	Machinery and Equipment	100	
	Note Payable		100
l.	Land	80	
	Cash		80
m.	Income Tax Expense	108	
	Income Taxes Payable		108
n.	Income Taxes Payable	91	
	Cash		91
o.	Dividends	30	
	Cash		30
p.	Sales	1,200	
	Income Summary		1,200
q.	Income Summary	1,048	
	Cost of Goods Sold.		560
	Salaries and Wages Expense		215
	Rent Expense		80
	Interest Expense		25
	Depreciation Expense.		60
	Income Tax Expense		108
r.	Income Summary	152	
	Retained Earnings		152
s.	Retained Earnings	30	
	Dividends		30

Required:
Prepare a statement of cash flows for 19x2 using the direct method.

P 14–10

*Statement of Cash
Flows—Indirect Method
(Challenging)*
L.O.6

Refer to the information given in Problem 14–9.

Required:
Prepare a statement of cash flows for 19x2 using the indirect method.

P 14–11
Statement of Cash
Flows—Direct Method
(Challenging)
L.O.3, 5

Gamen Company, Inc., has the following income statement for 19x2, comparative balance sheets at December 31, 19x1 and 19x2, and additional data:

Gamen Company, Inc.
Income Statement
For the Year Ended December 31, 19x2

Sales		$105,740
Cost of goods sold		68,731
Gross margin		$ 37,009
Expenses:		
Bad debt expense	$ 114	
Depreciation and amortization expense	870	
Interest expense	3,200	
Total expenses		4,184
Operating income before taxes		$ 32,825
Loss from sale of equipment		1,500
Income before taxes		$ 31,325
Income tax expense (34%)		10,651
Net income		$ 20,674

Gamen Company, Inc.
Comparative Balance Sheets
At December 31

	19x2	19x1
Assets		
Cash	$ 6,685	$ 4,300
Accounts receivable	18,505	12,800
Less: Allowance for doubtful accounts	(370)	(256)
Notes receivable	2,200	2,200
Inventory	60,569	17,300
Investments (long-term)	3,210	3,210
Property, plant, and equipment	114,771	92,771
Less: Accumulated depreciation	(8,310)	(9,770)
Intangible assets	520	550
Total assets	$197,780	$123,105
Liabilities and Stockholders' Equity		
Liabilities:		
Accounts payable	$ 60,800	$ 13,800
Interest payable	1,700	300
Income taxes payable	10,731	2,080
Short-term debt	13,600	13,600
Long-term debt	0	15,000
Total liabilities	$ 86,831	$ 44,780

	19x2	19x1
Stockholders' equity:		
Common stock ($5 par)	$ 12,500	$ 10,000
Contributed capital in excess of par	52,500	40,000
Retained earnings	45,949	28,325
Total stockholders' equity	$110,949	$ 78,325
Total liabilities and stockholders' equity	$197,780	$123,105

Additional data for 19x2:

a.   Cost of goods sold for the year was $68,731. Total sales were $105,470 of which $90,000 was paid in cash with the remainder on account.

b.   Cash of $10,035 collected on outstanding accounts receivable.

c.   Gamen maintains a 2% allowance for doubtful accounts on the year-end balance in accounts receivable.

d.   Equipment was sold for $9,700 cash. Equipment originally cost $13,500 and accumulated depreciation was $2,300 at date of sale.

e.   Inventory of $112,000 was purchased on credit.

f.   Payment of $65,000 to suppliers for merchandise purchased earlier on credit.

g.   Purchased a plant for $20,500 cash and the issuance of 500 shares of common stock at $30 per share.

h.   Retired $15,000 of long-term debt at year-end. Interest was also paid on the debt at the rate of 12%.

i.   Declared and paid dividends of $3,050.

j.   Interest expense for the period was $3,200.

k.   Depreciation on property, plant, and equipment was $840 for the period.

l.   Amortization expense on intangibles for the period was $30.

m.   Gamen is subject to a 34% tax rate on income before taxes.

Required:
Prepare a statement of cash flows for 19x2 using the direct method.

P 14–12
Statement of Cash Flows—Indirect Method (Challenging)
L.O.6

Refer to the information given in Problem 14–11.

Required:
Prepare a statement of cash flows for 19x2 using the indirect method.

P 14–13
Statement of Cash Flows—Direct Method
L.O.3, 5

Perlon, Inc., has the following income statement for 19x2, comparative balance sheets at 12/31/x1 and 12/31/x2, and additional data (in thousands).

Perlon, Inc.
Income Statement
For the Year Ending December 31, 19x2

	($000)
Revenues:	
Sales revenue	$37,000
Investment revenue	600
Total revenues	$37,600
Salary expense.	$ 5,000
Depreciation expense	4,640
Interest expense	2,500
	12,140
Income before taxes	$25,460
Income tax expense.	3,996
Net income.	$21,464

Perlon, Inc.
Comparative Balance Sheets
at December 31

	($000)	
	19x2	19x1
Assets		
Cash	$ 47,110	$12,800
Accounts receivable	10,190	21,440
Interest receivable	600	0
Long-term investment	7,500	0
Equipment (net)	63,220	61,560
Total assets	$128,620	$95,800
Liabilities and Stockholders' Equity		
Interest payable	$ 2,500	$ 0
Income tax payable.	2,646	2,350
Long-term note payable	42,400	38,400
Total liabilities	$ 47,546	$40,750
Common stock ($1 par)	$ 1,200	$ 1,000
Contributed capital in excess of par	26,600	22,000
Retained earnings	53,274	32,050
Total stockholders' equity	$ 81,074	$55,050
Total liabilities and stockholders' equity	$128,620	$95,800

Additional information for 19x2 (amounts in thousands):
a. Sales on credit amounted to $37,000.
b. Equipment was purchased by issuing a note for $4,000.
c. Common stock with total par of $200 was issued for cash of $2,500 and new equipment of $2,300.
d. A long-term investment in bonds costing $7,500 was purchased for cash.
e. Income tax expense for 19x2 was $3,996.

f. Depreciation expense for 19x2 was $4,640.

g. Cash dividends paid were $240.

Required:
Prepare a statement of cash flows for 19x2 using the direct method.

P 14–14
Statement of Cash
Flows—Indirect Method
L.O.6

Refer to the information given in Problem 14–13.

Required:
Prepare a statement of cash flows for 19x2 using the indirect method.

P 14–15
Statement of Cash
Flows—Indirect Method
(Challenging)
L.O.6

Trident Corporation's assistant controller roughed out the preliminary draft of a 12/31/x1 statement of cash flows:

Operations:

Net Income	$ 4,500,000
Add: Depreciation Expense	1,200,000
Cash from Operations.	$ 5,700,000

Other Cash Effects:

Issuance of Stock	$ 1,200,000
Issuance of Bonds	3,300,000
Payment of Dividends.	(900,000)
Payment for a Building	(1,215,000)
Net Other Cash Effects	$ 2,385,000
Cash Increase for Period	$ 8,085,000

The assistant controller is confused because the cash account shows a decrease of $3,165,000 for the period. As Trident's auditor you discover that the assistant controller failed to consider the following accounts:

Accounts Receivable

1/1/x1		Collections from	
Balance	$ 2,400,000	customers	$13,500,000
Sales	16,500,000		
12/31/x1			
Balance	$ 5,400,000		

Accounts Payable

		1/1/x1	
		Balance	$ 1,257,000
Payments	$17,250,000	Purchases	18,500,000
		12/31/x1	$ 2,507,000

Inventory

1/1/x1		Cost of goods sold	$9,000,000
Balance	$ 4,500,000		
Purchases	18,500,000		
Balance			
12/31/x1	$14,000,000		

Required:
Use the above information to construct a statement of cash flows in good form.

• **Appendix Problem** ——————————————————————————————

P 14–16
Worksheet for Preparing
Statement of Cash Flows
L.O.8

Pioneer Bakery, Inc., has the following comparative balance sheets for 19x1 and 19x2:

	19x2	19x1
Assets		
Current assets:		
Cash	$ 600	$ 400
Marketable securities	160	0
Accounts receivable (net)	1,680	1,160
Inventory	1,320	840
Prepaid insurance	200	100
Total current assets.	$3,960	$2,500
Plant, property, and equipment.	$2,260	$1,200
Less: Accumulated depreciation	220	100
	$2,040	$1,100
Total assets	$6,000	$3,600
Liabilities and Stockholders' Equity		
Current liabilities:		
Accounts payable	$1,060	$ 880
Accrued expenses	280	260
Dividends payable	140	0
Total current liabilities.	$1,480	$1,140
Bonds payable—long-term.	1,000	0
Total liabilities	$2,480	$1,140
Stockholders' equity:		
Common stock, no par	$2,400	$1,800
Retained earnings	1,120	660
Total stockholders' equity	$3,520	$2,460
Total liabilities and stockholders' equity	$6,000	$3,600

Pioneer Bakery's comparative income statement is as follows:

	Years Ended December 31	
	19x2	**19x1**
Net revenues.	$12,800	$8,000
Cost of goods sold	10,000	6,400
Gross profit	2,800	1,600
Expenses	2,000	1,040
Net income	$ 800	$ 560

Required:
Using the above information, prepare a working paper for Pioneer's statement of cash flows.

• CASES

C 14–1
Basic Purpose of
Cash Flow Statement
L.O.1

As assistant controller for Arrow Software, Inc., you are assigned to run an introduction to financial accounting workshop for programmers who have little or no financial accounting knowledge. After introducing the basic techniques and financial statements, you are asked the two following questions:

a. What is the key difference between the information found in an income statement and a statement of cash flows?
b. I notice that depreciation is added back to net income on the statement of cash flows. How does depreciation generate cash?

Required:
Write a one-paragraph answer to each question. Remember that these programmers have not studied accounting.

C 14–2
Using Cash Flow
Information to
Evaluate Performance
L.O.1, 5, 7

The following statement was made by the president of a publicly held corporation in a published annual report.

> Because of the depression in the international price of crude oil, the company saw further deterioration of sales and net income, both of which were 15% lower than the prior year. Net cash flow from operations was strong primarily because of tightening of credit which reduced our outstanding receivables and the adoption of accelerated depreciation for tax and book purposes as of January 1 which reduces cash flow for taxes by $8,400,000 and which resulted in the add back to net income of $20,000,000 as shown on the statement of cash flows.

Required:
Critique the logic behind the reasons given for the cash flow experience.

C 14–3
Interest and Dividends
as Investing Activities
L.O.3

While the majority of the FASB (four members) voted affirmatively for *SFAS No. 95*, three members dissented giving the following explanation: "... interest and dividends received are returns on investments in debt and equity securities that should be classified as cash inflows from investing activity.... Interest paid is a cost of obtaining financial resources that should be classified as a cash outflow for financing activities."

The current rule (*SFAS No. 95*) requires that interest and dividends received and interest paid be reported as cash flows from operating activities. What are some arguments for this treatment?

C 14–4
Direct versus
Indirect Method
L.O.6

Two formats are allowed for reporting cash flow from operations on the statement of cash flows: (1) the direct method, which shows major classes of cash receipts and payments such as cash received from customers and cash paid to employees summing to net cash flow from operating activities, and (2) the indirect method, which begins with net income and adds and subtracts amounts that are not the result of operating cash flows during the period. The sum of the net income number and the adjustments equals net cash flow from operating activity.

Required:
What are the advantages of the direct method and the indirect method?

C 14–5
Analysis of Cash Flows—Hershey Foods Corporation
L.O.2–4

Hershey Foods Corporation showed the following charts in a recent annual report.

Three-Year Sources of Cash and Short-Term Investments (in millions)

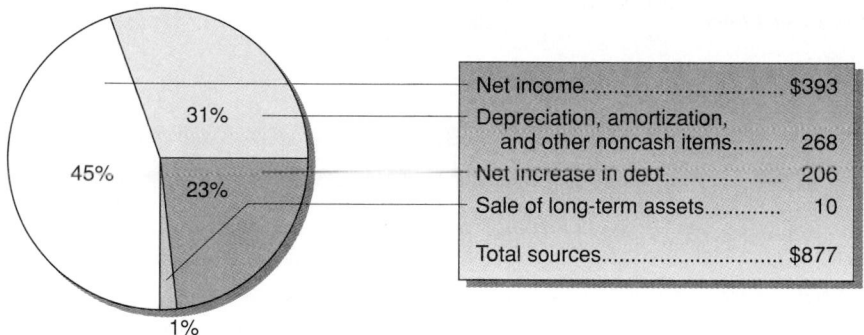

Net income.................................	$393
Depreciation, amortization, and other noncash items.........	268
Net increase in debt....................	206
Sale of long-term assets.............	10
Total sources..............................	$877

Three-Year Uses of Cash and Short-Term Investments (in millions)

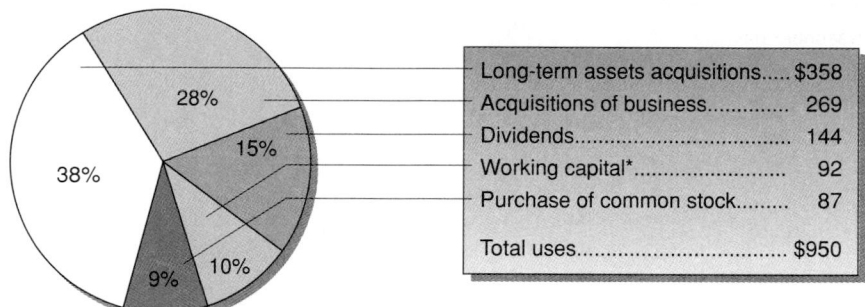

Long-term assets acquisitions.....	$358
Acquisitions of business.............	269
Dividends....................................	144
Working capital*..........................	92
Purchase of common stock.........	87
Total uses..................................	$950

*Net change in inventories, accounts receivable, prepayments, and accounts payable; that is, the increase in current assets not including cash and short-term investments over the increase in current liabilities for the three-year period.

Required:

1. Why are items such as depreciation shown as sources of funds?
2. If Hershey's book value of cash and short-term investments at January 1, 19x1, was $88,000,000, what was the book value of their cash and short-term investment on December 31, 19x3?
3. Construct a three-year summary statement of cash flows from the information given. Assume that cash is defined as cash plus short-term investments.

C 14–6
Recasting Financial
Analysis into a
Statement of Cash Flows
(Challenging)
L.O.3, 4, 6, 7

Morgan Investments and you are currently working on a corporate acquisition deal between your client, American Rental, Inc., and a privately owned regional rental company New England Rental, (NER). NER provides the following analysis of cash flows for the year just ended (in thousands):

Sources of Cash		Uses of Cash	
Net income	$5,327	Purchase of land.	$2,550
Sale of marketable equity securities	29	Payment of dividends	2,285
Issuance of long-term notes	300	Purchase of building	1,500
Issuance of common stock	750	Purchase of equipment	750
Depreciation expense	780	Increase in inventory	225
Decrease in accounts receivable	120	Decrease in taxes payable	75
Increase in account payable	75		
Total sources	$7,381	Total uses.	$7,385

Required:
1. Critique the categorization of "sources" and "uses" of cash in the analysis of cash flows presented.
2. Discuss the meaning of operating, investing, and financing transactions as shown on a statement of cash flows.
3. Recast the given analysis as a formal statement of cash flows.

C 14–7
Analysis of Cash Flows
L.O.3, 4, 6, 7

You are a bank lending officer and a potential customer has provided an income statement, a balance sheet, and the following cash flow analysis:

Net income	$ 3,750,000
Issuance of stock	1,000,000
Issuance of bonds	2,750,000
Payment of dividends	(750,000)
Purchase of building.	(1,012,500)
Net cash effects	$ 5,737,500

Upon scrutinizing the accounting records you determine that the following T account activities were ignored in the cash flow analysis:

Accounts Receivable

Beginning balance	$ 2,005,000		
Sales	13,750,000	Collections	$11,250,000
Ending balance	$ 4,505,000		

Accumulated Depreciation

	Beginning balance	$8,450,000
	Depreciation for year	1,000,000
	Ending balance	$9,450,000

Accounts Payable

Payments	$14,375,000	Beginning balance	$ 1,047,500
		Purchases	15,125,000
		Ending balance	$ 1,797,500

Inventory

Beginning balance	$ 3,750,000		
Purchases	15,125,000	Cost of goods sold	$7,500,000
Ending balance	$11,375,000		

Required:
1. Critique the cash flow analysis given.
2. Recast the analysis into a formal cash flow statement.

C 14–8

Analysis of Cash Flow Disclosure—Ralston Purina Company

L.O.2

Refer to the Ralston Purina Company (RPC) financial statements in Appendix E at the end of this book.

Required:
1. Identify the balance sheet items used in the definition of "cash and cash equivalents" in the statement of cash flows. What can you infer about the noncash items included?
2. Does RPC use the direct or indirect method to report the "operations" portion of the SCF? Explain.

Whitaker Corporation
Income Statement
For 1994

	1994	1993	Percent Change
Revenues			
Total revenues	$xx.x	$xx.x	xx.x%
Expenses			
Research and development	xx.x%	xx.x%	+xx.x
Advertising	xx.x	xx.x	−xx.x
Bad debts	xx.x	xx.x	−xx.x

Whitaker Corporation
Balance Sheet
12/31/94

	1994	1993	Percent Change
Current assets			
Total current assets.	$xx.x	$xx.x	xx.x%
Noncurrent assets			
Plant assets (net).	xx.x%	xx.x%	−xx.x
Intangible assets	xx.x	xx.x	+xx.x
Goodwill.	xx.x	xx.x	+xx.x
Current liabilities			
Total current liabilities.	xx.x	xx.x	xx.x
Noncurrent liabilities			
Total noncurrent liabilities	xx.x	xx.x	xx.x
Stockholders' equity			
Total stockholders' equity	xx.x	xx.x	xx.x

Whitaker Corporation
Cash Flow Statement
For 1994

	1994	1993
Operating activities		
Cash from operations	$xx.x	$xx.x
Investing activities		
Cash for investments	(xx.x)	(xx.x)
Financing activities		
Cash from financing	xx.x	xx.x

FINANCIAL STATEMENT COMPONENTS EMPHASIZED IN CHAPTER 15

15

Accounting Theory and Financial Statement Analysis

(Regarding) the timeliness of unexpected bad news. Financial outcomes which are less than expected by the financial statement users should be communicated as quickly as possible.

Merlin E. Dewing
KPMG Peat Marwick

· Learning Objectives

After studying Chapter 15, you should understand

1. The objectives of financial accounting and the qualitative characteristics of accounting information, pp. 775–78.

2. The importance of the elements of financial statements and recognition and measurement in financial statement analysis, pp. 778–79.

3. The common types of analysis used to evaluate financial statements—horizontal, vertical, vertical/horizontal, trend, and ratio analysis, pp. 784–89.

4. How to prepare accounting performance, market performance, liquidity, leverage, and activity ratios, pp. 789–97.

This chapter reviews the conceptual framework of accounting and introduces the fundamental concepts of financial statement analysis. To evaluate financial statements, you must understand their purposes and the underlying principles and concepts used to prepare them. Part A of this chapter ties together the concepts used throughout the text as the basis for accounting choices. This review will help you understand the structure underlying financial statements prepared in accordance with generally accepted accounting principles (GAAP). Part B of this chapter identifies sources of accounting data used to evaluate business entities and provides an introduction to analytical methods of evaluating financial statements.

PART A: ACCOUNTING THEORY—THE CONCEPTUAL FRAMEWORK OF ACCOUNTING

Throughout this textbook we have integrated the underlying theory that ties accounting practices together to form a cohesive body of knowledge. Without these underlying theoretical concepts, accounting would be a set of disjointed rules with no relation to one another. Some of the more obvious underlying concepts include the matching principle employed in the income measurement process and the principle of original (historical) costs that is used as a basis for the recognition and measurement of many balance sheet elements.

In Part A of this chapter, we discuss the theoretical framework that guides the development of accounting practice. This theoretical framework is perhaps best represented by the results of the FASB's Conceptual Framework Project, which was intended to aid the development of accounting practices. This project, initiated soon after the FASB was formed in 1973, has resulted in six *Statements of Financial Accounting Concepts (SFACs)* published between 1978 and 1985. The hierarchy shown in Exhibit 15–1 represents this

EXHIBIT 15–1

**Framework of
Accounting Theory**

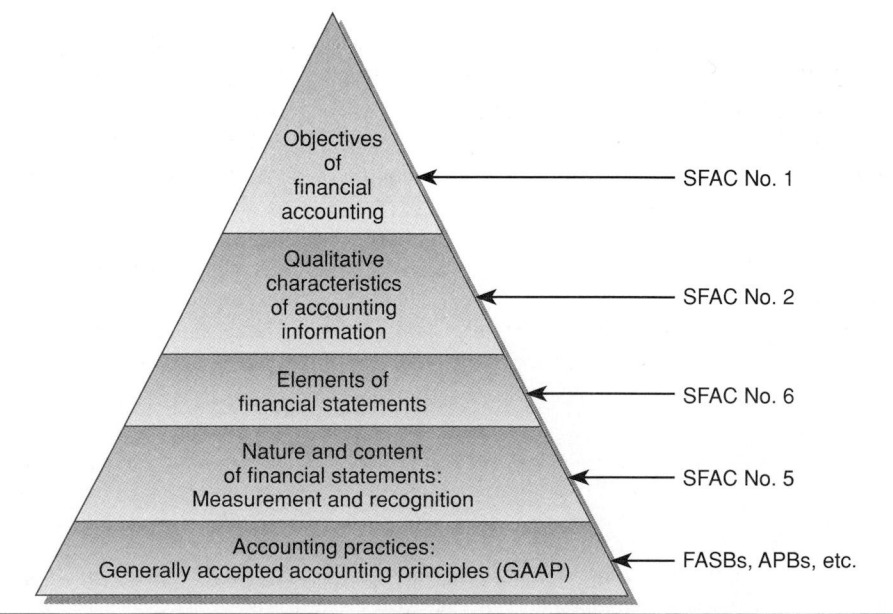

framework and its four related *Concept Statements* as they apply to business enterprises.[1] In this part of the chapter, you will study the first four components in the hierarchy—objectives of financial accounting, qualitative characteristics of accounting information, elements of financial statements, and measurement and recognition (nature and content of financial statements). The foundation of the hierarchy—generally accepted accounting principles (GAAP)—has been referred to throughout the text.

OBJECTIVES OF FINANCIAL ACCOUNTING

Objective 1
The objectives of financial accounting and the qualitative characteristics of accounting information.

The objectives of financial accounting are **to collect, measure, and communicate economic information for business decisions.** To accomplish these objectives, the goals of accounting include helping decision makers

1. **Assess the future cash-generating ability** of the entity or of some subset of the entity's operations.
2. **Evaluate the past performance** of the entity and its managers through the evaluation of the financial statements.[2]

The quality and value of the financial data provided by the accounting information system is based on the extent to which these goals and objectives are achieved.

The future cash-generating ability of an entity's overall operations and its individual components of operations is important for determining the value of the entity. In theory, the value of the entity is equal to the present value of the entity's expected future cash flows. As a result, information that helps predict future cash flows is important to decision makers for investing, credit granting, and other business decisions.

You can evaluate the past performance of an entity and its managers by analyzing the past financial statements of the entity. This evaluation process helps determine why the entity achieved its results, which in turn helps to provide expectations about future cash flows from operations. Since evaluating past performance helps predict future performance, past and current financial statements are important elements in achieving the overall objective of accounting. The combination of historical and forward-looking financial statement data helps management plan future operating decisions and also helps investors and creditors make investment and credit-granting decisions.

QUALITATIVE CHARACTERISTICS OF ACCOUNTING INFORMATION

To achieve its overall objective of guiding decision makers, accounting information must possess certain qualities. It is generally agreed that these qualities should be *relevance, reliability, comparability,* and *consistency.*[3] Although these four qualities have been discussed in earlier chapters, they are now reviewed in outline form, as presented in Exhibit 15–2.

Primary Qualities of Accounting Information

By studying Exhibit 15–2 you can see that the two primary qualities of accounting information are relevance and reliability. Although you already know some reasons why accounting information must be relevant and reliable, the discussion that follows focuses your attention on these two important qualities.

---

[1] *SFAC No. 4* pertains to nonbusiness organizations, which are discussed in Appendix D at the end of this text. *SFAC No. 6,* pertaining to elements of financial statements, replaced *SFAC No. 3* on the same subject.

[2] *Statement of Financial Accounting Concepts No. 1,* "Objectives of Financial Reporting by Business Enterprises" (Norwalk, Conn.: FASB, 1978).

[3] *Statement of Financial Accounting Concepts No. 2,* "Qualitative Characteristics of Accounting Information" (Norwalk, Conn.: FASB, 1980).

EXHIBIT 15–2

Qualities of Useful Accounting Data

Quality	Examples
Primary qualities:	

1. Relevance.
   a. Timeliness.
   b. Usefulness.
	1. Using information regarding inventory on hand provides useful information for the timely reordering of inventory, avoiding both lost sales from stockouts and excessive costs from carrying too much inventory.

2. Reliability.
   a. Measurability.
   b. Verifiability (or objectivity).
   c. Unbiasedness.
	2. The periodic physical counts of cash on hand, marketable securities, inventory, machines, and so on, enhance the reliability of the accounting data.

Secondary qualities:	
3. Comparability.	3. Reporting requirements (GAAP) help improve the comparability of operating income and other performance measures across firms.
4. Consistency	4. Using the same accounting methods each year enhances consistency.
Constraining qualities:	
5. Materiality considerations.	5. A company may have a policy of directly expensing small hand tools with a five-year life rather than recording them as an asset and depreciating them over five years because the differential effect on income is **not** material.
6. Cost-benefit considerations.	6. The cost of obtaining better estimates of the amount of oil or gas discovered may exceed the economic benefits of such data.

Relevance. Accounting data used in business decisions must be relevant, which means that the data should be both **timely** and **useful**. Information is **timely** if it is available before a critical decision is made, if it helps evaluate a future event or outcome of interest. For example, a report concerning new customer orders would be timely if it helped predict future sales and earnings. A net income figure is timely if it can be used in negotiations with a potential lender who wants to see past results *before* making a loan. Information is **useful** if it makes a difference in a decision context, if it helps reduce uncertainty about *future* events or outcomes of interest to the decision maker. For example, potential investors in a company may be more certain of the company's prospects for future profits, cash flows, and dividends after studying the company's most recent financial statements. Thus, relevant accounting information should be both timely and useful to decision makers.

Reliability. If decision makers are going to use accounting information to make decisions, this information must be reliable. **Reliable information** is characterized by data that are **measurable with a reasonable degree of precision,** free from bias, and verifiable.

The **measurability** attribute of reliable data is largely responsible for the dominance of historical cost measures in financial statements. The historical (or original) costs of assets and liabilities are in most cases easy to determine. These measures are also verifiable (or **objective**) and **unbiased** (or **neutral**) relative to other measures such as market value. For example, if we asked a dozen accountants to measure both the market value and the historical cost of a 10-year-old high rise apartment building, we would probably find the historical cost measures to be **more reliable.** Historical cost measures would probably be the same for all 12 accountants, reporting the original price of the apartment building as recorded 10 years earlier. This would be verifiable by looking up the documents support-ing the purchase (i.e., the legal sales documents, mortgage loans, etc.), and would be **unbiased** in that the 12 accountants would not introduce any systematic judgment error into the process. Alternatively, the 12 measures of market value would probably not agree, but would be apt to vary widely based on the judgments of the accountants. There would be relatively little evidence to help **verify** the market value measurements, and they could easily be biased by such things as knowledge that the reporting entity hopes to increase (or decrease) the value of the apartment building for some reason.

Reliable accounting data, then, are data that are verifiable, unbiased, and measurable with reasonable precision. Taken together, relevance and reliability are the primary quali-ties of accounting information—qualities that accounting data should have to be useful for decision-making purposes.

Secondary Qualities
of Accounting
Information

As indicated in Exhibit 15–2, the secondary qualities that accounting data should possess are comparability and consistency.

Accounting data are **comparable** when different companies experience the same or similar events and report the same results. For example, the comparability would be im-proved if all companies used the same depreciation method. Comparability is a "between entities" concept.

Consistency in accounting means that a given entity uses the same measurement proce-dures from year to year so that the same or similar events occurring in consecutive years are reported in the same manner. Consistency is a "within entity" concept. For example, the timing of revenue recognition must be **consistent** from year to year for each specific entity. If all entities in an industry recognized revenues at the same point (e.g., at the time of sale) over a number of consecutive accounting periods, revenue recognition would be **comparable** across entities and **consistent** within entities over time.

Constraining Qualities
of Accounting
Information

The constraining qualities of accounting information are considerations that might over-ride the primary and secondary qualities discussed above. Two constraining qualities are **materiality** and **cost-benefit** considerations.

Accountants strive for relevance, reliability, comparability, and consistency unless the amounts involved are immaterial. What is an immaterial amount? In some cases, account-ing policymakers have specified materiality limits. For example, special disclosures are required if a single customer represents 10% of sales. In most cases, however, a material amount is a subjective value based on the judgment of the preparer of the accounting data. As a general guideline, a material amount is an amount that could affect the decision of a reasonably knowledgeable user of accounting data. Professional judgment usually is the basis for materiality considerations.

Cost-benefit considerations suggest that the cost of providing the accounting data should not exceed the potential benefits that users will receive from the data. This means that some accounting information may be more costly to produce than their beneficial effects for users.

Cost-benefit considerations have had an important effect on accounting policy regard-ing whether or not companies should be required to disclose the effects of price changes on net income. (Accounting for changing prices is discussed in Appendix C of this text-book.) While policymakers believe that the impact of price changes on net income is rele-vant information, managers have argued that this information is too costly to produce. In many questions concerning cost-benefit considerations, exact measures of costs and bene-fits are difficult or impossible to obtain. As a result, cost-benefit issues, like materiality issues, are often resolved by the professional judgment of accountants.

In conclusion, for accounting data to be useful for business decisions, the data should possess the qualities of relevance, reliability, comparability, and consistency to the greatest feasible extent. The more closely accounting data reflect these qualities, the more valuable the data will be for business decision making. These four qualities provide accountants with guidance that gives valuable direction in helping to enhance the usefulness of accounting information.

You realize, of course, that relevance, reliability, comparability, and consistency are subjective qualities and do not lend themselves to precise identification or measurement. In other words, you cannot readily measure the amount of relevance, reliability, and so on, in a given accounting report or specific accounting data. However, professional judgments regarding the presence of these four qualities in financial accounting data have a significant effect on how informed users employ accounting in making business decisions.

ELEMENTS OF FINANCIAL STATEMENTS

Objective 2
The importance of the elements of financial statements and measurement and recognition in financial statement analysis.

The definitions of the elements of financial statements provide additional guidance for the preparation of useful accounting data. These elements (assets, liabilities, equity, investments by owners, distributions to owners, revenues, expenses, gains, and losses) and their definitions were presented throughout Part I of this textbook, and we referred to them several times to resolve measurement and reporting issues. Exhibit 15–3 reviews the elements of financial statements and their definitions.[4]

Recall from Chapters 1 and 2 that the definitions of assets and liabilities are very important, because all other financial statement elements can be defined in terms of assets and liabilities. To do this, remember that net assets are assets minus liabilities. After defining assets and liabilities, the other financial statement elements can be defined in terms of the related effect on net assets, as in Exhibit 15–3.

EXHIBIT 15–3

Elements of Financial Statements Defined

Element	Definition
Assets	Assets are probable future economic benefits obtained or controlled by a particular entity as a result of past transactions or events.
Liabilities	Liabilities are probable future sacrifices of economic benefits arising from present obligations of a particular entity to transfer assets or provide services to other entities in the future as a result of past transactions or events.
Equity	Equity is the residual interest in the assets of the entity that remains after deducting its liabilities. In a business enterprise, the equity is the ownership interest and equals the net assets of the business.
Investments by owners	Owner transactions resulting in an increase in net assets (e.g., owners' purchase of more stock).
Distributions to owners	Transactions between owners and the entity that result in a decrease in net assets (e.g., dividends).
Revenues	Increases in net assets resulting from operating activities.
Expenses	Decreases in net assets resulting from operating activities.
Gains and losses	Increases and decreases in net assets that are the result of nonowner events unrelated or indirectly related to normal operating activities.

---

[4]*Statement of Financial Accounting Concepts No. 6,* "Elements of Financial Statements of Business Enterprises" (Norwalk, Conn.: FASB, December 1980).

We can also relate the definitions of the elements of financial statements to the four qualities—relevance, reliability, comparability, and consistency—that accounting data should possess. For example, assets are probable future benefits that are controlled by an entity as a result of past transactions. To be recorded, asset measurements must be reliable; that is, asset measurements must be measurable with a reasonable degree of precision and be unbiased and verifiable. If you cannot reliably record assets, they are not assets in an accounting sense. Potential assets such as those represented by managerial talent, business location, customer relations, or research and development are not recorded in GAAP-based accounting statements even though they may represent "real" future benefits. When future benefits cannot be reliably estimated, they may not be recorded as assets.

RECOGNITION AND MEASUREMENT

Guidance as to when and how information about business transactions should be incorporated into the financial statements is provided by the *FASB Statement of Financial Accounting Concepts No. 5 (SFAC No. 5)*, "Recognition and Measurement in Financial Statements of Business Enterprises." This statement—the most specific of the concepts statements—has been integrated into various sections of earlier chapters.

Recall from Chapter 2 that in accounting, "to recognize" means "to record." In concept, *SFAC No. 5* provides guidance as to when to record and how to measure accounting data. For example, two key measurement and recognition issues involve revenues and expenses. We introduced these topics in Chapter 2, developed them in Chapters 3 through 5, and reviewed the more detailed aspects of revenue and expense recognition and measurement in Chapter 13. In essence, the underlying recognition and measurement concepts examined in *SFAC No. 5* have been fully integrated into earlier chapters. Since to be reported all financial statement data must meet the recognition (recording) and measurement criteria, the scope of these concepts includes the entire set of accounting data reported in the formal financial statements. Financial accounting data that **do not** meet recognition and measurement criteria yet are considered relevant are usually disclosed in the footnotes to the financial statements. This is commonly referred to as *disclosure* rather than formal financial statement *recognition*.

Although accounting theory aids the continuing development of accounting practice, it does not eliminate the need for professional judgments by policymakers or practicing accountants. Furthermore, the dynamic and complex nature of the business environment makes it unrealistic to expect accounting theory to provide a rigid framework for practice.

PART B: FINANCIAL STATEMENT ANALYSIS

Part B of this chapter examines the various sources of financial accounting information and some of the basic methods of analyzing accounting data within and among business entities.

SOURCES OF FINANCIAL DATA

Many sources and forms of financial data exist. In general, the data provided to and used by external users (investors, bankers, and so on) come from the same accounting information system as the data used by the entity's internal managers. The major difference is that external users generally use highly summarized and aggregated data about the entity, while most internal managers use detailed accounting reports about their specific

EXHIBIT 15–4

Relationship between Financial Accounting Information and Ownership Structure

Type	Ownership Structure/Size	Information Required or Needed
1	Publicly owned companies with stock traded on a public stock exchange.	Full disclosure of financial statements prepared in conformance with GAAP and independently audited as required by the SEC and all major stock exchanges.
2	Closely held companies *not* publicly traded; organized as a corporation, partnership, or proprietorship.	Disclosure requirements are not governed by SEC or other regulators but may be equivalent to SEC requirements, depending on the extent of nonowner (creditor) interests in the company and their demands. a. If no debt (no creditors other than suppliers, labor, and so on), no information need be provided to outsiders unless owners desire it. b. If material amount of debt (banks or public debt holders), creditors normally require that information be audited in conformance with GAAP resulting in disclosures like Type 1 companies.
3	Companies where managers are also owners and there are no significant outside interests.	Disclosures may be no more than the tax returns for these companies, which are not publicly available. However, financial services, such as Dun & Bradstreet, attempt to provide some financial data on all business entities.

area of authority and responsibility, because they are primarily concerned with subcomponents of the entity's overall operations.

The nature and source of financial accounting data may vary widely depending on the type of ownership structure of the entity and the interests of creditors. Exhibit 15–4 attempts to summarize the relationship between the ownership structure and the financial accounting information requirements.

For large publicly traded companies governed by SEC requirements, the primary financial accounting data sources are

1. Annual reports to stockholders (and proxy statements).
2. Quarterly reports to stockholders.
3. Securities and Exchange Commission (SEC) reports.

ANNUAL REPORTS TO STOCKHOLDERS (AND PROXY STATEMENTS)

A company's stockholders receive annual reports to help evaluate what the managers have accomplished with the resources entrusted to them. All publicly traded companies are required to prepare annual reports in accordance with GAAP, and most medium to large, closely held companies also prepare GAAP financial statements for creditors and/or internal users. The annual reports of publicly owned companies normally contain the elements outlined in Exhibit 15–5. The three main sections of the annual report are the management's discussion, the formal financial statements, and other financial and demographic data.

In recent years, a few companies have moved to a shortened version of the financial data normally found in annual reports. In these instances, the details of the formal finan-

EXHIBIT 15–5

**Content of
Annual Reports**

Section 1: Management discussion	Normally contains • Financial highlights • Letter to stockholders • Data on various business segments	
Section 2: Financial statements (audited)	Normally contains • Income statement (or earnings statement) • Balance sheet (or statement of financial position) • Statement of cash flows • Statement of changes in stockholders' equity • Footnotes to the statements • Management's report and independent auditor's report	
Section 3: Other data	Normally contains • Historical summary of key financial data for the past 5 to 10 years • List of members of the board of directors • List of top executives, office locations, plants, etc.	

cial statements needed to comply with GAAP and SEC requirements have typically been moved to the *proxy statement*. All stockholders usually receive the proxy statement before the annual stockholders' meeting and after they receive the annual report. The purpose of a proxy statement is to announce the time and place of the annual meeting and describe any agenda items to be voted on by the stockholders (e.g., who will be on the board of directors, selection of a CPA firm to conduct the audit, and so on). The proxy statement will usually include a stockholder ballot and other relevant data to help the stockholder decide how to vote.

Included as key components of Section 2 of the annual report are reports from management and from the independent (outside) auditor. The management report is not always present, but when included it usually contains a statement identifying management's responsibility for the financial statements and the system of internal controls for safeguarding the firm's assets. This report often identifies the audit committee of the board of directors and its role in hiring the independent auditor and maintaining the integrity of the company's financial reporting system. The report of the independent auditor, while normally addressed to the board of directors, provides useful information about the financial statements to all outside users and should be read whenever the financial statements are to be used as a basis for business decisions. For companies with publicly traded securities, the independent audit report is a required part of the financial statements. These two reports are usually found at the start or end of the formal financial statement data.

The Audit Report.   After the auditors conduct their audit, they issue an auditor's report or opinion as to whether the company's financial statements and accompanying footnotes fairly present the results of its operations and financial position. A "clean" or "unqualified" opinion, like that provided in Exhibit 15–6, informs owners that the auditors believe management's financial statements fairly present the results of the company's actual operations. The auditor's opinion provides the external users with a statement as to whether or not the financial statements of management included in the annual report were prepared in accordance with generally accepted accounting principles (GAAP). To provide some structure to how the audit is conducted, the CPA profession, through the American Institute of Certified Public Accountants (AICPA), has established generally accepted auditing standards (GAAS). In a "clean" opinion, the CPA states that the financial statements are "fairly present(ed)" in accordance with GAAP, and that the audit was conducted in accordance

EXHIBIT 15–6

**Annual Report
Disclosure of Auditor's
Opinion—Example**

Independent Auditors' Report

To Share Owners and Board of Directors
General Electric Company

We have audited the accompanying statement of financial position of General Electric Company and consolidated affliates as of December 31, 1992 and 1991, and the related statements of earnings and cash flows for each of the years in the three-year period ended December 31, 1992. These consolidated financial statements are the responsibility of the company's management. Our responsibility is to express an opinion on these consolidated financial statements based on our audits.

We conducted our audits in accordance with generally accepted auditing standards. Those standards require that we plan and perform the audit to obtain reasonable assurance about whether the financial statements are free of material misstatement. An audit includes examining, on a test basis, evidence supporting the amounts and disclosures in the financial statements. An audit also includes assessing the accounting principles used and significant estimates made by management, as well as evaluating the overall financial statement presentation. We believe that our audits provide a reasonable basis for our opinion.

In our opinion, the aforementioned financial statements appearing on pages 26–31 and 45–62 present fairly, in all material respects, the financial position of General Electric Company and consolidated affiliates at December 31, 1992 and 1991, and the results of their operations and their cash flows for each of the years in the three-year period ended December 31, 1992, in conformity with generally accepted accounting principles.

As discussed in note 6 to the consolidated financial statements, the company changed its method of accounting for postretirement benefits other than pensions in 1991.

KPMG Peat Marwick

KPMG Peat Marwick
Stamford, Connecticut

February 12, 1993

---

with GAAS. Note that a clean audit opinion, such as the one reported in Exhibit 15–6, includes a statement in the second paragraph describing the basic requirements of GAAS and the underlying limitations of the audit process. It states that the audit is designed to obtain "reasonable assurance" that the financial statements are "free of material misstatement." This does not represent a guarantee and cannot be viewed as such. We should also note that the audit report does not say whether management is doing a good job, but only indicates whether management has fairly disclosed the results of its activities.

In addition to "clean" opinions, auditors may issue three other types of opinons:

Qualified opinions. These state that except for some specified qualification the financial statements fairly present the entity's financial position in accordance to GAAP. Often the exception is explained in a footnote.

Adverse opinions. These state that the financial statements do not fairly present the entity's financial position in accordance with GAAP.

Disclaimer opinions. These state that the auditor does not express an opinion on the financial statements.

These three alternatives are relatively rare in practice, but when encountered they should alert the financial statement readers that something unusual may be present in the financial statements.

Quarterly Reports
to Stockholders

In addition to the annual reports, most publicly held companies also provide stockholders with quarterly financial statements. These interim reports contain less data than annual reports. The data *required* on a quarterly basis for publicly traded companies include the following.[5]

1. Income statement data:
   a. Sales.
   b. Income tax expense (estimated).
   c. Extraordinary items.
   d. Effect of changes in accounting principles.
   e. Net income.
   f. Earnings per share.
2. A discussion of the following, when appropriate:
   a. Seasonal nature of revenues and/or expenses.
   b. Change in method of computing estimated taxes.
   c. Discussion of any unusual items, disposals of segments, and so on.
   d. Discussion of any contingent obligations.
   e. Significant changes in the balance sheet.
   f. Discussion of any changes in accounting policies.

Some companies provide more than the required disclosures, including both a balance sheet and an income statement, while still other companies may also provide a statement of cash flows. However, unlike the annual report, which includes discussions by management, future plans, independent audit reports, and so on, the formal income statement is often the only financial statement provided in quarterly reports.

Securities and
Exchange Commission
(SEC) Reports

Over the past decade, the SEC adopted the policy of making its reports conform more to the annual and quarterly reports provided to owners of publicly held companies. The SEC, which has the authority to determine financial reporting requirements of publicly owned companies that are traded on U.S. stock exchanges, requires that these companies file financial statements with the SEC on an annual and quarterly basis. The annual report filed with the SEC is called Form 10-K, and the quarterly report is called Form 10-Q.

The SEC Forms 10-K and 10-Q are not really "forms" like those required for tax returns, but they are simply a set of guidelines describing the required disclosures. For most

---

[5]*APB Opinion No. 28,* "Interim Financial Reporting" (New York: AICPA, 1973).

companies, the 10-K and 10-Q are somewhat more detailed than annual and quarterly reports to stockholders. In addition to the information normally found in the quarterly and annual reports to shareholders, the 10-K and 10-Q also include data on inside ownership (stock owned by corporate management) and trades by insiders in the company's own stock, greater detail about management compensation, and several other items. Stockholders may request a copy of their company's 10-K and 10-Q.

Public companies must also file a Form 8-K with the SEC within 15 days of any major event that may have a significant effect on the entity. These 8-K reports are filed for major changes in ownership of an entity, when an entity files for bankruptcy, when a change is made in outside auditors, and for other similarly significant developments.

EVALUATING FINANCIAL STATEMENTS

So far in this chapter you have considered the nature, sources, and quality of formal accounting information. This section discusses the different methods used to evaluate financial statements. Remember that the evaluation of financial statements is worthwhile only if the quality of the underlying accounting data (discussed in Part A of this chapter) is at an acceptable level. For example, if the underlying data are **unreliable** (e.g., biased) or lacking **consistency** or **comparability**, then evaluating the resulting financial statements may produce useless information.

Financial reports may be evaluated using a number of different techniques. The following types of analysis are examined in this section:

Objective 3
The common types of analysis used to evaluate financial statements—horizontal, vertical, vertical/horizontal, trend, and ratio analysis.

1. Horizontal analysis—analysis of changes between the data of two consecutive years.
2. Vertical analysis—analysis of the data of a single year.
3. Trend analysis—analysis of data over three or more years.
4. Ratio analysis—analysis of one financial statement component relative to another component.

You may use these techniques separately or in conjunction with one another. While all these techniques are different in approach, they have one common feature in that they attempt to eliminate the size effects of dollar measures found in the financial statements. Size effects are eliminated by stating the financial statement data in terms of percentages or ratios, helping analysts make two fundamental types of comparisons:

1. Comparisons of a specific entity's performance from one period of time to another.
2. Comparisons of a number of different entities for a specific period of time.

Horizontal Analysis

The term horizontal analysis is used to describe any evaluation of financial statement data that looks at the change in a specific financial statement item from one period to another. Normally, accountants apply horizontal analysis to the financial reports of a specific entity. However, horizontal analysis could also be used with data summarized for an entire industry or for data on segments of a particular company. Horizontal analysis requires **two periods of data and evaluates the change in data items on a percentage basis.**

To illustrate horizontal analysis, study the summarized balance sheet and income statement data of Cybron G.T. Corporation given in Exhibit 15–7. The financial statement data of Cybron will serve as our example for several types of analysis. The Cybron

EXHIBIT 15–7

Financial Statement Data

Cybron G.T. Corporation
Balance Sheets
At December 31
(in millions)

Assets	19x7	19x6	Liabilities and Stockholders' Equity	19x7	19x6
Current assets:			Current liabilities:		
Cash	$ 7	$ 5	Accounts payable	$ 30	$ 35
Accounts receivable (net)	36	33	Notes payable	10	10
Inventory	42	48	Other payables	7	6
Prepaid insurance	3	2	Total current liabilities	$ 47	$ 51
Prepaid rent	6	9			
Total current assets	$ 94	$ 97	Noncurrent liabilities:		
			Bonds payable	$ 70	$ 70
Noncurrent assets:			Leases payable	23	25
Land	$ 20	$ 20	Total noncurrent liabilities	$ 93	$ 95
Buildings and equipment (net)	154	146	Total liabilities	$140	$146
Equity investments	38	34			
Intangible assets	9	8	Stockholders' equity:		
Total noncurrent assets	$221	$208	Common stock (par)	$ 98	$ 98
			Contributed capital in excess of par	21	21
			Retained earnings	56	40
			Total stockholders' equity	$175	$159
			Total liabilities and		
Total assets	$315	$305	stockholders' equity	$315	$305

Cybron G.T. Corporation
Income Statements
For the Years Ended December 31
(in millions)

	19x7	19x6
Sales (net)	$ 321	$ 303
Cost of goods sold	(230)	(215)
Gross margin on sales	$ 91	$ 88
Selling, general, and administrative expenses	(62)	(56)
Interest expense	(8)	(8)
Income from equity investments	7	6
Income before income taxes	$ 28	$ 30
Income tax expense	(8)	(12)
Net income	$ 20	$ 18

Other data (in millions, except per share data):

	19x7	19x6
Average number of shares of common stock	4	4
Cash dividends paid	$ 4	$ 4
Stock price per share, end of year	37.50	31.50
Net credit sales	276	241.8
Beginning net receivables	33	29
Beginning inventory	48	52
Beginning total assets	305	295

income statement below represents an example of horizontal analysis. (All percentages are rounded to a single decimal point.)

Cybron G.T. Corporation
Horizontal Analysis
Income Statements
For the Years Ending December 31
(in millions)

	19x7	19x6	19x7 Less 19x6 as a Percent of 19x6: % Increase (decrease)
Net sales.	$ 321	$ 303	5.9%
Cost of goods sold.	(230)	(215)	7.0
Gross margin	$ 91	$ 88	3.4
Selling, general, and administrative expenses	(62)	(56)	10.7
Interest expense.	(8)	(8)	—
Income from equity investments.	7	6	16.7
Income before income taxes	$ 28	$ 30	(6.7)
Income tax expense	(8)	(12)	(33.3)
Net income	$ 20	$ 18	11.1

Note that horizontal analysis may also be applied to other statements as well as the income statement.

Like all methods of analysis, horizontal analysis has both strong points and limitations. In its favor, horizontal analysis identifies how key variables change from one period to the next. Looking at the 19x7 and 19x6 dollar data, the only clear fact is that net sales, cost of goods sold, and gross margin all increased. Looking at the percentage change data, you can quickly see that cost of goods sold increased more (7.0%) than net sales (5.9%) in 19x7, resulting in only a 3.4% increase in gross margin.

Note the following limitations of horizontal analysis:

1. The percentages in the analysis are not intended to "add up" vertically.
2. Small base year numbers (near zero) may result in large change percentages.
3. Base year numbers of zero or of the opposite sign (+ or −) cannot be used to compute change percentages.

When you examine the results of horizontal analysis, remember these limitations. Horizontal analysis is designed to evaluate year-to-year changes in specific items of accounting data, thus providing financial analysis over time.

Vertical Analysis

The term vertical analysis describes any evaluation of financial statement data for a particular time period without comparison to other time periods. Some might think of vertical analysis as static analysis since only a single period's financial data is required.

Like horizontal analysis, vertical analysis restates dollar amounts to percentages. For balance sheet data, all items are usually expressed as a percent of total assets, with total assets equal to 100%. For income statements, all items are usually expressed as a percent of net sales, with net sales equal to 100%.

To illustrate vertical analysis, the following restatement could be made of the Cybron earnings data for 19x7 and 19x6:

Cybron G.T. Corporation
Vertical Analysis
Income Statements
For the Years Ending December 31
(in millions)

	19x7 Dollars	19x7 Percent	19x6 Dollars	19x6 Percent
Net sales	$ 321	100.0 %	$ 303	100.0 %
Cost of goods sold.	(230)	(71.7)	(215)	(71.0)
Gross margin	$ 91	28.3%	$ 88	29.0 %
Selling, general, and administrative expenses. . . .	(62)	(19.3)	(56)	(18.5)
Interest expense.	(8)	(2.5)	(8)	(2.6)
Income from equity investments.	7	2.2	6	2.0
Income before income taxes	$ 28	8.7%	$ 30	9.9 %
Income taxes	(8)	(2.5)	(12)	(4.0)
Net income	$ 20	6.2 %	$ 18	5.9 %

Note that in vertical analysis, percentages "add up," thus providing a view of the financial data stated in percentages rather than dollars. Vertical analysis reveals information such as the gross margin percentage (28.3% for 19x7) and effective tax expense rate on sales (2.5% for 19x7) at a glance. For the income statement, vertical analysis breaks down each cost or other revenue item in terms of each dollar of sales. For example, in 19x7, cost of goods sold averaged $0.717 per $1 of sales, while interest expense averaged $0.025 per $1 of sales.

Vertical/Horizontal Analysis

Accountants often follow vertical analysis with a horizontal analysis of the vertical percentage data. For example, once vertical analysis states everything as a percent of sales (or total assets, and so on) horizontal analysis may be used on these percentages. For the Cybron income statement data above, the following extension could be made:

Cybron G.T. Corporation
Vertical/Horizontal Analysis
Income Statement
For the Years Ending December 31

	Vertical Analysis 19x7	Vertical Analysis 19x6	Horizontal Analysis Percentage Change	Horizontal Analysis Relative Percentage Change Increase (Decrease)
Net sales	100.0 %	100.0 %	0.0 %	— %
Cost of goods sold	(71.7)	(71.0)	(0.7)	1.0
Gross margin	28.3 %	29.0 %	(0.7)%	(2.4)
Selling, general, and administrative expenses	(19.3)	(18.5)	(0.8)	4.3
Interest expense	(2.5)	(2.6)	0.1	(3.8)
Income from equity investments	2.2	2.0	0.2	10.0
Income before income taxes	8.7 %	9.9 %	(1.2)%	(12.1)
Income taxes	(2.5)	(4.0)	1.5	(37.5)
Net income	6.2 %	5.9 %	0.3 %	5.1

The first two columns simply report the results of vertical analysis, with no dollar data provided. Two forms of horizontal analysis for the percentages in the first two columns are reported in the last two columns of the example. Both the "percentage change" and the "relative change" columns provide horizontal analysis beyond that of the vertical analysis in the first two columns. The "percentage change" column is simply the 19x7 percent less the 19x6 percent. This tells us **how each income statement item changed from one year to the next as a percentage of net sales.** For example, gross margin on sales decreased by .7% of net sales (seven tenths of 1%, or .007) in 19x7 due to a .7% increase in cost of goods sold (from 71.0 to 71.7%). Selling, general, and administrative expenses went up .8% of sales, while interest expense went down .1% of sales.[6] Note that the "percentage change" column adds up, with positive changes (as they affect earnings) listed as positive percentages, and negative changes listed as negative percentages.

The last column in the above vertical/horizontal analysis of Cybron reports the **relative percentage change (RPC)** in each income statement item. Note that this is not the same as the first column in the horizontal analysis, which gives the percent change of the dollar amounts. The limitations of horizontal analysis cited earlier apply to this column of data. We expect the relative percentage change to be zero in cases where expenses are expected to vary directly with sales. For example, if marketing expenses are set to be 10% of sales each year, then the RPC should be zero. Positive RPCs indicate that an expense is relatively more than last year, and negative RPCs indicate that an expense has decreased as a percentage of sales compared to last year. The 4.3% RPC in selling, general, and administrative expense (SGA expense) is computed as follows:

$$\frac{\text{Percentage change}}{\text{19x6 (base year) percent}} = \frac{.8}{18.5} = 4.3\%$$

The selling, general, and administrative expense percentage increased from 18.5% of sales to 19.3% of sales, which is a 4.3% increase in SGA expense as a percent of 19x6 sales.

A partial vertical/horizontal analysis of Cybron's balance sheet data could be prepared as follows:

Vertical/Horizontal Analysis
Partial Balance Sheet Data
(total assets = 100%)

| | Vertical Analysis | | Horizontal Analysis | |
	19x7	19x6	Percentage Change Increase (decrease)	Relative Percentage Change Increase (decrease)
Liabilities:				
Accounts payable	9.5%	11.4%	(1.9)%*	(16.7)%[†]
Notes payable.	3.2	3.3	(0.1)	(3.0)
Other payables	2.2	2.0	.2	10.0
Total current liabilities	14.9%	16.7%	(1.8)%	(10.8)%

*9.5% − 11.4% = −1.9%
[†]−1.9%/11.4% = −16.7%

---

[6]Although the dollar **amount** of interest expense was the same for 19x7 and 19x6, it is not the same when stated as a percent of each year's net sales.

Note that total assets (which equal total liabilities plus stockholders' equity) equal 100% for balance sheet analysis. Accounts payable decreased from 11.4% of the balance sheet total ($35/$305) at the end of 19x6 to 9.5% ($30/$315) at the end of 19x7, resulting in a 1.9% (9.5% − 11.4% = −1.9%) decrease in the percentage of the balance sheet total represented by accounts payable. This change in accounts payable also represented a relative decrease of 16.7% (−1.9%/11.4%) in the proportion of the balance sheet total represented by accounts payable at the end of 19x6.

Horizontal analysis, vertical analysis, and vertical/horizontal analysis can be performed on any financial statement. Most forms of spreadsheet analysis performed by computer software will prepare these analyses automatically once the financial statement data are provided in the database.

Trend Analysis

The term trend analysis describes horizontal analysis over three or more time periods. Usually between 5 and 10 years of data are required for trend analysis. The objective of trend analysis, as the name implies, is to look for trends or patterns in the accounting data that might help predict future outcomes. Accounting income data are the most common object of trend analysis.

Accountants use many forms of trend analysis. Some techniques examine horizontal percentage over many years; some graphically plot the results obtained over the past 5 or 10 years on a weekly, monthly, quarterly, or annual basis; and still others use statistics to evaluate a series of historical data. Statistical methods of trend analysis include time-series analysis, regression analysis, and many other methods of evaluating the historical trends in elements of financial data. All of these techniques are based on the assumption that the historical trend in data is valuable for predicting the future. To the extent that this assumption is correct, trend analysis provides a useful tool for financial planning and forecasting.

In practice, accountants often combine trend analysis with other sources of information about future events when preparing financial plans. These methods are discussed in greater detail in most cost accounting and business statistics textbooks.

Ratio Analysis

Objective 4
How to prepare accounting performance, market performance, liquidity, leverage, and activity ratios.

A widely used method of evaluating financial data is ratio analysis, which **expresses the relationship between two numbers as a ratio of one to the other.** Analysts use many different types of ratios to evaluate financial data. Once these ratios are prepared, they may be used as the basis for further analysis, such as trend analysis, horizontal analysis, and so on.

The following five major categories of ratios will be discussed:

Overall performance measures:
1. Accounting performance ratios.
2. Market performance ratios.

Detailed performance measures:
3. Liquidity ratios.
4. Leverage ratios.
5. Activity ratios.

In each of these five categories, we examine several of the more commonly used ratios. Like the other types of analysis discussed above, these ratios eliminate the size effects of actual dollar measures and permit the analyst to make clearer comparisons within an entity over time and across entities at a given point in time.

Accounting Performance Ratios.   The evaluation process used by external and internal users of financial data normally includes one or more measures of overall performance.

The most common examples of these overall accounting-based performance ratios and their definitions are as follows:

---

1. Accounting performance ratios:

a. $\text{Earnings per share (EPS)} = \dfrac{\text{Net income} - \text{Preferred stock dividends}}{\text{Average shares of common stock outstanding}}$

b. $\text{Profit margin} = \dfrac{\text{Net income}}{\text{Net sales}}$

c. $\text{Return on assets (ROA)} = \dfrac{\text{Net income}}{\text{Average total assets}}$

You will frequently find these ratios used to express the performance of the entire entity or of its separate components.

Earnings per share (EPS).   External statement users and stockholders often refer to EPS as the single most important performance measure. As you recall from Chapter 13, EPS is the amount of earnings left after paying the preferred stock dividends, divided by the average number of shares of common stock outstanding during the period.[7] As such, EPS states the net income of a company on a per share of common stock basis.

Using the Cybron data from Exhibit 15–7, Cybron's EPS computations are

$$\text{EPS} = \frac{\text{Net income} - \text{Preferred stock dividends}}{\text{Average shares of common stock outstanding}}$$

$$\text{19x7 EPS} = \frac{\$20,000,000}{4,000,000 \text{ shares}} = \$5.00 \text{ per share}$$

$$\text{19x6 EPS} = \frac{\$18,000,000}{4,000,000 \text{ shares}} = \$4.50 \text{ per share}$$

Since Cybron has no preferred stock, preferred stock dividends are not deducted from net income. When a company has outstanding preferred stock, the declared dividends for the year are deducted from net income; and for cumulative preferred stock, the declared or undeclared dividends for the year are deducted from net income to compute EPS. As a result, EPS measures net income pertaining only to the common stockholders on a per share basis.

Profit margin.   The annual profit margin informs statement users what percentage of net sales remains as earnings after deducting all expenses. For Cybron, this margin is computed as

$$\text{Profit margin} = \frac{\text{Net income}}{\text{Net sales}}$$

$$\text{19x7 profit margin} = \frac{\$20,000,000}{\$321,000,000} = \underline{\underline{6.23\%}}$$

$$\text{19x6 profit margin} = \frac{\$18,000,000}{\$303,000,000} = \underline{\underline{5.94\%}}$$

---

[7] You may want to refresh your memory on EPS by reviewing pages 690–93 of Chapter 13.

Sometimes profit margins are computed using profit subtotals before the net income number. For example, the profit margin from operations would be computed by dividing operating income (net sales less operating expenses) by net sales, to eliminate the effects of nonoperating items on the profit margin measurement. In general, analysts feel that the higher the profit margin, the better the performance. However, it is not unusual for profit margins to be fairly small, below 5%, for large publicly owned companies.

Return on assets (ROA). The ratio most widely used by internal users is probably the return on assets (ROA) ratio. This ratio measures performance for the period relative to the amount of resources employed (average total assets) and informs users what they have earned relative to what they have invested in or loaned to the business entity. Return on assets is actually made up of two elements, profit margin and total asset turnover:

$$\frac{\text{Profit}}{\text{margin}} \times \frac{\text{Total asset}}{\text{turnover}} = \frac{\text{ROA}}{\text{ratio}}$$

$$\frac{\text{Net income}}{\text{Net sales}} \times \frac{\text{Net sales}}{\text{Average total assets}} = \frac{\text{Net income}}{\text{Average total assets}}$$

This ratio incorporates both the profitability of the business and a measure of how efficiently assets are used. Note that the ratio may be improved (increased) by either increasing profitability (more income per dollar of sales) or by increasing efficiency (either achieving more sales for a given amount of assets or reducing the amount of assets required to achieve the same sales). The ROA ratio is important and widely used because it incorporates **both** profitability and asset efficiency in its measure, whereas EPS and profit margin only focus on earnings. Most companies could increase their profit margins if they had unlimited assets available to them! ROA is sometimes computed based on operating income (before interest expense) instead of net income. This variation of ROA provides a return measure that is not affected by the sources of capital reported on the liabilities and shareholder' equity side of the balance sheet. In comparing two companies, the one with more interest-bearing debt and less stock would have lower net income (due to more interest expense) but the same operating income before interest expense, all else being equal.

For Cybron, the ROA ratios are

$$19\text{x}7 \text{ ROA} = \frac{\$20,000,000}{(\$315,000,000 + \$305,000,000)/2} = \frac{\$20,000,000}{\$310,000,000}$$

$$= \underline{.0645} \quad \text{or} \quad \underline{6.45\%}$$

$$19\text{x}6 \text{ ROA} = \frac{\$18,000,000}{(\$305,000,000 + \$295,000,000)/2} = \frac{\$18,000,000}{\$300,000,000}$$

$$= \underline{.06} \quad \text{or} \quad \underline{6.0\%}$$

For 19x7, the average total assets employed was computed as the ending 19x7 assets plus the ending 19x6 assets (also the **beginning** 19x7 assets) divided by 2, or $315,000,000 + $305,000,000 = $620,000,000/2 = $310,000,000. Cybron's ROA for 19x7 was 6.45% (or .0645). The average assets for 19x6 was $300,000,000 ($305,000,000 + $295,000,000 = $600,000,000/2 = $300,000,000; see "Other data" in Exhibit 15–7), resulting in a 6% ROA for 19x6. An increase in ROA is generally considered to mean improved performance. However, you should always try to understand the causes of such changes in ROA (or any other ratio).

There are two other accounting return measures that are often observed in practice: return on investment (ROI) and return on equity (ROE). As with most ratios, ROI may be defined many different ways. Sometimes it is measured the same as ROA, whereas in other cases the denominator is the sum of the average interest-bearing debt plus the average stockholders' equity, or some other amount representing "invested capital." ROE is generally defined as net income divided by the average shareholders' equity.[8]

Market Performance Ratios.   The following two commonly referenced performance ratios are based in part on the market prices of an entity's stock.

---

2. Market performance ratios:

$$a. \quad \begin{array}{c} \text{Price-to-earnings} \\ \text{or} \\ \text{P-E ratio} \end{array} = \frac{\text{Ending market price per share of common stock}}{\text{EPS}}$$

$$b. \quad \text{Dividend yield} = \frac{\text{Annual cash dividends per share}}{\begin{array}{c}\text{Ending market price} \\ \text{per share of common stock}\end{array}}$$

These two ratios describe the performance of the company relative to the market price of the company; they are aimed primarily at stockholders and other external users.

Price-to-earnings (P-E) ratio.   The price to earnings ratio, or P-E ratio, is perhaps the most popular measure of overall performance used by stock analysts. The P-E ratio describes the relation between a stock's year-end market price to the EPS for the period.[9] This ratio, also called the **earnings multiple,** expresses the company's year-end stock price per share as a multiple of the past year's earnings per share. For Cybron, these ratios would be

$$\text{P-E ratio} = \frac{\begin{array}{c}\text{Ending market price} \\ \text{per share of common stock}\end{array}}{\text{EPS}}$$

$$\text{19x7 P-E ratio} = \frac{\$37.50 \text{ per share}}{\$5.00 \text{ per share}} = \underline{\underline{7.5:1}}$$

$$\text{19x6 P-E ratio} = \frac{\$31.50 \text{ per share}}{\$4.50 \text{ per share}} = \underline{\underline{7.0:1}}$$

In the United States, P-E ratios average about 15 to 1. Low P-E stocks are generally considered to be less speculative and high P-E stocks are considered more speculative, all else being equal. P-E ratios vary among industries and are reported on a daily basis in the financial press.

Average P-E ratios in other countries vary considerably from those in the United States due largely to the differences in how earnings are measured. In Japan and Germany, where earnings are conservatively measured by U.S. standards, average P-E ratios are 38 and 20, respectively. In the United Kingdom the average P-E ratio is about 12, while in Mexico it

---

[8]ROE is clearly affected by the amount of debt relative to equity that is used to finance the firm's assets. The more debt that is used, the less will be the amount of equity. If the firm's ROA is greater than the borrowing rate, then in general ROE may be increased by using more debt and less equity to finance the firm.

[9]Note that for both the P-E ratio and the dividend yield we suggest using the year-end market price per share. However, other sources do not all agree on this share price, and some suggest that the average price for the past year or past month is more representative. When stock prices vary widely from day to day, some average may be preferred.

is about 10. Differences in the measurement of earnings explain much of the difference in P-E ratios around the world.

Dividend yield. The dividend yield measures the payment stockholders receive on their stock. The annual cash dividends per share divided by the ending stock price forms the basis for computing the dividend yield. For Cybron, the dividend yield percent calculations are as follows:

$$\text{Dividend yield percent} = \frac{\text{Annual cash dividends per share}}{\text{Ending market price per share of common stock}}$$

$$\text{19x7 dividend yield percent} = \frac{\$1.00}{\$37.50} = \underline{\underline{2.67\%}}$$

$$\text{19x6 dividend yield percent} = \frac{\$1.00}{\$31.50} = \underline{\underline{3.17\%}}$$

Making generalized statements about dividend yields is difficult. For Cybron, the dividend payment to common shares was $1 per share in both 19x7 and 19x6. Often annual dividends remain the same from year to year. However, if dividends stay constant and stock prices increase, then the dividend yield will drop, as in the Cybron example. Although higher dividend yields are often desirable, a decrease in the dividend yield is not necessarily bad news for stockholders. For example, a cut in current dividends could signal attractive growth opportunities that require cash now in order to generate even greater income and dividends in future periods.

Liquidity Ratios. In addition to the overall performance ratios discussed above, analysts can use many detailed financial ratios. Creditors often suggest that the most important of these detailed ratios are the liquidity ratios, which describe the resources of the company in terms of their convertibility to cash in a reasonably short time period. The two most common liquidity ratios are the following.

---

3. Liquidity ratios:

$$a. \quad \frac{\text{Current}}{\text{ratio}} = \frac{\text{Current assets (end of period)}}{\text{Current liabilities (end of period)}}$$

$$b. \quad \frac{\text{Quick}}{\text{ratio}} = \frac{\text{Cash + Temporary investments + Receivables}}{\text{Current liabilities}}$$

Current ratio. The current ratio measures the relationship between current assets and current liabilities. This ratio indicates whether the assets expected to be converted back to cash in the next year (or operating cycle) are greater than the liabilities expected to use cash in the next year (or operating cycle). A current ratio of less than 1.0 may signal financial problems, but this ratio can vary significantly from industry to industry. The current ratios for Cybron are computed as follows:

$$\text{Current ratio} = \frac{\text{Current assets}}{\text{Current liabilities}}$$

$$\text{19x7 current ratio} = \frac{\$94,000,000}{\$47,000,000} = \underline{\underline{2.0:1}}$$

$$\text{19x6 current ratio} = \frac{\$97,000,000}{\$51,000,000} = \underline{\underline{1.9:1}}$$

Note that these and many other ratios can be expressed several different ways. For example, the 19x7 current ratio could be stated as 2:1, or 2.0, or 200%.

The current ratio is a convenient way to describe the working capital position of a company for comparison with other companies in the same or similar industries.

Quick ratio. The quick ratio measures how quickly and easily a company's assets can be converted to cash in relation to its current liabilities. This ratio indicates whether a company's current liabilities can be paid with the company's current assets that can be quickly converted to cash. Normally, quick assets include cash, temporary investments, and net accounts receivable. Cybron's quick ratios are computed as follows:

$$\text{Quick ratio percent} = \frac{\text{Cash} + \text{Temporary investments} + \text{Receivables}}{\text{Current liabilities}}$$

$$\text{19x7 quick ratio percent} = \frac{\$43,000,000}{\$47,000,000} = \underline{91.5\%} \text{ (or .915:1)}$$

$$\text{19x6 quick ratio percent} = \frac{\$38,000,000}{\$51,000,000} = \underline{74.5\%} \text{ (or .745:1)}$$

The quick ratios show the improvement in Cybron's liquid position from the end of 19x6 to the end of 19x7.

Leverage Ratios. Leverage ratios are generally considered to be accounting measures of risk. The more financial leverage a company has, the higher the risk. The two primary leverage ratios are the following:

---

4. Leverage ratios:

a. $\text{Debt-to-equity ratio} = \dfrac{\text{Total liabilities}}{\text{Total equity}}$

b. $\text{Times-interest-earned ratio} = \dfrac{\text{Operating income before interest expense and taxes}}{\text{Interest expense}}$

Debt-to-equity ratio. The debt-to-equity ratio is the primary accounting measure of leverage. It can be measured in different ways. For example, some analysts only look at long-term debt to equity rather than total liabilities to equity. Others define leverage as the ratio of interest-bearing debt to equity, while still others divide one of the three measures of debt (total liabilities, long-term liabilities, or interest-bearing debt) by total assets instead of equity. The amount of leverage a company has is generally the main factor explaining the difference between ROA and ROE. If two firms had the same ROA but different ROE, the firm with the greatest leverage would generally have the higher ROE. Usually debt-to-equity ratios range between 1.0 and 5.0. For Cybron, the debt-to-equity ratios are:

$$\text{Debt to equity} = \frac{\text{Total liabilities}}{\text{Total stockholders' equity}}$$

$$\text{19x7 D/E ratio} = \frac{\$140,000,000}{\$175,000,000} = \underline{.80:1}$$

$$\text{19x6 D/E ratio} = \frac{\$146,000,000}{\$159,000,000} = \underline{.92:1}$$

Cybron's debt-to-equity ratio was less than 1.0 for both years, indicating a fairly conservative debt position. A ratio below 1.0 indicates that creditors have invested less than owners in the company's resources. All else being equal, a company with a debt-to-equity ratio below 1.0 would likely be able to borrow more funds at a lower rate of interest than a company with a ratio above, say, 2.5.

Times-interest-earned (TIE) ratio.   The times-interest-earned (TIE) ratio, a measure of operating income before interest expense and taxes over interest expenses, provides an estimate of a company's creditworthiness. Lower ratios suggest that a company finds it relatively difficult to make interest payments, whereas higher ratios suggest that a company may be able to take on more borrowing. For Cybron, the times-interest-earned ratios are computed as follows:

$$\text{Times-interest-earned (TIE)} = \frac{\text{Operating income before interest expense and taxes}}{\text{Interest expense}}$$

$$\text{19x7 TIE} = \frac{\$36,000,000}{\$8,000,000} = \underline{\underline{4.50}}$$

$$\text{19x6 TIE} = \frac{\$38,000,000}{\$8,000,000} = \underline{\underline{4.75}}$$

Cybron's interest expense was the same for both years, but its interest coverage ratio was higher in 19x6 due to higher pre-tax profits.

Activity Ratios.   Many different types of activity ratios can be used to help evaluate the efficient use of various asset investments. For example, the general idea behind turnover ratios is that more turnover signifies more efficient use of assets. Three common activity ratios are as follows:

---

5. Activity ratios:

$$a.\ \frac{\text{Receivable turnover}}{\text{ratio}} = \frac{\text{Net credit sales}}{\text{Average net accounts receivable}}$$

$$b.\ \frac{\text{Inventory turnover}}{\text{ratio}} = \frac{\text{Cost of goods sold}}{\text{Average inventory}}$$

$$c.\ \text{Asset turnover ratio} = \frac{\text{Net sales}}{\text{Average total assets}}$$

These three activity ratios may vary considerably from industry to industry. For example, you would expect inventory turnover to be more important to manufacturers who normally have sizable inventory than to service companies that normally have little inventory. Also, the investment in plant assets and total assets would probably be higher for manufacturing industries, making asset turnover lower in manufacturing industries than in service industries, which normally require relatively small investments in plant and equipment. A retailer who grants credit to customers may be expected to have lower receivables turnover than a wholesaler who provides supplies only to a few retail establishments. Since activity ratios may vary considerably, they are difficult to evaluate without considering industry averages.

Receivables turnover ratio.   The accounts receivable turnover ratio measures the ratio of net credit sales to net receivables, indicating how many times receivables "turn over" in a year. The higher the turnover ratio, the smaller the ratio of receivables to credit sales. If a company collected all of its accounts receivable every day, this ratio would be about 365, which is virtually the highest possible ratio. If receivables take an average of 100 days to collect, the ratio would be 3.65. A high receivables turnover ratio normally indicates good collection procedures. For Cybron, the receivables turnover ratios are

$$\text{Receivable turnover} = \frac{\text{Net credit sales}}{\text{Average net accounts receivable}}$$

$$\text{19x7 receivable turnover} = \frac{\$276,000,000}{\$34,500,000} = \underline{\underline{8.0}}$$

$$\text{19x6 receivable turnover} = \frac{\$241,800,000}{\$31,000,000} = \underline{\underline{7.8}}$$

While Cybron's receivables increased in 19x7, credit sales increased at a rate **greater than** 7.8 times the increase in receivables, resulting in an increase in the turnover rate from 7.8 to 8.0 for 19x7.[10]

Inventory turnover ratio.   Like most activity ratios, the inventory turnover ratio is generally considered better when it is higher than prior years, or on an increasing trend. For Cybron, the ratios are computed as follows:

$$\text{Inventory turnover} = \frac{\text{Cost of goods sold}}{\text{Average inventory}}$$

$$\text{19x7 inventory turnover} = \frac{\$230,000,000}{\$45,000,000} = \underline{\underline{5.11}}$$

$$\text{19x6 inventory turnover} = \frac{\$215,000,000}{\$50,000,000} = \underline{\underline{4.30}}$$

Cybron's increasing turnover ratio is due both to lower average inventory levels and to higher cost of sales. This could be caused in part by higher sales and in part by more efficient inventory stocking and ordering procedures, both of which would be positive factors in an evaluation of activity ratios. However, this increase could have also been caused by a change in inventory method during 19x7. It is helpful if you try to rule out artificial causes for changes in ratios. One way you can do this is to study the footnotes to the financial statements that describe the accounting policies the company uses.

Asset turnover ratio.   The asset turnover ratio estimates how efficiently a company used its assets in its revenue generating process, with larger ratios indicating greater efficiency. For Cybron, the asset turnover ratios are computed as follows:

$$\text{Asset turnover ratio} = \frac{\text{Net sales}}{\text{Average total assets}}$$

$$\text{19x7 asset turnover ratio} = \frac{\$321,000,000}{\$310,000,000} = \underline{\underline{1.04}}$$

$$\text{19x6 asset turnover ratio} = \frac{\$303,000,000}{\$300,000,000} = \underline{\underline{1.01}}$$

---

[10]This analysis of the change can also be directly computed by dividing the increase in net credit sales ($276,000,000 − $241,800,000 = $34,200,000) by the increase in average receivables ($34,500,000 − $31,000,000 = $3,500,000) or $34,200,000/$3,500,000 = 9.77. Since a 9.77 ratio for the change is greater than the first year's ratio of 7.8, we know the overall ratio must increase in the second year. See "Other data" in Exhibit 15–7 for 1/1/x6 balances.

EXHIBIT 15–8

Summary of Key Financial Ratios

Overall Performance Measures

1. **Accounting performance ratios:**

   a. Earnings per share (EPS) $= \dfrac{\text{Net income} - \text{Preferred stock dividends}}{\text{Average shares of common stock}}$

   b. Profit margin $= \dfrac{\text{Net income}}{\text{Net sales}}$

   c. Return on assets (ROA) $= \dfrac{\text{Net income}}{\text{Average total assets}}$

2. **Market performance ratios:**

   a. Price-to-earnings or P-E ratio $= \dfrac{\text{Ending market price per share of common stock}}{\text{EPS}}$

   b. Dividend yield percent $= \dfrac{\text{Annual cash dividends per share}}{\text{Ending market price per share of common stock}}$

Detailed Analysis Measures

3. **Liquidity ratios:**

   a. Current ratio $= \dfrac{\text{Current assets}}{\text{Current liabilities}}$

   b. Quick ratio $= \dfrac{\text{Cash} + \text{Temporary investments} + \text{Receivables}}{\text{Current liabilities}}$

4. **Leverage ratios:**

   a. Debt-to-equity $= \dfrac{\text{Total liabilities}}{\text{Total stockholders' equity}}$

   b. Times-interest-earned $= \dfrac{\text{Operating income before interest expense and taxes}}{\text{Interest expense}}$

5. **Activity ratios:**

   a. Receivable turnover ratio $= \dfrac{\text{Net credit sales}}{\text{Average net accounts receivable}}$

   b. Inventory turnover ratio $= \dfrac{\text{Cost of goods sold}}{\text{Average inventory}}$

   c. Asset turnover ratio $= \dfrac{\text{Net sales}}{\text{Average total assets}}$

The ratios we have studied in this section are summarized in Exhibit 15–8.

Limitations of Ratio Analysis.   Ratio analysis is very helpful for making comparisons of financial results within a firm over time and across groups of similar firms. However, it is extremely important to keep in mind the underlying limitations of financial accounting data. Two of the more pervasive limitations of financial accounting data are

1. The possibility that assets or liabilities may be over- or understated relative to their fair economic value.
2. The possibility that "assets" or "liabilities" broadly defined that have economic value may be missing from the balance sheet because of the narrowness of their GAAP definitions.

Though both of these limitations are expressed here in terms of assets and liabilities, they also have income and cash flow implications. An example of the first limitation is often found in the Plant, Property, and Equipment account, which when reported on a historical cost basis tends to be understated relative to fair values. As evidence, we usually find that these assets are written up to their fair value when a target firm is acquired by another. Also, as a result of acquisitions we often find goodwill recorded by the acquiring firm. This exemplifies the existence of off–balance sheet assets suggested by the second limitation, because goodwill is defined as the unrecorded net assets of the target firm.

The limitations of financial accounting have obvious implications for ratio analysis. To illustrate, assume that two companies are identical in all respects except that the plant assets of Company A are 10 years older than the identical plant assets of Company B, and are therefore recorded at a significantly lower historical cost. If both companies have the same sales and current period costs, which company will have the better return on assets (ROA)? The answer is Company A, since A will have higher net income **and** lower total assets than B. The higher income will result from lower depreciation on the lower (older) cost plant assets, and the lower cost plant assets will result in lower total assets. This gives Company A a superior ROA even though both companies are identical in terms of their current economic performance.

The ROA problem noted above is a classic example of what is often referred to as the "old plant/new plant" problem. Many companies use old, obsolete, fully depreciated equipment in their manufacturing operations because it makes their ROA look good. However, they may be increasing their probability of future failure when it becomes necessary for them to modernize plant assets to stay in business. The ratios used to evaluate firms must be used with caution, and only after careful consideration of the two general limitations in the underlying data noted above.

In addition to the limitations of the data upon which the ratios are based, it is important to realize that the ratios themselves have little meaning unless placed into the proper context. They will normally need to be compared to the previous years' ratios for the same company or to industry averages in order to be evaluated meaningfully. It is usually dangerous to make statements about the desirability of a particular value of a ratio without reference to an industry norm. A debt-to-equity ratio of 2.0 may be very safe in one industry and very risky in another. Library references such as *Value Line, Moody's Industry Surveys, Standard & Poor's,* and others should be referred to when attempting to evaluate the implications of a firm's financial statement ratios.

• SUMMARY

In this chapter you were given an overview of financial statement analysis. The chapter was divided into two parts. Part A discussed how accounting data should be evaluated to determine whether their quality justifies further analysis. Part B discussed (1) the various sources where accounting data useful for analysis purposes may be found, and (2) the various methods used to perform financial statement analysis on accounting data.

Part A essentially draws on our ability to apply accounting theory. The qualitative attributes identified by theorists are to be used to judge the quality of the accounting data. When accounting data are judged to be relevant, reliable, comparable, and consistent, the quality is judged to be high. However, these qualitative attributes are not readily observable, and assessing accounting quality requires professional judgment.

The various sources of accounting data discussed in Part B provide some insights into the types of analysis that are possible. The general-purpose financial statement data normally available to external users in annual reports provide the basis for most of the analysis performed by external users. However, SEC reports are also commonly used as a basis for financial statement analysis by sophisticated creditors and investors. Also, the many possible additional special reports not specifically illustrated in this chapter are subject to the same methods of analysis as those reports that provide the most common basis for analysis.

Part B concluded with an introduction to the various methods of financial statement analysis. The central advantage of these methods is in their ability to evaluate the relative performance of one company over many periods, as well as the relative performance of one company in comparison to others at the same point in time. These techniques, despite certain limitations noted in the chapter, add to the comparability of the accounting information and are extremely useful and widely used for performance evaluation purposes.

• DEMONSTRATION EXERCISE

The Rulkowski Company's comparative balance sheet at December 31, 19x2, and the income statement for the year 19x2 are as follows:

Rulkowski Company
Balance Sheet
At December 31

	19x2	19x1
Assets		
Cash	$ 25,500	$ 42,000
Accounts receivable	93,500	75,500
Inventory	63,000	75,000
Prepaid insurance	6,000	15,500
Investments (long-term)	0	25,000
Property, plant, and equipment (net)	180,000	120,000
Total assets	$368,000	$353,000
Liabilities and Stockholders' Equity		
Liabilities:		
Accounts payable	$ 38,500	$ 37,400
Accrued salaries payable	6,000	3,500
Notes payable, short-term	38,000	19,100
Mortgage payable (long-term)	80,000	105,000
Total liabilities	$162,500	$165,000
Stockholders' equity:		
Common stock	$120,000	$100,000
Contributed capital in excess of par	26,000	20,000
Retained earnings	59,500	68,000
Total stockholders' equity	$205,500	$188,000
Total liabilities and stockholders' equity	$368,000	$353,000

Rulkowski Company
Income Statement
For the Year Ended December 31

	19x2	19x1
Sales	$275,000	$255,000
Cost of goods sold	208,000	183,000
Gross margin	$ 67,000	$ 72,000
Expenses:		
Salaries expense	$ 10,000	$ 12,000
Rent expense	5,000	4,000
Depreciation expense	20,000	18,000
Other operating expenses	5,000	6,000
Interest expense	7,000	5,500
Total expenses	$ 47,000	$ 45,500
Income before taxes	$ 20,000	$ 26,500
Income tax expense	6,000	7,950
Net income	$ 14,000	$ 18,550

Required:

1. Prepare a vertical/horizontal analysis of the above financial statements for the Rulkowski Company. Assume all sales are on account.
2. Using the summary of ratios in Exhibit 15–8, prepare as many ratios as possible using the above information. During 19x1 and 19x2 Rulkowski Company averaged 50,000 and 55,000 shares of stock outstanding, respectively.

Requirement 1:

Rulkowski Company
Vertical/Horizontal Analysis
Balance Sheet
At December 31

	Vertical Analysis		Horizontal Analysis	
	19x2	19x1	Percentage Change Increase (decrease)	Relative Percentage Change Increase (decrease)
Assets				
Cash	6.9%	11.9%	(5.0)%	(42.0)%
Accounts receivable	25.4	21.4	4.0	18.7
Inventory	17.1	21.2	(4.1)	(19.3)
Prepaid insurance	1.7	4.4	(2.7)	(61.4)
Investments (long-term)		7.1	(7.1)	(100.0)
Property, plant, and equipment (net)	48.9	34.0	14.9	43.8
Total assets	100.0%	100.0%	0.0 %	

| | | | Horizontal Analysis | |
| | Vertical Analysis | | Percentage Change Increase (decrease) | Relative Percentage Change Increase (decrease) |
	19x2	19x1		
Liabilities and Stockholders' Equity				
Liabilities:				
Accounts payable	10.5%	10.6%	(0.1)%	(0.9)
Accrued salaries payable	1.7	1.0	0.7	70.0
Notes payable, short-term	10.3	5.4	4.9	90.7
Mortgage payable (long-term)	21.7	29.7	(8.0)	(26.9)
Total liabilities	44.2%	46.7%	(2.5)%	(5.4)
Stockholders' equity:				
Common stock	32.6%	28.3%	4.3 %	15.2
Contributed capital in excess of par	7.0	5.7	1.3	22.8
Retained earnings	16.2	19.3	(3.1)	(16.1)
Total stockholders' equity	55.8%	53.3%	2.5 %	4.7
Total liabilities and stockholders' equity	100.0%	100.0%	0.0 %	

Rulkowski Company
Vertical/Horizontal Analysis
Income Statement
For the Year Ended December 31, 19x2

| | | | Horizontal Analysis | |
| | Vertical Analysis | | Percentage Change Increase (decrease) | Relative Percentage Change Increase (decrease) |
	19x2	19x1		
Sales	100.0 %	100.0 %	0.0 %	— %
Cost of goods sold	(75.6)	(71.8)	(3.8)	5.3
Gross margin	24.4 %	28.2 %	(3.8)%	(13.5)
Expenses:				
Salaries expense	(3.6)%	(4.7)%	1.1 %	(23.4)
Rent expense	(1.8)	(1.5)	(0.3)	20.0
Depreciation expense	(7.3)	(7.1)	(0.2)	2.8
Other operating expenses	(1.8)	(2.4)	0.6	(25.0)
Interest expense	(2.6)	(2.1)	(0.5)	23.8
Total expenses	(17.1)%	(17.8)%	0.7 %	(3.9)
Income before taxes	7.3 %	10.4 %	(3.1)%	(29.8)
Income tax expense	(2.2)	(3.1)	0.9	29.0
Net income	5.1 %	7.3 %	(2.2)%	(30.1)

Requirement 2:

EPS: $19x2 = \dfrac{\$14,000}{55,000} = \$0.25$ $19x1 = \dfrac{\$18,550}{50,000} = \$0.37$

ROA: $19x2 = \dfrac{\$14,000}{(\$353,000 + \$368,000)/2} = 3.9\%$

Profit margin: $19x2 = \dfrac{\$14,000}{\$275,000} = 5.1\%$ $19x1 = \dfrac{\$18,550}{\$255,000} = 7.3\%$

Current ratio: $19x2 = \dfrac{\$25,500 + \$93,500 + \$63,000 + \$6,000}{\$38,500 + \$6,000 + \$38,000} = 2.28:1$

$19x1 = \dfrac{\$42,000 + \$75,500 + \$75,000 + \$15,500}{\$37,400 + \$3,500 + \$19,100} = 3.47:1$

Quick ratio: $19x2 = \dfrac{\$25,500 + \$93,500}{\$38,500 + \$6,000 + \$38,000} = 1.44:1$

$19x1 = \dfrac{\$42,000 + \$75,500}{\$37,400 + \$3,500 + \$19,100} = 1.96:1$

Debt-to-equity: $19x2 = \dfrac{\$162,500}{\$205,500} = .79:1$ $19x1 = \dfrac{\$165,000}{\$188,000} = .88:1$

Times-interest-
earned: $19x2 = \dfrac{\$27,000}{\$7,000} = 3.86$ $19x1 = \dfrac{\$32,000}{\$5,500} = 5.82$

Receivable
turnover: $19x2 = \dfrac{\$275,000}{(\$75,500 + \$93,500)/2} = 3.25 \text{ times}$

Inventory
turnover: $19x2 = \dfrac{\$208,000}{(\$75,000 + \$63,000)/2} = 3.01 \text{ times}$

Asset turnover: $19x2 = \dfrac{\$275,000}{(\$353,000 + \$368,000)/2} = .76 \text{ times}$

• KEY TERMS

Auditor's report or opinion. The report made by auditors after they conduct an audit; states whether the company's financial statements and notes fairly present the results of its operations and financial position.

Comparability. Accounting data are comparable when companies that experience the same or similar events report the same results.

Consistency. Accounting data are consistent when the entity uses the same measurement procedures from year to year, so that identical or similar events occurring in consecutive years are reported in the same manner from year to year.

Constraining qualities. Considerations that might override the primary and secondary qualities of accounting information, namely materiality and cost-benefit considerations.

Horizontal analysis. Any evaluation of financial statement data that looks at the change in a financial statement item between two periods.

Material amount. Amount that could affect the decision of a reasonably knowledgeable user of accounting data.

Proxy statement. Usually, a statement that announces the time and place of the annual meeting and describes any agenda items to be voted on by the stockholders.

Ratio analysis. Analysis in which the relationship between two numbers is expressed as a ratio of one to the other (see Exhibit 15–8 for summary of ratios).

Relevance. Information must be timely and helpful to users in making judgments about the future performance of an entity; **relevant** information is **timely** if it helps evaluate a future event or outcome of interest and **useful** if it helps reduce uncertainty about future events or outcomes of interest to the decision maker.

Reliability. Accounting information is reliable when it is unbiased, verifiable, and measurable with a reasonable degree of precision.

Trend analysis. Horizontal analysis over three or more time periods.

Verifiable. Accounting data produced by one accounting system are verifiable if they can be reproduced by another system or measurer.

Vertical analysis. Any evaluation of financial statement data for a particular time period without comparison to other time periods.

• SYNONYMS

Accounting principles; accounting practices; GAAP.

Auditor's opinion; auditor's report.

Objective information; verifiable information.

P-E ratio; P/E ratio; earnings multiple.

Ratio analysis; fundamental analysis.

Recognize; record.

Trend analysis; time-series analysis.

Unbiased; neutral.

Unqualified audit report; clean opinion.

• QUESTIONS

Part A

1. What is the objective of financial accounting?
2. How do financial statements help decision makers?
3. What four accounting qualities help financial statements achieve their objective?
4. What are two constraining qualities of accounting information?
5. How is relevant information identified?
6. How is reliable information identified?
7. What makes accounting information comparable?
8. What makes accounting information consistent?
9. What are the elements of financial statements?
10. Define five elements in terms of their effect on net assets.

Part B

11. Identify three separate sources of financial statement data.
12. Identify the three sections of an annual report.
13. Besides the formal financial statements, identify two other items of **financial** information found in most annual reports.
14. Identify three financial reports typically found in most publicly owned companies besides the formal financial statements.
15. Identify four types of analysis.
16. Define horizontal analysis.

17. Define vertical analysis.
18. Define trend analysis.
19. Define ratio analysis.
20. Identify and define two accounting performance ratios.
21. Identify and define two market performance ratios.
22. Identify and define two liquidity ratios.
23. Identify and define two leverage ratios.
24. Identify and define two activity ratios.
25. What ratio results when you multiply the profit margin ratio times the asset turnover ratio?

• EXERCISES

E 15–1
Reliability—
Balance Sheet
L.O.1, 2

Recall from the chapter that reliable information is measurable, verifiable, objective, and unbiased. The following balance sheet accounts are typically found in most companies. Each account is measured based on varying degrees of reliability. Using the following classifications, indicate the degree of reliability you believe to be present in each of the balance sheet accounts listed:

A = A *very reliable* account.
B = A *reliable* account.
C = A *relatively unreliable* account.

Balance sheet accounts:

a. Estimated warranty liability.
b. Cash.
c. Land.
d. Net accounts receivable.
e. Goodwill (net of amortization).
f. Marketable equity securities at lower of cost or market.

g. Accounts payable.
h. Buildings at original cost.
i. Buildings net of accumulated depreciation.
j. Inventory at lower of average cost or market.
k. Patents.
l. Bonds payable.

(Hint: In making your classifications, ask yourself whether the same account balances would have been arrived at if a dozen separate accountants had measured these account balances.)

E 15–2
Relevance—
Balance Sheet
L.O.1, 2

Recall from the chapter that relevant information is both timely and useful for decision making. Assume that you are evaluating financial statements **for purposes of making an equity investment** (between 20 and 50% ownership) in another company. Using the following classifications, indicate the degree of relevance of each of the listed balance sheet accounts for assisting you in your investment decision:

A = A *very reliable* account.
B = A *reliable* account.
C = A *relatively unreliable* account.

Balance sheet accounts:

a. Estimated warranty liability.
b. Cash.
c. Land.
d. Net accounts receivable.
e. Goodwill (net of amortization).
f. Marketable equity securities at lower of cost or market.

g. Accounts payable.
h. Buildings at original cost.
i. Buildings net of accumulated depreciation.
j. Inventory at lower of average cost or market.
k. Patents.
l. Bonds payable.

(Hint: In making your classifications, ask yourself how useful the information about each particular account balance would be in helping you make a buy/**not** buy decision.)

E 15–3
Elements of
Financial Statements
L.O.2

Based on your understanding of accounting theory, which of the following would qualify as an asset? Explain the amount, if any, and the justification for your answer.

1. A contract between the Denver Broncos and John Elway for exclusive service rights for the next three years. The present value of the contracted salary payments is $3 million.
2. A contract between Ford Motors and Donald Peterson, who will agree to be president for the next two years at a salary of $2 million per year.
3. The discovery of a vaccine to eliminate chicken pox, valued at $1 billion by competitors who wish to acquire the patent rights.

E 15–4
Comparability—
Balance Sheet
L.O.1, 2

Recall that comparable data are those that are meaningful when compared across firms. Assume you are doing a comparative analysis of a group of companies. Using the following classifications, indicate the degree of comparability present in each of the listed balance sheet accounts:

A = A *very comparable* account.
B = A *comparable* account.
C = A *relatively uncomparable* account.

Balance sheet accounts:

a. Estimated warranty liability.
b. Cash.
c. Land.
d. Net accounts receivable.
e. Goodwill (net of amortization).
f. Marketable equity securities at lower of cost or market.

g. Accounts payable.
h. Buildings at original cost.
i. Buildings net of accumulated depreciation.
j. Inventory at lower of average cost or market.
k. Patents.
l. Bonds payable.

E 15–5
Reliability
L.O.1, 2

Recall from the chapter that reliable information is measurable, verifiable, objective, and unbiased. Using the following classification, indicate the degree of reliability in each of the income statement accounts listed.

A = A *very reliable* account.
B = A *reliable* account.
C = A *relatively unreliable* account.

Income statement accounts:

a. Net sales.
b. Bad debt expense.
c. Goodwill amortization expense.
d. Depreciation expense—buildings.
e. Salaries expense.
f. Advertising expense.
g. Cost of goods sold (based on LIFO cost flow).

h. Cost of goods sold (based on FIFO cost flow).
i. Interest income.
j. Interest expense.
k. Realized loss on sale of marketable securities.
l. Unrealized loss on marketable securities.

E 15–6
Relevance and
Comparability
L.O.1, 2

The financial statements should include the following summary data:

a. Income from continuing operations.
b. Net income.
c. Cash flow from continuing operations.
d. Net cash flow.
e. Total assets.
f. Net assets.

Required:
1. Rank these six data items from 1 (*most* relevant) to 6 (*least* relevant) for purposes of selecting an investment from a group of investment grade (high quality) companies.
2. Rank these six data items from 1 (*most* comparable) to 6 (*least* comparable) for purposes of selecting an investment from a group of investment grade (high quality) companies.

E 15–7
Elements of
Financial Statements
L.O.2

Based on your understanding of accounting theory, which of the following would qualify as an asset or a liability? Explain your answers.

a. A customer advances your firm $20,000 cash for engineering services, which you plan to perform during the next fiscal year.
b. A customer falls while in your store and ruins five pieces of artwork that cost $15,000 and were being sold for $30,000. You sue for $30,000. The customer, who broke his leg in the fall, sues you for $100,000. Both cases are waiting to come to trial. Your insurance does not cover either possible loss.
c. Z Company, with office equipment recorded at $2.3 million, buys its 125 department-level managers each a $2.50 paperweight with the company's logo for their desk at work. Z Company reports $18 million in sales last year. The paperweights are expected to have a 10-year useful life.

E 15–8
Vertical Analysis—
Income Statements
L.O.3

The following condensed income statement data are taken from the year-end statements of Basic Elements Labs (in thousands):

	19x2	19x1
Sales	$1,850	$1,650
Cost of goods sold	1,320	1,240
Selling and administrative expense	216	187
Interest expense	120	105
Other gains (losses)	50	(28)
Income tax expense	62	25

Required:
1. Prepare comparative income statements for 19x2 and 19x1.
2. Evaluate the income statement data using vertical analysis to the nearest whole percent.
3. What is the profit margin for 19x2 and 19x1?

E 15–9
Vertical/Horizontal
Analysis—Income
Statements
L.O.3

Consider the data in Exercise 15–8 pertaining to Basic Elements Labs.

Required:
1. Prepare comparative income statements for 19x2 and 19x1.
2. Evaluate the income statement data using vertical/horizontal analysis as illustrated in the chapter. (Round answers to the nearest tenth of a percent.)

E 15–10
Horizontal Analysis—
Balance Sheets
L.O.3

Consider the following balance sheet data for Westwick, Inc. (in thousands):

	December 31	
	19x2	19x1
Cash	$ 356	$ 287
Receivables	420	530
Inventory	680	720
Other current assets	403	380
Land	600	600
Plant and equipment (net)	1,806	1,675
Total assets	$4,265	$4,192

	December 31	
	19x2	**19x1**
Accounts payable	$ 510	$ 488
Other current payables	420	540
Long-term debt	2,000	2,000
Common stock (par $10)	110	110
Other contributed capital	630	630
Retained earnings	595	424
Total liabilities and stockholders' equity	$4,265	$4,192

Required:
1. Prepare a horizontal analysis of the Westwick balance sheets for 19x2 and 19x1. Round all percents to a single decimal place (xx.x% or .xxx).
2. Assume that Westwick declared and paid dividends of $55,000 in 19x2. Compute EPS and dividends per share for 19x2.

E 15–11
Vertical Analysis—
Balance Sheets
L.O.3

Consider the balance sheet data of Westwick provided in Exercise 15–10 above.

Required:
Prepare a vertical analysis of these balance sheets as illustrated in the chapter. Let total assets equal 100%. (Round to xx.x% or .xxx.)

E 15–12
Vertical/Horizontal
Analysis—
Balance Sheets
L.O.3

Consider the balance sheet data of Westwick, Inc., provided in Exercise 15–10 above.

Required:
1. Prepare a vertical/horizontal analysis of these balance sheets as illustrated in the chapter. Let total assets equal 100%. (Round all answers to the nearest tenth of a percent.)
2. Evaluate the changes in the current accounts of Westwick (the current ratio). Did Westwick's current liquid position improve during 19x2? Explain your answer.

E 15–13
Ratio Analysis
L.O.4

The following data are taken from the records of the Taylor Wine Company as of the end of 19x2 (in thousands):

	19x2	19x1
Cash.	$ 185	$ 198
Accounts receivable	548	502
Allowance for bad debts	(16)	(14)
Wine inventory	832	786
Current prepaid expenses	54	46
Total current assets	$1,603	$1,518
Total current liabilities	1,122	1,139
Total long-term liabilities	2,000	2,000
Total stockholders' equity	1,800	1,700

Other data for 19x2:

Accounts Receivable Turnover Ratio	4.5
Inventory Turnover Ratio	3.2

Required:
Compute the following data:

a. Net sales for 19x2.
b. Cost of sales for 19x2.
c. Gross margin for 19x2.
d. Quick ratio for 19x2.
e. Current ratio for 19x2.
f. Asset turnover ratio for 19x2.

E 15–14
Ratio Analysis
L.O.4

Braxton Corporation reported the following data analysis for the most recent year:

Total asset turnover ratio	2.25 times
Average total assets	$8,000,000
Income tax expense	$2,100,000
Times interest earned	2.80 times
Gross margin as percentage of sales.	65%
Operating income before interest expense and tax as a percentage of sales	35%

Note that interest expense has not been deducted in computing operating income. Also, gross margin is sales less cost of goods sold only.

Required:
1. Prepare an income statement for Braxton that includes the following components:
 a. Sales.
 b. Cost of sales.
 c. Other operating expenses.
 d. Interest expense.
2. Compute the profit margin for the year.

E 15–15
*Ratio Analysis
(Challenging)*
L.O.4

Jansen, Inc., reported the following financial data for the most recent year of operations.

Income tax expense	$462,000
Income tax rate	30%
Return on assets	8%
Leverage (debt-to-equity) ratio	3.0 times
Asset turnover	1.8 times

Assume that Jansen's total assets were constant throughout the year.

Required:
Based on these facts, answer the following questions (not necessarily in order):

1. What is net income?
2. What are total assets?
3. What is total debt?
4. What are total sales?
5. What is pre-tax income?
6. What is stockholders' equity?

E 15–16
*Ratio Analysis—
General Electric*
L.O.4

The following data are summarized from General Electric financial statements and stock exchange data as of October 14, 1987 (the Wednesday before "Black Monday").

Market price per share of common stock	$61.375
Earnings per share, most recent four quarters combined	$ 3.85
Cash dividend per share, most recent four quarters combined	$ 1.32

Required:
1. Compute the price-earnings ratio for GE (round to two decimal places).
2. Compute the dividend yield ratio for GE (round to two decimal places).

E 15–17
Ratio Analysis—
Ford Motor Company
L.O.4

The following data are taken from the 1986 annual report of the Ford Motor Company.

Average total asset during 1986	$34.75 billion
Pre-tax operating income as a percentage of sales	8.08%
Pre-tax operating rate of return on average total assets	14.59%

Required:
Compute the following information based on the data provided above:

1. Pre-tax operating income (to nearest million).
2. Sales dollars (to nearest $100 million).
3. Total asset turnover (to nearest single decimal place).

• PROBLEMS

P 15–1
Relevance/Reliability/
Comparability
L.O.1

Consider the following facts. Each of 20 different companies owns a portfolio of stocks purchased at various dates over the past 12 years that consist of the exact same securities:

100 shares of X Company common.

200 shares of Y Company common.

300 shares of Z Company common.

150 shares of B Company common.

On December 31, 19x5, each of these 20 companies reports the value of this portfolio as a long-term asset at the lower-of-cost-or-market (LCM) value. The prices paid and current market value at the end of 19x5 were

Security	Range of Original Cost per Share	Market Value per Share
X common.	$10–$15	$18
Y common.	12– 18	14
Z common.	20– 27	29
B common.	45– 59	52

Required:
1. Discuss the relevance, reliability, and comparability of the LCM method.
2. Discuss the relevance, reliability, and comparability of the market value method.
3. Which method seems most relevant for comparison and performance evaluation?

P 15–2
Relevance/Reliability/
Comparability
L.O.1

Assume that two utility plants can each produce 100 million kilowatt-hours of energy per month, at capacity. Both plants run at 80% of capacity and charge an equal fee for each kilowatt of power. Plant A was built in 1946 at a cost of $10 million and is expected to last 80 years. Plant B was built in 1986 at a cost of $120 million and is expected to last 80 years. Straight-line depreciation is used by both. Assume that each plant is a separate entity, with separate shareholders, and so on. In 1990 each entity reports $4 million income from operations before depreciation and taxes. Each entity is subject to a 35% tax rate and has 1 million shares of stock.

Required:

1. Compute 1990 earnings per share and return on assets for each entity. (Assume no other assets.)
2. How relevant, reliable, and comparable are the net income and return on asset measures for these two plants?
3. Assume utility regulators allow utilities to set prices so that all utilities receive an equal return on assets. What problems do you foresee in such a regulatory system?

P 15–3
Relevance versus
Reliability
L.O.1

Banner Corporation is a closely held family business whose common stock is not publicly traded. Banner common stock has a par value of $10 per share. On November 1, 19x1, there are 100,000 shares outstanding, held by the Banner family. On November 2, 19x1, Banner Corporation issued 10,000 shares of stock in exchange for 50 acres of land that is to be used for a future operating location near Boyne Falls. Just prior to this transaction, Banner reported net assets of $2,850,000. The business was also appraised during the summer of 19x1, and the net assets were estimated to be worth between $4 and $5 million. The realtor who sold the land to Banner indicated that the owner had recently turned down an offer of $425,000 for the land before selling it to Banner for the stock.

Required:

1. Indicate the *most reliable* basis for recording the land on Banner's books. Explain why you believe this measure is the most reliable.
2. Indicate the *most relevant* basis for recording the land on Banner's books. Explain your choice.
3. What would you use as the recorded value of the land if you were Banner's accountant? Explain your choice.

P 15–4
Elements of
Financial Statements
L.O.2

Based on your understanding of accounting theory, how would the following situations be reflected in the financial statements, if at all?

a. B Company owns a fleet of oil tankers. In November 19x3 a tanker with a book value of $2 million sinks in a North Atlantic storm. In December 19x3 the insurance company agrees to pay B Company $3 million for the loss.
b. A forest fire destroys an apartment complex owned by Delta Corporation. The book value of the complex was $10 million and was about 30% of the assets owned by Delta Corporation. There was no insurance coverage for losses due to forest fire.
c. The city of Detroit agreed to not charge GM property taxes for a 30-year period for a site where a new plant was to be built. The property taxes would have been $530,000 in 19x3, the first year of the agreed tax waiver period.

P 15–5
Elements of
Financial Statements
L.O.2

Based on your understanding of accounting theory, how would you report the following items in the financial statements, if at all?

a. B Company buys a patent from its competitor for $50,000 cash. The patent has a remaining legal life of eight years. B Company does not intend to use the patent for production purposes.
b. C Company gives $250,000 (market value) of its own stock to a contractor who has agreed to build a new office building for C Company that will cost $8,000,000. The stock has a par value of $10,000.
c. The local government of Mayville is planning to build a new civic center on the site of your present downtown warehouse facility. The warehouse has a book value of $25,000 and the land originally cost $10,000. Mayville has agreed to pay you $350,000 for the land and warehouse at the beginning of the next fiscal year.

P 15–6
Ratio Analysis
L.O.4

Consider the condensed financial statement data for Garfield Fish, Inc., provided below (all amounts are in thousands):

Garfield Fish, Inc.
Balance Sheets
At December 31

	19x2	19x1	19x0		19x2	19x1	19x0
Cash	$ 21	$ 24	$ 20	Liabilities:			
Marketable securities	149	100	61	Accounts payable	$ 187	$ 193	$ 204
Receivables (net).	232	190	204	Taxes payable.	49	77	82
Inventory	229	244	260	Other current	63	39	68
Total current assets. . .	$ 631	$ 558	$ 545	Total current liabilities	$ 299	$ 309	$ 354
Plant and equipment (net) . . .	1,400	1,360	1,390	Long-term debt	1,020	985	985
Land	310	310	310	Common stock	680	680	680
				Retained earnings	342	254	226
Total assets	$2,341	$2,228	$2,245	Total liabilities and stockholders' equity	$2,341	$2,228	$2,245

Garfield Fish, Inc.
Earnings Statements
For the Years Ending December 31

	19x2	19x1
Revenues.	$4,508	$3,752
Cost of goods sold.	3,606	3,077
Gross margin	$ 902	$ 675
Other gains and (losses)	(14)	15
Interest expense.	(105)	(102)
Earnings before taxes	$ 783	$ 588
Income tax expense	(303)	(274)
Earnings	$ 480	$ 314

Par value for Garfield common stock is $1.00 per share. Market value of the stock was $2.75, $2.50, and $2.25 per share at the end of 19x2, 19x1, and 19x0, respectively.

Required:
Compute all of the ratios summarized in Exhibit 15–8 that are possible for 19x2 and 19x1 based on the data provided. (Round all ratios to two decimal places.)

P 15–7
Horizontal/Vertical
Analysis
L.O.3

Consider the data in Problem 15–6 pertaining to Garfield Fish, Inc.

Required:
1. Prepare a horizontal analysis of the balance sheet data for Garfield Fish, Inc., for 19x2 and 19x1.
2. Prepare a horizontal analysis of the income statement data for 19x2 and 19x1.
3. Prepare a vertical analysis of the income statement data for 19x2 and 19x1.
4. Prepare a vertical/horizontal analysis of the income statement data for 19x2 and 19x1.

P 15–8
Horizontal Analysis—
McDonald's
L.O.3

The following data are summarized from a recent income statement of McDonald's Corporation, the world's largest fast-food restaurant chain (in millions):

	Years Ended December 31	
	19x2	19x1
Revenues:		
Sales by company-operated restaurants	$3,106	$2,770
Revenues from franchised restaurants	1,037	924
Other revenues	97	66
Total revenues	$4,240	$3,760
Costs and expenses:		
For company-operated restaurants	$2,579	$2,278
For franchised restaurants	169	140
Total costs and expenses	$2,748	$2,418
Gross profit	$1,492	$1,342
General, administrative, and selling expenses	471	419
Interest expense	173	141
Income before taxes	$ 848	$ 782
Income tax expense	368	349
Net income	$ 480	$ 433
Net income per common share	$3.73	$3.32
Dividends per common share	0.65	0.59

Required:
Prepare a horizontal analysis for McDonald's similar to that illustrated in the chapter.

P 15–9
Vertical Analysis—
McDonald's
L.O.3

Consider the McDonald's income statement data provided in Problem 15–8.

Required:
Prepare a vertical analysis of each year's income statement data for McDonald's as illustrated in the chapter.

P 15–10
Vertical/Horizontal
Analysis—McDonald's
L.O.3

Consider the McDonald's income statement data provided in Problem 15–8.

Required:
Prepare a vertical/horizontal analysis of the McDonald's income statement as illustrated in the chapter.

P 15–11
Horizontal Analysis—
Ralston Purina
L.O.3

Consider the balance sheet of the Ralston Purina Company provided below.

Required:
Prepare a horizontal analysis of the balance sheet. To reduce computations, treat all of shareholders' equity as a single account (amount), including the redeemable preferred stock and the unearned ESOP compensation.

Ralston Purina Company and Subsidiaries

CONSOLIDATED BALANCE SHEET

September 30

(Dollars in millions)	1989	1988
Assets		
Current Assets		
Cash	$ 28.6	$ 23.8
Marketable securities	352.0	337.1
Receivables, less allowance for doubtful accounts	636.3	526.9
Inventories	677.8	559.9
Other current assets	126.3	94.7
Net assets of discontinued operations		152.1
Total Current Assets	1,821.0	1,694.5
Investments and Other Assets	795.1	638.0
Property at Cost		
Land	98.6	88.6
Buildings	612.9	598.5
Machinery and equipment	1,926.6	1,763.5
Construction in progress	80.2	81.1
	2,718.3	2,531.7
Accumulated depreciation	952.7	819.8
	1,765.6	1,711.9
Total	$4,381.7	$4,044.4
Liabilities and Shareholders Equity		
Current Liabilities		
Current maturities of long-term debt	$ 225.6	$ 60.3
Notes payable	142.0	150.2
Accounts payable and accrued liabilities	824.9	753.1
Dividends payable	33.8	25.6
Income taxes	89.5	92.6
Total Current Liabilities	1,315.8	1,081.8
Long-Term Debt	1,790.7	1,486.5
Deferred Income Taxes	172.9	142.6
Other Liabilities	242.0	243.6
Commitments and Contingencies		
Redeemable Preferred Stock – Series A 6.75% , $1 par value,		
authorized 4,600,000 shares – Issued 4,511,414 shares in 1989	500.0	
Unearned ESOP Compensation	(471.4)	
Shareholders Equity		
Preferred stock, $1 par value, authorized 1,400,000 shares – None outstanding		
Common stock, $.41⅔ par value, authorized 380,000,000 shares –		
Issued 114,604,912 in 1989 and 114,556,330 in 1988	47.8	47.7
Capital in excess of par value	261.8	252.0
Retained earnings	2,919.7	2,612.9
Cumulative translation adjustment	(33.3)	(33.3)
Common stock in treasury, at cost, 53,004,774 shares in 1989 and 46,358,013 in 1988	(2,350.1)	(1,766.5)
Unearned portion of restricted stock	(14.2)	(22.9)
Total Shareholders Equity	831.7	1,089.9
Total	$4,381.7	$4,044.4

The above financial statement should be read in conjunction with the Notes to Financial Statements on pages 21 to 30.

P 15–12
Vertical Analysis—
Ralston Purina
L.O.3

Consider the balance sheet of the Ralston Purina Company provided in Problem 15–11.

Required:
Prepare a vertical analysis of the balance sheet, stating all amounts as a percentage of total assets. To reduce computations, treat all of shareholders' equity as a single account, including the redeemable preferred stock and the unearned ESOP compensation.

P 15–13
Vertical/Horizontal
Analysis—
Ralston Purina
L.O.3

Consider the balance sheet of the Ralston Purina Company provided in Problem 15–11.

Required:
Prepare a vertical/horizontal analysis of the balance sheet as illustrated in the chapter letting total assets equal 100%. To reduce computations, treat all of sharcholders' equity as a single account, including the redeemable preferred stock and the unearned ESOP compensation.

P 15–14
Ratio Analysis—
Westinghouse
L.O.4

The following data are summarized from a recent annual report of Westinghouse Electric Corporation, a diversified technology-based corporation providing products and services for industrial, construction, and electric utility applications, and equipment for power generation.

Westinghouse Electric Corporation
Condensed Balance Sheet Data
At December 31
(in millions)

	19x2	19x1
Assets		
Cash and marketable securities	$ 598	$ 702
Receivables	1,905	2,032
Inventories	1,391	1,262
Prepaid and other current assets	741	625
Total current assets	$4,635	$4,621
Investments	894	762
Plant and equipment	2,189	3,300
Intangibles and other noncurrent assets	764	1,028
Total assets	$8,482	$9,711
Liabilities and Stockholders' Equity		
Accounts payable	$ 646	$ 625
Unearned revenues	1,129	1,097
Short-term debt	597	2,039
Other current liabilities	1,824	1,492
Total current liabilities	$4,196	$5,253
Long-term liabilities	1,252	1,190
Minority interest	24	33
Total stockholders' equity	3,010	3,235
Total liabilities and stockholders' equity	$8,482	$9,711

**Westinghouse Electric Corporation
Condensed Income Statement Data
For the Year Ended December 31
(in millions)**

	19x2	19x1
Sales	$10,731	$10,700
Cost of sales.	7,771	7,738
Depreciation and amortization	371	449
Interest expense	146	185
Other expenses (net)	1,643	1,534
Pre-tax income	$ 800	$ 794
Income tax expense	129	189
Net income	$ 671	$ 605

In addition to the condensed data above, Westinghouse reported that its weighted average number of shares of common stock outstanding for 19x2 and 19x1 were 157 million shares and 179 million shares, repectively. The market price of Westinghouse common was $55.75 and $44.50 per share at the end of 19x2 and 19x1, respectively.

Required:
1. Compute earnings per share for 19x2 and 19x1.
2. Compute the price-earnings ratio for 19x2 and 19x1.
3. Compute the quick ratio for 19x2 and 19x1.
4. Compute the debt-to-equity ratio for 19x2 and 19x1.
5. Compute the inventory turnover ratio for 19x2 only.

P 15–15
Ratio Analysis—Westinghouse
L.O.4

Consider the Westinghouse data provided in the previous problem.

Required:
1. Compute the return on assets ratio for 19x2.
2. Compute the profit margin for 19x2 and 19x1.
3. Compute the current ratio for 19x2 and 19x1.
4. Compute the times-interest-earned ratio for 19x2 and 19x1.
5. Compute the receivables turnover ratio for 19x2.
6. Compute the asset turnover ratio for 19x2.

P 15–16
Analysis of Performance—Westinghouse
L.O.3

Consider the Westinghouse data provided in Problem 15–14. Your objective in this problem is better to understand the improved net income of Westinghouse in 19x2 versus that of 19x1.

Required:
1. First, perform a vertical analysis of the two separate income statements for 19x2 and 19x1.
2. Which expenses decreased as a percentage of sales during 19x2 relative to 19x1?
3. Which expenses increased in 19x2?
4. What was the percentage increase in sales in 19x2 over 19x1?
5. What was the percentage increase in net income in 19x2 and 19x1?
6. Do you think cash flows from operations improved in 19x2? Explain.

P 15–17
Ratio Analysis—Ralston Purina
L.O.4

Consider the financial statements of the Ralston Purina Company (Appendix E). Include redeemable preferred stock and unearned ESOP compensation as debt.

Required:
Compute:

1. Return on assets for 1992.
2. The profit margin for 1992.

3. The current ratio for 1992.
4. The quick ratio for 1992.
5. The debt-to-equity ratio for 1992.
6. The times-interest-earned ratio for 1992.
7. The receivables turnover ratio for 1992.
8. The inventory turnover ratio for 1992.
9. The asset turnover ratio for 1992.

P 15–18
Trend Analysis
L.O.3

Consider the following data from the reports of Whetherwax, Inc. (in millions):

	19x5	19x4	19x3	19x2	19x1
Sales	$950	$838	$748	$687	$ 0
Cost of sales	710	630	560	515	0
Net accounts receivable	130	108	89	75	67
Net income	41	38	37	35	0

Assume that Whetherwax faced a constant tax rate throughout this four-year period.

Required:
1. Prepare a combination of horizontal, vertical/horizontal, and receivable turnover analysis to evaluate the performance of Whetherwax over the past four years.
2. What, if any, are your major concerns over the growth being experienced by Whetherwax?
3. What is the apparent trend in operating expenses?

P 15–19
Trend Analysis
L.O.3

The Bellstrom Furniture Company reported the following historical financial statement data (in millions):

	For the Year Ended			
	19x4	19x3	19x2	19x1
Sales	$203	$182	$96	$57
Cost of goods sold	138	119	58	38
Net income (loss)	45	35	15	(3)

	As of December 31				
	19x4	19x3	19x2	19x1	19x0
Inventory	$ 37	$ 33	$28	$14	$10
Net accounts receivable	71	59	26	12	10

Assume that Bellstrom has a 30% tax rate from 19x2 to 19x4 and that no taxes were paid in 19x1.

Required:
1. Prepare a combination of horizontal and vertical/horizontal analysis for income statement data over the past four years.
2. Prepare turnover ratios for the past four years.
3. Analyze the trends from your answers to parts 1 and 2 above. Should Bellstrom be concerned about any of its trends?

P 15–20
Ratio Analysis—
Leverage
L.O.4

The Modular Corporation reported the following data at the end of 19x1:

Assets	$400,000
Liabilities	100,000
Stockholders' equity	300,000
Interest expense	5,000
Net income	30,000
EPS (on 30,000 shares)	$1.00

During 19x2, the Modular Corporation expanded and financed the expansion with debt. The growth took place on the first day of 19x2, and the following results were reported at the end of 19x2:

Assets	$800,000
Liabilities	500,000
Stockholders' equity	300,000
Interest expense	45,000
Net income	70,000
EPS (on 30,000 shares)	$2.33

Income tax rate for both years is 30%.

Required:
1. Compute the following ratios before (19x1 data) and after (19x2 data) the expansion.
   a. Return on year-end assets (net income/ending assets).
   b. Return on year-end stockholders' equity (net income/ending stockholders' equity).
   c. Times-interest-earned (net income before interest expense and taxes/interest expense).
   d. Debt-to-equity ratio (liabilities/stockholders' equity).
2. What Modular has done with its debt financing of the expansion has had both positive and negative effects on the stockholders. What are some of the negative effects that could affect stockholders in future periods?

P 15–21
Ratio Analysis
L.O.4

The following condensed data are taken from the 19x3 annual report of Gotham, Inc. (in millions):

	Year Ended December 31	
	19x3	**19x2**
Sales	$387	$356
Cost of goods sold	212	193
Interest expense	8	8
Net income	20	17
Income tax rate	30%	30%

	December 31		
	19x3	**19x2**	**19x1**
Assets			
Current assets:			
Cash	$ 15	$ 13	$ 12
Accounts receivable	61	57	52
Inventories.	53	48	43
Other current assets	9	8	7
Total current assets.	$138	$126	$114
Plant and equipment	$127	$115	$120
Less: Accumulated depreciation	(39)	(36)	(40)
Net plant and equipment	$ 88	$ 79	$ 80
Total assets	$226	$205	$194

	December 31		
	19x3	**19x2**	**19x1**
Liabilities and Stockholders' Equity			
Current liabilities:			
Accounts payable	$ 47	$ 39	$ 36
Accrued liabilities.	18	19	20
Other current liabilities	12	15	13
Total current liabilities.	$ 77	$ 73	$ 69
Long-term liabilities	93	88	86
Total liabilities	$170	$161	$155
Stockholders' equity:			
Contributed capital	$ 20	$ 20	$ 20
Retained earnings	36	24	19
Total stockholders' equity	$ 56	$ 44	$ 39
Total liabilities and stockholders' equity	$226	$205	$194

Required:
1. Compute the following ratios for 19x3 and 19x2:
   a. Current ratio.
   b. Quick ratio.
   c. Debt-to-equity ratio.
   d. Times-interest-earned ratio.
   e. Accounts receivable turnover ratio.
   f. Inventory turnover ratio.
   g. Asset turnover ratio.
   h. Profit margin.
   i. Return on assets.
2. Compute the apparent amount of dividends for 19x3 and 19x2 declared and paid by Gotham, Inc.
3. Assume that Gotham's contributed capital consists of common stock with a par value of $100 per share that was sold for $200 per share at the time the company was formed. No sales have occurred since the original issuance. Compute EPS for 19x3 and 19x2.
4. Gotham common stock performed as follows:

	December 31	
	19x3	**19x2**
Market price per share	$450	$425

Compute the dividend yield for 19x3 and 19x2.

P 15–22
Analysis of Changes in Accounts (Challenging)
L.O.2

Refer to the financial statement data provided in Problem 15–21 pertaining to Gotham, Inc. The following additional data are obtained from the footnotes to Gotham's 19x3 annual report (in thousands):

	19x3	19x2	19x1
Bad debt expense	$ 937	$ 889	—
Depreciation expense	3,685	2,900	—
Gain (loss) on sale of depreciable assets.	(1,300)	1,500	—
Other data:			
Allowance for doubtful accounts, December 31	$ 1,935	$1,780	$ 1,520
New purchases of plant and equipment	15,000	5,000	12,000
New issuance of long-term debt	10,000	8,000	—
Amortization of premium/discount on long-term debt	0	0	0
Cash paid to retire long-term debt before maturity	4,580	5,000	—

Required:
1. Compute the amount of accounts receivable written off in 19x3 and 19x2. (Hint: Set up T accounts.)
2. Compute the cash received from the sale of depreciable assets in 19x3 and 19x2. (Hint: Use T accounts.)
3. Compute the pre-tax extraordinary gain or loss from the early retirement of long-term debt in 19x3 and 19x2. (Hint: Use T accounts.)

• CASES

C 15–1
Accounting Qualities
L.O.1

Accounting data are expected to have the qualities relevance and reliability. Evaluate the reliability of the following assets:

a. Cash.
b. Accounts Receivable.
c. Inventory.
d. Equipment (net of depreciation).
e. Equity Investment in Subsidiary.

C 15–2
Bad Debt Analysis
L.O.4

The Builtmore Products Company reported total accounts receivable of $468,000 at the end of 19x5 and $535,000 at the end of 19x6. The allowance for bad debts was $37,000 at the end of 19x5 and $49,000 at the end of 19x6. All sales were made on account during 19x6 except for $389,000 of cash sales. The accounts receivable turnover ratio for 19x6 was 3.8.

Required:
Compute Builtmore's net sales for 19x6.

C 15–3
Ratio Analysis
L.O.4

A newspaper report on Express Star, Inc., contained the following statements about the company's annual earnings:

The earnings for the current year resulted in a 12% return on total assets of $850 million, or 5 cents for each dollar of sales revenue. These earnings also resulted in a 25.5% return on average net assets for the past year.

Required:
Based on this information, compute the following data:

a. Average shareholders' equity.
b. Earnings.
c. Total revenues.
d. Asset turnover ratio.

C 15–4
Debt-to-Equity
L.O.4

In a recent report to shareholders, top management of Executech Software, Inc., identified a need for new sources of funds to support rapidly increasing sales. The president of Executech warned that additional long-term borrowing from banks would significantly increase the financial leverage of the company. The president expressed hope that additional stock could also be issued to reduce or offset the shareholder risk from additional borrowing. Explain the effects on leverage and "shareholder risk" from

a. Increases in borrowing.
b. Increases in stock issued.
c. Increases of equal size to both.

C 15–5
Accounting Risk
and Return
L.O.4

Consider two power generation companies in an unregulated market setting. Each company has a physical plant that cost $800 million to acquire in 19x1 and represents 80% of their total assets. Company A has total debt and equity equal to $500 million each. Company B is 100% equity (no debt) and is the exact same size as Company A. Company A is paying 8% per year on its debt. The tax rate for both companies is 40%. Over the past year, both companies reported income before interest and taxes of $80 million. In the coming year, the forecast of income before interest and taxes is uncertain, with estimates ranging between $30 million and $130 million.

Required:
Discuss the difference between Company A and Company B in terms of accounting leverage and return measures. Try to explain the relationship, if any, between the accounting measures of risk and return. (Which company has the highest expected return? Why? Which has the highest risk? Why?)

· **Evaluating Financial Statements** ────────────────────

C 15–6
Inventory Valuation—
LIFO versus FIFO—
General Mills
(Challenging)
L.O.2

The following footnote is taken from a recent annual report for General Mills Corporation:

Note Six: Inventories

The components of year-end inventories are as follows (in millions):

	May 31, 19x7	May 25, 19x6
Raw materials, work in process, and supplies	$156.4	$141.8
Finished goods	259.0	230.2
Grain.	24.7	24.7
Reserve for LIFO valuation method	(51.5)	(45.8)
Total inventories.	$388.6	$350.9

General Mills uses the LIFO method of valuing inventory. General Mills reported net income before taxes of $433 million and $317 million for fiscal 19x7 and 19x6, respectively. Cost of goods sold for fiscal 19x7 was $2,834 million. Assume that General Mills's income tax rate is 35% for all periods.

Required:
1. What would cost of goods sold have been for 19x7 if the General Mills LIFO Reserve account had not changed in fiscal 19x7?
2. What was the fiscal 19x7 tax savings attributable to the use of LIFO?
3. What is the total tax savings for all years before fiscal 19x7 attributable to LIFO?

C 15–7
Analysis of LIFO Inventory—Vader Corporation (Challenging)
L.O.2

The Vader Corporation reported the following partial income statement data (in millions):

| | For the Year Ended December 31 | |
	19x2	19x1
Cost of sales	$1,689.0	$1,557.0
Net income before tax	187.5	140.0
Income tax expense (40%)	75.0	56.0
Net income	112.5	84.0

The following balance sheet data (in millions) pertain to inventories, which are valued at FIFO during the year but converted to LIFO each year-end by way of adjustments to the LIFO Reserve account:

| | December 31 | |
	19x2	19x1
Inventories at FIFO	$597	$520
Less: LIFO Reserve	(86)	(75)
Inventories at LIFO	$511	$445

During 19x2 Vader liquidated some of its LIFO inventories, resulting in a decrease (debit) in the LIFO reserve of $10 million.

Required:
1. Compute the tax savings from using LIFO for 19x2 only, based on the data provided.
2. Compute the additional taxes paid in 19x2 because of the LIFO liquidations.
3. What was the dollar effect of 19x2 price changes on Vader's inventory value (amount and increase or decrease)?
4. What would cost of goods sold have been in 19x2 if there had been no 19x2 price changes in inventory and no LIFO liquidations?

C 15–8
Analysis of Sale of Plant Assets—Westinghouse
L.O.2

Consider the condensed financial statement data for Westinghouse presented in Problem 15–14. Assume that in 19x2 Westinghouse spent $440 million on new plant and equipment. Depreciation on plant and equipment in 19x2 was $320 million. Westinghouse disposed of plant and equipment during 19x2, resulting in a pre-tax gain on sale of $650 million. Westinghouse also wrote off plant and equipment with a net book value of $250 million during 19x2.

Required:
1. What was the net book value of the plant and equipment sold at a gain of $650 million?
2. What was the apparent cash flow from the disposal of these assets?

C 15–9
Receivables Valuation
L.O.2

Bradley Corporation is a wholesaler doing business with a group of retail stores in the Los Angeles area on a credit basis. Bradley reported the following balance sheet data as of the end of 19x4.

| | December 31 | |
	19x4	19x3
Accounts receivable—Retailers	$5,275,100	$2,967,800
Less: Allowance for bad debts	126,100	228,950
Net accounts receivable	$5,149,000	$2,738,850

Bradley estimates bad debt expenses at 0.5% (one half of 1%) of credit sales. All sales are on credit. Bradley has experienced significant increases in sales during the past few years, as noted in the following summary (in millions):

	For the Year		
	19x4	19x3	19x2
Credit sales	$40.85	$32.70	$26.35

Required:
1. Reconstruct the adjusting journal entry that was recorded at the end of 19x4 to reflect the year-end estimate for bad debt expense.
2. Assume there are no collections on accounts once they are written off. What was the amount of write-offs recorded by Bradley during 19x4?
3. What was the amount of cash collected on accounts receivable during 19x4?
4. As a banker who has made large loans to Bradley, you are responsible for evaluating Bradley's credit position. Do you feel Bradley's creditworthiness is improving or worsening? Answer "improving" or "worsening" and give support for your answer based **only** on the data provided—**do not** assume any additional facts.

C 15–10
Analysis of Equipment (Challenging)
L.O.2

Barth Corporation reported the following data:

	From the Balance Sheet as of December 31	
	19x9	19x8
Equipment at original cost	$239,500	$223,800
Less: Accumulated depreciation	64,600	62,000
Net equipment.	$174,900	$161,800

On January 1, 19x9, Barth sold some of its equipment, which had originally cost $26,000, for $5,000 cash. This sale resulted in a pre-tax loss of $8,000. No other equipment sales took place in 19x9. You may wish to use T accounts to help you solve this problem.

Required:
1. What was the amount of accumulated depreciation on the equipment sold in 19x9?
2. What was depreciation expense for 19x9?
3. What was the original cost of new equipment acquired during 19x9?
4. Assume that all equipment has **no** salvage value and is being depreciated on a straight-line basis (an equal amount of depreciation expense for each year of use). What is the estimated remaining useful life of Barth's equipment at the end of 19x9? (Round your answer to the nearest year. Label computations and show your work for credit.)

The environmental area causes problems not only for the current owner, but many acquisitions are stopped because environmental situations are found during the investigation.

Ronald L. Leach
Eaton Corporation

P·A·R·T

IV

Appendixes

Ethics and Accounting Judgments

When do you take bad news to regulators?
How do you audit "soft" management representations?
How do you know what will be interpreted as material to the user community?

Merlin E. Dewing
KPMG Peat Marwick

· Learning Objectives

After studying Appendix A, you should understand

1. The meaning and importance of ethical behavior, pp. 826–27.

2. Some common situations that threaten ethical behavior by accountants, p. 828.

3. Ethical considerations for each of the three groups of individuals in the environment of financial accounting (*a*) managers; (*b*) owners, creditors, and other financial statement users; and (*c*) auditors, pp. 829–37.

Note: This appendix can be covered as a reading assignment any time after the completion of Chapter 2. However, some of the end-of-appendix cases require knowledge of text material through Chapter 11.

**THE CONCEPTS
OF ETHICS AND
MORALS AND
THEIR BUSINESS
DIMENSIONS**

*Objective 1
The meaning and
importance of ethical
behavior.*

The objective of this appendix is to introduce important aspects of ethics in business and accounting and to demonstrate their application through a series of business cases. To discuss all relevant dimensions of ethics as related to accounting and financial reporting is beyond the scope of this text. However, ethics is so fundamental to accounting judgment and to a proper understanding of business decisions that an introduction to some of the key elements is warranted.

The dictionary definitions of the word *ethics* are a bit vague, starting usually with phrases sounding academic and impersonal, such as, "The study of standards of conduct and moral judgment."[1] Alternative definitions stress legalisms such as, "The rules or standards governing the conduct of the members of a profession."[2] While these definitions hint at personal responsibilities for decisions, we must look to the definition of *moral* to get closer to the role of the individual: "Of or concerned with the *judgment principles of right and wrong* in relationship to *human actions or characters.*"[3] In accounting and business we are concerned with both standards of conduct and the personal responsibility for the effects of decisions on other people and organizations.

In this appendix, we concentrate on the difficult decisions businesspeople have to make when there are perceived rights and wrongs on both sides of an issue and when guidelines or standards do not resolve the moral dilemma. Our purpose is to initiate thought about such conflicts and to demonstrate that certain approaches, though seldom providing absolute certainty, can help a person understand the nature of the trade-offs that must be made in many business and accounting settings.

Ethics relates to how people should behave in their dealings with other people and entities when the choice to be made has the potential to hurt or benefit others. To act in an ethical way is to choose an action that the decision maker believes is morally correct; that is, to choose what is believed to be right over what is believed to be wrong. There are many cases where most would agree on the morally correct choice, where we can easily determine who is benefited and who is hurt and where the degree of justice of the result is clear.

In cases of murder or robbery, the immorality of the act is apparent because an unjustifiable hurt has been inflicted on the victim. Personal morals, public opinion, and laws all more or less agree that such actions are immoral. In many business situations, however, we are confronted with ethical dilemmas that cannot be so readily categorized. For instance, a scientist involved in basic research on pesticides may sincerely believe that the research will help feed the world's people, but the resulting products may endanger wildlife and humans. Typically, such a scientist in a big organization does not have the ability to determine the way a product is marketed, labeled, or packaged. If he or she comes to believe that some harm is possible, should lines of responsibility be crossed in the business organization and traced to the ultimate effect? Is it ethical to rely on government regulators to make sure all such products are safe—regulators who may not know all the effects of the product? A start at answering such questions is to determine what the beneficial and the detrimental effects are and whether they are justified.

Business decisions affect individuals, entities, and even whole societies. Should all parties affected by a decision be viewed as capable of enjoying benefits and suffering harm? Who is hurt when a taxpayer is "over aggressive" in claiming deductions? Who

---

[1] *Webster's New World Dictionary of the American Language,* 2nd college edition (World Publishing Company, 1978).

[2] *The American Heritage Dictionary* (New York: Houghton Mifflin, 1982).

[3] *Ibid.*

benefits? Who is hurt when an insurance claim is exaggerated? Who benefits? In purely personal situations, the answers are reasonably straightforward, but what if you are the tax expert for a client who expects you to stretch the rules as far as possible, or what if you are the person responsible for making damage claims to insurance companies for your employer? Is it ethical to rely on the belief that it is up to the government or the insurance company to audit your returns or claims?

In addition to the problems created when an individual must consider the welfare of the organization as well as personal ethics, in some business settings we are confronted with even more ambiguous ethical decisions, where cultural norms may be in conflict. Consider the following case involving a U.S. company that is trying to start operations in an economically underdeveloped Eastern European country. You are heading up the management team assigned to deal with officials. You find that it is common practice for certain officials who approve business permits to take bribes. Such payments are clearly illegal, but it seems that all businesses pay them and that the government is fully aware of the practice. Your management back in the states wants the new venture to get off the ground and your reputation for being an up-and-coming executive is tied to your success in this assignment. Who besides you will benefit from your going along with the local custom? The society of the underdeveloped country will benefit from the expanded consumer choices your operations will provide and there will be good jobs for local workers. Of course, the bribe-taking officials will benefit from the cash they receive. Who is harmed? General disregard for the laws of the host country certainly does not bode well for the legal system. In addition, you find out that there are U.S. laws prohibiting the giving of bribes by U.S. firms in foreign countries, even when it is an accepted local custom. This case involves trading off legal and business considerations; and, of course, lawbreaking in any jurisdiction is a serious matter and should be avoided, no matter what the seeming justification.

Consider the following case involving cross-cultural frictions, which does not hinge on an illegality. A very profitable U.S. company has the opportunity to change its raw materials supplier from a relatively high-priced local firm to a low-priced foreign firm located in a country run by a notorious dictator. Who would be hurt by such a change? Employees of the domestic supplier in the local community may lose their jobs, but workers in the foreign country will be employed. Can it be said that the foreign society will be hurt by, in effect, support for its repressive regime? On the other hand, the company might, by being an important part of the foreign economy, be able to use its influence to improve conditions there. The owners of the company will benefit from higher profits, and the consumers of the company's products will benefit from lower costs.

The cases we have discussed up to now raise many questions and point to the ethical challenges in today's business environment. While our introduction does not give a formula or rule for making such decisions, three observations might be of help in approaching such issues. First, before a person can even hope to be ethical in a complex business situation, he or she must have the competence to understand the problem. Perhaps the most common form of unethical behavior in business occurs when individuals are unwilling to admit that they might not have an appropriate grasp of the facts, or the skills to act in a certain capacity. Second, a clear and honest listing of who benefits and who is harmed by a business decision would seem to be a prerequisite to deciding what the ethical choice should be. Third—and this is where judgment is most important—the justification for the effects must be assessed.

Ethics and Morals in an Accounting Setting

The above discussion of ethics helps us understand ethical behavior in a general sense, but how does ethics relate to accounting specifically? At first you might think that accounting in conformance with generally accepted accounting principles (GAAP) defines what is

Objective 2
Some common situations
that threaten ethical
behavior by accountants.

ethical, while non-GAAP accounting is unethical. However, as we will see, ethical choices in accounting involve more than merely determining whether the treatment of a particular transaction is in conformance with GAAP, or even if the overall financial statements are in conformance with GAAP. First, GAAP treatment is not always clear cut, and also it is not unusual that the issues involved go beyond the determination of GAAP. We will see that accounting decisions have the same potential for ethical conflict as do other business decisions.

In a study conducted by Touche Ross (now Deloitte & Touche), a major international CPA firm, key business leaders, deans of business schools, and members of Congress were asked to identify what conditions threaten to undermine ethical business behavior. Of the more than 1,000 respondents to the survey, 94% said that the business community is troubled by ethical problems. The four major areas of concern, identified in Exhibit A–1, include the emphasis on short-term accounting income, which ranked as the second most important area of concern, after concern with the perceived general deterioration of our institutions. Doing business in a multinational environment and pressures related to economic volatility also were seen as putting strain on business ethics.

In what follows, we focus first on the roles of accountants and some of the formal structures designed to guide ethical behavior. Later we discuss cases where choices about accounting reports create ethical dilemmas.

Our purpose is not to identify what is morally correct in accounting reporting. Instead, we attempt to identify some basic attributes of the financial reporting environment that frequently create the need for ethical choices. Although ethical standards and codes of conduct exist for both management accountants and independent public accountants,[4] these

EXHIBIT A–1

Most Threatening Conditions for American Business Ethics

Which conditions most threaten to undermine American business ethics today?
Rank them from first to fourth. (Ranking points: Possible, 4,000.)

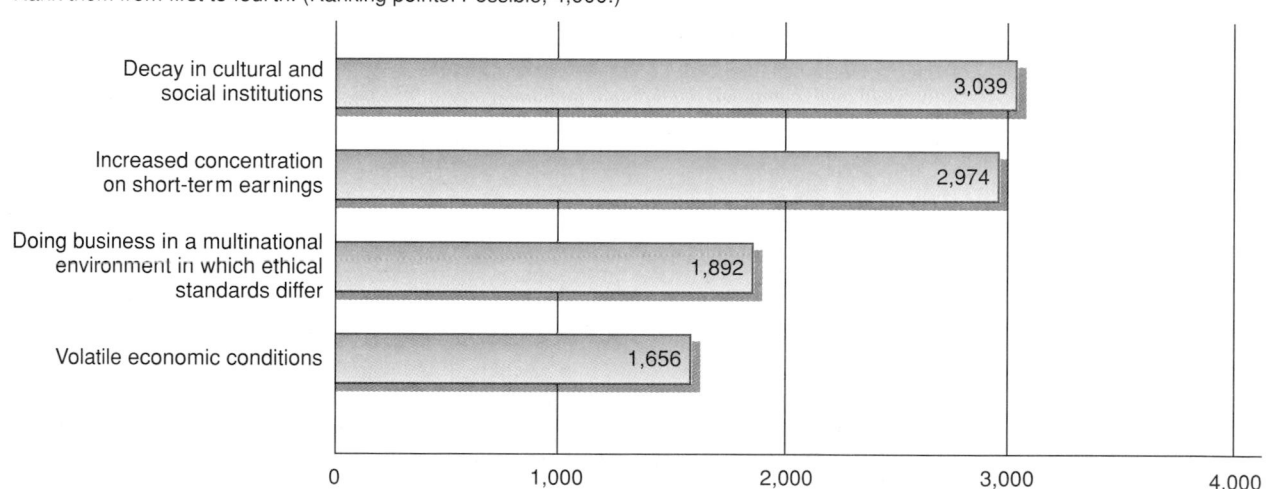

Source: *Ethics in American Business* (New York: Touche Ross and Company, 1988), p. 5.

[4]Specifically, the National Association of Accountants' (now called The Institute of Management Accountants) Management Accounting Practices Committee has issued in "Standards of Ethical Conduct for Management Accountants," *Statements on Management Accounting 1C,* which provides guidance for what is appropriate ethical behavior. Also, the AICPA has a *Code of Professional Conduct* (AICPA, 1988) providing similar guidance to public accountants.

sources fail to define what is morally correct behavior. The accountant must consider his or her specific charge, the environment, and the potentially conflicting benefits and harm to all parties related to or influenced by the decision at hand.

ENVIRONMENT OF FINANCIAL ACCOUNTING

Objective 3
Ethical considerations for each of the three groups of individuals in the environment of financial accounting: (a) managers; (b) owners, creditors, and other financial statement users; and (c) auditors.

We will discuss how ethical considerations affect these three key groups having special interests in accounting information:

1. Managers, including managerial accountants.
2. Owners, creditors, governments, and other "external" users.
3. Independent auditors.

In most privately held corporations, partnerships, and proprietorships, some overlap exists between managers and owners. As a result, the interests of these first two groups overlap significantly; and in some small businesses, there may be no real need for the third group—independent auditors—unless the owners decide to employ an auditor to verify the results of the company's information system independently or for consulting or income tax purposes. On the other hand, even small companies may have a need for an independent audit of their accounting statements, particularly if outsiders, such as bankers or other creditors, have a significant interest in the company. Therefore, although independent audits are only legally required of publicly traded companies, many closely held corporations, partnerships, and proprietorships also employ independent auditors for various reasons.

Auditor's Responsibility

In most large companies, there is a potential conflict of interests between managers and owners. Owners are generally assumed to be interested in maximizing their wealth; managers may concentrate on their own compensation and their consumption of resources. As a basis for performance evaluation, managers must then report back to the owners periodically on the results of operations. Published financial statements prepared in accordance with GAAP are an important reporting mechanism in this process.

To reduce the likelihood of inaccurate reporting in management's financial statements, independent public accountants are employed to verify that the periodic financial statements of management are, in fact, prepared in conformance with GAAP and "fairly state the position and results of operations" for the periods covered by the financial statements. The standard report provided by the independent auditor, illustrated in Exhibit A–2, gives owners some confidence that management's reports are properly stated.[5]

In essence, when owners are not involved in the management of a business, they hire (1) managers who administer the company's resources and prepare standard financial reports (e.g., balance sheets, income statements, and so on) to inform owners of their performance, and (2) independent accountants, who report to owners on the fairness of presentation of management's financial reports in conformance with GAAP. Note that independent accountants do not work for managers, and in fact must be unrelated to management.[6] Independent auditors, therefore, first must be competent to evaluate financial reports, and also they must be independent of management so that auditors are free to express their judgments about financial statements.

---

[5]Note the similarity between this example of an audit report and that disclosed in Exhibit 15–6 (page 782) of Chapter 15, Part B. The wording is similar in both examples, as well as in other "clean" (or unqualified) audit reports.

[6]Unrelated is used here to mean the auditor and manager have no mutually beneficial reasons for deceiving the owners. There are detailed professional standards that spell out which relationships between auditors and managers are violations of auditor independence. These are covered in detail in auditing texts.

EXHIBIT A–2

Standard Audit Report

Report of Independent Accountants

Coopers & Lybrand   certified public accountants

To the Board of Directors and Stockholders
Ford Motor Company

We have audited the consolidated balance sheet of Ford Motor Company and Subsidiaries at December 31, 1992 and 1991, and the related consolidated statements of income, stockholders' equity and cash flows for each of the three years in the period ended December 31, 1992. These financial statements are the responsibility of the company's management. Our responsibility is to express an opinion on these financial statements based on our audits.

We conducted our audits in accordance with generally accepted auditing standards. Those standards require that we plan and perform the audit to obtain reasonable assurance about whether the financial statements are free of material misstatement. An audit includes examining, on a test basis, evidence supporting the amounts and disclosures in the financial statements. An audit also includes assessing the accounting principles used and significant estimates made by management, as well as evaluating the overall financial statement presentation. We believe that our audits provide a reasonable basis for our opinion.

In our opinon, the financial statements referred to above present fairly, in all material respects, the consolidated financial position of Ford Motor Company and Sudsidiaries at December 31, 1992 and 1991, and the consolidated results of their operations and their cash flows for each of the three years in the period ended December 31, 1992, in conformity with generally accepted accounting principles.

As discussed in Notes 2 and 5 to the consolidated financial statements, the company changed its methods of accounting for postretirement benefits other than pensions and income taxes in 1992.

Coopers + LyBrand

400 Renaissance Center
Detroit, Michigan 48243
313–446–7100
February 8, 1993

Source: Ford Motor Company, *1992 Annual Report.*

Manager's
Responsibility

Managers are generally hired to manage business because of their special management skills (i.e., marketing, financing, operating, and so on). These managers have a legal and an ethical obligation to manage the business for the benefit of the owners. They also have an obligation to follow explicit and implicit contractual terms of employment. They are stewards for the owners and their stewardship over resources has an ethical dimension. Frequently contracts between the entity and its managers provide incentive clauses to encourage managers to earn profits for the owners. For example, bonuses to managers are often not paid unless management achieves some minimum level of profits. Also, in an effort to encourage key managers to act in the best interests of the owners, businesses often reward key managers with shares of stock if they perform well. By making managers part owners in the entity, some of their wealth becomes tied to the performance of the company.

In addition to the incentives in compensation agreements and the verification of management's financial statements by the independent auditors, various legal responsibilities govern the behavior of managers. One source of managers' legal responsibilities is defined by the Foreign Corrupt Practices Act (FCPA) passed by Congress in 1977. This act of Congress is broader than the name implies and covers the legal responsibilities of managers to control the entity's resources safely and report on the transactions and events that

EXHIBIT A–3

Formal Management Statement

Management's Financial Resposibility

Management is responsible for the preparation of the company's financial statements and the other financial information in this report. This responsibility includes maintaining the integrity and objectivity of the financial records and the presentation of the company's financial statements in conformity with generally accepted accounting principles.

The company maintains an internal control structure designed to provide, among other things, reasonable assurance that its records include the transactions of its operations in all material respects and to provide protection against significant misuse or loss of company assets. The internal control structure is supported by a staff of internal auditors who employ thorough auditing programs, by careful selection and training of financial management personnel, and by written procedures that communicate the details of the internal control structure to the company's worldwide activities.

The company's financial statement have been audited by Coopers & Lybrand, independent certified public accountants. Their audit was conducted in accordance with generally accepted auditing standards which included consideration of the company's internal control structure. The Report of Independent Accountants appears on page 37.

The Board of Directors, acting through its Audit Committee composed solely of directors who are not employees of the company, is responsible for determining that management fulfills its responsibilities in the preparation of financial statements and the financial control of operations. The Audit Committee appoints the independent public accountants, subject to ratification by the stockholders. It meets regularly with management, internal auditors, and independent accountants. The independent accountants have full and free access to the Audit Committee and meet with it to discuss their audit work, the company's internal controls, and financial reporting matters.

Harold A. Poling
Chairman of the Board

Stanley A. Seneker
Chief Financial Officer

Source: Ford Motor Company, *1992 Annual Report.*

affect the entity's resources.[7] Businesses need not be involved with foreign entities to be covered by the FCPA.

Management accountants have a special role in safeguarding the assets of the business (the stewardship function) in that they are charged with providing information that is timely and useful for business decision making. The information provided by management accountants helps other managers make internal business decisions regarding the operating, financing, and investment activities of the entity. Management accountants also prepare the publicly disclosed financial statements for use by outside creditors, stockholders, and other potential investors to use in their investment and credit-granting decisions. It is important to understand that management prepares and has the primary responsibility for the published financial statements. Exhibit A–3 shows an example of the formal management statement regarding its responsibility for the financial statements found in published annual reports. Hence, the management accountant is charged with developing an accounting information system that has the integrity, breadth, and detail needed to provide useful information for the business decisions of both internal and external users of accounting information.

ETHICAL JUDGMENT AND THE MEANING OF GAAP

One of the most important parts of the standard audit report is that which tells the owners (and other users) that the accounting reports of management are prepared in accordance with GAAP. The meaning of GAAP, however, is a matter of judgment. Sometimes a specific rule may apply to a transaction, but it is possible that no rule fits the facts exactly. In such cases accountants have a hierarchy of authoritative sources to consult. If a question

---

[7]For a discussion of the Foreign Corrupt Practices Act and its implications, see *Internal Control in U.S. Corporations* (New York: Financial Executives Research Foundation, 1980).

EXHIBIT A–4

Authoritative Sources for Determining What Procedures Constitute Generally Accepted Accounting Principles (GAAP)

Level One:

1. *FASB Statements* (1974 to the present)
2. *APB Opinions* (1960–73).
3. *AICPA Accounting Research Bulletins* (1953–59)
4. *FASB Interpretations* (1974 to the present)

Level Two:

1. *AICPA Accounting Interpretations* (1960–73)
2. *FASB Technical Bulletins*
3. *AICPA Statements of Position*

Level Three:

1. Documented prevalent industry practices and procedures
2. *FASB Concepts Statements*
3. *APB Statements*
4. Documented textbook procedures
5. Documented acceptance from other professional or academic literature

concerning whether something is a generally accepted accounting principle is not addressed by the first level of authority, the second level should then be considered, and so on, until some basis for choice can be established. Exhibit A–4 summarizes the three levels of authority that comprise GAAP.[8] In essence, to say that a practice or procedure is in conformance with GAAP requires either a specific reference to an authoritative source (e.g., *FASB Statements*), or a reference to the general use and acceptance of the practice or procedure.

While the sources of authoritative support for GAAP are voluminous, many specific transactions or adjustments encountered in practice are not explicitly addressed. These situations require in-depth knowledge of business practices, accounting theory, and professional judgment on the part of both management's internal accountants and the independent auditors. Ethical considerations are perhaps most important and most difficult to apply in these judgment situations. Where there is no direct authoritative guidance, managers may be inclined to account in a way that maximizes their own welfare. On the other hand, the auditor may disagree with management's judgment. In such uncertain situations where there is no clear authoritative basis, it may be difficult to convince management that a different accounting treatment is necessary to avoid a qualification of the audit opinion.

Two Cases Concerning GAAP and Ethical Judgments

To illustrate such reporting dilemmas, consider the following two cases, "Fly-by-Night Travel" and "20/20 Hindsight." Fly-by-Night is a new travel agency that specializes in booking flights to Florida over winter and spring breaks at deep discount fares. Its first four flights for spring break of 19x2 are sold out by December 31, 19x1. There is also a waiting list of 250 students who want tickets. Refund of ticket prices to students requires a cancellation notice by January 31, 19x2, for a full refund, and by February 28, 19x2, for a partial refund. The manager of Fly-by-Night is paid a salary based on reported net income and wants to include all bookings for the 19x2 spring break as sales revenue for the

---

[8]For a discussion of GAAP, see "The House of GAAP," *Journal of Accountancy* (June 1984), pp. 122–29. For authoritative reference to sources of GAAP, see *Statement on Auditing Standards No. 43* (New York: AICPA, 1982).

19x1 income statement instead of recording them as 19x2 sales. The owners of Fly-by-Night Travel have no other travel agencies (yet) but have employed you to audit this new venture as well as their other 35 unrelated business operations. You are not sure whether to permit Fly-by-Night to record sales revenues for these four sold-out flights in the 19x1 income statement. How do you decide?

Note that while GAAP does provide rather general directives as to when to recognize revenue, the ultimate decision is still based on professional judgment. The auditor must decide whether to disagree with the manager of Fly-by-Night, and if so, on what grounds. To disagree will cost the manager salary, providing economic incentives for the manager to argue in support of recording the revenue in 19x1. Who can be hurt by recording revenue in 19x1? If the financial statements are relied upon by creditors or stockholders and it turns out that the revenues are not legitimate, then those parties could be hurt. If the auditor forces the issue, the client may choose to change auditors; and, therefore, both the auditor and the audit firm may be harmed. How does one decide when ordinary sources do not specifically answer the question? Auditors could use industry practice as one basis for making a determination. Another pervasive approach to such gray areas is to reason by analogy. If GAAP covers a closely related type of transaction, the arguments may be compelling for the case at hand.

The Fly-by-Night case is but one example of the potential conflict of interests between owners, managers, and auditors. Each year there are literally thousands of conflicts whose resolutions have a material impact on the financial reports of publicly owned companies.

The second case, aptly named "20/20 Hindsight," focuses on a Senate hearing. Consider the following exchange between a U.S. senator and a senior partner of a CPA firm during a hearing before a congressional committee concerning the savings and loan crisis. The senator is referring to the chart shown here.

Senator: You are familiar with the MII, FSI, DLI affiliation as is shown on Chart A.

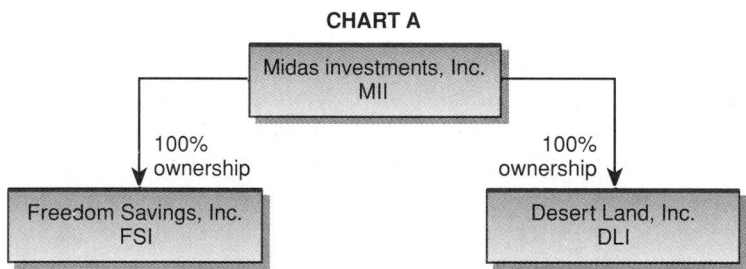

CPA: Yes, my firm was the external auditor of MII and subsidiaries from 1980 until we resigned from the engagement in 1988.

Senator: Now, I want you to verify that the series of transactions depicted in Chart B approximately describes the major cash flows within the group made up by MII and its subsidiaries during the period 1985–87.

As you know, our problem is that $300,000,000 of federally insured FSI depositor accounts will now have to be paid by the government because the notes FSI accepted and the land which is the collateral on those notes are now worth, on average, 10 cents on the dollar. Do you agree that this is in general what happened?

CPA: Yes, Senator, I believe that you have summarized the major features, but please keep in mind that we, as independent CPAs, didn't know back when FSI recorded those notes and DLI recognized the revenue on the sale of the land that the various land developers were not financially viable and that the land would decline in value. At the time, we believed that the sale met all GAAP requirements, and in the two years following we forced write-downs of the notes on FSI's balance sheet as we saw problems of collectibility emerge.

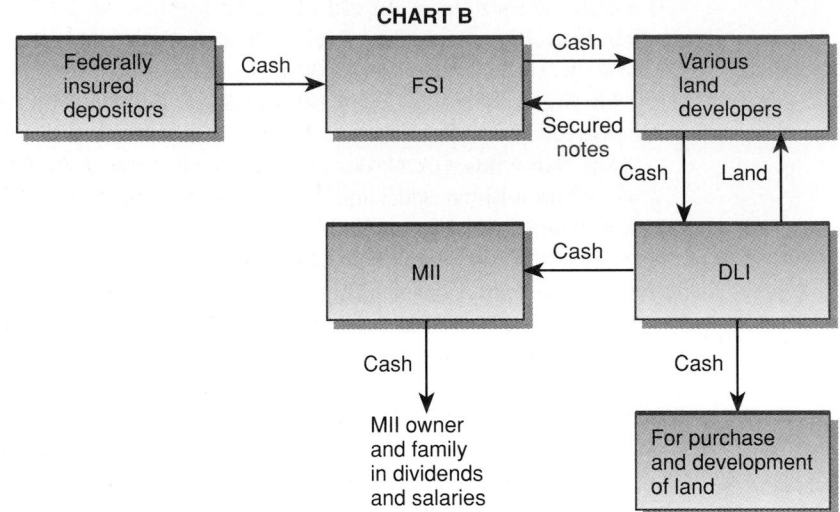

CHART B

Senator: Yes, but didn't you sketch out this pattern yourself before you gave clean opinions in 1986 and 1987? Couldn't you tell that this whole scheme of cash flows from insured depositors to the MII owners didn't seem quite right?

CPA: In hindsight, it looks obvious, but remember, Senator, that the regulations governing S&L investments were liberalized in the 80s to allow a great variety of investments and certainly many S&Ls were engaged in similar transactions, most of which were approved by the regulators at the time.

Senator: I always believed that before you issued a clean opinion on the overall financial statements you investigated the underlying economics of the transactions and made sure they were real and made economic sense.

CPA: I can assure you, Senator, that at the time we analyzed every major transaction—our working papers prove that—and we applied generally accepted auditing standards in all cases. In hindsight, we, like everyone else, see that land values were overstated and that cash actually flowed out of FSI to the parent company and because of a general collapse in the real estate market, the parent is now bankrupt. But we contend that your own regulators, in essence, approved of such transactions at the time; therefore, it was normal industry practice.

Senator: All I know, Sir, is that federally insured deposits were used to finance speculation and an extravagant lifestyle for a handful of corporate executives and their families and that your issuing a series of clean opinions was a contributing factor. You can say that you were in conformance with GAAP but I say that you had a professional responsibility to make sure that the economics were sound and that Federal Savings did not engage in such risky loans or at least that the cash could not flow from insured deposits to the owners' other business the way it did.

CPA: I respectfully disagree that we are responsible for the actions of the parties involved. We have the responsibility to determine if the financial statements were reported in conformance with GAAP, and we did that. If a business chooses to engage in risky loans and if the regulations allow that, we are not responsible for such losses.

Who was hurt by the downfall of FSI? Who benefited? Does this case involve an ethical dilemma for the CPA, the accounting profession, the owners of MII, Congress? Obviously, much of this case depends on the valuation of the land and the viability of the purchasers of the land. If these "sales" were not arm's length and in essence were just a scheme to divert cash from a federally insured entity to the owners of the parent company, and if the CPAs did not properly investigate the transactions, then a professional lapse certainly did occur. But can it be called an ethical lapse without a conscious decision to take a morally wrong course of action?

In both of these cases, there was pressure on the auditor to agree with management's interpretation of the appropriate accounting for the transactions at issue. Auditors must be both competent and independent so that they can judge for themselves what the appropriate treatment should be, and so that they will be free to report their positions regardless of management's desires.

To maintain an independent position as a representative of owners and other parties places an important responsibility on the auditor. A contributing environmental factor is that the auditor interacts relatively less with the true client (the owners, creditors, and general public) than with management when performing the audit. Nonetheless, auditors must maintain both an ethical and an independent attitude, particularly in gray areas where professional judgment is called upon to decide whether management's chosen accounting procedures are acceptable. Yet, without an ethical and independent posture, the services of the independent auditor are of no value to creditors, stockholders, or the public at large. As such, ethical and independent behavior and competence must be the hallmarks of the public accounting profession.

PROFESSIONAL ETHICS

Independent public accountants have met the challenges of a changing, increasingly more complex business environment. In the Touche Ross study noted earlier, participants were asked to identify the professions which they thought had the highest ethical standards. The results, reported here in Exhibit A–5, reveal that accountants are ranked second only to clergy in terms of their ethical standards and were perceived to be somewhat more ethical than both teachers and engineers. Still, the challenge to improve the quality of audit services continues, and the auditing profession has responded with changes in its ethical structure in an effort to meet these challenges.

EXHIBIT A–5

Most Ethical Professions

Which professions have the highest ethical standards?
Rank them from first to fourth. (Ranking points: Possible, 4,000.)

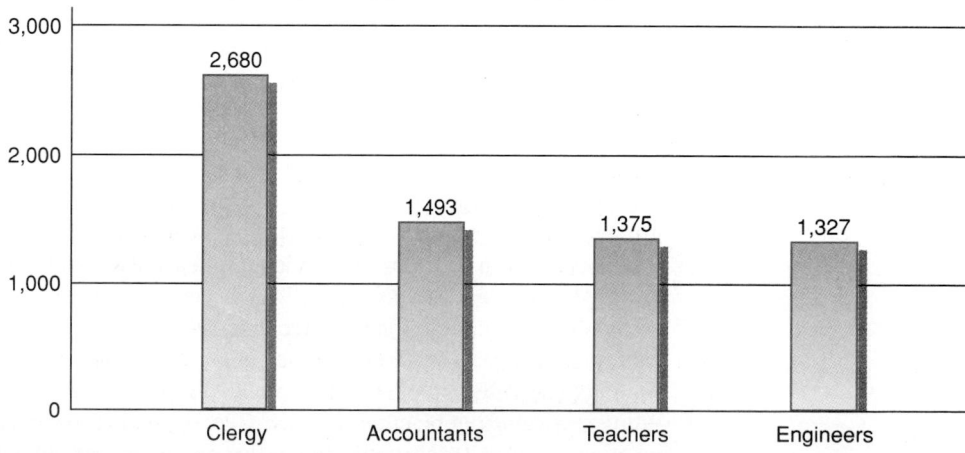

Source: *Ethics in American Business* (New York: Touche Ross and Company, 1988), p. 7.

EXHIBIT A–6

Most and Least Effective Measures for Encouraging Ethical Business Behavior

Which is the most effective measure for encouraging ethical behavior? Which is the least effective?

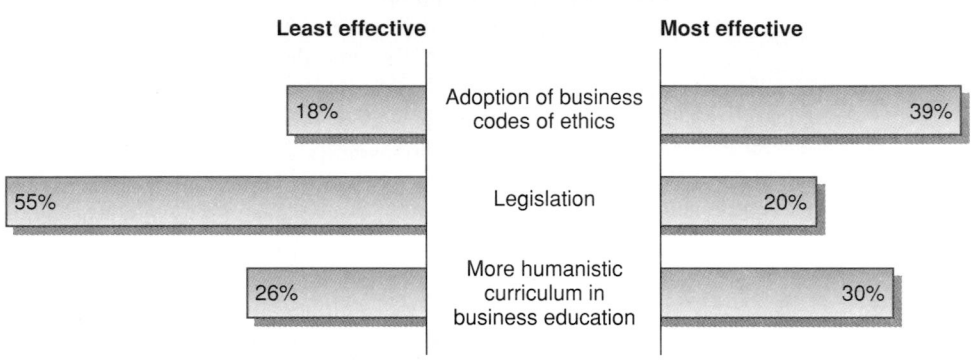

Percent of responses to question

Least effective		Most effective
18%	Adoption of business codes of ethics	39%
55%	Legislation	20%
26%	More humanistic curriculum in business education	30%

Source: *Ethics in American Business* (New York: Touche Ross and Company, 1988), p. 14.

Supporting Ethical Structure

What can be done to enhance ethical behavior in business and accounting? The participants of the Touche Ross study were asked to identify measures that were most and least likely to encourage ethical business behavior. The results, reported in Exhibit A–6, reveal a considerable amount of disagreement. The strongest response found that 55% of the participants thought **new legislation** would be the **least effective** way to encourage ethical behavior, while 20% thought it would be most effective. Codes of business ethics were considered to be the most effective way to encourage ethical behavior by 39% of the respondents, followed by 30% who felt business education could enhance ethical behavior.

To enhance the ethical behavior and independent image of the auditor, the public accounting profession and individual CPA firms have established several supporting structures. Most notable are

1. The profession's Public Oversight Board (POB) and the Peer Review Process.
2. The profession's Code of Professional Conduct and the AICPA's Professional Ethics Executive Committee.
3. Audit firms' quality control procedures.

The first two structures provide an audit quality assurance program (monitored by the POB) and a vehicle for resolving questions concerning ethical practices and positions. The third structure is used within each firm to assure that individual auditors perform in a professional manner.

The POB and the Peer Review Process

The Public Oversight Board (POB) and peer review process were established as an outgrowth of public concern over the ethical and independent behavior of the public accounting profession. In the mid-1970s, Congress conducted an investigation of the "Accounting Establishment," which was critical of the public accounting profession. Citing those rare cases of audit failure, Congress recommended more professional oversight of public accounting practices. As a result of the congressional inquiry and the 1976 staff report on its findings, the POB and peer review process were established. (Peer review calls for the auditing and reporting practices of each CPA firm conducting audits of publicly owned corporations—those firms with clients that are registered with the SEC—to be examined once every three years by another CPA firm.) Since the process began in 1979, thousands of peer reviews have been conducted. In most reviews, suggestions for improvements are

EXHIBIT A–7

The POB and the Peer Review Process

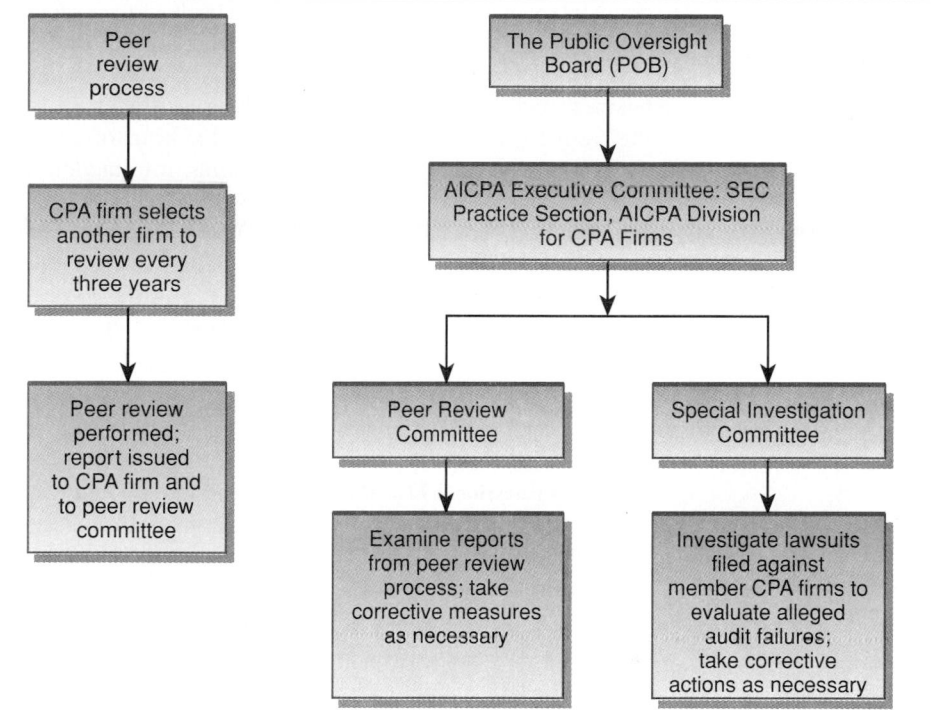

made, followed by responses to suggestions made by the firm being reviewed. A more complete diagram of the structure and procedures of the POB and the peer review process is provided in Exhibit A–7.

The Code of Professional Conduct and the AICPA's Professional Ethics Executive Committee provide a second major structure for accounting ethics. The Code of Ethics consists of 11 rules of conduct to guide auditors in determining appropriate behavior and to enhance the quality of audit services. The role of the Professional Ethics Executive Committee is to provide interpretations and rulings regarding the Code of Conduct. The committee is also in charge of the joint ethics enforcement program between the AICPA and the (50) individual state societies.

The audit practitioner, either as a firm or as an individual, has a great incentive to be perceived of as being both competent and independent. These attributes create the value of audit services, and, therefore, they create a self-governing mechanism at work in the auditing profession. Because auditors are keenly aware of the value of professional reputation, they establish many procedures to maintain ethical standards. One such procedure is to rotate auditors on specific client engagements. Another is to have staff who are not assigned to the specific client review the audit procedures and the resulting audit report. Auditing textbooks cover many similar procedures that are instituted in the private sector to promote professionalism.

• SUMMARY

While ethical considerations are important to the integrity of all activities of a business enterprise—from marketing to production to warranty service after the sale—they are the lifeblood of accounting. In particular, the practices of public accounting would not exist were it not for the independent ethical behavior of CPAs, and the value of managerial accountants would be diminished if they absolved themselves from the resolution of ethical dilemmas. Ethics, therefore, is a cornerstone of the accounting process.

This appendix discussed the structure and environmental factors affecting ethics in business and accounting. Judgments about justification of the harm and the benefit resulting from chosen courses of action lie at the heart of ethical decision making.

Accountants are charged with providing information about all types of relationships among people, business entities, not-for-profit entities, and governmental units. If their services are to enhance society, accountants must have competence and integrity. That is, financial statements must be viewed as being representative of underlying economic relationships. Accountants, who are charged with the creation and communication of such statements, must be considered both competent and ethical by all parties.

• KEY TERMS

AICPA's Professional Ethics Executive Committee. Group that provides interpretations and rulings regarding the Code of Professional Ethics and is in charge of the ethics enforcement program between the AICPA and the (50) individual state societies.

Code of Professional Conduct. Thirteen rules of conduct established to guide auditors in determining appropriate behavior and to enhance the quality of audit services.

Peer review process. Process by which the auditing and reporting practices of each CPA firm conducting audits of publicly owned corporations are examined once every three years by another CPA firm.

Public Oversight Board (POB). Structure that provides an audit quality assurance program and to resolve questions concerning practices and positions.

• CASES

C A–1
GAAP Disclosures
L.O.2, 3

United Mines, Inc., has copper and gold mining operations throughout the world. You as the new controller must decide on the amount of detailed geographical breakdown to show in the current year's financial statements. GAAP states that if at least 10% of sales or 10% of identifiable assets are related to a specific nondomestic geographical area then net revenue, operating profit, and identifiable assets for that foreign operation must be identified and disclosed in a footnote to the financial statement.

You have the following summary of operations (in thousands):

	U.S.	Argentine	Brazil	South Africa	Zimbabwe	Total
Sales.	57,570	14,780	28,600	40,500	21,400	162,850
Operating profit	5,400	1,800	3,500	6,900	2,100	19,700
Identifiable assets . . .	80,000	20,500	58,200	72,900	12,500	244,100

The president of the company tells you that because investment in South Africa is controversial and might offend some stockholders, she wants you to disclose the following breakdown of foreign operations (in thousands), which she says is in conformance with GAAP.

	U.S.	South America	Africa	Total
Sales	57,570	43,380	61,900	162,850
Operating profit	5,400	5,300	9,000	19,700
Identifiable assets	80,000	78,700	85,400	244,100

Required:

Assuming that the suggested disclosure is in conformance with GAAP, is there an ethical dilemma? Who can be hurt by the alternative chosen? Who can benefit?

C A–2
Banking
L.O.2, 3

You are a loan officer for First City Bank and you have the following dilemma. A minority-owned construction contractor has applied for a loan of $2,000,000 and has provided you with financial statements that show reasonably profitable operations and a reasonable balance sheet. The major item of value is a warehouse building that currently has a book value of $3,500,000, which would be the major collateral for the loan. You visit the sight and determine that it is a sound business and suitable for the purpose, but it is located in a part of town where property values have plummeted in recent years because of urban flight and arson. You consult a real estate expert and he says that the building has little resale value, perhaps only $800,000. Your problem is that if the loan is granted the building will be used profitably, and that a substitute in a more desirable part of town would cost in excess of $8,000,000. If the asset is revalued, the balance sheet ratios used in determining credit-worthiness will call for a rejection of the loan, but if the historic book value is maintained the loan will meet the technical hurdles. You consult a CPA who says that businesses do not revalue assets such as buildings to market value as long as it is expected that the assets will be utilized in the expected fashion and that the business is a going concern. Of course, ordinary depreciation is taken.

You believe that if the loan is not forthcoming there is grave doubt about the future of the business.

Required:

1. What is the ethical consideration in this case and how does accounting interact with it?
2. Who can be hurt and who can be helped by your decision and what is the justification for those possible effects?

C A–3
Accounting Judgment
L.O.2, 3

Zero Queen, Inc., owns 10 factories that manufacture sports equipment. You are auditing one of these plants, where they make ski equipment. The inventory records revealed the following data:

	Units of Inventory		
Item	Beginning Inventory	Made during Year	Ending Inventory
Pro K-3	1,000	13,500	600
Status RX7	2,800	36,500	2,000
ZQ 442	4,200	0	3,800
North Slop 88	3,600	45,000	2,900
Air Tuk 4ZK	1,800	53,000	2,000

The ZQ 442s represent about 40% of the reported cost of ending inventory. The material used to make these skis is no longer used in production. Newer makes use material that maintains its flexibility three times longer than the material used in the ZQ model. You recommend that the company write down the inventory or write it off. When presented with this suggestion, the controller tells you she is confident that all remaining units will eventually be sold at cost or above.

Required:

1. What is the ethical decision depicted in this exercise?
2. Identify factors that could convince you that the controller's judgment is morally correct.
3. Identify factors that could convince you that the controller's judgment is wrong.
4. Would you require a write-down of the inventory based on the facts provided?

C A–4
Ethical Behavior
L.O.2, 3

In January 1988, XYZ Publishing Company published a new introductory marketing textbook designed for the basic undergraduate marketing course taught in most colleges and universities. As is common practice in the textbook publishing industry, the company and its sales staff identified the people at each school who had recently taught the introductory marketing course and sent them a "desk copy" of the text (at no charge to the recipient) to encourage teachers to look their product over for possible selection as the book to be used in the introductory classes.

These desk copies were clearly stamped "complimentary copy—for professional use only—NOT for resale." This label is designed to keep the faculty from taking their desk copies and selling them to the "used" book salespersons who come to faculty offices offering to buy these desk copies for cash. Working in coordination with college textbook stores, these book salespersons then sell these desk copies to students as new books, or perhaps at a slight discount from the price of a new book.

The book introduced in January 1988 was for a fairly large market. A total of 5,000 complimentary copies were sent to marketing faculty as desk copies. For the first year of sales, the book sold 10,000 units, of which 4,000 were desk copies and 6,000 were units on which the publisher (and the authors) earned profits. Because the break-even point for this book is 8,000 units per year, XYZ is probably not going to revise the text and publish a second edition.

Required:
Identify at least one ethical dilemma in this case. Indicate what the appropriate (morally correct) choice should be from your viewpoint. Who are the "winners" and "losers" in this situation?

C A–5
Ethical Behavior
L.O.2, 3

In early January 19x8, the controller of the Wardel Corporation began to worry about the level of the corporation's profits for the most recently completed year. While the final results for 19x7 were not yet known, it appeared as though profits would not enable top management to maximize their bonus plan for 19x7. The 19x7 bonus plan is structured as follows:

Profit Range*	Bonus Pool
Below $20 million	0% of profits
$20–$29 million	2% of profits
$30–$39 million	3% of profits
$40–$49 million	4% of profits
$50 million or more	5% of profits

*Profit is net income before taxes and bonuses per GAAP (rounded to the nearest million).

The preliminary estimate by the corporate controller is that profits will be about $27 million. The controller has also made the following estimates of the effect on profits of certain possible year-end adjusting entries that are being considered:

Possible Adjustment	Effect on Profits
a. Change estimated life of factory building	+$10 million
b. Change estimate of warranty costs.	+ 3 million
c. Change amount of estimated bad debts.	+ 1 million
	+$14 million

The controller is in his last year of employment before retirement. His retirement plan provides an amount during each year of retirement that is based on the average of his last five years' income.

Required:
1. Identify the ethical dilemma in this case.
2. From the stockholders' point of view, what is the best, morally correct choice?
3. From the controller's point of view, what is the best, morally correct choice?
4. If you were the controller, what arguments could you make in support of the three possible adjustments?
5. Assume the controller makes all three adjustments and that profit turns out to be $39.6 million. As the independent auditor of Wardel Corporation, what would you do?

C A–6
Ethical Decisions
L.O.2, 3

Acquire Chemicals, Inc., (ACI) has been manufacturing sealants and adhesives at its plant just outside a major metropolitan area for 30 years. The state's Department of Natural Resources has started an investigation into accusations of illegal dumping of dangerous chemicals by ACI at its plant site and by the independent waste disposal company, Caper Sanitation, Inc., (CSI) that has been disposing of all of ACI's waste for the past eight years.

It is now February 10, 19x2, and you, as controller of ACI, are trying to decide whether some mention of the investigation is warranted in the annual report for the year ended 12/31/x1. Your independent auditor gives the following advice:

> The department's report will not be made public until at least June. We now have no way of knowing what the outcome will be, what their recommendation will be, what the cleanup costs, if any, will amount to, and we don't even know how much the insurance company or CSI would pick up if some cleanup is necessary. So, I say we are completely justified in ignoring this one for the time being. Companies are investigated all the time. If we mentioned every one before something reasonably concrete is known or at least some indication is given, our annual reports would be as thick as telephone books.

What your auditor doesn't know is that your sister-in-law, who works for the Department of Natural Resources, told you "off the record" that preliminary findings were that a massive cleanup would probably be necessary, both at the plant site and by CSI, which it turns out was not properly licensed for such work. There is no way for you to get official confirmation of her statement without violating her confidence. On your own, you have studied other cleanup cases in the state and you estimate that if what your sister-in-law says is true, the range of costs to the company would be from $25,000,000 to $75,000,000. ACI's net income for 19x1, a very profitable year, before consideration of the cleanup was just over $20,000,000.

You report directly to the president of the company and she has made it quite clear that she expects to see a healthy bottom line in the 19x1 income statement and in general an upbeat annual report, because she plans several major financing initiatives including bank borrowings and the issuance of preferred stock.

Required:
1. Who could be helped or hurt by mention of the investigation in the annual report?
2. What steps would you go through to determine the best course of action?
3. Assume that you decide to recommend a full discussion of all possible outcomes in the annual report, and the president of the company consults with and agrees with the auditor that no mention should be made. What steps would you take?

B

International Accounting

· Learning Objectives

After studying Appendix B, you should understand

1. How to measure and disclose foreign currency *transaction* gains and losses, pp. 845–48.
2. How to hedge to avoid *transaction* gains and losses, pp. 848–49.
3. How to measure and disclose *translation* gains and losses, pp. 849–51.
4. The general nature of differences between U.S. GAAP and foreign financial reporting rules, pp. 851–53.

Note: This appendix may be covered anytime after Chapter 6. It works well when combined with Appendix C on price changes, since both appendixes involve conversion of unlike measures to like measures on two somewhat different dimensions. This appendix is probably most effective if covered after Chapter 12 or toward the end of the course.

Throughout this text we have referred to the many differences and similarities in accounting standards of the United States and other countries. In many cases the standards employed by a country have their roots in its cultural and historical evolution. For example, the British accounting system remains the foundation of accounting in countries such as India, Australia, and other former British crown colonies long after they have become independent nations. Also, the conservative financial culture of Germany has resulted in its unique relationship between its largest corporations and their banks, with bankers having an influential role on boards of directors. These cultural differences and historical events have led to numerous differences among the GAAP of countries around the globe.

To help resolve these differences and to promote uniformity, the International Accounting Standards Committee (IASC) was formed in 1973 by accounting organizations in the United States, Canada, Mexico, Australia, Japan, the United Kingdom, France, West Germany, and the Netherlands. Today, more than 100 accounting organizations from 74 countries are effectively represented by the IASC, which has issued over 30 pronouncements identifying International Accounting Standards for financial reporting. At present these Standards have no authoritative support, but have been developed to facilitate the international effort to unify accounting methods, an effort referred to as harmonization.[1] Multinational firms often reference these standards in their financial reports.

One of the primary benefits of the IASC's efforts to achieve greater comparability is in international securities regulations, which facilitate the free flow of investment capital among nations. At present it is sometimes difficult to list U.S. corporations on foreign securities exchanges and vice versa because of differences in GAAP and other reporting or filing requirements. U.S. companies listed on U.S. stock exchanges are generally considered to have more stringent reporting requirements than companies listed on most foreign stock exchanges. As a result, foreign corporations that are permitted to list their securities on U.S. stock exchanges are a source of some controversy, with U.S. firms claiming that they are being unfairly treated by having to comply with more strict disclosure/reporting requirements. Similar controversies exist in other countries, too. Because of the lack of comparability created by differences in GAAP across countries there are many who now favor more uniform standards. They argue that greater uniformity will allow international capital markets to develop more rapidly and in an orderly way. Greater uniformity in accounting standards is expected to facilitate the free flow of investment capital around the world. The IASC's efforts to harmonize international standards are a step in this direction.

The differences in cultures and their related policy and procedural differences in accounting are considered in some detail in most of the texts on international accounting. As the international language of business, accounting is becoming more important than ever before. State-of-the-art communications and other technological developments continue to dissolve the age-old barriers of time and distance, increasingly making the world a single global marketplace. Like all markets, the global market needs relevant, reliable measures of financial position and performance that are comparable across all business entities, regardless of their country of origin. Accounting will need to keep pace with the ever-increasing need for financial information to facilitate international business decisions.

The remainder of this appendix focuses on the basic measurement issues raised by doing business around the world and dealing with many different currencies. In some

---

[1]It is interesting to note that another international group, the International Federation of Accountants (IFAC), was established in 1977 in an effort to harmonize, or unify, international auditing standards. To date, about 30 International Auditing Guidelines (IAGs) have been developed by the IFAC's International Auditing Practices Committee.

respects, this appendix and the next on price changes both address the same fundamental problem: How to prepare financial information meaningfully when more than one unit of measure is involved. In both cases, the solution is essentially the same: first convert unlike units of measure to like units of measure using a "conversion ratio," then perform whatever mathematical manipulations (e.g., adding or subtracting) are required to prepare more meaningful information. This basic process is illustrated in the pages that follow.

STRENGTH OF THE DOLLAR

What does it mean to have a strong or weak dollar? The strength of the U.S. dollar is measured by how many units of a foreign currency the dollar will purchase, known as its exchange rate. Exchange rates may fluctuate daily and are published each day in the financial press.

The exchange rate changes are based on the supply and demand of various currencies, which in turn are based on the relative demand for the respective countries' goods and services. If the change in exchange rates enables the dollar to purchase more Japanese yen, the dollar is said to be "stronger" against the yen, and the cost of Japanese goods in U.S. dollars should become cheaper, all else being equal. At the same time, the cost of U.S. goods in Japanese yen would become more expensive. Therefore, if you were spending U.S. dollars in Japan you would want the dollar to strengthen against the yen so your dollars would buy more. However, if you were exporting U.S. products to Japan, a stronger dollar would probably cause you to increase your selling prices in yen and therefore would reduce sales of your products. As a result, it is not obvious whether a stronger dollar is good news or bad news! As the U.S. dollar weakens against foreign currencies, we expect U.S. goods and services to be more attractive to foreign consumers, and foreign goods and services to be less attractive to U.S. consumers.

How are changes in exchange rates reflected in financial reports of U.S. companies doing business in foreign countries? Publicly owned businesses that operate in more than one country are called multinational corporations. The U.S. financial statements of multinational corporations report the position and operating results of both foreign and U.S. activities together, stated in U.S. dollars. The process of converting financial statements of those U.S. corporations with foreign businesses and subsidiaries into U.S. dollars for financial reporting purposes can result in two different types of gains and losses:[2]

1. Foreign currency **transaction** gains and losses.
2. Foreign currency **translation** gains and losses.

These two types of gains and losses are accorded different treatment by U.S. corporations, and each is explained in some detail in the sections that follow.

FOREIGN CURRENCY TRANSACTIONS

When U.S. companies purchase or sell goods or services with foreign companies, these transactions may result in a transaction gain or loss. If the transactions with foreign companies are expressed (i.e., paid off or settled) in terms of U.S. dollars, no transaction gains or losses will result for the U.S. company. However, when the transactions are expressed

---

[2]*Statement of Financial Accounting Standards No. 52*, "Foreign Currency Translation" (Norwalk, Conn.: FASB, 1981).

Objective 1
How to measure and
disclose foreign currency
transaction gains
and losses.

in terms of foreign currency (i.e., their contract calls for payment in foreign currency), the U.S. company is "exposed" to gains or losses from currency exchange rate fluctuations between the date the transaction is originally recorded and the date a cash settlement is made. If the dollar becomes **stronger** during the "exposed" period, a transaction **gain** will result for a U.S. company making **purchases,** whereas a transaction **loss** will occur for U.S. companies making **sales.**

Purchase:
Transaction Gain

To illustrate a transaction gain on a foreign purchase, assume that U.S.A., Inc., (a U.S. company) purchases German steel on June 2, 19x7, when the German mark is selling for U.S. $0.50 (1 mark = U.S. $0.50; or U.S. $1 = 2.00 marks). The purchase price of the steel is 200,000 marks. This purchase would be recorded on the U.S. company's books in U.S. dollars as follows:

```
19x7
June 2   Inventory—Steel (A) . . . . . . . . . . . . . . . . . . . .   100,000
               Accounts Payable—German (L) . . . . . . . . . . . .           100,000
         To record steel purchase: 200,000 marks at U.S. $0.50 each.
```

Assume that the account payable is settled in marks on June 30 when the exchange rate is U.S. $0.40 = 1 mark (the mark has become $0.10 cheaper, so the U.S. dollar is "stronger" against the mark). To pay off the payable still requires 200,000 marks, but the dollar cost of 200,000 marks is now only U.S. $80,000 (200,000 marks × $0.40 each = $80,000), resulting in a transaction gain of $20,000. The payment of the account payable on June 30, 19x7, would be recorded as follows:

```
19x7
June 30   Accounts Payable—German (L) . . . . . . . . . . . . . .   100,000
                Foreign Exchange Gain (R). . . . . . . . . . . . . . .           20,000
                Cash (A) . . . . . . . . . . . . . . . . . . . . . . .           80,000
          To pay account for German steel.
```

Note that if the terms of the purchase had been stated as U.S. $100,000 instead of 200,000 marks, the U.S. company would have been required to pay $100,000, and no foreign exchange gain or loss would have resulted for the U.S. company. (However, the German company would then have been "exposed" to an exchange gain or loss!)

Sale: Transaction Loss

To illustrate how sales have the opposite effect of purchases, assume that a U.S. company sold computer equipment to a German shipbuilder on June 2, 19x7 (mark selling for U.S. $0.50). The sale price is expressed as 300,000 marks, which is recorded by the U.S. company as follows:

```
19x7
June 2   Accounts Receivable—German (A). . . . . . . . . . . . . .   150,000
               Sales Revenue (R) . . . . . . . . . . . . . . . . . . .           150,000
         To record sale of computers for 300,000 marks.
```

On June 30, 19x7, the German company settles its obligation by paying 300,000 marks to the U.S. company, which have a dollar value of only U.S. $120,000 on that date (Exchange rate = U.S. $0.40 per mark on June 30, 19x7). The U.S. company would receive only U.S. $120,000 (300,000 marks × $0.40 each = $120,000) and would record a $30,000 foreign exchange loss as follows:

19x7			
June 30	Cash (A)	120,000	
	Foreign Exchange Loss (E)	30,000	
	Accounts Receivable—German (A)		150,000
	To record receipt of 300,000 marks.		

Once again, if the sale contract on June 2 called for payment of U.S. dollars, no gain or loss would have resulted for the U.S. company, and U.S. $150,000 would have been received regardless of exchange rate fluctuations.

Purchase Losses and Sales Gains

Note that in the examples above, the U.S. dollar is becoming stronger against the German mark, going from $0.50 per mark to $0.40 per mark. If the dollar had weakened, it would have resulted in a foreign exchange loss on the purchase and a foreign exchange gain on the sale. The effects of changing exchange rates on transaction gains and losses is summarized in Exhibit B–1. Whether a gain or loss occurs on a sale or purchase depends on whether the dollar becomes weaker or stronger between the date the sale/purchase is first recorded and the date it is settled. For cash sales or purchases in any currency, there would be no foreign exchange gains or losses, (because the date of first record is also the settlement date).

Unsettled Purchases and Sales

What if receivables or payables with foreign countries are not settled at year-end? Accounting rules require that "unrealized gains and losses" be measured and recorded for all unsettled foreign accounts as of the balance sheet date.[3] As a result, any unsettled receivables or payables would be adjusted at year-end to reflect year-end exchange rates, with gains or losses recorded as needed.

To illustrate unrealized gains and losses, assume that the following information regards the year-end receivables and payables of U.S.A., Inc.:

	Exchange Rate at Date Purchase/ Sales Recorded	Year-End Exchange Rate	Original Transaction Amount	Balance at Year-End before Adjustment
Receivables:				
Germany	$0.50 per mark	$0.40 per mark	30,000 marks	$15,000
Japan	0.01 per yen	0.02 per yen	2,000,000 yen	20,000
Payables:				
Swiss	1.50 per S. franc	1.20 per S. franc	12,000 S. francs	18,000

EXHIBIT B–1

Determining Transaction Gains and Losses

A. When the change in exchange rates between the original date a transaction is recorded and the settlement date (date paid) enables a U.S. dollar to buy:	B. Transactions expressed in the foreign currency that are:	
	B1. Credit sales will result in a transaction	B2. Credit purchases will result in a transaction
A1. More foreign currency (e.g., dollar becomes stronger).	Loss	Gain
A2. Less foreign currency (e.g., dollar becomes weaker).	Gain	Loss

[3]Ibid.

The unrealized gains and losses would be computed as follows:

	Original Transaction Amount	×	Year-End Exchange Rate	=	Year-End Amount in U.S.	−	Unadjusted Year-End Balance	=	Resulting Gain (Loss)
Receivables:									
Germany	30,000 marks	×	$0.40	=	$12,000	−	$15,000	=	$ (3,000)
Japan	2,000,000 yen	×	0.02	=	40,000	−	20,000	=	20,000
									$17,000
Payables:									
Swiss	12,000 S. franc	×	1.20	=	14,400	−	18,000	=	3,600
Net gain or (loss)									$20,600

U.S.A., Inc., would record the following year-end adjusting entry:

19x7				
Dec. 31	Accounts Payable—S. Franc (L)	3,600	
	Accounts Receivable—Japan (A)	20,000	
	Accounts Receivable—Germany (A).		3,000
	Foreign Exchange Gain—Unrealized (R)		20,600
	To record net unrealized gain on exchange rate changes.		

Disclosure

The total year-end balance in the foreign exchange gain or loss account from both realized and unrealized **transaction** gains and losses would be reported in the income statement below other gains and losses but before taxes on continuing operations, as follows:

U.S.A., Inc.
Partial Income Statements
For the Years Ending December 31
(in millions)

	19x7	19x6
Operating income	$287	$263
Other gains (losses)	11	(2)
Foreign exchange gains (losses)	(3)	6
Income before income taxes	$295	$267
Income tax expense	(67)	(48)
Net income	$228	$219

Often the net transaction gain or loss is not material enough to appear as a separate item in the income statement. In such cases, the amount of the transaction gain or loss for the period is often reported in the "Notes to Financial Statements." The footnotes in the Ralston Purina annual report provided in Appendix E illustrate such footnote disclosure.

HEDGING AGAINST GAINS AND LOSSES

Multinational corporations can hedge (or protect) against gains and losses from foreign exchange fluctuations in a number of ways. Hedging is like betting on each of two teams that are playing one another. One way to hedge against a foreign exchange loss from a **credit purchase** costing 200,000 Swiss francs (S. Fr.) would call for a **credit sale** for 200,000 Swiss francs to be made at the same time. The exchange gains or losses from the

Objective 2
How to hedge to avoid
transaction gains
and losses.

account payable and account receivable, both for S. Fr. 200,000, would offset one another as long as they were initiated on the same date and were outstanding for the same length of time. Although such exact offsetting is not usually possible, hedging against large gains or losses can be accomplished by keeping approximately the same balance in receivables and payables that must be settled in any given foreign currency.

When companies cannot keep their receivables in foreign denominations approximately equal to their foreign payables, they can still hedge against losses by purchasing or selling futures contracts. Futures contracts (also called forward exchange contracts) are rights to receive a specific amount of foreign currency in exchange for a fixed number of dollars at a specified future date. To illustrate, assume that a U.S. company purchased goods from Japan for 6 million yen on June 1, 19x1, on open account, to be paid on June 30, 19x1. The U.S. company could protect against exchange gains or losses by purchasing a futures contract on June 1, 19x1, to receive 6 million yen on June 30, 19x1. The purchase of this account receivable for 6 million yen would hedge the account payable for 6 million yen, preventing any gain or loss from the credit purchase. If foreign receivables are to be hedged, the U.S. company would **sell** futures contracts to other investors (e.g., foreign banks) to avoid exchange gains or losses. Of course, the easiest way to avoid transaction losses (and gains) is to negotiate all credit purchases and credit sales in terms of U.S. dollars rather than foreign currencies. This approach passes the concern over exchange rate fluctuations on to the foreign seller or buyer, who may then incur a gain or loss.

Hedging may be accomplished by (1) balancing foreign receivables with foreign payables and (2) buying or selling futures contracts to offset unhedged foreign receivables or payables. Some companies use these hedging strategies to avoid risk of foreign exchange losses. Others that are not hedged are said to be "exposed" to the risks of exchange losses. Still other companies are hedged in some foreign currencies and exposed in others.

FOREIGN CURRENCY TRANSLATION

The *transaction* gains or losses discussed above result from business transactions between U.S. companies and independent foreign companies. If the U.S. company owns a controlling interest in the foreign company, principles of consolidation in the United States require that the foreign company's financial results be reported as a part of the U.S. parent company's consolidated financial statements. The consolidation process first requires that the foreign subsidiary's financial statements be *translated* into U.S. dollars. This translation normally results in a translation gain or loss, which is accounted for in a different way than a transaction gain or lose.

Objective 3
How to measure and
disclose translation
gains and losses.

Translating foreign financial reports into U.S. dollars is guided by specific accounting rules. The following exchange rates are to be applied to this translation process:

Accounts	Exchange Rate
• All assets and liabilities ⟶	• **Current rate** at date of the balance sheet
• Stockholders' equity accounts **other than** retained earnings ⟶	• **Historical rate** from date item was originally recorded
• Retained earnings ⟶	• Not adjusted
• Income statement accounts ⟶	• **Average rate** for the period covered by the income statement

Application of these exchange rates will normally result in a balance sheet that is out of balance, necessitating a "plug" to a special account in the stockholders' equity section of the balance sheet. To illustrate the translation process, assume that Mardot Company is a wholly owned French subsidiary of the U.S. company Bardens, Inc. On January 1, 19x9, Mardot began its operations and was acquired by Bardens. The financial data of Mardot are stated in French francs (F. Fr.). The following exchange rate data are available on December 31, 19x9:

Time Period	Exchange Rates (U.S. $ per F. Fr.)
December 31, 19x9 (current)	$0.40
Historical rate for Mardot's stockholders' equity accounts.	0.44
Average for the year 19x9	0.42

The exchange rates are applied to the French company's income statement and balance sheet to convert them to U.S. dollars, as illustrated in Exhibit B–2. Several simplifying assumptions have been made in the example illustrated. Since Mardot is 100% owned and in its first year of operations, net income for 19x9 in U.S. dollars is the same as retained earnings in U.S. dollars at the end of 19x9. The ending retained earning balance would

EXHIBIT B–2

Translation of
Foreign Currency

**Mardot Company
Income Statement
For the Year Ended December 31, 19x9**

	French Francs	Exchange Rate	U.S. Dollars
Sales.	85,950,000	0.42	$ 36,099,000
Cost of goods sold.	(47,280,000)	0.42	(19,857,600)
Gross margin	38,670,000	0.42	$ 16,241,400
Other expenses	(21,440,000)	0.42	(9,004,800)
Other gains (losses)	(2,950,000)	0.42	(1,239,000)
Pre-tax income	14,280,000	0.42	$ 5,997,600
Tax expense	(6,830,000)	0.42	(2,868,600)
Net income	7,450,000	0.42	$ 3,129,000

**Mardot Company
Balance Sheets
December 31, 19x9**

	French Francs	Exchange Rate	U.S. Dollars
Cash.	1,900,000	0.40	$ 760,000
Receivables.	3,875,000	0.40	1,550,000
Inventory	6,620,000	0.40	2,648,000
Plant and equipment.	16,940,000	0.40	6,776,000
	29,335,000		$11,734,000
Payables	3,110,000	0.40	$ 1,244,000
Common stock	18,775,000	0.44	8,261,000
Retained earnings	7,450,000	See net income	3,129,000
Cumulative translation gains (losses)	0	Plug	(900,000)
	29,335,000		$11,734,000

normally be the beginning balance (in U.S. dollars), plus net income (in U.S. dollars), less dividends if any (in U.S. dollars). The plug needed to make the balance sheet (in U.S. dollars) balance—a $900,000 translation loss in this example—is the **cumulative** foreign currency translation gain or loss from all prior periods as of the end of 19x9. This is shown in a special account in the stockholders' equity section of the balance sheet.[4]

The role of this stockholders' equity account is similar to the role of the contra stockholders' equity account used to record unrealized losses on marketable equity securities held as a noncurrent asset (as discussed in Chapter 12). Cumulative unrealized foreign currency translation gains as well as losses can be recorded in this stockholders' equity account. Since 19x9 is the only year of operation, the cumulative loss of $900,000 is also the loss for the year 19x9. The **change** in this cumulative translation gain or loss account from the beginning of a year to the end of that year is the annual translation gain or loss. In the example given, the dollar strengthened against the French franc during 19x9, causing an unrealized translation loss of $900,000. Bardens' ownership of net assets in France during a period when the French franc fell in price against the dollar caused this translation loss.

INTERNATIONAL ACCOUNTING STANDARDS

Objective 4
The general nature of differences between U.S. GAAP and foreign financial reporting rules.

Accounting methods often differ between countries because of the different information needs of people in different countries and because of the different accounting conventions (or "habits") that have developed over time.[5] Variations in accounting methods sometimes result in substantive differences, while in other cases they are simply differences in the format of presentation. For example, U.S. firms show accumulated depreciation as a contra asset in their balance sheets, and Italian firms show accumulated depreciation on the liability side of their balance sheets! This format difference could affect the comparability of many financial statement ratios, such as return on assets, between U.S. and Italian firms, yet it is not an important difference in accounting methods. Examples of many of the more important accounting method differences have been noted through the text. Several other important differences are considered next.

Asset Costs

Differences in accounting methods between countries often lead to differences in how asset costs are measured, and in some cases whether they are measured at all. For example, firms in the United States include the full cost of manufactured inventories, which consists of direct material used, direct labor, and manufacturing overhead (consisting of such costs as factory supervisors' salaries and depreciation on factory buildings and equipment). This procedure, known as *full absorption costing,* is followed by many other countries too, including Japan and Great Britain. However, in some countries, for example, India, Denmark, and Chile, only the direct material and direct labor costs are included as an asset in inventory, with all manufacturing overhead costs charged against revenue in the period incurred.

In Chapter 8 of the text we noted that U.S. firms include some of the interest incurred on debt during the period when major long-term assets are being constructed as a cost of such assets. This procedure is similar to the normal treatment for interest during the

---

[4]See the stockholders' equity section of the Ralston Purina report in Appendix E for an example of this balance sheet disclosure.

[5]For example, in socialist and communist countries the accounting systems are usually very uniform across entities, with the government dictating a uniform set of accounts and accounting procedures in many cases. This is done to facilitate planning at the national level since the government is the primary user of accounting data in these countries.

construction period in over 30 countries, but it is not permitted for French or Belgian firms where all interest is expensed in the period incurred.

These examples point out but a few of the many differences in asset measurement between countries. At first glance it would seem that the use of financial ratios such as return on assets or return on stockholders' equity might enable us to evaluate a firm's relative performance and abstract away from the problems of different currencies in comparing firms from different countries. However, because the measurement of assets (or liabilities and equity) may also vary significantly from country to country, such comparisons must be made with caution. A thorough understanding of how differences in accounting methods affect the financial statements is needed before meaningful comparisons can be made across countries.

Using Reserves

One of the major differences between U.S. accounting procedures and those of other countries is in the use of "reserves" or "appropriations." Firms in the United States, under GAAP, use allowances, which are similar to reserves, to estimate bad debts and warranty costs, among other things. These allowances essentially reduce the net assets in the balance sheet and reduce income (via Bad Debt Expense, Warranty Expense, and so on) as well. Such reserves (or allowances) are used in an effort to better match revenues of a period with (actual and estimated future) expenses of the period. However, U.S. firms are not allowed to use reserves or appropriations to reduce current income for expected future problems or needs, such as self-insurance or possible shortfalls in future profits, as do many foreign firms.

In many foreign countries, these "set asides" are used to reduce income like an expense, with offsetting credits to reserves that appear either in stockholders' equity (like separate "appropriated" retained earnings accounts) or above stockholders' equity (like a liability). In some foreign firms up to 80% of stockholders' equity is made up of such reserves or appropriations. The purpose of these reserves varies, but their use often has the effect of smoothing the net income results over time. For example, Swedish companies may appropriate up to 40% of pre-tax profits as reserves, thereby avoiding the taxes on them and enabling the firm to call them back into income in later years when the firm is experiencing less profitable operations. In many countries the reporting rules make it difficult to determine the nature of changes in these reserves.

Exhibit B–3 illustrates the consolidated statement of income for Saab-Scania Group, the Swedish car and truck manufacturer. Notice that the "appropriations" of 1,344 million SEK (Swedish krona) are deducted from income before "income before taxes." Saab is setting aside 1,344 million SEK of 19x7 income to reserve for the items noted in their footnote 9, which is partially reproduced at the bottom of Exhibit B–3. The consolidated balance sheet of Saab-Scania is provided in Exhibit B–4. Note the large (10,328 million SEK) balance in Untaxed Reserves, as well as the Statutory Reserves (1,499 million SEK), which represent about 32% of Saab's total liabilities and stockholders' equity. These reserves and appropriations represent a common feature of financial statements in many foreign countries, but they are not allowed by U.S. GAAP.

• SUMMARY

The world is rapidly becoming one large marketplace. Multinational firms and multinational stock investors are becoming more commonplace, and are creating a greater need for the understanding international accounting. With the elimination or reduction of trade

EXHIBIT B–3

Saab-Scania Group Consolidated Statement of Income (in SEK millions)

		19x7		19x6	
Operating revenue	Sales		41,403		35,222
Operating expenses	Manufacturing, selling and administrative expenses		−37,163		−31,224
Operating income before depreciation			**4,240**		3,998
Depreciation according to plan			−1,377		−1,202
Operating income after depreciation			**2,863**		2,796
Financial income and expenses	Dividends	5		2	
	Interest income	1,222		909	
	Interest expenses	−791		−732	
	Currency differences	6	442	151	330
Income after financial income and expenses			**3,305**		3,126
Share of income of associated companies			240		163
Income before extraordinary income and expenses			**3,545**		3,289
Extraordinary income and expenses			85		38
Allocation to the Jubilee Fund for Group Employees			−50		—
Income before appropriations and taxes			**3,580**		3,327
Minority interest in subsidiaries' income			−44		−37
*Appropriations (Note 9)**			*−1,344*		*−1,204*
Income before taxes			**2,192**		2,086
Taxes, of which SEK 73 m. (22) is a tax to the wage-earner fund (profit-sharing tax)			−746		−780
Net income			**1,446**		1,306

*Note 9—Appropriations

		Group	
SEK millions		19x7	19x6
Reversed excess depreciation		**182**	139
Transfer to:			
General investment reserve		**−1,399**	−1,296
Inventory reserve		**−112**	−22
Contingency reserve		**−15**	−25
Internal profit reserve			
Group contribution received and given, respectively			
Total		**−1,344**	−1,204

barriers (i.e., tariffs on imports or exports) by more and more nations, business entities are freer to deal with anyone anywhere without having to consider economic barriers. This introductory discussion has highlighted the primary aspects of international accounting, and it should help you understand the fundamental impact of international operations on U.S.-based firms as well as the general nature of differences between U.S. and foreign business entities.

EXHIBIT B–4

Saab-Scania Group Consolidated Balance Sheet (in SEK millions)

		19x7		19x6	
Assets					
Current assets	Cash and marketable securities	5,927		5,113	
	Accounts receivable	5,807		4,944	
	Prepaid expenses and accrued income	687		521	
	Inventories	9,446	21,867	8,767	19,345
Blocked accounts with the Bank of Sweden			60		239
Obligations of the Kingdom of Denmark			76		101
Fixed assets	Long-term receivables	880		462	
	Shares, bonds and other securities	2,683		1,650	
	Property, plant and equipment, etc.	11,373	14,936	9,666	11,778
Total assets			36,939		31,463
Liabilities and stockholders' equity					
Current liabilities	Bank loans, etc.	1,478		1,289	
	Accounts payable, etc.	3,756		3,006	
	Accrued expenses and prepaid income	3,925		2,966	
	Other current liabilities	1,490		1,466	
		10,649		8,727	
	Advance payments from customers	2,800	13,449	2,679	11,406
Bond loans secured by the Kingdom of Denmark			75		100
Long-term liabilities	Long-term loans	3,803		2,947	
	Provision for pensions	2,146		1,962	
	Provision for vehicle damage guarantee	121	6,070	101	5,010
Minority interest in subsidiaries			323		287
Untaxed reserve			*10,328*		*8,992*
Stockholders' equity	Restricted stockholders' equity				
	Capital stock				
	67,894,192 common shares, par value SEK 25	1,697		1,212	
	240,000 preferred shares, par value SEK 25	6		6	
	Statutory reserves	*1,499*		*1,641*	
		3,202		2,859	
	Unrestricted stockholders' equity				
	Unappropriated earnings	2,046		1,503	
	Net income	1,446		1,306	
		3,492	6,694	2,809	5,668
Total liabilities and stockholders' equity			36,939		31,463

• KEY TERMS

Exchange rate. Number of units of foreign currency a U.S. dollar will purchase.

Futures contracts (forward exchange contracts). Agreements to exchange currencies with another country at a specified rate at a specified future date.

Harmonization. Effort on the part of international firms and setters of standards to unify accounting methods.

Hedge against gains or losses. To offset potential transaction gains or losses by purchasing or selling future contracts in the exposed currency.

Multinational corporations. Publicly owned businesses that operate in more than one country.

Transaction gain or loss. A gain or loss resulting from a change in the exchange rate between the functional currency and the foreign currency in which the transaction amount is expressed between the date the transaction is recorded and the date it is settled (paid).

Translation gain or loss. A gain or loss resulting from restating financial statements of a foreign subsidiary (investee) from a foreign (functional) currency to the reporting currency of the parent at the time financial statements are prepared.

• QUESTIONS

1. If the U.S. dollar is strengthening against the British pound, is it good news for those who buy from or for those who sell to Great Britain?
2. If the German mark is costing less to buy in U.S. currency, will it result in gains or losses among U.S. firms selling goods to German firms?
3. Where are transaction gains and losses reported by U.S. firms doing business with foreign companies?
4. How can U.S. firms avoid transaction gains or losses when doing business with foreign firms without hedging?
5. What does a hedge do for U.S. firms with foreign transactions?
6. Where are translation gains and losses reported?
7. At what exchange rate are income statement accounts translated?
8. At what exchange rate are assets and liabilities translated?
9. At what exchange rate are stockholders' equity accounts other than retained earnings translated?
10. What authority do international accounting standards (IASs) have?

• EXERCISES

E B–1
Transaction Gains/Losses
L.O.1

The Stripes Corporation exports some of its merchandise to France and also does business with a French exporter. The following transactions occurred during 19xx for Stripes:

19xx
June 21   Purchased goods on account for 85,000 francs.
      30   Sold goods on account to a French client for 12,000 francs.
July 30   Paid for June 21 purchase in cash.
Aug. 15   Received payment in cash for sale of goods from June 30.

The exchange rates on these dates were as follows:

Date	U.S. Dollar per Franc
June 21	0.18
30	0.19
July 30	0.17
Aug. 15	0.20
Dec. 31	0.21

Required:
Record these transactions on Stripes's books in U.S. dollars.

E B–2
*Transaction
Gains/Losses*
L.O.1

ITECK, Inc., a U.S. company, sold computers to Boyds, Ltd., an English company, for 400,000 pounds on December 1, 19xx. The sale was on open account, and Boyd was to make four installments of 100,000 pounds at the end of each month (no interest). Boyd paid the first 100,000 pounds on December 31, 19xx. The pound sold for $1.35 on December 1, 19xx, but had fallen to $1.25 by year-end.

Required:
1. Record the sale on December 1, 19xx, on ITECK's books.
2. Record the receipt of the first payment on December 31, 19xx.
3. Record any unrealized exchange gains or losses as of December 31, 19xx.
4. What would be reported on ITECK's 19xx pre-tax income as a result of the above entries?

E B–3
*Translation—
Income Statement*
L.O.3

Consider the consolidated income statement of Saab-Scania in Exhibit B–3. Assume that the average exchange rate during 19x7 was 6.3 krona per U.S. dollar.

Required:
Prepare Saab's 19x7 income statement in U.S. dollars, rounding each amount to the nearest million dollars.

E B–4
*Translation—
Balance Sheet*
L.O.3, 4

Assume that an Indian Corporation reported the following balance sheet at the end of 19x4 in pounds.

Bombay Hose, Inc.
Balance Sheet
December 31, 19x4
(in millions of pounds)

Assets		Liabilities and Stockholders' Equity	
Current assets	475,650	Liabilities:	
Plant and equipment	812,040	Current liabilities	495,100
Investments	196,190	Long-term debt	316,750
Intangibles	87,660	Total liabilities	811,850
		Stockholders' equity:	
		Paid-in capital	300,000
		Retained earnings	459,690
		Total stockholders' equity	759,690
		Total liabilities and stockholders'	
Total assets	1,571,540	equity	1,571,540

Assume that the appropriate current rate for translation to U.S. dollars is $3.75 per pound, and that the appropriate historical rate for all of stockholders' equity is $3.20 per pound.

Required:
1. Prepare a balance sheet for Bombay Hose, Inc., in U.S. dollars.
2. What is the ratio of current assets to current liabilities in pounds? In dollars?
3. What is the ratio of long-term debt to total assets in pounds? In dollars?

• PROBLEMS

P B–1
Translation Gains/Losses
L.O.3

The Ruhle Company was formed in Germany on January 1, 19x1, by a U.S. Corporation, Starstake, Inc. Ruhle is owned 100% by Starstake. During 19x1, the following exchange rates were noted:

Date/Period	Exchange Rate (U.S. $ per German mark)
January 1, 19x1.	$0.56
December 31, 19x1	0.60
Average for 19x1	0.58

Ruhle reported the following financial data at the end of 19x1:

Ruhle Company
Income Statement
For the Year Ended December 31, 19x1
(in German marks)

Revenues	24,789,640
Expenses	22,801,440
Operating income	1,988,200
Other gains.	483,800
Net income.	2,472,000

Ruhle Company
Balance Sheet
December 31, 19x1
(in German marks)

Assets		Liabilities and Stockholders' Equity	
Cash	2,805,000	Liabilities:	
Receivables	6,907,000	Payables	3,108,000
Inventory	10,518,000	Long-term notes	10,000,000
Plant assets	40,350,000	Total liabilities	13,108,000
		Stockholders' equity:	
		Common stock	45,000,000
		Retained earnings	2,472,000
		Total stockholders' equity	47,472,000
Total assets	60,580,000	Total liabilities and stockholders' equity.	60,580,000

Required:
Translate Ruhle's 19x1 income statement and year-end balance sheet into U.S. dollars.

P B–2
Translation Gains/Losses
L.O.3

Macadona Corporation was formed in Japan on January 1, 19x4, by a U.S. corporation, Micky Dees, Inc. Macadona is 100% owned by Micky Dees. During 19x4, the following exchange rates were noted:

Date/Period	Exchange Rate (U.S. $ per yen)
January 1, 19x4.	$0.0070
December 31, 19x4	0.0080
Average for 19x4	0.0075

Macadona reported the following financial statements at the end of 19x4:

Macadona Corporation
Income Statement
For the Year Ended December 31, 19x4
(in millions of yen)

Net sales	2,673
Cost of goods sold	(1,021)
Other costs and expenses.	(896)
Net income	756

Macadona Corporation
Balance Sheet
December 31, 19x4
(in millions of yen)

Assets		Liabilities and Stockholders' Equity	
Cash	971	Liabilities:	
Receivables	1,125	Payables	2,167
Inventory	3,081	Long-term notes	19,000
Plant assets	19,746	Total liabilities	21,167
		Stockholders' equity:	
		Capital stock.	3,000
		Retained earnings	756
		Total stockholders' equity	3,756
Total assets	24,923	Total liabilities and stockholders' equity . . .	24,923

Required:
Translate Macadona's income statement and balance sheet from yen to U.S. dollars.

P B–3
Transaction Gains/Losses
L.O.1

Sport Corporation purchases supplies from Britain and manufactures goods in the United States for sale to France. The following transactions occurred recently:

May 1   Purchased supplies on account for 28,000 pounds.
May 15   Sold goods on account for 180,000 French francs.
May 25   Sold goods on account for 420,000 French francs.
May 25   Purchased supplies on account for 50,000 pounds.
May 30   Collected on sale made May 15.
May 30   Paid for purchase made May 1.
May 31   Collected on the May 25 sale and paid for the May 25 purchase.

The exchange rates in May were as follows:

Date	U.S. Dollars per	
	French Franc	British Pound
May 1	$0.20	$1.50
May 15	0.21	1.55
May 25	0.22	1.60
May 30	0.24	1.65
May 31	0.24	1.65

Required:
Compute the exchange gains or losses on these transactions.

P B–4
Translation of Balance Sheet
L.O.3, 4

The following comparative balance sheet is for CAP Gemini Sogeti S.A., a large French multi-national company specializing in computer information systems, data processing, and systems consulting. The balance sheets are expressed in French francs. CAP's net income for 19x3 was 103,230,224 francs.

Assume the following exchange rates:

	Dollars per Franc
At December 31, 19x3	.18
Weighted average historical rate at the date stockholders' equity accounts other than retained earnings were created. . .	.20

Further assume that the amount of retained earnings in U.S. dollars (from the restated income statements of all prior years, which are not provided here) is U.S. $110,000,000.

Required:
1. Prepare a balance sheet in U.S. dollars for CAP Gemini Sogeti as of December 31, 19x3. (Round all amounts to the nearest thousand.)
2. What is the cumulative translation gain or loss?

P B–5
Translation of Balance Sheet
L.O.3, 4

Consider the consolidated balance sheet in Exhibit B–3 of Saab-Scania, the Swedish manufacturer of cars, trucks, and jet aircraft. Assume that one Swedish krona (SEK) is equal to $0.155 at the end of 19x7. Further assume that the appropriate historical rate for all stockholders' equity accounts (including retained earnings) is .172.

Required:
1. Prepare a December 31, 19x7, balance sheet for Saab in U.S. dollars.
2. What is the cumulative translation gain or loss?
3. Over Saab's life has the U.S. dollar strengthened or weakened against the krona?

CAP GEMINI SOGETI S.A.
Balance Sheet
At December 31, 19x3
(in French francs)

ASSETS	19x2	19x3
Cash	605,380,288	175,797,733
Accounts and notes receivable	1,638,604	1,992,975
Other receivables	3,928,532	21,128,225
Affiliated Companies	93,873,405	59,936,715
Other current assets	9,152,718	7,431,953
TOTAL CURRENT ASSETS	**713,973,547**	**266,287,601**
Consolidated investments in affiliates	304,772,518	1,051,336,405
Other investments	1,698,233	2,839,597
Other noncurrent assets	352,718,085	309,779,486
Property, plant and equipment, net of accumulated depreciation	18,730,402	19,220,862
Intangible assets	13,072,500	13,317,215
TOTAL NONCURRENT ASSETS	**690,991,738**	**1,396,493,565**
TOTAL ASSETS	**1,404,965,285**	**1,662,781,166**
LIABILITIES AND SHAREHOLDERS' EQUITY	**19x2**	**19x3**
Financial debt	643,822,248	850,386,245
Operating debt	11,263,967	13,022,034
Other current debt	23,698,961	29,659,734
Unrealized exchange gain	746,432	247,500
TOTAL CURRENT LIABILITIES	**679,531,608**	**893,315,513**
NONCURRENT LIABILITIES		
Provisions for risks and charges	30,408,077	20,709,595
SHAREHOLDERS' EQUITY		
Common stock, authorized and issued	70,687,500	77,837,800
Retained earnings	519,466,898	540,740,727
Foreign investment tax provision	33,747,307	26,947,307
Shareholders' equity	623,901,705	645,525,834
Net income for the year	71,123,895	103,230,224
Total shareholders' equity before appropriation of income	**695,025,600**	**748,756,058**
TOTAL LIABILITIES AND SHAREHOLDERS' EQUITY	**1,404,965,285**	**1,662,781,166**

• **CASES**

C B–1
Foreign Currency—
General Motors
L.O.3

Consider the following footnote disclosure from the 19x6 annual report of General Motors (GM). This footnote is describing details of GM's balance sheet account Accumulated Foreign Currency Translation and Other Adjustments appearing in the stockholders' equity section of the balance sheet. As noted, the account reflects holding gains or losses from translation of foreign currency discussed in Appendix B.

Excerpt from Footnote 15:

(dollars in millions)	19x6	19x5	19x4
Accumulated Foreign Currency Translation and other Adjustments:			
Balance at beginning of year:			
Accumulated foreign currency translation adjusments	$(675.0)	$(789.5)	$(661.8)
Net unrealized gains on marketable securities	130.0	71.7	91.3
Changes during the year:			
Accumulated foreign currency translation adjustments . . .	192.2	114.5	(127.7)
Net unrealized gains (losses) on marketable securities. . .	30.8	58.3	(19.6)
Balance at end of the year	$(322.0)	$(545.0)	$(717.8)

Required:

1. The cumulative **prior years'** effect of foreign currency translation adjustments have resulted in how much of a holding gain or loss as of January 1, 19x6? (Be sure to indicate amount as well as gain or loss.)
2. What was the effect of translation for 19x6? (Give amount and whether it was a gain or loss.)

C B–2
Foreign Currency—
Union Carbide
L.O.1, 3

Consider the following footnotes taken from a recent annual report of Union Carbide Corporation (UCC):

Excerpt from footnotes:

Foreign Currency Translation

The following is an analysis of Equity Adjustment from Foreign Currency Translation which reduces stockholders' equity:

Millions of dollars	
Balance at beginning of year	$(374)
Translation adjustments	34
Balance at December 31.	$(340)

Other Expense (Income)

The following is an analysis of Other Expense (Income):

Millions of dollars	
Investment income (principally from short-term investments)	$ (42)
Foreign currency adjustments	(3)
Net discount expense on sales of customer obligations to UCAR Capital Corporation	18
Special litigation costs	185
Costs relating to self-tender offer.	58
Sales and disposals of business and other assets	(63)
Other	20
Total	$173

Required:

1. What was UCC's translation gain or loss for the year?
2. What is the apparent gain or loss from **transaction** adjustments included in UCC's income statement account Other Expenses (Income)?
3. Did the U.S. dollar become stronger or weaker in the year reported in this case? Explain.

C B–3
French Balance Sheet
L.O.4

Consider the consolidated balance sheet and income statement of Pernod Ricard, the French manufacturer of liquors, wines, and soft drinks, reproduced on the following pages. (When Pernod uses the term *group,* it is the same as saying the consolidated parent company.)

Required:

1. Identify four differences between Pernod's balance sheet and those of U.S. firms.
2. What is the apparent exchange rate used for converting Pernod's assets from francs to dollars?

Pernod Ricard
Consolidated Income Statement
For the Years Ended December 31
(in millions)

	U.S. $ 19x3	F. Fr. 19x3	F. Fr. 19x2
SALES NET OF VAT	2,344	12,516	11,773
Excise taxes and duties	(339)	(1,812)	(1,757)
SALES NET OF TAX	2,005	10,704	10,016
Cost of sales	(838)	(4,476)	(4,246)
GROSS MARGIN	1,167	6,228	5,770
Outside services	(417)	(2,228)	(1,973)
INCOME FROM OPERATIONS	750	4,000	3,797
Taxes	(41)	(219)	(213)
Payroll	(386)	(2,059)	(2,019)
GROSS OPERATING PROFIT	323	1,722	1,565
Other income	25	131	106
Other expense	(33)	(173)	(140)
Depreciation	(68)	(362)	(336)
OPERATING PROFIT BEFORE INTEREST EXPENSE	247	1,318	1,195
Net interest expense	(15)	(82)	(91)
OPERATING PROFIT	232	1,236	1,104
Provision for employee profit-sharing	(15)	(78)	(69)
Gains (losses) on disposal of assets	5	26	40
Other income (expense)	(13)	(67)	(12)
INCOME BEFORE INCOME TAXES	209	1,117	1,063
Income taxes	(92)	(492)	(521)
Interest in earnings (losses) of equity companies	2	10	5
NET INCOME	119	635	547
Minority interests	(5)	(28)	(31)
GROUP INTEREST IN NET INCOME	114	607	516

Pernod Ricard
Consolidated Balance Sheet
At December 31
(in millions)

Assets	U.S. $ 19x3	F. Fr. 19x3	F. Fr. 19x2
CAPITAL ASSETS	**587**	**3,136**	**2,664**
Intangibles	46	245	539
Plant, property, and equipment	346	1,847	1,794
Goodwill	36	195	27
Financial investments	159	849	304
CURRENT ASSETS	**1,105**	**5,900**	**6,259**
Inventories	446	2,381	2,453
Customer and other receivables	575	3,069	2,865
Marketable securities	15	82	418
Cash	69	368	523
ACCRUED INCOME AND PREPAID EXPENSE	**18**	**97**	**83**
CURRENCY TRANSLATION ADJUSTMENT	**1**	**5**	**5**
TOTAL ASSETS	**1,711**	**9,138**	**9,011**

Liabilities and Shareholders' Equity			
SHAREHOLDERS' EQUITY	**718**	**3,835**	**3,907**
Of which Group interest in net income	114	607	516
MINORITY INTERESTS IN SHAREHOLDERS' EQUITY	**45**	**239**	**299**
Of which minority interest in net income	5	27	31
PROVISIONS FOR RISK AND EXPENSE	**46**	**245**	**199**
DEFERRED INCOME TAXES	**6**	**30**	**88**
DEBT	**895**	**4,780**	**4,514**
Financial debt	291	1,557	1,335
Containers on deposit	55	293	303
Accounts payable and other	452	2,414	2,279
Other debt	97	516	597
PREPAID INCOME AND ACCRUED EXPENSE	**1**	**6**	**1**
CURRENCY TRANSLATION ADJUSTMENT	**—**	**3**	**3**
TOTAL LIABILITIES AND SHAREHOLDERS' EQUITY	**1,711**	**9,138**	**9,011**

C B–4
*French Income
Statement*
L.O.4

Consider the income statement for Pernod Ricard provided in Case B–3. In its income statement, Pernod refers to "VAT," which is a tax (value added tax) paid by certain European firms based on the total value added to a product (both costs and profits). A VAT provides incentives for firms to cut costs and increase profits since they will be taxed on the total.

Required:
1. Does Pernod Ricard have equity-method investments in other firms (i.e., unconsolidated subsidiaries)?
2. Does Pernod Ricard have any consolidated subsidiaries?
3. How does "net income" reported ($119) differ from "net income" for a U.S. firm that has consolidated (but not 100% owned) subsidiaries?

C

Accounting for Changing Prices

· Learning Objectives

After studying Appendix C, you should understand

1. The limitations of the stable dollar assumption underlying the historical cost model, p. 866.
2. How to measure the effects of general price changes on accounting disclosures, pp. 868–70.
3. How to measure the effects of specific price changes and judge when they may be more relevant than general price changes, pp. 869–73.
4. How to measure monetary gains and losses and their effect on the business entity, pp. 875–77.

Note: This appendix introduces students to the measurement issues that reduce the relevance of the historical cost model, and also illustrates how to adjust for general and specific price changes. Based on the material provided, students should get an understanding of the nature of the problems created by changing prices and the methods that are available to adjust for the effects of general and specific price changes.

This appendix can be introduced anytime after Chapter 6. Two chapters where the effects of price change would be of more than average relevance would be after Chapter 6 (inventories) or after Chapter 8 (long-term assets).

Objective 1
The limitations of the
stable dollar assumption
underlying the historical
cost model.

This textbook introduces generally accepted accounting principles (GAAP) to students. For the most part, GAAP is based on the historical cost principle, which reports elements of financial statements at their original (historical) cost, less any depreciation, amortization, or depletion where appropriate. The major exception to historical cost within GAAP is the lower-of-cost-or-market (LCM) procedures which apply to marketable securities (Chapter 13) and to inventory (Chapter 6). The LCM procedures permit the use of current "market" values only if they are below historical cost.

Although historical cost-based financial statements are used to aid many business decisions, they are not without serious limitations in some decision-making situations. GAAP financial statements are based on the assumption that the dollar measurement unit is an equal unit of measure over all time periods, which is referred to as the stable dollar assumption. When prices do change, GAAP financial statements become more difficult to compare and evaluate. In this appendix, several concepts and procedures are introduced that should help you evaluate financial statements in periods of changing prices and compensate for these changing prices in the preparation or evaluation of a company's financial results. This appendix discusses the following:

1. Types of price changes.
2. The use of general and specific price changes:
   a. Constant dollar analysis using general price changes.
   b. Current cost analysis using specific price changes.
3. Monetary gains and losses.

Understanding the effects of price changes on financial statements is very important since it can significantly affect evaluations of a single company from year to year and evaluations comparing several companies at a single point in time. We will see from the examples presented here that consideration of the impact of price changes on GAAP financial statements may change our evaluations of how well a company is doing.

We begin by explaining the two basic types of price changes and how we can measure their effect on elements of financial statements.

TYPES OF PRICE CHANGES

While price changes may be defined and reported in various ways, all price changes can be expressed in the form of a price index. A price index is the ratio of current prices to some previous year's prices, with the previous year selected usually being referred to as the *base year.* The two basic types of price indexes are general price indexes and specific price indexes.

A general price index measures the changes in the prices of a group of items. The most common example of a general price index is the consumer price index (CPI), which measures the change in prices of all goods and services normally acquired by individual consumers. The CPI attempts to track the change in prices of a "market basket" of goods and services typically consumed by individual households. The price and price change for each good or service included in a general index such as the CPI is weighted in proportion to its relative importance to the "average" consumer. For example, housing prices may be weighted 20% of the total of all goods and services a consumer purchases; food, 25%; transportation, 15%; and so on. Another broad-based index is the gross national product (GNP) index, which measures the change in price of all items *produced* in the United States.

A specific price index measures the price and change in price of a specific good or service. The specificity of an index may vary, depending on what type of items are priced in the index. For example, one specific price index may measure hourly labor costs in general, while other more specific indexes may measure hourly skilled labor and hourly unskilled labor separately. The specific price index for a product or service is constructed by measuring its current cost over time. To illustrate, assume that the cost of steel is reported on the dates given as follows:

Date	Average Price per Ton of Cold Rolled Steel, 1/8″
12/31/x1	$1,900
12/31/x2	1,875
12/31/x3	2,150
12/31/x4	2,370

The price of steel can be stated in index form using the actual price reported in 19x1 of $1,900 per ton as the basis for comparison as follows:

Year	Actual Historical Cost Price per Ton	÷	Actual Price in 19x1 per Ton	=	Specific Price Index Stated as a Percent*
19x1	$1,900		$1,900		100.0%
19x2	1,875		1,900		98.7
19x3	2,150		1,900		113.2
19x4	2,370		1,900		124.7

*19x1 = Base year.

The specific price index can use any year as the base year, since a base year is simply a point in time used as the basis for price comparison. If you wish to know what current prices are compared to 1967, then 1967 would be the base year. It is most common for specific price indexes to use either the current year's prices or some arbitrary prior year's prices as the base year for preparing a specific price index. In the example above, 19x1 is the base year, and the specific price index measures prices for 19x1 to 19x4 **relative to** 19x1's prices.

Using General or Specific Price Changes

General and specific price indexes may be used to evaluate the impact of price changes on historical cost data. The financial statements prepared in accordance with GAAP on a historical cost basis are often referred to as nominal dollar financial statements because they do not differentiate the various dollar units that originate from transactions over many different accounting periods. The balance sheet, for instance, may sum dollar units from 35 years ago when 100 acres of land were purchased for $10,000 with dollar units from the current year when one acre of land is purchased for $10,000 without differentiating between these two $10,000 amounts. Since the nominal dollar amounts of these two transactions both have the same historical cost, GAAP would report their sum at $20,000. However, if we wish to account for the fact that prices have changed over the last 35 years, we can restate the value of the land using general or specific price changes, thereby developing new information which could be more relevant for certain types of business decisions. The examples that follow illustrate how we can use information about changing prices to restate financial report data, separating the effects of price changes from the real performance and position of the reporting entity. When price changes are large, these procedures are important for meaningful financial statement analysis.

Objective 2
How to measure the effects
of general price changes
on accounting disclosures.

Constant Dollar Analysis Using General Price Changes. Data that have been adjusted for the effects of changes in the general price index are called constant dollar data or **general price level adjusted (GPLA)** data. To illustrate constant dollar data, assume that SPA-Tech, Inc., reported the following historical summary of earnings per share (EPS) for the past five years:

SPA-Tech, Inc.
Historical Cost Results

	19x5	19x4	19x3	19x2	19x1
Earnings per share (EPS)	$3.30	$3.23	$3.15	$3.05	$3.00

These results reveal an increasing trend in earnings on a historical cost basis. However, assume that the general consumer price index from 19x1 to 19x5, measured using 1967 prices as the base (or reference) year, changed as follows:

End of Year	Consumer Price Index (CPI) (1967 = 100)
19x1	280.0
19x2	299.6
19x3	326.6
19x4	359.3
19x5	388.0

The historical results can now be examined on a constant dollar basis, which means that we can control for the effects of changes in the purchasing power of the dollar over time. We can restate the historical results in terms of uniform 1967 dollars, or uniform 19x5 dollars, or any other uniform measure desired. To restate all amounts to 1967 dollars, we would simply divide each year's historical data by the year-end CPI as follows (all amounts rounded to nearest cent):

SPA-Tech, Inc.
EPS Restatement—1967 Dollars

Year	Historical EPS Reported	×	1967 CPI Divided by Respective Year's CPI	=	Equivalent 1967 Constant Dollar Amount
19x5	$3.30	×	(100/388.0)	=	$0.85
19x4	3.23	×	(100/359.3)	=	0.90
19x3	3.15	×	(100/326.6)	=	0.96
19x2	3.05	×	(100/299.6)	=	1.02
19x1	3.00	×	(100/280.0)	=	1.07

In terms of 1967 dollars, we now see that EPS has actually been decreasing from 19x1 to 19x5! Restated in 1967 dollars (constant 1967 dollars), EPS has decreased from $1.07 per share in 19x1 to $0.85 per share in 19x5. This reversal of the trend first reported on a historical (nominal) basis, from $3.00 to $3.30 per share, results from the fact that general price changes increased more rapidly than EPS each year. For example, the change in the CPI during 19x2 was about 7% [(2.996 − 2.800)/2.800 = +.07], while the change in EPS during 19x2 was only about 2% [($3.05 − $3.00)/$3.00 = +.017]. The changes observed in the constant dollar or GPLA data are often referred to as "real changes," since they examine the reported earnings measures (e.g., $3.00 to $3.05) **after** removing the effects of general price changes.

Constant dollar data may be stated in other than base year dollars, which are 1967 dollars in the example above. Many analysts feel that restating all nominal dollars in terms of current year constant dollars is more appropriate than restating all amounts to some previous base year dollars. To restate the EPS data in 19x5 constant dollars requires adjusting all amounts except 19x5 as follows (rounded to nearest cent):

SPA-Tech, Inc.
EPS Restatement—19x5 Dollars

Year	Historical (nominal) Dollar Amount	×	19x5 CPI over Original Year's CPI	=	19x5 Constant Dollar Amount
19x5.	$3.30	×	(3.88/3.88)	=	$3.30
19x4.	3.23	×	(3.88/3.593)	=	3.49
19x3.	3.15	×	(3.88/3.266)	=	3.74
19x2.	3.05	×	(3.88/2.996)	=	3.95
19x1.	3.00	×	(3.88/2.800)	=	4.16

Notice that all prior years' EPS amounts are larger when restated in 19x5 dollars. Restatement of the historical cost data in this example to uniform constant dollars shows **the same decreasing trend in EPS** regardless of whether 1967 dollars, 19x5 dollars, or some other constant dollar is used as a reference point. The restated constant dollar EPS amounts tell the reader that the real trend in EPS has been decreasing in this example from 19x1 to 19x5 because increases in the CPI have outpaced increases in nominal dollar EPS amounts.

When these constant dollar results are compared among firms, it could give a different perspective to the evaluation of a firm's relative performance, as noted in the comparison of Company A and Company B in Exhibit C–1.

While Company A reveals steady real growth in constant dollar EPS measures, Company B actually appears to be on a declining constant dollar EPS trend since 19x3! Constant dollar analysis can add new insights to conventional accounting data, particularly in periods of rapidly changing prices.

Objective 3

How to measure the effects of specific price changes and judge when they may be more relevant than general price changes.

Current Cost Analysis Using Specific Price Changes. Constant dollar analysis adjusts nominal historical cost data for changes in general price levels, but not all accounting data are affected by general price changes. For example, what if your business is experiencing decreasing inventory costs in a period where prices in general are *increasing*? Would it make sense to increase the value of inventory to reflect general price increases? Many accountants feel that although constant dollar adjustments may be insightful for the evaluation of EPS, dividends per share, or other overall financial statement results, the effect of specific price changes may be more useful for assessing specific financial statement components whose prices are not changing at the same rate as the general price index. Specifically, inventory and plant, property, and equipment might be better evaluated by considering how they are affected by specific price changes.

EXHIBIT C–1

Comparison of EPS Performance of Company A and Company B

Year-End	Historical Cost EPS		×	19x5 CPI over the Original Year's CPI	=	19x5 Constant Dollar EPS	
	Company A	Company B				Company A	Company B
19x5 . . .	$8.35	$8.35		(3.88/3.88)		$8.35	$8.35
19x4 . . .	7.51	7.85		(3.88/3.593)		8.11	8.48
19x3 . . .	6.67	7.27		(3.88/3.266)		7.92	8.64
19x2 . . .	6.05	6.48		(3.88/2.996)		7.84	8.39
19x1 . . .	5.55	5.55		(3.88/2.800)		7.69	7.69

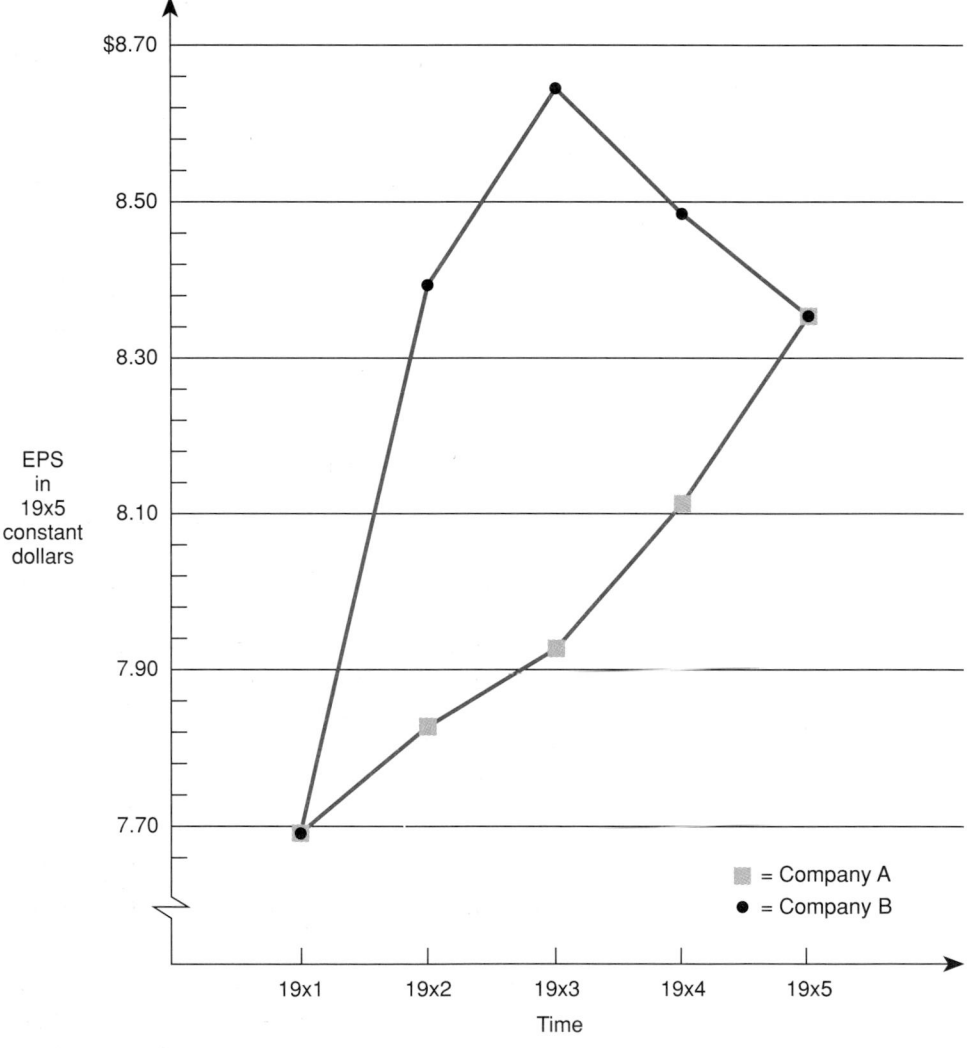

Historical cost accounting data that have been adjusted for the effects of specific price changes are called current cost data (also known as **replacement cost,** or **specific price level adjusted (SPLA)** data). These current cost data are prepared by using specific price indexes to convert historical cost amounts to current costs. The only difference between the current cost adjustment process and the constant dollar process illustrated earlier is the index. The current cost adjustments use a **separate specific price index** to convert each class of items (i.e., machinery, raw materials inventory, and so on) to its current costs, while the constant dollar model uses a single general price index for all conversions to constant dollars.

To illustrate current cost adjustments, assume that a retail carpet store has reported the following ending inventory values for its carpet inventory, which is valued on a FIFO basis.

Year-End	FIFO Value of Ending Inventory
19x4	$435,000
19x3	408,030
19x2	389,550
19x1	382,500

Further assume that the specific price index of carpeting has been increasing during this four-year period as follows:

Year-End	Specific Price Index for Carpeting (1967 ≡ 100)
19x4.	300
19x3.	290
19x2.	265
19x1.	250

By looking at the historical FIFO value only, it appears as though the quantity of inventory on hand at year-end has increased in each of the last three years since 19x1. However, using the information about specific price changes, we can see that the quantity of inventory (the "real" investment in inventory) actually decreased in 19x2 and 19x3 before increasing in a real sense in 19x4. Converting all of the year-end FIFO values to 19x4 current costs provides the following results:

Year-End	Ending Inventory		
	FIFO Value	× 19x4 Specific Index/Respective Year-End Index	= 19x4 Current Costs
19x4	$435,000	(300/300)	$435,000
19x3	408,030	(300/290)	422,100
19x2	389,550	(300/265)	441,000
19x1	382,500	(300/250)	459,000

The current cost measures computed above for the carpet inventory reveal a different pattern of "real" inventory change than the nominal FIFO values. The current cost measures show that there were decreases in the real quantity of inventory in both 19x2 and 19x3. The decrease is obscured because the increase in the specific index for carpet during 19x2 and 19x3 was greater than the increase in the FIFO inventory value. As a result, even though the total FIFO ending inventory value increased in both 19x2 and 19x3, the real quantity of carpet on hand actually decreased in both 19x2 and 19x3. In 19x4, both specific prices and real quantities increased.

Overall Effect of Specific Price Changes on Performance Measures

The effect of specific price changes on inventory in the example above may also be applied to other balance sheet items using other appropriate specific price indexes. These adjustments for specific price changes can be *very* important in measuring the performance of companies or parts of companies. The more long-term assets a company has, the greater the potential effect of specific price changes on a company's relative performance. To further illustrate how these specific price changes might affect performance measures, consider the following example:

> Company A and Company B are both lumber companies. Their primary assets are land and trees. Company A acquired most of its land in the 1920s at an average price of $200 per acre. Company B acquired most of its land in the 1970s at an average price of $2,000 per acre. Both companies started by borrowing half of the cost of the land initially, and have continued to maintain this same level of debt. The other half of the land cost was paid for from the sale of common stock. Assume that both companies have 100,000 acres of timberland and that each year they cut and sell 5,000 acres of timber and replant new seedlings on the harvested area. In 19x5, both companies reported net income of $5,000,000. By 19x5, the current cost of land for both companies was $2,300 per acre. Exhibit C–2 shows how, assuming there were no other specific price changes affecting these companies, historical cost performance measures can lead to incorrect comparisons. Exhibit C–2 also shows how current costs can result in more comparable performance ratios when results are very similar, as they were for companies A and B.

Based on the historical cost data, it looks as though Company A is much more efficient with its assets, since its ROA is more than four times that of Company B. Also, Company A has a much higher ROE than Company B. Yet according to the assumptions of this case, the companies are very similar in their assets and operations. The current cost comparison in Exhibit C–2 reveals the real similarity between companies A and B. The companies have identical ROAs of 1.9%. Also, since Company B is newer and has more debt, its ROE on a current cost basis is higher than that of Company A.

In Exhibit C–2, the increase in Company A's Land account from its historical cost of $200 per acre to its current cost of $2,300 per acre results in a *holding gain* of $2,100 per acre. A **holding gain** is the increase in the value of any asset over its original cost that results over time as the asset is held. **Holding losses** measure decreases in value over original cost. Inventory, buildings, and land often increase in value as they are held. In historical cost–based accounting, these holding gains are not recognized until the asset is sold. In current cost–based systems, holding gains or losses are recognized in income each period that the specific prices of assets change.

The example in Exhibit C–2 is simplified to illustrate the potential importance of current cost information in comparing one company to another (or one operating plant to another within the same company). However, the potential effect of specific price changes and their importance is very real. In capital-intense industries failure to consider the effects of specific price changes can lead to inappropriate operating, financing, and investing decisions that can eventually lead to bankruptcy. The U.S. steel industry provides an excellent example. Failure to consider the effects of specific price changes contributed to the demise of the United States as a world leader in steel production.

It should be noted that the failure of U.S. GAAP to require or permit financial statement adjustments and disclosures that adjust for general or specific price changes makes

EXHIBIT C–2

Comparison of Historical Cost and Current Cost Performance Measures

Historical Cost Balance Sheets
(in millions)

Company A

Assets:		Liabilities:	
Other assets . . .	$ 5	Other liabilities . .	$ 5
Inventory	25	**Debt**	10
Land	20	Total liab. . .	$15
		Stockholders' equity:	
		Capital stock . .	10
		Retained earnings	25
Total assets	$50	Total liabilities and stockholders' equity	$50

Return on assets (ROA) = $5/$50 = 10%
Return on equity (ROE) = $5/$35 = 14.3%

Company B

Assets:		Liabilities:	
Other assets . .	$ 5	Other liabilities. .	$ 5
Inventory	25	**Debt**	100
Land	200	Total liab. . .	$105
		Stockholders' equity:	
		Capital stock . .	100
		Retained earnings . . .	25
Total assets. . . .	$230	Total liabilities and stockholders' equity.	$230

ROA = $5/$230 = 2.2%
ROE = $5/$125 = 4.0%

Current Cost Balance Sheets
(in millions)

Company A

Assets:		Liabilities:	
Other assets . . .	$ 5	Other liabilities . .	$ 5
Inventory	25	**Debt**	10
Land	230	Total liab. . .	$ 15
		Stockholders' equity:	
		Plug total	245
Total assets	$260	Total liabilities and stockholders' equity	$260

$$ROA = \frac{\$5}{\$260} = 1.9\%$$

$$ROE = \frac{\$5}{\$245} = 2.0\%$$

Company B

Assets:		Liabilities:	
Other assets . .	$ 5	Other liabilities. .	$ 5
Inventory	25	**Debt**	100
Land	230	Total liab. . .	$105
		Stockholders' equity:	
		Plug total	155
Total assets. . . .	$260	Total liabilities and stockholders' equity.	$260

$$ROA = \frac{\$5}{\$260} = 1.9\%$$

$$ROE = \frac{\$5}{\$155} = 3.2\%$$

us the exception rather than the rule. Many other countries, including the United Kingdom, France, the Netherlands, and Sweden permit the revaluation of fixed depreciable assets in the balance sheet. Also, very few countries other than the United States do not permit depreciation expense reported in the income statement to exceed historical cost–based depreciation. It is fair to say that U.S.-based GAAP is more strictly tied to historical cost than GAAP of most other countries.

Monetary Items

Although constant dollar and current cost measurements may be useful and interesting when applied to certain elements of financial statement data, they are not appropriate for restating the current balances of those assets and liabilities that represent specific claims to receive (assets) or pay (liabilities) fixed money amounts. These balance sheet items represent **fixed claims to receive or pay money,** and are called monetary assets and monetary liabilities. Monetary assets such as cash and accounts receivable entitle the entity to receive a fixed money amount regardless of whether prices are increasing or decreasing. Yet these fixed claims to receive (in the case of monetary assets) or pay (in the case of monetary liabilities) specified money amounts are somehow affected by changing prices. As prices change, the values of some assets and liabilities change while the values of other assets and liabilities remain fixed. For example, the amount of cash you can receive from a customer with a $100 outstanding accounts receivable balance does not change over time. However, the amount of cash you can receive for the sale of inventory will normally increase as prices increase and decrease as prices decrease.

Cash and accounts receivable are examples of **monetary assets** because they represent **fixed claims to a specified number of dollars.** Inventory and land are examples of nonmonetary assets that do not represent fixed claims but instead represent assets whose values may change as prices change. Because most liabilities represent fixed claims to a specified number of dollars, most liabilities are monetary liabilities.

Typical examples of monetary and nonmonetary assets and liabilities are listed in the following table.

Assets	Liabilities and Stockholders' Equity
Monetary items:	**Monetary items:**
Cash	Accounts payable
Accounts receivable	Notes payable
Notes receivable	Salaries payable
Leases receivable	Taxes payable
Long-term investment in bonds	Bonds payable
	Dividends payable
Nonmonetary items:	**Nonmonetary items:**
Inventories	Estimated liabilities
Most investments in stocks	Health benefits payable
Land	Preferred stock
Building	Convertible bonds and stocks expected to be converted to common stock
Equipment	
Intangible assets	Common stock

These assets, liabilities, and stockholders' equity items are classified as monetary or nonmonetary depending strictly on whether they represent fixed claims to receive (or pay) a specified number of dollars that will not vary as prices change.

Monetary Gains and Losses

Although the recorded measures of monetary items do not change, their economic value to the company holding the asset or liability does change as prices change. For example, if you hold cash for one year and general price levels increase by 10% during that time, the cash will buy 10% less at the end of the year, resulting in a "monetary loss." Thus, if you hold monetary assets in a period of increasing prices, a **monetary loss** results. However, holding monetary liabilities in a period of increasing prices will result in **monetary gains** because you can pay off these liabilities with "cheaper dollars," dollars that can buy less than the dollars originally borrowed.

Monetary gains and losses (also called **purchasing power gains** or **losses**) resulting from the holding of monetary items in periods of changing prices are not reported in conventional GAAP financial statements, but their effects are measurable and may be of interest to decision makers.

Objective 4
How to measure monetary gains and losses and their effect on the business entity.

To illustrate, assume that Company X borrows $100,000 cash from Company Y at 0% interest on January 1, 19x9. (The effect of interest rates is examined in more advanced accounting texts.)[1] The general price index increases from 160 to 192 during 19x9, an increase of 20% [(192 − 160)/160 = 32/160 = .20 = 20%)]. On December 31, 19x9, Company X repays the $100,000 cash to Company Y. Because of the note payable to Company Y, Company X experienced a monetary gain of $20,000, the difference between the nominal dollar value and the constant dollar value of the note, computed as follows:

19x9	Note Payable	Nominal Dollars	×	Conversion Ratio	=	Year-End Constant Dollars (192)
Jan. 1	Beginning balance	$ 100,000	×	192/160	=	$ 120,000
Dec. 31	Change (repayment)	(100,000)	×	192/192	=	(100,000)
31	Ending balance	$ 0				$ 20,000
					−	0
	Monetary gain.					$ 20,000

The recorded value of the note payable remains at $100,000 on the books of Company X until paid at year-end. However, the value (or size) of the dollars used to repay the loan is not the **same** as those received on January 1! The dollars borrowed on January 1, 19x9, are size 160 index dollars, whereas the dollars used to repay the note on December 31, 19x9, are size 192 index dollars. In other words, it would take $192 at the end of 19x9 to buy the same things that $160 could have purchased at the start of 19x9, resulting in a 20% decline in purchase power [($160 − $192)/$160 = −.20 = −20%]. The purchasing power of the dollar has declined during 19x9, and the $100,000 cash at year-end will buy 20% less than the $100,000 cash at the start of the year. If Company X had taken the $100,000 cash on January 1 and invested it in the items making up the general price index (e.g., the "market basket" of goods and services), these items would be worth $120,000 at year-end. Company Y, holding a note receivable throughout 19x9, would have experienced a monetary loss of $20,000 from this loan.

---

[1]Interest rates on debt are generally established based on expected future inflation. As such, an interest rate may be viewed as consisting of two parts: one part to compensate the lender for expected future inflation plus a second part to provide the lender with a **real** return on his or her capital. A 10% interest rate might be based on 4% for expected inflation plus 6% for the real return. A borrower would only obtain a *real* benefit from a monetary gain if the actual rate of inflation exceeded the lender's expected rate of inflation. However, a monetary gain will still result in any case where there is a net monetary liability position in a period of inflation, as in the example later in this section. Without knowing the expected rate of *inflation* included in the lender's interest rate, it is not possible to determine whether monetary gains represent real gains to the borrower or real losses to the lender. This same uncertainty exists for monetary losses if the lender was expecting some unknown rate of deflation.

Note that in the example above, if Company X had simply held onto the $100,000 cash until the year-end repayment, it would have had a $20,000 monetary loss from holding cash to offset against the $20,000 monetary gain from the note payable. To illustrate how to compute the **net monetary** gain or loss for a company, assume the following data for the Tran Corporation:

Tran Corporation
Balance Sheet
December 31

Assets	19x7	19x6	Liabilities and Stockholders' Equity	19x7	19x6
Cash	$ 5,000	$ 8,000	Liabilities:		
Accounts receivable	28,000	22,000	Accounts payable	$ 5,000	$ 7,000
Inventory	42,000	45,000	Notes payable	40,000	40,000
Land	65,000	65,000	Total liabilities	$ 45,000	$ 47,000
			Stockholders' equity:		
			Common stock	$ 80,000	$ 80,000
			Retained earnings	15,000	13,000
			Total stockholders' equity	$ 95,000	$ 93,000
Total assets	$140,000	$140,000	Total liabilities and stockholders' equity. . . .	$140,000	$140,000

Assume that during 19x7, the general price index went from 150 at the start of the year to 200 by year-end, with the average price index equal to 180 during 19x7. Note that the average price level would be the sum of the daily price levels divided by 365 days and need not be exactly between the high and low price level for the year. Tran has two monetary assets (cash and accounts receivable) and two monetary liabilities (accounts payable and notes payable). In the previous example of Company X, note that the only change in the monetary account took place at the end of the year. Here we have several monetary accounts that could change daily. To simplify our analysis, *we assume that all account balance changes occurred evenly throughout the year,* unless otherwise stated. The total net monetary gain or loss for all four monetary accounts can be computed together, as follows:

	Monetary Liabilities		Monetary Assets		Net Monetary Liability
	(Accounts Payable + Notes Payable)	−	(Cash + Accounts Receivable)	=	
Beginning balance	($7,000 + $40,000)	−	($8,000 + $22,000)		
	$47,000	−	$30,000	=	$17,000
Ending balance.	($5,000 + $40,000)	−	($5,000 + $28,000)		
	$45,000	−	$33,000	=	12,000
Net increase (decrease) in net monetary liability					$ (5,000)

	Nominal Dollars	Conversion Ratio	Year-End Constant Dollars (200)
Beginning net monetary liability	$17,000	200/150*	$22,667
19x7 decrease in net monetary liability	(5,000)	200/180[†]	(5,556)
Ending net monetary liability	$12,000		$17,111
			− 12,000
Net monetary gain			$ 5,111

*End of period index/Beginning of period index.
[†] End of period index/Average of period index.

Since the Tran Company was in a net monetary liability position (monetary liabilities exceed monetary assets) throughout 19x7 (a period of general inflation), the difference between their nominal dollar and constant dollar net liability position results in a monetary gain.

While monetary gains and losses are not recorded or reported in GAAP financial statements, they may be computed from the comparative balance sheet data for any company, and might be useful for evaluating the management of a company. Since a monetary gain will result from being in debt during a period of inflation, and since most people believe we will continue to experience some inflation in the future, it would appear that being in debt would be a good strategy! However, the monetary gains from being in debt during a period of inflation must be weighed against the actual interest cost paid on the debt.

This example helps to illustrate the fundamental effects of price changes on monetary assets and liabilities, which may be summarized as follows:

1. In periods of inflation (increasing prices):
   a. Holding monetary assets results in a monetary (purchasing power) loss.
   b. Holding monetary liabilities results in a monetary (purchasing power) gain.

2. In periods of deflation (decreasing prices):
   a. Holding monetary assets results in a monetary (purchasing power) gain.
   b. Holding monetary liabilities results in a monetary (purchasing power) loss.

In general, increasing prices benefit companies that have a net monetary liability position. Alternatively, companies holding net monetary assets will incur monetary losses in periods of increasing prices.

DEPRECIATION AND PRICE CHANGES

In evaluating long-term assets in financial reports, an important aspect to consider is the effect of price changes throughout the useful lives of the assets. The longer the useful life of an asset, the greater the potential impact of price changes on its recorded book value. Over the last 40 to 50 years, most assets have experienced significant price increases. How do these price changes affect financial reports? To answer this question, consider the following example of two steel plants (dollar figures in thousands):

	Plant A	Plant B
Year assets purchased	1986	1979
Cost of assets.	$40,000	$10,000
Maximum production per year.	50 million tons	50 million tons
Annual cost of maximum production in 1988 excluding depreciation expense	$35,000	$35,000
Depreciation per year (straight line, 10 years)	$ 4,000	$ 1,000
Annual revenues per year at maximum production	$40,000	$40,000

Assuming maximum production, the 1988 income statements for each plant would be (in thousands):

	Plant A	Plant B
Revenues	$40,000	$40,000
Expenses:		
Material, labor, etc.	$35,000	$35,000
Depreciation	4,000	1,000
Total expenses.	$39,000	$36,000
Pre-tax income.	$ 1,000	$ 4,000
Income tax expense (40%)	400	1,600
Net income	$ 600	$ 2,400

Notice that both plants are identical in their operations except for the amount of depreciation charged and the related income tax effects. The depreciation difference occurs because Plant A was purchased in 1986 and is more expensive than Plant B purchased in 1979.

Several questions may be interesting to consider. Which plant is more profitable? Which plant provides more cash flow? If one of the two plants had to be closed, which one would you close? It seems that Plant B is more profitable than Plant A. However, since depreciation expense does **not** use cash, the cash flow from operations after taxes is higher for Plant A! If we assume that all revenues are for cash and all expenses other than depreciation use cash, the following results:

	Plant A	Plant B
Cash inflows (revenues)	$ 40,000	$ 40,000
Less cash outflows:		
Materials, labor, etc.	(35,000)	(35,000)
Taxes.	(400)	(1,600)
Net cash inflow	$ 4,600	$ 3,400

Plant A paid less taxes due to its higher depreciation expense and therefore had $1.2 million more net cash inflow from operations. This makes the question of which plant to close more difficult to answer. Plant A has higher cash flow, but Plant B has higher profits. However, both plants are equal in terms of their real operating performance even though historical cost measures of income fail to reveal this fact.

The effect of price changes on depreciable assets makes comparisons within a company and between companies more difficult. Between 1976 and 1984, companies were required to provide supplementary schedules reporting the effects of changing prices on plant assets and inventory. Today, these disclosures are voluntary and need not be reported. Exhibit C–3 provides an example of a voluntary disclosure. Exhibit C–4 provides an example of some of the disclosures previously required by *FASB Statement No. 33* and several other related pronouncements. In Exhibit C–3, we can see that Quaker Oats Company's net assets at historical cost and at current (replacement) cost differ significantly and vary over time. The difference in net asset values is $503.9 million in 1983, or 74% more than the historical cost–based values, compared with only a $365.8 million (44%) difference in 1986. This would suggest that either current costs have declined (i.e. price

EXHIBIT C–3

**Current Cost Annual
Report Disclosure—
Excerpt from Footnotes**

**The Quaker Oats Company and Subsidiaries
Comparison of Selected Supplementary Financial Data
Adjusted for the Effects of Changing Prices**

(in millions)

For the Years Ended June 30	1986	1985	1984	1983
Net assets at year-end:				
—Current cost	$1,196.9	$1,194.5	$1,548.7	$1,184.6
—Historical	831.1	824.8	758.6	680.7
Increase in the general price level over (under) increase in specific prices of inventories and property, plant, and equipment	$ (68.4)	$ (48.7)	$ (12.8)	$ (32.2)*

*Increase in general prices faster (slower) than specific price changes.

EXHIBIT C–4

**Former Disclosures for
Changing Prices**

**Standard Oil Company (Indiana)
Statement of Net Income
Adjusted for Changing Prices
For Year Ended December 31, 1984
(average 1984 dollars, in millions)**

	As Reported (historical cost)	As Adjusted for Changing Prices (current costs)
Total revenues	$29,008	$29,008
Purchases and operating expenses	**16,126**	**16,133**
Exploration expenses	1,286	1,286
Selling and administrative expenses	1,302	1,302
Taxes other than income taxes	3,825	3,825
Depreciation, depletion, and amortization	**2,090**	**2,651**
Interest expense	446	446
Total costs and expenses	25,075	25,643
Income before income taxes	3,933	3,365
Income taxes	1,750	1,750
Net income	$ 2,183	$ 1,615
Unrealized gain from decline in purchasing power of net amounts owed		$ 267

decreases) since 1983, or that the net assets on hand in 1986 are on average newer than those on hand in 1983.

In Exhibit C–4 we see that Standard Oil's 1984 net income on a current cost basis was $568 million less than on a historical cost basis ($2,183 less $1,615 = $568 difference). This decrease is in excess of half a billion dollars and would surely have a material effect on the measurement of Standard Oil's 1984 performance using such measures as return on assets (ROA) or return on equity (ROE). Standard Oil also reports a $267 million unrealized holding gain from its net monetary liabilities (not shown in Exhibit C–4). This suggests that the general price index in 1984 was higher than it was when Standard Oil's monetary liabilities were originally incurred. Therefore, paying these net monetary liabilities with 1984 dollars would have resulted in a purchasing power gain.

In some industries in which assets are, on average, rather old, the difference between historical cost depreciation expense and current cost depreciation expense can be large. It is possible that the additional depreciation expense on a current cost basis could change profits to losses if used to measure income. As a result, the current cost of depreciation should be considered in evaluating financial statements whenever possible.

• SUMMARY

Although current cost or constant dollar financial data are not currently required under GAAP, we should recognize the potential important effect of price changes on accounting data in making business decisions. Over time, a series of relatively small price changes can have a significant effect, particularly on the values reported in the balance sheet for long-term assets. We should not lose sight of the effects of changing prices on financial statements in making decisions about the performance of companies at a point in time or over time.

• KEY TERMS

Constant dollar. Data that have been adjusted for the effects of changes in the general price index; also called general price level adjusted (GPLA) data.

Current cost. Accounting data that have been adjusted for the effects of specific price changes; also called replacement cost or specific price level adjusted (SPLA) data.

General price index. A price index that measures the changes in the prices of a group of items.

Monetary assets. Fixed claims to receive a specified number of dollars.

Monetary liabilities. Fixed claims to pay a specified number of dollars.

Nominal dollar. Units of dollars that do not differentiate by accounting periods. GAAP financial statements are reported in nominal dollars.

Nonmonetary assets. Assets whose value may change as prices change.

Price index. The ratio of current prices to some previous year's prices, with the previous year selected usually referred to as the "base year."

Specific price index. A price index that measures the price and change in price of a specific good or service.

Stable dollar assumption. Assumption that the dollar is an equal unit of measure over all time periods.

• SYNONYMS

Constant dollar; general price level adjusted (GPLA).

Current cost; replacement cost; specific price level adjusted (SPLA).

Monetary gain (loss); purchasing power gain (loss).

• QUESTIONS

1. Identify two cases where GAAP permits market values of assets to be reported.
2. Give an example of a general price index and tell what it measures.
3. Give an example of a specific price index and tell what it measures.

4. If the general price index increased by 10%, what do we know happened to the price of automobile tires?

5. If the specific price index for automobile tires increased by 15%, what do we know happened to the general price index?

6. Assume there is no change in the general price index. If the specific price index for food increased by 10%, what else must have happened?

7. How many differently sized (indexed) dollars would typically appear in the balance sheet of a large publicly traded company? What is the effect of this on the comparability of one company's balance sheet with another?

8. Would it make more sense to restate the historical cost of ending inventory for specific price changes or general price changes? Explain.

9. Identify common examples of monetary assets and liabilities. Why are they monetary items?

10. What information is normally not available but is needed to measure the actual net monetary gain or loss that would result from borrowing $1 million at 10% annual interest per year during a period of inflation?

• EXERCISES

E C–1
Constant Dollar Measurements— Earnings
L.O.2

The Brazil Corporation reported the following earnings results for the past four years:

Year	Reported Earnings (in thousands)
19x4	$3,547
19x3	2,956
19x2	2,274
19x1	1,895

During this same time period, the economy experienced rapid inflation, with the value of the dollar decreasing by 25% per year, as follows:

Average for Year	General Price Index
19x4	244.1
19x3	195.3
19x2	156.3
19x1	125.0

Required:

1. Restate the Brazil Corporation's earnings results for each year using average 19x4 constant dollars. (Round answers to the nearest thousand.)

2. Did Brazil have real growth in earnings during any of the last three years?

E C–2
Monetary Gain or Losses
L.O.4

Jensen Corporation started 19x1 with cash of $175,000. At the end of 19x1 the cash balance had increased to $275,000. During 19x1 the consumer price index (CPI) went from 300 to 330. Assume that Jensen's changes in the cash balance and changes in the CPI both occurred evenly throughout 19x1.

Required:

1. Compute the monetary gain or loss that resulted from Jensen's holding cash during 19x1.

2. How would your answer to requirement 1 have changed if the CPI had decreased during 19x1?

E C–3
*Current Cost
Measures—Inventory*
L.O.3

Drasko Corporation reported the following data concerning its inventory:

December 31	Reported Book Value of Inventory at FIFO Cost	Specific Price Index at Year-End for Inventory
19x4	$850,000	229.9
19x3	825,000	209.0
19x2	770,000	200.0

The FIFO inventory value states the ending inventory at year-end prices each year.

Required:
1. Restate the reported value of the ending inventory for 19x3 and 19x2 in terms of 19x4 year-end current costs.
2. Did Drasko have a real increase in inventory during 19x4 or 19x3?

E C–4
*Constant Dollar
Measurements—EPS*
L.O.2

The Traster Corporation reported the following earnings over the past four years:

Year	Reported Earnings (in thousands)
19x4	$7,000
19x3	6,600
19x2	6,000
19x1	5,200

The general price index over this same period of time increased steadily, as follows:

Year-End	General Price Index
19x4	405
19x3	385
19x2	350
19x1	330

Required:
1. Restate Traster's earnings for 19x1 to 19x4 using 19x4 year-end constant dollars. (Round answers to the nearest thousand.)
2. In which years did Traster report real growth in earnings?

E C–5
Monetary Gain or Loss
L.O.4

Baily Corporation began 19x5 with accounts payable of $82,875. Baily made purchases on account of $473,800 evenly throughout 19x5, and payments on account of $465,300 evenly throughout 19x5. The consumer price index increased steadily from 320 at the start of 19x5 to 352 by the end of 19x5.

Required:
Compute the net monetary gain or loss attributable to accounts payable for 19x5.

E C–6
Monetary Gain or Loss
L.O.4

Arrow Corporation began 19x5 with accounts receivable of $95,000. Arrow recorded credit sales of $3,600,000 evenly throughout 19x5 and received $3,200,000 cash on accounts receivable evenly throughout 19x5. The consumer price index increased steadily from 320 at the start of 19x5 to 352 by the end of 19x5.

Required:
Compute the net monetary gain or loss from accounts receivable for 19x5.

• PROBLEMS

P C–1
Constant Dollar Measures—Earnings
L.O.2

The Red and White Companies have been in competition with one another for some time. Their operating results for the past several years are summarized as follows:

| | Earnings (in thousands) | |
Year	Red Company	White Company
19x4	$650,000	$325,000
19x3	558,382	298,465
19x2	542,118	289,481
19x1	526,329	263,164

Throughout this time period, Red Company has had twice as many assets and liabilities as White Company. The general price index has increased steadily over the past four years as follows:

Year	General Price Index
19x4	274.5
19x3	261.4
19x2	253.7
19x1	235.0

Required:
1. Recompute the reported earnings of both Red and White in 19x4 constant dollars for all four years.
2. In which years, if any, did Red Company experience a real increase in earnings?
3. In which years, if any, did White Company experience a real increase in earnings?
4. Which company appears to have the most consistent real growth in earnings?

P C–2
Current Cost Measurements— Inventory
L.O.3

The Waymire Corporation reported the following balances in their retail furniture inventory over the past several years:

Year	Ending FIFO Inventory Value
19x4	$737,124
19x3	702,023
19x2	644,058
19x1	596,350

During the same interval the specific price index of furniture costs from manufacturers to retail outlets (like Waymire), as reported by the Bureau of Labor, changed as follows:

Year	Specific Price Index— Retail Furniture
19x4	287.9
19x3	279.5
19x2	254.1
19x1	231.0

Required:
1. Compute the restated ending inventory balance for 19x1 to 19x4 in terms of 19x4 current costs.
2. In which of the last three years did Waymire have a real increase in inventory?

P C–3
*Constant Dollar
Adjustments
(Challenging)*
L.O.2

The following data summarize the financial statements of Parrot, Inc., as of December 31, 19x6. The index stated in parentheses to the right of each historical (nominal) dollar value indicates the general price index in effect when the original transaction giving rise to the item took place. (When more than one transaction affects an account balance, the index represents the weighted average index value.) The current general price index (at the end of 19x6) is 300.

Balance Sheet Data (in $000)

Cash	$ 130 (288)		Accounts Payable	$ 293 (275)
Accounts Receivable	286 (264)		Wages and Taxes Payable	346 (300)
Inventory	620 (180)		Long-Term Debt	2,500 (160)
Plant Assets	4,180 (160)		Common Stock	2,000 (140)
Land	1,200 (140)		Retained Earnings	1,277 (?)
	$6,416			$6,416

Required:

Prepare a general price level adjusted balance sheet for December 31, 19x6. Round all answers to the nearest thousand. (Hint: Treat retained earnings as a plug; do not try to price level adjust this balance.)

P C–4
*Price Changes
and Inventory
(Challenging)*
L.O.2, 3

During 19x1 Darren, Inc., purchased 10,000 units of product X for $10 each at a time when the general price index was 200. At the end of 19x4 these 10,000 units of product X were sold for $15 per unit, when the general price index was 280. An additional purchase of 10,000 units of product X was made at the end of 19x4 at a then-current cost of $13 per unit.

Required:

1. Compute cost of goods sold and gross profit for 19x4 for product X on a historical cost basis.
2. Repeat requirement 1 using current costs.
3. Repeat requirement 1 using constant dollars (general price level adjusted amounts).
4. Compare your answers in 1 and 2 above. What is the apparent "holding gain" included in gross profit in the historical cost income statement?
5. Which measure of gross profit do you believe to be the most relevant for measuring Darren's operating performance concerning product X during 19x4? Explain your answer.

P C–5
Monetary Gain or Loss
L.O.4

The Print Corporation reported the following comparative balance sheets:

**Print Corporation
Balance Sheet
At December 31**

	19x2	19x1		19x2	19x1
Assets			**Liabilities and Stockholders' Equity**		
Cash	$ 12,500	$ 10,000	Liabilities:		
Accounts receivable	21,350	30,000	Accounts payable	$ 18,300	$ 15,400
Inventory	41,400	39,800	Notes payable	60,000	60,000
Land	60,000	60,000	Total liabilities	$ 78,300	$ 75,400
			Stockholders' equity:		
			Common stock	$ 25,000	$ 25,000
			Retained earnings	31,950	39,400
			Total stockholders' equity	$ 56,950	$ 64,400
Total assets	$135,250	$139,800	Total liabilities and stockholders' equity. . . .	$135,250	$139,800

During 19x2, the consumer price index increased by 14% (.14), with the average increase for the year equal to 7% (.07).

Required (round all amounts to the nearest dollar):
1. Compute the net monetary gain or loss from monetary assets (combined) for 19x2.
2. Compute the net monetary gain or loss from monetary liabilities (combined) for 19x2.
3. Compute the total net monetary gain or loss for 19x2.

• CASES

C C–1
Current Costs—
LIFO Inventory
(Challenging)
L.O.3

The Weber Company uses the LIFO inventory method to account for its various product lines. During 19x7, Weber eliminated one of these product lines, causing it to liquidate its LIFO layers from beginning inventory. The beginning inventory for product Z on January 1, 19x7, was made up of the following layers:

Year Added	Units Added	×	Unit Price in Year Added	=	LIFO Cost
19x1	2,000		$10		$20,000
19x3	1,200		12		14,400
19x5	1,800		14		25,200
19x6	1,000		15		15,000
	6,000				$74,600

During 19x7 Weber acquired 2,500 units of product Z at $16 per unit for a total cost of $40,000. By the end of 19x7, all 8,500 units of product Z had been sold for $32 per unit.

Required:
1. Compute the gross margin (sales less cost of sales) from sales of product Z for 19x7.
2. Assume next that Weber did not have any beginning inventory of product Z at the start of 19x7, but that it purchased (for $16 each) and sold (for $32 each) 8,500 units during 19x7. Compute the gross margin from sales of product Z for 19x7.
3. Your answer to requirement 2 above is equivalent to the current cost measure of gross margin. What is the amount of holding gains included in the gross margin measured in requirement 1 above? In requirement 2?
4. If you were top management of Weber and were attempting to compensate the sales force for their efforts to sell product Z during 19x7, which gross margin measure do you think would be most equitable? Explain your choice briefly.

C C–2
Monetary Gains
and Losses
L.O.4

During 19x3 Weber Corporation borrowed $1 million from State Bank, signing a five-year, 10% note on January 1 of the year. The note calls for annual interest payments, with the principal to be paid at maturity. The corporation, which was owned by the Weber family, had never borrowed on a long-term basis before, and the president, John Weber, was nervous about doing so in 19x3 because of the changing economic climate. The inflation rate over the past three years (19x0 to 19x2) had been quite low, averaging about 2% per year. However, during 19x3 inflation began to climb, and by 19x4 it was up to about a 6% annual rate. Weber's chief accountant seemed happy with the increase in inflation and reported to John Weber at the end of 19x4 that the corporation was experiencing a large monetary gain from the $1 million bank loan. John Weber is having a difficult time understanding how being in debt can result in a gain. The financial statements do not report any such gain, but do report $100,000 interest expense in the 19x4 income statement.

Required:
1. Write a short note explaining to Mr. Weber how the recent inflationary trend might be viewed as a gain.
2. What information would you need to determine whether or not a real gain existed in this case?

C C–3
General versus
Specific Price Changes
L.O.2, 3

Assume that you are an investor who owns stock in about 25 large publicly traded corporations which you have held for the past five years. You invested $500,000 in these stocks five years ago because of their dividends, which is your major source of income. Over the past five years, your total dividends from these same investments have been as follows:

Year	Dividends Received
19x9	$67,350
19x8	63,200
19x7	61,940
19x6	60,015
19x5	57,330

Your accountant has frequently discussed the effects of changing prices on your investments with you. You understand that there are both specific price changes, which affect each of your companies somewhat differently, and general price changes which affect the economy as a whole. You realize that over the past five years there have been some rather significant general and specific price changes which have affected your investments. You begin to wonder whether you are really better off in 19x9 than you were in 19x5.

Required:
What general or specific price adjusted information might help you decide whether or not you are better off in 19x9 than you were in 19x5? Would general or specific price adjusted data be more useful to you? Explain your answer.

C C–4
General versus
Specific Price Changes
L.O.2, 3

Assume you are the chief operating officer for the Norfold plant of the Beldon Corporation. As the plant's top manager, you are held responsible for its performance by corporate management. The main asset controlled by your plant is inventory. Inventory costs have fluctuated widely over the past six years, with costs continuously experiencing rather large increases or decreases. The economy has experienced a steady increase in inflation over this same time period, causing selling prices to climb steadily. Your plant uses the LIFO method for costing inventories. You realize that the reported-asset value for inventory is not realistic since it consists primarily of costs from many years ago. This is having a serious effect on your analysis of your investment in inventory, inventory turnover ratios, etc. You would like to evaluate inventory using measures which better represent the current economic conditions. Most of your competitors are using the FIFO method of costing their inventory and are less affected by price changes.

Required:
What general or specific price adjusted information might best help you evaluate your investment in inventory over the past six years compared to both yourself (from year to year) and your competitors? Explain your answer.

D

Accounting for Not-for-Profit Entities

· Learning Objectives

After studying Appendix D, you should understand

1. The difference between not-for-profit and business entities, pp. 890–91.
2. The nature of fund accounting, including fund accounting statements and types of funds, pp. 891–98.
3. The three key features of fund accounting—modified accrual accounting, accounting for encumbrances, and accounting for budgets, pp. 895–903.

Note: This appendix could be covered anytime after Chapter 8. It is probably best to cover this appendix near the end of the course if inclusion is elected.

ACCOUNTING FOR NOT-FOR-PROFIT ENTITIES—FUND ACCOUNTING

Objective 1
The difference between not-for-profit and business entities.

Although this textbook has concentrated on profit-seeking business entities, a great many resources in the United States are controlled by approximately 1,000,000 not-for-profit entities which include federal, state, and local governments; universities; hospitals; religious organizations; and various public service organizations (e.g., the United Way). These organizations are also frequently referred to as nonbusiness entities. In this appendix you will learn some of the basic concepts of accounting for not-for-profit entities.

Not-for-profit entities are organizations established to provide goods and/or services on a nonprofit basis. As you know, business entities are established to provide goods and/or services at a profit. The lack of a profit motive may seem like a minor difference separating business entities from nonbusiness entities; however, this profit motive difference is associated with major differences in the accounting systems of business and nonbusiness entities.

The three major categories of entities using not-for-profit systems are

1. Federal, state, and local governmental units.
2. Hospital and health care entities.
3. Colleges and universities.

Specialized accounting standards and special-interest groups affect the accounting information systems of these three groups of not-for-profit entities. For example, the Municipal Finance Officers Association has established a National Council on Governmental Accounting (NCGA) which has published several statements on financial reporting principles.[1] Special-interest groups like the NCGA have in some cases helped formulate generally accepted accounting principles (GAAP) for not-for-profit entities.

In 1984, the Financial Accounting Foundation (which is also the "parent" of the FASB) organized the Government Accounting Standards Board (GASB) to establish GAAP for governmental units. In its first GASB statement, *GASB No. 1*, "Authoritative Status of NCGA Pronouncements and AICPA Industry Audit Guide," the GASB recognized the authority of the pronouncements of these two unrelated organizations (NCGA and AICPA) in establishing GAAP. The AICPA (American Institute of Certified Public Accountants) has also been influential in defining GAAP for hospitals, colleges, and universities. In general, the GASB is now responsible for formulating GAAP for governmental units, while the FASB remains involved in establishing GAAP for hospitals, colleges, universities, and most other not-for-profit organizations. Still many other organizations play an important part in the establishment of GAAP for not-for-profit entities. Although we cannot adequately cover GAAP for all not-for-profit entities in this appendix, we do introduce the basic underlying concepts.

GAAP for not-for-profit entities is changing rapidly, with standard setting becoming more active during the past two decades. This increased activity reflects a greater public awareness and concern with how efficiently the vast amounts of resources controlled by the not-for-profit organizations are being utilized. With the federal government alone spending over $1 trillion a year, this increased interest is surely warranted. The expected trend for the future is to make not-for-profit accounting systems more like those of business entities, moving toward a more complete accrual accounting approach to permit costs and benefits to be assessed by taxpayers, insurers, patients, and other providers of funds to not-for-profit entities.

Accounting systems for nonbusiness entities are typically referred to as fund accounting systems. The term *fund* used in nonbusiness accounting has a special meaning, as

---

[1]For example, see NCGA, "Government Accounting and Financial Reporting Principles, Statement 1" (Chicago: Municipal Finance Officers Association of the United States and Canada, 1979).

defined in the sections to follow. Three key features of most fund accounting systems that differ from accounting for profit-oriented businesses include the following:

1. A modified accrual system.
2. A different type of a liability, called *Reserve for Encumbrance*, which is formally recorded when funds are committed (e.g., a purchase agreement).
3. Budgets that are formally recorded in the accounting system.

We begin with a general discussion of the nature of fund accounting. Then, we examine the above three key features that make fund accounting systems different from profit-oriented business accounting. We conclude with a brief discussion of reporting for multiple funds and evaluating not-for-profit entities.

NATURE OF FUND ACCOUNTING

A fund is an accounting entity within the larger nonbusiness entity with a self-balancing set of accounts that is usually defined by its purpose. Like any entity, a fund consists of resources, which equal the claims against these resources. In fund accounting, fund assets are those resources controlled by the fund that are available to carry out the specified purpose(s) of the fund.[2] Fund liabilities represent those claims or other uses or proposed uses of fund assets that have yet to be paid.[3]

In business entities, the difference between assets and liabilities is called *owners' equity;* however, in nonbusiness entities, fund assets less fund liabilities is known as the fund balance. Thus, the fund balance represents the difference between the resources available to carry out the activities of the fund and the claims against these resources. The statement reporting the resources, claims, and balance of the fund is the balance sheet, which looks much like the balance sheet of any business entity.

Objective 2
The nature of fund accounting, including fund accounting statements and types of funds.

Whereas the financial statements of profit-oriented business entities include an income (or earnings) statement, no income statement is prepared for not-for-profit entities. Instead, the not-for-profit accounting system uses a statement of revenues, expenditures, and changes in fund balance (SRECFB), which focuses on the flow of resources into and from the fund and reconciles changes in the fund balance sheet during the period. Also referred to by other names, such as activity statement or statement of inflows and outflows, the SRECFB identifies the sources of resources coming into the fund and their uses for a specified period of time. If sources exceed uses during the period, the "fund balance" in the balance sheet increases much like retained earnings increases with net income. If uses exceed sources during the period, the "fund balance" decreases.

Many nonprofit entities (e.g., city or state governments) are required by law to maintain a positive fund balance. However, the federal government has for some time had a large negative fund balance that we refer to as the national debt or deficit. Deficit spending by the federal government means that the uses of funds exceed the sources of funds for a specified period of time. Often, federal deficit spending is financed by the issuing of U.S. government debt; for example, the federal government issues U.S. Treasury Bonds.

Fund Accounting Statements

To illustrate the fund balance sheet and SRECFB, consider the balance sheet and SRECFB of Pioneer City High School (Exhibit D–1). For fund assets, Pioneer reports cash and receivables from various funding agencies available for running the operation of the high school. The fund liabilities are unpaid expenditures necessary for operating the school.

---

[2]See *Statement of Financial Accounting Concepts No. 6,* "Elements of Financial Statements" (Norwalk, Conn.: FASB, 1985).
[3]Ibid.

EXHIBIT D–1

Fund Accounting Statements

Pioneer City High School
Balance Sheet
At December 31

	19x2	19x1
Assets:		
Cash	$ 23,200	$ 19,800
Taxes receivable	187,950	162,800
Federal funding receivable	71,240	68,440
State funding receivable	13,010	9,960
Total assets	$ 295,400	$ 261,000
Liabilities:		
Accounts payable	$ 105,420	$ 108,990
Salaries and benefits payable	86,940	63,430
Fund equity:		
Fund balance	103,040	88,580
Total liabilities and fund equity	$ 295,400	$ 261,000

Pioneer City High School
Statement of Revenues, Expenditures, and Changes in Fund
Balance for the Years Ending December 31

	19x2	19x1
Revenues:		
From property taxes	$2,897,205	$2,599,603
From federal agencies	383,291	382,000
From state agencies	200,000	200,000
From school fund-raising activities	185,200	173,550
Total revenues	$3,665,696	$3,355,153
Expenditures:		
For faculty salaries	$1,488,960	$1,376,220
For administration salaries	370,469	330,105
For student aid	187,500	182,500
For the library	310,000	300,000
For texts, supplies, and other	1,294,307	1,162,738
Total expenditures	$3,651,236	$3,351,563
Net increase in fund balance	$ 14,460	$ 3,590

The SRECFB reports the sources of the revenues received by Pioneer City High School Fund and how the school has used these resources. Note that the 19x2 increase in fund balance ($14,460) represents the excess of revenues less expenditures and the change in the fund balance between 19x2 and 19x1 ($103,040 − $88,580 = $14,460).

The purpose of the Pioneer City High School Fund is to account for the day-to-day operations of the high school. As a result, the statements of this fund only report on these responsibilities. Other funds (entities) may also exist for activities such as Pioneer City

Elementary School, Pioneer City Fire Department, Pioneer City Police, Pioneer City Public Library, and so on.

Also, within a given entity, special-purpose funds might exist that require separate fund accounting. For example, within the Pioneer City High School Fund, there may be special funds for band, athletics, or the drama club. These funds may report separately, and they may also be included in the overall statements illustrated in Exhibit D–1. Similarly, Pioneer City might report separate statements for the high school fund, fire department fund, and so on, or it might report a single set of statements for all activities under its jurisdiction. This is similar to the separate/combined reporting that business entities use when a parent company has a number of 100% owned subsidiaries (see Chapter 12 on investments).

No rule exactly states when an activity should be reported as a separate fund or as part of a fund. A separate set of fund accounts and statements may be prepared for any specific activity. The domain of a fund and what it accounts for depends on the specified purpose or *charge* of the fund's activity.

Types of Funds

Objective 2
The nature of fund accounting, including fund accounting statements and types of funds.

Although any not-for-profit entity may include many separate funds, accountants have identified and defined categories of funds to help determine the type of fund involved and its related accounting system attributes. Different types of funds have somewhat different accounting attributes. In governmental accounting, the GASB has identified seven types of funds, while colleges and universities usually use six different types of funds. The titles and brief descriptions of these types of funds are summarized in Exhibit D 2.

Since this textbook only introduces the basic concepts of not-for-profit accounting, we will not give detailed explanations and examples of all the various types of funds that can be found in not-for-profit entities. Instead, we will summarize all the different fund categories into three types of funds and discuss their basic aspects as follows:

1. General funds (or unrestricted funds).
2. Special-purpose funds.
3. Revenue-producing funds.

General Funds (or unrestricted funds). Most not-for-profit entities have a fund that is viewed as a general fund and is commonly known as an **unrestricted fund.** As the name implies, a general fund accounts for all activities that the entity (e.g., city) is responsible for that have not otherwise been assigned to another fund (e.g., a special-purpose fund). A general fund usually has the broadest set of responsibilities and the most diverse set of activities. If an entity has no revenue-producing funds or special-purpose funds, then the general fund accounts for all of the entity's activities.

Special-Purpose Funds. As implied by the name, special-purpose funds have specific responsibilities. These funds are specifically limited in their authority and responsibility. Some are designed to only account for expenditures, others are accountable only for inflows of resources, and still others do both. The following are common examples of special-purpose funds:

Plant asset funds—These funds account for the long-term assets of a nonbusiness entity once they are acquired. One of the primary objectives of these funds is to facilitate the timing of when assets must be replaced, repaired, or renewed. This group of funds includes capital projects funds and plant funds as described in Exhibit D–2.

Investment funds—These funds contain resources of the nonbusiness entity invested in stock, bonds, and so on, to generate income for use by the entity. In those cases where the originally invested amount cannot be spent, the fund is called an endowment fund. Other funds that could be included in this category are trust and agency funds, annuity funds, and income funds.

EXHIBIT D–2

Types of Funds

Government accounting systems:

1. General fund—for all activities not accounted for elsewhere.
2. Special revenue funds—funds accounting for specific sources of revenues.
3. Capital project funds—funds accounting for acquisition of major capital assets.
4. Debt service funds—funds accounting for payments of interest and principal on long-term debt.
5. Enterprise funds—funds operating similar to a business enterprise, to provide some public goods or services usually with fees for users.
6. Internal service funds—funds operating to provide some service to another fund (e.g., government printing office).
7. Trust and agency funds—funds responsible for holding resources to be used by some outside (private) agency or other governmental unit.

College and university funds:

1. Current funds—funds established to carry out the operations of the college or university (e.g., food service, housing, instruction).
2. Loan funds—funds established to account for loans to students, faculty, and other school organizations.
3. Plant funds—funds established to account for the acquisition, renewal, and replacement of facilities, and the repayment of debt incurred to acquire the facilities.
4. Endowment funds—funds established to account for resources received from donors, and the disbursement of the income from these resources for general or specific purposes as stipulated by the donor.
5. Annuity and income funds—funds accounting for donated resources, making payments to individuals in a stipulated way.
6. Agency funds—funds for which the college or university is a custodian on behalf of an individual student or faculty member or some group (usually affiliated with the school).

Debt service funds—These funds are established for the purpose of paying the interest and principal on the debt (bonds or notes) of the nonbusiness entity. Usually resources are transferred from a general fund or an investment fund to the debt service fund so that interest and principal payments can be made.

Special-purpose funds can be grouped in many possible ways. One special-purpose fund is distinguished from another by the specific charge or task assigned to the fund describing the purpose of the fund and the authority and responsibility of the fund's managers.

The performance of special-purpose funds is evaluated on the basis of how well the funds achieve their purpose. Usually, when a specified purpose for a fund is not being achieved, the fund managers will request more resources or modify its operations in another way. However, the relationship between a fund's resources and its ability to accomplish its purpose is not always clear, making management performance evaluation more difficult in a not-for-profit entity than in its profit-seeking counterpart.

Revenue-Producing Funds. While general and special-purpose funds employ special-fund accounting procedures (illustrated in this chapter), revenue-producing funds do not. A revenue-producing fund may employ the conventional full accrual accounting system employed by profit-seeking entities. The major difference between the financial statements of revenue-producing funds and those of business entities is the use of a fund balance in place of owners' equity. Examples of revenue-producing funds include enterprise funds, possibly internal service funds, and certain current funds or loan funds (see Exhibit D–2), depending on the structure and purpose of the fund.

Whenever a nonbusiness entity conducts activities that involve receiving revenues based on the provision of some service or product, the entity may elect to establish a separate **revenue-producing fund** to account for these activities. Revenue-producing funds, similar to the enterprise funds described in Exhibit D–2, may be designed to lose money in that revenues are not expected to cover expenses. It is becoming more popular to identify those funds with distinguishable revenue-producing activities as revenue-producing funds and to account for them on a full accrual system just as for-profit entities. This approach allows users of financial statements to evaluate the fund's costs and benefits. The increased use of revenue-producing funds is expected to enhance the efficient use of public funds (e.g., taxes) because they provide a clearer picture of the net cost (or benefit) of each activity.

To illustrate, assume that the state capital has a central copy center for copying all types of state government documents (i.e., an internal service fund). Assume that the copy center is accounted for as a revenue-producing fund, with fees for copy services charged to each state government unit using these services. If the copy center is established as a revenue-producing fund with user fees charged to those who use the copy services, the efficiency of the government's copy center may be compared to that of other local private (for-profit) copy services. If a local private copy service could do the same job at a lower cost to the state government (and the taxpayers), state officials might consider switching to a private copy service (eliminating the government-run service) as a source of cost savings to the public.

Without information provided by a revenue-producing fund using conventional business (accrual) accounting systems, an evaluation of a fund's effectiveness or efficiency in its use of public resources is difficult, if not impossible. Therefore, revenue-producing funds are viewed as a means of improving the efficiency of certain nonprofit operations.

Not-for-profit entities use many types of funds. These funds may be categorized in other ways than the system described above, which places all funds into three broad categories. Since revenue-producing funds are capable of operating on a full accrual accounting system like that discussed elsewhere in this textbook, the remainder of this appendix focuses on the fundamental accounting procedures applicable to general funds and special-purpose funds.

MODIFIED ACCRUAL ACCOUNTING

Objective 3
The three key features of fund accounting — modified accrual accounting, accounting for encumbrances, and accounting for budgets.

The modified accrual method of accounting is the first key feature of fund accounting systems mentioned at the beginning of this appendix. Most general- and special-purpose funds use a modified accrual system rather than the full accrual system employed by most businesses or the cash system used by many individuals for tax purposes.

As illustrated throughout this textbook, **accrual accounting recognizes revenues as they are earned and matches expenses with revenues.** On the other hand, the **cash basis of accounting recognizes revenues as cash is received and expenses as cash is paid.** Since most fund accounting activities are not involved in the process of generating revenues by providing goods or services as we normally understand that process, the full accrual method is not applicable. Also, the cash basis of accounting has limitations caused by differences in the timing of when cash is actually needed and when cash inflows occur. This inconsistency between inflows and outflows could result in overspending or underspending if funds were run on a cash basis. The most common solution to these problems is to use a modified accrual system for fund accounting.

The modified accrual system recognizes revenues as soon as their amount is known and their collectibility is reasonably assured. This revenue recognition point often coincides with when revenues are billed, since at the billing date the goods or services have been provided or another event (e.g., the passage of time) has already occurred, giving rise to the right to collect revenues. For example, property tax revenue, city water revenue, and other city services (e.g., trash collection) are normally recognized at the time they are billed. Also, tuition revenue may be recognized at the time it is billed. Alternatively, some revenues such as sales taxes, late fees or fines (e.g., libraries), user permits (e.g., parks), and licenses (e.g., fishing, drivers'), are recognized when cash is received.

In a modified accrual system, **expenditures recognition** takes the place of expense recognition under the matching concept employed in an accrual system. Expenditures occur when the fund recognizes outflows of resources through payments. Note that in a full accrual system, **expense** recognition does not occur until resources are consumed. Hence, **expenditure recognition in not-for-profit systems often precedes expense recognition** in the conventional full accrual system. For example, if supplies were purchased on account for $1,000, the accrual (for-profit) example would record an asset (supplies) and a liability (accounts payable), whereas the modified accrual system used by not-for-profit entities would record an expenditure and a liability. We will illustrate this difference between for-profit and not-for-profit entities more completely in the examples that follow.

Revenues—Modified Accrual

To illustrate the modified accrual system, assume that Pioneer City assesses property taxes on all homes and businesses once a year. The assessed value of all property and the tax rate per $1,000 of assessed value are known on the first day of each fiscal year when tax bills are sent out. Note that when revenues for the year are known or reasonably estimable at the start of the year, they may be recorded on the first day of the year even if the revenue bills are not sent out until later in the year.

On July 1, 19xx, the start of the current fiscal year for Pioneer City, collectible taxes of $44,890,000 are billed to property owners. Assume that estimated uncollectible taxes are 2% of this total. The following entry would be recorded on July 1, 19xx:

19xx			
July 1	Property Taxes Receivable (A)	44,890,000	
	Allowance for Uncollectible Taxes (XA)		897,800
	Property Tax Revenue (R)		43,992,200
	To record property tax revenue for fiscal year.		

The asset, Property Taxes Receivable, and the contra asset, Allowance for Uncollectible Taxes, would be reported in the balance sheet. The Property Tax Revenue account would be reported in the SRECFB as a revenue.

Expenditures—Modified Accrual

Unlike the matching procedures used for expense recognition, the modified accrual basis reports expenditures for outflows of resources as soon as the fund becomes obligated to pay for goods or services. In other words, an expenditure is recorded, regardless of when the benefits resulting from the expenditure are to be used.

Exhibit D-3 compares the modified accrual system with the accrual accounting system. Note that fund assets are seldom created by the acquisition of goods or services by a fund. **Assets of a fund are those resources available for carrying out the stated purpose of the fund.** The acquisition of supplies is viewed as an expenditure that has accomplished an objective of the fund (e.g., to buy supplies enabling the fund to repair school desks, projectors, driveways, and so on). The supplies are not considered assets because modified accrual accounting considers the supplies as no longer available for acquiring the goods and services. Instead, the supplies are expenditures reported in the SRECFB. In general, expenditures in the modified accrual system precede expensing in an accrual system. Also, the modified accrual system has few year-end adjustments.

EXHIBIT D–3

Comparison of Modified Accrual and Accrual Methods

Event	Fund Accounting—Modified Accrual		Business Accounting—Accrual	
Buy supplies on October 1, 19x0.	Expenditures 7,500		Supplies Inventory. 7,500	
	Cash.	7,500	Cash	7,500
On June 30, 19x1, record use of $5,000 of supplies during year.	No entry.		Supplies Expense 5,000	
			Supplies Inventory. . . .	5,000
Purchase insurance on facilities for the next 18 months on January 1, 19x1, for cash of $2,400.	Expenditures 2,400		Prepaid Insurance. 7,500	
	Cash.	2,400	Cash	7,500
Six months' worth of insurance used— adjusting entry on June 30, 19x1.	No entry.		Insurance Expense 5,000	
			Prepaid Insurance. . . .	5,000

New standards continue to reduce the differences between full accrual accounting and the modified accrual accounting allowed for not-for-profit entities. For many years, not-for-profit entities recorded expenditures for depreciable capital assets, such as furniture, fixtures, equipment, and so on, in the year of acquisition and did not record depreciation expense like accrual accounting (e.g., as in Chapter 8). However, the FASB issued a statement requiring not-for-profit entities governed by FASB standards (e.g., schools and hospitals) that also issue general-purpose financial statements to record depreciation on long-term depreciable assets.[4] Although GASB has not ruled on this issue for government entities, the trend is toward a more complete accrual system for all not-for-profit entities.

If a not-for-profit entity with a December 31 year-end used the modified accrual basis for a depreciable-type asset purchased on June 30, 19x1, for $60,000 cash, the entry would be

```
19x1
June 30   Expenditures . . . . . . . . . . . . . . . . . . . . . . . . . .   60,000
              Cash. . . . . . . . . . . . . . . . . . . . . . . . . . .            60,000
          To record the purchase of an asset.
```

At the end of 19x1, no asset would be reported on the balance sheet. If this asset had a five-year life and no salvage value, *an accrual accounting system* (using straight-line depreciation), would have recorded the following entries in 19x1:

```
19x1
June 30   Asset . . . . . . . . . . . . . . . . . . . . . . . . . . . . .   60,000
              Cash. . . . . . . . . . . . . . . . . . . . . . . . . . .            60,000
          To record the purchase of an asset.

Dec. 31   Depreciation Expense (E) . . . . . . . . . . . . . . . . . .   6,000
              Accumulated Depreciation (XA). . . . . . . . . . . . . .            6,000
          To record depreciation: $60,000/5 years = $12,000/year =
          $1,000/month.
```

[4]*Statement of Financial Accounting Standards No. 93*, "Recognition of Depreciation by Not-for-Profit Organizations" (Norwalk, Conn.: FASB, 1987).

The year-end balance sheet would report a net asset of $54,000 ($60,000 − $6,000), and expenditures would be $54,000 less than in the modified accrual system. While most government entities (e.g., cities, states) still employ the modified accrual system, schools and hospitals now are required to use accrual techniques for depreciable assets.

ACCOUNTING FOR ENCUMBRANCES

Objective 3
The three key features
of fund accounting—
modified accrual
accounting, accounting
for encumbrances, and
accounting for budgets.

The second key feature of a fund accounting system is that the fund recognizes commitments to spend fund resources before an accrual system would recognize them. This early recognition of commitments is called encumbrance accounting. Encumbrances are like expenditures in that they indicate that fund resources have been spoken for. Encumbrances are recorded at the time funds are committed, before the recording of expenditures. The objective of encumbrance accounting is to prevent the fund from making commitments of fund resources in excess of the fund balance. An encumbrance is recorded like an estimated expenditure and is later converted from an encumbrance to an expenditure when the amount becomes known and an obligation exists. When these estimated future expenditures are recorded as encumbrances, fund managers can tell how much of the fund's resources have been spoken for at any point in time.

To illustrate encumbrance accounting, assume that Pioneer City High School orders 50 new lockers on June 15, 19xx. An encumbrance is recorded on the date the order is placed, with the lockers expected to cost about $35 each at this time. The lockers arrive on September 1, 19xx, and the total actual invoice price is then determined to be $1,825, or $36.50 each. The encumbrance is converted to an expenditure on September 1, 19xx, the time the actual cost of the obligation is known. Assume that the high school pays the invoice on September 30, 19xx. The four entries to record (1) the encumbrance, (2) the actual obligation, and (3) the payment are as follows:

19xx		
June 15	Encumbrances (E)	1,750
	Reserve for Encumbrances (L)	1,750
	To record estimated expenditure: 50 units at $35 each.	
Sept. 1	Reserve for Encumbrances (L)	1,750
	Encumbrances (E)	1,750
	To reverse estimated expenditure.	
1	Expenditures (E)	1,825
	Accounts Payable (L)	1,825
	To record actual invoice for expenditure.	
30	Accounts Payable (L)	1,825
	Cash (A)	1,825
	To record payment for lockers.	

The June 15 entry records an encumbrance, which appears like an expenditure in the SRECFB (e.g., at June 30, 19xx), as an outflow or use of fund resources. The encumbrance represents the **estimated** cost of the 50 new lockers. Encumbrance accounts are closed to the fund balance at the end of each accounting period and are listed in the SRECFB with expenditures of the same category (e.g., equipment). Note that the debit to encumbrances of $1,750 on June 15, 19xx, would be closed to the fund balance on June 30, 19xx (the fiscal year-end for Pioneer City High School). The credit to encumbrances for $1,750 on September 1, 19xx, would leave a credit balance in the encumbrances account until other new encumbrance debits (like that on June 15) were added to its balance. At the end of any fiscal year, the balance in most encumbrance accounts will usually be net debit; but, if credit balances exist, they would offset the debit balances in the appropriate expenditures accounts.

The credit to Reserve for Encumbrances establishes a balance sheet account that represents an **estimated fund liability** which is reported in the balance sheet as a component of the fund balance until it is reversed on September 1, 19xx. As a result, the fund balance reported in the balance sheet has two components: (1) reserve for encumbrances and (2) fund balance (unencumbered).

Exhibit D–4 illustrates how the reserve for encumbrances and the fund balance appear in the balance sheet. In Pioneer's June 30 financial statements, the Reserve for Encumbrances account would alert the financial statement reader that funds of approximately $42,103 had been committed but not yet spent. In general, fund managers should have fund assets greater than or equal to fund liabilities plus Reserve for Encumbrances to prevent deficit spending.

ACCOUNTING FOR BUDGETS

Objective 3
The three key features of fund accounting— modified accrual accounting, accounting for encumbrances, and accounting for budgets.

The third key feature of a fund accounting system is that the annual budget is formally recorded in the accounting records. While budgets are important accounting tools for both profit and not-for-profit entities, budgets have an added significance for not-for-profit entities. For example, in state and local governments, budgets often define the legal limit on expenditures (plus encumbrances) for specific fund activities. In most government entities, budgets establish spending limits that may not be exceeded without formal legislative approval for modification of the budget. As a result, the accounting records are designed to permit continuous comparison between **budgeted** revenues and expenditures and **actual** revenues and expenditures.

EXHIBIT D–4

Balance Sheet Disclosure of Fund Balance

Pioneer City High School
Balance Sheet
June 30, 19xx

Assets

Cash	$ 18,120
Taxes receivable	99,650
Federal funding receivable.	13,105
State funding receivable.	8,650
Total assets	$139,525

Liabilities and Fund Equity

Liabilities:	
Accounts payable.	$ 47,350
Salaries and benefits payable	19,730
Total liabilities	$ 67,080
Fund equity:	
Reserve for encumbrances.	**$ 42,103**
Fund balance	**30,342**
Total fund equity	$ 72,445
Total liabilities and fund equity	$139,525

To illustrate how budgets are recorded in the accounting records, assume that the Pioneer City High School has budgeted revenues of $3,800,000 for 19x2 and budgeted expenditures (normally called appropriations) of $3,600,000 for 19x2, resulting in a budgeted increase in the fund balance of $200,000 for 19x2 ($3,800,000 − $3,600,000 = $200,000). On the first day of the new budget year, the following entry would be recorded:

(a)	Estimated Revenues	3,800,000	
	Appropriations		3,600,000
	Fund Balance		200,000
	To record the budget for the year.		

These three new budget accounts are like revenue and expenditure accounts in that they are nominal (or temporary) in nature and must be closed out at the end of each accounting period. Entry *a* in Exhibit D–5 shows a more detailed example of the summary entry provided above for the Pioneer City High School's annual budget. Note that debit/credit balances in the entry to record the budget are the opposite of **actual** revenues and expenses. For example, budgeted revenues have debit balances while actual revenues have credit balances.

Next, assume that actual revenues for 19x2 are $3,700,000 and that actual expenditures are $3,580,000. The following entries, which summarize these actual results for the year, are provided in somewhat greater detail in *b* and *c* of Exhibit D–5:

(b)	Cash (and/or Receivables)	3,700,000	
	Revenues		3,700,000
(c)	Expenditures (and/or Encumbrances).	3,580,000	
	Cash (and/or Payables; and/or Reserve for Encumbrances) . .		3,580,000

The following T accounts would be reported prior to closing:

Nominal Accounts

Estimated Revenues		Revenues	
(a) 3,800,000			(b) 3,700,000

Appropriations		Expenditures/Encumbrances	
	(a) 3,600,000	(c) 3,580,000	

Balance Sheet Accounts

Cash		Fund Balance	
(b) 3,700,000	(c) 3,580,000		(a) 200,000

At the end of 19x8, the following closing entries would be made to eliminate both the budget accounts and the actual accounts with the difference between actual revenues and actual expenditures ($3,700,000 − $3,580,000 = $120,000) left in the balance sheet account, Fund Surplus:

(d)	Revenues	3,700,000	
	Fund Balance	100,000	
	Estimated Revenues		3,800,000
	To close revenues and budgeted revenues.		

(e) Appropriations   3,600,000

      Expenditures/Encumbrances   3,580,000

      Fund Balance   20,000

      To close expenditures, encumbrances, and budgeted
appropriations.

The detailed entries for the summary entries in *b, c, d,* and *e* are also provided in Exhibit D–5 on the following page. After posting these entries, the following balances would result:

Nominal Accounts

Estimated Revenues				Revenues			
(a)	3,800,000	(d)	3,800,000	(d)	3,700,000	(b)	3,700,000
			0				0

Appropriations				Expenditures/Encumbrances			
(e)	3,600,000	(a)	3,600,000	(c)	3,580,000	(e)	3,580,000
			0		0		

Balance Sheet Accounts

Cash				Fund Balance			
(b)	3,700,000	(c)	3,580,000			(a)	200,000
				(d)	100,000	(e)	20,000
	120,000						120,000

The budget accounts have been eliminated and would not appear in any of the year-end statements. Budget accounts are only used for interim reporting purposes, to reveal how actual revenue and expenditures are doing compared to the budgeted amounts. This helps keep not-for-profit entities within their budgeted (or authorized) spending limits, reducing the chance of unexpected deficit spending.

EVALUATING NOT-FOR-PROFIT ENTITIES

Some concern exists over the limitations of the accounting systems for not-for-profit entities. Without a "bottom-line" profit measure, it is difficult to compare and evaluate the effectiveness and efficiency of a not-for-profit entity. Though the measurement of net income for businesses is not without its limitations, it does afford users some basis for comparing and evaluating the relative performance of business entities. Without the benefit of such a bottom-line measure, how can the effectiveness and efficiency of various not-for-profit entities be compared and evaluated?

Many important decisions concerning the allocation and use of public and private resources must be made by not-for-profit entities without the aid of uniform or comparable measures of effectiveness and efficiency. Each nonprofit entity, such as a fire department, is established for a specific purpose, such as fire prevention and control. It is often difficult to determine how successful the entity is at accomplishing its purpose. (For example, if you put out more fires this year than last, is it good or bad?) It is even more difficult to compare the success of one type of fund (e.g., fire department) with another (e.g., police

EXHIBIT D–5

Detailed Journal Entries for 19x2	**Budget entry:**

(a)　Estimated Property Tax Revenues . . . . 　2,900,000

　　　Estimated Federal Program Revenues . . . . 　400,000

　　　Estimated State Program Revenues . . . . 　300,000

　　　Estimated Fundraising Revenues . . . . 　200,000

　　　　　Appropriations—Faculty Salaries . . . . 　　　　1,900,000

　　　　　Appropriations—Administrative Salaries . . . . 　　　　350,000

　　　　　Appropriations—Student Aid . . . . 　　　　150,000

　　　　　Appropriations—Library . . . . 　　　　350,000

　　　　　Appropriations—Texts, Supplies, etc. . . . . 　　　　850,000

　　　　　Fund Balance . . . . 　　　　200,000

　　　　To record the annual budget.

Summary entries of actual events:

(b)　Cash . . . . 　3,200,000

　　　Receivable from Property Taxes . . . . 　250,000

　　　Receivable from Federal Programs . . . . 　125,000

　　　Receivable from State Programs . . . . 　125,000

　　　　　Revenues from Property Taxes . . . . 　　　　2,880,000

　　　　　Revenues from Federal Programs . . . . 　　　　400,000

　　　　　Revenues from State Programs . . . . 　　　　291,000

　　　　　Revenues from Fundraisers . . . . 　　　　129,000

　　　　To record summary entry for revenues for the year.

(c)　Expenditures—Faculty Salaries . . . . 　1,895,000

　　　Expenditures—Administrative Salaries . . . . 　345,000

　　　Expenditures—Student Aid . . . . 　85,000

　　　Encumbrances—Student Aid . . . . 　45,000

　　　Expenditures—Library . . . . 　260,000

　　　Encumbrances—Library . . . . 　140,000

　　　Expenditures—Texts, Supplies, etc. . . . . 　695,000

　　　Encumbrances—Supplies and Other . . . . 　115,000

　　　　　Cash . . . . 　　　　3,237,000

　　　　　Accounts Payable . . . . 　　　　105,000

　　　　　Salaries and Benefits Payable . . . . 　　　　38,000

　　　　　Reserve for Encumbrances . . . . 　　　　200,000

　　　　To record summary entry for expenses for the year.

To close budget accounts against actual accounts:

(d)　Revenues from Property Taxes . . . . 　2,880,000

　　　Revenues from Federal Programs . . . . 　400,000

　　　Revenues from State Programs . . . . 　291,000

　　　Revenues from Fundraisers . . . . 　129,000

　　　Fund Balance . . . . 　100,000

　　　　　Estimated Property Tax Revenues . . . . 　　　　2,900,000

　　　　　Estimated Federal Program Revenues . . . . 　　　　400,000

　　　　　Estimated State Program Revenues . . . . 　　　　300,000

　　　　　Estimated Fundraising Revenues . . . . 　　　　200,000

　　　　To close budget accounts.

EXHIBIT D–5   (*concluded*)

(*e*) Appropriations—Faculty Salaries	1,900,000	
Appropriations—Administrative Salaries	350,000	
Appropriations—Student Aid	150,000	
Appropriations—Library	350,000	
Appropriations—Texts, Supplies, etc.	850,000	
Expenditures—Faculty Salaries		1,895,000
Expenditures—Administrative Salaries		345,000
Expenditures—Student Aid		85,000
Encumbrances—Student Aid		45,000
Expenditures—Library		260,000
Encumbrances—Library		140,000
Expenditures—Texts, Supplies, etc.		695,000
Encumbrances—Supplies and Other		115,000
Fund Balance		20,000
To close expenditures, encumbrances, and budgeted appropriations.		

department) since each is established for a different purpose and with different objectives. While for-profit businesses have the virtue of a common objective—to earn profits for owners—not-for-profit entities seldom have common objectives or objectives that are readily measurable using accounting data. As a result, not-for-profit entities are frequently considered to be inefficient and ineffective at utilizing resources. This complaint seems to be particularly problematic in government entities where those providing funds (the public by way of income, property, and some other taxes) are only remotely influential in important decisions such as how much funding is required, for what purposes, and whether the existing level of funding is being efficiently and effectively utilized.

Because of the frustration with these limitations of not-for-profit accounting systems, more emphasis is being placed on using revenue-producing funds to account for activities whenever possible. Application of business accounting methods (especially full accrual accounting) to those activities of not-for-profit entities that generate some revenue from products or services is viewed by many as the primary tool to enhance the effectiveness of accounting information. It is hoped that improvements in accounting for nonbusiness entities may make for more rational social decisions.

• SUMMARY

This appendix introduced the basic concepts of accounting for not-for-profit entities. We examined the nature of fund accounting and noted the differences and similarities of fund accounting statements and the statements of profit-oriented businesses. The fund accounting balance sheet is similar to that of a business, except that owners' equity is replaced by a fund balance. The statement of revenues, expenditures, and changes in fund balance (SRECFB) reports on the nature of balance sheet changes for a period of time.

The three key features that help to differentiate fund accounting are (1) the modified accrual method, (2) the use of encumbrances, and (3) the formal recording of budgeted amounts. Each of these key features was illustrated in the chapter.

We concluded with a discussion on reporting for multiple funds and on evaluating fund accounting statements. This introduction to fund accounting, though brief, should be helpful for reading financial reports of not-for-profit entities and understanding some of the fundamental differences between business and not-for-profit accounting systems. Advanced accounting texts usually provide more detailed coverage of accounting for not-for-profit entities.

• DEMONSTRATION EXERCISE

Paradise City realizes revenues from two sources, property taxes from city property owners and income taxes from employees within the city. During fiscal year 19x1, the following information is available for Paradise City government:

a. On January 1, 19x1, budgeted property tax revenue for the year is $15,481,685. Budgeted income tax revenue is $10,900,000. Paradise budgets expenditures for the year to be $26,100,000.

b. Paradise City bills property owners $15,960,500 for property taxes. Historically 3% of those taxes are not collected.

c. During the year, property tax collections total $15,725,000 and income tax collections total $10,461,300. All payments are received in cash.

d. Encumbrances for 19x1 total $9,860,500 of which $8,900,000 has been received and included in actual expenditures for the year. Expenditures for the year total $25,000,950 of which $22,105,000 has been paid in cash and the remainder is in accounts payable.

Required:

1. Prepare the journal entries to record Paradise City's 19x1 budget.
2. Prepare the journal entries to record actual revenues, encumbrances, and expenditures for 19x1.
3. Prepare the journal entries to close the appropriate accounts at the end of 19x1.

Solution:

Requirement 1:

19x1			
Jan. 1	Estimated Property Tax Revenue	15,481,685	
	Estimated Income Tax Revenue	10,900,000	
	Appropriations.		26,100,000
	Fund Balance		281,685
	To record the budget for the year.		

Requirement 2:

Property Taxes Receivable	15,960,500	
Allowance for Uncollectible Taxes		478,815
Property Tax Revenue		15,481,685
To record property tax revenue for the year.		
Cash	26,186,300	
Property Taxes Receivable		15,725,000
Income Tax Revenue.		10,461,300
To record collections of property taxes and income tax revenue for the year.		
Encumbrances	9,860,500	
Reserve for Encumbrances		9,860,500
To record encumbrances for the year.		

Reserve for Encumbrances.	8,900,000	
Encumbrances		8,900,000
To reverse estimated expenditures for the year.		
Expenditures	25,000,950	
Cash.		22,105,000
Accounts Payable		2,895,950
To record expenditures for the year.		

Requirement 3:

19x1
Dec. 31

Property Tax Revenues	15,481,685	
Income Tax Revenues	10,461,000	
Fund Balance.	439,000	
Estimated Property Tax Revenues.		15,481,685
Estimated Income Tax Revenues		10,900,000
To close revenues and budgeted revenue accounts.		

Dec. 31

Appropriations.	26,100,000	
Encumbrances		960,500
Expenditures		25,000,950
Fund Balance		148,550
To close expenditures, encumbrances, and budgeted appropriations accounts.		

• KEY TERMS

Appropriations. Budgeted expenditures for nonbusiness entities.

Business entities. Organizations established to provide goods and/or services at a profit.

Charge. Purpose of a specific fund.

Encumbrance accounting. Early recognition of commitments.

Endowment fund. An investment fund in which the original amount invested is not allowed to be spent.

Fund accounting systems. Accounting systems used by nonbusiness entities.

Fund assets. Resources controlled by fund that are available to carry out the specified purpose(s) of the fund.

Fund balance. Difference between fund assets and fund liabilities in a nonbusiness entity.

Fund liabilities. Claims or other uses or proposed uses of fund assets that have yet to be paid.

General fund. Fund that accounts for all activities the entity is responsible for that have not otherwise been assigned to another fund; also called unrestricted fund.

Government Accounting Standards Board (GASB). Organization whose task is to establish uniform accounting standards (GAAP) for governmental units.

Modified accrual system. Accounting system used in nonbusiness entities that recognizes inflows of resources as soon as their amount and collectibility are reasonably assured and recognizes outflows when a commitment of resources is made by the fund.

Not-for-profit entities. Organizations established to provide goods and/or services on a nonprofit basis; also called nonbusiness entities.

Revenue-producing fund. Fund a nonbusiness entity elects to establish when it conducts activities that involve taking in revenues based on the provision of some service or product.

Special-purpose fund. Fund with limited authority and responsibility designed for specific responsibilities.

Statement of revenues, expenditures, and changes in fund balance (SRECFB). Statement that identifies the sources of funds coming into the fund and the uses of the resources of the fund for a specified period of time.

• SYNONYMS

Encumbered; restricted (fund balance).

Fund purpose; fund charge.

General fund; unrestricted fund.

Not for profit; nonbusiness; nonprofit.

Unencumbered; unrestricted (fund balance).

• QUESTIONS

1. What is a fund and how is it usually defined? Give an example.
2. What are fund assets and liabilities?
3. What is the fund balance?
4. What is deficit spending?
5. What are the three broad categories of funds?
6. Which broad category of funds employs the same accounting procedures as business entities? Why?
7. What is the fundamental difference between general funds and special-purpose funds?
8. Identify three types of special-purpose funds.
9. What are three key features of a fund accounting system?
10. In the modified accrual system used for fund accounting, when are inflows of resources recognized? When are outflows recognized?
11. What is an encumbrance and when is it recorded?
12. What is the role of budgets in a fund accounting system?
13. What are the two primary budget accounts?
14. What is the major limitation in evaluating the performance of most funds?

• EXERCISES

E D–1
Recording Revenues
L..O. 3

The city of Westbranch estimated its gross revenues from property taxes for the coming year ending June 30, 19x6, to be $3,875,000. In the past few years uncollected property taxes were about 2% of those levied. On August 31, 19x5, tax bills of $3,875,000 were sent to property owners in West-branch. Cash collections between July 1, 19x5 (the start of the fiscal year), and August 31, 19x5, for property taxes were $1,000,000. (These were actually collected in advance of the billing.) Property taxes for the 19x5–x6 year, still uncollected at June 30, 19x6, were $56,300.

Required:
1. Record the July 1, 19x5, entry for property taxes, if any.
2. Record collections of the first $1,000,000 of taxes.
3. Record the entry for the August 31, 19x5, billing, if any.

E D–2
Recording Revenues
L.O.3

Millvale City estimated total property tax revenue to be $985,000 for the year starting July 1, 19x8. The expected uncollectible taxes are 1% of the total taxes. Millvale also has had revenue from parking tickets in the past. This revenue has varied between $4,000 and $1,800 over the past five years.

Required:
Record any entries required or implied by the above data. Be sure to date the entries.

E D–3
Recording Expenditures
L.O.3

The city of Westbranch has the following selected transactions for the year:

a. Westbranch officials obtained $5,000 of furniture for city offices on open account on July 1, 19x6. Payment for the furniture took place on July 20, 19x6. The fiscal year ends June 30. The furniture has a five-year expected life and no salvage value.

b. Westbranch officials purchased a new city car with a four-year life and no salvage value for $18,000 cash on June 29, 19x7.

c. Westbranch officials purchased $1,500 of office supplies on open account on June 30, 19x7. The supplies are expected to last for six months.

Required:

1. Record the journal entries for the year ending June 30, 19x7, for these three events using the modified accrual procedures of a fund accounting system (i.e., do not record depreciation).

2. Record the journal entries for the year ending June 30, 19x7, for these three events assuming conventional accrual accounting had been used. Use straight-line depreciation where necessary.

E D–4
Recording Expenditures
L.O.3

Selected events from the records of the Howell Public School District, which has a fiscal year-end of September 30, are

a. Pays first annual interest payment of $20,500 on school bonds on June 30, 19x7.

b. On August 20, 19x7, purchases, on account, $2,400 of art supplies for all elementary schools. Payment is made on the due date, October 10, 19x7. Half of the supplies are used by September 30, 19x7.

c. On September 1, 19x7, $15,000 of monies received from a federal grant is spent to purchase 10 computers with expected useful lives of five years each for the high school computer lab.

Required:

1. Record the journal entries required by these events assuming a modified accrual system is used by Howell.

2. What is the total expenditure to be reported for the year ending September 30, 19x7, for these three events using the modified accrual procedures of a fund accounting system?

3. What would be reported as an expenditure (expense) for the year ending September 30, 19x7, if conventional accrual accounting had been used? Assume that all depreciable assets have no scrap value and employ straight-line depreciation.

E D–5
Recording Encumbrances
L.O.3

On June 15, 19x3, Knollville officials ordered a new fire truck. The estimated cost of the truck, fully equipped, was $38,000. Several companies were involved in building the truck and the final cost of $42,875 was not known until September 30, 19x3, when the truck was delivered. Knollville's fiscal year ends on June 30.

Required:

1. Record the entries necessary to account for the acquisition of the fire truck.

2. In which fiscal year will the fire truck appear as an expenditure? Explain.

E D–6
Recording Encumbrances
L.O.3

Rural School District orders five new buses on August 28, 19x3. The assistant superintendent of finance estimates the total cost of the buses to be $280,000. When the buses are delivered, on December 1, 19x3, the actual invoice amount is $259,632. The district's fiscal year ends on September 30.

Required:

1. Record the journal entries necessary to account for the acquisition of the buses.

2. In which fiscal year will the buses appear as an expenditure? Explain.

E D–7
Accounting for Budgets
L.O.3

Cedarville has a June 30 fiscal year-end. The budget for the coming year calls for revenues of $4,500,000 and appropriations of $4,350,000. During the year, actual revenues were $4,800,000 and expenditures were $4,300,000. Encumbrances at year-end (June 30, 19x4) were $250,000.

Required:

1. Record the entries for the budgeted revenues and appropriations.
2. Record the actual revenues and expenditures. Assume that revenues and expenditures were all for cash.
3. Record encumbrances.
4. Record the closing entries for eliminating the budget accounts and the other nominal accounts.
5. What is the change in the fund balance for the year ending June 30, 19x4?

E D–8
Accounting for Budgets
L.O.3

The city of Ishpeming has a September 30 fiscal year-end. The budget for the coming year calls for revenues of $16.8 million and appropriations of $16.1 million. During the year, actual revenues were $16.5 million and expenditures were $16.2 million. Encumbrances at September 30, 19x2, were $350,000.

Required:

1. Record the entries for the budgeted revenues and appropriations.
2. Record the actual revenues and expenditures. Assume that revenues and expenditures were all for cash.
3. Record encumbrances.
4. Record the closing entries to eliminate the budget accounts and the other nominal accounts.
5. What is the change in the fund balance for the year ending September 30, 19x2?

E D–9
Multiple Choice
L.O.2, 3

1. What type of account signals financial statement readers that funds are being earmarked to pay for goods or services that are ordered but not yet received?
   a. Appropriations.
   b. Reserve for Encumbrances.
   c. Encumbrances.
   d. Expenditures.
   e. Contingent Liabilities.
2. In fund accounting systems—
   a. The budget accounts appear in the balance sheet at year-end.
   b. The budget accounts appear in the SRECFB for the period.
   c. Some budget accounts appear in the balance sheet and some appear in the SRECFB.
   d. Budget accounts do not appear in either the balance sheet or the SRECFB.
3. In governmental accounting, when a legislative body designates that a certain amount of funds may be spent for a specific purpose (e.g., fire protection)—
   a. It is referred to as an appropriation.
   b. It becomes part of that government's budget accounts.
   c. It is the legal limit that may be spent for that purpose without further legislative approval.
   d. All of the above.
   e. None of the above.
4. When estimated revenues are less than actual revenues for the year—
   a. The fund balance must be negative.
   b. The fund balance must report a decrease for the year.
   c. The fund balance cannot increase for the year.
   d. All of the above.
   e. None of the above.
5. If the budget called for estimated revenues to exceed appropriations by $48,000 and actual revenues exceeded expenditures and encumbrances by $60,000, the fund balance for the period will—
   a. Increase by $12,000.
   b. Decrease by $12,000.
   c. Increase by $48,000.
   d. Increase by $60,000.
   e. None of the above.

E D–10
Multiple Choice
L.O.2

1. In governmental entities, a fund that behaves like a regular business entity is referred to as—
   a. A profit center.
   b. A general fund.
   c. An enterprise fund.
   d. An internal service fund.
2. Virtually every government has—
   a. A debt service fund.
   b. A general fund.
   c. An enterprise fund.
   d. A capital projects fund.
3. The two broad categories of funds employed by not-for-profits that are usually on a modified accrual basis are—
   a. General funds and special-purpose funds.
   b. Special-purpose funds and revenue-producing funds.
   c. General funds and revenue-producing funds.
   d. All of the above.
   e. None of the above.
4. Examples of funds that could be considered revenue producing are—
   a. Enterprise funds and internal service funds.
   b. Debt service funds and capital project funds.
   c. Agency funds and plant asset funds.
   d. Endowment funds and enterprise funds.
   e. All of the above.
5. The purpose of a general fund is—
   a. To raise funds for other funds.
   b. To pay government salaries.
   c. For miscellaneous purposes.
   d. To account for all activities not accounted for by other funds.
   e. None of the above.

• PROBLEMS

P D–1
*Encumbrance
Accounting*
L.O.3

The Mason County Road Commission reported the following balances at June 30, 19x1:

Account	Balance Debit (credit)
Reserve for Encumbrances	$ 38,600
Expenditures	263,100
Encumbrances	18,600

Required:
Use T accounts to help you answer the following questions:

1. What was the apparent beginning balance in the Reserve for Encumbrances account?
2. What is the total amount to be charged against revenues in 19x1?
3. If revenues during 19x1 are $300,000, what is the change in the total fund equity during 19x1?

P D–2
Balance Sheet
L.O.3

The general fund of Ski Town USA reported the following account balances at June 30, 19x1, just before closing journal entries were prepared:

	Pre-Closing Trial Balance	
	Debit	Credit
Revenues		$330,500
Taxes Receivable	$ 47,600	
Allowance for Uncollectible Taxes		3,100
Accounts Payable		6,300
Notes Payable		58,800
Notes Receivable	39,500	
Appropriations		315,000
Encumbrances	3,500	
Estimated Revenues	320,000	
Reserve for Encumbrances		13,000
Fund Balance		35,300
Expenditures	314,300	
Cash	37,100	
Totals	$762,000	$762,000

Required:
1. Prepare the necessary closing journal entries for all temporary accounts.
2. Prepare Ski Town USA's balance sheet at June 30, 19x1.

P D–3
Budgets/Closing Entries
L.O.3

The following account balances (all with normal balances) were available from the Jonville City ledger at the end of fiscal 19x3:

Appropriations	$356,000
Encumbrances	39,500
Expenditures	279,800
Estimated Revenues	340,000
Revenues	318,600
Reserve for Encumbrances	36,900
Fund Balance	8,200

Required:
1. Prepare the necessary closing entries.
2. What is the new fund balance at the end of 19x3?

P D–4
Encumbrance Accounting
L.O.3

The Town of Dent reported the following comparative balance sheet data (in millions):

	December 31	
	19x2	19x1
Fund equity:		
Reserve for encumbrances	$ 59.6	$ 84.3
Fund balance	163.2	118.9
Total fund equity	$222.8	$203.2

During 19x2, encumbrances of $189.9 million were charged against revenues. Also during 19x2 bills for goods and services totaling $237.8 million were received for items originally recorded as encumbrances of $214.6 million. Cash payments of $200 million were made during 19x2 on these billed amounts.

Required: (Hint: You may find a T account helpful.)
1. What is the change in fund equity during 19x2?
2. Record the encumbrances incurred in 19x2.
3. Record the reversal of encumbrances that occurred in 19x2.
4. Record the expenditures for the actual cost of encumbered goods and services in 19x2.
5. Record the payments made in 19x2.

E

1992 Annual Report— Ralston Purina Company

RALSTON PURINA COMPANY AND SUBSIDIARIES

The following discussion is a summary of the key factors management considers necessary in reviewing the Company's results of operations, liquidity, capital resources, and operating segment results.

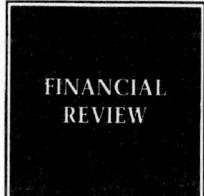

This discussion should be read in conjunction with the Business Segment Information and the Consolidated Financial Statements and related notes beginning on pages 12 and 16, respectively.

Highlights and Outlook

Net earnings were $313.2 million, or $2.75 per primary share for the year compared to $391.9 million, or $3.34 per primary share in 1991. Included in net earnings in 1992 is an extraordinary loss on early retirement of debt of $7.5 million, after taxes, or $.07 per primary share. Net earnings in 1992 included $32.9 million, after taxes, or $.31 per primary share for the restructuring of international battery manufacturing, agricultural, and bakery operations, offset by a gain on sale of assets. In 1991, the Company recognized $28.1 million, after taxes, or $.25 per primary share for the restructuring of international battery, bakery and baby food operations and costs related to environmental matters. Excluding the effect of these provisions in both 1992 and 1991 and the extraordinary loss in 1992, net earnings decreased $66.4 million or $.46 per primary share in 1992, primarily due to reduced operating profit for the Human and Pet Foods segment and higher net interest costs, partially offset by improved Other Consumer Products segment results.

In 1991, net earnings decreased $4.4 million although primary earnings per share increased $.11. Included in net earnings of 1990 are provisions of $12.9 million, after taxes, or $.11 per primary share, for costs of restructuring pet food operations and certain litigation costs. Excluding the effect of these provisions and the aforementioned 1991 provisions, net earnings and primary earnings per share increased $10.8 million and $.25 on improved battery products' results partially offset by declines in pet foods and baby foods.

Fully diluted earnings per share decreased $.53 to $2.59 for 1992. In 1991, fully diluted earnings per share increased $.09 over 1990. A reduced number of shares outstanding favorably impacted earnings per share.

Net earnings in the fourth quarter of 1992 were $28.0 million compared to $87.5 million in 1991. Excluding the portion of the previously discussed reserves and gain recognized in the fourth quarter, net earnings and primary earnings per share for the fourth quarter of 1992 declined $40.9 million or $.33 due to reduced operating profit for the Human and Pet Foods segment and higher net interest costs.

The Company's businesses operate principally in the packaged goods industry which accounts for approximately 90% of operating earnings. The human and pet food industries in which the Company competes domestically are mature and non-cyclical with strong cash flows. Competition is intense in these industries and growth depends on innovative new product introductions and focused advertising and promotion spending. Consolidation of the retail industry and growth of the mass merchandiser segment has resulted, and will continue to result, in significant changes in the product distribution pattern and trade promoting and pricing practices of the Company.

OPERATING RESULTS

Included in the period under review are the following acquisitions that affect comparability of operating results for the periods.

Fiscal 1992

In 1992, the Company acquired two battery products businesses, operating primarily in the United Kingdom, Spain and Portugal, which have been included in the Company's Other Consumer Products segment results since the date of acquisition.

Fiscal 1990

In November 1989, the Company acquired the Beech-Nut baby food business which has been included in the Company's Human and Pet Foods segment results since the date of acquisition.

In December 1989, the battery products group acquired the remaining interest in its Mexican subsidiary which is now being reported on a consolidated basis.

In June 1990, the Company acquired the remaining interest in the Keystone Resort operations.

Net Sales

Net sales increased $376.6 million or 5% in 1992, primarily due to acquisitions, increased international volume and domestic pricing growth in battery products, Agricultural Products volume increases and price increases in bakery products. In 1991, net sales increased 4% over 1990 on battery products volume growth, expanding international pet food operations and the consolidation of the resort operations. Comments on sales changes by business segment may be found on pages 12 and 13 of this report.

Gross Profit

Consolidated gross profit increased 4% in 1992 following a 5% increase in 1991. Cost of products sold as a percentage of sales was 54.5% in 1992 compared to 53.9% in 1991 and 54.4% in 1990. The increase in 1992 was primarily attributable to unfavorable product mix in the Human and Pet Foods segment and a decline in Agricultural Products margins after increasing in 1991. The decline in 1991 reflected improved product mix and cost containment in the battery products business.

Cost of products sold in the Human and Pet Foods and Agricultural Products segments, and to a lesser extent Other Consumer Products, depends upon commodity market prices. Prices may fluctuate widely due to weather conditions, government regulations, economic climate or other unforeseen circumstances. The Company manages exposure to changes in the agricultural commodities markets by hedging certain of its ingredient requirements.

Operating Expenses

Selling, general and administrative expenses increased 9% in 1992 and 1991 primarily as a result of higher distribution costs in both years and, in 1992, acquisitions. In 1991, business development spending in support of expanding international operations also contributed to the increase. Advertising and promotion expenses have remained at 12% of sales.

Interest Expense and Other Income/Expense

Interest expense increased in 1992 to $242.9 million compared to $208.7 million in 1991 and $207.7 million in 1990. The increase in 1992 resulted from higher average borrowings. Other expense included the previously mentioned restructuring provisions and gain. The increases in restructuring provisions and translation and exchange losses in 1992 were more than offset by the gain on sale of assets. In 1991, other expense increased $13.5 million over 1990 primarily due to the additional provisions recorded in 1991 and lower investment income.

Income Taxes

Income taxes, which include federal, state and foreign taxes, were 40.8% of pre-tax earnings before extraordinary item in 1992 and 39.5% in 1991 and 1990. Provisions for restructuring in certain countries did not result in a tax benefit due to a tax loss situation or the particular tax statutes of that country, resulting in a higher overall tax rate in 1992. Other than the aforementioned item, the Company's tax provisions generally reflect statutory tax rates.

Earnings Available to Common Shareholders

Earnings available to common shareholders are reduced by preferred stock dividends of $21.0 million in 1992, $20.7 million in 1991 and $20.5 million in 1990, net of tax benefit.

LIQUIDITY AND CAPITAL RESOURCES

Sources of Liquidity

Cash flow from operations is the Company's primary source of liquidity. Management continues to have a strong orientation on cash flows and the effective use of excess cash flows. In addition, the Company uses financial leverage to minimize the overall cost of capital and maintain adequate operating and financial flexibility. Management monitors leverage through its interest coverage ratio (defined as earnings before interest expense, income taxes and extraordinary item divided by interest expense), debt to internal funds ratio (defined as long-term debt divided by earnings adjusted for non-cash items) and long-term debt as a percentage of total capitalization. The ratios as a group demonstrate the Company's liquidity strength due to its strong cash flow generation.

Dollars in millions	1992	1991	1990
Cash Flow from Operations	$577.9	$711.1	$640.3
Interest Coverage	3.2	4.1	4.2
Debt to Internal Funds	3.7	2.9	3.1
Long-Term Debt as a Percent of Total Capitalization	72%	70%	75%

On a current equity market basis, long-term debt as a percent of total capitalization was 31% at September 30, 1992 compared to 28% at September 30, 1991. For purposes of the long-term debt ratio, the guarantee of the ESOP debt is treated as long-term debt and redeemable preferred stock and related unearned compensation are treated as capital. The historical cost basis ratio is significantly influenced by the large amount of stock repurchased by the Company.

The Company's working capital requirements for inventories and receivables are influenced by changes in raw material costs, the availability of raw materials and seasonality, and as a result, may fluctuate widely. The Company has traditionally used short-term debt to finance these seasonal and other working capital requirements and, from time to time, to finance capital expenditures on a temporary basis. In addition, the Company is currently using short-term debt to minimize its overall cost of debt. Bank lines of credit provide future credit availability and support the sale of commercial paper. Payment for lines of credit is effected primarily through fees. At September 30, 1992 the total unused lines of credit were $300.9 million. In addition, the Company has $178.1 million remaining from a previous shelf registration.

Working capital (current assets less current liabilities) was $35.0 million at September 30, 1992 compared to $481.6 million and $246.3 million at September 30, 1991 and 1990, respectively. The decline in working capital is primarily due to lower marketable securities and higher short term borrowings used to finance the European acquisitions.

Investing Activities

Capital expenditures were $325.4 million, $404.3 million and $342.1 million in fiscal years 1992, 1991 and 1990, respectively. Projected capital expenditures of $366 million in 1993 are expected to be financed with funds generated from operations.

The acquisition of the European battery operations in 1992 and the Beech-Nut baby food business in 1990 represented significant investments.

Financing Activities

Long-term financings are arranged as necessary to meet the Company's capital or other requirements, with the timing of issue, principal amount and form depending on the prevailing securities markets and general economic conditions. The Company received $250.0 million, $207.6 million and $229.6 million in proceeds from new debt issuances offset by payments on long-term debt of $172.7 million, $49.2 million and $237.1 million in 1992, 1991 and 1990, respectively. The Company also increased short-term obligations by $399.2 million in 1992.

The Company returned a significant amount of cash to its common shareholders during the three years ended September 30, 1992 through common stock dividends and common stock repurchases. These outflows totalled $358.6 million and $123.3 million for stock repurchases and dividends, respectively, in 1992 compared to $45.5 million and $113.8 million in 1991 and $536.3 million and $103.7 million in 1990. As of November 16, 1992, 379,000 shares of the current Board of Directors' authorization for the purchase of up to four million shares remain outstanding.

Environmental Matters

The operations of the Company, like those of other companies engaged in similar businesses, are subject to various federal, state, and local laws and regulations with respect to environmental matters, including regulations intended to protect public health and the environment, including air and water quality, underground fuel storage tanks, and waste handling and disposal. The Company has approximately 440 underground fuel storage tanks at various locations throughout the United States which are subject to federal and state laws and regulations establishing requirements for testing, upgrading or replacement of such tanks and, where necessary, remediation of associated contamination. The Company is presently in the process of testing and evaluating, and, if necessary, removing, replacing or upgrading such tanks in order to fully comply with applicable laws and regulations. In addition, the Company has received notices from the U.S. Environmental Protection Agency, state agencies, and/or private parties seeking contribution, that it has been identified as a "potentially responsible party" (PRP), under the Comprehensive Environmental Response, Compensation and Liability Act, as amended, and may be required to share in the cost of cleanup with respect to approximately 24 disposal sites. The Company's ultimate liability in connection with those sites is dependent on many factors including the volume of material contributed to the site, other PRP's and their financial viability and remediation methods and technology to be used. Management continually reviews the facts and circumstances surrounding such environmental matters and, if necessary, provides reserves to cover the probable ultimate cost. While it is difficult to quantify with certainty the potential financial impact of actions regarding environmental matters, particularly remediation, shared cleanup costs at Superfund sites, and future capital expenditures for environmental control equipment, in the opinion of management, the ultimate liability arising from such environmental matters, taking into account established accruals for estimated liabilities, will not have a material adverse effect on the financial position or results of operations of the Company as of and for the period ended September 30, 1992.

Pending Accounting Pronouncements

In December, 1990, the Financial Accounting Standards Board (FASB) issued Statement No. 106, "Employers' Accounting for Postretirement Benefits Other Than Pensions". The Company currently provides health and life insurance benefits for its retired employees who meet specified age and years of service requirements, and provides other postretirement benefits to certain management employees. The statement will require the Company to accrue the costs of postretirement benefits over the employees' active service periods. The Company is required to adopt the statement no later than fiscal 1994. The estimated obligation may be recognized as expense in the year of adoption or amortized as a component of postretirement benefit expense over a period of up to twenty years. The Company is currently evaluating these options.

Based on preliminary actuarial assumptions and assuming the statement is adopted in October 1993, as required, the non-cash, after tax transition obligation charge is estimated between $130 million and $200 million. Once adopted, assuming recognition of the estimated obligation at the date of adoption, annual after tax postretirement expense is expected to increase $5 million to $10 million, per year.

In February 1992, the FASB issued Statement No. 109 "Accounting for Income Taxes." This statement requires the use of the liability method of accounting for deferred income taxes. The statement is required to be adopted no later than fiscal 1994. The Company has not completed its evaluations to determine the impact of this statement on its consolidated financial statements.

Inflation

Management recognizes that inflationary pressures may have an adverse effect on the Company through higher asset replacement costs and related depreciation and higher material costs. The Company tries to minimize these effects through cost reductions and productivity improvements as well as price increases to maintain reasonable profit margins. It is management's view, however, that inflation has not had a significant impact on operations in the three years ended September 30, 1992.

RALSTON PURINA COMPANY AND SUBSIDIARIES

BUSINESS SEGMENT INFORMATION

Summarized financial information on a worldwide basis by business segments for the three years ended September 30, 1992 is set forth below. During these years the segments comprised the following:

Human and Pet Foods		**Other Consumer Products**		**Agricultural Products (International)**
Bakery products	Other specialty	Battery products	Dietary soy protein,	Animal feeds
Pet foods	grocery products,	All-seasons resort	fiber food ingredi-	
Cereals	including crackers,		ents and polymer	
Baby food products	cookies and snacks		products	

Included in the period under review are the following items which affect comparability of operating results for the periods.

Human and Pet Foods

Includes bakery restructuring provisions of $13.7 million in 1992.

Includes $29.2 million in 1991 for restructuring and environmental costs in bakery products and realign-

ment of certain cookie and cracker and baby food manufacturing operations.

Includes pet food restructuring provisions and litigation settlements of $21.4 million in 1990.

Other Consumer Products

Includes battery products manufacturing restructuring provisions of $53.3 million and gain on sale of assets of $41.5 million in 1992.

Includes battery products restructuring and environmental costs of $16.7 million in 1991.

Agricultural Products

Includes $12.0 million restructuring provision in 1992.

Comments, amounts and percentages in the remaining Business Segment discussion exclude the effects of the items discussed above.

HUMAN AND PET FOODS

Sales in the Human and Pet Foods segment increased 2% in 1992, primarily on higher pricing in bakery products, increased cereal sales and higher international pet food volume. Cereal sales increased in 1992 as higher volumes in store brands and higher prices in other categories were partially offset by volume declines in the children's category. Domestic pet food sales were flat compared to the prior year as volume increases in dog food and dry cat food brands were offset by unfavorable selling prices and product mix in dog food and volume declines in soft-moist cat foods.

In 1991, sales for the segment increased slightly on additional international pet food sales, higher volumes and prices in store brand cereals and higher prices in branded cereals. Partially offsetting these increases, domestic pet food sales declined slightly on volume declines in most major categories. Bakery products' sales were even with the prior year as price increases offset volume declines in both the bread and sweet baked goods categories.

Operating profit of the Human and Pet Foods segment declined 14% in 1992. Domestic pet food

operating profit declined on unfavorable product mix. In addition, lower margins, higher advertising and promotion expense in dog food and continuing substantial volume declines in the soft-moist cat category contributed to the decline. Cereal operating profit was off significantly as volume declines in children's cereals and start up costs associated with a new plant more than offset volume improvements in store brand cereals. Bakery products' operating profit declined in both bread and sweet baked goods largely on the shift to private label bread sales from higher margin brands. Bakery products have been under intense competitive pressure with limited ability to raise prices. Higher distribution costs associated with a high fixed cost distribution structure also adversely affected results.

Operating profit for the fourth quarter of 1992 declined 32%. Slightly more than half of the pet food and cereal operating profit decline in the quarter was due to higher recorded advertising and promotion expenses as a result of lower than expected volumes. In addition, lower dog food margins, cat food volume declines and intense competitive pric-

ing pressure in cereal markets negatively impacted the quarter. Bakery products operating profit for the quarter declined as unfavorable bread product mix was partially offset by higher volume in sweet baked goods.

In 1991, operating profit declined 4%. Domestic pet food operating profit declined on lower volumes and higher advertising and promotion behind line extensions and new products in dog food while cat food operating profit was flat on lower volumes and an unfavorable product mix offset by reduced advertising and promotion. Domestic cereal operating profit increased on higher margins and volume growth in all categories, except children's cereals, partially offset by higher manufacturing costs. Bakery products' operating profit was flat for the year on improved margins offset by lower volume. Operating profit in baby foods declined significantly in the year on a sharp volume reduction and higher advertising and promotion spending and manufacturing costs. International human and pet food operating profit declined from the prior year due to additional spending in developing new markets in the Asia Pacific region and Europe.

OTHER CONSUMER PRODUCTS

Sales for the segment increased 9% in 1992 on the acquisition of European operations, strong international volume growth and improved domestic pricing in battery products, and volume growth in soy protein products. In 1991, sales increased 9% over the prior year on strong volume growth, improved product mix and favorable exchange rates in the battery products business and the consolidation of resort operations.

Operating profit for the segment increased 8% in 1992 due to improved domestic battery products performance on lower manufacturing costs and favorable prices, and the incremental revenue earned through the introduction of a new ski slope. In addition, soy protein product earnings improved on volume increases partially offset by an unfavorable product mix and higher marketing costs asso-

ciated with new market penetration. Internationally, battery products operating profit declined primarily on substantially reduced results in Europe on an unfavorable product mix and lower margins. Higher advertising and promotion expense in battery products operations, primarily domestic, also affected earnings.

In 1991, operating profit for the segment increased 16%. Domestically, the battery products business was up significantly on strong volume growth and improved product mix as increased alkaline battery volume and margins more than offset declines in the carbon zinc brands. Internationally, operating profit was up principally on volume growth in the Asia Pacific region and Europe and favorable exchange rates. Operating profit of the soy protein products business was down in 1991 on lower

export volume partially offset by favorable exchange rates and product mix.

Domestically, the battery products business continues to face intense competition. While carbon zinc batteries dominate on a worldwide basis, there is a rapid shift to alkaline batteries in more developed markets such as the U.S., Canada, Europe and Japan. Internationally, the acquisition of strong European brands positions the battery products business well for continued international growth. Restructuring of the international battery manufacturing operations initiated in 1992 is projected to significantly reduce production costs beginning in 1995. The soy protein products business faces slower recoveries in certain key export markets while incurring additional costs associated with production capacity expansion.

RALSTON PURINA COMPANY AND SUBSIDIARIES

AGRICULTURAL PRODUCTS

Sales increased 12% in 1992 on increased volume in most geographic areas. Operating profit declined 12% in 1992 on lower margins in Korea, Canada and Europe, partially offset by improved margins in Central and South America and higher volumes in Europe. In 1991, sales increased slightly from the prior year on volume growth. Operating profit was down 9% in 1991 as a result of depressed economic conditions in certain South American countries.

BUSINESS SEGMENT FINANCIAL INFORMATION

Dollars in millions	1992	1991	1990
Sales by Product Lines and Segments			
Human and Pet Foods			
Bakery Products	$2,016.0	$1,966.2	$1,956.5
Pet Foods	1,733.7	1,724.8	1,701.0
Cereals	562.6	531.8	507.6
Other	246.0	250.4	217.5
Subtotal	4,558.3	4,473.2	4,382.6
Other Consumer Products			
Battery Products	1,798.0	1,659.0	1,541.5
Soy Protein Products	288.1	255.0	261.8
Other	75.0	64.7	8.9
Subtotal	2,161.1	1,978.7	1,812.2
Agricultural Products	1,033.0	923.9	906.6
Total	$7,752.4	$7,375.8	$7,101.4
Operating Profit			
Human and Pet Foods	$ 508.9[a]	$ 579.5[d]	$ 611.2[f]
Other Consumer Products	264.6[b]	239.0[e]	219.8
Agricultural Products	26.0[c]	43.2	47.4
Total	799.5	861.7	878.4
Unallocated Corporate and Miscellaneous Expenses	(14.5)	(5.2)	(15.7)
Interest Expense	(242.9)	(208.7)	(207.7)
Earnings before Income Taxes and Extraordinary Item	$ 542.1	$ 647.8	$ 655.0
Assets at Year End			
Human and Pet Foods	$1,650.6	$1,602.4	$1,489.6
Other Consumer Products	2,690.3	2,192.0	2,210.6
Agricultural Products	345.0	309.3	290.8
Subtotal	4,685.9	4,103.7	3,991.0
Corporate Assets	464.6	528.4	403.5
Total	$5,150.5	$4,632.1	$4,394.5
Depreciation Expense			
Human and Pet Foods	$ 118.5	$ 107.7	$ 103.8
Other Consumer Products	103.1	87.6	74.7
Agricultural Products	16.3	14.7	12.7
Property Additions			
Human and Pet Foods	155.3	191.9	136.3
Other Consumer Products	125.3	136.2	154.0
Agricultural Products	27.3	46.5	40.7

[a] Includes restructuring provisions of $13.7.
[b] Includes restructuring provisions of $53.3, offset by gain on sale of property of $41.5.
[c] Includes restructuring provisions of $12.0.
[d] Includes restructuring provisions and environmental costs of $29.2.
[e] Includes restructuring provisions and environmental costs of $16.7.
[f] Includes restructuring provisions and litigation settlement of $21.4.

Export sales and sales between business segments were immaterial. No single customer accounted for 10% or more of sales. Minority interests in earnings of certain subsidiaries and the Company's equity in earnings of unconsolidated 20% through 50% owned companies were not significant and have been included in operating profit.

RALSTON PURINA COMPANY AND SUBSIDIARIES

**BUSINESS
SEGMENT
INFORMATION**

GEOGRAPHIC SEGMENT FINANCIAL INFORMATION

Financial information by geographic location for the past three years is set forth below.

Dollars in millions	1992	1991	1990
Sales			
United States	$5,340.0	$5,209.7	$5,083.7
Europe	964.1	813.7	764.3
South & Central America	647.0	555.0	515.1
Asia Pacific	525.1	508.2	419.9
Other	276.2	289.2	318.4
Total	$7,752.4	$7,375.8	$7,101.4
Operating Profit			
United States	$ 681.0	$ 715.3	$ 715.6
Europe	(4.5)[a]	54.0[e]	55.9
South & Central America	22.1[b]	28.2	32.8
Asia Pacific	97.8[c]	54.8	49.9
Other	3.1[d]	9.4[f]	24.2
Total	$ 799.5	$ 861.7	$ 878.4
Assets			
United States	$2,895.7	$2,877.6	$2,791.2
Europe	1,061.0	550.6	564.6
South & Central America	248.6	218.3	205.2
Asia Pacific	332.8	323.5	287.1
Other	147.8	133.7	142.9
Total	$4,685.9	$4,103.7	$3,991.0

[a] *Includes restructuring provisions of $53.6.*
[b] *Includes restructuring provisions of $11.7*
[c] *Includes gain on sale of property of $41.5, and restructuring gains of $9.5.*
[d] *Includes restructuring provisions of $9.5.*
[e] *Includes restructuring provisions of $7.1.*
[f] *Includes restructuring provisions of $8.6.*

RALSTON PURINA COMPANY AND SUBSIDIARIES

RESPONSIBILITY FOR FINANCIAL STATEMENTS

The preparation and integrity of the financial statements of Ralston Purina Company are the responsibility of its management. These statements have been prepared in conformance with generally accepted accounting principles and in the opinion of management fairly present the Company's financial position, results of operations and cash flows.

The Company maintains accounting and internal control systems which it believes are adequate to provide reasonable assurance that assets are safeguarded against loss from unauthorized use or disposition and that the financial records are reliable for preparing financial statements. The selection and training of qualified personnel, the establishment and communication of accounting and administrative policies and procedures, and an extensive program of internal audits are important elements of these control systems.

The report of Price Waterhouse, independent accountants, on their audits of the accompanying financial statements is shown below. This report states that the audits were made in accordance with generally accepted auditing standards. These standards include a study and evaluation of internal control for the purpose of establishing a basis for reliance thereon relative to the scope of their audits of the financial statements.

The Board of Directors, through its Audit Committee consisting solely of nonmanagement directors, meets periodically with management, internal audit and the independent accountants to discuss audit and financial reporting matters. To assure independence, Price Waterhouse has direct access to the Audit Committee.

REPORT OF INDEPENDENT ACCOUNTANTS

To the Shareholders and Board of Directors of Ralston Purina Company

In our opinion, the accompanying consolidated balance sheet and the related consolidated statements of earnings, of shareholders equity and of cash flows present fairly, in all material respects, the financial position of Ralston Purina Company and its subsidiaries at September 30, 1992 and 1991, and the results of their operations and their cash flows for each of the three years in the period ended September 30, 1992, in conformity with generally accepted accounting principles. These financial statements are the responsibility of the Company's management; our responsibility is to express an opinion on these financial statements based on our audits. We conducted our audits of these statements in accordance with generally accepted auditing standards which require that we plan and perform the audit to obtain reasonable assurance about whether the financial statements are free of material misstatement. An audit includes examining, on a test basis, evidence supporting the amounts and disclosures in the financial statements, assessing the accounting principles used and significant estimates made by management, and evaluating the overall financial statement presentation. We believe that our audits provide a reasonable basis for the opinion expressed above.

Price Waterhouse

St. Louis, Missouri
November 2, 1992

RALSTON PURINA COMPANY AND SUBSIDIARIES

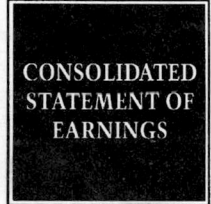

**CONSOLIDATED
STATEMENT OF
EARNINGS**

Dollars in millions except per share data

Year ended September 30	1992	1991	1990
Net Sales	$7,752.4	$7,375.8	$7,101.4
Costs and Expenses			
Cost of products sold	4,223.1	3,974.3	3,864.1
Selling, general and administrative	1,784.9	1,643.3	1,511.8
Advertising and promotion	931.3	870.5	845.1
Interest	242.9	208.7	207.7
Other (income)/expense, net	28.1	31.2	17.7
	7,210.3	6,728.0	6,446.4
Earnings before Income Taxes and			
Extraordinary Item	542.1	647.8	655.0
Income Taxes	221.4	255.9	258.7
Earnings before Extraordinary Item	320.7	391.9	396.3
Extraordinary Item - Loss on			
Early Retirement of Debt	(7.5)		
Net Earnings	313.2	391.9	396.3
Preferred Stock Dividend, Net of Taxes	21.0	20.7	20.5
Earnings Available to Common Shareholders	$ 292.2	$ 371.2	$ 375.8
Earnings per Share -			
Primary			
Earnings before Extraordinary Item	$ 2.82	$ 3.34	$ 3.23
Extraordinary Item	(.07)		
Net earnings	$ 2.75	$ 3.34	$ 3.23
Fully Diluted			
Earnings before Extraordinary Item	$ 2.65	$ 3.12	$ 3.03
Extraordinary Item	(.06)		
Net earnings	$ 2.59	$ 3.12	$ 3.03

*The above financial statement should be read in conjunction with the Notes to Financial Statements on
pages 20 to 28.*

RALSTON PURINA COMPANY AND SUBSIDIARIES

Dollars in millions except per share data

September 30	1992	1991
ASSETS		
Current Assets		
Cash	$ 23.6	$ 21.0
Marketable securities	35.9	136.5
Receivables, less allowance for doubtful accounts	833.9	672.0
Inventories	775.7	735.5
Other current assets	111.2	110.5
Total Current Assets	1,780.3	1,675.5
Investments and Other Assets	1,063.8	772.9
Property at Cost		
Land	158.8	147.0
Buildings	798.7	738.7
Machinery and equipment	2,662.0	2,340.4
Construction in progress	145.5	216.4
	3,765.0	3,442.5
Accumulated depreciation	1,458.6	1,258.8
	2,306.4	2,183.7
Total	$5,150.5	$4,632.1
LIABILITIES AND SHAREHOLDERS EQUITY		
Current Liabilities		
Current maturities of long-term debt	$ 76.0	$ 66.3
Notes payable	508.1	110.8
Accounts payable and accrued liabilities	1,057.8	917.1
Dividends payable	39.7	38.3
Income taxes	63.7	61.4
Total Current Liabilities	1,745.3	1,193.9
Long-Term Debt	2,111.3	2,071.3
Deferred Income Taxes	192.0	197.3
Other Liabilities	292.0	274.4
Commitments and Contingencies		
Redeemable Preferred Stock-Series A 6.75%, $1 par value,		
issued 4,600,000 shares in 1992 and 4,587,506 shares in 1991	509.8	508.4
Unearned ESOP Compensation	(355.1)	(397.0)
Shareholders Equity		
Preferred stock, $1 par value, None outstanding		
Common stock - $.10 par value, issued 114,670,049 shares in 1992		
and $.41 2/3 par value, issued 114,660,791 shares in 1991	11.5	47.8
Capital in excess of par value	117.4	81.4
Retained earnings	1,192.1	1,032.8
Cumulative translation adjustment	19.3	(38.0)
Common stock in treasury, at cost, 10,930,851 shares		
in 1992 and 4,161,781 in 1991	(676.1)	(321.1)
Unearned portion of restricted stock	(9.0)	(19.1)
Total Shareholders Equity	655.2	783.8
Total	$5,150.5	$4,632.1

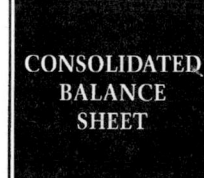

CONSOLIDATED
BALANCE
SHEET

The above financial statement should be read in conjunction with the Notes to Financial Statements on pages 20 to 28.

RALSTON PURINA COMPANY AND SUBSIDIARIES

CONSOLIDATED STATEMENT OF CASH FLOWS

	Dollars in millions		
Year ended September 30	**1992**	1991	1990
Cash Flow from Operations			
Earnings before extraordinary item	**$320.7**	$391.9	$396.3
Adjustments to reconcile earnings to net cash flow provided by operations			
Depreciation and amortization	**292.4**	259.7	236.4
Deferred income taxes	**(11.8)**	10.5	18.8
Gain on sale of property	**(41.5)**		
Changes in operating assets and liabilities used in operations			
Increase in accounts receivable	**(113.4)**	(31.2)	(25.2)
Decrease (increase) in inventories	**26.1**	(45.0)	39.2
Decrease (increase) in other current assets	**8.0**	(16.0)	16.2
Increase (decrease) in accounts payable and accrued liabilities	**73.2**	131.6	(22.9)
Increase (decrease) in other current liabilities	**11.7**	12.9	(15.8)
Other, net	**12.5**	(3.3)	(2.7)
Net cash flow from operations	**577.9**	711.1	640.3
Cash Flow from Investing Activities			
Property additions	**(325.4)**	(404.3)	(342.1)
Proceeds from the sale of property	**62.0**	9.2	19.1
Acquisition of businesses	**(315.2)**		(55.0)
Other, net	**(30.2)**	4.3	(46.2)
Net cash used by investing activities	**(608.8)**	(390.8)	(424.2)
Cash Flow from Financing Activities			
Proceeds from sale of long-term debt	**250.0**	207.6	229.6
Principal payments on long-term debt, including current maturities	**(172.7)**	(49.2)	(237.1)
Net increase (decrease) in notes payable	**399.2**	(221.8)	201.8
Proceeds from sale of stock	**2.9**	10.5	3.7
Treasury stock purchases	**(358.6)**	(45.5)	(536.3)
Dividends paid	**(157.7)**	(147.9)	(137.5)
Net cash used by financing activities	**(36.9)**	(246.3)	(475.8)
Effect of Exchange Rate Changes on Cash	**(30.2)**	(28.9)	(8.5)
Net (Decrease) Increase in Cash and Cash Equivalents	**(98.0)**	45.1	(268.2)
Cash and Cash Equivalents, Beginning of Year	**157.5**	112.4	380.6
Cash and Cash Equivalents, End of Year	**$ 59.5**	$157.5	$112.4

The above financial statement should be read in conjunction with the Notes to Financial Statements on pages 20 to 28.

RALSTON PURINA COMPANY AND SUBSIDIARIES

CONSOLIDATED STATEMENT OF SHAREHOLDERS EQUITY

Three years ended September 30, 1992	Number of Shares (In thousands)		Amount (Dollars in millions)					
	Common Stock	Common Stock in Treasury	Common Stock	Capital in Excess of Par Value	Retained Earnings	Cumulative Translation Adjustment	Common Stock in Treasury	Unearned Portion of Restricted Stock
Balance October 1, 1989	114,605	(53,005)	$47.8	$261.8	$2,919.7	($33.3)	($2,350.1)	($14.2)
Treasury stock purchased		(6,310)					(536.3)	
Common stock issued on conversion of debentures	16			.2				
Activity under stock plans		367		23.2			.1	(23.2)
Market value adjustment on restricted stock				5.4				(5.4)
Amortization of restricted stock								11.8
Translation adjustments						7.6		
Net earnings					396.3			
Dividends declared on common stock					(105.5)			
Dividends declared on preferred stock, net of taxes					(20.5)			
Balance September 30, 1990	114,621	(58,948)	47.8	290.6	3,190.0	(25.7)	(2,886.3)	(31.0)
Effect of two-for-one stock split		55,734		(212.5)	(2,402.9)		2,615.4	
Balance September 30, 1990, restated	114,621	(3,214)	47.8	78.1	787.1	(25.7)	(270.9)	(31.0)
Treasury stock purchased		(879)					(45.5)	
Common stock issued on conversion of debentures	40			.3				
Activity under stock plans		(69)		2.6	(6.2)		(4.7)	.4
Market value adjustment on restricted stock				.4				(.4)
Amortization of restricted stock								11.9
Translation adjustments						(12.3)		
Net earnings					391.9			
Dividends declared on common stock					(119.3)			
Dividends declared on preferred stock, net of taxes					(20.7)			
Balance September 30, 1991	114,661	(4,162)	47.8	81.4	1,032.8	(38.0)	(321.1)	(19.1)
Effect of change in par value			(36.3)	36.3				
Treasury stock purchased		(6,778)					(358.6)	
Common stock issued on conversion of debentures	9			.1				
Activity under stock plans		9		(.1)	(7.1)		3.6	.6
Market value adjustment on restricted stock				(.3)				.3
Amortization of restricted stock								9.2
Translation adjustments						57.3		
Net earnings					313.2			
Dividends declared on common stock					(125.8)			
Dividends declared on preferred stock, net of taxes					(21.0)			
Balance September 30, 1992	114,670	(10,931)	$11.5	$117.4	$1,192.1	$19.3	($ 676.1)	($ 9.0)

The above financial statement should be read in conjunction with the Notes to Financial Statements on pages 20 to 28.

RALSTON PURINA COMPANY AND SUBSIDIARIES

Dollars in millions except per share data

SUMMARY OF ACCOUNTING POLICIES

NOTES TO FINANCIAL STATEMENTS

The Company's significant accounting policies, which conform to generally accepted accounting principles and are applied on a consistent basis among years, are described below:

Principles of Consolidation - The consolidated financial statements include the accounts of the Company and its majority-owned subsidiaries. All significant intercompany transactions are eliminated. Investments in affiliated companies, 20% through 50%-owned, are carried at equity.

Minority interests in earnings of consolidated subsidiaries and the Company's share of the net earnings of unconsolidated companies carried at equity are included in selling, general and administrative expenses.

Foreign Currency Translation - Foreign currency financial statements of foreign operations where the local currency is the functional currency are translated using exchange rates in effect at period end for assets and liabilities and average exchange rates during the period for results of operations. Related translation adjustments are reported as a separate component of shareholders equity. For foreign operations where the U.S. dollar is the functional currency and for countries which are considered highly inflationary, translation practices differ in that inventories, properties, accumulated depreciation and depreciation accounts are translated at historical rates of exchange and related translation adjustments are included in earnings. Gains and losses from foreign currency transactions are generally included in earnings.

Financial Instruments - The Company enters into interest rate swap and cap agreements in the man-agement of interest rate exposure. The differential to be paid or received is normally accrued as interest rates change and is recognized over the life of the agreements. In addition, in order to hedge foreign currency exposures on firm commitments, the Company regularly enters into forward foreign currency contracts. Gains and losses resulting from these instruments are recognized in the same period as the underlying hedged transaction.

Cash equivalents for purposes of the statement of cash flows are considered to be all highly liquid investments with a maturity of three months or less when purchased. Cash flow from hedging transactions are classified in the same category as the cash flow from the item being hedged.

Marketable Securities are valued at cost which approximates market.

Inventories are valued generally at the lower of average cost or market. The Company hedges certain of its grain and commodity purchases as considered necessary to reduce the risk associated with market price fluctuations. Gains and losses on hedges of future grain and commodity purchases are recognized in the same period as the related purchase transaction.

Property at Cost - Expenditures for new facilities and those which substantially increase the useful lives of the property, including interest during construction, are capitalized. Maintenance, repairs and minor renewals are expensed as incurred. When properties are retired or otherwise disposed of, the related cost and accumulated depreciation are removed from the accounts and gains or losses on the dispositions are reflected in earnings.

Depreciation is generally provided on the straight-line basis by charges to costs or expenses at rates based on the estimated useful lives of the proper-ties. Estimated useful lives range from 3 to 25 years for machinery and equipment and 10 to 50 years for buildings.

Intangible Assets, which are included in Investments and Other Assets, represent the excess of cost over the net tangible assets of acquired businesses and are amortized over estimated periods of related benefit ranging from 5 to 40 years.

Income Taxes - Deferred income taxes are recognized for the effect of timing differences between financial and tax reporting. No additional U.S. taxes have been provided on earnings of foreign subsidiaries expected to be reinvested indefinitely. Additional income taxes are provided, however, on planned repatriations of foreign earnings after taking into account tax-exempt earnings and applicable foreign tax credits.

Earnings per Share - Primary earnings per share are based on the average number of shares outstanding during the year (106,314,000 in 1992, 111,189,000 in 1991 and 116,308,000 in 1990). Fully diluted earnings per share assumes the conversion of the Series A 6.75% Preferred Stock (Redeemable Preferred Stock) and other dilutive securities into Company common stock. For purposes of calculating fully diluted earnings per share, net earnings have been adjusted for the additional contribution to the Company's employee stock ownership plans and their related trust (ESOP) that would have been required had the Redeemable Preferred Stock been converted as of the beginning of the period.

All related common per share information and average share data has been restated, for all periods presented, to reflect the effects of the two-for-one stock split declared in 1991.

BUSINESS SEGMENT INFORMATION

The business segment financial information and geographic segment financial information sections appearing on pages 13 and 14 herein, are an integral part of these financial statements.

ACQUISITIONS

On July 15, 1992, the Company completed the purchase of Ever Ready Limited from Hanson, PLC, London for $245.2 in cash. On February 18, 1992, the Company acquired the consumer battery products business of Sociedad Espanola Del Acumulador Tudor, a battery products manufacturer based in Spain and Portugal for $70.0 in cash.

On November 3, 1989, the Company acquired the assets and assumed certain liabilities of the Beech-Nut baby food business from affiliates of Nestle Enterprises, Inc. for $55.0 in cash.

These acquisitions were accounted for using the purchase method of accounting, and accordingly, the results of operations are included in the consolidated statement of earnings from the date of acquisition.

In June, 1990, the Company acquired the assets and assumed the current liabilities and outstanding long term debt of the remaining 50 percent ownership interest in the Company's Keystone resort operations. The Keystone resort operation was formerly accounted for as an investment under the equity method.

Assuming these acquisitions had occurred as of the beginning of their respective fiscal years, they would not have had a material effect on net sales, net earnings or earnings per share.

Dollars in millions except per share data

RALSTON PURINA COMPANY AND SUBSIDIARIES

INCOME TAXES

The provisions for income taxes consisted of the following:

	1992	1991	1990
Currently payable			
United States	$173.2	$185.4	$179.2
State	19.3	21.2	20.2
Foreign	34.0	39.5	37.7
Total current	226.5	246.1	237.1
Deferred			
United States	(13.6)	17.1	18.1
Foreign	3.8	(7.3)	3.5
Total deferred	(9.8)	9.8	21.6
	216.7	255.9	258.7
Income tax benefit - extraordinary item	4.7		
Income taxes	$221.4	$255.9	$258.7

Deferred income taxes, reflecting timing differences between financial and tax reporting, relate primarily to depreciation, deferred incentive compensation, pensions and self-insurance reserves.

The source of pre-tax earnings follows:

	1992	1991	1990
United States	$465.8	$529.2	$528.6
Foreign	64.1	118.6	126.4
	529.9	647.8	655.0
Extraordinary loss	12.2		
Pre-tax earnings	$542.1	$647.8	$655.0

Income taxes were 40.8% of pre-tax earnings in 1992 and 39.5% in 1991 and 1990. A reconciliation of income taxes with the amounts computed at the statutory federal rate follows:

	1992	1991	1990
Computed tax at 34% statutory rate	$180.2	$220.3	$222.7
State income taxes, net of federal tax benefit	12.7	14.0	13.3
Foreign tax in excess of (less than) domestic rate	23.9	(.1)	8.2
Other, net	(.1)	21.7	14.5
	$216.7	$255.9	$258.7

The Company has recognized no tax benefit for certain foreign operating losses. Of such losses, approximately $60 is expected to be available to offset future income in those foreign jurisdictions. These loss carryforwards expire primarily from 1993 to 1997.

In February 1992, the FASB issued Statement No. 109, "Accounting for Income Taxes." This statement requires the use of the liability method of accounting for deferred income taxes. The statement is required to be adopted no later than fiscal 1994.

The Company has not completed its evaluations to determine the impact of this statement on the consolidated financial statements.

INCENTIVE COMPENSATION

The Company's 1988 Incentive Stock Plan (1988 Plan), adopted in January 1988, replaces the 1982 Incentive Stock Plan (1982 Plan). Reserved shares of stock under the 1982 Plan, which will continue until granted awards are exercised or terminated,

will be used for the 1988 Plan. No additional awards may be granted under the 1982 Plan.

The 1988 Plan provides that eligible employees may receive stock option awards and other stock awards payable in whole or part by the issuance of stock. Stock option awards are issued at an option price at

least equal to the fair market value of the shares at the date of grant. Since option prices are equal to market value, no charge is made against earnings. Proceeds from the exercise of stock options are credited to the appropriate capital accounts.

RALSTON PURINA COMPANY AND SUBSIDIARIES   *Dollars in millions except per share data*

NOTES TO FINANCIAL STATEMENTS	Changes in incentive and nonqualified stock options outstanding are summarized as follows:	
		SHARES UNDER OPTION
	Outstanding October 1, 1991 ($5 15/16 to $44 5/8 per share)	2,931,569
	Granted ($44 3/8 to $52 3/8 per share)	1,206,350
	Exercised ($5 15/16 to $40 7/8 per share)	(132,336)
	Cancelled	(22,960)
	Outstanding September 30, 1992 ($10 1/8 to $52 3/8 per share)	3,982,623
	Exercisable at September 30, 1992	696,773

At September 30, 1992 and 1991, there were 4,259,259 and 5,435,668 shares available for future awards, respectively.

In addition, at September 30, 1992 and 1991, 877,030 and 1,157,570 shares of restricted stock awards were outstanding, respectively. Restrictions on shares of restricted stock issued to eligible employees lapse over periods ranging from three to ten years provided continued employment and, in certain cases, minimum stock price requirements are met. Compensation cost is recognized over this vesting period. Charges to earnings were $9.6 in 1992, $12.6 in 1991, and $12.7 in 1990.

PENSION PLANS AND OTHER POSTRETIREMENT BENEFITS

The Company has several noncontributory defined benefit pension plans covering substantially all full-time employees in the United States, who are not participating in a multiemployer pension plan, and certain employees in other countries. The plans provide retirement benefits based on years of service and earnings. It is the Company's practice to fund pension liabilities in accordance with the minimum and maximum limits imposed by the Employee Retirement Income Security Act of 1974 (ERISA) and federal income tax laws. The Company also contributes to jointly administered multiemployer defined benefit pension plans covering certain of its union employees.

Certain foreign pension arrangements, which include various retirement and termination benefit plans, some of which are required by local law or coordinated with government-sponsored plans, are not material in the aggregate and are not included in these disclosures.

Pension cost and other retirement savings plan costs included the following components:

	1992	1991	1990
Defined benefit plans			
Service cost for benefits earned during the year	**$30.7**	$ 27.4	$ 25.6
Interest cost on projected benefit obligation	**57.9**	53.4	51.3
Return on plan assets	**(78.9)**	(142.4)	76.8
Net amortization and deferral	**(14.3)**	52.4	(162.5)
	(4.6)	(9.2)	(8.8)
Multiemployer plans	**55.6**	54.5	52.4
Defined contribution plans	**33.5**	34.4	30.7
Total	**$84.5**	$ 79.7	$ 74.3

The following table presents the funded status of the Company's principal defined benefit plans and amounts recognized in the balance sheet at September 30:

	1992	1991
Actuarial present value of:		
Vested benefits	**($ 575.0)**	($526.2)
Nonvested benefits	**(48.6)**	(51.9)
Accumulated benefit obligation	**(623.6)**	(578.1)
Effect of future salary increases	**(206.2)**	(166.6)
Projected benefit obligation	**(829.8)**	(744.7)
Plan assets at fair value	**1,017.0**	930.4
Plan assets in excess of projected benefit obligation	**187.2**	185.7
Unrecognized net gain	**(59.3)**	(69.1)
Unrecognized prior service cost	**13.7**	2.0
Unrecognized net asset at transition, net of amortization	**(30.2)**	(35.0)
Prepaid pension cost included in Investments and Other Assets	**$ 111.4**	$ 83.6

The assumptions used in determining the information above, which reflect weighted averages for the component plans, were as follows:

	1992	1991
Discount rate	**7.8%**	8.0%
Rate of increase of future compensation levels	**5.4%**	6.0%
Long-term rate of return on assets	**9.4%**	9.4%

Dollars in millions except per share data

RALSTON PURINA COMPANY AND SUBSIDIARIES

Assets of the plans consist primarily of listed common stocks and bonds, including 1,700,900 shares of the Company's common stock with a market value of $74.8 at September 30, 1992.

Substantially all full-time administrative and non-union production employees in the United States are eligible to participate in the Company-sponsored leveraged ESOP. The Company makes a matching contribution of up to 100% of the participant's contribution based on specified limits of the participant's salary.

The cost of the ESOP is recognized as incurred and was $32.2 for 1992, $30.2 for 1991, and $29.0 for 1990. Company contributions include $6.1 in 1992, $6.3 in 1991 and $6.1 in 1990 of additional employer contributions necessary to meet the debt service requirements of the leveraged ESOP's long-term debt as discussed in the Long-Term Debt note on page 24.

The Company currently provides health care and life insurance benefits for its retired employees who meet specified age and years of service requirements. The cost of health care benefits is recognized as incurred. The cost of life insurance benefits is recognized as insurance premiums are paid. The cost of such benefits were $7.1 in 1992, $5.4 in 1991, and $5.2 in 1990. Coincident with the adoption of the FSOP, the Company is phasing out its subsidy of medical benefits for future retirees. The Company currently anticipates continuing to provide all, or some portion of, the subsidy for retirement medical benefits for current retirees and a limited group of active employees.

The Company also provides other postretirement benefits to certain management employees. The estimated cost of such benefits payable in the future are accrued over the life of the participant.

In December 1990, the FASB issued Statement No. 106, "Employer's Accounting for Postretirement Benefits Other Than Pensions". The statement requires the Company to accrue the costs of postretirement benefits over employees' active service periods. The Company is required to adopt the statement no later than fiscal 1994. The estimated obligation may be recognized as expense in the year of adoption or amortized as a component of postretirement benefit expense over a period of up to twenty years.

Based on preliminary actuarial assumptions and assuming the statement is adopted in October 1993, as required, the non-cash, after tax transition obligation charge is estimated between $130 and $200. Once adopted, assuming recognition of the estimated obligation at the date of adoption, annual after tax postretirement expense is expected to increase $5 to $10, per year.

NOTES PAYABLE

Information relative to short-term debt borrowings for the three years ended September 30, 1992 follows:

	1992	1991	1990
Notes payable			
Ending balance	$452.6	$110.8	$277.0
Weighted average interest rate	9%	21%	14%
Outstanding during period[a]			
Maximum	$563.8	$407.1	$518.5
Average	294.4	196.4	234.5
Weighted average interest rate	11%	15%	15%
Commercial paper			
Ending balance	$ 55.5		$ 66.7
Weighted average interest rate	4%		8%
Outstanding during period[a]			
Maximum	$101.2	$153.2	$145.0
Average	37.1	63.9	36.6
Weighted average interest rate	4%	7%	8%

[a] *Based on month-end balances.*

Notes payable include borrowings in highly inflationary economies. The real effective cost of local currency borrowing in these economies is expected to be substantially less due to devaluation of the applicable local currencies against the U.S. dollar.

On September 30, 1992, total unused lines of credit were $300.9.

RALSTON PURINA COMPANY AND SUBSIDIARIES

Dollars in millions except per share data

LONG-TERM DEBT

The detail of long-term debt as of September 30 follows:

	1992	1991
Debentures		
7.70% due 1996	$ 5.6	$ 10.2
9 1/2% due 2016	264.9	277.1
9 3/8% due 2016	175.0	175.0
10.45% due 2018		126.0
9 1/4% due 2009	200.0	200.0
9.30% due 2021	200.0	200.0
8 5/8% due 2022	250.0	
Other Debt		
ESOP debt guarantee	355.1	397.0
Medium-term Notes, 7.75% to 10.18%	121.0	121.0
12 3/4% Swiss Franc Bonds due 1994[a]	50.1	50.1
11 3/4% Notes due 1995	132.3	132.3
9% Notes due 1996	200.0	200.0
12% Notes due 1996	38.8	38.8
7 3/4% Notes due 1998	30.4	34.8
Capitalized lease obligations, 4.0% to 12.0%	13.2	14.7
Industrial revenue bonds, 5 1/2% to 12 3/4%	77.9	81.4
Other	73.0	79.2
	2,187.3	2,137.6
Less current portion	(76.0)	(66.3)
	$2,111.3	$2,071.3

[a]*Represents the equivalent principal amount and approximate effective interest rate of the 5 3/8% Bonds under related currency exchange arrangements.*

Aggregate maturities on all long-term debt, exclusive of debentures held in treasury, are $47.8, $193.9, $221.7 and $107.2 for the years ending September 30, 1994 through 1997, respectively. These aggregate maturities do not include the future maturities of the ESOP debt guarantee.

To fund its purchase of the Company's preferred stock, the Trust for the Company-sponsored ESOP borrowed $500.0 principal amount in ten-year 8.25% notes (ESOP loan). The ESOP loan is unconditionally guaranteed by the Company and is included in the Company's consolidated balance sheet as long-term debt, along with a corresponding Unearned ESOP Compensation. Both the long-term debt and the unearned ESOP compensation will be reduced as employee and employer contributions to the ESOP are used to reduce the outstanding ESOP loan. During 1992 and 1991, the ESOP incurred $31.9 and $35.2, respectively, of interest expense on the ESOP loan.

Dollars in millions except per share data

RALSTON PURINA COMPANY AND SUBSIDIARIES

REDEEMABLE PREFERRED STOCK

At September 30, 1992, the Company had 10,600,000 shares of $1 par value preferred stock authorized, of which 4,600,000 shares were authorized as Series A 6.75% Preferred Stock and issued to the Company's ESOP. Series A 6.75% Preferred Stock has a guaranteed minimum value of $110.83 per share and is convertible into the Company's common stock at the ratio of approximately two-for-one. The shares have preference in liquidation and each share has one voting right. Dividends are cumulative, compounded and payable semi-annual-

ly. In accordance with financial reporting requirements of the Securities and Exchange Commission, the Series A 6.75% Preferred Stock has been classified outside of permanent equity as Redeemable Preferred Stock.

Preferred stock shares are held, on behalf of the ESOP, by the ESOP's trustee and are allocated to individual participants' accounts based on the amount of employee and employer matching contributions to the ESOP. Dividends on unallocated

Redeemable Preferred Stock are used to fund the debt service requirements of the ESOP.

The trustee, as holder of preferred stock, may convert its shares into Company common stock at any time, or may require the Company to redeem the preferred stock shares, under certain limited circumstances, at the guaranteed minimum price, in cash or common stock. The Company may elect to redeem the preferred stock, under limited circumstances, in cash or common stock.

SHAREHOLDERS EQUITY

On January 17, 1986 the Board of Directors declared a dividend distribution of one share purchase right (Right) for each outstanding share of the Company's common stock. The terms of the Rights were subsequently amended on May 26, 1989. Each Right entitles a shareholder to purchase from the Company one common share at an exercise price of $75 per share subject to antidilution adjustments. The Rights, however, become exercisable only at the time a person or group acquires, or commences a public tender offer for, 20% or more of the Company's common stock. If an acquiring person or group acquires 20% or more of the Company's common stock, the price will be further adjusted so that holders of Rights (other than the acquiring person or group) may purchase common stock at one-third of its then market price. In

the event that the Company merges with, or transfers 50% or more of its assets or earning power to, any person or group after the Rights become exercisable, holders of Rights may purchase, at the exercise price, common stock of the acquiring entity having a value equal to twice the exercise price. The Rights can be redeemed by the Board of Directors at $.05 per Right only up to the date a person or group acquires 20% or more of the Company's common stock. Also, following the acquisition by a person or group of beneficial ownership of at least 20% but less than 50% of the Company's common stock, the Board may exchange the Rights for common stock at a ratio of one share of common stock per Right. The Rights expire on January 27, 1996. At September 30, 1992, 122,485,802 shares of the Company's common

stock have been reserved for issuance upon exercise of the Rights.

At September 30, 1992; there were 9,200,000 shares of common stock reserved for conversion of Redeemable Preferred Stock, 28,806 shares of common stock reserved for conversion of the 5 3/4% subordinated debentures, convertible at 130.434 shares for each $1,000 principal amount, and 9,517,798 shares reserved under various employee incentive compensation and benefit plans.

Also, in conjunction with the shareholder approved reduction in the par value of the Company's common stock, as reflected on the consolidated balance sheet, the shareholders approved an increase in the number of authorized common shares of stock from 380,000,000 to 600,000,000.

RALSTON PURINA COMPANY AND SUBSIDIARIES

Dollars in millions except per share data

COMMITMENTS AND CONTINGENCIES

NOTES TO FINANCIAL STATEMENTS

The Company is a party to a number of legal proceedings in various state, federal and foreign jurisdictions. These proceedings are in varying stages and some involve highly complex questions of fact and law. The amount of the Company's liability, if any, from these proceedings cannot be determined with certainty; however, in the opinion of management, based upon the information presently known, the ultimate liability of the Company, if any, arising from the pending legal proceedings, as well as from asserted legal claims and known potential legal claims which are probable of assertion, should not have a material adverse effect on the consolidated financial position of the Company at September 30, 1992.

Other Contingencies

The Company had outstanding, at September 30, 1992, interest rate swap agreements effectively converting French franc, Australian dollar and Swiss franc variable rate debt having an equivalent U.S. dollar value of $109.3 into fixed rate debt. These agreements mature between fiscal 1995 and 1996 and result in a weighted average fixed interest rate of 9.4%. Also, at September 30, 1992, the Company had interest rate swap agreements effectively converting Belgian franc fixed rate debt having an equivalent U.S. dollar value of $25.8 into variable rate debt. These agreements mature in six months.

At September 30, 1992, the Company had forward foreign exchange contracts to purchase or sell the equivalent of $390.0 of foreign currency principally denominated in European, Canadian and Asian currencies. The contracts generally range from one month to one year and are for the purpose of hedging balance sheet and operating income currency exposures.

The counterparties to interest rate swap agreements and forward foreign currency contracts consist of a number of major international financial institutions. The Company continually monitors its positions and the credit ratings of its counterparties, and limits the amount of agreements it enters into with any one party. While nonperformance by these counterparties exposes the Company to potential credit losses, such losses are not anticipated due to the control features mentioned.

At September 30, 1992, the Company had third party guarantees outstanding in the aggregate amount of approximately $38.8. These guarantees relate to financial arrangements with customers, suppliers, and other business relationships. The Company sells certain of its trade accounts receivable and notes receivable to others subject to defined limited recourse provisions, which include repurchase by the Company of delinquent notes receivable. The Company is responsible for collection of the accounts and remits the proceeds to the purchaser on a monthly basis. During 1992, the Company sold, on average, accounts receivable totaling $53.5 each month. At September 30, 1992, $11.5 of transferred receivables were outstanding and subject to recourse provisions.

At September 30, 1992, the Company's primary concentration of credit risk related to approximately $54.0 of trade accounts receivable due from several highly leveraged customers. Consideration was given to the financial position of these customers when determining the appropriate allowance for doubtful accounts.

Lease Commitments

Future minimum rental commitments under non-cancellable operating leases in effect as of September 30, 1992 were: 1993—$31.2, 1994—$24.3, 1995—$15.6, 1996—$10.5, 1997—$7.5, thereafter—$36.2.

Total rental expense for all operating leases was $70.1 in 1992, $66.8 in 1991 and $64.5 in 1990.

OTHER INCOME AND EXPENSE

Other (income)/expense, net consists of the following:

	1992	1991	1990
Translation and exchange (gain)/loss	$ 18.6	$ 11.0	$ 15.7
Investment income	(15.6)	(18.4)	(31.8)
Gain on sale of assets	(41.5)		
Provisions for restructuring, environmental costs and litigation settlement	79.0	45.9	21.4
Miscellaneous	(12.4)	(7.3)	12.4
	$ 28.1	$ 31.2	$ 17.7

Dollars in millions except per share data

RALSTON PURINA COMPANY AND SUBSIDIARIES

SUPPLEMENTAL EARNINGS STATEMENT INFORMATION

	1992	1991	1990
Maintenance and repairs	$206.5	$197.4	$183.5
Research and development	77.4	73.6	66.4

SUPPLEMENTAL BALANCE SHEET INFORMATION

	1992	1991
Receivables (current)-		
Trade	$ 741.1	$596.4
Notes and other	119.0	95.1
Allowance for doubtful accounts	(26.2)	(19.5)
	$ 833.9	$672.0
Inventories-		
Raw materials and supplies	$ 250.6	$239.9
Work in process	73.3	76.5
Finished products	451.8	419.1
	$ 775.7	$735.5
Other Current Assets-		
Prepaid expenses	$ 83.4	$ 87.2
Deferred income tax benefits	27.8	23.3
	$ 111.2	$110.5
Investments and Other Assets-		
Intangible assets (net of accumulated amortization:		
1992-$239.3 and 1991-$199.8)	$ 722.1	$486.3
Investments in affiliated companies	18.3	14.7
Deferred charges and other assets	323.4	271.9
	$1,063.8	$772.9
Accounts Payable and Accrued Liabilities-		
Trade accounts payable	$ 461.9	$473.9
Incentive compensation, salaries and vacations	121.1	112.4
Accrued interest	67.1	67.8
Restructuring reserves	105.5	42.6
Other items	302.2	220.4
	$1,057.8	$917.1
Other Liabilities-		
Self-insurance reserves	$ 107.3	$ 90.8
Minority interests	19.5	16.2
Deferred compensation and other	165.2	167.4
	$ 292.0	$274.4

SUPPLEMENTAL CASH FLOW STATEMENT INFORMATION

	1992	1991	1990
Interest paid	$224.4	$184.2	$200.3
Income taxes paid	220.4	232.0	250.2

RALSTON PURINA COMPANY AND SUBSIDIARIES

NOTES TO
FINANCIAL
STATEMENTS

Dollars in millions except per share data

ANALYSIS OF BALANCE SHEET CHANGES

	1992	1991	1990
Allowance for Doubtful Accounts-			
Balance, beginning of year	$ 19.5	$ 21.3	$ 11.4
Provision charged to expense	15.1	9.5	17.1
Writeoffs, less recoveries	(8.4)	(11.3)	(7.2)
Balance, end of year	$ 26.2	$ 19.5	$ 21.3
Property at Cost-			
Balance, beginning of year	$3,442.5	$3,153.9	$2,718.3
Additions	325.4	404.3	342.1
Acquisitions	50.2[a]		128.0[b]
Disposals	(103.2)	(90.4)	(75.4)
Foreign translation	50.1	(25.3)	40.9
Balance, end of year	$3,765.0	$3,442.5	$3,153.9
Accumulated Depreciation-			
Balance, beginning of year	$1,258.8	$1,121.4	$ 952.7
Depreciation provision	254.7	221.0	204.1
Disposals	(75.3)	(74.1)	(51.5)
Foreign translation	20.4	(9.5)	16.1
Balance, end of year	$1,458.6	$1,258.8	$1,121.4

[a] *Represents property at acquisition of Ever Ready Limited and Tudor.*
[b] *Represents property at acquisition of the Beech-Nut baby food business, Keystone resort operations, and the Mexican battery products operations. Keystone and the Mexican battery products operations were previously accounted for under the equity method.*

Dollars in millions except per share data

Fiscal 1992	First	Second	Third[a]	Fourth[b]
Net sales	$2,029.2	$1,866.3	$1,856.9	$2,000.0
Gross profit	958.4	848.8	841.0	881.1
Earnings before extraordinary item	130.7	86.1	75.9	28.0
Net earnings	130.7	86.1	68.4	28.0
Earnings per common share-				
Primary				
Earnings before extraordinary item	1.14	.76	.68	.22
Net earnings	1.14	.76	.61	.22
Fully diluted				
Earnings before extraordinary item	1.06	.71	.64	.22
Net earnings	1.06	.71	.58	.22
Dividends paid per common share	.26875	.30	.30	.30
Market price range of common stock	58 3/8- 47 3/4	58 7/8- 50 5/8	50 3/4- 43 7/8	50- 43 1/2

Fiscal 1991	First	Second	Third[c]	Fourth[d]
Net sales	$1,956.8	$1,823.6	$1,763.3	$1,832.1
Gross profit	910.0	849.0	805.8	836.7
Net earnings	135.3	98.4	70.7	87.5
Earnings per common share-				
Primary	1.17	.84	.59	.74
Fully diluted	1.09	.78	.56	.70
Dividends paid per common share	.23125	.26875	.26875	.26875
Market price range of common stock	54 3/16- 46 1/8	59 1/2- 46	60 1/8- 49	53 3/8- 48

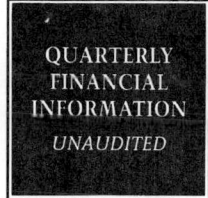

QUARTERLY FINANCIAL INFORMATION
UNAUDITED

[a] *Earnings for the third quarter of 1992 were reduced by $5.7 million or $.05 per primary share due to provisions for restructuring expenses.*

[b] *Earnings for the fourth quarter of 1992 were reduced by $27.2 million or $.26 per primary share due to provisions for restructuring expenses, partially offset by unusual gains on disposition of property. Slightly more than a quarter of the net earnings decline was due to higher recorded advertising and promotion expense as a result of lower than expected volume.*

[c] *Earnings for the third quarter of 1991 were reduced by $19.5 million or $.18 per primary share due to provisions for restructuring expenses and costs relating to environmental matters.*

[d] *Earnings for the fourth quarter of 1991 were reduced by $8.6 million or $.07 per primary share due to provisions for restructuring expenses.*

· *Index*